PROCEEDINGS OF THE FIFTH CHINA-JAPAN CONFERENCE ON SHIELD TUNNELLING

第五届中日盾构隧道技术交流会

第5回日中シールド技術交流会

论文集

主 编 何川
副主编 耿萍 王剑宏

Edited by
Chuan HE
Ping GENG &Jianhong WANG

西南交通大学出版社
SOUTHWEST JIAOTONG UNIVERSITY PRESS
Chengdu · China

Cataloguing in Publication (C I P) Data

Proceedings of the Fifth China-Japan Conference on Shield Tunnelling / Editor in Chief Chuan HE. －Chengdu : Southwest Jiaotong University Press, 2009.9

ISBN 978-7-5643-0441-6

Ⅰ. 5th… Ⅱ. HE… Ⅲ. Tunnel Engineering－Shield(Tunnel)－International Conference－Proceedings Ⅳ. U455.43-53

Archival Library of Chinese Publications CIP Data Nunber (2009) No.164487

Proceedings of the Fifth China-Japan Conference on Shield Tunnelling

Chuan HE

Ping GENG & Jianhong WANG

*

Responsible Editors: Xiao YANG Fang WAN

Cover Design: BENGE

Published by Southwest Jiaotong University Press

No.111, 1st North Erhuan Road, Chengdu 610031, China

Tel: 086-028-87600533

http: //press.swjtu.edu.cn

Printed by Sichuan Senlin Printing Co. Ltd.

*

First Edition in Sep, 2009

First Printing in Sep, 2009

ISBN 978-7-5643-0441-6

Price: ¥200.00 元

主办单位（主催者）

西南交通大学
成都地铁有限责任公司

早稲田大学

支持单位（後援）

中国土木工程学会
及其隧道及地下工程分会
中国岩石力学与工程学会
及其隧道掘进机工程应用分会
中国公路学会隧道工程分会

日本トンネル技術協会

日本土木学会トンネル工学委員会

承办单位（開催者）

西南交通大学

参办单位（共催者）

中铁二院工程集团有限责任公司
中铁二局股份有限公司
中铁西南科学研究院有限公司
成都畅达通地下工程科技发展有限公司
同济大学
北京交通大学
中铁第四勘察设计院集团有限公司
北京城建设计研究总院有限责任公司
广州地铁设计研究院有限公司
上海隧道工程股份有限公司
中铁隧道集团有限公司
中铁十三局集团有限公司
中铁十一局集团有限公司
广东华隧建设股份有限公司
中铁二十三局集团有限公司

長岡技術科学大学
金沢工業大学
長岡工業高等専門学校
東京地下鉄株式会社
メトロ開発株式会社
みずほ情報総研
パシフィックコンサルタンツ株式会社
日本シビックコンサルタント株式会社
大成建設株式会社
清水建設株式会社
株式会社ハザマ
株式会社銭高組
三菱重工地中建機株式会社
株式会社 IHI

组织委员会（主催委員会）

主　席（主　席）

陈春阳　小泉　淳

大会执行主席（大会執行主席）

何　川

副主席（副主席）

伍勇	范平志	蔺安林	朱颖	何义斌	唐志成
梅志荣	郭陕云	白云	蒋树屏	李乔	钱永久
高波	余喧平	张丕界	陈建	朱丹	史海鸥
叶建兴	徐润泽	王广忠	方启超	田宝华	曹大明
孙亮	王剑宏	杉本光隆	藤木育雄	水上博之	斉藤正幸
西村高明	眞鍋尚				

委　员（委　員）

邱延峻	张文桂	杨宁	赵彦灵	张雪	阎勇建
马文义	熊朝辉	吕强	孙谋	刘向阳	仇文革
王明年	杨其新	周晓军	巫锡勇	蒋关鲁	陈寿根
耿萍	曾艳华	孙建生	陈复兴	王波	田中弘
三浦正昭	守山亨	橋本博英	西方浩樹	和気輝幸	上野登紀夫
沼澤憲二郎	小梶敬	斎木公嗣良			

学术委员会（学術委員会）

顾　问（顧　問）

孙钧	钱七虎	刘建航	卢耀如
施仲衡	周丰峻	郑颖人	梁文灏

主　席（主　席）

王梦恕　小泉淳

副主席（副主席）

何川	肖中平	白云	杨秀仁	刘思宁	于波
张海波	朱合华	袁大军	肖明清	郭信君	朱伟
洪开荣	杨国祥	卿三惠	彭立敏	牟锐	张成
易觉	侯刚	李林	张玉川	王守慧	华明
吴圣宏	张厚美	吴旭	王剑宏	李黎明	赵唯坚
杉本光隆	木村定雄	田中弘	岩波基	名倉浩	清水幸範

委　员（委　員）

林家祥	郭小红	刘广钧	张志强	漆泰岳	晏启祥
耿萍	韩向阳	杨书江	崔勤	王洪波	罗世培
李志南	赖伟文	王国义	任庆铨	王华伟	郭俊
毛麒麟	段绍和	何达兵	李有道	张延	刘高峰
徐敏	张稳军	王波	陈复兴	陈剑	官林星
守山亨	深田和志	大塚努	沼田敦	入田健一郎	岡村直利

SPONSORED BY

Southwest Jiaotong University
Waseda University
Chengdu Metro Co.,Ltd.

SUPPORTED BY

China Civil Engineering Society
Chinese Society for Rock Mechanics and Engineering
Tunnel Engineering Branch, China Highway & Transportation Society
Japan Tunnelling Association
Tunnel Engineering Committee, Japan Society of Civil Engineering

ORGANIZED BY

Southwest Jiaotong University

CO-OPERATED BY

China Railway Eryuan Engineering Group Co.,Ltd.
China Railway Erju Co.,Ltd.
Southwest Research Institute Co.,Ltd of CREC
Chengdu Changdatong Underground Engineering Sci-Tech Development Co.,Ltd.
Tongji University
Beijing Jiaotong University
China Railway Siyuan Survey and Design Group Co.,Ltd.
Beijing Urban Engineering Design & Research Institute Co.,Ltd.
Guangzhou Metro Design & Research Institute Co.,Ltd.
Shanghai Tunnel Engineering Co.,Ltd.
China Railway Tunnel Group Co.,Ltd.
China Railway 13th Bureau Group Co.,Ltd
China Railway 11th Bureau Group Co.,Ltd.
China Tunnel Construction Co.,Ltd. Guangdong
China Railway 23th Bureau Group Co.,Ltd
Nagaoka University of Technology
Kanazawa Institute of Technology
Nagaoka National College of Technology
Tokyo Metro Co., Ltd.
Metro Development Corporation
Mizuho Information & Research Institute, Inc.
Pacific Consultants Co., Ltd.
Nippon Civic Consulting Engineers Co., Ltd.

Taisei Corporation
Shimizu Corporation
Hazama Corporation
Zenitaka Corporation
Mitsubishi Heavy Industries Tunneling Machinery & Geotechnology Co., Ltd.
IHI Corporation

ORGANIZING COMMITTEE

CHAIRMEN

Chunyang CHEN
Atsushi KOIZUMI

EXECUTIVE CHAIRMAN

Chuan HE

VICE-CHAIRMEN

Yong WU
Ying ZHU
Zhirong MEI
Shuping JIANG
Bo GAO
Jian CHEN
Jianxing YE
Qichao FANG
Liang SUN
Ikuo FUJIKI
Takaaki NISHIMURA
Pingzhi FAN
Yibin HE
Shanyun GUO
Qiao LI
Xuanping YU
Dan ZHU
Runze XU
Baohua TIAN
Jianhong WANG
Hiroyuki MINAKAMI
Takashi MANABE
Anlin LIN
Zhicheng TANG
Yun BAI
Yongjiu QIAN
Pijie ZHANG
Haiou SHI
Guangzhong WANG
Daming CAO
Mitsutaka SUGIMOTO
Masayuki SAITO

COMMITTEE MEMBERS

Yanjun QIU
Yanling ZHAO
Wenyi MA
Mou SUN
Mingnian WANG
Xiyong WU
Ping GENG
Fuxing CHEN
Masaaki MIURA
Hiroki NISHIKATA
Kenjiro NUMASAWA
Wengui ZHANG
Xue ZHANG
Zhaohui XIONG
Xiangyang LIU
Qixin YANG
Guanlu JIANG
Yanhua ZENG
Bo WANG
Toru MORIYAMA
Teruyuki WAKI
Takashi KOKAJI
Ning YANG
Yongjian YAN
Qiang LV
Wenge QIU
Xiaojun ZHOU
Shougen CHEN
Jiansheng SUN
Hiroshi TANAKA
Hirohide HASHIMOTO
Tokio UENO
Koshiro SAIKI

ACADEMIC COMMITTEE

CONSULTANTS

Jun SUN
Yaoru LU
Yingren ZHENG
Qihu QIAN
Zhongheng SHI
Wenhao LIANG
Jianhang LIU
Fengjun ZHOU

CHAIRMEN

Mengshu WANG
Atsushi KOIZUMI

VICE-CHAIRMEN

Chuan HE
Xiuren YANG
Haibo ZHANG
Mingqing XIAO
Kairong HONG
Limin PENG
Jue YI
Yuchuan ZHANG
Shenghong WU
Jianhong WANG
Mitsutaka SUGIMOTO
Motoi IWANAMI
Zhongping XIAO
Sining LIU
Hehua ZHU
Xinjun GUO
Guoxiang YANG
Rui MOU
Gang HOU
Shouhui WANG
Houmei ZHANG
Liming LI
Sadao KIMURA
Hiroshi NAGURA
Yun BAI
Bo YU
Dajun YUAN
Wei ZHU
Sanhui QING
Cheng ZHANG
Lin LI
Ming HUA
Xu WU
Weijian ZHAO
Hiroshi TANAKA
Yukinori SHIMIZU

COMMITTEE MEMBERS

Jiaxiang LIN
Zhiqiang ZHANG
Ping GENG
Qin CUI
Zhinan LI
Qingquan REN
Qilin MAO
Youdao LI
Min XU
Fuxing CHEN
Toru MORIYAMA
Atsushi NUMATA
Xiaohong GUO
Taiyue QI
Xiangyang HAN
Hongbo WANG
Weiwen LAI
Huawei WANG
Shaohe DUAN
Yan ZHANG
Wenjun ZHANG
Jian CHEN
Kazuyuki FUKADA
Kenichiro IRITA
Guangjun LIU
Qixiang YAN
Shujiang YANG
Shipei LUO
Guoyi WANG
Jun GUO
Dabing HE
Gaofeng LIU
Bo WANG
Linxing GUAN
Tsutomu OOTSUKA
Naotoshi OKAMURA

前　言

随着中国社会和经济的长足发展，城市地铁已经在社会公共功能中扮演越来越重要的角色，水下隧道也正在改变着越江跨海通道“唯桥是举”的局面，高速铁路、高速公路、水利工程面临大型隧道工程的挑战。中国作为目前世界上隧道工程建设数量最多、规模最大、技术难度最复杂、发展最快的国家，如何采用安全、高效的先进隧道技术，是非常重要的课题。现代盾构隧道技术顺应了时代的步伐，必将在中国的基础设施建设等领域发挥越来越重要的作用。日本是世界上盾构隧道技术最发达的国家之一，成功建成了以东京湾横断公路隧道为代表的数量巨大的各类盾构隧道工程。积极开展中日间盾构隧道技术的交流将会极大地推动两国在该领域的学术与技术进步。

由王梦恕院士、小泉 淳教授、朱合华教授、何 川教授、袁大军教授等中日学者提议，中国西南交通大学、同济大学、北京交通大学与日本早稻田大学等单位共同发起的蜚声中日两国隧道工程界的“中日盾构隧道技术交流会”自 2003 年在北京召开首届会议以来，已历时四届，日益受到了中日两国及其他国家和地区同行的重视。第五届中日盾构隧道技术交流会更是得到了中日两国 5 个相关学（协）会、30 多家大学及研究机构与企业、多名著名专家学者的大力支持，于 2009 年 9 月 16 日—19 日在位于天府之国的百年老校——西南交通大学召开。

本次交流会论文集共收录论文 93 篇，其中中方 68 篇，日方 25 篇，是历届交流会收录论文最多的一次，反映了两国在大型越江海盾构隧道、城市地铁盾构隧道等方向的最新进展，涉及设计和施工、建设对环境的影响与控制、防灾减灾、重大工程实录等多方面的内容，相信论文集不仅可作为了解目前中日两国盾构隧道科技动态的一个窗口，同时也必将成为该领域中日两国广大科技工作者进行学术探讨和交流的一个园地。在此，谨向积极参加论文撰写投稿、为论文集编辑与出版成功付出辛勤汗水的中日两国科技工作者深表谢意。

大会执行主席

西南交通大学　博士生导师

教育部长江学者特聘教授

何 川

2009 年 9 月

まえがき

中国の社会および経済は長期的な発展を続ける中で，地下鉄は都市の公共施設の一部としてその機能が都市生活にますます重要となっています．河川下や海底下のトンネルの建設によって，従来の川と海を横断するときに必ずしも橋を架ける必要となくなり，高速鉄道，高速道路および水利施設の建設に長大トンネルへ多くの挑戦がなされています．現在の中国はトンネル工事の数が世界の中で一番多く，かつ，最大規模のトンネルや技術面でもっとも複雑なトンネルが造られ，その建設スピードもまた最速です．安全かつ有効な最先端のトンネル技術をいかに利用するのが現段階の最大課題となってきています．現在のシールド技術は時流に適合したトンネル技術であり，中国の地下インフラの建設にはますます重要な役割を果たしています．一方，日本はシールドトンネルの最先端の技術を発展させた国の一つとして，東京湾横断道路トンネルをはじめ数多くシールドトンネルの建設に成功しました．日中間のシールドトンネル技術交流を積極的に行うことにより，両国の当該分野での学術および技術の進歩が大きく促進されることを期待しています．

日中シールド技術交流会は，王夢恕中国工程院 院士，小泉　淳教授，朱合華教授，何　川教授および袁大軍教授などが提案し，中国側での西南交通大学，同済大学および北京交通大学と日本側での早稲田大学と共同で発足し，2003年の北京での第1回目以降，現在までに４回開催され，今や日中両国のみならず，そのほかの国や地域にも拡大される機運にあり，トンネル技術者にとっての大きなイベントとなりつつあります．第５回日中シールド技術交流会は，日中両国の五つの学協会，三十余の大学や研究機構，企業，さらに，数多く著名な専門家や学者などからのご支援を得て，2009年9月16日～19日に“天府之国－四川”の百年以上の歴史を有する西南交通大学で開催されます．

今回の交流会の論文集には，中国側68篇、日本側25篇の合計93編の論文が収められています．これは今までの日中シールド技術交流会の中でもっとも多く，日中両国の最近の河川下や海底下のシールドトンネル，地下鉄などのシールドトンネルにおける設計，施工，環境対策および換気防災などに関する最新技術や，それらの研究成果ならびに重大プロジェクト事業の情報が集録されています．本論文集が日中両国の最新シールドトンネル技術の発信源となるとともに，将来的にも日中両国の技術者らの情報交換と技術交流の場となることを確信しています．ここに，論文投稿にご協力いただいた方々および本技術交流会開催の準備ならびに論文集の編集や発刊に協力していただいた日中両国の皆様に心より感謝申し上げます．

2009 年 9 月

主催委員会　大会執行主席
西南交通大学　教授
何　川

Preface

With the rapid development of society and economy in China, urban metro has been playing an increasingly important role in public service. While bridge might be the only means of transportation across rivers and seas in the past, under-water tunnel now represents an inspiring alternative. High-speed railway, expressway, and hydraulic works face the challenge of large-scale tunnel construction. China is a country where tunnels have been highly developed in terms of the number and scale of tunnels being constructed, and the complexity of the technology. It has been a critical topic in China to research into how to improve the safety and efficiency of tunnel technology. Shield tunnel technology, as the safest and most efficient tunneling technology to date, is expected to be more and more popular in the field of infrastructure construction. Being one of the most advanced countries in shield tunnel technology, Japan has built up a large number of shield tunnel constructions of various types, for instance, the Tokyo-Bay Tunnel. It is hoped that the China-Japan Conference on Shield Tunneling will greatly improve academic and technical development in this field in both China and Japan.

China-Japan Conference on Shield Tunnelling was inaugurated in Beijing in 2003 at the proposal of Academician Mengshu WANG, Professor Atsushi KOIZUMI, Professor Hehua ZHU, Professor Chuan HE and Professor DajunYUAN and sponsored by Southwest Jiaotong University, Tongji University, Beijing Jiaotong University, and Waseda University, etc. The conference has held sessions and has become a reputable research and academic event in the field of tunnel engineering in China, Japan and many other countries and regions. The Fifth China-Japan Conference on Shield Tunneling will be held in Southwest Jiaotong University on September 16-19, 2009. The conference has won supports from five related societies, more than 30 universities, research institutions and enterprises as well as a large number of famous experts and scholars in China and Japan.

The 2009 conference receives more submissions than any of the 4 previous sessions. The proceedings at the 2009 conference include 93 articles, among which 68 are submitted by Chinese scholars and 25 by Japanese scholars. These articles reflect the recent development of large-scale under-water shield tunnel and urban metro shield tunnel, etc. both in China and Japan, involving design and construction, the impact on environment and control, disaster prevention and reduction, and major project cases, etc. It is believed that the proceedings will not only be a window to China-Japan shield tunnel development, but also be an arena for academic discussion and communication for the broad mass of scientific and technological workers from the two countries. Here, we express our deepest gratitude to those who worked for the composition, compilation and publication of the conference proceedings.

Professor Chuan HE
Executive Chairman, Organizing Committee
Southwest Jiaotong University
P.R. of China
2009.9

目　录

结构与设计

Structural Analysis Method Considering Contact Pressure Between Segment Lining and Expansive Ground ······ 3
何 川　周济民　封 坤　谢 俊

Design of Composite Segment for Underground Discharge Channel ······ 10
张稳军　小泉 淳

Study on Crack Opening Displacement of Shield Tunnel in Longitudinal Direction ······ 20
张志强　何 川　乔卖青

Research on Mechanical Behavior of Segment Joint of Large Section Shield Tunnel ······ 27
邹育麟　何 川　封 坤　夏松林

南京长江隧道盾构管片分块设计 ······ 33
肖明清　韩向阳　薛光桥

玻璃纤维筋混凝土围护桩在盾构端井头的应用研究 ······ 39
陈 中　马文义　肖中平

成都地铁盾构法区间隧道设计施工关键技术 ······ 48
林 刚　罗世培　郭 俊　邹永尧

基于渗流-应力耦合的水下盾构隧道结构特性研究 ······ 61
谢红强　何 川

富水砂层土压平衡盾构施工地表沉降性状研究 ······ 69
丁洲祥　袁大军　吴全力　周 峻　肖 衡

深埋盾构隧道抗震分析的近似解析法 ······ 79
晏启祥　马婷婷　何 川　汪 东

埋深和地层条件对盾构隧道地震响应的影响分析 ······ 83
江英超　聂 亮　耿 萍　何 川

成都膨胀土地层地铁区间隧道盾构法可行性分析 ······ 89
胡 茜　罗世培　牟 锐　邹永尧

大型水下盾构隧道管片衬砌结构劣化研究现状及展望 ······ 99
王士民　何 川　晏启祥

盾构隧道设计常用计算方法的归纳与比较 ······ 105
孙文昊　殷怀连

软土层中水下盾构隧道复合衬砌列车振动响应分析 ······ 110
陈松洁　彭立敏　丁祖德

南京长江隧道管片接头三维有限元分析 ······ 119
郭 瑞　何 川　苏宗贤　彭志忠

城市地铁盾构隧道管片设计与分析 ······ 126
梅江兵

水下盾构隧道管片衬砌结构受埋深影响的力学特性研究 ······ 131
周济民　何 川　郭德平　谭 准
既有盾构隧道上方开挖卸载后隧道力学特征研究 ······ 137
杨 征　林 刚
浅谈盾构隧道管片的破损与修复 ······ 145
梁艳文　廖少明
水下盾构隧道施工及运营阶段抗浮计算方法探讨 ······ 152
郭德平　何 川　周济民　耿 萍
日本におけるシールドトンネルの設計法の変遷と性能規定の提言 ······ 159
木村 定雄　山本 努
都心部における非開削切拡げ施工時の載荷挙動に関する研究 ······ 170
岩波 基　千代啓三　大澤拓洋
施工時荷重がセグメント挙動に与える影響の定量的評価方法に関する検討 ······ 180
松本 貴士，Auttakit Asanprakit，陳 剣，杉本 光隆
重複円形シールドトンネルの応答変位法における地盤ばねに関する考察(その 2:地盤反力) ······ 194
徐 敏　眞鍋 尚
シールド工法により構築する水道トンネルの構造設計および合理化について ······ 204
王 剣宏，小泉 淳
計測変位から覆工安全性を評価する逆解析方法とその適用 ······ 217
呉 旭　中村 敦　桜井 春輔
大断面分割シールド工法（ハーモニカ工法）の構造研究 ······ 225
趙 唯堅　服部佳文　三木洋人
円形立坑開口部側壁厚の下限値の簡易設定について ······ 235
陳 復興　荒木 繁雄　岡田 一郎　斉藤 正幸　小泉 淳
コンクリート中詰め合成セグメントの地下鉄トンネルへの適用検討 ······ 245
入田 健一郎　西井 成実　沼澤 憲二郎　藤木 育雄
営業線直下・小土被り条件下におけるシールドトンネルの計画と施工について ······ 258
足立邦靖　沼澤憲二郎
性能規定に基づく既設地下鉄シールドトンネルの保有性能評価手法の検討 ······ 267
横山 正浩　木村 定雄　山本 努
テールシールがセグメントリングの断面力に与える影響に関する研究 ······ 278
鈴木雄士　高橋正朗　小泉 淳

设备与施工

小覆土水底隧道盾构掘进泥水压力研究 ······ 289
袁大军　黄清飞　尹 凡　王 胤　王华伟
超长距离超大直径盾构隧道若干关键施工技术研究及应用 ······ 295
杨国祥　林家祥　王吉云
大伙房输水工程特长隧洞施工方法优化与 TBM 选型研究 ······ 304
梅志荣　张军伟　唐 与　章元爱
扰动地层塌陷隧道原位修复综合技术 ······ 314
余暄平　朱卫杰

成都地区富水砂卵石地层盾构机选型及其适应性探讨 ……325
张 延 肖中平
富水砂卵石地层土压平衡盾构施工关键技术 ……334
李 林
素混凝土连续墙在盾构始发端头加固施工中的应用 ……344
易 觉 姜自明 王家星
富水砂卵石地层土压平衡盾构带压换刀研究 ……348
刘向阳 陈 强
卵石地层盾构掘进机刀盘刀具适应性分析及对策 ……359
彭健成 吴惠明 阮关荣
富水砂卵石地层土压平衡盾构关键施工技术 ……368
王明胜 章龙管
北京地区砂卵石地层盾构掘进参数分析 ……375
郭玉海 李兴高 袁大军
地铁盾构隧道扩挖车站方案初探 ……383
罗世培
盾构先行条件下拓展地铁车站的施工过程风险分析 ……389
路美丽 刘维宁 张新金
砂卵石地层盾构刀盘选型、刀具组合配置设计研究 ……395
黄清飞 袁大军 王梦恕 肖 衡
盾构隧道数字化远程监控系统的研究与实现 ……409
袁 钊 李晓军 高小庆 杨文威 陆晓龙
土压平衡式盾构壁后注浆量的影响因素分析 ……415
刘泉维 钟小春 左 佳 闵凡路 韩月旺
软土盾构隧道工程综合效益评估 ……422
尹 玫 芮 易 闫治国
南京长江隧道冲槽段大直径泥水盾构开挖面稳定研究 ……428
王 胤 袁大军 肖 衡 黄清飞 刘泉维
ＩＨＩ シールド最新技術 ……434
団野 均
伸縮カッターを用いた大断面複合円形シールドの掘進管理実績と評価 ……443
大塚 努 沼田 敦
シールドテール内形状保持装置（TKS）の効果 ……452
藤木 育雄 大塚 努 吉成 寿男 守山 亨
日立造船におけるシールド掘進機の新技術・新製品 ……459
花岡 泰治 富木 広志
シールドマシーンの後退と岩盤掘進対応型 マシーンへの地中における改造 ……466
金野 正一
泥水式シールドによる複合地盤の掘削 ……472
田中 善広 野村 朝雄 三野 秀作 山内 健二
開削工法による道路シールドトンネル分合流部の築造 ……480
三木 章生
FFU 横矢板を用いたシールド機の直接発進到達 ……489
竹中 計行 深田 和志 中川 達也

试验与监测

青草沙水源地原水工程输水隧道衬砌管片接头试验……501
朱合华 顾 赟 丁文其 闫治国
水压条件对水下盾构隧道结构内力 影响的模型试验……508
封 坤 何 川 夏松林 邹育麟
地下工程预制化结构接头力学特性试验研究……515
王明年 魏龙海 李志业 刘惠敏 贾永刚
管片背后注浆效果无损检测试验研究……521
曹大明 黄 亮 温佐彪
盾构隧道管片土体之间接触应力测试分析……526
李兴高 袁大军 吴晓军
地铁施工过程自动安全监测系统的应用及展望……532
曹大明 段 强
砂卵石地层盾构法施工地面滞后塌陷成因初探……540
张治国 曹大明 黄 亮
某地铁岩溶注浆浆液配比试验研究……544
杨秀竹 赵国旭 孙成伟 雷金山
盾构隧道近距离穿越地下管线施工监测分析……549
王荣劲 曹大明
大直径盾构隧道壁后注浆无损探测技术研究……553
刘 浩
泥水盾构开舱时泥浆配制及泥膜形成试验研究……559
闵凡路 朱 伟 王守慧 钟小春
盾构壁后注浆浆体收缩规律及对间隙参数的影响……565
左 佳 钟小春 王华伟 朱 伟
北京砂卵石地层泥水盾构泥浆特性试验研究……573
于 娇 袁大军 叶旭洪 黄清飞 李建华
通信用シールドとう道の補修に関する実験的な研究……580
官 林星 入江 浩志 島田 徹 小泉 淳
補剛リブを設けた大深度地下水道管の外水圧による座屈挙動に関する実験的研究……586
天野 裕基 王 剣宏 小泉 淳

工程案例

杭州庆春路过江隧道工程设计……597
肖明清 焦齐柱 张 迪 孙文昊
台湾超高压地下电缆隧道潜盾施工案例探讨……603
李文权 吴福祥 张达德 王义夫 陈聪海
土压平衡盾构近距离穿越污水管施工技术……615
杨书江
土压平衡复合型盾构双级螺旋输送机对喷涌的控制技术……621
雷金山 刘德智 杨秀竹

大直径泥水盾构在中硬岩地层中的施工难点及对策 …… 627
刘广钧 姚永勤 常 鑫 王冬胜
大型盾构输水隧洞技术应用研究 …… 632
张 弢 王 雷 杨文明
盾构采用辅助工法通过硬岩段施工技术的研究与应用 …… 638
王家祥 贯 科
新建盾构隧道下穿运营隧道的相互影响研究 …… 646
夏炜洋 何 川 汪 洋 汪 波 晏启祥
配合盾构法修建三条平行隧道地铁车站横向通道时车站结构力学行为研究 …… 651
张海波 何 川
上海世博电力隧道盾构下穿地铁1号线施工控制分析 …… 657
付昱凯 丁文其 高小庆
黄土地区修建地铁区间平行盾构隧道数值模拟分析 …… 664
高云龙 何 川 方 勇 汪 洋
武汉长江隧道盾构下穿武九铁路沉降影响分析 …… 673
季大雪
大型水下隧道水喷雾系统灭火的模拟分析 …… 679
张玉春 何 川 曾艳华 孙晓琴
越江盾构隧道纵向排烟的数值模拟研究 …… 683
曾艳华 方 伟 何 川
地铁盾构隧道下穿铁路桥结构安全分析 …… 689
张 增 林 刚 张 庆
盾构超浅覆土近距离上穿运营地铁施工风险与对策 …… 697
李 金 廖少明 梁艳文
软土盾构隧道渗漏水成因分析 …… 705
芮 易 李晓军 尹 玫 王 帅
世界最大級ϕ14.27 mの泥土圧シールドの適用 …… 710
三浦 正昭 田中 淳一
長距離・多急曲線シールド掘進の計画と実績 …… 719
元永 隆章 中野 修吾

Contents

STRUCTURE AND DESIGN

Structural Analysis Method Considering Contact Pressure Between Segment Lining and Expansive Ground ······ 3
Chuan HE, Jimin ZHOU, Kun FENG, Jun XIE

Design of Composite Segment for Underground Discharge Channel ······ 10
Wenjun ZHANG, Atsushi KOIZUMI

Study on Crack Opening Displacement of Shield Tunnel in Longitudinal Direction ······ 20
Zhiqiang ZHANG, Chuan HE, Maiqing QIAO

Research on Mechanical Behavior of Segment Joint of Large Section Shield Tunnel ······ 27
Yulin ZOU, Chuan HE, Kun FENG, Songlin XIA

The Segment's Division Design of Nanjing Yangtze River Tunnel ······ 33
Mingqing XIAO, Xiangyang HAN, Guangqiao XUE

Researching of Gfrp Concrete Fender Piles of Shield Launching Shafts ······ 39
Zhong CHEN, Wenyi MA, Zhongping XIAO

Key Technique for Design and Construction of Shield Sectional Tunnel of Chengdu ······ 48
Gang LIN, Shipei LUO, Jun GUO, Yongyao ZOU

Study on Structural Characteristics of Subriver Shield Tunnel Based on Seepage-Stress Coupling ······ 61
Hongqiang XIE, Chuan HE

Study on Ground Settlement Behavior of Epb Shield Tunnel in Water-Rich Sandy Layers ······ 69
Zhouxiang DING, Dajun YUAN, Quanli WU, Jun ZHOU, Heng XIAO

An Approximate Analytic Method for Aseismic Analysis of Deep-Buried Shield Tunnel ······ 79
Qixiang YAN, Tingting MA, Chuan HE, Dong WANG

Analysis of Depth and Ground Condition of Shield Tunnel on Its Seismic Response ······ 83
Yingchao JIANG, Liang NIE, Ping GENG, Chuan HE

Feasibility Analysis of Shield Driving Method Used in Interzone Tunnel in Expansive Soils in Chengdu Metro ······ 89
Qian HU, Shipei LUO, Rui MU, Yongyao ZOU

Research Status and Prospect on the Deterioration of the Segment Structure in Large Underwater Shield Tunnel ······ 99
Shimin WANG, Chuan HE, Qixiang YAN

Generalization and Comparsion of Common Calculation Methods on Design of Shield Tunnel ······ 105
Wenhao SUN, Huailian YIN

Analysis of Train Vibration Response of Underwater Shield Tunnels in Soft Soil ······ 110
Songjie CHEN, Limin PENG, Zude DING

Three Dimensional Finite Element Analysis on Segment Joint of Nanjing Yangtze River Shield Tunnel ······ 119
Rui GUO, Chuan HE, Zongxian SU, Zhizhong PENG

Design and Analysis of Segement in Urban Shield Tunnel ······ 126
Jiangbing MEI

Research on Mechanical Behavior of Lining Structure Influenced by Embedded Depth of Submarine Shield Tunnel ······ 131
Jimin ZHOU, Chuan HE, Deping GUO, Zhun TAN

Study on Mechanical Characteristics of Shield Tunnel with Excavation above ······ 137
Zheng YANG, Gang LIN

An Introduction to the Damage and Repair of Sheild-Tunnel Segment ······ 145
Yanwen LIANg, Shaoming LIAO

Discussion on Anti-Upward Moving Calculation Method of Submarine Shield Tunnel During the Construction and Service Stages ······ 152
Deping GUO, Chuan HE, Jimin ZHOU, Ping GENG

Trends of Modern Design Methods of Shield Tunnels in Japan and Advance of Performance Based Design Codes ······ 159
Sadao KIMURA, Tsutomu YAMAMOTO

A Study on Behavior of the Structures and the Surrounding Ground Applied Non-Open Cut Method in the Metropolitan Area ······ 170
Motoi IWANAMI, Keizo CHISHIRO, Takuhiro OHSAWA

Study on the Quantitative Method for Assessing the Influence of Construction Loads on Segment Behavior ······ 180
Atsushi MATSUMOTO, Asanprakit AUTTAKIT, Jian CHEN, Mitsutaka SUGIMOTO

Considerations of the Coefficient of Subgrade Reaction on Seismic Deformation Method of Double-O-Tube Shield Tunnel (Part Ⅱ: Subgrade Reaction) ······ 194
Min XU, Takashi MANABE

Structural Design and Rationalization for Water Convey Tunnel Built by Shield-Driven Tunneling Method ······ 204
Jianhong WANG, Atsushi KOIZUMI

A Back Analysis Procedure of Tunnel Lining Assessment and Its Applications ······ 217
Xu WU, Atsushi NAKAMURA, Shunsuke SAKURAI

Development of the Shield Method Construction Structures for Large Section Tunnel by Joining Small Section Tunnels Together ······ 225
Weijian ZHAO, Yoshifumi HATTORI, Hiroto MIKI

A Simplified Method to Determine the Minimum Thickness of Opening Reinforcement for a Circular Vertical Shaft ······ 235
Fuxing CHEN, Shigeo ARAKI, Ichiro OKADA, Masayuki SAITO, Atsushi KOIZUMI

Study on Application of Pre-Casting Concrete Composite Segments in Subway Tunnel ······ 245
Kenichiro IRITA, Narumi NISHII, Kenjiro NUMASAWA, Ikuo FUJIKI

Epb Shield Tunneling for Shallow Twin Tunnels under Railway in Operation ······ 258
K.NUMAZAWA, K.ADACHI

A Study of Evaluation Methods of Keeping Performance of Subway Shield Tunnels Base on Performance Criterion ······ 267
Masahiro YOKOYAMA, Sadao KIMURA, Tutomu YAMAMOTO

Effect of Sealing Material at the Tail of Shield Machine on the Segmental Lining ······ 278
Takeshi SUZUKI, Masaaki TAKAHASHI, Atsushi KOIZUMI

EQUIPMENT AND CONSTRUCTION

Study on Slurry Pressure During Shield Tunneling in Shallow Cover and Underwater Ground ···················· 289
Dajun YUAN, Qingfei HUANG, Fan YIN, Yin WANG, Huawei WANG

Research and Application of Some Key Construction Techniques for Shield Tunnel with Super-Large Diameter and Super-Long Distance ······························· 295
Guoxiang YANG, Jiaxiang LIN, Jiyun WANG

Study on Optimization of Construction Method and Tbm Lectotype Technology of Super-Long Tunnel ······· 304
Zhirong MEI, Junwei ZHANG, Yu TANG, Yuanai ZHANG

The Comprehensive Repairing Technology for Collapsed Tunnel in Disturbed Soils in Its Original Site ······ 314
Xuanping YU, Weijie ZHU

Study on Shield Machine Type Selection and Applicability in Water-Rich Cobble Ground Chengdu Area ···· 325
Yan ZHANG, Zhongping XIAO

Study on Driving of Earth-Pressure Balanced Shield Machine in Water-Rich Cobble Ground ··················· 334
Lin LI

The Application of Plain Concrete Diaphragm Wall in the Shield Launching Soil Reinforcement ················ 344
Jue YI, Ziming JIANG, Jiaxing WANG

The Research of Changing Cutter Tools under Air Presure for Epb Excavating in Water Sand and Gravel Staratum ······························· 348
Xiangyang LIU, Qiang CHEN

Cutter Adaptability Analysis and Countermeasures for Shield Machine in Gravel Stratum ························ 359
Jiancheng PENG, Huiming WU, Guanrong RUAN

Key Technology for Epb Shield Boring in Water-Rich Sand/Gravel Ground ······························· 368
Mingsheng WANG, Longguan ZHANG

Analysis of Shield Tunneling Parameters in Sanfy Cobble Ground in Beijing Area ······························· 375
Yuhai GUO, Xinggao LI, Dajun YUAN

Exploratory Study on Scheme for Enlargement of Station in Metro Shield Tunnel ······························· 383
Shipei LUO

Construction Risk Analysis of the Expanded Metro Station Under Shield Running Tunnel ························ 389
Meili LU, Weining LIU, Xinjin ZHANG

Study on Shield Cutting Wheel Type Selection and Cutting Tool Combination Disposition in Sandy Cobble Stratum ······························· 395
Qingfei HUANG, Dajun YUAN, Mengshu WANG, Heng XIAO

Research and Implementation of Shield Tunnel Digital Remote Monitoring System ······························· 409
Zhao YUAN, Xiaojun LI, Xiaoqing GAO, Wenwei YANG, Xiaolong LU

Study on the Factors Influencing on Backfill Grouting Quantity of Epb Shield ······························· 415
Quanwei LIU, Xiaochun ZHONG, Jia ZUO, Fanlu MIN, Yuewang HAN

Comprehensive Benefit Evaluation on Shield Tunnel Engineering in Soft Soil ······························· 422
Mei YIN, Yi RUI, Zhiguo YAN

Study on Cutting Face Stability of Yangtze River Tunnel during Large Diametre Slurry Shield Tunneling in Stamping Notches ······························· 428
Yin WANG, Dajun YUAN, Heng XIAO, Qingfei HUANG, Quanwei LIU

The Latest Ihi Shield Technology ······ 434
Hitoshi DANNO
Results and Evaluation of the Control over Driving the Shield Machine with a Large Flat Circle Section by Excavation Method of Adjustable Cutter ······ 443
Tsutomu OOTSUKA, Atsushi NUMATA
Efficacy of Position Retaining System for Shield Tunnel Segment ······ 452
Ikuo FUJIKI, Tsutomu OOTSUKA, Hisao YOSHINARI, Toru MORIYAMA
New Technologies and Products of Hitachi Zosen Shield Tunneling Machines ······ 459
Yasuharu HANAOKA, Hiroshi TOMIKI
Shield Machine Shift Back and Underground Remodelling for the Excavation of Rock Ground ······ 466
Shouichi KONNO
Application of Slurry Pressure Balance (Spb) Tunneling Method under Challenging Project Conditions ······ 472
Yoshihiro TANAKA, Asao NOMURA, Shusaku MINO, Kenji YAMAUCHI
Construction of Enlarging Road Shield Tunnel for the Open-Cut Method ······ 480
Akio MIKI
Departing and Arriving Directly of Shild Machine with FFU Horizontal Lagging ······ 489
Kazuyuki TAKENAKA, Kazuyuki FUKADA, Tatsuya NAKAGAWA

EXPERIMENT AND MONITORING

Introduce to the Joint Test of the Shield Tunnel's Lining Structure in Qingcaosha Water Conveyance Project ······ 501
Hehua ZHU, Yun GU, Wenqi DING, Zhiguo YAN
Model Test on the Impact of Water Pressure on Mechanical Characteristics of Underwater Shield Tunnel ······ 508
Kun FENG, Chuan HE, Songlin XIA, Yulin ZOU
Study on the Joint Mechanics Characters of the Prefabricated Structure by Model Test ······ 515
Mingnian WANG, Longhai WEI, Zhiye LI, Huimin LIU, Yonggang JIA
The Study on Nondestructive Testing Experiment of the Effect of Grouting Behind Shield Tunnel Segment ······ 521
Daming CAO, Liang HUANG, Zuobiao WEN
Measurement and Analysis of Contact Stress Between Shield Tunnel Segment and Soil ······ 526
Xinggao LI, Dajun YUAN, Xiaojun WU
The Application and Prospect of the Automatic Safety Monitoring System in Subway Construction Process ······ 532
Daming CAO, Qiang DUAN
Exploration of the Causes of Lagging Subsidence in Sandy Cobble Stratum by Shield Method ······ 540
Zhiguo ZHANG, Daming CAO, Liang HUANG
Experimental Study on Mixture Ratio of Grout for Filling Solution Cavity and Soil Cave under One Subway ······ 544
Xiuzhu YANG, Guoxu ZHAO, Chengwei SUN
The Monitoring Analysis on the Construction of Shield Tunnel Crossing Underground Pipiline in Short Distance ······ 549
Rongjin WANG, Daming CAO

Study on Non-Destructive Detection of Backfill Grouting in Large-Diameter Shield Tunnel 553
Hao LIU
Study on Adjusting Slurry Property When Opening the Pressure Cabin of Slurry Shield 559
Fanlu MIN, Wei ZHU, Shouhui WANG, Xiaochun ZHONG
Analysis on the Impact of Gap Parameters for Grout Deformation Properties of Shield Tunnel 565
Jia ZUO, Xiaochun ZHONG, Huawei WANG, Wei ZHU
Tests Study on Mud Fluid Properties of Slurry Shield in Beijing Sandy Cobble Stratum 573
Jiao YU, Dajun YUAN, Xuhong YE, Qingfei HUANG, Jianhua LI
Experimental Test on Communication Cable Tunnel Constructed by Shield Tunneling Method for Maintenance 580
Linxing GUAN, Hiroshi IRIE, Toru SHMADA, Atsushi KOIZUMI
Experimental Study on Buckling of Stiffed Steel Pipe under External Water Pressure for Deep Water Supply Tunnel 586
Yuki AMANO1, Jianhong WANG1, Atsush KOIZUMI

ENGINEERING CASE

Design of Qingchun Rode Rive-Crossing Tunnel in Hangzhou 597
Mingqing XIAO, Qizhu JIAO, Di ZHANG, Wenhao SUN
Construction Case Study on the Shield Tunnel for 345kV Power Cables In Taiwan 603
Wenchuan LEE, Fuhsiang WU, Tathechang DAVE, Yihfu WANG, Tsunghai CHEN
Short-Distance Across Sewage Pipe Construction Technique of Epb Shield 615
Shujiang YANG
Control Techniques of Spewing by Two-Stage Screw Conveyor in Epb Composite Shield 621
Jinshan LEI, Dezhi LIU, Xiuzhu YANG
Consruction Difficulty and Countermeasure of Major Diameter Slurry Shield in Medium-Hard Rock Condition 627
Guangjun LIU, Yongqin YAO, Xin CHANG, Dongsheng WANG
Appllied Research on Water Delivery Tunnel of Large Scale Shield 632
Tao ZHANG, Lei WANG, Wenming YANG
The Study and Application of Shield Method in Composite Formation Using Auxiliary Construction Technology through Hard Rock Above 638
Jiaxiang WANG, Ke JIA
Interaction Influence Between Running Tunnel and New Shield Tunnel in Stage of Construction and Operation 646
Weiyang XIA, Chuan HE, Yang WANG, Bo WANG, Qixiang YAN
Study on Mechanical Behave of Three Parallel Tunnels Metro Station Cross Passage Based on Shield Tunnel with Natm 651
Haibo ZHANG1, Chuan HE
Study on Construction Control of Shanghai World Expo Power Tunnel Under-Passing through Metro Line 657
Yukai FU, Wenqi DING, Xiaoqing GAO
Numerical Simulation Analysis of Subway Interzone Parallel Shield Tunnel Construction in Loess Area 664
Yunlong GAO, Chuan HE, Yong FANG, Yang WANG

Settlement Analysis of Wuhan Yangtze River Shield Tunnel Crossing Wuhan-Jiujiang Railway ········ 673
Daxue JI

Simulation of Fire Extinguishment by Water Spray System of Large-Scale Underwater Tunnel ········ 679
Yuchun ZHANG, Chuan HE, Yanhua ZENG, Xiaoqin SUN

The Research of Numerical Simulation for Longitudinal Smoke Extraction in River-Crossing Shield Tunnel ········ 683
Yanhua ZENG, Wei FANG, Chuan HE

Analysis on Structure Safty of a Shield Tunnel under Passing Railway Bridge in Metro Construction ········ 689
Zeng ZHANG, Gang LIN, Qing ZHANG

Construction Risk and Coutermeasures of Shield Tunneling Crossing above Running Tunnel at Shallow Depth ········ 697
Jin LI, Shaoming LIAO1, Yanwen LIANG1

Cause Analysis of Shield Tunnel Leakage In Soft Soil ········ 705
Yi RUI, Xiaojun LI, Mei YIN, Shuai WANG

Application of ϕ 14.27 m Largest Earth Pressure Balance Shield Machine to the Waitan Road Tunnel in Shanghai China ········ 710
Masaaki MIURA, Junichi TANAKA

Planning and Records of Shield Tunnel Excavation with Long Distances and Multi Cute Curves ········ 719
Takafumi MOTONAGA, Shugo NAKANO

PART ONE

STRUCTURE AND DESIGN

结构与设计

STRUCTURAL ANALYSIS METHOD CONSIDERING CONTACT PRESSURE BETWEEN SEGMENT LINING AND EXPANSIVE GROUND

Chuan HE, Jimin ZHOU, Kun FENG, Jun XIE

Department of Underground Engineering, Southwest Jiaotong University, Chengdu 610031, Sichuan, China

Abstract: Expansive ground is clay soil or rock which exhibits significant volume changes because of mineral moisture variation. The design of shield tunnel lining in saturated expansive ground is a difficult task. Difficulties are generally met for characterization of expansive ground and for prediction of the response for tunnel excavation and support loading. In this paper, temperature-stress coupling model is adopted to simulate swelling behavior considering different expansion rates and distribution locations by generating a volumetric strain increment measured from laboratory tests. Research results show that the swelling contact pressure is distinguished to the force tested in laboratory because of different boundary conditions. The swelling contact pressure varies with different distribution patterns of expansive ground. In the calculation of lining internal force, considering swelling pressure, the value of calculated bending moments and displacement have a great increase, but the changes of axial forces and shear forces are little.

Key words: tunnel lining; expansive ground; swelling contact pressure; numerical simulation; temperature -stress coupling model

1. INTRODUCTION

Expansive ground is clay soil or rock which exhibits significant volume changes because of mineral moisture variation. Shield tunnels constructed in these ground are subjected to large uplift forces caused by swelling pressure and it is possible to induce cracking even destruction of the lining. The design of tunnels in a saturated expansive ground is a difficult task. Difficulties are generally met for characterization of expansive ground and for prediction of the response to tunnel excavation and support loading.

The swelling mechanism is a combination of physic-chemical reaction involving water and stress relief. The physic-chemical reaction with water is usually the major contribution but it can only take place simultaneously with, or following, stress relief (ISRM, 1983). As far as the identification of the swelling potential, a wide variety of index tests have been proposed. Soil suction is the most relevant soil parameter for characterization of the swelling behavior to the lining. Due to the different boundary conditions, the swelling contact pressure is distinguished to the force tested in laboratory. To study the effects of different expansion rates and distribution locations on actual structure, temperature-stress coupling model was adopted to simulate swelling by generating a volumetric strain increment measured from laboratory tests.

2. NUMERICAL MODELING OF CONTACT PRESSURE

Expansive ground swells upon absorption of water and shrink upon evaporation of water. Humidity stress field and temperature stress field are based on the same theory, whose governing equations are similar (Xu Han, 2007). Therefore, it is feasible to simulate volumetric strain increment with the change of temperature.

There are a lot of noncontiguous problems in tunnel engineering such as interaction and discontinuities and interfaces inside the material. As a noncontiguous element, the use of contact model can simultaneously consider radial and tangential friction characteristic between the tunnel lining and expansive ground.

Supported by the National High Technology Program of China (863 Program, 2006AA11Z116); Science and Technology Program of Ministry of Railway of China (2007G036、2006G007B)

2.1 Temperature-stress Coupling Model

The total strain of the swelling soils consists of elastic and swelling components. The strain components in incremental form can be written as

$$\varepsilon = \varepsilon_e + \varepsilon_t \tag{1}$$

where the elastic strain increment (ε_e) is related to the stress increment (σ) as

$$\varepsilon_e = \frac{\sigma}{D} \tag{2}$$

where the fourth-order tensor (D) is the elasticity matrix given for elastic modulus (E) and poisson's ratio (v).The swelling strain rate in the principal direction (ε_t) is related to the humidity linear expansion coefficient (β) and variation of water content (θ), which is equivalent to the temperature increment (ΔT) and linear expansion coefficient (α) as follows,

$$\varepsilon_t = \beta\theta = \alpha \cdot \Delta T \tag{3}$$

Solving swelling force must first form a temperature field strain, and then calculate the obtained temperature-structural field coupling model. In general engineering, computing the temperature field to transient thermal analysis, and as a hot load to carry out stress analysis. Based on energy conservation theory, the matrix form of transient thermal balance equation is as

$$[C]\{T'\} + [K]\{T\} = \{Q\} \tag{4}$$

where $[K]$ is the conductivity matrix related to the thermal conductivity coefficient, convection coefficient, radiation rate and the shape factor; $[C]$ is specific heat matrix; $\{T\}$ is node temperature vector; $\{Q\}$ is node heat transfer vector.

The size of temperature expansion is controlled by the temperature rise rate. After receiving the results of temperature field, temperature change of each node element will be imposed as a hot load to stress field analysis, and then the stress of notes is obtained (Zhang Sherong, 2008).

$$\begin{cases} \sigma_x = \dfrac{E}{1-\mu^2}\left[\dfrac{\partial u}{\partial x} - z\dfrac{\partial^2 w}{\partial x^2} + \mu\dfrac{\partial v}{\partial y} - z\mu\dfrac{\partial^2 w}{\partial y^2}\right] + \dfrac{\alpha E \Delta T}{1-\mu} \\ \sigma_y = \dfrac{E}{1-\mu^2}\left[\dfrac{\partial u}{\partial y} - z\dfrac{\partial^2 w}{\partial y^2} + \mu\dfrac{\partial v}{\partial x} - z\mu\dfrac{\partial^2 w}{\partial x^2}\right] + \dfrac{\alpha E \Delta T}{1-\mu} \\ \tau_{xy} = \dfrac{E}{2(1-\mu)}\left[\dfrac{\partial u}{\partial y} + \dfrac{\partial v}{\partial x} - 2z\dfrac{\partial^2 w}{\partial x \partial y}\right] \end{cases} \tag{5}$$

where μ is poison's ratio and ΔT is temperature rise rate.

2.2 Contact Model

The segments transfer the pressure to the surrounding rock mass and are also pressed by the rock reaction force at the same time, which is considered as a contact relationship. Theoretically the contact analysis should meet with the normal contact and the tangential contact conditions, and the former can't be penetrated (Zhuang Zhuo, 2002). The relationship of contact is shown in Fig.1 (l_{AB} is the minimum distance between two contact surfaces).

In the numerical calculation, contact principle, including normal spring, shear spring and the frictional forces is derived by the penalty function method as follows,

$$l_n = \min \alpha l_{AB}, \quad \alpha = \begin{cases} 1, & (x_B - x_A)\cdot n_A \leqslant 0 \\ 0, & (x_B - x_A)\cdot n_A > 0 \end{cases} \tag{6}$$

$$|\tau| \leqslant \mu p + c \tag{7}$$

where l_n is defined as the amount of ingression and τ is equivalent shear stress.

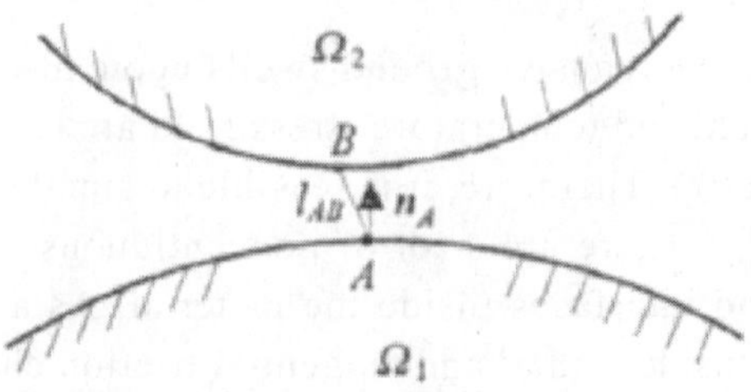

Fig.1 Relationship of contact

3. CASE STUDY

3.1 Project Overview

Recently, many tunnels have been noted for their susceptibility to swelling. The swelling problem is also encountered during the construction of metro engineering in Chengdu, as shown in Fig.2. Taking shield tunnel of No.2 metro as an example, swelling behavior was computed by using above numerical modeling. The test site was carried out along metro shield tunnel, where the overburden depth is about 10 m and the groundwater level is about 3 m below the ground surface. The geological survey report shows that free swelling ratio is 20%~80% and the swelling force is 70 kPa~125 kPa of expansive ground. Numerical simulation assumed that the swelling ratio is 50% and swelling force is 100 kPa. Tab.1 summarizes the characteristics of both the soil and the lining.

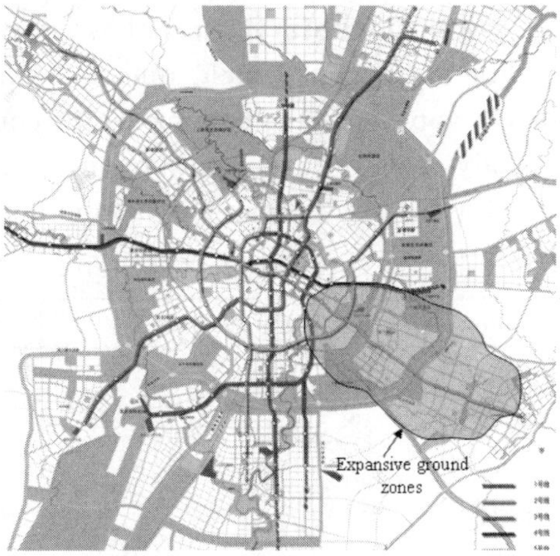

Fig.2 Chengdu Metro network with expansive ground zones

Tab.1 Properties of geometrical and structure

geometrical	unit weight γ/ (kN/m^3)	cohesion c/ (MPa)	friction angle φ/ ($^\circ$)	young's modulus E/ (MPa)	poisson's ratio v
soil	20	50	23	35	0.30
lining	25	—	—	34 500	0.25

The dimensions, numbering and arrangement of the segment are shown in Fig.3. Segment external diameter is 6 m; internal diameter is 5.4 m; width is 1.5 m; and thickness is 0.3 m. One segment ring consists of 1 key segment (K), 2 adjacent segments (B) and 3 standard segments (A). The key segment deviate 18° from vertical direction. Each segment is connected by M24 curved bolts.

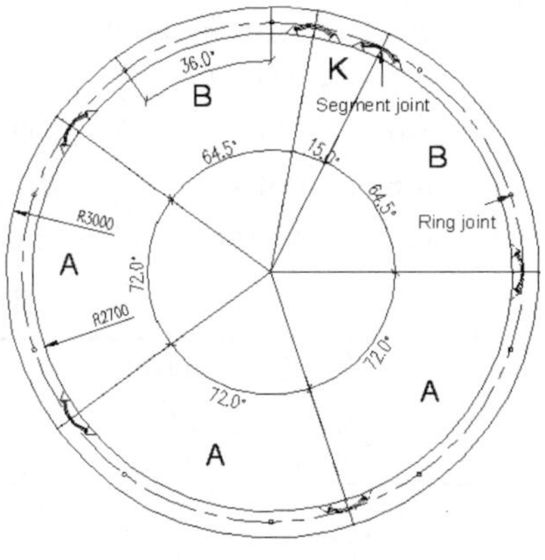

Fig.3 Segment arrangement and numbering (mm)

3.2 Finite Element Mesh

With the application of FEM, temperature-stress coupling model is applied so as to simulate the swelling behavior by generating a volumetric strain increment measured from laboratory tests in a given zone of the model. The lateral boundaries of the model are located at a distance 4D from the tunnel axis in order to minimize their interaction with the tunneling construction. The model adopts Plane42 element to simulate elastic plane strain. Element birth and death technique is applied to simulate tunnel excavation and analyze stress redistribution (Fig.4a). The contact calculation model of stratum-structure mode is built with Targe169 and Conta171 element (Fig.4b).

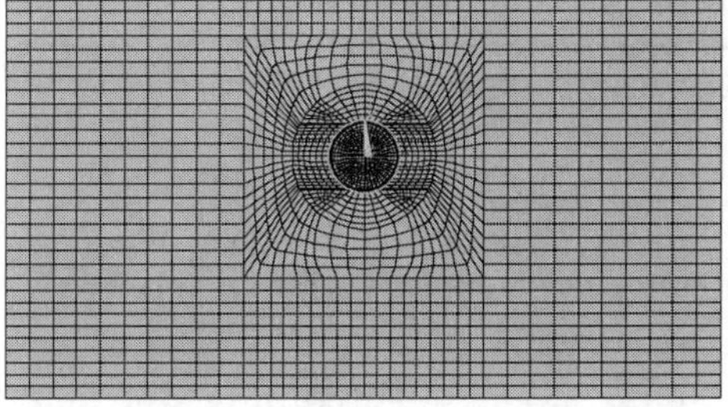

(a) Finite element mesh of numerical model

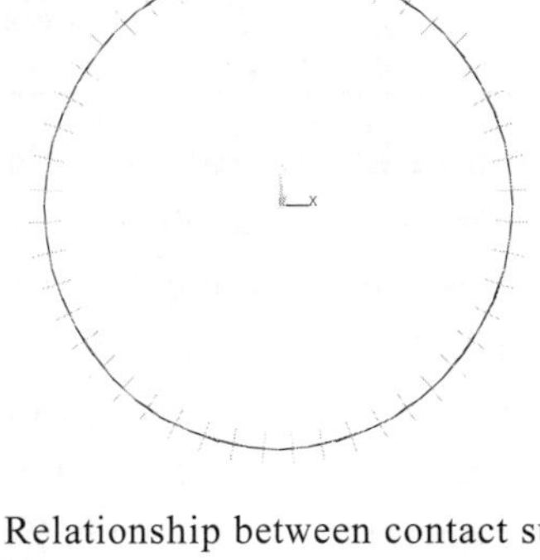

(b) Relationship between contact surfaces

Fig.4 Calculation models

3.3 Numerical Simulation of Working Types

For most metro shield tunnel, no matter what kind of computing model selected, the larger bending moment appears at the bottom, which controls the design of reinforced concrete lining section. In this paper, the analysis of swelling pressure on the shield lining should give consideration to the negative working types of the lining. Tab.2 shows the distribution of expansive ground in different areas.

Tab.2 Numerical simulation of working types

Number	Distribution pattern	Description	Number	Distribution pattern	Description
Sf_01	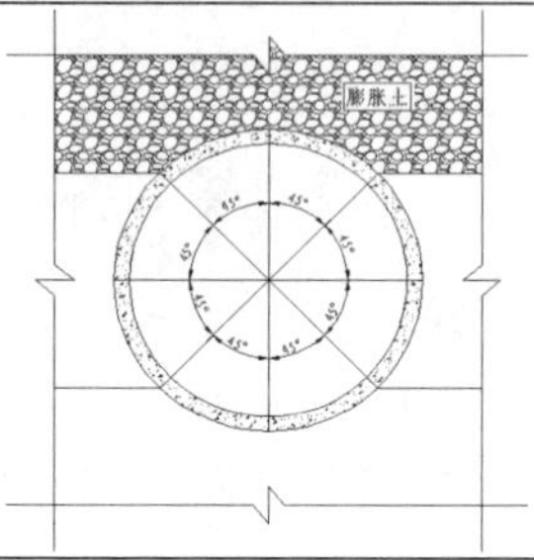	upper scope of 90°	Sf_03	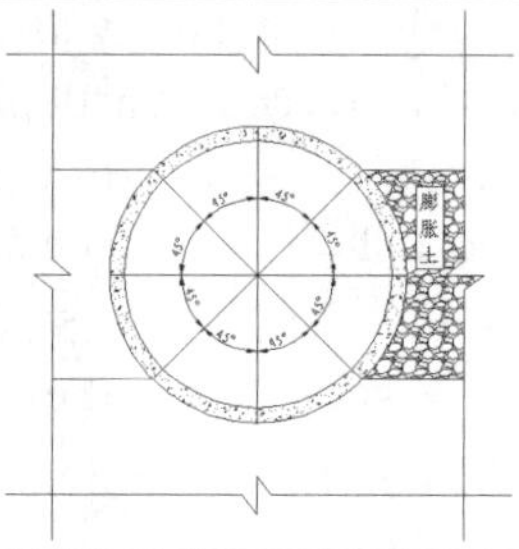	left or right scope of 90°
Sf_02	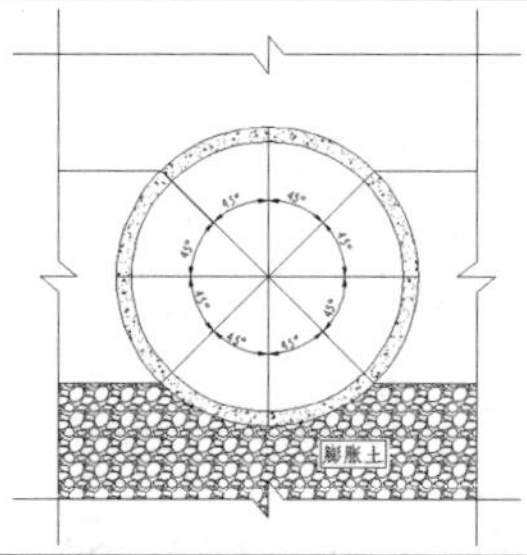	lower scope of 90°	Sf_04	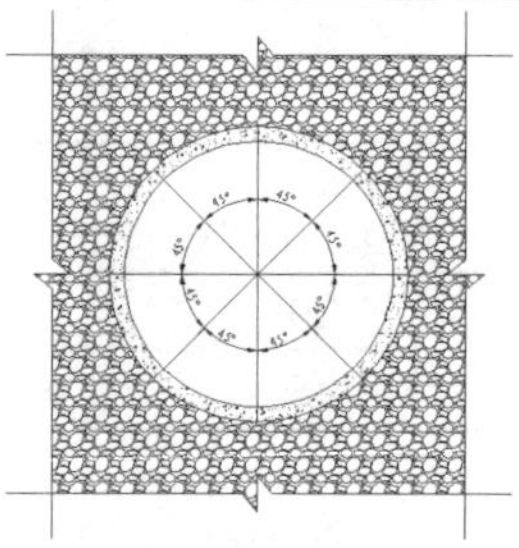	all scope

3.4 Results and Analysis

According to four kinds of working types listed in Tab.2, the results of swelling contact pressure are shown in Tab.3. The distribution modes of contact pressure along the lining segment are quadratic parabola. At the junction site between the expansive ground and non-expansive ground, swelling contact pressure appears the phenomenon of small-scale distortion. It is also clear that the results of swelling contact pressure vary with different lining stiffness and boundary conditions.

Tab.3 Results of swelling contact pressure

Number	Swelling contact pressure / (kpa)		Distribution maps	Number	Swelling contact pressure / (kPa)		Distribution maps
	max	min			max	min	
Sf_01	49.4	20.1		Sf_03	20.4	2.1	
Sf_02	28.7	10.9		Sf_04	6.0	2.8	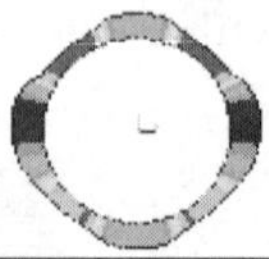

3.5 Calculation of Lining Internal Forces

The lining structure of shield tunnel is composed of several segments and joints. In the design of the cross-section forces subjected to a definite external loading, beam-spring model is usually employed (Koizumi Chun,1978 and Zhu Hehua, 1998). Two parallel segment rings are modeled, where each ring consists of beam elements representing the segments. Rotational spring elements with a rotational stiffness coefficient k_θ represent the segment joints which connect the segments in the circumferential direction, and shearing spring elements with a shearing stiffness coefficient k_s, which represents the ring joints which connect adjacent segment rings. The support of the ground that surrounds the tunnel is modeled by a continuous spring support with a coefficient of sub grade reaction k_r in a normal direction, which is not effective as the tensile spring support (Mashimo, 2003 and Zeng Dongyang, 2004). The beam-spring model is shown in Fig.5.

As mentioned above, there is a significant difference between the swelling contact pressure on the lining structure and the swelling force measured from laboratory tests. Swelling contact pressure varies with the different distribution patterns of the expansive ground. In the calculation of lining internal force, if the distribution of expansive ground is unclear, it is safe to select the most adverse condition (Sf_01). Because expansive ground is at the bottom of the tunnel lining in Chengdu metro, the calculation selects the condition of Sf_02. The value of swelling contact pressure is 30kPa. Earth pressure and swelling contact pressure pattern are shown in Fig.6.

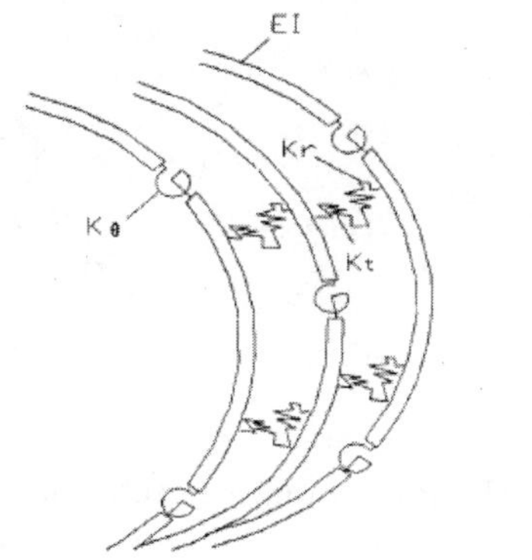

Fig.5 Beam-spring model

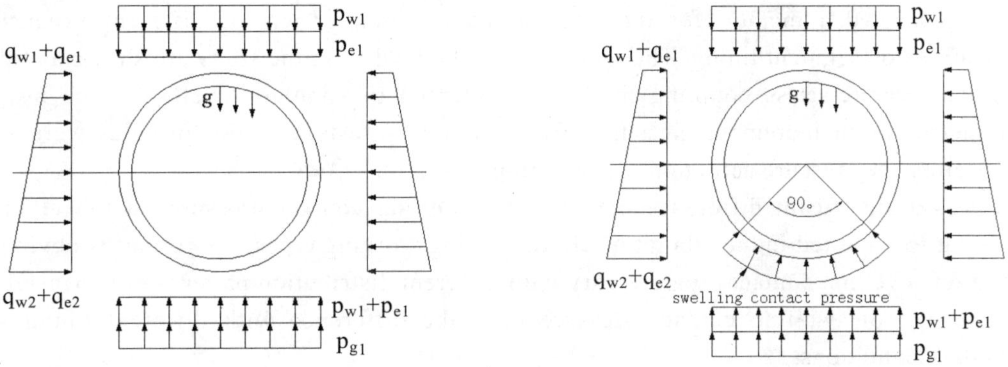

Case 1- non-swelling contact pressure

Case 2- swelling contact pressure

Fig.6 Pressure acting on segment lining

Tab.4 and Fig.7 show the comparison of lining internal forces and displacement of two cases. The calculation results are illustrated as follows: when taking consideration of swelling contact pressure, the value of the calculated bending moments and displacement is approximately 50% larger than the other case; the value of axial forces and shear forces have a slight increase.

Tab.4 Results of lining internal forces and displacement

number	Bending moment (kN · m)		Axial force (kN)		Shear force (kN)		Displacement (mm)
	max	min	max	min	max	min	
Case 1	98.2	−59.6	975	407	109.1	−104.7	2.535
Case 2	134.7	−89.0	1087	437	116.4	−142.1	3.539

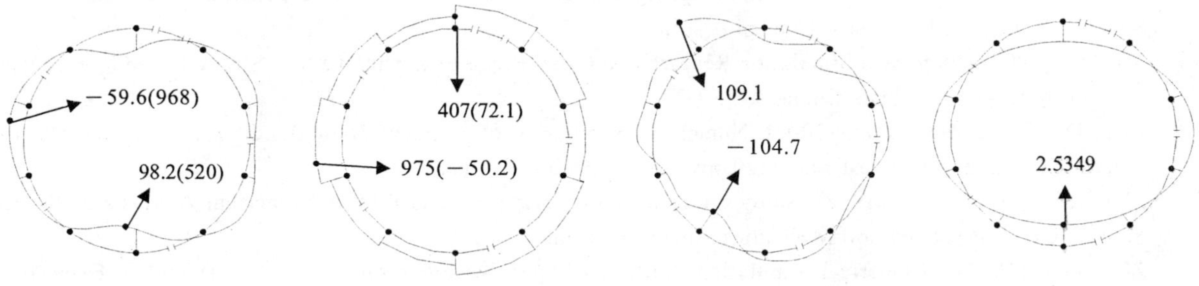

Bending moments (kN · m)　　Axial forces (kN)　　Shear forces (kN)　　Displacement (mm)

Case 1

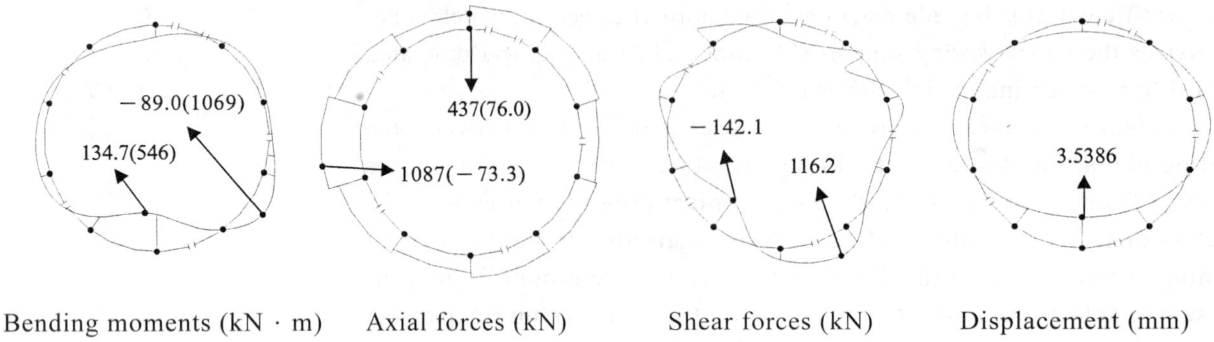

Case 2

Fig 7 Distribution maps of lining internal forces and displacement

4. CONCLUTIONS

The paper presented a method for interpreting the swelling effects of different expansion rate and distribution locations on segment lining. The main results obtained from the study are shown as follows:

(1) The temperature-stress coupling model was adopted to simulate swelling force by generating a volumetric strain increment measured from laboratory tests. Simple formulas were suggested for calculating the pressure acting on tunnel lining.

(2) There is a significant difference between the swelling contact pressure on tunnel lining and the swelling force tested in the laboratory. In the setting working types, the former is obviously less than the latter, swelling contact pressure vary with different distribution patterns of expansive ground.

(3) The results of swelling contact pressure have the difference with different lining stiffness and boundary conditions.

(4) In accordance with the design of the segment lining of a transit shield tunnel, the paper adopts beam-spring model to calculate bending moments, axial forces, shearing forces and displacements in two cases. When taking consideration of swelling pressure, the value of the calculated bending moments and displacement are approximately 50% larger than the other case; axial forces and shear forces have a slight increase.

From these results, it will be desirable to take great account of the influence of swelling contact pressure. The reinforcement must be enforced to control the development of lining cracks in the design.

References:

[1] Chen, F.H. (1988), Foundations on Expansive Soils. Development in Geotechnical Engineering, New York, USA.

[2] Isrm. (1983), "Characterisation of Swelling Rock", Commission on Swelling Rock. Pergamon Press. Oxford, U.K.

[3] Koizumi Chun, Murakami Pok Chi. (1978), Plan of the Dutch Resistance Agencies a lie Against Allah [C], Civil Society Sets Papers Report, Japan.

[4] Mashimo, H. (2003), Evaluation of the Load on Shield Tunnel Lining in Gravel, Tunnelling and Underground Space Technology, Tsukuba, Japan.

[5] Su Zongxian, He Chuan. (2007), Shell-Spring-Contact Model for Load and Structure Interaction, Journal of Southwest Jiaotong University, Chengdu, China.

[6] Xu Han. (2007), Numerical Simulation Research on Canal Slope of Expansive Soil Strengthened by Geogrid, Rock and Soil Mechanics, Wuhan, China.

[7] Zeng Dongyang, He Chuan. (2004), Numerical Simulation of Segment Joint Bending Stiffness of Metro Shield Tunnel, Journal of Southwest Jiaotong University, Chengdu, China.

[8] Zhu Hehua, Tao Lubin. (1998), Study on Two Beam-Spring Models for the Numerical Analysis of Segments in Shield Tunnel, Rock and Soil Mechanics, Shanghai, China.

[9] Zhou kun. (2007), "Numerical Simulation Study On Expansive Force Of Lining For Tunnel In Expansive soil", Southwest Jiaotong University Master Degree Thesis, Chengdu, China.

[10] Zhang Sherong. (2008), Finite Element Analysis of Ice Thermal Expansive Pressure Acting on Aqueduct Structure, Journal of Tianjin University, Tianjin, China.

[11] Zhuang Zhuo. (2002), "Nonlinear Finite Elements for Continua and Structures", Tsinghua University Press, Beijing, China, pp.467-483, 495-509.

Bio-data:

Chuan HE was born in June 1964 and obtained the Dr. Eng. in the Waseda University. Currently, Dr. HE is the director of Department of Underground Engineering in Southwest Jiaotong University, the doctor supervisor, the professor of Changjiang Scholar Programm, Ministry of Education of PRC. He has been engaging in the teaching and research of tunnel engineering for many years. He specializes in design theory of modern shield tunnel, structural design of subway, construction technique of tunnel under complicated condition, tunnel ventilation control system.

Tel: +86-28-87601932

E-mail: chuanhe21@163.com

DESIGN OF COMPOSITE SEGMENT FOR UNDERGROUND DISCHARGE CHANNEL

Wenjun ZHANG[1], Atsushi KOIZUMI[2]

[1]*Advanced Research Institute for Science and Engineering, Waseda University, Tokyo 169-8555, Japan;*
[2]*Department of Civil and Environmental Engineering, Faculty of Science and Engineering, Waseda University, Tokyo 169-8555, Japan*

Abstract: Composite segment has been widely used in deep shield tunnel. However, the present design for composite segment based on the theory of reinforced concrete cannot appropriately reflect the excellent properties of composite segment. Therefore, the rational design method of composite segment is required. In this paper, the proposed mechanical model is used to design the most complicated composite segment called as closed composite segment for underground discharge channel based on the limit state design method. As a result, the reduction of segment thickness is obtained using Closed-composite segment and this indicates that composite segment is suitable for decreasing muck, construction period and the outside diameter of the shield machine. In general, the costs of construction, risk, and maintenance will be decreased

Key words: composite segment; confinement effect; Slip effect; limit state design method

1. INTRODUCTION

It is well known that the segments production cost accounts for a large part of the total shield tunnel construction cost. One of the effective methods is to design the segments more efficiently for reducing the shield tunnel construction cost. The common design method for shield segments is to determine firstly the load acting on the tunnel lining, then determine the material and the cross sectional dimensions of the segments by structural calculations. Therefore, it is important to evaluate the load accurately. In structural calculation, the stress in each part of a segment is usually calculated with a design model, by taking account of the structural property of segmental lining and interaction between the ground and lining. According to the calculation result of member forces, the safety of the most critical sections must be checked using the limit state design method or the allowable stress design method. The safety factors should be based on the ground loading and defined in accordance with the structural requirements and codes (eg. national standard specification for design and construction of concrete structures). Therefore, construction procedure and performance of underground structures should be linked with the safety factors.

The present design for composite segment based on the theory of reinforced concrete cannot appropriately reflect the excellent properties of composite segment and causes the production cost of composite segment increasing. For decreasing the production the production cost of composite segment increasing, it is necessary to give a rational design of composite segment based on the studies of mechanical behavior. In this paper, a rational design method of composite segment will be described based on the previous study on composite segment of the authors.

In order to get an overview of the proposed design method of composite segment, the following sections include calculation of loads, structural calculation, and check of safety of segmental lining.

2. CALCULATION OF LOADS

In general, To take the relationship of the outer diameter of a tunnel and overburden, soil condition, and ground water level effects into account, the design earth pressure and water pressure are calculated by guideline of design segment of JSCE[1].

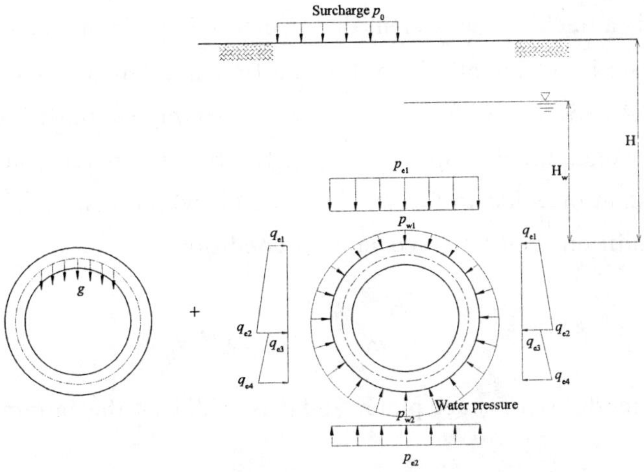

Fig.1 Model of calculation of the loads

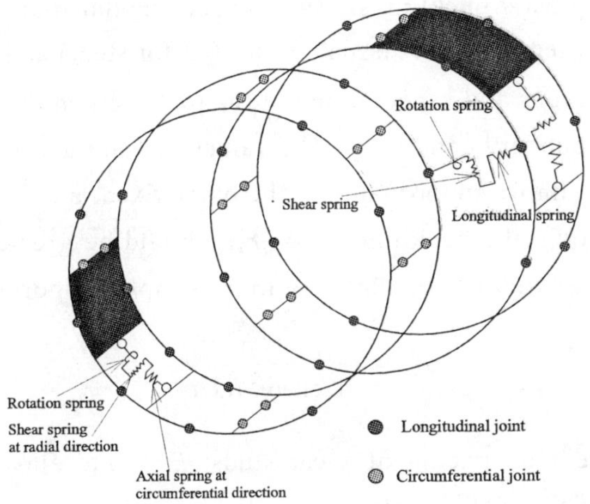

Fig.2 Structural models of the segmental lining

However, the subsurface of big cities is already crowded with underground facilities such as railroads, and tunnels for electricity, gas, communications, sewage and drainage, and conduits. For this reason, newly constructed tunnels must be constructed deeper year by year in order to avoid those conduits. Therefore, those tunnels always locate in alternation of soil hard strata, and are below ground water table. Underground water will fill around the tunnel, because the holes are left in back grouting procedure. It can be seen that the modeling method for the earth and pore water pressures is rational shown in Fig.1.

3. STRUCTURAL CALCULATION

As present, the uniform rigidity ring model has been applied. The circumferential joint is assumed to have the same rigidity as that of the segment, the moment for the design of joint is overestimated, and that occurring at the segment is not calculated correctly. Therefore, it is difficult to design the bending moment at the joint area.

For the above reason, the beam-spring model and the shell-spring were proposed and applied in design of segmental lining nowadays. In the beam spring model, segments are modeled using beams. The circumferential joints are modeled using the rotation of springs and their rigidities are expressed by the constants of the springs concerning the bending moments. The longitudinal joints are modeled using shear springs to simulate the relative displacement occurring between the two adjacent rings in the longitudinal direction. However, the bending moment distribution along the width of a ring is non-uniform due to the split effect of the longitudinal joints. Therefore, the shell-spring model shown in Fig.2 is applied, in which tunnel lining is modeled using shell, and the joints are modeled using springs.

4. CHECK OF SAFETY OF SEGMENTAL LINING

According to the calculation result of member forces, the safety of the most critical sections must be checked using the limit state design method or the allowable stress design method. These are as follows:

1) Section with the maximum positive moment.
2) Section with the maximum negative moment.
3) Section with the maximum axial force.

The safety of the lining against the thrust force of the shield jacks should be checked. Meanwhile, Durability (anticorrosive performance) and cutoff performance should be checked.

5. DESIGN OF COMPOSITE SEGMENT

In the design of composite segment, the following design rules must be ensured.

5.1 Width to Thickness Ratio

Elastic buckling stress for a rectangular plate subjected to an axial compression can be computed by Eq. (1), where ν is a Poisson's ratio (0.3 for steel) and k is a bucking coefficient that is determined from boundary conditions and aspect ratios of the plate. When the plate is sufficiently long, the coefficient k depends only on the boundary conditions. The values of k are given as 4.0, 5.42, and 6.97 for both edges simply supported, one edge simply supported with the other fixed, and both edges fixed, respectively [2]. In order to prevent elastic buckling, the buckling stress, F_{cr}, should be greater than or equal to the yield stress, f_{sy}, which results in the limit of width to thickness ratio for simple support conditions and for fixed support condition:

$$F_{cr} = k\frac{\pi^2 E_s}{12(1-\nu^2)(s/t)^2} \tag{1}$$

where s is spacing of shear studs; E_s is the elastic modulus of steel plate; and t is taken as the minimum thickness of skin plates.

Zhang[3] studied that stress of the buckled top skin plate still increases as the applied load increases, and is greater than the post-buckling stress calculated by Eq.(2). Considering the design tendency to safety side, according to Guideline of buckling design of JSCE code [4], the post-buckling stress f'_{ud} is calculated as:

$$f'_{ud} = (t/s)\sqrt{E_s f_{sy}} \tag{2}$$

5.2 Confined Concrete

Montoya et al.[5] proposed a concrete confinement model for steel tube confined concrete is adopted in limit state. The stress σ_c is related to the strain ε_c using the following formula:

$$\sigma_c = \frac{f_{cc}}{A\left(\dfrac{\varepsilon_c}{f_{cc}}\right)^2 - B\left(\dfrac{\varepsilon_c}{f_{cc}}\right) + C + 1.0} \tag{3}$$

where f_{cc} is peak axial stress for confined concrete; A is shape factor; $B = 2\dfrac{A}{E_{\mathrm{sec}}}$; $C = \dfrac{A}{E_{\mathrm{sec}}^2}$; $E_{\mathrm{sec}} = \dfrac{f_{cc}}{\varepsilon_{cc}}$; and ε_{cc} is the strain corresponding to f_{cc}.

5.3 Shear Stud and Steel Plate

Shear stud can be bonded to the steel element using an automatic welding procedure. The most important dimension is the diameter of the shank d_{sh} which varies from about 13 mm to about 22 mm. The diameter of the head is usually about 1.5 d_{sh}, and the height of the connector is usually greater than 4 d_{sh}, in order to ensure that the connector does not pull out of the concrete element. The weld collar has a diameter of about 1.3 d_{sh}, and a height of about 0.3 d_{sh}. The minimum spacing of connectors in a composite segment is controlled by this concrete bearing zone because it is necessary to ensure that these zones do not overlap, otherwise the dowel strengths of the connectors will be reduced. This is achieved in design through detailing rules which require that the longitudinal spacing of stud shear connectors is greater than about 5 d_{sh}, and that the lateral spacing is greater than about 4 d_{sh}. The distance from the edge of the stud to the edge of the steel plate is greater than about d_{sh} [6].

The design axial capacity and the design bending capacity of the member cross-sections subjected to axial load and bending moment can be calculated using the state of stress and strain distribution shown in Fig.3. M_{ud}, N'_{ud} can be calculated by Zhang and Koizumi proposed method [7-9].

The number of shear studs can be calculated using Eqs.(4) and (5). Axial force and shear force of members can be determined based ultimate limit state shown in Fig.4 and Fig.5.

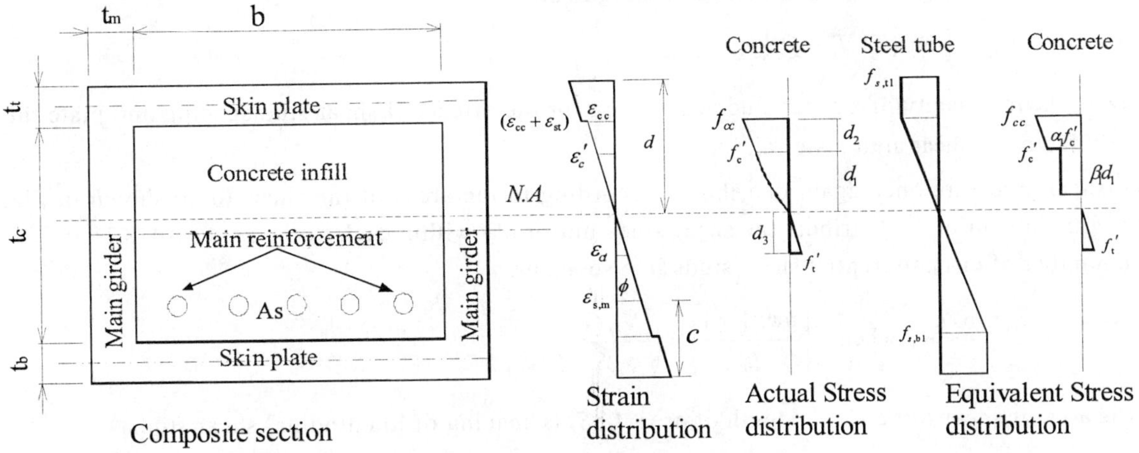

Fig.3 Transition of ultimate limit states for Closed-composite segment [7]

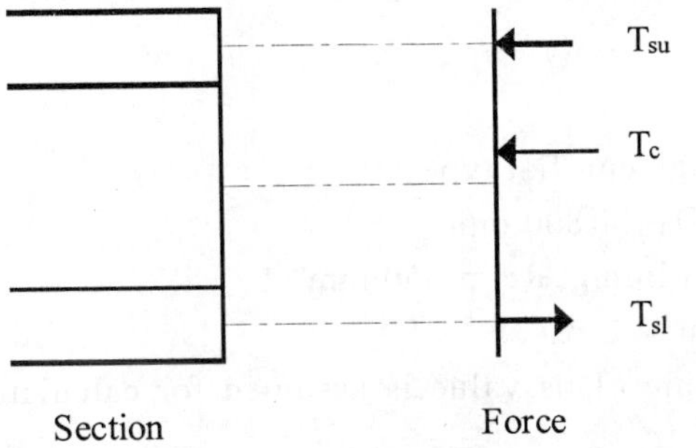

Fig.4 Resultant axial force in each element

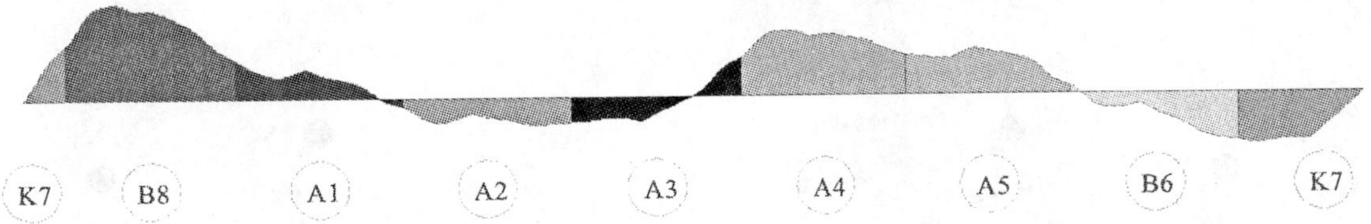

(a) Segmental ring arrangement

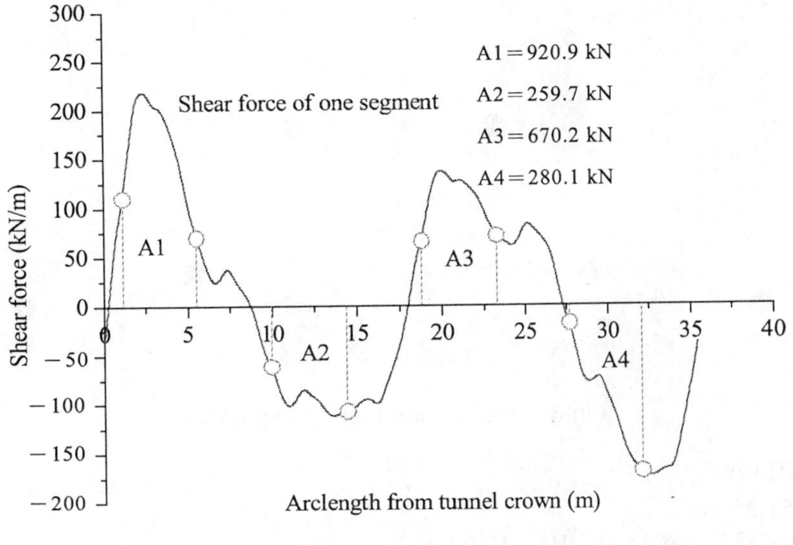

(b) Shear force distribution

Fig.5 Distribution of connectors in segment with distributed loads

The numbers of longitudinal shear studs in a segment:

$$N_{SL} = \{\min(T_{su}, T_c)/Q_u\}\gamma_m \tag{4}$$

where Q_u is shear capacity of a shear stud accounting for the effects of shear stud spacing and plate thickness; γ_m is safety factor of shear stud material.

The shear studs are once again distributed according to the areas of the shear force shown in Fig.5. It is also standard convention to distribute the shear studs uniformly within each of the zones A1-K7.

The number of circumferential shear studs in a segment:

$$N_{SC} = \frac{L_i}{S_L} \quad \text{when} \quad \left\{\frac{\max(A_i)}{L_i}\right\} = \left(\frac{N_{SL}Q_u}{\gamma_m S_L}\right) \tag{5}$$

where A_i is area of shear force; L_i is length of area A_i; S_L is spacing of longitudinal shear studs.

6. DESIGN EXAMPLE

The design example is the Underground Discharge Channel. The Closed-composite segment is designed in the following design example.

6.1 Dimensions of Segment

Type of segment: Composite segment, flat type

Diameter of segmental lining: D_0=11 800 mm

Radius of centroid of segmental lining: Rc=5 650 mm

Width of segment: B=2 000 mm

Thickness of segment: t=250 mm (This value is assumed for calculating loads acting on the segmental lining)

Assembling type of segments: Staggered pattern (Fig.6)

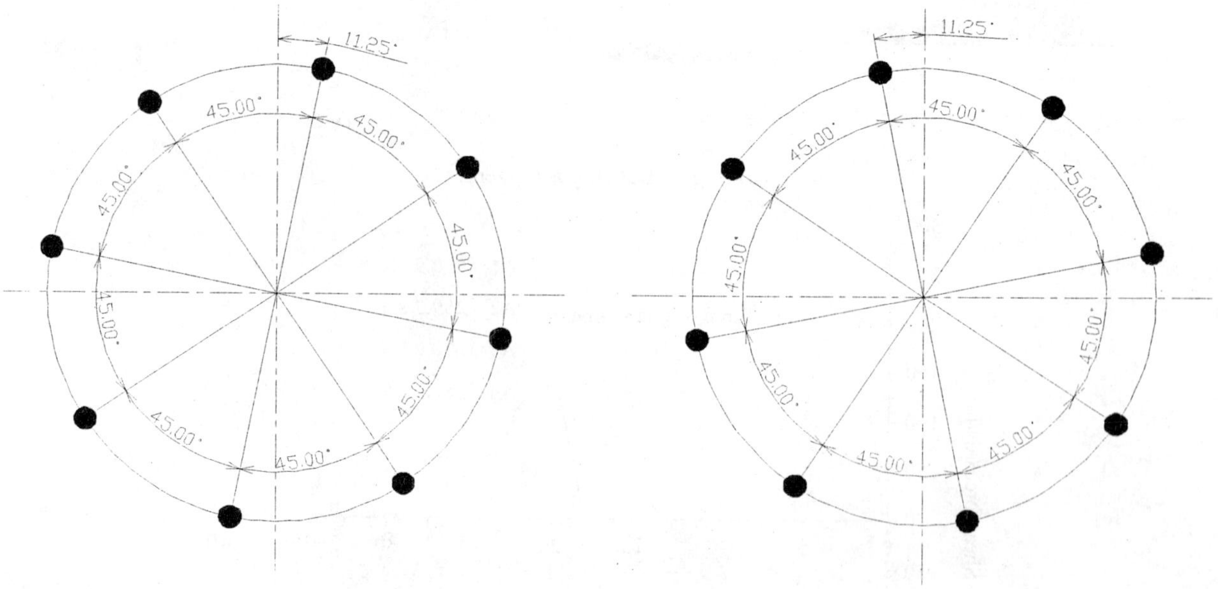

Fig.6 Assembling type of segments

6.2 Ground Conditions

Overburden: H=51.35 m

Groundwater table: G.L. − 6.33 m Hw=45.02 m

Surcharge: P_0=3.1×10×1.0=31 kN/m^2 (Height of flood=3.1 m)

Soil condition: Alternation of soil strata (Clay, Sandy, and Gravel)

Unit weight of soil, submerged unit weight of soil, and angle of internal friction of soil, and *N* value are shown in Fig.7.

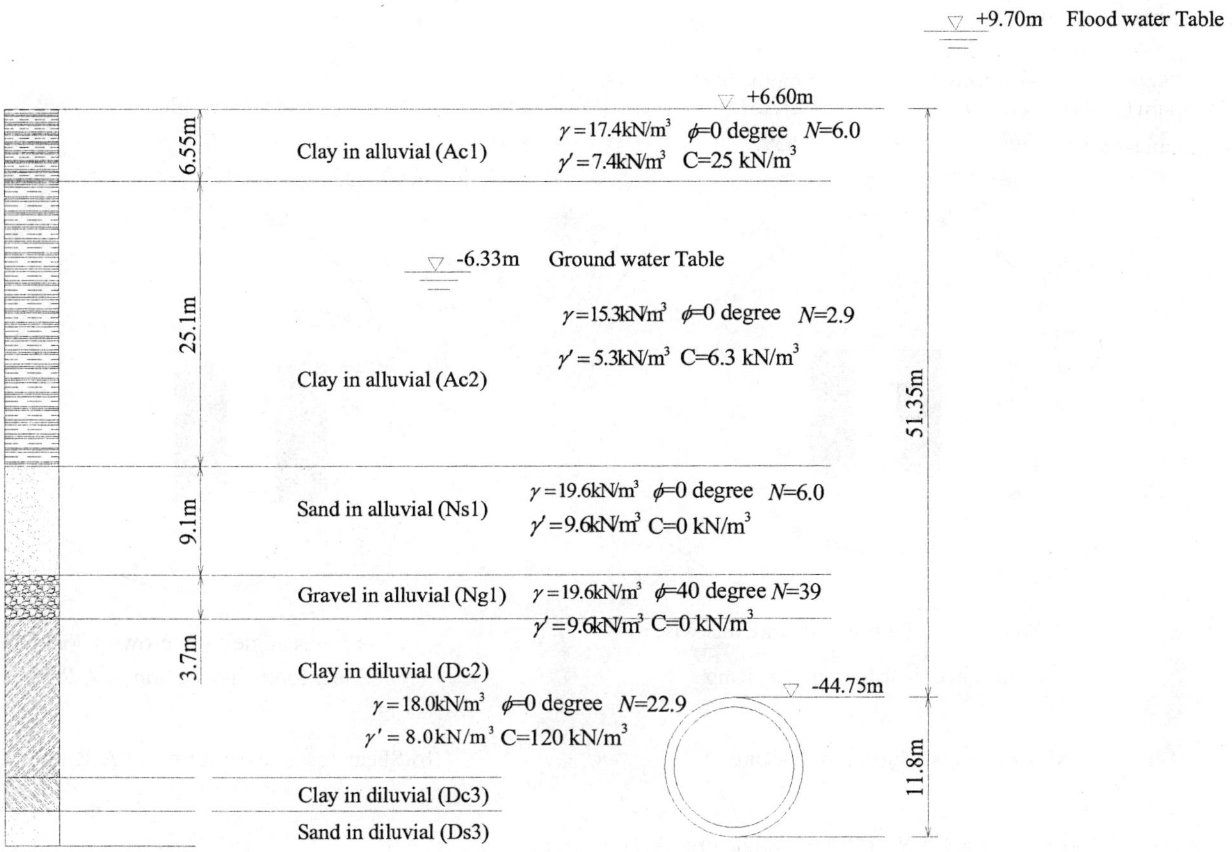

Fig.7 Ground condition

6.3 Load Conditions

The forces applying on tunnel lining are calculated based on combined load case shown in Tab.1.

Tab.1 Combined load case

Load case	Tunnel condition	Earth pressure		Groundwater table		Inner water pressure		Self weight	Subgrade reaction
		Large	small	High	Low	Normal	Abnormal		
1	No inner water pressure	×		×				×	×
2	No inner water pressure	×			×			×	×
3	Normal inner water pressure	×			×	×		×	×
4	Normal inner water pressure		×		×	×		×	×
5	Abnormal inner water pressure	×			×		×	×	×
6	Abnormal inner water pressure		×		×		×	×	×

6.4 Calculation of Member Forces

The member forces are calculated by Shell-Spring model shown in Fig.2. The segments are assembled in a staggered pattern shown in Fig.6.

Fig.8 and Fig.9 show the distributions of bending moment, axial force, and shear force in A-Ring and B-Ring, respectively.

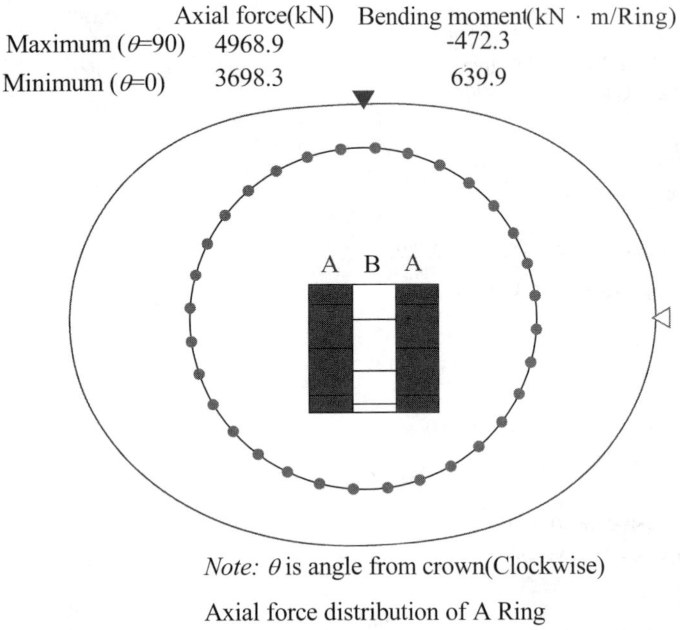

(a) Axial force distribution of A-Ring

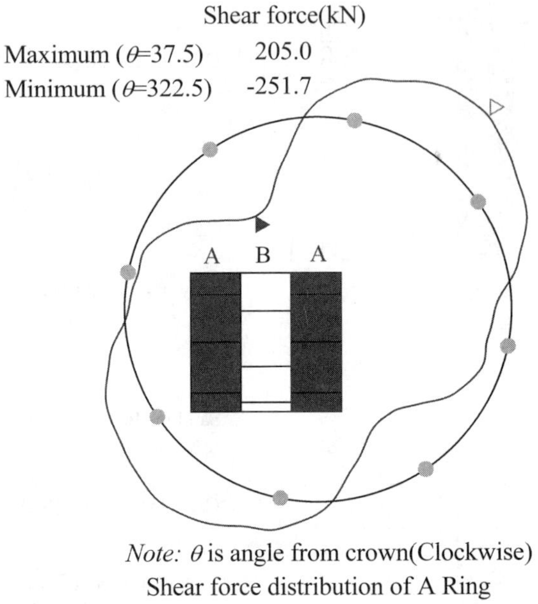

(b) Shear force distribution of A-Ring

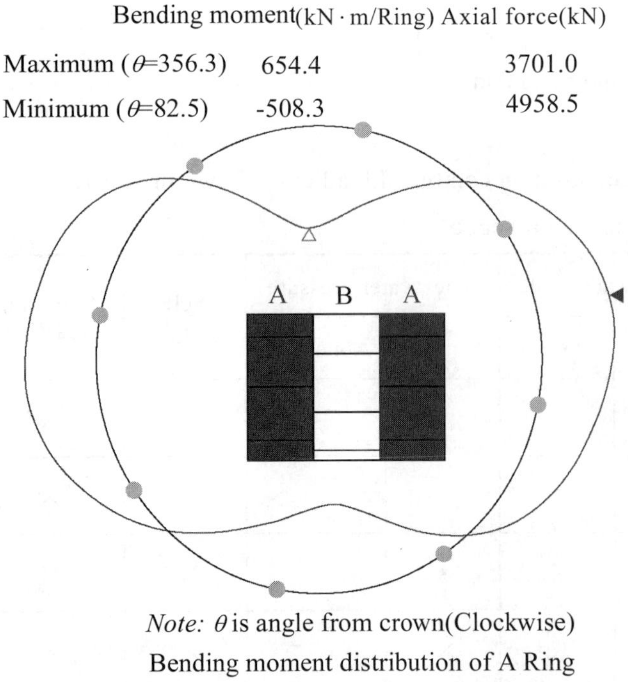

(c) Moment distribution of A-Ring

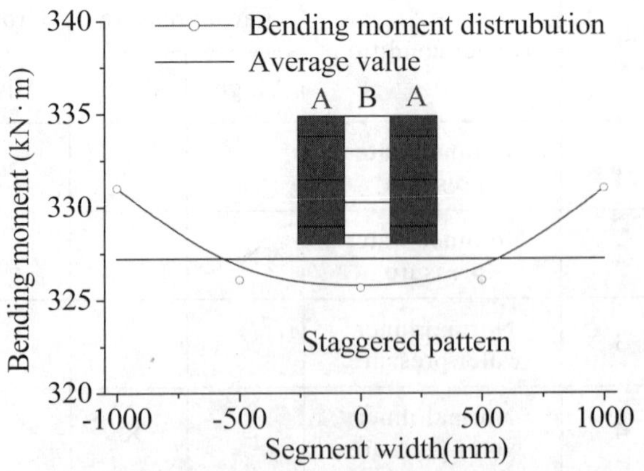

(d) Moment distribution along width of A-Ring

Fig.8 Distributions of member forces of A-Ring in circumferential direction

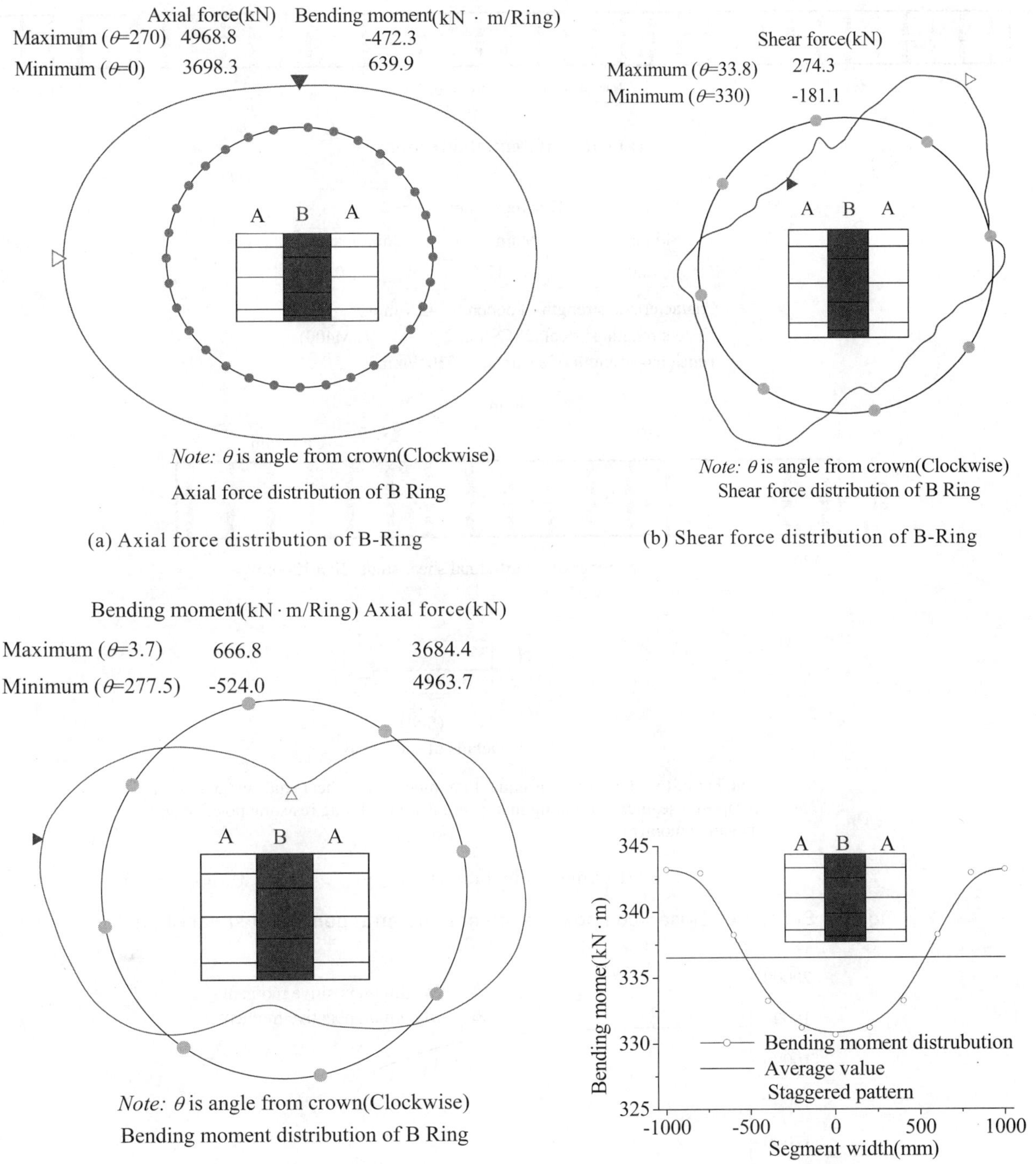

(a) Axial force distribution of B-Ring (b) Shear force distribution of B-Ring

(c) Moment distribution of B-Ring (d) Moment distribution along width of B-Ring

Fig.9 Distributions of member forces of B-Ring in circumferential direction

Fig.10 shows the design cross-section of Closed-composite segment based on the previous rules.

Axial force-moment interaction diagram of cross-section is described by Fig.11. Therefore, as a rule, the safety for combined axial load and bending moment is examined by confirming that the point (M_d, N_d) is located inside of the (M_{ud}, N'_{ud}) curve. It can be seen that both Section A and Section B are safe.

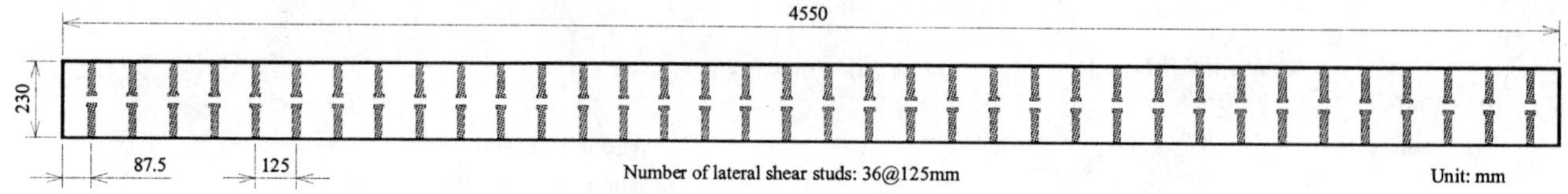

(a) Circumferential direction

Thickness(mm)		
Skin plate	Main girder	Joint plate
6.0	12.0	12.0

Characteristic strength of concrete: 42N/mm2
Yield strength of steel: 235N/mm2 (SM400)
Tensional strength of shear stud: 530N/mm2

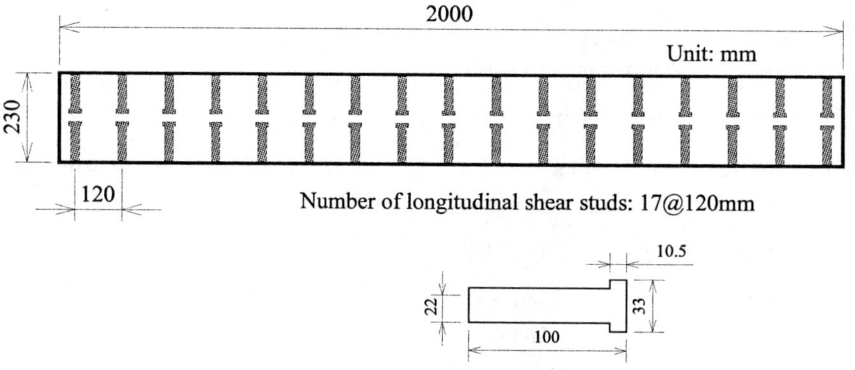

(S=4)
Details of shear stud

Note: Number of top shear studs is equal to number of top shear studs in the design of composite segment for taking in accout the tunnel lining resisting positive and negative moment

(b) Longitudinal direction

Fig.10 Section of Closed-composite segment and arrangement of shear studs

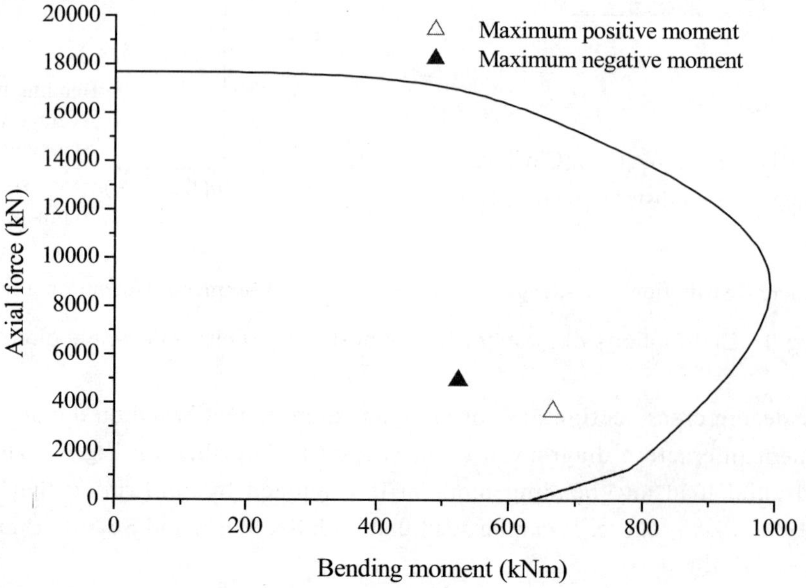

Fig.11 Axial force-moment interaction diagram of Closed-composite segment

7. CONCLUSION

The reduction of segment thickness is obtained using Closed-composite segment and this indicates that Closed-composite segment is suitable for decreasing muck, construction period and the outside diameter of the shield machine. In general, the costs of construction, risk, and maintenance will be decreased

References:

[1] Japanese Society of Civil Engineers (JSCE). Standard specifications for tunneling-2006, Shield tunnels, 2007.

[2] Galambos TV. Guide to stability design criteria for metal structures.5th ed. New York: Wiley, 1998.

[3] Wenjun, Zhang. Study on mechanical behavior and design of composite segment for shield tunnel, Ph.D. Dissertation, Waseda Univ., Tokyo, 2009.

[4] Japanese Society of Civil Engineers (JSCE). Buckling design guideline, 2005.

[5] Montoya, E. Behavior and analysis of confined concrete, Ph.D. Dissertation, Univ. of Toronto, Toronto, 2003.

[6] Deric J Oehlers, Mark A Bradford. Composite steel and concrete structural members, UK: Pergamon, Elsevier Science, 1995.

[7] Wenjun, Zhang, Atsushi, Koizumi. Flexural behavior of composite segment, Journal of JSCE, 2009, Vol.65, No2,246-263. (In Japanese)

[8] Wenjun, Zhang, Atsushi, Koizumi. Flexural rigidity of closed composite segment, Proceedings of the International Symposium on Tunnelling for Urban Development, ITA, Pattaya, Thailand, 2007, pp.205-212.

[9] Wenjun, Zhang, Atsushi, Koizumi. Stiffness and deflection of composite segment for shield tunnel, Tunnelling Technology & The Environment, TAC, Canada, 2008, pp.95-105.

Bio-data:

Wenjun ZHANG joined Waseda University in Japan in 2005 to initiate research, as a Research Associate in Faculty of Science and Engineering. He joined Waseda University in Japan in 2008 as a researcher in Advanced Research Institute for Science and Engineering (RISE). He joined Nippon Civic Consulting Engineers Co.,Ltd in 2009.

Wenjun ZHANG is a reviewer of Journal of Structural Engineering of ASCE international journal (USA) and Tunneling and Underground Space Technology international journal (UK).

His academic pursuits are fundamental and applied research of structural engineering mechanics and tunneling technology, including mechanical behavior of composite structure under combined loads, risk management, drilling technology and support of tunnel and caverns in complex grounds, numerical modeling.

STUDY ON CRACK OPENING DISPLACEMENT OF SHIELD TUNNEL IN LONGITUDINAL DIRECTION

Zhiqiang ZHANG, Chuan HE, Maiqing QIAO

Department of Underground Engineering, Southwest Jiaotong University, Chengdu 610031, Sichuan, China

Abstract: Compared with the case of the cast in situ concrete with a uniform bending rigidity of NATM tunnel, the rigidity of shield tunnel lining composed of segments connected by bolts in longitudinal direction and transverse direction are quite different. The increasing attention is focused on the likelihood of water leakage caused by the longitudinal excessive deformation of undersea tunnel i.e. excessive crack opening displacement in view of its far less longitudinal rigidity. In this paper, the 3D numerical analyses are firstly conducted to investigate the distribution ranges of longitudinal uneven deformation. Based on this, taking the differential settlements as displacement boundary, the crack opening displacements of the aimed shield tunnel in longitudinal direction are studied by establishing longitudinal shell-spring-contact model. The results provide a reference for the lining longitudinal design of Nanjing highway tunnel across Yangtze River.

Key words: shield tunnel; longitudinal deformation; COD (crack opening displacement); 3D numerical analyses

1. INTRODUCTION

Nowadays shield tunneling is one of the popular tunneling methods, especially in increasingly bad and difficult undersea geological conditions. Usually, shield tunnel is designed by only considering the lateral deformation. However, the increasing cases show that the behavior of deformation and load bearing of shield tunnel in soft ground are influenced not only laterally in cross section but also longitudinally. The measured records of operated metros in Shanghai show potential damage of shield structure due to the longitudinal settlement, especially the uneven settlement (H.W. Huang et al., 2006). Water leakage due to excessive crack opening displacement has result in deterioration of tunnel structure and shortening of the tunnel life. Based on the fact that the shield tunnel is commonly regarded as one dimension and thin long structure with many weak points on the longitudinal and transverse direction, the model that the rings and the joints in the longitudinal direction are regarded as a continuous beam is often utilized to analyze roughly longitudinal deformation of the tunnel in most subway shield tunnel design. Researchers such as Chen and Wen (2003), Lin (2001), Zang and Huang (2003) can benefit from the simplified equivalent model in considering the cross section of subway shield tunnel with 5.2m nominal diameter. Unfortunately, the simplified equivalent model can not adapt to the case of large section shield tunnel such as Nanjing highway tunnel across Yangtze River with 14.45 m external diameter, that is because the size effect in cross section is not permitted to be neglected. In deed, the shield tunnel lining behaves three dimensionally.

By establishing a three dimensional elastic equivalent rigidity model for the whole shield tunnel, the longitudinal uneven deformation rule and mechanical characteristics of super long shield tunnel can be generally obtained at the cost of less modeling effort and computational time. Furthermore, through establishing the longitudinal shell-spring-contact model which reflects the joint effects of shield tunnel segment both in radial and longitudinal, and taking the differential settlements above as the following displacement boundary, the crack opening displacements of the aimed shield tunnel in longitudinal direction are reached. As a result, the safety of shield tunnel due to the longitudinal uneven deformation is given.

Supported by the National High Technology Program of China (863 Program, 2006AA11Z116); Science and Technology Program of Ministry of Railway of China (2007G036、2006G007B)

2. DESCRIPTION OF THE WORK

Nanjing Changjiang tunnel, as the secondary highway tunnel across Yangtze River, is presently the largest section shield tunnel in China. The highway tunnel across Yangtze River starts from the north end of Puzhu Road, extends towards south along North Bingjiang Road, passes through Yangtze River to Mei Zizhou entrance, leaves Youcha Bridge to pass through South Bingjiang Road, and finally enters Weiqi Road. The total length of main line is 5 853 m. The mileage of shield tunnel is K3+600~K6+590, i.e. the length is 2 990 m. Fig.1 shows Geologic Profile of Nanjing Changjiang tunnel.

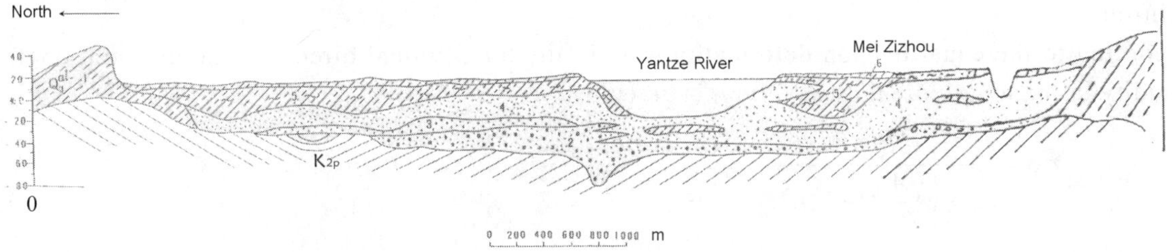

Fig.1 Geologic Profile of Nanjing Changjiang tunnel

(Q_3^{al}): 1. Brown Silty Clay 2. Gravel and Cobble Layer 3. Gray Mid Sand and Coarse Sand
(Q4al): 4. Gray Silty and Fine Sand 5. Gray and Brown Organic Soft Clay in Brown Silty Clay 6. Brown Silty Clay

3. MODELING IN THE LONGITUDINAL DIRECTION OF SHIELD TUNNEL

3.1 Presentation of the Equivalent Rigidity Model in the Longitudinal Direction

In the longitudinal structure design of shield tunnel, the segment lining is simulated by the beam-spring model. In order to achieve the deformation characteristics and structural performance in the longitudinal direction of super long segmental tunnel linings, a realistic consideration of these issues is presentation of the equivalent rigidity model in the longitudinal direction. For the equivalent rigidity models, considering segments are simulated by the beam-spring structure model in which the beam elements and spring elements are positioned alternately, the beam element for the segment is estimated by the equivalent longitudinal tension-compression rigidity, the equivalent shear rigidity and the equivalent bending rigidity (He Chuan 1999), as shown in Fig.2～Fig.4.

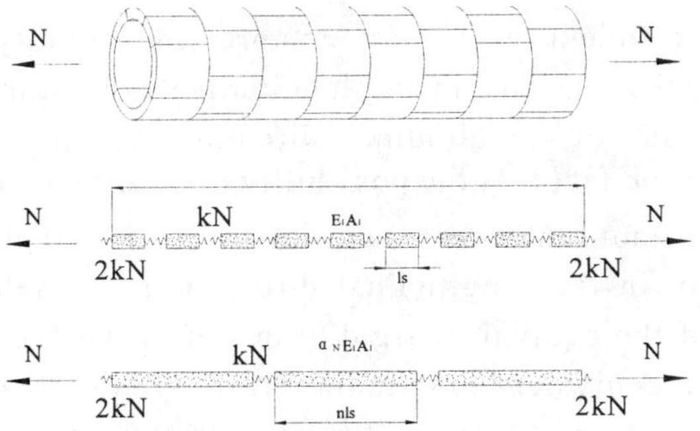

Fig.2 Calculation of the equivalent tension-compression rigidity in the longitudinal direction

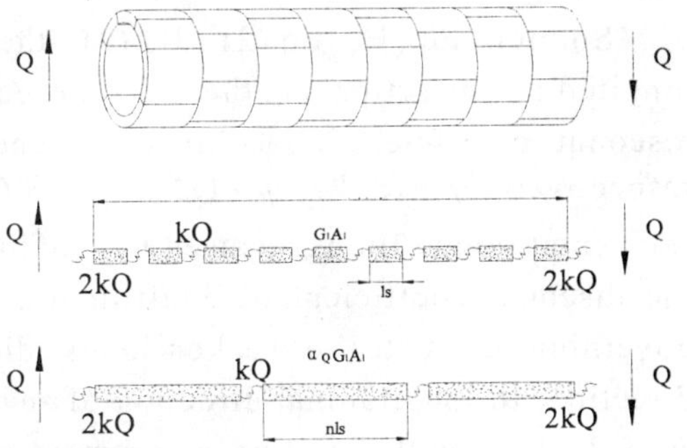

Fig.3 Calculation of the equivalent shear rigidity in the longitudinal direction

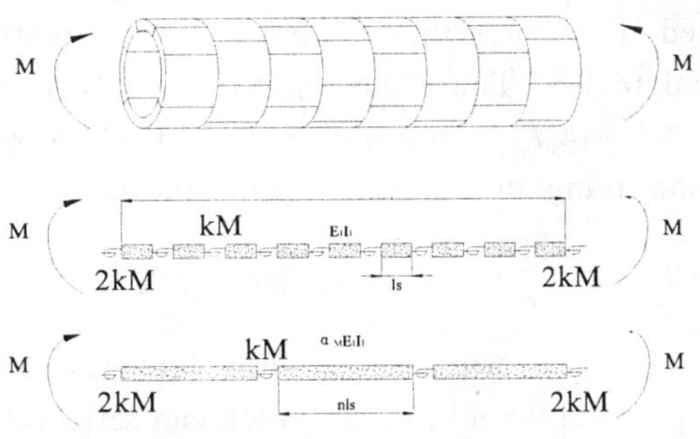

Fig.4 Calculation of the equivalent bending rigidity in the longitudinal direction

According to the equal tension deformation rule in the longitudinal direction, the discount coefficient of tension-compression rigidity in the longitudinal direction η_N is given by

$$\eta_N = \frac{K_u}{K_u + \frac{E_c A_c}{B}(1 - 1/n)} \qquad (1)$$

Where E_c, A_c, B, n designate the Young's modulus of reinforcement concrete segment, cross section area, width of the segment, rings of segment, respectively. While the length of segmental tunnel linings is enough long, n goes to infinite.

According to the equal tension deformation rule in the longitudinal direction, the discount coefficient of shear rigidity in the longitudinal direction η_Q is given by

$$\eta_Q = \frac{K_v}{K_v + \frac{G_c A_c}{B}(1 - 1/n)} \qquad (2)$$

Where G_c designates the shear modulus of reinforcement concrete segment.

According to the equal tension deformation rule in the longitudinal direction, the discount coefficient of equivalent bending rigidity in the longitudinal direction η_M is given by

$$\eta_M = \frac{K_{\theta 1}}{K_{\theta 1} + \frac{E_c I_c}{B}(1 - 1/n)} \qquad (3)$$

Where E_c, I_c designate the Young's modulus of reinforcement concrete segment, the moment of inertia, respectively.

For Nanjing Changjiang tunnel, the strength grade of reinforcement concrete segment is C60, liner diameter of the tunnel is 13.3 m, thickness of the segment is 600 mm, width of the segment is 2 m. Each ring of tunnel lining is composed of 10 segmental linings, which are connected together by the bolts in the transverse direction of tunnel. The linings are arranged in stagger in the longitudinal direction of tunnel, there are 42 bolts which connected two consecutive rings of linings in the longitudinal direction of tunnel. The diameter of the bolt is M30.

Solving Eq.(1), Eq.(2), Eq.(3), the discount coefficient of tension-compression rigidity in the longitudinal direction η_N, the discount coefficient of shear rigidity in the longitudinal direction η_Q, the discount coefficient of equivalent bending rigidity in the longitudinal direction η_M are obtained respectively. η_N=1.37%, η_Q=1.2%, η_M =3.67%. Based on the fact that the possibility of potential damage of segmental tunnel linings caused by bending effect is far more than the situations caused by other factors, the discount coefficient of equivalent bending rigidity in the longitudinal direction η_M is selected as governing parameter to weaken longitudinal rigidity of the equivalent rigidity model in the longitudinal direction. In longitudinal direction of segment ring, the equivalent longitudinal rigidity is represented as $\eta_M E_c I_c$. In lateral direction of segment ring, due to the decrease of rigidity at segment circumferential joints, a coefficient of effective ratio of lateral bending rigidity (η_c<1) is introduced to evaluate rigidity of joints, a ring is treated as uniform, but less rigid (solid ring with equivalent bending rigidity). Considering the segment rings being arranged in stagger in the longitudinal direction, the reasonable value of the coefficient η_c can be taken equal to 0.7. Thus, the equivalent lateral rigidity is represented as $\eta_c E_c I_c$. Furthermore, the ratio of $\eta_c E_c I_c$ to $\eta_M E_c I_c$ is approximately 20. It shows that the equivalent rigidity of segment linings for Nanjing Changjiang tunnel in the longitudinal direction is far less than in lateral direction.

3.2 Numerical Simulation

According to analysis of the discount coefficients of equivalent rigidity above, there is a need to establish an anisotropic rigidity model of segmental tunnel linings which can reflect the difference of equivalent rigidity in the lateral direction and in the longitudinal direction.

3.2.1 Longitudinal continuous beam with ground springs model

The segment linings with joints are simulated by the longitudinal continuous beam with ground springs model in which the longitudinal discount coefficient η_M and the lateral discount coefficient η_c can be taken equal to 0.7 and 0.12, respectively. As shown Fig.5, the interaction between the segment lining and ground is represented by modeling the ground by spring. Based on the elastic foundation theory, the stiffness of ground spring $k_c = k_0 \cdot D \cdot L$, Where k_0, D, L designate the coefficient of ground reaction, the external diameter of tunnel, the length of beam element, respectively. Herein the length of beam element is taken equal to the width of segment B, i.e. L=B=2 m.

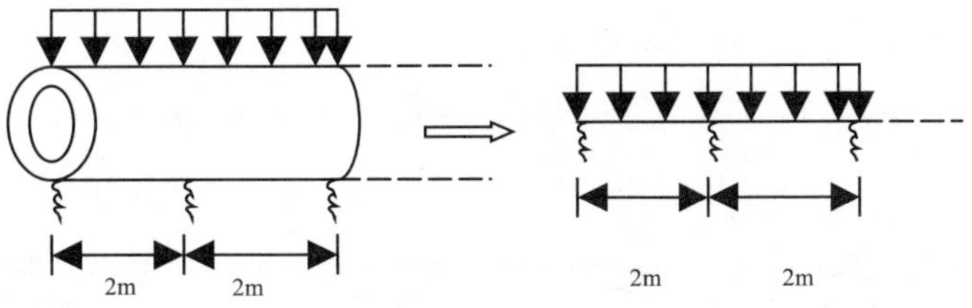

Fig.5 Longitudinal continuous beam with ground springs model

3.2.2 Three-dimensional elastic foundation model

Considering the longitudinal structural performance is related to the cross structural performance of tunnel, the segment linings with joints are simulated by a shell-spring model in which the longitudinal discount coefficient η_M and the lateral discount coefficient η_c can be taken equal to 0.7 and 0.12, respectively. As shown Fig.6, the interaction between the segment lining and ground is represented by modeling the ground springs covered over around circumference of each ring. Based on Winkler's assumption, these ground springs are independent and each ground spring reaction is only related to its radial deformation, the stiffness of each ground spring $k_{3c} = k_0 \cdot (\pi Dt/n)$, Where k_0, D, t, n designate the coefficient of ground reaction, the external diameter of tunnel, the width of shell element in the longitudinal direction, the total number of shell elements in each ring, respectively. Herein the width of shell element in the longitudinal direction is taken equal to the width of segment B, i.e. t=B=2 m.

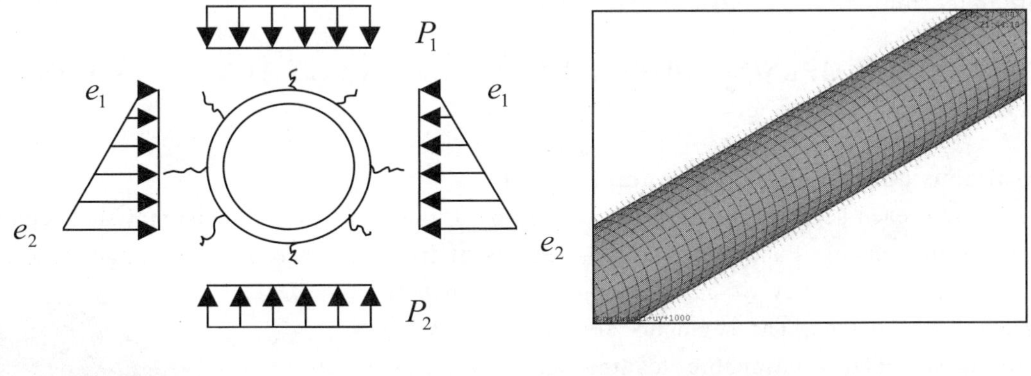

Fig.6 3D shell-spring model with ground springs covered over around circumference of each ring

3.3 Comparison of Results of Two Longitudinal Equivalent Rigidity Models

Tab.1 summarizes the parameters of the lining and the four class soils in the mileage of K3+600~K6+590 during shield construction across Yangtze River. The lining is assumed to be governed by a linear-elastic behavior with Young's modulus E=36 GPa and a Poisson's ratio ν=0.17. The stiffness of ground springs are determined from the coefficient of ground reaction k listed in Tab.1. The vertical soil pressure was calculated according to the relaxation pressure formula of Terzaghi. In real calculation, soil and water are considered in separation or together are determined by the soil permeability factor Kv.

Tab.1 Properties of geo-materials used in numerical simulation

Geomaterial	E (GPa)	v	γ (kN/m³)	K₀(MPa/m)	Kv(cm/s)
lining	36	0.20	25		1×10^{-7}~1×10^{-9}
Organic silty clay	3.09	0.40	17.3	5	3×10^{-6}
Silty sand	12.19	0.40	19.2	12	2×10^{-5}~3×10^{-4}
Sility and Fine sand	12.07	0.40	18.5~19.1	12~27	4×10^{-3}~6×10^{-3}
Gravel	16.20	0.36	20.5	41	3×10^{-2}

The comparison of the lining displacements based on two longitudinal equivalent rigidity model is given in Fig.7. The horizontal axis represents the shield tunneling mileage while the vertical axis represents the lining deformation.

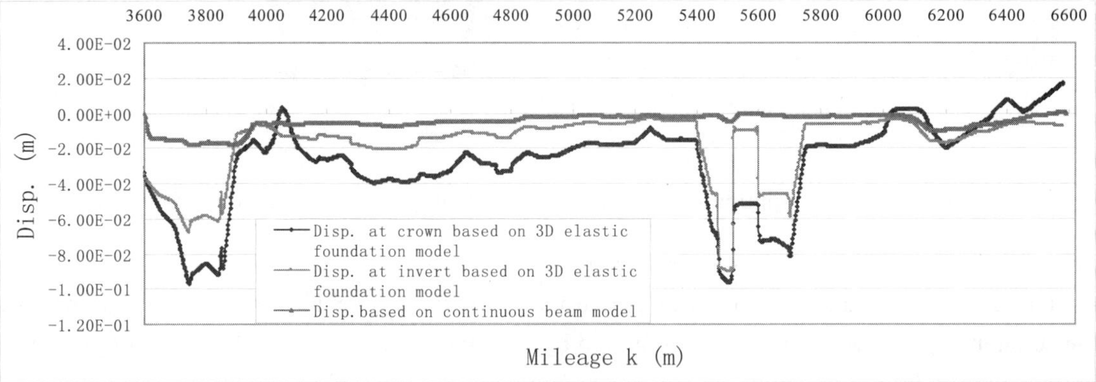

Fig.7 Comparison of the lining displacements based on two longitudinal equivalent rigidity models

From Figure 7, it is easy to find that the lining displacement based on continuous beam model is less than the results based on 3D elastic foundation model in most section of tunnel. The continuous beam model can not reflect effectively the "obvious" uneven deformations caused by uneven and sudden change ground, such as in the section from clay stratum to Sility and Fine sand stratum. Moreover, the continuous beam model only reflects the settlement trend of tunnel to some extent. Conversely, the reasonable displacement rule are achieved by 3D elastic foundation model, since in the model the circumferential springs cut off automatically when they are in tension.

4. STUDY ON CRACK OPENING DISPLACEMENT OF SHIELD TUNNEL IN LONGITUDINAL DIRECTION

4.1 Three-dimensional Shell-spring-contact Model

In this research, each segmental lining is modeled by a mesh of three-dimensional shell elements. Each shell element has four nodes. Each node has six degrees of freedom. In order to arrange longitudinal joint elements and guarantee accuracy of calculation, each segmental lining are meshed 4 divisions. The segments are assembled with alternating joints to obtain reasonable loading and controlled deformation, as shown in Fig.8.

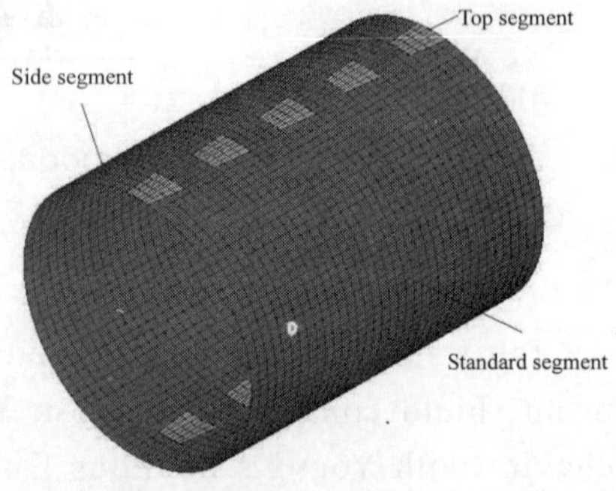

Fig.8 3D shell-spring-contact model with the segment rings being arranged in stagger in the longitudinal direction

Considering segmental joint having the mechanical behavior of shear resistance, bending resistance and compression resistance, the shear, rotation and compression of the spring elements are described by shear stiffness in radial direction, shear stiffness in tangential direction, rotational stiffness, and axial stiffness, respectively.

Similarly, longitudinal joints demonstrate also the mechanical behavior of shear resistance, bending resistance and compression resistance. Thus, the shear spring elements are still described by shear stiffness in longitudinal direction, shear stiffness in tangential direction. Considering bending deformation in longitudinal direction of shield tunnel, the tension spring elements are set at the place of the joints to simulate the tension of the segments in longitudinal direction. At the same time, the compression spring element which can simulate the compression resistance of concrete, are set at the nodes of the contact faces of the rings. The combined action of the two kinds of element can equal to the action of the bending resistance of the segments in the longitude direction which just like the reality so that the element of the bending resistance can be omitted.

4.2 Calculation of Crack Opening Displacement of Shield Tunnel in Longitudinal Direction

Through investigating longitudinal differential settlements along the whole Nanjing highway tunnel, as shown in figure 7, it is easy to find that the mileage 3 946 to 4 002 and the mileage 5 400 to 5 500 need to be concerned, because of the differential settlements values is up to 9.22 cm and 9.80 cm, respectively.

According to the 3D shell-spring-contact model, taking the differential settlements as displacement boundary, the maximum values of crack opening displacements and the additional moments of the aimed shield tunnel in longitudinal direction are obtained, as listed in Tab.2.

Tab.2 The maximum values of COD and additional moment due to longitudinal differential settlements

Mileage(m)	Length(m)	Differential settlements values (cm)	The maximum COD (mm)	The maximum additional moments (kN · m/m)	
				longitudinal	transverse
3946-4002	56	9.22	5.49	54.76	−255.6
5400-5500	100	9.80	1.90	24.9	−56.4

Compared with the results of the two aimed zones of shield tunnel, the more disadvantageous distribution of additional moments and crack opening displacement are caused by the differential settlements of 9.22 cm occurred the length of 56 m, but the differential settlements of 9.8 cm occurred the length of 100 m.

From table 2, the differential settlements of 9.22 cm occurred the length of 56 m result in the maximum transverse additional moment to be 255.6 kN · m/m (see Fig.9), the maximum longitude additional moment to be 54.76 kN·m/m and the maximum crack opening displacement to be 5.49 mm (see Fig.10). It is easy to find that the maximum value of transverse additional moment is more than the longitude value. It represents that the design of main structure of the shield segment tunnel must take account of the transverse additional moment caused by uneven settlements.

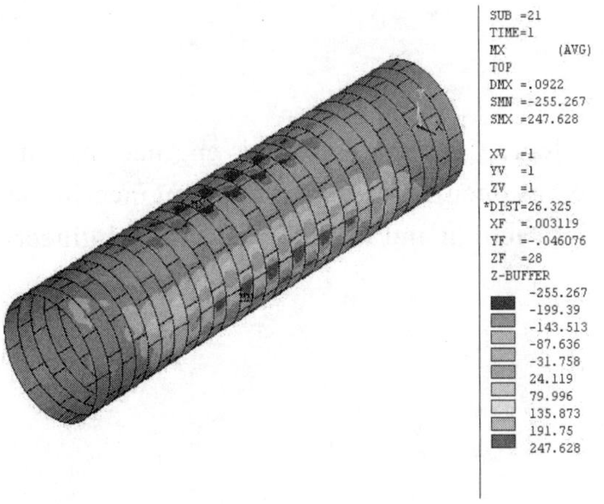

Fig.9 Transverse additional moment due to longitudinal differential settlements of 9.22 cm

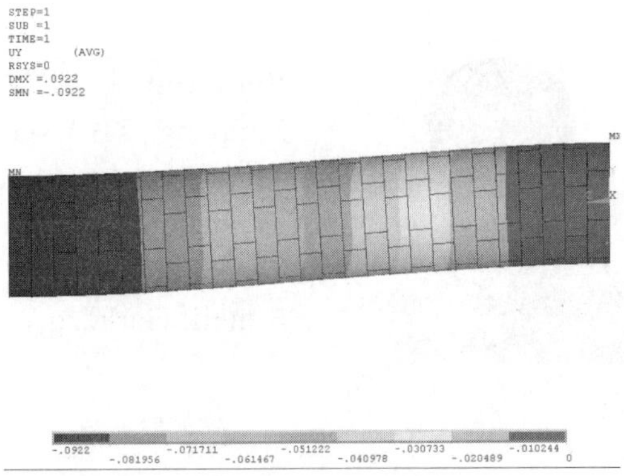

Fig.10 Crack opening displacement due to longitudinal differential settlement of 9.22 cm

5. CONCLUSIONS

Based on the construction of Nanjing highway tunnel across Yangtze River, this paper investigates the longitudinal deformation and structure mechanical characteristic of shield tunnel by establishing two longitudinal equivalent rigidity models. The following conclusions can be drawn:

(1) Considering the more possibility of potential damage of segmental tunnel linings mainly caused by bending effect, it is reasonable that the discount coefficient of longitudinal bending rigidity be selected as governing parameter to establish longitudinal equivalent rigidity model.

(2) For super long shield tunnel with large section, the prediction based on the continuous beam model only gives a relatively plain and mild curve of longitudinal deformation. Through establishing a three dimensional elastic equivalent rigidity model for the whole length, the reasonable results of longitudinal uneven deformation can be generally obtained at the cost of less modeling effort and computational time.

(3) By using the longitudinal shell-spring-contact model which reflects the joint effects of shield tunnel segment both in radial and longitudinal, and taking the differential settlements which is obtained by the macro-model above, as the following displacement boundary, the crack opening displacements of the aimed shield tunnel in longitudinal direction are reached.

(4) It must not be neglected that the effect of longitudinal uneven deformation on mechanical behavior of super long shield tunnel, and the transverse additional moment caused by uneven settlement is more than the longitude additional moment. As a result, the transverse additional moment must be taken into account in the design of main structure of shield segment tunnel.

(5) In case of excessive crack opening displacement caused by longitudinal uneven deformation, some effective measures for controlling water leakage should be considered in segment joint treatment.

References:

[1] Chen, B. and Wen, Z.Y., (2003). Elasto-plastic analysis for the effect of longitudinal uneven settlement. Proceedings of the ITA World Tunnelling Congress (2003). Rotterdam, pp.969- 974

[2] Lin, Y.G., (2001). Study on the longitudinal structure and deformation of subway shield tunnel. Doctor Dissertation, Shanghai, Tongji University.

[3] He Chuan.(1999).A study on the seismic behavior in the longitudinal direction of shield tunnels. Doctor Dissertation, Tokyo, Waseda University, pp.61-65

[4] H.W. Huang, (2006). L. Xu and J.L. Yan. The longitudinal model test of shield tunnel. Tunnelling and Underground Space Technology, Volume 21, Issues 3-4, Pages 418-419

[5] Zang, X.L. Huang, H.W and Xu Ling, (2003). The Study on the longitudinal settlement and structure behaviour of shield tunnel in soft ground. Collection of Papers from 2003 Shanghai International Symposium on Tunnel Engineering: pp257-265.

Bio-data:

Zhiqiang ZHANG obtained a Ph.D. degree in underground engineering at the Chongqing University in 1996. From 2003 he has been Professor of civil engineering at the Southwest Jiaotong University, specializing in teaching and research of tunnel engineering.

Tel: +86-28-87601115

E-mail: clarkzzq@sina.com

RESEARCH ON MECHANICAL BEHAVIOR OF SEGMENT JOINT OF LARGE SECTION SHIELD TUNNEL

Yulin ZOU, Chuan HE, Kun FENG, Songlin XIA

Department of Underground Engineering, Southwest Jiaotong University, Chengdu 610031, Sichuan, China

Abstract: Based on the idea of typical strip method in higher concrete structure design, the joint detail structure of the concrete liner is solved by demixing firstly and then synthesizing. Meanwhile, the mechanical behavior of segment joint of shield tunnel is studied comparatively with the contact mechanics model of 3D FEM. It has been concluded that the typical strip method is a feasible method to calculate joint. Finite element method is proposed to be a major means of analysis, fitted and complemented with strip method. The flexural rigidity value range of segment joint of Shiziyang shield tunnel is probable 2.6×10^5 kN · m/Rad ~ 10×10^5 kN · m/Rad.

Keywords: segment joint; typical strip method; FEM; comparative study; mechanical behavior

With the rapid development of China's economic level and the gradual improvement of shield technology, shield tunnel technology has widely applied in underground engineering. Joint is the most important component in universal segment lining which has typically nonlinear. Its structure controls both the bearing capacity and the whole deformation of lining structure.

This paper uses the idea of typical strip method in higher concrete structure design for reference and solves the joint detail structure of the concrete liner by demixing firstly and then synthesizing. Then it sets Shiziyang shield tunnel which is China's under construction Guangzhou-Shenzhen-Hongkong high-speed railway as an example, whose segment joints are analyzed by 3D FEM on its contact mechanics. Finally, it carries out a comparative analysis of segment joint's force mechanics laws and makes out the preliminary flexural rigidity's value range of segment joint of Shiziyang shield tunnel for the reference of design and construction.

1. TYPICAL STRIP METHOD

Fig.1 illustrates the segment joint mechanical model of not setting liner or not considers the role of liner joint (HE 2007). Concrete segment is deformed and flexed like simply supported beam by the effect of moment M and uniform surface force P. Typical strip method is usually used to analyze concrete and pre-stressed concrete section (ZHAO 1999). The main principle is dividing into a number of bands or blocks, in the premise of plane-section. The change of section's geometric characteristics and mechanical properties are counted by using two basic condition of the balance of force and moment, through numerical iteration count. Fig.2 illustrates the force analysis of typical strip method.

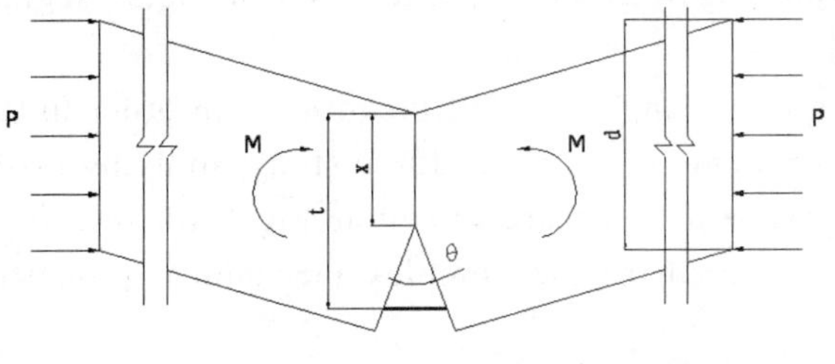

Fig.1 Sketch of Mechanical model of Segment Joint

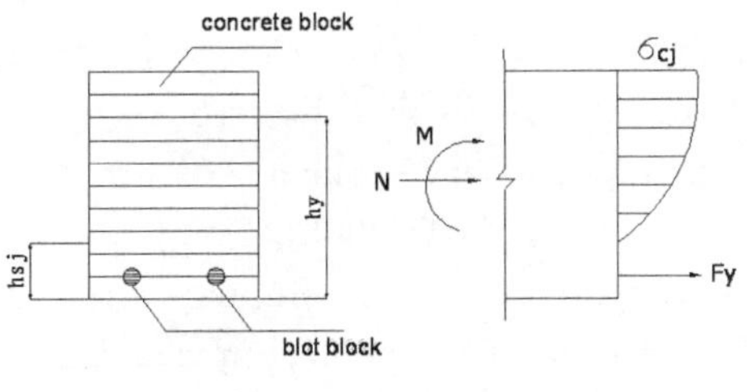

Fig.2 Sketch of Force Analysis of Strip Method

Supported by the National natural science Foundation of China (50778154); Science and Technology Program of Ministry of Railway of China (2007G036、2006G007B)

Based on the theory of typical strip method, this paper makes out segment joint mechanical property's "strip method" by using C++ to compile corresponding numeration program. In composite effect of axial force and moment, from section static equilibrium, it can be concluded as follows.

$$N=\sum_{j=1}^{m}\sigma_{cj}A_{cj}+\sum_{j=1}^{m}\sigma_{sj}A_{sj} \qquad M=\sum_{j=1}^{m}\sigma_{cj}A_{cj}(h_N-h_{cj})+\sum_{j=1}^{m}\sigma_{sj}A_{sj}(h_N-h_{sj})$$

In the formula: A_{cj} ——area of the number j layer of concrete segmentation zone section;

A_{sj} ——area of the number j bolt;

σ_{cj} ——stress of the number j layer of concrete segmentation zone section;

σ_{sj} ——stress of the number j bolt;

h_{sj} ——distance from the number j bolt to the bottom;

h_{cj} ——distance from the number j layer of concrete segmentation zone section enter of gravity to the bottom;

h_N ——distance from moment reference axis to the bottom of section.

The specific steps of computer program are listed as follows.

(1) a number N is confirmed;

(2) a compression region concrete edge strain ε_{cm} is selected as iterative original strain. For pre-strain concrete section, it can iterate from the beginning of a negative value, adding a proper increment value every time;

(3) for every given ε_{cm}, a neutral axis height Kh_0 is assumed; on the basis of plane section supposition, deformation compatibility equation and the stress-strain relation of block material, passim section's strain is decided; numerical integration method making section resistance axial force and resistance moment is used, which are checked to meet the balance equation; if they not to meet, the neutral axis height in accordance with the regularity is adjusted, after successive iterations to find out the value Kh_0 to meet the balance equation;

(4) bending moment equilibrium equation is used to make out M;

(5) plane section supposition and deformation compatibility equation are used to make out sectional curvature, stress and strain of every block, and the height of compression region, then make out the sectional corner;

(6) successively increasing in the value ε_{cm} and return to Step 2 to calculate the corresponding M and Φ so on, until ε_{cm} meet ultimate compressive strain;

(7) transforming value N and repeat step 2～6, they can be obtained different values N corresponding to the mechanical properties of section.

2. FINITE ELEMENT MODEL

This paper takes Shiziyang shield tunnel of Guangzhou-Shenzhen-Hongkonghigh-speed railway as an example, which is being under construction in china, whose lining structure segment ring is composed of 8 (5+2+1) segments, and there are 6(or 2 group) circle bolts of type M36, ranking 6.8 connecting segments. Segment's internal diameter is 9.8 meters long, external diameter is 10.8 meters long, and the thickness is 0.5 meter thick. The corresponding centre of the circle of the standard blocks and the adjacent ones is $49°5'27.27''$, and the corresponding centre of the circle of the capping block is $16°21'49.09''$, illustrated in Fig.3. Segment breadth is 2.0 meters wide. Concrete's strength grade is C50.

Account shows that the error of one of three breadth is less than 1% of full breadth, so in order to save time, using geometry symmetry of structure, this account selects one of three breadth to study, applying load to symmetry side(PENG 2008). Computational model and impose restriction are shown as Fig.4. Meanwhile, in order to more accurately simulate the junction of adjacent segment of the complex mechanical properties, analyze uses 3D FEM contact mechanics.

FEM model uses Solid Element that can better deal with material's non-linear character and reflect the performance of concrete's crushing and cracking to simulate segment concrete, and applies another Solid Element to simulate joint bolt, meanwhile makes use of Aim Side Element and Interface Element to simulate the side to side contact condition of nut and gasket, gasket and concrete, screw and concrete. FEM model is shown as Fig.5.

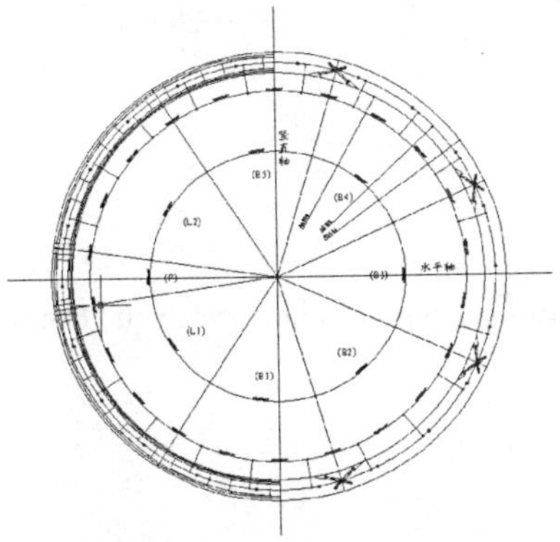

Fig.3 Sketch of Structure of Segment Lining

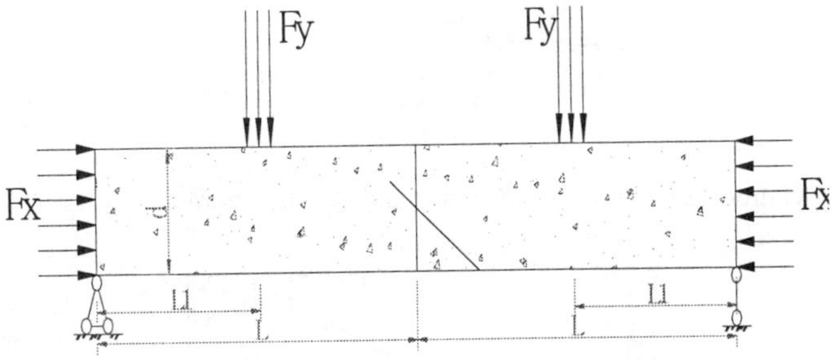

Fig.4 Sketch of Computational Model and Applied Load of Joint

(a) Segment Model of Overall Plan (b) Segment Model of Semi-Profile (c) Connect Bolt

Fig.5 Sketch of FEM Model

Bolt, considering yielding, adopts perfect elastic-plastid relationship and Biso material constitution. In the account, pre-stress section which is made of multi-pre-stress elements, is selected to simulate Pre-Tightening Force that is added to the connect bolt in the actual project. Reinforced concrete uses non-linear elastic material of national design specification. Failure Criterion applies Concer Matnum constitution. Yield Criterion uses Von Mises Kinematics Hardening constitution. Gasket uses non-liner big deformation material, considering the coexistence form of joint gasket contact and concrete direct contact.

3. COMPARISONS AND ANALYSIS OF MECHANICAL PROPERTY

The same segment joint's structure is calculated by FEM and typical strip method respectively. First, the calculated curve of the relationship between theta and bending moment is compared, illustrated as Fig.6 and Fig.7. From the overall level, the trends of the calculated results using FEM and typical strip method are comparatively consistent. But we can see that the flexural rigidity's value from FEM is always bigger than that from typical strip method through a detailed analysis.

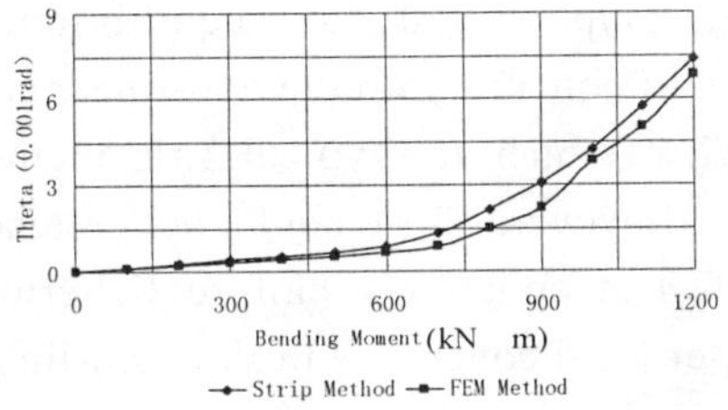

Fig.6 the relationship between theta and bending moment when N=4 000 kN

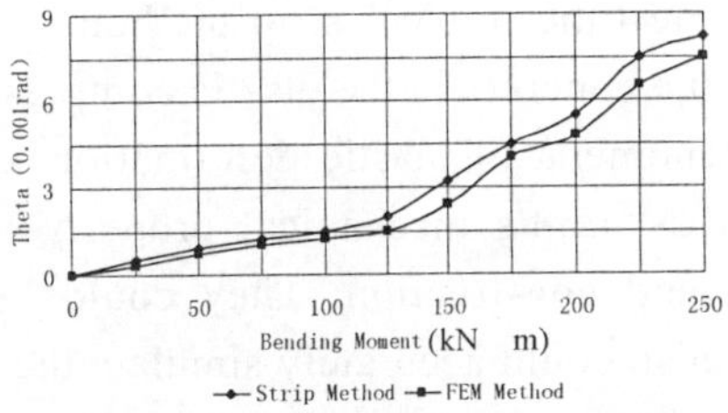

Fig.7 the relationship between theta and bending moment when N=2 000 kN

The joint mechanics parameters in the condition of N = 4 000 kN is selected to be the object for analysis in the calculation. The relationship between bending moment and 4 control parameters of joint's maximum stretches, height of stretch, section concrete's maximum compressive stress and bolt tensile stress is compared studied. The compared results are shown as Fig.8.

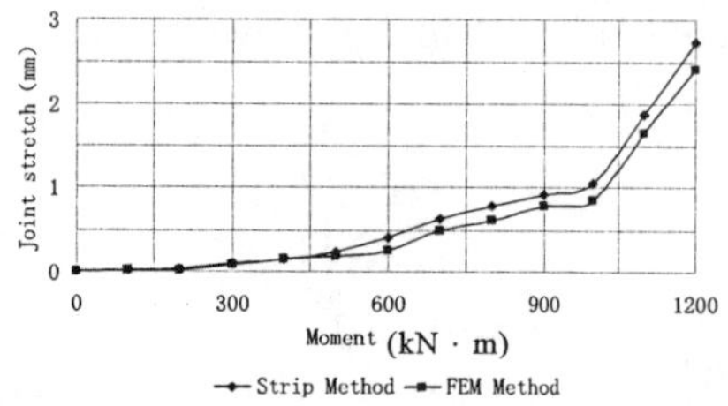

(a) Relationship between joint stretch and bending moment

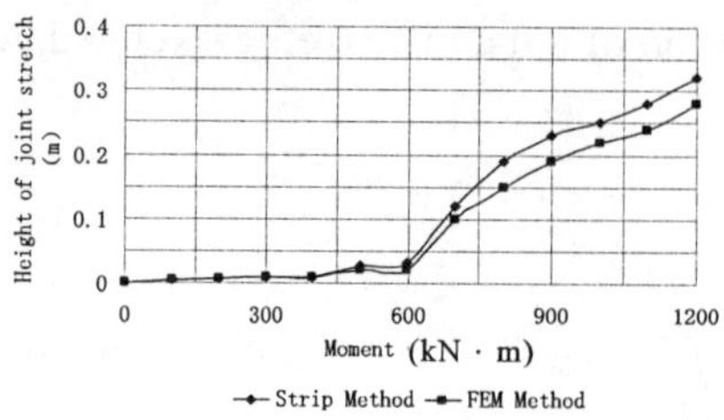

(b) Relationship between height of joint stretch and bending moment

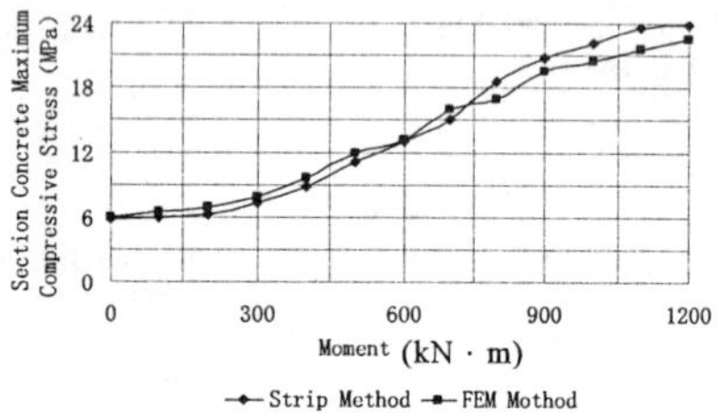

(c) Relationship between section concrete compressive stress And bending moment

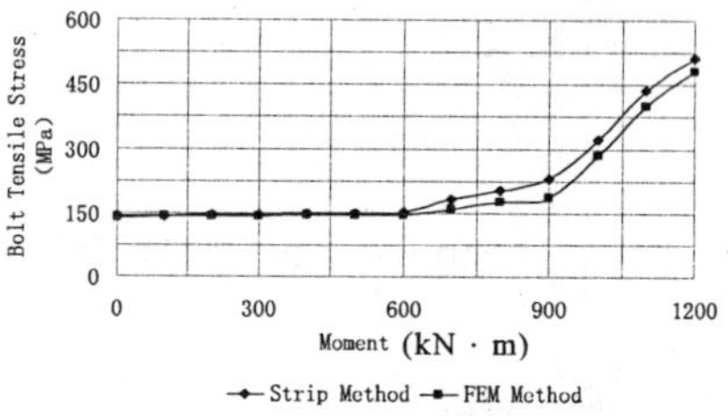

(d) Relationship between bolt tensile stress and bending moment

Fig.8 the relation curves comparison diagram about two kinds of algorithms of other related parameters when N=4000KN

When bending moment is smaller than 600 kN · m , joint's corner, joint stretch, the height of joint stretch, and bolt tensile stress are increasing slowly from the graph's analysis. Meanwhile, they are performing linear relation. And joint section concrete's maximum compressive stress is increasing fast and also performing linear relation. At this time, the calculated results of typical strip method and FEM are relatively consistent. When bending moment is bigger than 600 kN · m, the four are increasing fast and gradually performing non-linear relation. Moreover, joint section concrete's maximum compressive stress is increasing slowly and performing non-linear relation. When axial force is fixed and bending moment is less small, segment joint is under the condition of small eccentricity of total cross section compression, and concrete is in the elastic compression phase through analysis. When bending moment is bigger than one certain value, joint is turning faster evidently. That is to say, joint is under the condition of local compression and large eccentricity, and local compression concrete is in the non-linear elastic-plastic phase. At this time, the calculated results of typical strip method and FEM turn to be different.

From the specific analysis, the corner, stretch, height of the stretch of the joint which is calculated by the FEM model is appreciably smaller on the same moment in the vicinity of demarcation between large and small eccentricity. Moreover, the result of section concrete compression force and bolt stress is basically consistent. The reason from the analysis is that the calculation is limited by the FEM software calculation theory and the mesh generation, adding the bolt pretension force of 100 kN. The most important reason is that there is a contact penetration phenomenon in FEM model leading the smaller data than trip method, shown as Fig.9.

At the same time, typical strip method uses plane-section assumption and static equilibrium condition is established in the concrete in the elastic compression stage. As part of concrete into the non-linear stage, it would appear the phenomena of plastic deformation, crushing and crack of concrete. Typical strip method could not correctly express joint's mechanical property in this condition. However, FEM could better adapt to joint's specific form and construction. They could better define reinforced concrete's Failure Criterion and Yield Criterion, and also could accurately simulate the characteristics after local concrete entering non-linear phase.

Bending stiffness is an important performance indicator of segment joint. What's more, it is the essential important mechanical parameter of the integral domain segment lining structure calculation model. It is most feasible by using segment joint experimentation to ascertain flexural rigidity. But the expenditure of experimentation is expensive. However, it is can not only reduce the expenditure but also exactly apply in the design and a preliminary analysis by using typical strip method and FEM to determine segment joint's flexural rigidity from a qualitative point of view. In order to better reflect the character of local concrete entering non-liner stage, this paper make use of FEM to determine segment joint's flexural rigidity(M-θ curve), shown as Fig.10. And the relation curves of θ-M-N in three-dimension are also shown as Fig.11.

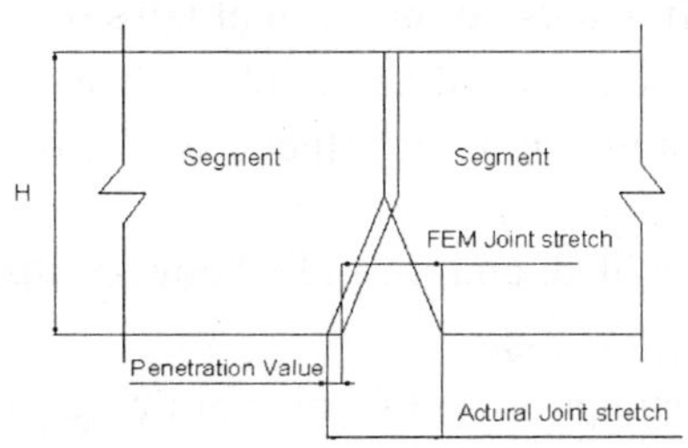

Fig.9 Sketch of penetrating phenomenon in the contract part of FEM

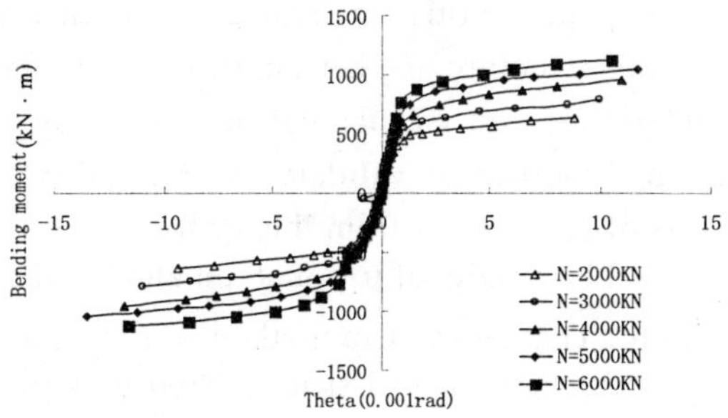

Fig.10 Sketch of joint M-θ curve

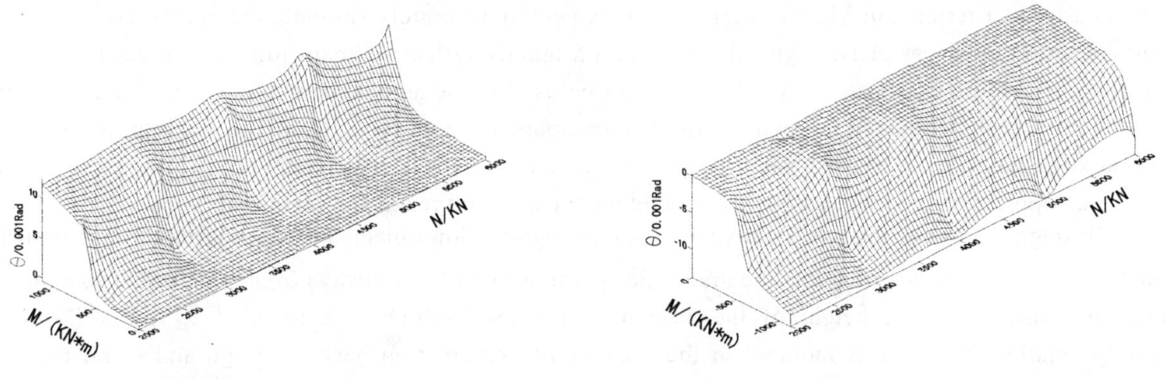

(a) Sketch of positive curve (b) Sketch of negative curve

Fig.11 the relation curves of θ-M-N in three-dimension

It can be seen that the relationship between bending moment and theta showing a clear non-linear and flexural rigidity is not a constant value. But it is closely related with the level of axial force. When axial force is bigger, the flexural rigidity is bigger. Positive and negative bending moment's curve shape is similar as bolt in the location of face is almost in the middle. Negative flexural rigidity is generally slightly larger than the positive one. When the axial force is constant, the joint theta is increasing simultaneously as bending moment value increases. When the bending moment is small, the joint rotates slowly, that because segment joint is under the condition of small eccentricity of total cross section compression. When moment is bigger than one certain value, joint is turning faster evidently. That is to say, joint is under the condition of local compression's large eccentricity, and local compression concrete which is in non-linear elastic-plastic phase is in the secant rigidity obviously.

Basing on Shiziyang shield tunnel under the ocean depth of a large state and the requirement of joint stretch (less than 3 millimeter), the list of reference value calculated flexural rigidity of joint bending moment is shown as Tab.1. Calculation can first take the minimum as start. Then joints at the results of the bending moment need a further amendment to its re-calculation of flexural rigidity. And the segment of the internal forces in the calculation must give serious consideration to joint flexural rigidity of the non-linear.

Tab.1 Reference value of joint flexural rigidity

Axial force N (kN)	The possibility of bending moment's range (kN·m)	Recommended positive flexural rigidity K_θ^+ (MN·m/Rad)	Recommended negative flexural rigidity K_θ^- (MN·m/Rad)
2 000	300～500	260～600	280～650
3 000	350～600	300～700	340～750
4 000	400～650	420～800	480～850
5 000	450～700	500～900	540～950
6 000	500～800	550～1 000	600～1 000

4. CONCLUSIONS

This paper builds mechanical properties calculation model of shield tunnel segment joint on the basis of joint detail structure and certain supposition and predigest. It makes out movement laws of section's geometric characteristics and mechanical properties by joint section moment and axial force change through computer program. In order to validate the reliability of theory formula, it is concluded as follows by comparative analysis of two results from theory formula and contact mechanics.

(1) The results of trip method and FEM are totally coincided, and it can be believed that they are holding consistent. That shows trip method is a feasible joint calculation mode.

(2) Because typical strip method uses plane-section assumption and static equilibrium condition which is established in the concrete in the elastic compression stage. When analyzing section's internal force's distribution, it can not consider segment joint's flexural rigidity reduced, segment 3D size effect and other factors as the port weakness. FEM could better adapt to joint's specific form and construction. They could better define reinforced concrete's Failure Criterion and Yield Criterion, and also could accurately simulate the characteristics after local concrete entering non-linear phase. Typical strip method mainly reflect segment joint in the elastic stage of the internal force distribution, whose analyzed results can be used in the actual segment structure and a preliminary qualitative analysis. It is advised that when calculate complex segment joint, FEM can be used as a major mean and typical strip method can be used as a supplementary. In other words, it is to say that trip method can be used as fitting and supplement data when FEM can not educe local region result for various reasons.

(3) Through the use of the comparative analysis of segment joint mechanical properties by the typical strip method and FEM, we can see that the flexural rigidity value of FEM is always bigger than that of typical strip method. The corner, stretch, height of the stretch of the joint which is calculated by the FEM model is appreciably smaller on the same moment in the vicinity of demarcation between large and small eccentricity. Moreover, the result of section concrete compression force and bolt stress is basically consistent. When the bending moment is small, the joint rotation speed is slower. But the joint rotation speed has noticeably accelerated when the bending moment is greater than a certain value. When the segment joint bending moments is small, axial pressure on the joint theta is less. While the larger bending moment, axial pressure on the joint theta effects become more apparent. Basing on Shiziyang shield tunnel under the ocean depth of a large state, and the requirement of joint stretch (less than 3 millimeter), the preliminary area of segment liner joint flexural rigidity value is 2.6×10^5 kN · m/Rad ~ 10×10^5 kN · m/Rad through the use of FEM and the reference to related projects.

References:

[1] He Chuan, Zeng Dongyang (2007). Research on the Structural Design of Shields Tunnels And Influences on the Environment in Construction [M]. Chengdu: Southwest Jiaotong University Publishing House, 2007: 20-21 .

[2] Peng Zhizhong (2008). Prototype Test on Mechanical Behavior of Segment Joint of Shields Tunnels With Large Span River-Sea [M]. Chengdu: Southwest Jiaotong University, 2008.

[3] Zhao Guofan (1999). Higher Reinforced Concrete Structure Study [M]. China's hydropower house, 1999.6.

Bio-data:

Yulin ZOU, male, born in Feb.1984, Chongqing, Master of Engineering, research direction: the design theory of tunnels and underground.

E-mail: zouyulin_617@163.com

南京长江隧道盾构管片分块设计

肖明清　韩向阳　薛光桥
中铁第四勘察设计院集团有限公司，湖北　武汉　430064

【摘　要】　南京长江隧道在我国盾构隧道发展史上具有历史里程碑意义，对于这种超大直径的盾构隧道，科学、合理的划分管片对保证结构安全和防水效果、增强施工的便利性等均有重大意义。本文针对南京长江隧道拟定了四种分块方案，并且通过对这四种分块方案在力学特征、拼装效果、施工便利性等方面进行了综合分析比选，最终推荐采用 9+1 分块（1/3 封顶块）模式，实践证明，这种管片分块封顶块重量较轻、施工便利、拼装效果好，非常适合于像南京长江隧道此类的超大直径盾构管片划分。
【关键词】　南京长江隧道；盾构隧道；管片分块

THE SEGMENT'S DIVISION DESIGN OF NANJING YANGTZE RIVER TUNNEL

Mingqing XIAO，Xiangyang HAN，Guangqiao XUE
China Railway Siyuan Survey and Design Group Co.,Ltd., Wuhan 430064, Hubei, China

Abstract: The Nanjing Yangtze River Tunnel is a landmark in the history of shield tunnel development in China. For a shield tunnel with such a super-large diameter, scientific and reasonable segment division is of great significance to ensure the structural safety, waterproofing effect, and also to improve the convenience of construction. In the paper, four different segment division programs were designed for The Nanjing Yangtze River Tunnel, and a comparative study was made on the four programs in aspects of mechanical characteristics, segment erection, convenience of construction, etc. Finally, 9+1 sub-blocks (1 / 3 wedge-shaped segment) mode was adopted in The Nanjing Yangtze River Tunnel. Practice has proved that, this wedge-shaped segment has the property of light weight and construction convenience. This mode is suited to the shield tunnel, which has a super-large diameter like the Nanjing Yangtze River Tunnel.
Key words: The Nanjing Yangtze River Tunnel; shield tunnel; segment division

1　南京长江隧道概况

南京长江隧道工程是连接南京浦口区与河西新城区的市内快速通道，位于长江一桥、在建的长江三桥之间，上距长江三桥 9 km，下距长江一桥 10 km。

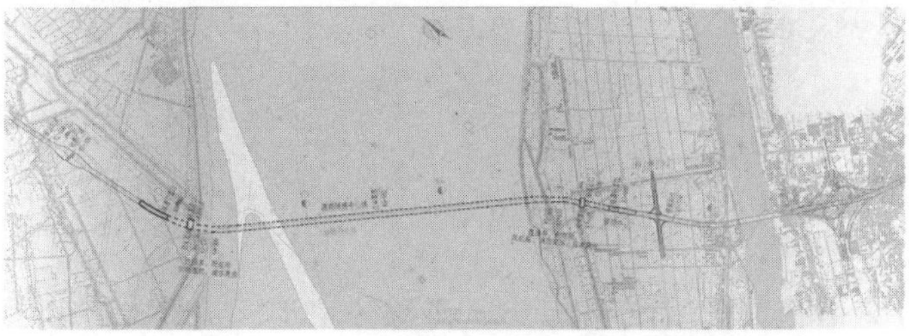

图 1　南京长江隧道工程平面示意图

基金项目：863 计划（2006AA11Z116）；铁道部课题（2007G036、2006G007B）

隧道全长约 3 930 m，其中盾构段长度 3 022 m。采用双管单层形式，双向六车道，道路等级为城市快速路，设计行车速度为 80 km/h。盾构隧道内径 13.3 m，外径 14.5 m。圆形衬砌环采用环宽 2 m、厚 0.6 m，采用 9+1（1/3）小封顶分块模式。

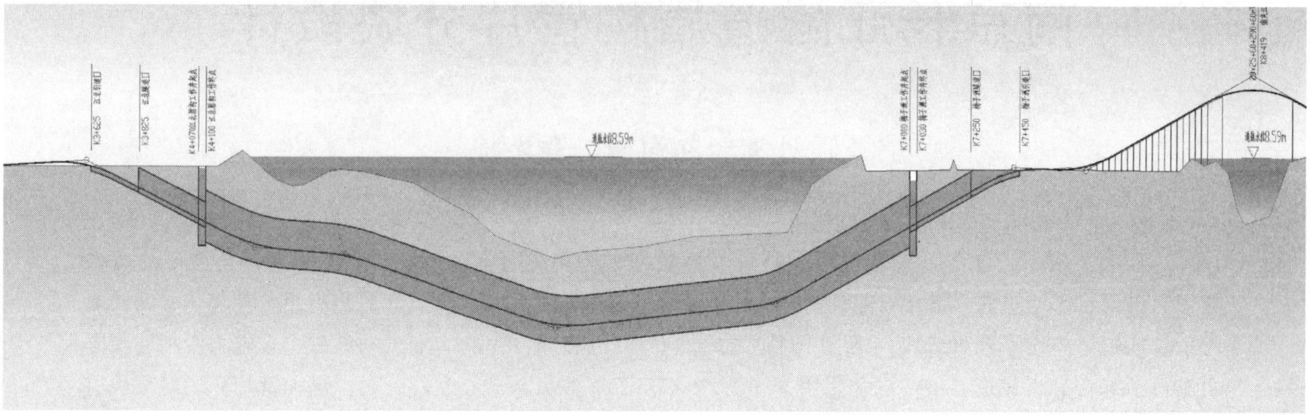

图 2　南京长江隧道工程纵断面示意图

2　南京长江隧道管片分块方案的拟定

根据国内外同等直径水平的盾构管片分块情况，结合南京长江隧道特殊的地质条件、防水要求、盾构机施工要求等提出以下分块模式：

方案一：9 块等分模式、1/2 错缝，采用 9 块等分模式，每块管片的中心线圆心角度为 40°，详细分块形式为 6B(40°)+ 2L(40°)+ F(40°)，见图 3 所示。

方案二：11 块等分模式、1/2 错缝，采用 11 块等分模式，每块管片的中心线圆心角度为 32°44′，详细分块形式为 8B(32°44′)+ 2L(32°44′)+ F(32°44′)，见图 4 所示。

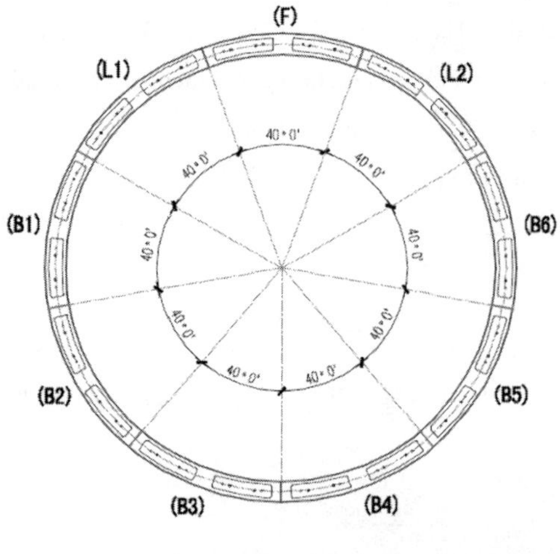

图 3　分块方案一示意图

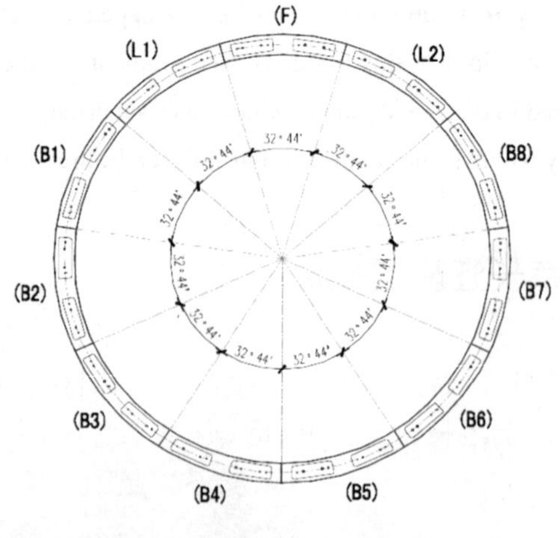

图 4　分块方案二示意图

方案三：9+1 模式、1/3 错缝，采用 9+1 模式，详细分块形式为 7B(38°34′)+2L(38°34′)+F(12°51′)，见图 5 所示。

方案四：9+1 模式、1/2 错缝，采用 9+1 模式，详细分块形式为 7B(37°54′)+2L(37°54′)+F(18°57′)，见图 6 所示。

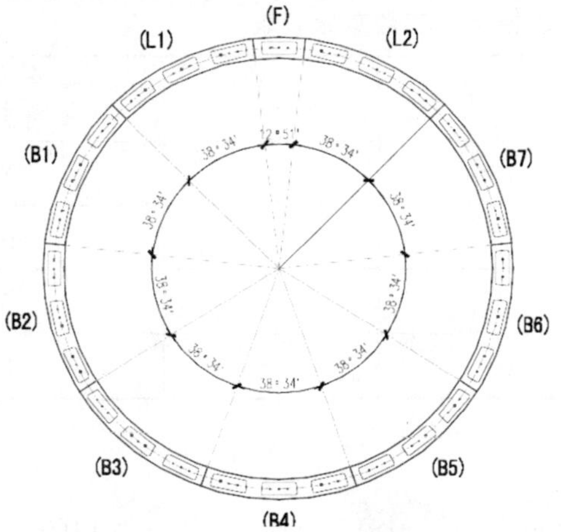

图 5 分块方案三示意图

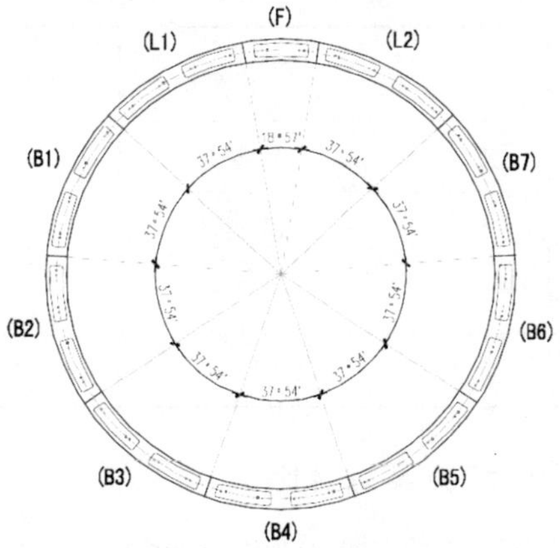

图 6 分块方案四示意图

3 南京长江隧道管片分块方案的比选

3.1 比选思路

针对前面拟定的四种管片分块方案，设计采用相同的计算断面，对各个方案不同拼装组合进行计算，取最不利拼装组合的行管片结构内力和变形计算结果进行分析。根据计算结果，综合考虑施工、造价和防水等因素来确定所采用的分块形式。

3.2 不同分块方案内力计算结果

经计算、各分块方案的单点最大变形量、最大正负弯矩和相应的轴力见表 1 所示。

表 1 五种管片分块方案的结构内力和变形分析比较表

（最不利拼装位置）

编号	对应分块形式	单点最大变形 (mm)	最大正弯矩 (kN · m/环)	最大正弯矩对应轴力(kN/环)	最大负弯矩 (kN · m/环)	最大负弯矩对应轴力(kN/环)
方案一	9 等分、1/2 错缝	20.403	1 900.4	6 555.8	1 110.3	8 328.6
方案二	11 等分、1/2 错缝	20.657	1 836.6	6 592.1	1 035.1	8 205.7
方案三	9＋1、1/3 错缝	20.553	1 840.5	6 569.1	1 083.4	8 379.9
方案四	9＋1、1/2 错缝	20.570	1 899.0	6 573.1	1 104.9	8 310.5

由表 1 可以看出，在管片最不利拼装条件下，9 块等分模式的刚度比其他四种管片模式要大，故其变形较小、内力较大。11 块等分模式的刚度比其他四种管片模式要小，故其变形较大、内力较小。

3.3 不同分块方案其他特征

同时，管片的分块还应该考虑盾构的拚装能力、螺栓的数量、千斤顶的数量与布置。各分块方案的比较见表 2、表 3。

表 2 各分块方案管片长度与重量比较表

序号	方案号	分块方式	封顶块		邻接块		标准块	
			中心弧长(mm)	重量(kN)	中心弧长(mm)	重量(kN)	中心弧长(mm)	重量(kN)
1	方案一	9 等分、1/2 错缝	4 529	135.4	4 529	135.4	4 529	135.4
2	方案二	11 等分、1/2 错缝	3 706	110.8	3 706	110.8	3 706	110.8
3	方案三	9＋1、1/3 错缝	1 456	43.5	4 367	130.6	4 367	130.6
4	方案四	9＋1、1/2 错缝	2 145	64.1	4 291	128.3	4 291	128.3

表 3 各分块方案千斤顶、螺栓、错缝角度数量比较表

序号	方案号	分块方式	错缝方式	千斤顶组数	螺栓个数	错缝拼装的位置数量（个）
1	方案一	9 等分	1/2	18	36	8
2	方案二	11 等分	1/2	22	44	10
3	方案三	9+1 模式	1/3	28	42	5
4	方案四	9+1 模式	1/2	19	38	0

3.4 不同分块方案综合比选

结构刚度而言：结构整体刚度大，对结构变形的控制有利，对结构的防水也是有利的。方案一（9 块等分）的分块方式的弯矩值为 1 900.4 kN · m，整体刚度最大；方案二（11 等分）的分块方式的弯矩值为 1 836.6 kN · m；整体刚度最小；其余方案居中。

从盾构机的拼装能力比较：方案一（9 块等分）的分块方式的单块重量标准块与封顶块均为 135.4 kN，重量最大；方案二（11 块等分）的分块方式的单块重量标准块与封顶块均为 110.8 kN；方案三（9+1 模式、1/3 错缝）的分块方式标准块为 130.6 kN、封顶块为 43.5 kN，封顶块的重量最小。相比之下，就拼装方便程度而言，方案三 C（9+1 模式、1/3 错缝）的分块方式较为方便；方案一（9 块等分）的分块方案相对略难；其余方案居中。

从分块的数量比较：如果管片分块多，施工时拼装方便，但是分块多螺栓安装工序多。管片分块少，安装节奏快，防水缝少。因此，在盾构机拼装能力允许的前提下，分块数量越少，结构越有利，相比之下，方案一（9 块等分）的分块方案较好；方案二（11 块等分）的分块方案较差；其余方案居中。

从千斤顶的布置来看，各方案的布置均满足要求。

上述四种方案，方案三块等分的分块方式在分块的数量上、千斤顶的布置上均较为合理，其结构整体刚度也较大。

综合以上分析，设计分块方式推荐采用方案三。本分块方案的优点在于：① 封顶块重量较轻，施工便利；② 采用 1/3 封顶块设置，无需切削角，封顶块的自锁能力强；③ 能够实现全环错缝拼装，结构变形小，纵向刚度大；④ 该分块结构可以采用全环 44 颗螺栓布置，纵向螺栓布置数量合理，设置灵活。

4 南京长江隧道管片设计

根据上述研究结论，推荐采用 9＋1 分块模式，该衬砌环由一块封顶块 F、两块邻接块 L1、L2 和七块标准块 B1～B7 拼接组成，其特征是所述封顶块 F 的分块角度为 360 /28=12.857 1°，标准块和邻接块的分块角度均为 360 /28×3=38.571 4°，在衬砌环全环沿圆周方向均匀布置 28 组纵向螺栓，其中一组纵向螺栓位于封顶块 F 两侧分块线 1 夹角中央。在上述 28 组纵向螺栓中，相邻两组之间，一组可以采用两颗纵向螺栓，另一组可以采用一颗纵向螺栓，一颗一组的纵向螺栓位于衬砌环全环沿圆周方向分为 28 等份的角度平分线 2 上，两颗一组的两个纵向螺栓分别位于衬砌环全环沿圆周方向分为 28 等份的角度平分线两侧。

目前，南京长江隧道左线已经贯通，右线也将即日到达江南井。从目前的力学测试、防水测试、拼装效果、施工难易程度等来看，南京长江隧道的管片分块设计是科学、合理的，施工效果也是相当不错的，实践证明 9+1 的 1/3 小封顶方案也非常适合于此类直径大小的隧道。

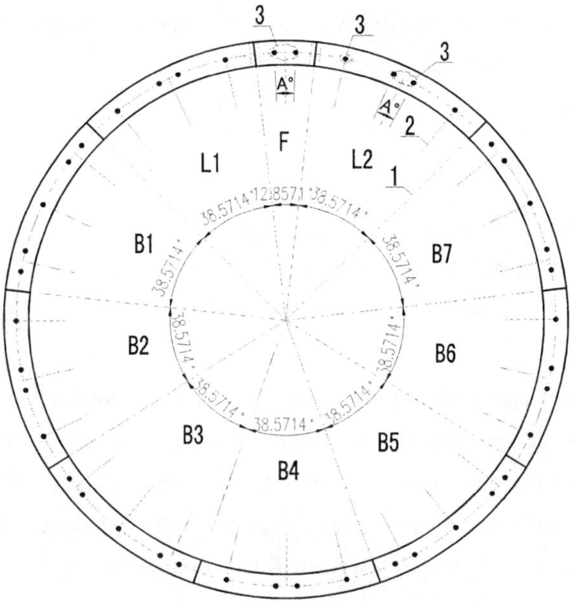

图 7　南京长江隧道管片分块设计图

1—分块线；2—28 等分线；3—纵向螺栓

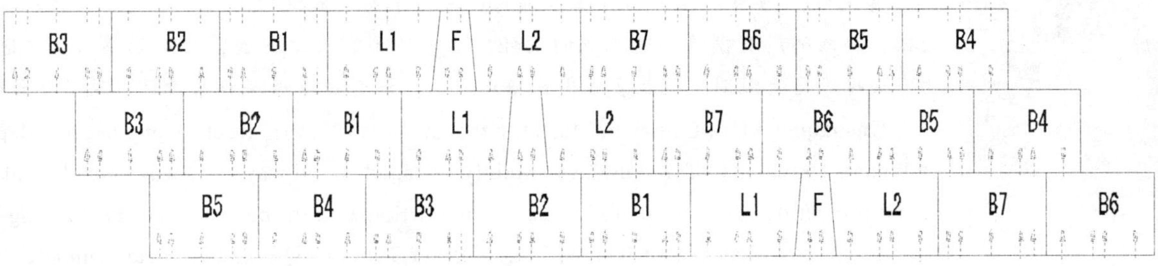

图 8　南京长江隧道管片错缝拼装示意图

参考文献（References）：

[1]　张凤祥，朱合华等. 盾构法隧道. 北京：人民交通出版社，2004：310-332.

[2]　何川，曾东详. 盾构隧道结构设计及施工对环境的影响[M]. 成都：西南交通大学出版社，2007.

作者简介（Bio-data）：

肖明清，1970 年生，男，教授级高工，博士研究生，现任中铁第四勘察设计院集团有限公司副总工程师。主要从事高速铁路隧道及越江隧道工程的理论研究与设计。在越江隧道领域：主持了武汉长江隧道、南京长江隧道、狮子洋隧道等多条水下隧道的研究和设计；在高速铁路领域：主持了武广客运专线、郑西客运专线、杭长客运专线、向蒲铁路等多条铁路的设计及科研工作。

Mingqing XIAO,(1970—), candidate for doctor's degree, senior engineer (professorship) , Served as Deputy Chief Engineer of China Railway Siyuan Survey and Design Group CO., LTD., mainly engaged in High-speed railway tunnel and River-crossing tunnel engineering design and theoretical research. In the field of High-speed railway tunnel, he presided over the design and research of Wuhan-Guangzhou Passenger Dedicated Line, Zhenzhou-Xian Passenger Dedicated Line, Hangzhou-Changsha Passenger Dedicated Line, Xiangtang-Putian railway, etc. In the field of River-crossing tunnel, he presided over the design and research of the Wuhan Yangtze River Tunnel, Nanjing Yangtze River Tunnel, and Shiziyang tunnel, etc.

Tel: 027-51156624（office）

E-mail: tsyxmq@vip.163.com

韩向阳，1970 年生，男，高级工程师，硕士，毕业于北京交通大学，现任中铁第四勘察设计院集团有限公司城建院副院长；主要从事水底隧道、复杂山岭隧道的设计与理论研究，担任了南京长江隧道的总设计师，并主持了南京纬三路长江隧道、郑西客运专线等项目的设计工作。

Xiangyang HAN, Senior Engineer, Master, Graduated from of Beijing Jiaotong University. Served as Vice-president of the Urban Rail Transit & Architectural Design & Research Institute of China Railway Siyuan Survey and Design Group CO., LTD. Mainly engaged in River Tunnel, complex mountain tunnels design and theoretical research, assume as chief engineer of Nanjing Yangtze River tunnel and presided over the design and research of Nanjing Weisan Road Yangtze River Tunnel, Zheng(Zhou)-Xi(an) Passenger Dedicated Line, etc.

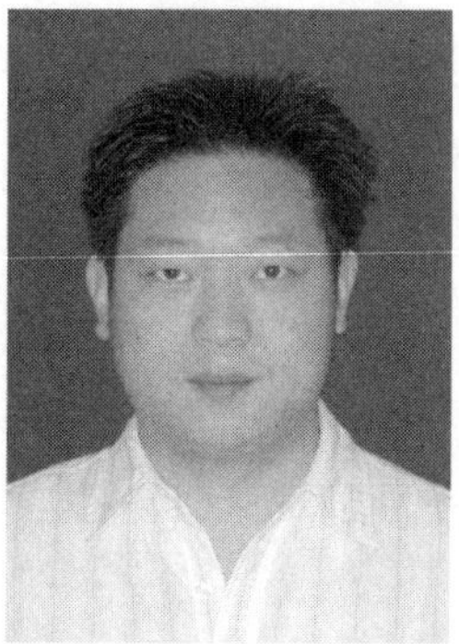

薛光桥，1979 年生，男，工程师，硕士，毕业于武汉理工大学结构工程系；主要从事地铁、公路隧道及铁路隧道工程的设计，参与了南京长江隧道、武汉鹦鹉洲过江通道、琼州海峡跨海通道规划、杭长客运专线塘江隧道、沪通铁路等工程的设计以及多项科研工作。

Guangqiao XUE, Engineer, Master, Graduated from of the structure engineering department of Wuhan University of Technology, Mainly engaged in subway, highway tunnels and railway tunnel project design and theoretical research. Participated in the design of the Nanjing Yangtze River Tunnel, Wuhan Parrot Island Yangtze River Tunnel, Qiongzhou Strait Tunnel, Qiantang River Tunnel of Hang(zhou)-Chang(sha) Passenger Dedicated Line, Shanghai-Nantong railway.

玻璃纤维筋混凝土围护桩在盾构端井头的应用研究

陈 中 马文义 肖中平
成都地铁有限责任公司，四川 成都 610031

【摘 要】 结合成都地铁1号线一期工程的工程实例，提出采用玻璃纤维筋替代传统盾构进（出）洞门附近围护桩中的钢筋，实现盾构机直接切削桩体进（出）洞的新理念，实践证明，该方案与传统的先人工破除洞门端墙附近钢筋混凝土围护桩，然后盾构机再进（出）洞的方案相比，具有经济实用、安全可靠和环保高效等特点。本文还结合科研试验成果，提出了玻璃纤维筋的设计参数取值及其圆形围护桩的设计计算方法，并将现场实测内力数据值与设计值进行了比较分析，填补了国内地铁设计领域上的一块空白，可为今后类似工程的结构设计和玻璃纤维筋混凝土构件设计规范制订提供参考借鉴。
【关键词】 玻璃纤维筋（GFRP）；围护桩；计算方法；现场测试

RESEARCHING OF GFRP CONCRETE FENDER PILES OF SHIELD LAUNCHING SHAFTS

Zhong CHEN，Wenyi MA，Zhongping XIAO
ChengDu Metro Co.,Ltd., Chengdu 61003, Sichuan, China

Abstract: With the example from first-stage construction of Chengdu Metro Line 1, this article puts forward a new idea to substitute the traditional reinforced steel bar with glass fiber reinforced polymer at shield launching shafts to realize the shield machine get into/out of the tunnel by cutting the pipe body directly. The reality proves that this method is more economical, safer, more reliable, more environment-friendly, and more efficient than the traditional way. Combined with the scientific research achievements, the article also puts forward the design parameter of GFRP and the design method of its round fender piles. It analyses and compares the data of the on-site survey with the design data, which is the first of its kind of the metro design field, and provides some reference for similar design and for the setting of GFRP design specifications.
Key words: glass fiber reinforced plastics (GFRP); fender piles; calculating method; on-site test

1 工程概述

成都地铁1号线一期工程线路穿越在成都市中心南北交通骨干道路下方，北起红花堰站，南至新会展站（如图1所示），线路全长18.15 km，均为地下线。全线共设车站17座，其中换乘站7座，站间距最长为1 452.4 m（海洋公园站—新会展站），最小站间距为779 m（锦江宾馆站—小天竺站），平均站间距1 097.088 m。线路北端红花堰车站附近设皂角树车辆段及综合维修基地，会展中心站附近设控制中心一座，在皂角树车辆段及火车南站附近各设主变电所一座。

结合线路埋深、周边建（构）筑物、道路交通、地质条件等，红花堰站—火车南站区间隧道采用盾构法施工，其余区间隧道全部采用明挖法施工。其中：

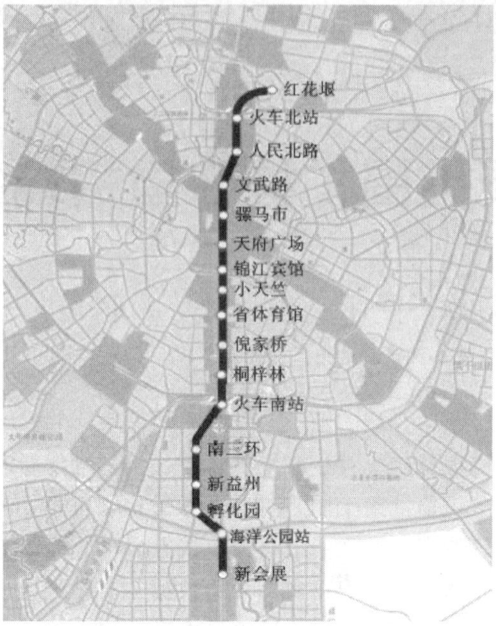

图 1 成都地铁 1 号线一期工程平面示意图

采用盾构法施工地段（红花堰站—火车南站）线路穿越成都市主城区，线路埋深约 10.1 m～19.9 m，在人民北路站—文武路站区间和锦江宾馆—小天竺区间两次穿越府河，在火车北站和火车南站两次穿越铁路站场股道。区间隧道主要穿越埋深为 7.0 m～15.0 m 中密～密实的卵石土地层，层厚 2.75 m～13.6 m。卵石单轴极限抗压强度 55.1 MPa～165 MPa，粒径一般为 5 cm～8 cm，含量约占 55%～80%，部分粒径 8 cm～12 cm，含少量漂石，最大粒径达 21 cm，勘探期间曾发现最大粒径达 67 cm。卵石中充填物以黏性土、中砂、砾石为主，含量约 10%～35%。地层渗透系数 K=12.5 m/d～48.5 m/d，枯水期地下水位埋深 3 m～5 m，丰水期埋深 2 m～4 m，水质无腐蚀性。盾构法隧道左线累计全长 9 175.174 m，右线累计全长 9 316.796 m，全线盾构法隧道累计单线延长米为 18 491.970 m。

2 方案来由

根据全线工程筹划，成都地铁 1 号线一期工程盾构从四处始发，其中红花堰站、省体育馆站和火车南站系利用车站端头作为始发井，骡马市站至天府广场站之间的盾构井为独立的盾构工作井。有六个车站盾构过站，共设四处起吊井，一处盾构转场，一处调头（如图 2 所示）。全线在盾构始发端头，过站、起吊、转场车站两端头以及独立始发工作井两端头共设 44 个盾构隧道洞门。

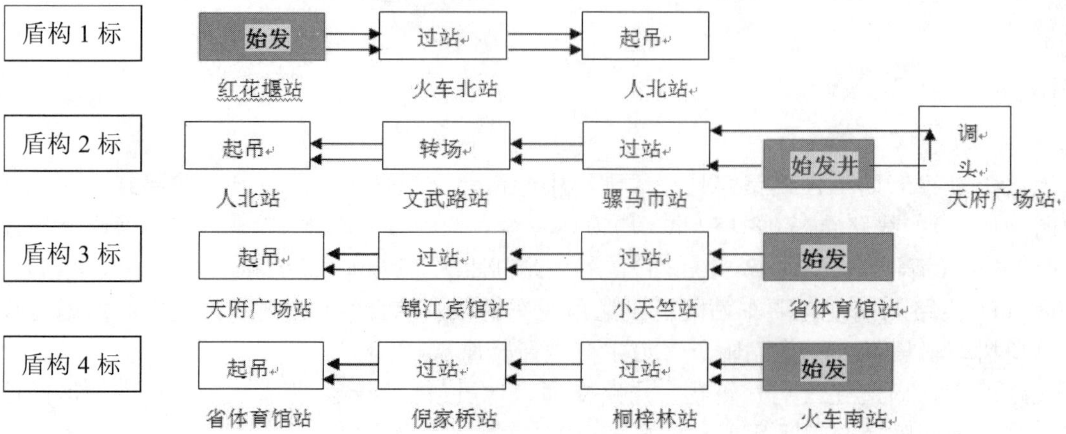

图 2 盾构掘进路线示意图

盾构进出洞是盾构法隧道施工过程中的关键工序之一。为确保进出洞作业安全，传统做法是先在盾构端头井附近区域先进行人工降水，然后施作盾构端井钢筋混凝土围护桩并用注浆等措施对桩后的土体进行加固，在盾构机进出洞前，由于盾构机无法直接切削围护桩中钢筋，需先人工破除盾构机穿越范围内盾构端头井围护桩并切割其中的钢筋。在此过程中，由于盾构机始发、到达部位的作业环境恶劣，同时由于破除桩体使土体暴露，极易出现土体失稳、基坑坍塌，导致地表下沉并造成地下管线和附近建筑物损坏等事故，特别在埋深较大的情形下危险性更大，容易造成人身伤亡事故。

为此，成都地铁公司组织西南交大、中铁二院工程集团有限责任公司等单位进行了科研立项并开展了许多卓有成效的研究，采用玻璃纤维筋（Glass Fiber Reinforced Plastics，以下简称 GFRP）围护桩替代传统的钢筋混凝土围护桩（如图 3、图 4 所示），盾构进出洞时，可以直接破除桩体（如图 5 所示），有效地规避了传统施工方法的作业风险，同时还具有保护环境、提高工效和节省工程投资的优点，这在国内尚属首次并且得到成功运用，其研究成果也填补了国内地铁设计领域上的一块空白。

图 3　盾构端头井 GFRP 桩施工现场

图 4　GFRP 桩入孔后的现场情况

图 5　盾构进洞直接切削 GFRP 桩情况

3　GFRP 计算参数的选定及其圆形围护桩的计算方法

3.1　GFRP 计算参数的选定

3.1.1　抗拉强度设计值及弹性模量

根据玻璃纤维筋拉拔试验，可测试出玻璃纤维筋的极限抗拉承载力 F_u，从而根据公式（1）～（7）计算出极限抗拉强度值、抗拉强度标准值、抗拉强度设计值以及弹性模量。对不同直径的样本试验值进行汇总如表 1 所示。

表 1 不同直径玻璃纤维筋试验结果表

直径 (mm)	样本数	有效直径	抗拉强度平均值 f_u(MPa)	抗拉强度标准值 f_{fu}^* (MPa)	抗拉强度设计值 f_{fu} (MPa)	弹性模量 E(GPa)	极限应变平均值 ε_u (%)	极限应变标准值 ε_{fu}^* (%)	极限应变设计值 ε_{fu} (%)
10	11	9.7	520.1	490.8	343.5	30.8	2.07	1.87	1.31
12	6	11.7	540.9	497.2	348.1	33.0	2.18	2.03	1.42
16	9	15.6	485.45	482.6	313.79	34.5	2.08	1.57	1.21
18	3	17.6	511.7	460.6	322.4	36.3	2.07	1.10	0.77
22	16	21.5	644.5	507.5	355.2	32.1	2.04	1.13	0.79
25	18	24.5	665.5	577.5	404.3	34.5	2.02	0.89	0.63

抗拉强度设计值和极限应变设计值按下式计算:

$$f_u = \frac{F_u}{A} \tag{1}$$

$$EA = \frac{\Delta F}{\Delta \varepsilon} \tag{2}$$

$$E = \alpha \cdot \frac{L}{A} \tag{3}$$

$$f_{fu} = C_E \cdot f_{fu}^* \tag{4}$$

$$f_{fu}^* = f_u - 3f_\sigma \tag{5}$$

$$\varepsilon_{fu} = C_E \cdot \varepsilon_{fu}^* \tag{6}$$

$$\varepsilon_{fu}^* = \varepsilon_u - 3\varepsilon_\sigma \tag{7}$$

式中 f_u——极限抗拉强度;

F_u——极限抗拉承载力;

f_{fu}——抗拉强度设计值;

f_{fu}^*——抗拉强度标准值;

ε_{fu}——极限应变设计值;

ε_{fu}^*——极限应变标准值;

A——单根纤维筋名义横截面面积;

E——杨氏弹性模量;

EA——单根纤维筋的拉伸刚度;

α——试验荷载－应变曲线在拉伸承载力为 20%～60% 时的斜率;

$\Delta F, \Delta\varepsilon$——在拉伸承载力为 20%～60% 时对应的荷载、应变之差;

L——纤维筋测试区原始长度;

C_E——工作条件系数，参照欧美经验和围护桩的工作环境取 0.7;

f_u、ε_u——样本极限强度、极限应变的平均值;

f_σ、ε_σ——样本极限强度、极限应变的标准差。

通过对玻璃纤维筋抗拉强度、弹性模量和极限应变的的统计分析，并考虑到纤维筋强度的离散性和产品质量的不断稳定和提高，成都地铁在进行盾构端头井围护桩计算时，玻璃纤维筋的抗拉强度标准值 f_{fu}^* 取 500 MPa（保证率不小于 99.87%），抗拉强度设计值为 350 MPa；弹性模量 E_f 为 34 GPa。

3.1.2 锚固长度

（1）理论公式

根据国外一些试验结果表明，GFRP 筋与混凝土的黏结机理类似于钢筋与混凝土，GFRP 基本锚固长度计算公式如下:

$$l_{bf}=\frac{d\cdot f_{fu}}{K_1} \tag{8}$$

式中　K_1—是常数，取 18.5。

根据美国 ACI318-M96 和加拿大 CAS A23.3-94 标准，对于普通混凝土，基本锚固长度还应乘以 1.08～1.38 的锚筋位置修正系数 K_2（本文取 1.20）。

另外，根据实验，混凝土保护层厚度取 2 倍 GFRP 筋直径所测得的黏结强度与混凝土保护层厚度为 1 倍直径的黏结强度的比值范围是 1.2～1.5，因此，基本锚固长度还应乘以混凝土保护层厚度修正系数 K_3（1.2～1.5），结合实验具体情况，本文取 1.5。即：

$$l_{bf}=\frac{d\cdot f_{fu}}{K_1}\cdot K_2\cdot K_3 \tag{9}$$

另外，根据我国现行《混凝土结构设计规范》(GB 50010－2002)，受拉钢筋的锚固长度的计算公式为

$$l_a=\alpha\cdot f_y/f_t\cdot d \tag{10}$$

式中　l_a——受拉钢筋的锚固长度；

f_y——普通钢筋的抗拉强度设计值；

f_t——混凝土轴心抗拉强度设计值；

d——钢筋的公称直径；

α——钢筋的外形系数。

由公式（9）和（10）得出玻璃纤维筋与钢筋基本锚固长度之比为：

$$\frac{l_{bf}}{l_a}=\frac{f_{fu}\cdot f_t\cdot K_4\cdot K_5}{K_3\cdot f_y\cdot \alpha} \tag{11}$$

对于 C30 混凝土，ϕ22 的 GFRP 筋和普通钢筋，有

$$\frac{l_{bf}}{l_a}=\frac{350\times1.43\times1.20\times1.50}{18.5\times300\times0.14}=1.16 \tag{12}$$

（2）实验情况及结果

对直径ϕ10、ϕ12、ϕ22、ϕ25 的 GFRP 螺纹筋分别按 150 mm、200 mm 和 250 mm 三种不同锚固深度进行了锚固力实验，并与 ϕ22 直径的 HPB335 月牙普通钢筋锚进行了试验对比，实验中筋材锚固部分采用 C30 混凝土，自由端粘贴钢管。

根据实验结果：对于ϕ10、ϕ12 直径的 GFRP，在三种锚固深度下，均被拉断，而 ϕ25、ϕ22 直径的玻璃纤维筋，在三种不同锚固深度下的试验综合结果如表 2 所示。

表 2　ϕ25 玻璃纤维筋和 ϕ22 玻璃纤维筋（钢筋）锚固力实验结果

筋材直径(mm)-类型	锚固深度(mm)	破坏时油压(MPa)	拉力(kN)	粘结力(MPa)	锚固破坏形态	对应筋材应力(MPa)
25-GFRP	150	22.0	193.12	≥15.49	混凝土破坏	429.5
25-GFRP	200	36.0	297.6	≥19.0	纤维筋拉断	661.8
25-GFRP	250	36.0	285.7	≥15.20	纤维筋拉断	635.41
22-GFRP	150	18.0	142.9	14.63	纤维筋拔出	423.51
22-GFRP	200	28.0	222.2	17.07	纤维筋拔出	658.80
22-GFRP	200	26.0	206.3	15.85	混凝土破坏	611.74
22-GFRP	250	26.0	230.15	≥14.14	纤维筋拉断	682.31
22-Steel	200	28.0	225.38	17.31	钢筋拔出	668.21
注：钢筋类型栏后缀为“GFRP”表示玻璃纤维筋，后缀为“Steel”表示钢筋						

通过 GFRP 与同直径ϕ22 的钢筋 C30 混凝土锚固试验结果比较，在埋深 200 mm 的情况下，钢筋都

被拔出，此时钢筋对应的锚固黏结力为 17.31 MPa。玻璃纤维筋被拔出的情况，对应的黏结力为 14.14～17.07 MPa 之间。钢筋与 GFRP 锚固力之比为 1.0～1.2 之间。

由于 GFRP 抗拉强度离散性较大，需要大样本去测定其锚固长度，在实际应用中，应采用较大的安全系数来保证 GFRP 与混凝土的黏结可靠性。结合理论推导公式，本次研究成果建议 GFRP 基本锚固长度按取同直径钢筋锚固长度的 1.2 倍。

3.1.3 最小配筋率

根据纯弯梁的破坏模式，以及与现行《钢筋混凝土设计规范》的衔接，本次科研成果提出了 GFRP 最小配筋率的计算公式如式（13）～（14），并结合实验情况，列出了几种直径 GFRP 的最小配筋率，如表 3 所示。

配筋率：
$$\rho_{\mathrm{f}}=\frac{A_{\mathrm{f}}}{bh_0} \tag{13}$$

最小配筋率：
$$\rho_{\mathrm{fb}}=\alpha_1\cdot\beta_1\cdot\frac{f_{\mathrm{c}}}{f_{\mathrm{fu}}}\cdot\frac{\varepsilon_{\mathrm{cu}}}{\varepsilon_{\mathrm{cu}}+\varepsilon_{\mathrm{fu}}} \tag{14}$$

式中 A_{f}——玻璃纤维筋的面积；

b——截面宽度；

h_0——截面有效高度；

α_1——混凝土平均应力与混凝土强度的比值，建议值为 0.85；

β_1——混凝土受压区等效应力高度与中心轴高度的比值，取值范围 0.85～0.65，建议值为 0.80；

f_{c}——混凝土抗压强度设计值；

$\varepsilon_{\mathrm{cu}}$——混凝土的极限压应变；

表 3 C30 玻璃纤维筋混凝土的最小配筋率

直径 d(mm)	有效直径 d_{b}(mm)	系数 α_1	系数 β_1	混凝土抗压强度设计值 f_{c}	纤维筋抗拉强度设计值 f_{fu}	混凝土的极限应变 $\varepsilon_{\mathrm{cu}}$(%)	拉应变设计值 $\varepsilon_{\mathrm{fu}}$(%)	最小配筋率 ρ_{fb}(%)
10	9.7	0.85	0.80	14.3	343.5	0.33	1.31	0.57
12	11.7	0.85	0.80	14.3	348.1	0.33	1.42	0.53
18	17.6	0.85	0.80	14.3	322.4	0.33	0.77	0.90
22	21.5	0.85	0.80	14.3	355.2	0.33	0.79	0.80
25	24.5	0.85	0.80	14.3	404.3	0.33	0.63	0.83

3.2 GFRP 圆形桩的计算方法

由于盾构端头井围护桩属于确保盾构进出洞期间的一种临时地下结构，结合《地铁设计规范》（GB 50157—2003）等有关国家规范要求，在设计时，只需对其进行承载力能力极限状态进行设计，而无需进行正常使用极限状态进行设计。在实际设计过程中，偏于保守将 GFRP 围护桩按照纯弯构件进行受正截面受弯、斜截面抗剪的计算和配筋。其中正截面弯曲应力主要由纵向主筋承担，而斜截面抗剪应力主要由横向箍筋承担。

根据研究成果，GFRP 筋圆形围护桩承载力能力极限状态设计时采用的计算公式如下：

3.2.1 正截面受弯承载力计算

玻璃纤维筋圆形截面承载力设计按现行《混凝土结构设计规范》（GB 50010—2002）第 7.2.6 条有关圆形截面受弯构件的正截面受弯承载力计算公式进行，但应对弯矩设计值乘以不少于 1.4 的修正系数。

3.2.2 斜截面受剪承载力计算

玻璃纤维筋混凝土结构斜截面受剪承载力设计值 V_f 可按公式（15）～（19）计算：

$$V_{\mathrm{f}}\leqslant V_{\mathrm{fc}}+V_{\mathrm{fv}} \tag{15}$$

其中：

$$V_{fc} = \alpha_c V_c \tag{16}$$

$$V_{fv} = \frac{A_{fv} f_{fv} b_0}{s} \tag{17}$$

$$f_{fv} = 0.002E_f \leqslant f_{fb} \tag{18}$$

$$f_{fb} = \left(0.05\frac{r_b}{d} + 0.3\right) f_{fu} \leqslant f_{fu} \tag{19}$$

式中 V_f——斜截面受剪承载力设计值；

V_{fc}——构件斜截面上混凝土的受剪承载力设计值；

V_{fv}——构件斜截面上箍筋的受剪承载力设计值；

α_c——构件中玻璃纤维筋对混凝土的受剪承载力影响系数，对于 C30 混凝土构件 α_c 值的参考值范围是 0.6～0.7；

V_c——普通钢筋混凝土构件斜截面上混凝土的受剪承载力设计值，按现行《混凝土结构设计规范》(GB 50010—2002)的规定计算；

A_{fv}——玻璃纤维箍筋的面积；

s——沿构件长度方向的箍筋间距；

b_0——玻璃纤维筋圆形箍筋桩的等效高度，对于围护桩可以对应现行《混凝土结构设计规范》(GB 50010—2002)的有关部分取值；

r_b——玻璃纤维箍筋的弯曲半径；

f_{fb}——玻璃纤维筋弯曲段的抗拉强度；

f_{fu}——玻璃纤维筋的抗拉强度设计值；

E_f——玻璃纤维筋的弹性模量。

4 工程设计及现场测试情况

成都地铁 1 号线一期工程盾构端头井基本为地下二层三跨钢筋混凝土框架结构型式，结构底板位于埋深 14 m～18 m 的砂卵石地层中，围护桩采用钢筋混凝土人工挖孔灌注桩（桩径 1 200 mm，桩间距 2.4 m）和 GFRP 混凝土人工挖孔灌注桩（洞门端墙附近）相结合的形式。

在先期结合作科研的一些站点（如火车南站和后子门盾构井），GFRP 混凝土桩采用疏排布置（见图 3），桩的竖向和横向受力钢筋全部采用 GFRP，而在后面设计的工点，结合前期科研测试成果、现场施工情况和经济性考虑，作了些优化，如将桩由疏排改为密排，桩的竖向和横向受力钢筋只在尚门范围附近采用 GFRP，在洞门上部和下部均采用普通钢筋。目前成都地铁盾构端头井围护桩的具体布置和配筋基本如图 6 所示。

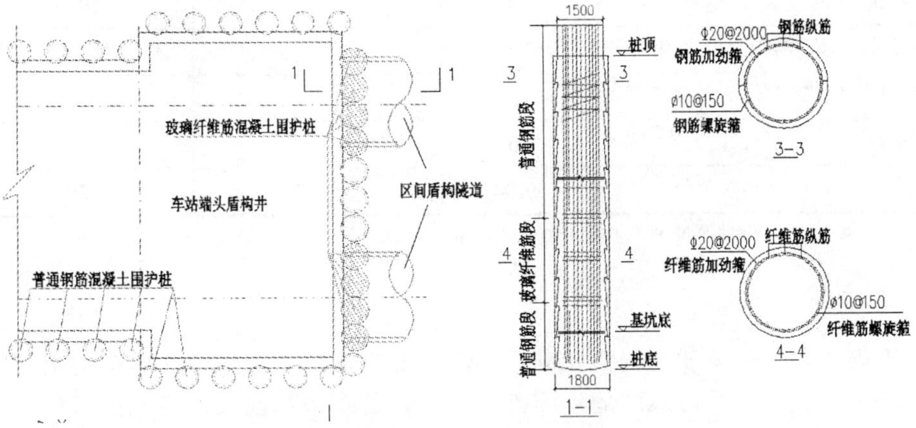

图 6 典型工程设计实例图

通过火车南站和后子门的围护桩现场实测数据表明，GFRP 围护桩在施工过程中，和钢筋围护桩弯矩值的变化趋势基本一致，最大弯矩都出现在最不利工况处（即基坑开挖到底和拆除横撑这两个特殊工况之间），但是在最不利工况时所产生的最大弯矩没有超过 200 kN · m，火车南站的最大弯矩仅是设计弯矩的 8%，后子门最大弯矩是设计弯矩的 11%，火车南站设计轴力为 680 kN，实测最大轴力为 336 kN，是设计值的 49%，后子门设计轴力为 675 kN，实测最大轴力为 250 kN，是设计轴力的 37%。究其原因，主要是测试内力数据是通过在降水条件下测得的应变读数为初始值计算到的，而设计内力值除了考虑水压力，还考虑了围护桩灌注混凝土后相对于初始值的应变增量的计算内力。

5 经济和社会效益分析

5.1 经济效益

通过成都地铁 1 号线一期工程洞口成本比较显示（见表 3）：单个洞口玻璃纤维筋围护桩的综合成本可较钢筋围护桩节省约 14 万元，节省工期约 30 天。在此，需要作说明的是，这个成本比较是在盾构井不需要再作端头加固，桩体筋材全部采用玻璃纤维筋的条件下得出的。随着科研工作的深化和结合 1 号线施工现场的施工经验，成都地铁 2 号线在对其进行了优化设计，桩体只在洞门及其周边范围采用玻璃纤维筋，其余部分还是采用普通钢筋（如图 13 所示），另外，由于成都地铁区间隧道主要穿越砂卵石地层，该地层富含砂层和黏土，车站在降水施工过程中，盾构井端头地层已经松弛，致使在盾构机进（出）洞时，地面出现较为严重的沉陷甚至陷坑，影响地面交通，因此，成都地铁 2 号线普遍采用了对围护桩后进行土体加固，主要方式是在桩后 3 m，隧道顶上部 3 m，洞门两侧各 3 m，隧道底部以下 1 m 范围内进行旋喷加固。综合上述因素，客观上讲，目前成都地铁端头井采用玻璃纤维筋围护桩方案较传统钢筋围护桩方案每个洞可节约 5 万左右，节省工期约 15 天。但对于国内其他城市，若盾构端头井附近地层为黏土、泥岩等不透水层，表 4 所示数据仍然具有很好的参考价值。

从总体来说，玻璃纤维筋桩比钢筋桩具有综合成本低，整体经济效益良好的特点，它可以有效地简化施工工序，提高施工效率。

表 4 盾构区间单个盾构进（出）洞主要成本比较表

比较项目	钢筋桩	玻璃纤维筋桩	差异 工期/人工	费用差异
围护桩筋材成本及加工（万元）	2.54	5.27		-2.73
出洞前桩外加固费用(万元)	11.0	0		11.0
出洞前桩外加固工期（天）	20	0	20/	
出洞前桩后加固需人数（人）	10	0	/10	
出洞前凿除桩体费用(元)	5.5			5.5
出洞前凿除桩体工期（天）	10		10/	
出洞前凿除桩体需人数（人）	10		/10	
一个盾构出口计 (元)	19.04	5.27	30/20	13.77

说明：费用中已包含施工所需要的各种费用包括材料费、人工费、机械费等。

5.2 社会效益

采用玻璃纤维筋桩替代传统盾构端头井洞门端墙处的钢筋桩，避免了在盾构进出洞时需人工凿除围护桩的复杂工序和影响人身安全健康的危险因素。另外，若在渗水性较差的地层（如黏土、黄土、泥岩等）中施工，不需要对桩后土体进行加固，还可以减少地面施工对地面交通和周边环境的影响。因此，具有良好的社会综合效益。

6 结语与展望

（1）文中有关 GFRP 的相关设计参数和对 GFRP 圆形围护桩的计算方法，通过成都地铁 1 号线一期工程实践证明是可行的，可为今后类似工程设计提供参考借鉴。

（2）通过成都地铁 1 号线的工程实践证实，用玻璃纤维筋替代盾构机进出洞附近围护桩中的钢筋，既可以提高盾构进出洞时的安全性，又节省了材料、时间，具有明显的经济效益。同时由于工期的缩短和安全性的提高，减少了对地面和环境的干扰，特别是减少了灾害性的事故发生，改善了施工环境，具有长远的社会效益。同时本科题的研究成果对我国已经和即将修建地铁的 34 个城市中盾构隧道进出洞具有同样的应用价值和指导意义。

（3）尽管玻璃纤维筋具有抗拉强度高、耐腐蚀、非磁性或非导电等等许多优点，国内外也有广泛的应用领域和卓有成效的研究成果。但到目前为止，国内外对在地铁领域系统的研究和应用甚少，缺乏玻璃纤维筋的相关设计参数和纤维筋混凝土结构的设计依据，笔者希望通过介绍玻璃纤维筋在成都地铁中的一些研究应用成果，为国内业界同仁在地铁领域作进一步的研究起到抛砖引玉的作用。

参考文献（References）：

[1] 《地铁设计规范》(GB 50157—2003)，北京：中国计划出版社，2003.

[2] 《混凝土结构设计规范》(GB 50010—2002)，北京：中国建筑工业出版社，2002.

[3] 成都地铁公司，西南交通大学，铁道第二勘察设计院.《玻璃纤维筋(GFRP)在盾构端头井围护桩中的应用研究》科研报告，2006.12.

[4] 高丹盈. 纤维聚合物筋混凝土的黏结机理及锚固长度的计算方法. 水利学报，2000（11）：70-78.

[5] 罗毅. 玻璃纤维筋混凝土构件的设计原理. 华南理工大学学报：自然科学版，2004，32（10）：71-75.

作者简介（Bio-data）：

陈中，男，1974 年 10 月 30 日出生，高级工程师，硕士，成都地铁有限责任公司建设事业部总体室经理，曾从事过铁路、公路隧道和地铁的设计和施工现场管理工作，主持过“应用 ANSYS 进行盾构管片的内力分析及二次开发”、“铁路隧道计算机辅助设计系统（RTCADS）”计算软件开发等科研工作。目前在成都地铁从事业主的工程计划和设计技术管理工作。

Zhong CHEN, male, born on October 30, 1974，Senior Engineer, Master, Overall Work Office Manager of Construction Department，Chengdu Metro Co., Ltd. He has engaged in railway, highway and subway tunnel design and construction site management for years, and was in charge of the research tasks such as "Application of ANSYS to carry out the internal force analysis and secondary development of the shield segment", and the software development of "Computer-aided design system of the railway tunnel (RTCADS) calculation". The author is currently engaged in project and design management at Chengdu Metro Co., Ltd.

E-mail: chen10301204@163.com

马文义，男，成都地铁有限责任公司，建设事业部部长，高级工程师。

Wenyi MA, Male, Director of Construction Department, Chengdu Metro Co., Ltd.

肖中平，男，成都地铁有限责任公司，副总经理，西南交通大学兼职教授。

Zhongping XIAO，Male，Vice General Manager，Chengdu Metro Co., Ltd. Part-time Professor.

成都地铁盾构法区间隧道设计施工关键技术

林 刚 罗世培 郭 俊 邹永尧
中铁二院工程集团有限责任公司，四川 成都 610031

【摘 要】 盾构法为成都地铁区间隧道的主要施工方法。目前地铁 1 号线区间隧道已成功交验；2 号线一期工程区间隧道已完成所有的施工图设计，其中三个盾构标段已成功始发；2 号线西延线区间隧道已完成初步设计并通过了专家评审。笔者通过参与地铁 1、2 号线盾构区间隧道全过程的设计和现场配合施工，根据对成都地铁盾构区间隧道设计施工的认识总结出几个关键点，以期能为成都以后的盾构隧道建设提供一定的参考，并能为盾构技术的发展作一份贡献。
【关键词】 成都地铁；盾构隧道；设计施工；关键技术

KEY TECHNIQUE FOR DESIGN AND CONSTRUCTION OF SHIELD SECTIONAL TUNNEL OF CHENGDU

Gang LIN， Shipei LUO，Jun GUO，Yongyao ZOU
China Railway Eryuan Engineering Group Co.,Ltd., Chengdu 610031, Sichuan, China

Abstract: the shield method is a main construction method for sectional tunnel of Chengdu Metro. At present the inspection has been done for the sectional tunnel of Chengdu Metro Line I and all construction drawings for sectional tunnel of Chengdu Metro Line II have been finished, in which three shield lots have been excavated. By participating in the complete design and on-site coordination of construction of sectional tunnel of Chengdu Metro Line I, II, several key points of design and construction have been summarized based on the knowledge about the design and construction of shield sectional tunnel of Chengdu Metro, in the expectation of providing references for shield design and construction in Chengdu in the future and contribution to development of shield technique.
Keywords: chengdu metro; shield tunnel; design and construction; key technique

1 引 言

成都市轨道交通网由 7 条线路组成，目前 1 号线一期工程区间隧道已成功交验；2 号线一期工程区间隧道已完成所有的施工图设计，其中三个盾构标段已成功始发；2 号线西延线区间隧道已完成初步设计并通过了专家评审。地铁 1 号线一期工程 16 个区间隧道有 11 个采用盾构法施工，地铁 2 号线 24 个区间隧道有 23 个采用盾构法施工，可见盾构法为成都地铁区间隧道的主要施工方法。笔者通过参与地铁 1、2 号线盾构区间隧道全过程的设计和现场配合施工，根据对成都地铁盾构区间隧道设计施工的认识总结出几个关键点，以期能为成都以后的隧道建设提供一定的参考，并能为盾构技术的发展作一份贡献。

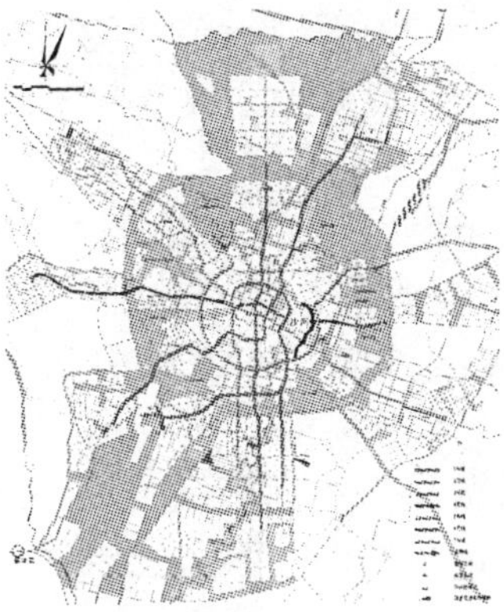

图 1 成都市快速轨道线网规划图

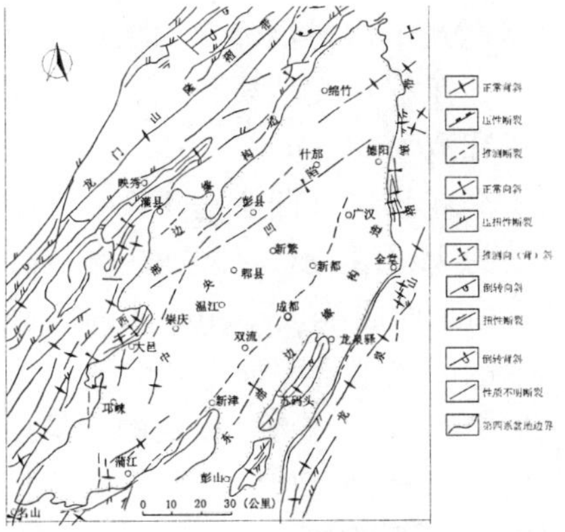

图 2 成都平原及周边构造纲要图

2 工程地质特点

成都平原为一断陷盆地，西部的大邑—彭县—什邡和东部的蒲江—新津—成都—广汉两条隐伏断裂将断陷盆地分为西部边缘构造带、中央凹陷和东部边缘构造带三部分。地铁 1、2 号线位于东部边缘构造带，以沙河为界，沙河以西区间隧道主要位于砂卵石地层中、以东区间隧道主要位于具有膨胀性的黏土或泥岩地层中。

砂卵石地层有以下特点：① 地下水位高，勘察期间最高水位达到地下 3.9 m；② 砂卵石地层分布广且复杂，砂卵石地层分布深度 1.6～29 m，在卵石层的任意深度均可能有 1～2 m 的砂层透镜体；③ 卵石分布不均，全线卵石含量 10%～15%，但局部区间可达 50% 以上；④ 卵石尺寸大、强度高，大部分尺寸 40～50 cm、最大达到 67 cm，单轴抗压强度 50～150 MPa、最大达到 206 MPa。

膨胀性岩（土）层具有以下特点：① 黏土为微透水层，透水性、富水性均较差，地下水主要为上层滞水和泥岩裂隙水；② 膨胀岩（土）遇水软化、膨胀、崩解，失水开裂、收缩；成都市大气影响急剧深度为 1.35 m，大气影响深度为 3.0 m；③ 膨胀力大，黏土膨胀力 100～200 kPa、最大达到 300 kPa，泥岩膨胀力 60～160 kPa、最大达到 500 kPa。

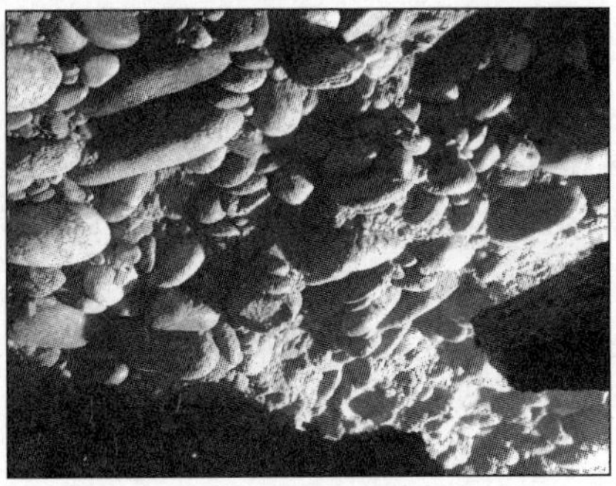

图 3 砂卵石地层盾构开仓情况

图 4 地表膨胀土

3 设计施工关键技术

3.1 盾构管片

3.1.1 *砂卵石地层*

（1）结构设计

成都地铁 1、2 号线均为 B 型车，盾构区间隧道内径根据 Φ5 200 mm 建筑限界，综合考虑施工、测量和设计拟合误差以及不均匀沉降等因素取为 5 400 mm，根据国内已建地铁区间盾构隧道工程经验以及成都砂卵石地层具体工程水文地质条件，盾构区间隧道采用单层钢筋混凝土平板型衬砌，接头为弯螺栓；管片厚度经综合研究取为 300 mm。

一环管片由 1 个封顶块（圆心角 15°）、2 个邻接块（圆心角 64.5°）和 3 个标准块（圆心角 72°）管片组成，纵向接头为 10 处，按 36° 等角度布置；在平面曲线半径小于等于 400 m 的曲线段采用 1.2 m 的管片幅宽，在直线和平面曲线大于 400 m 的区间段采用 1.5 m 的管片幅宽；错缝式拼装，管片环采用“直线＋左右转弯环”的方式拟合平面曲线。

结构计算采用“荷载－结构”模式的“梁－弹簧”模型，计算中考虑了环纵向接头位置与刚度、错缝环间相互咬合效应以及隧道与周围土体间的相互作用，抗震设计标准：7 度、乙类、三级。

（2）地震损害及处理措施

2008 年 5 月 12 日，汶川发生里氏 8.0 级构造大地震，震中映秀位于成都西北方向、距离约 70 km。成都有强烈震感，初步判断成都地震烈度为 6 度。地震发生时，1 号线盾构区间已完成约 1/3 的掘进工作，地震对已建盾构隧道结构的损害主要表现为新增错台、螺栓松动（其中一处环向螺栓被拉脱约 1/3）、环纵缝渗漏水和局部破损几个方面。

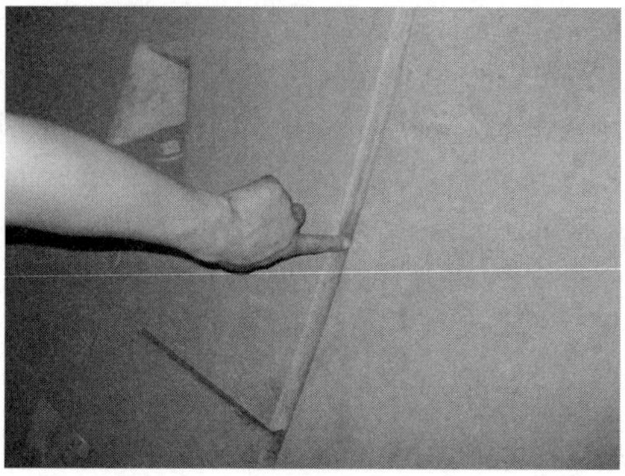

图 5　盾构管片错台情况

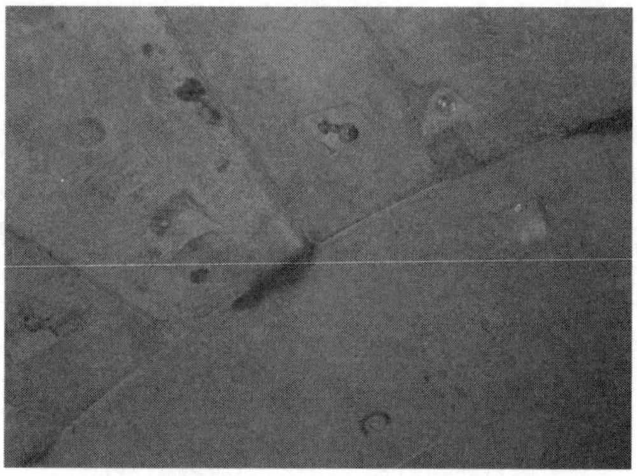

图 6　盾构管片渗水及环向螺栓拉脱

采用“梁－弹簧”模型对部分和全部管片纵向螺栓失效进行了数值模拟对比分析计算（工况 1，所有纵向螺栓均正常工作；工况 2，盾构管片 12 点、1 点、2 点共 3 处位置纵向螺栓失效；工况 3，所有纵向螺栓均失效），计算结果表明：如果纵向螺栓变形过大或被剪坏，管片变形将增大，整体性和防水效果将有所降低，但结构仍满足受力要求。因此，对于新增管片错台，可不作特殊处理。

对于栓杆没变形的松动螺栓，处理措施为直接拧紧；对于少部分栓杆变形（或栓杆被拉出）的螺栓，处理措施为更换新螺栓。若为吊装孔渗漏水，采用通过管片吊装孔向渗水位置处注浆的方法进行处理；若为二次注浆后仍继续渗漏水点，采用通过在管片相应位置处钻孔注浆的方法处理；若环纵缝渗漏水，采用在环纵缝相应位置处钻孔注浆的方法处理。现场局部破损的管片采用满足相关技术要求条件的工艺进行修复处理。

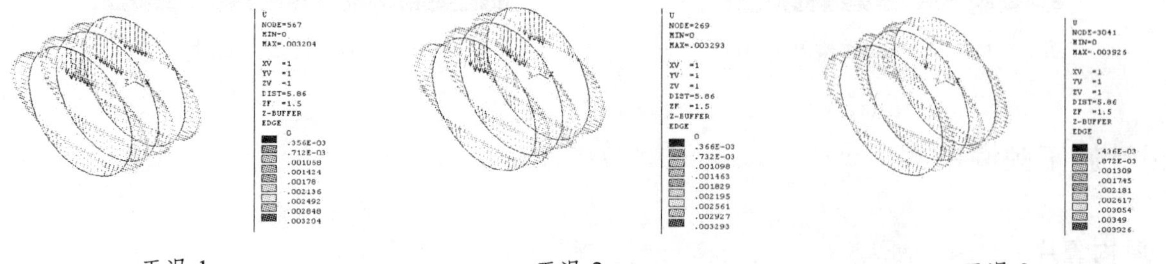

工况 1　　工况 2　　工况 3

图 7　三种工况结构变形图（m）

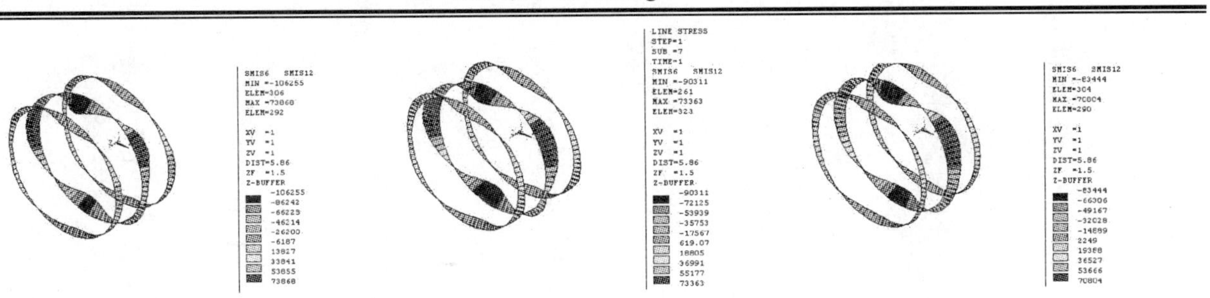

工况 1　　　工况 2　　　工况 3

图 8　三种工况结构弯矩图（kN · m）

3.1.2　膨胀岩土地层

（1）膨胀力和膨胀接触压力

按照《岩土工程基本术语标准》(GB/T 50279—98)，膨胀力的定义为：土体在不允许侧向变形下充分吸水，使其保持不发生竖向膨胀所需施加的最大压力值。因此由于膨胀土膨胀效应而作用于实际结构上的力与膨胀力不同，为便于区分，称之为膨胀接触压力。

采用平面单元模拟隧道和地层，接触对单元模拟隧道与地层间的相互作用力，对膨胀力和膨胀接触压力进行了研究。通过对典型工况的综合分析，得出以下结论：作用于结构的膨胀接触压力约为膨胀力的 50%，且膨胀接触压力一般呈抛物线分布。

表 1　典型工况膨胀接触压力计算结果

工况	1	2	3	4
膨胀土分布	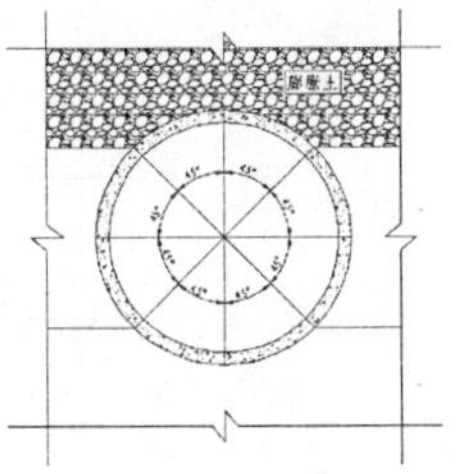	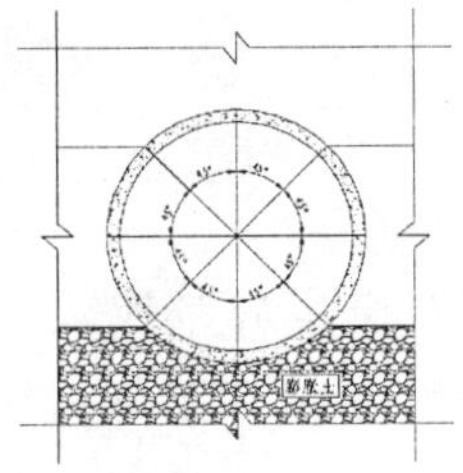	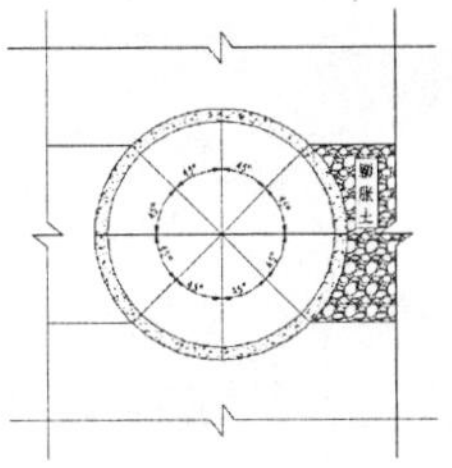	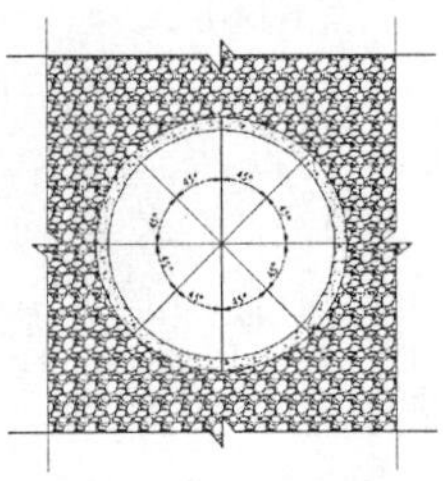
膨胀接触压力云图	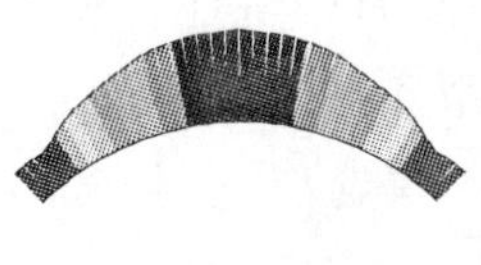		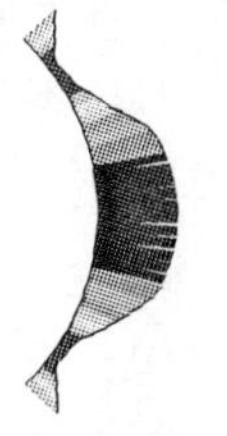	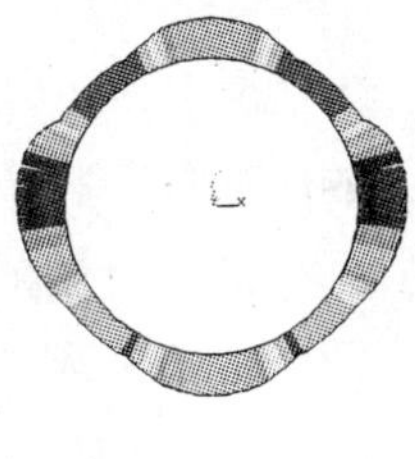

（2）“荷载－结构”模式结构外力分析

与国内外许多盾构隧道一致，成都地铁区间盾构隧道结构设计计算分析以“荷载—结构”模式为主。作用在隧道上方的土层压力，根据隧道覆土深度，当覆土深度较小时采用全土柱荷载，当覆土深度较大时采用卸载拱理论(太沙基公式为主体)计算确定，但当计算荷载值小于 2D（D 为隧道外径）覆土荷载时，取 2D 覆土荷载；作用在隧道下方的荷载，根据荷载平衡原理，为上方荷载与结构自重的和。

当结构周围分布有膨胀土时，若将膨胀接触压力与外荷载作简单叠加作为设计外荷载的话，显然结构设计偏于保守，因此对不同的膨胀土分布时结构的设计外荷载进行了研究，主要研究结果为：① 当膨胀土位于结构下方且膨胀接触压力小于上方荷载与结构自重的和时，可不考虑膨胀土的附加力学效应；② 当膨胀土位于结构上方或一侧时，应考虑膨胀土的附加力学效应；③ 当膨胀土位于结构四周时，只考虑上方膨胀接触压力大于下方膨胀接触压力的工况。

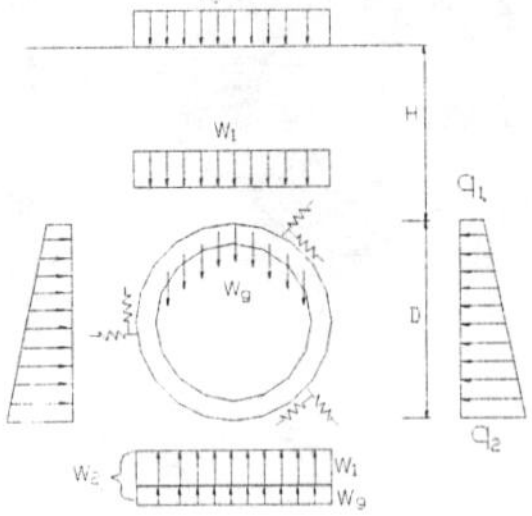

图 9　一般地层荷载 - 结构模式

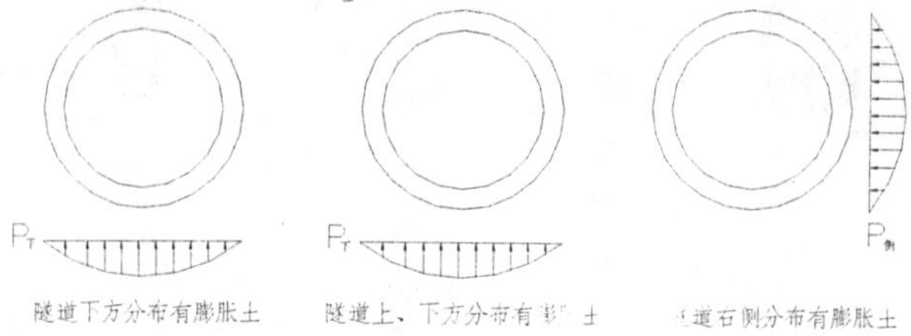

图 10　膨胀土与膨胀力分布关系

（3）结构设计

由于 1 号线和 2 号线沙河以东盾构区间均采用内径 5 400 mm、外径 6 000 mm 的平板型钢筋混凝土管片，考虑到成都后续地铁区间盾构机的通用性、管片模板加工、管片厂现场管理等因素，膨胀土地层盾构管片宜尽量采用统一的结构尺寸。

根据以上设计原则，在膨胀力、结构外荷载研究成果的基础上对盾构管片结构做了进一步研究，研究表明：膨胀岩土段盾构区间采用与砂卵石地层一致的管片结构尺寸基本可行，但须采取以下特殊设计：① 根据膨胀土分布进行分段配筋；② 根据计算结果，特定地段选用Ⅲ级钢筋；③ 特殊地段该错缝式拼装为通缝式拼装。

3.2　盾构机

3.2.1　*砂卵石地层*

（1）试验段及前期

由于成都长距离富水砂卵石地层在国内甚至全世界都比较特殊，盾构机的形式及相应配置几乎无成熟的经验可参考，因此 1 号线选择了两个盾构先行开工标段作为富水砂卵石地层试验段，试验段包括 3 台加泥式土压平衡盾构机和 1 台泥水平衡盾构机。针对地层特点，盾构机在以下方面做了针对性设计：① 具备处理大粒径卵石和漂石的能力，土压平衡盾构机采用了较多数量的滚刀（包括双刃滚刀），同时还考虑了滚刀、刮刀、齿刀、羊角刀的不同组合及布置，泥水平衡盾构机还在泥水平衡仓的底部，排泥管的前面安装了颚板式破碎机；② 具有能够在砂砾石地层中长距离掘进的能力，盾构机设计过程中适当增加了刀盘的开口率，优化了开口形状及布置，刀盘、刀具、螺旋出土器、泥水输送系统等均采用了耐磨材料或堆焊了耐磨层；③ 具有处理高地下水的能力，土压平衡盾构机采用了两段式螺旋输送管。

通过以上措施，对砂卵石采用以“破碎排出”为主的指导思想和“适当超压”的掘进模式，区间盾构隧道实现了成功始发和掘进，但在接下来的几个月时间里，盾构区间突出表现了以下几方面的问题：① 由于大部分卵石均在“破碎”后再排入土仓（排泥管），因此刀具、刀盘磨耗比预期严重，每隔 120～150 m 就需换刀一次；② 综合进度不理想，加泥式土压盾构的综合进度为 120 m/月，泥水盾构的综合进度为 110 m/月；③ 盾构换刀风险和对环境的影响都较大，该阶段盾构换刀主要有洞内和地面两种，洞内换刀主要采用地面管井降水配合地面和洞内注浆等辅助措施，由于浆液在地层扰动前注入困难，因此掌子面稳定性较差，而地面换刀采用挖孔桩或旋喷桩，挖孔桩工期长且费用高，旋喷桩加固效果不理想，且以上两种方法对交通干扰都较大；④ 刀盘结泥饼，局部地段夹杂厚度不均的粉细砂层，在受到大推力和大扭矩时，易固结成坚硬的泥饼，该地层反应敏感，清仓后地层损失较大；⑤ 由于砂卵石比例大且中石英含量较大，泥水盾构排泥系统易堵塞且磨损大。

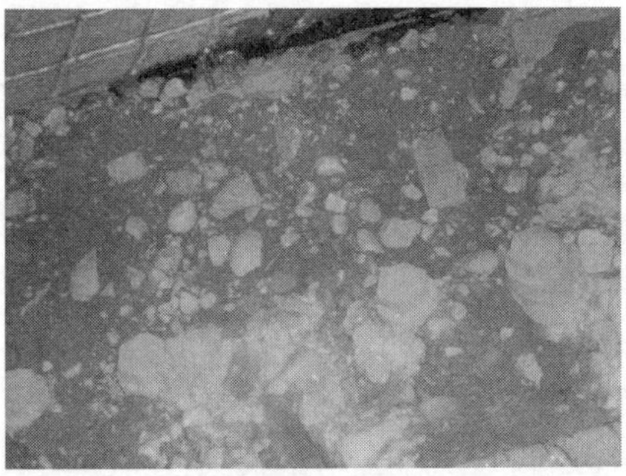

图 11　土压平衡盾构试验段前期碴土

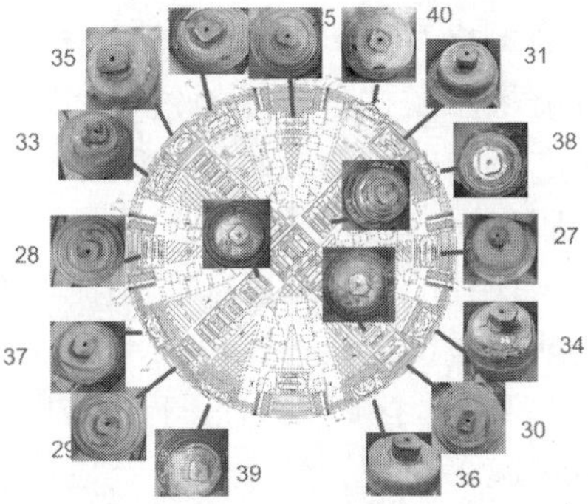

图 12　土压平衡盾构试验段刀具磨损情况

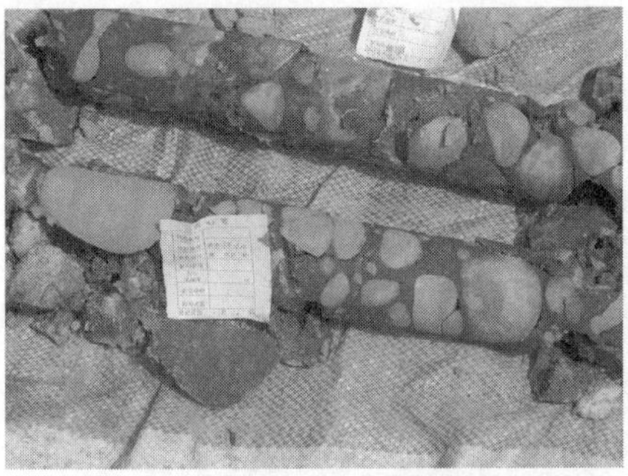

图 13　砂卵石地层旋喷桩岩芯

图 14　土压平衡盾构试验段刀盘中心泥饼

（2）中后期

根据试验段遇到的实际情况，通过参建各方的研究和交流，最后对以上问题有了统一的认识，决定主要从以下几方面进行改进：① 砂卵石应以“排出为主，破碎为辅”，可通过提高刀盘开口率（1 号线盾构 3 标将刀盘开口率由 25%提高到 29%）、刀具进行段差设计，适当减少滚刀数量，最大限度的发挥刮刀作用，新造盾构机应优选小幅面板＋辐条式刀盘，设计与刀盘配套的螺旋出土器；② 为减小盾构换刀对地面交通的影响，经过室内及现场多次试验，1 号线盾构区间砂卵石地层后期主要采用洞内带压换刀的方式，为减小施工风险，新购盾构机可考虑选用刀盘开口封闭装置；③ 为防止刀盘结泥饼、减少刀盘刀具磨损，对碴土改良系统注入材料（膨润土、泡沫、聚合物、水等）和注入时机、注入量等进行分段针对性研究；④ 严格控制地层损失率，一般段采用“土压平衡”、过建构筑物段采用“适当超压”的掘进模式，地层损失率控制在 3%以内，一般段碴土量以体积作为主要的控制指标、控制性建构筑物段还增加了质量控制指标。

图 15　上海地铁小幅面板＋辐条式刀盘

图 16　都灵地铁具有开口封闭装置的刀盘

通过以上针对性改进，1 号线中后期盾构区间在以下几方面得到了明显改善：① 盾构掘进速度明显度提高，综合进度为 180 m/月，最快达到 350 m/月；② 换刀距离明显加大，平均可达 400m；③ 刀盘结泥饼现象得到明显改善。

3.2.2 膨胀岩土地层

国内目前采用盾构法修建地铁区间隧道的城市较多，盾构设备资源相对紧张，因此在盾构选型时，我们尽量考虑所选的盾构机对成都砂卵石地层也应有一定的适应性。

由于膨胀岩具有浸水膨胀、风化开裂崩解；膨胀土具有吸水膨胀、失水收缩，再吸水再膨胀和再失水再收缩的可逆性变形特性，考虑到泥水盾构机泥水系统在施工过程中会对膨胀岩土有不利的影响，因此膨胀岩土地层盾构选型不建议采用泥水平衡式盾构机，而应优先考虑土压平衡式盾构机。

2 号线东段盾构区间 70% 位于膨胀岩、30% 位于膨胀土地层，因此设计的盾构机应适应软硬两种地层，根据盾构施工原理，黏土段刀具应以齿刀和刮刀为主、泥岩段刀具应以滚刀为主，所以盾构机应同时配置软土和硬岩两套刀具，施工过程中齿刀和滚刀应根据具体地层情况互换。该种刀具设计在铁路狮子洋隧道盾构机设计中已取得成功经验。

由于膨胀岩土段地下水较少，刀盘整体开口率可适当加大到 35%；同时为防止刀盘结泥饼，刀盘中心开口率可作进一步加大到 40%；碴土改良材料应优先考虑聚合物，慎用膨润土、水。

图 17 基岩岩面破坏图

图 18 齿刀、滚刀可互换的狮子洋隧道盾构机刀盘

3.3 盾构端头井

盾构进出洞是盾构法隧道施工过程中的关键工序之一，传统做法：在盾构进出洞前对井壁背后的土体进行加固，降水条件下采用人工凿除围护结构并切割其中的钢筋。由于围护结构凿除过程中结构自身破坏、结构背后土体暴露、地下水较难控制、地层土体损失等原因，施工过程中极易出现地层塌方而导致工程事故。

地铁 1 号线盾构区间共有始发和到达洞门各 22 个，盾构通过区域端头井围护结构均采用玻璃纤维筋，盾构进出洞时，在降水条件下盾构机直接切割围护结构而无需提前拆除盾构端头井临时端头墙围护结构，该方法避免了盾构进、出洞时端头井失稳工程事故的发生，增加了工程的安全性，同时取消了盾构井端头部地层加固的费用，取得了良好的技术经济效益。2 号线盾构端头井也将继续采用该种围护结构，同时该法也已在深圳、广州等城市地铁盾构端头井中被成功推广应用。

图 19 盾构达到直接切削玻璃纤维筋桩情况

图 20 玻璃纤维筋桩现场测试

3.4 盾构过建构筑物

3.4.1 总体情况

1 号线区间盾构隧道成功下（侧）穿了大量建（构）筑物，根据建（构）筑物种类，主要可分为以下几类：① 房屋，盾构隧道从火车北站站北居民小区、火车北站行包大楼、冶金宾馆（50 年代）等既有房屋下方穿过，其中隧道顶距冶金宾馆桩基础只有 0.75 m、隧道侧墙至行包房建筑物基础的最小距离只有 2 m；② 市政隧道，盾构隧道从罗天区间人防通道、天府隧道、滨江路隧道、小省区间人行过街通道等市政隧道下方穿过，其中盾道顶距滨江路隧道桩底只有 3.9 m、距小省区间人行过街通道底只有 2.0 m；③ 城市桥梁基础，盾构隧道从万福桥、锦江大桥、二环路人南立交桥、机场立交桥等城市桥梁基础侧（或下方）穿过，其中隧道侧墙与人南立交桥桩基础的水平净距只有 0.7 m；④ 城市河流，盾构隧道从沙河、府河、南河等城市河流正下方穿过，其中隧道顶与南河河床的距离只有 7 m；⑤ 市政管线，盾构隧道通过区域地下管线纵横，主要包括水管、煤气管、电力、通信电缆管等，其中省倪区间近 200 m 隧道与平行的市政污水管间的净距只有 1.0～2.0 m；⑥ 铁路股道，盾构隧道从火车北站和南站铁路股道下穿过，与铁路股道的距离约 8 m。

2 号线区间盾构隧道也将下（侧）大量建（构）筑物，根据建（构）筑物种类，主要有：① 房屋，盾构隧道将下穿白果林片区（多数为八九十年代 5~7 层的砖混或框架房屋，条形或柱下独立基础，密度大）、春熙路片区（成都市的商业中心区，房屋高，筏板或柱下独立基础，密度大）和秀水园小区等房屋；② 市政隧道，盾构隧道将下穿红星隧道、金河人防工程等市政隧道；③ 城市桥梁基础，盾构隧道将下（侧）穿羊犀线立交桥、摸底河桥、中医学院站立交桥、十二桥等城市桥梁基础；④ 城市河流，盾构隧道将从摸底河、西郊河、沙河、秀水河等城市河流下方穿过；⑤ 市政管线，盾构隧道通过区域地下管线密集，主要有水管、煤气管、电力、通信电缆管等；⑥ 铁路桥基，盾构隧道将侧下穿西环铁路立交桥基础；⑦ 高压铁塔基础，盾构隧道还将下侧穿 110 kV 高压铁塔基础。

3.4.2 设计施工原则

盾构下（侧）穿建构筑物的主要设计原则：① 综合考虑建（构）筑物结构形式、现状及与盾构隧道关系、地质条件及周边环境等因素，因地制宜，拟定相应的技术措施，以确保盾构施工安全和建（构）筑物、地下管线的正常使用；② 若建（构）筑物（或基础）位于盾构隧道破裂面影响范围内，原则上需要在盾构通过前对建（构）筑物（或基础）及破裂面影响范围内的地层进行加固，但若其本身具有防护措施、或者施工承包商具有类似工程的水平和经验保证，则主要通过控制盾构掘进参数来确保盾构施工安全和建（构）筑物的正常使用；③ 经综合判定需对建（构）筑物（或基础）地层进行预加固处理，但地面不具备实施条件或效果不甚理想的，采用在预制管片上增加注浆孔的方式通过洞内二次及三次注浆方式保证地层稳定及建（构）筑物的正常使用；④ 一般情况下，地表沉降应控制在 30 mm 以内，并以 20 mm 作为安全警界值，但当下穿建（构）筑物时，控制值应满足相关规范及相关权属部门的要求。

3.4.3 主要工程措施

工程措施以减少盾构施工过程中的地层变形和建（构）筑物变形作为主要目的，具体如下：

（1）施工过程控制

① 控制盾构参数

根据盾构穿越及上覆地层情况，设定适当的掘进参数并进行严格控制（主要包括刀盘和土舱压力、排土量和推进速度、螺旋机转速、千斤顶总推力等）以此确保开挖掌子面的稳定、尽量减少对地层扰动和开挖过程中的地层损失，其中将排土导致的地层损失率严格控制在 3%以内。

② 同步和二次注浆

在管片衬砌环脱出盾尾瞬间立即同步注浆并适当加大注浆量，以及时充分地填充衬砌与地层之间的空隙，在盾构完成拼装约 10 环处再以同步注浆层和围岩之间孔隙为主要填充对象（即突破同步注浆层）进行二次注浆，以弥补同步压浆的不足，必要时重复二次注浆。

③ 曲线段施工

为减少盾构在曲线段施工的超挖及其导致的不利影响，曲线段适当降低掘进速度，及时纠偏并严格控制纠偏幅度，加大盾尾同步注浆和洞内二次注浆量。

（2）地面注浆加固

综合考虑地质、周边环境、建（构）筑物结构形式及与盾构隧道的关系，盾构到达前对需要且具备施工条件的建（构）筑物地基进行地面注浆预加固处理。

注浆加固一般采用袖阀管，施工承包商也可结合自身经验和设备，在满足加固范围及相关技术要求的前提下，采取其他注浆方式。注浆材料以水泥浆液为主，特殊情况下选水泥－水玻璃浆液；注浆参数，包括注浆孔的布置、浆液配比、注浆压力、注浆顺序、注浆时间和注浆量等，经现场试验确定，并在注浆施工过程中根据监测反馈信息进行优化。

图 21　地表注浆孔

图 22　洞内注浆管

（3）洞内注浆加固

需对建（构）筑物地基作预加固处理，但不具备地面实施条件或者地面实施效果不甚理想时，采用洞内注浆加固地层的措施。

将盾构管片邻接块和标准块的注浆孔由 1 个增加为 3 个，盾构通过后，利用注浆孔（吊装孔）设注浆管，对盾构隧道拱顶和拱肩一定范围内的地层立即进行注浆加固。注浆管可选用 $\phi42\times3.5$ mm 的钢花管，长度一般为 3.5 m。注浆材料以水泥浆液为主，特殊情况下选水泥－水玻璃浆液；注浆参数，包括浆液配比、注浆压力、注浆顺序、注浆时间和注浆量等，经现场试验确定，并在注浆施工过程中根据监测反馈信息进行优化。

（4）地面补偿注浆

盾构始发及到达、通过建构筑物前换刀及检修后重启动、曲线段施工、下（侧）穿建构筑物时易出现较正常掘进段更多的超挖量，地层损失后易出现较大数量级的地层沉降，（严重时）不仅破坏既有建（构）筑物，甚至导致地面塌陷。盾构在以上特殊段掘进过程中，在采取施工过程控制、地面注浆加固、洞内注浆加固等各项技术措施的同时，为保证砂卵石地层的密实度、降低施工风险，将地面补偿注浆作为以上措施的有效补充措施。

地面补偿注浆采取通过地面在地层特定位置预埋注浆管的方式完成，注浆材料以水泥浆液为主，特殊情况下选水泥－水玻璃浆液；注浆参数经现场试验确定，并在注浆施工过程中根据监测反馈信息进行调整。

（5）针对性设计

对于结构特殊且施工过程中风险较高的建构筑物，采用特殊的针对性措施。

（6）监控量测

盾构施工及相关工程措施施工过程中，针对相应范围内的隧道结构、地层地表、建构筑物及地下管线，进行系统全面的监控量测，实行信息化施工。根据监测反馈信息，调整、优化各项施工参数，以确保盾构施工安全和建（构）筑物、地下管线的正常使用，必要时采取应急措施。

3.4.4　典型实例

（1）盾构下穿冶金宾馆

1 号线骡马市—天府广场站左线盾构区间正下穿冶金宾馆。该宾馆建于上世纪 90 年代，四层钢筋混凝土框架结构，人工挖孔端承桩基础，桩底埋深 8.6 m～13.08 m，盾构隧道拱顶埋深约 13 m，与基础的净距为 0.45 m～4.65 m。

图 23 冶金宾馆照片

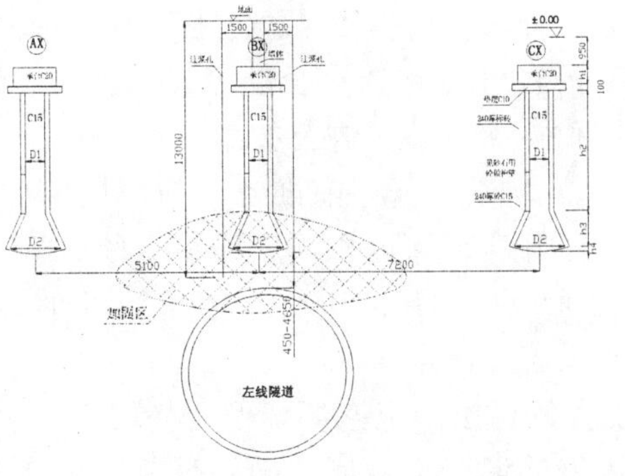

图 24 盾构隧道与基础关系及加固区域

盾构不但成功下穿了冶金宾馆，同时还保证了下穿期间宾馆正常营业。盾构下穿冶金宾馆主要采取了以下措施：① 控制施工过程：提前换刀，保证盾构安全快速通过，派专人严格监控出土量（保证地层体积损失率在 2%以内），保证同步注浆量（每环至少达到 8 m^3），选用双液速凝浆液；② 地面注浆预加固：通过袖阀管将桩底与隧顶之间地层进行预加固，并预留地面补偿注浆条件；③ 地面补偿注浆；④ 加强结构设计：将该段盾构管片主筋由 $\phi16$（$\phi18$）上调为 $\phi25$，将螺栓机械性能由 5.6 级上调为 8.8 级，将该段盾构管片拼装方式由错缝式拼装调整为通缝式拼装。⑤ 加强监测：派专人实行 24 小时监测，每小时监测一次，同时将测量结果及时反馈控制室。

（2）盾构侧穿锦江大桥

1 号线小天竺—锦江宾馆盾构区间将下穿南河，考虑到对南河锦江大桥的保护，区间从锦江大桥西侧下方通过，但由于大桥南北两侧均有重要建筑物，优化线路后，盾构隧道与桥梁基础的最小水平距离仍只有 2.043 m。

锦江大桥位于人民南路中段，建于 1958 年，为跨度 17.15 m 的三跨连续拱桥，桥长 51.45 m，桥面宽 50 m，台阶形扩大基础，厚 3 m，最下层为 110 级混凝土基础，其余二阶为 50 级水泥砂浆砌条石基础，桥墩为 50 级水泥砂浆砌城砖，拱部为 100 级水泥砂浆砌城砖拱。

图 25 锦江大桥照片

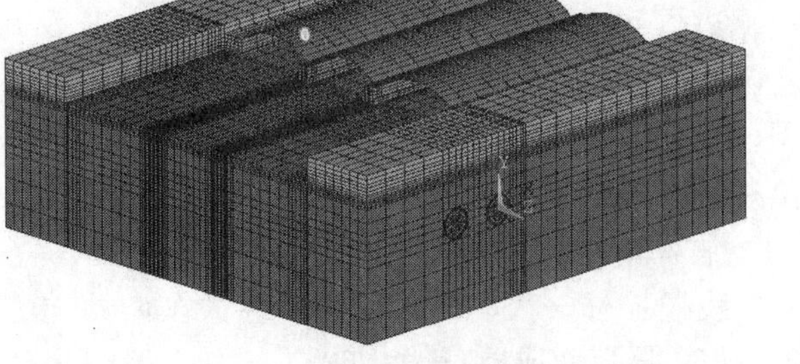

图 26 有限元数值模拟网格

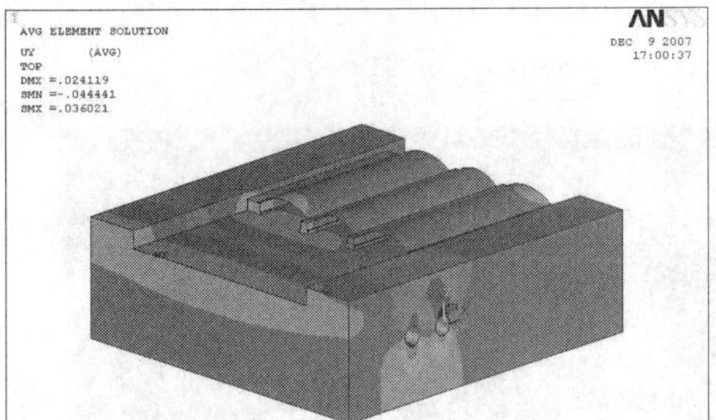

图 27 FEM 典型工况地层位移云图

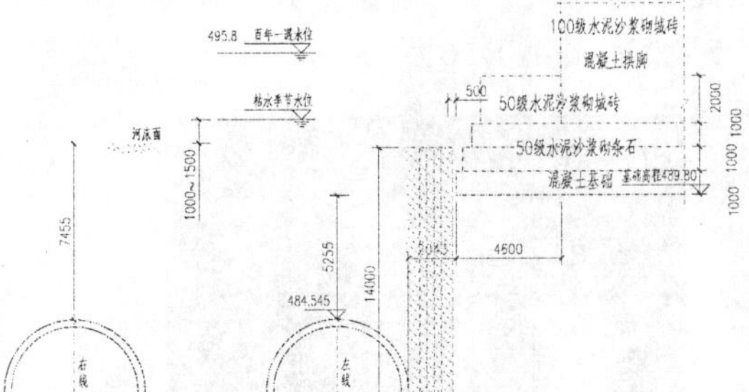

图 28 盾构隧道与桥墩关系及旋喷桩加固情况

根据监测资料，盾构下穿全过程，大桥基础水平及竖向位移均小于 1 cm。盾构侧下穿锦江大桥主要采取了以下措施：① 选择适合的工程措施：盾构通过前对主要的工程措施，地面注浆加固、钢管桩＋注浆隔断、钻孔隔断桩等，进行技术、经济对比研究，综合各方意见，最后选择了旋喷桩隔断法作为主要的工程措施；② 做好下穿前准备：与产权单位充分沟通，提前做好盾构纠偏及换刀作业；③ 做好过程控制：重点做好穿越河堤和河床浅覆土段盾构参数的控制，优选泥浆泡沫等碴土改良剂，同时做好盾尾密封及防喷涌；④ 加强监测：派专人 24 小时监控，备足机动设备、材料、人员，以保证大桥安全。

（3）盾构下穿污水管

1 号线省体育馆—倪家桥、倪家桥—桐梓林区间 1 km 范围内上方有一管径为 ϕ1 200 mm 的污水管，该污水管为钢筋混凝土带形基础，每节管长 2 000 mm、壁厚 100 mm，平口相接，接口采用水泥砂浆封堵，砂浆内埋 $20^{\#}$ 10×10 镀锌铁丝网，铁丝网埋入封堵砂浆 100 mm。污水管位于盾构隧道上方 1.2 m，与左、右线的水平净距分别为 6.49 m，3.51 m。

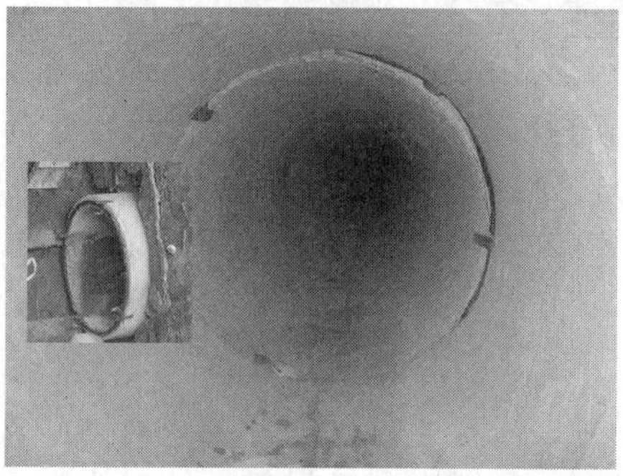

图 29 改迁后的污水管连接

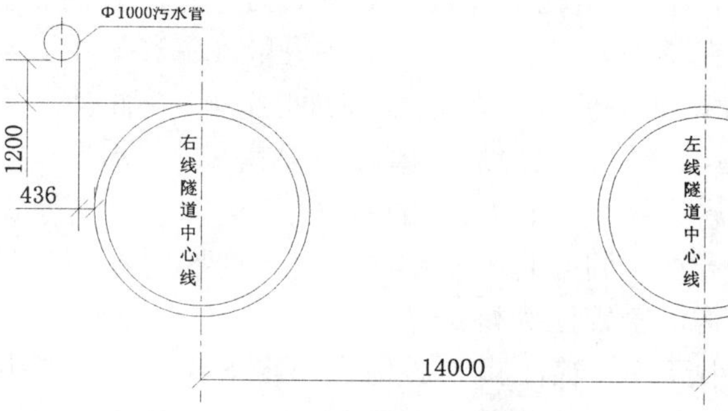

图 30 盾构隧道与改迁后的污水管关系

由于省体育馆站施工，对车站附近 240 m 范围内省体育馆～倪家桥区间污水管进行了改迁，改迁后管径变为 ϕ1 000 mm，接口采用宽 50 mm、长 200 mm 的工字形钢板卡槽连接。污水管与右线盾构隧道的最小水平净距为 0.436 m，最小竖直净距为 1.2 m。

盾构区间下（侧）穿污水管，主要采取了以下措施：① 做好盾构快速通过的准备：提前 30 m 对盾构设备进行全面检查及保养，做好筹划，确保有计划有步骤的带压进仓换刀；② 控制施工过程：严格控制过污水管段掘进参数，包括刀盘转速、推力、出土量、盾构机压力波动、同步注浆量等；③ 地面预埋注浆管，根据实际情况进行地面补偿注浆：共布设 27 个地面补偿注浆孔，其中最密处每隔 5 m 布置一个；④ 做好管片选型，保证管片拼装质量；⑤ 加强监测：每 5 m 布设一个测点，监测内容包括地表沉降、土体位移、地下水位和污水管流量及水位等，同时在地面派专人 24 小时不间断巡查；⑥ 做好污水截流应急预案。

（4）盾构下穿铁路股道

1 号线桐梓林—火车南站区间下穿火车南站 10 条线间距约 5 m 的平行铁路股道，其中 $10^{\#}$ 股道已废弃，$3^{\#}$ 和 $5^{\#}$ 股道为成昆正线，60 轨，其余股道为到发线、站线，50 轨，均为混凝土轨枕，碎石道床。

地铁区间隧道中心线间距 15 m，与铁路股道平面呈 86° 交叉，隧道顶距股道净距为 7.448 m。根据现场及铁路部门意见，盾构隧道通过前需对未废弃的铁路股道进行扣轨加固处理，具体为：$3^{\#}$ 股道采用 D24 梁、$5^{\#}$ 股道采用 D16 梁、其余用工字钢束梁（一束采用 4 根 56b 型工字钢）。

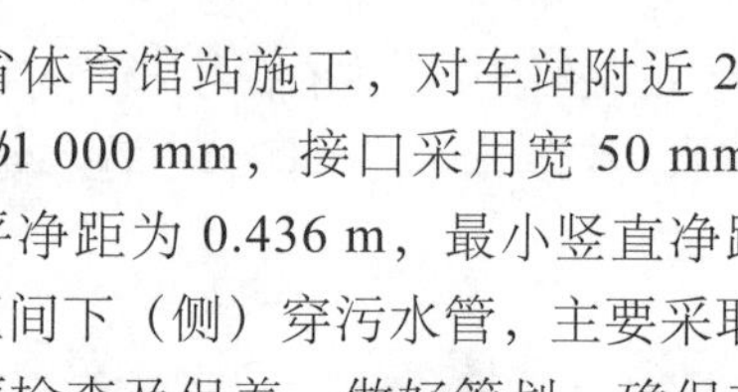

图 31 火车南站铁路股道扣轨

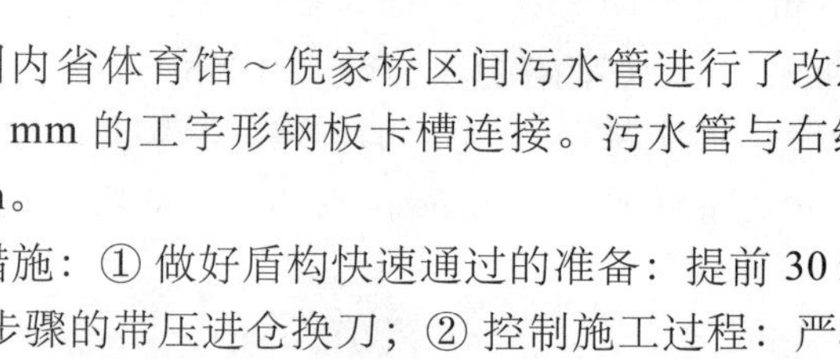

图 32 交叉隧道空间关系图

(5) 空间交叉隧道

地铁 2 号线西延线犀浦站与大铁实现了同台同向换乘，由于大铁行车方向与地铁相反，因此线路需进行换边，综合考虑各边界条件后，决定在犀浦站的下一个站西区站后盾构区间进行线路换边，因此西区—外语学院约 600 m 盾构区间为空间交叉隧道，交叉隧道的空间关系如图 32 所示。

对空间交叉隧道进行综合研究后，决定采取如下措施：① 盾构到达前，对重叠隧道地层进行加固处理；② 根据成都砂卵石层特点、周边环境及盾构机实际情况，采用先修下侧隧道，后修上侧隧道的施工顺序；③ 优化盾构掘进和注浆参数，严格控制出土量，将地层损失率控制在 2%～3%以内；④ 制定全面细致的施工组织，避免在该段区间进行换刀作业和检修设备，为盾构顺利掘进创造条件；⑤ 及时盾尾注浆、适时采用穿越同步注浆层的二次或三次注浆，并根据实际情况对先建隧道采用地表跟踪注浆和在管片上增设二次注浆孔；在后建隧道通过前，视具体情况在先建隧道内架设移动临时支撑等工程措施；⑥ 在后建盾构施工过程中，视情况可考虑对隧道穿越范围局部区域实施管井降水；⑦ 盾构施工过程中，进行全面、系统的监控测量；⑧ 根据计算结果，加强下侧隧道结构。

3.5 产、学、研

1 号线盾构区间由成都地铁公司、中铁二院、西南交通大学、同济大学、中铁隧道局、中铁十三局等组成了《成都地铁盾构区间设计施工关键技术研究》科研小组；成都地铁公司、中铁二院、西南交通大学等组成了《玻璃纤维筋在盾构端头井中的应用》（该科研成果 2008 年获成都市科技进步二等奖）；2 号线盾构区间由成都地铁公司、西南交通大学、中铁二院等组成了《膨胀岩土地区修建地铁盾构工程综合技术研究》科研小组，以上科研成果直接指导了 1，2 号线区间的设计和施工。

图 33 盾构科研室内试验台架

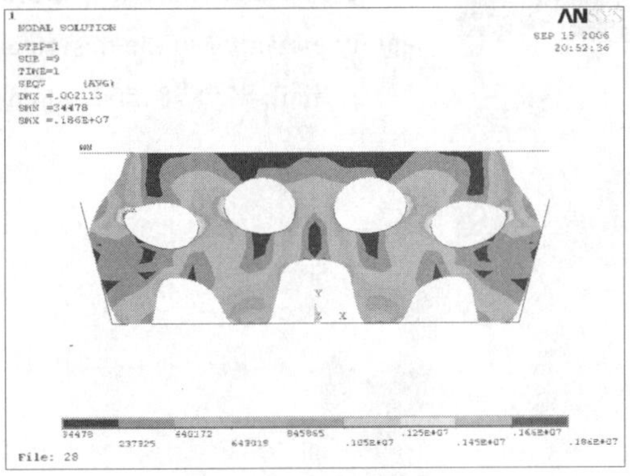

图 34 FEM 典型工况密封垫应力云图

4 结 语

本文根据笔者参加成都地铁 1、2 号线盾构区间隧道全过程的设计和现场配合施工，对成都地铁 1、2 号盾构区间盾构管片、盾构设备及配套、盾构端头井及盾构下（侧）穿建（构）筑物等做了一个简单的总结介绍，目前成都地铁 2 号线盾构区间正处于全面开工阶段，1 号线南延线盾构区间、4 号线盾构区间也将全面开始初步设计，同时国内的地铁、公路、铁路、水下、电力等盾构隧道建设正如火如荼，希望本文能为成都以后的盾构隧道建设提供参考验，并能为国内外类似地层条件下盾构隧道的修建提供借鉴，为盾构隧道的技术发展作一份贡献。

参考文献（References）：

[1] 林刚，倪娟，罗世培. 地铁结构地震破坏分析及设计关键技术[J]. 现代隧道技术，2009(4).
[2] 林刚，罗世培. 玻璃纤维筋在盾构端头井围护结构中的应用[J]. 铁道工程学报，2009(8).

[3] 铁道第二勘察设计院，西南交通大学建筑勘察设计研究院. 成都地铁 1 号线一期工程初步设计[R]
[4] 铁道第二勘察设计院. 成都地铁 1 号线一期工程施工图设计[R]
[5] 中铁二院工程集团有限责任公司，西南交通大学建筑勘察设计研究院. 成都地铁 2 号线一期工程初步设计[R]
[6] 中铁二院工程集团有限责任公司. 成都地铁 2 号线一期工程施工图设计[R]
[7] 中铁二院工程集团有限责任公司. 成都地铁 2 号线二期工程（西延伸线）初步设计[R]
[8] 成都地铁公司，中铁二院工程集团有限责任公司，西南交通大学.《玻璃纤维筋在盾构端头井中的应用》[R]
[9] 成都地铁公司，西南交通大学，同济大学，中铁二院工程集团有限责任公司，中铁隧道局，中铁十三局等.《成都地铁盾构区间设计施工关键技术研究》[R]
[10] 成都地铁公司，西南交通大学，中铁二院工程集团有限责任公司.《膨胀岩土地区修建地铁盾构工程综合技术研究（中间报告）》[R]
[11] 成都地铁 1 号线盾构 1～4 标段，《成都地铁 1 号线盾构区间施工技术交流材料》[R]

作者简介（Bio-data）：

林刚，男，汉族，1976 年 8 月生，工学博士，高级工程师。2005 年毕业于西南交通大学地下工程系，现任职于中国中铁二院工程集团有限责任公司，主要从事隧道工程设计及科研工作。

Gang LIN, male, the Han Nationality, born in August,1976, doctor of engineering, senior engineer. Graduated from the Department of Underground Engineering of Southwest Jiaotong University in 2005 .Now working in the China Railway Eryuan Engineering Group Co.,Ltd, mainly engaging in the design and research work in the field of tunnel engineering.

E-mail: 429878450@qq.com

基于渗流-应力耦合的水下盾构隧道结构特性研究

谢红强[1,2]　何　川[2]

[1]四川大学 水利水电学院，四川　成都　610065
[2]西南交通大学 地下工程系，四川　成都　610031

【摘　要】 高水压是影响水下盾构隧道施工期结构特性的重要因素，其本质上是掘进过程中渗流场-应力场耦合效应对管片结构内力的改变。结合国内某过江盾构隧道工程，引入渗流-应力耦合模型，采用三维有限元法，对水下盾构隧道的掘进施工进行全过程模拟，揭示施工过程中围岩及结构的渗流场、应力场及位移场分布规律，并将数值模拟结果与现场量测值进行比较，计算结果与实测值吻合较好，所得结论可对类似工程提供参考。

【关键词】 盾构隧道；结构特性；液固耦合；有限元法

STUDY ON STRUCTURAL CHARACTERISTICS OF SUBRIVER SHIELD TUNNEL BASED ON SEEPAGE-STRESS COUPLING

Hongqiang XIE[1,2], Chuan HE[2]

[1]*College of Hydraulic & Hydroelectric, Sichuan University, Chengdu 610065, Sichuan, China*

[2]*Department of Underground Engineering, Southwest Jiaotong University, Chengdu 610031, Sichuan, China*

Abstract: High water pressure is one of significant factors which affect structure characteristics of sub-river shield tunnel during construction stage. Essentially, it is coupling action of seepage and stress field which change the internal force of segment structures. Combined with subriver shield tunnel in China, coupling model of seepage and stress field is introduced and 3D finite element method is applied to simulate overall process of tunneling for subriver shield tunnel, so as to reveal the distribution laws of seepage, stress and displacement field. At the same time, numerical simulation data are compared with results of in-situ test, and well in agreement.

Key words: shield tunnel; structural characteristic; liquid-solid coupling; FEM

1 引　言

随着世界各国经济联系的日益加深，对修建水下隧道，实现各大陆陆路相通，已提到了议事日程。到目前为止，世界上已修建了许多水底隧道，其结构形式以水底深埋暗挖隧道或盾构隧道或沉管隧道为主，而国内也开始了水下隧道的修建，如已建的南京地铁玄武湖盾构隧道、上海崇明隧道、重庆长江排水盾构隧道以及在建的武汉过长江盾构隧道、过松花江隧道等，对于此类水下隧道的修建而言，无论采用矿山法、盾构法还是沉管法，隧道在高水压条件下的结构稳定性问题都是隧道建设中的一个关键技术问题，甚至是工程成败与否的控制性因素，这就涉及到隧道围岩及结构场与高水压条件下渗流场之间的相互作用问题，即应力场与渗流场的耦合效应。

近年来，国内外在渗流－应力耦合方面开展了大量的工作，主要集中在岩石渗透率、孔隙水压力分

基金项目：国家自然科学基金（50778154）；铁道部课题（2007G036、2006G007B）

布等方面[1~3]，而在隧道液固耦合方面，国内外也开展一些工作，杨明举[4]通过对地下水封裸洞储气工程应力场、渗流场以及储气场各自特性及相互作用研究，建立了地下水封储气耦合的数学模型；黄涛，杨立中[5]提出了渗流与应力耦合环境下裂隙围岩隧道涌水量预测计算的确定性数学模型方法（包括理论解析法、经验解析法和水文地质数值模拟法）；李宗利[6]以简单的圆形隧洞为研究对象，考虑渗流场作用对其弹塑性解析解进行了研究；李廷春，李术才[7]依据流固耦合理论，应用三维快速拉格朗日法进行数值分析了厦门开挖后的应力分布、洞周位移、塑性区、孔隙水压力分布等结果。而对于盾构隧道，特别是水下盾构隧道的渗流-应力耦合方向的研究，国内则刚刚起步。

对于水下盾构隧道而言，渗流场与应力场的耦合作用是一个相对复杂的问题，不仅表现在工程岩/土体的渗流场和应力场都是随时间、空间变化的，两者耦合作用又处于一种复杂的动态变化过程中，尤其在施工期间，掘进过程引起的液固耦合效应主要表现在围岩及水压对管片结构内力的改变[8]。已建的重庆长江排水盾构隧道工程受地质条件、水文条件及工期的控制，选择采用盾构施工法修建，隧道将主要穿越单轴抗压强度从 7.3 MPa 到 69.4 MPa 的软硬程度差异极大的砂岩和泥岩层，顶部与长江最高水位差约 60 m，在施工及使用阶段隧道均将承受极高的水压（0.6 MPa），施工条件十分困难，且隧道主体结构体系复杂、未知因素众多，而目前国内在修建同类水下隧道上刚刚起步，经验欠缺，尚无同类水下隧道的先例。为了解决水下隧道工程修建关键技术问题，确保施工期安全，并在环境保护、建成后可靠性等诸多方面取得成效，开展高水压作用下水下盾构隧道的结构力学特性及施工控制技术研究对于该工程具有重要的技术支持，并为同类隧道的设计、施工提供重要参考。

2 水下隧道渗流场与应力场耦合分析的数学模型

2.1 渗流 – 应力耦合的数学模型[9]

高水压隧道的渗流场与应力场耦合分析的数学模型可表示为：

$$\begin{cases}[K]\{\phi\}+\{Q\}=[S]\dfrac{\mathrm{d}\phi}{\mathrm{d}t}\\ \Delta\varepsilon_V=\dfrac{n\gamma}{E_w}\Delta\phi\\ \{\sigma\}=[D]\left[\{\varepsilon\}+\{\Delta\varepsilon_V\}\right]\end{cases}\tag{1}$$

式中 $[K]$——总渗透矩阵；

$[Q]$——源（汇）项列阵；

$[S]$——贮水矩阵；

$\{\sigma\}$——岩体的应力列阵；

$\{\varepsilon\}$——不考虑渗透压力的应变矩阵；

$\Delta\varepsilon_V$——渗透水压力引起岩体变形的应变列阵；

$\Delta\phi=\phi-\phi_0$——静水头差；

$[D]$——弹性矩阵，可用下式表示：

$$[D]=\frac{E(1-\nu)}{(1+\nu)(1-2\nu)}\begin{vmatrix}1 & A & A & 0 & 0 & 0\\ & 1 & A & 0 & 0 & 0\\ & & 1 & 0 & 0 & 0\\ & \text{对} & & B & 0 & 0\\ & \text{称} & & & B & 0\\ & & & & & B\end{vmatrix}\tag{2}$$

式中 $A=\dfrac{\nu}{1-\nu}$；$B=\dfrac{1-2\nu}{2(1-\nu)}$。

2.2 有限元数值解法

渗流场与应力场耦合分析的有限元解法及步骤为：

①假设应力场 $\sigma_{ij}^0=0$，求得均质岩体的渗透系数，即 $K_0\left(\sigma_{ij}^0=0\right)=K_0(x,y,z)=K_0$ 为常数，按有限元法求解渗流场，得出水头分布 $\phi_1(x,y,z)$；

②根据水头分布 $\phi_1(x,y,z)$，分别求出各结点处的静水压力 $P_{s1}(x,y,z)$、动水压力 $P_d(x,y,z)$ 和渗透体力 $f_1(x,y,z)$；

③根据静水压力 $P_{s1}(x,y,z)$、动水压力 $P_d(x,y,z)$ 和渗透体力 $f_1(x,y,z)$，按有限元法求解应力场分布 $\sigma_{ij}^1(x,y,z)$ 和应变场 $\varepsilon_{ij}^1(x,y,z)$ 分布，并求出体积应变场 $\varepsilon_V^1(x,y,z)$；

④根据 $\sigma_{ij}^1(x,y,z)$ 和 $\varepsilon_V^1(x,y,z)$，求出应力场改变所引起渗透系数变化 K_1 和水头压力变化 ΔP；

⑤重复①～④步，直至迭代满足以下要求：

$$\begin{cases}\left|\phi_{n+1}(x,y,z)-\phi_n(x,y,z)\right|\leqslant\varepsilon_\phi\\ \left|\sigma_{ij}^{n+1}-\sigma_{ij}^n\right|\leqslant\varepsilon_\sigma\end{cases}\tag{3}$$

式中 $\phi_n(x,y,z)$、$\phi_{n+1}(x,y,z)$——第 n 次迭代和第 n+1 次迭代求得的渗流场水头分布；

ε_ϕ——水头的求解精度；

$\sigma_{ij}^n(x,y,z)$、$\sigma_{ij}^{n+1}(x,y,z)$——第 n 次迭代和第 n+1 次迭代求得的应力张量场分布；

ε_σ——应力的求解精度。

3 水下盾构隧道渗流-应力耦合的有限元模型

3.1 计算模型及计算参数

为了实现与现场试验成果对比，双场耦合有限元计算选择水下盾构隧道现场测试剖面（K0+600 m）为目标计算对象。计算范围的选取以能消除边界效应为原则，充分考虑河床的真实地形、地质条件和隧址区长江水与围岩及隧道主体结构的相互作用过程，选取的模型范围为：沿隧道轴线方向，以目标断面为对称，各选取 100 m，即隧道里程 K0+500 m～K0+700 m（X 轴方向，南岸指向北岸为正）；顺长江水流方向，以隧道轴线为对称，上、下游各取 70 m（Y 轴方向，上游指向下游为正）；铅直方向向上取至河床表面，向下取至弱透水层一定深度（▽60.00 m）（Z 轴方向，竖直向上为正）。对所选取的计算区域进行有限元的结构离散，采用 8 节点等参单元模拟围岩及主体结构，计算模型共离散 29 825 个节点，27 136 个单元，三维有限元模型参见图 1。

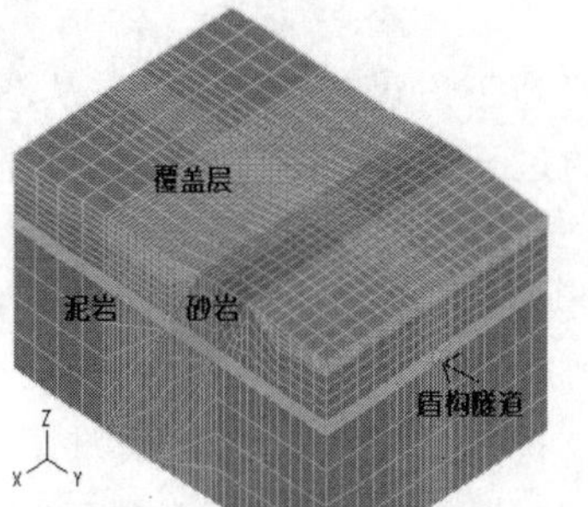

图 1 三维有限元计算模型

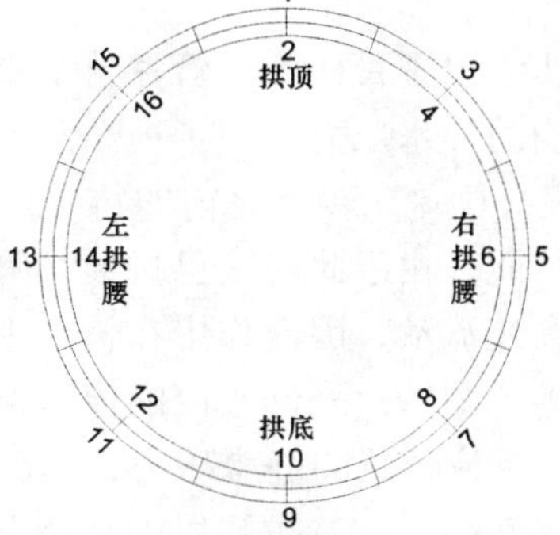

图 2 目标断面管片特征点

计算中对砂岩、泥岩及覆盖层等地质围岩体采用 DP 模型进行模拟，管片混凝土则按弹性计算，围岩及结构的物理力学参数参见表 1。

表 1 围岩及结构计算参数

岩性	容重（kN/m^3）	弹模（GPa）	泊松比	凝聚力（MPa）	内摩擦角（°）	孔隙率（%）	渗透系数（cm/s）
卵石土	20.0	0.40	0.40	0.02	30	50	1.0×10^{-1}
泥岩	25.2	6.36	0.33	1.85	35	7	2.0×10^{-4}
砂岩	26.5	8.82	0.15	6.27	62	10	4.1×10^{-3}
C50 混凝土	25.0	35.0	0.15	—	—	0.1	1.0×10^{-9}

为了研究水下盾构隧道掘进施工过程中，前方水体（长江水、基岩裂隙水等）与围岩及结构的相互动态关系，故而在流固耦合计算中对盾构隧道的掘进施工过程进行动态数值模拟，从而探明施工过程中围岩及主体结构应力、变形及水压力动态变化特征及相互影响关系，水下盾构隧道施工过程参见图 3。

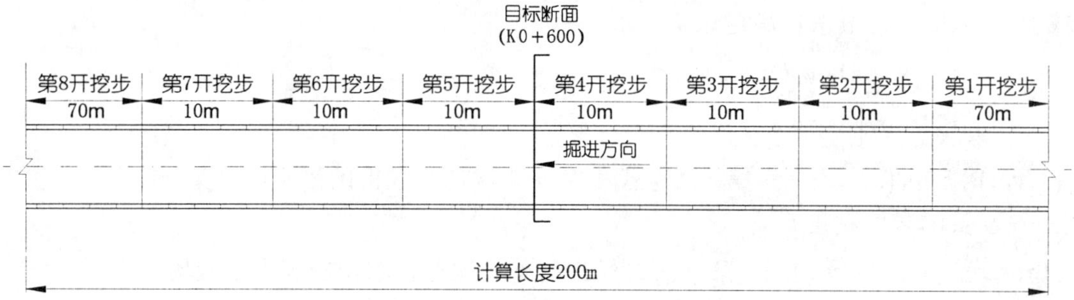

图 3 水下盾构隧道施工过程模拟示意图

3.2 计算边界条件

对水下盾构隧道进行液固双场耦合分析时，其计算边界条件分为两种，即应力边界条件和渗流边界条件。结合水下盾构隧道的地形、地质、水文条件及隧道的施工过程，本次耦合计算的边界条件按如下定义，即应力边界为：模型两侧和底部为法向约束，顶部为自由边界，初始应力场取自重应力场；渗流边界条件为：模型两侧及底部不透水（假定与外界无水量交换），顶部边界为河床，承受实际长江水压力水头（根据现场监测，典型断面施工时的长江水位基本维持在 175.0 m 左右，因此计算模拟假定在 175.0 m 长江水位条件下进行），盾构隧道衬砌与围岩接触，衬砌内表面为零水压力边界（衬砌混凝土假定极弱透水），隧道开挖面则根据泥水式盾构机泥浆流量，设置为定流量边界。

4 施工期渗流-应力耦合计算成果分析

4.1 围岩及管片衬砌的渗流场分布特征

表 2 和图 4 给出了目标断面管片特征点的水压力量值及随施工进度的变化曲线。从图表中可以看出，作用在管片结构的外水压力经历了一个从无到有，从小到大的过程，即：盾构脱环前，作用在管片上的水压力为零（表 2 中施工步 4 之前的特征点水压力实际为围岩水压力值）；在盾构脱环后，水压力迅速作用到管片上，然而，由于此时（已拼装）管片接近前方存在大量水量交换的掌子面，管片外表面的水流在掘进过程中高速流动，因而作用在管片上的外水压力值一般较小；随着盾构掘进的深入和目标管片离掌子面越来越远，则管片外部水流的流速减缓，甚至接近静止状态，则外水压力值基本不变并达到最大值（等于或小于相应位置的静水压力，量值比值约为 0.9～1.0）。从管片外水压力的环向分布来看，基本呈现拱顶低、拱底高，左右拱腰居中且呈左右对称。无论是管片外水压力随施工进度的变化规律还是环向分布特征，耦合结果与现场跟踪实测结构具有较好的一致性。

表 2　不同施工步管片特征点水压力量值（单位：MPa）

特征点	拱　顶		右拱腰		拱　底		左拱腰	
	1-外侧	2-内侧	5-外侧	6-内侧	9-外侧	10-内侧	13-外侧	15-内侧
初始状态	0.43	0.44	0.45	0.45	0.46	0.46	0.45	0.45
施工步 1	0.42	0.42	0.45	0.45	0.48	0.48	0.45	0.45
施工步 2	0.41	0.42	0.45	0.45	0.48	0.47	0.45	0.45
施工步 3	0.41	0.41	0.44	0.44	0.47	0.47	0.44	0.44
施工步 4	0.33	0.00	0.36	0.00	0.42	0.00	0.34	0.00
施工步 5	0.37	0.00	0.40	0.00	0.45	0.00	0.39	0.00
施工步 6	0.41	0.00	0.45	0.00	0.48	0.00	0.45	0.00
施工步 7	0.41	0.00	0.45	0.00	0.48	0.00	0.45	0.00
施工步 8	0.41	0.00	0.45	0.00	0.48	0.00	0.45	0.00

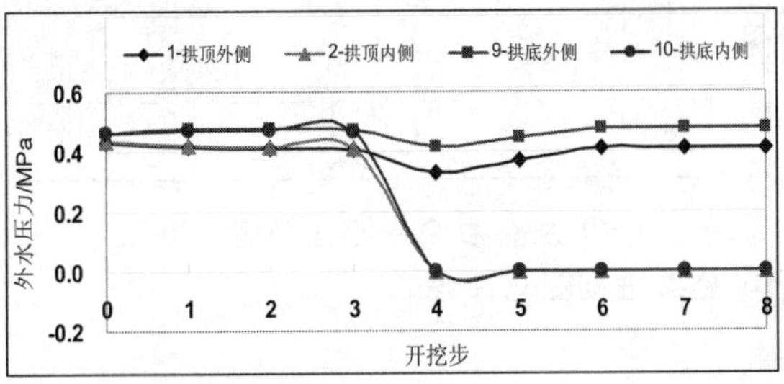

（a）拱顶和拱底

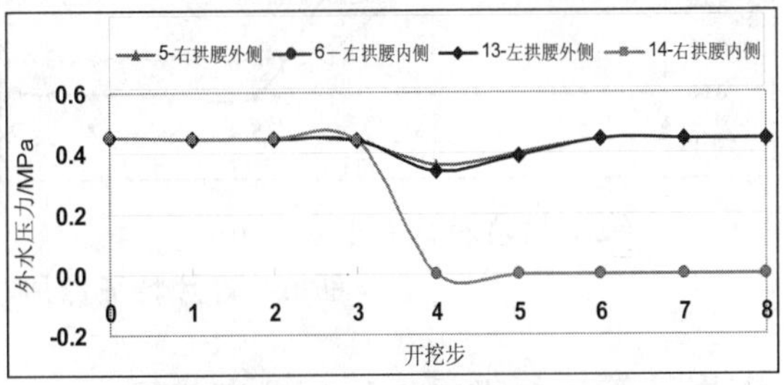

（b）左、右拱腰

图 4　典型特征点孔隙水压力随施工进度变化曲线

4.2　围岩及管片衬砌的应力场分布特征

表 3 给出了目标断面管片特征点的主应力量值；图 5 给出了管片特征点主应力量值随施工进度的变化曲线。从图和表中可以看出，管片结构上的应力值也经历了从小到大直至稳定的一个过程，即：盾构脱环前，管片上的应力实际为自重应力，量值较小（表 2 和表 3 中施工步 4 之前的特征点应力实际为围岩应力）；在盾构脱环后，围岩压力迅速作用到管片上，对最大主应力而言：管片拱顶和拱底的内、外侧的最大主应力均增大，而拱腰内侧和外侧的最大主应力均增大，拱顶和拱底的增幅较大；而对最小主应力，拱顶和拱底的外侧的最小主应力增大，内侧最小主应力降低，左右拱腰的内外侧最小主应力均增大。当目标断面距前方施工一定距离后，管片结构上的主应力均趋于稳定，其中拱顶的最大主应力为 2.56 MPa，最小主应力为 0.32 MPa；左、右拱腰最大主应力为 5.24 MPa，最小主应力为 0.45 MPa；拱顶的最大主应力为 2.81 MPa，最小主应力为 0.44 MPa。

表 3　不同施工步管片特征点主应力量值（单位：MPa）

特征点	拱　顶				右拱腰				拱　底				左拱腰			
	1-外侧		2-内侧		5-外侧		6-内侧		9-外侧		10-内侧		13-外侧		14-内侧	
	σ_1	σ_3	σ_1	σ_3	σ_1	σ_3	σ_1	σ_3	σ_1	σ_3	σ_1	σ_3	σ_1	σ_3	σ_1	σ_3
初始状态	0.70	0.24	0.67	0.24	0.78	0.27	0.78	0.27	0.91	0.30	0.86	0.30	0.78	0.27	0.78	0.27
施工步 1	0.70	0.25	0.67	0.24	0.78	0.27	0.78	0.27	0.91	0.30	0.86	0.31	0.78	0.27	0.78	0.27
施工步 2	0.70	0.24	0.68	0.24	0.78	0.27	0.78	0.27	0.91	0.30	0.86	0.31	0.78	0.27	0.78	0.27
施工步 3	0.71	0.24	0.68	0.24	0.79	0.27	0.79	0.28	0.92	0.30	0.87	0.31	0.79	0.27	0.79	0.28
施工步 4	2.85	0.28	2.66	0.12	1.48	0.38	2.55	0.30	2.92	0.35	2.78	0.25	1.48	0.38	2.55	0.30
施工步 5	2.53	0.32	2.56	0.08	2.45	0.43	5.22	0.26	2.81	0.44	2.54	0.00	2.45	0.43	5.22	0.26
施工步 6	2.52	0.32	2.56	0.08	2.46	0.44	5.24	0.27	2.81	0.44	2.54	0.00	2.46	0.44	5.24	0.27
施工步 7	2.51	0.32	2.56	0.08	2.46	0.44	5.24	0.27	2.81	0.44	2.54	0.00	2.46	0.44	5.24	0.27
施工步 8	2.51	0.32	2.56	0.08	2.46	0.45	5.24	0.27	2.81	0.44	2.54	0.01	2.46	0.45	5.24	0.27

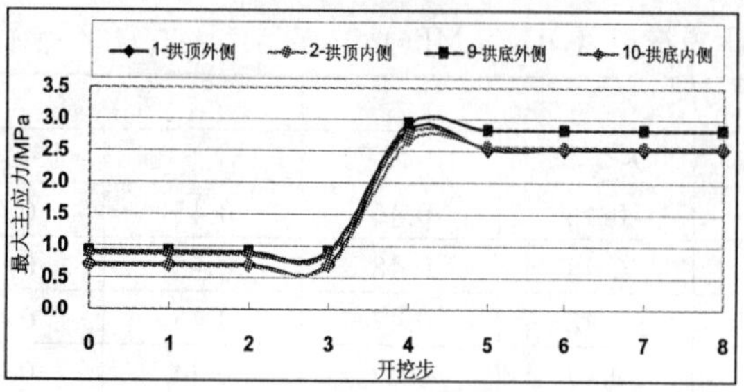

（a）拱顶和拱底大主应力

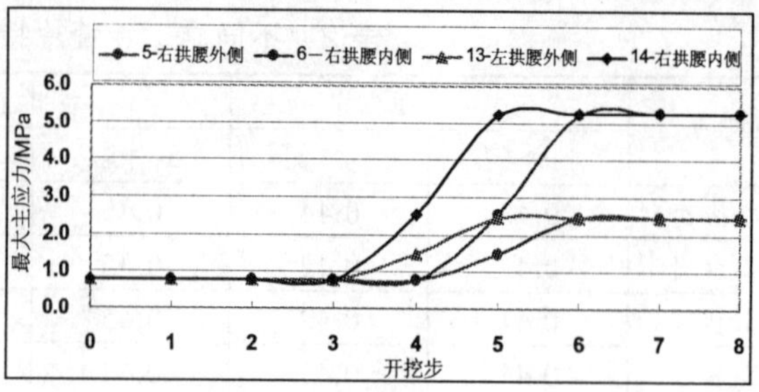

（b）左、右拱腰大主应力

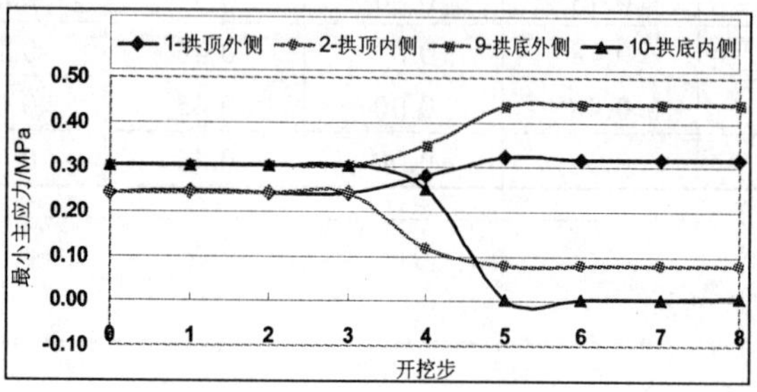

（c）拱顶和拱底小主应力

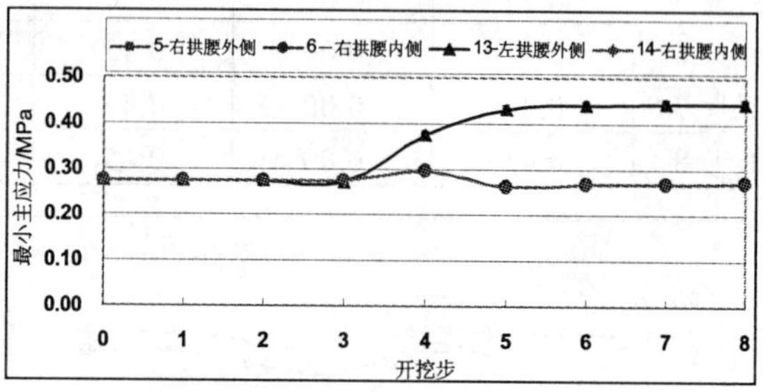

（d）左、右拱腰小主应力

图 5　管片特征点最小主应力随施工进度变化曲线

4.3　围岩及管片衬砌的位移场分布特征

图 6 给出了目标断面管片特征点变形随施工进度的变化曲线，从图中可以看出，隧道管片结构上的变形以拱顶下沉和拱底上拱的变形为主，拱腰变形以水平外扩变形为主，但在量值上较拱顶和拱底变形要小得多；从施工进度上看，随着施工的深入，无论是拱顶、拱底还是拱腰，其整体变形均呈增大的趋势，仅在变形增幅上有所差异；这种因开挖引起的变形增量在盾构掘进到前方一定距离后便趋于稳定。

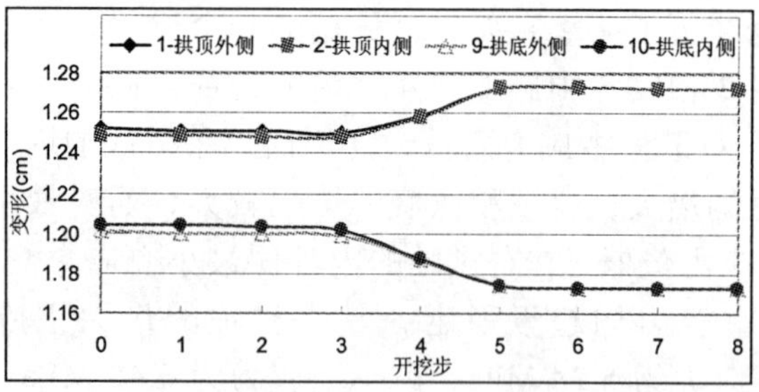

（a）拱顶和拱底

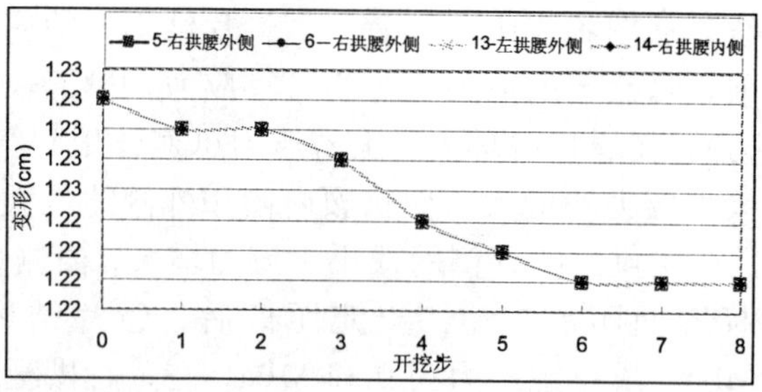

（b）左、右拱腰

图 6　管片特征点变形随施工进度变化曲线

4.4　施工期现场测试结果与液固耦合计算的对比分析

图 7 给出了施工期隧道管片外水压力环向分布对比图，从图中可以看出，两种手段所获得的水压力无论在分布上还是在量值上都有所差异，现场测试的外水压力在管片环向呈不对称分布，量值较数值计算值小，但水压力极值差较大，这主要在于测试值受现场条件的影响较大（同步注浆不均匀性及裂隙分布不均匀性）；而数值计算中因未考虑同步注浆及裂隙分布的影响，水压力的分布左右侧基本呈对称分布，且水压力极值差不大。从水压力随施工进度变化的对比（图 9）可以看出，数值模拟和实测的水压力值随施工进度的变化规律基本相似，但数值计算的规律性更强，而量值上则是数值计算的要大一些。

图 8 给出了施工期隧道管片应力的环向分布对比图。从图中可以看出，现场跟踪试验与流固耦合计算所得管片应力的空间分布规律基本相似，拉应力和压应力的分布部位基本相同，但由于实测值受现场因素（同步注浆不均匀性、管片破损等）的影响，分布规律较数值模拟要差得多，且量值上现场测试值

要大一些（应力集中、管片破损等）。

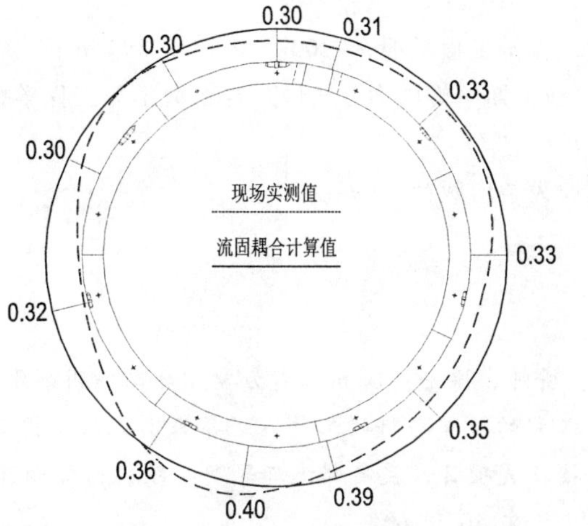

图 7　管片外水压力环向分布对比图

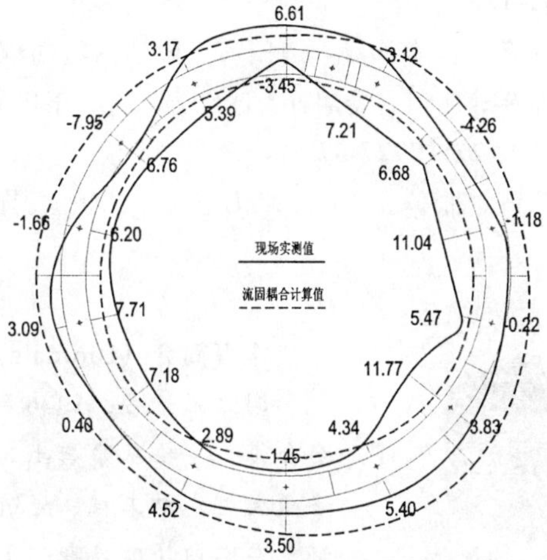

图 8　管片应力环向分布对比图

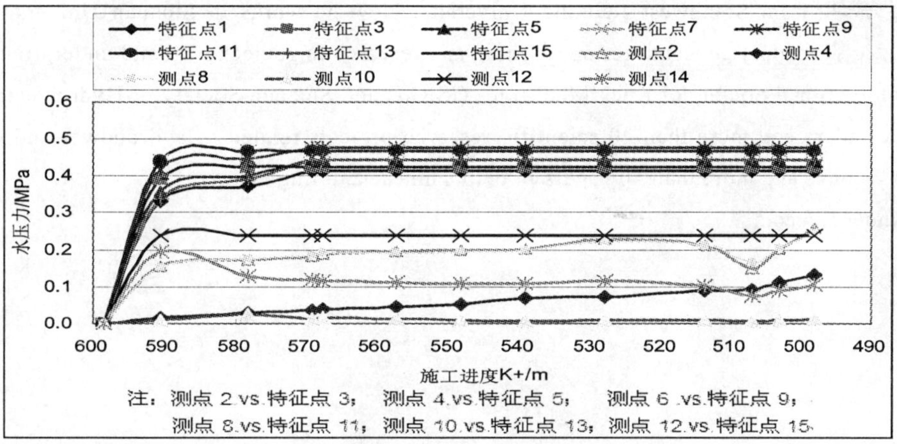

图 9　管片外水压力随施工进度变化对比图

5　结　语

结合国内某高水压过江盾构隧道的工程实际情况，从渗流场与应力场的耦合机理及分析方法出发，引入渗流场～应力场耦合的数学模型及相应的数学解法，采用三维有限元法，获得施工期水下隧道围岩及结构的渗流场、应力场及位移场分布特征，并对数值模拟结果和实测结果进行了对比分析，从而为水下盾构隧道的设计及施工期主体结构稳定性评价提供直接的参考依据。

参考文献（References）：

[1] Biot M A. General solution of the equation of elasticity and consolidation for porous material [J]. Jour. Appl. Mech., 1956(78): 91-96.

[2] Verruijt. Elastic storage of aquifers [A]. In: Flow Through Porous Media [C]. R J M. New York: Tiho Wiley, 1969, 5-65.

[3] Killsall P C et al. Evaluation of excavation induced changes in rock permeability [J]. Int. J. Rock Mech. Min. Sci., 1984(3).

[4] 杨明举．地下水封裸洞储存 LPG 耦合问题的变分原理及应用[J]．岩石力学与工程学报，2003(4).

[5] 黄涛．渗流场与应力场耦合环境下裂隙围岩型隧道涌水量预测的研究[D]．西南交通大学博士论文，1997.

[6] 李宗利，任青文等．考虑渗流场影响深埋圆形隧洞的弹塑性解[J]．岩石力学与工程学报，2004，23(8)：1291-1295．

[7] 李廷春，李术才等．厦门海底隧道的流固耦合分析[J]．岩土工程学报，2004，26(3)：397-401．

[8] 夏炜洋，何川，晏启祥，谢红强. 高水压岩质盾构隧道施工期结构内力分析[J]. 岩石力学与工程学报，2007，26（增 2）：3727-3731

[9] 仵彦卿，张倬元. 岩体水力学导论[M]. 成都：西南交通大学出版社，1994.

作者简介（Bio-data）：

谢红强，男，1976 年 12 月生，讲师，博士，国际岩石力学学会与四川省水力发电学会会员，主要从事岩土工程、隧道工程的教学与科研工作。近年来，先后主持或参与 20 多项大型水电工程、隧道工程的科技攻关项目，获省部级二等奖 1 项，出版专著、教材 2 部，在国内外顶级期刊上发表中英文论文 40 余篇。

Hongqiang XIE (1976—), obtained PhD degree in Bridge and Tunnel Engineering (2006) from Southwest Jiaotong University. Now he works in Sichuan University as Lecturer and mainly concentrates on teaching and research in geotechnical and underground engineering. He is the member of International Society of Rock Mechanics (ISRM) and Sichuan Society of Hydroelectric Engineering. In recent years, he has undertaken more than 20 scientific research projects related to hydropower and tunnel engineering and is the author of 2 books and more than 40 papers in both Chinese and English.

E-mail: alex_xhq@126.com

富水砂层土压平衡盾构施工地表沉降性状研究

丁洲祥[1] 袁大军[1] 吴全力[2] 周 峻[1] 肖 衡[1]

[1]北京交通大学 土建学院，北京 100044

[2]中交隧道工程局有限公司，北京 100088

【摘 要】 土压平衡盾构隧道在富水砂性土地层施工时，由于其流塑性差、含水量高、渗透系数大，容易产生扰动液化或流砂，往往伴随较大的沉降。通过掺入添加剂可以改善砂土的流动性和保水性，容易形成工作面动态土压平衡，有效控制地层沉降变形。结合广州市轨道交通三号线北延段盾构施工情况，通过现场监测和理论分析，研究了土压平衡盾构施工对富水砂层地面沉降的影响规律。盾构掘进对沉降的影响范围大约为断面前后 20 m，即 3D 距离内。盾构通过期间和盾尾注浆阶段的沉降量约占总沉降量的 75%。所得成果对今后土压平衡盾构长距离穿越复杂条件下的砂土地层施工有参考意义。

【关键词】 土压平衡盾构；盾构隧道；砂层；地表沉降

STUDY ON GROUND SETTLEMENT BEHAVIOR OF EPB SHIELD TUNNEL IN WATER-RICH SANDY LAYERS

Zhouxiang DING[1], Dajun YUAN[1], Quanli WU[2], Jun ZHOU[1], Heng XIAO[1]

[1]School of Civil Engineering, Beijing Jiaotong University, Beijing 100044, China;

[2]CCCC Tunnel Engineering Co. Ltd., Beijing 100088, China

Abstract: During the earth pressure balanced (EPB) shield tunnel excavation in water-rich sandy layers, a series of unfavorable conditions such as construction-induced liquefaction, quicksand and the related excessive ground settlement often occur due to the poor plastic liquidity, high water content and substantial seepage coefficient of sandy layers. The fluidity and water retention ameliorate for sandy layers by mixing additives, helping to establish dynamic earth pressure balance at work face and to reduce effectively ground settlement by EPB shield construction. The EPB shield excavation carried out in the north-extension part for Guangzhou Metro Line 3 was studied in this paper, from the points of view of both site monitoring and theoretical investigation on ground deformation behavior during and post construction. The influence range of shield execution on ground settlement covers back and forth of shield head about 20 meters, equivalently three times of shield diameter. The settlement arising during shield excavation and grouting at shield toe accounts for 75%. The investigation results provide valuable reference for EPB shield tunnel excavation in wide-spread and complex-conditioned sandy layers.

Key words: EPB shield machine; shield tunnel; sandy layers; ground settlement.

1 引 言

当前城市建设、公用设施和各种交通日益繁杂，市区明挖隧道施工对城市生活干扰问题非常严重。在这种条件下采用盾构法则具有明显优点和经济合理性[1]，目前采用盾构法施工的隧道已成为新一轮隧道建设的发展趋势。在众多盾构机型中，土压平衡式盾构是现今国内应用最多的一种盾构型式，图 1 给出了其基本原理图。

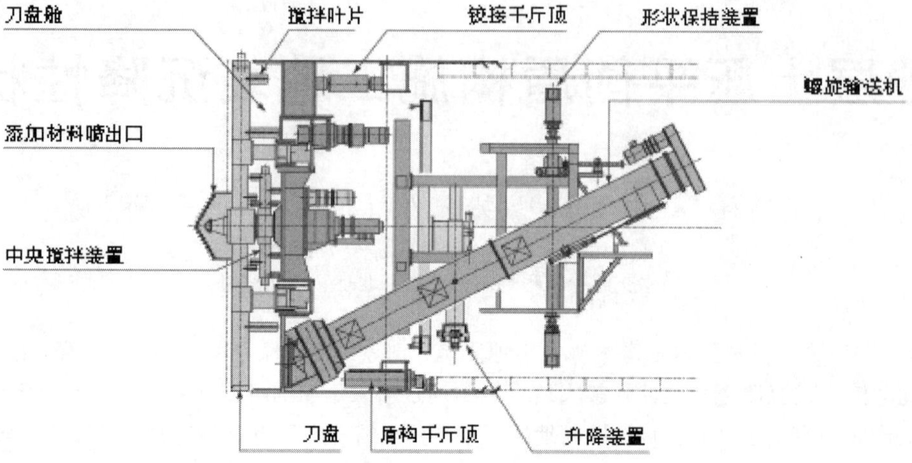

图 1　土压平衡盾构示意图

在土压平衡盾构施工过程中周围土体的主应力状态不断发生改变。盾构机向前推进使前方土体处于受压加荷状态，盾壳与周围土体还存在剪切作用，盾构机脱离衬砌后，由于衬砌与开挖面间间隙的存在，开挖面周围的土体处于卸荷状态，而在注浆过程中注浆压力使开挖面土体处于加压状态。处在这些复杂的应力状态下，部分土体的极限状态受到破坏，从而对周围土体产生扰动，诱发土体变形和沉降。国内外对盾构施工引起的地层变形问题已有大量研究成果[2-10]，对土体沉降变形规律的认识也不断深入，目前的研究方法主要有经验公式法[2]、理论分析法[3]、室内模型试验法[4]和数值模拟法等。现有计算分析方法大都只考虑土体损失引起的土体位移，而对土体中应力场变化引起的扰动研究较少。由于盾构施工引起土体位移和扰动的影响因素很多，无论是经验公式法，还是模型试验等方法，通常都难以全面考虑盾构掘进的各种内因（土层物理力学特性等）和外因（辅助工法、壁后注浆和施工管理等）。因此，结合盾构施工动态监测数据，研究相应的地层沉降特性具有重要的实际意义。

本文结合广州市轨道交通三号线北延段盾构施工情况，通过理论分析和现场监测，充分利用国内外类似条件下的工程经验，对富水砂层中盾构施工地层沉降性状及其机理进行研究，为解决相关的技术难题和类似工程提供有益参考。

2　工程概况

广州地铁三号线是实现城市总体规划，拉开城市布局，加快城市向南发展的战略线路，在南面到达番禺广场后将折向东，穿过广州新城后直达海鸥岛，还将在 2010 年广州亚运会前，往北延伸至广州白云国际机场，为亚运会服务，届时全线将达 84 公里，成为广州地铁中最长的线路。本设计所依托的课题在广州市轨道交通三号线北延段（新机场线）高增至新机场南区间开展研究，线路总长 3 832.981 单线米。其中盾构区间线路总长 3240.489 单线米，其中含有富水砂层的达到 1 784 m，占盾构区间线路总长的 55%，区间途径农田、鱼塘、菜地及市政道路和绿化带，地处广花冲积盆地，盾构始发段为溶岩发育区，并有孤石发育，靠近机场管线分布较多，由于地质条件和环境条件的复杂，对工程安全和质量以及对周边环境的影响提出了很高的要求。如何减少广州市轨道交通三号线北延段盾构隧道施工对周边环境的影响，是地铁盾构隧道施工的重大课题。特别是大部分在含水量特别丰富，厚度大，连通好，和地表水水力联系密切，渗透性强的长距离全砂层中推进，这在广州地铁土压盾构施工中还是首次，如何保证施工作业的安全和施工的正常进行是工程的关键。

3 监测断面的布置

3.1 监测孔布置

通过对广州轨道交通三号线北延段（高增至新机场南区间）11 标的隧道平、纵断面图地层条件和地面地形的研究，考虑盾构穿越砂层时为风险控制点需加强监测，再考虑到机场的特殊地形和实际可行性，在机场高速中间的绿化带上选取监测断面，共选取两个监测断面，分别位于 YCK27+430 和 YCK27+610 位置，不妨依此称为断面 1（图 2）和断面 2（图 3）。

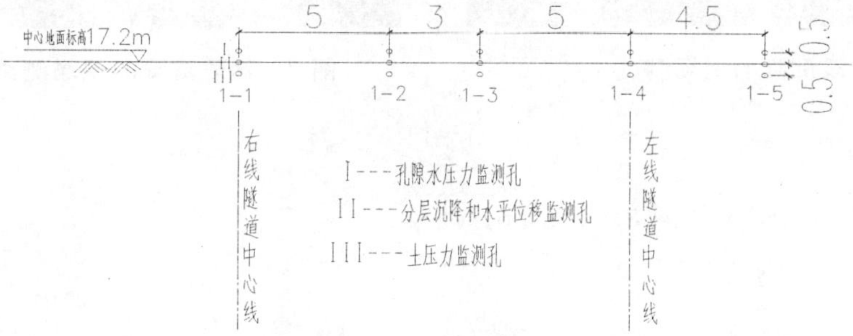

图 2 断面 1 监测孔平面布置图

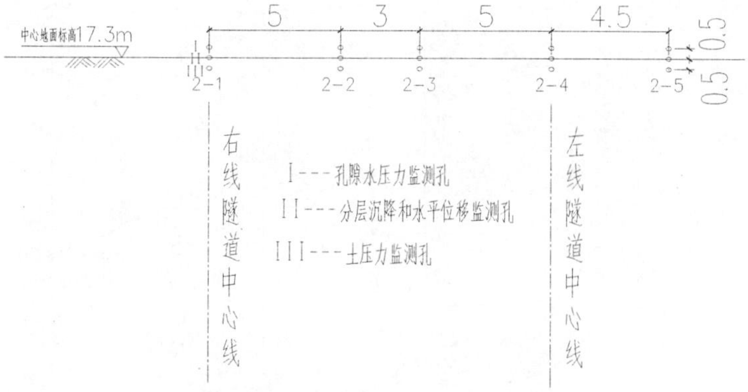

图 3 断面 2 监测孔平面布置图

断面 1 和断面 2 在布置上类似，以右线隧道中心线为基准，向右共设置 5 处监测孔。每处预设 3 个监测孔成一列，从上往下依次为孔隙水压力监测孔，分层沉降和水平位移监测孔，以及土压力监测孔。隧道中心线监测孔的现场照片图 4 所示，图 5 至图 7 是分层沉降以及地表沉降的现场测试照片。

图 4 隧道中心线监测孔的布置

图 5 分层沉降的现场测试

图 6 地表沉降的现场测试 1

图 7 地表沉降的现场测试 2

3.2 监测断面地质

断面 1 和断面 2 的地层情况如图 8（a），（b）所示。

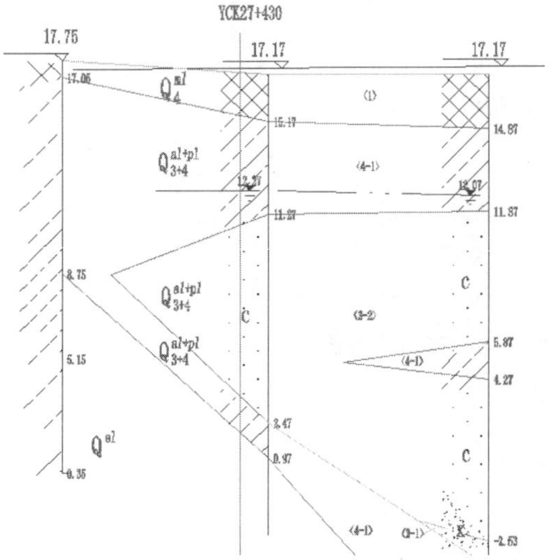

（a）断面 1 地质图

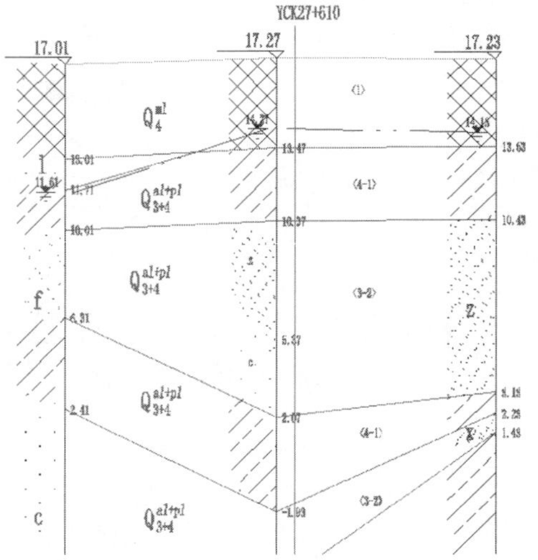

（b）断面 2 地质图

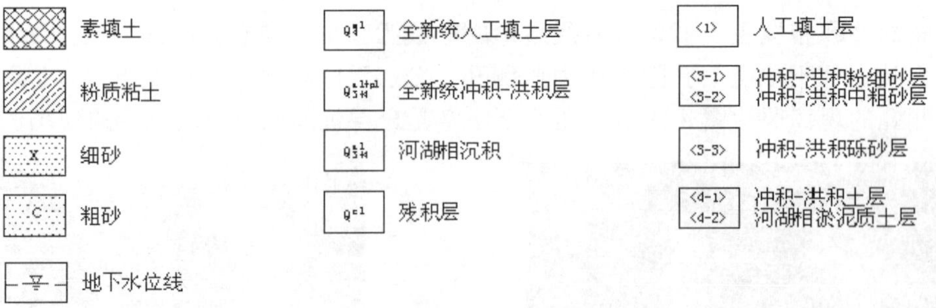

（c）地质图图例

图 8 监测断面 1 和 2 的地质剖面图

4 地表沉降的理论分析

4.1 地表沉降机理

盾构施工引起的地表沉降是由多种因素产生的，它既与地层情况、土(岩)的性质、地下水、隧道的埋深及截面特性等客观因素有关，也与施工方法、技术水平等主观因素密切相关。即使地层情况相同，但采用的施工方案和质量不同，相应的地表沉降也会有很大的差异。也即，施工因素(如开挖时土压平衡力的大小、衬砌后注浆是否及时及注浆填充率的大小)对地表沉降具有重要的影响。

按照沉降的产生机理，可将其分为以下三部分：① 隧道周围土体中超孔隙水压力消散产生的主固结沉降，超孔隙水压力是由于盾构施工引起的；② 土体的蠕变引起的变形，也就是通常所说的次固结沉降；③ 地铁运营过程中，列车行驶所产生的循环动荷载，以及列车振动对周围土体产生的影响也会促进隧道长期沉降的发展。

因初始应力状态改变造成土层变形、地层损失、降水引起的固结变形均是造成地表沉降的主要因素。由于固结引起的沉降在土体变形发生的初期占主导地位，直到超孔隙水压力消散完毕为止，然后，土体的蠕变特性成为超孔隙水压力消散完毕之后土体发生沉降的主要原因。也就是说，隧道的长期沉降是由固结和蠕变共同引起的，而且在其发展过程中很难将二者区分开来。

按照盾构掘进时间来分，可将地表沉降分为以下几个阶段[5]：

（1）先行沉降——盾构的开挖面到达之前早已产生的沉降，主要是由于地下水位降低产生的固结沉降。

（2）开挖面前沉降（沉降）——开挖面通过之前产生的沉降或隆起，是对开挖面的土水压力的控制压力不足而引起的弹塑性变形。

（3）通过时沉降（隆起）——盾构通过时产生的地基变形，其原因有超挖、偏离中线施工、盾壳与周围土体之间的摩擦等。

（4）盾尾空隙沉降（隆起）——这是由于产生盾尾空隙时应力释放引起的弹塑性变形。若壁后注浆压力过大，附加的土压力（附加土压力）也会引起隆起。

（5）后续沉降——这是盾构通过后长时间内继续产生的沉降现象，当为软弱的黏性土地基时有所发现，可以认为伴随着盾构掘进的土体松动、扰动等是其产生的原因。

4.2 理论计算

1969 年 Peck 在分析大量地表沉降观测数据的基础上，提出了地表沉降槽符合正态分布曲线的概念[2]，见图 9。他认为地层变形由地层损失引起，施工引起的地面沉降是在不排水的条件下发生的，从而假定地表沉降槽体积等于地层损失体积；地层损失量与盾构种类、操作方法、地层条件、地面环境及施工管理严格程度有关，一般很难准确估计。

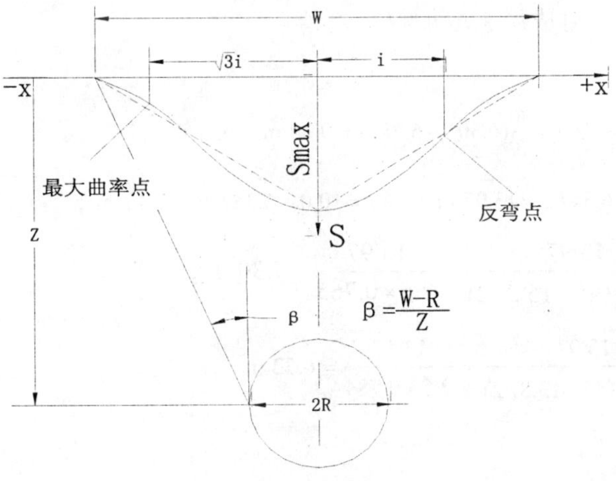

图 9 沉降槽横向分布图

对两个监测断面进行理论计算，采用 Peck 公式，YCK27+430 断面和 YCK27+610 断面的覆土厚度和地质参数见表 1。

表 1　计算断面地质参数

<table>
<tr><th>里　程</th><th>地质名称</th><th colspan="2">深度/m</th><th>天然重度 γ/ (KN/ m³)</th><th colspan="2">内摩擦角 φ/ °</th><th>备注</th></tr>
<tr><td rowspan="3">CK27+430</td><td>①素填土</td><td>1.82</td><td rowspan="3">H=10.8</td><td>18.5</td><td>10.5</td><td rowspan="3">加权内摩擦角 φ=15.2</td><td rowspan="3">隧道穿越粗砂、粉质黏土</td></tr>
<tr><td>②粉质黏土</td><td>4.63</td><td>18.9</td><td>11.6</td></tr>
<tr><td>③粗砂</td><td>4.35</td><td>20.1</td><td>21.6</td></tr>
<tr><td rowspan="3">CK27+610</td><td>①素填土</td><td>3.79</td><td rowspan="3">H=10.0</td><td>18.5</td><td>10.5</td><td rowspan="3">加权内摩擦角 φ=13.8</td><td rowspan="3">隧道穿越中砂、粗砂、粉质黏土</td></tr>
<tr><td>②粉质黏土</td><td>3.10</td><td>18.9</td><td>11.6</td></tr>
<tr><td>③中砂</td><td>3.11</td><td>20.1</td><td>22.2</td></tr>
</table>

横向分布地面沉降估算公式为:

$$s(x) = s_{\max} \exp\left(-\frac{x^2}{2i^2}\right) \tag{1}$$

$$s_{\max} = \frac{V}{\sqrt{2\pi} i} \tag{2}$$

$$i = \frac{Z}{\sqrt{2\pi} \tan\left(45^\circ - \varphi/2\right)} \tag{3}$$

式中　$s(x)$——沉降量（mm）;

$s_{\max}$——最大沉降量（mm）;

x——距隧道中心线处距离（m）;

i——沉降槽宽度系数（m），由查图表或公式求得;

V——盾构隧道单位长度地层损失（m^3/m）;

Z——地面至隧道中心深度（m）;

φ——土的内摩擦角，对成层土取加权平均值。

其中地层损失

$$V = \frac{\pi}{4}(D_{挖}^2 - D^2) = \frac{\pi}{4}(6.30^2 - 6.28^2) = 0.20\ \mathrm{m}^3/\mathrm{m}\ ;$$

$$Z_1 = 10.8 + 6.34/2 = 13.97\ \mathrm{m}\ ;\quad Z_2 = 10.0 + 6.34/2 = 13.17\ \mathrm{m}\ ;$$

$$i_1 = \frac{13.97}{\sqrt{2\pi} tg(45 - 15.2/2)} = \frac{13.97}{2.5 \times 0.765} = 7.30\ \mathrm{m}\ ;$$

$$i_2 = \frac{13.97}{\sqrt{2\pi} tg(45 - 13.8/2)} = \frac{13.17}{2.5 \times 0.784} = 6.72\ \mathrm{m}\ .$$

沉降槽理论计算值见表 2。

表 2　沉降槽理论计算值

里　程	覆土厚度 H（m）	地层损失 V（m^3/m）	沉降槽宽度系数 i（m）	最大沉降量 S_{max}（mm）
CK27+430	10.8	0.20	7.30	10.93
CK27+610	10.0	0.20	6.72	11.87

理论沉降槽曲线图如图 10 和 11 所示。

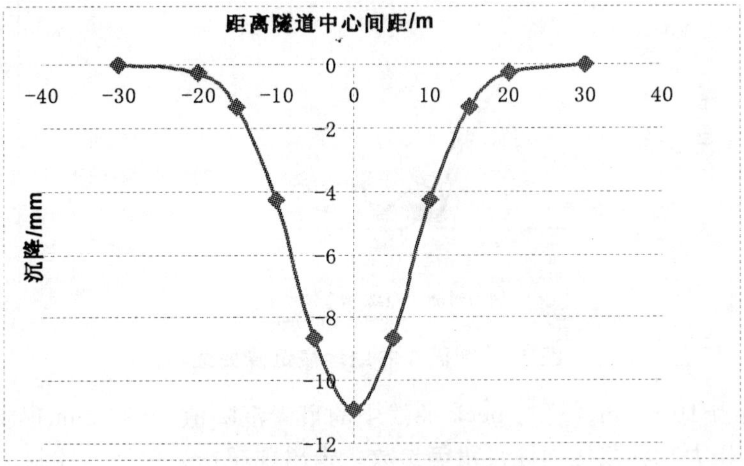

图 10 断面 1 横向沉降槽理论值

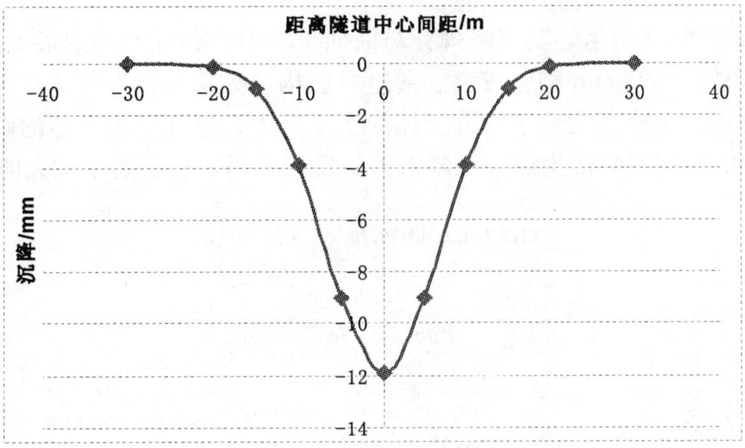

图 11 断面 2 横向沉降槽理论值

通过利用 Peck 公式进行预估，在不考虑盾构超挖或欠挖（超压或欠压）的理想情况下，断面 1 的理论最大沉降值为 10.93 mm，断面 2 的理论最大沉降值为 11.87 mm，横向影响范围在隧道中心两侧约 20 m 以内，即隧道 3D 范围内。

5 地表沉降的实测结果分析

5.1 断面 1 数据分析

断面 1 的右线监测结果如图 12，从监测结果来看，在切口距断面 20 m 左右（3D）时，盾构开始有沉降发生，在距断面 7.5 m 之前的沉降都很小，这是由于后方土体的开挖，而且土仓压力设置与前方开挖面土水压力和相当，没有引起前方土体的隆起。在盾构接近和通过断面时，沉降速率加快，这段主要是由于盾构刀盘前进过程中引起的土层损失以及盾壳前进时的摩擦引起土体扰动，从而产生土体沉降。在盾尾脱出后，由于盾尾间隙的形成以及盾尾注浆未及时发挥作用，此时的沉降最快。在切口过断面 21 m 以后，沉降速率变缓，到切口过断面 44 m 后，沉降基本稳定。在切口过断面 16.5 m 以前，隧道轴线上和距隧道轴线 5 m 处的沉降基本一致，在切口过断面 16.5 m 以后，沉降出现差异，最终沉降相差 2 mm。

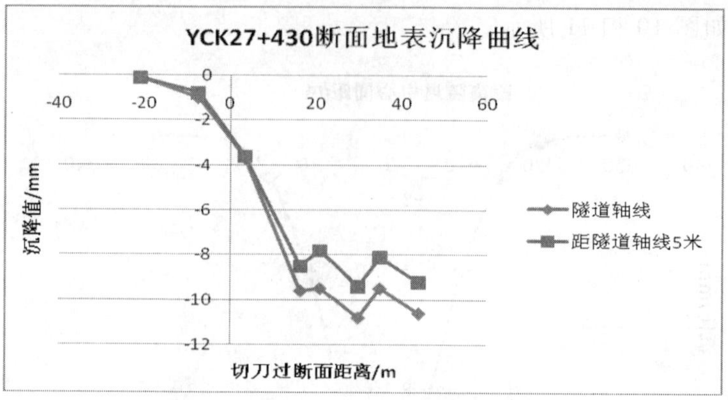

图 12 断面 1 右线地表沉降曲线

沉降监测的最大值为 10.8 mm，这与 peck 曲线中的最大沉降值 10.93 mm 很相近，说明在此段推进时，很好地控制了土仓压力和注浆压力注浆量等参数，未出现超挖，较好地控制了地表沉降的发展。

5.2 断面 2 数据分析

断面 2 的监测结果如图 13 所示，其沉降规律与断面 1 类似，但此断面的最大的沉降值为 22.4 mm，与 peck 的理论最大沉降值 11.93 mm 相差较大。通过对盾构参数的分析发现，在通过此断面时盾构掘进速度较快，盾构欠压推进，土仓压力小于前方土体的水土合力，这样引起土体的沉降较大。再加上快速通过断面后，较大范围的盾尾间隙产生后，注浆来不及发挥作用，也引起了较大的土体沉降。

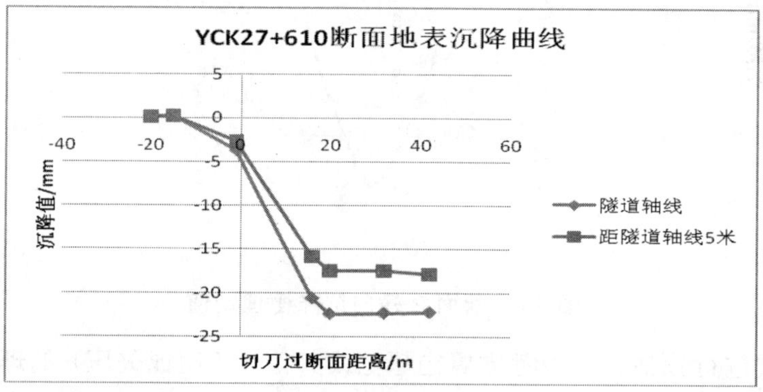

图 13 断面 2 右线地表沉降曲线

5.3 讨 论

（1）盾构推进沉降分布百分比及影响范围。

盾构推进各阶段的沉降百分比见图 14。

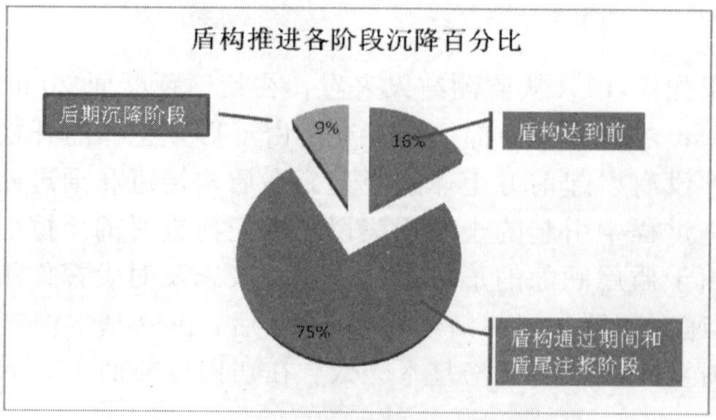

图 14 盾构推进各阶段沉降百分比

从百分比图可以看出，对于砂土为主的土层，前期沉降占到了 16%，而主要的沉降集中在盾构通过期间和盾尾注浆阶段，占了 75%，后期沉降只占 9%，表明盾构在通过期间和盾尾注浆阶段的参数设置很重要，比如土仓压力的控制，注浆量和注浆压力的设定等。

在盾构距断面 20 m 时，沉降开始发生，在盾构过断面 20 m 后，沉降趋于稳定，盾构掘进对沉降的影响范围大约为断面前后 20 m，即 3D 距离内。

（2）砂土在扰动后的固结速率较快

由监测结果可以看出，在盾构刀盘过断面 20 m 后的地表沉降都已经趋于稳定，这是由于沉降主要是由超孔隙水压力消散产生的主固结沉降，而砂土的含水量高，连通性好，渗透系数较大，在扰动减弱后，超孔隙水压力会迅速消散，因此砂土在扰动后固结速率较快。盾构通过期间的和盾尾通过后的弹塑性变形远大于土体蠕变压缩的次固结沉降。

（3）砂土在扰动持续时间较长的情况下容易发生液化

由于砂层颗粒与颗粒之间吸引力相对很小，几乎没有连接，且含水量较高，所以在循环荷载作用的一开始，就产生一个较大的瞬间变形。主要原因是颗粒受到挤压后，孔隙体积被压缩，孔隙比减小，此时部分有效应力发生转移，由超孔隙水压力来承担，土骨架强度降低，土体产生残余变形。随着振动次数增多，土体结构经过一段时间的调整仍不能适应新的压力环境，而在这过程中，孔隙水压力不断上升，有效应力不断下降，最后导致土体强度丧失，也即砂层达到了液化状态。在砂性土层中盾构推进时，因盾构前进、盾构内部设备的振动和其他等因素，容易使周围的砂土发生液化，这在推进速度较慢和推进持续时间较长等情况下更加明显。砂土发生液化后，不可避免地造成土体的沉降。

因此盾构在通过富水砂层时，应尽量快速通过，不要停留时间过长。

6 结　论

通过对广州地铁 3 号线北延段盾构隧道施工现场监测和理论分析，本文研究了富水砂层地区土压平衡盾构工法引起的地面沉降变形规律，主要得到以下初步认识：

（1）在流塑性差、含水量高的砂土地层中，很难建立土压平衡盾构工作面的平衡关系，地面变形控制较为艰难。同时，砂土混合物的 C、Φ值增大，造成推进过程中主刀盘扭矩及千斤顶推力增加，施工进展较慢，加剧了盾构机切削刀头和面板的磨损。

（2）土压平衡盾构机穿越砂层时，其掘进参数宜适当提高盾构机的推进速度，低刀盘转速，严密监测地表沉降情况，确保平、稳、快速通过砂层。此外，向刀盘、土舱喷注泡沫剂实现渣土改良，有利于降低刀盘扭矩，减小千斤顶顶推力，并可以减轻刀盘的磨损。

（3）在盾构距监测断面 20 m 时，地表沉降开始发生，在盾构过断面 20 m 后，沉降趋于稳定，盾构掘进对沉降的影响范围大约为断面前后 20 m，即 3D 距离内。

（4）对于砂土为主的土层，前期沉降约占总沉降量的 16%，而盾构通过期间和盾尾注浆阶段的沉降量约占 75%，后期沉降只占 9%，这表明盾构在通过期间和盾尾注浆阶段的参数设置很重要，比如土仓压力的控制，注浆量和注浆压力的设定等。

致　谢：

中交隧道局三公司的王建军总工和罗兴元经理等人在现场测试过程中提供了一定的帮助和配合。参与现场监测工作的还有杨志新、赵光和尹凡等硕士生。还要感谢在机场高速公路绿化带作业面受限等艰难条件下，钻机工人们为埋设监测仪器付出的辛勤劳动。

参考文献（References）：

[1] 刘建航，侯学渊. 盾构法隧道[M]. 北京：中国铁道出版社，1991.

[2] PECK R B. Deep excavations and tunneling in soft ground [A]. State of the Art Report. Proceedings of the 7th International Conference on Soil Mechanics and Foundation Engineering [C]. Mexico City, 1969, 225-290.

[3] LOGANATHAN N, POULOS H G. Analytical prediction for tunneling-induced ground movement in clays [J]. Journal of Geotechnical and Geoenvironmental Engineering, 1998,124(9):846-856.

[4] 徐前卫，朱合华，廖少明. 砂土地层盾构法施工的模型试验设计研究[J]. 地下空间与工程学报，2006，2(3)：361-364，368.

[5] 日本地盘工学会著. 盾构法的调查、设计、施工[M]. 牛青山等译. 北京：中国建筑工业出版社出版，2008.

[6] 张凤祥，朱合华，傅德明. 盾构隧道[M]. 北京：人民交通出版社，2004.

[7] 卓普周.土压平衡式盾构施工地层沉降控制[D]. 成都：西南交通大学硕士学位论文，2003.

[8] 徐俊杰. 土压平衡盾构施工引起的地表沉降分析[D]. 成都：西南交通大学硕士学位论文，2004.

[9] 卢瑾. 软土地层中盾构法开挖引起的地表沉降研究. 南京：河海大学硕士学位论文，2007.

[10] 王涛. 盾构隧道施工的环境效应影响研究[D]. 杭州：浙江大学硕士学位论文，2007.

[11] 刘昌. 盾构施工引起地表沉降的研究[D]. 西安：西安建筑科技大学硕士学位论文，2007.

[12] LIAO Shao-ming, LIU Jian-Hang, WANG Ru-Lu, etc. Shield tunneling and environment protection in Shanghai soft grond [J]. Tunnelling and Underground Space Technology, 2009, 24:454-465.

作者简介（Bio-data）：

丁洲祥（1976—），男，讲师，博士，博士后，主要从事岩土与地下工程方面的研究。E-mail：dingzhouxiang@163.com。学术简历主要为：1999 年于西安公路交通大学获交通土建工程（地下工程与隧道工程）专业学士学位；2002 年于长安大学获岩土工程专业工学硕士学位；2005 年于浙江大学获土木工程专业博士学位。2008 年于同济大学土木工程博士后流动站出站。近年来，先后主持了国家自然科学基金项目、中国博士后科学基金项目和国家重点实验室项目等若干项目，并获得省部级科技进步二等奖项目 2 项。

Zhouxiang DING, male, lecturer, Ph.D., post-doctor in Civil Engineering. He completed his undergraduate studies at Chang'an University in 1999 with a B.S. in Civil Engineering (Underground Space and Tunneling Branch), followed by a M.S. in Geotechnical Engineering there. In 2005, He obtained his Ph.D. degree at Zhejiang University in Civil engineering. He conducted his postdoctoral research work in Tongji University, Shanghai, China. DING is interested in tunneling and underground space technology, and the related geotechnical mechanics and numerical simulation techniques. In recent years, he has been project leaders in a series of scientific research projects funded by National Science Foundation of China, China Postdoctoral Foundation, State Key Laboratory of China and so on. And he obtained second prize twice for the Provincial and/or Ministry Science and Technology Achievement Award.

E-mail: dingzhouxiang@163.com

深埋盾构隧道抗震分析的近似解析法

晏启祥　马婷婷　何 川　汪 东

西南交通大学 地下工程系，四川　成都　610031

【摘　要】　目前国内抗震分析普遍采用地震系数法或数值分析法，缺乏简便易行的公式解析法，且现有方法大多只能考虑剪切波的作用。本文基于深埋隧道福季耶娃法抗震分析基本理论，提出了同时考虑 P 波、S 波作用的盾构隧道抗震分析近似解析法及其计算流程，简化了圆形盾构隧道抗震分析的繁杂性，供隧道领域设计与施工单位参考。

【关键词】　福季耶娃法；深埋盾构隧道；抗震分析；近似解析法

AN APPROXIMATE ANALYTIC METHOD FOR ASEISMIC ANALYSIS OF DEEP-BURIED SHIELD TUNNEL

Qixiang YAN，Tingting MA，Chuan HE，Dong WANG

Department of Underground Engineering, Southwest Jiaotong University, Chengdu 610031, Sichuan, China

Abstract: At present, the seismic coefficient method or numerical analytical method is usually used in aseismic analysis in China. A simple and feasible formula analytic method is required. Moreover, most current methods can only take the effect of shear wave into consideration. Based on deep-buried tunnel Fotieva aseismic analysis theory, an approximate analytic method and its calculation process for aseismic analysis of shield tunnel are provided in this paper. The effects of P wave and S wave are both taken into consideration in the method, and the aseismic analysis of shield tunnel is simplified. Using this method, references can be provided for tunnel design and construction.

Key words: fotieva method; deep-buried shield tunnel; aseismic analysis; approximate analytic method

1 引　言

目前，国内隧道工程的抗震设计方法有地震系数法、反应位移法、质量弹簧法、动力有限元法等。现行《铁路工程抗震设计规范》（GB 50111—2006）、《公路工程抗震设计规范》（JTG D70—2004）都规定隧道工程的抗震设计应采用静力法,即地震系数法进行计算，特别重大的隧道工程应配合动力时程有限元法进行验算。1997 年颁布的《核电厂抗震设计规范》中规定对于地下隧道采用反应位移法进行抗震计算。在我国地下铁道设计中，由于研究工作开展不够，目前规范对抗震设计尚无具体规定。总体上看，国内隧道相关抗震规范基本上采用地面结构的地震系数法。然而地震系数法用于深埋隧道的抗震计算存在诸多问题，如随着埋深的增大其顶部的水平地震力急剧增大，其计算结果显然与工程实践不符。前苏联专家福季耶娃提出的拟静力法，给出了隧道远场 P 波、S 波的等代荷载，可用于解决深埋隧道的抗震设计问题[1]。然而，在等代荷载确定后，需要采用连续介质地层结构有限元静力模型进行不同体波入射方向下四种等代荷载组合的分析计算，然后绘制不同组合下衬砌内力的包络线，最后获得四种组合中的最大包络线进行抗震设计。本文提出的抗震分析近似解析法省却了有限元静力分析，且对于深埋圆形盾

基金项目：863 计划（2006AA11Z116）；铁道部课题（2008G010A、2008G028B）

构隧道，体波的入射方向变化只会导致隧道衬砌具体位置内力量值的变化，不会影响其包络线形状和大小的变化，故而不需要考虑入射方向与隧道的相互关系，只需进行四种荷载组合的计算即可，有鉴于上述原因，这种近似解析法将大大简化深埋圆形盾构隧道抗震分析的复杂性。

2 近似解析公式及流程

福季耶娃法将地震反应的动力学问题比拟成围岩在无限远处承受一定荷载的弹性力学平面问题，其原理是：对于 P 波和 S 波，当波长大于隧道洞径的 3 倍，且隧道埋深较大（大于洞径的 3 倍），隧道长度大于洞径的 5 倍时，假设围岩属于线弹性变形介质，地震作用引起隧道围岩应力的计算，可归结为有加固孔口周围应力集中的线弹性理论动力学问题。根据线弹性动力学，福季耶娃提出 P 波的等代荷载为[1]：

$$\sigma_x^{(\infty)} = \pm\frac{1}{2\pi}K_C\gamma_G C_P T_O \tag{1}$$

$$\sigma_y^{(\infty)} = \frac{\mu_G}{(1-\mu_G)}\sigma_x^{(\infty)} \tag{2}$$

式中 K_C——与地震烈度有关的地震系数；

$K_C = a/g$——（a 为地震加速度，g 为重力加速度）；

γ_G——围岩的容重；

T_O——围岩质点震动的卓越周期；

μ_G——围岩的泊松比；

C_P——弹性压缩波在地层中的传播速度，$C_P = \sqrt{\frac{(1-\mu_G)}{(1+\mu_G)(1-2\mu_G)}\cdot\frac{E_G}{\rho_G}}$，$\rho_G$ 为围岩的密度，E_G 为围岩弹性模量；x，y 方向的应力以拉为正，压为负。S 波的等代荷载为：

$$\tau_{xy}^{(\infty)} = \pm\frac{1}{2\pi}K_C\gamma_G C_S T_O \tag{3}$$

式中 C_S——弹性剪切波在地层中的传播速度，$C_S = \sqrt{\frac{1}{2(1+\mu_G)}\cdot\frac{E_G}{\rho_G}}$，其他物理量意义同上。

隧道周边远场正应力和剪应力已知后，可利用下述公式[2]计算 P 波荷载作用下圆形隧道结构的衬砌内力，其中 θ 为从 y 正向进行顺时针旋转的夹角：

$$M(\theta) = \frac{R^2\sigma_y^{(\infty)}}{4}(1-K)(1-2a_2^* + 2b_2^*)\cos 2\theta \tag{4}$$

$$N(\theta) = \frac{R\sigma_y^{(\infty)}}{2}[(1+K)(1-a_0^*) + (1-K)(1+2a_2^*)\cos 2\theta] \tag{5}$$

式中 K——横向荷载与竖向荷载的比，$K = \sigma_x^{(\infty)}/\sigma_y^{(\infty)}$；$a_0^* = \frac{C^*F^*(1-\mu_G)}{C^*+F^*+C^*F^*(1-\mu_G)}$

$a_2^* = \beta b_2^*$；$b_2^* = \frac{C^*(1-\mu_G)}{2[C^*(1-\mu_G)+4\mu_G-6\beta-3\beta C^*(1-\mu_G)]}$；

$F^* = \frac{E_G R^3(1-\nu_s^2)}{E_s I_s(1-\mu_G^2)}$；$C^* = \frac{E_G R(1-\nu_s^2)}{E_s A_s(1-\mu_G^2)}$；$\beta = \frac{C^*(6+F^*)(1-\mu_G)+2F^*\mu_G}{3C^*+3F^*+2C^*F^*(1-\mu_G)}$；

I_s——隧道衬砌断面惯性矩；

E_s——隧道衬砌的弹性模量；

ν_s——隧道衬砌的泊松比；

R——圆形衬砌中轴线半径。

S 波荷载作用下，圆形隧道衬砌结构内力可按以下公式计算[3]:

$$M(\theta)=\frac{3E_sI_s\Delta D_{G\max}^s}{2R^2(1-\nu_s^2)}\cos\left[2\left(\theta+\frac{\pi}{4}\right)\right] \tag{6}$$

$$N(\theta)=-\frac{3E_sI_s\Delta D_{G\max}^s}{R^3(1-\nu_s^2)}\cos\left[2\left(\theta+\frac{\pi}{4}\right)\right] \tag{7}$$

式中，$\Delta D_{G\max}^s=\dfrac{4(1-\mu_G)R\tau_{xy}^{(\infty)}}{G_G(1+\alpha_s)}$；$\alpha_s=\dfrac{6E_sI_s(1+\mu_G)(3-4\mu_G)}{R^3E_G(1-\nu_s^2)}$，$G_G$ 为围岩地层剪切模量；

其它符号的含义同上。

对于不同的地震波入射角，在 P 波和 S 波的等代荷载作用下均可用解析法求出隧道衬砌内力。对于轴对称的圆形盾构隧道衬砌，其在不同地震波入射角条件下，隧道具体位置的衬砌内力会发生改变，但其内力包络线图的形状和大小不变，因此，只需考虑等代荷载的 4 种组合即可，即：$\sigma_{压}+\tau_{剪}$, $\sigma_{压}-\tau_{剪}$, $\sigma_{拉}+\tau_{剪}$, $\sigma_{拉}-\tau_{剪}$, 如图 1。

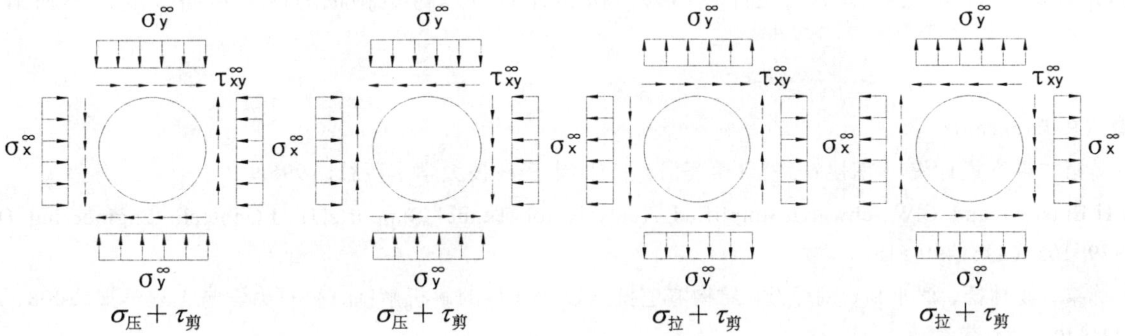

图 1　深埋圆形隧道抗震计算荷载组合示意

3　计算实例

某深埋圆形盾构隧道的衬砌外径为 6.0 m，厚度为 0.3 m，重度为 25 kN/m^3，弹性模量为 32.5e9 N/m^2，泊松比为 0.2；围岩弹性模量 3.13e8 N/m^2，重度 21.4 kN/m^3，泊松比 0.18，围岩质点震动的卓越周期为 0.6 s。计算地震烈度取为Ⅶ度（0.15g）。根据上述解析公式，可得到 S 波等代荷载作用及 4 种组合情况下的衬砌结构内力，其弯矩和轴力分别如图 2～5 所示，在图 4 和图 5 中，实线、点线、点画线、虚线分别代表 $\sigma_{压}+\tau_{剪}$, $\sigma_{压}-\tau_{剪}$，$\sigma_{拉}+\tau_{剪}$, $\sigma_{拉}-\tau_{剪}$ 四种荷载组合的计算结果。

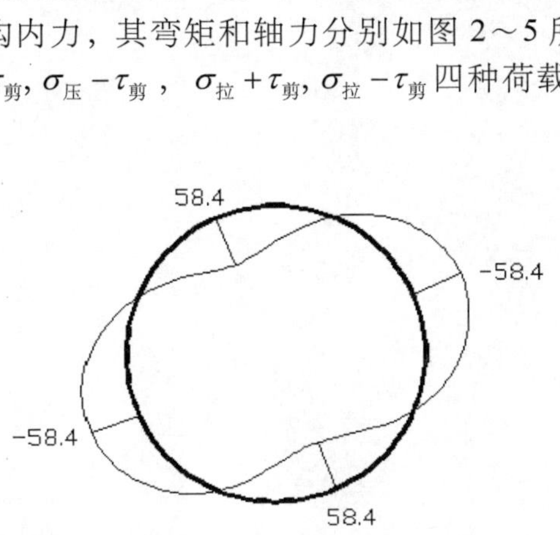

图 2　S 波等代荷载作用下的弯矩 M（单位：kN · m）

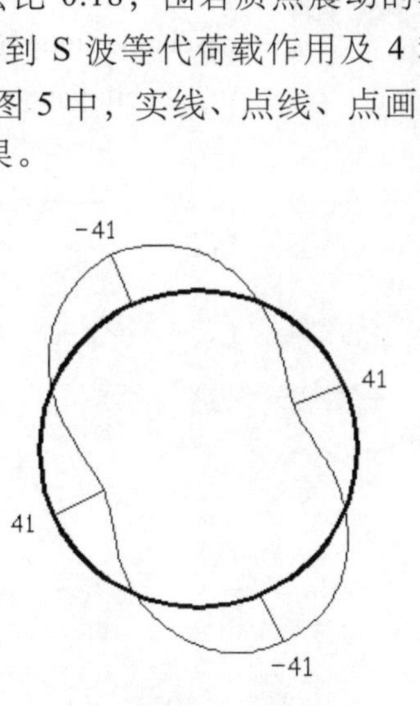

图 3　S 波等代荷载作用下的轴力 N（单位：kN）

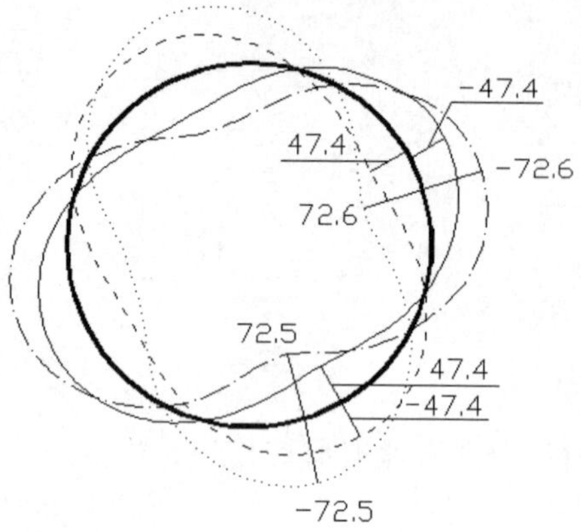

图 4 四种荷载组合的弯矩 M 对比（单位：kN · m）

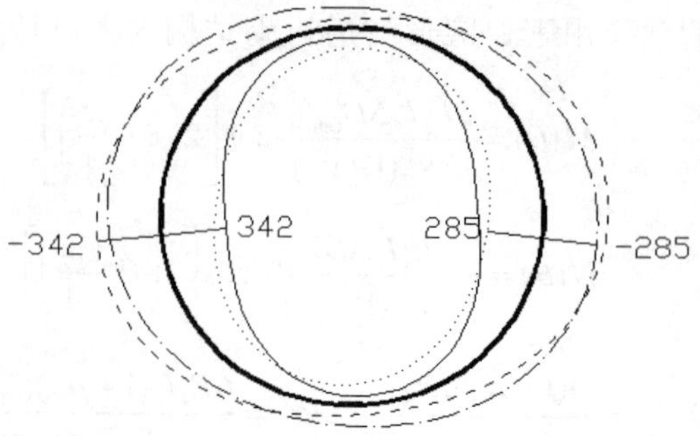

图 5 四种荷载组合的轴力 N 对比（单位：kN）

从图 4 和图 5 中可以看出：$\sigma_{压}-\tau_{剪}$，$\sigma_{拉}+\tau_{剪}$ 计算所获得的弯矩和轴力包络线图形状相似，数值相同，只是旋转了 90°；$\sigma_{压}+\tau_{剪}$, $\sigma_{拉}-\tau_{剪}$ 计算所获得的弯矩和轴力表现出相同的特征；在上述分析条件下，弯矩包络线的最值 $\sigma_{压}-\tau_{剪}$，$\sigma_{拉}+\tau_{剪}$ 比 $\sigma_{压}+\tau_{剪}$, $\sigma_{拉}-\tau_{剪}$ 略大,相反的，轴力包络线的最值 $\sigma_{压}+\tau_{剪}$, $\sigma_{拉}-\tau_{剪}$ 比 $\sigma_{压}-\tau_{剪}$，$\sigma_{拉}+\tau_{剪}$ 略大。基于上述计算结果，抗震计算可以弯矩和轴力两种包络线的最不利组合进行设计。

参考文献（References）:

[1] 铁道第二勘察设计院.《南昆铁路》（第三册）[M]. 电子科技大学出版社. 1996.9

[2] H.H.Einstein and C.W.Schwartz.Simplified Analysis for Tunnel Supports[J]. J.Geotech. Engineering Division, 1979, 105（4）: 499-518.

[3] 张栋梁，杨林德，谢永利，刘保健. 盾构隧道抗震设计计算的解析解[J]. 岩石力学与工程学报. 2008，27（3）: 543-549.

作者简介（Bio-data）:

晏启祥，男，1971 年 10 月出生，副教授，毕业于四川大学岩土工程系，并获博士学位。现执教于西南交通大学，主要从事盾构隧道抗震研究。

Qixiang YAN（1971—), male, assistant professor, obtained his PhD degree in geotechnical engineering from Sichuan University. Now He works in Southwest Jiaotong University, carrying on aseismic study of shield tunnels.

E-mail: yanqixiang@tom.com

埋深和地层条件对盾构隧道地震响应的影响分析

江英超　聂亮　耿萍　何川

西南交通大学　地下工程系，四川　成都　610031

【摘　要】　基于反应位移法，通过改变隧道埋深和地层条件参数，对地铁区间盾构隧道进行了不同条件下的模拟分析，分析了埋深和地层条件对结构内力的影响规律，同时对参数进行了灵敏度分析。结果表明，地震时，在一定埋深范围内，处于均匀性地层的盾构隧道结构内力随埋深增加变化不大，而地层条件对盾构隧道的结构内力与变形有显著影响。

【关键词】　盾构隧道；结构抗震设计；反应位移法；灵敏度分析

ANALYSIS OF DEPTH AND GROUND CONDITION OF SHIELD TUNNEL ON ITS SEISMIC RESPONSE

Yingchao JIANG，Liang NIE，Ping GENG，Chuan HE

Department of Underground Engineering, Southwest Jiaotong University, Chengdu 610031, Sichuan, China

Abstract: Based on seismic deformation method, this paper analyses internal force of metro shield tunnels under different conditions by altering tunnel depth, ground conditions, and have summarized the varying regularity of internal forces as well as the sensitivity analysis of each factor. The result shows that internal forces have no obvious change as the depth increasing while the alteration of ground conditions has obvious effect on the internal forces and deformation of shield tunnel.

Key words: shield tunnel; seismic structural design; seismic deformation method; sensitivity analysis

1　引　言

地下结构由于受到周围土体或者岩体的约束作用，在地震作用下自振特性表现得不很明显，一直被认为具有较好的抗震性能（相对地面结构），因此，在很长的一段时间内，地下结构的震害问题远没有地面结构那样得到重视。1995 年日本阪神大地震，“5·12”汶川大地震，部分隧道结构受到了较严重的破坏[1-4]。近年来，随着城市化进程的加快，国内有很多城市开始兴建地下铁道。综合目前已建城市地铁区间隧道工程，盾构隧道具有以下特点：衬砌环采用单层装配式预制钢筋混凝土管片，纵向和环向接头多，接头力学行为复杂；埋深较小，一般属于浅埋。结合我国现行地震烈度区划图，我国百万以上人口的特大城市中有 70%位于 7 度和 7 度以上的地震设防区[5]。由于地铁属于抗震城市中生命线工程的核心建筑，按照建筑抗震设计规范，应在符合本地区抗震设防烈度基础上提高一度[6]。因此，进行盾构隧道的抗震设计具有重要意义。

2　分析方法与原理

随着对地下结构在地震荷载下响应特征的研究，更加符合地下结构内力的反应位移法得以提出，并

基金项目：863 计划（2006AA11Z116）；铁道部课题（2008G010A、2008G028B）

在实际工程上得到应用。何川、小泉 淳基于振动台试验和动力分析证实了盾构隧道采用反应位移法的有效性[7]；曾德顺、奚爱华等应用反应变位法，研究了隧道埋深、剪切波速、弹性地基刚度等因素对隧道轴向变形和弯曲变形的影响及其相互关系[8]；耿萍、何川等采用反应位移法对大型水下盾构隧道进行了地震响应分析[9]。

反应位移法的基本思想是由于地下结构在地震中自身很难单独起振，结构的加速度与周围地层基本保持一致，本身振动中的惯性力对结构影响较小，地下结构主要受所在位置地层的地震变位支配。根据反应位移法，输入地震力主要考虑地层最不利相对变形、地层剪力（周围剪力）以及结构自身的惯性力等三种地震作用,在结构与地层间设置可反映综合考虑地层特性的弹簧来体现结构与地层相互作用关系，据此求得结构物的应力。分析模型如图 1 所示[7]。基于反应位移法概念明确、计算简便，能较好的反映地震对地下结构的影响，因此本文利用反应位移法，以国内典型地铁区间盾构隧道为例，分析埋深和地层条件对盾构隧道地震响应的影响。

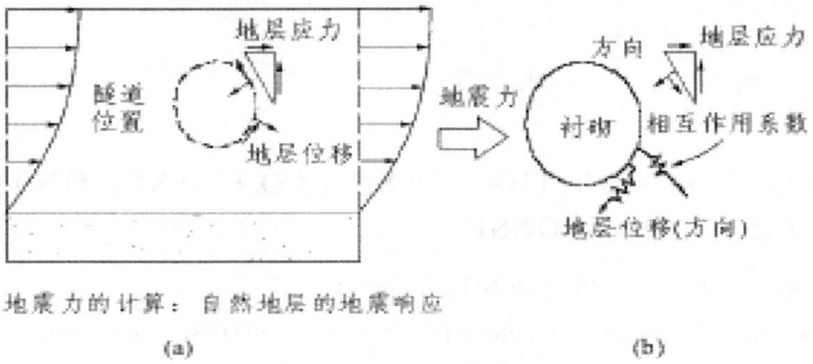

图 1　反应位移法模型

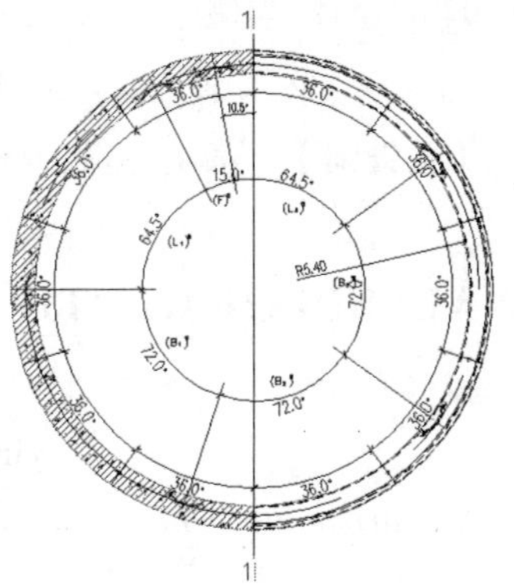

图 2　管片结构示意图

3　分析过程及结果

3.1　计算模型及计算流程

以成都地铁区间盾构隧道衬砌环为例，结构如图 2 所示。所选结构为单层装配式预制钢筋混凝土管片衬砌环，混凝土标号为 C40。管片外径 6.0 m，内径 5.4 m，幅宽 1.5 m，分块采用“1+2+3”模式，采用错缝拼装方式。为简化计算，采用对管片衬砌环的抗弯刚度作折减的匀质等价圆环进行计算，刚度折减系数取为 0.8[4]。

在地震作用下，作用在盾构隧道结构上的荷载还应同时包括常时土水压力等荷载值。本文仅单独分析地震力引起的盾构的结构内力。

在进行计算时，将非均一的地层简化成单一地层进行分析计算，根据公式 1 和公式 2[10]可以计算出等效地层的单位体积重度和弹性剪切波速。成都地层物理力学参数如表 1 所示。

$$\gamma = \frac{\sum_{i=1}^{n} \gamma_i h_i}{\sum_{i=1}^{n} \gamma_i} \tag{1}$$

$$v_{sd} = \frac{\sum_{i=1}^{n} h_i}{\sum_{i=1}^{n} \frac{h_i}{v_{sdi}}} \tag{2}$$

表 1　地层物理力学参数

土层名称	厚度 h/m	Vs/(m/s)	γ/(kN/m³)
素填土	3.982 8	120	18.5
粉土	2.962 4	170	18.5
卵石土	8.007 6	420	23
细沙	3.296 4	270	19
漂石层	10.722 9	580	22.5
泥岩	4.881 4	560	20

地震作用引起地层位移随深度的变化模式简化为正弦波分布，如图 3。按 7 度基本地震烈度，考虑 100 年发生概率为 2%，从基底进行单向水平激振。

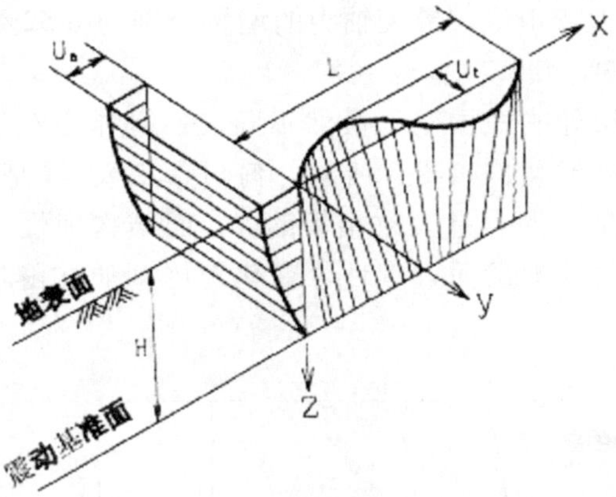

图 3　地层变形模式

以成都地铁为例选取不同计算埋深来分析地震作用下结构内力随埋深的变化规律;并同时进行成都、南京、西安三种地层条件为对象的计算分析。

3.2　埋深对盾构隧道结构内力的影响

根据表 1 数据，基岩震动面选在泥岩顶面，埋深为 29 m。横断面计算埋深为 15 m，地层的固有周期 T_s=0.581 s，速度反应谱 S_u=0.0879 m/s，动剪切模量 G=0.1 326 GPa。

根据盾构隧道埋深较浅的特点，结合城市地铁埋置深度，分别选择埋深为 2D、2.5D、3D、3.5D、4D（D 为隧道衬砌结构中心线的直径），纵向取单位长度进行计算分析。

根据反应位移法，将地震剪应力分解为径向应力和切向应力直接作用到结构上，将地震响应分析中的强制位移从地层弹簧末端输入（如图 1），可得到分析断面的内力值。以埋深 3D 为例，结构的典型内力图如图 4 和图 5 所示。根据不同埋深下结构的内力值，绘制成内力分布图，如图 6 和图 7 所示。

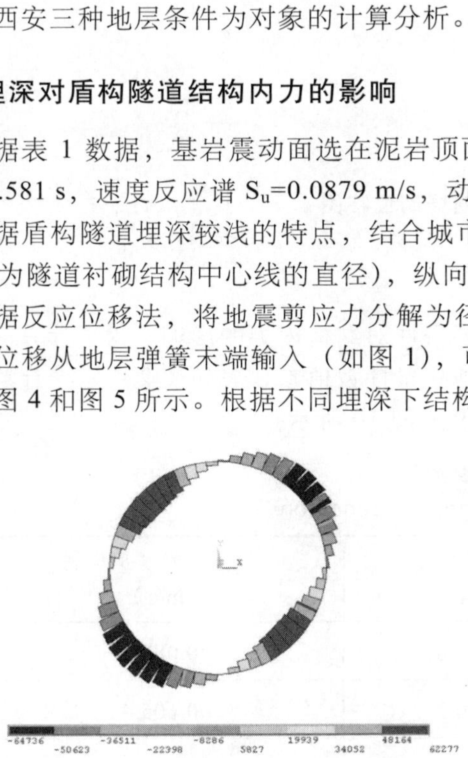

图 4　结构轴力图（单位：N）

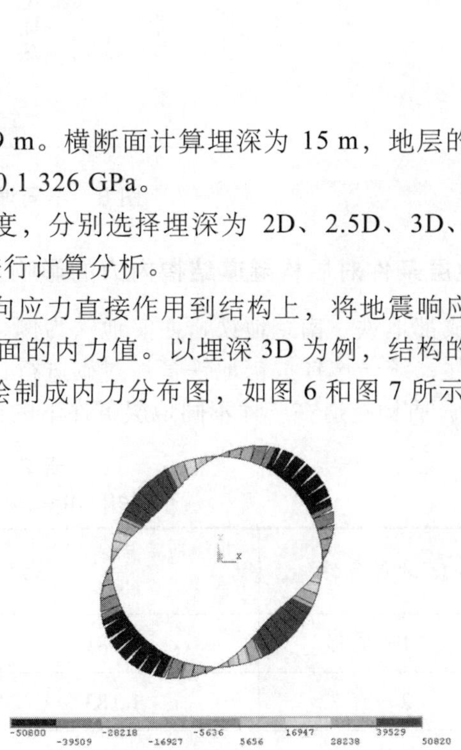

图 5　结构弯矩图（单位：N · m）

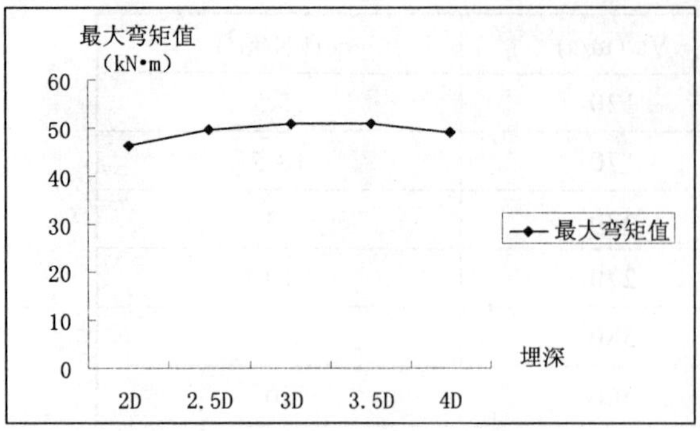

图 6 不同埋深条件下最大弯矩值图

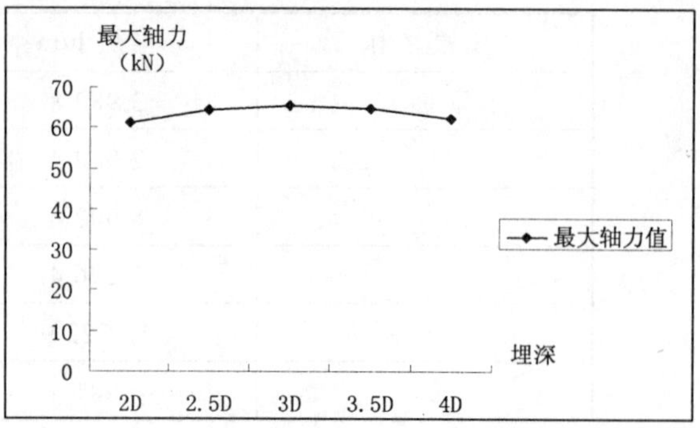

图 7 不同埋深条件下最大轴力图

由计算结果可以看出，随着埋深的增加，结构的最大弯矩值和最大轴力均未发生明显的变化。例如，从埋深 2D 到 2.5D 变化时，最大弯矩值和最大轴力的增量分别为 6.52%和 3.36%，当埋深从 3.5D 到 4D 变化时，相应的增量分别为 5.03% 和 3.74%。

分析其原因如下：不同埋深处的地层变位虽然不同，但是作用在结构上的相对强制位移（顶部与底部的位移差）随埋深增加变化不大，如图 8 所示。何川、小泉 淳基于振动台试验研究结果也证实，周边剪切力和强制位移分别产生的内力是大致相等的[7]，而结构惯性力引起的结构内力相对较少。因此，在一定埋深范围内，对均匀性地层而言，埋深变化对区间盾构隧道这类结构的内力不会产生明显的影响。

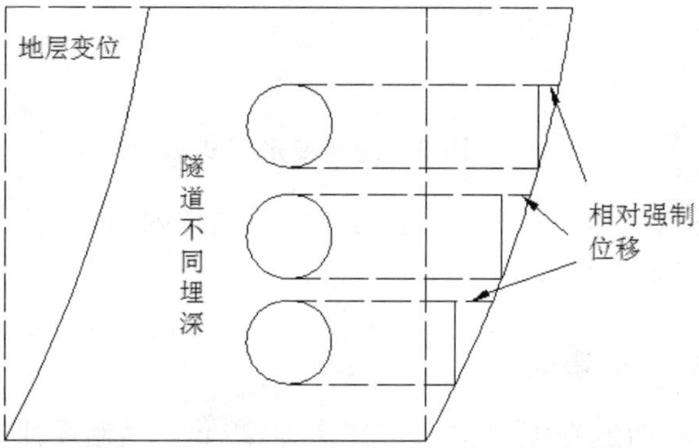

图 8 不同埋深下隧道的相对强制位移图

3.3 地层条件对盾构隧道结构内力的影响

以成都地铁、南京地铁、西安地铁为例，研究改变地层条件对结构内力的影响。为了计算简便和增强可比性，统一选择成都地铁管片衬砌进行计算分析。各地层条件数值参数表如表 2 所示，计算埋深选择 15 m。盾构隧道在三种不同地层条件下的内力分析如图 9 和图 10 所示。

表 2 地层条件数值参数表

Table2 the parameter of the ground condition

地层条件	地层固有周期 (s)	动剪切模量 (GPa)	震动面速度反应谱 (m/s)
1—成都	0.581	0.132 6	0.087 9
2—南京	1.183	0.030 2	0.105 4
3—西安	0.991	0.048 5	0.105 4

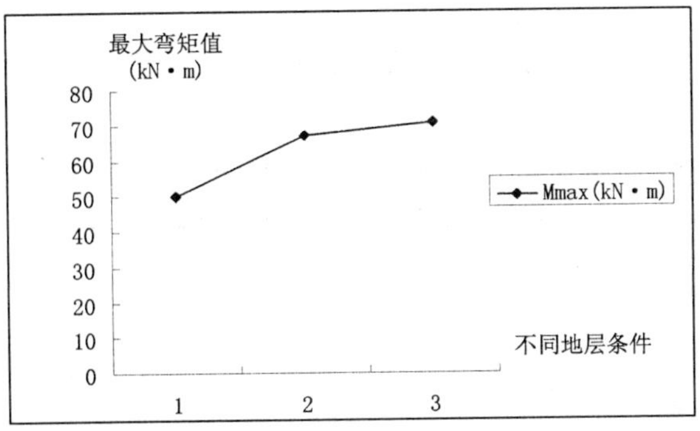

图 9　不同地层条件下最大弯矩值图

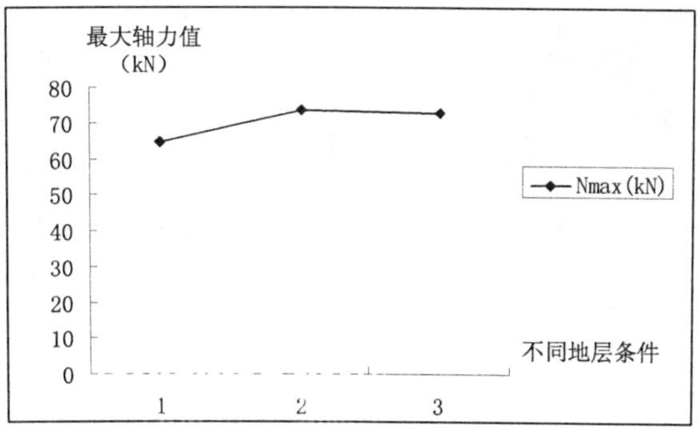

图 10　不同地层条件下最大轴力图

根据图 9 和图 10 计算结果可知，地层条件改变后，结构的内力发生了较大的变化。以最大弯矩值和最大轴力为例，成都、南京和西安的比值分别为 1：1.21：1.23 和 1：1.34：1.41。这是因为，成都地区地层主要以砂卵石为主，简化计算后地层的固有周期低，地震作用时，地层对加速度的放大效应较小，地层的绝对变位以及隧道顶部与底部的相对位移量均较小。这与南京地层以粉土为主，西安地层以黄土为主不同，因此导致结构内力的差别较大。总体而言，在固有周期低的地层中盾构隧道结构内力明显降低，反之亦然。

4　结　论

本文采用反应位移法对地铁盾构隧道横断面进行了结构内力计算分析。由计算结果可知：

（1）对于均匀性地层，在一定埋深范围内，地震引起的不同深度地层的变位虽然不同，但对盾构隧道的相对强制位移差别不大，结构最大内力值随埋深增加变化不大。

（2）不同地层条件下，结构内力的变化差别较大。土层的固有周期低，动剪切模量大的地层，结构的内力较小。地层条件对盾构隧道结构内力有着明显的影响。

（3）地震作用对结构内力有着不可忽略的影响。常时荷载作用下，结构弯矩值一般为 130 kN·m～200 kN·m，在地震荷载单独作用下，结构最大弯矩值能达到 70 kN·m,为常时荷载作用下的 1/3～1/2。因此，在隧道抗震设计中必须考虑地震对结构的影响，避免造成隧道结构的破坏。

参考文献（References）：

[1] 郑永来，杨林德. 地下结构震害与抗震对策[J]. 工程抗震，1999，18(4):23-28.

[2] 王瑞民，罗奇峰. 阪神地震中地下结构和隧道的破坏现象浅析[J]. 灾害学，1998，13(2):63-66.

[3] 钱七虎，何川等. 隧道工程动力响应特性与汶川地震隧道震害分析及启示[J]. 汶川大地震工程震害调查分析与研究，2009：773-778.

[4] 何川，曾东洋. 盾构隧道结构设计及施工对环境的影响[M]. 成都：西南交通大学出版社，2004.

[5] 何海健，刘维宁等. 地下铁道抗震研究的现状与探讨[J]. 中国安全科学学报，2005，15(8):3-7.

[6] 中华人民共和国国家标准. 建筑抗震设计规范（GB 50011—2001）. 北京，2001：14.

[7] HE Chuan, KOIZUMI Atsushi. Study on Seismic Behavior and Seismic Design Methods in Transverse Direction of Shield Tunnels [J], An International Journal, Structural Engineering and Mechanics, 2001, 11(6): 651-662.

[8] 曾德顺，奚爱华等. 反应变位法在区间隧道抗震设计中的应用[J]. 工程力学（增刊），1999：774-778.

[9] 耿萍，何川等. 水下盾构隧道抗震设计分析方法的适应性研究[J]. 岩石力学与工程学报，2007，26:3625-3630.

[10] 川岛一彦. 地下构造物の耐震设计[M]. 鹿岛出版社，1995.

作者简介（Bio-data）:

江英超，男，1986.10 出生，2009 年 7 月毕业于西南交通大学土木工程学院，获工学学士学位。现为西南交通大学桥梁与隧道专业硕士研究生。

Yingchao JIANG (1986—) , male, graduated from School of Civil Engineering in Southwest Jiaotong University and got the bachelor's degree in July, 2007. Now he is pursuing the master's degree in the major of bridge and tunnel engineering.

E-mail: yingchaojiang@gmail.com

聂亮，男，1986.02 出生。2009 年 7 月毕业于西南交通大学土木工程学院，获工学学士学位。现为西南交通大学桥梁与隧道专业硕士研究生。

Liang NIE(1986—), male, graduated from School of Civil Engineering in Southwest Jiaotong University and got the bachelor's degree in July, 2007. Now he is pursuing the master's degree in the major of bridge and tunnel engineering.

E-mail: koy0272@yahoo.com.cn

成都膨胀土地层地铁区间隧道盾构法可行性分析

胡 茜　罗世培　牟 锐　邹永尧

中铁二院工程集团有限责任公司，四川　成都　610031

【摘　要】 成都地铁 2 号线工程部分区间将穿越由黏性土、卵石、泥岩组成的具有膨胀性的覆盖层，该土层具有吸水膨胀软化，失水收缩开裂的特性，采用盾构法通过国内外实例不多，无完全成熟的经验。本文从各个方面对盾构法隧道在膨胀土地层中的应用进行了可行性分析，如：盾构机选型、盾构隧道结构受力、盾构隧道防渗漏水对策、如何预测及控制盾构施工对环境的影响以及盾构法与矿山法施工的综合对比分析，提出一些建议供参考。

【关键词】 地铁区间隧道；盾构法；膨胀土；有限元法

FEASIBILITY ANALYSIS OF SHIELD DRIVING METHOD USED IN INTERZONE TUNNEL IN EXPANSIVE SOILS IN CHENGDU METRO

Qian HU，Shipei LUO，Rui MU，Yongyao ZOU

China Railway Eryuan Egineering Group CO.LTD, Chengdu 610031, Sichuan, China

Abstract: some section of Chengdu Metro will cross the cover of expansive soil consisting of clayed soil, cobble and mud. This soil stratum has the characteristics of expansion and softening on water absorbing, and shrinkage cracking on water losing. The subway tunnels are built by using shield driving method in these strata has not mature experience at home and abroad. Therefore it is necessary to analyze how to use shield driving method in Chengdu Metro. The contents in this paper enumerated as follows: the type choosing of shield machine, structure stress and anti- leaking of shield tunnel, forecasting and controlling the circumstantial impact of shield construction. Finally the mining method is contrasted with the shield driving method.

Key words: interval tunnel in metro; shield driving method; expansive soil; FEM

1　引　言

我国在城市地铁的修建中，由于盾构施工法以其良好的防渗漏水性、施工安全快速、对周围环境的影响极小等优点，在地下铁道的建设中已成为重要的可选施工方法之一，在许多场合已成为首选方法。在上海、广州、深圳、北京、成都、天津等城市已建地下铁道中，区间隧道大量采用盾构法施工，但穿越地层大多为冲积层黏土、砂黏土、软岩等，在这些地层中采用盾构法施工国内外已有较为成熟的经验[1,2]。但成都地铁 2 号线一期工程根据部分区间将穿越由黏性土、卵石、泥岩组成的具有膨胀性的覆盖层，该土层具有吸水膨胀软化，失水收缩开裂的特性，采用盾构法通过国内外实例不多，无完全成熟的经验。

2　成都膨胀土（岩）地层工程地质及水文地质概况

根据地质勘察报告，2 号线位于膨胀土、岩地层的区间其工程范围内的地质情况大致分为三部分，上部由第四系全新统人工填土（Q_4^{ml}）：<1-1>杂填土、<1-2>素填土等组成；中部由第四系中、下更新统冰水沉积（Q_{2-1}^{fgl}）：<4-2>黏土、<4-3>粉质黏土、<4-5-3>中砂、<4-7-1>含卵石黏土、<4-7-2>含黏土卵石等组成；下部为白垩系上统灌口组（K_{2g}）：<5-1>全风化泥岩、<5-2>强风化泥岩、<5-3>中等风化泥岩等组成。其中部分膨胀土、膨胀岩地层的有关膨胀性指标如下表 1：

根据成都区域水文地质资料及地下水的赋存条件，地下水主要有四种类型：一是赋存于黏土层之上的上层滞水，二是赋存于黏土中的裂隙水，三是第四系松散土层（含黏土卵石）的孔隙水，四是基岩裂隙水（基岩溶孔溶隙裂隙水）。其中上层滞水与黏土的裂隙水的水位浅，水量受季节性变化明显，难以形成贯通的自由水面；而含黏土卵石（厚度约 0.5～13.2 m），其水量、水位不稳定，大气降水和区域地表水为其主要补给源，具中等渗透性，根据区域水文地质资料，渗透系数（K）为 1.0～4.0 m/d，对工程有一定的影响；第四种基岩裂隙水由于基岩为白垩系灌口组紫红色泥岩，是地下水的流动将石膏溶蚀，并顺溶蚀孔或裂隙形成网络状的风化带溶蚀孔和溶隙形成的，为地下水的补给、储集、径流创造了良好的通道和空间，该含水层地下水富集规律性较差，在一定条件下，某些地方可形成富水块段。泥岩渗透系数（K）一般为 0.027～2.01 m/d，区段大部分泥岩的含水量甚微，对地铁盾构施工影响较小，但不排除区段局部地段有富水条件，储藏有一定裂隙水[3]。

图 1　现场膨胀土实例

表 1　膨胀土、膨胀岩相关指标的统计值（部分区间）

区　间	阶地	岩土层		试验值 自由膨胀率 (%)	试验值 蒙脱石含量 (%)	试验值 阳离子交换量 CEC（NH4＋）(mmol/kg)	试验值 膨胀力 (kPa)	膨胀力标准值 (kPa)
站东广场—东洪路	Ⅲ级阶地	膨胀土	(4-2)黏土	40 ~ 82	7.6~18.9	152~293	24~365	190
			(4-7-1)含卵石黏土	40~64	7.5~17.9	172~273	75~286	155
		膨胀岩	(5-1)全风化泥岩	36~47	6.5~12.2	152~215	38~263	165
			(5-2)强风化泥岩	24~37			12~146	141
			(5-3)中等风化泥岩	22~35			13~162	77
东洪路—东部副中心	Ⅲ级阶地	膨胀土	(4-2)黏土	41 ~ 64	8.6 ~ 18.8	195 ~ 289	52 ~ 280	182
		膨胀岩	(5-1)全风化泥岩	35 ~ 48	6.2 ~ 12.4	153 ~ 236	10 ~ 160	102
			(5-2)强风化泥岩	23 ~ 33			45 ~ 102	74
			(5-3)中等风化泥岩	18 ~ 37			24 ~ 202	76

3　盾构机的适应性分析

目前国内地铁中最常用的盾构主要为土压平衡式盾构与泥水式盾构，均为密封式盾构，工作原理是利用泥水压力或土压力保持开挖面稳定，防止开挖面坍塌，同时有效控制开挖面的变形，从而防止地层被扰动[4]。目前按照经验两者适用土层的区别主要有以下两方面[5]:

（1）透水性：泥水盾构适用于透水性较高的地层，土压平衡式盾构则用于透水性较低的地层。一般的，当土层渗透系数>1×10^{-7} m/s 时，泥水盾构适于进行掘进；当土层渗透系数<1×10^{-4} m/s 时，土压平衡式盾构适于进行掘进；渗透系数处于两者之间时，两者均适用。如图 2 所示。

（2）土壤颗粒级配：这两种盾构适用的土壤级配范围如图 3:

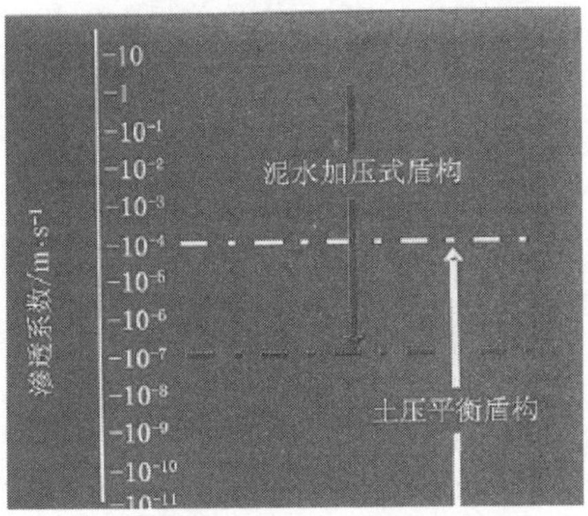

图 2　适于泥水盾构、土压平衡盾构开挖土壤渗透系数范围图

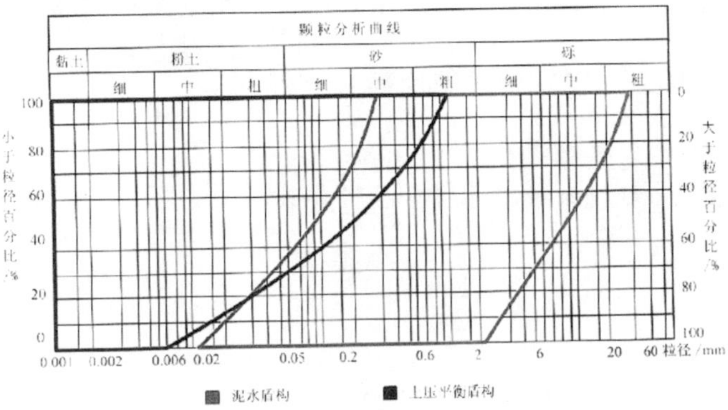

图 3　适于泥水盾构、土压平衡盾构开挖土壤颗粒级配范围图

根据 2 号线膨胀土（岩）区间地段的地质工程条件及水文条件描述，膨胀土（岩）地层主要为黏土及泥岩层，土层渗透系数小，地下水主要为裂隙水，局部富集，因此加泥式土压平衡式盾构较适宜。但应注意，加泥式土压平衡盾构机在黏性土地层中掘进时常会发生刀盘黏附导致增大阻力和螺旋输送机的黏附堵塞，在具体选型时应注意在刀盘形式、开口率、刀具、增加添加剂注浆位置等考虑解决方法。

4　盾构法隧道的结构分析与防水对策

4.1　盾构隧道结构设计

成都地铁 1 号线一期工程根据线路情况以及成都的砂卵石地层特点，对管片结构的设计如下[6]:

（1）分块模式：采用 6 分块模式（如图 4），其分块设计为 3B(72°)+2L(64.5°)+F(15°)，一环内纵向布置 10 个螺栓，环向 12 个螺栓，即每个接缝布置 2 个。其螺栓均采用弯螺栓，螺栓为 M27 型（用于 1.5 m 幅宽管片）或 M24 型（用于 1.2 m 幅宽管片），如图 5 所示。

图 4　管片分块图

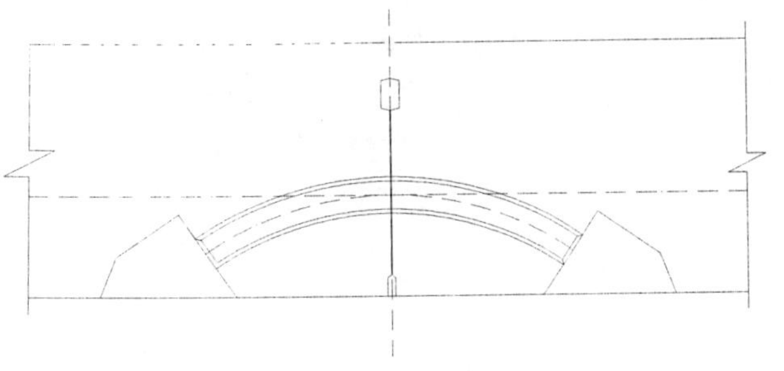

图 5　管片螺栓图

（2）管片几何参数：隧道内半径 $R_1=2.7$ m；管片厚度 $h=0.3$ m；隧道中心半径 $R_2=2.85$ m；隧道

外半径 $R_3=3$ m。管片幅宽采用 1.5 m（直线地段或大于 400 m 曲线半径的曲线地段）或 1.2 m（小于或等于 400m 曲线半径的曲线地段）。

（3）管片拼装方式：为直线＋左转＋右转形式（楔形量 38 mm），采用两环一组的错缝拼装方式，第一环封顶块在拱顶正上方、第二环封顶块从拱顶正上方右偏或左偏 18°。

对于成都地铁 2 号线一期工程，大部分区间仍然处于砂卵石地层，只有部分区间位于膨胀土（岩）地层，因此对于位于膨胀土（岩）地层的区间，上述管片结构设计如果适合，并且满足受力要求，则可以节约管片模板成本，产生经济效益，因此下面对于膨胀土（岩）管片受力进行重点分析。

4.2 膨胀土（岩）地层管片受力分析

4.2.1 荷载－结构模式

管片受力一般采用荷载－结构模式[7]~[9]进行分析，该模式如图 6 所示：

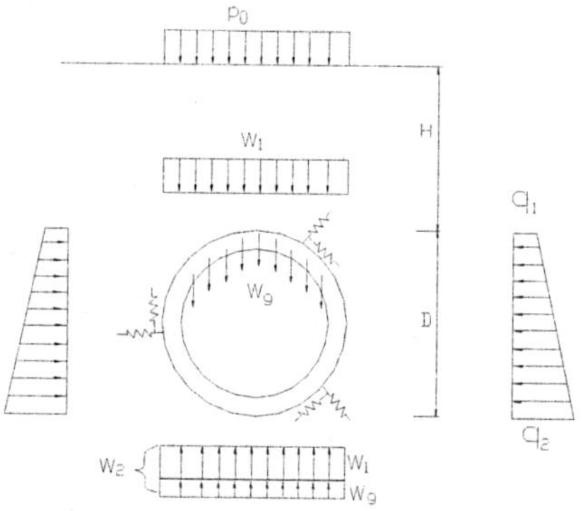

图 6 荷载－结构模式

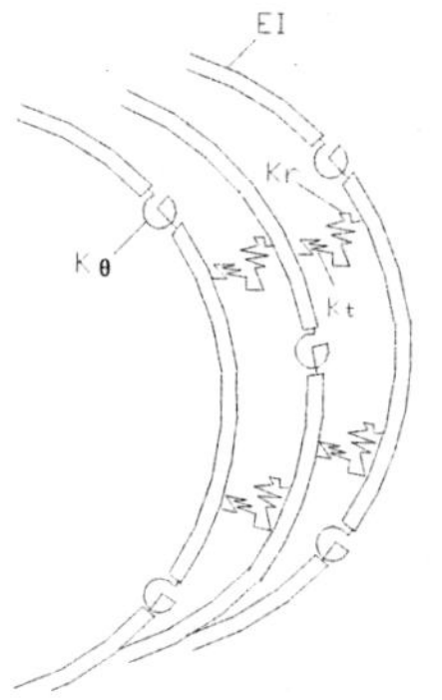

图 7 盾构管片衬砌环梁－弹簧力学模型

（1）结构：

在一衬砌圆环内，具体考虑环向接头的位置和接头的刚度，用曲梁单元模拟管片的实际状况，用接头抗弯刚度 K^{θ} 来体现环向接头的实际抗弯刚度，见图 7。为错缝式拼装时，因纵向接头将引起衬砌圆环间的相互咬合作用，此时根据错缝拼装方式，除考虑计算对象的衬砌圆环外，将对其有影响的前后的衬砌圆环也作为对象，采用空间结构进行计算，并用圆环径向抗剪刚度 Kr 和切向抗剪刚度 Kt 来体现纵向接头的环间传力效果。根据国内外研究成果，结合成都地铁 2 号线一期工程建设实际情况和所选用的管片结构尺寸、内力分布情况、接缝衬垫厚度等实际影响因素，力学分析中环向接头正抗弯刚度 k_{θ}^{+} 取 5×10^4 kN · m/rad，负抗弯刚度 k_{θ}^{-} 取 3×10^4 kN · m/rad，同时本力学分析假定环间接头（纵向接头）不产生错动，盾构环的纵向接头抗剪刚度 Kr 和 Kt 均取无穷大[10]。

（2）荷载：

① 土压力：在确定作用在隧道上方的土层压力方面，国内外视地层情况，主要采用卸拱理论(太沙基公式为主体)和按全部地层压力计算土层压力的方法（国内目前一般采用 2D 为分界），当盾构隧道埋深在 2D（D 为隧道外径）以内时，作用在隧道上方的土层压力取全土层压力；当盾构隧道埋深在 2D 以上时，作用在隧道上方的土层压力根据卸载拱理论取值。

② 地基反力：将周边地基模型化为地基弹簧，当管片在土体一侧产生变位时，作为压缩弹簧起作用，当管片在隧道内侧产生变位时，就作为不起作用对待。

③ 膨胀力：

相比于普通地层，膨胀土（岩）地层由于它的特性，还需要考虑膨胀力荷载的产生。根据 2 号线区间穿越膨胀土（岩）地层的实际情况，膨胀力荷载主要可分为以下几类：①全环均有膨胀力荷载；②在隧道局部产生膨胀力荷载。如图 8 所示。

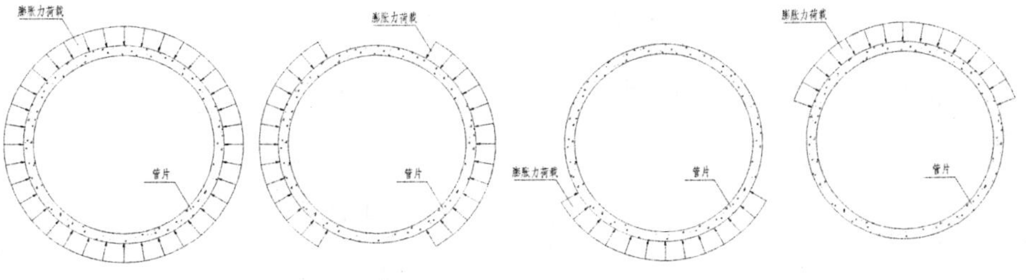

图 8　膨胀力荷载形式分类

4.2.2　计算分析

由于隧道为圆形结构，工况一全环都有膨胀力荷载，类似于静水压力，对于管片结构只是增加轴力，并不产生弯矩，实际是有利工况；工况二与工况一类似，由于水平侧土压力小于垂直土压力，因此腰部增加膨胀力荷载，对于管片结构受力更加均匀，也是有利工况（如果膨胀力荷载分布范围宽以及数值过大，会引起管片结构的弯矩分布反转，则为不利工况，实际情况中未出现）。

工况三，隧道下方有膨胀力荷载，采用荷载－结构模式，对于下方荷载如何取值是需要考虑的，普通工况荷载－结构模式中下方荷载是“上部荷载＋管片自重”之和，管片结构处于平衡体系；对于本工况如果将普通工况下方荷载与膨胀力直接叠加进行计算，则与实际不符，因为当下方膨胀力发生时，下部荷载就变为“主动加荷”的一方，当膨胀力小于管片衬砌所受的径向压力时，对于管片结构受力应不会产生影响，而当膨胀力大于管片衬砌所受的径向压力时，则会产生“膨胀力增量”，此时才会对管片结构受力有影响[11]。因此可采用梁－弹簧模型单独考虑下部“膨胀力增量”的作用，将普通工况得到的内力与“膨胀力增量”产生的内力进行叠加得到该工况管片内力。其具体最不利工况是在站东广场站—东洪路站区间出现，下部膨胀力荷载最大为 165 kPa，见表 1，计算结果见图 9。

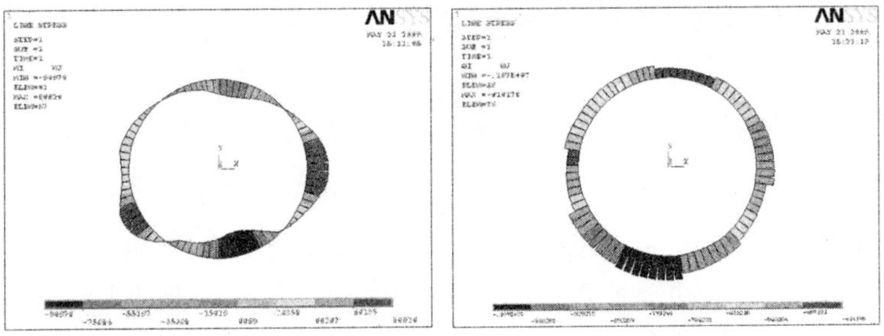

（a）弯矩图（N · m）　　（b）轴力图（N）

图 9　隧道下方有膨胀力荷载管片结构内力图

工况四，隧道上方有膨胀力荷载，对于荷载－结构模式，与工况三不同的是，上方的膨胀力荷载与上部荷载应进行叠加，此时下部荷载为“被动荷载”，仍可取下方荷载＝“上部荷载＋管片自重”，建立一个平衡体系进行计算，与实际较符合。具体最不利工况是在东洪路站—东部副中心站区间出现，该处覆土 12 m 左右，其最大膨胀力标准值为 182 kPa，管片内力计算结果与普通工况对比见图 10，根据该结果进行加强配筋，仍然无法满足受力要求，因此对于该特殊地段最后采用通缝拼装，并将钢筋由Ⅱ级提高到Ⅲ级。

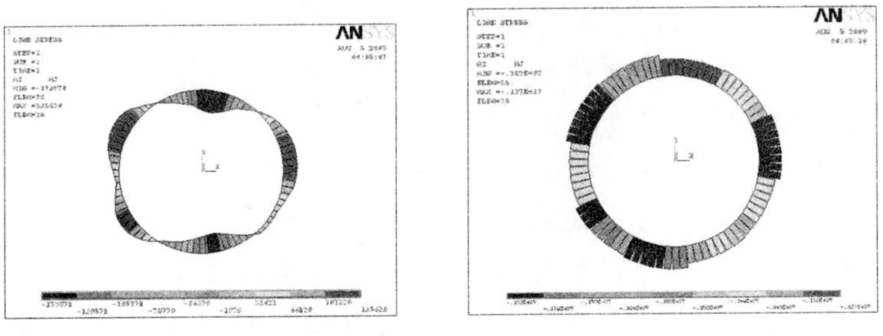

（a）弯矩图（N · m）　　（b）轴力图（N）

图 10　隧道上方有膨胀力荷载管片结构内力图

由以上受力分析可知，盾构法隧道断面满足安全、经济的要求。

4.3 膨胀土（岩）地层盾构隧道防水分析

对于盾构法隧道结构，其防水体系[12]见表 2:

表 2 盾构法区间防水设计体系表

<table>
<tr><td rowspan="5">防水体系</td><td rowspan="3">衬砌结构自防水</td><td>混凝土抗渗等级</td><td>管片混凝土采用 C50、不小于 S12。</td></tr>
<tr><td>裂缝控制</td><td>裂缝宽度不大于 0.20 mm，且不得有贯穿裂缝。</td></tr>
<tr><td>耐腐蚀要求</td><td>有侵蚀性区段，混凝土的抗侵蚀系数不小于 0.8。</td></tr>
<tr><td>接缝防水</td><td colspan="2">管片接缝防水采用在密封垫沟槽内设置橡胶密封垫，手孔及吊装孔（注浆孔）采用遇水膨胀橡胶圈止水，管片接缝、手孔及吊装孔要求不得渗水。</td></tr>
<tr><td colspan="3">管片外注浆</td></tr>
</table>

对于膨胀土（岩）地层中的盾构隧道，考虑膨胀土（岩）吸水膨胀、失水收缩的特性，一是在选择同步注浆及二次注浆材料时应尽量不改变盾构周围膨胀土（岩）的原状，根据成都地区已有的在膨胀土（岩）地区修建构筑物的经验，细砂对于膨胀土（岩）是比较好的缓冲材料，可考虑采用砂浆作为同步注浆材料；二是可借鉴盾构隧道穿越江河的经验，每隔一段距离（10～20 m 左右）盾构隧道打一道“环箍”，使隧道形成间断的止水隔离带，避免区间纵向形成水的通道[13]。

根据以上分析可知，在特殊地段采用改变管片拼装方式、提高管片含钢量以及提高钢筋等级等措施后，沿用 1 号线的管片结构设计对于成都地铁 2 号线一期工程膨胀土（岩）区段是可行的。

5 盾构法施工过程中的环境影响预测和控制

5.1 盾构法区间地表沉降控制标准

采用盾构法在软土地层中建造隧道，会引起周围地层移动，即使采用当前最先进的盾构技术，也难以完全防止这些移动。地层移动一方面直接引起地下结构物的变位，影响其使用，当变位不均匀时还会产生附加应力；另一方面，地层移动在地表引起沉降，这种沉降往往是不均匀的，当不均匀沉降过大时就会对地面建筑物产生影响。目前国内一般认为地表沉降标准为 10～30 mm，即地表下沉最大值不大于 30 mm，地表隆起不大于 10 mm。

5.2 盾构法区间地表沉降控制措施

对于在膨胀土（岩）地层中的盾构隧道，主要可采用以下措施：

（1）为了减少地表沉降对地面及地面建筑物的危害，必须对土体变形进行施工监测。

（2）保持盾构开挖面的稳定。

盾构开挖面的稳定可以通过优化掘进参数控制。掘进参数主要有：刀盘和土舱压力、排土量、推进速度、旋转机转速、千斤顶总推力、注浆压力与时间、注浆量方式、浆体性能、盾构坡度、盾构姿态和管片拼装偏差等。为施工参数优化，必须熟练掌握盾构机的操作，根据地面变形曲线进行实测反馈，以验证选择施工的合理性或据以再调整优化施工参数。

（3）同步注浆和二次注浆。

为了减少和防止地面沉降，在盾构掘进中，要尽快在脱出盾构后的衬砌背面环形建筑空隙中充填足量的浆液材料。根据地质条件，确定浆液配比，注浆压力、注浆量及注浆的起止时间同步注浆能达到预期效果起关键作用。二次注浆则可以弥补同步注浆的不足，是减少地表沉降的有效辅助手段。

（4）地层加固法

地层加固法分为注浆法和高压喷射搅拌法两种。前者是向周围地层注入固结性浆液；后者是向地层喷射注浆的同时搅拌地层使土体与浆液混合在一起然后固结。两者的目的都是固结地层，提高地层的强度和防渗性能。进而抑制盾构通过时的松动范围，从而防止地层变位。

6 矿山法浅埋暗挖施工

6.1 国内已有的工程实例及经验

在膨胀土（岩）区间修建矿山法隧道，国内在公路隧道以及铁路隧道中均有实例，如：襄渝线的董家沟隧道、七里沟隧道、梅七线的崔家沟隧道、南昆铁路上车湾 2 号隧道等等，上述隧道采用矿山法修建既有成功的，也有失败的[14]，但通过不断的摸索，目前国内在膨胀土（岩）地区修建矿山法隧道，有以下方面成功的经验总结：

（1）优化断面形式，越接近圆形越有利；

（2）减少围岩含水量的变化：隧道开挖后及时喷射混凝土封闭洞壁及掌子面，及时注浆封闭透水层的通路；

（3）防止底鼓的发生：

① 采用大曲率、大厚度的钢筋混凝土仰拱；② 预留较大的变形量，允许围岩产生一定的变形；③ 采用合理的施工方法和施工工艺，如七里沟隧道就采用了“慢进快封强支护”的微、超短台阶加临时支撑开挖法。采用上台阶全部人工开挖，人工出碴，中下台阶机械配合开挖。开挖前先施作一环超前小导管，再施作一环系统锚管（径向锚杆）。开挖中，坚持上台阶每天量测一次，中下台阶一天二次，随时掌握拱部的沉降量和边墙的收敛量，并依靠抢拼施工循环速度加强中下台阶收敛的控制。

6.2 成都膨胀土（岩）地层矿山法浅埋暗挖施工

6.2.1 隧道断面拟定

对于地铁隧道，矿山法主要是以马蹄形隧道建筑限界为基础，综合考虑施工工期、使用期结构的安全性、可行性，以及施工误差、测量误差、结构容许沉陷、结构受力及变形的需要确定结构横断面的合理拱轴线及结构尺寸。考虑到隧道所处地层为膨胀土（岩），结合上述成功经验，隧道内轮廓按 150 mm 加宽、加高设计，并加大仰拱的曲率，尽量使隧道轮廓圆顺，如图 11 所示。

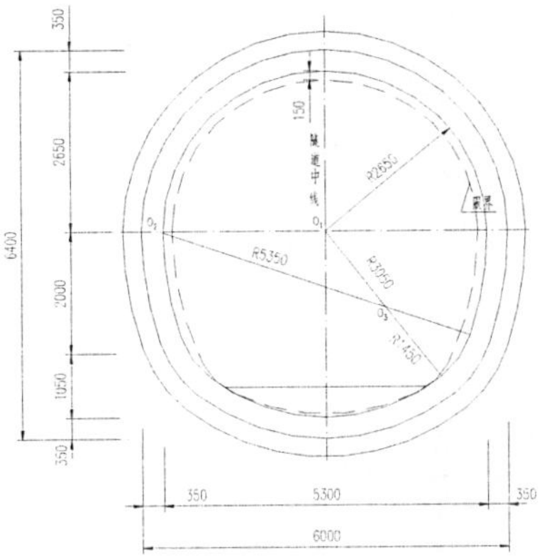

图 11　膨胀土（岩）地层矿山法隧道断面

6.2.2 主要支护参数、辅助工程措施及施工方法

目前中国内地地铁中的矿山法隧道一般采用浅埋暗挖法进行设计，该工法具有“管超前，严注浆、短进尺、强支护、早封闭、勤量测”的十八字方针[15]，与上述膨胀土（岩）地层中修建矿山法隧道的成

功经验是一致的。

因此对于处于成都膨胀土（岩）地层的矿山法隧道，其超前支护采用复合式衬砌结构（即以锁脚锚杆、钢筋网、喷射混凝土和钢架为初期支护并辅以小导管），采用模筑钢筋混凝土衬砌作为二次衬砌，初期支护与二次衬砌间设全封闭防水隔离层，并在隧道全环刚架设 4 处锁脚锚杆。施工方法选用上下台阶法进行开挖，为减少地面沉降，开挖进尺控制在 1 m 以内，拆除临时支撑纵向长度控制在 5 m 以内，一般采用人工或机械开挖，当采用爆破开挖时，应采用光面微震微差爆破，严格控制爆破振动速度，尽量减少对围岩的干扰；开挖后及时支护，及时封闭成环，见表 3。

表 3 矿山法隧道支护参数、辅助工程措施及施工方法表

衬砌类型	衬期支护				辅助措施	二次衬砌	施工方法	预留变形量（mm）
	锁脚锚杆	钢筋网	喷射早强混凝土	格栅钢架 180	ϕ42 超前小导管			
单线	ϕ32 自进式锚杆，L=3.5	ϕ8 钢筋网，@0.2 m ×0.2 m，全环单层布置	C25、S6 喷射早强混凝土 0.3 m	间距 0.8 m	L=3.5 m，环向 0.3 m，纵向 2.4 m 拱部布置	C30、S8 模筑钢筋混凝土、厚 0.35 m	环形台阶法	80

6.2.3 *矿山法隧道衬砌受力分析*

（1）数值模型

计算模型如图 12。

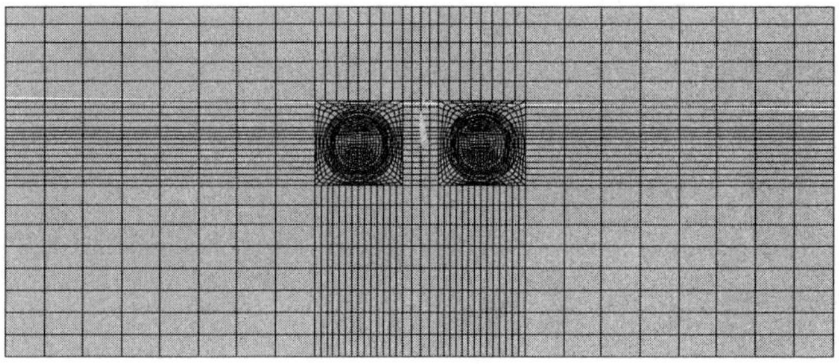

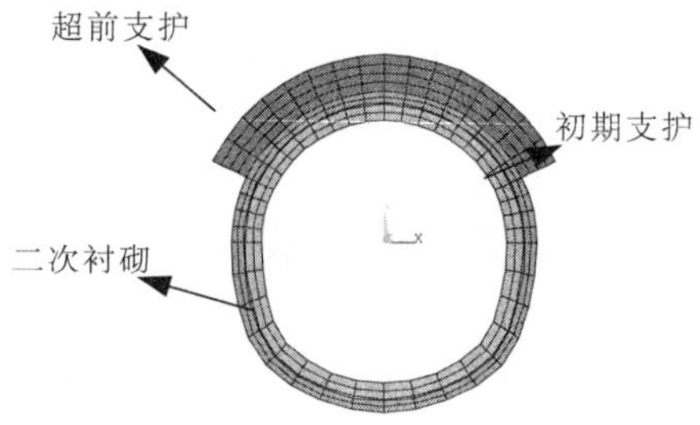

图 12 矿山法隧道数值模型

（2）计算结果分析

根据支护参数以及地层参数进行分析计算，得到以下结果（见表 4）。

表 4 二次衬砌结构内力值

工况	膨胀力大小（kPa）	膨胀土高度（m）	最大正弯矩 (kN · m)	对应轴力 (kN)	对应剪力（kN）	最大负弯矩 (kN · m)	对应轴力 (kN)	对应剪力（kN）	最大变形量 (mm)
1	0	无	75.8	463.6	9.1	55.8	585.5	32.6	2.08
2	35	1	105.2	483	11.7	86.2	628.6	27.7	3.09
3		2	101.3	490.2	11.4	82	633.4	28.5	3.42
4		3	97.5	492.8	11.3	82.9	634.5	30.8	3.48
5		4	95.7	493.6	11.3	83.8	634.9	31.6	3.3
6		5	93	498.1	11.1	81.6	636.9	35.5	2.73
7		6	79.4	533.2	9.6	61.7	658.9	39.2	2.06
8	165	1	166.2	693.5	16.7	140.1	885.3	19.3	5.8

由以上结果表明，对于矿山法隧道，当拱底局部 1 m 存在膨胀力时，衬砌结构的最大正负弯矩值为最大。量值上与无膨胀力状态的二次衬砌结构内力值相比，最大正弯矩为后者的 1.39 倍，最大负弯矩为

后者的 1.54 倍，且内力集中于仰拱和拱脚部位。随着膨胀土的膨胀范围不断加大，管片衬砌结构的最大弯矩值和最大剪力值均趋于减小，而轴力水平趋于提高。说明对于局部区域膨胀的膨胀土区域，尤其是拱底局部土体的膨胀，对结构影响较大。因此工况 8 为最不利工况，其内力见图 13。根据该结果进行配筋计算，可以满足要求。

由以上受力分析可知，矿山法隧道断面满足安全、经济的要求。

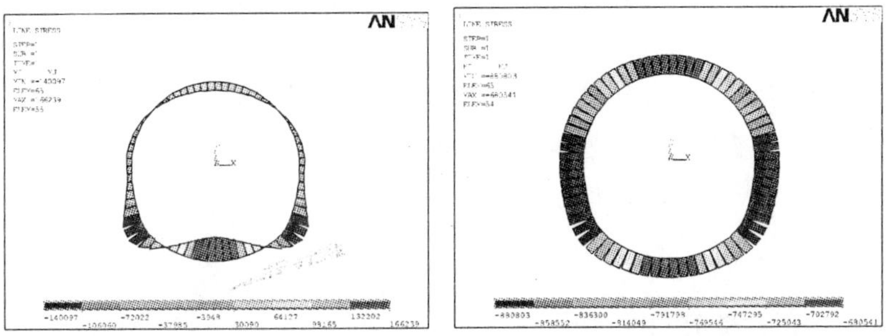

（a）弯矩图（N·m）　　（b）轴力图（N）

图 13　拱底有膨胀力矿山法隧道二次衬砌结构内力图

7　成都膨胀土（岩）地层中盾构法与矿山法施工综合对比分析

在成都 2 号线东段膨胀土（岩）区间修建地铁隧道，盾构法与矿山法均可行，现将两种工法进行对比分析：

对于盾构工法，其优点是掘进速度快，沉降控制较好，对环境影响小，施工安全；管片为预制结构，质量易控制，并且可以及时封闭成环，适应地层变形能力较强；其同步注浆以及二次注浆可以起缓冲、止水、阻水的作用。存在问题是后期运营维护费用高、可修补性弱。

对于矿山法隧道，其优点是在隧道运营阶段的维护和后期修补方面具有较强的优势。但存在问题是进尺慢，沉降控制受人为因素影响大，区间过建构筑物风险较大；并且施工中超欠挖现象难以控制，容易出现衬砌结构厚度不均、衬砌受力状态不良的现象。

8　结　论

通过以上各方面的分析，可以得出结论，对成都膨胀土（岩）地层，区间隧道采取盾构法施工无论技术上，经济上和社会效益上，都是可行的，并且较之于矿山法，无论是施工期间的安全性、对环境的影响程度、隧道主体长期使用的可靠性等等方面，盾构法均是一种优先的选择。

参考文献（References）：

[1] 地下铁道新技术文集 2003，西南交通大学出版社，2003 年.

[2] 隧道和地下工程第 10 界科技动态报告会报告文集，西南交通大学出版社，2000 年.

[3] 成都市勘察测绘研究院，成都地铁 2 号线一期工程（1 标段）详细勘察阶段天府广场站—经干院站区间岩土工程勘察报告（正式），2009 年.

[4] (日)地盘工学会著，牛清山等，译．盾构法的调查 · 设计 · 施工．北京：中国建筑工业出版社，2007.

[5] (日)土木学会编，朱伟，译．隧道标准规范（盾构篇）及解说[M]．北京：中国建筑工业出版社，2001.

[6] 中铁二院工程集团有限责任公司地下铁道设计研究院，成都地铁 1 号线一期工程区间施工图，2006.

[7] 朱合华、陶履彬．盾构隧道衬砌结构力学分析的梁—弹簧系统模型[J]．岩土力学，1998，19(2)：26-32.

[8] 李围，何川．地铁区间盾构隧道管片衬砌结构设计探讨，中国土木工程学会地下工程学会第十三届年会，北京：现代隧道技术增刊，2004.

[9] 李围，何川．盾构隧道管片结构纵向设计梁－地层弹簧模型研究[J]. 2005年全国博士生学生论坛－土木建筑学科论文集，东南大学主办，2005.

[10] 曾东洋．盾构隧道衬砌结构力学行为及施工对环境的影响研究．西南交通大学研究生学位论文，2005.

[11] 何川，罗世培．膨胀岩土地区修建地铁盾构工程综合技术阶段研究报告，2009年.

[12] 成都地铁2号线一期工程区间施工图，中铁二院工程集团有限责任公司地下铁道设计研究院，2009年.

[13] 周文波．盾构法隧道施工技术及应用[M]．北京：中国建筑工业出版社，2004.

[14] 董新平．膨胀岩隧道施工技术研究现状．北京：世界隧道，2000（5）：60-63.

[15] 王梦恕．地下工程浅埋暗挖技术通论[M]. 合肥：安徽教育出版社，2004.

作者简介（Bio-data）：

胡茜，女，汉族，1979年9月生，工学硕士，工程师。2006年毕业于西南交通大学地下工程系，现任职于中铁二院工程集团有限责任公司地下铁道设计研究院，主要从事地铁工程设计及科研工作。

Qian HU, female, the Han Nationality, born in September,1979, master of engineering, engineer, graduated from the Department of Underground Engineering of Southwest Jiaotong University in 2006. Now she works in China Railway Eryuan Engineering Group Co.Ltd, mainly engaging in the design and research work in the field of metro engineering.

E-mail: 125109@qq.com

大型水下盾构隧道管片衬砌结构劣化研究现状及展望

王士民　何 川　晏启祥
西南交通大学 地下工程系，四川　成都　610031

【摘　要】 大型水下盾构隧道管片衬砌结构劣化问题是一个从细观到宏观的跨尺度问题，同时又是一个包含了连续、非连续、连续与非连续耦合以及连续向非连续转化的多态问题，其劣化过程是一个包括损伤、破坏直到灾变失稳的渐进性过程，目前对其的研究尚不充分。本文首先介绍了大型水下盾构隧道管片衬砌结构劣化的研究背景，然后从耐久性研究和裂缝产生原因分析及控制两方面阐述了目前的研究现状，最后通过讨论指出了大型水下盾构隧道管片衬砌结构劣化问题的一个重要研究方向。

【关键词】 水下盾构隧道；管片衬砌结构；劣化

RESEARCH STATUS AND PROSPECT ON THE DETERIORATION OF THE SEGMENT STRUCTURE IN LARGE UNDERWATER SHIELD TUNNEL

Shimin WANG，Chuan HE，Qixiang YAN
Department of Underground Engineering, Southwest Jiaotong University, Chengdu 610031, Sichuan, China

Abstract: The deterioration of the segment structure in large underwater shield tunnel is a multi-scale problem from microscopic to macroscopic. And it contains continuous, discontinuous, the cohesion of continuous and discontinuous and the conversion from continuous to discontinuous problems at the same time. The deterioration process is progressive process that contains damage, crack and failure. The research on the deterioration of the segment structure in large underwater shield tunnel is just at the beginning and is not enough by now. In this paper, the research background of the deterioration of the segment structure in large underwater shield tunnel is introduced. Then the research status is expounded from two sides. One is the structure durability and the other is the generation reasons and control methods of the crack in the segment structure. At the end, the direction of the research on the deterioration of the segment structure in large underwater shield tunnel is pointed out through discussion.

Key words: underwater shield tunnel; segment structure; deterioration

1　研究背景

我国上海市于 1966 和 1984 年分别修建了外径 10.22 m 的打浦路越江隧道和外径 11.30 m 的延安东路越江隧道，由此开始了我国大型水下隧道建设的历史[1]。仅上海就先后修建了延安东路南沿线隧道、大连路隧道、复兴东路隧道、翔殷路隧道和上中路等越江隧道，而位于长江上游的重庆也在 2005 年完成了外径 6.32 m 的排水工程越江隧道；目前，国内开工建设的还有南京长江公路隧道、武汉长江公路隧道、杭州庆春路公路水底隧道、上海崇明越江隧道、广州狮子洋隧道；另外，上海市长江西路、军工路、龙

基金项目：国家自然科学基金（50778154）；铁道部课题（2007G036、2006G007B）

耀路越江隧道、钱塘江第十通道隧道工程、武汉地铁过江隧道、大连湾海底隧道、哈尔滨松花江越江隧道以及长沙湘江隧道等隧道也进入了开工前期的工程可行性研究阶段。据不完全统计，在未来 10 年内，我国将有数十座大型水下隧道需要开工建设。随着我国城市化进程的加快，大城市的交通、环境以及文物保护等问题日益突出，为了满足城市功能的需要，我国的城市轨道交通工程建设已逐渐进入高潮，已有 23 个城市正在建设或即将建设地铁等轨道交通项目，近期规划建设 61 条线路，约 1 700 公里长，总投资达到 6 000 亿元以上，建设规模和速度已居世界首位。

在大批盾构隧道修建的同时，与之相伴的是，盾构隧道管片衬砌结构在管片制造、施工以及运营阶段不可避免地会出现管片裂缝、渗漏水、钢筋锈蚀、混凝土腐蚀老化甚至剥落、掉块等不同程度的病害。1973～1975 年建造的阿联酋迪拜 Shindagha 海底隧道，1986 年就不得不维修，维修费用是建造费的两倍；上世纪 70 年代建成的香港地铁部分区间隧道，在 90 年代就发现内排钢筋严重锈蚀，导致混凝土保护层的剥落，影响到正常使用。日本对部分铁路和公路隧道病害的调查表明，有 70%的隧道发生衬砌裂损病害，其他病害如渗漏、基底下沉和底鼓也很常见[2]。日本的铁路隧道相继发生 3 次重大的混凝土掉块事故，引起了日本运输省的重视。1999 年 6 月 27 日，山阳新干线福岗隧道发生衬砌混凝土剥落，造成列车破损的重大事故；10 月 9 日，山阳新干线北九州隧道的边墙上端又发生混凝土剥落事故；11 月 28 日，室兰本线礼文宾隧道再次发生重达 2 吨的拱部衬砌混凝土的剥落，造成货物列车脱轨事故。香港地铁不得不花费大量资金，在不能影响正常运营的十分苛刻的条件下，采用特殊施工措施及工具，利用晚间收车的短短几个小时内，花费几年的时间，采用超高压水刀铲除保护层及内排钢筋，然后喷射钢纤维混凝土或植筋后再扎内排钢筋以聚合物混凝土加以修复。打浦路隧道在运营了 36 年后，也存在隧道衬砌结构混凝土劣化、钢筋和管片螺栓锈蚀及渗漏水等现象 [3]。广州地铁隧道投入运营不到 1 年后，在 2007 年 11 月 2 日发现了左线 1662 环～1724 环隧道段环号为偶数的管环管片 11 点位的管片内表面出现了不同程度的纵向裂纹，该受损隧道段施工时间为 2005 年 12 月 17 日～12 月 28 日[4]。

如果对盾构隧道的病害不及时进行治理，会导致衬砌结构的进一步破坏乃至失稳，将会造成严重的损失。然而众所周知，通常对于盾构隧道管片衬砌结构病害的治理费用是相当高的，国外学者曾用“五倍定律”对其进行了形象的描述：设计阶段对钢筋防护方面节省 1 美元，那么就意味着发现钢筋锈蚀时采取措施将追加维修费 5 美元，混凝土表面顺筋开裂时采取措施将追加维修费 25 美元，严重破坏时采取措施将追加维修费 125 美元[5]。日本一些有识之士提出“2020 年的警钟”，即“日本将从土建大国变成修缮大国”。2020 年的结构维修费和改建费，仅建设省就超过 2 兆亿日元，是现在的 3 倍，维修费将成为国家财政的巨大负担[6]。

2 研究现状

管片作为盾构隧道的结构主体，同时也是组成衬砌结构的基本单元，其材料性能、结构设计方法以及耐久性对隧道结构耐久性和使用寿命具有决定性的影响[7]；并且隧道工程项目投资巨大，如果一旦由于管片破坏导致工程过早破坏，将造成巨大的损失。与普通的盾构隧道相比，对大型水下盾构隧道管片衬砌结构具有以下显著的不同之处[8]：① 大型水下隧道管片衬砌结构通常要承受几十米甚至上百米高水头的渗透压力，以及深厚土层围压的长期持续作用，致使衬砌结构所承受的外界荷载以及边界条件更为复杂多变；② 钢筋混凝土管片衬砌结构随不同截面位置和各种不利荷载组合，分别呈大、小偏心受压作用，若干控制截面还将局部承受不利的拉弯受力，并处于允许的限裂和裂控状态；③ 江水或海水以地下水渗流的方式作用并长期腐蚀管片衬砌，同时，江（海）水经土层中化学成分的物化反应过程之后，亦会对管片衬砌形成腐蚀作用，从而造成管片衬砌结构的损伤劣化。上述三点中前两点使大型水下盾构隧道管片衬砌结构出现不利荷载及边界条件组合的几率显著增加，而第三点则在长期作用下降低了管片衬砌结构的力学性能指标。可以看出，大型水下盾构隧道管片衬砌结构更容易出现破坏失稳事故的发生，而且一旦出现破坏失稳事故，水下盾构隧道所造成的生命财产损失更是难以估计的，对水下盾构隧道的修复也是非常困难并耗资巨大。

因此，近年来国内外针对大型水下盾构隧道的研究和成果也是颇多的，研究主要集中在以下两个方面：

（1）结构耐久性和健康诊断

日本曾以东京湾越湾高速公路盾构隧道为对象进行了耐久性与防蚀性的研究，另外，用于评定侵蚀性环境对钢筋混凝土影响程度的量测技术在国外已有了较大的发展，如日本在隧道施工中采用了一些检测特殊量的光纤传感器，其中光纤 pH 传感器用于检测混凝土由于各种化学变化，诸如硫酸盐的侵蚀、酸化过程、钢筋腐蚀等造成的退化过程，同时开发出了隧道检查和诊断专家系统（TIMES-1），该系统包括四种设备，主要用于找出隧道内表面变形或开裂可能的原因，显示需要进一步检查的项目和为用户提供有关隧道维修有用的信息[9]。丹麦 Storebelt 海峡隧道也采用了相当多的结构监测设施，用以监测与结构的耐久性问题及结构性能有关的选定参数，例如在隧道管片内的钢筋上，装上专门研制的抗腐蚀元件以警报侵蚀性（despassivating）物质从外界侵入时的情况；此外，采用振弦式应变仪量测应变的变化，振弦式测压计量测外界水压，同时设置一些控制点以量测隧道断面几何形状的变化。这样就可使结构性能的蜕化过程得以实时监控，以便及时采取防治措施[5]。荷兰采用整套传感器系统对 Westerschelde 隧道耐久性进行了长期监测，监测体统包括无线应变计、渗漏检测仪、多环电极和参考电极等众多测试元器件[10]。我国在水底隧道耐久性方面也有一定研究。杨林德[11,12]利用蒙特—卡罗法(MC)模拟计算了管片构件耐久性失效风险值，通过对管片结构体系各类风险因素的层次化分析（Analytical Hierarchy Process, AHP），确定了隧道结构的耐久性失效风险等级并提出了耐久性失效风险的防治措施及对策。乔宗昭[13]以上海长江隧道为例，通过对水底盾构隧道工程所在地的环境条件分析，提出了水底隧道的耐久性设计的总体要求、设计构思及具体使用要求，并提出了耐久性设计方案的风险水平方案。 武汉理工大学[14]针对武汉长江隧道工程高压富水的环境要求，以提高构件的耐久性，延长其服役寿命为主要目标，引入功能梯度材料设计原理，提出了功能梯度混凝土管片形式（Functionally Graded Concrete Segment, 简称 FGCS）。伍振志[5]结合上海长江隧道工程，针对越江盾构隧道衬砌裂损管片混凝土中氯离子运移规律及裂缝对管片结构耐久性损伤、管片上覆土层中氯离子运移规律及其对管片侵蚀的影响、隧道接缝防水密封垫的耐久性等关键问题进行了研究，建立了越江盾构隧道钢筋混凝土管片衬砌和接缝防水密封垫结构体系耐久性的研究方法和理论框架体系。孙钧院士[8]结合崇明长江隧道对盾构管片衬砌结构的耐久性设计进行了系统的研究，讨论了管片衬砌结构的腐蚀机理、影响耐久性的主要因素、接头螺栓和填缝防水材料的耐久性等问题，建立了一种耐久性设计基本方法，并从耐久性设计的角度对崇明长江隧道结构的服务寿命进行了预测，提出了提高隧道管片衬砌耐久性的综合防治措施。为解决盾构隧道管片衬砌结构强度的历史老化和衰减问题提供了一条新的思路。

（2）盾构隧道管片衬砌结构裂缝产生原因分析及控制

盾构隧道管片在制作、隧道施工和运营期间都不可避免的会出现裂缝。

管片在制作过程中，由于振捣棒的挤压作用，管片混凝土水化产生的蒸汽和水分容易集中在模具的侧板和管片侧面的结合处，在管片在钢模中凝固时失水会导致管片表面微裂缝的产生。同时，由于自身重力和振捣等因素的影响，混凝土凝固时在模具内不可能分布得很均匀，在分布不均匀的地方凝固速度也不完全相同，就会形成一定数量的小裂缝。另外，温度和湿度的变化也会导致裂缝的产生[15-17]：管片入模后，较大的温差会使混凝土内外凝固很不均匀，从而产生较大的温度应力，而此时混凝土还未完全凝固，强度比较低，在巨大的温度应力作用下很容易出现裂缝。同样，管片从蒸汽养护模具里取出到入水池养护的过程中，暴露在空气中导致温度应力过大也会产生裂缝。另外，如果空气中的湿度比较小，混凝土表面也会因失水太快而出现收缩裂缝。

在盾构隧道施工过程中，管片在运输、吊装以及千斤顶推进等荷载作用下均可能产生裂缝，其中常见的裂缝成因有：管片环面不平整或千斤顶撑靴重心偏位[18,19]、盾构机姿态控制与曲线段不匹配、管片间相对扭转[20]。

在隧道运营期间，各种动、静荷载作用也会导致裂缝的产生。同时，各种环境因素和外部条件，包括温度变化（水泥水化热、冰冻）湿度变化、酸碱度、基础变形（膨胀地层、湿陷地层、地基差异等）

以及碳化收缩和内部钢筋锈胀等都会使结构承受一定的应力而使管片开裂。

管片裂缝按成因又可以分为两种类型[21]：由变形引起的裂缝和由外荷载（各种动、静荷载）直接引起的裂缝和次应力引起的裂缝。前者的特征是结构要求变形，当受到约束和限制时产生内应力，应力超过一定数值后产生裂缝，裂缝出现后变形得到满足，内应力松弛。这种裂缝宽度大、内应力小，对荷载的影响小，但对耐久性损害大。尤其是动荷载引起的裂缝不能自愈合，有利于混凝土的中性化作用，混凝土的中性化作用不仅发生在裂缝壁上，而且发生在钢筋表面与混凝土接触受到破坏的区域[22]。据国内外调查资料，工程结构产生属于变形（温湿度、收缩与膨胀、不均匀沉降）引起的裂缝约占 15%～20%，属于荷载引起的裂缝约占 80%～85%。

目前部分学者对盾构隧道衬砌管片裂缝的成因进行了比较详细的分析和归类，也为裂缝的控制及修复提供了较好的指导[23-33]。钟长平[23]叙述了广州地铁一号线黄沙站—长寿路站区间隧道泥水盾构掘进施工中出现的有规律性的管片开裂现象，重点分析了开裂产生的原因及应对措施，为类似工程设计与施工时参考和借鉴。于利红[24]根据在上海地铁 1 号线和 2 号线隧道施工的经验，对几种常见的管片破碎现象作了分析，并提出了针对性措施。竺维彬等[18]通过实例分析分别对管片生产、盾构施工及使用过程中管片开裂原因进行了研究，并提出了相应的对策。黄威然等[25]根据广州、南京地铁管片生产的经验,从介绍混凝土配合比、生产工艺和管片构造等方面入手，着重分析了裂纹产生的原因，并提出了相应的解决方法。韩小鸣[26]结合山西省万家寨引黄工程中的 TBM 隧洞开挖工程的实际，从衬砌管片的生产、运输、安装、维护等环节分析了造成 TBM 隧洞衬砌管片损坏的主要原因，并有针对性地提出了预防及修补措施。秦建设[27]从分析盾构机与管片相互作用入手，研究了盾构机姿态与衬砌走向不协调导致管片错台及混凝土开裂问题，并给出了相关建议。梁仲元等[28]通过对实际管片破损和裂缝的分析和有限元模拟，由计算出相关的应力集中区域推断出典型破损和裂缝的产生原因，并为下一步裂缝试验分析提供了参考依据。董明钢等[19]针对盾构管片在拼装过程中经常发生的破裂现象，通过现场调查和有限元计算，分析了引起盾构管片拼装过程中破裂的主要影响因素，对于目前工程中常见的管片施工开裂现象进行定量的解释。陈俊生、莫海鸿[20,28]等通过三维有限元模拟对施工过程中部分管片螺栓孔附近出现开裂或破损的现象进行了数值模拟研究，证明该开裂不是由于管片间相对弯曲位移产生的，而是由管片间相对扭转引起的。宋书显[29]结合武汉长江隧道盾构管片施工过程中的实际经验,介绍了盾构大体积管片施工过程中不同裂纹类型、形成原因及控制重、难点,对关键工序及关键工艺进行重点介绍,并简要介绍了常见问题及其对策和预防措施。丁庆军、蔡茂涛等[30-32]结合武汉市长江过江隧道管片生产的实际情况，针对大直径、大手孔钢筋混凝土管片在生产过程中裂缝产生的位置及其特点，从材料配合比、设备、生产工艺与养护制度等几个方面分析了裂缝产生的原因，并对混凝土配合比及管片生产工艺等方面进行了改进。荣耀[33]将海底隧道衬砌简化为偏心受压混凝土构件，对其进行了小比尺模型相似试验，得到了裂缝产生和扩展的表现形态，应用逻辑模糊理论进行了海底隧道温度裂缝模糊的控制，结合可靠度理论进行了裂缝控制模糊随机可靠性分析，并提出了限制最大裂缝宽度的设计建议值。

3 讨 论

目前针对地下结构耐久性的研究是相当不充分的，并且研究内容和手段大多同上部结构几无差别。其中针对大型水下盾构隧道的研究主要集中于材料层面和耐久性实时监测方面，机理研究较为欠缺。而盾构隧道衬砌结构管片裂缝方面的研究分析都只是针对一个或几个盾构隧道工程，未能就盾构隧道衬砌结构裂缝产生机理以及扩展机制进行系统分析,因此其对工程实践的意义仅仅停留在经验借鉴的层面上,难以从理论层面上揭示盾构隧道衬砌结构损伤破坏等劣化问题的本质。

综上所述，目前对大型水下盾构隧道管片衬砌结构劣化方面的研究还处在初级阶段，缺乏对管片衬砌结构从损伤到破坏直至灾变的整个劣化过程的定量分析方法及相应的预测理论。

大型水下盾构隧道管片衬砌结构劣化问题是一个从细观到宏观的跨尺问题，同时又是一个包含了连续、非连续、连续与非连续耦合以及连续向非连续转化的多态问题，其劣化过程是一个包括损伤、破坏直到灾变失稳的渐进性过程。近年来，随着计算科学与技术、试验方法与技术的发展，采用理论分析、模型试验、数值试验和现场试验测试等手段的综合研究方法，从多尺度角度出发，结合损伤力学、断裂力学等多学科交叉技术，开展对大型水下盾构隧道管片衬砌结构劣化机理及劣化过程的精细化研究，将会成为今后大型水下盾构隧道研究的一个重要方向。

参考文献（References）:

[1] 张凤祥，朱合华，傅德明. 盾构隧道[M]. 北京：人民交通出版社，2004.

[2] 何川，佘健. 高速公路隧道维修与加固[M]. 北京：人民交通出版社，2006.

[3] 袁勇，李剑等. 既有打浦路越江隧道的现状与补修方法初探[C]. 第五届混凝土结构耐久性科技论坛论文集，2006.

[4] 陆永芳. 盾构隧道管片衬砌裂纹病害整治技术[J]. 山西建筑，2008，34(17)：325-326.

[5] 伍振志. 越江隧道耐久性研究[D]. 上海:同济大学博士学位论文，2007.

[6] 关宝树. 隧道维修管理要点集[M]. 北京:人民交通出版社，2004.

[7] 王信刚,马保国,王睿. 跨江海盾构隧道管片的研究进展[J]. 现代隧道技术，2008，45(3)：1-6.

[8] 孙钧. 崇明长江隧道盾构管片衬砌结构的耐久性设计[J]. 建筑科学与工程学报，2008，25(1)：1-9.

[9] 工藤泉，郭树棠. 耐久性与防蚀性的研究—东京湾越湾公路盾构隧道[J]. 隧道译制丛，1994(10)：20-28.

[10] M.L. Post, F.W.J.van de Linde, E.J.C. Rademarker.The Westerchelde tunnel-using a sensor-based system for durability monitoring for the tunnel lining[J]. Tunneling and underground space technology，2004(19)：325.

[11] 杨林德，黄慷. 越江通道工程盾构隧道耐久性失效风险评估[J]. 地下空间，2004，24(1)：1-4.

[12] 黄慷，杨林德. 崇明越江盾构隧道工程耐久性失效风险研究[J]. 现代隧道技术，2004，41(2)：8-13

[13] 乔宗昭，朱祖熹，范益群，等. 水底盾构法公路隧道耐久性设计[C]. 全国第六届混凝土耐久性学术交流会论文集，2004：3-16.

[14] 马保国，高英力，王信刚. 盾构隧道功能梯度混凝土管片保护层设计及性能研究[C]. 第五届混凝土结构耐久性科技论坛论文集，2006.

[15] 赵军，王大海. 地铁隧道混凝土管片的孔洞和裂缝控制[J]. 城市轨道交通研究，2005（4）:75-77

[16] 孙宗军，李永利，刘松玉，等. 地铁衬砌混凝土管片防温裂试验研究及有限元分析[J]. 特种结构, 2003, 20(4): 45-47.

[17] 孙宗军，刘松玉，吴京荣等. 隧道管片生产阶段防裂措施及温度场数值模拟[J]. 公路交通科技，2004, 21（3）: 64-66.

[18] 竺维彬，鞠世健. 盾构隧道管片开裂的原因及相应对策[J]. 现代隧道技术，2003，40(1)：21-25.

[19] 董明钢，张雷，姚海明，冯紫良. 盾构管片拼装过程中破裂现象的可靠度分析[J]. 地下空间与工程学报，2006，(2)：916-920，925.

[20] 陈俊生，莫海鸿，梁仲元. 盾构隧道施工阶段管片局部开裂原因初探[J]. 岩石力学与工程学报，2006， 25(5): 906-910.

[21] 伍振志，杨林德，时蓓玲，等. 裂缝对隧道管片结构耐久性影响及其模糊评价[J]. 地下空间与工程学报，2006，3(2)：224-228.

[22] 朱元祥，候应武，屈文俊.混凝土结构裂缝处的碳化分析[J].西北建筑工程学院学报，1998 (4)：34-38.

[23] 钟长平. 广州地铁盾构隧道管片开裂原因分析[J]. 广东土木与建筑，2000，(4)：93-95.

[24] 于利红. 隧道施工过程中管片破碎现象分析及防治[J]. 地下工程与隧道，2002，(4)：37-39.

[25] 黄威然，竺维彬. 盾构隧道混凝土管片表面裂纹成因及防治[J]. 现代隧道技术，2003，40(3)：47-50.

[26] 秦建设，朱伟，陈剑. 盾构姿态控制引起管片错台及开裂问题研究[J]. 施工技术， 2004，33(10)：25-27.

[27] 梁仲元，陈俊生，莫海鸿，竺维彬. 广州地铁盾构施工阶段管片开裂原因初探[J]. 广东土木与建筑，2004，(4)：23-25.

[28] J.S.Chen, H.H.Mo. Numerical study on crack problems in segments of shield tunnel using finite element method[J]. Tunneling and Underground Space Technology，2009，(24)：91-102.

[29] 宋书显. 盾构大体积管片裂纹分析[J]. 隧道建设，2006，26 (5): 56-59，73.

[30] 丁庆军，曾波，彭波，等. 大手孔隧道混凝土管片裂纹的成因分析及改善措施[J]. 混凝土，2006，(7)：59-60，68.

[31] 蔡茂涛，丁庆军，曾波. 大直径、大手孔钢筋混凝土管片裂缝问题探析[J]. 混凝土与水泥制品，2007，(1)：28-32.

[32] 蔡茂涛，丁庆军. 武汉长江隧道管片生产中出现裂缝的分析及控制[J]. 施工技术，2007，36(4)：73-77.

[33] 荣耀. 海底隧道衬砌裂缝控制关键技术研究[D]. 上海：同济大学博士学位论文，2007.

作者简介（Bio-data）:

王士民(1978—)，男，博士，2008 年毕业于同济大学地下建筑与工程系结构工程专业（地下结构方向），现任西南交通大学地下工程系讲师，主要从事地下结构损伤劣化机理及数值模拟方法方面的研究工作。

Shimin WANG (1978—), male, Ph.D., Graduated from department of geotechnical engineering, Tongji University in 2008, work in department of geotechnical engineering Southwest Jiaotong University as a lecturer at present; engage in the research on the damage mechanism and numerical simulation of underground structure.

E-mail: neumining@163.com

何川，1964 年生，工学博士（早稻田大学）。西南交通大学地下工程系主任、博士生导师、教育部长江学者特聘教授。长期从事隧道与地下工程的教学与科研工作。主要研究领域为：现代盾构法隧道设计理论、地下铁道结构设计、特殊隧道结构施工控制、高速公路隧道运营控制。

Chuan HE was born in June 1964 and obtained the Dr. Eng. in the Waseda University. Currently, Dr. HE is the director of Department of Underground Engineering in Southwest Jiaotong University, the doctor supervisor, the professor of Changjiang Scholar Programm, Ministry of Education of PRC. He has been engaging in the teaching and research of tunnel engineering for many years. He specializes in design theory of modern shield tunnel, structural design of subway, construction technique of tunnel under complicated condition, tunnel ventilation control system.

Tel: +86-28-87601932

E-mail: chuanhe21@163.com

盾构隧道设计常用计算方法的归纳与比较

孙文昊 殷怀连

中铁第四勘察设计院集团有限公司，湖北 武汉 430063

【摘 要】 对盾构隧道设计中常用的衬砌内力计算方法进行了归纳，并对荷载结构模型中多种具体的计算方法进行了分类。以南京地铁 2 号线为背景，对几个典型断面，采用目前最为常用的三种计算方法—修正惯用法、梁弹簧模型法及质圆环法分别进行了内力计算，并对计算结果以及造成计算结果差别的原因进行了分析，得出几点结论，可供相关的技术人员参考。

【关键词】 盾构隧道；计算方法；归纳；比较

GENERALIZATION AND COMPARSION OF COMMON CALCULATION METHODS ON DESIGN OF SHIELD TUNNEL

Wenhao SUN，Huailian YIN

China Railway Siyuan Survey and Design Group CO., LTD, Wuhan 430063, Hubei, China

Abstract: The calculation methods of shield tunnel is generalized in this paper, and many type specific calculation methods in load-structure model are classified. Based on Nanjing Metro Line 2, three kinds of common calculation method—modified usual calculation method, beam-spring model calculation method and modified solid ring calculation method are applied to calculate the endogen force of shield tunnel respectively. By comparing the calculation result and analyzing the reason, some research conclusions have been reached in the expectation of providing references for technicians.

Key words: shield tunnel; calculation method; generalization; comparsion

1 前 言

盾构法隧道在世界范围内都有应用，但不同国家所采用的盾构隧道衬砌内力计算方法各不相同。根据国际隧道协会（I.T.A）隧道结构设计模型研究组总结的结果，目前用盾构法开挖的软土质隧道的设计方法主要归纳为以下四种设计模型：① 经验类比法；② 收敛—限制法；③ 荷载—结构模型；④ 连续介质模型（地层结构模型）[1]。

目前我国常用的盾构隧道衬砌设计模型主要有经验类比法和荷载—结构法。在工程的前期研究阶段一般可以采用经验类比法确定结构尺寸；在初步设计和施工设计阶段多用荷载—结构模型对衬砌结构内力进行计算；在特殊条件下也会采用地层结构模型进行分析，但很少用于结构设计。总的来看，目前盾构隧道设计中，荷载—结构模型仍然是最常用的结构计算方法。但是，由于目前国内尚无相关规范对盾构隧道的结构计算进行系统的指导，所以不同的设计机构所采用的具体计算方法也各不相同，甚至有时对同一座隧道的同一断面内力计算结果相差也很大。下面对国内常用的几种荷载——结构模型进行比较分析。

2 荷载-结构模型的分类

任何理论计算都需要对工程原型进行一定程度的简化或假定处理，在盾构隧道的荷载—结构模型中，

基金项目：863 计划（2006AA11Z116）；铁道部课题（2007G036、2006G007B）

根据对衬砌结构和结构上作用的荷载采用不同的处理方式，又可以衍生出多种具体的计算方法：

（1）根据对结构（主要指管片接头和衬砌环刚度）处理方法的不同，可以分为均质圆环法、多铰圆环法、弹性铰法。

（2）根据对荷载（主要指地基抗力）的处理方法不同，可以分为自由变形圆环法、假定弹性抗力法(如三角形分布法（见图 1）和前苏联的布加耶娃法)、地基弹簧法（见图 2)。

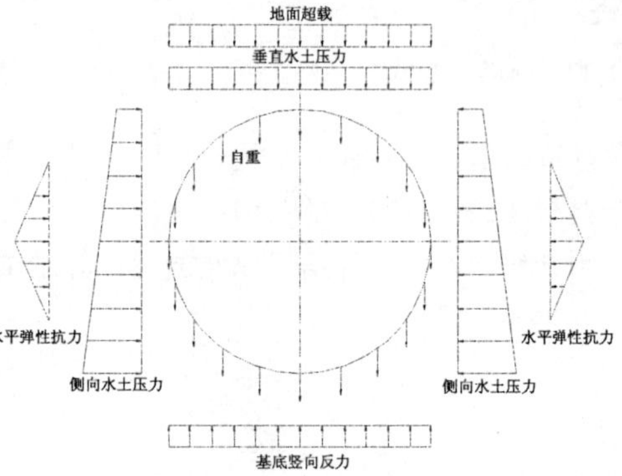

图 1　惯用荷载系统

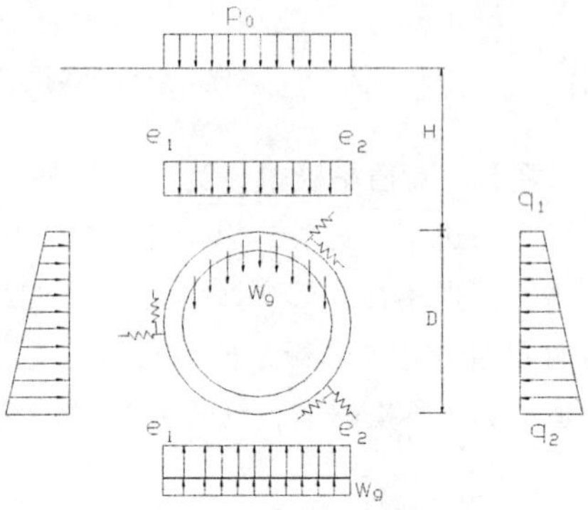

图 2　地基弹簧荷载系统

上述的对接头的处理方法和对荷载的处理方法是可以任意组合的。事实上，由于对结构及荷载的处理方法不止上述几种，从理论上说至少可以组合出十几种计算方法。

另外，近几年来有学者对壳—弹簧模型进行了研究[2] [3]，即在荷载结构模型下，用厚壳单元模拟管片结构，用弹簧单元模拟接头及螺栓作用的一种计算方法；并有学者提出了壳—弹簧—接触模型[4]，该模型是在地层结构模型下，在壳—弹簧模型的基础上，考虑管片与地层间的接触条件，从而更为精确地模拟实际状态的一种计算方法。由于上述计算模型提出较晚，目前在实际工程中尚未得到应用，故未作比较研究，下面仅对被技术人员广泛接受并常用几种组合形式进行比较分析。

2.1　惯用法及修正惯用法[5]

惯用计算法即把管片环简化为与管片主截面具有相同刚度的弹性均质圆环，并采用以三角形抗力为特征的惯用荷载系统进行计算的方法。修正惯用计算法也中将管片衬砌圆环考虑为弹性匀质圆环，并用小于 1 的刚度折减系数η来体现环向接头的影响，不具体考虑接头的位置，即仅降低衬砌圆环的整体抗弯刚度。当采用通缝拼装方式时，其分析结果就作为设计值；而当为错缝拼装时，由于环与环间的纵向接头的咬合作用，出现附加弯矩值，用附加弯矩增大系数ξ来表示，即用于管片主截面设计的弯矩为（$1+\xi$）M，用于接头设计的弯矩为（$1-\xi$）M。惯用法的荷载系统如图 1 所示。

2.2　梁-弹簧模型法

梁-弹簧模型是指对于管片衬砌环，用梁单元模拟管片结构，用旋转弹簧来模拟接头，并用抗弯刚度 K_θ 来体现环向接头的抗弯刚度。这种模型在计算中可以具体考虑环向接头的位置以及由接头引起的管片环的刚度降低。当采用错缝拼装时，因纵向接头将引起衬砌圆环间的相互咬合作用，此时，除考虑计算目标环外，将对其有影响的前后二衬砌圆环也作为研究对象，并用径向抗剪刚度 K_r 和切向抗剪刚度 K_t 来体现纵向接头的环间传力效果，计算模型如图 3 所示。该计算模型目前在国内多采用地基弹簧来模拟地基抗力，如图 2 所示。

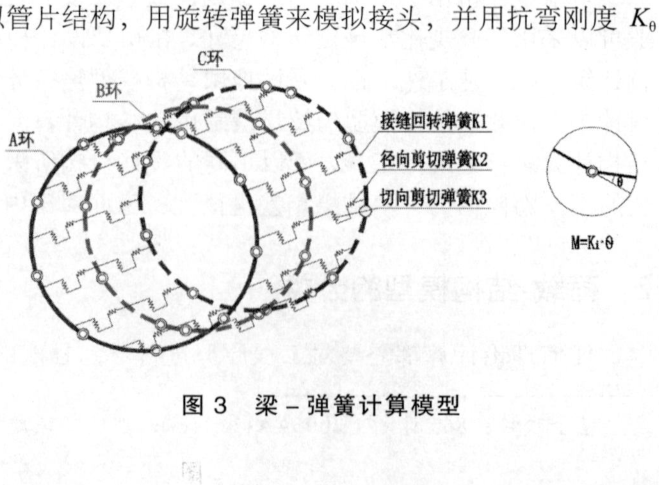

图 3　梁－弹簧计算模型

2.3 修正匀质圆环法

如图 4 所示，该计算方法结构模型与修正惯用法相同，也是将管片衬砌圆环考虑为弹性匀质圆环，并用小于 1 的刚度折减系数η来体现环向接头的影响，不具体考虑接头的位置，即仅降低衬砌圆环的整体抗弯刚度；当采用错缝拼装方式时，用附加弯矩增大系数ξ来模拟由于环间的纵向接头的咬合作用引起的附加弯矩值。与修正惯用法不同的是，其荷载系统中的地基抗力不采用三角形假定抗力，而是用地基弹簧模拟。这一计算方法其他资料未见提及，笔者根据计算特点，为其命名为修正匀质圆环法。

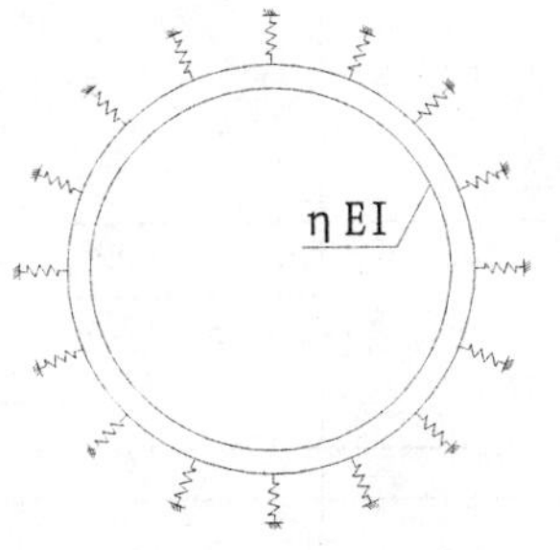

图 4 修正匀质圆环计算模型

3 不同模型计算结果比较分析

3.1 计算条件

为了研究上述三种计算模型计算结果的差别，结合南京地铁二号线一期工程的工程实例，对三个区间隧道同时用三种方法进行了计算。本次计算根据沿线的地质条件和埋深不同共选取了四个具有代表性的断面，分别用修正惯用法、修正匀质圆环法和梁-弹簧模型进行了计算，断面选取及土层参数（根据地质勘查报告）见表 1。

表 1 计算工况及参数

截面编号	覆土厚度（m）	隧道所在土层	侧压力系数 λ	地基抗力系数 K（MN/m^3）	贯入度 N
1	16.8	淤泥质粉质黏土	0.65	7	2.5
2	8.5	粉土	0.45	10	13
3	13.7	粉细砂	0.4	20	6
4	9.5	淤泥质粉质黏土	0.65	6.5	2

其他计算参数如下：

(1) 管片几何参数：

隧道内径 5 500 mm；管片厚度 350 mm；幅宽 1 200 mm

(2) 材料参数：

C50 钢筋混凝土弹模 $E=3.45\times10^{10}$ Pa；泊松比 $\mu=0.22$

(3) 匀质圆环法修正系数：$\eta=0.75$；　$\xi=0.30$

(4) 梁－弹簧模型：

径向抗剪刚度：$K_r=1\times10^9$ (N/m/m)

切向抗剪刚度：$K_t=1\times10^9$ (N/m/m)

接头转动刚度：$K_\theta^+=3.0\times10^4$ (kN.m/rad/m)；$K_\theta^-=1.5\times10^4$ (kN.m/rad/m)

相邻环错缝角度：45 度

3.2 计算结果比较分析

四个具有代表性断面的内力计算结果如表 2 所示，其中计算弯矩比值是以梁-弹簧模型计算结果为基准值 M。由表中可见，采用修正惯用法计算的管片最大正弯矩在 1、4 断面的黏土层约为（1.05～1.07）M，在 2、3 断面的砂土层约为（1.18～1.27）M；而在 1、4 断面的最大负弯矩为（0.65～0.67）M，在 2、3 断面的最大负弯矩为（0.75～0.87）M。

表 2　内力计算结果及各模型计算弯矩比值汇总表

截面编号	计算模型	最大正、负弯矩及对应轴力				计算弯矩比值	
		M_{max} (kN·m)	N (kN)	M_{min} (kN·m)	N (kN)	最大正弯矩	最大负弯矩
1	修正惯用法	172.5	491.1	151.9	678.6	1.05	0.84
	修正匀质圆环	168.2	595.0	152.7	811.1	1.02	0.84
	梁-弹簧	164.8	217.81	181.0	800.8	1	1
2	修正惯用法	90.2	362.0	74.9	474.2	1.27	1.14
	修正匀质圆环	80.6	440.5	71.7	567.8	1.14	1.09
	梁-弹簧	70.8	336.7	65.8	576.2	1	1
3	修正惯用法	125.0	573.4	102.0	721.5	1.18	0.98
	修正匀质圆环	113.7	701.3	93.7	864.0	1.08	0.90
	梁-弹簧	105.6	450.5	104	869.2	1	1
4	修正惯用法	124.0	385.3	107.0	521.2	1.07	0.88
	修正匀质圆环	118.2	467.4	104.2	628.0	1.02	0.85
	梁-弹簧	115.4	198.3	122	627.3	1	1

从以上的计算结果可以看出，在不同土质和不同埋深条件下，采用修正惯用法计算得到的衬砌环最大正弯矩比采用全周地基弹簧的梁-弹簧模型和修正匀质圆环模型的最大正弯矩大。造成这种偏差的主要原因在于修正惯用法所采用的假定三角形分布地基抗力与全周地基弹簧计算出的地基抗力分布相差较大。

图 5 和图 6 分别示出了截面 2 处采用梁-弹簧模型和修正惯用法模型计算得到的地基抗力分布图形。由图可以看出，不仅假定三角形地基抗力的最大值偏小，且向拱顶、拱底两个方向递减的很快，这使得总地基抗力更小。在竖直方向荷载和水平水土压力相同的情况下，地基抗力偏小，则造成拱顶正弯矩偏大。

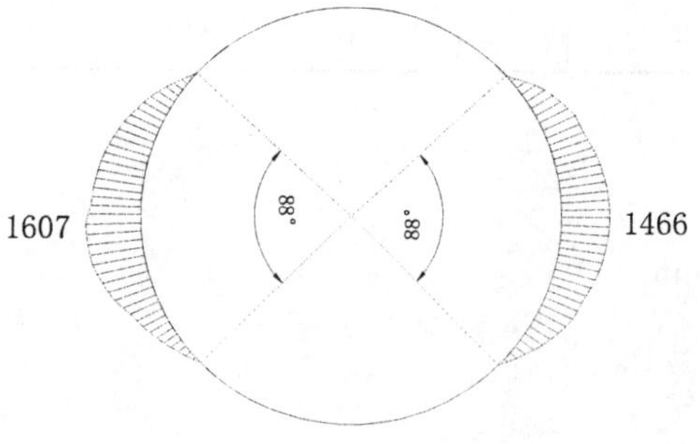

图 5　地基抗力值(单位:N)（**梁－弹簧模型**）

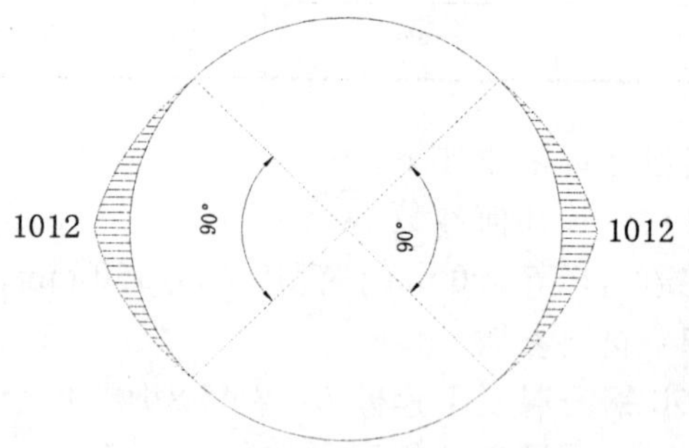

图 6　地基抗力值(单位:N)（**惯用法模型**）

对梁-弹簧模型和修正匀质圆环模型来说，由于采用的荷载模型相同，在刚度折减系数η和附加弯矩增大系数ξ取值适当的情况下二者计算出的最大正弯矩很接近。但是在梁-弹簧模型中，由于目前对纵向螺栓的剪切刚度研究很不充分，因此计算偏于安全考虑，均取无穷大（例如本次计算取为$K_r = K_t = 1\times10^9$ (N/m/m)），这使得轴力分布很不均匀，且在最大弯矩处轴力最小，因此绝大多数情况下梁-弹簧模型计算结果更不利。

4　结论及建议

根据以上分析，可以得出如下结论：

（1）在相同地层参数条件下采用修正惯用法计算出的管片内力正弯矩偏大，且随着埋深的增加，这种偏大趋势愈加明显。另外，在标贯值 N 相同，地层抗力系数 k 值相近的条件下，国内地质资料提供的侧向土压力系数λ取值与惯用法推荐采用的λ[5]相比偏小。这就是说在相似的地层条件下，同样用修正惯用法计算，采用地质勘察资料提供的λ值计算得到的弯矩要比采用惯用法推荐采用的λ值计算得到的弯矩偏大。

（2）修正匀质圆环法和梁-弹簧模型计算得到的弯矩结果总的来说较为接近，由于修正匀质圆环法在计算过程中不必考虑接头刚度、纵向螺栓位置等因素，所以计算过程较为简单，对于工程设计来说较为实用。

（3）梁-弹簧模型从理论上说能更为精确的计算出管片内力，并可同时得到管片的剪力及螺栓的剪力，但是计算过程相对较为复杂，且确定管片接头刚度、纵向螺栓连接刚度的准确值较为困难。

根据对南京地铁二号线及其他盾构隧道管片内力计算经验，并参考国内一些盾构隧道的管片内力现场实测资料，目前采用的几种管片内力计算方法得到的结果都是足够安全的。但安全储备有多大，是不是存在建筑浪费等问题还有待设计和研究人员进行进一步的研究。

参考文献（References）：

[1] 刘建航，侯学渊主编. 盾构法隧道[M]. 北京：中国铁道出版社，1991.

[2] 胡志平，罗丽娟，蔡志勇. 盾构隧道管片衬砌的平板壳-弹性铰-地基系统模型[J]. 岩土力学, 2005, 26(9): 1403-1408.

[3] 谢卓雄. 盾构隧道壳-弹簧模型与梁-弹簧模型计算比较[J]. 广东公路勘察设计, 2007, 128(4): 16-18.

[4] 苏宗贤，何川. 盾构隧道管片衬砌内力分析的壳-弹簧-接触模型及其应用[J]. 工程力学, 2007, 24(10): 131-136.

[5] [日]土木学会编　隧道标准规范（盾构篇）及解说　中国建筑工业出版社，2001.

作者简介（Bio-data）：

孙文昊，1975 年生，男，工程师，硕士，毕业于西南交通大学地下工程系；主要从事地铁、公路隧道及铁路隧道工程的设计与理论研究，参与了武汉长江隧道、杭州庆春路过江隧道、钱江隧道、沪通铁路以及南京地铁 2 号线、北京地铁 10 号线等工程的设计以及多项科研工作。

Wenhao SUN,Engineer, Master, Graduated from of the School of Civil Engineering of Southwest Jiaotong University. Mainly engaged in subway, highway tunnels and railway tunnel project design and theoretical research. Participated in the design of the WuhanYangtze River Tunnel, Qingchun Road River-crossing Tunnel (Hangzhou), Qiantang River Tunnel, Shanghai-Nantong railway, Nanjing Metro Line 2 and Beijing Subway Line 10.

E-mail: sunwenhao_w@163.com

殷怀连，1972 年生，男，高级工程师，本科，毕业于西南交通大学地下工程系，现任中铁第四勘察设计院集团有限公司地下工程设计研究室主任；主要从事山岭隧道以及 TBM 法隧道工程的设计与理论研究，参与了宜万铁路、向蒲铁路及贵广铁路等项目的设计。

Huailian YIN, Senior Engineer, Graduated from of the School of Civil Engineering of Southwest Jiaotong University. Served as manager of the Tunnel Engineering Design Institute of China Railway Siyuan Survey and Design Group CO., LTD. Mainly engaged in mountain tunnels and TBM tunnel engineering design and theoretical research. Participated in the design of the Yichang-Wanzhou railway, Xiangtang-Putian railway and Guizhou-Guangzhou railway.

软土层中水下盾构隧道复合衬砌列车振动响应分析

陈松洁　彭立敏　丁祖德

中南大学　隧道工程系　湖南　长沙　410075

【摘　要】　采用激振函数模拟高速列车竖向振动荷载，采用 Byrne 孔压体变模型描述可液化地层的动力特性，运用二维弹塑性有限差分方法对狮子洋盾构隧道在列车振动荷载作用下的动力响应进行分析，重点考察管片内侧无内衬与有内衬两种计算工况下隧道地基土层的孔隙水压力、有效应力以及隧道结构变形、内力（轴力、剪力、弯矩）的区别。计算结果表明：在软土层中水下盾构隧道的管片内增加内衬，能够较为显著地减小隧底软土层的 PPR 值，且离隧底振源越近，减小幅度越大，降低了软土层液化的可能性；对隧道衬砌结构的位移、变形以及结构所受内力的影响较小。

【关键词】　盾构隧道；激振函数；软土；液化

ANALYSIS OF TRAIN VIBRATION RESPONSE OF UNDERWATER SHIELD TUNNELS IN SOFT SOIL

Songjie CHEN，Limin PENG，Zude DING

School of Civil Engineering and Architecture, Central South University, Changsha 410075, Hunan, China

Abstract: Using Excitation function to simulate high-speed train vertical vibration,using Byrne pore pressure model to describe the dynamic properties of liquefied strata, using two-dimensional elastic-plastic finite-difference method to analyze the response of shield tunnel under train vibration, the Study focused on no lining or having lining the foundation soil pore water pressure, effective stress and deformation of the tunnel structure, the internal force(axial force, shear, bending moment). The results show that underwater shield tunnel in the soft which increase linings can more significantly reduce the the PPR of the soft soil, and local oscillator from the nearer end of the tunnel, reducing the rate of more large, reducing the possibility of soft soil liquefaction; the impact of the tunnel lining structure displacement, deformation and internal is very little.

Key words: shield tunnel; shock excitation function; soft soil; liquefaction

1 引　言

近年来，盾构法施工被越来越多地应用到水下隧道的建设中，然而盾构法隧道是一种由预制管片通过纵向和横向螺栓拼装起来的结构形式，存在接缝多、接头处易损、整体性差、动力响应复杂等弱点[1-3]。水下隧道所经地层的地质构造一般比较复杂，地下水较发育，当越江隧道主体下卧土层为饱和砂性土或饱和软黏性土时，在振动环境下容易发生液化或震陷等病害，最终使得隧道结构产生过量的位移、变形而失效破坏。

基金项目：铁道部科技研究开发计划项目（2006G007-B）

地下结构振动响应研究方法根据是否考虑孔隙水压变化对土体动力特性的影响，可分为总应力法和有效应力法。与总应力法相比，有效应力法可直接求得孔隙水压力和预测土体液化的可能性，更加合理地反映了地震作用过程中土层动力性质的变化。本文基于有效应力分析法，采用 Byrne 孔压体变模型对狮子洋隧道盾构段在可液化地层中的列车振动响应规律进行分析。

2 工程概况

狮子洋隧道位于广深港客运专线东涌站至虎门站区间，是国内第一条高速铁路水下隧道，也是目前世界上行车速度目标值最高的水下高速铁路隧道。隧道全长 10 800 m，其中盾构段长 9 340 m，内径 9.8 m，外径 10.8 m，管片厚度 500 mm。狮子洋隧道纵剖面设计见图 1。

根据标准贯入试验结果，狮子洋盾构隧道里程 DIK33+723～DIK34+700、DIK42+510～DIK43+200 段存在轻微至严重液化的可能性[4]。为了改善隧道支护结构的抗振性能，减小列车荷载作用下砂土及软土产生的变形以及振动，狮子洋隧道在经过软土和沙层段的隧道管片内部增加了 25 cm 厚度的内衬。为了分析软土沙层段增加内衬后的减振效果，在盾构出口端选择 DIK42+855 断面进行计算分析。该断面处隧道工程主要穿越粘性土、淤泥质土等软土层，隧底粘性土层厚度达 5.6 m，该断面地质剖面见图 2。

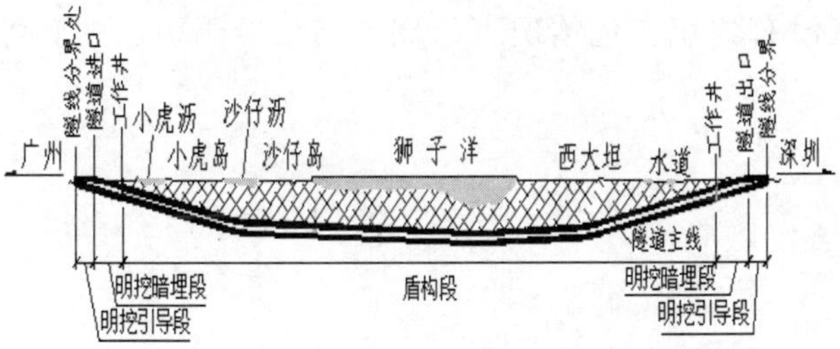

图 1 狮子洋隧道纵断面示意图

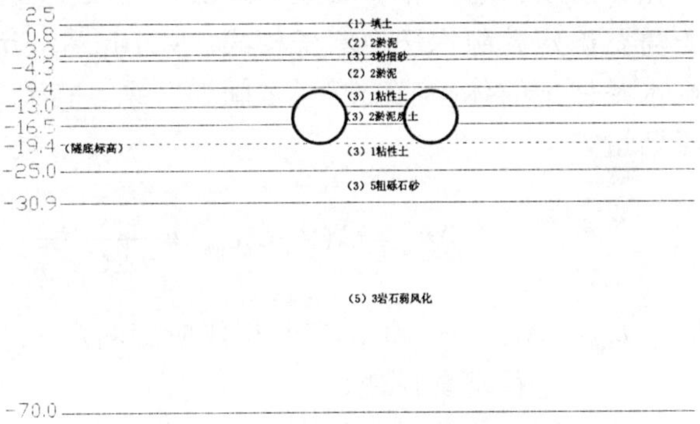

图 2 DIK42+855 计算断面地质剖面示意图

3 计算原理与计算条件

3.1 列车荷载

列车在不平顺的轨道上行驶，竖向激振荷载可用一个激振力函数来模拟，其表达式为[5-7]:

$$F(t) = p_0 + p_1\sin(\omega_1 t) + p_2\sin(\omega_2 t) + p_3\sin(\omega_3 t) \quad (1)$$

式中 p_0 ——车轮静载；

p_1, p_2, p_3 ——振动荷载。

令列车簧下质量为 M_0，则相应的振动荷载幅值为:

$$p_i = M_0 a_i \omega_i^2 \quad (i=1,2,3) \quad (2)$$

式中 a_i ——典型矢高；

ω_i ——对应车速下不平顺振动波长的圆频率，其计算式为:

$$\omega_i = 2\pi v / L_i \quad (i=1,2,3) \quad (3)$$

式中 v ——列车的运行速度；

L_i ——典型波长。

国外所研制的高速车辆的轴重一般为 16～17 t[6]，这里取轴重为 17 t，簧下质量 M_0=750 kg。考虑到狮子洋高速铁路隧道的运行标准，不平顺振动波长和矢高分别取为：L_1=10 m，$a1$=3.5 m；L_2=2 m，a_2=0.4 m；L_3=0.5m，a_3=008m。由此得到的列车振动荷载时程见图 3（图中只给出了前 0.5 s 的时程）。

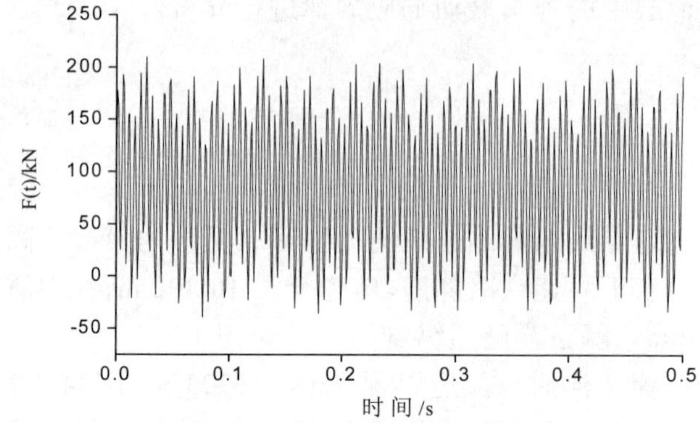

图 3 列车振动荷载时程

3.2 孔隙水压力模型

孔隙水压力增大和有效应力降低是导致土层液化的根本原因，在用有效应力法进行动力反应分析时，首先需要确定孔隙水压力增长模式。Martin 和 Finn 等[8]根据饱和砂土在不排水条件下的孔隙水压力增量与排水条件下的体积应变增量之间的关系，得到试样在没有体积变化情况下，周期剪切一周引起的孔隙水压增量：

$$\Delta\varepsilon_{vd}=C_1(\gamma-C_2\varepsilon_{vd})+\frac{C_3{\varepsilon^2}_{vd}}{\gamma+C_4\varepsilon_{vd}} \tag{4}$$

式中 ε_{vd}、$\Delta\varepsilon_{vd}$ ——体积应变和体应变增量；

γ ——循环剪应变；

$C_1\sim C_4$ ——由排水周期剪切试验确定的试验参数。

基于上述思想，Byrne 提出一个更为简明的孔压计算模型（Byrne 孔压体变模型）[9]：

$$\frac{\Delta\varepsilon_{vd}}{\gamma}=C_1\exp\left[-C_2\left(\frac{\varepsilon_{vd}}{\gamma}\right)\right] \tag{5}$$

一般情况下，参数 C_1、C_2 满足以下关系：

$$C_2=0.4/C_1 \tag{6}$$

$$C_1=7600D_r^{-2.5} \tag{7}$$

式中，D_r 为砂土相对密度。大量试验表明，相对密度与标贯击数 $N_{63.5}$ 存在以下关系：

$$D_r=15(N_{63.5})^{0.5} \tag{8}$$

所以

$$C_1=8.7(N_{63.5})^{-1.25} \tag{9}$$

Byrne 孔压体变模型可以反映地震持续时孔隙压力上升对土体性质的影响情况，因此可液化土层的动力特性采用此模型描述。

3.3 材料本构关系及计算参数

土层材料性质采用弹塑性本构关系，屈服条件满足 Mohr-Coulomb 屈服准则，相关参数见表 1；管片采用弹性曲梁单元模拟，管片接缝的影响通过折减结构的抗弯刚度来考虑(折减系数取 0.75)，材料参数见表 2。

表 1 土层材料参数

土 层	天然重(kN/m^3)	变形模量(MPa)	泊松比	黏聚力(kPa)	内摩擦角(°)	标贯击数(击)	渗透系数(m/d)
(1)填土	18.0	7.5	0.31	19.5	26.8	3	0.9
(2)2 淤泥	16.8	2.0	0.41	11.0	7.1	3	0.000 1
(3)1 黏性土	19.2	5.0	0.35	36.0	20.0	9	0.003 2
(3)2 淤泥质土	17.6	2.0	0.41	14.6	6.4	5	0.000 1
(3)3 粉细砂	19.5	20.0	0.28	0.0	30.0	15	5.0
(3)5 粗砾石砂	20.0	30.0	0.31	0.0	35.0	26	15.0
(5)2 岩石强风化	22.0	600	0.26	80.0	40.0	54	1.2
(5)3 岩石弱风化	26.0	2530	0.23	150	50.0	80	0.8

表 2 管片材料参数

弹性模量（GPa）	密度(kg/m^3)	泊松比
26.3	2 600	0.167

3.4 动力边界条件

为消除散射波在截断边界上的反射，较好地模拟远场地球介质的弹性恢复性能，模型两侧和底部分别采用自由场边界和 Lysmer 和 Kuhlemeryer 提出的黏滞边界，其原理可参见文献[10,11]。

3.5 计算范围

DIK42+855 断面隧道埋深约 12.5 m，该断面计算模型取水平方向为 X 轴，铅直向上方向为 Y 轴，计算范围取 $-50.0\ \text{m} \leqslant X \leqslant 50.0\ \text{m}$，$-70.0\ \text{m} \leqslant Y \leqslant 2.5\ \text{m}$，两条主隧道中心线间距为 21 m，有无内衬两种计算工况下模型的网格及梁单元的划分相同，计算模型的网格划分见图 4，左洞管片梁单元的单元节点编号和单元编号见图 5。为了模拟两列车交汇运行，计算时两个隧道同时施加竖向列车荷载。

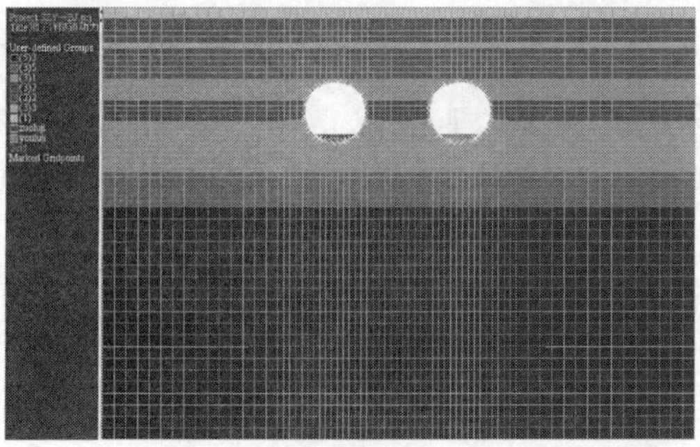

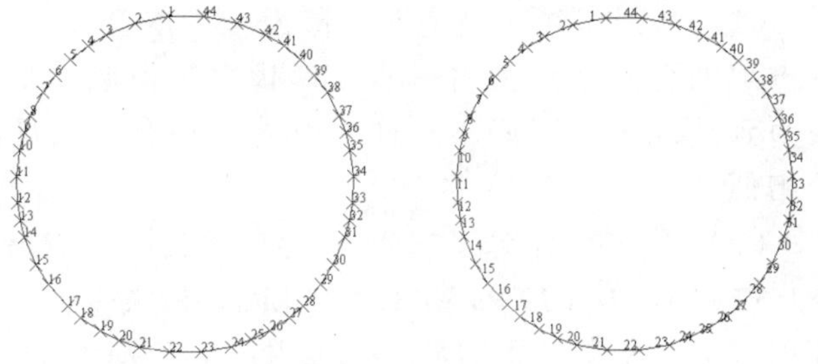

（a）管片节点编号　　（b）管片单元编号

图 4 DIK42+850 计算断面地质剖面示意图

图 5 DIK42+850 断面隧道衬砌结构网格划分

4 计算结果分析

4.1 孔隙水压力变化分析

动力荷载作用下孔隙水压力的发展变化是影响土体变形及强度变化的重要因素。图 6 给出了列车荷载作用 2.5 s 时，隧道拱底以下 1 m 处各土层的孔隙水压力变化时程曲线。

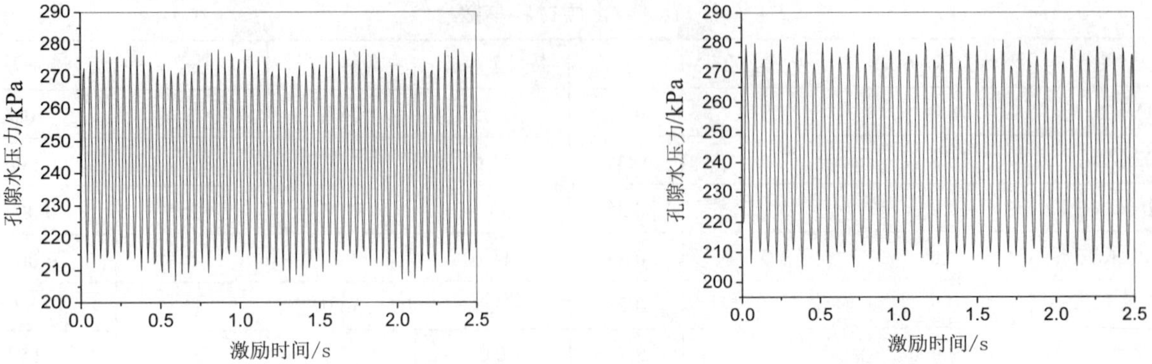

（a）无内衬 （b）有内衬

图 6 隧道拱底以下 1 m 处土层的孔隙水压力变化时程曲线

在评判土体抗液化能力或是否液化时，一般采用超孔隙水压与初始有效应力之比 *PPR*（Pore Water Pressure Ratio）作为判据，表 3 列出了列车经过隧道时不同埋深土层的 PPR 值，PPR 值越大说明发生液化的可能性越大，当 PPR=1 时，表示该土层将发生液化。

表 3 列车荷载作用下各土层的超孔隙水压力与初始有效应力之比 PPR

土层类别	与隧道拱底的相对距离	无内衬计算工况下 PPR	有内衬计算工况下 PPR	增加内衬后 PPR 值减小百分比
(3)1 黏性土	拱底以上 12 m	0.127 0	0.120 2	−5.35%
(3)2 淤泥质土	拱底以上 6 m	0.040 5	0.043 2	+6.66%
(3)1 黏性土	拱底处	0.702 2	0.543 3	−22.63%
(3)1 黏性土	拱底以下 2 m	0.358 0	0.284 4	−20.56%
(3)5 粗砾石砂	拱底以下 8 m	0.145 2	0.124 3	−14.39%

注：负号“−”代表减小，正号“+”代表增加。

从以上图表计算结果可以看出：

（1）当列车经过隧道时，隧道土层的孔隙水压力随着列车的反复加载、卸载而不断上升、下降；各土层的孔隙水压力时程曲线形状比较相似，基本上是由多个简谐波叠加而成，只是各土层孔隙水压力到达峰值的时间不一样；无内衬和有内衬两种计算工况下各土层的孔隙水压力时程曲线形状比较相似；

（2）无内衬计算工况下，隧道拱底以下 1 m、2 m 和 8 m 处各土层的最大孔隙水压力分别为 281.67 kPa、286.79 Pa 和 323.45 kPa，最大变幅分别为 101.96 kPa、74.90 kPa 和 50.96 kPa；有内衬计算工况下，相同位置的最大孔隙水压力分别为 282.43 kPa、289.08 Pa 和 325.46 kPa，最大变幅分别为 101.70 kPa、70.46 kPa 和 47.21 kPa，最大变幅比不加内衬计算工况分别减小 0.26 kPa、4.44 kPa 和 3.75 kPa，说明增加内衬能小幅度减小隧底各土层超孔隙水压力；

（3）无内衬计算工况下，位于隧道拱底、拱底以下 2 m 和 8 m 处的 PPR 值分别为 0.702 2、0.358 0 和 0.1452；有内衬计算工况下，相同位置的 PPR 值分别为 0.543 3、0.284 4 和 0.124 3，比无内衬计算工况下分别减小 0.158 9、0.073 6 和 0.020 9，减小百分比分别为−22.63%、−20.56%、−14.39%。说明增加内衬能够减小隧底软土层的 PPR 值，且离隧底振源越近，减小幅度越大；

（4）两种计算工况下，各土层的超孔隙水压力与初始有效应力的比值均小于 1，说明在列车单次交汇条件下土体尚达不到发生液化的条件。

4.2 衬砌结构位移变化分析

列车经过隧道时，由列车振动荷载引起的衬砌结构顶部和底部位移时程曲线如图 7 所示。从图中可以看出：

（1）列车振动荷载致使隧道结构产生振动，结构顶部和底部在列车荷载作用下做上、下受迫运动，结构有整体下沉的趋势，隧道拱底沉降约为拱顶沉降的 2 倍；无内衬和有内衬两种计算工况下，结构顶部和底部的位移时程曲线非常相似；

（2）在无内衬计算工况下，隧道拱顶的位移振动幅值约 0.22 mm，拱底的位移振动幅值约 0.36 mm，隧道的竖向位移收敛值最大约 0.29 mm；在有内衬计算工况下，隧道拱顶的位移振动幅值约 0.26 mm，拱底的位移振动幅值约 0.35 mm，隧道的竖向位移收敛值最大约 0.27 mm；计算结果显示增加内衬对衬砌结构的位移和变形几乎没有影响。

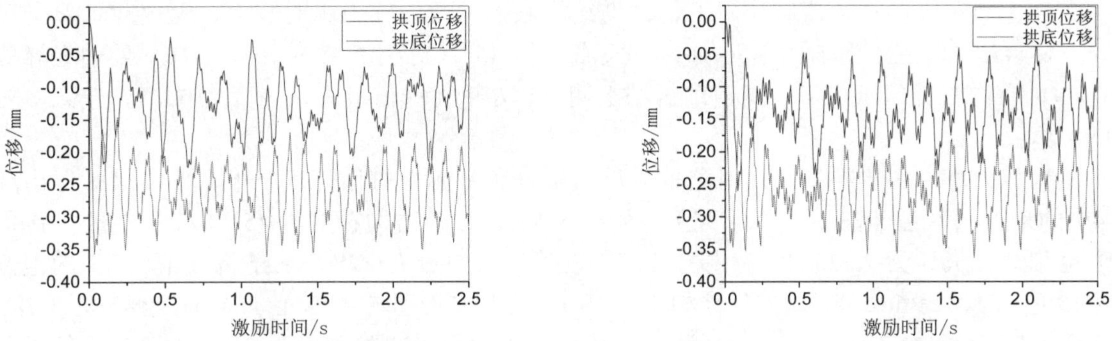

（a）无内衬　　（b）有内衬

图 7　列车荷载作用下衬砌结构的位移时程曲线

4.3 衬砌结构内力变化分析

列车振动荷载作用 2.5 s 时刻的结构内力分布如图 8 至图 10 所示。

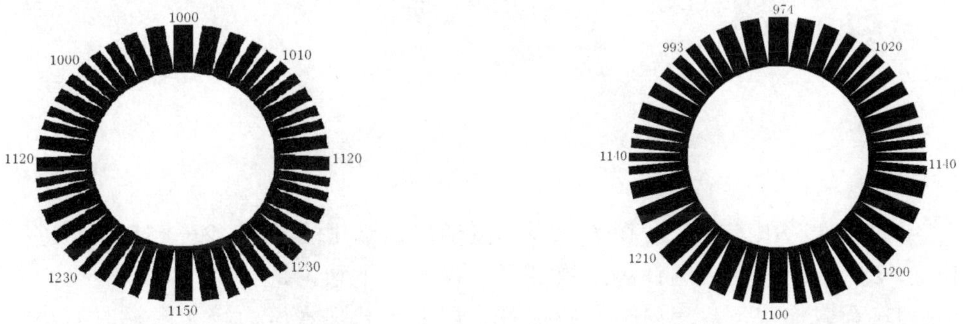

（a）无内衬　　（b）有内衬

图 8　列车荷载作用 2.5 s 时刻衬砌结构的轴力分布图（单位：kN）

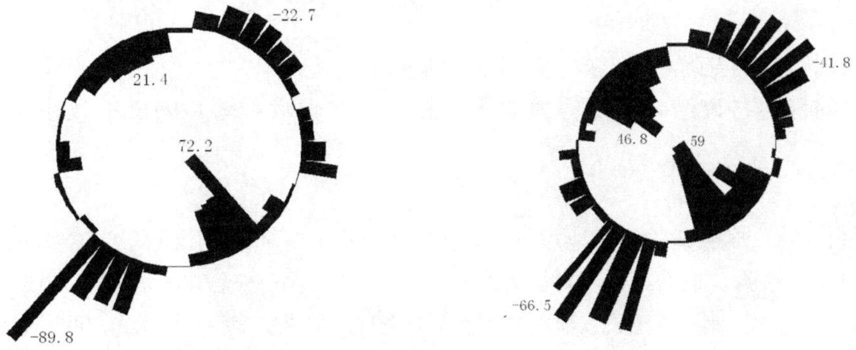

（a）无内衬　　（b）有内衬

图 9　列车荷载作用 2.5s 时刻衬砌结构的剪力分布图（单位：kN）

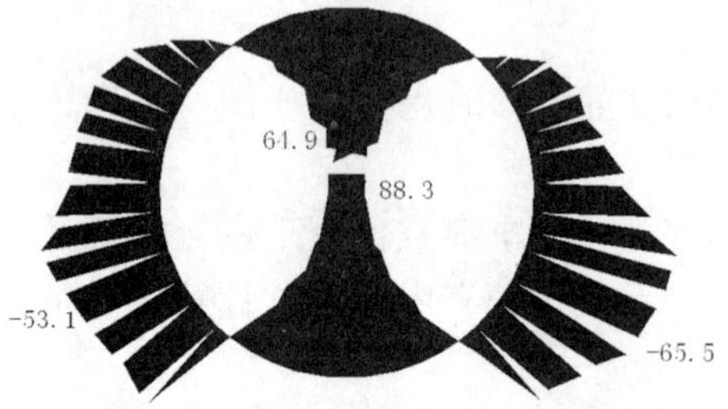

(a) 无内衬

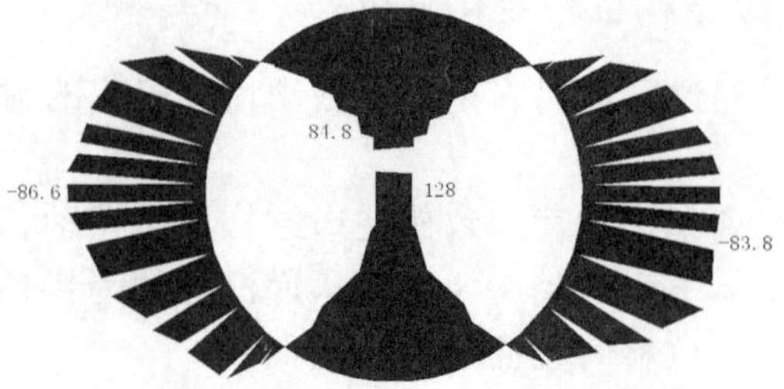

(b) 有内衬

图 10 列车荷载作用 2.5 s 时刻衬砌结构的弯矩分布图（单位：kN · m）

依据以上内力图可知：

（1）在高速列车竖向振动荷载作用下，衬砌结构底部承受的轴力相对较大，无内衬计算工况下，隧道结构左下侧 45°（对应于图 5 中单元 16）以及右下侧 45°（对应于图 5 中单元 28）处轴力峰值最大，为 1 230 kN；有内衬计算工况下，隧道结构左下侧 45°处轴力峰值最大，为 1 210 kN，较无内衬计算工况小 20 kN；

（2）结构剪力基本关于结构竖向对称轴呈反对称分布，无内衬计算工况下，剪力最大值出现在结构左下侧 46°的地方（对应于图 5 中单元 17），为 89.8 kN，另外结构右下侧 45°（对应于图 5 中单元 28）处的剪力也相对较大，为 72.2 kN；有内衬计算工况下，剪力最大值出现在结构左下侧 45°的地方（对应于图 5 中单元 16），为 66.5 kN，另外结构左上侧 37°（对应于图 5 中单元 7）、右上侧 40°（对应于图 5 中单元 39）、右下侧 45°（对应于图 5 中单元 27）处的剪力也相对较大，为 72.2 kN；计算结果显示，加内衬计算工况下隧道结构的左上方和右上方剪力增大了约 1 倍；

（3）结构弯矩基本关于结构竖向对称轴成对称分布，结构顶部、底部以及左、右侧等地方的弯矩较大，无内衬计算工况下，剪力最大值出现在结构拱底处（对应于图 5 中单元 22），为 88.3 kN · m；有内衬计算工况下，剪力最大值出现在相同位置，为 128 kN，相比无内衬工况增大了约 50%；

（4）无内衬和有内衬两种计算工况下，列车荷载作用下衬砌结构内力分布形式相近，总体上看内衬对衬砌结构所受内力影响不大。

5 结 论

通过运用二维弹塑性有限差分法对狮子洋盾构隧道出口端里程 DIK42＋855 断面进行分析，对比管片内无内衬和增加 25 cm 厚的内衬的计算结果，可以得出以下结论：

（1）在竖向列车荷载作用下，有内衬时隧底各土层的超孔隙水压力较无内衬时有小幅度的减小；增加内衬对减小隧底各软土层的 PPR 值有较好的效果，离隧底振源越近，PPR 值的减小幅度越大，效果越明显，说明增加内衬能够降低列车荷载作用时隧道结构的振动，提高隧底各软土层的抗液化能力，提高车辆的运行安全性。

（2）增加内衬对隧道衬砌结构位移与变形的影响非常小。

（3）增加内衬对隧道衬砌结构所受剪力的影响较大，对轴力和弯矩的影响较小。

参考文献（References）：

[1] 刘晶波，李彬，谷音. 地铁盾构隧道地震反应分析[J]. 清华大学学报(自然科学版)，2005， 45（6）：757-760.

[2] 王秀英，刘维宁，张弥．地下结构震害类型及机理研究[J]．中国安全科学学报，2003，13(11)：55-58.

[3] 何海健，刘维宁，王霆. 地下铁道抗震研究的现状与探讨[J]. 中国安全科学学报，2005，(08)：3-7.

[4] 铁道第四勘察设计院. 广深港客运专线广州至深圳段狮子洋隧道定测工程地质勘察报告[R]. 2006.

[5] 潘昌实，G.N.Pande. 黄土隧道列车动荷载载响应有限元初步数定分析研究[J]. 土木工程学报，1984，17(4):19-28.

[6] 李亮，张丙强，杨小礼. 高速列车振动荷载下大断面隧道结构动力响应分析[J]. 岩石力学与工程学报，2005，24(23)：4259-4265.

[7] 梁波，蔡英. 不平顺条件下高速铁路路基的动力分析[J]. 铁道学报，1999，21(2)：84-88.

[8] Martin G R.，Finn W D L，Seed H B. Fundamentals of liquefaction under cyclic loading[J]. Journal of Geotechnial Engineering, ASCE, 1975, 101(5): 423-438.

[9] BYRNE P A. cyclic shear-volume coupling and pore-pressure modelfor sand[C]// Proceedi –ngs of the 2nd International Conference on Recent Advances in Geotechnical Earthquake Engineering and Soil Dynamics. St. Louis，Missouri：[s.n.]，1991：47-55.

[10] Lysmer J, Kuhlemeyer R L. Finite dynamic model for infinite media [J]. Journal of the Engineering Mechanics, ASCE, 1969, 95 (4)：859-877.

[11] Lysmer J，Waas G. Shear waves in plane infinite structures[J]. Journal of Engineering Mechanics，1972，98(1)：85-105.

作者简介（Bio-data）：

陈松洁，男，1985 年 12 月生，汉族，江苏省泗阳县人。2002 年 9 月至 2006 年 6 月就读于江南大学，2007 年 9 月考入中南大学，现为隧道工程系硕士研究生，主要从事地下结构动力方面的研究。

2007 年以来作为主要参加人员完成了三个铁道部科研课题："武广客运专线浏阳河隧道邻近结构物地层及结构物变形控制技术研究"、"武广客运专线线下工程变形监测方案及典型区段试验研究"和"狮子洋隧道地震及列车振动响应分析"。2008 年 8 月—2009 年 3 月作为项目负责人主持了深圳地铁 2 号线 2201 标段的监测工作。

Songjie CHEN, male, Han nationality, was born in December 1985 in Siyang County Jiangsu Province. Learning at Southern Yangtze University from September 2002 to June 2006, admitted to the Central South University in September 2007, now is a graduate majoring in tunnel engineering, the primary research is on Underground Structural Dynamics.

As a major researcher, He has participated in three research projects which were conducted by Chinese Ministry of Railways since 2007. These projects are listed here:

-Technology of deformation control in structure formations & structures adjacent to Liuyang River tunnel in Wuhan-Guangzhou Line.

-Deformation monitoring program work of underground engineering and experimental study of typical sections in Wuhan-Guangzhou Line.

-Response analysis of seismic and train vibration in Shiziyang Tunnel.

As a project leader, I presided the monitoring work of Section 2,Shenzhen Metro Line 2 from August 2008 to March 2009.

E-mail:2maosongzi@163.com

彭立敏，男，1956 生，湖南省澧县人。1986 年 7 月获桥梁与隧道工程硕士学位，2000 年 5 月获桥梁与隧道工程博士学位，2001 年 6 月被中南大学聘为博士生导师。1986 年 8 月至 1988 年 6 月任助教；1988 年 7 月至 1994 年 5 月任讲师；1994 年 6 月至 2000 年 5 月被聘为副教授；2000 年 6 月晋升为教授。1992—1994 任土建学院隧道教研室副主任；1994—2004：任土建学院隧道工程系(教研室)主任；现任中南大学土木建筑学院副院长。

1990 年以来主持或作为主要参加人员完成省部级科研课题 10 多项及 30 多项横向课题，获鉴定成果 6 项，获省部级科研三等奖奖励 4 项。陆续在全国各级学术期刊上发表科研论文 60 余篇，其中有 20 余篇被 SCI、EI、ISTP 收录，有 3 篇分获湖南省优秀学术论文奖励。 主编专业教材两本和出版学术专著一部（《交通隧道工程》;《地下铁道》;《公路连拱隧道技术》）。

E-mail:plmcsu@yahoo.com.cn

丁祖德，男，汉族，1979 年 12 月生，湖南省汉寿县人，现为中南大学土木建筑学院博士研究生。

主要学习与工作经历如下：1999—2003 年长沙理工大学河海工程学院本科阶段学习，土木工程专业；2003—2005 年中交四航局工作，任技术主管；2005—2008 年长沙理工大学土木与建筑学院硕士阶段学习，岩土工程专业；2008 至今，中南大学土木建筑学院博士阶段学习桥梁与隧道工程专业。

E-mail:dzdvsdt@163.com

南京长江隧道管片接头三维有限元分析

郭 瑞 何 川 苏宗贤 彭志忠

西南交通大学 地下工程系，四川 成都 610031

【摘 要】 盾构隧道管片接头作为管片衬砌环的特殊构造部分，其力学特性的明确至关重要。本文采用三维有限元法对南京长江盾构隧道管片环向接头的受力特征进行了数值模拟计算，分析研究了不同荷载作用下管片接头的变形、转角以及接头端面混凝土和连接螺栓的受力情况，获得了接头的抗弯刚度和受力特征，并将计算结果与接头荷载试验测试结果进行了对比。研究结果为南京长江隧道整体结构力学分析提供了重要基础资料，并可为同类大型越江海盾构隧道工程管片接头的设计提供参考。

【关键词】 盾构隧道；管片接头；有限元分析；荷载试验；抗弯刚度

THREE DIMENSIONAL FINITE ELEMENT ANALYSIS ON SEGMENT JOINT OF NANJING YANGTZE RIVER SHIELD TUNNEL

Rui GUO，Chuan HE，Zongxian SU，Zhizhong PENG

Department of Underground Engineering, Southwest Jiaotong University, Chengdu 610031, Sichuan, China

Abstract: It is very important to analyze the mechanical characteristics of segment joint which as special part of fabricated segment lining structure of shield tunnel. The numerical simulation of circumferential segment joints of Nanjing Yangtze River shield tunnel was carried out with 3D FEM (finite element method). The deformation, rotational angle of a segment joint and mechanical behavior of face-joint and connecting bolt under different working conditions were investigated. The bending stiffness and mechanical characteristics of segment joint were obtained. The results can offer important basic data for the mechanical Analysis of the whole structure of Nanjing Yangtze River shield tunnel, and can provide references for segment joint design of similar super-large river-crossing shield tunnel.

Key words: shield tunnel; segment joint; finite element method analysis; load test; bending stiffness

1 引 言

盾构隧道装配式衬砌结构是由管片体通过管片间接头相互连接而成，接头既影响着管片内力传递分布，又要承担自身力学和防水作用。大量实践表明，接头的力学形态将对衬砌结构的受力产生重要影响[1]，对接头的分析研究极为关键。目前，研究管片接头的方法主要有理论解析算法、有限元数值模拟法和试验方法三种。对于试验方法，因其费时且不经济，故不可能在每条隧道设计之前都进行试验，即使进行试验，也满足不了前期的设计需要；理论解析算法以某些假设为前提，得到的接头参数往往比较粗糙，而且对接缝端面、螺栓、手孔等局部情况不能精确模拟；而随着有限元理论的成熟，数值解可以为工程提供较为精确的数据，提高设计质量和效率，被广泛应用[2]。

盾构隧道管片接头力学特性指标分析是一个较为复杂的三维空间问题，既受宏观整体上的受力特征（如轴力和弯矩作用下的结构弯曲）影响，还受局部受力特征（如接头端面、连接螺栓、螺栓孔、手孔等）

基金项目：863 计划（2006AA11Z116）；国家自然科学基金（50778154）

影响。在较小空间范围内分析由不同材料（如管片混凝土、连接螺栓、橡胶衬垫）组装而成结构体的力学特性将不可避免地涉及到行为非线性、面－面接触、材料非线性等诸多问题，如何合理正确模拟各类材料及结构特性是管片接头有限元计算的重点和难点[1, 3]，本文采用三维有限元法对南京长江盾构隧道管片接头进行了数值计算，分析了其抗弯刚度及受力特征，并与接头加载试验结果进行了比较。

2 有限元模型的建立

2.1 研究对象

本文所研究的南京长江隧道是我国在建的穿越长江的水下超大断面公路隧道，隧道顶部与长江最高水位差约 60m，将是目前国内水压力最大和直径最大的城市隧道。

盾构隧道主体结构外径 ϕ14.5 m，内径 ϕ13.3 m，管片厚度 600 mm，幅宽 2.0 m，衬砌环分成 10 块，7B(标准块 38.57°)+2L(邻接块 38.57°)+F(封顶块 12.86°)，每环环向布置 30 颗螺栓，即每纵缝 3 颗，纵向（环缝）布置 42 颗螺栓。螺栓均采用斜螺栓连接方式，环向螺栓采用 M36 型 6.8 级，纵向采用 M30 型 8.8 级。管片接头主要采用有传力面的接缝形式，即中间不加衬垫，混凝土直接接触，内外使用防水橡胶作止水条，南京长江隧道管片纵缝（环向接头）及连接螺栓构造见图 1 所示。

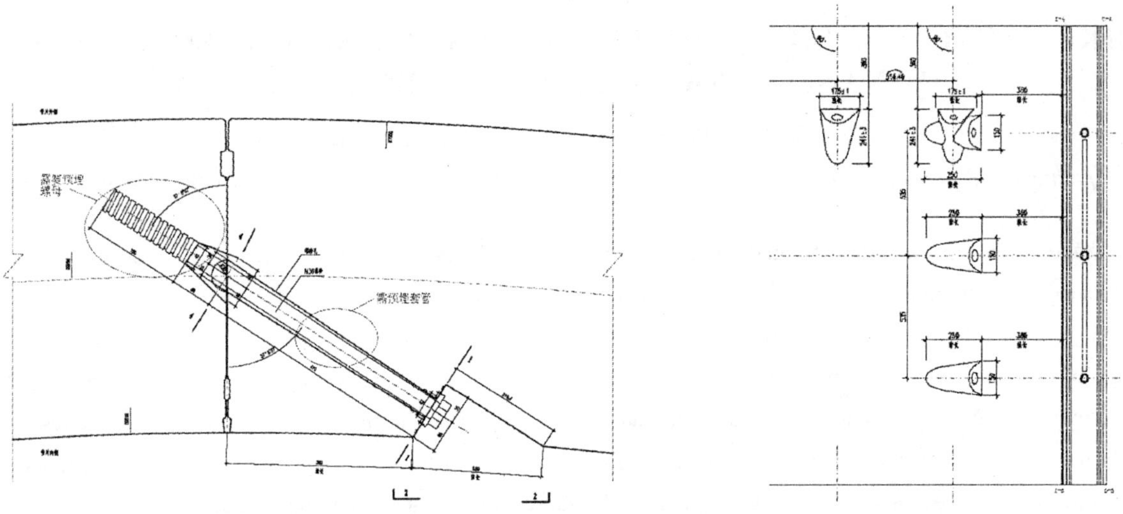

(a) 纵缝及环向螺栓　　(b) 环向螺栓手孔分布

图 1　纵缝及环向螺栓构造图

2.2 单元选择及材料特性

模型中涉及的单元类型及材料参数如下：

（1）实体单元

模型中选用 8 节点空间六面体单元模拟管片体，采用一定形函数来克服传统的形函数在纯弯时产生的虚假剪切。将混凝土和钢筋材料作为连续整体式考虑，混凝土本构关系计算参数按《公路隧道设计规范》(JTG D70－2004) 和《混凝土设计规范》(GB50010－2002) 取值。

（2）梁单元

选用 2 节点空间梁单元模拟连接螺栓，该单元可模拟任意形状截面，可施加初应力以模拟螺栓的预紧力，螺栓材料采用双线性等向强化模型，该模型能够模拟螺栓屈服后应力尚能增长的特性。

（3）衬垫单元

防水橡胶和软木衬垫采用 8 节点衬垫单元模拟，橡胶材料的力学性能与加载历史有关，在本模型中，假设橡胶的卸载曲线为线性，加载沿原卸载的路径发展，材料的曲线方程[1], [4]为：σ=378.39$\varepsilon^{3.0892}$。从后面的计算可发现，止水条橡胶对结构刚度的影响很小。

（4）接触单元

接头端面混凝土直接接触采用面-面接触单元模拟，用单元高斯点判断接触状态，由于螺栓与螺栓孔壁间隙约 3 mm，当变形较小时不发生接触，在此不模拟螺栓与螺栓孔壁的接触问题，在螺栓两头与混凝土管片连接的部位以共用节点方式进行模拟，中间段不与混凝土单元发生联系。

2.3 模型与加载

全幅宽模型见图 2(a)，共有单元 27 473 个，节点 26 013 个；1/3 幅宽模型见图 2(b)，共有单元 9 454 个，节点 10 835 个。虽然螺栓间距并非 1/3 幅宽，但经计算发现采用 1/3 幅宽模型与全幅宽模型的结果相差不到 1%，为了节省计算时间，采用 1/3 幅宽模型计算，单块管片长度取 2.2 m，管片厚度及接头端面尺寸均与实际相同，接缝构造详图见图 3 所示，接缝附近的单元网格进行了加密。

管片接头边界条件及加载见图 4 所示。边界条件为：模型一端采用固定铰支座，另一端采用可动铰支座，管片体两侧面布置链杆约束。图中 N 为施加的轴向荷载，方向穿过中部接头面的中心，N 值即为管片接头处的轴力，F_y 为上部压力荷载，用来实现管片接头处的弯矩。

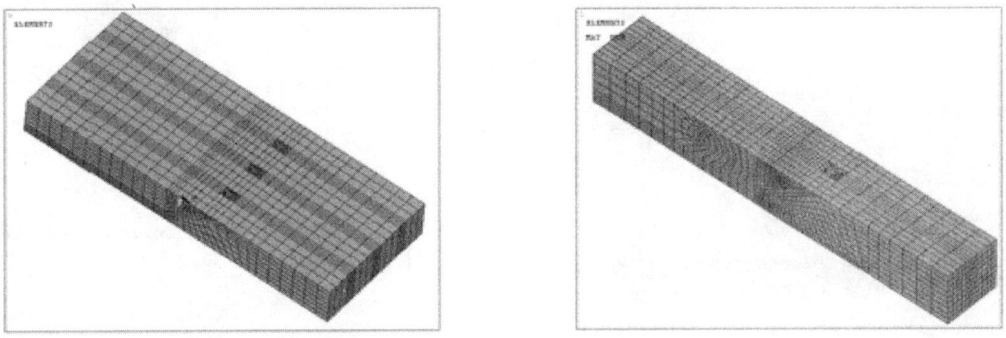

(a) 全幅宽　　(b) 1/3 幅宽

图 2　管片接头模型

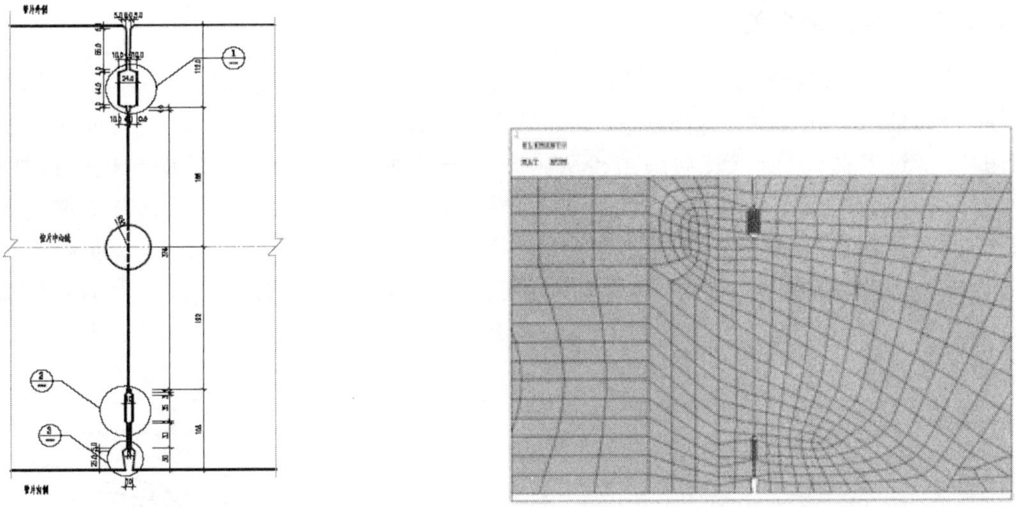

(a) 实际接缝构造　　(b) 模型中的接缝

图 3　管片接头构造图

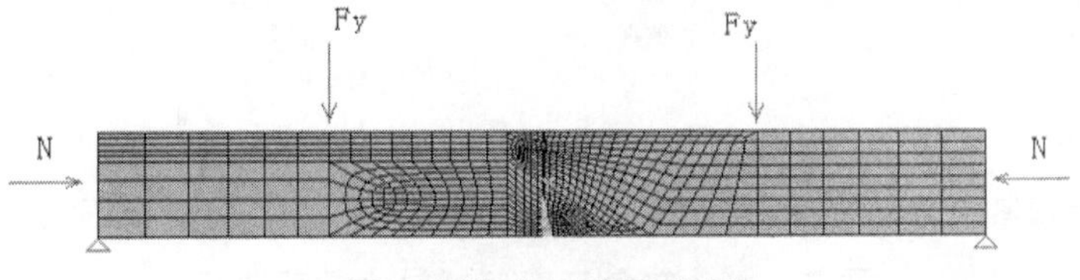

图 4　接头加载示意图

3　计算结果及分析

根据南京长江隧道管片的受力范围，即接头轴力绝大部分处于 3 500～8 000 kN 范围内，弯矩处于 −800 kN · m～+1000 kN · m 范围内，选取了轴力为 3 000 kN，4 000 kN，5 000 kN，6 000 kN，7 000 kN 和 8 000 kN 六组轴力荷载工况进行计算，得到了如下结果。

3.1　接头张开量与弯矩、轴力关系

管片接头张开情况见图 5 所示，各轴力下接头的最大张开量与弯矩关系曲线见图 6，图中弯矩考虑了由于管片挠度而产生的附加弯矩。可以看出，轴力一定时，在弯矩较小时，接缝张开量很小，且该现象随着轴力的增大持续更久，但随着弯矩增大到一定程度后，接缝张开量随着弯矩的增大迅速增大；而在弯矩一定时，接缝张开量随轴力的增大而减小。在同等荷载情况下，负弯时的接缝张开量略小于正弯时张开量。

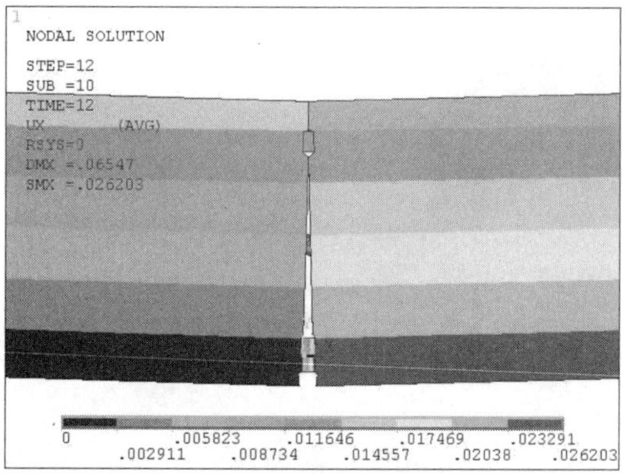

图 5　数值模拟张开情况示意图

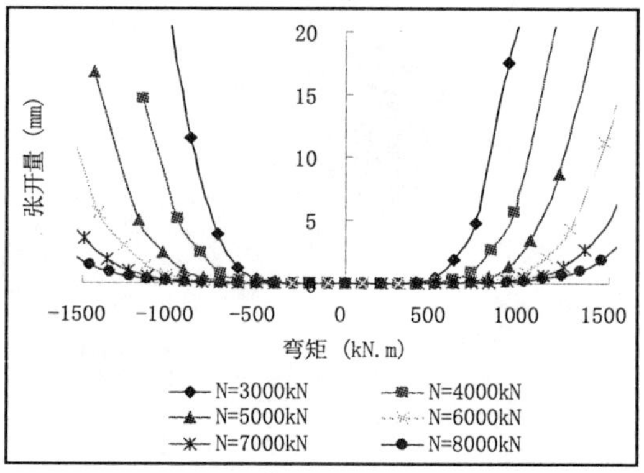

图 6　接头张开量与弯矩、轴力关系曲线

3.2　接头转角与弯矩、轴力关系

各轴力下接头的转角与弯矩关系曲线见图 7 所示，(a)为没有施加螺栓预紧力的情况，(b)为施加 100 MPa 预应力的情况，由于接头受力后接头面的形状并非像假设中的两个平面，而是从受压区平面到脱离区平面的一个过度曲面，所以转角是由接头张开量与其对应管片厚度位置曲线进行线性拟合得出的。

可以看出，在轴力一定时，弯矩较小时，接头转角随弯矩近似呈线性增长，弯矩增大到一定程度后呈非线性增长，而且轴力水平越大，曲线线性段保持越长，抗弯刚度也越大；正、负弯矩作用下曲线形状类似，正负抗弯刚度差别不大，说明斜螺栓对接头正负弯曲特性影响较小，可近似看作直螺栓作用。对比图 7(a)和图(b)可看出，有螺栓预紧力的接头在初始段抗弯刚度要大，后面段的形态大致相同，有预紧力的抗弯刚度要稍大一些。

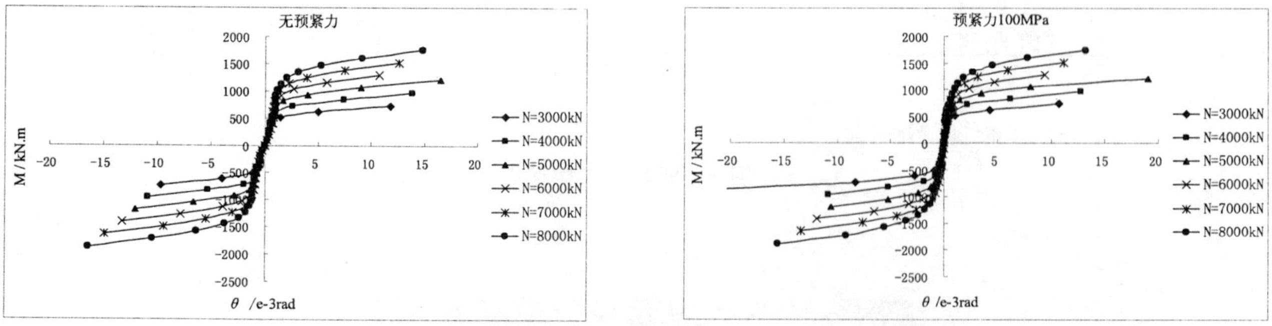

(a) 无预紧力时　　(b) 预紧力为 100 MPa 时

图 7　接头转角与弯矩、轴力关系曲线

3.3 接头抗弯刚度

根据南京长江隧道受力的大致状况和接缝张开要求（防水要求<2 mm 控制）进行估计，给出接头的计算刚度参考值见表 1，从表中可以看出，在接头可能性较大的弯矩范围内，其抗弯刚度的可能取值范围很大，这将大大地影响着整体结构的计算内力，在管片的内力计算中有必要认真考虑接头抗弯刚度的非线性。

表 1　接头计算刚度参考值

轴力 N(kN)	可能的弯矩 M 范围(kN·m)	正抗弯刚度 $K_{\theta+}$(kN·m/rad)	负抗弯刚度 $K_{\theta-}$(kN·m/rad)
3 000	300~600	120~900	150~900
4 000	400~700	310~1 000	350~1 000
5 000	450~800	550~1 000	630~1 100
6 000	550~900	650~1 100	740~1 100
7 000	600~1 000	680~1 200	760~1 200
8 000	700~1 100	750~1 200	830~1 200

3.4 混凝土与螺栓应力

接头在抗弯过程中端面混凝土最大压应力和螺栓最大拉应力情况见图 8 和图 9 所示，螺栓采用 6.8 级 M36 高强螺栓，其屈服强度为 480 MPa，混凝土采用 C60 高性能混凝土，其抗压强度设计值为 27.5 MPa、标准值为 38.5 MPa。

可以看出，在轴力一定时，当弯矩较小时，端面混凝土最大压应力和螺栓最大拉应力均小于设计值，当弯矩达到与图 6 所示的接缝张开量为 2 mm 所对应的弯矩时，端面混凝土最大压应力均已超过 C60 混凝土的抗压强度设计值，连接螺栓最大拉应力均未超过 6.8 级螺栓的屈服强度。端面混凝土最大压应力总是先于螺栓达到设计值，即有可能在螺栓屈服前混凝土被压坏，轴力越大越明显，这种情况类似于在钢筋混凝土截面设计原理中的超筋梁脆性破坏。M36 的螺栓存在较大的富余承载能力，接头的破坏与否主要取决于混凝土的抗压性能和螺栓预埋套筒的抗拔能力，因此可考虑使用 M30 螺栓以节约钢材。

同时，在计算中发现连接螺栓最大拉应力值均出现在有预埋套筒端预埋套筒口位置，实际工程中此位置螺栓孔设置成喇叭型和预埋套筒采用非刚性的铁或钢制套筒而是高分子材料制成的套筒是合理的。

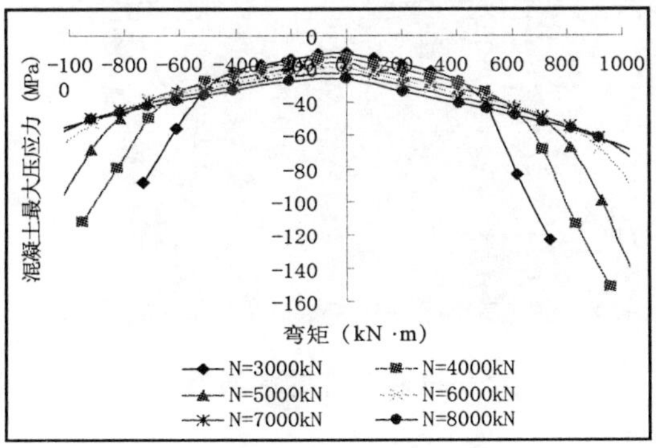

图 8　端面混凝土最大压应力

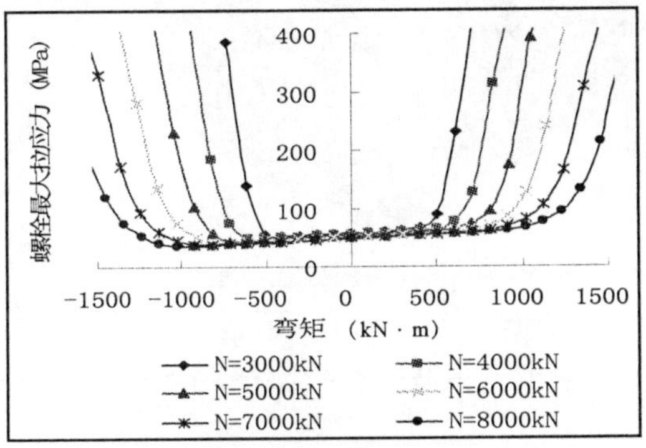

图 9　螺栓最大拉应力

4 与试验结果比较

4.1 抗弯刚度比较

将数值模拟计算结果与参考文献 5 中南京长江隧道管片接头抗弯加载试验结果比较，图 10 为管片接头加载示意图，图 11 为试验得到的转角与弯矩、轴力关系曲线，与数值计算结果图 7 比较可得，两曲线图的形状相同，量级一致，数值计算的曲线斜率略大于试验结果，即数值计算的抗弯刚度大于试验结果的抗弯刚度，这是由于接缝附近和螺栓与混凝土结合点附近单元划分不够细致，结构模型整体偏硬；而现场试验的结果可能偏小，主要由于测量误差、位移测针偏转后接触点偏位和螺栓未预紧等因素造成，真实值应在两者之间。

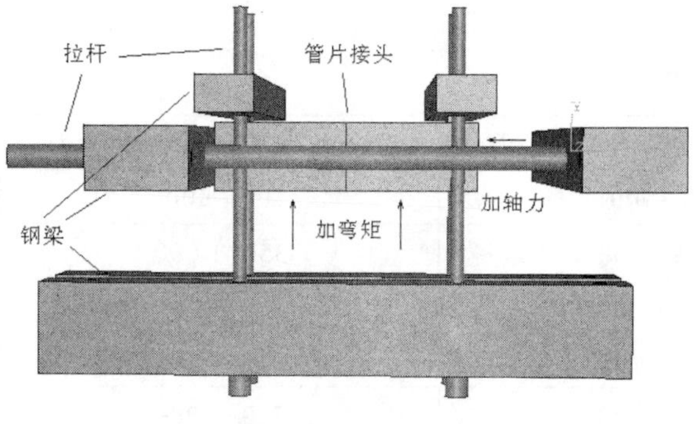

图 10 管片接头抗弯加载示意图

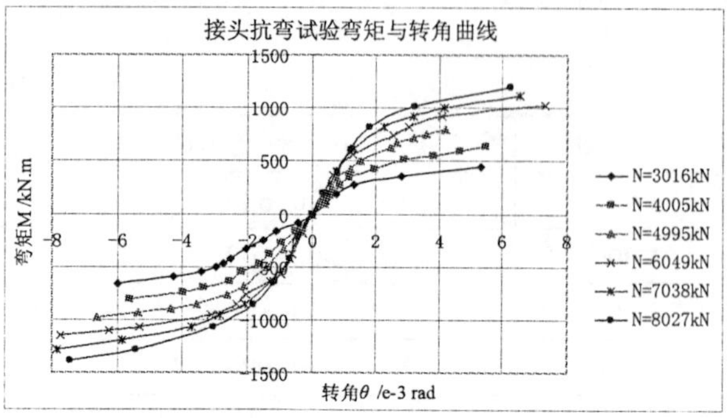

图 11 接头抗弯试验弯矩与转角关系曲线

4.2 破坏特征比较

对于轴力 N=3 000 kN 荷载工况，当弯矩 M=1075.14 kN · m 时，经数值模拟计算接缝张开 24.6 mm，图 12 为接头端面第一主应力图，其拉应力已远大于混凝土的抗拉应力。图 13 为接头破坏试验（轴力 N=3 500 kN，弯矩 M=1432 kN · m）时的接头端面破坏情况，可以看出，数值模拟接头受拉部位与试验拔坏的部位一致（注意管片试件在试验时倒置，外弧面朝下内弧面朝上，与计算模型相反）。

由于螺栓预埋套筒埋设深度合理、端面布设构造钢筋以及混凝土实际抗压强度远大于设计值（因为其设计值是以概率统计理论为基础给出的，往往比实际承载力小），接头破坏时先是钢筋屈服，然后受压区混凝土受压破坏、最后螺栓被拔出和受压区混凝土彻底压溃几乎同时出现，结构设计是合理的延性破坏。

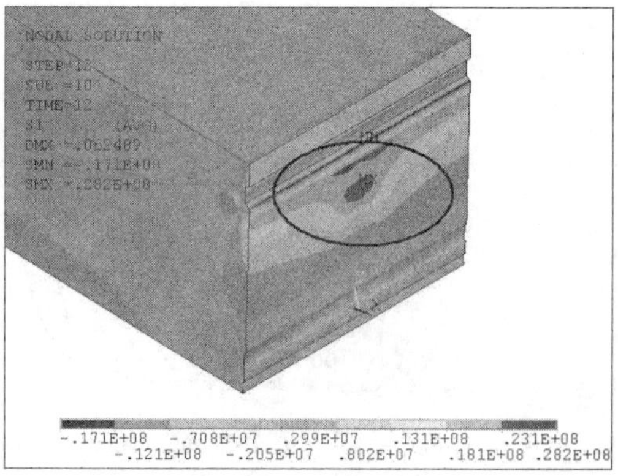

图 12 混凝土第一主应力（单位：Pa）

图 13 接头试验破坏的端面情况

5 结 论

通过以上分析，可得出以下结论：

（1）通过数值计算，为南京长江隧道整体结构计算提供了重要参数—接头抗弯刚度 K_θ（表 1），接头抗弯刚度呈明显非线性，具体数值与诸多因素有关，最为密切的是承受的弯矩和轴力，在隧道整环结构计算中需将各接头的抗弯刚度应反复调整，使其取值与接头处所受的弯矩、轴力协调一致。

（2）从计算结果和破坏情况看，M36 的螺栓存在较大的富余承载能力，接头的破坏与否主要取决于混凝土的抗压性能和螺栓预埋套筒的抗拔能力，因此可考虑使用 M30 螺栓以节约钢材。

（3）混凝土的实际抗压强度往往明显大于其设计值或标准值，管片接头破坏是延性破坏，受压区混凝土压坏的同时螺栓也进入了屈服状态。

（4）通过对数值模拟结果与试验结果进行比较，数值模拟的接头抗弯刚度略大于试验结果，接头的破坏特征一致，充分说明了数值模拟方法的可靠性和合理性。

参考文献（References）：

[1] 何川，曾东洋. 盾构隧道结构设计及施工对环境的影响[M]. 成都：西南交通大学出版社，2007.

[2] 苏宗贤. 超大断面水下盾构隧道原型结构试验及结构分析模型研究[博士学位论文][D]. 成都：西南交通大学，2008.

[3] 张建刚. 大断面水下盾构隧道的相似模型试验及结构内力分析[博士学位论文][D]. 成都：西南交通大学，2008.

[4] 曾东洋，何川. 地铁盾构隧道管片接头抗弯刚度的数值计算[J]. 西南交通大学学报，2004，39(6)：744-74.

[5] 彭志忠. 南京长江隧道管片接缝力学行为研究[硕士学位论文][D]. 成都：西南交通大学，2008.8.

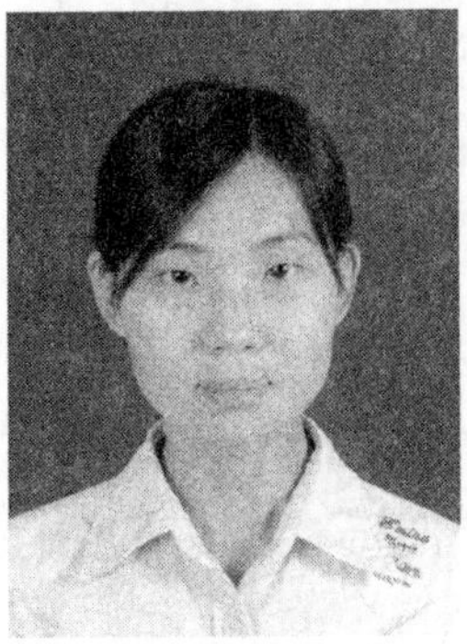

作者简介（Bio-data）：

郭瑞，女，1980 年 9 月生，在职博士研究生，现任西南交通大学土木工程学院讲师，主要从事隧道与地下工程方向研究。

Rui GUO (1980—) lecturer, a candidate for doctor's degree in the major of Bridge and Tunnel Engineering in Southwest Jiaotong University. She obtained a Master's degree in Municipal Engineering, and then became a teacher of Hydraulics Department in her University. She specializes in the highway and subway tunnel engineering.

E-mail:ruiguo@swjtu.cn

城市地铁盾构隧道管片设计与分析

梅江兵
中铁第四勘察设计院集团有限公司，湖北　武汉　430063

【摘　要】　盾构管片设计合理与否对盾构施工便利性、隧道使用寿命、工程造价与运营安全等至关重要。盾构管片的设计包括分块、厚度、楔形量、接缝、连接、配筋等，本文结合郑州轨道交通 1 号线管片设计的心得与体会，与大家一起探讨，欢迎批评指正。
【关键词】　管片；厚度；分块；接缝

DESIGN AND ANALYSIS OF SEGEMENT IN URBAN SHIELD TUNNEL

Jiangbing MEI
China Railway Siyuan Survey and Design Group Co., LTD, Wuhan 430063, Hubei, China

Abstract: The rationality of Segment design greatly relates to the convenience of shield construction, the life of tunnel, engineering cost and operational safety. Segment design includes block design, thickness, wedge, joints, connection, and reinforcement and so on. This paper is based on segment design experience of Zhengzhou urban rail transit line 1.
Key words: segment; thickness; wedge; joints

1　引　言

近年来我国城市轨道交通迅猛发展，盾构是城市轨道交通地下区间的主要工法，对工程进度、造价等影响大，本文结合郑州轨道交通 1 号线盾构隧道进行管片设计与分析。

2　工程概况

郑州地铁 1 号线呈东西走向,一期工程线路全长约 25.2 km，18 个区间采用盾构法施工。

郑州轨道交通 1 号线大致以京广铁路为界，以西处于黄土塬间冲洪积平原，局部为黄土沟谷型人工湖。沿线地形变化较大，最大标高 123.68 m，最低标高 102.74 m，最大高差 20.94 m；以东处于黄河冲洪积平原，沿线地形局部变化较大，最大标高 101.92 m，最低标高 82.98 m，最大高差 18.94 m，局部为沟谷和河流分布。地下水位西端埋深大，约地下 10～18 m；东端埋深浅，约地下 2 m。

3　管片厚度设计

目前国内地铁管片主要有 350 mm 与 300 mm 两种厚度，确定管片厚度要根据全线的工程地质情况、隧道覆土厚度，对管片配筋与裂缝进行试算与验算。根据 1 号线隧道覆土厚度、工程地质与水文地质条件，计算管片配筋，选择合适的管片厚度。取郑州轨道交通 1 号线东部、中部、及西部三个代表性区段不同深度的典型断面进行计算。如果全线采用两种厚度的盾构管片，虽然可以解决部分内力大的区段配筋量大的矛盾，但引起很多新的问题，如盾构机施工的局限性，只能在同管片厚度区段施工，否则进行较大的改造，工程造价高，管片制造模具需要量增大，工程投资增加等。所以有条件时应尽量设计为相同厚度的管片，模具应尽量采用一种，这样便于施工与管理。

郑州火车站站以西代表性区段 12 m 覆土区段，覆土均按饱和容重计算,地下水位地下 10~18 m，年变动 1～2 m。

3.1 隧道上覆土土层参数

表 1 隧道上覆土层参数表

上覆土层名称	层厚(m)	土的黏聚力 c(kPa)	土的内摩擦角 φ (°)	土的容重 γ (kN/m^3)
1 杂填土	0.8	12	16	19．9
2 粉土	2.5	12	16	19.9
3 粉土	1.9	14	19	19.9
4 粉土	1	8.6	11	19．7
5 粉土	1	16.5	17	21.1
6 粉土	1.6	15.2	14	20.1
7 细砂	3.1	0	18	20

3.2 隧道埋深段土层参数

表 2 隧道埋深段土层参数表

土层类别	土层厚度(m)	计算容重(kN/m^3)	侧压力系数 K_0	水平抗力系数(MPa/m)	垂直抗力系数(MPa/m)
细砂 7	1.3	20	0.5	28	32
粉土 8	1.4	20	0.56	22	23
细砂 8-1	1.8	20	0.49	25	28
粉土 8	1	20	0.56	22	23
粉质黏土 9	3	20	0.58	34	37

3.3 采用均质圆环模型计算管片内力结果

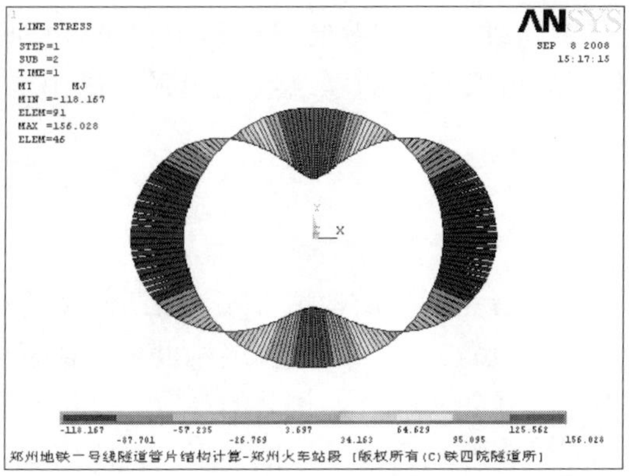

图 1 衬砌结构计算弯矩图（单位：kN · m）

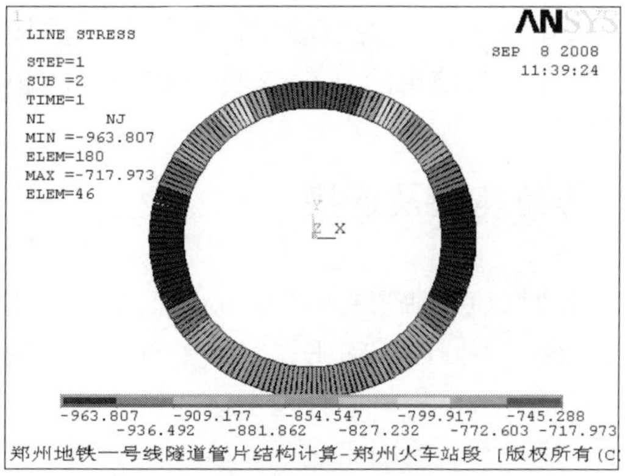

图 2 衬砌结构计算轴力图（单位：kN）

1 号线东段、西段计算结果见下表，计算过程由于篇幅限制，不做赘述。

3.4 配筋表

表 3 正常使用极限状态配筋表(管片按照 1.2m 宽度进行配筋计算，弯矩相应乘了 1.2)

项　目	b	h	c	正常使用状态		排数	第一排			主筋	裂缝宽度	计算配筋率
				Mk	Nk		n1	d1	间距			
	mm	mm	mm	kN · m	kN			mm	d	mm_2	mm	%
火车站以西 12 m 覆土管片内侧（泰沙基）	1 200	300	30	187.2	717.9	1	8	22	6.26	3041	0.191	0.97
火车站以西 18 m 覆土管片内侧（泰沙基）	1 200	300	30	196.8	984.7	1	8	22	6.26	3041	0.169	0.97
东区 15 m 覆土内侧	1 200	300	30	246.2	832.9	1	10	25	3.96	4909	0.160	1.57

根据计算结果，管片含钢量 160 kg/m^3 左右，裂缝宽度均小于 0.2 mm，管片厚度 300 mm 能满足工程要求。

4 管片的环宽与分块设计

衬砌环的分块及宽度主要由管片的制作、防水、运输、拼装、隧道总体线形、地质条件、结构受力性能、盾构掘进机选型等因素确定。衬砌环环宽越大，即管片宽度越宽，隧道结构的纵向刚度越大，抗变形能力越强；衬砌环接缝越少，因而漏水环节、螺栓数量越少；施工速度越快，费用越省；但盾构机千斤顶的行程要大，施工难度亦有一定提高；在小半径曲线上，管片的设计拟合误差大。本工程盾构隧道最小曲线半径为 300 m，拟合误差很小。与环宽 1.2 m 的管片相比，采用环宽 1.5 m 的管片有以下优点：一方面，减少了 20% 的环向接缝数量，降低了接缝漏水的几率，提高隧道防水质量；另一方面，降低了接缝止水材料和连接螺栓的使用量；此外还可减少 20% 的拼装时间。综合考虑管片的制作、运输、拼装、曲线施工及综合经济效益等因素，采用了 1.5 m 的环宽。

地铁隧道管片分块数为六块（3A+B+C+K）。

5 管片楔形量设计

楔形量主要与隧道曲线半径及管片环宽相关，计算时采用隧道曲线最小半径，楔形量Δ=L(管片宽度)*D（管片外径）/R（曲线半径）=1.5*6.0/300=0.03，管片楔形量取值时考虑施工误差等，须有一定的富余量，楔形量取 45 mm（双面楔形）。1 号线还设有联络线，但其最小曲线半径为 160 m，长度 300 m，覆土厚度约 20 m，主要地层为粉土粉砂层，联络线上有古代商城遗址，不允许采用明挖施工，采用盾构法施工要求楔形量大，需单独设计模具，且盾构铰接装置要做特殊处理与改装，这样工程投资增加约三百万元，而且今后使用的几率较低，这样很不经济，经比选该区段及类似的联络线区段采用矿山法施工。

6 环、纵缝构造及连接

管片接缝构造包括密封垫槽、嵌缝槽及凹凸榫的设计，其中前者为通用的构造方式，而凹凸榫的设置与否在不同时期、不同区域的工程实践中有着不同的理解。凹凸榫的设置有助于提高接缝刚度、控制不均匀沉降、改善接缝防水性能，也有利于管片拼装就位，但与此同时增加了管片制作、拼装的难度，是拼装和后期沉降过程中管片开裂的因素之一，客观上又削弱了管片防水性能。1 号线管片设计推荐不设置凹凸榫。

管片环面外侧设有弹性密封垫槽，内侧设嵌缝槽。管片之间及衬砌环间的连接方式，从力学特性来看，可分为柔性连接及刚性连接。实践证明，刚性连接不仅拼装麻烦、造价高，而且会在衬砌环中产生较大的次应力，带来不良后果。因此，本管片设计采用柔性连接。

按螺栓连接形状又可分为弯螺栓连接、直螺栓连接、斜螺栓连接和榫槽加销轴等方式。弯螺栓连接的接头具有一定的自由度，十分方便安装。弯螺栓在德国、法国、英国、新加坡、丹麦等许多国家的地铁交通项目及国内地铁中广泛应用，这种接头系统都非常成功。直螺栓和斜螺栓是近年来发展起来的管片连接形式，其手孔体积小，管片强度损失很小，而且容易实现机械快速安装，但安装难度较高，施工误差要求较小。

本设计管片块与块、环与环之间采用在国内应用比较成熟的弯螺栓连接。环与环之间 16 个 M30，块与块之间 12 个 M30，强度等级 5.8 级，性能等级 C 级。

7 楔形衬砌环之间相互组合

盾构隧道在曲线上是以若干段折线（最短折线长度为一环衬砌环宽）来拟合设计的光滑曲线。设计和施工是采用楔形衬砌环与直线衬砌环的优选及组合进行线路拟合的。根据线路转弯方向及施工纠偏的需要，设计左转弯、右转弯楔形衬砌环及直线衬砌环。设计时根据线路条件进行全线衬砌环的排列，以使隧道设计拟合误差控制在允许范围之内。盾构推进时，依据排列图及当前施工误差，确定下一环衬砌类型。由于采用的衬砌环类型不完全确定，所以给管片供应带来一定难度。

目前欧洲较为流行通用管片。它只采用一种类型的楔形衬砌环，盾构掘进时通过盾构机内环向千斤顶的传感器的信息确定下环转动的角度，管片衬砌环是可以 360°旋转的。由于它只需一种管片类型，可降低管模成本，但是通用管片拼装难度较高，需要有经验的盾构机操作人员；考虑地铁建设规模较大，管片模具使用寿命有限（每套模具约制作 1 000 环管片）等因素，大规模生产地铁管片基本不会增加模具的成本；综合以上考虑，本线路推荐采用：左转弯+右转弯+直线环。

衬砌环的拼装形式有错缝、通缝两种拼装形式。错缝拼装能使圆环接缝刚度分布趋于均匀，减少结构变形，可取得较好的空间刚度，但衬砌环较通缝拼装内力大，且管片制作精度不够时容易在推进过程中被顶裂，甚至顶碎。通缝拼装施工难度小，衬砌环内力较错缝衬砌环小，可减少管片配筋量，但衬砌空间刚度稍差。

国内有通缝拼装的实例，但后期管片变形大，经实测局部达到了 150 mm 之多，结合本线区间地质条件，推荐采用错缝拼装，错缝角度 22.5°。

8 防水设计

8.1 防水混凝土

混凝土强度等级及抗渗等级：C50、S10。

8.2 接缝防水设计

（1）弹性密封垫防水

弹性密封垫的材料选择首先应能满足防水要求的各项技术指标。目前国内、国际采用的材料大体分为三种：氯丁橡胶与遇水膨胀橡胶复合型、遇水膨胀橡胶和三元乙丙橡胶，此外，还发展有三元乙丙橡胶与遇水膨胀橡胶的复合型。

弹性密封垫作为隧道防水的主要防线，其选择必须慎重，从结构和防水材料的耐久性和耐腐蚀性角度出发，确定选用三元乙丙橡胶弹性密封垫。

封顶块纵向插入时要求采用减摩润滑剂，防止止水条错位过大甚至完全错开而影响防水效果。

弹性密封垫必须由足够黏结力的黏接剂固定于管片上，这对封顶块、邻接块的纵缝管片面尤其重要。

（2）嵌缝防水

在弹性密封垫寿命期满之后，虽然无法更换密封垫，但作为第二道防水线的嵌缝材料是容易剔除并重新嵌填新嵌缝密封胶，保证隧道长期防水效果。

嵌缝范围：进出洞 20～30 m、联络通道两侧各 8～10 m 处等变形量大的衬砌环段进行整环嵌填，其余区段则在拱顶 45°范围和拱底 90°范围内嵌填。

嵌缝材料：嵌缝槽密封材料采用单组份水溶性聚氨脂密封胶，由嵌缝枪嵌填处理。

（3）螺栓孔及吊装孔的防水

螺栓孔防水采用可更换的遇水膨胀橡胶密封圈，利用压密和膨胀双重作用加强防水。

当吊装孔和注浆孔结合使用时，为减少注浆孔作为隧道渗水的薄弱环节，在吊装孔的管片外侧 30 毫米的素混凝土，当需要进行衬砌背后二次注浆时，将吊装孔素混凝土破开，作为注浆孔使用。注浆孔设置一道水膨胀螺孔密封圈加强防水。

（4）管片其他部位防水

管片角部应粘贴未硫化的丁基橡胶腻子薄片。管片通缝拼装后形成的“十”形缝及错缝拼装后形成“T”形缝是防水的一个薄弱环节，因此要求在管片角部粘贴橡胶薄片，以加强角部防水，包括防止同步注浆浆液的漏入。

管片配筋设计分区段进行计算，在本文就不做详述。

9 结 论

郑州轨道交通 1 号线盾构隧道管片设计，综合考虑了沿线地层特点，选取了代表性断面进行受力计算，并结合兄弟城市地铁隧道设计施工经验，在管片厚度、宽度、连接、接缝等方面进行了一些优化。部分土层透水性中等，难以界定作为透水层或不透水层，采用水土分算或合算对计算结果影响较大，建议分别进行水土分算与合算，然后比对计算结果。有条件时应进行一些科研课题研究，选取代表性地层断面，量测出管片钢筋应力等，以校核设计计算，指导后续设计。

管片模具设计应综合考虑盾构掘进施工的便利性、工程的经济性等因素，设计前应充分熟悉全线线路的平纵断面，考虑管片使用时的通用性与特殊条件下的适用性，有些城市推荐采用通用环，有些城市推荐采用左右转弯+直线环，各有优缺点，必要时进行一些调研工作，进行比选，本文仅代表本次设计的意见。

参考文献（References）：

[1] GB 50157—2003 地铁设计规范[S]．北京：中国计划出版社，2003.

[2] GB 50446—2008 盾构法隧道施工与验收规范[S]．北京：中国建筑工业出版社，2008.

[3] GB 50299—1999 地下铁道工程施工与验收规范（2003 年版）[S]．北京：中国建筑工业出版社，2008.

[4] 张凤祥，朱合华，傅德明．盾构隧道[M]．北京：人民交通出版社，2004.

作者简介（Bio-data）：

梅江兵（1976 年 10 月出生），男，中国地质大学（武汉）双学位毕业，工程师，主要从事岩土工程设计与施工、隧道与地下空间工程设计与施工工作。

Jiangbing MEI（1976.10—）, engineer. He got the double degree of China University of Geosciences. Mainly he engaged in the design and construction of Geotechnical Engineer, tunnel and underground space Engineer.

E-mail: mjb3008@126.com

Telephone: 13018063259

水下盾构隧道管片衬砌结构受埋深影响的力学特性研究

周济民　何　川　郭德平　谭　准
西南交通大学 地下工程系，四川　成都　610031

【摘　要】 在进行水下盾构隧道设计时，合理确定隧道的埋置深度十分重要，不仅对结构安全性起着决定性作用，还是决定水下隧道长度和造价的主要因素。通过调研国内外水下盾构隧道相关技术资料，分析确定了已建水下盾构隧道埋置深度的范围；采用梁—弹簧模型对不同埋置深度条件下盾构隧道管片的力学特性进行系统研究，从结构受力的角度分析了不同隧道外径、不同地层、不同水压条件下隧道合理埋置深度的取值方法。研究成果可为类似的工程设计提供参考。

【关键词】 水下隧道；盾构隧道；埋置深度；管片内力

RESEARCH ON MECHANICAL BEHAVIOR OF LINING STRUCTURE INFLUENCED BY EMBEDDED DEPTH OF SUBMARINE SHIELD TUNNEL

Jimin ZHOU，Chuan HE，Deping GUO，Zhun TAN
Department of Underground Engineering, Southwest Jiaotong University, Chengdu 610031, Sichuan, China

Abstract: In the design of submarine shield tunnel, it is very important to determine the reasonable embedded depth of the tunnel. The cover thickness not only plays a decisive role on the safety, but also decides the length of the tunnel and the construction costs. Through surveying constructed submarine shield tunnel's information at home and abroad, analyzing and confirming the scope of embedded depth. Considering the factors of different diameter, different strata and different water pressure, the mechanical behavior of lining structure is analyzed by beam-spring model. From the view of internal forces of segment, reasonable embedded depth is discussed. The research result can provide reference to the design of similar projects.

Key words: submarine tunnel; shield tunnel; embedded depth; internal forces of segment

1 引　言

自1843年第一座盾构法隧道 ——Times河水底隧道完工以来，盾构法作为一种主要的隧道施工工法，在世界范围内的城市市政工程、跨越江河及海湾（峡）等方面得到了快速发展。近年来，一大批大型跨江海水下盾构隧道的建设，把我国水下隧道的建设规模和修建技术推进到了新的高度，水下盾构隧道合理埋置深度的确定成为隧道建设者们所面临的新问题[1,2]。

水下隧道的埋置深度，即隧道在河床下的岩土覆盖厚度。合理确定隧道的埋置深度是修建水下盾构隧道的关键技术之一：一方面，如果覆盖层厚度太小，水下盾构隧道工作面就有面临塌方、涌水、开挖面支护压力不易控制以及隧道上浮等问题，会导致辅助工法的投入增大；另一方面，覆盖层厚度太大将增加水下隧道的长度、结构内力和变形值，从而影响水下隧道的建设费用[3,4]。本文在广泛收集国内外已

基金项目：国家自然科学基金（50778154）；铁道部课题（2007G036、2006G007B）

建水下盾构隧道设计资料的基础上，分析确定出水下盾构隧道埋置深度的范围，开展了不同埋置深度条件下盾构隧道结构受力的数值分析，研究成果可供类似工程参考。

2 国内外水下盾构隧道埋置深度的调查

国外在跨江海水下隧道的建设上起步较早,在水下隧道建设方面积累了大量的工程实例和实践经验，而且那些大型隧道无论是在建设规模上，还是复杂性上都处于当时地下工程新技术的前列，其中最具代表性的有：外径 8.4 m 的英法海峡隧道、外径 14.14 m 的日本东京湾横断公路隧道、外径 13.8 m 的德国易北河第四隧道、外径 14.5 m 的荷兰绿色心脏隧道、外径 11.1 m 的荷兰西斯凯尔特公路隧道、外径 8.5 m 的丹麦斯多贝尔特海峡隧道等。

国内上海市于 1966 和 1984 年分别修建了外径 10.22 m 的打浦路越江隧道和外径 11.30 m 的延安东路越江隧道，由此开始了我国大型水下隧道建设的历史；上世纪 90 年代又先后修建了外径均为 11.0 m 的延安东路南沿线隧道、大连路隧道、复兴东路隧道三条越江隧道；近年又完成了外径 11.36 m 的翔殷路和外径 14.5 m 的上中路两条越江隧道,重庆也在 2005 年完成了外径 6.32 m 的排水工程越江隧道,2008 年竣工的外径 11.0 m 的武汉长江隧道被誉为“万里长江第一隧”。目前，正在建设中的水下盾构隧道包括南京长江公路隧道、杭州庆春路公路水底隧道、上海崇明越江隧道、广深港铁路客运专线珠江狮子洋高速铁路隧道等。

虽然国内外已修建或正在修建的水下盾构隧道工程情况各有差别，但是也有很多共同的特点。隧道合理埋置深度的确定可以参照已建隧道的工程设计资料，尤其是对于位于相同的工程地质和水文地质区域内的隧道而言，已建成隧道成功的设计和施工经验是待建隧道值得借鉴的。国内外已建的水下盾构隧道埋深的调查情况如图 1 所示。

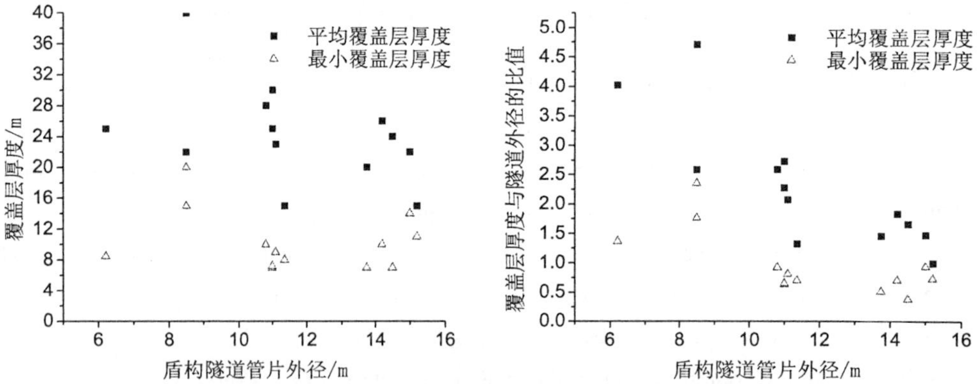

图 1 国内外水下盾构隧道埋置深度的调查情况

根据已建工程实例来看，水下盾构隧道的平均埋置深度并没有随着隧道外径的加大而有显著增长，大多数隧道的平均埋深在 20~30 m 之间（除去早期修建的英法海峡隧道，隧道平均埋深达到了 40 m）。而水下隧道的最小覆盖层厚度（除开水底松散沉积物厚度）与隧道外径的大小紧密相关，尤其是对于外径超过 10 m 的大断面盾构隧道而言，最小覆盖层厚度随着隧道外径的加大而增长，设计一般控制在（0.5～1.0）D 之间。

3 管片衬砌结构受埋深影响的力学特征

3.1 计算对象

从对国内外水下盾构隧道的调研情况可知，目前我国主要存在 3 种典型断面的水下盾构隧道：① 小直径（D=6 m 左右）地铁盾构隧道，以南京地铁下穿玄武湖隧道、武汉地铁过长江盾构隧道为代表；② 大直径（D=11 m 左右）盾构隧道，此类隧道有两种用途：一类为两车道的公路隧道，以武汉长江隧道、上海翔殷路越江隧道等为代表，另一类为单线高速铁路隧道，以广深港狮子洋隧道为代表；③ 特大直径（D=15 m 左右）公路隧道，此类隧道多为三车道公路隧道，以南京长江隧道、上海崇明越江隧道、上海上中路越江隧道等为代表。

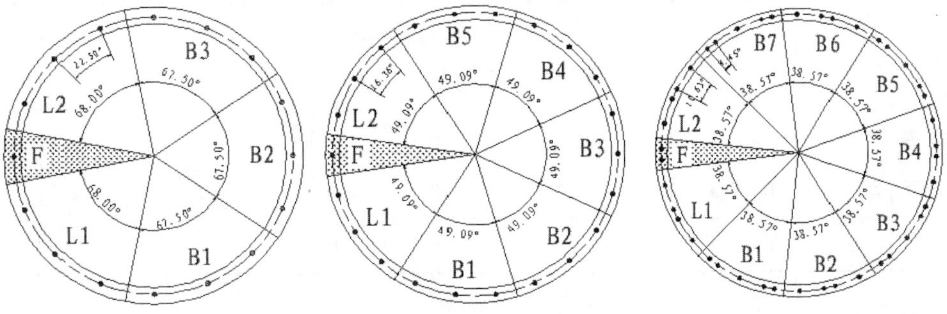

武汉地铁过长江隧道　　广深港狮子洋隧道　　南京长江隧道

图 2　三座隧道的管片分块图

针对上述分析的 3 种断面形式，选取武汉地铁过长江盾构隧道、广深港狮子洋高速铁路隧道、南京长江公路隧道为计算依托工程。在具体的计算过程中，均取出三环管片进行空间计算，检算目标环为中间一环，封顶块在左侧水平位置，相邻环按照错缝 180° 考虑。三座隧道的横断面结构形式见图 2，管片衬砌的结构参数见表 1。

表 1　三座隧道的管片衬砌结构参数

隧道名称	外径（m）	厚度（m）	幅宽（m）	分块方式	环向接头抗弯刚度（kN·m/rad）	
武汉地铁过江隧道	6.2	0.35	1.5	3+2+1	8.0×10^4	-5.0×10^4
广深港狮子洋隧道	10.8	0.50	2.0	5+2+1	4.0×10^5	-5.0×10^5
南京长江隧道	14.5	0.60	2.0	7+2+1	6.0×10^5	-7.5×10^5

3.2　计算模型

对于盾构法水下隧道管片衬砌结构计算模型的选择，应该注意隧道所处的地质条件、地下水的作用以及隧道本身的特征这些问题。对于荷载较为明确的盾构隧道，可以采用荷载结构模型下的梁-弹簧模型进行计算，同时采用日本修正惯用法进行复核[5]。对于硬岩条件下的管片衬砌结构计算，建议采用地层结构模型，考虑地层与管片间的相互作用和盾构掘进引起的开挖效应，推荐采用地层-壳-弹簧模型进行计算[6]。

梁-弹簧模型法在计算过程中引入抗弯刚度、抗剪刚度等接头力学参数，可以对任意管片环组装方式和接头位置下的衬砌环变形和内力等进行计算，较好地反映了接头对管片环刚度的局部影响以及衬砌环的错缝拼装效应。本次计算主要研究埋深变化对衬砌结构受力的影响，为避免采用不同的计算模型对结果产生附加影响，故采用梁-弹簧模型进行计算。

3.3　计算荷载

目前，我国已建的水下盾构隧道在江心处穿越的土层主要为砂性土层（南京、武汉过江隧道）、黏性土层（上海过江隧道）和岩质地层（狮子洋隧道），选取这三种代表性地层分别进行计算，其物理力学参数如表 2 所示。河床面以上取 20～40 m 共 3 种水位高度进行对比分析。荷载的计算采用 Terzaghi 松动土压力理论，隧道荷载模式见图 3。当地层为砂性土层时，其作用于盾构隧道管片结构上的荷载按水土分算考虑，水面以下的土采用浮容重进行计算；当地层为黏性土层时，其作用于盾构隧道管片结构上的荷载按水土合算考虑，水面以下的土采

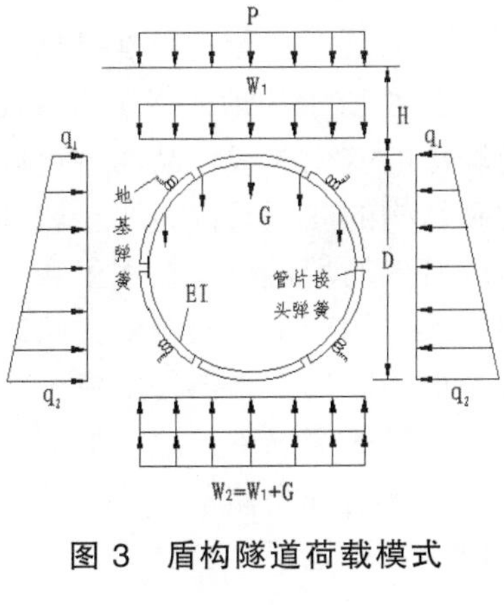

图 3　盾构隧道荷载模式

用饱和容重进行计算；当地层为岩质土层时，根据岩层的渗透系数 10^{-4}～10^{-3} cm/s 作为分界值，本次计算按照水土分算考虑。

表 2 水下盾构隧道穿越典型地层的物理力学参数

地层特征	水土分/合算	含水率 Ω（%）	孔隙比（e）	天然重度（kN/m²）	粘聚力（c/kPa）	内摩擦角 φ（°）	侧压力系数（λ）	基床系数	
								水平 K_H（Mpa）	垂直 K_V（Mpa）
砂性土层	水土分算	30	0.83	19.0	0	30	0.33	25	30
粘性土层	水土合算	34	0.94	18.5	28.5	12	0.60	15	20
岩质地层	水土分算	3.0	0.06	22.0	0	40	0.20	180	200

3.4 计算结果与分析

3.4.1 隧道直径对合理埋置深度的影响

图 4 所示为在砂性土层条件下，地面以上水头高为 30 m 时，不同直径隧道的衬砌结构变形及内力随埋深的变化曲线。从图中可以看出，随着埋深加大，三种直径隧道的变形及内力的增长曲线均表现为先陡后缓，二者之间呈非线性，究其原因，当埋深增加到一定深度时，隧道上方形成一个自然拱，此时埋深增加对于作用在管片的土荷载增速减慢，只有外周径向水压力的增加使管片的最大弯矩增长减慢。经比较分析，三种直径隧道上方形成塌落拱高度所对应的埋深是不同的，对于小直径隧道，埋深大于 2D 时，最大弯矩和变形基本保持不变，轴力的增长使最大偏心距有明显的减小，表明此种情况下，小直径隧道在深埋时对于结构受力是有利的；对于大直径和超大直径的隧道，埋深大于（1~1.5）D 时，最大偏心距开始随着埋深的增加略有降低，但结构的内力和变形并没有收敛，而是一直线性增加，此时仅从结构受力优化和降低配筋率的角度看，大直径隧道浅埋是合适的。

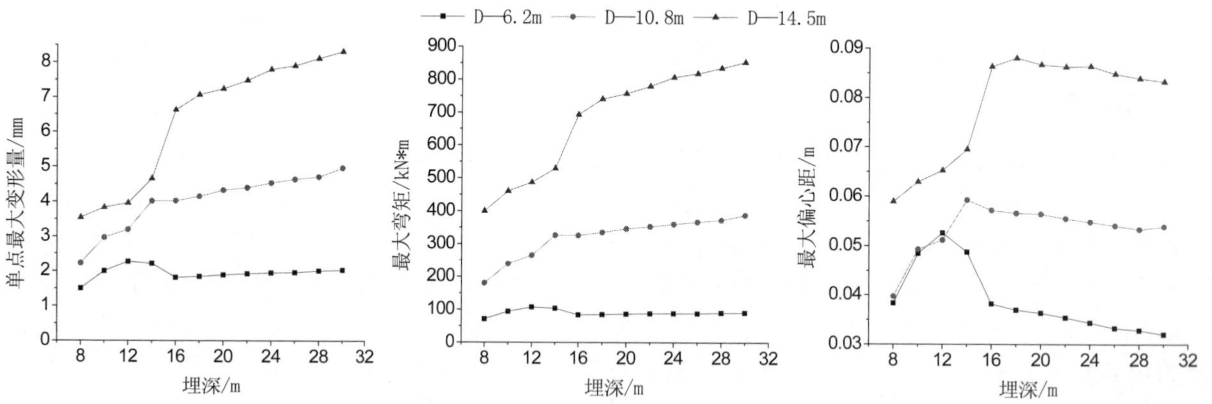

图 4 不同直径的隧道衬砌结构变形及内力随埋深的变化曲线

3.4.2 地层条件对合理埋置深度的影响

图 5 所示为地面以上水头高为 30 m，外径 10.8 m 的隧道在不同的地层条件下衬砌结构变形及内力随埋深的变化曲线。从图中可以看出，地层条件的差异对于计算结果的影响很大，黏性土地层中，隧道衬砌结构的变形及内力明显较其他两种地层大，且随着埋深的增加线性增长，这是由于软黏土地层不能形成有效的塌落拱，在水土合算及侧压力系数小于 1 的情况下，埋深的增大会使水土压力共同增长，从而导致结构产生不利的受力状态，可见，黏性土地层中隧道应尽量浅埋，但对于大断面隧道，当上下水头差很高时，如果隧道上覆土压较小，可能会发生隧道上浮的情况；岩质地层中，围岩自承能力强，在水土分算的情况下，埋深的变化对于结构的变形及内力影响不大，最大偏心距还略有减小，管片结构受力有较高的安全储备，此时结构受力不是确定埋深的决定因素；砂性土层中的计算结果介于两者之间，类似于岩质地层。

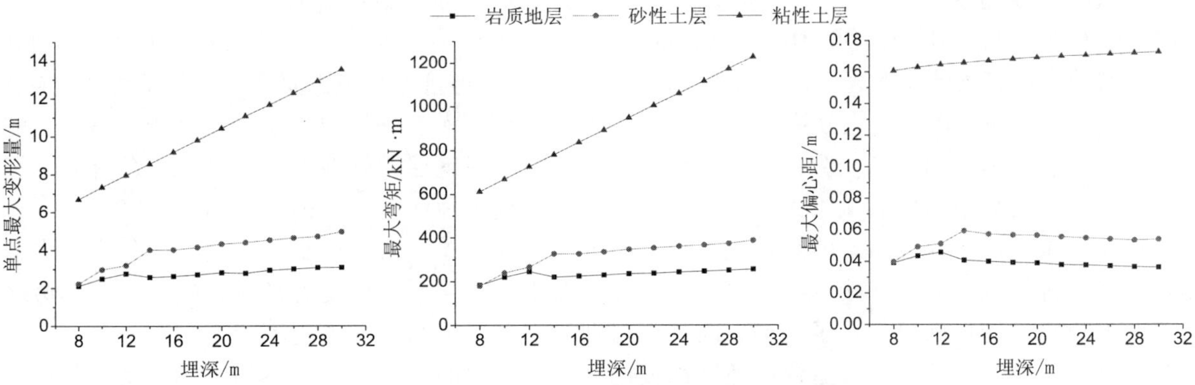

图 5 不同地层条件下衬砌结构变形及内力随埋深的变化曲线

3.4.3 水位对合理埋置深度的影响

图 6 所示为在砂性土层条件下，外径 10.8 m 的隧道在不同水压力作用时衬砌结构变形及内力随埋深的变化曲线。从图中可以看出，对于采用水土分算的透水性地层，水压力变化对于衬砌结构内力及变形的影响并不是很大，当隧道埋深大于 1D 时，由于竖直土压和水平土压基本恒定，变化的部分只是非均匀水压的大小，随着径向作用水压的增加，提高了结构的轴力和整体刚度，管片截面的最大偏心距水平降低，在结构受力允许的范围内对结构是有利的。设计时为安全考虑，对于水土分算的情况，应取最低水位进行计算。

对于水土合算的黏性土地层，由于水压通过土压间接作用于结构，水平方向的水压也按侧压力系数进行了折减，虽然高水位提高了结构的轴力和刚度，但是竖直土压和水平土压差也在增大，弯矩增长速度要比轴力增长速度快，管片偏心距增大，因此高水位成为最不利工况。

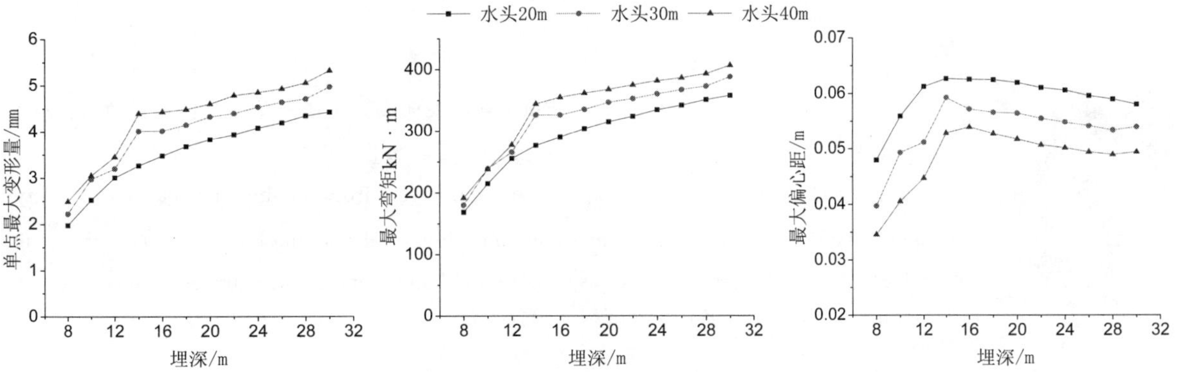

图 6 不同水位下衬砌结构变形及内力随埋深的变化曲线

从以上的分析可以得出，地层条件不同时，水土分/合算对于管片内力影响显著，对于判定某一断面属于分算模式还是合算模式时应该慎重。对于一般的水下盾构隧道来说，上覆地层并不是单层、均质的，渗透系数不同的地层可能出现互层现象，设计前必须准确地调研好，盲目采用水土合算过于保守，浪费资源；不切实际地采用水土分算，结构安全性得不到满足。设计时应针对实际工程灵活考虑，使设计达到既经济、又安全的目的。

4 结 论

本文调研了国内外已建水下盾构隧道的技术资料，采用梁—弹簧模型对于水下盾构隧道管片衬砌结构受埋深影响的力学特征进行了研究，得出如下结论：

（1）国内外已建的盾构法水下隧道的平均埋置深度与隧道外径关系不大，大约在 20 m～30 m 之间；

而最小覆盖层厚度随着隧道外径的加大而增长，一般控制在(0.5~1.0)D之间。

（2）砂性土层中不同外径的隧道衬砌结构的变形和内力随埋深增加呈非线性增长，小直径隧道在深埋时对于结构受力是有利的，大直径和超大直径的隧道在满足隧道抗浮和施工安全等条件下浅埋是合适的。

（3）地层条件不同时，水土分算/合算对于计算结果影响显著，黏性土地层采用水土合算时，隧道衬砌的变形及内力与埋深同步增长，此时隧道应尽量浅埋；岩性地层和砂性土层采用水土分算时，埋深的变化对于结构的变形及内力影响不大，此时结构受力不是确定埋深的决定因素。

（4）外水压力对于计算结果的影响主要与地层的渗透性有关。对于透水地层而言，外水压力的增加会提高衬砌结构的轴力和整体刚度，同时降低了偏心距水平，对于结构受力是有利的；对于非透水性地层而言，水压通过土压间接作用于结构，高水位时埋深越大对于结构受力越不利。

综上所述，控制水下盾构隧道合理埋置深度因素是多方面的，它不仅关系到结构的受力与稳定，还影响着整个工程的造价，笔者重点从结构受力的角度进行了粗浅分析,希望能对类似工程的设计有微薄的参考价值，也希望得到专家的批评与指导。

参考文献（References）：

[1] 孙钧. 海底隧道工程设计施工若干关键技术的商榷[J]. 岩石力学与工程学报，2006，25(8)：1513-1521.

[2] 王梦恕，皇甫明. 海底隧道修建中的关键问题[J]. 建筑科学与工程学报，2005，22(4)：1-4.

[3] 蒋树屏，刘元雪，谢锋，等. 重庆市朝天门两江隧道越江段盾构法合理覆盖层厚度研究[J]. 岩石力学与工程学报，2007，26(6)：1188-1193.

[4] 宋超业，周书明，谭志文. 水下盾构隧道合理覆盖层厚度的探讨[J]. 现代隧道技术，2008，增刊：47-51.

[5] 何川，曾东洋. 盾构隧道结构设计及施工对环境的影响[M]. 成都：西南交通大学出版社，2007. 51-68.

[6] 苏宗贤，何川. 盾构隧道管片衬砌内力分析的壳-弹簧-接触模型及其应用[J]. 工程力学，2007，24(10)：131-136.

作者简介（Bio-data）：

周济民，男，1984年10月出生，2007年毕业于西南交通大学，获得学士学位，现就读于西南交通大学，攻读博士学位，主要研究方向为隧道与地下工程。

Jimin ZHOU (1984—), graduated in Civil Engineering from Southwest Jiaotong University in 2007 and obtained a Bachelor's degree in the same time. Now he is studying for the Ph.D dergree in the magor of Bridge and Tunnel Engineering. His specialize in highway and subway tunnel engineering.

E-mail：zhoujm84@126.com

既有盾构隧道上方开挖卸载后隧道力学特征研究

杨 征　林 刚

中铁二院工程集团有限责任公司，四川　成都　610031

【摘　要】 以某市轨道交通建设工程为背景，采用计算机数值模拟分析手段，分析了隧道上方开挖卸载对隧道结构受力和变形的影响，研究了隧道横向和纵向结构受力和变形的变化规律，并结合已有工程实例的经验教训，提出了合理的施工方法。

【关键词】 盾构隧道；上方开挖；力学特征

STUDY ON MECHANICAL CHARACTERISTICS OF SHIELD TUNNEL WITH EXCAVATION ABOVE

Zheng YANG，Gang LIN

China Railway Eryuan Engineering Group Co.Ltd, Chengdu 610031, Sichuan, China

Abstract: Based on engineering construction in some city, this paper Analyzed the mechanical characteristics of the shield tunnel with excavation and unloading above by numerical simulation, and studied the force and deformation of the structure of the tunnel. Combined with the experiences and lessons from the previous project, a reasonable method of the construction was put forward.

Key words: shield tunnel; excavation above; mechanical characteristics

1 引 言

近年来，随着城市轨道交通建设的快速发展，在既有隧道上方进行开挖施工的情况也越来越普遍。某市轨道交通一盾构区间全长 1 248 m，其中里程 CK19＋745～CK20+010 范围内在盾构隧道施工结束后将修建一规划的人工湖。该段隧道顶部埋深 13～15 m，人工湖采用明挖法施工，湖底深约 4 m。

已建地铁隧道对其自身的变形要求非常高，过大的变形沉降会影响地铁的运营安全；人工湖施工过程实际上是一卸载过程，隧道上方的卸载必定会对隧道结构产生不利影响。因此为保证地铁运营安全，有必要研究人工湖开挖全过程隧道结构的力学行为及变形情况。

2 数值模拟研究[1, 2]

2.1 模型简介

本次采用 ANSYS 有限元软件进行模拟计算，采用 shell63 壳单元模拟混凝土管片，solid45 三维实体单元模拟土体。模型尺寸为：80×50×400（m），满足边界距隧道结构大于等于 3D 的相关要求；模型上边界为自由面，左、右、下边界为面约束，模型共计单元 69 014 个，节点数目 71 152 个。建模情况如图 1、图 2 所示。

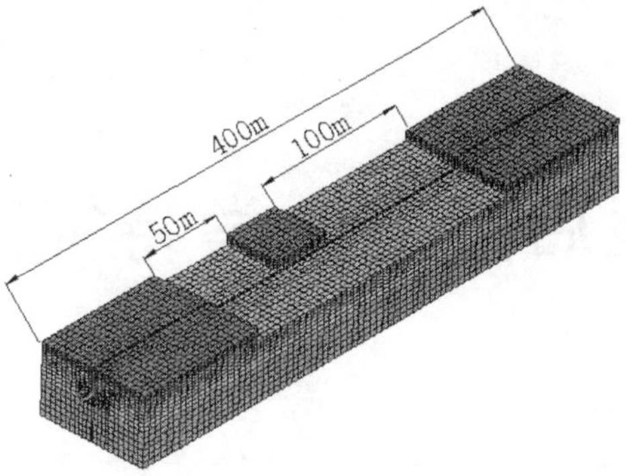

图 1 三维有限元模型

图 2 有限元模型中隧道及开挖土体

隧道底板以上地层自上而下分别为杂填土、淤泥质土、灰色粉质黏土夹粉砂、粉质黏土，地层物理力学参数指标如表 1 所示，计算严格按照工程勘查报告，采用弹塑性本构关系和 Drucker－Prager 屈服准则进行计算。

计算步骤如下：自重固结，盾构法施工左线隧道，拼装左线隧道管片，盾构法施工右线隧道，拼装右线隧道管片，明挖法施工人工湖。

表 1 隧道所处地层物理力学性质表

材　料	γ（kN/m^3）	c（kPa）	φ（°）	E（MPa）
填　土	17.2	19	11.5	4
灰色淤泥及淤泥质土	16.9	13	11.5	2.2
灰色粉质黏土夹粉砂	18.3	18	18.7	4.5
灰色粉质黏土	18	17	17.1	4.25
混凝土 C50	25	—	—	34 500

2.2 盾构隧道在人工湖施工后的分析

（1）变形分析

如图 3 为隧道在人工湖开挖前的变形云图，图 4 为隧道在人工湖开挖 4m 后的变形云图，图 5 为隧道在人工湖未开挖前的沉降和偏移，图 6 为隧道在人工湖开挖 4 m 后的沉降和偏移。由图可以看出在人工湖未开挖前，双线隧道纵向沉隆均很小，最大隆起值仅为 5 mm 左右，而且左右线隧道纵向沉降都很均匀。而在人工湖开挖 4 m 后，隧道不均匀沉降变形明显加大，最大隆起值达到了 18 mm。

由于人工湖中部左线隧道上方有一小块土体未开挖，隧道沉降和偏移曲线在此均出现了反弯，左线隧道的不均匀沉降程度比右线大，而但左右线横向偏移程度缺差别不大，最大偏移均为 3 mm 左右。

图 3 隧道在人工湖开挖前的变形云图（单位：m）

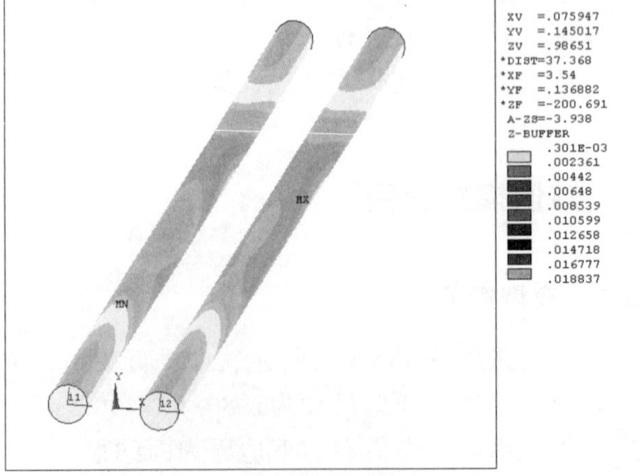

图 4 隧道在人工湖开挖后的变形云图（单位：m）

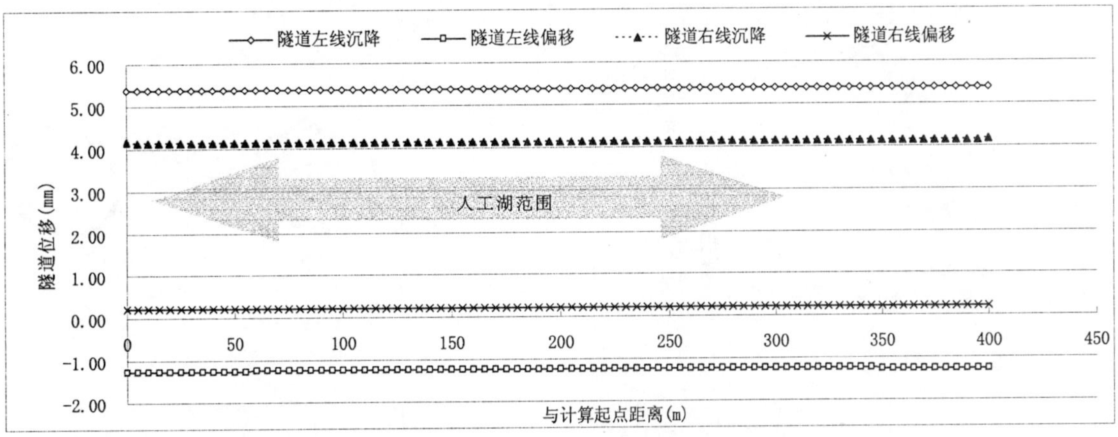

图 5　隧道在人工湖开挖前的沉降和偏移

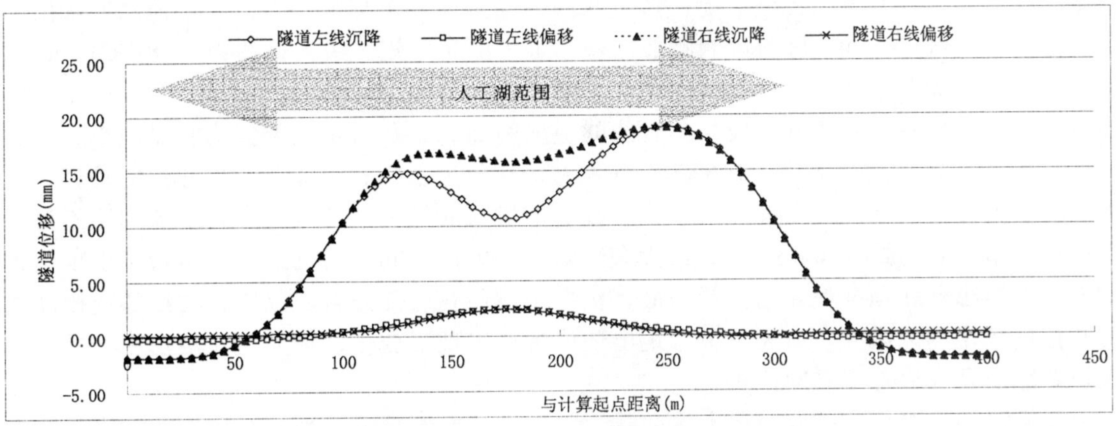

图 6　隧道在人工湖开挖 4 m 后的沉降和偏移

由以上分析可知，隧道上方土体的开挖会导致隧道上方土体卸载，下部未开挖的土体产生应力释放，出现回弹，地层随之隆起，造成隧道的隆沉。当上方非对称开挖时，由于隧道两侧侧部压力不对等，会出现隧道向侧压力小的一方的横向偏移。

（2）隧道横断面受力分析

图中正弯矩代表隧道内侧受拉，负弯矩代表隧道外侧受拉，以下各图同。

如图 7 为人工湖开挖前双线隧道横断面弯矩图，图 8 为开挖后隧道横断面弯矩图，图 9 为开挖后隧道横断面弯矩的变化，图 10 为非对称开挖处横断面弯矩形状。

图 7　开挖前隧道横断面弯矩(单位：N · m)

图 8　开挖 4 m 隧道横断面弯矩(单位：N · m)

图 9 开挖 4 m 隧道横断面弯矩变化(单位：N · m)

图 10 非对称开挖隧道横断面弯矩

由图 7 可以看出，在开挖人工湖之前，隧道纵向各横断面弯矩基本一致，隧道顶部底部出现最大正弯矩，最大值约为 188 kN · m，隧道两侧腰部出现了最大的负弯矩，最大值约为－181 kN · m。由图 8、图 9 可以看出，人工湖开挖 4 m 后，双线隧道纵向各横断面弯矩变化不一。

在隧道上方有土体对称开挖的地段，左右线隧道横断面的正负弯矩最大值均明显减小，最大正弯矩为 150 kN · m 左右，最大负弯矩为－146 kN · m 左右。在隧道上方有土体非对称开挖的地段，左右线的弯矩出现了较大的差异，如图 8、图 9 所示，左线隧道横断面最大正负弯矩与开挖前相比不仅未减小，反而略微增加，最大正弯矩 196 kN · m，最大负弯矩－189 kN · m，而且最大正负弯矩出现位置出现了变化，最大正弯矩出现在顶部偏左的位置，最大负弯矩出现在底部偏右的位置；右线隧道横断面最大正负弯矩与开挖前相比明显减小，最大正负弯矩出现位置也出现了变化，最大正弯矩出现在顶部偏左的位置，最大负弯矩出现在底部偏右的位置。

由以上分析可知，对称开挖段由于土体卸载，结构横断面弯矩值减小，对盾构管片纵缝的受力和防水是有利的，但是非对称开挖段隧道两侧的土体侧压力不对等，造成隧道弯矩形状发生偏转，左右线隧道弯矩差异较大。

如图 11 为人工湖开挖前双线隧道横断面轴力图，图 12 为开挖后隧道横断面轴力图，图 13 为开挖后隧道横断面轴力的变化，图 14 为非对称开挖处横断面轴力形状。

图 11 开挖前隧道横断面轴力(单位：N)

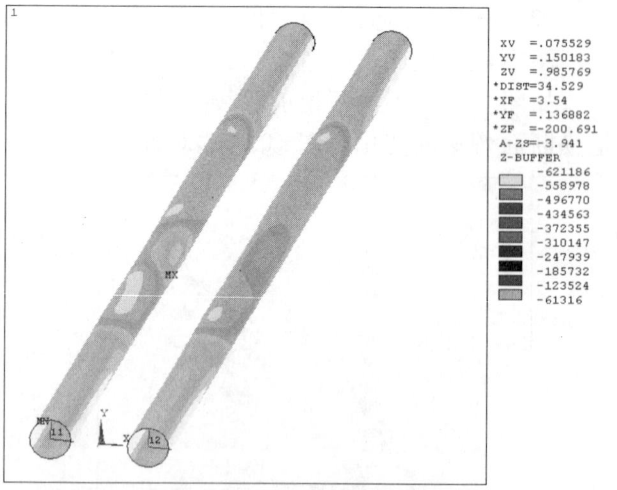

图 12 开挖 4 m 后隧道横断面轴力(单位：N)

由图 11 可以看出，在开挖人工湖之前，隧道纵向各横断面轴力基本一致，最小轴力出现在隧道顶部和底部，最小值约为 360 kN，最大轴力出现在隧道两侧腰部，最大值约为 608 kN。由图 12、图 13 可以看出，人工湖开挖 4 m 后，双线隧道纵向各横断面轴力变化不一。

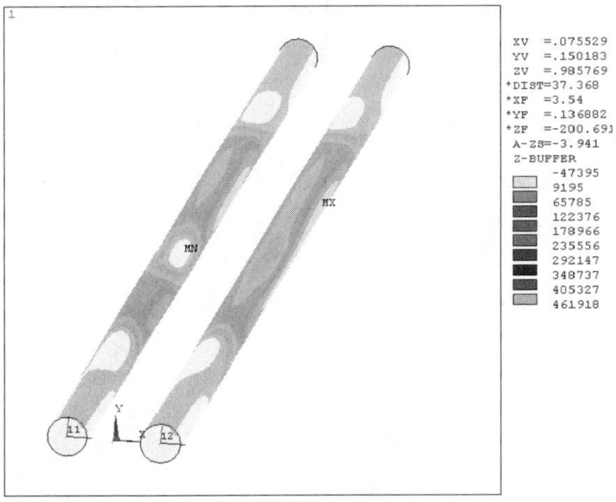

图 13　开挖 4m 隧道横断面轴力变化(单位：N)

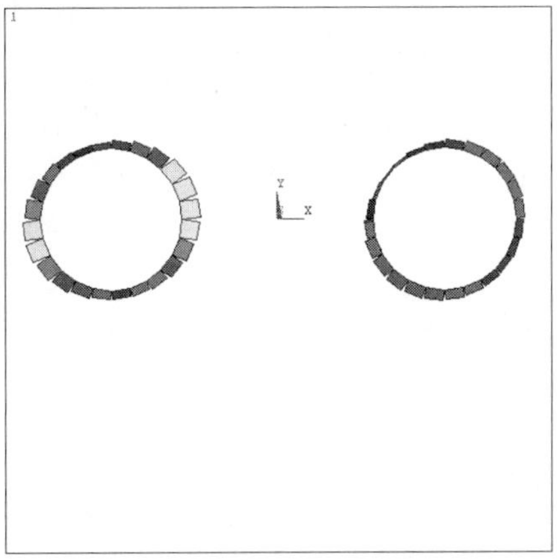

图 14　非对称开挖隧道横断面轴力

在隧道上方有土体对称开挖的地段，左右线隧道横断面的轴力值均明显减小，最大轴力仅为 310 kN 左右。在隧道上方有土体非对称开挖的地段，左右线的弯矩出现了较大的差异，如图 13、图 14 所示，左线隧道横断面最大轴力未减小，反而略微增加，最大轴力 621 kN；右线隧道横断面最大轴力开挖前相比明显减小。

值得注意的是，当人工湖开挖 4 m 后，双线隧道横断面轴力的不均匀程度增加较多，如图 14 所示，在非对称开挖地段，双线隧道尤其是右线隧道顶部偏左位置的轴力值减少较多，这对隧道结构的受力和防水是不利的。

(3) 人工湖开挖后隧道纵向应力分析

图中正应力代表拉应力，负应力代表压应力，以下各图同。

如图 15 为人工湖开挖前双线隧道 Z 向应力图，图 16 为开挖 4 m 后隧道 Z 向应力图，图 17 为开挖后隧道 Z 向应力的变化。

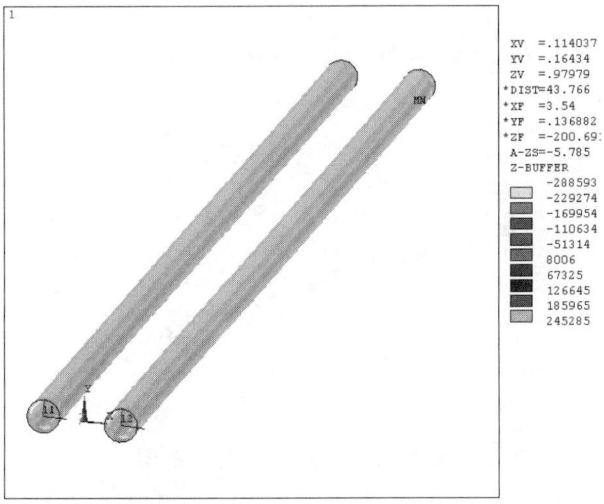

图 15　开挖前隧道 Z 向应力(单位：Pa)

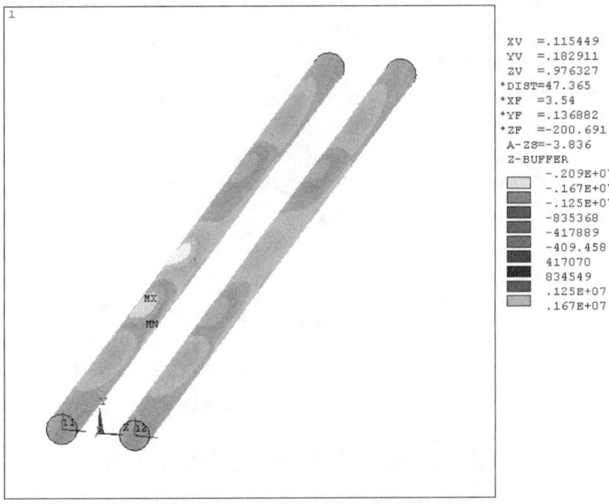

图 16　开挖 4 m 后隧道 Z 向应力(单位：Pa)

如图 15 所示，人工湖开挖前，双线隧道纵向 Z 向应力很均匀，而且值很小，最大拉应力约 0.24 MPa，最大压应力约 0.28 MPa。如图 16、图 17 所示，人工湖开挖 4 m 后，双线隧道的 Z 向应力不均匀程度增加较快，而且其绝对值增大较多，最大拉应力约 1.6 MPa（超过了混凝土的抗拉极限），最大压应力约 −2 MPa，说明双线隧道出现了不均匀沉降。最大拉应力出现在人工湖开挖段隧道顶部，最大压应力出现在人工湖开挖段隧道底部，说明这个范围内的隧道出现上拱，由于人工湖两侧的土体未开挖，所以这种上拱趋势受到了约束，从而出现了隧道上部受压下部受拉的现象。

如图 16 所示，左线隧道某段顶部出现了最大压应力，而与之相邻段的隧道顶部均是最大的拉应力，这是由于左线隧道上方人工湖中存在未开挖土体，相邻段隧道上拱趋势受到约束，从而导致隧道顶部纵向应力曲线在这里出现了反弯。

如图 17 所示，双线隧道应力变化程度最大的地段是人工湖开挖地段和人工湖中的未开挖地段，由于此处孤岛的存在，导致左线隧道的应力变化更加复杂，孤岛下方的隧道上部应力由拉应力变为压应力。

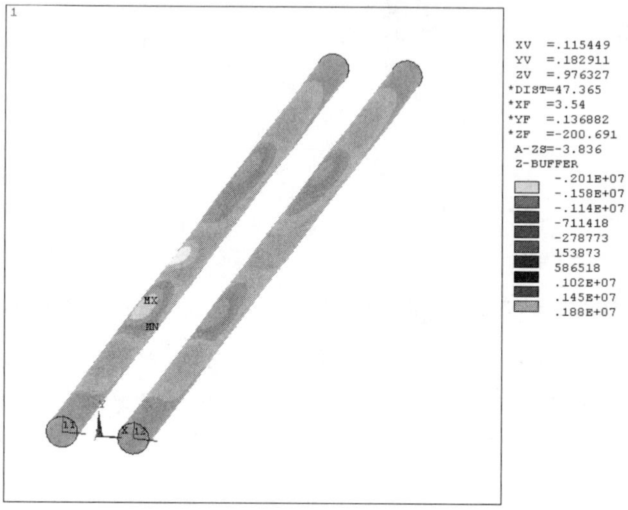

图 17 开挖 4 m 后隧道 Z 向应力的变化(单位：Pa)

2.3 人工湖开挖深度对隧道纵向受力和变形的影响

如图 18 为隧道变形与开挖深度关系图，图 19 为隧道 Z 向最大应力与开挖深度关系图，由图可知，随着开挖深度的增加，隧道最大隆起值增加较快，而最大偏移值变化不明显，当开挖深度为 4 m 时，最大偏移约 19 mm，最大偏移约 2 mm，但当开挖深度达到 8 m 时，最大偏移值接近 5 mm，而最大隆起值接近 40 mm。由于的隧道不均匀沉降和偏移，隧道 Z 向最大正负应力增加也较快，说明隧道纵向产生了较大的弯矩。

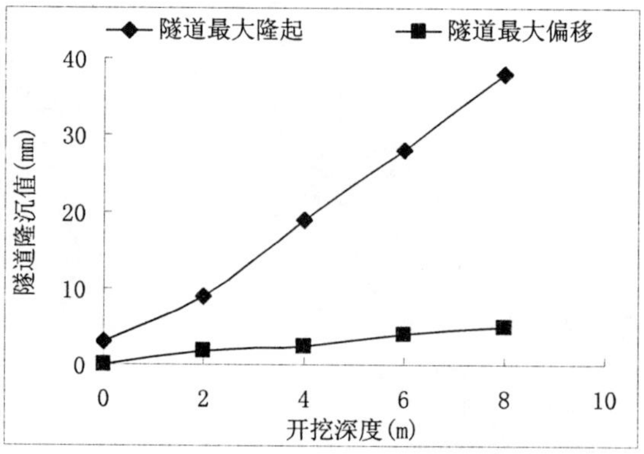

图 18 隧道变形与开挖深度关系图

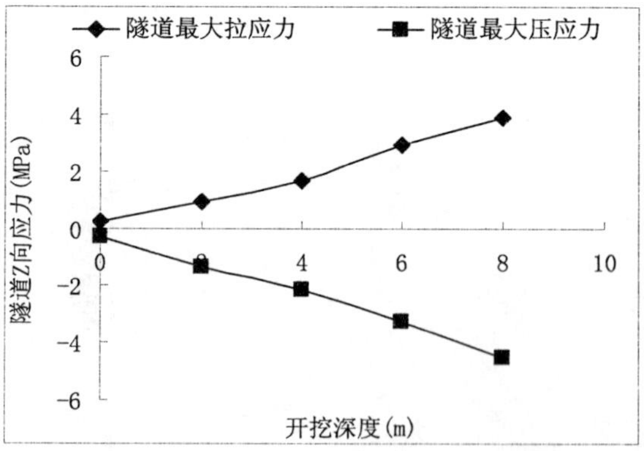

图 19 隧道 Z 向最大应力与开挖深度关系图

3 工程实例处理经验

3.1 号线上方开挖立交工程基坑[3]

上海东方路下立交工程基坑开挖位于已运营的地铁隧道 2 号线之上：地铁隧道覆土 9.3 m，大多位于灰色淤泥质黏土中；深基坑工程开挖宽度达 18 m、深达 6.5 m，基坑坑底距隧道顶部的最近距离只有 2.8 m，空间关系如图 20 所示。

基坑施作时，采取了如下措施：① 隧道上方进行深层搅拌桩加固和双液注浆加固，如图 21 所示；② 实行分层分段开挖，先挖一薄层，结合隧道隆起和沉降监控不断调整每层开挖厚度；③ 采用先进的监测系统，信息化施工。通过以上措施，成功地将运营地铁隧道的位移控制在 20 mm 之内。

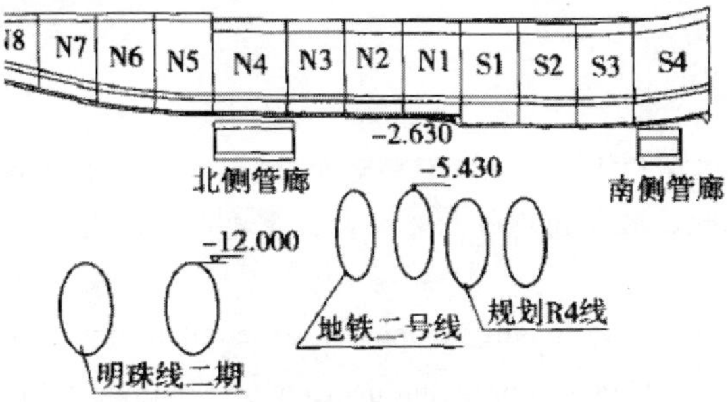

图 20　基坑与隧道位置关系

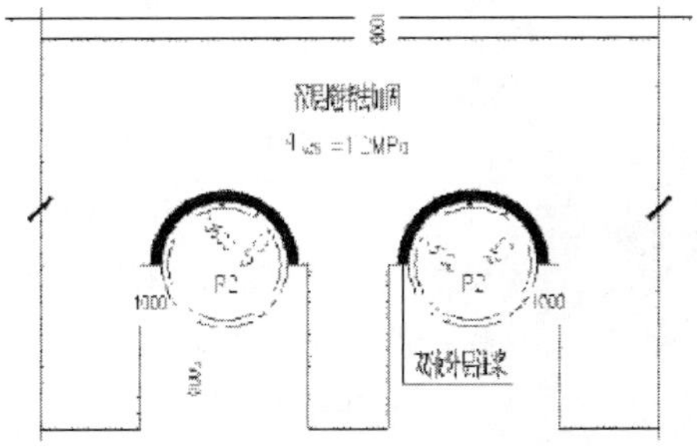

图 21　隧道上方加固示意图

3.2　号线上方开挖淮海路车站通道[4]

淮海路车站北风井位于车站北端头井西侧，为地下一层结构，南北长约 50 m，东西宽约 30 m，面积约 1 300 m^2。基坑开挖深度 9 m，坑底距隧道顶约 7.5 m。北风井基坑下方是营运中的地铁 1 号线隧道。基坑开挖深度较深，土方的土体开挖后，卸载超过 160 kN/m^2，对地铁 1 号线安全影响极大。

为了控制施工卸载、控制隧道上浮，施工时采取技术措施如下：① 隧道两侧设深层搅拌桩内插 H 型钢围护，隔断地层，减少对隧道的影响。围护结构与底板结构联结形成"门"式抗浮结构；② 基坑内采用深层搅拌桩加固；③ 分层分块分区挖土；④ 通道底板修筑完成后进行反压；⑤ 尽可能减小施工扰动；⑥ 加强施工监测。

通过以上措施，隧道最终上浮最大值为 3.6 mm，隧道收敛监测值小于 3 mm，通道施工取得了成功。

由以上两个成功的工程实例的处理不难看出，在既有盾构隧道上方进行大面积开挖，施工过程中要尽量减少扰动，分层分段开挖，加强监控量测，必要时还要对隧道上方地层进行加固，防止隧道隆起量过大。

4　结论及施工建议

通过对数值模拟和工程实例分析不难得出如下结论：

（1）土体卸载后隧道产生了较大的隆起，为保证地铁运营安全，对地铁隧道的隆沉值必须有一定限制。《地铁设计规范》（GB 50157—2003）中对隧道纵向的不均匀沉降并未有具体规定，上海地区《地铁隧道保护条例》规定，地铁结构设施的绝对沉降量及水平位移≤20 mm。从本次数值模拟分析的结果看，该人工湖开挖深度为 4 m 时，隧道的最大隆起值与以上标准基本接近。

（2）人工湖开挖中心、边缘覆土高度突变处下方的隧道的变形、横断面受力、变形会发生突变，施工过程中要重点加强对这些部位的监测。

（3）非对称开挖方式对隧道的结构受力影响较大，采用非对称开挖方式时，开挖后隧道两侧尚未开挖的土体会造成隧道两侧的侧压力不一致，从而导致横断面内力、变形重分布，而且最值都有较大变化，不利于隧道的安全和受力，开挖过程中要尽量采取对称开挖的方式。

（4）施工过程中要尽可能减小扰动。并采用信息化施工，加强对既有隧道监测，若隧道隆起值较大，必要时采取搅拌桩加固、注浆加固等措施对隧道上方及侧部土体进行加固，限制隧道的纵向变形。

参考文献（References）：

[1]　李文婷，王如路，余占奎．软土盾构隧道局部卸载的理论与三维有限元分析[J]. 四川建筑科学研究，2008，(10)：103-107.

[2] 余占奎,黄宏伟等. 软土盾构隧道纵向设计综述[J]. 地下空间与工程学报，2005(4): 315-318.
[3] 李志高,曾远,刘浩,王毅斌. 基坑开挖引起下方地铁隧道位移的控制措施[J]. 铁道建筑技术，2005(5): 33-36.
[4] 青二春,廖少明. 地铁隧道上方大面积卸载下的变形及控制模式研究[D]. 同济大学硕士学位论文,2007(3):92-95.

作者简介（Bio-data）：

杨征，男，汉族，1982年7月生，工学硕士，助理工程师。于2007年毕业于西南交通大学地下工程系，现任职于中国中铁二院工程集团有限责任公司，主要从事隧道及地下工程的设计及研究工作。

Zheng YANG (1982—), male, the Han Nationality , master of engineering, assistant engineer, graduated from the Department of Underground Engineering of Southwest Jiaotong University in 2007.Now he works in China Railway Eryuan Engineering Group Co.Ltd , mainly engaging in the design and research work in the field of tunnel and underground engineering.

E-mail: 4943893874@qq.com

浅谈盾构隧道管片的破损与修复

梁艳文 [1] 廖少明 [2]

[1]同济大学 地下建筑与工程系，上海 200092

[2]同济大学 岩土及地下工程教育部重点实验室，上海 200092

【摘 要】 盾构隧道的长期服役性能与衬砌管片的耐久性有很密切的关系。本文通过对上海某区间盾构隧道衬砌管片损伤的实地调查，首次对盾构隧道衬砌管片各种破损状况进行了分类；并从施工的角度初步提出了盾构隧道衬砌管片破损等级、破损修复方案、破损修复效果检验方法以及建立管片破损修复档案等管片破损修复建议，以期推动盾构隧道管片破损修复的规范化。

【关键词】 盾构隧道；管片；破损；修复

AN INTRODUCTION TO THE DAMAGE AND REPAIR OF SHEILD-TUNNEL SEGMENT

Yanwen LIANG [1]， Shaoming LIAO[2]

[1]*Department of Geotechnical Engineering, Tongji University, Shanghai 200092, China;*

[2]*Key Laboratory of Geotechnical and Underground Engineering of Ministry of Education, Tongji University, Shanghai 200092, China*

Abstract: The durability of the shield tunnel is closely related to the assembly quality of segment. By site investigation on certain section in Shanghai Shield Tunnel, the damage forms of shield-tunneling segment was firstly classified according to the actual damage situations of the segment damage level. And, some suggestions, such as:the damage level, the repairing schemes, the method of inspecting the repairing effect , and establishement of the damage files, were put forward. All ot these were hoped to improve the standardariztion of damage repairing of shield tunnel segment.

Key words: shield tunnel; segment; damage; repair

1 前 言

目前，全国地铁建设已步入建设高峰期，盾构隧道衬砌将要使用大量钢筋混凝土管片。开裂和破碎是钢筋混凝土管片最常见的一种质量通病。当然这里提到的开裂均是我们肉眼可见的宏观开裂，大多细小微观上的开裂对工程结构的美观、承载能力、安全性和耐久性不会有大的影响。当开裂较深较宽时，会影响管片的美观和抗渗性能，诱发内部钢筋的锈蚀和加速混凝土的老化，从而损害盾构隧道管片的承载能力、安全性和耐久性。

管片破损的现象在国内外的盾构隧道施工中时有发生，例如：瑞士 Sorrenberg 内燃气隧道掘进阶段，管片出盾尾后发生严重开裂；广州地铁 1 号线和 2 号线在施工阶段部分区间段管片出现开裂；上海地铁 7 号线和 9 号线施工阶段出现部分管片开裂的现象。根据对某在建轨道交通盾构隧道管片破损的现场调查分析，上行线总共统计的 162 环管片中 157 环发生破损，占 97%；下行线总共统计的 140 环中 91 环发生破损，占 65%。

下图 1 是盾构隧道管片破损情况的部分图片。

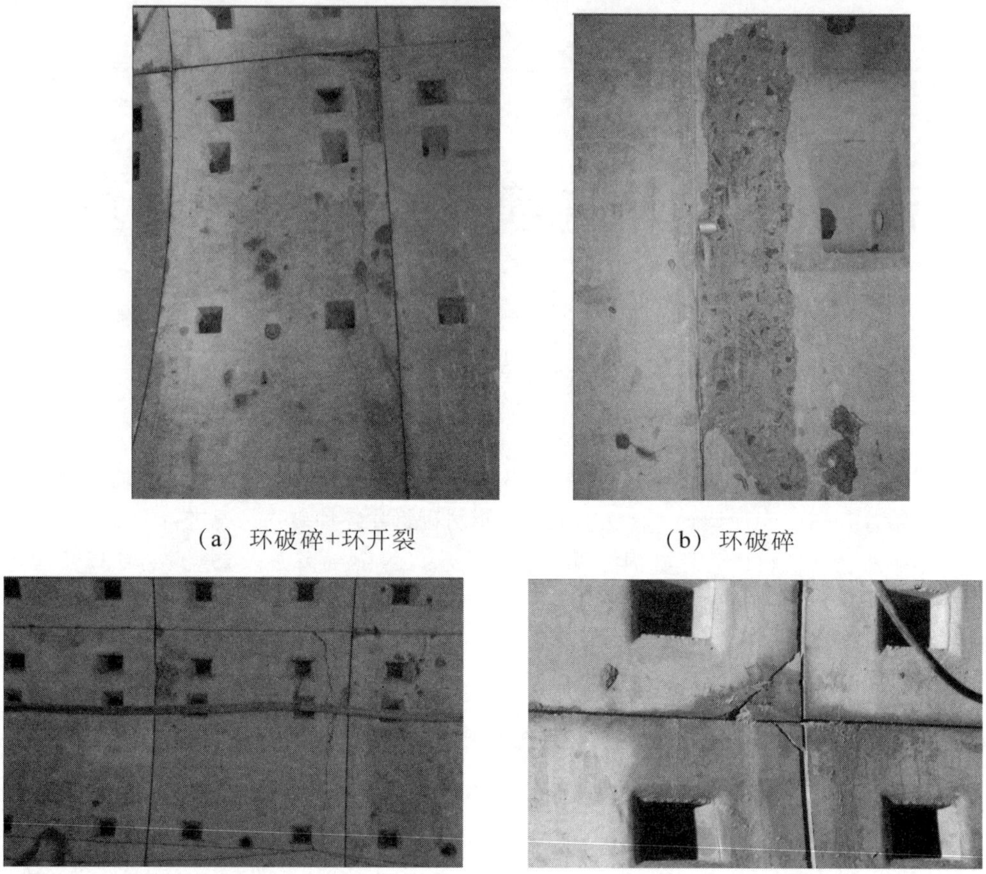

(a) 环破碎+环开裂　(b) 环破碎

(c) 环开裂　(d) 角破碎

图 1　管片各种破损图片

钢筋混凝土结构的承载能力与使用寿命有图 2 的关系。曲线①和②分别代表了老化和伤病的盾构隧道的使用寿命曲线，其使用寿命分别为 OA 和 OB。在 C 点时修复，则形成了曲线③，使盾构隧道的使用寿命延长至 OE；而在 D 点时修复，就形成曲线④，使盾构隧道的使用寿命延长至 OF。显然，OE>OF>OA，这说明老化和伤病的盾构隧道的使用寿命是受修复时间影响的，且早修复要比晚修复好[1]。

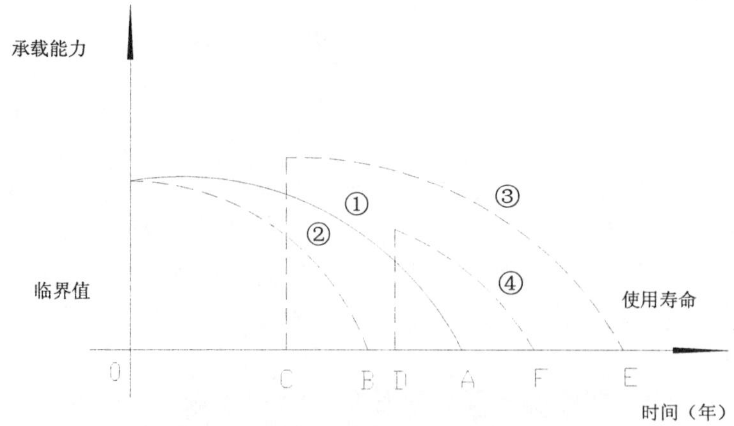

图 2　结构的承载能力与使用寿命示意图[1]

因此，在施工和后期运营期间管片的开裂、破碎的修复问题将成为地下施工研究中一个不可忽视的课题。从耐久性来讲，修复后的使用寿命将大于修复前的使用寿命；从经济的角度来讲，修复的费用肯定要低于重建的费用；从时间来讲，对破碎和开裂的部分进行修复所用的时间也要少于拆除重建的时间。目前相关规范中对施工引起的管片开裂及修复没有明确的规定，造成实际修复施工比较混乱。因此，通过调查工程制定相关规范或规程对管片进行针对性修复以确保管片修复的长期耐久性是十分必要的。

2 管片破碎与开裂的原因分析

在预制钢筋混凝土管片拼装衬砌结构中，我们经常可以看到部分管片开裂或破碎，这些开裂或破碎大多位于隧道中平面以上，而又以拱顶部位最多。管片开裂或破碎以不同的形状和不同的位置出现在隧道中。为区别这些开裂或破碎，我们结合开裂或破碎出现的位置和形状给之命名与归类。如：

- 角破碎分为前角破碎和后角破碎；
- 环破碎分为前环破碎和后环破碎；
- 纵破碎分为前纵破碎和后纵破碎；
- 开裂分为前纵开裂，后纵开裂，前环开裂，后环开裂，中环开裂和中纵开裂。

以上所说的“前”、“中”和“后”均是相对开裂或破碎的管片而言的。“前”和“后”是以盾构机的前进方向为准的，管片靠近盾构机刀盘的一端即为管片的“前”端，则相对的另一端即为“后”端；“中”是指管片中部。而“纵”和“环”是相对于隧道而言的。“纵”是指沿着隧道轴线的方向；“环”是指沿着管片环向的方向。目前还没有在隧道中发现开裂贯穿管片的前后，故在此不做命名。图 3 和图 4 是隧道盾构中钢筋混凝土管片开裂或破碎的形式（一种或几种的组合）：

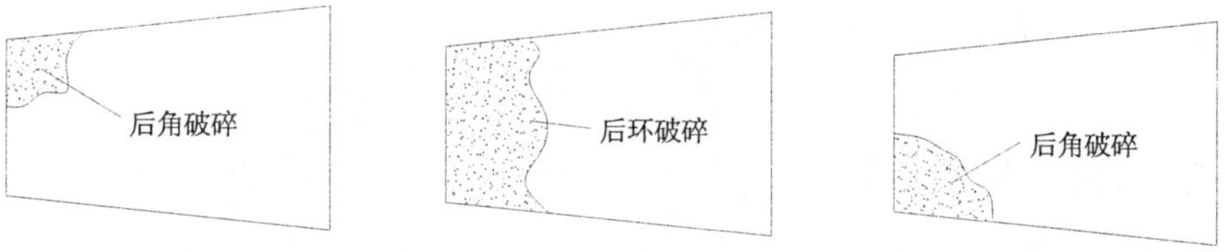

图 3 封顶块破碎示意图

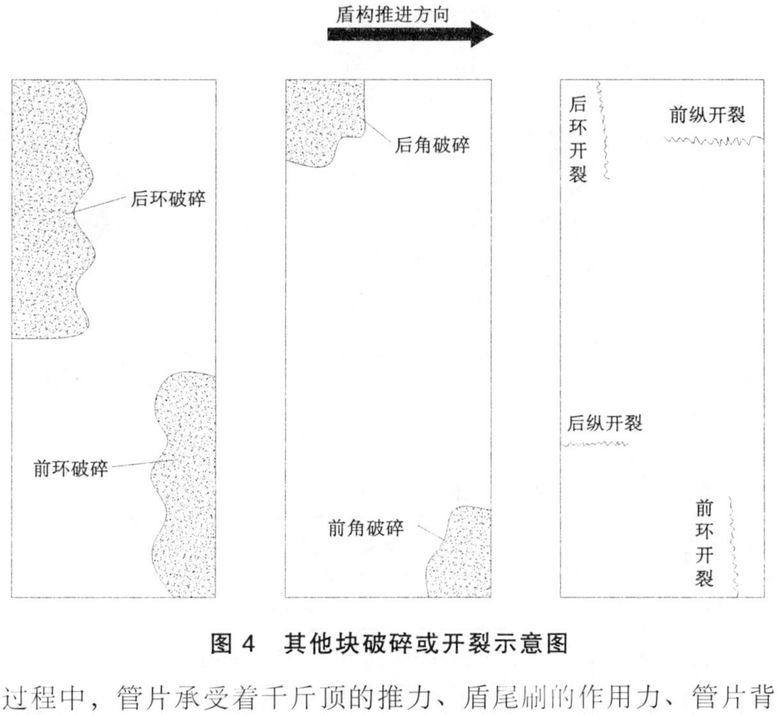

图 4 其他块破碎或开裂示意图

在盾构掘进施工过程中，管片承受着千斤顶的推力、盾尾刷的作用力、管片背部的浆液压力、管片之间的相互挤压作用力以及管片和连接螺栓之间的挤压力等。混凝土管片开裂或破碎，究其根本原因，无外乎是钢筋混凝土管片所受应力过大，超出钢筋混凝土管片本身的抵抗能力。它表现为：① 管片符合设计强度但外荷载过大或实际工作状态处于设计的不利情况；② 管片制作不合格。

在施工过程中，应力过大会因不同的地质情况和不同的盾构机施工参数而以不同的形式表现出来。

通过现场施工跟踪，我们发现钢筋混凝土管片开裂或破碎可能是由以下原因造成：

（1）管片的构造设计不合理，包括接头位置、钢筋布置和配置不合理等；

（2）钢筋混凝土管片在预制阶段把关不严或工艺不合理导致管片的密实度与强度未达到设计要求；

（3）管片运输阶段的擦碰造成管片破损；

（4）管片环面受千斤顶纵向局部压载或偏心压载。拼装机拼装过程中，千斤顶与管片轴线有一定交角出现局部压载或偏心压载导致管片开裂[2]；

（5）钢筋混凝土管片壁后的注浆压力的分布不均匀导致拼装好的管片局部应力集中以致真圆度下降造成管片开裂；

（6）盾构推进过程中千斤顶总推力过大是致使管片开裂或破碎的最直接原因。当总推力过大造成应力集中时，对于养护不好的管片可能开裂；

（7）盾构壳体横向挤压管片环。盾构机的轴线与管片环的轴线夹角较大时，盾尾壳体挤压位于盾尾的管片导致管片开裂；

（8）管片环面不平整造成纵向挤压应力集中。造成管片环面不平整主要有：管片制作精度误差管片纠偏时贴片不平整，盾构机推进时各区的千斤顶推力大小不等，管片之间的环缝压缩量不一致等原因。因管片环面不平整，盾构机千斤顶作用于管片上将产生较大的劈裂力矩造成管片开裂[3]；

（9）盾构隧道的纵向不均匀沉降导致隧道横向内应力集中造成管片开裂[4]；

（10）隧道使用过程中的管片老化以致破损。

3 管片破碎与开裂的评定标准

目前，规范中对出场管片的规定较为明了，而对施工过程中的管片破损情况的规定较少，有的仅仅只做定性说明，更多的则是对隧道圆环平面位置、环直径椭圆度、圆环高程以及错台等情况进行规定，这就导致现行的管片破损评定与修复比较混乱，无法可依，不利于管片破损修复技术的发展。

盾构隧道衬砌管片破损的原因较为复杂，难以对管片破损进行严谨定量分类，这给施工人员准确判断管片破损程度和性质变化情况提出了很高的要求。很大一部分情况下，施工人员在未了解施工破损情况的下即对不同的管片破损情况采用相同的施工修复方案，与科学施工的要求严重不符。图 5 是某区间盾构隧道内管片破损现场调查情况图。

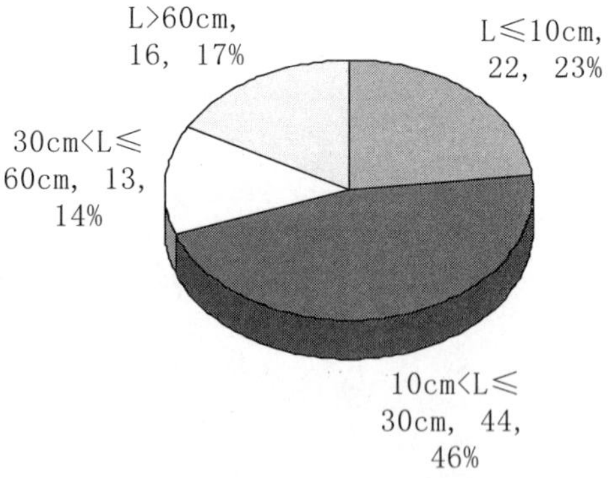

图 5 某区间盾构隧道内管片破损现场调查情况图

基于以上情况，本文建议将钢筋混凝土管片受损程度进行分类[5]。

表 1 管片受损程度分类表[5]

等级	破损名称	开裂长度（h,l）	破碎面积（s）
一级	轻微损伤	h≤0.1 H；l≤0.1 L	s≤10% S
二级	中度损伤	0.1 H<h≤0.5 H; 0.1 L<l≤0.5 L	10% S≤s≤20% S
三级	重度损伤	0.5 H<h≤0.7 H; 0.5 L<l≤0.7 L	20%S≤s≤40% S
四级	危险损伤	0.7 H<h≤H; 0.7 L<l≤L	40% S≤s≤60% S

表 1 中每个等级的 3 个表达式中任意一个符合即属于此种等级，以管片破损测量最大值为标准定等级。其中 h：开裂的深度；H：管片的厚度；l：开裂的长度；L：内环弧长； s：破碎面积；S：管片内表面面积。

4 管片修复[5, 6, 7]

4.1 管片修复原则

修复开裂或破碎的钢筋混凝土管片，总的修复是经济、强度、防水、防锈和美观。经济就是要求修复开裂或破碎的管片的费用要大大低于重建费用；强度就是要求新旧混凝土黏结要牢固，修复所用材料的强度要高于管片强度，修复位置修复后强度不低于管片强度；防水就是要求修复后的管片一定要能达到盾构隧道的防水要求，修复后不能有管片渗漏水的现象；防锈就是要求修复前和修复中做好钢筋混凝土管片内衬钢筋的防锈措施，以免后期由于钢筋的锈蚀而导致混凝土开裂；美观就是要求修复的管片表面平整，没有突出物，且拼装缝要相互连通。

4.2 修复步骤

钢筋混凝土管片的修复工作要在已拼装好的条件下进行，它比正常拼装一环管片要复杂的多、困难的多，因此对于管片修复要有一个周密的人员安排和施工计划。一般来讲，管片修复的工作程序可分为管片修复前的评定等级、管片修复方案的确定、管片修复施工、管片修复验收四个步骤。

（1）管片修复前的等级评定：

修复前的等级评定是对开裂或破碎管片进行修复工作的基础。它包括：资料的收集、现场检测和测量、开裂或破碎定级等工作内容。在鉴定工作中必须尽可能多的收集调查、实测资料，以便对管片现状作出较客观的评价。

（2）管片修复方案的确定：

对开裂或破碎管片进行修复，其修复方案的选择，将直接影响到修复工程的质量和经济性。在选择修复方案时首先应对照评定等级，再认真听取设计单位和施工单位的意见，选择修复最可靠，对使用功能影响最小，施工最方便，加固费用最省、所需时间最短的加固方案（特别是大面积的管片开裂或破碎的情况则更要注意），并且要考虑管片修复不能和正常施工冲突。而后根据以上原则进行结构计算，选择修复材料，绘制修复施工图，安排修复人员。

（3）管片修复施工：

管片修复很多时候都是在不停工的情况下进行的，因此修复施工是一项专业性很强的技术。修复施工时，必须充分考虑到其复杂性和特殊性，认真做好施工组织设计，选择具有专业经验和信誉良好的施工队，严格按图施工，确保工程质量，全面实现设计者的意图，满足使用功能。

（4）管片修复验收：

管片修复完工之后，应由主管部门组织专业技术人员进行验收。为了保证修复效果，对一些重要部位，还需采取检测对修复效果进行检验。

4.3 不同破损等级的对应修复方案

对于开裂或破碎的钢筋混凝土管片的修复的总的方法是：将严重损伤的混凝土铲除掉，修补孔洞和缺损，采用等强原则对管片进行加固，保证管片原有承载力。修复前，应尽量使管片卸荷，使加固获得更好的效果。建议按管片受损等级进行修复。

一级：轻度损伤

因管片受损较轻，开裂或破碎都较小。① 修复裂缝可以采用压力灌浆法。首先用高压水将裂缝内粉灰冲洗掉；然后将环氧树脂、聚酯树脂及丙烯酸树脂等其他黏结类材料在一定压力下注入到裂缝内部；

对宽度较细、深度较浅的裂缝，可用低压注入方式；对宽度较宽、深度很深的裂缝，可用高压注入方式；然后进行表面粉刷装修即可。② 修复破碎，则要首先清除掉破碎的块，然后用高压水冲洗破碎面，而后在破碎面涂抹混凝土强力修补胶以增加新旧混凝土之间的黏结力，使新旧混凝土结合更密实，最后用等强素混凝土进行修复并加强养护。

二级：中度损伤

此级裂缝较宽较深，破碎面积较大，管片内衬钢筋部分露出，管片损伤较为严重，修复处理要涉及到钢筋防锈的问题，因此修复方案要更为严谨。① 对于开裂，由于裂缝较宽较深，需要将裂缝处混凝土凿开（主要是将裂缝处松动的混凝土凿掉），然后高压水流将裂缝里面的粉灰冲洗掉，待干燥后对钢筋进行防锈处理（即在钢筋上涂抹氨基甲酸乙酯树脂用以防锈），而后在裂缝内填充密封材料，最后向裂缝内压入无收缩或膨胀水泥砂浆，并做好养护工作。② 修复破碎部分，首先清除掉松散的混凝土，并用高压水流冲洗破碎面，将破碎面存留的混凝土碎块和粉灰清理干净，待破碎面干燥后对钢筋进行防锈处理，然后在旧混凝土破碎面上混凝土修补胶以增加新旧混凝土之间的黏结力，最后使用碳纤维配套树脂将碳纤维布作为补强材料粘贴在混凝土结构表面，共同受力以提高管片的承载力，并做好后期养护工作。

三级：重度损伤

此级开裂很深很宽，破碎面积较大，处理要特别对待。此级钢筋混凝土一旦发生损伤就要对管片卸荷，且立刻采用早强混凝土水泥砂浆管片破碎进行封闭（至于开裂，则要用硫酸盐超早强水泥浆压入裂缝），待情况稳定后，再做处理。

四级：危险损伤

此级损伤非常严重，管片已破坏，丧失承载能力，建议进行更换。更换时为防止壁后土体的坍方，建议采用冻结法首先对壁后土层进行冻结，待冻结强度达到要求后方可拆除损坏的管片，然后更换新管片，最后在拼装缝中注入环氧树脂凝胶，封闭拼装缝以防地下水通过拼装缝渗漏到隧道中。

4.4 修复效果检验与验收

由于盾构隧道衬砌管片的个体相对较小，若采用对修复好的部分进行直接取芯检测，会抵消修复的效果，所以盾构隧道衬砌管片修复效果检验宜采用无损检测技术。综合各种检测技术，建议超声波法结合回弹法来监控和检验[8]修复情况。检验合格，方能通过验收，并记入电子档案已备案。

4.5 建立修复电子档案

为了便于后期排查和推动管片破损修复技术的发展，建议对管片的破损程度、管片的修复方案、管片的修复效果情况建立电子综合档案。

5 结　语

本文初步分析了盾构隧道管片在施工过程中的破损原因，并对破损的不同情况进行归类。在此基础上根据现场调查进一步制定了盾构隧道管片破损等级和破损等级评定方法，由此针对不同破损等级制定不同管片修复方案。最后提出管片破损修复效果检验方法和建立修复电子档案的管片破损管理方法。希望本文对推动盾构隧道衬砌管片破损修复的施工技术的发展有所帮助。

参考文献（References）：

[1] 袁广林，袁迎曙，吴庆安. 钢筋混凝土结构的加固与修复[J]. 混凝土与水泥制品，1997(4).

[2] 廖少明，闫治国，宋博. 钢纤维管片接头局部应力的数值模拟试验. 岩土工程学报，2006，28：5.

[3] 竺维彬，鞠世健. 盾构隧道管片开裂的原因及相应对策[J]. 现代隧道技术，2003.

[4] 廖少明，白廷辉，彭芳乐. 盾构隧道纵向沉降模式及其结构响应. 地下空间与工程学报，2006，2.

[5] 张耀宇．钢筋混凝土结构火灾受损鉴定与修复．消防技术与产品信息，2007(9).
[6] 孟建国，于翠云．混凝土结构裂缝的成因、危害性评估及其修复方法．铁道建筑技术，2006(增).
[7] 中华人民共和国国家标准．盾构法隧道施工与验收规范．GB 50446—2008.
[8] 肖云风，周先雁．钢管混凝土无损检测技术研究．无损探伤，2008，32：5.

作者简介（Bio-data）：

梁艳文，男，1980/09，2005 年毕业于石家庄铁道学院，获得学士学位。现为同济大学土木工程学院地下建筑与工程系隧道及地下建筑工程专业硕士研究生。

Yanwen LIANG（1980—）, Male, graduated from Institute of Givil Engineeting, Shijiazhuang Railway Institute in 2005 and obtained a bachelor's degree in the same time. Now he is studying in Tongji University for Master degree ,majored in Geotechnical Engineering.

E-mail: tomliang870@163.com

水下盾构隧道施工及运营阶段抗浮计算方法探讨

郭德平 何川 周济民 耿萍
西南交通大学 地下工程系，四川 成都 610031

【摘 要】 水下盾构在浅覆土和大断面情况下抗浮问题日益凸显，但现行规范未对抗浮设计做出明确的规定。本文从工法特点、地层渗透性和应力重分布等方面分析和探讨了盾构隧道产生上浮的机理，并根据隧道建设和运营中可能遇到的上浮情况将抗浮计算分为施工和运营两个阶段。用荷载分项系数、安全系数和浮力折减系数来分别考虑各种抗浮效应、安全储备以及围岩的透水性。对不同的抗浮效应组合推导出了相应的最小覆土厚度计算式。

【关键词】 盾构隧道；水下隧道；抗浮设计；分项系数；施工与运营

DISCUSSION ON ANTI-UPWARD MOVING CALCULATION METHOD OF SUBMARINE SHIELD TUNNEL DURING THE CONSTRUCTION AND SERVICE STAGES

Deping GUO，Chuan HE，Jimin ZHOU，Ping GENG
Department of Underground Engineering, Southwest Jiaotong University, Chengdu 610031, Sichuan, China

Abstract: It's very important for a shallow covering or a large scale across-section underwater shield tunnel to anti-upward move，but the standing criterion does not make clear how to deal with the design problem. Based on construction method's characteristics, stratum's permeability and stress redistribution etc, the paper analyzes the upward moving mechanism of the shield tunnel and discusses the calculation methods. According to situations that maybe encounter during the tunnel's construction and service stages, anti-floating calculation has been subdivided into the construction stage and service stage. Partial Coefficients for Loads, the safety factor and buoyancy reduction factor are been introduced to respectively consider the variety of anti-upward effects, the safety reserves and the stratum's permeability. For different combinations of anti-floating effect, formula of the minimum cover thickness is been derived.

Key words: shield tunnel; submarine tunnel; anti-upward design; partial coefficients; construction and operation

1 引 言

世界发达国家自 20 世纪 30 年代起，就开始修建海峡海底隧道，由于盾构技术的不断进步和盾构法施工所具有地面影响小、机械化程度高、安全、劳动强度低、进度快等优点，在修建水下隧道时盾构工法越来越多的被采用。但在施工中，隧道管片经常会出现局部或整体上浮，表现为管片错台、裂缝、破损，乃至轴线偏位等现象[1]，尤其是对于大断面或浅覆土水下隧道，上浮问题显得尤为突出，因此必须进行抗浮计算（或验算）。

2 水下盾构隧道上浮机理

根据盾构工法开挖的特点可知：开挖直径 D>盾壳外径 D_0>管片外径 d，由此在管片与土体间形成了建筑间隙$\Delta=D-d$，正是此间隙的存在，为同步注浆浆液、泥浆或者水进入提供了可能性，对于不同的地质情况将产生不同的力学行为过程。

基金项目：国家自然科学基金（50778154）；863 计划（2006AA11Z116）

对于软弱地层来讲，围岩在自重和水平侧压力作用下将填充建筑间隙，表现为施工对地层的扰动。由于地层受到扰动加剧了浆液（或水）向管片周围渗透，当包裹衬砌环的浆液产生的浮力大于抗浮作用时就会产生上浮现象。衬砌环的上浮对地层产生挤压效应使地层发生位移甚至隆起，地层应力发生重分布。随着地层应力的释放和调整最终衬砌环和地层达到平衡状态。

对于围岩稳定性较好的地层来讲，由于地层基床系数较大，受力变形较小，建筑间隙能保持一定时间，衬砌环脱离盾尾后马上受到浆液（或水）的包裹，这种情况下的浮力相对于软弱地层情况而言会更快的作用到衬砌环上，衬砌环也会对上覆土产生挤压效应，影响地层的应力分布并最终趋于稳定，不同之处在于地层挤压位移较小，衬砌环更快的处于受力平衡状态。

从上述分析可知水下盾构隧道的上浮受工法特征、浆液性质、地层渗透性、地层应力重分布等因素的影响。根据盾构隧道所处的不同时期，将抗浮计算分为：施工阶段和运营阶段。

3 水下盾构隧道抗浮要求

3.1 上覆土最小厚度

由于地下结构抗浮设计是一个比较复杂的问题，对其中的一些问题存在不同认识。目前《地铁设计规范》（GB 50157—2003）只要求进行抗浮验算，并未对抗浮设计及计算做出明确的规定。参考《地铁设计规范》（GB 50157—2003）和《建筑结构荷载规范》（GB 50009—2001），建议隧道抗浮计算采用极限状态法设计，其表达式为[2]：

$$\gamma_F \lambda S \leqslant \gamma_G R \tag{1}$$

式中 R——综合抗浮效应组合，如上覆土重力、管片自重、隧道内部静荷载、土的抗剪强度、管片环间摩擦力、螺栓的抗剪强度；

S——综合浮力效应组合，如水、注浆浆液、泥浆、注浆压力所产生的浮力；

γ_G——荷载分项系数，荷载效应对结构抗浮有利时取 0.9；

γ_F——抗浮安全系数，目前尚无统一规定，宜参照类似工程，根据各地的实践经验确定，也可以参照城市地铁采用的安全系数，见表 1。

λ——浮力折减系数。置于渗透系数较小的粘性土地层中的隧道，可结合当地工程经验，对浮力作适当折减；置于砂性土地层中的隧道，折减系数取 1，按全水头确定作用在结构上的浮力。

表 1 城市地铁采用的抗浮安全系数

城市地铁	不计侧壁摩擦阻力时	计侧壁摩擦阻力时
上海	1.05	1.10
广州、南京、深圳、北京	1.05	1.15

3.2 管片环结构受力要求

管片的结构设计多采用荷载-结构模式，常用的结构计算模型有：（修正）惯用法、多铰圆环模型、梁-弹簧模型，上述模型的共性为：外荷载由围岩产生 ，计算示意简图如图 1。当考虑浆液浮力或同步注浆压力所产生的浮力时，管片环除受到围岩所产生的荷载以外，还受到非均布压力作用，如图 2 所示。对结构的安全性需用承载能力极限状态法进行验算，表达式为：

$$\gamma_0 S \leqslant R \tag{2}$$

式中 γ_0——结构重要性系数，建议取 1.1；

S——内力组合设计值，代表轴力设计值、弯矩设计值、剪力设计值；

R——结构构件承载力设计值，代表截面对于轴力、弯矩、剪力的抵抗能力[3]。

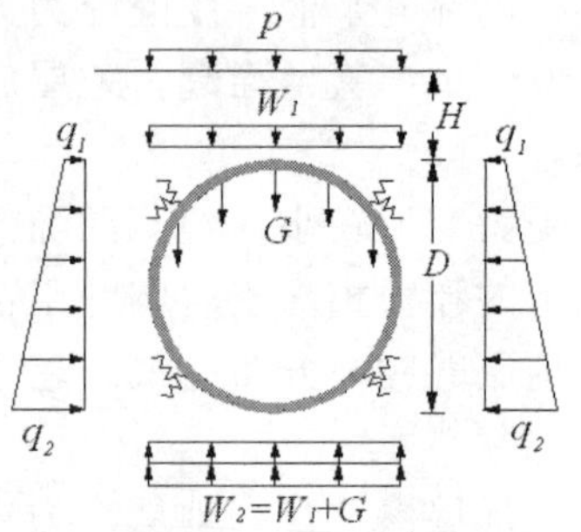

图 1 荷载结构模型示意图

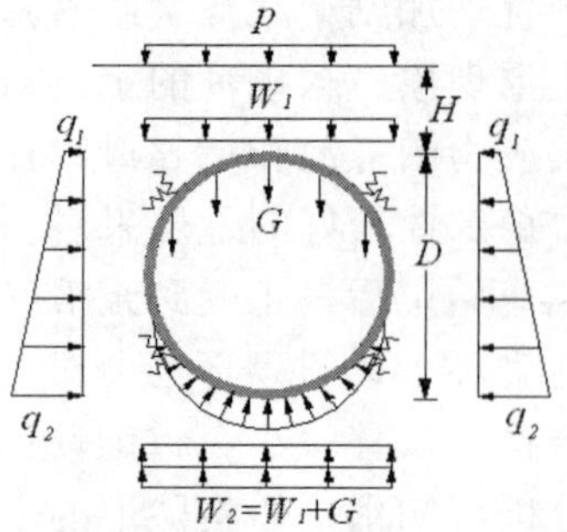

图 2 考虑浮力作用的荷载结构模型示意图

4 水下盾构隧道施工阶段抗浮计算

施工阶段浮力的计算方法根据产生浮力原理的不同可以分为：注浆压力产生的浮力和管片排开未凝固注浆浆液或泥浆所产生的浮力。

4.1 注浆压力产生的浮力

对于不同的围岩状况，建筑间隙是不同的。在土质较好的硬质土中，管片脱离盾尾后，其建筑间隙可能在一定时间内完整存在，此时注浆浆液能全部包裹整环管片，注浆压力分布形式可以假设为如图 3 所示的整环均匀分布形式或图 4 所示整环非均匀分布形式。

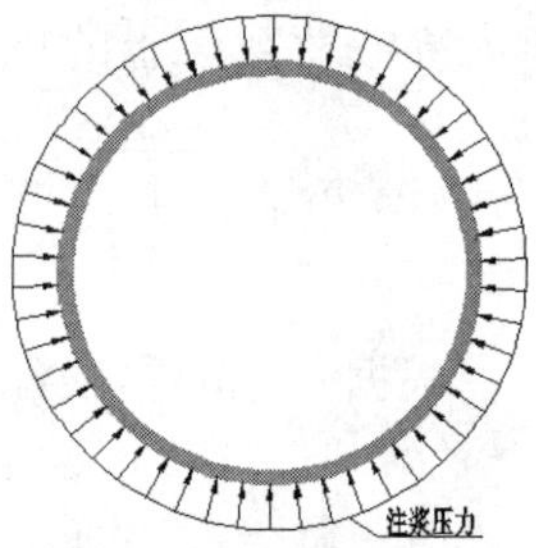

图 3 整环均匀分布

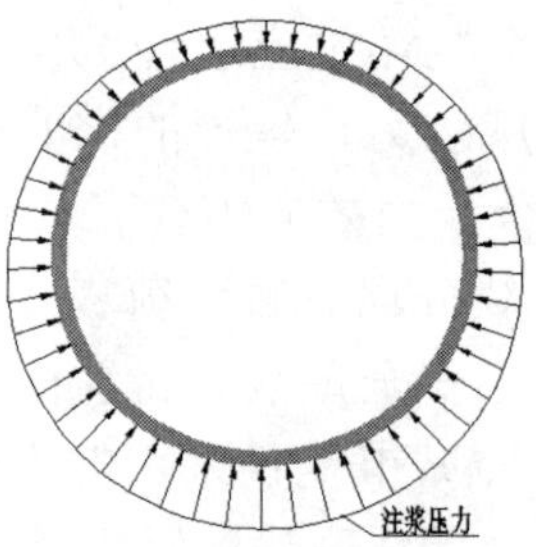

图 4 整环非均匀分布

对于土质一般的情况，上部和两侧土体在重力作用下会向管环靠拢，建筑间隙被填充。若把盾构隧道在纵向上看成是一两端固定的梁，在浮力作用下纵向上发生向上的挠曲，则会在管片环下侧形成新的空隙，如图 5 所示。此时的注浆压力分布形式为扇形，如图 6 所示。

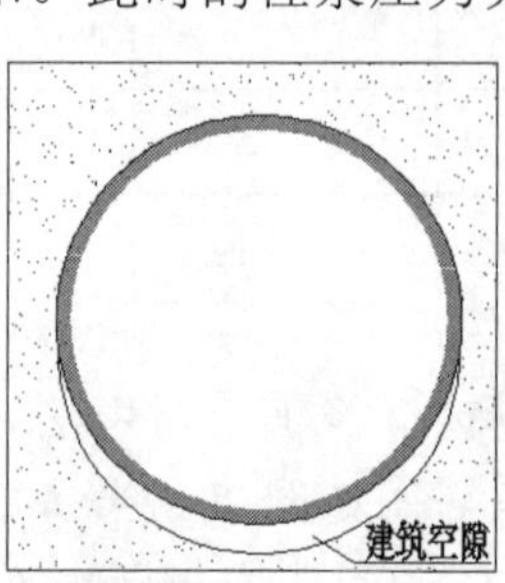

图 5 建筑空隙示意图

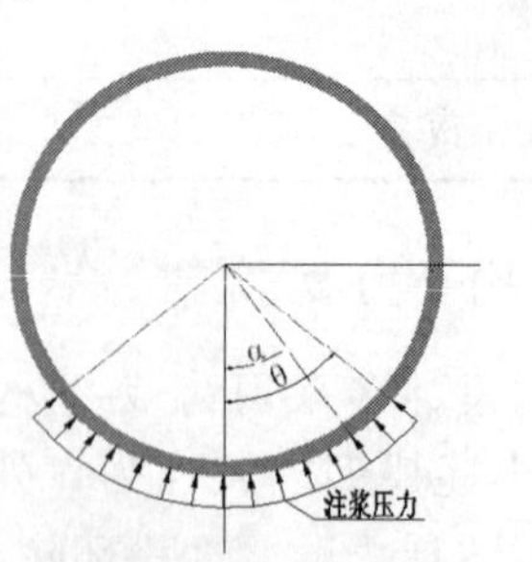

图 6 注浆压力扇形分布示意图

对比分析上述注浆压力分布形式可知：当注浆压力按扇形分布时形成的向上合力较大，如果施工阶段注浆压力所形成的浮力取此较大值为“上浮力”进行抗浮计算，计算结果相对于其他注浆压力分布形式会偏于安全。

扇形注浆压力形成的向上合力计算式为：

$$F_{浮1} = \int_{-\theta}^{\theta} PR\cos\alpha \mathrm{d}\alpha = 2PR\sin\theta \qquad (0<\theta<\pi/2) \tag{3}$$

式中 P——施工中所用注浆压力；

θ——注浆浆液分布区域边界与竖向的夹角[4]。

4.2 排开浆液产生的浮力

假设刚脱离盾尾的管片环(一环或数环)被注浆浆液（或者是泥浆）全部包裹住，根据阿基米德原理可知浮力的大小等于排开液体重力，计算式如下：

$$F_{浮2} = \pi R^2 \gamma_j \tag{4}$$

这是一种较为理想的情况，只有在土质较好的硬质土中可能会出现。因为在一般情况下，管片脱离盾尾后，在上覆土自重以及侧压力作用下，管片周围的全部或部分土体会马上向管片靠拢，根本形不成完整的浆液环[4]。

4.3 施工阶段最小覆土厚度

上覆土重力、管片自重、隧道内部静载、管片环间摩擦力和由于土体被上浮隧道挤压而发挥出的土体抗剪强度以及管片环间由于有相对运动趋势或相对运动而发挥出的纵向螺栓抗剪强度均可在结构的受力中起到抗浮作用。由于隧道内部的静载相对较小，将其作为安全储备在计算中不予考虑；盾构隧道不论是在建设中还是在运营中，管片错台都会对隧道防水产生重大危害，在运营期也会影响轨（路）面的平顺性，所以在抗浮计算中不应利用纵向螺栓的抗剪强度。鉴于上述分析，根据抗浮效应组合的不同，施工阶段的抗浮计算分为以下四类。以注浆压力产生的浮力 $F_{浮1}$ 为例进行计算，要计算 $F_{浮2}$ 对应的施工阶段最小覆土厚度时只需将浮力做相应替换即可。

（1）不考虑管片环间的摩擦力及上覆土的剪切强度。

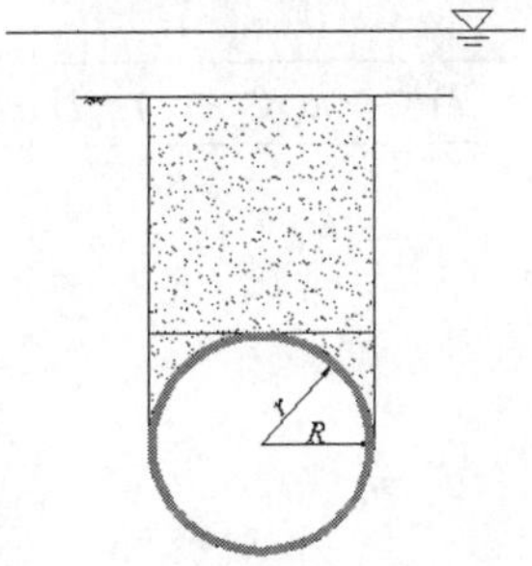

图 7 上覆土重力计算简图

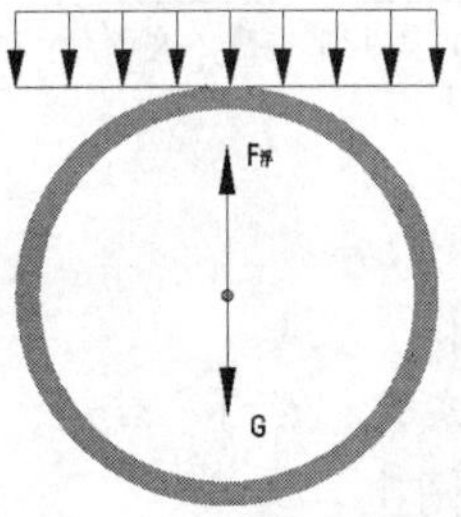

图 8 管片受力示意图

单位长度管片自重 G 为：

$$G = \pi(R^2 - r^2)\gamma_c \tag{5}$$

单位长度管片上部土体有效重量为：

$$W = \gamma'\left[2Rd - \left(2 - \frac{\pi}{2}\right)R^2\right] \tag{6}$$

由力的平衡可知，管片稳定的条件为：

$$\gamma_G(W+G) \geqslant \gamma_F \lambda \cdot 2PR\sin\theta \tag{7}$$

此时满足抗浮要求的上覆土最小厚度计算公式如下：

$$d \geqslant \frac{\gamma_F \lambda \cdot 2PR\sin\theta - \gamma_G\left[\gamma'(2-\pi/2)R^2 - \pi(R^2 - r^2)\gamma_c\right]}{2\gamma_G \gamma' R} \tag{8}$$

式中 R 为管片外径；r 为管片内径；γ_c 为管片重度；γ_w 为水的重度；γ' 为土的浮重度。其余符号意义同前。

（2）考虑上覆土的剪切强度。

若盾构隧道产生上浮，上覆土因被挤压产生剪切变形或破坏，假设劈裂面为垂直直线，根据摩尔-库仑强度理论可知在破裂面上会存在剪应力，其分布形式和大小如图 9、图 10 所示。

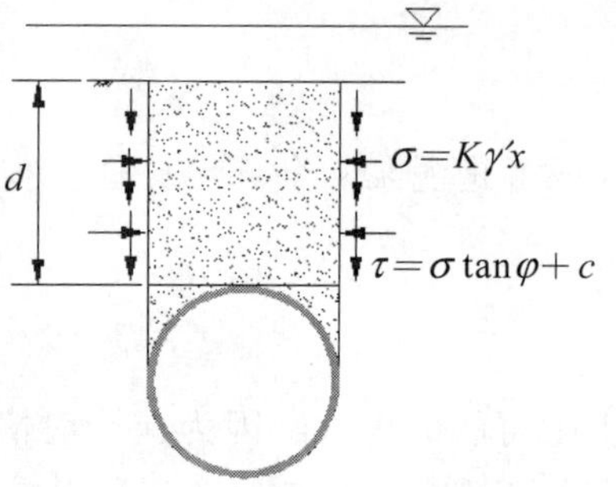

图 9　剪应力分布形式示意图

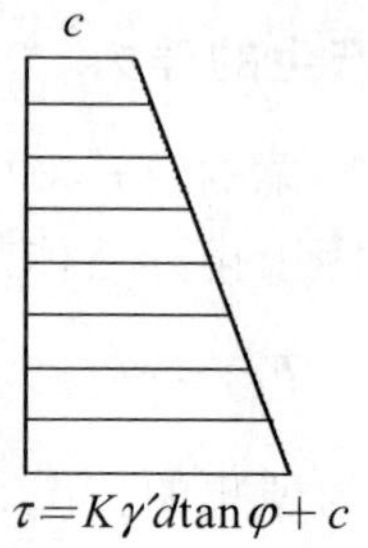

图 10　剪应力大小示意图

由力的平衡可知：

$$\gamma_G(W+G+F_\tau)\geqslant \gamma_F\lambda\cdot 2PR\sin\theta \tag{9}$$

其中 F_Z 为剪应力的合力：

$$F_\tau=(c+K\gamma' d\tan\varphi+c)d/2 \tag{10}$$

将式（2）、（4）、（5）、（9）代入式（8），有如下不等式：

$$\left(\frac{1}{2}\gamma_G K\gamma'\tan\varphi\right)d^2+\gamma_G(2\gamma' R+c)d-2\gamma_F\lambda PR\sin\theta-\gamma_G\left[\gamma'\left(2-\frac{\pi}{2}\right)R^2-\pi(R^2-r^2)\gamma_c\right]\geqslant 0 \tag{11}$$

解不等式，得此时满足抗浮要求的上覆土最小厚度为下：

$$d\geqslant\frac{\sqrt{\gamma_G^2(2\gamma' R+c)^2+2\gamma_G K\gamma'\tan\varphi\{\gamma_F\lambda\cdot 2PR\sin\theta+\gamma_G[\gamma'(2-\pi/2)R^2-\pi(R^2-r^2)\gamma_c]\}}-\gamma_G(2\gamma' R+c)}{\gamma_G K\gamma'\tan\varphi} \tag{12}$$

式中 c ——土的粘聚力；

φ ——内摩擦角；

K ——侧压力系数，$K=1-\sin\varphi$；

其余符号意义同上。

（3）考虑管片环间的摩擦力。

管环脱离盾尾后，会受到浮力作用，当其中一环或者相邻几环相对于其他环有向上的浮动趋势或者发生了相对运动，那么将会在环间产生摩擦力，此摩擦力的大小决定于纵向连接螺栓的预紧力和接触面的状况。参考叶飞等人在参考文献[4]中提出的计算式，并对其进行改进后，得到此时满足抗浮要求的上覆土最小厚度计算公式如下：

$$d\geqslant\frac{\gamma_F\lambda\cdot 2PR\sin\theta-\gamma_G\left[\gamma'(2-\pi/2)R^2-\pi(R^2-r^2)\gamma_c-2\sum_{i=1}^{n}N_i\mu/B\right]}{2\gamma_G\gamma' R} \tag{13}$$

式中 n ——管片环间纵向螺栓的数量；

N_i ——每个环间纵向螺栓施加的紧固力；

μ ——管片环间的摩擦系数；

B ——管片环宽度；

其余符号意义同上。

④ 同时考虑管片环间的摩擦力及上覆土的剪切强度。

$$d \geqslant \frac{\sqrt{\gamma_G^2(2\gamma' R+c)^2+2\gamma_G K\gamma'\tan\varphi\left\{\gamma_F\lambda\cdot 2PR\sin\theta+\gamma_G\left[\gamma'(2-\pi/2)R^2-\pi(R^2-r^2)\gamma_c-2\sum_{i=1}^{n}N_i\mu/B\right]\right\}}-\gamma_G(2\gamma' R+c)}{\gamma_G K\gamma'\tan\varphi} \tag{14}$$

式中各符号意义同前。

对比分析上述四类抗浮计算方法可知：第一类计算方法只考虑盾构隧道上覆土的重力，计算所得的最小覆土厚度最大，结果偏于安全；第四类计算方法较全面的考虑了起抗浮作用的因素，计算所得最小覆土厚度最小，结果偏于经济；第二和第三类计算方法介于两者之间。

5 水下盾构隧道运营阶段抗浮计算

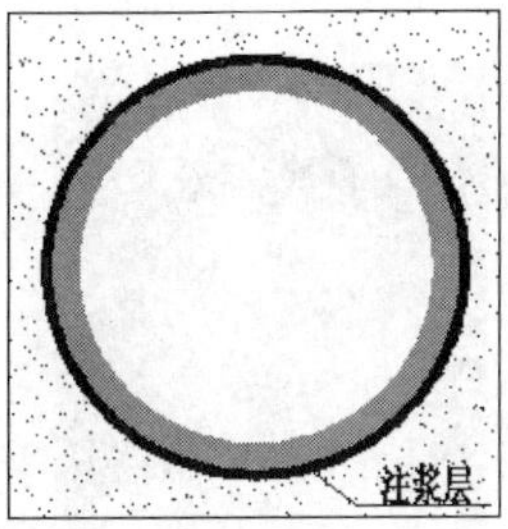

图 11 注浆层示意图

在运营阶段考虑大自然的营造力，为避免建成后的隧道由于长年的河床冲刷和水流的下切作用使覆土减薄而引起隧道上浮，产生路（轨）面变形，管片错台，衬砌开裂，漏水等病害，进行运营阶段的抗浮计算也是必要的。由于最终形成的同步注浆层形状受地层和施工等因素影响很大，带有一定随机性。偏于安全考虑，将注浆层考虑为厚$\varDelta$（$\varDelta=D-d$）的一层均匀外壳，注浆层如图 11 所示。此阶段浮力大小为考虑注浆层后所排开水受到的重力。

则运营阶段的浮力可由下式求得：

$$F_{浮3}=\pi(R+\varDelta/2)^2\gamma_w \tag{15}$$

当不考虑管片环间的摩擦力及上覆土的剪切强度时，运营阶段满足抗浮要求的上覆土最小厚度计算式为：

$$d \geqslant \frac{\gamma_F\lambda\cdot\pi(R+\varDelta/2)^2\gamma_w-\gamma_G\left[\gamma'(2-\pi/2)R^2-\pi(R^2-r^2)\gamma_c\right]}{2\gamma_G\gamma' R} \tag{16}$$

6 结论和建议

（1）水下盾构隧道需进行抗浮设计（或验算），尤其是对于浅覆土地段。水下盾构隧道的上浮受工法特性、浆液性质、地层渗透性、地层应力重分布等因素的影响。对于不同的地层状况，上浮响应会出现不同的现象。

（2）建议采用以概率论为基础的分项系数法来考虑上覆土重力、管片自重、隧道内部静荷载、土的抗剪强度、管片环间摩擦力等抗浮效应，用浮力折减系数来考虑不同地层的渗透性差异。

（3）对于不同的地层性质注浆压力的分布形式会有很大差异，在施工阶段计算注浆压力产生的浮力时，建议采用注浆压力为扇形分布的形式，这样是偏于安全的。

（4）上覆土重力、管片自重、隧道内部静载、土的抗剪强度、管片环间摩擦力、螺栓的抗剪强度在结构的受力中均可以起到抗浮作用，因隧道内部的静载值相对较小，建议将其作为安全储备在抗浮计算中不予考虑。鉴于防水和避免错台的发生，在抗浮计算中本文认为不应利用螺栓的抗剪强度来抵抗浮力。

（5）只考虑盾构隧道上覆土的重力和管片自重，计算所得的最小覆土厚度最大，结果偏于安全；考虑上覆土的重力、管片自重、管片环间的摩擦力及上覆土的剪切强度，计算所得最小覆土厚度最小，结果偏于经济；其余两种计算方法介于两者之间。

（6）由于河床冲刷、水流的下切作用等自然营造力使上覆土减薄而有可能引起隧道上浮，因此隧道运营阶段的抗浮计算也应予以关注。此时抗浮计算在隧道外径的基础上还应考虑注浆层厚度。

参考文献（References）：

[1] 王选祥.构隧道管片上浮机理及控制技术[J]. 铁道建筑，2009，5：52-55.

[2] 宋超业，周书名，谭志文. 水下盾构隧道合理覆盖层厚度的探讨[J]. 现代隧道技术,2008 增刊：47-51.

[3] 中华人民共和国建设部. GB 50009—2001 建筑结构荷载规范[S]. 中国建筑工业出版社，2001.

[4] 叶飞,朱合华,丁文其等. 施工期盾构隧道上浮机理与控制对策分析[J]. 同济大学学报(自然科学版)，2008，36(6)：738-743.

[5] 中华人民共和国建设部. GB 50157—2003 地铁设计规范[S]. 北京中国计划出版社，2003.

作者简介（Bio-data）：

郭德平，男，1983 年 9 月出生，2008 年毕业于西南交通大学，获得学士学位，现就读于西南交通大学，攻读博士学位。主要研究方向为隧道与地下工程。

Deping GUO (1983—), male, graduated from School of Civil Engineering, Southwest Jiaotong University in 2008 and obtained a bachelor's degree in the same time. Now he is studying for the Ph.D.degree in Southwest Jiaotong University. He specializes in highway and subway tunnel engineering.

E-mail: guodeping99@gmail.com

日本におけるシールドトンネルの設計法の変遷と性能規定の提言

木村　定雄[1]　山本　努[2]

[1]金沢工業大学地域防災環境科学研究所，石川県白山市　924-0838

[2]東京地下鉄株式会社　工務部，東京都上野　110-8614

本論文は，日本における過去のシールドトンネル構造物の設計法の変遷を整理するとともに，トンネル構造物の性能規定を策定するための基本的指針を述べたものである．日本では1960年代の高度経済成長とともに社会資本が急速に整備された．この時代は一定の性能をもつ多くの構造物を建設する要請があり，構造物の設計法は許容応力度設計法がこれを担った．トンネルなどの地下構造物もこの例外ではなかった．現在では，この時代につくられたトンネル構造物がほぼ同時に老朽化してきており，新設の構造物や既存の構造物にかかわらず，その目的に応じた性能を適切に評価し，これを維持するための設計法を整備する必要がある．トンネル構造物の性能規定はそのために欠かすことのできない基準となるものでる．

キーワード：トンネル；設計法；性能規定；維持管理；アセットマネジメント

TRENDS OF MODERN DESIGN METHODS OF SHIELD TUNNELS IN JAPAN AND ADVANCE OF PERFORMANCE BASED DESIGN CODES

Sadao KIMURA[1]，Tsutomu YAMAMOTO[2]

[1]Department. of Civil and Environmental Engineering, Institute of Disaster and Environmental Science, Kanazawa University of Tech., Ishikawa Hakusan 924-0838, Japan

[2]Tokyo Metro Co., Ltd. Infrastructure Maintenance Dept., Tokyo 110-8614, Japan

Abstract: This paper presents recent trends of design methods and a basic scheme in order to decide performance based design codes for shield tunnels. In Japan, construction of the urban infrastructure was substantially advanced in the 60's, along with high economic growth. It was a request that a lot of structures constructed with a constant allowable performance, therefore the allowable stress design method was adopted as the design method of the structure in this age, and urban infrastructures (tunnels) are not the exception. To date, the urban tunnels which were constructed in this age have deteriorated almost simultaneously. Consequently, it is necessary to establish a design method in order to evaluate the required performance which accommodates to the objective of the urban tunnel whether new construction or existing. The performance based design codes of the urban tunnel become guideline for the establishment of the performance based design methods.

Key word: tunnel; design; performance based design; maintenance; asset-management

1　日本におけるシールドトンネル設計法の変遷

日本では，1960年代からの高度成長時代にあわせて，わが国の社会資本整備が急速に進展した．この時代では，まずは短期間で大量の公共施設構造物の建設を優先する必要があり，構造物の設計も単純化，簡便化，さらには規準化されて一般に適用されてきた．仕様規定や許容応力度設計法はこの時代を担った設計法と言える．その結果，ある程度の品質と性能をもつ構造物を大量に構築することが可能になった．しかし一方で，構造物の設計法は固定化され，構造物の利用形態や需要の変化，または多様化する構造物の機能に対応できる設計法の進展を妨げてきた向きがある．ここで，とくに都市部のトンネル工法であるシールド工法によって造られるトンネルの設計法に着目して，近年の動向を土木学会が制定した規準類の変遷からみてみる．

1964 年, シールドトンネルの設計法と施工法の規準として「シールド工法指針」から制定された. 1977 年,「シールド工法指針」は「トンネル標準示方書(シールド工法編)」に規準が格上げされた．その後，示方書は数度の改訂を経て，とくに経験的技術の進歩が顕著な施工技術がこれらの示方書に反映されてきた．一方，トンネル構造物の設計法には 1964 年から長きにわたり許容応力度設計法が採用されてきている．許容応力度設計法は，材料特性，部材特性，構造物特性，外力特性，などの構造計算上のすべての不確実性を材料強度の安全率で評価するものであり，設計実務の簡便化が図られ，大量のトンネル構造物の建設の時代においては，ある一定以上の性能を照査し確保する設計法として有益であった．

21 世紀に入って，2006 年に改訂された示方書では，限界状態設計法が採用され，その基本的な考え方が示された．限界状態設計法の採用は，長きにわたって適用されてきた許容応力度設計法からの大きな転換となった．

限界状態設計法は，トンネルの構造安定性能，耐久性能および耐震性能に対して限界状態を設け，それを照査する設計法である．しかし，トンネルの建設当初に成された設計行為が「みなし型設計」であり，対象となるトンネル構造物に作用する地圧の不確実性や供用過程において変化する環境作用等の設計上の取り扱い，ならびに個々のトンネル構造物の目的に応じて定まる各種要求性能に対する設計の考え方が，限界状態設計法では明確にすることができない．

2　構造物の目的に応じた使用性能を重視する設計の必要性

21 世紀をむかえた現在では，これまでに造られてきた構造物がほぼ同時期に集中して老朽化してきている．一方，人口推計をみると，わが国の人口は 21 世紀中に急激に減少することが予測されることから，将来の社会資本整備のあり方や整備に要する財源の減少などの課題がでてきている．したがって，今後の社会資本整備では，構造物を新設する技術とともに，既設の構造物を維持管理して長く供用する技術の重要性が指摘されている. すなわち, 社会資本となる構造物を構築する行為から, 個々の構造物の利用目的に応じて効率的に構造物を使う行為への転換が求められている．地下構造物も例外ではなく，今後の地下利用を考える上で，構造物の設計概念を転換する必要がある．

したがって，構造物の建設を前提とした構造安全性のみを重視した従来の設計法から構造物の目的に合致した機能を精査し，構造物の維持管理段階においても適用できる設計法(Life Cycle Design Methods [1])を整備する必要がある．

例えば，1999 年 6 月，山陽新幹線福岡トンネルの覆工コンクリートの一部がはく落し，新幹線を損傷させた [2]．このケースでは，トンネルの構造物としての構造安定性は問題ではなく，鉄道トンネルの目的に応じて定まる使用上の安全性や利便性を確保することが問題となったのである．一方，トンネル内に利用者が入らない電力や通信などのトンネルであれば，覆工コンクリートのはく落は，喫緊の問題とはならない．このように，トンネルに要求される性能はトンネルの利用目的に応じて個々に異なる．

さらに，地下構造物は地上構造物とは異なり，一度構築したらそれを安易に放棄することができない構造物である．すなわち，種々の理由により使用しない地下空間をそのままに放置すると将来にわたり地盤沈下や近接構造物基礎の変状等によって周辺環境に悪影響を及ぼすおそれがある．

このように，個々のトンネル構造物の上手な「ものづかい」を強く意識し，トンネル構造物の使用性を性能として位置づけ，計画，設計，施工，維持管理のすべての段階でそれを評価できる手法を吟味することが求められる．

このような既設構造物の維持管理にかかわる国際標準としてISO13822[3)]が発効されている．この規格では構造信頼性とリスクの概念を基にした既設構造物(建物，橋梁，他)の評価の基本的な考え方が，①予期される用途の変更や修復，設計供用寿命の延長，②管理者や保険会社などから要求される信頼性のチェック，③経過時間に依存する荷重・作用による劣化，④アクシデンタル・アクションによる損傷等に分けて示されている．しかしながら，構造物が有する本来の目的を反映した機能や使用性能の評価が言及されるには至っていない．

したがって，今後はトンネル構造物を造る時のみならず，その供用過程においても構造物の目的を前提とした各種要求性能の定義化とその照査方法を検討する必要がある．また，このようにして構築された性能規定と照査方法を基本としたトンネルのマネジメントシステムを早期に構築することが望まれる．

3　構造物設計法の国際標準化とわが国の包括設計コード

従来，わが国では，道路，河川，港湾，または建築等の設計基準はそれぞれの施設構造物がもつ歴史，文化，地域性ならびに経験的な伝統によって，構造物の種類に応じて個別に策定されてきた．一方，海外でも同様の個別設計がなされてきていたが，近年では，構造物の設計の基本と体系を示したISO2394[4)]や前述した既存構造物の性能評価を示したISO13822[3)]が包括設計コードとして発効されている(図-1参照)．わが国でもこれを見習い，2002年に国土交通省から「土木・建築にかかる設計の基本」[5)]が発効された．

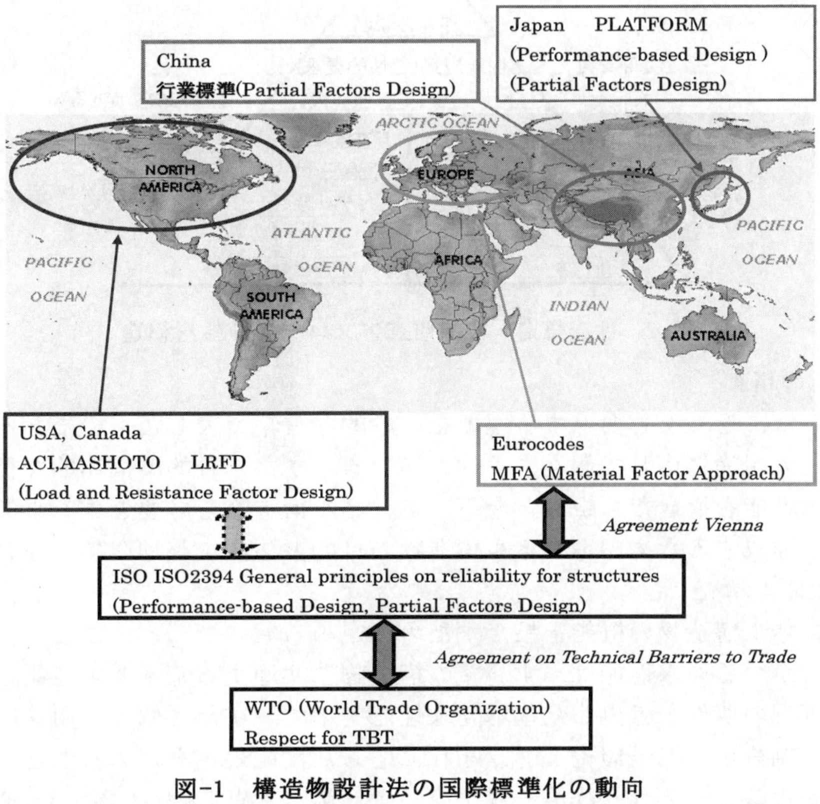

図-1　構造物設計法の国際標準化の動向

これに従い，個別の構造物の設計基準を策定する際に，設計規準のコードライターが依るべき策定の原則や用語を統一する必要性から，2003 年に土木学会から「包括設計コード(Principles, guidelines and terminologies for structural design code drafting founded on the performance based concept ver.1.0), (通称：PLATFORM)」[6)]が発表された．包括設計コード(PLATFORM) は，Comprehensive design code あるいは base code であり，その策定の狙いは以下のとおりである．

① わが国の優れた土木設計技術を海外にわかりやすく発信する．

② 日本に参入しようとする国外技術者には，非関税障壁とならない．

③ 後に続く若い技術者に日本の構造物設計の基本的な考え方を体系的かつ分かりやすく伝えていく．

わが国の包括設計コード(PLATFORM)は，主に structural design を対象として「性能照査型設計法」という新しい設計概念を導入している．既に，鋼構造分野，コンクリート分野，地震分野，地盤工学分野等，多くの機関では，PLATFORM に基づく，個別の固有基本設計コードの改訂作業が進んでいる[7),8)]．

以上のように，構造物設計の標準化にあたって，ISO2394 や Euro0 の海外の包括設計コードを見据えながら，わが国では「性能規定」に基づいた設計コードの体系が整備されつつあり，トンネル構造物を主とする地下構造物設計のコードライターは，この設計体系を早い時期に認識し，過去の設計の経験と良き伝統を反映したトンネル構造物の包括設計コード，個別基本設計コードを策定する必要がある．

4　トンネル構造物の包括設計コード・固有設計基本コードの考え方[9)]

前述したトンネル構造物の特殊性と過去の設計体系[10)]の経緯を考慮し，トンネル構造物の包括設計コード・固有設計コードの体系化を図るためには，図-2 に示す各 Phase を精査することがまず必要となる．以下には各 Phase の基本的な考え方を述べる．

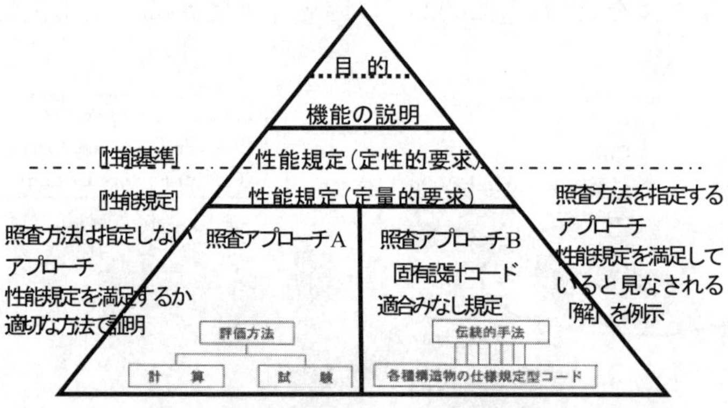

図-2　性能規定・性能照査アプローチの階層構造

(1) 目的と機能の精査

構造物の目的とは，それを必要とする理由を一般的な言葉で表したものである．トンネル構造物を対象とすると，その用途に応じて個々に目的が異なる．また，目的の具体的な役割を説明したものが機能であり，要求性能を導きだす根拠となる．トンネル構造物を必要とする事業の目的を定めた法令およびその目的を達成するためのトンネル構造物の目的と機能を整理して表-1 に示す．

(2) 基本要求性能の精査

要求性能はトンネル構造物の機能を果たすために定めるものである．ここで，安全性，使用性，環境性，経済性にかかわる要求性能は，すべての構造物に共通する基本要求性能となる．以下には，トンネル構造物に固有の要件を考慮した基本要求性能を示す．また，個々の用途に応じた要求性能は基本要求性能を基に細分化し，階層化して，それに応じた性能規定を定めることになる．ここでは，利用者，管理者，周辺の人をそれぞれ第一者，第二者，第三者とし(表-2 参照)，それら対象と基本要求性能との関連を表-3 に示すように位置づけている[11)]．

表-1 トンネル構造物の目的と機能

用途	トンネル構造物の目的と機能 (参考とした法律)
道路	車両を所定の速度で安全・円滑・快適に走行させることができ,所定の供用期間中にそれを維持・管理できる.(道路法・第一条)
鉄道	列車を所定の速度で安全・円滑・快適に運行させることができ,所定の供用期間中にそれを維持・管理できる.(鉄道事業法・第一条),(鉄道に関する技術上の基準を定める省令・第二十四条)
電力	所定のケーブル条数を収納し送電ができ,所定の供用期間中にそれを維持・管理できる.(電気事業法・第一条)
通信	所定の電気通信用ケーブルを敷設・撤去でき,所定の供用期間中にそれを維持・管理できる.(電気通信事業法・第一条)
ガス	所定のガス導管を設置でき,所定の供用期間中にそれを維持・管理できる.(ガス事業法・第一条)
下水	所定の雨水・汚水を通水,貯留させることができ,所定の供用期間中にそれを維持・管理できる.(下水道法・第一条)

表-2 第一者,第二者,第三者の考え方

第一者	移動などの目的を達成するためにトンネル(構造物)を利用する人または物.道路トンネルでは車の運転者・同乗者・輸送される荷物,鉄道トンネルでは乗客・貨物,電力・ガス・下水道・地下河川トンネルでは電気・ガス・水そのものまたはケーブル・管路などがこれにあたる.
第二者	トンネルを供用・管理する事業主体,関係機関やそれに従事する人や組織.
第三者	トンネルの施工または供用により影響を受ける周辺の人・建物・交差構造物など.

表-3 基本要求性能とその対象の位置づけ

対象 \ 性能		安全性に関する性能		使用性に関する性能
第一者	利用者 (運転者, 乗客, ガス管等)	①利用者の安全性能 ③構造安定性能	④耐久性能	②利用者の使用性能
第二者	管理者 (事業主体, 保守管理者等)	⑥維持管理性能		⑤管理者の使用性能 ⑥維持管理性能
第三者	周辺の人等	⑦周辺への影響度		⑦周辺への影響度

① 利用者の安全性能。

② 利用者の使用性能。

③ 構造安定性能。

④ 耐久性能。

⑤ 管理者の使用性能。

⑥ 維持管理性能。

⑦ 周辺への影響度。

なお,個々の目的に応じたトンネルの具体的な要求性能の考え方は以降で詳説する.

(3) 設計照査の手続き

トンネル構造物の性能規定に基づく設計照査の手続きを検討するうえでは,前述のトンネル構造物の特殊性や過去の設計法における良き経験的技術を反映するとともに,以下に示す事項を十分に検討する必要がある.

① 新規のトンネル構造物の性能照査方法を検討することはもとより,あわせて,使用に供されている既存のトンネル構造物の性能も新規構造物と同等に照査できる方法を検討する必要がある.すなわち,構造物のライフサイクルを念頭にデザインし,それを基に構造物をマネジメントするための手法を整備する必要がある.

② 従来の個別設計コードでは，構造物の力学的能力を照査することが設計とされてきた．一方，トンネル構造物の用途に応じた使用性は異なる．したがって，力学的観点のみならず，規定化された使用性にかかわる性能についてもその照査方法を整備する必要がある．

a) 照査アプローチA：従来から行われてきた設計方法とは異なり，構造物の性能照査に用いる方法に制限はなく，広く設計・施工・補修・補強への新技術の導入や新規企業の参入を可能とする照査アプローチである．このため，設計者は当該構造物の性能規定を一定のある適当な信頼性で満足することを証明しなければならない．この照査アプローチを採用する場合は，その照査手法や照査結果を適切に審査する機関を設置するなどして，定められた性能規定を満足しているか否かを「適切な手順(事業者，設計者のいずれとも利害関係を有さない当該構造物の設計に関する分野の専門技術に精通した者からなる委員会など)」で評価・判定することが必要となる．現状，「事業者(管理者)，設計者の両者から独立し，中立な立場にある第三者機関」としての審査機関に関する議論，および事業者(管理者)，設計者ならびに審査官の責任範囲に関する議論などが十分ではなく，照査アプローチAを採用するにあたっては，これら議論に待つところが多い．

b) 照査アプローチB：包括設計コードに基づいて，「適切な手順」に従って作成されたトンネル構造物の包括設計コード，または固有設計基本コードに基づく性能照査アプローチである．したがって，照査アプローチBを採用するための各種設計コードを整備する必要がある．トンネル構造物を対象とする場合，地山作用など不確実性が高い等の特徴がある．したがって，適合みなし規定および具体的な照査方法として「部分係数による設計法」によることが適切と考えられる．また，部分係数による設計法は構造物，または構造部材の力学的な性能のみの設計照査方法であることから，トンネル用途に応じた使用性能に関する照査方法は別途検討する必要がある．

5 目的に応じたトンネル構造物の要求性能 [12),13)]

(1) 要求性能の考え方

道路，鉄道，上下水道，電力，通信など様々な用途に供されるトンネルの要求性能は，その目的に応じて基本要求性能の枠で個々に具体化される．一方，トンネル構造物の場合，その施工法によって構造設計の考え方が大きく異なる[14)]ことから，これを十分に考慮して要求性能を具体化する必要がある．すなわち，比較的地山が良く自立性の高い地盤の場合に採用される山岳トンネル工法では，トンネルとなる空間を形成する構造主体は自然地山そのものであり，この能力を最大限に利用して人工的に支保する考え方で構造設計がなされる．これに対し，都市トンネル工法に代表されるシールド工法では，地山の自立性がほとんど期待できない場合に採用され，この場合の構造主体は人工的な構築物となる．このことが，トンネル構造物の構造設計を難しいものにしている大きな一因である．このため，トンネル工法によって異なる主たる要因を整理する必要がある．表-4 はトンネル工法の違いによって異なる要因を整理した例(道路トンネルの場合)である．したがって，要求性能の精査にあたっては施工法の違いも考慮する必要がある．

表-4 トンネル工法の違いによる要因の差異の例 (道路)

	山岳工法	シールド工法
建設場所	主に山岳部，郊外等 (トンネル内の凍結を考慮する)	主に都市部 (トンネル内の凍結は考慮しない)
坑口	基本的に坑門が存在する	基本的に坑門がない
施工時荷重	一般的に施工時荷重は考慮不要	施工時荷重により変状を生じることがある 施工時に切羽安定のために対策を要する
覆工構造	覆工コンクリートは一般に構造部材でない (基本的に無筋コンクリート構造)	覆工(セグメント)が構造部材である (鉄筋コンクリート，鋼構造，合成構造)
路盤	インバートがない場合は路盤が変状することがある．この場合，走行安定性に影響する．	セグメントを組み合わせた閉合構造であるため，変状することはない．

(2) 要求性能の具体例

基本要求性能をもとに要求性能の具体を考える．表-5はシールド工法による鉄道トンネルの要求性能を整理した例[12),13)]である．要求性能の大項目は基本要求性能とその説明である．中項目は大項目を評価するための事象を，さらに小項目は中項目をより詳細に評価するための事象を示している．したがって，要求性能の小項目の事象をすべて満足すれば大項目で示した性能を満たすこととなる．一方，小項目に示される事象をみると，事象そのものを直接的に評価できるものとそうでないものとがある．また，定量的評価が可能な事象と曖昧で定性的評価をせざるを得ない事象とが存在することがわかる．このため，個々の性能を具体的に照査するにあたっては，トンネル構造物の計画設計段階，施工段階，維持管理段階(供用段階)の各々の段階で具体的な事象を評価するための照査指標を設けて照査することになる．

表-5　細分化された要求性能の例（シールド工法・鉄道）

目的(機能)	性能(要求性能)			
	大項目		中項目	小項目
所定の供用期間中，車両を安全・快適・円滑に走行させることができる	利用者の安全性能	利用者が安全に利用できる	安全に走行できる	良好な線路線形を確保できる
				走行安全性を確保できる
				建築限界を確保できる
			利用者の安全を直接脅かさない	剥落が生じない
				漏水が生じない
			非常時に利用者が安全に避難できる	非常時に防災設備が確実に稼働する
				防災設備を適切に配置できる
	利用者の使用性能	利用者が快適に利用できる	乗り心地がよい	線形が適切、乗り心地を悪化させる軌道変位を起こすようなトンネル変位が生じない
			利用者に不快感・不安感を与えない	利用者が不快感・不安感を持つような漏水・ひび割れが見られない
	構造安定性能	想定される荷重に対して安定する	常時作用する荷重に対して安定する	常時作用する荷重に対して必要な耐荷性能を有する
				想定される地盤沈下に対して必要な追従性を有する
				浮力に対して安定しており，必要な重量を有する
			必要な耐震性能を有する	供用期間中に想定される地震動に対して覆工が必要な耐震性能を有する
				地震時に液状化等で浮き上がらない
			想定される荷重の変化に対して安定する	供用期間中に想定される近接施工による影響や周辺環境の変化等、荷重条件の変化に対して必要な耐荷性能を有する
			想定される施工時荷重に対して安定する	施工時に想定される荷重に対して必要な耐荷性能を有する
	耐久性能	想定される劣化要因に対して耐久性がある	防食性がよい	鉄筋・鋼製セグメント・継手金物等、鋼材の防食性がよ
				耐久性を脅かす有害なひび割れがない
			コンクリートが劣化しない	コンクリートが侵食・劣化しない
			止水性がよい	覆工・諸設備の劣化原因となる漏水が生じない
	管理者の使用性能	管理者が適切に供用(使用)できる	必要な需要を満足する	必要な線路数と諸設備を収容できる内空断面が確保できる
				必要な列車速度を出せる線形が確保できる
			列車が安定的に運行できる	列車運行に関わる諸設備の機能を支障するような剥落が生じない
				列車運行に関わる諸設備の機能を支障するような漏水が生じない
			列車運行のための諸設備が確実に稼動できる	列車運行に関わる諸設備を適切に配置・使用できる
				トンネル内の水が適切に排水され諸設備に影響しない
	維持管理性能	適切な維持管理が確実に行える	安全・容易に点検できる	日常の巡回・点検が安全・容易にできる
			安全・容易に補修・補強ができる	対策工の足場の設置と，資材置場の確保ができる
				内空断面に補修・補強余裕が確保されている
	周辺への影響度	周辺への影響度が最小限に抑えられる	地下水への影響が少ない	地下水位変動が許容範囲内である
				周辺への地下水汚濁影響が許容範囲内である
			周辺地盤への影響が少ない	地表面の沈下・隆起が許容範囲内である
			周辺の物件への影響が少ない	近接建物・埋設物等への影響が許容範囲内である
			周辺での振動・騒音が少ない	施工中・供用中に周辺での振動・騒音が許容範囲内である

6　性能規定に基づくマネジメント[15)]

(1) 性能規定に基づくマネジメントの考え方

性能規定に基づくマネジメントとは，トンネルのライフサイクルを念頭において，計画，調査・設計，施工，維持管理のすべての段階において，要求性能を基準にそれを評価する指標を定めて性能照査を行い，これに基づいて戦略的なマネジメントを実施するというものである．図-3 は性能規定に基づくマネジメント手法の流れを示したものである．

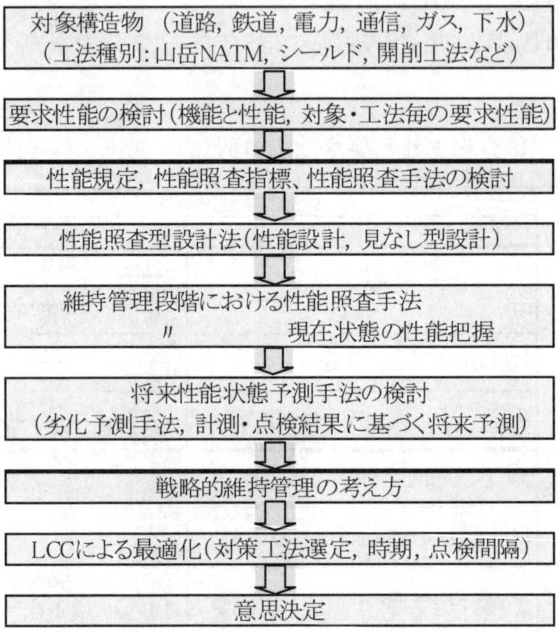

図-3　性能規定に基づくマネジメントの流れ

性能規定に基づくマネジメントにおいては，トンネルの用途(目的)に応じて，計画設計段階，施工段階，維持管理段階(供用段階)の各々の段階で同一の要求性能に対して性能照査することが基本となる．ここでは，とくに既設のトンネル構造物の維持管理段階に着目してその考え方を論じる．

従来から既設トンネル構造物の維持管理では個々に基準を設けて点検・評価・対策がとられている[16)]．しかしながら，これらの維持管理は基本的に個々の不具合事象に対策を講じる行為であり，性能規定を明確にして性能を照査したうえで対策を講じるという行為とはなっていない．また，将来的な対策は限られた予算制約の中で適宜検討されているのが実状である．

一方，性能規定に基づくマネジメントでは現在状態の性能照査に基づいて将来状態を予測し，管理者の戦略に基づいて LCC の最適化手法を適用して対策時期や対策工選定を意志決定するところに大きな違いがある．ただし，性能照査にあたっての照査項目は従来からの点検項目と大きく異なるわけではなく，個々の点検項目が要求性能を照査するための性能照査指標，または性能照査代替指標となる．

図-4 に基本要求性能に対する性能照査手法の基本的な考え方を示す．図中には基本要求性能に対応して定量的評価が可能な性能照査指標の例を示してある．また，性能照査指標の中には"部材耐力"や"ひび割れ"など，トンネルの点検や計測によって得られたデータから解析や統計的手法を援用して指標を評価する項目もある．一方，前述のように，性能照査指標の中には定量的評価が可能なものとそうでないものとがある．したがって，総合的な性能照査は 5 段階程度の照査基準を設けたレイティング手法によることが現実的である．これにより，対象となるトンネル構造物の用途，トンネル工法，事業者の戦略およびサービスアビリティー等の条件によって，各要求性能の優先度を重み付けすることが可能となる．また，定量的評価が困難な性能照査指標は，階層分析法などを適用してそれを定量的に取り扱うことになる．このような性能照査をトンネル延長のスパンごとに，あるいはトンネルごとに実施することによってトータル性能インデックスが求められる．これにより，トンネル構造物の性能を一元的に管理することが可能となる．

要求性能	性能照査指標	照査手法（判定基準策定）		重み付け
		数值評価	レイティング	
利用者の安全性能	内空形状寸法，内空変位，ひび割れ，線形視距，漏水など	B	5段階	w1
利用者の使用性能	内空変位，ひび割れ，線形視距，漏水など	B	5段階	w2
構造安定性能	部材耐力，継手耐力，継手変形性能，	A	5段階	w3
耐久性能	部材品質，ひび割れ，漏水	A	5段階	w4
管理者の使用性能	内空形状寸法，ひび割れ，線形視距，防災設備規模，漏水	B	5段階	w5
維持管理性能	内空形状寸法	B	5段階	w6
周辺への影響度	騒音振動，地盤変動，漏水質，地下水変動	B	5段階	w7

数值評価A: 計測，数值解析等により積極的に数值化する

数值評価B: 計測可能な項目以外は，判定基準に照合しレイティング．

◆ 部材毎の評価
◆ 性能毎の評価
◆ AHP等による重み付けによる統合
◆ 性能照査型評価法の確立

トータル性能インデックス

図-4　要求性能に対する性能照査手法の考え方

(2) 将来状態の予測

性能規定に基づくマネジメントでは，供用目標期間あるいはそれを越えた実質使用期間において，必要最小限のコストによってトンネルの性能を確保することが求められる．その概念を示したのが図-5である．性能水準の低下に応じて要求性能を確保するよう予防保全や予防管理[17]の施策を図る必要がある．しかしながら，トンネル構造物は既述のように不確実性の高い地盤中に構築される構造物であることなどから，その性能の評価には相当の不確実性を内包することが多い．このため，平均的な保有性能が要求性能を満足していても，図-6に示す損傷確率を考慮すると要求性能を満足しないことが生じるおそれもあり，このような場合には緊急対策を講じる必要がある．したがって，トンネル構造物においては，保有性能を確認するための点検を頻繁に行い，局所的にも重要な要求性能を満たさなくなる寸前に補修などを施す予防管理[17]を適用することが適切であると考えられる．また，点検頻度は保有性能の現在状態から将来状態を推定する精度に大きく影響する．図-7はその概念を示したものである．点検頻度が極端に少ない場合には不確実性が増大することになる．推定精度の低下は予防管理施策に直接的に反映されるため，点検頻度は対象となるトンネルのサービスアビリティーに応じて適切に設定する必要がある．

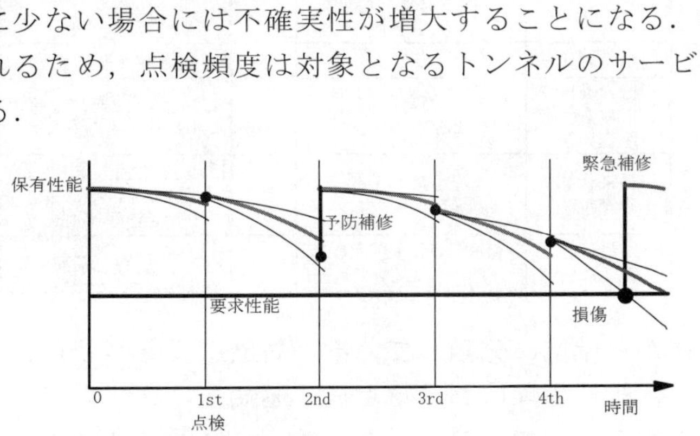

図-5　維持管理の最適化戦略の概念

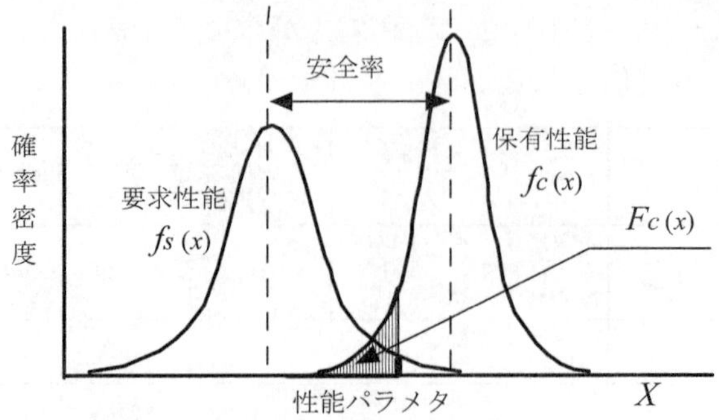

図-6 損傷確率の概念

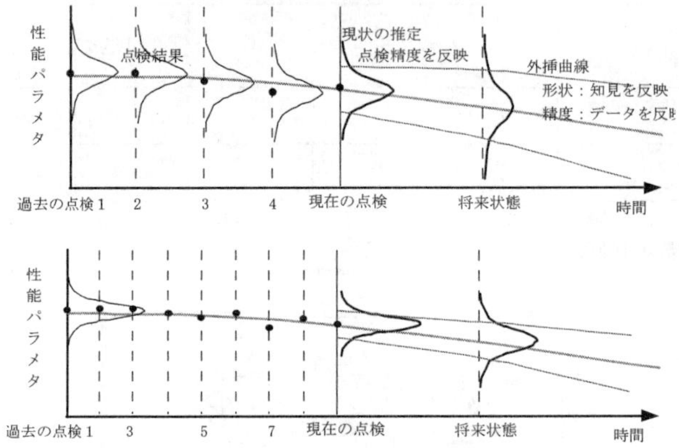

図-7 点検頻度と状態推定精度

(3) トンネルのサービスアビリティー

トンネル構造物のサービスアビリティーは，対象となるトンネルの用途，社会的機能，管理者の事業規模や財源などによって異なる．このため，個々のトンネルの社会的役割や重要性に応じてサービスアビリティーが異なることが想定される．したがって，個々のトンネルのサービスアビリティーを設定し，それに応じたマネジメント手法を検討する必要がある．表-7 はサービスアビリティーを反映したサービスレベルとその基本的なマネジメントの考え方を示したものである．

表-7 サービスアビリティーに応じたマネジメントの考え方

サービスレベル	**低位** 交通量小，劣化進行低 山間部	⟺	**高位** 交通量大，劣化進行高 重要路線，緊急輸送路
性能規定	利用者の安全性能・使用性能，構造安定性能，耐久性能 管理者の使用性能，維持管理性能，周辺への影響度		
性能照査指標	極力数値化が可能な指標を選定		
設計法	見なし型設計		性能設計
モニタリング	点検＋必要に応じて 簡易計測		点検＋計測
健全度評価法	レイティングが基本		性能照査型評価法
維持管理段階における性能照査手法	点検（＋簡易計測）結果によるレイティング		計測を主体とした数値化指標による照査
将来状態予測手法	確定論的予測 （残存耐力）		信頼性，確率論的手法などによる不確実性を考慮した予測法
LCC最適化による意思決定	点検，補修を想定した LCC		LCC最適化を実施

サービスレベルは高位から低位に分類している．高位に位置づけられるトンネルは，社会的重要性がとくに高く，このため，維持管理における点検や連続モニタリングを詳細に行い，可能な限り定量化された指標で性能照査するものである．一方，低位に位置づけされるトンネルは，社会的必要性

はあるものの，使用頻度が低かったり，管理者の予算制約がとくに厳しいなどの条件があるものである．このようなサービスアビリティーの違いは，それを管理するうえでのマネジメント手法にも反映されるべきである．

参考文献（References）：

[1] 例えば，水谷，清水，木村：トンネル構造物のライフ・サイクル・デザイン手法の構築(1)，土木学会第58回年次学術講演会概要集，VI-131, 2003.9.

[2] トンネル安全問題検討会報告書，運輸省，2000.2.

[3] ISO：ISO13822 Bases for design of structures- assessment of existing structures 1st edition, 2001.12.

[4] ISO：ISO2394 General principles on reliability foe structure 3rd edition, 1998.6.

[5] 国土交通省：土木・建築にかかる設計の基本，2002.10.

[6] Principles, guidelines and terminologies for structural design code drafting founded on the performance based concept ver.1.0)，JSCE, 2003.

[7] 地盤工学会：包括基礎構造物設計コード，地盤コード21 ver.1, 2000.3.

[8] 地盤工学会：地盤工学会基準 JGS4001-2004, 性能設計概念に基づいた基礎構造物等に関する設計原則, 2006.3.

[9] 木村定雄：構造物設計法の国際標準化の動向とトンネル構造物の性能規定化の必要性，土木学会平成19年度全国大会研究討論会，研-14資料，pp.3-10, 2007.9.

[10] 例えば，土木学会：2006年制定トンネル標準示方書(山岳工法・同解説，シールド工法・同解説，開削工法・同解説)，2006.7.

[11] 畑生浩司，栗木実，野城一栄，鈴木尊，粥川幸司：トンネルのデザインとマネジメント(その２)-トンネルの機能と要求性能についての考察-，土木学会第58回年次学術講演会概要集，VI-167, 2007.9.

[12] 佐野信夫：トンネルの機能と性能についての考察，土木学会平成19年度全国大会研究討論会，研-14資料, pp.11-14, 2007.9.

[13] 木村定雄，安田亨：トンネルの性能規定化の動向とマネジメント，サマースクール2008テキスト，建設マネジメント勉強会，pp.109-120, 2007.8.

[14] 土木学会：都市NATMとシールド工法の境界領域：トンネルライブラリー第11号，2003.10.

[15] 安田亨，畑生浩司，内藤幸弘，野田賢治：トンネルのデザインとマネジメント(９)-トンネルの性能照査型マネジメント手法の検討-，土木学会第58回年次学術講演会概要集，VI-174, 2007.9.

[16] 例えば，土木学会：トンネルの維持管理，トンネルライブラリー第14号，pp.5-7, 2005.7.

[17] 中村一樹，細沼宏之，高田充伯，大津宏康，小林潔司：トンネルアセットマネジメント，サマースクール2007テキスト，pp.143-152, 2007.8.

著者紹介（Bio-data）：

木村　定雄　　教授　博士(工学)　技術士(建設)　トンネル工学・建設マネジメント

Sadao KIMURA　Professor　Dr. Eng.　P.E.(Japan)　Tunnel Engineering and Management

s.kimura@neptune.kanazawa-it.ac.jp

Tel. +81 76-274-7704

Fax. +81 76-274-7102

都心部における非開削切拡げ施工時の載荷挙動に関する研究

岩波　基[1]，千代啓三[2]，大澤拓洋[1]
[1]長岡工業高等専門学校，長岡　940-8532
[2]株式会社熊谷組，東京　162-8557

東京地下鉄副都心線では，路線の最深部にポンプ室を構築した．ポンプ室の構築では，トンネル内から曲線パイプルーフを施工した後，非開削工法で切り広げる PSS-Arch 工法を採用した．施工中，セグメントや曲線パイプルーフ，変形防止鋼材の計測[1)]を実施し，その特徴をまとめた[2)]．さらに，FEM 解析や多リングはり・ばねモデルで解析を行い，構造物に生じた現象の再現を試みた．その結果，横断面 2 次元 FEM 解析だけでは，構造物の挙動を表現できないとの知見が得られた[2),3)]．これらの知見のもとに，本論文はトンネル縦断面についても 2 次元 FEM 解析を行い，曲線パイプルーフに作用する掘削解放力を推定し，構造物に対する載荷メカニズムを検討するものである．

キーワード：シールドトンネル；非開削工法；曲線パイプルーフ；計測

A STUDY ON BEHAVIOR OF THE STRUCTURES AND THE SURROUNDING GROUND APPLIED NON-OPEN CUT METHOD IN THE METROPOLITAN AREA

Motoi IWANAMI[1], Keizo CHISHIRO[2], Takuhiro OHSAWA[1]
[1]*Nagaoka National College of Technology, Nagaoka 940-8532, Japan;*
[2]*KUMAGAI GUMI CO.,LTD. Tokyo 162-8557, Japan*

Abstract: The pumping station was designed at the deepest point in the whole route of the Fukutoshin line. PSS-Arch method was applied to it, in which t the curved pipe roofs were inserted and then inner area was excavated. Segments were measured, pipe roofs and internal supports were curved during construction, and features of their behaviors were picked out. Furthermore, the phenomena were reproduced by 2-dimensional FEM analysis and beam-spring model. As a result, the conclusion has been got that 2-dimensional cross section analysis couldn't explain them completely. So, this paper investigated 2-dimensional longitudinal section FEM analysis to estimate released forces and a load carrying mechanism to structures.

Key words: shield tunnel; non-open cut construction; curved steel pipes; measurements

1　はじめに

東京地下鉄（株）では，地下鉄副都心線池袋～渋谷間 8.9 km の建設を行った（図-1）．この中で，路線延長全体で最深部となる雑司が谷駅と西早稲田駅間の中間地点付近にポンプ室を構築した．

中間ポンプ室は，交通量の激しい都道部交差点直下であり，かつ，土被りは約 33 m で，トンネル直上には NTT とう道や東電シールドが輻輳するという厳しい条件下での施工が求められた．このため，シールドトンネル内から曲線パイプルーフを地盤内に先行して挿入し，これを支保工として内部を掘削する非開削工法（PSS-Arch 工法）を採用した．

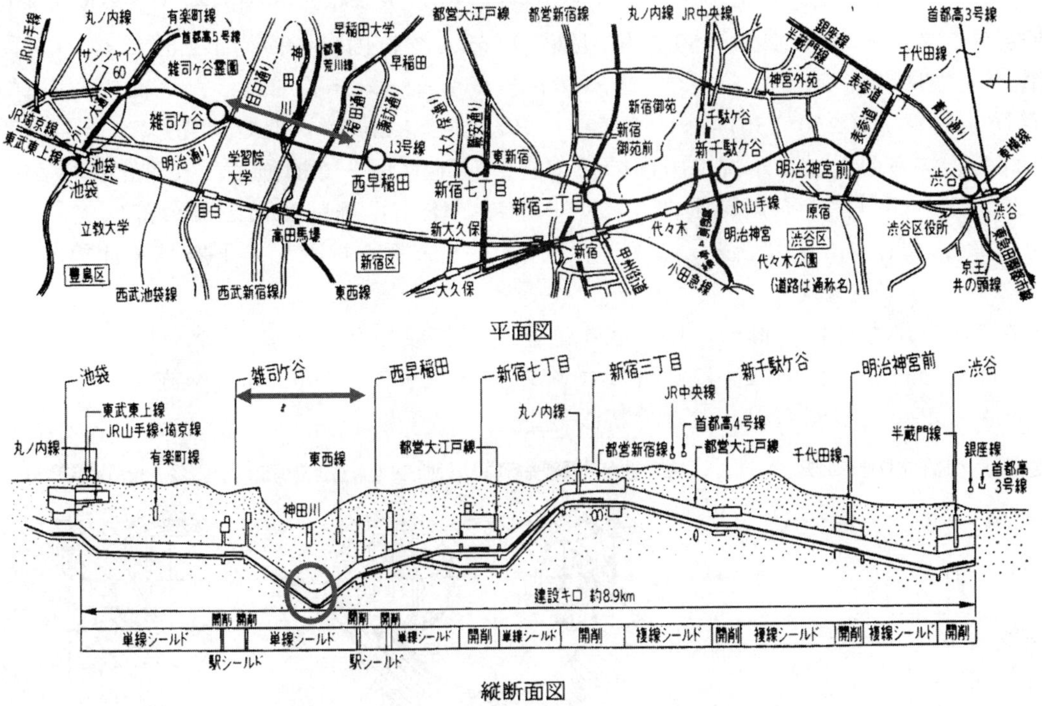

図-1 地下鉄 13 号線路線平面・縦断図

施工にあたり，セグメントや曲線パイプルーフ，変形防止鋼材の挙動を確認するために計測 [1)]を実施し，その特徴をまとめた．さらに，横断面２次元 FEM 解析や多リングはり・ばねモデルで解析を行い，構造物に生じた現象を再現することを試みた．その結果，通常の FEM 解析だけでは，構造物に対する載荷メカニズムを表現できないという知見を得た [2),3)]．そこで，本論文では，トンネル断面方向だけでなく，トンネル縦断方向についても２次元 FEM 解析を行い，曲線パイプルーフに作用する掘削解放力を推定して構造物に生じた現象を再現し，構造物に対する載荷メカニズムを検討するものである．

2 施工方法の概要

2.1 中間ポンプ室の仕様

中間ポンプ室の概要を図-2 に示す．中間ポンプ室は，幅 7.2 m，高さ 7.05 m で中床版を有した２階構造であり，約 4.4 m の離隔をもった２本の単線トンネルの間に設置された．単線トンネルは，曲線パイプルーフや変形防止鋼材の設置を考え，鋼製セグメントとしており，厚さ 270 mm，外径 φ 6 600 mm であり，リング幅は一般部と同じ 1 600 mm である．

2.2 施工手順

施工手順を図-3 を用いて概説する．

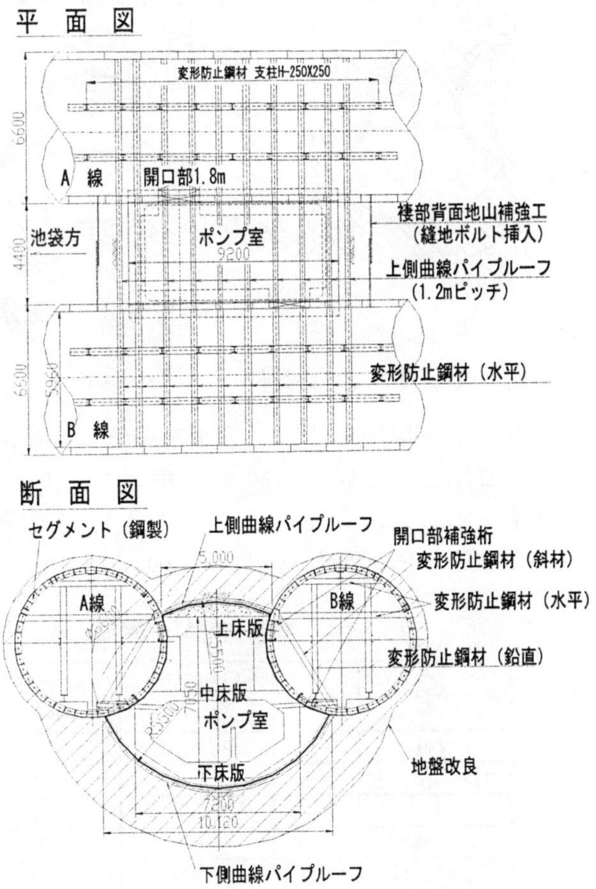

図-2 中間ポンプ室施工概要図

① ディープウェル工法とウェルポイント工法を併用し，トンネル下端の高さまで地下水位を下げた．

② 曲線パイプルーフ（□-250×250 の角型鋼管）を A 線坑内から，約 1.2 m ピッチで挿入した．掘削は，鋼管の先端に装備したウォータージェットとバキューム装置で行った．曲線パイプルーフの設置後，変形防止鋼材（H-250×250）をパイプルーフと同じ 1.2m ピッチで設置した．

③ 中間ポンプ室のトンネル掘進方向の褄部を，縫地ボルトで補強し，安定化をはかった．

④ セグメント開口部から斜め上向きに掘り進み，上半を掘削した．開口部は図-2 のように，A 線に 1 箇所設け，幅は 1.8 m である．また，掘削後，上床版を打設し，上床版と曲線パイプルーフの間は，コンクリートで充填した．

⑤ 上半二次掘削を行い，側壁と中床版を逆巻きで打設した．

⑥ 下半掘削を行い，掘削直後に吹付けコンクリート（厚さ 100 mm）を施工した．

⑦ 下床版とポンプ室側壁を逆巻きで打設した．

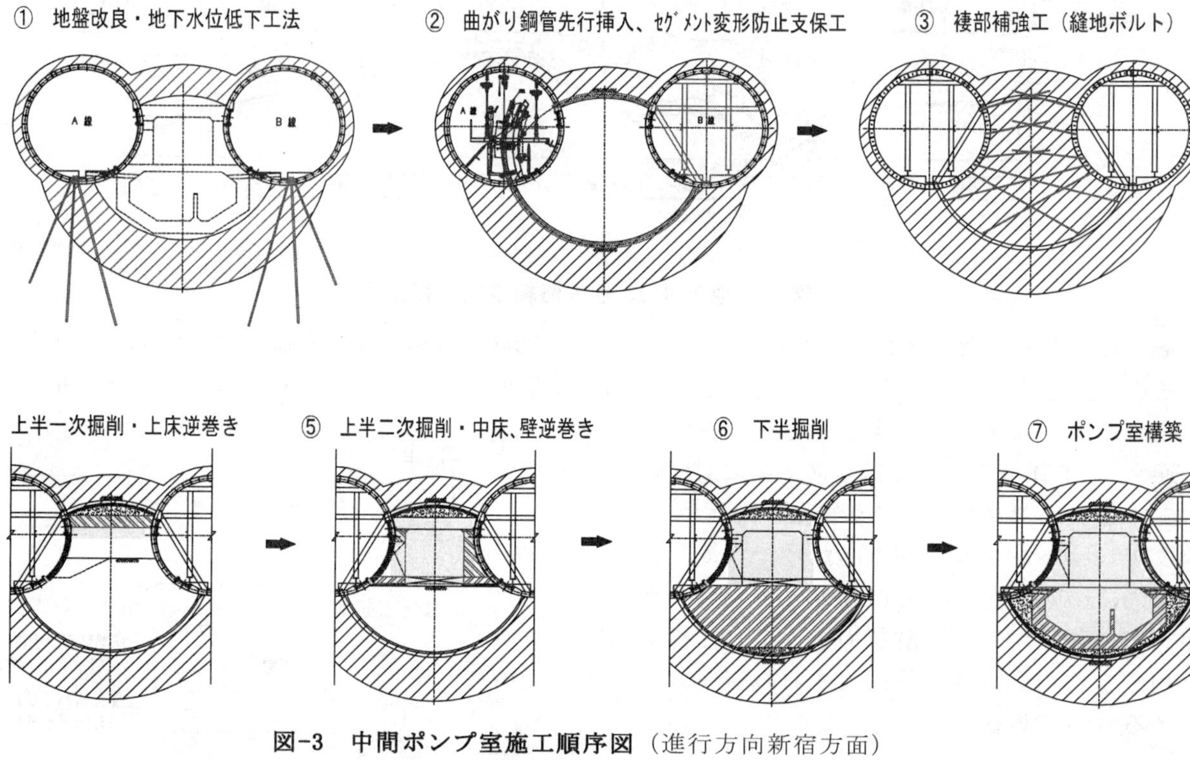

図-3 中間ポンプ室施工順序図（進行方向新宿方面）

2.3 地質条件・施工条件

トンネル掘削箇所は，第 4 紀更新世洪積層上総層群砂質土層（Kas1）と粘性土層（Kac1）が互層となって堆積している（図-4）．ポンプ室上半は，上総層粘性土層（Kac1），ポンプ室下半側は上総層砂質土（Kas1）が存在する．Kac1 と Kas1 の各層の物性値を表-1 に示す．土被りはポンプ室天端で約 33 m，地下水圧は掘削底版で約 0.32 MPa であった．

表-1 地盤物性値一覧表

項目	単位	上総層粘性土 (Kac1)	上総層砂質土 (Kas1)
N値	—	30～50	50以上
単位体積重量	kN/m^3	17	18
粘着力	kN/m^2	260	0
内部摩擦角	°	0	42
変形係数	kN/m^2	54,400	75,300
透水係数	cm/sec	—	1×10^{-3}

写真-1 曲がり鋼管

3　計測工の概要

3.1　計測項目

掘削時の構造物への影響を確認するため，セグメント，曲線パイプルーフと変形防止鋼材のひずみ計測を行った．計測位置や測点数は，図-5のとおりである．また，計測したひずみ値の初期値は，セグメントの開口部撤去を行う直前の値とした．

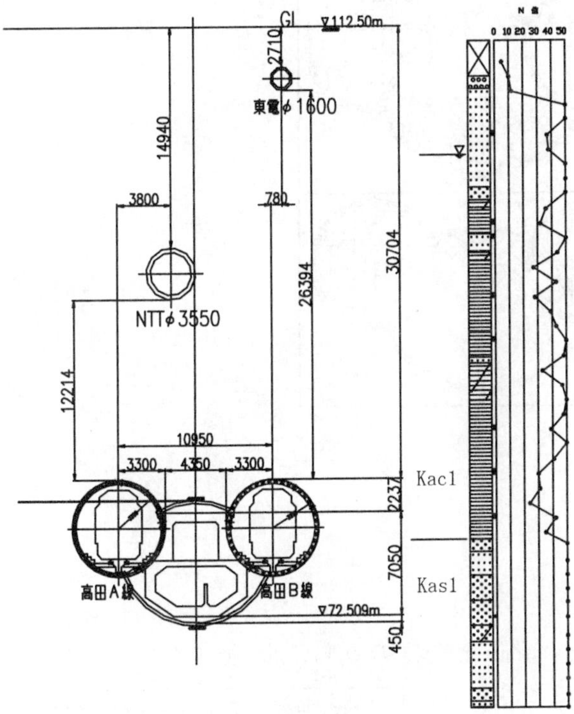

図-4　地質条件概要図

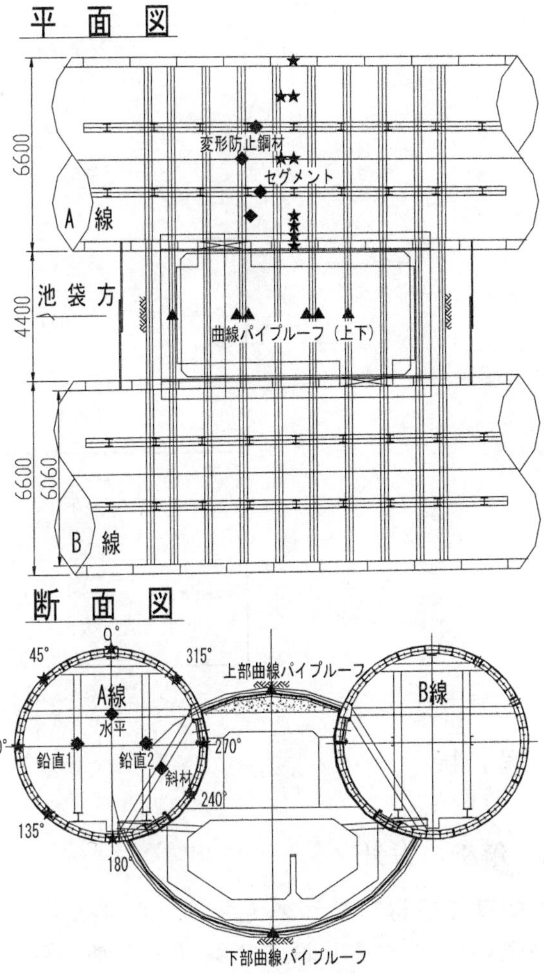

図-5　計測位置図

3.2　計測結果の概要

表-3に示すように，初期値のほか，①上半一次掘削後，②上半二次掘削後，③上半三次掘削後，④下半掘削後の4つのステップの施工段階に着目し，部位ごとにまとめた結果[3)]を以下に記す．また，鋼材およびセグメントの軸力と曲げモーメントは1m幅あたりの値に換算している．

・上半掘削では，背面が掘削された位置のセグメントの軸力が解放されている．一方，地山側のセグメントと変形防止鋼材は，ほとんど変形しておらず，地山の主働的な土圧が作用していない可能性がある．

・曲線パイプルーフ間のセグメントは，背面地山が掘削されると軸力が解放され，その一部が変形防止鋼材（斜材）に伝達されている．

・下半掘削では，下側曲線パイプルーフを含めたすべての部材にほとんど影響がなく，周辺地盤は堅固で自立性が高く，土砂による側面や下面からの主働的な土圧はきわめて小さいと考えられる．

表-3　着目した施工段階の説明

施工段階	状態図
①上半一次掘削 天端～-2.0m セグメント開口部設置 上半一次掘削 パイプサポート間土留	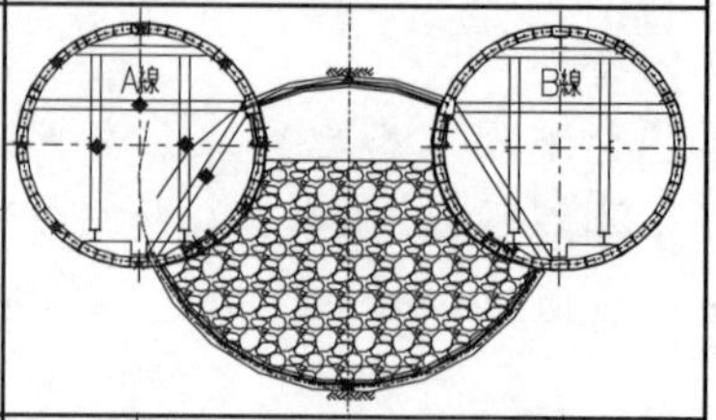
②上半二次掘削 -2.0～-3.0m (上床版打設前) 上半二次掘削 パイプサポート間土留	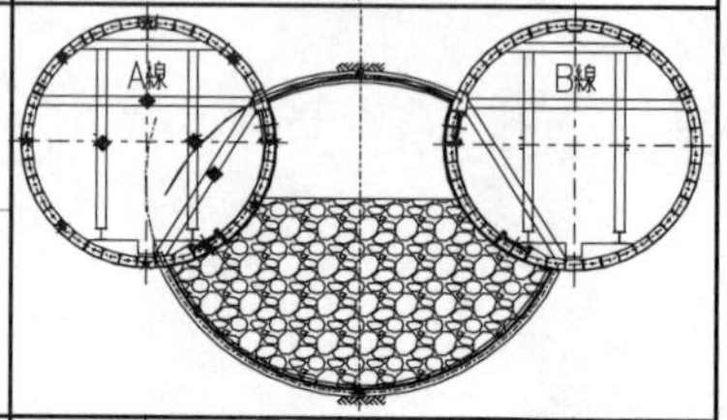
③上半三次掘削 -3.0～-5.0 (中床版打設前) 上床版打設 上半三次掘削	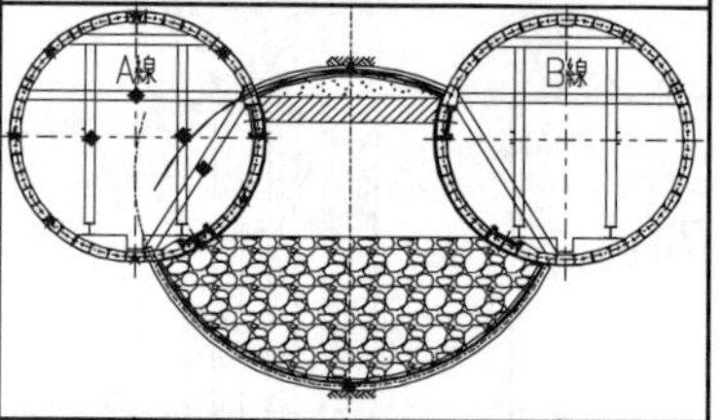
④下半掘削 側壁・中床スラブ打設 下半掘削・吹付け	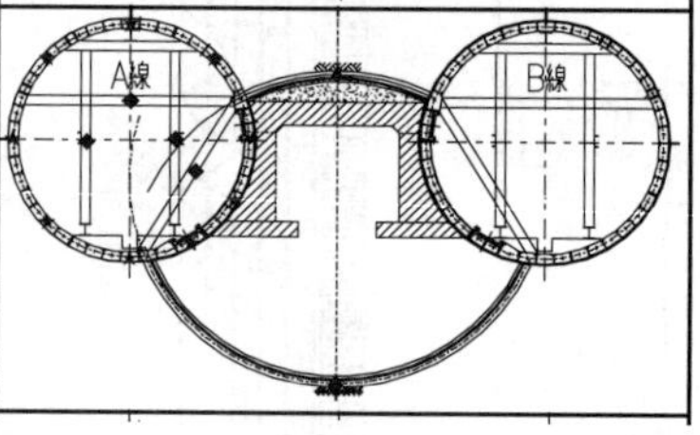

4　解　析

4.1　解析の方針

前章で確認したセグメント，曲線パイプルーフ，変形防止鋼材のうち，曲線パイプルーフとポンプ室側のセグメントおよび斜材の挙動を解析によって表現することを試みる．

千代らの論文[3)]では実際の挙動を再現することができなかった．ポンプ室の延長が 9.4 m であり，トンネル方向のアーチ効果が解析上で無視できないことが考えられる．そこで，千代らの論文で実施したトンネル横断面の 2 次元 FEM 解析を行う前に，ポンプ室をトンネル掘進方向と平行な断面でモデル化した 2 次元 FEM 解析を行い，掘削応力解放率を算出し，横断面 2 次元 FEM 解析に適用することとした．なお，トンネル掘進方向の 2 次元 FEM 解析で，土圧を受ける鋼管の挙動を表現するため，鋼管を支持するばねを骨組み解析を用いて算出した．解析の手順を図-6 に示す．

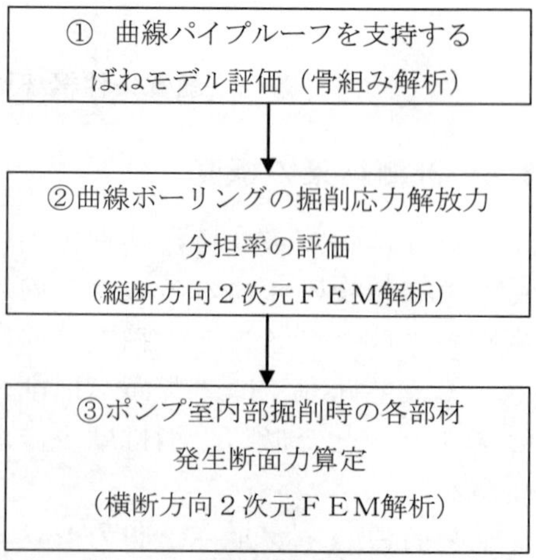

図-6　解析の手順

上下の曲線パイプルーフをそれぞれヒンジアーチとしてモデル化し，土圧相当の分布荷重を載荷して中央部の変位を算出する．そして，変位と分布荷重から各曲線パイプルーフ中央部のばね値を算定する．

②曲線パイプルーフの掘削解放力分担率の評価

ポンプ室中央のトンネル掘進方向断面を２次元 FEM 解析のモデルで評価し，自重載荷時の初期応力，曲線パイプルーフの施工，鋼管および①で算定したばねモデル設置そしてポンプ室内部掘削の４段階の施工ステップで解析を行う．次に，施工完了時の曲線パイプルーフ周辺における鉛直方向地盤応力度と初期応力度との比率で曲線ボーリングが分担する掘削解放の割合を求める．この値を，トンネル横断方向の２次元 FEM 解析に掘削解放率として用いる．解放率の合計は 100%にならないことで，地山のアーチ効果等を表現されていると言える．

③ポンプ室内部掘削時の各部材発生断面力算定

②で算定した解放率を用いてトンネル横断方向２次元 FEM 解析を実施し，各施工ステップの曲線パイプルーフ，セグメントおよび変形防止鋼材の断面力を算定する．

4.2 解析条件

(1) 地山の物性値

解析では地盤は弾性とし，地山の物性値は表-4 の値を使用する．また，一般にリバウンドを生じる地盤では変形係数を大きくしたほうが計測値に一致することが経験的に知られている．このため，除荷時の変形係数として載荷時の 3 倍の値を使用した事例にならった．また，千代らの解析結果 [3)]も比較して記載するので，変形係数を 6 倍した値も記す．

表-4 地山の物性値

	単位体積重量 γ(kN/m³)	変形係数 E(kN/m²)	ポアソン比 ν	側方土圧係数*)
上総層粘性土 (Kac1)	17	54,400	0.35	0.54
上総層砂質土 (Kas1)	18	75,300	0.35	0.54
上総層砂質土 (Kas1')**)	18	225,900	0.35	0.54
上総層砂質土 (Kas1'')***)	18	451,800	0.35	0.54

*)側方土圧係数=ν/(1-ν)
**)FEM解析におけるKas1'の変形係数は，Kas1の3倍とする.
***)前報の解析ではKas1''の変形係数をKas1の6倍とした.

(2) 部材の物性値

表-5～8 に，構築コンクリート，セグメント，H 鋼および曲線パイプルーフの物性値をそれぞれ示す．

曲線パイプルーフは，鋼管と中詰材の合成構造とし合成物性値を使用した．計測ひずみより断面力を算出する時には，軸力は鋼管と中詰材で分担し，曲げモーメントは鋼管のみで受け持つものとした．

表-5 構築コンクリートの物性値

項目	設計基準強度 (N/mm²)	変形係数E (kN/m²)	ポアソン比
吹付けコンクリート	18	3.4×10^6	0.2
ポンプ室躯体	24	2.5×10^7	0.2
ポンプ室躯体 中床版開口部 開口比:8.0/9.4	24	2.1×10^6	0.2

表-6 セグメントの物性値（1.6m 幅）

	1リングあたり	1mあたり
セグメント外径(m)	6.600	—
セグメント幅(m)	1.600	—
セグメント高さ(mm)	270	—
変形係数(kN/m²)	2.1×10^8	
ポアソン比ν	0.3	
断面積A(m²)	2.533×10^{-2}	1.583×10^{-2}
断面二次モーメントI(m⁴)	1.982×10^{-4}	1.239×10^{-4}

表-7 H鋼の物性値（H-250×250@1.2m）

		1本あたり	1mあたり
変形係数E	(kN/m²)	2.1×10^{8}	
ポアソン比		0.3	
断面積A	(m²)	9.143×10^{-3}	7.619×10^{-3}
断面二次モーメントI	(m⁴)	1.070×10^{-4}	8.917×10^{-5}

表-8 曲線パイプルーフ鋼管の物性値（1.2m ピッチ）

			1mあたり
合成物性値	変形係数E	(kN/m²)	4.583×10^{7}
	断面積A	(m²)	5.191×10^{-2}
	断面二次モーメントI	(m⁴)	3.089×10^{-4}
照査用物性値	軸力Nの分配率	鋼管	0.623
		中詰	0.377
	鋼管断面積As	(m²)	7.056×10^{-3}
	中詰断面積Ac	(m²)	4.485×10^{-2}

4.3 曲線パイプルーフを支持するばねモデルの評価

図-6において太線で囲んだ上側曲線パイプルーフと下側曲線パイプルーフをそれぞれヒンジアーチの骨組構造でモデル化して，ばね値を算出する．なお，曲線パイプルーフは□-250×250×9の角形鋼管にコンクリートを中詰めした表-8の合成物性値を用いた．

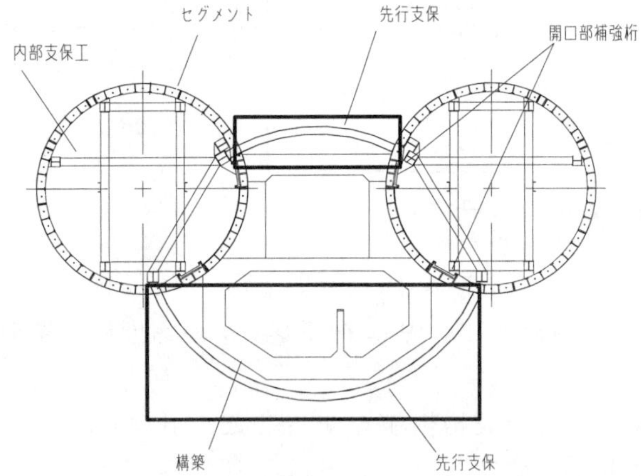

図-7 検討対象先行支保工

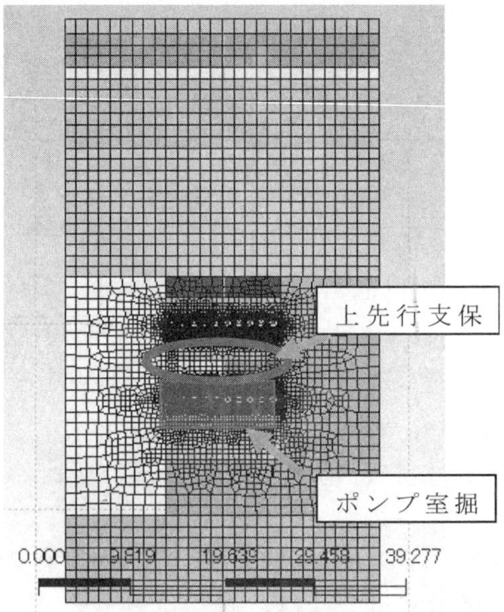

図-8 縦断方向モデル

(1) 上側曲線パイプルーフ

全土被り相当の鉛直応力度の鋼管ピッチ 1.2 m 分である 328 kN/m を載荷した．中央部の変位が 6.515 mm であった．この結果から，ばね値は 1 本あたり 50,290 kN/m と評価した．

(2) 下側曲線パイプルーフ

鉛直力 427 kN/m と水平力 214 kN/m とを載荷した．その結果，中央部が 4.332 mm 変位した．このことから，ばね値は 1 本あたり 9,857 kN/m と評価した．

4.4 曲線パイプルーフの掘削解放力分担率の評価

ポンプ室中央のトンネル掘進方向断面を図-8のようにモデル化し，施工完了時の曲線パイプルーフ周辺における鉛直方向地盤応力度と初期応力度との比率で曲線パイプルーフ掘削解放応力の分担率を算定した．

(1) 上側曲線パイプルーフ

初期応力状態と掘削後の鋼管周辺における鉛直応力度の平均値を算出し，鋼管とポンプ室の掘削により解放される土圧のうち鋼管に作用する比率を α で示す.

以上の結果から初期鉛直応力度 σ_{0v} が 559.9 kN/m^2 で，掘削後の鉛直応力度の平均値 $\overline{\sigma}_{iv}$ が 454.5 kN/m^2 となり，上曲線パイプルーフに作用する掘削解放力の分担率 α は 81%となった.

(2) 下側曲線パイプルーフ

初期鉛直応力度 σ_{0v} が 709.0 kN/m^2 で，掘削後の鉛直応力度の平均値 $\overline{\sigma}_{iv}$ が 180.3 kN/m^2 となり，下側曲線パイプルーフに作用する掘削解放力の分担率 α は 25%となった.

4.5 ポンプ室内部掘削時の各部材発生断面力算定

計測結果から確認したセグメント，曲線パイプルーフそして変形防止鋼材の挙動を，(4)で求めた解放率を用い，トンネル横面方向の 2 次元 FEM 解析モデルによる解析によって表現することを試みる.

(1) 解析モデル

解析モデルを図-9,10 に示す．なお，図では寸法や支保工を記入するため半断面で示したが，解析は全断面で行っている．本モデルでは，全土被りを考慮し，水平方向に掘削幅の約 5 倍，下方向にトンネル径の約 2 倍の解析領域とし，境界条件

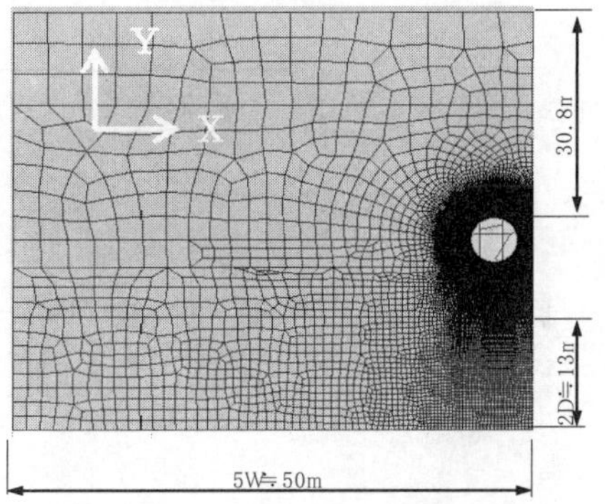

図-9 横断方向 2 次元 FEM 解析モデル

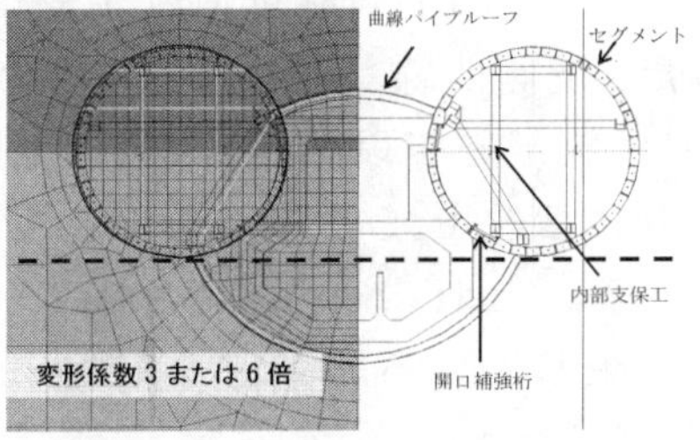

図-10 横断方向 FEM 解析モデル（拡大図）

は下端が X,Y 方向固定，左右端は X 方向固定，Y 方向自由とした.

(2) 解析ケース

解析ケースを表-9 に示す．千代らの論文 [3)]の解析条件と比較して，曲線パイプルーフ施工の影響を考慮したケースと，さらに，変形防止鋼材およびセグメントの曲げ剛性を 1/10 に低下させたケースについて解析を実施した.

表-9 解析

	掘削下地盤剛性	鋼管解放力分担率	内部支保工・セグメントの剛性
case1	6倍	無視	低下無し
case2	3倍	考慮	低下無し
case3	3倍	考慮	低下考慮（1／10）

(3) 解析ステップ

解析は，実際の施工手順にあわせ，上半掘削，上床版打設，側壁打設，下半掘削などの施工ステップ順に解析を行う．また，「4.4 曲線パイプルーフの掘削解放力分担率の評価」の結果に基づき，上半 1 次掘削では掘削解放率を 81%に，下半掘削では掘削解放率を 25%とした．その他の掘削では，解放率は全て 100%として解析を実施した.

5　計測結果

上記の方法で解析した結果と実測値を比較する．解析値は，曲線パイプルーフと変形防止鋼材を設置したステップで計算された値を初期値とし，上半1～3次掘削および下半掘削の各施工段階での値を初期値からの変化量で示して，実測値と比較する．

(1) 曲線パイプルーフ

図-11 に上下曲線パイプルーフにおける曲げモーメントと軸力の解析値と実測値とを比較して示す．上側曲線パイプルーフの軸力は，施工段階①「上半一次掘削」で case2 と case3 の解析値が実測値とほぼ一致するが，その後，実際には生じていない水平荷重によって解析値が圧縮力が実測値より大きな値となっている．これに対して，case1 の解析値は全ての施工段階で実測値の 3～4 倍となった．上側曲線パイプルーフの曲げモーメントについては，実測値も解析値も施工段階①「上半一次掘削」で正曲げ側に変化し，その後，顕著な変化が見られないという点で傾向が一致している．ただし，case2 と 3 の解析値は，実測値よりやや大きい値となり，case1 の解析値は実測値より 3～4 倍の値となった．下側曲線パイプルーフの軸力については，case1 の解析値が施工段階④「下半掘削」で軸力の解析値が圧縮側に変化している点を除いて，実測値とよく一致している．これに対して，case2 と case3 の解析値では施工段階②「上半２次掘削」以降，軸力は大きく生じている結果となった．

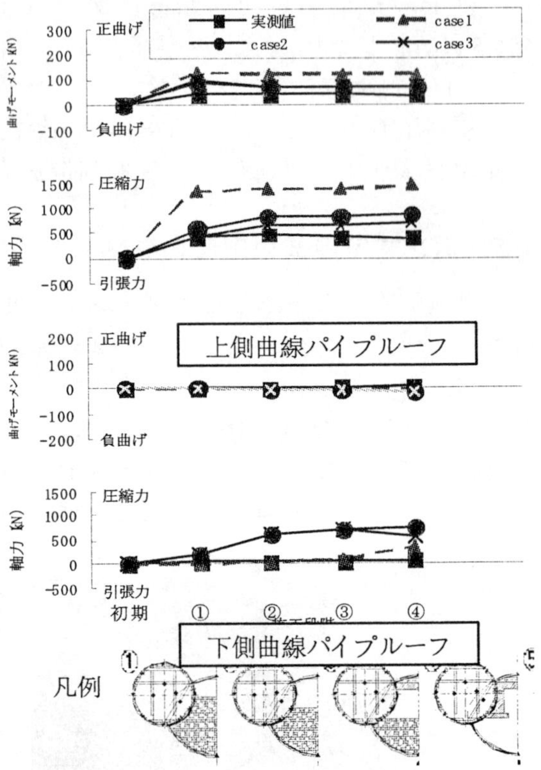

図-11　実測値と解析値との比較（曲線パイプルーフ）

(2) セグメント

セグメントポンプ室側の 240° と 270° では，case2 と case3 における軸力の解析値は，比較的実測値と一致している．施工段階①と②ではやや差あるが生じるが，③以降で良く一致している．これに対して，case1 の解析値は実測値と違いが大きい．

240° と 270° の曲げモーメントでは，case2 と case3 の解析値は，施工段階①と②で，はらみだしによる影響が表現できず，計測値より小さい値となっているが，③と④での変化は良く一致している．曲げモーメントでも case1 の解析値と実測値の挙動が異なっている．

315° では，軸力については全ての解析値と実測値とがほぼ一致しているが，曲げモーメントでは，全ての解析値が実測値と差がある．180° では全ての解析値が負曲げに変化しており，ほとんど変化のなかった実測値と異なる変化となっている．これは，解析では下半掘削による荷重の受け替えとリバウンドの影響が断面力に反映したが，実測値ではこれらの影響が非常に小さかったためと思われる．

(3) 変形防止鋼材（斜材）

斜材の解析値は全てのケースで，施工段階②以後，実測値の 3～4 倍となっている．ただし，施工段階①では case2 と case3 の軸力の解析値と計測値は一致している．

また，施工段階④「下半掘削」時に，case1 と case2 の解析値で，斜材と鉛直１の軸力が圧縮側に変化しており，実測値と異なっている．

実測値は，ほとんど変化のなかったが，解析値では変化が大きいものが多く異なる動きとなっている．

6 まとめ

本研究により得られた知見と課題を以下にまとめる.

・施工段階①「上半１次掘削」で，曲線パイプルーフと変形防止鋼材の軸力において，case2 と case3 の解析値と実測値がよく一致している．このことから，曲線パイプルーフの構築時の横断方向の応力解放による影響とトンネル掘進方向のアーチ効果を考慮して，得られた掘削解放率を用いてトンネル横断方向の２次元 FEM 解析のモデルに用いることにより，３次元的な効果を反映した計算が可能となった.

・水平荷重の受け替えやリバウンドにともなう上向き荷重による構造物の挙動は，トンネル縦断方向の事前解析を行う解析方法よりも，掘削下部地盤の変形係数を初期剛性の６倍にして行った解析結果の方が実測値に近い値を示した.

・ボルトおよび溶接による鋼材の接合部や計測位置の断面が異なることによる影響で変形を吸収するので，実際に発生する断面力は解析値より小さくなると考える.

・非開削工法による地下空間切拡げは，モデルが複雑であり，発生する断面力を正確に推定することは難しいが，より合理的な設計法の策定が可能となるように本研究を推進していく予定である.

謝辞：本論文のまとめるにあたって貴重なご意見をくださった早稲田大学　小泉　淳先生，日本シビックコンサルタント（株）　斉藤正幸氏に深甚なる謝意を表します.

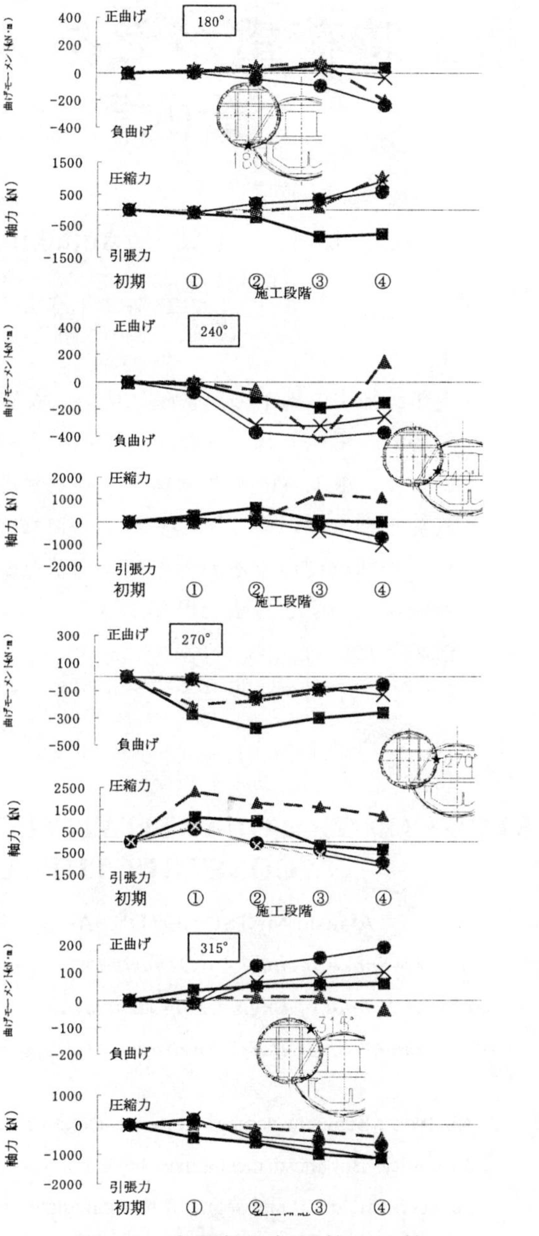

図-12　実測値と解析値の比較

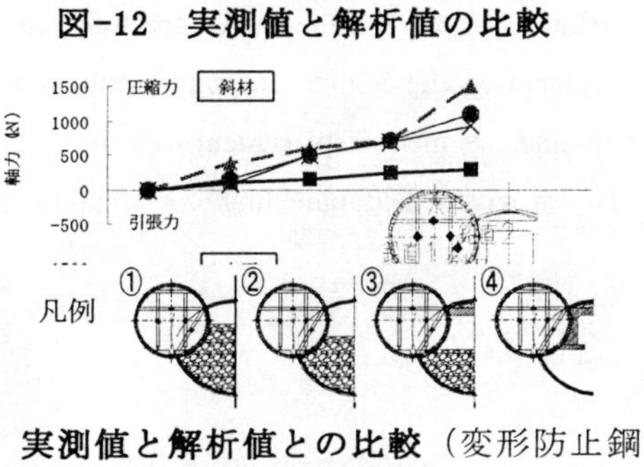

図-13　実測値と解析値との比較（変形防止鋼材）

参考文献（References）:

[１]　荻野　竹敏，村松　泰ほか：地下鉄 13 号線（副都心線）中間ポンプ室（その２）（PSS－Arch 工法の計測結果のまとめ），第 62 回年次学術講演会講演概要集，6-012，2007.

[２]　辻　雅之，村松　泰ほか：都心部における非開削地下空間施工法の仮設設計に関する一考察，トンネル工学論文集，第 17 巻，pp.93-103，2007.

[３]　千代　啓三，辻　雅行ほか：都心部での非開削切拡げ施工の計測結果と解析に関する一考察，トンネル工学論文集，第 18 巻，pp.89-110，2008.11.

著者紹介（Bio-data）:

岩波　基，博士(工)；長岡工業高等専門学校 教授；1987 年早稲田大学大学院修了；構造工学，トンネル工学.

Motoi IWANAMI, Dr.Eng.; Nagaoka National College of Technology ,Professor, ; M.Eng.,Waseda University, Japan(1987); Fields: Structure Engineering, Tunnel engineering.

E-mail: miwanami@nagaoka-ct.ac.jp

施工時荷重がセグメント挙動に与える影響の定量的評価方法に関する検討

松本　貴士[1]，Auttakit　Asanprakit[2]，陳　剣[3]，杉本　光隆[3]
1. 日本シビックコンサルタント株式会社 地下空間設計部，東京　116-0013
2. 長岡技術科学大学大学院 工学研究科，長岡新潟　940-2188
3. 長岡技術科学大学 環境建設系，長岡新潟　940-2188

近年，都市の地下の過密化に伴い，大深度および急曲線におけるシールドトンネルの施工が増加している．また，コスト縮減の流れを受け，セグメントの薄肉化および幅広化が進んでいる．これらにより，施工時にセグメントに発生する応力は以前より増大する傾向にあり，セグメントにひび割れなどの損傷が多く発生するようになっている．本研究では，シールド機動力学モデルのシールドテール部に作用する力のモデルを改良し，シールド掘進中にセグメントに作用する施工時荷重を定量的に推定する方法を提案するとともに，セグメントの変位計測データを用いて同手法の妥当性を検証した．

キーワード：シールドトンネル；施工時荷重；セグメント挙動；シールド動力学モデル；三次元有限要素法

STUDY ON THE QUANTITATIVE METHOD FOR ASSESSING THE INFLUENCE OF CONSTRUCTION LOADS ON SEGMENT BEHAVIOR

Atsushi MATSUMOTO[1]，Asanprakit AUTTAKIT[2]，Jian CHEN[3]，Mitsutaka SUGIMOTO[3]
1. Geo-Space Technology Department, Nippon Civic Consulting Engineers Co. Ltd., Tokyo 116-0013, Japan;
2. Graduate School of Engineering (Doctoral Program), Nagaoka University of Technology, Nagaoka 940-2188, Japan;
3. Department. of Civil and Environmental Engineering, Nagaoka University of Technology, Nagaoka 940-2188, Japan

Abstract: Segment damage during excavation at sharp curve due to construction loads gives heavy influence on tunnel durability. But these mechanism have not yet been made clear quantitatively. In this paper, at first, the contact force between shield tail and segment was calculated by a modified kinematic shield model with shield-segment interaction in detail. By using the measured jack force and the obtained contact force, the segment displacement was analyzed by 3D segment model with a ground reaction curve. Finally, the performance of its model was discussed, comparing the obtained segment displacement with the measured one.

Key words: shield tunnelling; construction loads; segment behavior; kinematic shield model; 3D-FEM

1　はじめに

近年，都市の地下空間では，構造物の輻輳化や施工可能空間の狭隘化により，シールドトンネルの大深度化や急曲線化が進み，加えてコスト縮減の流れを受け，シールドトンネルの急速施工化，セグメントの薄肉化，および，幅広化などが進んでいる．これらのことから，施工時にセグメントに作用する荷重は以前よりも増大する傾向にあり，施工中のトンネルに発生する不具合が顕在化してきている．しかし，施工時にセグメントに作用する荷重については，定量的な検討を含め，未解明な点が多いのが現状である[1].

施工時荷重に関する研究としては，現場計測データをもとにした研究と数値解析による研究が行われている．前者については，有泉ら[2][3]，吉本ら[4]，中村ら[5]が，シールドジャッキ力，テールシール圧，グリス圧，裏込め注入圧や接合セグメントが，施工時にセグメントに作用する荷重に与える影響を明らかにするとともに，設計上の考え方や，セグメント断面力を用いてセグメント外荷重を推定する手法を提案している．一方，後者については，田嶋ら[6][7][8]，Leendertse ら[9]が，セグメントをソリッド要素で，継手をばね要素でモデル化した３次元 FEM 解析により，シールドジャッキ使用状況やセグメント組立誤差等が，セグメント発生応力に与える影響を解析している．しかし，前者はシールド全体の力の釣合いを考慮に入れた検討となっていないこと，後者はセグメント組立誤差がセグメント発生応力に与える影響を把握することを主な目的としていて，急曲線部始点近傍のセグメント挙動を数値解析した研究は今までなかった．

そこで本研究では，これまで開発，検証してきたシールド機動力学モデル[10]を用いてシールドの挙動をシミュレーションすることにより施工時荷重を推定するとともに，得られた施工時荷重を外力としたシールドトンネルの 3 次元 FEM 解析を行い，FEM 解析により得られたセグメント変位分布とセグメント変位計測結果[11]を比較することにより，施工時荷重がセグメント挙動に与える影響の定量的評価方法を検討することを目的とする．

2　現場計測

2.1　現場概要

検討対象のトンネルは，図-1 の路線平面図に示すように，R=17.3 m～50.0 m の急曲線部を 5 個所含む，延長 2 840 m，内径 4 000 mm の下水道シールドトンネルである．シールドの掘削管理データの計測区間（以下，計測区間と呼ぶ）は，R=17.3 m の左曲線を含む区間であって，中折れ機構を有する泥土圧式シールドを用いて，土被り約 13.5 m，地下水位 G.L.-4.15 m で掘削された．計測区間の地層構成は，砂層，砂礫層を主体とする上総層群を基盤層として，下位より東京層，厚い層厚を有する沖積層が分布し，図-2 の地質縦断図に示すように，計測区間のトンネル横断面には，N 値が 0～2 である下部有楽町層粘性土層上部 Ylcu と，N 値が 0～6 である下部有楽町層粘性土層下部 Ylcl の境界面が現れる．表-1，表-2，表-3 に現場概要，セグメント諸元，地盤物性値を，それぞれ示す．

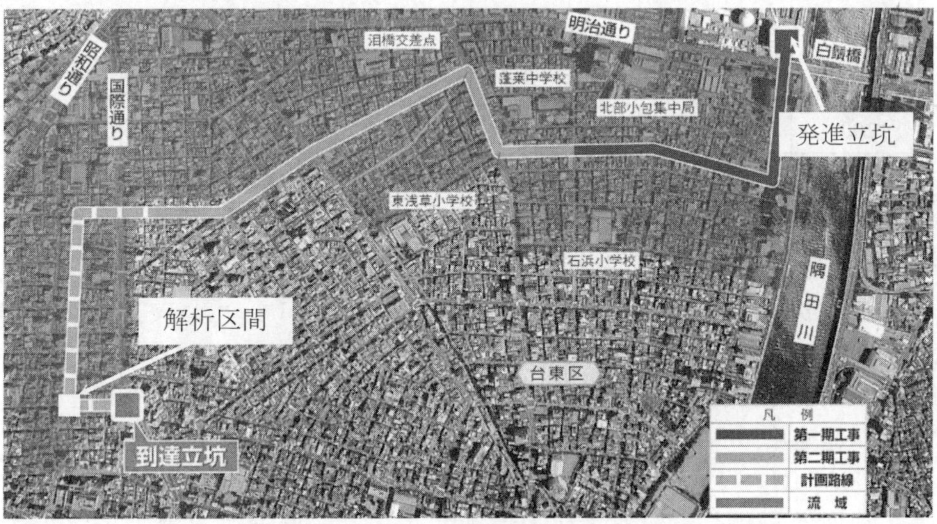

図 1　路線平面図

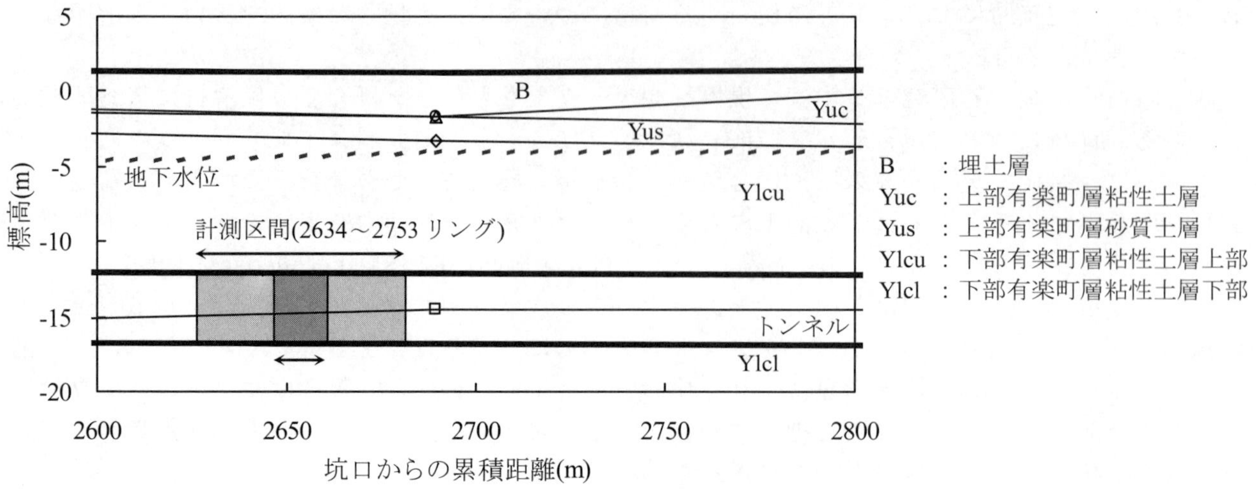

図 2　地質縦断図

表 1　現場概要

地盤	地層	下部有楽町層
	N 値	0～6
	土被り	約 13.5 m
	地下水位	G.L.-4.15 m
トンネル線形	掘進延長	2840 m
	最小曲線半径	17.3 m
	勾配	下り 0.06%
シールド	外径	4 700 mm
	全長	7 200 mm
	テールシール	ワイヤブラシ式×3
	中折れ装置	V 中折れ

表 2　セグメント諸元

線形	直線部	直線部	曲線部
Ring No.	2650～2655	2656～2667	2668～2752
種類	鋼製セグメント		
幅(mm)	1200	300	300
外径(mm)	4550	4550	4480

表 3　地盤物性値

地層	Ylcu	Ylcl
N値	0～2	0～6
単位体積重量(kN/m^3)	16.20	16.20
静止土圧係数	0.882	0.787
地盤反力係数(kN/m^3)	2772	8316

2.2　シールドの掘進管理データ

図-3 に，シールドの制御，挙動に関する計測データを示す．この図から，距離 2 652 m 付近で，ジャッキ推力 F_{3r} が 6.0 MN～7.3 MN と安定しているにもかかわらず，掘進速度 V_s が 0.043 m/min から 0.018 m/min へと急減していること，テール部が曲線始点を通過中である距離 2 657 m 付近で，掘進速度 V_s が約 0.02 m/min と変動していないにもかかわらず，ジャッキ推力 F_{3r} が 6.1 MN から 8.3 MN へと急増していることがわかる．これらは，取込率が直線部で約 1.02，曲線部で 0.75～1 程度と変化し，切羽土圧が増加したこと，曲線始点部でテールクリアランスが減少したことのためであると考えられる．

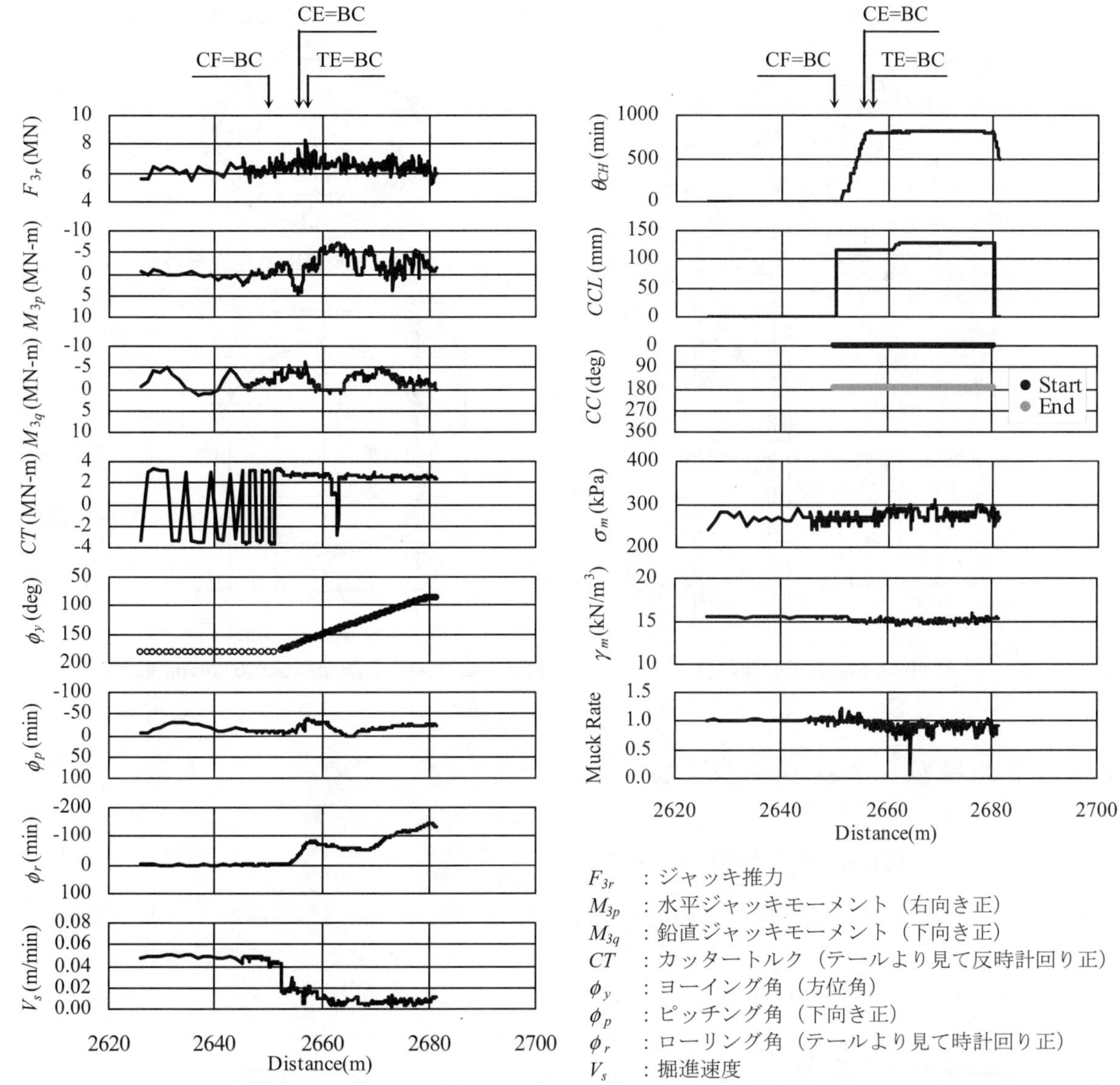

CF=BC：カッターフェイスが曲線始点部を通過中
CE=BC：エレクター中心が曲線始点部を通過中
TE=BC：テールエンドが曲線始点部を通過中

F_{3r} ：ジャッキ推力
M_{3p} ：水平ジャッキモーメント（右向き正）
M_{3q} ：鉛直ジャッキモーメント（下向き正）
CT ：カッタートルク（テールより見て反時計回り正）
ϕ_y ：ヨーイング角（方位角）
ϕ_p ：ピッチング角（下向き正）
ϕ_r ：ローリング角（テールより見て時計回り正）
V_s ：掘進速度
θ_{CH} ：中折れ角（左折れ正）
CCL ：コピーカッター長さ
CC ：コピーカッター使用範囲
（インバートをゼロとし，テールより見て時計回り正）
σ_m ：切羽圧
γ_m ：チャンバー内泥水密度
Muck Rate：取込み率

図 3　シールドの掘進管理データ

2.3　セグメント変位計測データ

図-4 に示すように，セグメントの変形，変位が最も発生すると想定される曲線始点から 2 リング手前のリング継手面（2 664～2 665 リング継手面）で，図-5 に示す 8 点の変位をトータルステーション 2 台とユニバーサル内空変位計[12]で計測した．本論文に用いた 2 671 リング掘進時のセグメント断面変位の実測値を坑口側より切羽側を見た状態で図-6 に示す．なお，セグメント断面変位は 40 倍にして表示している．また，図-6 の計測時は，2671 リング掘進中で，ジャッキストローク 1 510 mm（急曲線掘進のため，シールドジャッキ固定端を移設した 1 100 mm を含む），シールドのエレクター中心点が計画線形上の距離程 2 656.731 m に位置し，テールエンドが 2 666 リング（ラッパ形状外径調整セグメント）を通過中である．この図より，セグメントは縦長に変形し，セグメント全体が曲線外側に剛体変位していることがわかる．

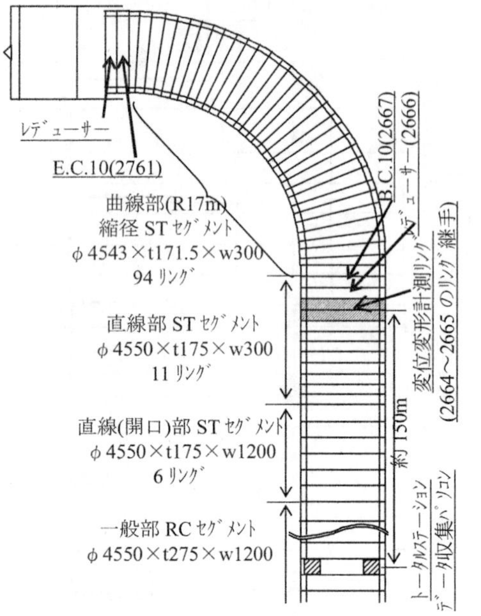

図 4　トンネル覆工計測位置

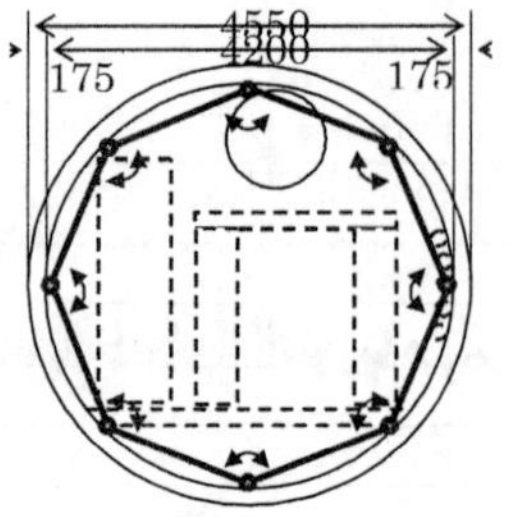

図 5　トンネル覆工内空変形計測

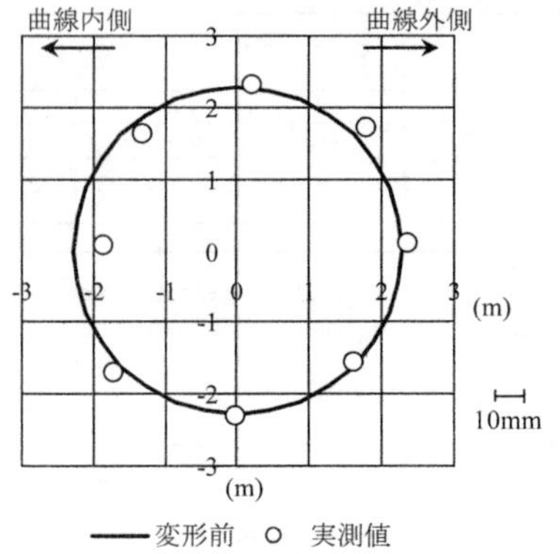

図 6　セグメント断面変位(2671Ring 掘進時)

3　シールドの挙動シミュレーション

3.1　シールドテール部における作用力のモデル

シールドからセグメントに作用する施工時荷重を検討する場合には，詳細なシールドテール部における作用力（以下，シールドテール作用力と呼ぶ）モデルが必要となる．そこで，本研究では，既存のシールドテール作用力モデル[10]を図-7 に示すように改良した．すなわち，シールドテール作用力を，

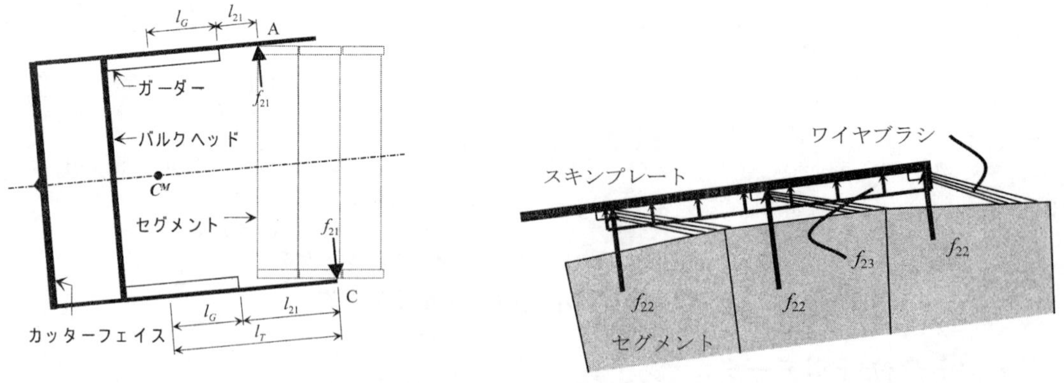

(a) シールドテールとセグメントの競りによる作用力　(b) ワイヤブラシとグリースによる作用力

図 7　シールドテールに作用する力

f_{21}：シールドテールとセグメントの競りによる作用力

f_{22}：ワイヤブラシによる作用力

f_{23}：ワイヤブラシ間に充填されているグリスによる作用力

に分類するとともに，以下の仮定を用いた．

(1) セグメントは剛体で，真円である．

(2) シールドテールがセグメントと競った場合，シールドテールはガーダー端部を支点とする片持ち梁として挙動する．

(3) ワイヤブラシによって発生する力は，ワイヤブラシがセグメントに接触する位置のテールクリアランスに依存し，ワイヤブラシに沿った線荷重として作用する．

(4) ワイヤブラシ間に充填されたグリスによって発生する力は，グリス注入圧とグリスの流動抵抗で，分布荷重として作用する．

シールドが曲線部を掘進しているなどの理由で，テールクリアランスの周方向分布に偏りがある場合，テールクリアランスが大きい所で裏込め注入材がテールシールに回り込んで固化し，有効なテールクリアランスが減少し，競りが発生しやすくなることがある[1]．そこで，シールドテールとセグメントの競りによる作用力f_{21}，ワイヤブラシによる作用力f_{22}を，図-8に示すテールクリアランスと作用力の関係で表現した．ここで，Δtcは，裏込め注入材がテールシールに回り込み固化したことによるテールクリアランス減少量で，指定したワイヤブラシから後方のワイヤブラシに対して，周方向に分布して設定できるようにした．

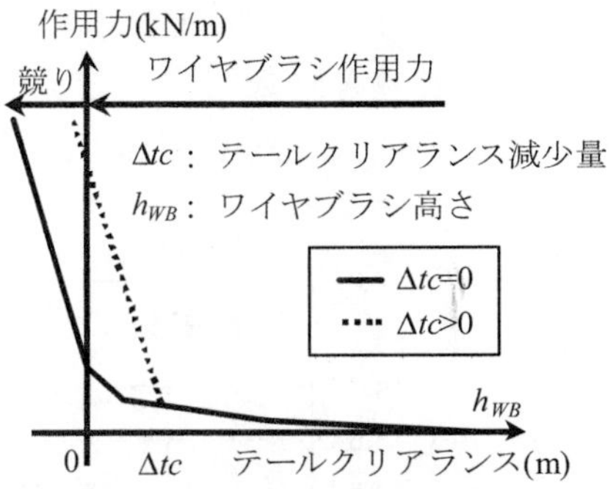

図8 テールクリアランスと競り，ワイヤブラシによる作用力の関係

3.2 解析条件

グリスの流動抵抗については，具体的な値が不明であるため，ワイヤブラシ間に充填されているグリスによる作用力f_{23}のうち，グリスの流動抵抗をゼロとし，解析を行った．これは，シールドテールとセグメントの競りによる作用力f_{21}と，ワイヤブラシによる作用力f_{22}に，グリスの流動抵抗を含めたことになる．

掘削半径とシールド半径の差による全周余掘り，および，コピーカッターによる余掘りには，取込めなかった掘削土や泥水，掘削壁面から剥落してくる土砂が入り込むため，100%有効にはならない．そこで，パラメータ解析を実施し，余掘り低減率を表-4のように設定した．

表4 余掘り低減率

掘進 Ring No.	角度(deg)	低減率
余掘り 2657～2683	全周	1
コピーカッター 2657～2670	0	0.400
	30	0.400
	40	0.000
	140	0.000
	150	0.400
	210	0.400
	220	0.000
	320	0.000
	330	0.400
コピーカッター 2671～2683	0	1.000
	30	1.000
	40	0.000
	140	0.000
	150	0.300
	210	0.300
	220	0.000
	320	0.000
	330	1.000

表5 テールクリアランス減少量Δtc

掘進 Ring No., 範囲	角度(deg)	Δtc(m)
2671～2672, ワイヤブラシ3段目	0	0.000
	30	0.000
	60	0.100
	120	0.040
	150	0.000
2673～2717, ワイヤブラシ3段目	0	0.000
	30	0.000
	60	-0.020
	120	-0.020
	150	0.000

さらに，裏込め注入材が回り込み固化したことによるテールクリアランス減少量Δtcをゼロとして，シールドの挙動のシミュレーションを行うと，「2.2 シールドの掘進管理データ」で述べた図-3のシールド推力と掘進速度の関係を再現できなかったこと，シールド推力が急増する直前のシールドテール端部におけるテールクリアランス（以下，テールエンドクリアランスと呼ぶ）分布の解析値は，シールド左側で最大となり，約100mmであったことから，2671~2717リングにΔtcを表-5のように設定した．ワイヤブラシのばね値は，既往の実験データ[13]を基に，パラメータ解析で決定した．

3.3 シールドの挙動

図-9 に，トンネル計画線形とシールド機動力学モデルによるシールドの挙動のシミュレーションにより得られたシールド軌跡の縦断図，平面図を示す．これらの図より，縦断線形は，距離程 2 658 m までは計画値と一致しているが，距離程 2 658 m 以降で計画値より上方となり，シミュレーション終了時で計画値より約 0.15 m 上方となった．平面線形は，直線部，曲線部とも計画線形とよく一致していることがわかる．

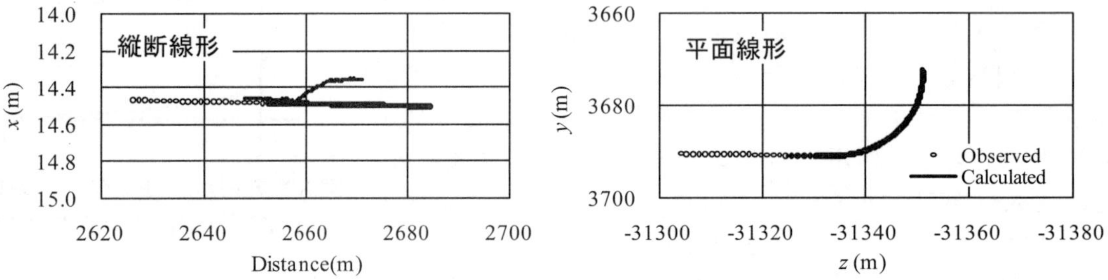

図 9　シールド軌跡

図-10 に，ヨーイング角 .$_y$，ピッチング角 .$_p$，掘進速度 V_s の実測値と計算値を示す．これらの図より，ヨーイング角，ピッチング角，掘進速度の計算値は直線部，曲線部とも実測値とよく一致していることがわかる．

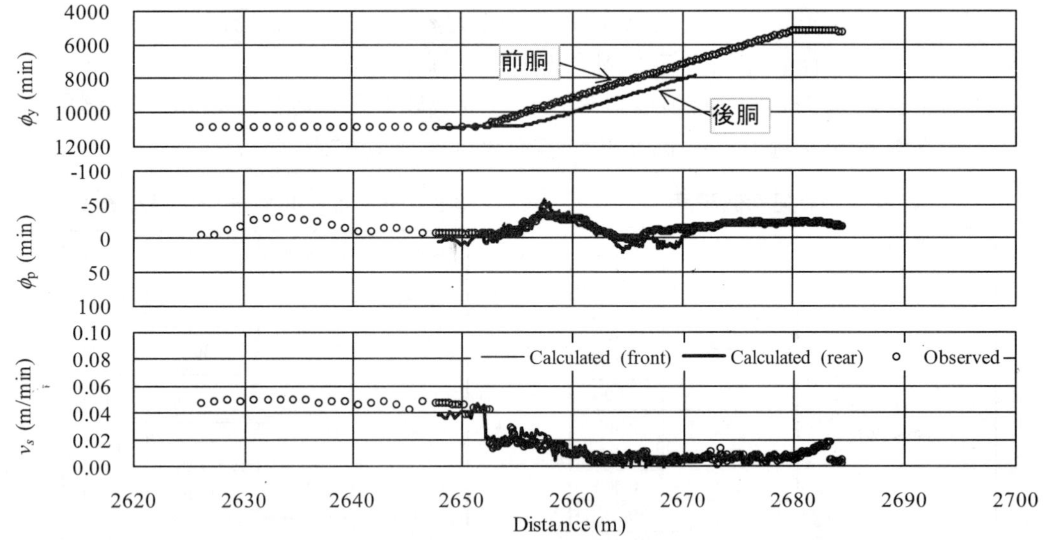

図 10　シールド挙動

3.4 シールドテールとセグメントの位置関係

図-11 に，シールドの挙動シミュレーションにより得られた，テールクリアランスとテールエンドクリアランスの経時変化を示す．この図から，距離程 2 655 m 付近で，クラウン部のテールクリアランスの変化と関係なく，インバート部のテールクリアランスが増加している．同様に，左スプリングラインのテールクリアランスに対応して，右スプリングラインのテールクリアランスが増加している．そして，距離程 2 654 m~2 656 m で，右スプリングラインのテールエンドクリアランスが減少し，左スプリングラインのテールエンドクリアランスが増加している．さらに，距離程 2 658 m 以降で，左スプリングラインのテールエンドクリアランスがマイナスとなり，競りが発生していることがわかる．これらは，距離程 2 655 m 付近で，テール部がラッパ形状外径調整セグメントを通過中であること，距離程 2 654m~2 656 m で，中折れ角が 500~800 min 程度で，右向きのジャッキモーメントを使用していることと対応していると考えられる．また，距離程 2 654 m~2 656 m における左スプリングラインのテールエンドクリアランス増加時に，ワイヤブラシに裏込め注入材が回り込み，その後，距離程 2 657 m 付近で，ジャッキモーメントが左向きへ変化するとともに，左スプリングラインのテールエンドクリアランスが減少し，これらのためにシールドテール作用力が増加し，それに伴い掘進抵抗が増加し，距離程 2 657 m 付近でジャッキ推力が増加したと考えることができる．

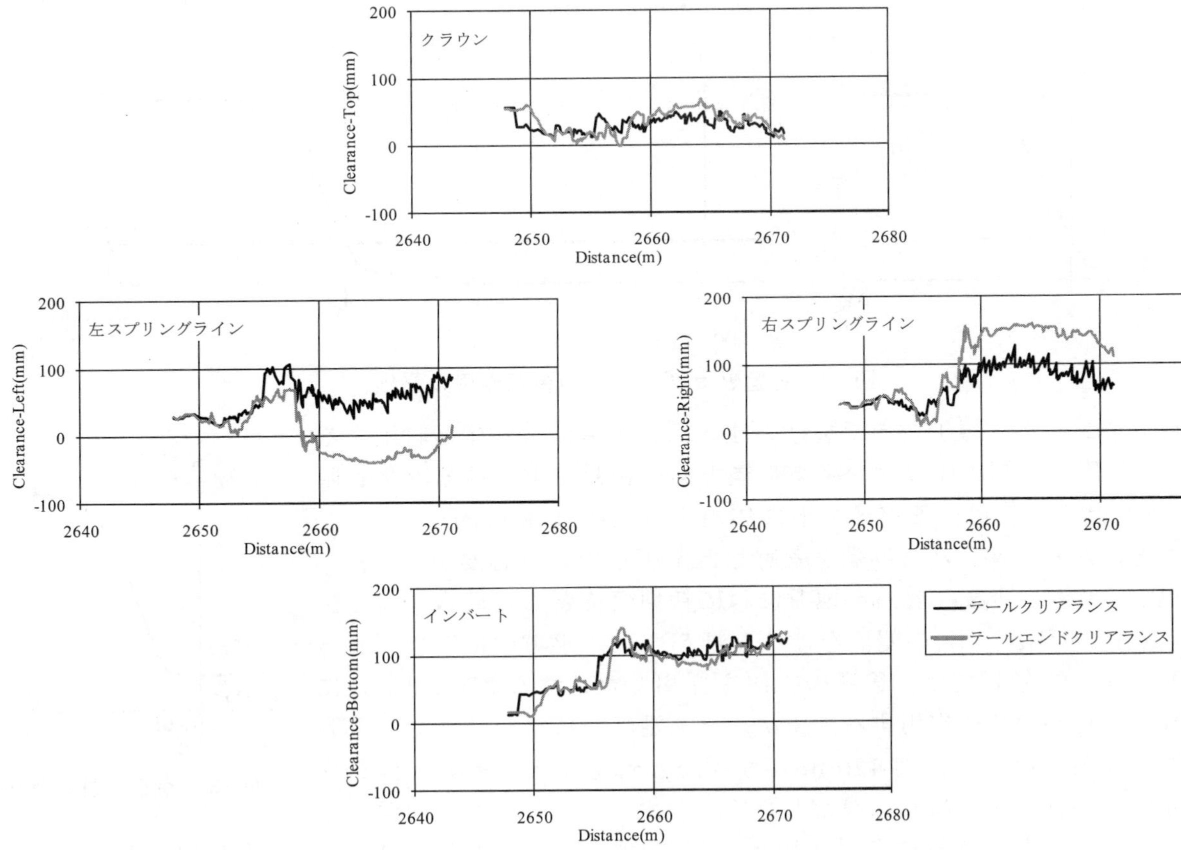

図 11　テールクリアランスの経時変化

4　セグメント変位解析

シールド機動力学モデルを用いて得られた施工時荷重を用いて，3 次元 FEM 解析によりセグメント変位を求め，計測されたセグメントの断面変位との比較を行った．

4.1　地盤とセグメントの相互作用モデル

本解析では，地盤とセグメントの相互作用モデルとして，図-12 に示す地盤反力曲線の特性を有する全周ばねモデルを用いた．図中のδ_nは初期掘削面からセグメント外周面への距離（外向き正），σ_nはセグメントに作用する土圧で，セグメントの変位に関係無く定まる設計土圧σ_{n0}と，セグメントの変位よって生じる土圧変化$\Delta\sigma_n$との和で表される．ここで，σ_{n0}は地盤ばねにプレストレスト力を導入することにより，$\Delta\sigma_n$は非線形地盤ばねで表現できる．したがって，このモデルでは，地盤が受働側となる場合のみだけでなく，地盤が主働側となる場合にも地盤反力が変化する．なお，地盤を土水一体として扱う場合には，全土圧を土圧σ_nとし，土水分離として扱う場合には，有効土圧を土圧σ_nとし，水圧をトンネルに直接載荷すればよい．また，この地盤ばねモデルを用いれば，初期応力解析が不要になるとともに，トンネル全体のトンネル横断方向の剛体変位を表現できる．

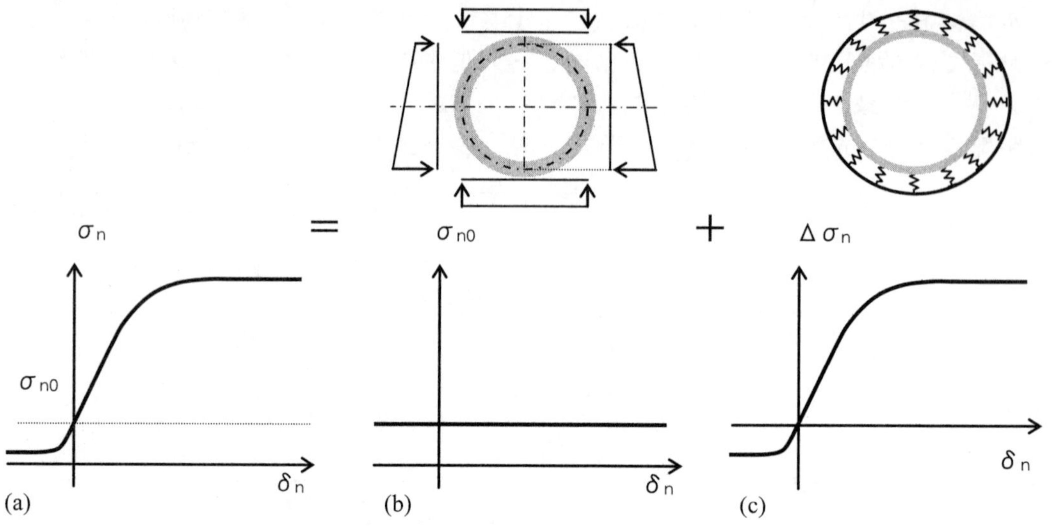

図 12　地盤とセグメントの相互作用の評価

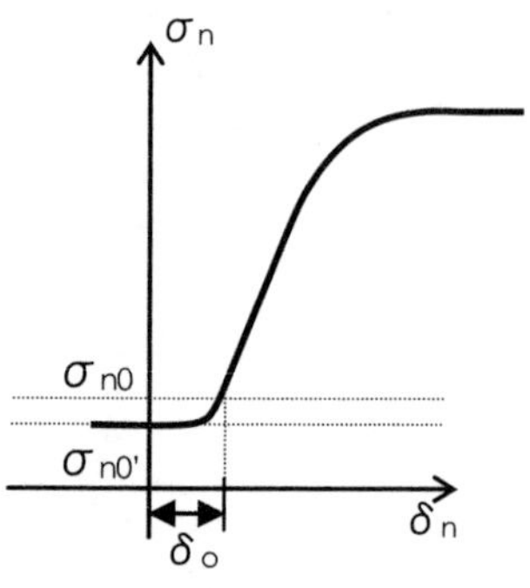

図 13　ゆるみ量の評価

さらに，シールド覆工背面の裏込め注入は，圧密により体積収縮する[14]（以下，体積収縮に伴うトンネル半径方向の相対変位をゆるみ量と呼ぶ）．こうした場合には，セグメントに作用する土圧は静止土圧より小さくなることがあるため，ゆるみ量を考慮した土圧を用いる必要がある．これを表現するには，ゆるみ量δ_0を地盤ばねに初期変位として導入する方法と，図-12(a)に示す$\delta_n-\sigma_n$の関係をゆるみ量δ_0だけ水平方向にシフトする方法があるが，本解析では，後者の方法を採用した．すなわち，図-13に示すように，δ_n=0の時に作用する土圧σ_{n0}'を地盤ばねにプレストレスト力として導入するとともに，図-12(c)に示す$\delta_n-\Delta\sigma_n$をゆるみ量δ_0だけシフトした非線形特性を地盤ばねに設定した．こうすることにより，地盤がゆるみ量δ_0だけ変位したときに設計土圧σ_{n0}が作用するようになる[15]．こうした地盤ばねの特性は，シールド機動力学モデルの地盤ばねの特性と同じである．

4.2　解析モデル

セグメント断面変位を表現するためには，シールドからセグメントに作用するジャッキ推力，シールドが変位することにより生じるテール作用力，セグメント周辺地盤を考慮しなければならない．また，シールドの変位を表現するためには，シールドのカッターフェイスに作用する切羽抵抗，シールド周辺地盤，セグメントから作用するジャッキ推力を考慮しなければならない．そこで，本研究では，これらの影響を評価するために，テール作用力f_2によるセグメントの横断方向の変形と，ジャッキ推力f_3によるトンネル全体の軸直角方向の剛体変位を分けて解析モデルを開発した．ここで，セグメント周方向剛性および周方向曲げ剛性と等価な剛性をシェル要素に，トンネル全体の軸方向曲げ剛性と等価になるようにリング継手部の軸方向ばねを設定した．図-14に解析モデルの概要図を示す．

ジャッキ力の影響範囲は20m程度と言われていることから，解析範囲は切羽側端部の2670リングから後方30mとし，周方向，軸方向ともに一様剛性のシェル要素でモデル化し，地盤中にある部分を地盤ばねで支えた．また，トンネル坑口側節点を鉛直ローラー，地盤ばねの地盤ばね外側節点を剛結とした．また，セグメント周面の周方向，軸方向摩擦を表現するために，シェル要素と地盤ばねの間にインターフェイス要素を設定した．このインターフェイス要素は，垂直，せん断方向ともに，相対変位と応力が線形関係にあるが，せん断応力の上下限は，Mohr-Coulomb型の摩擦則で規定される．このインターフェイス要素のせん断相対変位u_tとせん断応力t_tの関係を図-15に，解析条件は表-6に示す．

なお，本解析の対象地盤は粘性土層なので，法線方向応力として全応力を用いた．

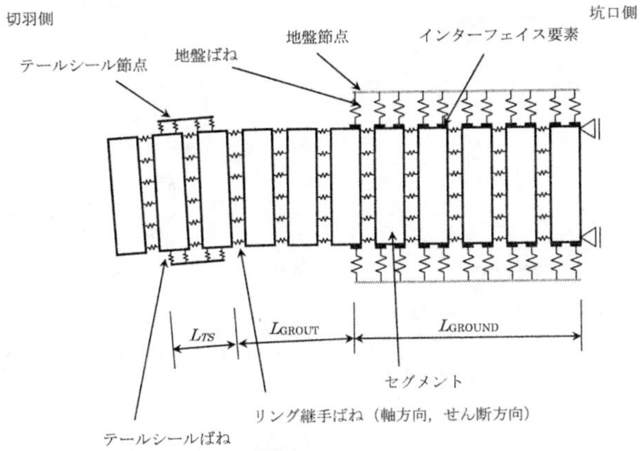

(a) 変形解析モデル

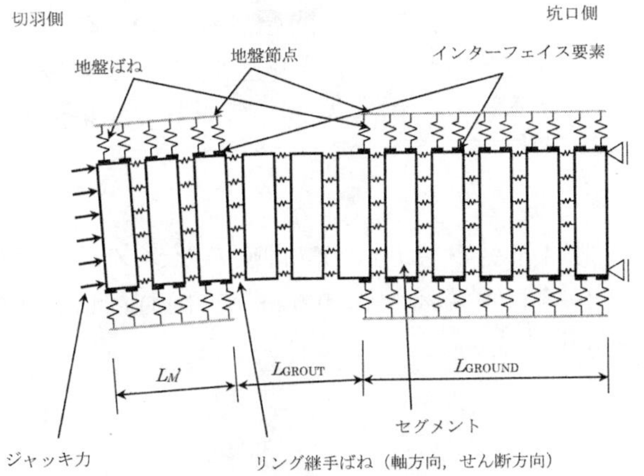

(b) 変位解析モデル

図 14　解析モデルの概要図

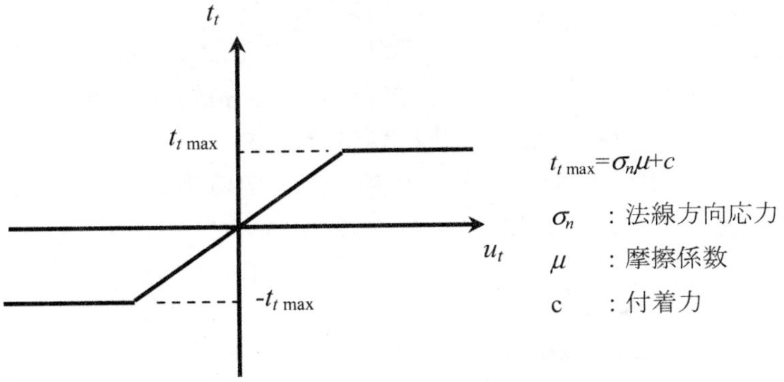

図 15　インターフェイス要素のせん断方向の特性

表 6　解析条件

モデル		L_M(m)	7.200
		L_M'(m)	1.200
		L_{TS}(m)	0.746
		L_{GROUT}(m)	1.800
		L_{GROUND}(m)	27.000
セグメント		幅(m)	0.300
		図心半径(m)	2.12175
		厚さ(m)	0.1430
	軸方向	ヤング率(kN/m^2)	6.646E+08
		ポアソン比	0.300
		せん断剛性係数(kN/m^2)	2.556E+08
	周方向	ヤング率(kN/m^2)	3.323E+07
		ポアソン比	0.300
		せん断剛性係数(kN/m^2)	1.278E+07
	半径方向	ヤング率(kN/m^2)	3.323E+07
		ポアソン比	0.300
		せん断剛性係数(kN/m^2)	1.278E+07
その他	インターフェイス要素		
		垂直剛性(kN/m^3)	1.00E+10
		せん断剛性(kN/m^3)	2.77E+03
		摩擦係数	0.200
		付着力(kN/m^2)	0.000
	リング継手		
		軸方向ばね(kN/m)	4.954E+05
		半径方向ばね(kN/m)	3.217E+07
		接線方向ばね(kN/m)	3.787E+07
	テールシール		
		圧縮ばね値(kN/m)	7.500E+04

図-14(a)の変形モデルには，2671リング掘進時のテールクリアランス分布と2670リング掘進完了時のテールクリアランス分布より，2670リング掘進完了から2671リング掘進時へのシールドテールの変位を求め，テールシール節点に強制変位として与えた．図-16に各断面の強制変位量分布を示す．一方，図-14(b)の変位モデルには，施工時荷重として，セグメントの切羽側端部に2671リング掘進時に計測されたジャッキ力を，ジャッキ中心と2670リングのセグメント中心を結ぶ方向に作用させた．図-17に，2671リング掘進時のジャッキパターンとジャッキ推力を示す．なお，土水圧，セグメント自重は，両モデルに与えた．

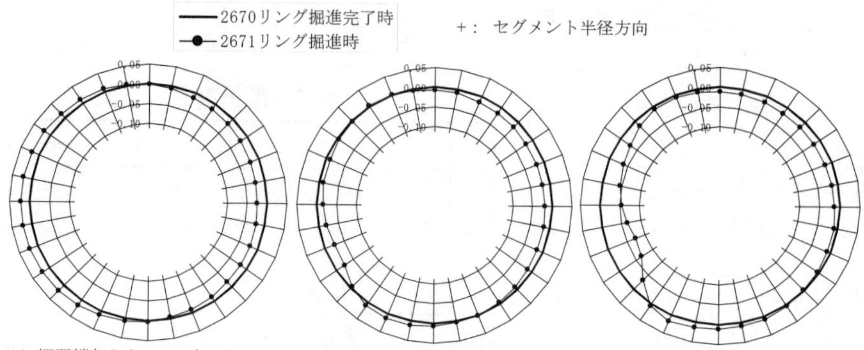

(a) 切羽端部から 0.6m 坑口側　(b) 切羽端部から 0.9m 坑口側　(c) 切羽端部から 1.2m 坑口側

図 16　各断面の強制変位量(m)

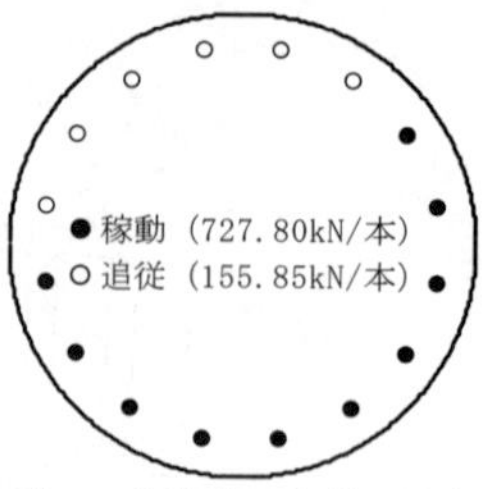

作用方向：ジャッキ中心−セグメント中心

図 17　ジャッキパターン(テールより見た)とジャッキ推力

4.3　解析手順

セグメントの断面計測は，2666リング組立後，シールド停止中から開始されているので，計測されたセグメントの断面変位は，施工時荷重載荷前を初期値(変位ゼロ)とした施工時荷重載荷後の変位である．そこで，以下の手順で，変形，変位を対象とした解析を行い，両者を足し合わせ，解析結果を得た．

(1) 施工時荷重を載荷せず，解析を行う．

(2) 施工時荷重を載荷し，解析を行う．

(3) (2)で求めた計測断面変位(セグメント切羽側端部から 1.8 m 坑口側)のセグメント変位から，(1)で求めた計測開始時点の計測断面位置(セグメント切羽側端部から 0.6 m 坑口側)のセグメント変位を減じて．2671 リング掘進時のセグメント変位を算出する．

4.4　セグメント断面変位

図-18に，計測断面におけるセグメント断面変位の計算値と計測値を，坑口側より切羽側を見た状態で示す．なお，変位は40倍にして表示している．また，セグメントの変形量（鉛直内空－水平内空，＋：縦長），水平方向変位量（＋：右側への変位），鉛直方向変位量（＋：上側への変位）を図中に示す．この図より，解析値は，セグメントが縦長に変形し，曲線外側に剛体変位する挙動を再現できていること，縦長の変形量は，計測値で10.8 mm，解析値で9.8 mmで，解析によりセグメントの変形を概ね表現できていること，また，セグメントの水平方向剛体変位は，計測値で2.6 mm右側，解析値で1.7 mm右側で，解析によりセグメントの曲線外側への剛体変位を概ね表現できていることがわかる．これらは，図-16に示した強制変位量から，シールドテールエンド（セグメント切羽側端部から1.2 m坑口側）の曲線内側で，圧縮の強制変位が最大であり，それにともなって，大きなシールドテール作

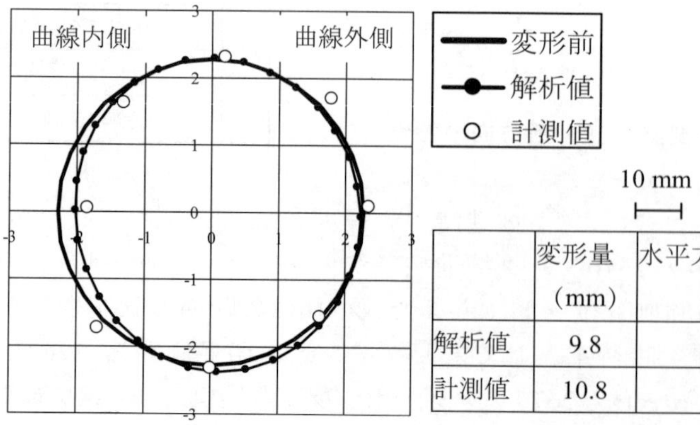

	変形量 (mm)	水平方向変位量 (mm)
解析値	9.8	1.7
計測値	10.8	2.6

図 18　セグメント断面変位(変位 40 倍)

用力が作用していること，自由端であるセグメント切羽側端部に図-17に示したジャッキ推力が作用し，セグメント切羽側端部に曲線外向きの水平力が作用していること，セグメントの横断方向の変形性能を表現するために，セグメント周方向剛性，セグメント周方向曲げ剛性と等価な剛性を，トンネル全体の軸直角方向の剛体変位を表現するために，トンネル全体の軸方向曲げ剛性と等価になるようにリング継手部の軸方向ばねを設定したことのためであると考えられる．

図-19に，セグメント法線方向変位分布を，セグメントのインバート部で切断したスキンプレート展開図上に示している．横軸0，360degはセグメントインバート部で，坑口側より見て時計回りに展開している．また，図の上端はセグメント切羽側端部，下端はセグメント坑口側端部で，トンネル外側への変位が正である．この図より，以下のことがわかる．

(1) テールシールばねに与えた圧縮強制変位量が最大となるセグメント切羽端部より 1.2 m 坑口側の左スプリングライン付近で，トンネル内側への最大変位が発生している．

(2) セグメント背面の裏込め注入材が固結している区間 L_{GROUND} は，変位量は小さく，切羽側から 13.0 m（距離 17.0 m）で，変位は収束している．

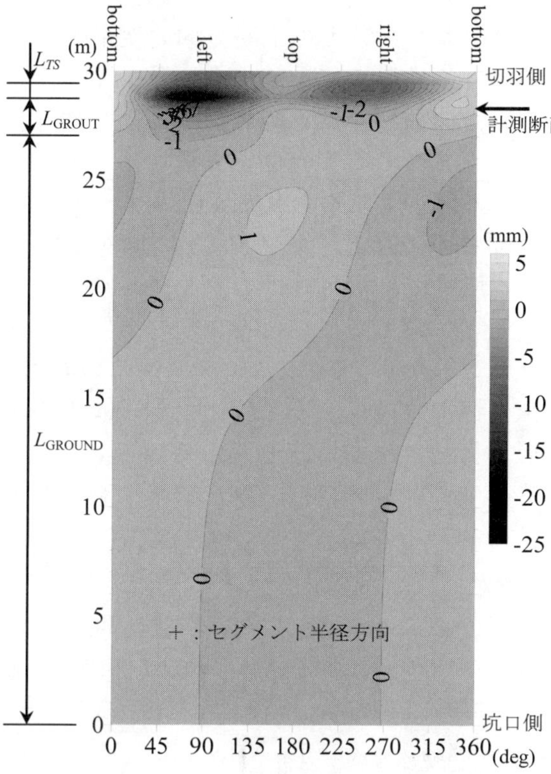

図 19　セグメント法線方向変位分布

これらは，図-18のセグメント断面変位で述べたように，切羽側から1.2 m（距離28.8 m）の曲線内側で，大きなシールドテール作用力が生じていること，地盤ばねがセグメントの変位を抑制していることのためであると考えられる．

4.5　テール作用力

解析より得られたテールシールばねの軸力を基に，シールドの変位によりシールドテールからセグメントに作用する応力の平均値を算出したところ，9 829 kN/m^{2}となった．セグメントスプリングライン位置の鉛直土圧は約180 kN/m^{2}なので，このシールドテールに作用している応力は，鉛直土圧の50倍以上の大きい応力となっている．

5　まとめ

本論文では，より詳細なシールドテール作用力を表現できるように改良したシールド機動力学モデルを用いて，シールドの挙動をシミュレーションすることにより施工時荷重を推定した．さらに，得られた施工時荷重を外力とし，シールド機動力学モデルの地盤ばねと同じ特性を有する地盤ばねで支えられたシールドトンネルの 3 次元モデルを用いて，3 次元 FEM 解析を行い，得られたセグメント変位分布とセグメント変位計測結果を比較することにより，施工時荷重がセグメント挙動に与える影響の定量的評価方法を検討した．以上より得られた結論を以下に記す．

(1) 施工時荷重の影響が見られた現場のシールド挙動を再現できたことから，改良したシールドテール作用力モデルは妥当である．

(2) 軟弱地盤中の急曲線では，シールドの挙動はシールドテール作用力の影響を大きく受けるが，シールド機動力学モデルは，シールドテール，セグメントの変形を考慮できない．このため，シールド機動力学モデルを軟弱地盤中の急曲線に適用する場合には，セグメントの変形を考慮するために，マイナスのテールクリアランス減少量を与えるといった工夫が必要である．

(3) セグメントの横断方向の変形性能を表現するために，セグメント周方向剛性，セグメント周方向曲げ剛性と等価な剛性を，トンネル全体の軸直角方向の剛体変位を表現するために，トンネル全体の軸方向曲げ剛性と等価になるようにリング継手部の軸方向ばねを設定することによって，計測されたセグメント断面変位を表現することができた．

(4) 解析より得られたシールドテールに発生する応力は 9829 kN/m^2 で，セグメントスプリングライン位置の鉛直土圧より 50 倍以上の大きい応力となった．

本解析では，2671 リング掘進時のジャッキ推力，シールド挙動から，2671 リング掘進時に計測されたセグメント断面変位を表現した．しかし，セグメント断面変位計測は，2666 リング組立後より行われたことから，2671 リング掘進時の計測結果は，2667 リング掘進から 2671 リング掘進までの，各リング掘進時のジャッキ推力，シールド挙動によるシールドテール作用力によるセグメントの変位，変形が累積されていると考えられる．シールドテール作用力を適切に評価するためには，各リング掘進時のセグメント変位，変形を足し合わせて評価できるモデルが必要と考えられる．

参考文献（References）:

[1] 土木学会トンネル工学委員会技術小委員会シールドトンネル施工時荷重検討部会：トンネル・ライブラリー17　シールドトンネルの施工時荷重，土木学会，2006.

[2] 有泉毅，岡留孝一，五十嵐寛昌，長屋淳一：シールド洞道に働く施工時荷重に関する分析，トンネル工学研究論文・報告集，Vol.9，報告 36，1999.

[3] 有泉毅，岡留孝一，長屋淳一：シールド洞道に働く荷重計測結果とその分析(その２)，トンネル工学研究論文・報告集，Vol.9，報告 37，1999.

[4] 吉本正治，阿南健一，大塚正博：シールドトンネルの施工時荷重の照査方法に関する一提案，土木学会論文集，No.756，6-62，pp.131-144，2004.

[5] 中村益美，足立一郎，大迫健一，松浦將行：大深度急曲線シールド工事における施工時荷重の実態と分析，下水道協会誌，Vol.41，No.495，pp.127-139，2004.

[6] 田嶋仁志，岸田政彦，団昭博，斉藤正幸：現場施工データに基づく大断面シールド機の挙動解析，トンネル工学研究論文・報告集，Vol.14，報告 51，2004.

[7] 田嶋仁志，岸田政彦，深井直光，斉藤正幸：三次元 FEM モデルを用いたシールドトンネルの施工時荷重に関する検討，トンネル工学研究論文・報告集，Vol.14，報告 52，2004.

[8] 田嶋仁志，春日清志，深井直光，団昭博，斉藤正幸：セグメント挙動計測に基づいた大断面シールドトンネルにおける施工時荷重の影響検討，トンネル工学報告集，Vol.15，pp.293-300，2005.

[9] W.L. Leendertse, P.S. Javanovic, C.B.M. Blom: Using 3D FEM models for predicting damage during assembling of shield driven tunnel lining of the Green Heart Tunnel, Modern Tunneling Science and Technology, Proc. Of IS-Kyoto, pp.653-656, 2004.

[10] 杉本光隆，Aphichat Sramoon：施工実績に基くシールド機動力学モデルの開発，土木学会論文集，No.673/III-53，pp.131-144，2004.

[11] 譽田孝宏，粥川幸司，杉本光隆，中村益美，岡田章：急曲線シールド掘進に伴うトンネル覆工挙動の現場計測，トンネル工学報告集，Vol.15，pp.347-354，2005.

[12] 橋本正，藤原正明，中山淳，坂田啓二，岩切琢哉，西田修：連結ユニバーサル変位計の開発，第２回最近の地盤計測技術に関するシンポジウム発表論文集，pp.11-14，2000.

[13] 中村益美，沢里能雄，小林豊，李黎明：テールブラシの施工時荷重を考慮した実験的検討，土木学会第 59 回年次学術講演会，6-041，2004.

[14] 杉本光隆，佐藤豊，入中島克明：シールドトンネルに用いる可塑状裏込め注入材の圧密挙動に関する研究，

土木学会論文集，No.788/V-67，pp.127-137，2005.
[15] 岡崎麻里，杉本光隆，A. Sramoon：大深度地下シールドトンネル用セグメントの設計方法に関する一考察，土木学会第 58 回年次学術講演会，3-433，2003.

著者紹介（Bio-data）：

松本　貴士（まつもと　あつし）
所属　日本シビックコンサルタント株式会社
　　　地下空間設計部　シールド Gr.
最終学位　工学博士（シールド機動力学モデルによる施工時荷重の評価方法に関する研究）
Atsushi MATSUMOTO
NIPPON CIVIC CONSULTING ENGINEERS Co.,LTD.
Geo-Space Technology Department　Shield Gr.
Doctor of Engineering (Research on evaluation method of execution loads by shield kinematic model)
E-mail　matsumoto@nccnet.co.jp

重複円形シールドトンネルの応答変位法における地盤ばねに関する考察(その 2:地盤反力)

徐 敏 眞鍋 尚
みずほ情報総研㈱ ｻｲｴﾝｽｿﾘｭｰｼｮﾝ部 東京都千代田 101-8443 日本

論文要旨：シールドトンネル耐震解析におけるはりーばねモデルによる応答変位法ではトンネル・地盤間の相互作用を地盤ばねでモデル化する．本論では重複円形シールドトンネルに対し，カモメ部セグメントを含む，周辺の地盤反力の適切な設定について検討した．3 次元動的 FEM 解析方法による結果と比較を通して，重複円形シールドトンネルの応答変位法における地盤ばね様々な方法によって求める解析結果の比較を行い，算定方法について議論する．

キーワード：応答変位法；地盤反力係数；重複円形シールドトンネル；3 次元動的 FEM；M-K 法

CONSIDERATIONS OF THE COEFFICIENT OF SUBGRADE REACTION ON SEISMIC DEFORMATION METHOD OF DOUBLE-O-TUBE SHIELD TUNNEL (Part Ⅱ : SUBGRADE REACTION)

Min XU，Takashi MANABE
Science Solutions Division, Mizuho Information & Research Institute, Inc. Chiyoda-ku,Tokyo 101-8443, Japan

Abstract: In the seismic deformation method to shield tunnel, the ground displacement is one of the external load by earthquake; and it is subjected to ground spring on beam-spring model based on M-K method. In comparison with to results of 3D dynamic FEM analysis, it is has been appeared that results of double-o-tube shield are errors around wing segments. In this paper, the validity of ground-springs around wing segments of double-o-tube shield tunnel is discussed on seismic deformation method based on M-K method. In particular, the coefficient of subgrade reaction is effectively estimated through discussion in details of the deformation of the ground obtained by 3D dynamic FEM analysis.

Key words: seismic deformation method; coefficient of subgrade reaction; double-o-tube shield tunnel, 3D dynamic analysis; M-K method

1 はじめに

シールドトンネルの応答変位法では，地震時におけるセグメントと地盤間の相互作用を地盤ばねでモデル化する．しかしながら，これまでこの地盤ばね定数の算出方法には確立されたものがなく，重要な検討課題の一つとなっている．

著者らは重複円形シールドトンネルに対し，3 次元動的 FEM と 2 次元はりーばねモデルの応答変位法の解析を行い，2 次元はりーばねモデルについては，既往の接線方向のせん断応力が完全に伝達されてない場合の地盤ばね定数を含む，接線方向のせん断応力が完全に伝達される場合の地盤ばね定数と FEM 解析より算定した地盤ばね定数をそれぞれ用いて行った解析結果と 3 次元動的 FEM 解析結果と比較した [1]．その結果は重複円形シールドトンネルに対し，地盤ばね定数の算定について注意が必要であることが分かった．

本論では FEM 解析モデルによる地盤ばね定数の算定方法に注目し,重複円形シールドトンネルの一般部とカモメ部にそれぞれの方法より地盤ばね定数を推定し，応答変位法による解析を行い，3 次元動的 FEM 解析方法によって得られた結果と比較する．地盤反力について，①FEM 解析モデルによる単位強制変位法（以下 δ=1 m 法と呼ぶ），②FEM 解析モデルによる単位荷重法（以下 F＝1 kN 法と呼ぶ），③2 次元弾性理論より地盤の接線方向のせん断応力が覆工に完全に伝達されない場合の理論解 [1)]（以下 Full-slip 法と呼ぶ），④2 次元弾性理論について地盤の接線方向のせん断応力が覆工に完全に伝達される場合の理論解 [1)]（以下 No-slip 法と呼ぶ），の 4 つの算定方法について検討した．

2　重複円形シールドトンネルに対する応答変位法[1)]

半無限水平成層地盤でのシールドトンネルの耐震解析には，はりーばねモデル [2)]による応答変位法は比較的簡便な計算手法であり，地中構造物の耐震設計によく用いられている．この手法では図 1 に示すような一次元重複反射理論より得られた地震時地盤変位をばね先変位で入力，周面せん断力を直接に作用させ，解析を行う．図 2 に示すような地盤に図 3 に示すような中心は地下 14.0 m における外径 3.15 m の重複円形シールドトンネルに対し，著者らはこれまでに 3 次元動的 FEM と 2 次元はりーばねモデルの応答変位法による解析結果の比較を行った．3 次元動的 FEM 解析方法によって得られた結果と比較すると，カモメの部分を除くトンネル一般部では両手法の解析結果がほぼ一致するが，カモメの部分の断面力に差が現れることが分かった． 2 次元はりーばねモデルについては，図 1 に示すような既往の Full-slip 法の地盤反力係数を含む，No-slip 法の地盤反力係数を算定し，それぞれの解析を行った．それぞれの解析結果と 3 次元動的 FEM 解析結果と比較し，カモメ部の差が小さくが，一般部の差が大きくなった．

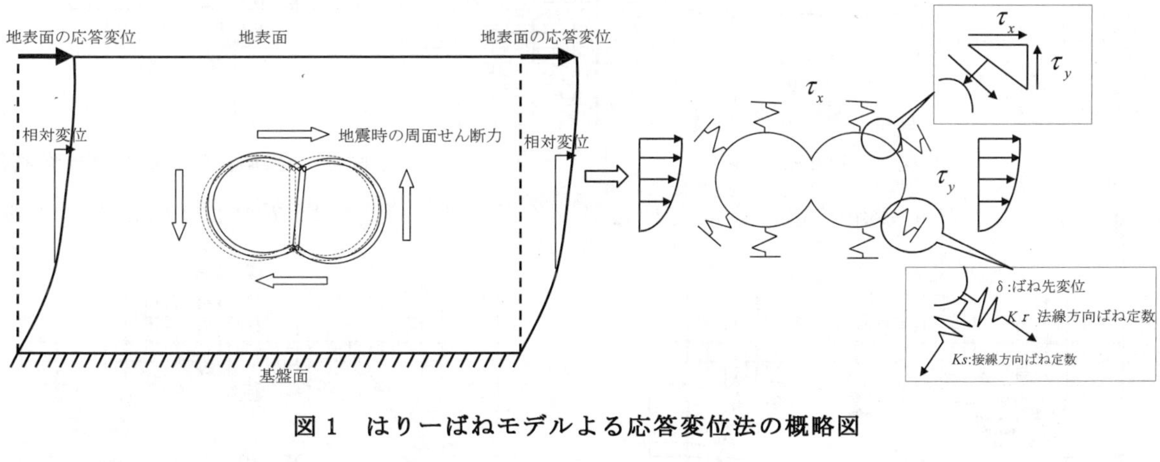

図 1　はりーばねモデルよる応答変位法の概略図

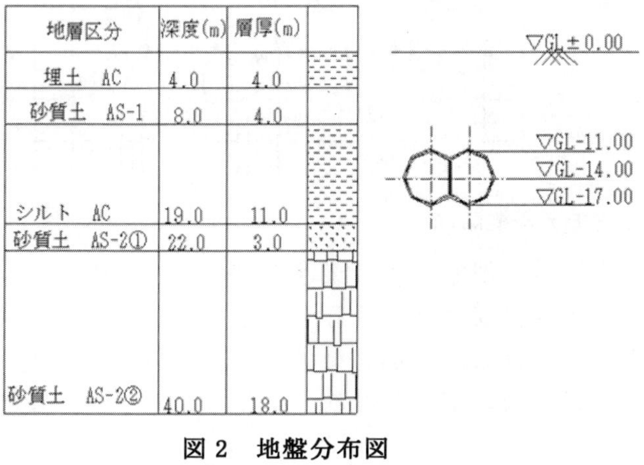

図 2　地盤分布図

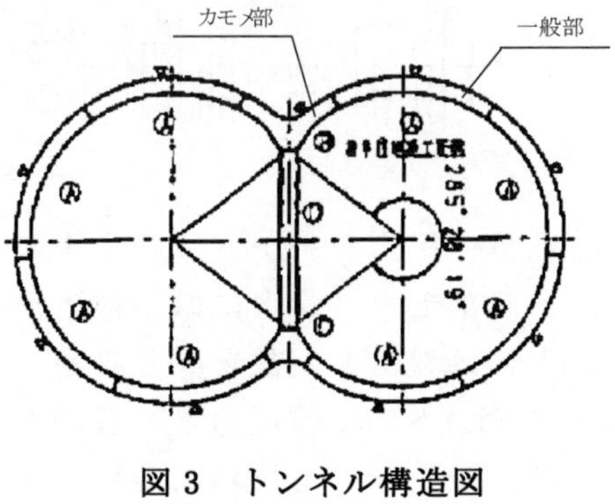

図 3　トンネル構造図

以上のことから，重複円形シールドトンネルの応答変位法の解析では，一般部とカモメ部の地盤反力係数の設定について異なる推定方法から算定する必要があることがわかった.

3 地盤反力係数の算定方法

地盤反力係数の求め方にはいくつかの方法がある．ここでは① δ =1 m 法，②F＝1 kN 法，③Full-slip 法，④No-slip 法，の 4 つ算定法より地盤反力係数を求め，それぞれの結果を用いて応答変位による解析（Case1～Case4）を行い，3 次元動的 FEM（Case5）の結果と比較し，地盤反力の算定方法について検討する．

3.1 δ =1 m 法（Case1）

ここでは，図 4 に示すような空洞地盤の FEM 解析モデルを作成し，空洞各点に単位の強制変位を作用させ [3]，その際に生じている反力から地盤に接しているセグメント周辺の地盤ばね定数を算定した．前回の解析 [1] には水平方向のみ（図 4 に示される全体座標系の X 方向）を考慮し，地盤反力算定したが，今回は水平および鉛直（図 4 に示される全体座標系の Y 方向）のそれぞれの方向に単位強制変位を与え，地盤反力を求める．求めた全体座標系の地盤反力を図 5 に示すようなトンネルの要素系（接線-法線方向の座標系）に変換し，Case1 の地盤ばね定数として，応答変位法による解析を行った．

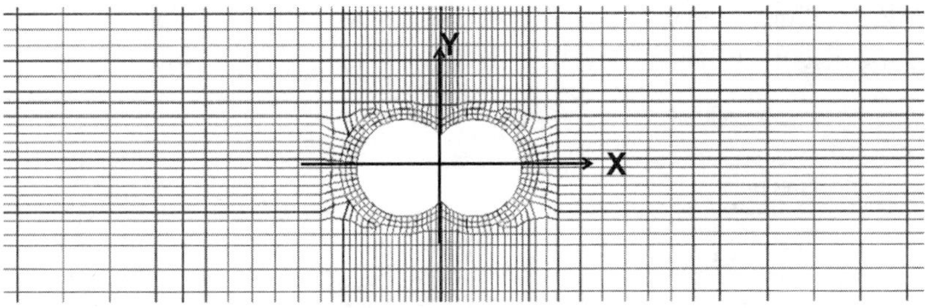

図 4　FEM モデル

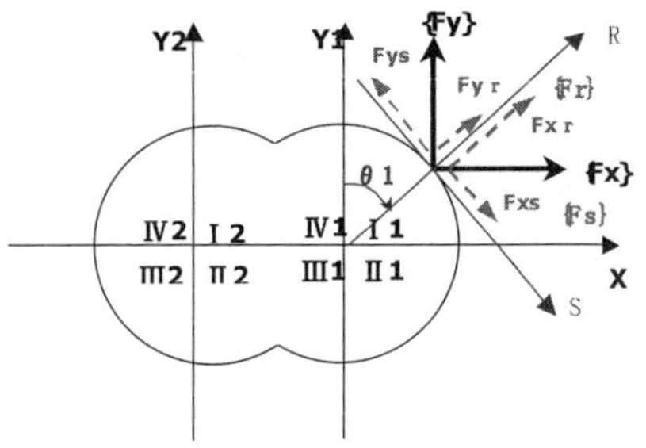

図 5　全体座標系および要素座標系

図 6 に示すような δ =1 m 法による推定した空洞各点の地盤反力は図 7 および図 8 に示す。δ =1m の場合.

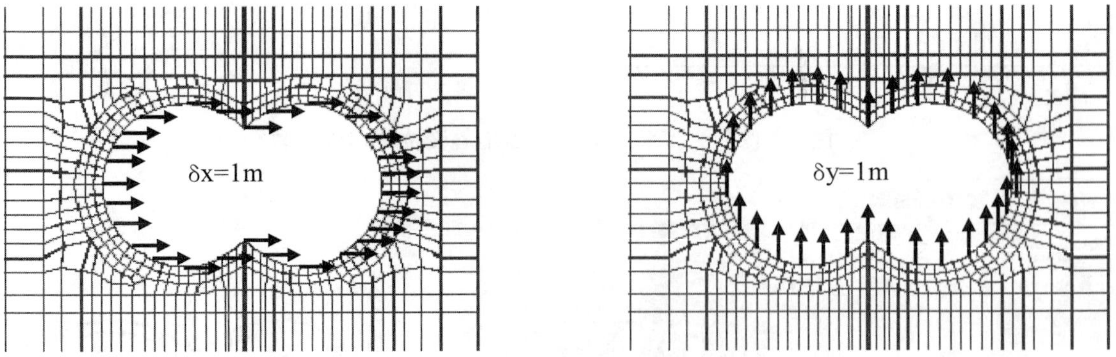

図 6　δ =1 m 法モデル概略図

には重複円形シールドトンネルの一般部セグメントの地盤反力は深さによって大きくなる．すなわち，一般部セグメントには重複円形の左および右の地盤反力は反対称となる．同じ深さにおけるセグメントの地盤ばね定数を同じ設定すればよいと考えられる．しかしながら，同じ深さにおけるカモメ部セグメントの地盤反力と一般部セグメントの地盤反力は不同となり，異なる地盤ばね定数を設定しなければならないと思われる.

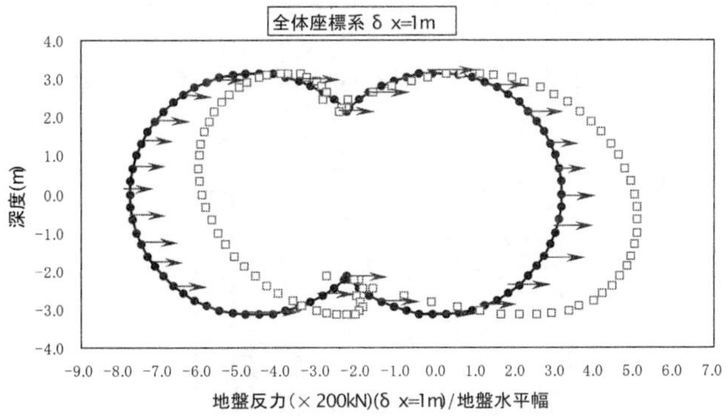

図 7　全体座標系 δ x=1m による地盤反力

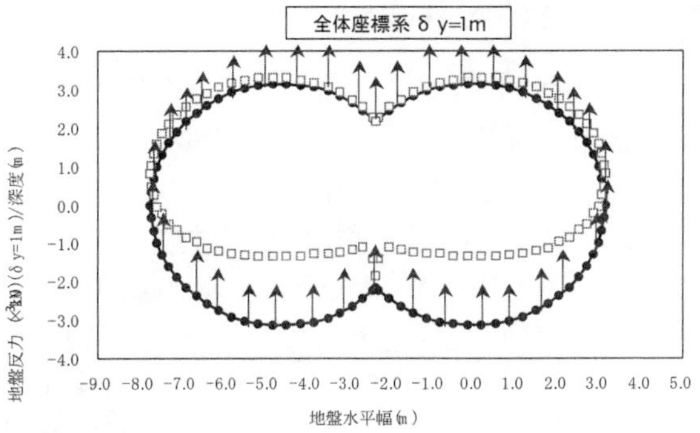

図 8　全体座標系 δ y=1m による地盤反力

ここで，応答変位法における地盤ばね定数として，X，Y 方向の地盤反力をセグメント要素座標系に変換し，絶対値を取り上げ，推定した地盤ばね定数の分布を図 9,図 10 に示す．図 9 に示すようにシールドトンネルを５つの部分に分け，各部各点の地盤反力の平均値を求め，その平均値より地盤ばね定数を求め，応答変位法による解析を行う．求めた地盤ばね定数を表 1 に示す．

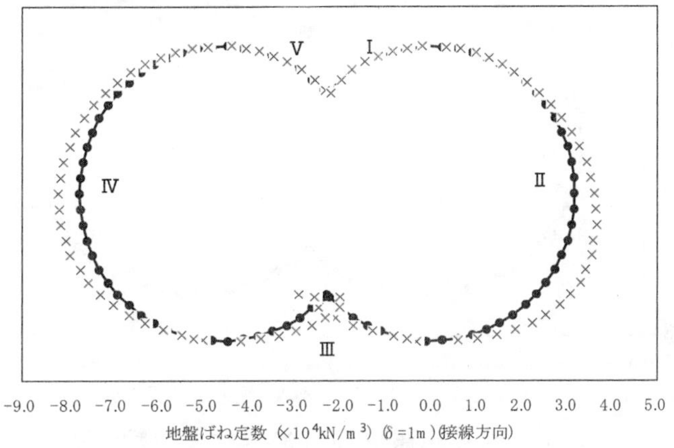

図 9　δ =1m 法による算定した接線方向地盤ばね定数分布図

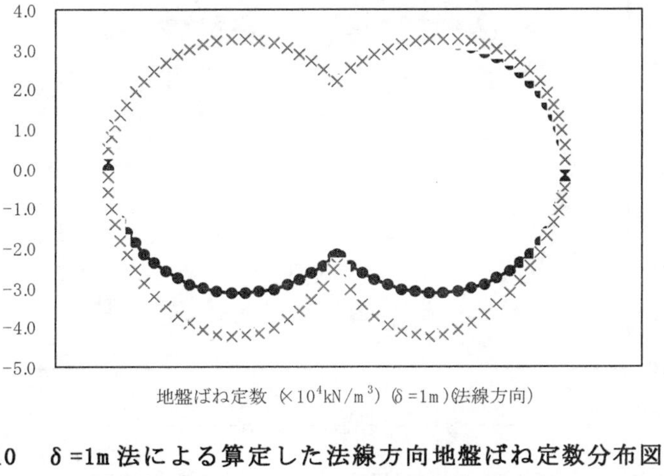

図 10　δ =1m 法による算定した法線方向地盤ばね定数分布図

表 1　δ =1m 法による算定した地盤ばね定数(kN/m^3)

δ =1m 法	I	II	III	IV	V
接線方向	5.200×10^2	3.550×10^3	1.420×10^4	3.098×10^3	4.471×10^2
法線方向	5.342×10^2	4.290×10^3	2.240×10^4	4.708×10^3	5.758×10^2

3.2　F=1 kN 法(Case2)

次に，図 11 に示すような単位荷重を空洞各点に作用させ[4)]，地盤変位の値を算出する．推定した空洞各点の地盤変位を図 12 および図 13 に示す。

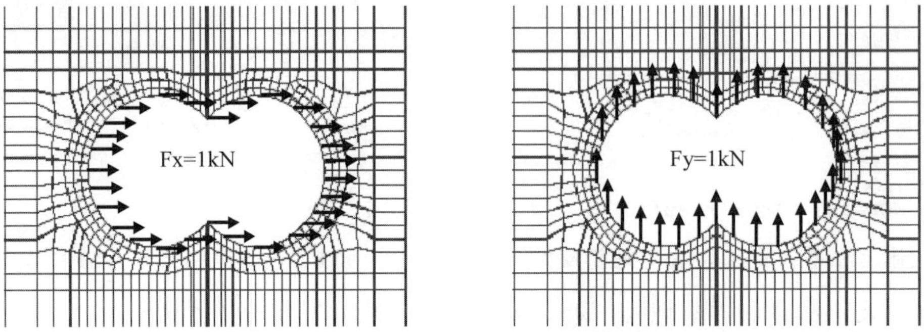

図 11　F＝1 kN 法モデル概略図

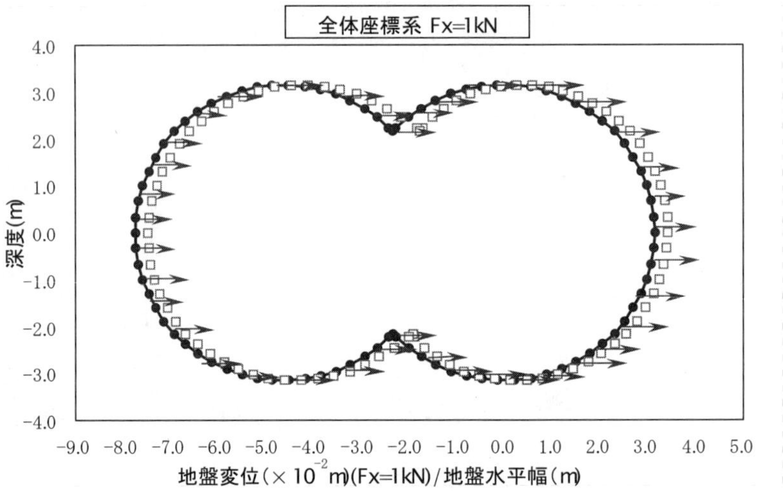

図 12　全体座標系 Fx=1 kN による地盤変位

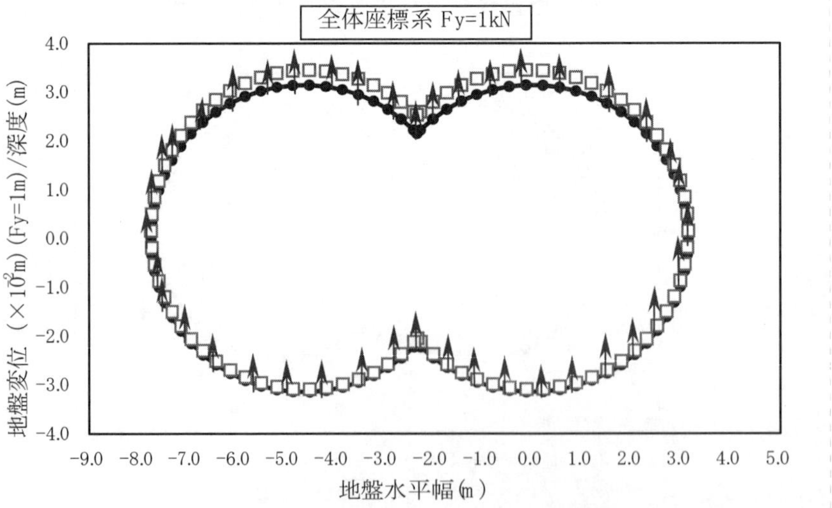

図 13　全体座標系 Fy=1kN による地盤変位

ここで，応答変位法における地盤ばね定数として，X，Y 方向の地盤反力をセグメント要素座標系に変換し，絶対値を取り上げ，推定した地盤ばね定数の分布を図 14，図 15 に示す．Case1 の場合と同様に各点の値によって図 9 に示すような 5 つの部分に分け，各部の地盤ばね定数の平均値を求め，応答変位法による解析を行う．求めた地盤ばね定数を表 2 に示す．

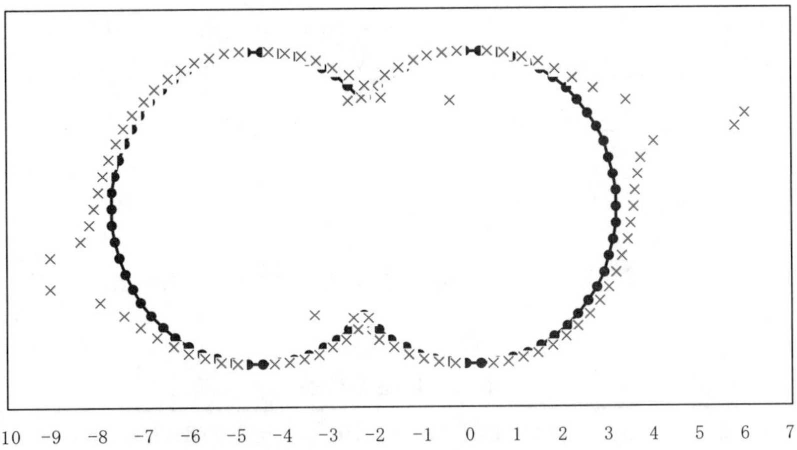

図 14　F=1kN 法による接線方向の地盤反力係数分布図

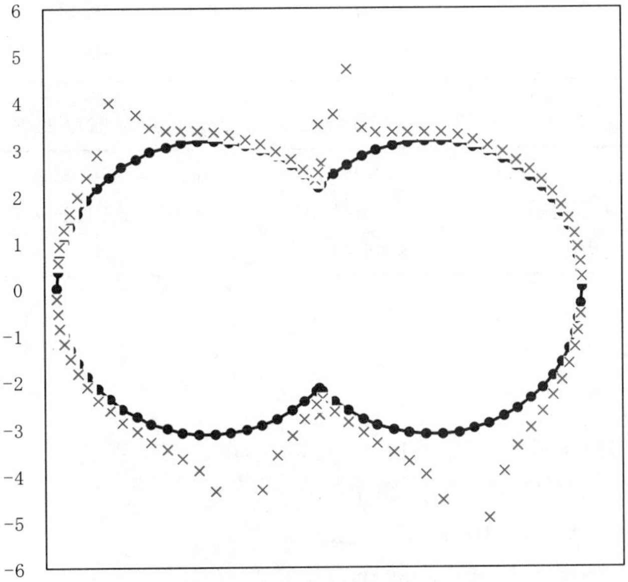

図 15　F＝1 kN 法による法線方向の地盤反力係数分布図

表 2　F＝1 kN 法による算定した地盤反力係数(kN/m^3)

F= 1 kN 法	I	II	III	IV	V
接線方向	1.360×10^3	5.282×10^3	4.384×10^4	1.147×10^4	4.305×10^3
法線方向	7.580×10^3	7.918×10^3	2.286×10^4	8.243×10^3	1.492×10^3

3.3 Full-slip 法(Case-3)および No-slip 法(Case-4)

Full-slip 法の算定式は各種の設計指針 [5)]で比較的よく用いられている．その算定式は式(1)に示される．

$$K_r = \frac{3E}{(1+\nu)(5-6\nu)R}, K_s = \frac{1}{3}K_r \tag{1}$$

ここに，K_r:法線方向地盤反力係数(kN/m^3)，K_s:接線方向地盤反力係数(kN/m^3)，E：地盤の変形係数(E=2(1+ν)G)（kN/m^2），R:セグメントの図心半径(m)，ν:ポアソン比である．

また，No-slip 法の算定式は式(2)，(3)に示される．

法線方向： $$K_r = \frac{(13-12\nu)E}{R(1+\nu)(3-4\nu)} \quad (2)$$

接線方向： $$K_s = \frac{(11-12\nu)E}{R(1+\nu)} \quad (3)$$

以上の方法によって,表 3 に示すような地盤条件を用いて, Full-slip 法および No-slip 法で求めた地盤ばね定数を表 4 に示す．

表 3　地盤物性値

地層		厚さ（m）	単位体積重量 γ（kN/m^3）	せん断剛性 G（kN/m^2）	ポアソン比 ν
埋土	AC	4	14	11 181	0.497
砂質土	AS-1	4	19	7 933	0.497
シルト	AC	11	17	8 672	0.496
砂質土	AS-2①	3	20	5 940	0.482
砂質土	AS-2②	18	20	79 420	0.482

表 4　Full-slip 法および No-slip 法による算定した地盤ばね定数(kN/m^3)

	Full-slip	No-slip
接線方向	2.856E+03	2.918E+04
法線方向	8.569E+03	4.011E+04

4　計算結果および考察

算定したそれぞれの地盤反力係数（Case1～Case4）を用いて応答変位法による解析を行った．図 15 に示す位置のそれぞれ発生断面力と 3 次元動的 FEM 解析（Case5）の発生断面力を表 5～表 10 に示す．Case1 の断面力分布を図 16 に示す.各々のケースの断面力分布傾向はほぼ同じである.表 5～表 10 に示す解析結果より，位置①における上端カモメ部セグメントの曲げモーメントは 3 次元動的 FEM の曲げモーメントと比較し，ほぼ同じが，軸力およびせん断力の差が現れた．位置②における上端カモメ部と一般部接続のところには，断面力の差が現れた．位置③，④，⑤における一般部セグメントには曲げモーメントはほぼ同じが，軸力およびせん断力の差が現れた．位置⑥における下端カモメ部と一般部接続のところには，断面力がほぼ同じである．

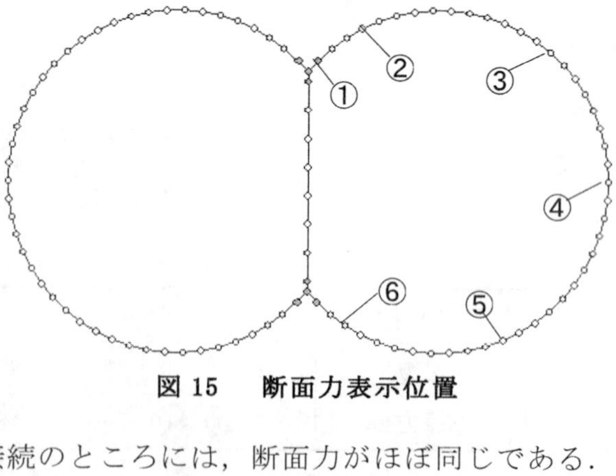

図 15　断面力表示位置

表 5　位置①断面力の比較

位置	Case	曲げモーメント（kN・m）	軸力（kN）	せん断力（kN）	備考
①	1	173.850	-60.824	-28.414	δ =1 m 法
	2	175.890	-64.951	-34.957	F=1 kN 法
	3	167.770	-67.083	31.636	Full-slip 法
	4	176.800	-111.870	50.926	No-slip 法
	5	171.720	-138.630	19.676	3 次元動的 FEM

表 6　位置②断面力の比較

位置	Case	曲げモーメント（kN・m）	軸力（kN）	せん断力（kN）	備考
②	1	105.45	-18.781	128.93	δ =1 m 法
	2	102.67	-21.343	132.72	F=1 kN 法
	3	98.516	-25.535	126.990	Full-slip 法
	4	91.305	-59.722	141.070	No-slip 法
	5	138.470	-130.730	50.651	3 次元動的 FEM

表 7　位置③断面力の比較

位置	Case	曲げモーメント（kN・m）	軸力（kN）	せん断力（kN）	備考
③	1	-71.94	69.744	52.302	δ =1 m 法
	2	-70.378	72.986	49.215	F=1 kN 法
	3	-68.418	66.615	48.012	Full-slip 法
	4	-67.077	138.170	37.464	No-slip 法
	5	-141.700	125.620	6.3407	3 次元動的 FEM

表 8　位置④断面力の比較

位置	Case	曲げモーメント（kN・m）	軸力（kN）	せん断力（kN）	備考
④	1	-18.146	17.198	86.342	δ =1 m 法
	2	-20.143	15.377	86.335	F=1 kN 法
	3	-19.005	14.347	83.802	Full-slip 法
	4	-24.847	10.065	90.942	No-slip 法
	5	-32.455	40.799	103.600	3 次元動的 FEM

表 9　位置⑤断面力の比較

位置	Case	曲げモーメント（kN・m）	軸力（kN）	せん断力（kN）	備考
⑤	1	85.673	-46.454	-131.96	δ =1 m 法
	2	85.708	-58.568	-129.87	F=1 kN 法
	3	83.348	-51.284	127.100	Full-slip 法
	4	81.310	-143.600	133.620	No-slip 法
	5	107.92	-102.31	99.174	3 次元動的 FEM

表 10　位置⑥断面力の比較

位置	Case	曲げモーメント（kN・m）	軸力（kN）	せん断力（kN）	備考
⑥	1	-103.310	166.350	61.371	δ =1 m 法
	2	-101.46	164.400	56.928	F=1 kN 法
	3	-103.010	151.330	58.658	Full-slip 法
	4	-96.818	189.080	53.602	No-slip 法
	5	-119.450	117.240	82.134	3 次元動的 FEM

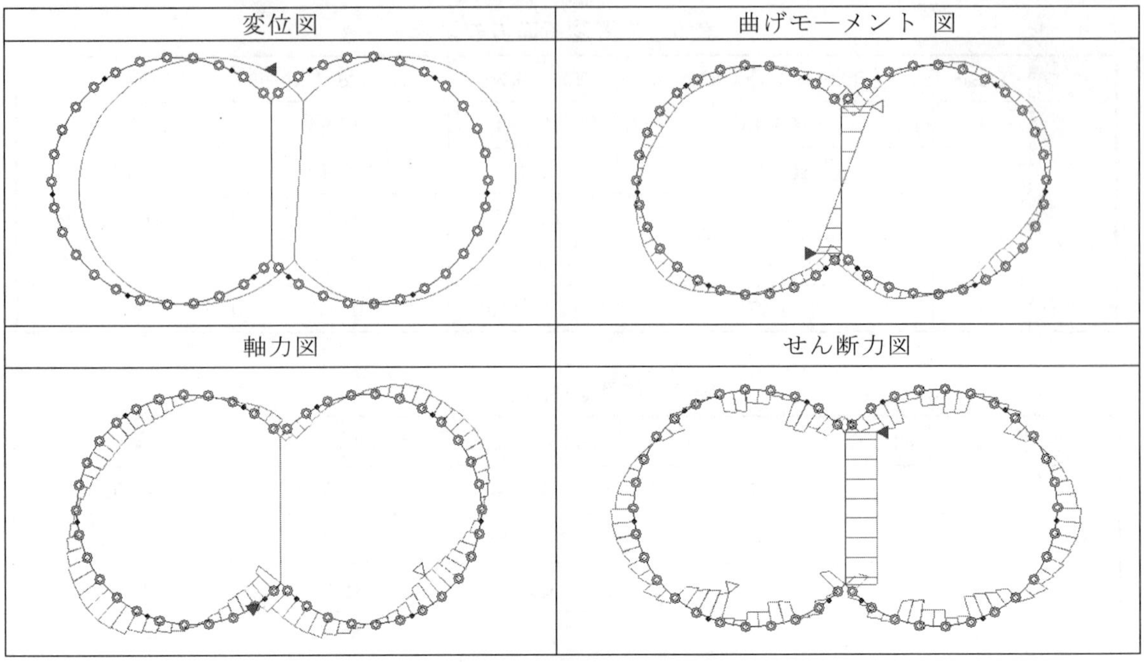

図 16 断面力分布図

5 おわりに

本論では，重複円形シールドトンネルに対する応答変位法における地盤ばね定数を適切な設定するに関する検討を行った．重複円形シールドトンネルに対し，3 次元動的 FEM と 2 次元はりーばねモデルの応答変位法の解析を行った．2 次元はりーばねモデルについては，FEM 解析より水平方向のみ単位強制変位を与えるケースと，鉛直方向のみ単位強制変位を与えるケースと，水平方向のみ単位荷重を作用させるケースと，鉛直方向のみ単位荷重を作用させるケースを設定し，それぞれのケースによる地盤ばね定数を求め，応答変位法による解析結果と 3 次元動的 FEM 解析結果と比較した．

その結果，重複円形シールドトンネルの一般部セグメントの地盤反力は．深さによって大きくなる．すなわち，地盤の深さによって応答相対変位が小さくなるが，地盤反力係数は大きくなることがわかった．また，一般部セグメントには重複円形の左および右の地盤反力は反対称となる．同じ深さにおけるセグメントの地盤ばね定数を同じ設定すればよい，同じ深さにおけるカモメ部セグメントの地盤反力と一般部セグメントの地盤反力は不同となり，異なる地盤ばね定数を設定しなければならないと判明した．重複円形シールドトンネルの応答変位法における地盤ばねは簡便な手法より地盤ばね定数を算定する可能性があると検証したが，このばねを精度よく解析し，その特性を明らかにする必要があると思われる．

参考文献（References）:

[1] 徐敏・眞鍋尚，重複円形シールドトンネルの応答変位法における地盤ばねに関する考察，第 4 回日中シールド技術交流会論文集，pp46 ～ 52, 2007.

[2] 村上博智・小泉淳，シールドセグメントリングの耐荷機構について，土木学会論文報告集，No.727, 1978 年.

[3] 土木学会編，開削トンネルの耐震設計，トンネル・ライブラリ-9，丸善（株）.

[4] 川島一彦，地下構造物の耐震設計，鹿島出版会，1995 年.

[5] たとえば，鉄道総合技術研究所，鉄道構造物設計標準・同解説シールドトンネル，1997.

著者紹介（Bio-data）：
徐敏(工学修士)
所属：みずほ情報総研株式会社 ｻｲｴﾝｽｿﾘｭｰｼｮﾝ部
業務：地下構造物の解析
Min Xu, (Master of Engineering), Science Solutions Division,
Mizuho Information & Research Institute, Inc.
Main work: Seismic Earthquake Analysis of Underground Constructions,
Shield tunnel, etc.
Email: min.xu@mizuho-ir.co.jp

眞　鍋　尚 (博士(工学))
所属：みずほ情報総研株式会社 ｻｲｴﾝｽｿﾘｭｰｼｮﾝ部
業務：地下構造物の解析.
Takashi MANABE, (Dr. Eng), Science Solutions Division, Mizuho Information & Research Institute, Inc.
Main work: Numerical Analysis of Underground Constructions, Nonlinear structural analysis
Email: takashi.manabe@mizuho-ir.co.jp

シールド工法により構築する水道トンネルの構造設計および合理化について

王　剣宏，小泉　淳

早稲田大学　理工学術院　社会環境工学学科，東京　169-8555

近年，地球の気候変動や都市化の進展などにともない，世界各地で水不足の問題が生じている．一方，早期に建設された水道施設は老朽化によりその機能が低下し，施設の維持管理費用の増加や補修補強が必要となり，場合によっては更新せざる得ない状況も出てきている．近代都市における最重要な機能の一つは水道であり，都市内に水を安定的に供給するために，送水幹線と立坑により複数の配水基地と浄水場を連絡する有機的なネットワークの建設が急務となっている．本研究は，シールド工法により建設する水道幹線トンネルの構造方式を検討し，その設計および計算方法を提案するともに，数値解析により空管時と満管時におけるトンネルの覆工および内挿管の挙動を考察し，提案する設計法の妥当性を検討するものである．また，合理的な水道トンネルを構築するために，建設時のみならず，将来の供用時を含めてもっとも合理的と思われる水道トンネルの構造を検討して，その最適な構造を提案するものである．

キーワード：水道トンネル；シールド工法；分離型構造；覆工設計；座屈設計；内水圧；全体照査；構造合理化

STRUCTURAL DESIGN AND RATIONALIZATION FOR WATER CONVEY TUNNEL BUILT BY SHIELD-DRIVEN TUNNELING METHOD

Jianhong WANG，Atsushi KOIZUMI

Department. of Civil and Environmental Engineering, Faculty of Science and Engineering, Waseda University, Tokyo 169-8555, Japan

Abstract: The water scarcity problem is becoming serious with the Global Warming and rapid urbanization. On the other hand, many aged public water supply utilities deteriorate so heavily that has to conduct its rehabilitation or regeneration. To ensue that high quality water is available for people and business, it is required to develop the water supply network system composed of the water treatment plan, water distribution station and water convey tunnel. In this article, the water main tunnel built by shield-driven method is focused and its structural design and rationalization are discussed. The structural design method is proposed in terms of the separated type and integrated type structures, and its validation is verified through a design example using numerical analysis. Meanwhile, the behavior of segment linings and steel liners are investigated as well as the parametric study on influence of backfill material and segmental joint type. Moreover, the structural rationalization of the water tunnel is investigated through comparison between two type structures in terms of safety, cost and future maintenance.

Key words: water tunnel; shield tunnel; segmental lining; structural design; liner design; rationalization

1　はじめに

近代的な都市機能を維持する重要なものの一つが水道である．都市部に水を安定的に供給するためには，水源の確保，水源から都市部への送水幹線，浄水場などの水道施設と配水基地，水道幹線と支線，各家庭への送水管など，各種のインフラストラクチャーが必要となる．早期に建設された水道施設は老朽化などにより機能が低下し，施設の維持管理費用の増加や補修補強が必要となり，場合によってはその更新を行わざるを得ない状況も出てきている．例えば，ニューヨークでは現有の水道管網を合理的に再構成する目的で，1970 年から 2020 年までに 3 段階で合計 96.6 km，直径 7.3-6.0 m の第三水道トンネルを建設しており，また，東京の区部では送水管網の有機的なネットワーク化を図るために，33km の東南幹線の建設に着手し，これによって，城南地区と城東地区間の相互の水供給機能を実現するとともに，三郷浄水場と金町浄水場の送水区域を拡大し，より信頼性の高い送水システムを構築中である．

一方，都市部では各種の地上構造物に加えて，その地下にも多くの施設が建設されてきており，新たな水道管路施設を建設するには，都市部のより深い地下を使用せざるを得ない状況になってきている．そのような水道用のトンネルでは，建設コストのみならず，将来の維持管理や補修・補強，さらにはその更新などについても，あらかじめ十分に考えておかなければならない．都市部の深い地下に，このような水道施設の構築を実現するためには，水道用トンネルの構造から検討する必要がある．

水道用のトンネルの構造は，従来から 2 つの構造に大別される．水道管を敷設するためのトンネルは開削工法やシールド工法などによりを構築されるが，その後，トンネルの内側に支持架台を設けて，その上に鋼管やダクタイル管を載せて収容する構造（以降，独立構造と呼ぶ）と，図-1a に示すように，トンネルの内側に管を挿入し，両者の間に間詰めをして一体化する構造（以降，一体型構造と呼ぶ）とがある．独立構造の場合は，水道管には内水圧が作用するだけで構造的には単純で問題もほとんどない．しかし，この場合にはトンネル内に支持架台や管路を収容することになるため，大きなトンネル断面が必要となり，とくに深い地下に構築する場合には不経済であるため，本研究では検討対象としない．一方，一体型構造の場合にはトンネル断面は小さくてすむが，内挿管は内水圧だけでなくトンネルに作用する土水圧の変動やトンネルの変形などの影響を受け，また逆に，トンネルは管内の水流による振動や水圧の変動，水温の影響などを直接受ける．そのため，これらをあらかじめ考慮に入れて設計しておかなければならず，トンネル覆工および内挿管は両者ともにその構造が重厚にならざるを得ない．最近の研究では大深度の高水圧下のトンネルに収容する管路に，その安全性と合理性を確保するために，図-1b に示すように，トンネルと内挿管との間に間詰めをしないで，それぞれ独立の構造とする分離型構造が提案されている．この構造は前述した独立構造のものと基本的な考え方は同じであるが，トンネルの内径と内挿管の外径との差を可能な限り小さくしようとするものである．経済性にすぐれていること，必要に応じて一次覆工と内挿する鋼管を併行して施工することができ，工期の短縮やコストの縮減が図られることなどが，机上の検討や各種の実験および解析から確認されてきている．しかし，トンネル内への長期にわたる漏水は内挿管に高い外水圧を作用させる可能性がある．このような状態で，補修や補強のために給水を止めれば，その高い外水圧により内挿管が座屈する可能性が十分に考えられる．著者らはすでに一体型構造および分離型構造に対して，それぞれの座屈挙動を実験や数値解析により解明し，実用性の高い内挿管の座屈設計方法を提案している．一方で，内水圧を受けるトンネル覆工の挙動には未解明な課題も多く，内挿管とセグメント覆工との間の相互作用の評価やそれらの全体としての安全評価がほとんど検討されていない実状にある．また，現在でも水道トンネルの構造設計はほんど「トンネル標準示方書」と「水門鉄管技術基準」に準じて行われ，構造計算および設計方法はまだ確立していない現状である．

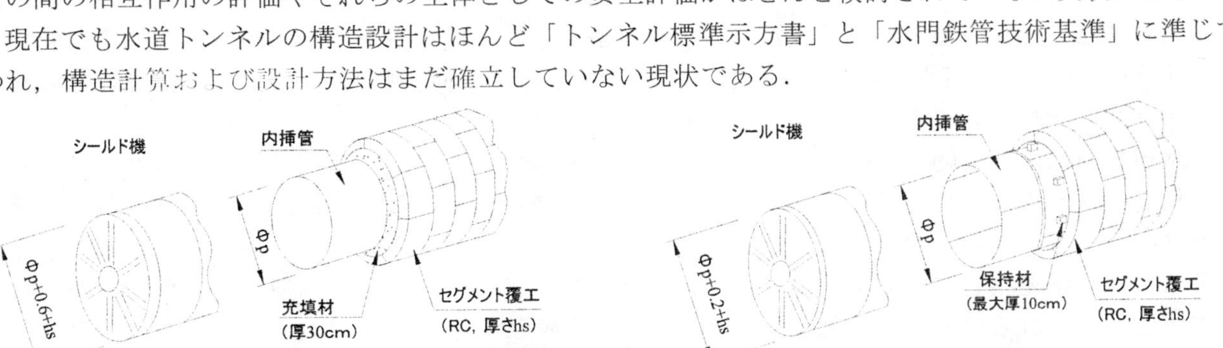

a) 一体型構造（従来からの方式）　　b) 分離型構造（提案する方式）

図-1　水道トンネルの構造

本研究は，シールド工法によって構築されるトンネルを対象に，図-1 に示した一体型構造と分離型構造の両者について，その覆工構造であるセグメントに対する適切な評価や詳細な検討を行ったものである．まず，一体型構造の場合と分離型構造の場合の設計および計算方法を提案し，その設計法の妥当性を検討する．それとともに，空管時と満管時の荷重によるトンネル覆工および内挿管の挙動を考察する．また，一体構造ではセグメントと内挿管との間の充填材の影響を，分離型構造ではセグメント継手の剛性の影響を考察する．最後に，建設時のみならず，将来の供用時を含めて水道トンネルの合理的な構造について検討を加える．

2　設計方法の検討および設計例

2.1　設計方法

一般的に，水道トンネルはトンネル覆工と内挿管により構成され，荷重と構造とも複雑であるため，単純な理論式や一般の計算式を用いて設計することはほとんど不可能である．また，水道トンネルの設計には，主に 2 つの状況が考えられる．①内挿管内に水圧がないとき（空管時）で，外部荷重（土圧，水圧など）のみが作用する状況と，②内挿管内に水圧が作用しているとき（満管時）で，外部荷重と同時に内部荷重が作用する状況である．本研究では，水道トンネルの構造設計において，図-2 に示す設計方法を提案して，その適用性や妥当性を検討する．図中の 2）は水道トンネルの基本的な設計を，3）は構造全体の安全照査を示すもので，以降，前者を基本設計，後者を全体照査と略称する．

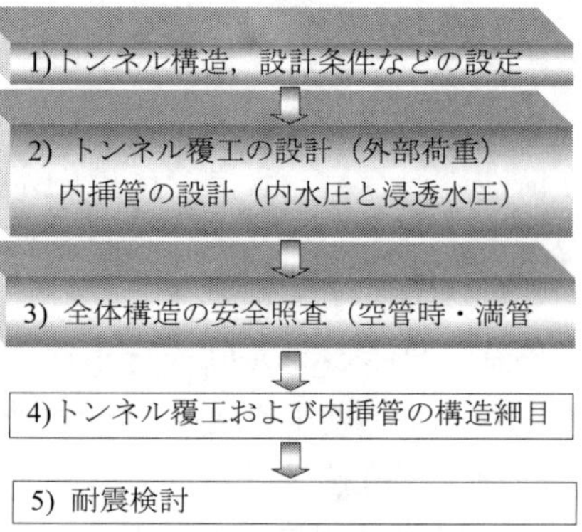

図-2　水道トンネルの設計方法

基本設計は荷重として外部荷重と内部荷重を対象に，全体照査は空管時と満管時とに分けて考える．外部荷重は従来の覆工設計に用いる荷重を対象とし，内部荷重は内挿管の設計に用いる内水圧と，長期にわたってトンネルと内挿管とに間に浸透する水圧(以下，浸透水圧と呼ぶ)を対象にする．内水圧は一般に最大静水圧と水撃圧とを水道管の設計荷重としているが,ここでは長期荷重として水道管内の最大静水圧のみを考える．浸透水圧は高水位の地下水圧に安全係数を考慮したものを用いた．また，満管時の荷重は内水圧と，安全側を考慮して最小土水圧荷重を外部荷重として用いる．

セグメントの設計計算法は,大別して慣用計算法,修正慣用計算法およびはり－ばね構造モデルによる計算法があるが，慣用計算法,修正慣用計算法では内部荷重を受ける場合に断面力を算定することができないことから，本研究でははり－ばね構造モデルによる計算法を用いた．この計算法は設計の実務にもよく使われており，継手の剛性や地盤条件などを評価でき，シールドトンネルの挙動を忠実的に再現することが可能である．また，この計算法を用いれば，トンネルと内挿管との間に間詰めを行う場合(一体型)も両者間の位置決めを保持材のみで行う場合(分離型)も検討でき，空管時と満管時の水道トンネル全体構造の安全照査が可能である．

水道の断面は一般的に水理設計により決定するものであるが，本研究では分離型と一体型のトンネル構造の比較の容易性を考えて，両者のトンネル外径を同じに仮定した．まず，設計荷重を算定してセグメント覆工と内挿管の設計を行う．つぎに，トンネル覆工と管とを一体とした一体構造と両者を分離した分離型構造について検討を行い，セグメント継手の影響や一体型構造に用いる間詰材について考察し，それらの安全性を評価するともに，設計方法の妥当性を検証する．最後に，設計した水道トンネルの経済性と安全性とに考察を加え，合理的な水道トンネル構造を提案する．なお，本研究では構造細目や耐震検討については省略した．

2.2 検討の対象

検討の対象としたシールドトンネルは外径 6 000 mm で，覆工には短ボルト継手形式の幅 1 000 mm，厚さ 250 mm の RC 平板形セグメントを用い，地盤条件は図-3 に示すとおりの軟弱地盤を想定した．図-4 はセグメントリングの形状寸法を示したものである．使用材料は，表-1 に示すように，一体型構造の充填材にはエアミルクを，分離型構造の保持材にはゴムを，内挿管には溶接構造用圧延鋼材を用いる．

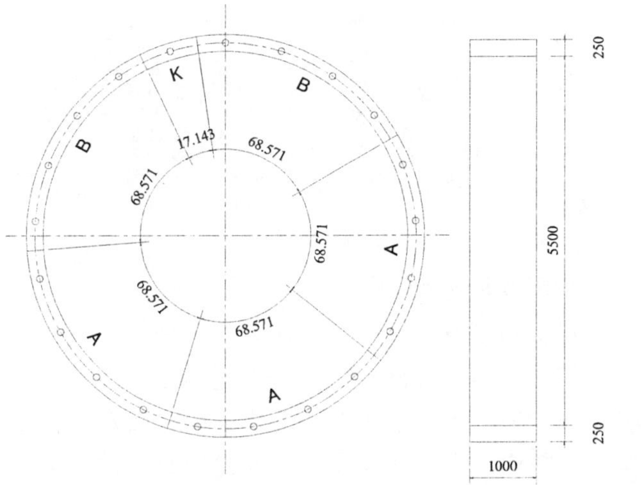

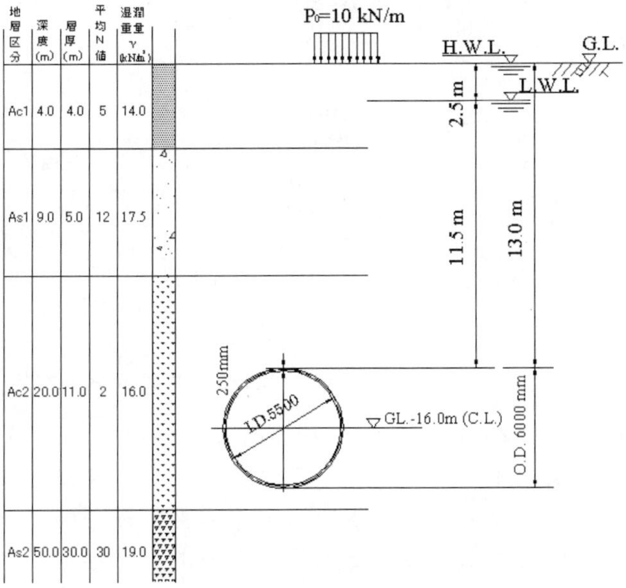

図-3 地盤条件およびトンネルの位置　　**図-4 セグメントリングの形状寸法**

表-1 使用材料

部材	材　　料	ヤング係数（N/mm^2）	許容応力度（N/mm^2）
ｾｸﾞﾒﾝﾄ覆工	コンクリート（基準強度 42）	3.30E+04	16
	鉄筋（SD345）	2.10E+05	200
	ボルト（強度区分 10.9）	2.10E+05	380
2 次覆工	管材（SS400）	2.10E+05	135
	一体型間詰材料（エアミルク）	200[1)]	—
	分離型保持材（ゴム）	8.4	—

1).那珂道水路事故調査報告書

セグメントリングとトンネル周辺地盤との相互作用を地盤ばねで評価するほかは，トンネル標準示方書「シールド工法」・同解説に準じて外部荷重を定めた．トンネル周辺の地盤が軟弱粘土（Ac），平均 N 値は 2 程度としたため，側方土圧係数は λ=0.8，地盤反力係数は k = 0 と仮定した．また，鉛直荷重は全土被り荷重とし，土水一体として算出した．その結果は図-5 に示すとおりである．鋼管の設計においては，内水圧が供用時の静水圧 0.3 MPa，浸透圧が地下水圧に安全係数 1.5 倍を乗じたもの 0.24 MPa とする．ただし，地下水圧は高水位の場合を考える．

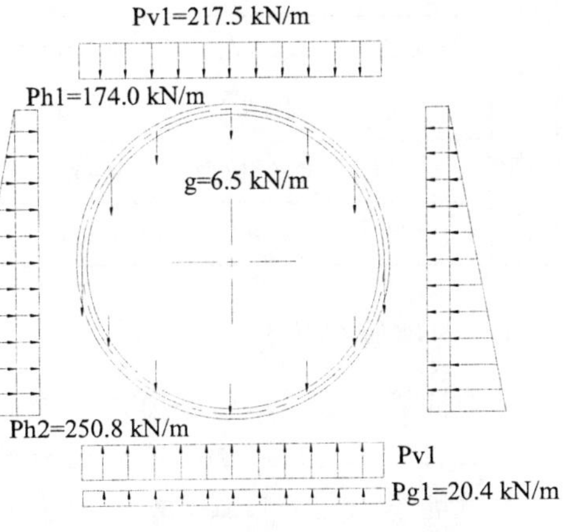

図-5 設計荷重（外部荷重）

2.3 セグメントの設計

はりーモデルにより断面力を算定して，セグメント本体部と継手部における最大断面力に対して応力度の照査を行う．照査断面は，図-6a)に示すようにリング継手のボルトボックスの断面欠損を考慮した T 形断面と，図-6b）に示すようにボルトを鉄筋と見なした継手部の矩形断面である．鉄筋のかぶりは，トンネルの内外面ともに腐食環境と考え，35mm とした．また，セグメントにひび割れが発生すると同時に鉄筋が降伏して圧縮側コンクリートが脆性破壊するのを避けるために，引張鉄筋比は 0.59%とした．

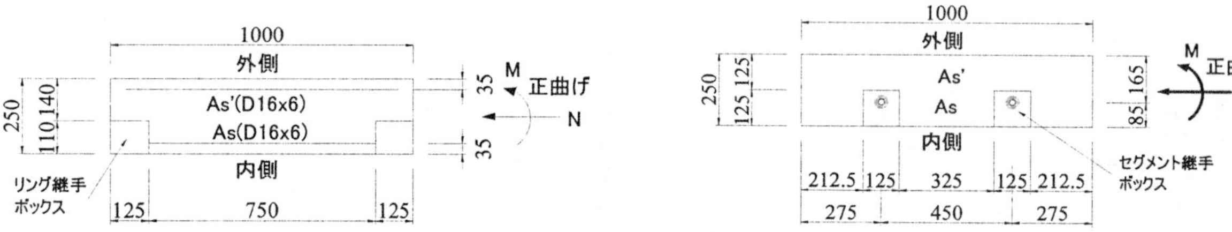

(a) セグメント本体部　　(b) 継手部

図-6　セグメント本体と継手部の応力度照査断面

表-2 は許容応力度の照査結果を示したものである．表-2 からセグメント本体と継手はともに許容応力度以下になっていることがわかる．なお，セグメントの応力度が許容応力度に比べてかなり低くなっているのは，内水圧による影響をあらかじめ考慮したためである．また，各応力の比較から継手部の応力はセグメント本体の応力より小さく安全側であるため，トンネル全体の安全照査にはセグメント本体のみを対象として行う．

表-2　セグメントと継手部の応力度照査の結果

	セグメント本体部			セグメント継手部		
正曲げ	最大曲げﾓｰﾒﾝﾄ M (kN・m)	55.3		最大曲げﾓｰﾒﾝﾄ M (kN・m)	32.9	
	軸力 N (kN)	587.7		軸力 N (kN)	603.9	
	ｺﾝｸﾘｰﾄの応力度 σ_c (N/mm^2)	8.0	<16	ｺﾝｸﾘｰﾄの応力度 σ_c (N/mm^2)	5.8	<16
	鉄筋の圧縮応力度 σ_s' (N/mm^2)	89.8	<200	ボルトの応力度 σ_b (N/mm^2)	16.9	圧縮
	鉄筋の引張応力度 σ_s (N/mm^2)	64.8	<200			
負曲げ	最大曲げﾓｰﾒﾝﾄ M (kN・m)	53.8		最大曲げﾓｰﾒﾝﾄ M (kN・m)	7.6	
	軸力 N (kN)	688.1		軸力 N (kN)	665.6	
	ｺﾝｸﾘｰﾄの応力度 σ_c (N/mm^2)	8.1	<16	ｺﾝｸﾘｰﾄ圧縮応力度 σ_c (N/mm^2)	3.1	<16
	鉄筋の圧縮応力度 σ_s' (N/mm^2)	98.4	<200	ボルトの応力度 σ_b (N/mm^2)	40.7	圧縮
	鉄筋の引張応力 σ_s (N/mm^2)	19.3	<200			
せん断	最大せん断力 S (kN)	49.8		最大せん断力 S (kN)	33.9	
	せん断応力度 τ (N/mm^2)	0.3	<0.71	せん断応力度 τ (N/mm^2)	44.5	<270

2.4 内挿管の設計

内挿管の設計は管の厚さを決定するために行われる．一般にそれは内水圧の大きさにより決まるが，ここではそれに加えて，浸透水圧による管の座屈も考慮して管厚を決定している．内水圧による管厚は簡単に定められるが，浸透水圧による座屈挙動は管の構造によって異なる．ここでは一体型構造と分離型構造に対して，以下に示す順番で管の厚さを設計した．

(1) 内水圧による厚さの算定

一般的に内水圧が円管に作用する場合は,管の軸力が卓越するので，管厚は式（1）で求める．

$$t = \frac{P_i D_i}{2\sigma_a} \tag{1}$$

ここで，管の内径を D_i=5.5 m，設計内水圧を P_i =0.3 MPa とすれば，管の円周方向応力度が許容応力度 σ_a 以下になる最小管厚は t=6.5 mm となる．

(2) 一体型構造の場合の浸透水圧による管の座屈設計

一体構造の場合は，トンネル覆工と内挿管の間はエアミルクやコンクリートなどにより充填されるため，これらの間詰め材によって管の変形は拘束される．このような場合の管の座屈は一般的にシングルローブ座屈と考えられ,従来から Jacobsen や Amstutz の座屈式を用いて座屈計算が行われる．しかし，著者らの研究によると，Jacobsen の理論式は Amstutz のより安全側の結果が得られやすい．これは充填の不完全性や温度変化などの原因で，管と覆工との間にはすき間ができるが，この正確的な評価が困難であることから，ここでは欧米諸国と同じく Jacobsen の座屈式を用いることとした．Jacobsen の理論式は式（2）に示すとおりである．同式中のすき間量 Δ は，内水圧による管の拡径量 1.8 mm，打設による温度上昇 30°場合の管の拡径量 1.0 mm，および Amstutz の計算式の場合のすき間量の 1.1 mm を考慮して，これらの最大値 1.8 mm を設計すき間量とした．

$$R'/t = \sqrt{\frac{\left[(9\pi^2/4\beta^2)-1\right]\left[\pi-\alpha+\beta(\sin\alpha/\sin\beta)^2\right]}{12(\sin\alpha/\sin\beta)^3\left[\alpha-\pi\Delta/R'-\beta(\sin\alpha/\sin\beta)\left[1+\tan^2(\alpha-\beta)/4\right]\right]}} \tag{a}$$

$$P_{cr}/E = \frac{9\pi^2/4\beta^2-1}{12(R'/t)^3(\sin\alpha/\sin\beta)^3} \tag{b} \quad (2)$$

$$f_y/E = \frac{h}{2R'}\left(1-\frac{\sin\beta}{\sin\alpha}\right)+\frac{P_{cr}R'}{E^{*}t}\frac{\sin\alpha}{\sin\beta}\left[1+\frac{4R'\beta\sin\alpha\tan(\alpha-\beta)}{\pi\ t\sin\beta}\right] \tag{c}$$

ここに，R':トンネル覆工の内半径, R:内挿管の半径，Δ:すき間量，2α: 座屈前の管の円心における座屈変形部の角度，f_y: 降伏強度，2β: 座屈後の管の円心における座屈変形部の角度，t: 管厚である.

設計浸透水圧を地下水の最大水圧である P=0.24 MPa とすれば，式（2）により算出した管厚は最小 t=14 mm となる．

(3)分離型構造の場合の浸透水圧による管の座屈設計

分離型構造の場合は，セグメントによる内挿管への拘束がないため，基本的に自由管の座屈として考えてよい．自由管には補剛材がない場合（以下，一般鋼管と呼ぶ）と一般鋼管を補剛した場合(以下，補剛管と呼ぶ)とが考えられ，高い外水圧が作用する場合や大口径の管の場合には補剛管を用いる方が有利である．補剛材がない一般鋼管の場合に，設計浸透水圧 P=0.24 MPa に対して Von.Mises の無限長管の座屈式（式（3））を用いて計算すると，管の最小厚さが t=44.2 mm 必要となる．そのため，分離型構造の場合には補剛管を用いることとした．

$$P_{cr} = \frac{Et^3}{4(1-\nu^2)R^3} \tag{3}$$

補剛管の座屈は，補剛材や補剛間隔により全体座屈と局部座屈があるため，座屈計算は著者らが提案した二段階座屈計算法を用いる．また，全体座屈は管軸方向に長く発生する座屈形態であるから，座屈設計は全体座屈を避けて局部座屈が発生するように設計することとした．二段階座屈計算法は，まず，座屈が全体座屈となるか局部座屈となるかを判断し，つぎに，その結果に応じて座屈荷重を計算する方法である．式(4)および式（5）はそれぞれ全体座屈の場合の座屈荷重，局部座屈の場合の座屈荷重を計算する式であり，二段階座屈計算法はこの２つの座屈荷重を比較することにより座屈形態を判断し，小さい方を座屈荷重として求めるものである．補剛材の剛性や間隔を変えることにより，どちらの座屈形態を選択するかを決めることができる．

$$P_{cr}^{G}=\frac{Et^{3}}{4(1-\nu^{2})R^{3}}+\frac{3EI_{r}}{SR^{3}} \tag{4}$$

$$P_{cr}^{L}=\frac{Et}{(n^{2}-1)R}\left[\frac{t^{2}(\alpha^{2}+n^{2}-1)^{2}}{12(1-\nu^{2})R^{2}}+\frac{\alpha^{4}}{(\alpha^{2}+n^{2})^{2}}\right] \tag{5}$$

ここに，I_r は限界補剛材の有効断面２次ﾓｰﾒﾝﾄ，n は局部座屈の波数，S は補剛間隔であり，また，これらの式中で，

$$\alpha=\frac{\pi R}{S},\quad n=\sqrt[8]{\frac{3\alpha^{4}}{K}},\quad K=\frac{t^{2}}{12(1-\nu^{2})R^{2}}$$

である．

設計浸透水圧 P=0.24 MPa に対して，肉厚 7 mm の鋼管を用いて，局部座屈が発生するように設計すると，補剛間隔は S=1.0 m，限界補剛材の断面は高さ×厚さ（hr×tr）＝75×40 mm となる．補剛材がない一般鋼管に換算すると，管の厚さはわずか te=10 mm である．

一体型構造の場合と分離型構造の場合の内挿管の設計結果をまとめると，それぞれ図-7a) および b)に示すような断面が得られる．

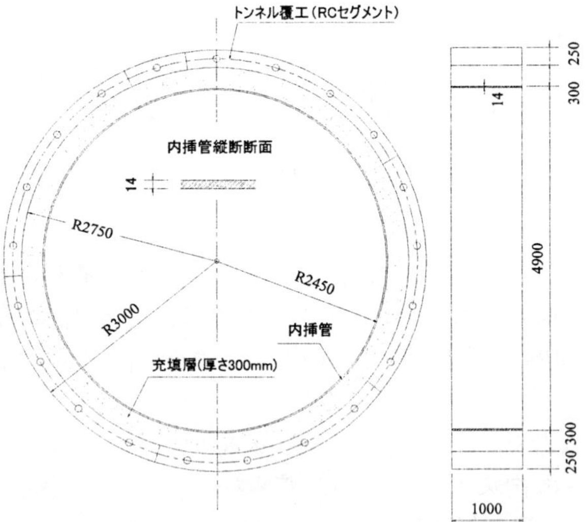

(a)　一体型構造

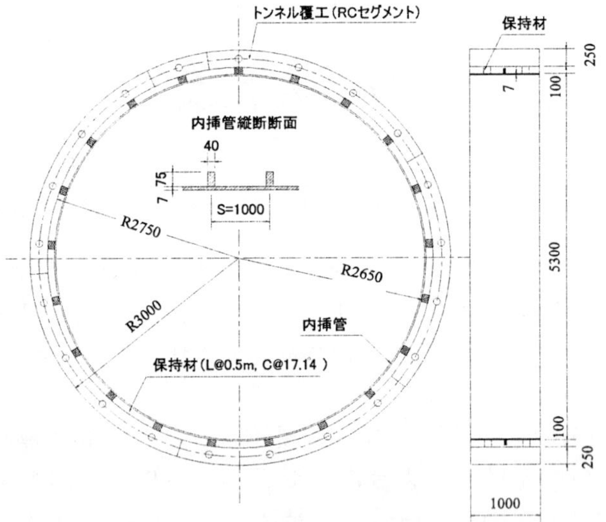

(b) 分離型構造

図-7　水道トンネルの全体構造断面

3　水道トンネルの安全性の照査およびその考察

水道トンネルの安全性の照査は，セグメントと内挿管により構成されたトンネルの全体断面を対象として行う．すでに述べたように，セグメントリングははり－ばねモデルで評価し，内挿管はソリッドリングに，充填層または保持材はばね部材にそれぞれ評価して，２層リング構造として解析した．解析には解析ソフト Moleman を用いた．ばね部材のばね定数は，充填材または保持材の材料の弾性係数 E，厚さおよびそれらの分布面積から算定した．また，応力度の照査はセグメントと管それぞれについて行った．すなわち，断面力の計算結果から，セグメントのコンクリート，内側鉄筋および

外側鉄筋の応力度，管の応力度をそれぞれに算定した．また，一体型構造の場合は充填材，分離型構造の場合はセグメント継手に対して，それぞれの影響を検討した．最後に，設計時の最大応力度と比較して，水道トンネル全体の構造の安全性を考察し，提案した設計法の妥当性を検討している．以下にはそれらの詳細を述べる．

3.1　一体型構造の場合

内挿管の設計では管とセグメントの間にエアミルクを用いて充填すること多いが，ここではそれに加えて，コンクリートを用いる場合，何も充填しない場合の3とおりの状況について，空管時と満管時のトンネル覆工および内挿管への影響を考察する．なお，エアミルクの場合には弾性係数は E=220 N/mm^2，コンクリートの場合は E=33 kN/mm^2，何も詰めない場合は E=0 N/mm^2 としてトンネル覆工と内挿管に発生する応力度を計算した．計算結果は図-8 の a)～d)に示すとおりである．

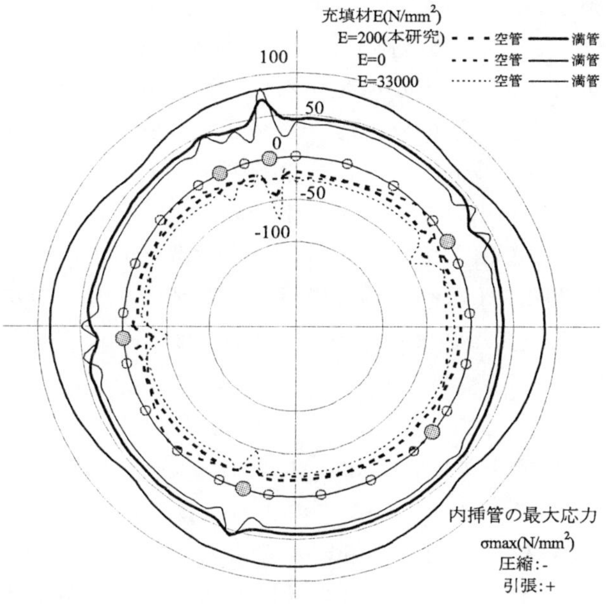

(a) 内挿管

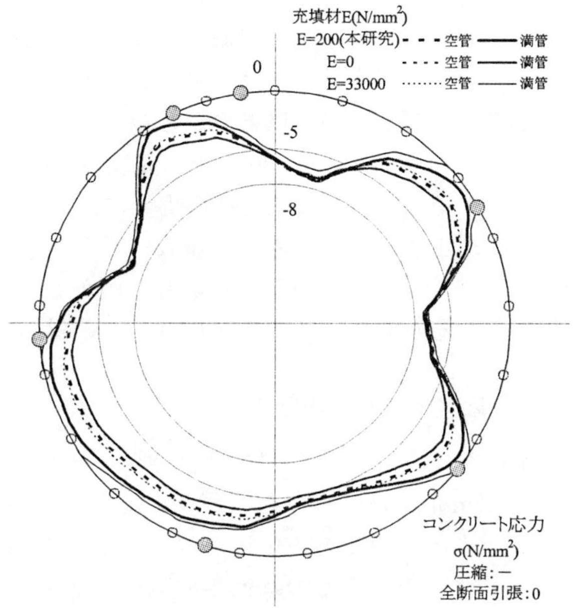

(b)　セグメントのコンクリート

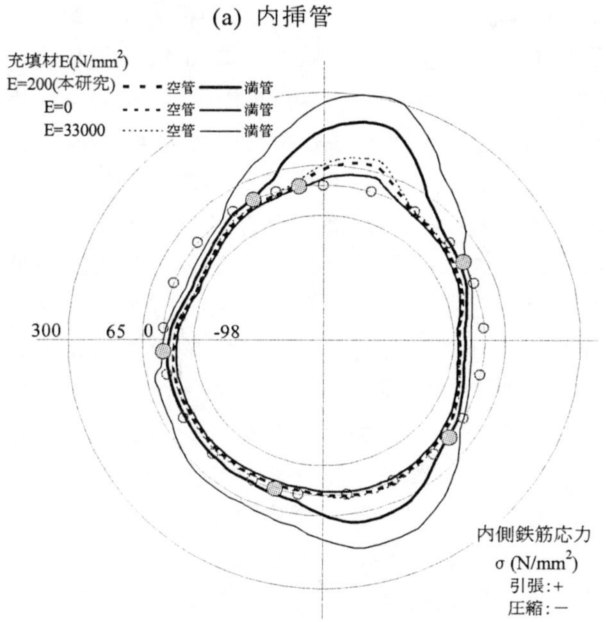

(c) セグメントの内側鉄筋

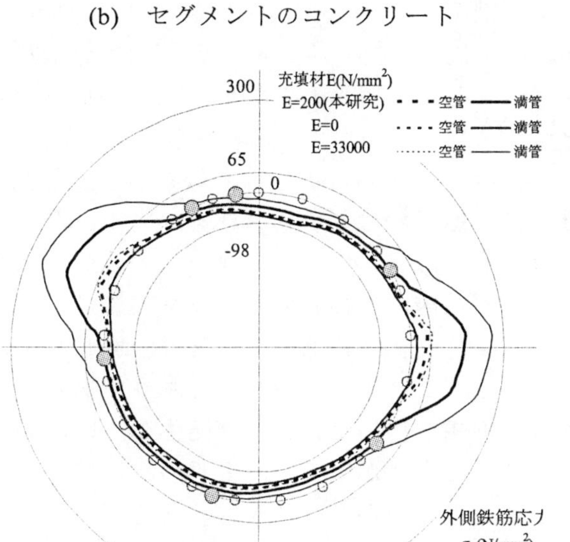

(d) セグメントの外側鉄筋

図-8　応力度分布

図-8から，空管時の場合は充填材料の弾性係数が異なってもトンネル覆工と内挿管の応力度にはあまり差がないが，満管時の場合は充填材の弾性係数が大きくなるにつれセグメント覆工の応力度が大きくなり，逆に内挿管の最大応力度が小さくなることがわかる．これはセグメント覆工と内挿管との間に充填層を介して相互作用が発生し，充填材が硬くなればその相互作用が強くなるためと考えられる．また，内挿管は内水圧による軸引張力に強く，一方で曲げモーメントには弱い構造であり，図-8のa)から，セグメント継手の剛性が低いと内挿管には大きな曲げ応力度が生じ，充填材が硬くなるほど継手部の応力度の変化が大きくなることがわかる．一方，セグメント継手部以外の内挿管の応力度は充填材が硬いほうが空管時で大きく，満管時で小さくなる傾向がある．これは充填層の材料の硬いほうが外部荷重を管に伝達しやくなる一方で，内水圧による管径の拡張を拘束する効果があるためと考えられる．図-8のb),c),d)をみると，セグメント覆工の応力度は充填材の硬さによって変化するが，分布形状は継手の位置によってほぼ決まることがわかる．

エアミルクを用いた場合には，セグメントを設計したときの最大応力度に比べ，コンクリートと鉄筋の圧縮応力度はすべて小さくなっているが，鉄筋の引張応力度はかなり大きく，また，内水圧が大きくなると増加することから，外部荷重のみを考えてセグメントを設計できないことがわかる．また，コンクリートを充填する場合には，セグメント覆工の一部に全断面引張の状況が発生する．これは覆工の耐久性を考える上で問題となる．以上のことから，充填層をもつ一体型構造の場合は，セグメント覆工と内挿管との間に相互作用が発生し，内水圧と充填材の剛性によってはその全体構造大きな影響を与えることがわかった．したがって，一体型構造の場合には，単純に外部荷重を用いてセグメントを設計し，また，内水圧および浸透水圧を用いて内挿管を設計することができず，その相互作用をあらかじめ考慮して水道トンネル全体の設計を行う必要があることがわかる．また，設計内水圧が高い場合には，セグメント覆工の安全性を確保するために，できるだけ軟らかい材料を用いて充填する必要があるものと思われる．

3.2 分離型構造の場合

本研究で考えた分離型構造は，セグメント覆工と内挿管との間に一定のすき間を保つために，補剛材より25mm高い保持材を等ピッチで円周や軸方向に設けるものである．このような構造はトンネル覆工と内挿管との間で力の伝達が少ないことから，両者間の相互作用も小さいと考えられる．全体構造にもっとも影響を与えるのは継手の剛性と思われる．そのため，セグメント継手として，短ボルト継手，ヒンジ継手および剛継手の３種類の継手剛性を考慮して検討を行うこととした．内挿管をトンネル内の所定の位置に保持するための保持材は，図-7に示したように，トンネル軸方向に0.5m，円周方向にリング継手と同じピッチで設置した．これらの構造に対して，空管時と満管時の断面力を計算し，内挿管とセグメントに発生する応力度を算出した．図-9のa)～d)はその算出結果を示した応力度分布図である．

図-9のa)から，内挿管の最大応力度は空管時が小さく，満管時にも管の許容応力度以下であり，継手による影響はクラウン部を除いてほとんどないことがわかる．また，セグメント継手をヒンジとした場合にはリングのクラウン部の変形が大きくなり，そこに設置した保持材を通して力が内挿管に作用するため，内挿管のクラウン部の最大応力度が大きくなったものと思われる．一方，セグメントのコンクリートと鉄筋の応力度は，空管時と満管時とでほぼ同じであることが，図-9のb)，c)，d)からわかる．これは，予想したとおりであり，セグメント覆工と内挿管の間に力の伝達があまりなく，両者間の相互作用がほとんど発生していないことを示している．しかし，セグメント覆工では継手の剛性による影響が大きく，継手の剛性が小さくなると応力度の変化が激しくなり，断面内の最大応力度と最小応力度がともに大きくなる傾向がある．したがって，このような軟弱地盤に水道トンネルを構築する場合には，高い剛性を有するセグメント継手を用いることが望まされる．

分離型構造の場合は，セグメント覆工と内挿管の最大応力度は，ともに基本的な当初設計の最大応力度より小さい．また，満管時の引張応力度はほとんど増加せず，とくに，セグメント継手の剛性が大きくなるほど，空管時の応力度と満管時の応力度との差が小さくなる．これらことから，分離型構造では，外部荷重によりセグメント覆工を設計し，内水圧と浸透水圧により内挿管を設計すれば，水道トンネルは全体として安全側になるものと思われる．

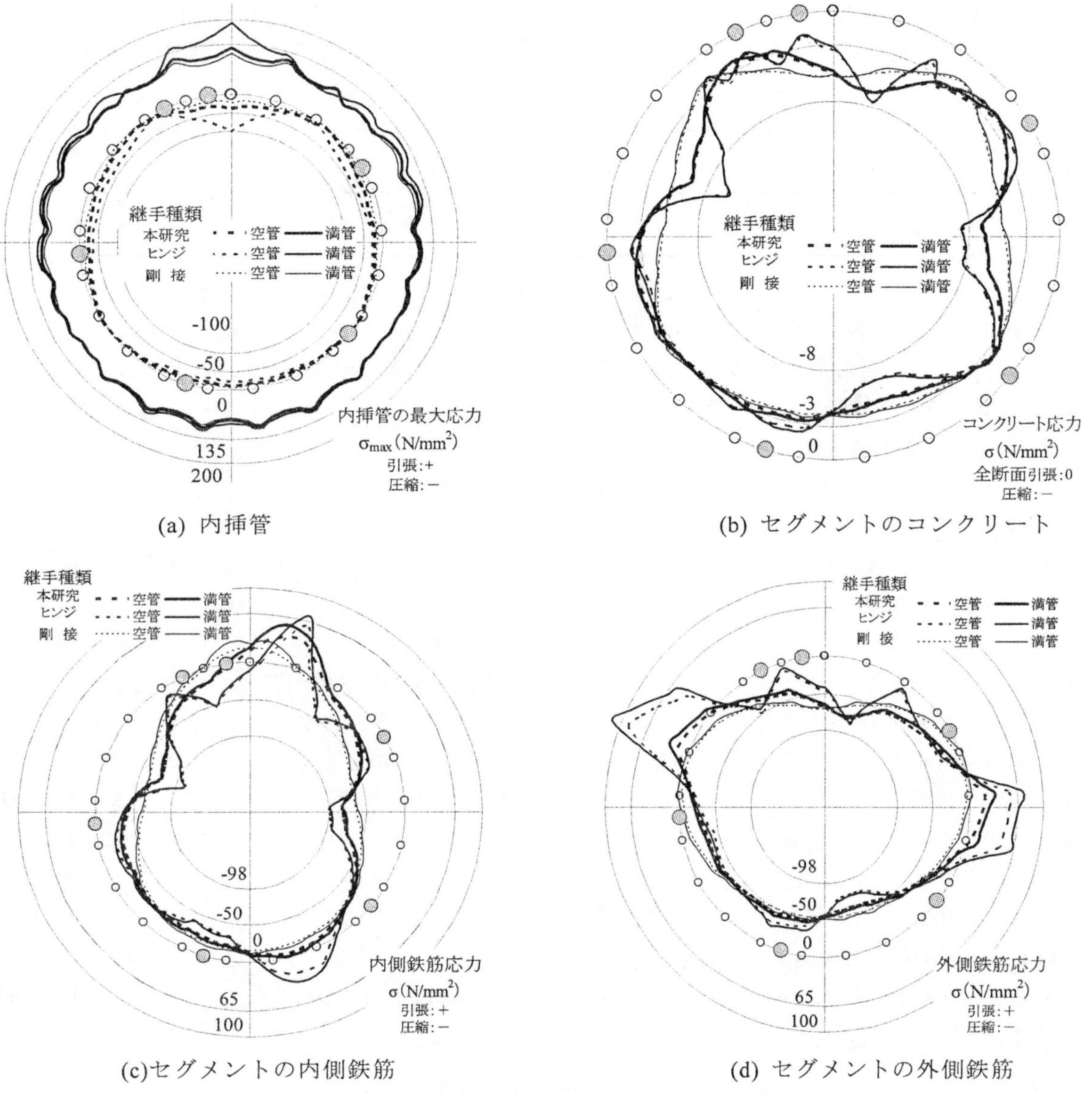

(a) 内挿管

(b) セグメントのコンクリート

(c)セグメントの内側鉄筋

(d) セグメントの外側鉄筋

図-9　応力度分布

4　水道トンネル構造の合理化

(1) 構造の安全性

以上の検討から，従来の一体型構造の場合は充填層を介して相互に力の伝達があるため，セグメント覆工と内挿管の設計には外部荷重と内水圧との両方を設計の当初から考慮する必要がある．また，設計内水圧が大きい場合は，セグメント覆工には全断面が引張となることが予想され，トンネルの長期にわたる耐久性などを考えると問題があるものと思われる．一方，分離型構造の場合は，覆工と内挿管との間に剛性の低い保持材を設置すれば，両者間の相互作用がほとんど発生せず，それぞれの設計を分けて行うことができる．

したがって，分離型構造は一体型構造より単純であり，水道トンネルの構造として有利である．また，セグメント覆工と内挿管の安全性を確保しやく，設計上からも分離型構造のほうが容易である．

(2) 経済性

一体型構造の場合は充填材の費用や充填に要する工費や工期が必要であり，また，充填層の厚さ分だけトンネルの径を大きくせざるを得ないため，建設コストが高くなる．また，トンネル覆工と内挿管との間の間詰めをすき間なく行うことは非常に困難であり，施工上からも問題が多い．一方，分離型構造の場合は，内挿管の位置を保持するための保持材を設置すればよく，経済性も施工性も問題が少ない．また，セグメント覆工への内水圧の影響が少ないため，より経済的な覆工構造を設計できる．

表-3　コスト縮減効果例

項　目	工期	工事費
一体型構造（従来方式）	45.1 ヶ月	39.3 億円
分離型構造	32.3 ヶ月	35.3 億円
経済効果	12.8 ヶ月	4.0 億円

これら２つの構造の経済性について，「水道技術研究センター」らが行った大深度水道管布設技術の研究の結果の一例は表-3 に示すとおりである．この例は水道管径が 2．4m，敷設延長が 3000m のケースである． この表から，従来の一体型構造と比べ，分離型構造のほうが，約 30%の工期の短縮と，約 10%の工事コストの縮減が可能であることがわかる．この例ではセグメントに同じものを用いているが，設計内水圧を P=1.6 MPa とした本研究の検討結果からみると，一体型構造の場合にはセグメント覆工はより重厚とならざるを得ないため，そのコスト分だけでももっと増えるものと思われる．

(3) 維持管理

一般的に水道トンネルは立坑間の距離が長く，大きなトンネル内に管路を敷設した独立構造の場合を除いて，その点検や維持管理などが十分にできない．これは一体構造や分離型構造の従来からの大きな課題である．内挿管内を空にすれば，管内からの目視による点検は可能であるが，内挿管の外側の状況は把握できない．現在，小型カメラやファイバカメラなどを用いた検査技術が発達してきており，この新しい技術を水道トンネルに利用するためには，トンネル覆工と内挿管との間のすき間を利用することが必要である．水道トンネルを分離型構造として構築すれば，セグメント覆工と内挿管の間のすき間が有効に使える可能性がある．これは水道の供用中でも可能であるため，漏水や腐食の状況を評価でき，補修箇所の確定や適切な補修方法の検討を可能にする．また，分離型構造はセグメント覆工と内挿管がそれぞれ独立していることから，管の補修は比較的容易と思われる．このような技術を長い距離にわたって用いるためには，さらに多くの技術開発が必要と思われるが，将来の供水事業に不可欠なものと考えられる．

表-4 は一体型構造の場合と分離型構造の場合との安全性，経済性および将来性を分類してまとめた表である．この表から，すべての面において，一体型構造より分離型構造のほうがより合理的な構造であることがわかる．

表-4　一体型と分離型構造の合理性について

検討項目			一体型構造	分離型構造
安全性	セグメント覆工	基本設計	OK	OK
		全体照査	危険側 / 必要	安全側 /必要ない
	内挿管	基本設計	OK	OK
		全体照査	安全側 / 必要ない	
経済性	セグメント覆工	材料，形状寸法	同様	
	内挿管	形状寸法	外径 Φ＝4.9m，肉厚 t＝14mm	外径 Φ＝5.3m，肉厚 te＝10mm
	充填・保持材	材料及び寸法	エアミルク・コンクリート（厚さ 300mm）	ゴム　軸@0.5m，円周@17.14 度（100×100×100）
	最大導水能力	断面	18.86 m^2	22.06 m^2
	工期		長い	短い
	コスト		高い	低い
維持管理	監視，検査		長期間の断水が必要	運営のままで可能
	補修・更新	計画・補修方法	要素多く / 困難	要素少ない / 簡単
		実行	困難/ 所要時間長い	容易 / 所要時間短い

5　結論および今後の課題

本研究は，大口径水道トンネルを対象として，分離型構造と一体型構造の設計を実施し，両者の設計結果を用いてそれらの比較を行ったものである．本研究から得られた知見を示せば，以下のようになる．

(1) 一体型構造はトンネル覆工と内挿管との間で充填層を介して相互作用が発生する．その相互作用は充填材の剛性や充填性の良否による影響があり，構造的に複雑で，セグメント覆工も内挿管も構造が重厚にならざるを得ない．

(2) 分離型構造は構造的に明確であり，トンネル覆工は外部からの土水圧などに対して，また，内挿管は内水圧と浸透水圧に対してそれぞれ設計すればよく，両者間の相互作用の影響がほとんどないため，土水圧や内水圧などが変動しても相互に影響を与えないという利点をもつ．また，トンネル覆工が内水圧を直接受けないこと，内挿管に補剛管を用いれば管の肉厚を小さくすることができることなどから，経済的な水道トンネルを構築することが可能である．

(3) 提案した設計法は分離型構造と一体型構造の両者に適用できる妥当な設計法であることを確認した．分離型構造の場合には，セグメント覆工に外部荷重を，内挿管に内部荷重（内水圧と浸透水圧）を作用させて，それぞれ独立設計すればよいが，一体型構造の場合には，基本設計を行った上で，両者の相互作用を考慮した全体構造の安全照査を行う必要がある．

(4) 大口径水道トンネルに分離型構造を用いることによって，安全で経済的な水道トンネルを設計することが可能であり，将来の維持管理にも有利であることから，分離型構造は合理的な構造であると考えられる．

本研究は水道トンネルの常時の設計のみを行ったものであり，今後は地震時の挙動などについても検討する必要がある．また，分離型構造に対しての実験的な検証が必要であり，とくに保持材の材料や設置方法による影響，その具体的な施工方法などについてさらに検討する必要がある．また，分離型構造の場合に確保できるすき間を利用して水道管への浸透水圧を減少する方法や，すき間の維持管理への活用についても今後の課題と考えている．

参考文献（References）:

[1] 土木学会：トンネル標準示方書「シールド工法・同解説」，東京，2006 年．

[2] 国土交通省関東地方整備局: 導水路施設評価検討委員会参考資料，pp. 6-10，2004.

[3] 財団法人 水道技術研究センター：平成 15 年度　大深度水道管のコスト縮減に関する研究報告書，pp. 1-37，2003.

[4] 王　剣宏, 小泉　淳 :大深度地下水道管の外水圧による座屈に関する理論的研究, 土木学会論文集 A, Vol.64, No.3，pp.588-602，2008.7.

[5] Berti, D., Stutzman, R., Lindquist, E., and Eshghipour, M.: Buckling of steel tunnel liner under external pressure, *J. Energy Engng.*, Vol. 124, No.3, pp. 55–89, 1998.

著者紹介（Bio-data）:

王　剣宏　博士（工学）助手
早稲田大学理工学術院
社会環境工学学科
1998 年武漢水利電力大学学部卒
2005 年早稲田大学　修士修了
2008 年早稲田大学　博士修了
専門分野：地下空間、都市建設、

構造設計、シールドトンネル、
水道管路構造、立坑など、
Jianhong WANG (Dr. Eng.)　Research Associate
Dept. of Civil and Environmental Engineering,
Faculty of Science and Engineering, Waseda University
Research fields: Underground space, Urban construction,
Structural design, Shield tunnel, and Water pipeline, etc.
Email:wangjh2003@aoni.waseda.jp

小泉　淳　博士（工学）教授
早稲田大学理工学術院
社会環境工学学科
専門分野：地下空間、都市建設、
構造設計、シールドトンネル、
セグメント、立坑など、
Atsushi KOIZUMI (Dr.Eng.) Professor
Dept. of Civil and Environmental Engineering, Faculty of Science and Engineering, Waseda University
Research fields: Underground Space, Urban construction,
Structural design, Shield tunnel, and Segment, Shaft, etc.
Email: koizumi@waseda.jp

計測変位から覆工安全性を評価する逆解析方法とその適用

呉　旭 [1]　中村　敦 [2]　桜井　春輔 [3]

[1] 応用地質㈱技術センター，埼玉 331-8688

[2] 鉄道運輸機構北陸新幹線建設局，長野 380-8566

[3] 財団法人建設工学研究所，神戸 657-0064

本論文は，時間依存的変形を有するトンネルを対象に計測変位から覆工安全性を評価するFEM逆解析方法を示すとともに，膨張性トンネルの覆工補強の適用例を紹介する．この方法では，トンネルの覆工に発生する変位（残留変位）が３つ以上与えれば，残留変位と計算変位の誤差二乗和を最小となるよう覆工に作用する見かけの解放応力がFEM逆解析より求められ，それに対応した覆工の変形と応力が計算されることになる．具体的な膨張性トンネルの適用例においては，残留変位が掘削時の計測変位から双曲線近似で推定され，FEM逆解析により求めた覆工の応力は計測結果と概ね整合し，提案方法の適用性が示された．

キーワード：逆解析；FEM；観測的方法；トンネル覆工；安全性評価

A BACK ANALYSIS PROCEDURE OF TUNNEL LINING ASSESSMENT AND ITS APPLICATIONS

Xu WU [1]，Atsushi NAKAMURA [2]，Shunsuke SAKURAI [3]

[1] *Technical center, OYO Corporation, Saitama 331-8688;*

[2] *Hokuriku Bureau of Construction, JRTT, Nagano 380-8566;*

[3] *Construction engineering research institute foundation, Kobe 657-0064*

Abstract: A back analysis procedure of tunnel lining assessment is presented and its application to evaluation of the safety of tunnel lining in squeezing ground is illustrated. In the procedure, the deformation and stresses in tunnel lining are calculated by a FEM analysis in which observed and calculated displacements in the lining are fitted in the sense of least-square method. For a tunnel excavated in squeezing ground, the residual displacements can be estimated from the data observed during tunnel excavation, thus the stresses in the tunnel lining can be determined using the procedure.

Key words: back analysis; FEM; observed method; tunnel lining; safety assessment

1　はじめに

日本の山岳トンネルの覆工は，坑口や断層破砕帯等の特殊な地形地質または水圧や近接施工等の影響を受ける区間を除いて，一般的に30cm巻厚のプレーンコンクリートを設置するのが標準となっている[1]．これは，トンネル掘削による地山の応力再配分がロックボルトや吹付けコンクリート等の支保工と地山と一体化で受け持っており，覆工の施工は原則的に支保の変形が収束してから行われることから，覆工の耐荷力はトンネルの安全余裕として考えているためである．しかし，時間依存的な変形挙動の顕著な膨張性地山におけるトンネルでは，切羽通過後長時間を経過しても変位が僅かながら観測され，工期の制約から変位が収束していない段階で止む得なく覆工を施工する場合がしばしばある．このように変位が進行している状態で覆工を施工する場合には，標準のプレーンコンクリートの安全性が懸念され，スチールファイバー混入等覆工補強の要否を検討する必要がある．

また，供用中のトンネルとりわけ長大トンネルや海底トンネルの維持管理のため，覆工の変位を計測し覆工の安全性を評価することが求められている．しかし，このように覆工の計測変位から安全性を検討する方法は必ずしも確立されていない．従来では，緩み荷重や土かぶり荷重等の考え方に基づいて骨組モデルは一般的に用いられるが，覆工を地山から分離してモデル化し，荷重の推定や地山バネ係数の設定等には多くの課題が残されている．

本論文は，時間依存的変形を有するトンネルを対象に計測変位から覆工安全性を評価する FEM 逆解析方法を示すとともに，膨張性トンネルの覆工補強の適用例を紹介する．この方法では，トンネルの覆工に発生する変位（残留変位）が３つ以上与えれば，残留変位と計算変位の誤差二乗和を最小となるよう覆工に作用する見かけの解放応力が FEM 逆解析より求められ，それに対応した覆工の変形と応力が計算されることになる．具体的に膨張性トンネルの適用例においては，残留変位は掘削時の計測変位から双曲線近似で推定され，FEM 逆解析により求めた覆工の応力は計測結果と概ね整合したことから，提案方法の適用性が示される．

2　逆解析方法の概要

トンネルは，ほかの地中構造物と同様，覆工に作用する荷重が地山の変形に支配され明確に規定できないことから，変位の計測データからトンネルの安全性を評価することが望ましい[2]．

桜井は[3]，NATM 工法の情報化施工を目的に，掘削時の変位計測から地山の見かけ弾性係数と初期地圧を求める逆解析方法を開発したとともに，限界ひずみの考え方に基づいて掘削による地山の安定性を評価する方法を提案した．桜井の方法は，現在日本の NATM 工法の情報化施工において広く適用され大きな役割を果たしている．ただし，これらの場合では掘削時の地山の変形挙動を検討対象としていることから，初期地圧の解放が地山の変形の原因として考えておりその初期地圧の鉛直成分が土かぶり圧に等しいと仮定し，見かけの地山の弾性係数は未知としている．

これに対して本論文では，掘削後のトンネルの変形挙動を検討対象としていることから，計測変位から覆工応力を求めるのが目的であり地山の弾性係数は既知とするが，見かけの解放応力の全成分は未知としている．

以下では，平面ひずみモデルを例に FEM 逆解析方法の概要を示す．トンネルの覆工と地山を一体化としてモデル化する．FEM により離散化された応力釣合い方程式は，式（１）で表される．

$$[K]\{\Delta u\}=\{\Delta f\} \tag{1}$$

ここで，$[K]$は剛性マトリックスであり，覆工と地山の材料定数および幾何形状より，次のように計算される．

$$[K]=\sum_{e=1,N_e}\int[B]^T[D][B]dv_e \tag{2}$$

$\{\Delta u\}$は節点変位ベクトルであり，計測点での既知変位 Δu_i とその以外の未知変位 Δu_j に分けることができる．また，$\{\Delta f\}$は節点力ベクトルであり，覆工と地山との境界面において見かけの解放応力 $\Delta\sigma_{ij}$ の関数として，式（３）のように計算することができる．

$$\{\Delta f\}=\sum_{k=1,Nex}\int[B]^T\{\Delta\sigma\}dv_{ex} \tag{3}$$

従来，式（1）右辺の節点力ベクトル$\{\Delta f\}$を与えて，左辺の節点変位ベクトル$\{\Delta u\}$を求めるのが一般的であり，いわゆる順解析というものである．しかし，ここでの問題は，式（1）左辺の節点変位ベクトル$\{\Delta u\}$の一部分が計測変位Δu_iとして既知ではあるが，右辺の節点力ベクトル$\{\Delta f\}$は見かけの解放応力$\Delta\sigma_{ij}$の関数で未知であることから，FEM逆解析と呼ぶこととする．

具体的には，2次元問題において見かけの解放応力$\Delta\sigma_{ij}$は３つの成分（$\Delta\sigma_x,\Delta\sigma_y,\Delta\tau_{xy}$）を有し，３つ以上の計測変位$\Delta u_i$が与えれば（$i=1,m\ \ m\geqslant 3$），計測変位と解析変位の誤差二乗和を最小となるよう見かけの解放応力$\Delta\sigma_{ij}$の３つの成分（$\Delta\sigma_x,\Delta\sigma_y,\Delta\tau_{xy}$）が一意的に求められ，それに対応した覆工の変位と応力を計算することができる．これらの詳細な定式化については，付録に示す．

3　膨張性地山におけるトンネルの覆工補強

3.1　概要

飯山トンネルは[4]，北陸新幹線（長野～金沢間）長野県と新潟県の県境に位置する延長約22.2 kmの長大トンネルである．東北新幹線の八甲田トンネル（延長約 26.5 km）と岩手トンネル（延長約25.8 km）に次いで日本の３番目長い陸上長大トンネルである．2000年6月着工から６つ工区に分けて施工を進め9年半の歳月をかけて2008年1月に貫通した．

飯山トンネルの地質は，図－1の地質縦断図に示すように下位より新第三紀の寺泊層，椎谷層，西山層，灰爪層，第四紀の小国層および新規火山噴出物などからなる．これらの地層は富倉背斜に支配され，背斜軸付近に寺泊層，椎谷層が分布しその両側には対称的に西山層，灰爪層が分布している．このような褶曲構造にある脆弱な堆積軟岩は原油やガスを胚胎し，トンネル掘削により周辺地山は強度不足による塑性変形およびガス圧による地山の押し出しが顕著に現れ，内空変位が数十cmを越えた顕著な膨張性区間は多く出現した．そのため新たに多重支保工法を適用し可燃性ガス対策を駆使しながら掘削工事を進めて来た．

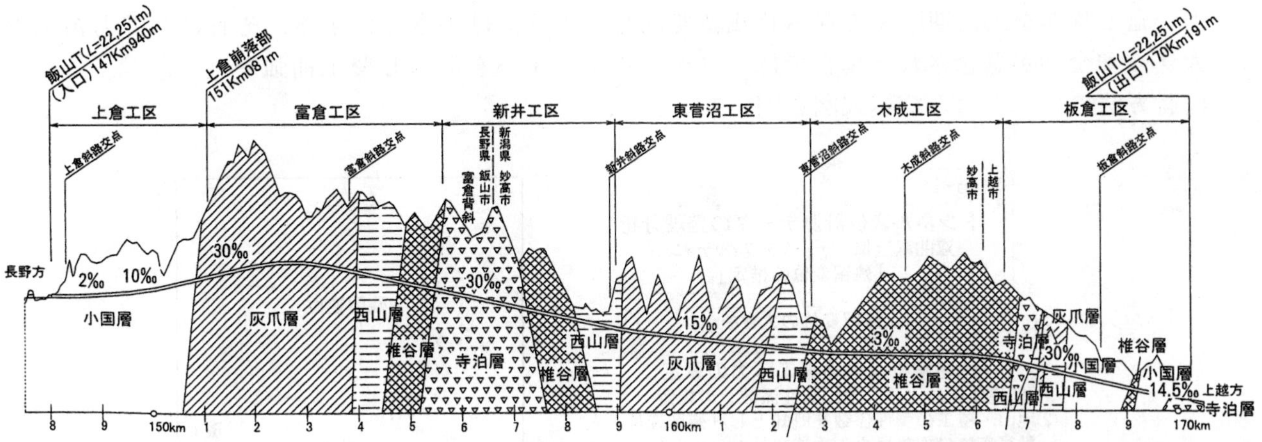

図1　飯山トンネルの地質縦断図

一方，もう一つの問題として膨張性の顕著な区間においては，掘削完了後長時間を経過してもトンネルの変位が収束しないことから，覆工の施工時期や補強検討が必要となった．そこで，東菅沼工区を最初の検討対象とし，変位が収束していない段階で覆工を施工する場合に覆工の安全性を評価する方法を検討した[5]．そして地質条件を踏まえて検討した結果はほかの施工区間にも適用された．

東菅沼工区は飯山トンネルのほぼ中間部に位置しており，土かぶりは最大450mで延長3800mである．地質は図－2の地質縦断図に示したように，砂岩優勢の灰爪層が大部分を占めているが，泥岩優勢の西山層と椎谷層は両端に分布している．当該工区においてトンネル掘削時の変位は富倉工区，木成工区等に比べ小さいものの，インバート閉合後半年経過しても，内空変位が約2 mm/月の速度で進行していた．そこで，掘削時の計測変位から双曲線近似で覆工施工後の残留変位を推定し，FEM逆解析により覆工の応力を求め，計測結果と比較することにより提案方法の適用性を検討した．

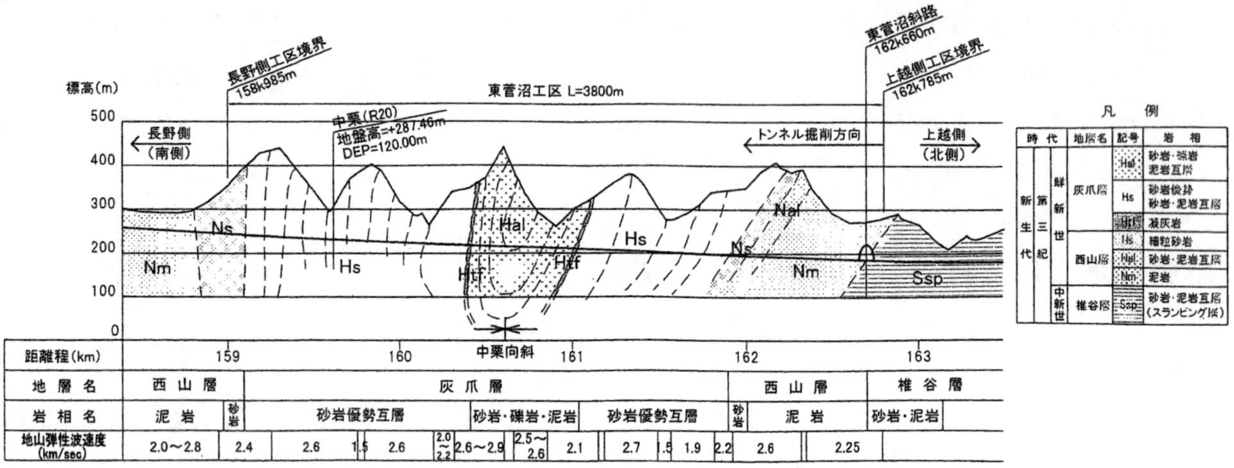

図２　東菅沼工区の地質縦断図

3.2　検討方法

変位が収束していない段階で覆工を施工する場合に，覆工の安全性を評価する方法は以下に示す．

①　トンネル掘削時の計測変位から覆工の施工時期に応じて残留変位を双曲線法から推定する．

②　残留変位をインプットデータとして，FEM 逆解析により覆工に作用する見かけの解放応力を求め，それに対応した覆工の変形と応力を計算する．

③　覆工応力の大きさとりわけ引っ張り応力の有無に対して覆工の安全性を照査する．

④　施工時期を工期期限まで遅らせ残留変位をできるだけ小さくにする．それにしても覆工の応力が大きく安全性が懸念される場合では，スチールファイバを混入し覆工補強を行う．

検討方法のフローおよび模式図を図－3 に示す．

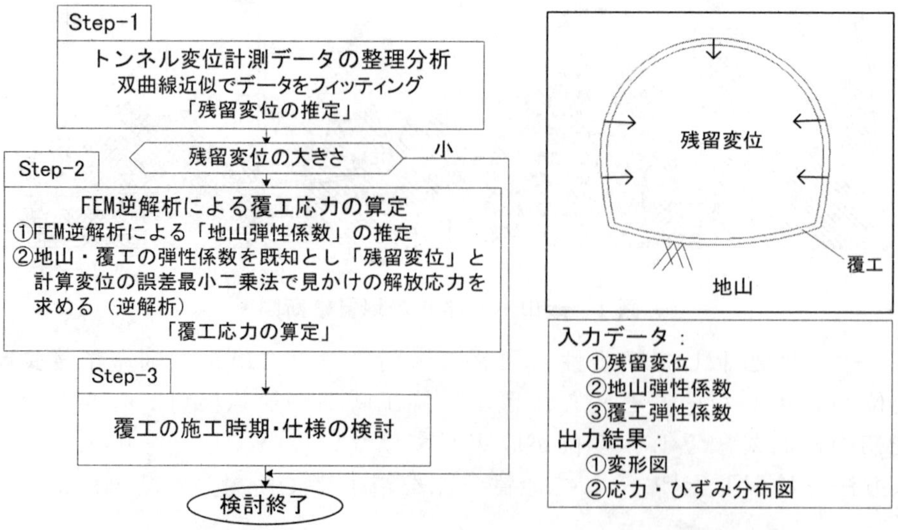

(a) 検討フロー　　(b) 模式図

図－3　覆工補強検討の考え方

3.3 計算例

（1）残留変位の推定

トンネル掘削時の計測変位データから残留変位を推定する例を以下に示す．

まず計測変位に対してデータフィッティンクを行う．飯山トンネルの計測変位の多くは，式(4)に示す双曲線を用いて良くフィッティンクすることができる．

$$u(t)=\frac{t}{a+bt} \tag{4}$$

ここで，$u(t)$は計測変位，tは経過時間，$1/a$は初期変位速度，$1/b$は収束変位．非線形最小二乗法を用いて計測変位からパラメータのaとbが求められる．

そして，覆工の施工時期Tに応じて，残留変位$\Delta u_i(T)$は式(5)より推定される．

$$\Delta u_i\left(T\right)=u_i\left(\infty\right)-u_i\left(T\right)=1/b_i-u_i\left(T\right) \tag{5}$$

表－1と図－4は，実際のある断面の計測変位から残留変位を推定した結果を示したものである．

表－1　残留変位の推定結果

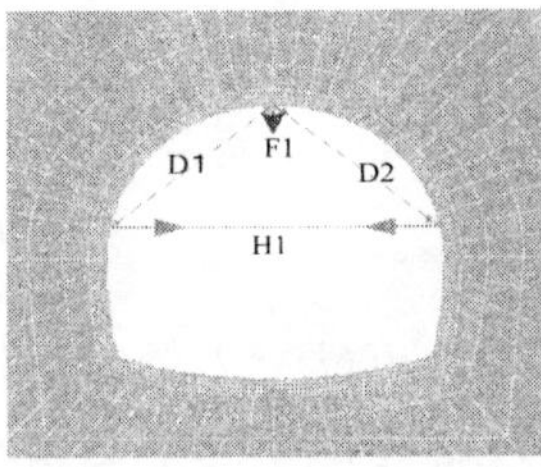

	計測値(mm)	推定値(mm)		残留変位(mm)
	(255日経過)	覆工施工時点(620日経過)	最終収束値	
天端沈下　F1	28	28.3	28.4	0.1
上半内空　H1	140.5	145	147.1	2.1
左斜め　D1	40.3	40.6	41	0.4
右斜め　D2	44.2	45.1	45.7	0.6

図－4に示したように，計測変位のデータに対して双曲線のフィッティンクは非常によく再現している．この結果より，覆工の施工時期に応じて推定された残留変位は上半内空 2.1mm，天端沈下 0.1 mm 左右斜めの内空それぞれ 0.4 mm と 0.6 mm である．

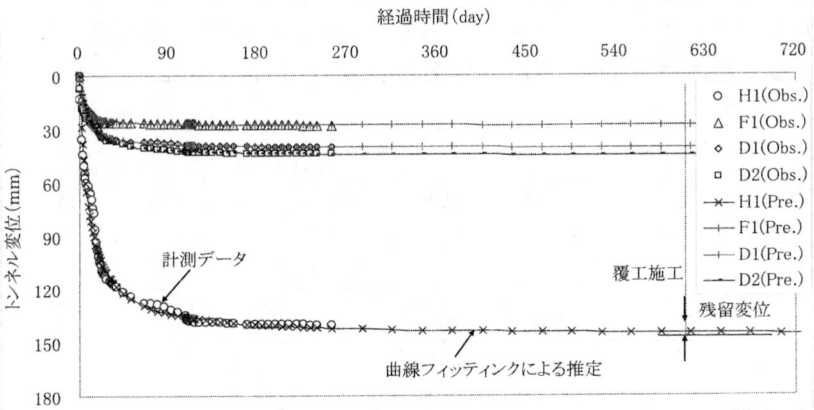

図－4　計測変位のデータと推定された残留変位

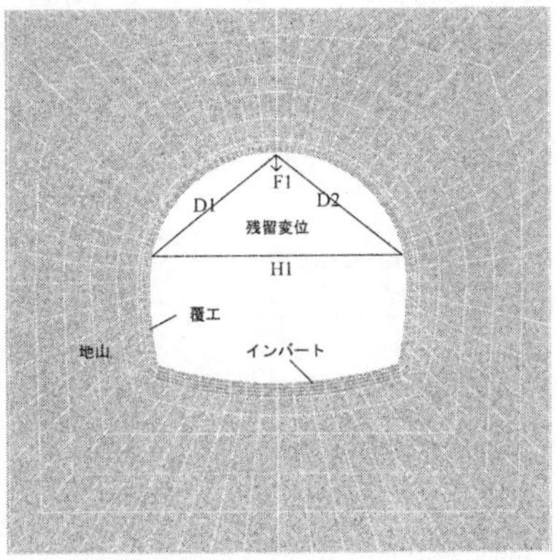

図－5　FEM 逆解析モデル

（2）覆工応力の逆解析

前項に示した残留変位をインプットデータとして，FEM逆解析より覆工の応力を求める例を以下に示す．

FEM逆解析のモデルは，図－5に示すように覆工と地山を一体化して離散化したものである．境界条件は地山の外周において変位を固定とする．覆工と地山の弾性係数およびポアソン比が既知としてそれぞれ与える．地山の弾性係数は100 N/mm^2，ポアソン比は0.3である．覆工の弾性係数は22,000 N/mm^2,ポアソン比は0.2である．

残留変位をインプットデータとして入力しFEM逆解析を行うことにより，残留変位と計算変位との誤差二乗和を最小となるように覆工に作用する見かけの解放応力が求められ，そして対応した覆工の変形と応力が計算されることになる．

逆解析の結果から覆工の変形および主応力の分布図をそれぞれ図－6(a)(b)に示す．図－6(a)に示したように残留変形を受けた覆工は,SL付近では大きな曲げ変形が発生している．この変形モードに対応した覆工応力は，図－6(b)に示したように天端付近では覆工の横断面においてほぼ一様な圧縮応力が発生しているが，SL付近では横断面の内側では僅かながら引っ張り応力が発生し外側ではやや大きな圧縮応力が発生している．

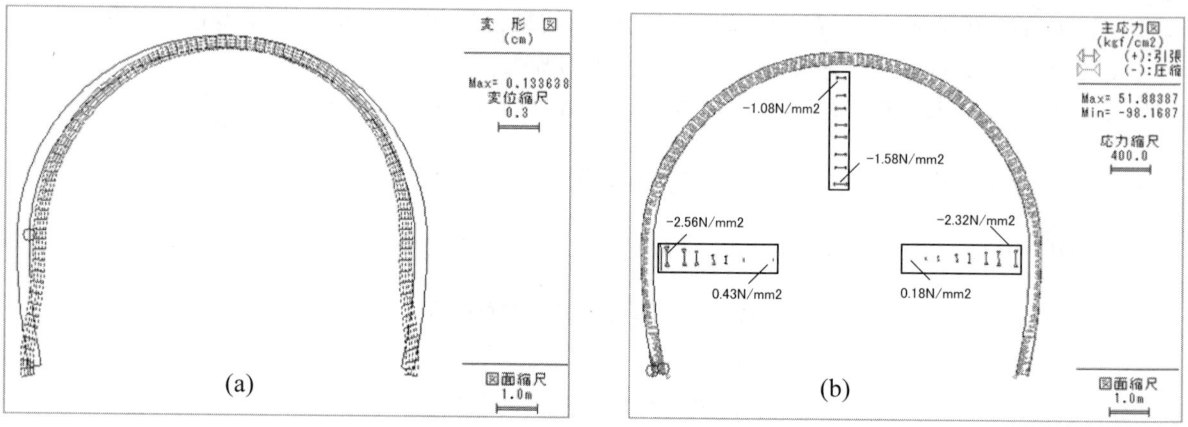

図-6　FEM逆解析による覆工の変形(a)と応力(b)

一方，現場で計測した覆工の応力は図－7に示す．図－7に示したように，天端での横断面にはほぼ一様な圧縮応力が発生したことに対して，SLでの横断面には左右とも曲げ応力が卓越するような応力分布が示され，特に左のSL横断面の内側には引っ張り応力が発生した．このように覆工応力の計測結果は概ね逆解析から求めた結果と定性的に整合した．

さらには，定量的に覆工応力の計測値と解析値との比較を図－8に示す．全般的には解析値の方が計測値よりやや大きいものの，計測値にかなり近い結果を与えており両者は概ね一致した．特に一番大きな引っ張り応力が計測された左SLでの横断面の内側では，解析値と計測値がほぼ一致した．また，右SLでの横断面の外側では，計測された一番大きな圧縮応力も解析値と同程度であった．

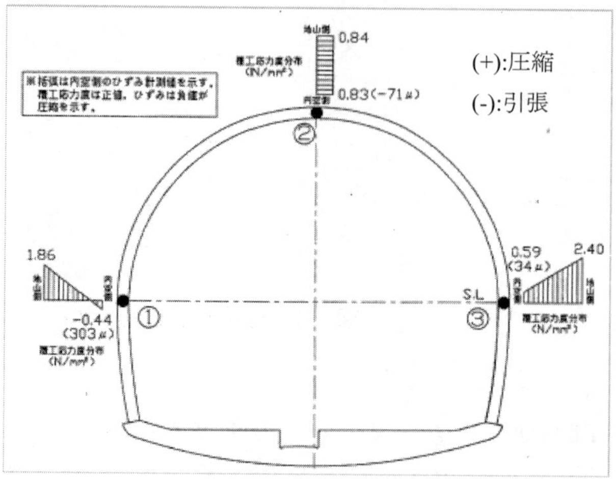

図-7　覆工応力の計測結果

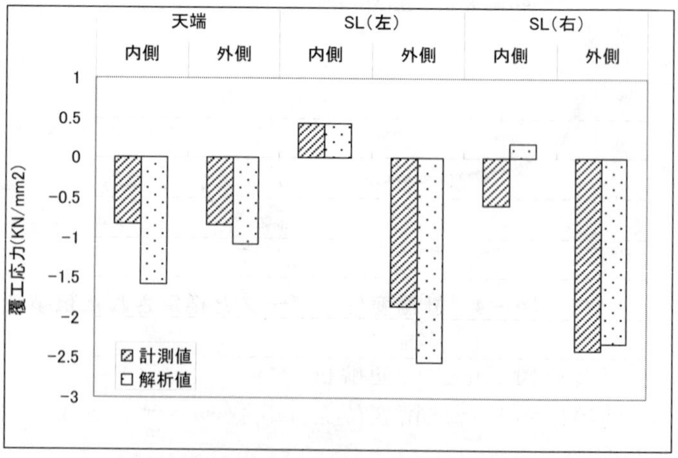

図-8　計測値と解析値との比較

このようにFEM逆解析から求めた覆工応力は計測された応力と比べ，横断面の応力分布および内外縁の応力値が概ね一致した．このことから，提案する方法は概ね妥当であり適用性があると考えられる．

実際に，上述した方法を用いて東菅沼工区における変位の収束性の悪い代表断面に対してそれぞれ覆工応力の逆解析を行った．解析結果から覆工の横断面の内側に引っ張り応力が発生するかどうかを踏まえたうえ，周辺地山の地質条件等を総合的に考慮して覆工補強の要否を判断した．

4 結論

本論文は,時間依存的変形を有するトンネルを対象に計測変位から覆工安全性を評価する FEM 逆解析方法を示し，膨張性トンネルの覆工補強の適用例を紹介した．

この方法では，トンネルの覆工に発生する変位（残留変位）が３つ以上与えれば，残留変位と計算変位の誤差二乗和を最小となるよう覆工に作用する見かけの解放応力が FEM 逆解析より求められ，それに対応した覆工の変形と応力が計算されることになる．具体的な膨張性トンネルの覆工補強の適用例においては，残留変位はトンネル掘削時の計測変位から双曲線近似で推定され，FEM 逆解析により求めた覆工の応力は計測結果と概ね整合した結果が得ており，提案方法の適用性が示された．

残留変位をインプットデータとして FEM 逆解析より覆工応力を求める方法は,多くの仮定があるものの計測変位が利活用され非常に簡便であることから，今後の更なる実証ができれば供用中のトンネルの維持管理にも適用できると考えられる．

参考文献（References）：

[1] 日本土木学会．トンネル標準示方書「山岳工法」・同解説〈2006 年制定〉．2006, pp.94-101.

[2] K. Kovari, Ch. Amstad. Decision Making and Field Measurements in Tunnelling, 25th OYO Anniversary Lecture Meeting, 1979, pp.1-44.

[3] 桜井春輔，武内邦文.トンネル掘削時における変位計測結果の逆解析法，土木学会論文集，1982，第 337 号，pp.61-69.

[4] 光木香, 小幡芳文. 北陸新幹線飯山トンネル地質調査最終報告, トンネルと地下, 2000, Vol. 31, No. 7: 53-61.

[5] 中村敦，小野利昭，亀谷英樹，呉旭．膨張性地山での二次覆工の現状評価と設計手法の提案（北陸新幹線飯山トンネル東菅沼工区），トンネルと地下，2007，Vol. 38, No. 4: 39-47.

著者紹介（Bio-data）：

呉　旭（Xu WU）

現職　応用地質(株)技術センター グループリーダー

工学博士

略歴　1994 年名古屋大学大学院地圏環境工学 博士課程修了，

同大学工学部機械情報システム工学科助手を経て現職

専門　地盤工学,地盤防災

北陸新幹線における合理的なトンネル施工方法や青函トンネルの維持管理等の検討業務に従事した他，トンネルと地すべりとの相互作用や地盤災害対策などの研究にも携われている．地質や地盤の力学問題に関する解析が得意．

Dr. Wu is currently a group leader of geotechnical division in OYO Corporation. He has over decades of experience in geotechnical consulting, practical tunneling applications, research and academia. He has worked with JRTT for consulting the tunneling in complex geological conditions in Hokuriku Shinkansen. He also has expertise in investigation and analysis of landslides, countermeasure of ground hazards, especially in the development and application of numerical models in geotechnical mechanics.

付録:

計測変位からトンネル覆工の応力を求める FEM 逆解析の定式化

FEM により離散化された応力釣合い方程式は，式（1）で表される．

$$[K]\{\Delta u\}=\{\Delta f\} \quad (1)$$

まず，節点変位ベクトル $\{\Delta u\}$ を，既知の計測変位 Δu_i（$i=1,m$）とその以外の節点変位 Δu_j（$j=1,n$，$n=N-m$，N は総自由度数）に分けて並べ，離散化モデルの応力釣りあり方程式（1）は，式（2）のように書き換えられる．

$$\begin{bmatrix} [K]_{m\times m} & [K]_{m\times n} \\ [K]_{n\times m} & [K]_{n\times n} \end{bmatrix} \begin{Bmatrix} \{\Delta u\}_{m\times 1} \\ \{\Delta u\}_{n\times 1} \end{Bmatrix} = \begin{Bmatrix} \{\Delta f\}_{m\times 1} \\ \{\Delta f\}_{n\times 1} \end{Bmatrix} \quad (2)$$

これより計測変位と節点力の関係が次のように求められる．

$$[K]_{m\times m}\{\Delta u\}_{m\times 1}+[K]_{m\times n}[K]_{n\times n}^{-1}\left(\{\Delta f\}_{n\times 1}-[K]_{n\times m}\{\Delta u\}_{m\times 1}\right)=\{\Delta f\}_{m\times 1} \quad (3)$$

一方，節点力ベクトル $\{\Delta f\}$ は，解放応力 $\Delta\sigma$ の線形関数であるため，式（4）で表せる．

$$\{\Delta f\}_{m\times 1}=[P]_{m\times 3}\{\Delta\sigma\}_{3\times 1}\ ;\ \{\Delta f\}_{n\times 1}=[Q]_{n\times 3}\{\Delta\sigma\}_{3\times 1} \quad (4\,\text{a,b})$$

式（4 a,b）を式（3）に代入し整理すれば，式（5）が導かれる．

$$\{\Delta u\}_{m\times 1}=[A]_{m\times 3}\{\Delta\sigma\}_{3\times 1} \quad (5)$$

ただし，$[A]_{m\times 3}=\left([K]_{m\times m}-[K]_{m\times n}[K]_{n\times n}^{-1}[K]_{n\times m}\right)^{-1}\left([P]_{m\times 3}-[K]_{m\times n}[K]_{n\times n}^{-1}[Q]_{n\times 3}\right)$

この式（5）は，計測変位 Δu_i と解放応力 $\Delta\sigma_{ij}$ の関係式であり，逆解析の基本式である．

一般的に3つ以上の計測変位を与える場合では，最小2乗法を用いて式（5）から未知な解放応力 $\Delta\sigma_{ij}$（$\Delta\sigma_x,\Delta\sigma_y,\Delta\tau_{xy}$ 3つの成分）は，次のように求めることができる．

$$\{\Delta\sigma\}_{3\times 1}=\left([A]_{m\times 3}^{T}[A]_{m\times 3}\right)^{-1}[A]_{m\times 3}^{T}\{\Delta u\}_{m\times 1} \quad (6)$$

さらには，式（5）より計測変位以外の節点変位 Δu_j も計算されることになり，全体の離散化モデルの変位，応力およびひずみが得られる．

著者の一人は，以上に示した逆解析のアルゴリズムを FEM 解析プログラムに取り込むことにより，計測変位から覆工の応力を求める解析システムを開発した．

大断面分割シールド工法（ハーモニカ工法）の構造研究

趙 唯堅 服部佳文 三木洋人

大成建設株式会社 〒163-060 東京都新宿区西新宿 1-25-1

要旨：大断面分割シールド工法（ハーモニカ工法, Harmonica Tunneling Method）は，推進工法により小断面の単体トンネルを逐次隣接させながら掘削した後，鋼殻内に躯体を構築し，内部に残置される鋼殻を撤去し大断面トンネルを構築する工法である．本論文は，ハーモニカ工法によるトンネル構造の特徴に着目し，設計合理化の第１ステップとして，仮設鋼殻の不連続部が本体構造に及ぼす影響を実物大構造実験より把握し，併せて本体構造の簡易設計方法を提案したものである．

キーワード：非開削工法；ハーモニカ工法；アンダーパス；鋼殻；構造設計

DEVELOPMENT OF THE SHIELD METHOD CONSTRUCTION STRUCTURES FOR LARGE SECTION TUNNEL BY JOINING SMALL SECTION TUNNELS TOGETHER

Weijian ZHAO，Yoshifumi HATTORI，Hiroto MIKI

Taisei Corporation, 1-25-1, Nishi-Shinjuku, Shinjuku, Tokyo 163-0606, Japan

Abstract: We are developing a new technique of building a large tunnel by piling up small shield tunnels, as a way of making underpasses at the intersection between a railway and a roadway, or between two roadways.

A tunnel is divided into several sections as if mouthpiece of a harmonica and each section is built individually, and then they are connected together. The miniaturization of machines makes it possible to build a tunnel which is shallow ground.

We suggest the Structural design method of a large cross-section tunnel which constructed by this method in this paper.

Key words: Non-Open-Cut method; harmonica tunneling method; underpass; steel segments; steel reinforced concrete; structural design

1 はじめに

近年，東京，大阪など大都市の再生事業の一環として，交通渋滞の解消や防災施設の充実などが重要課題として取り上げられ，都市部の交通渋滞解消策の一つとして，幹線道路の交差点や道路・鉄道交差部でのアンダーパスによる立体交差化が進められている．

これまで，市街地におけるアンダーパスの建設は主に開削工法によって行われてきたが，地上部施工ヤードの確保や，工事期間中における車線規制，工事に伴う新たな交通渋滞，施工期間の長期化，周辺環境の悪化などの問題が深刻であり，事業の実施を困難にしている場合が多い．

一方，アンダーパスを非開削工法で施工する場合，従来適用されてきた PCR 工法や HEP&JES 工法などの外殻先行型の工法[1]は，最適施工距離は 100 m 以下で，曲線施工ができず，開放型掘削のため切羽の安定や地下水対策など施工上の課題を抱えている．また，全断面シールド工法では，施工距離・曲線対応・切羽の安定・地下水対策などの面で長けているが，低土被り下での施工・テールボイドによる地上への影響，および経済性に課題を残している．

これらの課題を合理的に解決する非開削工法として，矩形の大断面トンネルを複数の小断面に分割し，それぞれを小型の掘削機を使用して繰返し掘削した後，その内部にトンネルの躯体を作り上げる「大断面分割シールド工法」を開発した[2]．掘削を完了した坑口の形状が，ハーモニカの吹き口に似ていることからこの工法を「ハーモニカ工法」(Harmonica Tunneling Method)と命名した（図 1）．

図 1　ハーモニカ工法のイメージ

ハーモニカ工法は施工法的発想から生まれたものであることから，これまで掘削，方向制御，止水，本体構築など，施工に関する多くの要素技術が開発・適用されてきた．一方，ハーモニカ工法の構造は施工法の制約を受け，現状では必ずしも最適なものとはなっていない．その一つは，小断面分割掘削時の支保工である鋼殻は単なる仮設であり，大断面トンネルの本体構造に有効利用されていないことが挙げられる[3) 4)]．これまで累積 6 件の適用実績はあるが，いずれも鋼殻は，仮設としての取り扱いとなり，本体構造として考慮されていない．そのため，鋼殻構造高の空間はデッドスペースとなり，中に充填されているコンクリートも大きなロスとなった．

ハーモニカ工法の優位性を高めるためには，施工技術のみならず，仮設構造と本体構造，継手，構造解析，せん断補強方法，耐震性能評価などを含めた構造技術の開発も併せて行い，設計の合理化を図る必要がある．本稿は，ハーモニカ工法によるトンネル構造の特徴に着目し，構造合理化の第 1 ステップとして，埋めこみ鋼殻の不連続部が本体構造に及ぼす影響を検討するために試設計に基づく実物大構造実験を行い，その結果をもとに本体構造の簡易設計方法を提案したものである．

2　ハーモニカ工法の概要

2.1　施工手順

ハーモニカ工法による断面の分割数は，構築されるアンダーパスの寸法，掘削機・函体の運搬条件，コストや工期などを勘案して決定する．分割数を増やすと，掘削機械が小型になり安価になるが，段取り替え回数が増し工期が長期化し，鋼殻の重量も増える．ここでは，矩形トンネルの断面を上下 2 分割，横 3 分割の合計 6 分割とした断面について施工手順を説明する（図 2）．

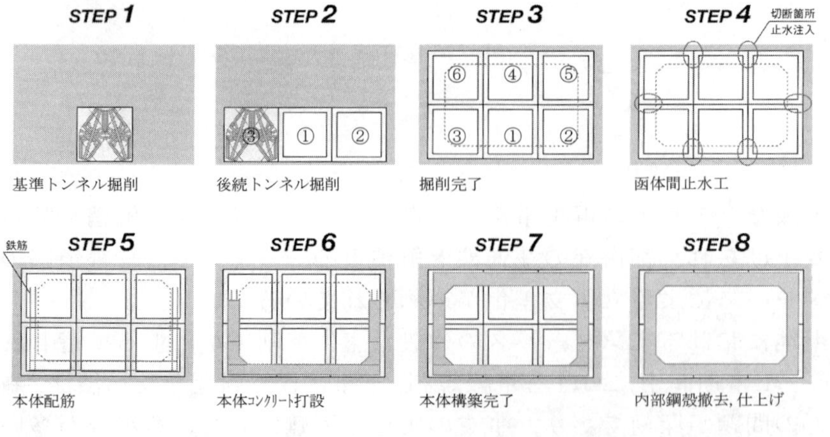

図 2　ハーモニカ工法の施工手順

始めに，下段中央より基準トンネルを掘削して基準函体を構築する（STEP1）．この基準函体はアンダーパスの位置管理基準となるため慎重な施工が要求される．引続き基準函体をガイドに隣接するトンネルを掘削する（STEP2）．次に構台を組み立て，上段トンネルを順次掘削し，トンネル全体の掘削を完了する（STEP3）．外周部で函体間の隙間に止水処理をした後，鋼殻（スキンプレート・縦リブ）を部分的に解体し（STEP4），底版・側壁・上床版の順序で鉄筋を組み立て（STEP5），コンクリートを打設して（STEP6），大断面トンネルの本体を構築する（STEP7）．最後にコンクリート硬化後，内部に残された鋼殻を切断・撤去し仕上げを行って完成となる（STEP8）．

2.2 ハーモニカ工法の特徴

ハーモニカ工法は，既存の外殻先行型工法と比較して，以下の特長がある．

① 尺取掘削方式を採用することで，100 m を超える距離の掘削が可能である．

② 曲線施工が可能である．

③ 小断面推進工事が完了すると，トンネル掘削が全て完了するため，内部掘削が不要である．

④ 密閉型の掘削機で切羽管理が行えるため，地表面に与える影響が少ない．

また，全断面シールド工法と比較した場合，以下の特長がある．

① 小型掘削機を使用するため，全断面シールドマシンに比べ安価である．

② 掘削時のトンネル単体が小断面のため，低土被りでの施工が可能である．

③ 函体同士を接触させながら推進方式による掘削を行うため，テールボイドが少なく，地表面に与える影響が少ない．

④ 小型掘削機を使用するため，施工時の作業基地占用が小規模となる．

2.3 掘削機械

土被りが低い箇所での施工を想定しているため，掘削機の形式は主として切羽の安定に優れ地表面への影響が少ないとされる密閉型土圧式シールド機を使用する．また，函体同士を接触させながら掘削を行うため，掘削方法はテール内でセグメントを組立てるシールド方式ではなく，立坑内で鋼殻を供給する推進方式を採用している．

写真 1　掘削機の

掘削機のカッタ形状は矩形断面の未掘削部分を少なくできる揺動型カッタと，補助的にコーナーカッタを装備する（写真 1）．100m を超える距離を施工する場合，掘削機は前胴・後胴に分け推進ジャッキにて接続し，尺取虫方式で掘進を行う．さらに，曲線施工を行う場合は，線形に合致した鋼殻の使用と，中折れ装置の付いた掘削機械の使用により施工することが可能である（縦断 190R の実例がある）．

2.4 鋼殻

ハーモニカ工法では，小断面トンネルの覆工として鋼殻を使用する．この鋼殻は，外周部を覆うスキンプレート，施工時に土水圧などの外力に抵抗する役目を果たす主桁，および推力を伝える部材である縦リブから構成される（写真 2）．また，トンネル本体構築時（図 2 の STEP6～STEP7）トンネル外周部のスキンプレートを外型枠としてコンクリートを打設するため，完成時には，縦リブを含めて外周側の鋼殻主桁は躯体コンクリートの中に埋められている．

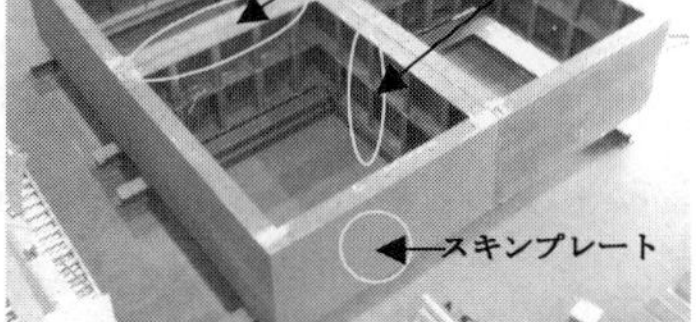

写真 2　鋼殻

掘進精度を上げるために，鋼殻間にガイドとなる特殊構造の継手を設けている．継手の形状はレール（雄，Y 形）と溝（雌，C 形）の組み合わせを基本として，鋼殻の 2 方向の姿勢制御を可能にしている（写真 3，図 3）．継手の配置位置は鋼殻の隅角部とし，隣接鋼殻との間で最低 2 箇所を設けており，掘進方向で貫通している．

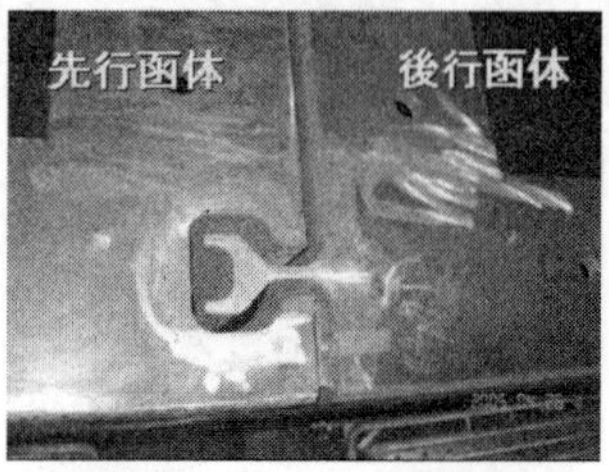

写真 3　ガイド継手

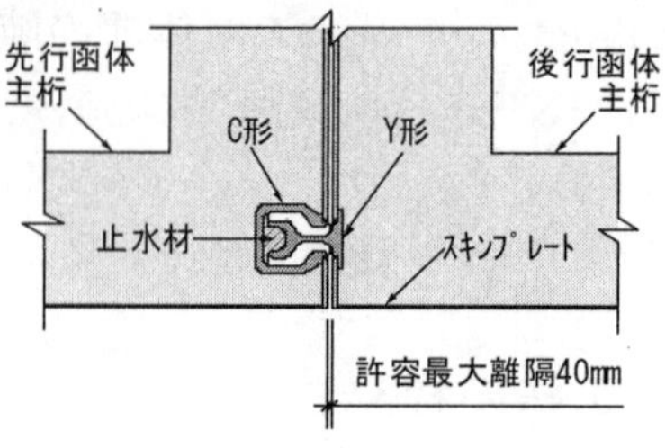

図 3　ガイド継手（兼止水）

この継手には鋼殻推進時のガイドのみならず，C と Y の間に止水材を注入して止水機能をも持たせている（図 3）．なお，注入箇所はトンネル本体外周部にあたる場所のみとし，止水材料として水中分離しないアクリル系のものを採用している．

3　ハーモニカ工法によるトンネル構造の特徴と課題

3.1　構造的特徴と設計フロー

ハーモニカ工法の構造的特長はその施工上の特徴から決定される．すなわち，小断面単体トンネル掘削時の鋼殻構造と，完成時の鉄筋と外周側鋼殻主桁を補強材とするコンクリート構造となる．構造設計は，単体トンネル構築段階と本体構造完成段階に分け，それぞれの段階の荷重を考慮して行う（図 4）．

単体トンネル時の構造は，施工時荷重に耐えられる主桁，縦リブ，スキンプレート，および継手からなる鋼殻構造である．

鋼殻フレームの断面力算定は，単体トンネルの各施工段階の荷重（土水圧,裏込め注入圧など）および隣接鋼殻の影響を考慮して剛性一様の骨組みモデルにより行い（図 5），部材の応力度照査は，鋼殻一般部断面とボルト継手部断面に分けてそれぞれ行う．

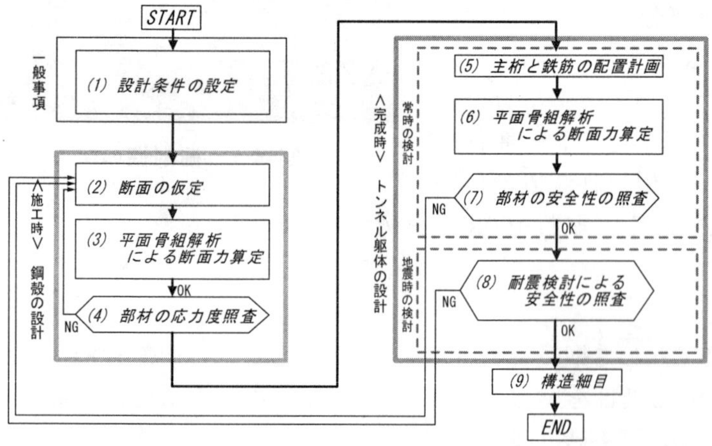

図 4　設計フロー

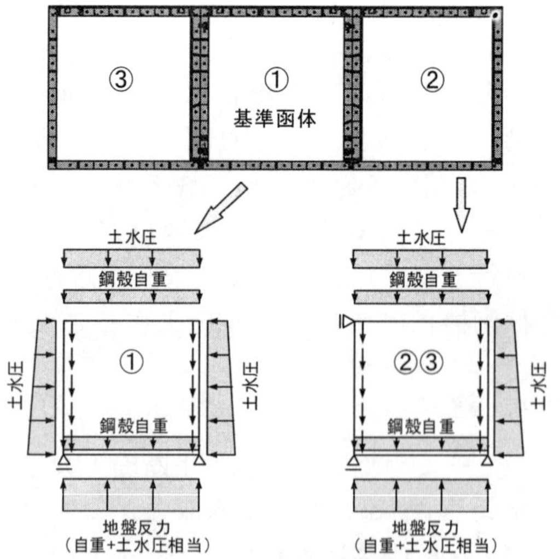

図 5　施工時仮設鋼殻の設計

完成段階では，鋼殻の内側に複鉄筋を配置した鉄筋コンクリート構造が基本となり，躯体に埋められている鋼殻を無視している（図 6）．これは，隣接鋼殻の主桁同士は接合しておらず，ガイド継手の仕様から最大 40mm 程度の離隔が発生する可能性もあるためである．

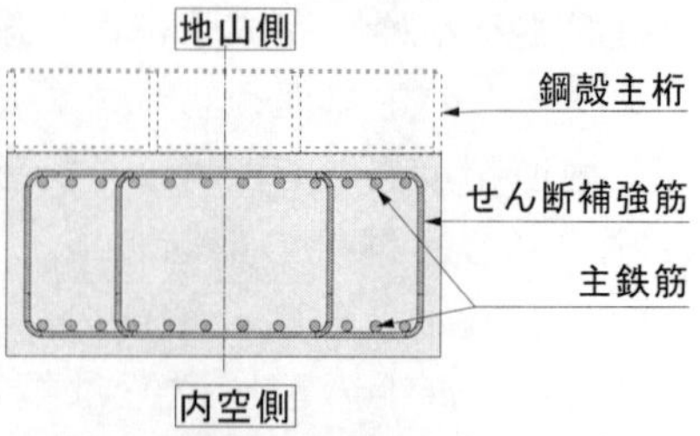

図 6　鋼殻を無視した RC 断面

トンネル本体の構造解析は,照査レベルと限界状態に応じて適切な解析モデルと解析理論を適用する必要がある．使用性および断面破壊安全性の照査を行う場合には，一般の地下構造物と同様に，剛性一様の骨組みモデルに線形解析を適用し,発生断面力に対して通常の鉄筋コンクリート(以下 RC)理論により断面照査を行う（図 7）．耐震設計においては部材の非線形挙動を考慮する．

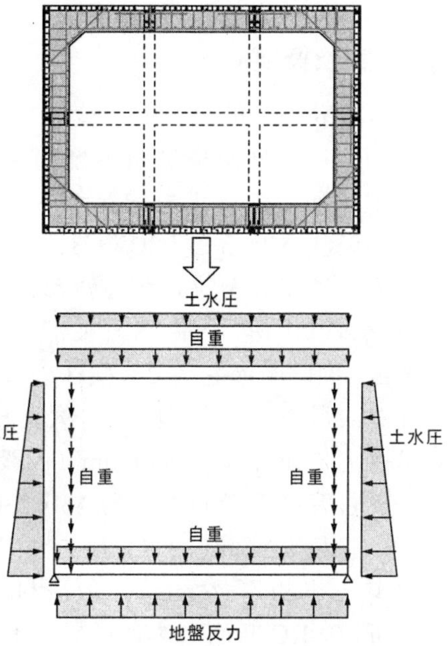

図 7　完成時トンネル躯体の設

3.2　構造合理化の課題

トンネルの完成段階では,コンクリートはスキンプレートの内面まで打設され，外周側の鋼殻主桁は躯体中に残される．この主桁を本体コンクリートの補強材に，縦リブを主桁のシアコネクタとしてコンクリートと一体化させ，トンネル内側の補強鉄筋と組合わせた鉄骨鉄筋コンクリート（以下 SRC）構造を構成することで，施工時の仮設材としての鋼殻を有効利用でき，後施工の主鉄筋や配力筋を減らし,構造の合理化やコスト縮減を図ることができる[5]．

しかし，外周部の鋼殻と鋼殻の間では主桁が不連続となっている．また，その間にガイド兼止水継手があるため，この最大 40mm になる隙間はコンクリートで埋めることができず，ほぼ主桁高さの範囲で圧縮応力も伝達することができない．すなわち，トンネル完成時の本体構造として断面変化部（主桁とほぼ主桁高さ範囲のコンクリートが不連続）が存在することになる（図 8）.

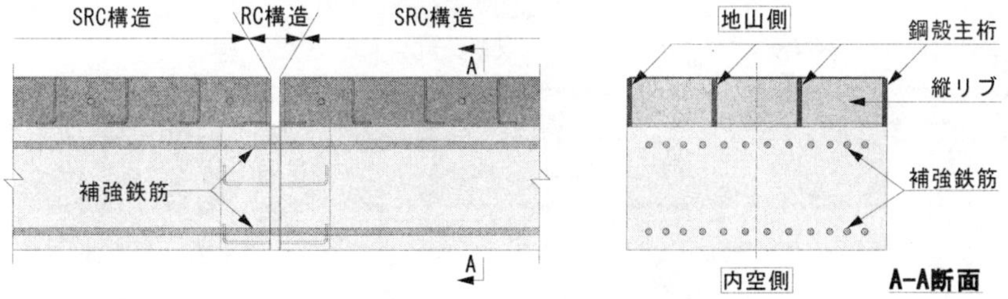

図 8　完成時トンネル躯体の断面変化部

現状では，主桁より内側にかぶりを確保して補強鉄筋を配置しているが，断面高さも補強材の量と位置も変化しており，一般部と異なった挙動を示すと考えられる．従って，通常荷重時の設計検討はともかく，レベル 2（以下 L2）地震時のようなトンネル躯体の非線形挙動を検討する場合には，一般部と断面変化部を区別して，その影響を考慮するようにモデル化する必要がある．

そこで，ハーモニカ工法の構造・設計合理化を以下に示す 3 つの形態（3 つのステップ）に分けて考えることとする．

第 1 形態（第 1 ステップ）: 鋼殻主桁同士が接合されず，引張・圧縮ともに不連続部を有する場合の鋼殻本設利用の効果の把握．

第 2 形態（第 2 ステップ）: 鋼殻主桁同士が接合されていないが，圧縮応力のみ伝達できるように隙間がコンクリートで充填されている状態の効果の把握．

第 3 形態（第 3 ステップ）: 鋼殻主桁同士が接合され，隙間もコンクリートで完全充填され，引張・圧縮ともに不連続部をなくした鋼殻の本格利用．

第 1 形態は現状の構造に対する設計の合理化，第 2 形態は横長の矩形トンネルで正曲げ（内空側引張）を受ける上・下床版のスリム化にかなり有効と思われる．そして，第 3 形態は完全なる鋼殻の本設利用を実現したもので，断面変化によるひび割れ集中もかなり改善される．

本研究では，次に述べる実験および解析的検討により，上記第 1 形態（第 1 ステップ）の効果を検証する．

4 断面変化部の実物大構造実験

4.1 実験概要

本実験の目的は，断面変化部のひび割れ・変形性状や鋼殻と主鉄筋間の応力伝達状況を確認し，断面の不連続性が構造耐力と剛性に及ぼす影響および鋼殻本体利用の効果を把握するとともに，その特性を設計に反映させることである．

供試体諸元を決定するため，土被りが 4.2 m，矩形トンネルで内空の最終出来形寸法が幅 7.8 m×高さ 10.8 m，掘削断面を縦 2×横 3 の 6 分割を想定して本格的な試設計を行った（図 9）．試設計の結果，上下床版，側壁ともに躯体厚さ 800 mm（仮設鋼殻を含む）となった．うち仮設鋼殻の断面高さが 230 mm（鋼殻リング幅 1.2 m，主桁 22 mm×224 mm を 1 リング 4 本配置，スキンプレート板厚 6 mm），仮設材の高さを引いた桁高 570 mm の RC 断面が本体の設計有効断面，設計有効断面の内側（内空側）に D32，外側（地山側）に D29 の鉄筋をそれぞれ 1 リング 12 本づつ配置した．

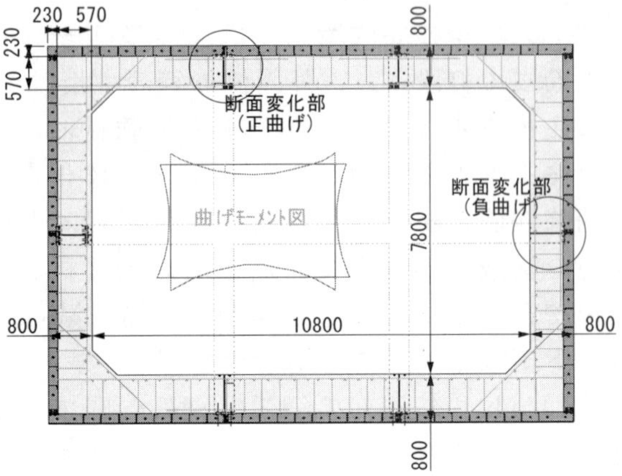

図 9 試設計したトンネル諸元

本実験では，寸法効果の影響を避け，確実な実験データを得るために，試設計で得られた断面を忠実に再現し，奥行き幅を 1 リングの 1.2 m とした実物大の供試体を製作して実施した（図 10）．

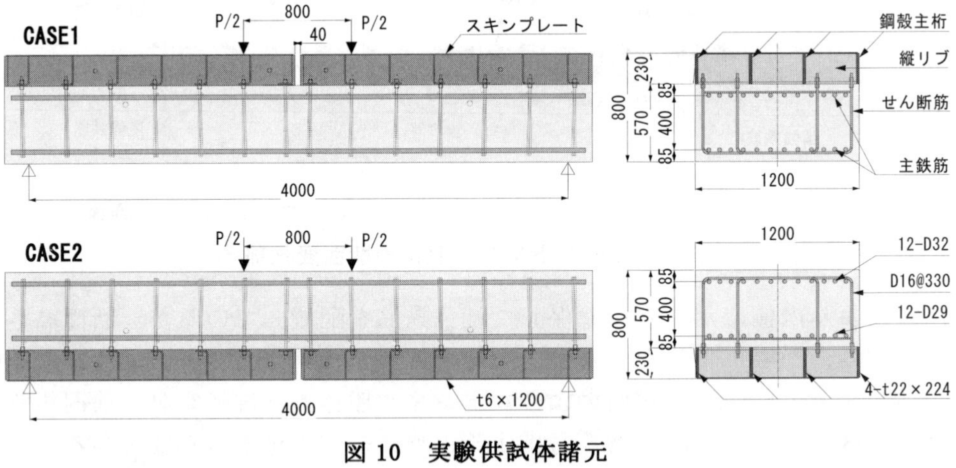

図 10 実験供試体諸元

供試体幅 1.2 m，供試体長 4.36 m，支間長 4.0 m，載荷点距離 800 mm の対称 2 点載荷としている．供試体の中央部には，鋼殻が不連続かつ掘削時 40 mm の函体離隔が発生しコンクリートが充填されない状態を模擬して，幅 40 mm×高さ 230 mm（＝主桁高さ）の隙間を設けた（図 10）．

せん断補強鉄筋は縦リブのピッチに併せて 1 断面 4 本の D16@330 とした．RC 構造では，主鉄筋に沿う付着割裂破壊の防止・緩和や，斜めひび割れ発生後のトラス機構を確保するために，一般的に，部材の軸方向を補強する主鉄筋を，横方向を補強するせん断補強鉄筋が取り囲むように配置する．ハーモニカ工法では，既存の鋼殻と新たに配置するせん断補強鉄筋を如何に連結するかは，鋼殻を本体利用するにあたってのもう 1 つの課題である．本研究では，著者らが過去に提案し首都高川崎縦幹線トンネル工事で実験によって検証を行った連結方法と同様に，せん断補強鉄筋にネジ節鉄筋を使用し，内空側には主鉄筋を取囲み，地山側にはナットにより縦リブに固定した（写真 4）．

写真 4 供試体製作状況

使用材料は，鉄筋はSD345，鋼材はSM490A，コンクリート設計基準強度は30 N/mm^{2}であった．また，材料試験結果の平均値を取って，鉄筋降伏強度は 379 N/mm^2，鋼材降伏強度は 340 N/mm^2，コンクリートシリンダ圧縮強度は 45 N/mm^2，コンクリートのヤング率は 25 kN/mm^{2}であった．

トンネル躯体の断面変化部（鋼殻隣接部）の位置によって，発生曲げモーメントは正曲げ（内空側引張）と負曲げ（地山側引張）があるため，両者の挙動が確認できるように，本実験では同一構造で正曲げ（CASE1）と負曲げ（CASE2）の 2 ケースを実施することとした（図10）．載荷は油圧ジャッキを使用して単調漸増載荷とした（写真 5）．

写真 5　載荷実験状況

4.2　実験結果および考察

各ケースのひび割れパターンを示す（図 11）．ひび割れ発生荷重はいずれも 290 kN 弱であり，計算値の 313 kN より若干低く，隙間による応力集中の影響が僅かにあったと思われる．また，CASE1 に比べ，CASE2 のほうは若干ひび割れの本数が多かったが，これは CASE1 の実験では，載荷装置の不具合で部材が降伏を過ぎた程度で載荷を中止し，供試体が破壊に至らなかったためである．

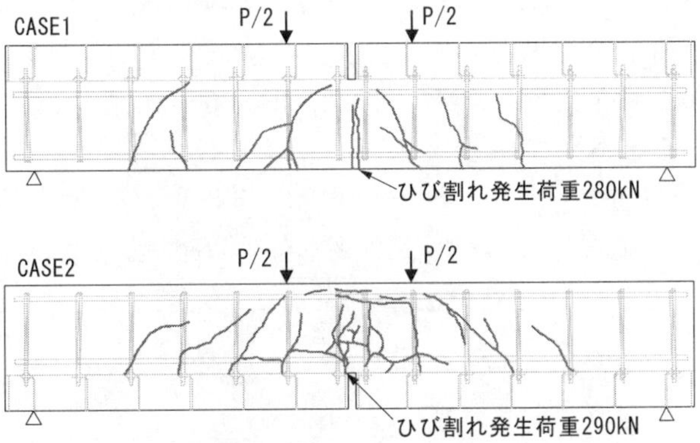

図 11　最終ひび割れ状況

載荷実験では，荷重，変位を含めて，材料のひずみなど種々計測したが，紙面の関係でここに荷重－変位関係のみについて示し考察する．まず，CASE1 と CASE2 の結果を比較するとともに，それぞれの設計許容荷重と設計終局荷重を同時に示した（図 12）．一見して，隙間による断面欠損が圧縮ゾーンにあっても（CASE1），引張ゾーンにあっても（CASE2），梁の曲げ剛性がほとんど変わらないが，断面変化部（RC 部）の引張鉄筋量で CASE2 が CASE1 の約 8 割程度しかないことから考えると，剛性については，鋼殻が引張側にあるほうが効果的であると言える．一方，曲げ降伏荷重に関しては，ほぼ断面変化部の引張鉄筋量と同じ比率で CASE2 が CASE1 の約 8 割程度となった．なお，それぞれの設計終局耐力に対して，実験結果のほうは約 4 割ほど大きく，鉄筋の実強度と特性値（345 N/mm^2）との差を考慮しても約 2 割弱大きかったため，耐力を支配する狭い構造変化部に対して，剛域に近い左右一般部の影響が何らかあったのではないかと推測される．

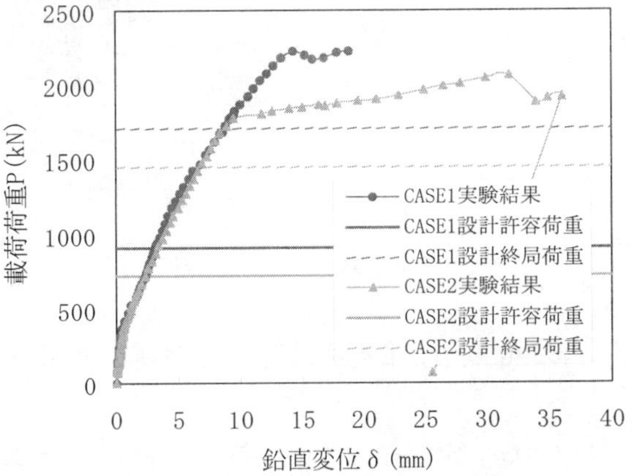

図 12　実験結果

上記実験結果を 2 種類のシミュレーション解析と比較した．解析手法の 1 つは，実験供試体に対する 2 次元非線形 FEM 解析，もう 1 つは断面変化部がなく桁高 h=800 mm または h=570 mm の剛性一様の梁に対して，Fiber モデルを適用した骨組み解析である（図 13）．ハーモニカ工法の場合は，躯体断面に比べ鋼殻主桁の桁高が相対的に低く，鉄骨による累加効果が小さいため，主桁を同図心の鉄筋に換算して取り扱った．また，いずれの解析モデルでも，鉄筋をバイリニア，コンクリートを 2 次放物線＋水平直線モデルを用い，材料強度と弾性係数は実験値を使用した．なお，コンクリートの引張強度を無視した．

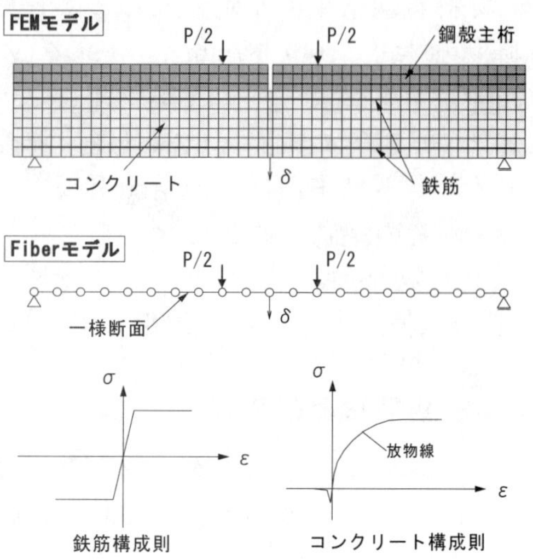

図 13　解析モデル

解析結果は実験ケースごとに示す（図 14）．まず，FEM モデルと h=570 mm 剛性一様の Fiber モデルではほぼ同様な結果が得られたが，CASE2 の降伏前の曲げ剛性に関しては僅かの違いが認められた．鋼殻が引張ゾーンにあったほうは剛性へ寄与する効果があるようである．次に，CASE1 と CASE2 の実験結果は，剛性，耐力ともに h=800 mm と h=570 mm 剛性一様梁の解析結果の間に来ているが，より h=570 mm の結果に近寄っており，梁の挙動は断面変化部に支配されていることが認められる．一方，実験結果と h=570 mm 剛性一様梁の解析結果との差は左右一般部の鋼殻本体利用の効果としても認められた．なお，圧縮応力が伝達される第 2 形態や鋼殻主桁同士も完全に接合される第 3 形態を実現すれば，h=800 mm 剛性一様梁の解析結果のように倍以上の剛性と耐力増加が期待できると考えている．

以上より，断面変化部は鉄筋により容易に補強できること，破壊荷重は鋼殻を無視した RC 断面による設計耐力以上を有していること，および鋼殻本体利用の効果はあったことが確認された．

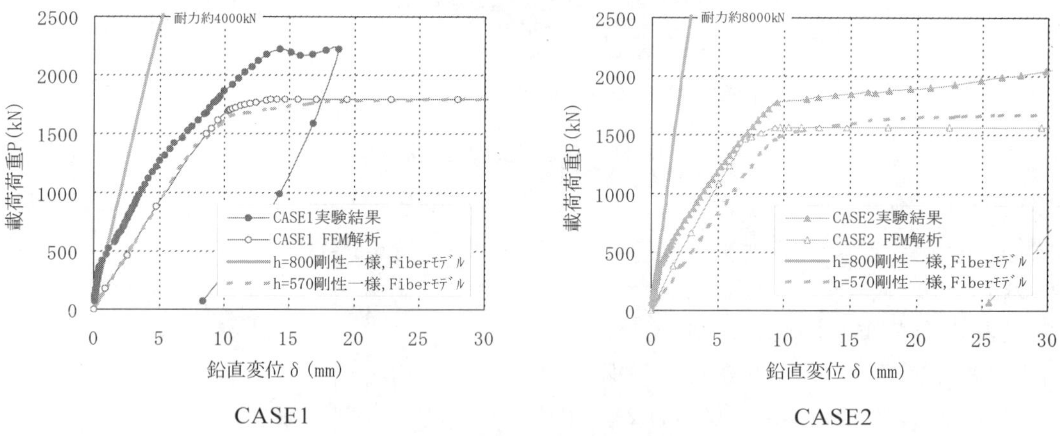

図 14　実験と解析の比較

5　断面変化部を考慮した本体構造の簡易設計方法

4 章の実験結果で分かるように，今回の試設計では，鋼殻が埋め込まれ大きな桁高を有する一般部 SRC 断面と，桁高が比較的小さく鉄筋のみで補強している断面変化部とでは，剛性のみならず曲げ耐力も 2 倍以上の差がある．使用性および断面破壊安全性の照査を行う場合には，このことを無視して，とにかく断面変化部を基準とした剛性一様の RC 断面に簡略して構造解析を行ってよいが，トンネルの耐震性能照査を行う場合には，断面変化の事実は無視できなくなる．すなわち，トンネル形状や施工分割などによって隅角部よりも断面変化部は先行して塑性ヒンジを形成する可能性があるため，過大見積りでも過小見積りでもなく，トンネル躯体各部の剛性や耐力を，非線形を考慮して忠実に評価しなければならない．一方，4 章に示したとおり，Fiber モデルや FEM モデルなど高度な解析手法を駆使すれば，これら構造変化の影響の評価は可能であるが，手法が煩雑のため設計実務には向いていない．

ここで，L2耐震検討において部材の曲げモーメントと曲率の関係（M-ϕ関係）が適用可能な骨組み解析手法を提案する．本解析手法では，ハーモニカ工法によるトンネル本体の一般部と断面変化部を，それぞれ梁要素と，梁端を結ぶ回転バネ要素で表す．梁要素には鋼殻を含むSRC断面のM-ϕ関係を与え，回転バネ要素には，要素実験またはFEM解析の結果との対比により同定されたM-θ関係を与える．ここに，梁バネモデルの構成（図15）と4章に記述した実験CASE1を例とした計算結果（図16）を示す．そして，ハーモニカ工法の耐震検討における簡易解析モデル（図17）は，応答変位法による地盤変位をトンネル構造物に与えた静的解析に用いるものであり，動的解析を行う場合には部材の履歴モデルが必要である．

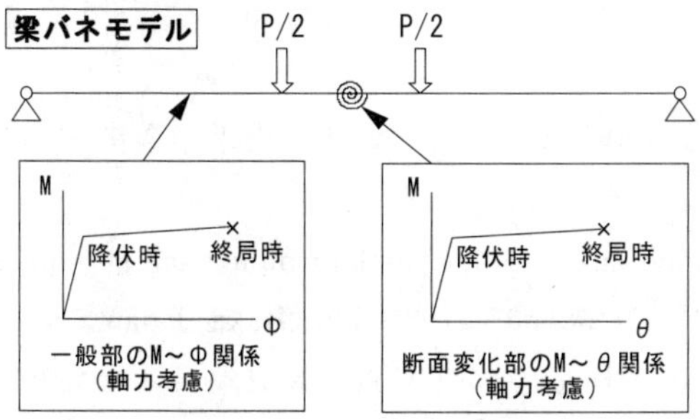

図15　梁バネモデル

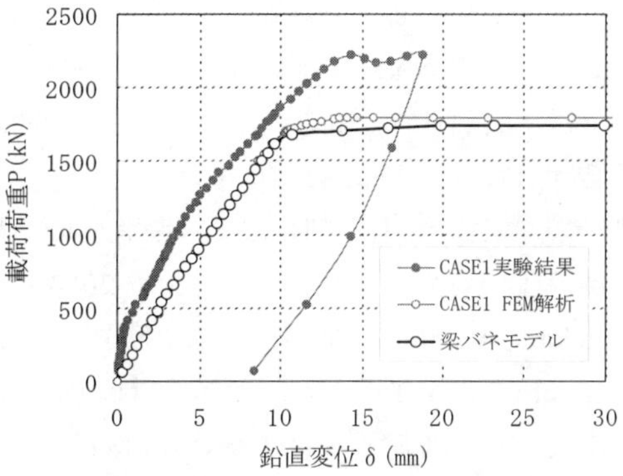

図16　梁バネモデルの解析例（CASE1）

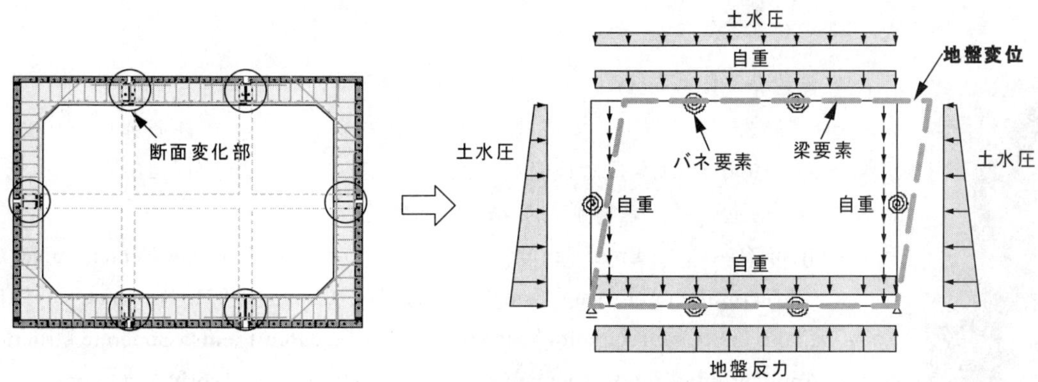

図17　ハーモニカ工法の耐震検討における簡易解析モデル

6　まとめ

本研究では，ハーモニカ工法におけるトンネル構造の特徴に着目し，設計合理化の道筋として鋼殻の本体利用に関する3つの形態（ステップ）を提案した．そして，第1形態（第1ステップ）について，試設計に基づく実物大構造実験を行い，断面変化部が本体構造に及ぼす影響，および鋼殻本体利用の効果を把握した．断面変化部は鉄筋で容易に補強できること，RC断面による設計は安全側であること，および仮設鋼殻が本体構造の耐力と剛性に寄与したことが確認された．また，断面変化部を回転バネにモデル化した簡易耐震解析手法を提案した．

ハーモニカ工法の優位性を高めるには，鋼殻の本体利用は重要な課題であり，またそれによる躯体桁高縮小の効果は非常に大きいと思われる．今後，第2形態，第3形態へと順次取り組んでいく予定である．第3形態のような鋼殻の完全有効利用を実現するには，主桁の接合方法が鍵の技術になるが，著者らが過去に考案した支圧方式接合は方法の1つとして考えられる（図18）[6]．

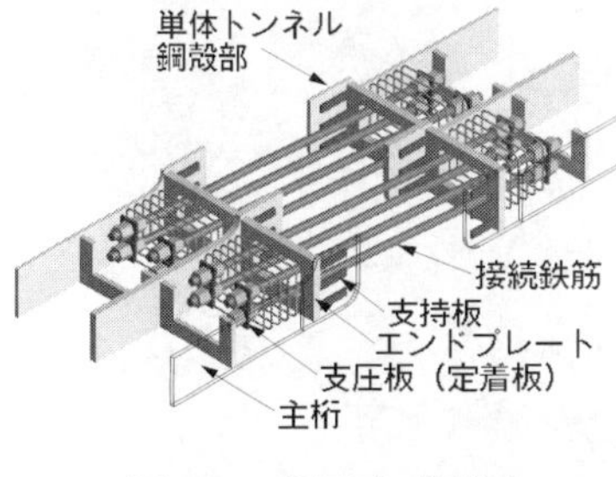

図18　支圧方式接合

ハーモニカ工法の適用実績は増え，それに伴い曲線施工や新しい止水方法などの施工技術もまた進化している．ハーモニカ工法の機動性を生かして，今後，大断面，大深度・高水圧の場合やトンネル分岐部への適用拡大に向けて，鋼殻の本体利用による構造・設計の合理化は更なる重要な技術として位置づけられよう．

参考文献（References）：

[1] 小林和雄, 佐藤大介: 非開削工法による幹線道路の立体交差計画, 建設コンサルタンツ協会『Civil Engineering Consultant』Vol.218，pp50-53，2003.1.

[2] 湯口正樹，潮田悦郎，金子研一，植田堅朗，大畑 裕：大断面分割シールド工法の開発，大成建設株式会社技術センター報 No.36，pp21-1~21-4，2003.

[3] 湯口正樹，服部佳文，真柴 浩：大断面分割シールドの開発(その２，土木学会第 59 回年次学術講演会講演概要集（VI），pp125-126，2004.9.

[4] 大畑 裕，植田堅朗，若林正憲，進藤芳典：大断面分割シールドの開発(その３，土木学会第 59 回年次学術講演会講演概要集（VI），pp127-128，2004.9.

[5] M.Tanaka, K.Mori, Y.Abe, W.Zhao, K.Kano, O.Mochizuki：Huge underground tunnel constructed by Multi-micro Shield Tunneling, fib2002 Osaka Congress, E-318, October 13 -19, 2002, Osaka, Japan.

[6] 三桶達夫，趙 唯堅，加納宏一：MMST 工法によるトンネル構造の部材実験，大成建設株式会社 技術センター報 No.36，pp18-1~18-5，2003.

著者紹介（Bio-data）：

趙 唯堅，工学博士；大成建設株式会社技術センター主任研究員；1982 年中国同済大学卒業；1996 年日本長岡技術科学大学博士課程修了；専門分野：コンクリート工学，耐震工学，構造工学，新材料新工法，複合構造.

Weijian ZHAO, Dr.Eng.; Senior Research Engineer, Technology Center, Taisei Corporation; B. Eng., Structural Engineering, Tongji University, China (1982); Dr. Eng., Civil Engineering, Nagaoka University of Technology, Japan (1996); Research Fields: Concrete structures, Seismic design, Application of innovative new material for structures, Hybrid Structures.

E-mail: zhao@sakura.taisei.co.jp

円形立坑開口部側壁厚の下限値の簡易設定について

陳 復興[1] 荒木 繁雄[2] 岡田 一郎[2] 斉藤 正幸[2] 小泉 淳[3]
[1]D&C 構造解析サービス株式会社，松戸 271-0092
[2]日本シビックコンサルタント株式会社，東京 116-0013
[3]早稲田大学 理工学術院 社会環境工学学科，東京 169-8555

立坑側壁の開口部においては，土圧・水圧の作用を受けて，開口部周辺に応力集中が生じる．また，軸力が卓越する一般部とくらべて，開口による面外変形も生じ，応力状態は複雑となる．本文は，鉛直方向応力と水平方向応力の比による開口部周辺の応力集中の変化に注目して，側壁壁厚の下限値の設定方法を提案する．経済設計を得るために壁厚を対象とするパラメータスタディを実施される場合，この下限値を参考にし，設計コストを軽減することを期待する．
キーワード: 最小壁厚，立坑，開口補強

A SIMPLIFIED METHOD TO DETERMINE THE MINIMUM THICKNESS OF OPENING REINFORCEMENT FOR A CIRCULAR VERTICAL SHAFT

Fuxing CHEN[1], Shigeo ARAKI[2], Ichiro OKADA[2], Masayuki SAITO[2], Atsushi KOIZUMI[3]
[1]Department. of Ground Structure, D&C Structural Analysis Services co., LTD, Matsudo 271-0092, Japan;
[2]Nippon Civic Consulting Engineers co. , Tokyo 116-0013, Japan;
[3]Department. of Civil and Environmental Engineering, Waseda University, Tokyo 169-8555, Japan

Abstract: Around the opening area of the shaft wall, the stress concentration will appear under the load of soil pressure and water pressure. Because of the opening, the bending moment become to be serious, and the stress state of the shaft will become to be more complex than ordinary section. In this paper, the attention is focused on the effect of vertical/horizontal stress ratio on the stress concentration. An approximate relationship between the minimum thickness of the shaft wall and the diameter was proved. It is hoped to reduce the design cost during parameter study of the thickness of the shaft wall to get an economical design.
Key words: minimum thickness; vertical shaft; opening reinforcement

1 はじめに

円形立坑の外壁は，土圧・水圧に対してリングコンプレッション効果で抵抗することが期待できることから，地盤条件が悪い場合や大深度掘削の場合において，矩形よりも構造上有利である．しかし，偏圧が作用する場合あるいは開口により構造上不連続となる場合，軸力のみならず，大きな曲げモーメントとせん断力が生じ，断面を算定する場合には十分な検討が必要となる．

本報告文では理論分析に基づき，円形立坑開口部側壁の「壁厚下限値」の存在を明らかにする．ここで言う「壁厚下限値」とは，「側壁はある厚さ以下の値を取ると，開口部の引張応力が大きくなり，設計計算上成立が難しくなる下限値」のことを指す．

本報告文の後半では，参考資料[1]にまとめた坊主山立坑の三次元解析の結果を踏まえて，円形立坑の三次元的な挙動を把握し，設計計算上の注意点を明らかにする．

2　シールド開口部側壁の「壁厚下限値」

2.1　立坑側壁の応力状態と平面応力問題の板の相似性

図1に示す開口無しの立坑を仮定する．半径方向より一様な荷重を受ける立坑は，任意深さの水平リングには軸力のみが生じ，曲げモーメントとせん断力は生じない．円周方向の応力 σ_H は壁厚方向に均一分布となる．鉛直方向応力 σ_V については，壁面と地盤の摩擦力を無視し，すべての壁重量が底版に作用することを仮定すれば，鉛直方向応力も簡単に計算できる．図-1に示すように立坑の初期応力状態は同図右側に示す同じ応力状態を有する平板と相似であると考えられる．

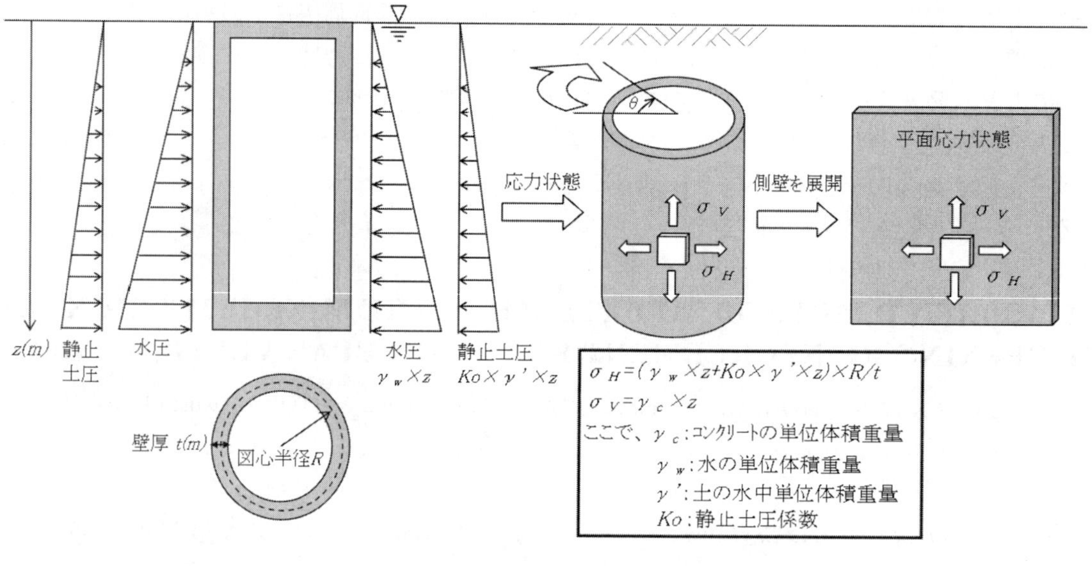

図-1　開口部無しの円形立坑と平面応力問題の板の相似性

逆に考えると，図-2に示すように，平面応力状態の平板に円孔を開けた後の応力状態は，円孔の径が小さければ，円筒に同じ径の円孔を開けた後の応力状態と相似である．

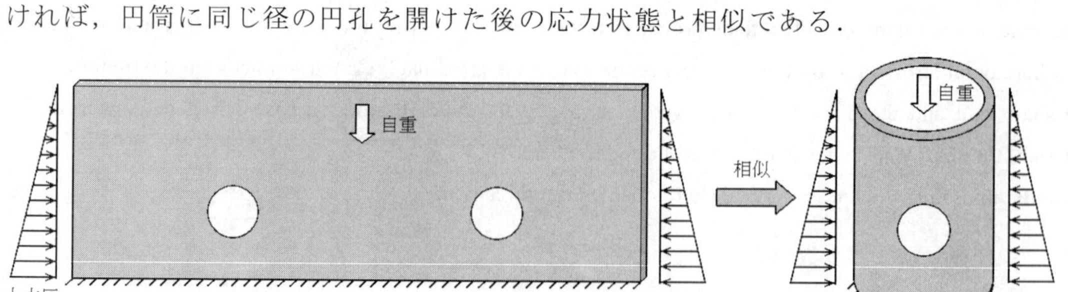

図-2　円孔を持つ板の挙動と開口部がある立坑の相似性

図-3～6に，水圧と自重を受ける平板と開口円筒のFEM解析モデルと応力状態の解析例を示す．図-5,6から分かるように，円孔周りの応力状態はよく似ている．また，表-1に示すように，最大値もほぼ一致している．以上より，平板モデルの応力挙動で立坑の開口部の応力挙動を定性的に説明できると判断できる．

表-1　最大応力比較

	最大応力 kN/m^2	比率
理　論　解	6490	-
平板モデル	6949	1.1
円筒モデル	7661	1.2

注:理論解=3× $\sigma_H - \sigma_V$=3×2330-500=6490

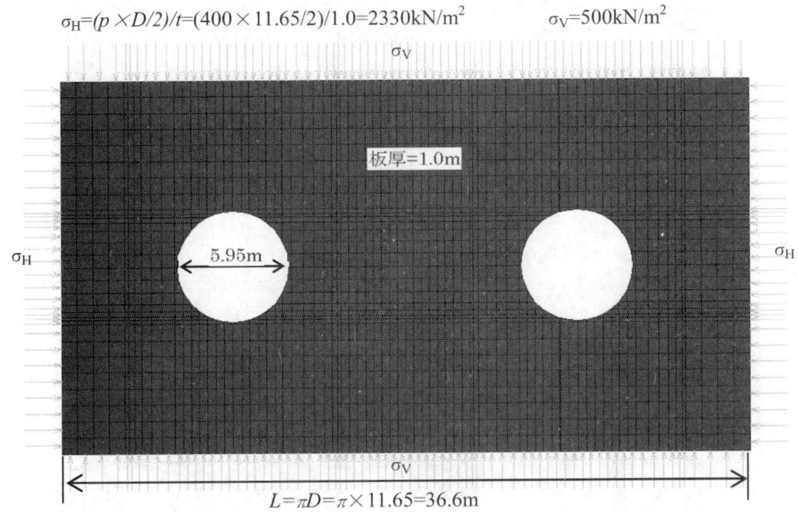

図-3　平板モデル（平面応力要素）

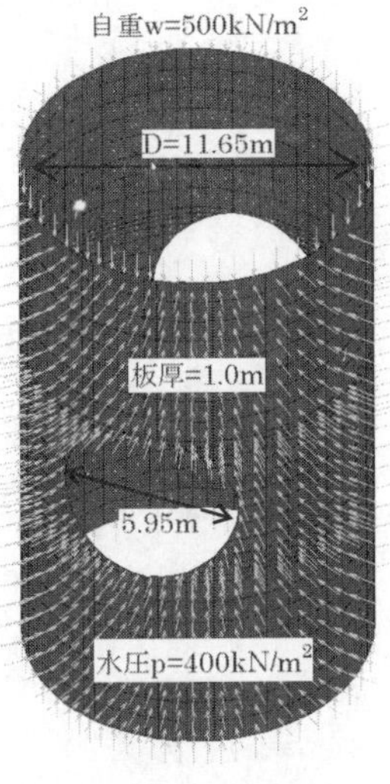

図-4　円筒モデル

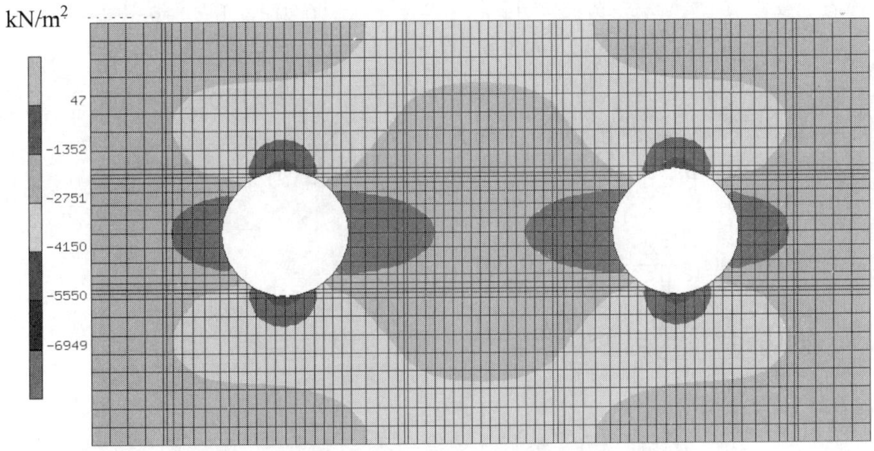

図-5　平板の水平方向応力（平面応力要素）

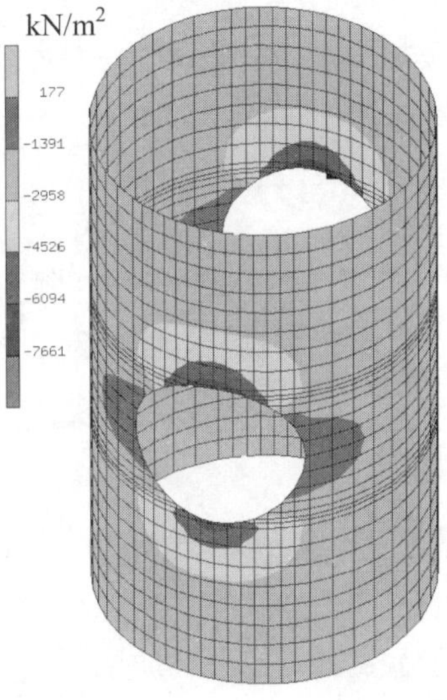

図-6　円筒の円周方向応力

2.2　無限板に円孔が掘削された場合の理論解

図-7 に示すように，等方等質の無限板に初期応力 σ_H, σ_V の作用のもとで半径 a の円孔が掘削された場合を考えると，円孔近傍の任意点（r, θ）における応力 σ_r, σ_θ, $\tau_{r\theta}$ は次式で与えられる．

式(1)は平面ひずみ問題の理論解であり，厳密的に言えば，図 2 に示す平面応力問題と違う．しかし，コンクリートの場合，式(2)，(3)が示すように両問題における σ～ε マトリックスの差が小さく，土木設計問題に関しては，許容範囲内であると判断できる．なお，本報告文の目的は，理論と実際が厳密に一致するといった設計手法を確立させることではなく，円形立坑の開口部挙動を定性的に把握することと設計時の注意点を明らかにすることである．したがって，式(1)の平面応力問題への適用は，支障がないと判断した．

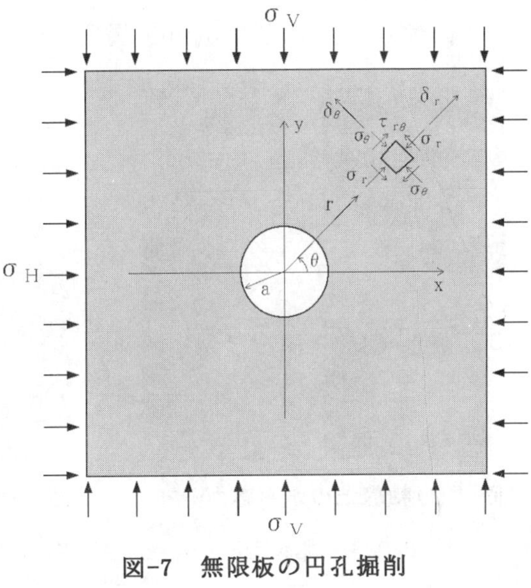

図-7　無限板の円孔掘削

$$
\left.
\begin{aligned}
\sigma_r &= \frac{\sigma_H+\sigma_V}{2}\left(1-\frac{a^2}{r^2}\right)+\frac{\sigma_H-\sigma_V}{2}\left(1-\frac{4a^2}{r^2}+\frac{3a^4}{r^4}\right)\cos(2\theta)\\
\sigma_\theta &= \frac{\sigma_H+\sigma_V}{2}\left(1+\frac{a^2}{r^2}\right)-\frac{\sigma_H-\sigma_V}{2}\left(1+\frac{3a^4}{r^4}\right)\cos(2\theta)\\
\tau_{r\theta} &= -\frac{\sigma_H-\sigma_V}{2}\left(1+\frac{2a^2}{r^2}-\frac{3a^4}{r^4}\right)\sin(2\theta)
\end{aligned}
\right\} \quad (1)
$$

注：圧縮応力は正
　　引張応力は負

・平面応力状態（コンクリート材料のポアソン比 ν=0.17）

$$
\begin{Bmatrix}\sigma_x\\ \sigma_y\\ \tau_{xy}\end{Bmatrix} = \frac{E}{1-\nu^2}\times\begin{bmatrix}1 & \nu & 0\\ \nu & 1 & 0\\ 0 & 0 & (1-\nu)/2\end{bmatrix}\begin{Bmatrix}\varepsilon_x\\ \varepsilon_y\\ \gamma_{xy}\end{Bmatrix} = \frac{E}{0.97}\times\begin{bmatrix}1 & 0.17 & 0\\ 0.17 & 1 & 0\\ 0 & 0 & 0.42\end{bmatrix}\begin{Bmatrix}\varepsilon_x\\ \varepsilon_y\\ \gamma_{xy}\end{Bmatrix} \quad (2)
$$

・平面ひずみ状態

$$
\begin{Bmatrix}\sigma_x\\ \sigma_y\\ \tau_{xy}\end{Bmatrix} = \frac{E(1-\nu)}{(1+\nu)(1-2\nu)}\times\begin{bmatrix}1 & \nu/(1-\nu) & 0\\ \nu/(1-\nu) & 1 & 0\\ 0 & 0 & (1-2\nu)/2(1-\nu)\end{bmatrix}\begin{Bmatrix}\varepsilon_x\\ \varepsilon_y\\ \gamma_{xy}\end{Bmatrix} = \frac{E}{0.93}\times\begin{bmatrix}1 & 0.20 & 0\\ 0.20 & 1 & 0\\ 0 & 0 & 0.40\end{bmatrix}\begin{Bmatrix}\varepsilon_x\\ \varepsilon_y\\ \gamma_{xy}\end{Bmatrix} \quad (3)
$$

以下，式(1)に示す無限板の掘削問題の理論解を用い，立坑の開口部の挙動を議論する．まず，鉛直圧係数 $\beta=\sigma_V/\sigma_H$ を導入し，$\sigma_V=\beta\cdot\sigma_H$ を式(1)に代入すると式(4)のようになる．

$$
\begin{aligned}
\sigma_r &= \frac{\sigma_H}{2}\left[(1+\beta)\left(1-\frac{a^2}{r^2}\right)+(1-\beta)\left(1-\frac{4a^2}{r^2}+\frac{3a^4}{r^4}\right)\cos(2\theta)\right]\\
\sigma_\theta &= \frac{\sigma_H}{2}\left[(1+\beta)\left(1+\frac{a^2}{r^2}\right)-(1-\beta)\left(1+\frac{3a^4}{r^4}\right)\cos(2\theta)\right]\\
\tau_{r\theta} &= -\frac{\sigma_H}{2}(1-\beta)\left(1+\frac{2a^2}{r^2}-\frac{3a^4}{r^4}\right)\sin(2\theta)
\end{aligned} \quad (4)
$$

式(4)より明らかなように，β の値，すなわち立坑鉛直方向応力と円周方向応力の比の大きさによって開口部の応力状態は大きく変化する．図-8～10 に鉛直圧係数 β が変化する場合の，円孔周辺応力状態の理論解を示す．

（1）β=0（鉛直応力 σ_V=0）場合の円孔周辺応力分布（注，青色＝圧縮応力，赤色＝引張応力）

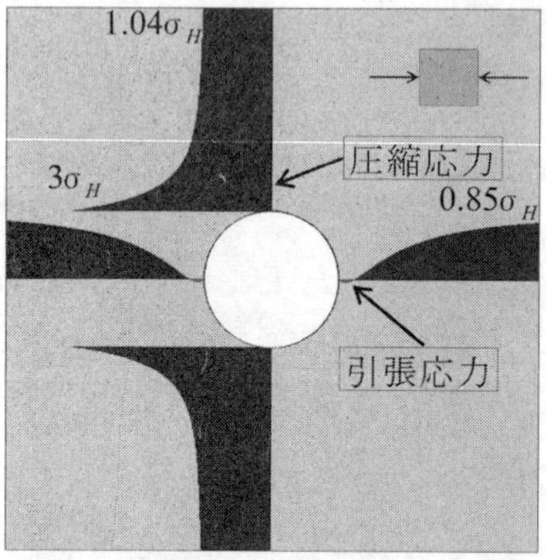

図-8(1)軸線上の水平応力分布

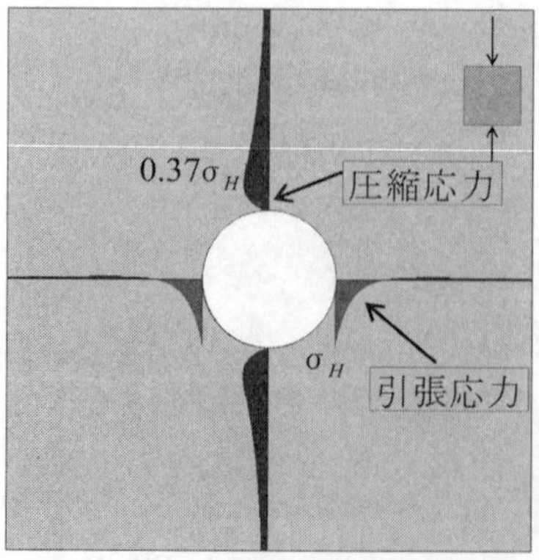

図-8(2)軸線上の鉛直応力分布

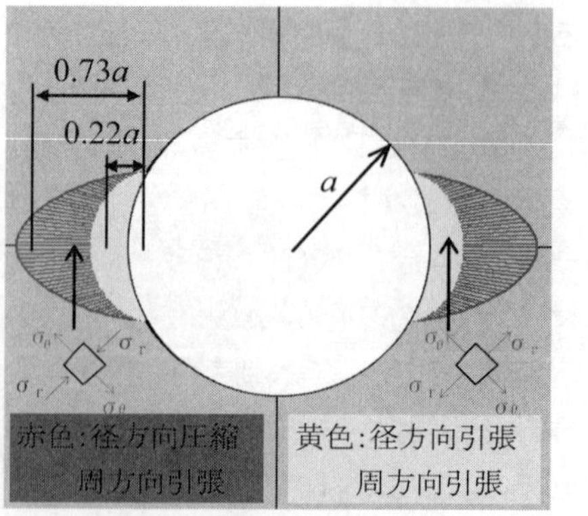

図-8(3)引張応力発生領域

（2）β=1/3（鉛直応力 $\sigma_V=\sigma_H/3$）場合の円孔周辺応力分布（注：引張応力が発生しない）

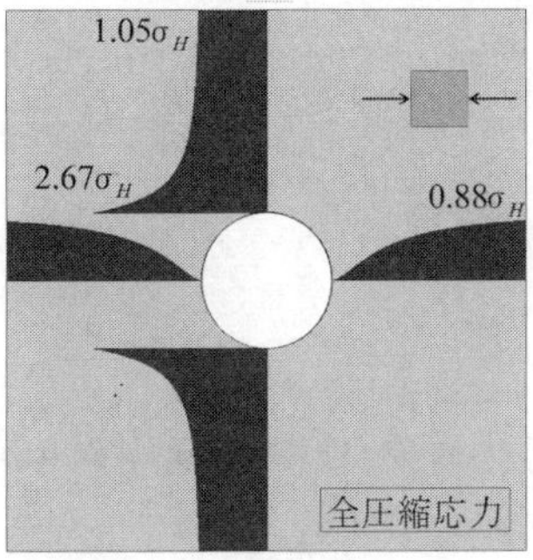

図-9(1)軸線上の水平応力分布

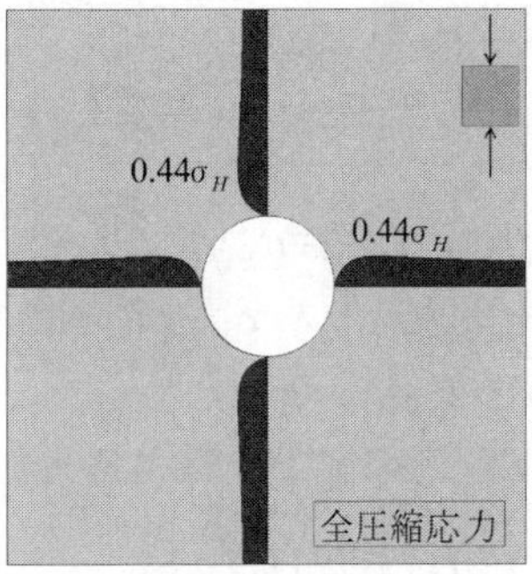

図-9(2)軸線上の鉛直応力分布

（3） β=1（鉛直応力 $\sigma_V=\sigma_H$）場合の円孔周辺応力分布（注：引張応力が発生しない）

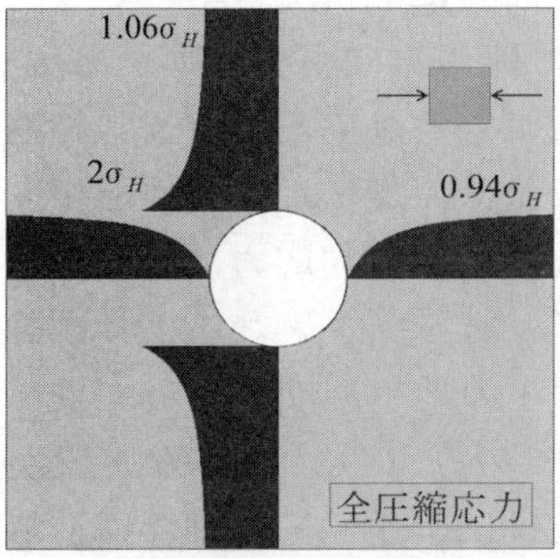

図-10(1)軸線上の水平応力分布

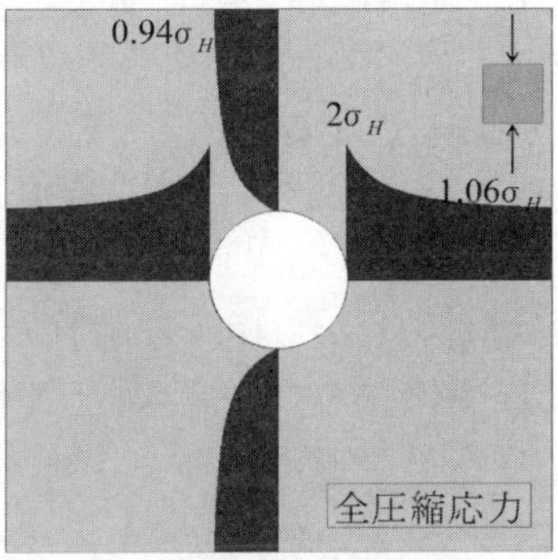

図-10(2)軸線上の鉛直応力分布

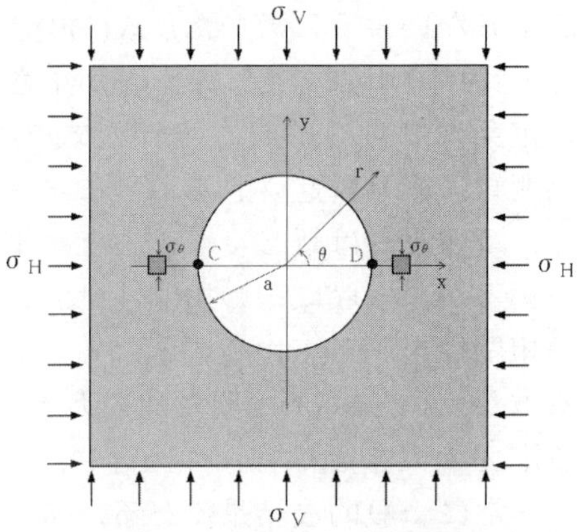

図-11 開口部ｽﾌﾟﾘﾝｸﾞﾗｲﾝ位置の鉛直力

図-8～10 より，β=0（鉛直方向応力 $\sigma_V=0$）の場合，スプリングライン位置付近では引張応力を生じ，β=1/3,1 になると，引張応力を生じないことが分かる．

2.3 シールド開口部側壁の「壁厚下限値」の決め方

鉛直圧係数 β が小さい場合, 図 11 に示す開口部スプリングライン位置の *C,D* 点の鉛直方向応力 σ_θ は引張応力となる．式(4)に θ=0°，a/r=1 を代入すると，式(5)のようになる．

$$\sigma_\theta = \sigma_H(3\beta - 1) \tag{5}$$

式(5)から明らかなように，スプリングライン位置の鉛直方向応力 σ_θ が引張応力を生じない条件は，

$$\sigma_\theta = \sigma_H(3\beta - 1) \geqq 0$$

であるため，式(6)である．

$$\beta \geqq 1/3 \tag{6}$$

すなわち，鉛直応力が水平応力の 1/3 倍以上の値となれば，円孔のスプリングライン位置に鉛直方向の引張応力が生じない．

図-1 に示す計算モデルを用い，σ_V，σ_H を算出するために，以下のように計算条件を設定する．

・開口部上下端から一定の範囲で σ_V，σ_H の変化を無視し，開口部中心の応力を用いる．
・水の単位体積重量：γ_w=10 kN/m^3
・ｺﾝｸﾘｰﾄの単位体積重量：γ_c=25 kN/m^3
・地盤の水中単位体積重量：γ'=20 kN/m^3 －10 kN/m^3=10 kN/m^3
・静止土圧係数：*Ko*=0.5
・偏土圧：考慮しない

・土圧：深度と比例

以上の条件を用い，σ_V，σ_H をそれぞれ以下のように算出する．

$\sigma_V=25\times z$

$\sigma_H=(10+0.5\times10)\times z\times(D/2+t/2)/t$

$\beta=\sigma_V/\sigma_H=1/3$ として σ_V と σ_H を消去すると，

$25\times z=\{15\times z\times(D/2+t/2)\}/3$

となり，t と D について整理すると，開口部に引張応力が生じない壁厚は式(7)となる．

$$t=D/9=0.11D \tag{7}$$

ここに，D は立坑内径．

式(7)は，円形立坑と平板の相似性を利用し，無限板の理論解に基づき，開口部の鉛直方向に引張応力が生じないように導いた．式(7)の本質は，同式で決めた壁厚以上の値を用いれば，開口により発生した応力集中（引張応力）の影響が小さくなり，通常範囲の鉄筋量で立坑断面力に抵抗できるという一つの安定条件である．逆に，壁厚が式(7)で決めた値より小さい場合，開口部に鉛直方向引張応力が発生し，また開口により誘起される曲げモーメントが大きくなるため，これに抵抗できる鉄筋設計は通常範囲を超え，断面設計は難しくなることが十分考えられる．厳密には，壁厚下限値は深度・地盤条件と相関関係があるが，一般にその相関性は弱いので，無視できると判断した．立坑の水平方向応力は地下水圧と強い相関性を示していることから，計算条件は図-1 から極端に離れた場合，$\sigma_V=\sigma_H/3$ となるように計算する方がよい．式(7)は開口部の大きさには無関係であり，実際，「弾性体中の地下掘削によって誘起される応力の大きさは空洞の大きさよりもむしろその形によってきまるのである．」[2]のような定説があり，非常に一般的な結果である．開口部の大きさの影響は，壁厚を決めた後に実施する詳細な構造解析の中で考慮される．表-2 に示す立坑設計の実績データに式(7)で計算した結果を併記し，図-12 に示す．

表-2　立坑実績データと下限値の比較

出典	立坑名	工法	内径 D(m)	下部側壁厚(m)	下限値 (0.11D)
首都圏外郭放水路インフォメーションHP	第1立坑	地中連壁	31.6	3.3	3.5
	第2立坑		31.6	3.3	3.5
	第3立坑		31.6	3.3	3.5
	第4立坑		25.1	3.3	2.8
	第5立坑	ケーソン	15.0	2.0m<	1.7
銭高組HP	未掲載	ケーソン	9.0	1.2	1.0
―	坊主山立坑	ケーソン	9.85	1.3（三次元FEM解析結果）	1.1

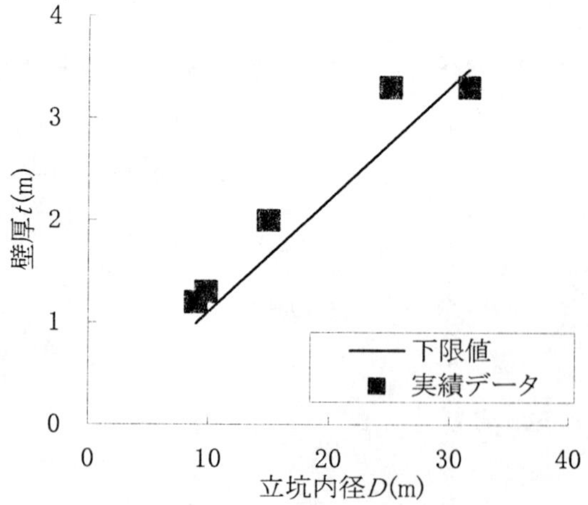

図-12　実績データと下限値の比較

以上より，壁厚の下限値の存在を明らかにした．これらが一つの目安として円形立坑の設計業務に役立つことが期待される．

3　三次元 FEM 解析により検証

3.1　検討条件

図 13 に示す坊主山立坑を検討対象とする．以下，本立坑の概要と開口部側壁の設計結果を示す．

【施工方法】: 圧入オープンケーソン工法

【構造条件】: 仕上がり内径 φ9.850m

コンクリート fck=24N/mm^2

鉄 筋 規 格 *SD345*

【開口部壁厚】: 1.8m

【荷重条件】: 静止土圧

静水圧

偏荷重は静止土圧の20%

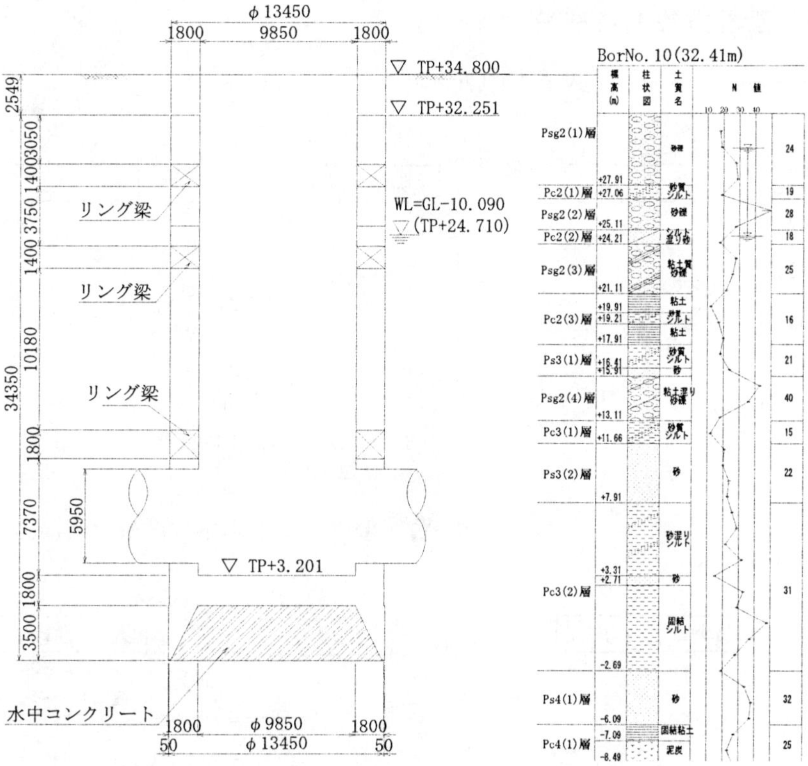

図-13 坊主山立坑断面図

3.2 三次元 FEM 解析モデル

三次元 FEM 解析は，立坑全体をシェル要素でモデル化し，立坑の三次元形状効果が自動的に考慮できる．図-14 に坊主山立坑の三次元シェルモデルを示し，壁厚パラメータを表-3 に示す．また，作用させる荷重は，図-15～16 に示す完成時荷重を用いる．

表-3 壁厚パラメータ

No.	壁厚 t_1(m)	底版厚 t_2(m)	図心径 Dc(m)	鉛直圧係数 $\beta=\sigma_V/\sigma_H$
1	0.60	0.60	11.65	0.19
2	0.80	0.80	11.65	0.25
3	1.00	1.00	11.65	0.32
4	1.20	1.20	11.65	0.38
5	1.40	1.40	11.65	0.44
6	1.60	1.60	11.65	0.51
7	1.80	1.80	11.65	0.57

注: σ_V、σ_Hは開口部中心位置で評価する

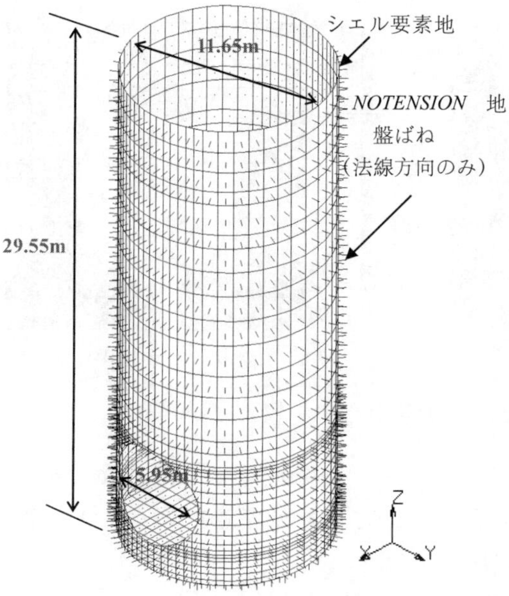

図-14 FEM 解析モデル図

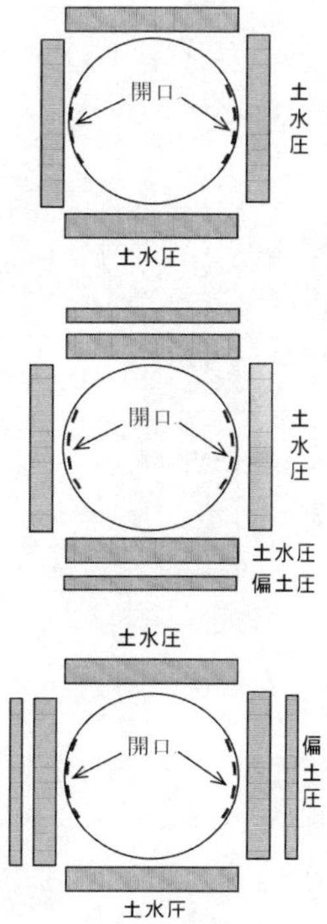

図-15 作用荷重パターン

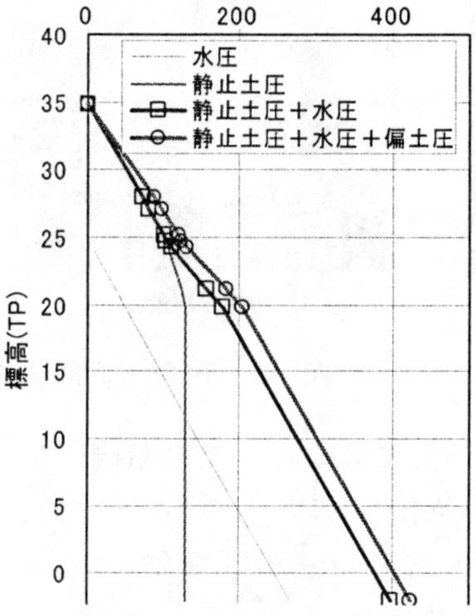

図-16 深度方向荷重分布

3.3 設計方法開口部最大断面力

開口部の水平方向最大断面力，鉛直方向最大断面力を図-17，図-18 に示す．

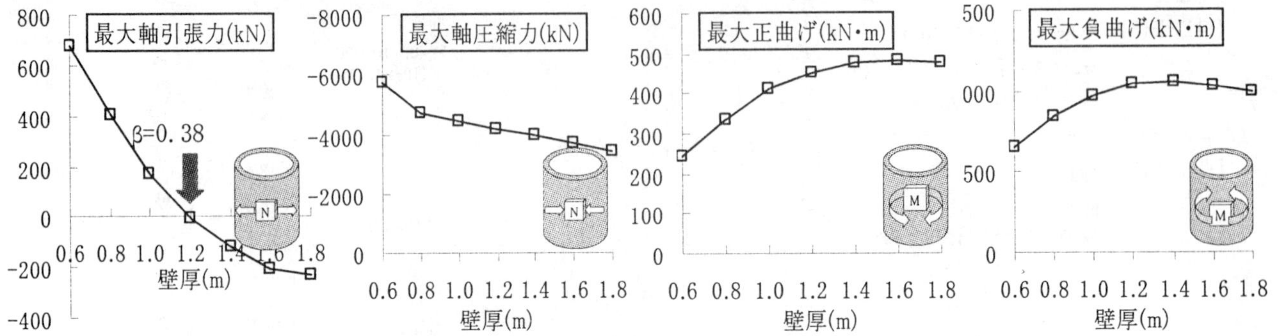

図-17 壁厚による水平方向最大断面力の変化

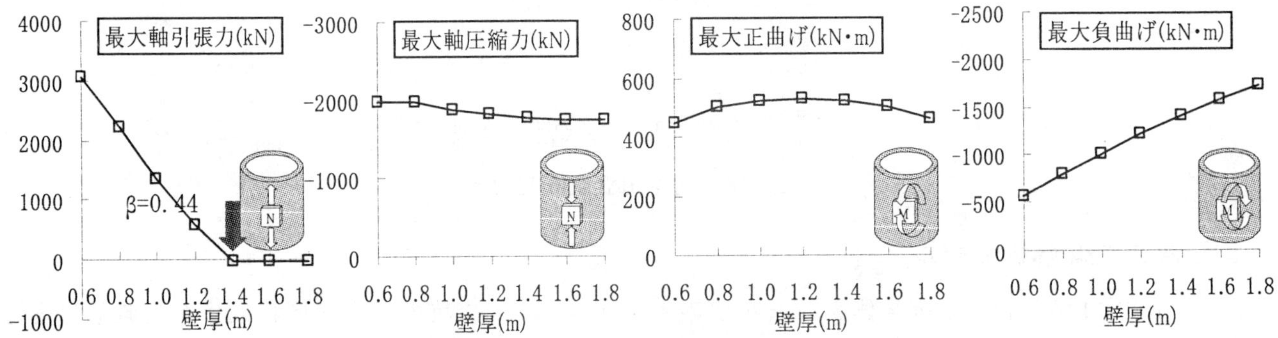

図-18 壁厚による鉛直方向最大断面力の変化

3.4 開口部の応力集中

図-19 に示す開口部の円周方向応力の色コンター図から分かるように，開口部の上下端に応力集中が生じている．側壁が厚くなれば最大応力は減り，また分布範囲も広がることから，設計上有利となる．

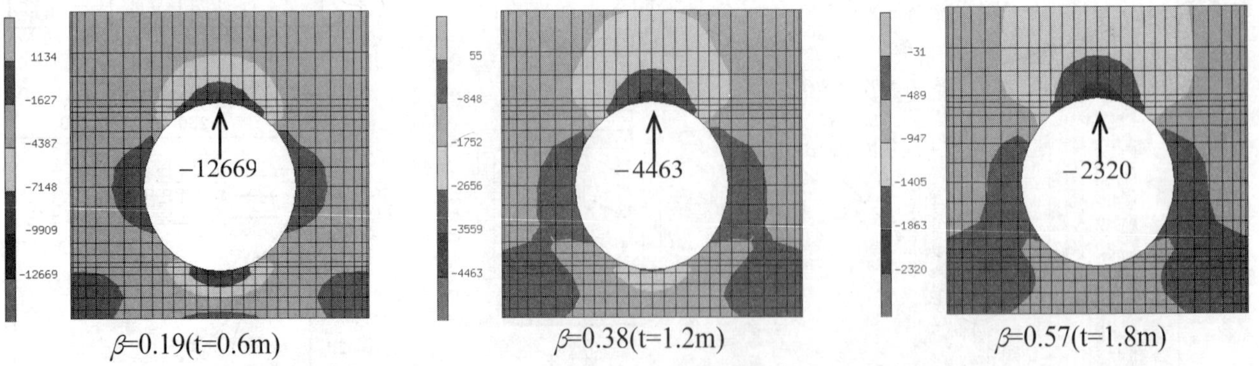

図-19 円周方向応力の色コンター図（荷重パターン 2，側壁の中心層，単位：kN/m^2）

図-20 に開口部の鉛直方向応力の色コンター図を示す．同図から分かるように，開口部のｽﾌﾟﾘﾝｸﾞﾗｲﾝ位置で応力集中が生じており，側壁が薄い場合，大きい鉛直方向引張応力が生じていることが確認できる．側壁が厚くなれば応力集中は緩和され，引張応力も小さくなる．

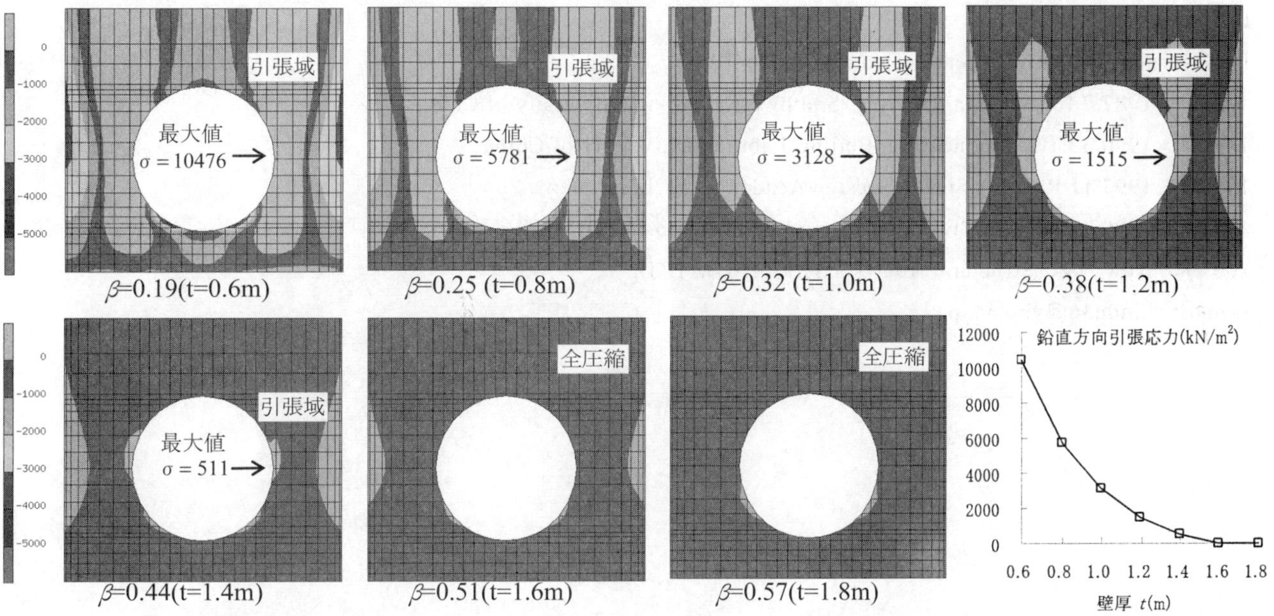

図-20　鉛直方向応力の色コンター図と変化図（荷重パターン２，側壁の中心層，単位：kN/m²）

4　まとめ

・　円形立坑開口部側壁厚の下限値の存在を明らかにした．すなわち，鉛直圧比 β＝1/3 を超えるように壁厚を設計する．これは円形立坑実務設計の参考となる．

・　立坑の自重は開口部の応力状態に大きく影響することが説明できた．荷重として取り扱われてきた立坑自重はシールド開口部に有利に働くことを証明した．

・　ケーソン工法立坑の場合，鉛直荷重は原則として基礎底面地盤の反力のみで抵抗させるものとするが，周辺地盤が良質な場合，地盤鉛直方向せん断抵抗を考慮してもよい[3]．開口部設計においては，周面地盤せん断抵抗を考慮すると，躯体鉛直方向軸力が減り，開口部の応力状態が厳しくなるため，安全側の設計となる．このため，FEM 解析時には，周面地盤鉛直せん断抵抗を考慮する必要がある．

参考文献（References）:

[1]　陳復興：3 次元 FEM 解析手法を用いる円形立坑開口部の最適化設計，23 回 *NCC* 社内論文，2005.11

[2]　E.ｲｻﾞｸｿﾝ著・高橋彦治・小林芳正共訳：ﾄﾝﾈﾙ技術者のための岩盤力学入門，pp.25，鹿島出版会

[3]　道路橋示方書・同解説　Ⅳ下部構造編，pp.298，H14.3（社）日本道路協会

著者紹介（Bio-data）:

陳復興

D&C 構造解析サービス株式会社　　社長

1983.9～1987.7 中国西南交通大学　鉄道工学部

1987.7～1990.3 中国北京交通大学　土木工学部

1990.4～1993.11 中国鉄道部専門設計院

1993.12～2007.7 日本シビックコンサルタント株式会社

2007.8～現在 D&C 構造解析サービス株式会社

Fuxing CHEN

D&C Structural Analysis Services co., LTD President

1983.9～1987.7 Railway Engineering, Southwest Jiaotong University of China.

1987.7～1990.3 Civil Engineering, Beijing Jiaotong University of China .

1990.4～1993.11 Railway Special Design Academy of China.

1993.12～2007.7 Nippon Civic Consulting Engineers co., LTD.

2007.8～Now D&C Structural Analysis Services co., LTD.

E-mail: chindu36@ybb.ne.jp

コンクリート中詰め合成セグメントの地下鉄トンネルへの適用検討

入田　健一郎 [1]　西井　成実 [1]　沼澤　憲二郎 [2]　藤木　育雄 [3]

[1] 清水建設株式会社 土木事業本部，東京　105-8007

[2] 京王電鉄株式会社 鉄道事業本部，東京　182-0026

[3] メトロ開発株式会社 技術部，東京　103-0001

京王電鉄（株）は，京王線調布駅付近の交通渋滞緩和のため，調布駅部および京王本線，相模原線の当該駅付近の地下化を行っている．清水建設 JV は，一連の中で京王本線に 2 本，相模原線に 2 本，計 4 本の地下鉄シールドトンネルを構築中である．4 本のシールドトンネルは，主に RC セグメントの一次覆工で構成され，トンネル同士の離間は 0.4 m～1.0 m程度で併設しており，さらにトンネルは営業線直下を低土被りで構築される．
相模原線の平面線形は，地下鉄シールドトンネルとしては急曲線の曲線半径 R=160 m 程度の線形で，上下線の離間が小さい．当初，この急曲線の上下線の区間にもＲＣセグメントを配置することになっていたが，先行トンネルである上り線の構築後，後行トンネル（下り線）の掘進および施工が，先行トンネルに影響を与えることが懸念された．この影響を考慮し，相模原線の先行トンネル急曲線部のセグメントには，RC セグメントに比較して損傷の可能性が低いコンクリート中詰め合成セグメントが採用されている．
本報告では，この合成セグメントの採用にあたり，その特長，構造検討や各試験について概要を述べるものである．

キーワード：シールドトンネル；合成セグメント；構造設計；単体曲げ試験；継手曲げ試験

STUDY ON APPLICATION OF PRE-CASTING CONCRETE COMPOSITE SEGMENTS IN SUBWAY TUNNEL

Kenichiro IRITA[1], Narumi NISHII[1], Kenjiro NUMASAWA[2], Ikuo FUJIKI[3]

[1]Div. of Civil Engineering, Shimizu Corporation, Tokyo 105-8007;

[2] Railway Management Headquarters, KEIO Corporation, Tokyo 182-0026;

[3]Div. of Civil Engineering, Metro-Development Corporation, Tokyo 103-0001

Abstract: Keio Corporation is conducting to move Chofu Station, a part of Keio Main Line, and one of Sagamihara Line near this station to underground to reduce traffic jam around Keio Chofu Station. Shimizu Corporation JV is building four subway shield tunnels in total, two of Keio Main Line and two of Sagamihara Line. Four shield tunnels consist of a primary lining of the RC (reinforced concrete) segmental lining, and adjacent tunnel's clearance is only 0.4m～1.0m, and each tunnel will be constructed under the operating railway lines with shallow overburden.
The horizontal alignment of Sagamihara Line is composed of a sharp curve with radius of about 160m, shield tunnels of the up and down track are very close to each other. It was studied that RC segments were applied into the section of both track of this sharp curve at first, but after the construction of the up track which was a preceding tunnel, it was concerned that the execution of the succeeding tunnel (the down track) had various influences on preceding tunnel. In consideration of this influences, the pre-casting concrete composite segments were employed as the segments in sharp curve portion of the preceding tunnel of Sagamihara Line, in order to resolve the possibility of the damage by the influences in comparison with the RC segments.
This report describes a summary about the feature, structure examination and various test of this composite segment for the adoption in sharp curve portion.

Key word: shield tunnel; composite segment; structural design; segment bending test; joint bending test

1　はじめに

京王電鉄（株）は，京王線調布駅付近の交通渋滞緩和のため，調布駅部および京王本線，相模原線の当該駅付近の地下化を行っている．清水建設 JV は，一連の中で京王本線に２本，相模原線に２本，計４本の地下鉄シールドトンネルを構築中である．４本のシールドトンネルは，主にコンクリート系セグメント(以下, RC セグメントと呼ぶ.)の一次覆工で構成され，トンネル同士の離間は 0.4 m～1.0 m 程度で併設しており，さらにトンネルは営業線直下を低土被りで構築される．

相模原線の平面線形は，地下鉄シールドトンネルとしては急曲線の曲線半径 R=160 m 程度の線形で，上下線の離間が小さい．当初，この急曲線の上下線の区間にも RC セグメントを配置することになっていたが，先行トンネルである上り線の構築後，後行トンネル（下り線）の掘進および施工が，先行トンネルに影響を与えることが懸念された．この影響を考慮し，相模原線の先行トンネル急曲線部のセグメントには，RC セグメントに比較して損傷の可能性が低いコンクリート中詰め合成セグメントが採用されている．本論文では，コンクリート中詰め合成セグメントの地下鉄シールドトンネルへの適用にあたり，その設計，性能確認試験の概要を報告する．

2　工事概要

2.1　工事概要

京王線調布駅付近立体交差工事は，京王線の柴崎駅～西調布駅間約 2.8 km の区間と相模原線の調布駅～京王多摩川駅間約 0.9 km の区間を地下化することにより，18 箇所の踏切道を解消するとともに，８箇所の都市計画道路を立体化するものである．

コンクリート中詰め合成セグメントを適用する第４工区（清水 JV）では、調布駅から京王線と相模原線に分かれる V 字区間の地下化をシールド工法によって行う．工事区間は調布駅西側から鶴川街道までの 379 m の京王線，および調布駅西側から品川通りまでの 424 m の相模原線の区間である．この工事では，１台のシールド機を使用して京王線と相模原線の上下４本，総延長 1,606 m のシールドトンネルを構築する．このうちコンクリート中詰め合成セグメントは，相模原線の先行トンネル（上り線）の急曲線部（曲線半径 165 m）に配置する（図１参照）．

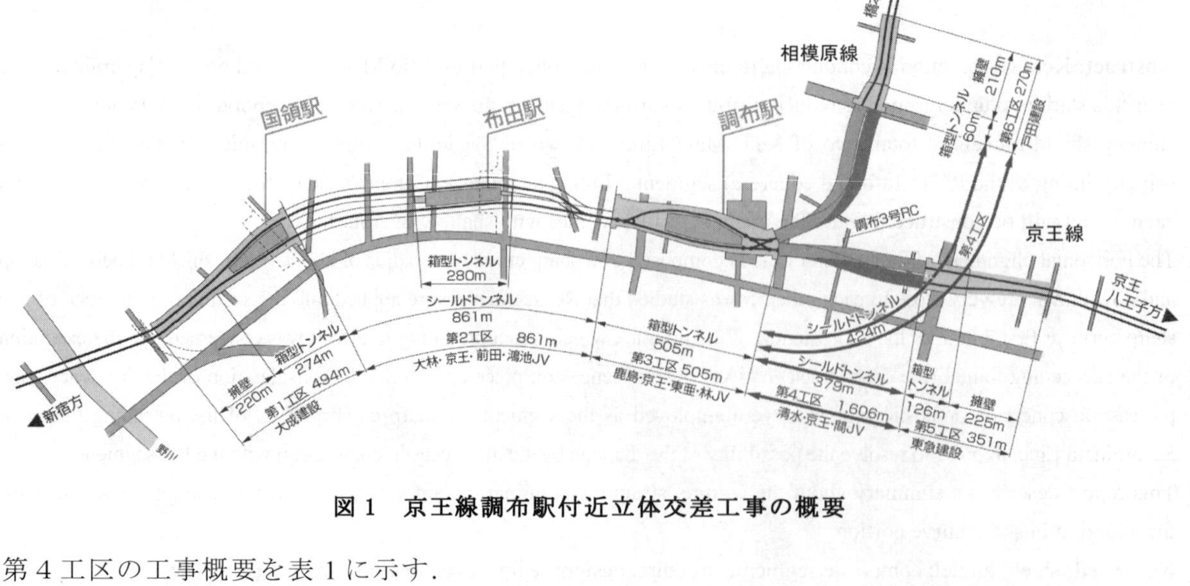

図１　京王線調布駅付近立体交差工事の概要

第４工区の工事概要を表１に示す．

表１　工事概要

工事件名	調布駅付近連続立体交差工事（土木）第４工区その３
発注者	京王電鉄株式会社
工事場所	東京都調布市小島町１丁目～小島町２丁目間
工期	2008 年 9 月 30 日～2012 年 6 月 30 日
工事内容	シールド工法（泥土圧シールド工法） 単線シールド総延長 1,606 m のうち，京王線 379 m×2 線（上下線），相模原線 424 m×2 線（上下線）
シールド機	泥土圧シールド，シールド機外径ϕ6,850 mm を１台使用， 立坑にてＵターンを３回実施
トンネル構造	セグメント外径ϕ6,700 mm，覆工厚 300 mm コンクリート系セグメント（RC 平板形，幅 1.4 m，急曲線部 1.2 m），コンクリート中詰め合成セグメント（幅 1.2 m）
線形	最大勾配 3.5%，最小平面曲線半径 160 m，最小土被り 4.3 m
土質	立川礫層，上総層群砂質土，砂固結シルト互層

2.2　施工手順

シールド機は、鶴川立坑より発進し，京王線上り線を掘進（1 本目）後、調布西立坑地下 3 階に到達する．ここでシールド機を回転して相模原線上り線を掘進（2 本目）する．品川立坑に到達後回転して，相模原線下り線を掘進（3 本目）し，調布西立坑地下 2 階に再度到達する．ここでシールド機は最後の回転を行い，京王線下り線を掘進（4 本目）して鶴川立坑に到達する（図２参照）.

掘進の特徴としては，営業線の直下を低土被り（最小土被り 4.3 m=0.64D）での掘進，最大礫径 ϕ300 mm 程度が想定される立川礫層の存在，上下線の最小離隔が 424 mm と超近接の併設トンネルの構築が挙げられる．さらに、相模原線では最小曲線半径 160 m の急曲線を掘進する．以上より難易度の高い施工が要求されている工事である．

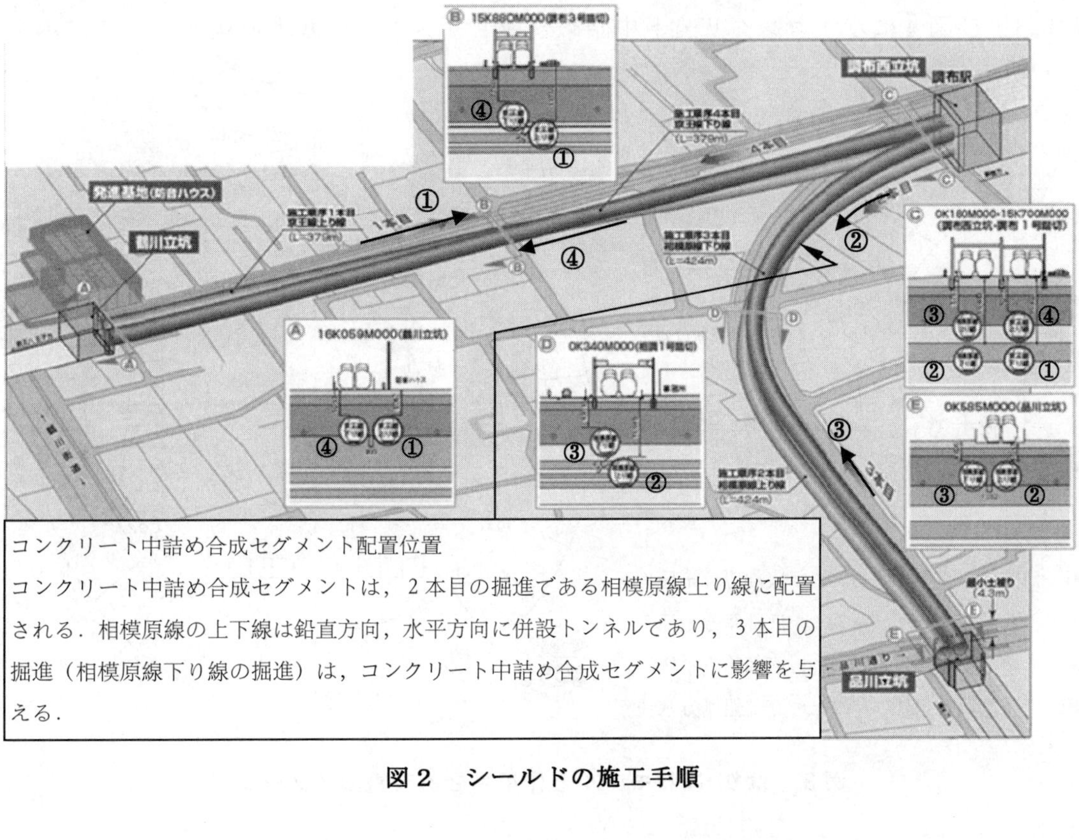

図２　シールドの施工手順

3　コンクリート中詰め合成セグメントの設計

当初，相模原線の急曲線部の上り線，下り線には，両方ともコンクリート系セグメント（以下，RC セグメントと呼ぶ.）の配置が計画されていた．RC セグメントの設計では以下の検討が行われた．

① 自重，土圧，水圧に対する横断方向の検討（常時の検討）

② 下り線（後行）のトンネルの構築が上り線（先行）のトンネルに与える影響の検討（併設トンネルの検討）

③ 急曲線掘進時のシールドの推力や片押しによるトンネル縦断方向の検討（急曲線検討）

④ 下り線（後行）の急曲線掘進が，構築された上り線（先行）トンネルに与える影響検討（急曲線施工時の併設トンネルの影響）

これらの検討より耐荷性能を確認している RC セグメントではあるが，1m を下回る上下線の離間および急曲線部の土質が礫層であること，鉄道の平面曲線として曲線半径 160m は最小曲線であることより，下り線（後行トンネル）施工が，上り線（先行トンネル）に与える影響は重大であることを考慮し，さらに，仮に RC セグメントを配置して，これが損傷した場合，維持・補修等によりトンネルのライフサイクルコストが増大することを回避するため，急曲線部の上り線への RC セグメントの配置は見送られた．割れ，欠けなどの損傷，これに起因するトンネル内部への漏水の懸念がある RC セグメントに対し，これらの不具合を避けることができると考えられるコンクリート中詰め合成セグメントの適用を検討した．

3.1　自重，土圧，水圧に対する横断方向の検討

コンクリート中詰め合成セグメントの自重，土圧，水圧に対する横断方向の検討は，RC セグメントの設計を踏襲して実施した．設計条件のうち，荷重の算定に用いる土質条件等，地下水位は RC セグメントの設計と同様である．

構造解析モデルには，はり-ばねモデルを用いた．はり-ばねモデル（図３参照）による構造計算には，表３および図４に示すコンクリート中詰め合成セグメントの基本形状と，表４に示すパラメータを入力した．

記号説明

Pe1 ：頂部鉛直土圧，Pe2 ：底部鉛直土圧

qe1 ：頂部側方土圧，qe2 ：底部側方土圧

Pw1 ：頂部鉛直水圧，Pw2 ：底部鉛直水圧

qw1 ：頂部側方水圧，qw2 ：底部鉛側方水圧

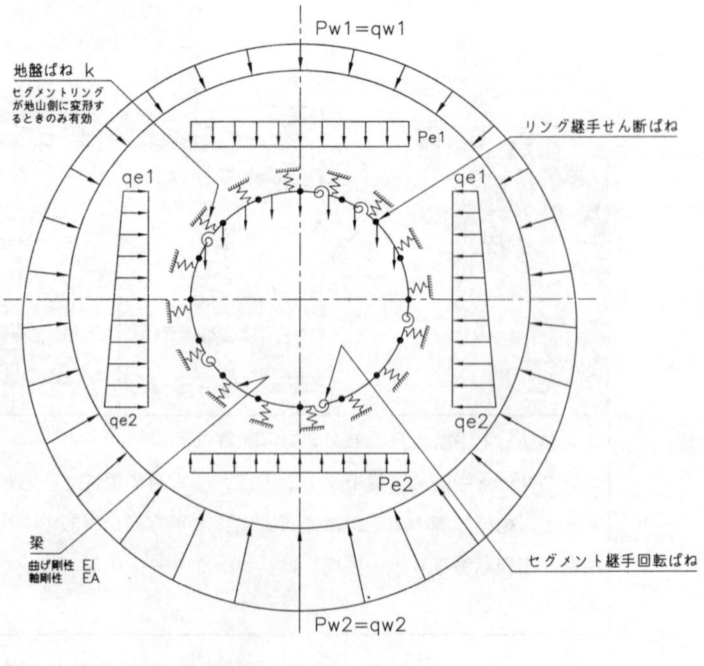

図３　はり-ばねモデルと作用させる荷重のイメージ

表 3　コンクリート中詰め合成セグメントの形状寸法

項目	記号	単位	値など
セグメント外径	Do	(mm)	6 700
セグメント内径	Di	(mm)	6 100
覆工厚	h	(mm)	300
セグメントの分割数	n	-	6 分割
セグメント継手の形式	-	-	ボルト締結式（ボルトおよび埋込みナット）
リング継手の形式	-	-	ボルト締結式（ボルトおよび埋込みナット）

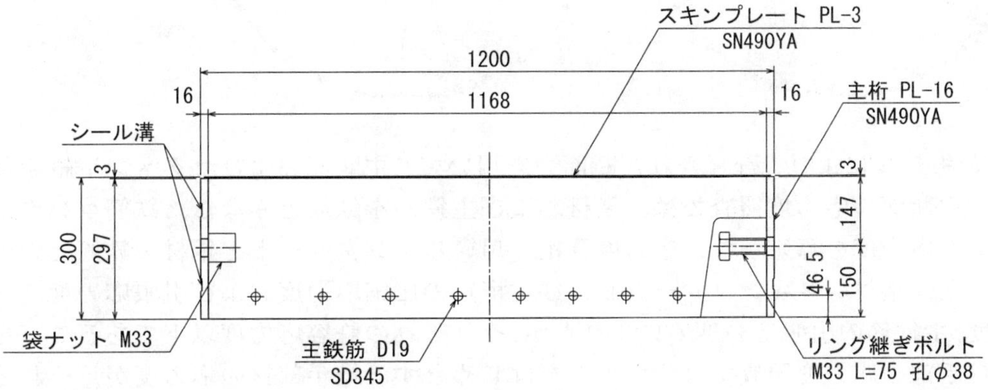

図 4　主断面の形状寸法

表 4　はりーばねモデル入力パラメータ

項目			記号	単位	値
図心径			Dc	(mm)	6 400
コンクリートの設計基準強度			f'ck	(N/mm^2)	42
コンクリートのヤング係数			Ec	(kN/m^2)	3.6×10^7
鋼材のヤング係数			Es	(kN/m^2)	3.6×10^8
主断面の断面積			A	(m^2)	4.049×10^{-1}
主断面の断面係数			I	(m^4)	3.016×10^{-3}
セグメント継手回転ばね	正曲げ	第一勾配	Km1	(kN·m/rad)	∞
		第二勾配	Km2	(kN·m/rad)	3.04×10^4
		第一勾配から第二勾配に移行するときのモーメント	Mx	(kN·m)	42.517
	負曲げ	第一勾配	Km1	(kN·m/rad)	∞
		第二勾配	Km2	(kN·m/rad)	3.22×10^4
		第一勾配から第二勾配に移行するときのモーメント			42.061
リング継手せん断ばね	法線方向せん断ばね		Ksn	(kN/m)	1.076×10^6
	接線方向せん断ばね		Kst	(kN/m)	7.362×10^6
地盤反力係数			k	(kN/m^3)	1.4×10^4

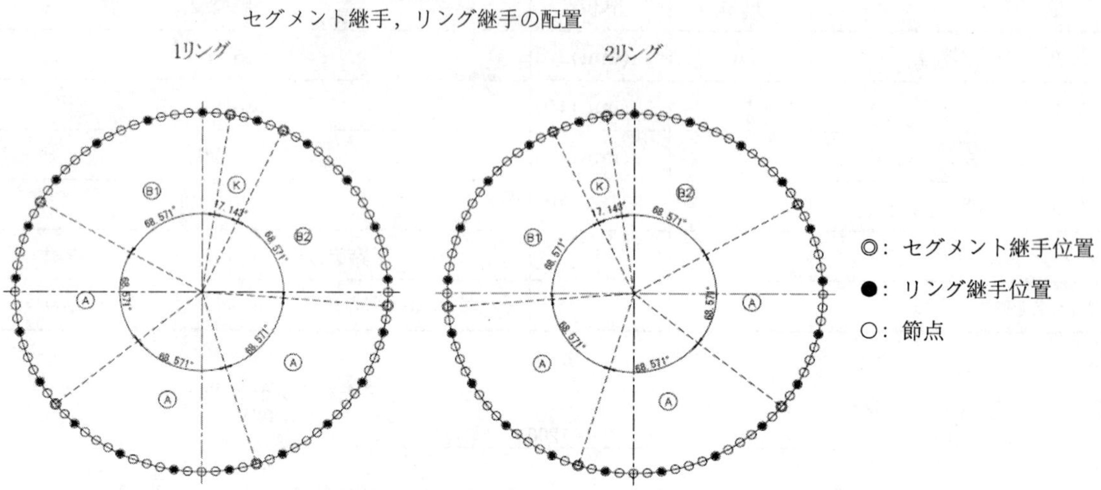

はり-ばねモデルにより，計算された断面力を用いて，主断面およびセグメント継手部の応力度照査を行った．主断面の応力度照査では，鋼材および主鉄筋を鉄筋とみなした鉄筋コンクリートの応力算定理論により応力度を算定した．応力度算定に用いるコンクリートと鋼材・鉄筋とのヤング係数比は n=15 とした．鋼材（スキンプレートおよび主桁）の圧縮応力度および引張応力度，コンクリートの圧縮応力度, 主鉄筋の引張応力度のいずれもが, それぞれの許容応力度以下であることを確認した．セグメント継手部の応力度照査では，ボルトをはじめとする継手部材の応力度が，それぞれの許容応力度以下であることと確認した．

また，本セグメントを RC セグメントとみなして，これにシールドのジャッキ推力（装備推力）が作用するときの検討を行った．ジャッキ推力 1 本当たりの装備推力 2 000 kN が，偏心量 10 mm で，偏心軸圧縮力としてセグメントに作用するときのコンクリートに発生する圧縮応力度は，その短期許容応力度の半分以下であることを確認した．

3.2　急曲線掘進時のシールドの推力や片押しによるトンネル縦断方向の検討（急曲線検討）

曲線半径 R=165 m の急曲線においては，シールドは，直線を掘進しているときとは異なるジャッキパターンでセグメントに推力を作用させ（片押し），その反力により旋回力を得て掘進すると考えられる．直線部とは異なるジャッキパターンと推力とにより，セグメントにはトンネル縦断方向にモーメントと軸力が作用する．

既往の施工事例では，偏ったジャッキパターンと過大な推力により，セグメントのリング継手が破断したり，これらの影響によりセグメントが損傷したりする例が見受けられた．

本検討では，中折れ機構を有するシールドではあるが，安全側にジャッキパターンが最も片押しになるジャッキパターンで，急曲線部を掘進すると想定し，シールドの後方に組み立てられるコンクリート中詰め合成セメントを対象としてその構造検討を行った．

検討フローを図 5 に示す．

構造解析モデルを図 6 に示す．コンクリート中詰め合成セメントが配置される急曲線の平面線形を反映し，セグメントリングで構築されたシールドトンネルの縦断方向においてリング継手の剛性低下を考慮した等価剛性を有する弾性床上のはりモデルを作成した．このはりモデルでは，推力が作用しているセグメント先端から 4 リングの区間は，裏込め注入材の未固化を考慮して地盤ばねを設置していない．また，セグメント先端にはセグメントリングとシールドとの干渉を考慮したばねを設置した．

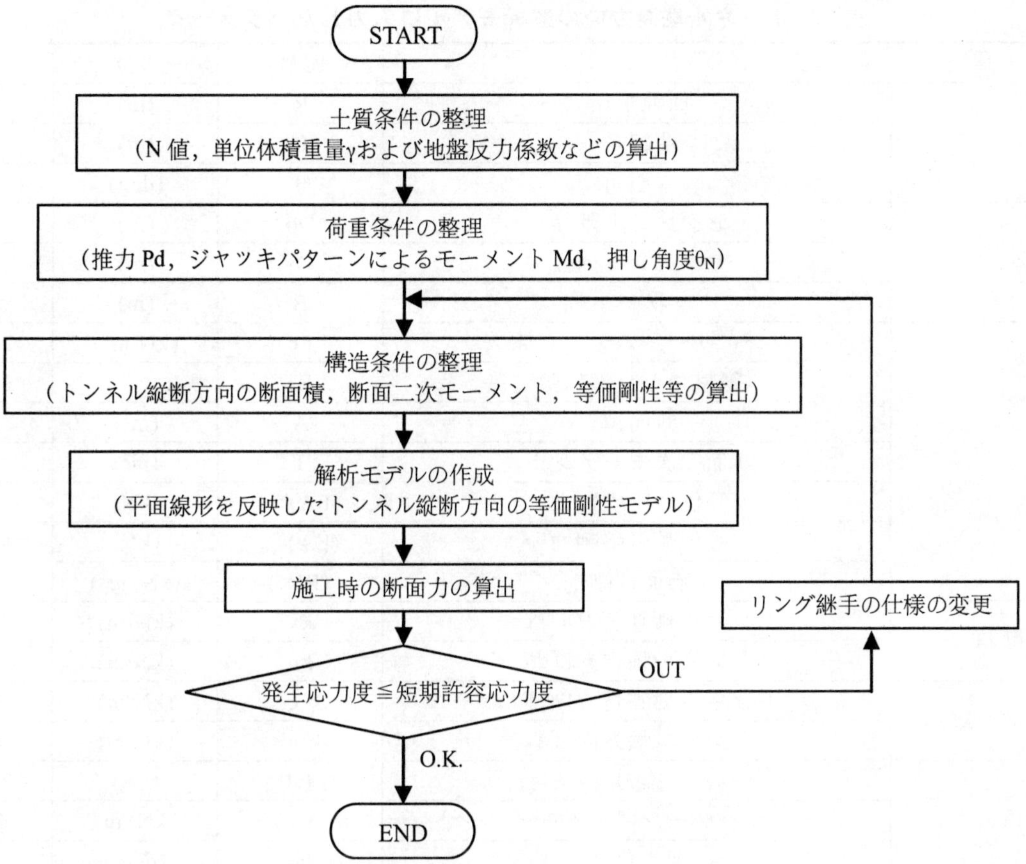

図５　急曲線検討のフロー

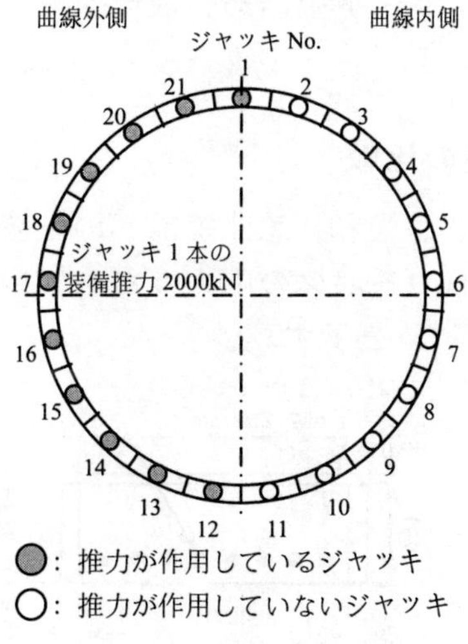

図７　ジャッキパターン

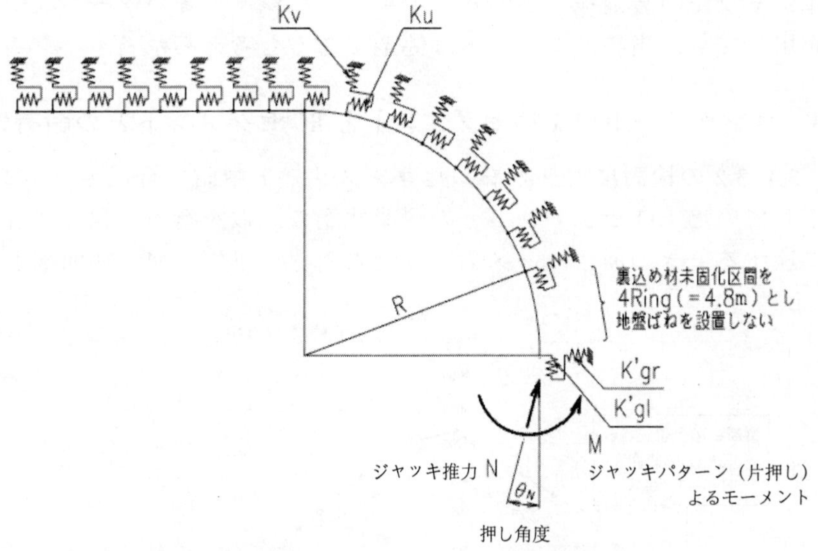

図６　トンネル縦断方向の構造解析モデルとジャッキパターン

構造解析モデルに入力したパラメータを表５に示す.

構造解析で得られたトンネル縦断方向の断面力により，リング継手部の部材の応力度照査を行った．応力度照査の結果，セグメントリングとシールドマシンとのトンネル軸直角方向の干渉により，リング継手ボルトのせん断応力度が増大したが,ボルトの短期許容応力度以下であることを確認した。また、その他の応力度として，コンクリートの圧縮応力度，リング継手ボルトの引張応力度およびリング継ぎボルトに発生する引張力に伴う継手板（主桁）の曲げ応力度は，おのおのの短期許容応力度に対して十分安全であることを確認した.

表5　トンネル縦断方向の解析モデルに入力したパラメータ

項目		記号	単位	値
線形	曲線半径	R	(m)	165
	曲線長	L	(m)	180.514
	中心角	θ	(deg)	62.683
セグメント形状	セグメント外径	Do	(m)	6.700
	セグメント内径	Di	(m)	6.100
	セグメント幅	B	(m)	1.200
剛性	コンクリートのヤング係数	Ec	(kN/m^2)	2.468×10^7
	鋼材のヤング係数	Es		2.468×10^8
	断面積	A	(m^2)	6.856
	断面二次モーメント	I	(m^4)	30.95
	等価軸圧縮剛性	$(EA)^C_{eq}$	(kN)	2.468×10^8
	等価軸引張剛性	$(EA)^T_{eq}$	(kN)	4.585×10^5
	等価曲げ剛性	$(EI)_{eq}$	$(kN\cdot m^2)$	6.880×10^7
地盤ばね	トンネル軸直角方向ばね	kv	(kN/m)	2.15×10^5
	トンネル軸方向ばね	ku	(kN/m)	2.26×10^5
シールド機のばね	トンネル軸直角方向ばね	k'gr	(kN/m)	5.67×10^5
	トンネル軸方向ばね	k'gl	(kN/m)	1.70×10^5
荷重	推力	Pd	(kN)	2.200×10^4
	ジャッキパターンによるモーメント	Md	(kN·m)	4.143×10
	押し角度	θ_N	(deg.)	1.6

ジャッキの装備推力が図6に示すようなジャッキパターンでコンクリート中詰め合成セグメントに作用しても，当該セグメントは健全であると考えられる.

3.3　コンクリート中詰めセグメントとRCセグメントとの耐荷性能の比較

3.1, 3.2 の検討により設計したコンクリート中詰め合成セグメントと，当初，急曲線部への配置を予定していたRCセグメントとの耐荷性能の比較を行う．図7に主断面の各部材の応力度が許容応力度に達するときの曲げモーメント－軸力曲線（以下，M－N曲線と呼ぶ.）を示す.

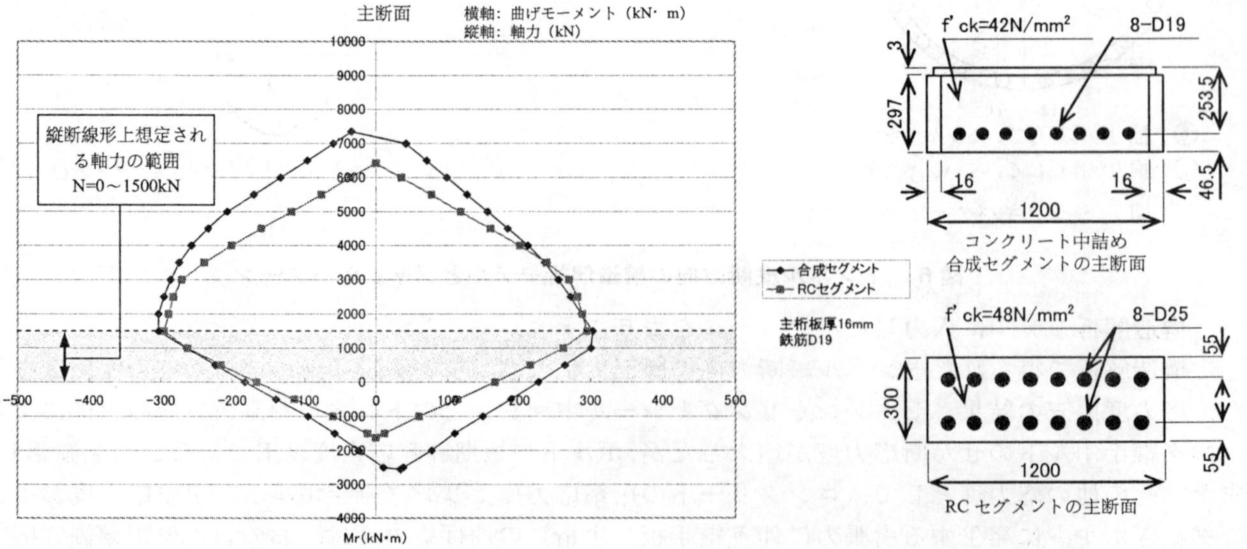

図7　主断面の部材の応力度が許容応力度に達するときの曲げモーメント-軸力曲線

図７でコンクリート中詰め合成セグメントの主断面のＭ－Ｎ曲線は，概ねRCセグメントのこれを包絡しているが，正曲げの軸力2 000～3 500 kNの範囲で，RCセグメントの主断面のＭ－Ｎ曲線がコンクリート中詰め合成セグメントのこれを超過している．しかしながら，コンクリート中詰め合成セグメントが配置される区間で想定させる軸力は0～1500kNであり，この軸力の領域では，本セグメントの主断面のＭ－Ｎ曲線がRCセグメントのこれを超過している．よって，指定の区間に配置される本セグメントの主断面に関する耐荷性能は，RCセグメントより優れていることが分かる．セグメント継手の耐荷性能についても同様の状況である．

コンクリート中詰め合成セグメントの耐荷性能がRCセグメントのそれを上回ること，本セグメントの剛性は，RCセグメントの剛性より10%程度大きいが概ね同等であることより，RCセグメントに対して実施し、安全性を確認していた以下の検討を，コンクリート中詰め合成セグメントの設計実務では省略した．

・下り線（後行）のトンネルの構築が上り線（先行）のトンネルに与える影響の検討（併設トンネルの検討）

・下り線（後行）の急曲線掘進が構築された上り線（先行）トンネルに与える影響検討（急曲線施工時の併設トンネルの影響）

4　性能確認試験

設計により設定された部材仕様を持つコンクリート中詰め合成セグメントが，所定の性能を有することを確認するために性能確認試験を実施した．性能確認試験では，①単体曲げ試験，②継手曲げ試験，③ジャッキ推力試験，④リング継手引張試験を行った．ここでは，性能確認試験のうち，主要な単体曲げ試験について詳述し，他の試験はその概要を述べることとする．

4.1　単体曲げ試験

単体曲げ試験の目的と、それを確認するための項目を表６に示す．

表６　単体曲げ試験の目的と確認項目

試験	主目的	確認事項
単体曲げ試験	セグメント本体部 性能確認	合成構造として挙動すること 所定の性能（剛性、耐力）を発揮すること

単体曲げ試験の概要と主断面の構造を図８，図９に示す．セグメント１ピースを供試体とし，そのスパン中央部に２線載荷を行う．

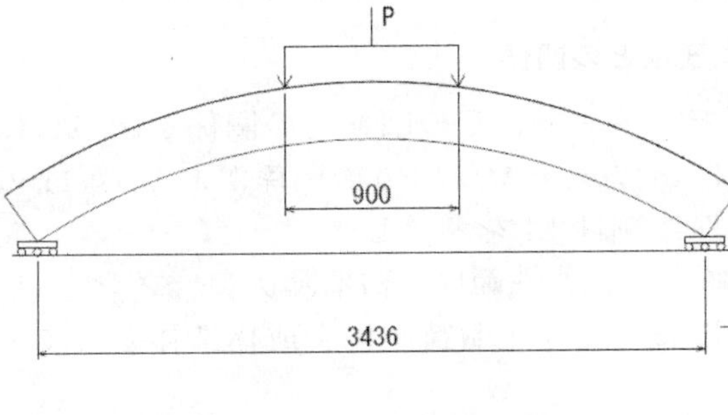

図８　単体曲げ試験の概要

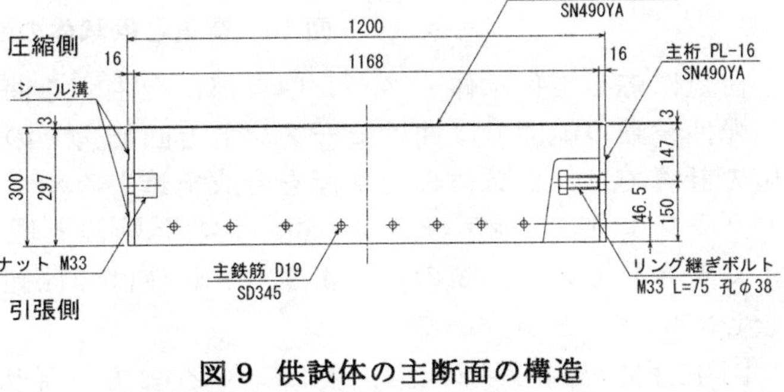

図９　供試体の主断面の構造

載荷は，供試体部材が許容応力度に達する荷重，降伏応力度に達する荷重を超え，供試体が破壊に達する（荷重の増加が見られなくなる）まで継続して行った．

供試体の作成に用いた材料およびその規格値，材料試験値（特性値）を表 7 に示す．

表 7　材料およびその規格値，材料試験値

部位		仕様		材料規格値		材料試験値		
		寸法	材質 (JIS)	静弾性係数 ($\times 10^7$kN/m^2)	降伏点または設計基準強度 (N/mm^2)	降伏点強度 (N/mm^2)	引張強度 (N/mm^2)	静弾性係数 (N/mm^2)
鋼殻	主桁	t=16	SM490YA	21	360	398.0	542.0	210,000
	継手板	t=3.0	SM490YA	21	360	398.0	542.0	210,000
	スキンプレート	t=16	SM490YA	21	360	378.0	528.0	210,000
コンクリート		—	—	3.6	42	58.3（圧縮強度）		29,370
鉄筋	周方向鉄筋	D19	SD345	21	345	382.6	582.0	210,000
ボルト・ナット		M33	（10.9）	21	940	-	-	-

図 10 に荷重と供試体の鉛直変位との関係を示す．載荷荷重は，許容レベル荷重（部材の応力度が許容応力度に達するときの荷重），降伏荷重レベル（部材の応力度が降伏応力度に達するときの荷重），終局荷重レベル（中詰めコンクリートひずみが 3500μ に達し、圧壊するときの荷重）を順次超え，最大荷重 1 060 kN に達している．その後，載荷荷重は若干低下したが，その後も供試体は 1 000 kN 程度の荷重を保持しながら変形し，高い変形性能を保有することを示した。また，最大載荷荷重の許容レベル荷重に対する比率は 3.02（=1 060/351）であり，供試体の終局耐力は十分な安全率（3.02）を持っている．したがって，供試体は，十分な耐荷性能を有していることが確認できた．

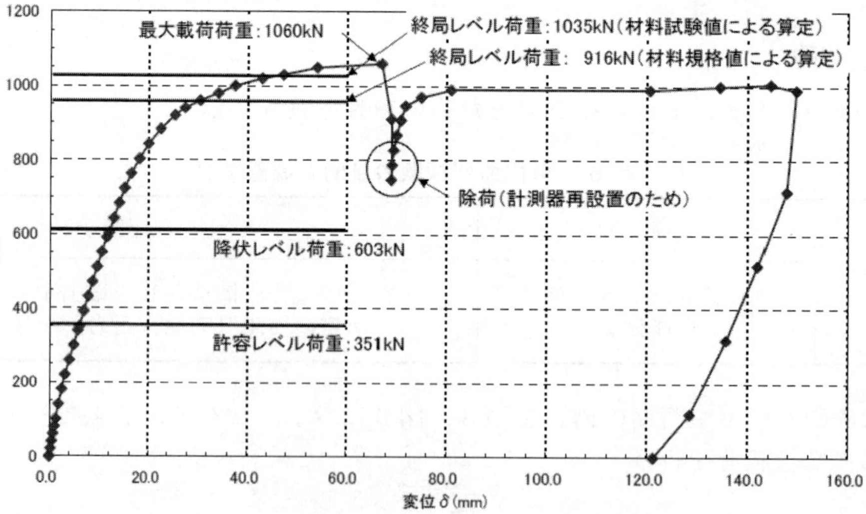

図 10　荷重と供試体の鉛直変位との関係

荷重に応じて供試体のスパン中央部に発生する曲げモーメントとその回転角の関係を図 11 に示す．弾性挙動の範囲では曲げモーメントと回転角との間に $dy^2/dx^2 = M/EI = \phi$ の関係がある.図 11 の理論値の計算では，供試体の主断面を合成構造とみなした曲げ剛性 EI を考慮した．

グラフより，計測データから得られた試験値と理論値とは，弾性範囲（初期降伏モーメント以下）でよく整合している．このことより，供試体は弾性範囲において荷重載荷時に合成構造体としての挙動をしていたことが分かる．

図 12 に，部材が降伏応力度に達するまで（降伏荷重レベル）の 3 段階の荷重に対する，供試体のスパン中央部の部材のひずみ分布を示す．グラフの縦軸は圧縮縁からの距離である．コンク

リートのひずみに若干差異があるが，各荷重における鋼殻（スキンプレートまたは主桁），コンクリートおよび鉄筋のひずみの分布は，概ね直線に沿っている．このことより，主断面の部材のひずみ分布は平面保持の仮定を満足しており，供試体の主断面は合成構造とみなすことができると考えられる．

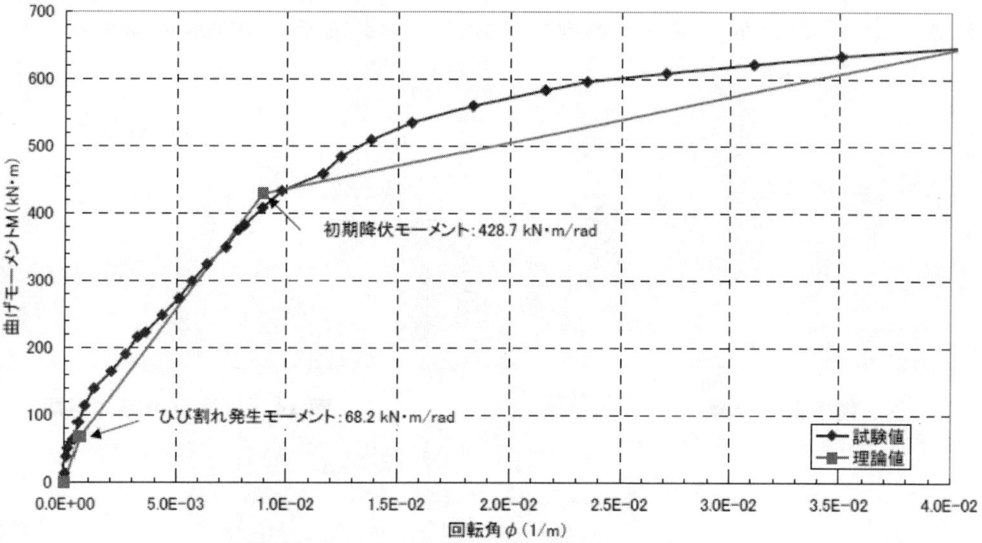

図 11　曲げモーメントと回転角との関係

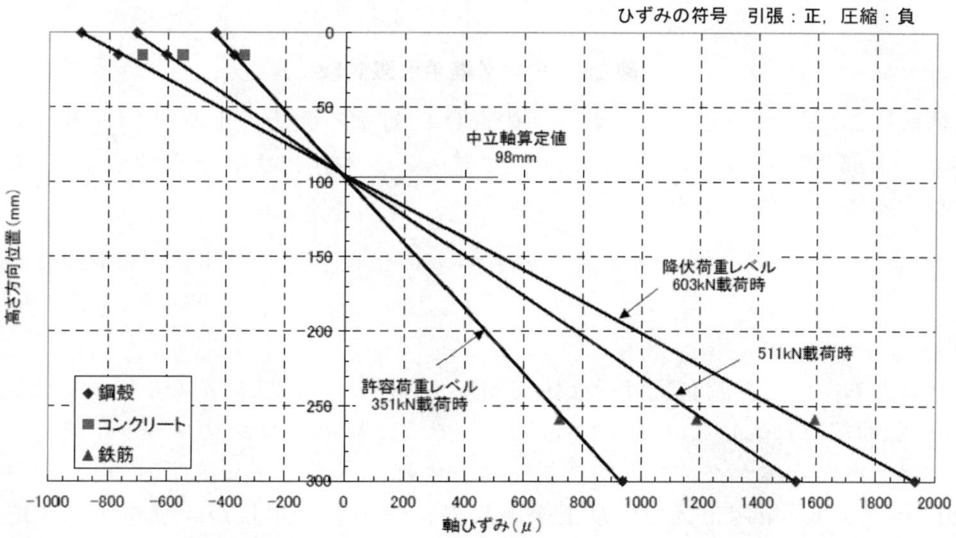

図 12　ひずみの分布

なお，単体曲げ試験後の供試体を写真 1 に示す．供試体内面のひび割れはトンネル周方向に約 130 mm 間隔で分散して発生しており，特定箇所に集中することはない。これは RC セグメントのひび割れ発生の状況に類似している。

図 10～12 の試験結果より，供試体は合成構造体とみなすことができ，その耐荷性能は合成構造の耐力を十分有することが確認できた．

また，ひび割れは特定の箇所に発生せず分散し，RC セグメントで単体曲げ試験を実施した場合のひび割れの発生状況

写真１　単体曲げ試験後の供試体

と類似しており，鉄鋼製セグメントとしての高い耐荷性能と，RC セグメントに類似した分散したひび割れ発生状況，換言すれば供試体内部でのスムーズな応力の伝達という，合成セグメントの特長の２面性が見られたと思われる．

4.2 他の試験の概要

図 13～15 に，継手曲げ試験，ジャッキ推力試験，リング継手引張試験の概要を示す．

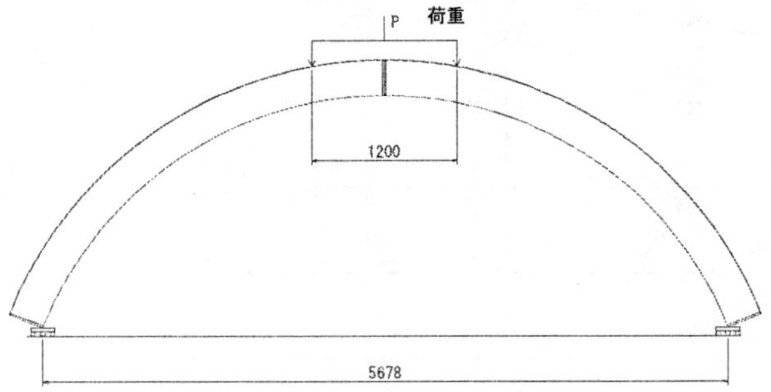

図 13 継手曲げ試験

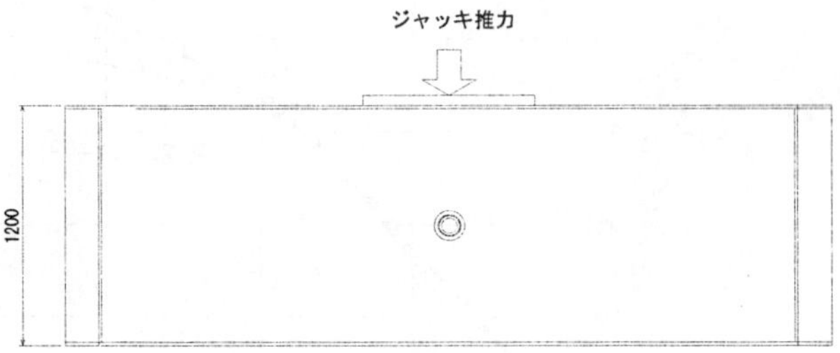

図 14 ジャッキ推力試験

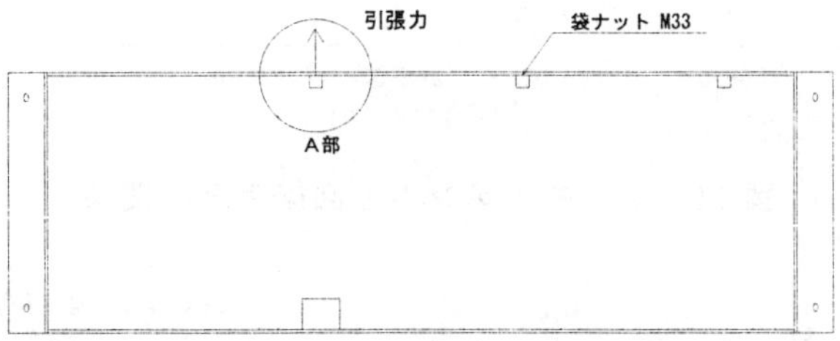

図 15 リング継手引張試験

いずれの試験においても，セグメント継手の曲げに対する耐力，セグメント本体の圧縮耐力，リング継手の袋ナット部(ボルトボックスを設けずセグメント本体にナットを埋設する)の引張耐力は，所定の耐力を有することを確認できた．

5 まとめ

以上の検討により，京王線調布駅付近立体交差工事のうち，第四工区（清水 JV）の相模原線上り線（先行トンネル）急曲線部において，地下鉄トンネルでは，初めてコンクリート中詰め合成セグメントを採用することとなった．本セグメントの特長を考慮すればさまざまな箇所への適用が期待できる．

現在（2009 年 7 月)，第四工区では京王線上り線シールド 1 本目が，調布西立坑地下 3 階に到達しつつある．

本セグメントを配置する予定の相模原線上り線シールド 2 本目の掘進は 2009 年 9 月から 2010 年２月を予定している．京王電鉄（㈱)，JV 職員をはじめ関係各位の総力を挙げて，４本のシールドトンネルの完工に努める所存である．

最後に，コンクリート中詰め合成セグメントの本工事への適用に向けて，御指導御協力を賜った，パシフィックコンサルタンツ（株）清水氏，新日本製鐵（株）の広沢氏，中島氏に改めて謝意を表します．

参考文献（References)：

[1] 財団法人 鉄道総合技術研究所編：鉄道構造物等設計標準・同解説 シールドトンネル，2002.
[2] 小泉 淳ら:急曲線施工用セグメントの設計法について，土木学会論文集 No.448/Ⅲ-19, 1992,06 pp111-120.

著者紹介（Bio-data）:

氏　名：入田健一郎

誕生日：1966 年 10 月 14 日生（年齢 42 歳）

所　属：清水建設株式会社　土木技術本部　シールド統括部　課長

専　門：シールドトンネル，セグメント設計他

Name (Age, Birthday): Kenichiro IRITA (42 years old, 14 Oct. 1966), supervisor of Shield Tunneling Engineering, dev. of Civil Engineering, Shimizu Corporation.

Specialized fields: design of segmental linings and other underground structures.

営業線直下・小土被り条件下におけるシールドトンネルの　計画と施工について

足立邦靖[1]　沼澤憲二郎[2]

[1](株)大林組京王布田 JV 工事事務所，東京 182-0022

[2]京王電鉄(株)調布工事事務所，東京 182-0022

論文要旨：

新宿を起点とする京王線は、東京都西部地域を中心に神奈川県北部にも跨る 84.7 km の路線において、1 日約 174 万人の旅客を輸送しており、首都圏交通の大動脈の一翼を担っている。

東京都、調布市および京王電鉄株式会社では、交通事故や慢性的な道路渋滞などの交通諸問題の抜本的解決を図るとともに、分断化されていた市街地を一体化することにより地域を活性化させる目的で、2003 年より調布駅付近で連続立体交差事業を施行している。同事業は、延長 3.7 km に渡り営業線の直下で地下化工事を行うもので、駅部および掘割部は開削工法、駅間はシールド工法を採用し、早期完成に向けて現在工事を進めている。

本稿では、本事業のうち国領駅～調布駅間の上下線、延長 861 m×2 本のシールド工事を紹介する。

キーワード：営業線直下掘進；小土被り施工；併設シールドトンネルの施工

EPB SHIELD TUNNELING FOR SHALLOW TWIN TUNNELS UNDER RAILWAY IN OPERATION

K.NUMAZAWA[1]，K.ADACHI[2]

[1]Keio Corp. Chofu Construction Office, Tokyo 182-0022, Japan;

[2]Obayashi Corp. Keio Buta JV, Tokyo182-0022, Japan

Abstract: The Keio Line, which is a private railway line of 84.7km long operated by the Keio Corporation, covers the western area of the Tokyo Metropolitan City and the northern part of the Kanagawa Prefecture. The daily passenger transmission is approximately 1.7 million, and the line contributes as a part of the main transportation network in the metropolitan area.

The development of the area along the railway line has raised concerns on daily traffic congestions that must have caused increase in traffic accidents. In order to eliminate the concern and to additionally stimulate vigorousness of the areas by unifying the cites and the towns split by the line, the Tokyo Metropolitan Government, the Chohu City Government and the Keio Corporation have started a 8-years project since 2003 to divert the 3.7km of Keio Line from the ground level to underground. The project consists of three underground stations, the transition slopes by open-cut method and tunnels by an Earth Pressure Balanced (EPB) shield machine, and the shield tunnel is constructed just under beneath the existing operating railway line.

This report introduces a part of the project that has construction of the twin tunnels with the length of 861m each (from Kokuryo Station to Chohu Station) by an EPB shield machine.

Key word: tunnel construction under operating railway line; shallow tunnel construction; twin shield tunnels construction

1 はじめに

1.1 事業概要

東京都、調布市および京王電鉄株式会社では、交通事故や慢性的な道路渋滞などの交通諸問題の抜本的解決を図るとともに、分断化されていた市街地を一体化して地域を活性化させる目的で、2002年2月に都市計画決定を受け、2004年9月より調布駅付近で連続立体交差事業を施行している。同事業は、京王線の柴崎駅～西調布駅間約 2.8 km の区間と相模原線の調布駅～京王多摩川駅間約 0.9 km の区間を地下化することにより、18 箇所のいわゆる“開かずの踏切”を解消するとともに 8 箇所の都市計画道路を立体化するもので、駅部および掘割部は開削工法、駅間はシールド工法を採用し、早期完成に向けて現在工事を進めている。

表－1 に事業概要、図－1 に事業全体平面図を示す。

表－1　事業概要

事業目的	鉄道と道路の連続立体交差工事・鉄道の地下化工事		
事業名称	京王電鉄京王線（柴崎駅～西調布駅）及び同相模原線（調布駅～京王多摩川駅間）連続立体交差工事		
事業区間	京王線の柴崎駅～西調布駅間の 2.8 km、相模原線の調布駅～京王玉川駅間の 0.9 km　合計 3.7 km		
構造形式	地下方式	駅施設	国領駅・布田駅・調布駅
事業者	東京都・調布市・京王電鉄㈱	発注者	京王電鉄㈱
事業期間	2004 年 9 月～2013 年 3 月		

今回報告する「調布駅付近連続立体交差工事第 2 工区シールド工事」は、国領駅～調布駅間の 861 m を泥土圧（気泡）シールドにて施工する。シールドトンネルは上下線 2 本からなり、延長 1,722 m（L=861 m×2 本）を 1 台のシールド機で U ターン施工を行う。今回のシールドトンネルは、国領駅～布田駅間は並列配置であるが、将来の線増線（急行線）を調布駅に接続する計画であることから、調布駅手前のスパイラル区間を経て調布東立坑では完全な縦列配置となる。

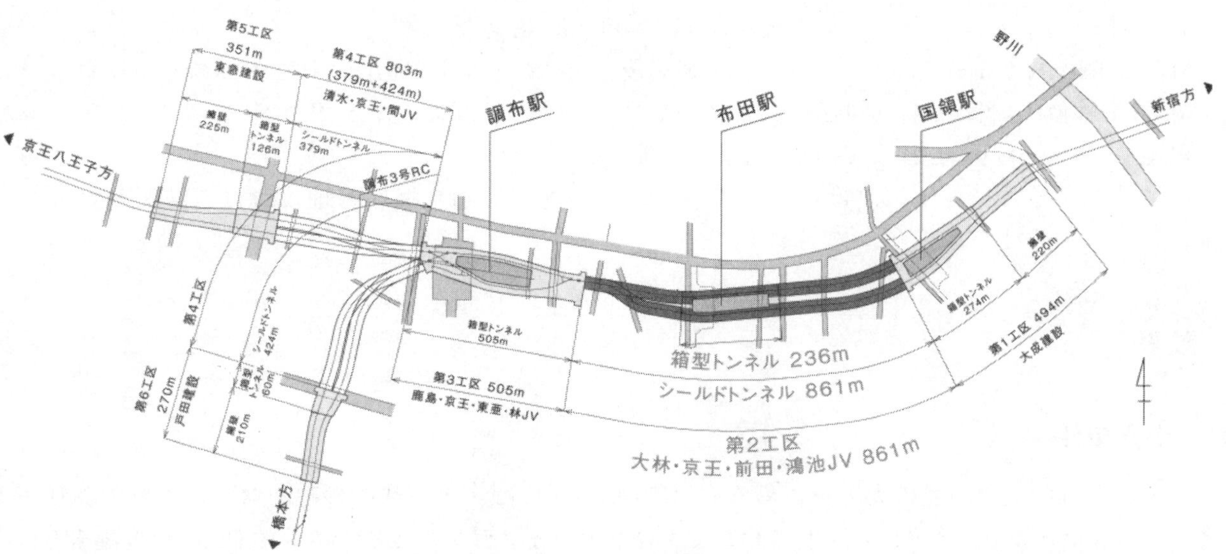

図－1　事業概要図

第２工区シールド工事概要を表－２に、第２工区平面図を図－３に示す。

表－２　第２工区シールド工事概要

工事名称		調布駅付近連続立体交差工事（土木）第２工区 その４の３工事（シールド工事）		
施工者		大林・京王・前田・鴻池建設共同企業体		
工期		平成20年３月～平成22年３月		
工事内容	掘削工法	泥土圧（気泡）シールド工法	トンネル延長	L=1,722 m（上り線 L=861 m　下り線 L=861 m）
	線形	平面：最小 500R、縦断：2～35‰		
	トンネル外径	φ6,700 mm	シールド機外径	φ6,850 mm
	掘削土量	64,000 m^3（地山）		
	セグメント	（トンネル部）RC（EXP）セグメント：外径 6,700×内径 6,100×幅 1,400×桁高 300　697Ring （トンネル部）SFRC セグメント　：外径 6,700×内径 6,100×幅 1,400×桁高 300　185Ring （布田駅部）　ダクタイルセグメント：外径 6,700×内径 6,200×幅 1,250×桁高 250　387Ring		
	土質	立川礫層（Tag），上総層群（Ks1，Ksc）		
	土被り	小土被り【上り線】5.0～13.7m,　【下り線】4.7～6.0m　最小土被り 0.69D		

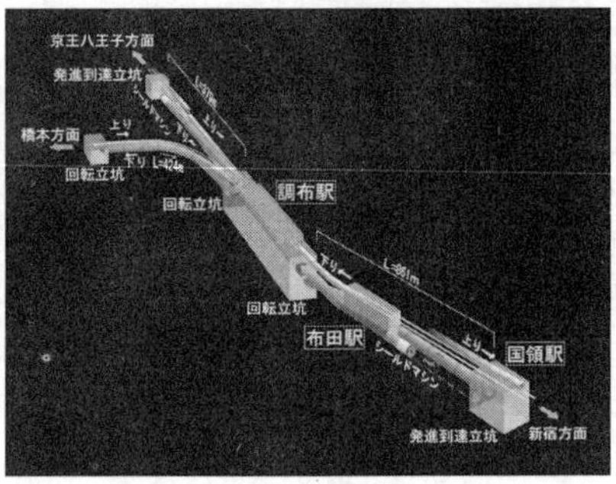

図－２　事業全体イメージ図

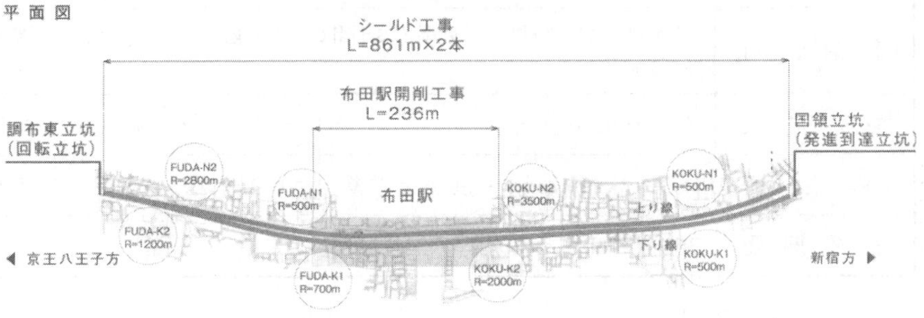

図－３　第２工区平面図

本シールド工事の特徴を以下に示す。

1) 営業線の直下を小土被り（最小土被り 4.7 m/0.69 D）で縦断方向に連続して掘進する。
2) 掘削対象地盤は立川礫層が主体のため、バインダー分が少なく最大礫径 300 mm が想定される。
3) 地下水位はシールド掘削断面に対し不飽和で季節変動する。
4) 上下線のシールドトンネルの最小離隔が 400 mm と近接している。
5) 中間駅となる布田駅部では、シールド通過後、並列シールドの切開きにより駅舎を築造する。
6) 営業線直下の調布東（回転）立坑において、約 300 t のシールド機を回転・扛上する。

以上に示すとおり、これまで日本国内でも例を見ない極めて厳しい条件のシールド工事といえる。今回は、このような条件下における泥土圧シールドの施工計画、掘進管理における課題と対策、施工実績について報告する。

2　設計

2.1　土質条件

シールド掘削対象地盤の大半を占める立川礫層（Tag）は、玉石状の砂礫を含む砂礫層であり、玉石の最大径は 300 mm で、いずれの深度においても径 200 mm クラスの玉石が 3～10 個/m^3 程度混入し、バインダー分が 5%以下という特徴を有している。また、透水係数はおおむね 10^{-2}～10^{-1} cm/s を示している。

上総層群砂質土層（Ks1）は、比較的均質な細砂～粗砂が互層状をなしており、所々に粘性土薄層を介在する。N 値は最上部で 20～40 程度であるが、概ね 50 以上の非常に締まった地層である。

上総層群粘砂性土層（Ksc）は、固結シルトと砂の互層で、N 値は 35～50 以上を示し、多くは 50 以上の非常に硬い地層である。

また、地下水位は GL-5.5～-7.3 m であり、トンネル断面の上半部から天端付近まで季節変動する。

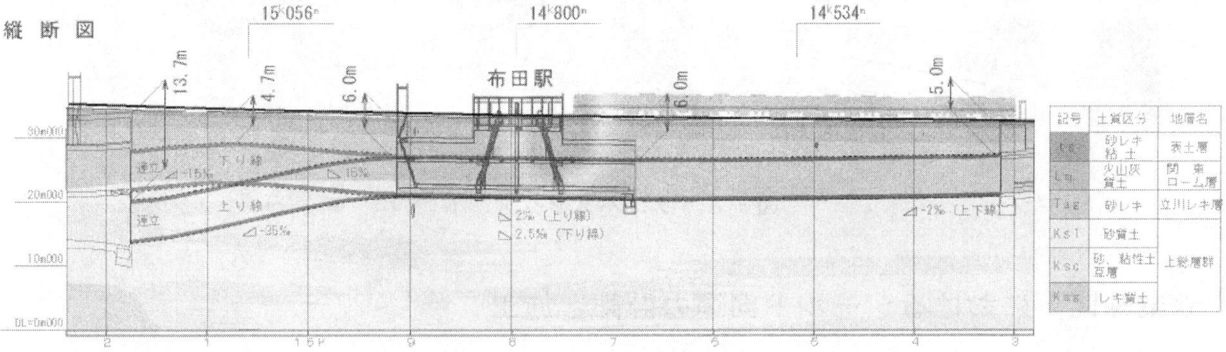

図－4　土質縦断図

2.2　トンネル構造

本シールドでは，３種類のセグメントを以下のように使い分けて使用している．

・トンネル部（軽構造／小土被り部）　RC(EXP)セグメント※1

・トンネル部（重構造／大土被り部）　SFRC（鋼繊維補強高流動コンクリート）セグメント※2

・布田駅部　（駅舎切開き部）　ダクタイルセグメント

※1 EXP セグメント：Exfoliation Prevention Segment　耐アルカリガラス繊維シートをセグメント内面に埋設した剥離防止セグメント

※2 SFRC セグメント：Steel Fiber Reinforced Concrete Segment　鋼繊維補強高流動コンクリートセグメント

図－5　EXP セグメント

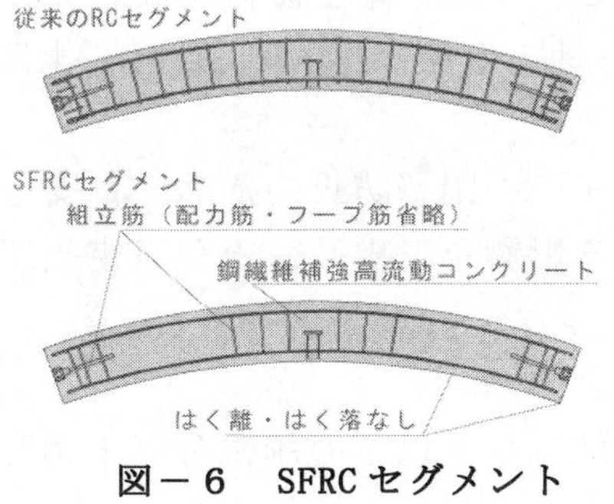

図－6　SFRC セグメント

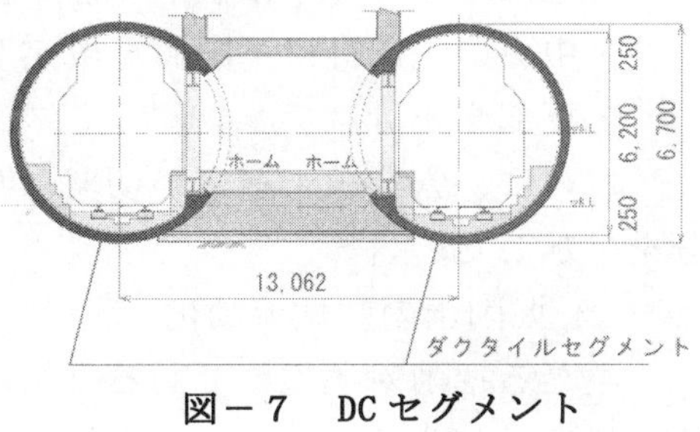

図－7　DC セグメント

RC セグメントと SFRC セグメントは、機械的な位置決めと締結を同時に完了する内面平滑型「ワンパスセグメント」を採用し、セグメントの組立て時間を大幅に短縮した。特長を以下に示す。

1) ピース間は先付け水平コッター（楔式継手)、リング間はプッシュグリップ 3（ピン式継手）

2) 組立ピースをスライドするだけで組立完了するため、高速施工に対応できる

3)ボルトボックスが無く断面が一様で剛性が高いことから、高い耐久性を有する

4)継手がトンネル内面に露出しないため、腐食環境に曝されない

トンネル供用後のコンクリートの剥離、剥落、落下を防止するため、RC（EXP）セグメントとSFRC（鋼繊維補強高流動コンクリート）セグメントを採用した。

DCセグメントは開口部に鋼製柱と縦桁を設置するためD型（受台付）セグメント構造とした。

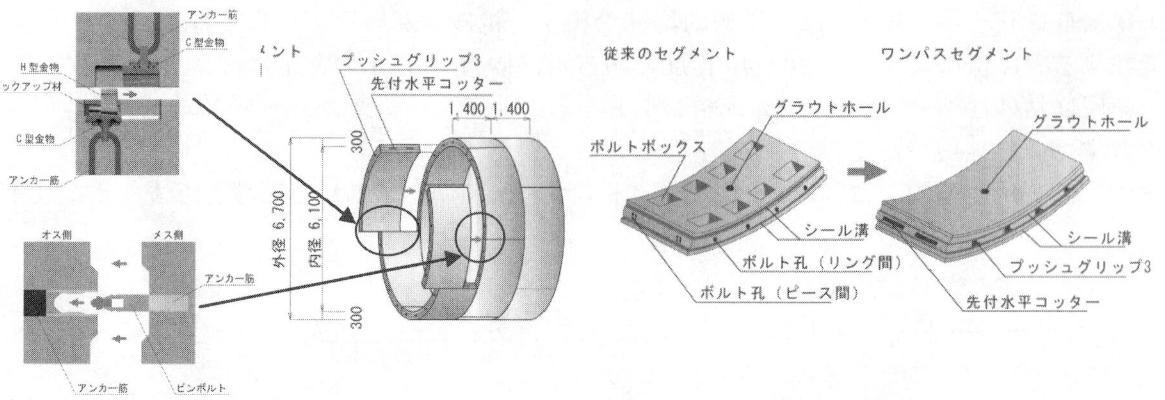

図－8　ワンパスセグメント

3　営業線直下におけるシールド掘進の計画と施工

営業線直下において軌道の安全を確保してシールド掘進するためのポイントは、
①切羽の安定　②排土量の管理　③計測管理　である。
以下に、管理方法および上り線における管理結果を報告する。

3.1　切羽の安定

(1) 土圧管理

小土被り条件下では当然ながら土被り圧が小さく、土圧係数から求められる静止土圧との差も小さくなる。そのため、切羽土圧の許容幅が狭くなり、わずかな管理誤差でも周辺地盤に影響を与える可能性がある。従来以上に繊細な切羽土圧の調整を行うために、以下の対策を講じた。

・チャンバー内に土圧計を6箇所（上部・中央・下部　各2箇所）配置した
・上部土圧計をメインの管理土圧とし、下限値と上限値を設定した
・上部土圧計の下限値は「静止土圧+地下水圧+予備圧」とし、上限値は「土被り圧」とした
・中央の土圧計は下限値を設定した
・下部土圧計はチャンバーとスクリューの閉塞防止のための目安とした

さらに、営業線の運行が切羽に与える影響を考慮し、上記設定土圧に列車荷重による動的荷重成分を付加した。

(2) 掘削土の塑性流動化

主たる掘削対象地盤である立川礫層はシルト以下の細粒分が不足しているため、ベントナイト系加泥材を添加することでこれを補うとともに、気泡を添加することにより、安定したチャンバー内の塑性流動および排土性状の確保とカッタートルクと推力の低減を図ることとした。注入量・注入位置は掘進状況および排土状況に応じて調整することとした。

3.2　排土量の管理

本工事のような礫地盤では延伸式の連続ベルトコンベヤによる土砂搬出が最も効率的であることから、坑内の土砂搬出には連続ベルトコンベヤを、掘削土砂の垂直搬送には垂直ベルトコンベヤを採用した（図－9）。切羽に近い後続台車上の中継コンベアに体積式のレーザースキャナと重量式のベルトスケール設置した（図－9）。排土量の管理は統計的手法を用いて行い、過去20リングを対象として$\pm 3\sigma$を管理値とし、掘進中はリアルタイムグラフで監視することにより、異常の有無にすぐ対応できるシステムを構築した。

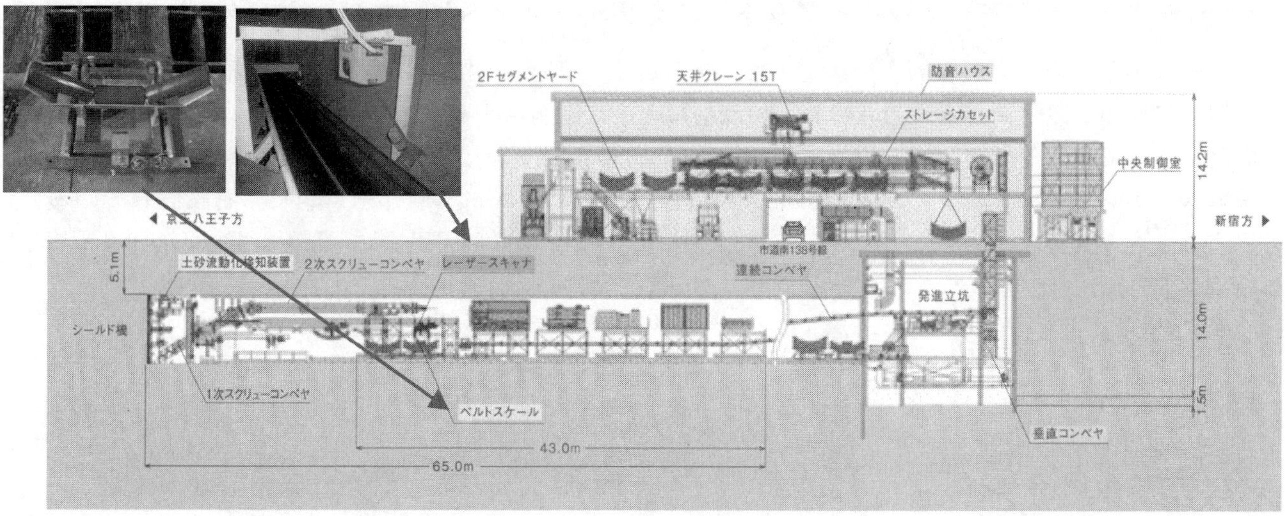

図－9　土砂搬出設備と計測装置

3.3　計測管理

軌道の安全確認、および、変化する条件の中での掘進管理の妥当性確認を目的として、24 時間の自動計測による情報化施工を行うこととした。計画・実施した主な計測項目は以下の通りである。

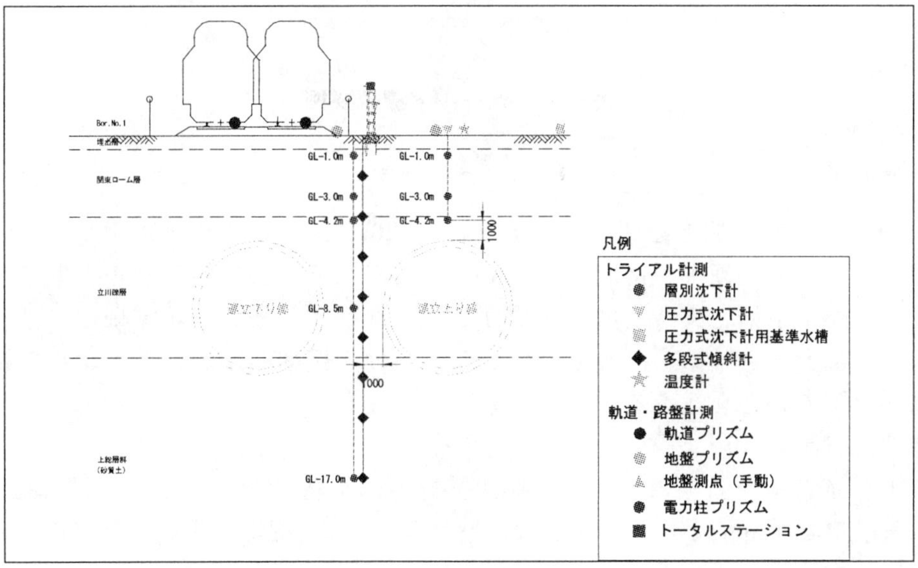

図－10　計測概要図

(1) トライアル計測

周辺地盤に影響を与えない掘進管理方法を早期に確立するため、発進立坑から約 90mまでの初期掘進区間においてトライアル計測を 3 断面設置した。トライアル計測断面①、②で得られたデータにより掘進管理方法を見直し、断面③にてその妥当性を検証してから軌道直下に進入することとした。

(2) 軌道および地盤計測

軌道の安全確認と、地盤の変状を掘進管理へリアルタイムにフィードバックし地盤変状を最小限に抑えるため、トータルステーションによる自動計測を実施した。測定箇所は、上下線の内軌側レールとシールド直上地盤とし、測定ピッチは 10 m とした。

3.4　シールド機の対策（カッタービット、スクリューコンベヤ、コピーカッター）

シールド形式は、立川礫層への対応、小土被り掘進、発進基地用地等を考慮して泥土圧シールド工法を採用している。カッタヘッド形状は、立川礫層に対して破砕よりも取り込みを優先してスポークタイプを採用し、玉石を取込むスクリューコンベアは内径φ850 mm（排土可能礫径φ500 mm）のリボン式スクリューコンベアを採用し、確実なプラグゾーンを確保するため2次スクリューコンベヤを設置している。

また、地表面の沈下を極力抑えるため、シールド機には同時注入管を設置せず、形状保持装置上部を二又にすることでセグメントから早期に裏込注入が可能な構造とした。

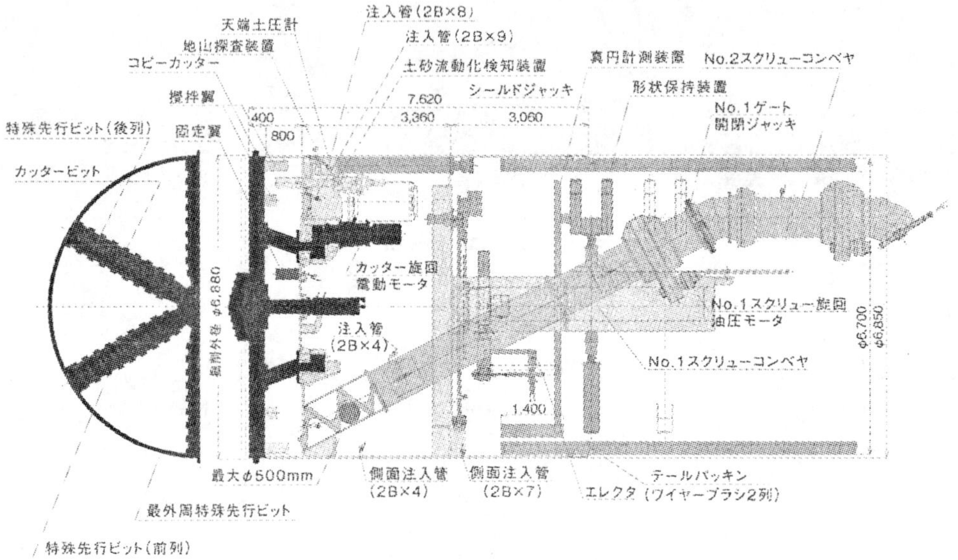

図－11　シールド機概要図

3.5　上り線の掘進結果

2008年6月末にシールド掘進を開始した上り線は、2009年1月に無事到達した。上り線の掘進は、営業線直下に進入する前の初期掘進区間（区間A）、営業線直下におけるシールド掘進を行った本掘進区間（区間B）、軌道を工事桁と支持杭にて仮受けし一次掘削完了後シールド掘進を行った布田駅部区間（区間C）の3つに大別される。それぞれの区間における掘進結果およびそれらの結果より得られた下り線掘進にむけての課題を述べる。

①初期掘進結果（区間A）

発進直後のトライアル断面①における層別沈下計の沈下量はシールド機先端通過時で-1 mm、シールド機テール通過時で-7 mm という結果となった（図－12）。測定結果は、地表面からの深度に関わ

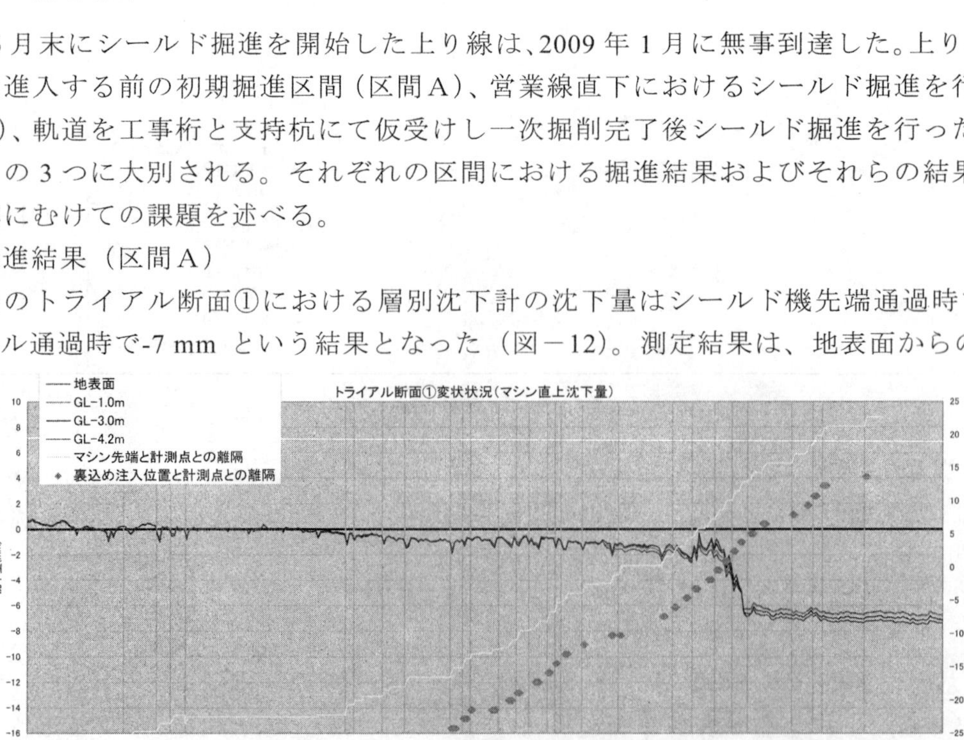

図－12　トライアル断面①計測結果

らず同様の挙動を示していることから、小土被りにおける掘進の場合地盤が硬質であっても地表面まで影響がダイレクトに伝達することがわかった。

トライアル断面① の結果を考慮し、管理土圧のうち、静止土圧および予備圧の考え方を再検討した後、再度トライアル断面②および③において設定土圧の妥当性を再検証した。図－13 にトライアル断面② 近傍を掘進した時の層別沈下計の計測結果を示す。変状はシールド機先端通過時で-1 mm、シールド機テール通過時で-3 mm となり、管理土圧の考え方は適正と評価し、この管理方針に基づき本掘進を行うこととした。トライアル断面③においても変状は±1 mm と良好であった。

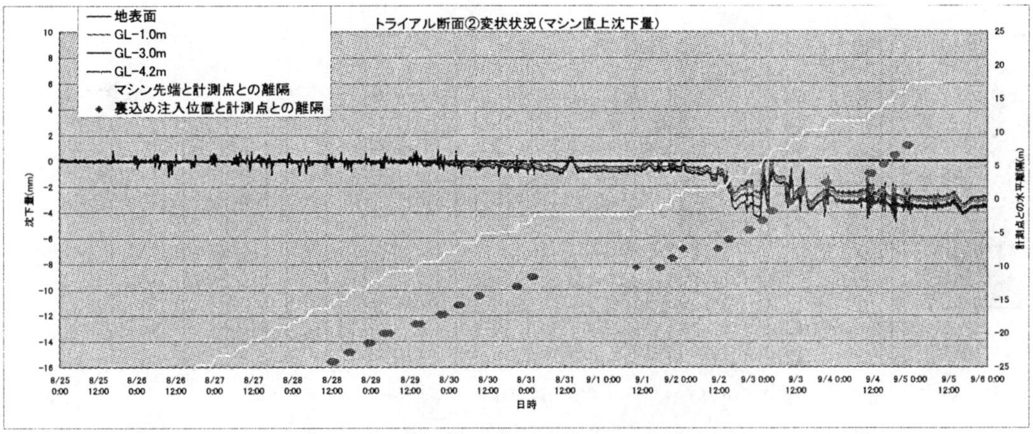

図-13　トライアル断面②計測結果

②本掘進結果（区間Ｂ）

本掘進では、全線を通して軌道および路盤の変状は管理目標値の±5 mm 以内で掘進することができ、初期掘進により得られた管理土圧の設定思想が全線において妥当であったことが確認された。

掘削添加材については、地山状況に応じて加泥材と気泡の比率を調整し掘進することで、安定して掘進することが可能であった。

③布田駅部掘進結果

布田駅部開削工事は全体工程短縮のため、上り線シールド通過時には図－１４に示すように一次掘削（G.L.-3.5 m）まで終了しており、最小土被り 2.4 m でのシールド掘進となった。切羽土圧が低すぎると土被りの大きい民地や道路に影響を与え、高すぎるとシールド直上に位置する土留杭に変状を与えることが懸念されたため、さらに狭い幅での切羽土圧の管理が要求された。そこで、管理土圧を上部土圧計において、下限：静止土圧+水圧+予備圧、上限：下限値＋20 kPa と設定し掘進を行った。

本区間通過時の変状測定結果を図-１５に示す。仮橋上駅舎の変状は管理目標値（±5 mm）以内であり掘進管理方法が妥当であることが確認できた。

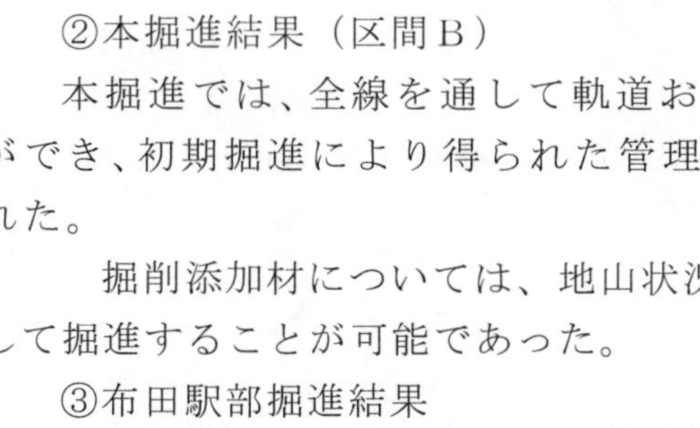

図-14　布田駅部標準断面図

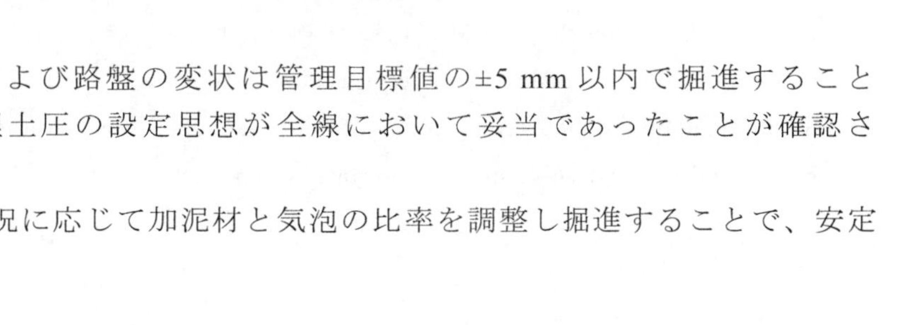

図-15　仮橋上駅舎変状計測結果

4　おわりに

2009年1月に上り線が到達した本工事は、シールド機の回転・扛上・艤装を経て、2009年4月に下り線の掘進を開始し、現在施工中である。

1日も早い地下化実現に向けて、上り線の施工で得られたデータと知見をもとに日々改善を図り、2009年秋の下り線到達を目指している。

著者紹介（Bio-data）：
氏名：足立　邦靖，職位：工事長，最終学位：工学学士（土木工学）
専門分野：シールドトンネル
職務内容：調布駅付近連続立体交差工事（土木）第2工区　シールド工事
これまでの主な経歴：地下鉄都営三田線（6号線）シールド工事
八潮共同溝シールド工事
地下鉄副都心線（13号線）南池袋A線シールド工事
Name：Kuniyasu ADACHI，Employment title：Construction Manager
The final degree：Engineering bachelor（Civil engineering）
Specialized field：Shield tunnel
Job content：Shield tunneling in the second work section for continuous grade separation structure construction near Chofu Station
Career：Shield tunneling for Mita Line of Toei Subway No.6
Shield tunneling for Yashio multi-service tunnel）
Shield tunneling in the A Line Section of South Ikebukuro for Fukutoshin Line of Tokyo Metro Subway No.13）
E-mail address：adachi.kuniyasu@obayashi.co.jp

性能規定に基づく既設地下鉄シールドトンネルの保有性能評価手法の検討

横山　正浩[1]　木村　定雄[1]　山本　努[2]

[1]金沢工業大学　環境土木工学科　地域防災環境科学研究所，〒924-0838　石川県白山市八束穂 3-1

[2]東京地下鉄株式会社　工務部，〒110-8614　東京都台東区東上野 3-19-6

既存の構造物の性能評価の考え方を示した ISO13822 が国際標準として発効されている．著者らは地下鉄シールドトンネルの性能規定に基づく性能評価手法について検討してきている．本文では日本土木学会で検討されている要求性能に基づき，維持管理段階を対象として，既存の地下鉄シールドトンネルの性能評価を行い，現在実施されている既存トンネルの健全度評価との整合性を分析した．その結果，AHP を用いることで，既存の地下鉄シールドトンネルの保有性能を総合的に評価できる可能性が示された．

キーワード：シールドトンネル；性能規定；維持管理；Analytic Hierarchy Process

A STUDY OF EVALUATION METHODS OF KEEPING PERFORMANCE OF SUBWAY SHIELD TUNNELS BASE ON PERFORMANCE CRITERION

Masahiro YOKOYAMA[1], Sadao KIMURA[1], Tutomu YAMAMOTO[2]

[1]*Kanazawa Institute of Technology Department of Civil and Environmental Engineering Institute of Disaster and Environmental Science3-1 Yatsukaho, Hakusan, Ishikawa 924-0838, Japan;*

[2]*Tokyo Metro Co., Ltd.Infrastructure Maintenance Dept.3-19-6 Higashi-ueno, Taitou-ku, Tokyo 110-8614, Japan*

Abstract: This paper presents a study of evaluation method of keeping performance of existing shield tunnels base on performance criterion. The ISO13822 have been established as the international standard for evaluation of existing structures, and efforts are continuing to coordinate Japanese design criteria with this standard. In this paper, based on the performance requirements for subway shield tunnels called for by a committee of the Japan Society of Civil Engineers, we evaluation a total performance index using AHP and assess its utility for quantitative evaluation of tunnels at the maintenance stage. As a result, we show that the total performance index using AHP was consistent with current inspection and evaluation methods and appropriate for comprehensive assessment of performance maintenance of existing subway shield tunnels.

Key words: shield tunnels; performance based design; maintenance; analytic hierarchy process

1　はじめに

構造物の設計体系が国際標準化へ移行を進める中，土木学会から「包括設計コード 1)」が発効された．ここでは「性能照査型設計法」という新しい設計概念が導入され，日本では「性能規定」に基づく設計コードの体系が土木・建築分野で整備されつつある．トンネル分野でも性能規定に基づくトンネルの設計体系が整備されてきている[3]．「性能規定」とは，構造物の用途に応じて計画段階，設計段階，施工段階および維持管理段階で要求される性能を明確にし，要求性能とその照査の基本を定める行為である．これまで土木学会トンネル工学委員会「トンネル構造物の設計法の将来像と国際標準への対応に関する検部会」では，トンネル構造物の目的・機能から要求性能を定義するとともに，その照査方法の検討を行なってきている[4]．また，同検討部会では，既存構造物の戦略的なマネジメントを実施するため，性能規定に基づくマネジメント手法の考え方も論じられている[3,4] 一方，既存構造物の性能評価の考え方を示した ISO13822[5] がグローバルスタンダードとして発効されており，国際的に既存構造物を評価する仕組みづくりが検討されてきている．

ここで，既存のトンネル構造物の性能照査法の確立においては，現在実施されているトンネル構造物の健全度を評価する点検評価手法との整合を図る必要があると考えられる．現在実施されているトンネルの点検評価法(以下，現行法)では，健全度判定の基準[2]に基づいて，トンネルの変状を確認し，表 1 に示すようなレイティングによる判断区分を適用して補修や補強の対策を判断している[6]．

表 1　現行の健全度評価の判定区分（鉄道シールドの場合）[2]

判定区分	構造物の状態
A	運転保安、旅客及び公衆などの安全ならびに正常運行の確保を脅かし、またはそのおそれのある変状等があるもの
AA	運転保安、旅客及び公衆などの安全ならびに正常運行の確保を脅かす変状等があり、緊急に措置を必要とするもの
A1	進行している変状等があり、構造物の機能が低下しつつあるもの、または、大雨、出水、地震等により構造物の性能を失うおそれなあるもの
A2	変状等があり、将来それが構造物の性能を低下させるおそれのあるもの
B	将来、健全度Aになるおそれのある変状等があるもの
C	軽微な変状があるもの
S	健全なもの

本研究では，まずは既存の地下鉄シールドトンネルの保有性能を評価することを具体的に試みた．すなわち階層分析法（Analytic Hierarchy Process：以下 AHP[7,8]）を用いて定量的に保有性能を評価した．また，保有性能評価結果と現行法の判定結果とを比較してその整合性を分析した．その上で，AHP を用いた既存の地下鉄シールドトンネルの保有性能評価手法の有効性を検討した．

2　既存トンネルの保有性能の評価・照査の考え方

(1)サービスアビリティーと保有性能の評価・照査

トンネル構造物のサービスアビリティによって既存トンネルの保有性能評価・照査手法は異なると考えられる．表 2 はトンネルのサービスアビリティのレベルとそれに対応するマネジメント手法の基本的な考え方を示したものである．トンネル構造物のサービスアビリティは対象となるトンネルの用途ならびに個々のトンネルの社会的役割や重要度に応じて異なる[2]．サービスアビリティが低いトンネルでは中長期的に管理を行うため，レイティングなどによって簡易的に保有性能を評価・照査し，これに基づき今後の対策を検討するのが有効であると考えられる．一方，サービスアビリティが高い地下鉄トンネルでは，レイティングによってトンネルの路線や区間ご

表 2　サービスアビリティに応じたマネジメントの考え方

サービスレベル	低位 交通量小，劣化進行低 山間部	⇔	高位 交通量大，劣化進行高 重要路線，緊急輸送路
性能規定	利用者の安全性能・使用性能，構造安定性能，耐久性能 管理者の使用性能，維持管理性能，周辺への影響度		
性能照査指標	極力数値化が可能な指標を選定		
設計法	見なし型設計		性能設計
モニタリング	点検＋必要に応じて簡易計測		点検＋計測
健全度評価法	レイティングが基本		性能照査型評価法
維持管理段階における性能照査手法	点検（＋簡易計測）結果によるレイティング		計測を主体とした数値化指標による照査
将来状態予測手法	確定論的予測 （残存耐力）		信頼性，確立論的手法などによる不確実性を考慮した予測法
LCC最適化による意思決定	点検，補修を想定したLCC		LCC最適化を実施

との総合的な保有性能を一元的に評価するとともに，より詳細なモニタリングと性能評価・照査法を検討する必要がある．

(2)維持管理段階におけるトンネルの要求性能

既存の鉄道シールドトンネルの要求性能を表 3 に示す [4]．ここで，大項目はトンネルの用途にかかわらない基本要求性能である．また，中項目および小項目は基本要求性能を鉄道シールドトンネルの用途に応じて細分化して具体的にしたものである．

表 3　要求性能(鉄道シールドトンネル)

要求性能				
大項目		中項目	小項目	
利用者の安全性能	利用者が安全に利用できる	安全に走行できる	良好な線路線形を確保できる	1
			走行安全性を確保できる	2
				3
				4
			建築限界を確保できる	5
		利用者の安全を直接脅かさない	剥落が生じない	6
			漏水が生じない	7
		非常時に利用者が安全に退避できる	防災設備を適切に配置・使用でき、利用者の避難経路が確保されている	8
利用者の使用性能	利用者が快適に利用できる	乗り心地が良い	線形が適切、乗り心地を悪化させる軌道変位を起こすようなトンネル変位が生じない	9
		利用者に不快感・不安感を与えない	利用者が不快感・不安感を持つような漏水・ひび割れが見られない	10
構造安定性能	想定される荷重に対して安定する	常時作用する荷重に対して安定している	常時作用する荷重に対して必要な耐荷性能を有している	11
				12
				13
		必要な耐震性能を有している	供用期間中に想定される地震動に対して、必要な耐震性能を有している	14
		想定される荷重の変化に対して安定する	供用期間中に想定される近接施工による影響や周辺環境の変化等、荷重条件の変化に対して必要な耐荷性能を有する	15
				16
		想定される施工時荷重に対して安定する	施工時に想定される荷重に対して必要な耐荷性能を有する	17
耐久性能	想定される劣化要因に対して耐久性がある	防食性がよい	鉄筋・鋼製セグメント。継手金物等の鋼材の発錆速度が最小限に抑えられている	18
				19
				20
		コンクリートが劣化しない	覆工のコンクリートが浸食・劣化しない	21
		止水性が良い	覆工・諸設備の劣化原因となる漏水が最小限に抑えられている	22
管理者の使用性能	管理者が適切にトンネルを供用(使用)できる	必要な需要を満足できる	必要な線路数を収容できる内空断面の確保　必要な列車速度を出せる線形の確保	23
		列車が安定的に(定時に)運行できる	列車運行に関わる諸設備の機能を支障するような剥落・漏水が生じない	24
				25
				26
		列車運行のための諸設備が確実に稼働できる	列車運行に関わる諸設備を適切に配置・使用できる	27
			トンネル内の水が適切に排水され諸設備に影響しない	28
維持管理性能	適切な維持管理が確実に行える	安全・容易に点検できる	日常の巡回・点検が安全・容易にできる	29
		安全・容易に補修・補強ができる	補修・補強工事の足場仮設・資材仮置が大きな支障なくできる　内空断面に補修・補強余裕が確保されている	30
周辺への影響度	周辺への影響度が最小限に抑えられる	地下水への影響が少ない	地下水位変動が最小限である　周辺への地下水汚濁影響がない	31
				32
				33
		周辺地盤への影響が少ない	地表面の沈下・隆起が最小限である	34
				35
		周辺の物件への影響が少ない	近接建物・埋設物等への影響が許容範囲である	36
		周辺での振動・騒音が少ない	列車走行等による周辺での振動・騒音が最小限である	37

3　既存シールドトンネルの保有性能の評価手法

(1)トータル性能インデックスによる保有性能の評価

鉄道シールドトンネルの路線や区間ごとの総合的な保有性能を一元的に評価するため,AHP[7),8)] を採用した．式（1）に保有性能を表わすトータル性能インデックス(Total Performance Index：以下 *TPI*)の定義[9)]を示す．*TPI* は各要求性能小項目に対する性能評価基準値(P_i)と重み係数(C_i)の積によって表される．

$$TPI = \sum_{i}^{n} P_i \cdot C_i \tag{1}$$

ここで　TPI =トータル性能インデッ　クス

P_i = 性能評価値

C_i = 要求性能の重み係数

n = 要求性能評価項目の数

(2) 性能評価基準と重み係数の設定

要求性能項目と性能評価基準との関係を表 4 に示す．また，性能評価値を決めるための性能評価基準を表 5-1 および表 5-2 に示す．表中の性能照査代替指標は要求性能小項目を具体的に評価するための代替指標である．モニタリング項目は性能照査代替指標にかかわる計測・観察項目である．保有性能評価は 5 段階の性能評価基準を設けている．また，性能評価基準の設定は既存の点検評価要領[10)] を参考とした．とくにひび割れなどの変状は定量的評価が難しいく，このように定量化が困難なモニタリング項目も 5 段階の基準で評価する[11)]．また，性能評価基準は 1 点から 15 点の配点とした．なお，表 5-1 および表 5-2 中の無記入覧は，本調査で保有性能評価の対象から除外した項目である．

表 4　性能評価基準のイメージ(利用者の安全性能を抜粋)

要求性能			重み係数	Ci	配点 Pi	性能評価基準				
大項目	中項目	小項目				1	3	5	7	15
利用者の安全性能	安全に走行できる	良好な線路線形を確保できる								
		走行安全性を確保できる				健全			劣化	
		建築限界を確保でき								
	利用者の安全を直接脅かさない	剥落が生じない								
		漏水が生じない								
	非常時に利用者が安全に退避できる	防災設備を適切に配置・使用でき、利用者の避難経路が確保されている	AHPで設定							

重み係数(C_i)は，鉄道シールドトンネルに精通する 18 名の高度技術者のアンケートによって定めた．AHP は過去の技術体系と技術者の経験情報を考慮した意思決定モデルによって，保有性能が評価できる手法である．重み係数は 1.000 点に近いほど重要度が高くなる．表 6 は鉄道シールドトンネルの重み係数を定めた結果である．

(3) AHP による鉄道シールドトンネルの保有性能評価

単線の中子形セグメントリング区間と二次覆工区間の 2 種類の地下鉄シールドトンネル区間を対象として *TPI* を求めた．*TPI* の算定にあたっては，図 1 に示す既存の地下鉄シールドトンネルの点検評価結果である覆工展開図を用いた．中子形セグメントリング区間では 350 リング，また，二次覆工区間では 58 スパンを対象とした．*TPI* の算定にあたっては，中子形セグメントリング区間では 1 リングごとに，二次覆工区間では 1 スパン(10 m)ごとに数値化して評価した．*TPI* は最も健全なもので 1 点，また変状が厳しく劣化した状態のもので 15 点となる．

表 5-1　性能評価基準(鉄道シールドトンネル)

番号	性能照査代替指標	モニタリング項目	性能評価基準 配点 ： 1 問題ない・健全・もしくは健全と想定される場合（S，C）	性能評価基準 配点 ： 3 日常点検にて注意・継続監視が必要（B）
1	軌道変位量(走行安全性の影響有無)	軌道変位量	−	−
2	トンネル線形の変位量	水準測量，トンネル中心測量	−	−
3	走行安全を脅かす範囲(軌道直上等)のセグメント・二次覆工のひび割れ・浮き，鉄筋の腐食等の状況	ひび割れ・腐食等の位置・長さ・幅・範囲：目視，可視画像 浮きの範囲：打音，赤外線カメラ ﾊﾟﾀｰﾝ：変状展開図 進行性：マーキング，写真撮影，ひび割れ計 鉄筋の腐食状況：自然電位，分極抵抗，はつり目視	・走行安全を脅かす範囲（軌道直上等）に剥落の危険性がないリング ・リブにひび割れはあるが剥落の恐れがない 二次覆工 ・はつり出しがある ・剥落危険範囲にひび割れが発生している（枝状ののひび割れ，短いひび割れ，一つのひび割れ変状に２本以下の亀裂が交わっているとき）	
4	軌道への漏水かかり状況	漏水の位置・量：目視 漏水の水質：水質検査	・軌道への漏水かかりがない ・軌道上に漏水がない	・軌道への漏水かかりがあるが、滴下量が少なく、水質も問題ない ・軌道上（剥落危険範囲）に漏水がある
5	建築限界外余裕量	建築限界車測定，光波測距儀	−	−
6	利用者に安全を脅かす範囲(ホーム・コンコース天井等)のセグメント・二次覆工のひび割れ・浮き等の状況	ひび割れ等の位置・長さ・幅・範囲：目視，可視画像 浮きの範囲：打音，赤外線カメラ ﾊﾟﾀｰﾝ：変状展開図 進行性：マーキング，写真撮影，ひび割れ計	利用者に安全を脅かす範囲に剥落の危険性がない リング ・リブにひび割れはあるが剥落の恐れがない 二次覆工 ・はつり出しがある ・剥落危険範囲にひび割れが発生している（枝状ののひび割れ，短いひび割れ，一つのひび割れ変状に２本以下の亀裂が交わっているとき）	・利用者の安全性を脅かす範囲に剥落の危険性はないが、 ・変状に進行性がある，・変状の進行性の有無が確認されていない リング ・前回の点検では確認されていないひび割れが多く発生している 二次覆工 剥落危険範囲に ・３つ以上のひび割れが重なっている場合 ・亀甲状のひび割れ模様であるがひび割れは閉合していない
7	利用者に安全を脅かす範囲(ホーム・コンコース天井等)の漏水発生状況	漏水の位置・量：目視	・利用者に安全を脅かす範囲に漏水の発生がない ・軌道上に漏水がない	
8	建築限界外余裕量(防災設備との離隔，避難の空間)	建築限界車測定，目視検査	−	−
9	軌道変位量(乗り心地の影響有無)	軌道変位量，列車動揺測定	−	−
10	利用者から見える範囲(ホーム・コンコース天井等)の漏水・ひび割れの発生状況	目視	・利用者から見える範囲(側壁)にひび割れ，漏水，エフロレッセンス，ジャンカが見られない	・利用者から見える範囲(側壁)にひび割れ，漏水，エフロレッセンス，ジャンカが見られる
11	トンネル内空変位量	内空変位量：内空変位計，光波測距儀	−	−
12	セグメント・二次覆工のひび割れ・損傷の発生状況(構造的変状の有無)	ひび割れ・損傷等の位置・長さ・幅・範囲：目視，可視画像 浮きの範囲：打音，赤外線カメラ ﾊﾟﾀｰﾝ：変状展開図 進行性：マーキング，写真撮影，ひび割れ計 鉄筋の腐食状況：自然電位，分極抵抗，はつり目視	・構造的に問題となるようなひび割れ・損傷が見られない ・ひび割れがない	・将来、構造的に問題となる可能性のあるひび割れ・損傷が見られる リング ・単独的なひび割れがある
13	変形解析等による覆工の応力度または断面力	変位：内空測定，目開き・目違い量測定 部材の歪・応力：歪測定 覆工の強度，変形特性：強度試験（ﾎﾞｰﾘﾝｸﾞ，反発硬度法，打撃・打診法，ｱﾝｶｰ引抜き法），弾性係数試験	−	−
14	解析等による耐震性能，損傷レベル	材料の特性値：設計上の材料の特性値，実構造物のひずみ測定・強度試験・動弾性係数試験	−	−
15	トンネル内空・線形の変位量	天端沈下量：水準測量，光波測距儀 内空変位量：内空変位計，光波測距儀 線形変位量：水準測量，光波測距儀 ひび割れパターン：目視	−	−
16	影響解析等による覆工の応力度または断面力	変位：内空測定，目開き・目違い量測定 部材の歪・応力：歪測定 覆工の強度，変形特性：強度試験（ﾎﾞｰﾘﾝｸﾞ，反発硬度法，打撃・打診法，ｱﾝｶｰ引抜き法），弾性係数試験	−	−
17	維持管理段階では評価されない	−	−	−
18	セグメント・二次覆工のひび割れ・浮き等の有無	ひび割れ・剥離等の位置・長さ・幅・範囲：目視，可視画像 浮きの範囲：打音，赤外線カメラ ﾊﾟﾀｰﾝ：変状展開図 進行性：マーキング，写真撮影，ひび割れ計	・鉄筋腐食に起因するようなひび割れ・錆汁・浮き等が見られない	・鉄筋腐食が原因とも考えられるひび割れ、浮き等が軽微に見られるが、進行性が確認できていない ・リングに数本ひび割れがあるがつながっていない 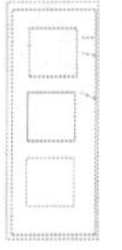
19	鉄筋・継手金物等の腐食状況	露出鋼材の腐食状況：目視，腐食減厚測定 コンクリート中の鋼材の腐食状況：自然電位，分極抵抗，電磁波レーダー，はつり目視 進行性：写真撮影，錆汁の状況	・鋼材腐食が認められない	−
20	かぶり・中性化残り・塩化物濃度・含水率等の劣化指標	かぶり深さ：ＲＣﾚｰﾀﾞｰ､はつり出し､スケール 中性化残り：中性化深さ測定 塩化物濃度：塩化物イオン濃度測定 含水率：含水率測定 環境条件：飛来塩分測定，漏水中の塩分濃度、雨かかり状況、日射状況、温度・湿度	・かぶりが一定以上（概ね20～30㎜）あり、中性化残りが十分かつ塩化物イオン濃度が低く、塩分飛来・漏水・滞水等が認められない（＝劣化予測しても相当年数、鋼材腐食発生限界に達しない）	・かぶりが一定以上（概ね20～30㎜）あり、中性化残りが十分あるが、漏水・滞水・雨かかり等により、腐食速度が遅くなる恐れがある。（中性化：深さ限界、高含水率または乾湿繰り返し） ・かぶりが一定以上あり、中性化深さが鋼材発生限界以上になっているが、漏水・滞水・乾湿繰り返し等は見られない。（中性化：深さ限界以上、紙含水率） ・かぶりが一定以上あり、塩化物濃度が鋼材腐食限界以下だが、飛来塩分・塩分含有漏水等がある（塩害：限界濃度以下、塩分供給あり）
21	セグメント・二次覆工のひび割れ・浸食等の状況	・ひび割れ：ゲルの滲出・腐食・スケーリング等の位置・長さ・幅・範囲・深さ：目視、打音、減厚測定 パターン：変状展開図，　　・進行性：マーキング、写真撮影、ひび割れ計 覆工コンクリートの物性劣化状況：強度試験、弾性係数試験、物性試験（アルカリ量・骨材の反応性・微細構造・化学組織等） 環境条件：漏水中の有害物質濃度、水分供給状況、日射状況、	−	−
22	漏水の発生状況	漏水の位置・量：目視 漏水の水質：水質検査 漏水の変動状況：センサー測定	・漏水がない	・漏水が見られるが、水質に問題ない周辺環境である （沿岸、河川交差、工場近接等ではない） ・漏水があることで新たなひび割れ発生時に漏水がひび割れに進入する恐れがあるため３点とする
23	維持管理段階では評価されない	−	−	−
24	列車運行に関わる諸設備に影響する範囲のセグメント・二次覆工のひび割れ・浮き等の状況	ひび割れ等の位置・長さ・幅・範囲：目視、可視画像 浮きの範囲：打音、赤外線カメラ パターン：変状展開図 進行性：マーキング、写真撮影、ひび割れ計	・列車運行に関わる諸設備に影響する範囲に剥落の危険性がない	・利用者の安全性を脅かす範囲に剥落の危険性はないが、 ・変状に進行性がある ・変状の進行性の有無が確認されていない
25	列車運行に関わる諸設備に影響する範囲の鋼材の腐食状況	露出鋼材の腐食状況：目視，腐食減厚測定 コンクリート中の鋼材の腐食状況：自然電位，分極抵抗，電磁波レーダー，はつり目視 進行性：写真撮影，錆汁の状況	・列車運行に関わる諸設備に影響する範囲に腐食が見られない (評価が困難なため評価しない)	・利用者の安全性を脅かす範囲に腐食の危険性はないが、 ・変状に進行性がある ・変状の進行性の有無が確認されていない (評価が困難なため評価しない)
26	列車運行に関わる諸設備に影響する範囲の漏水状況	漏水の位置・量：目視 漏水の水質：水質検査	・列車運行に関わる諸設備に影響する範囲に漏水がない	・列車運行に関わる諸設備に影響する範囲に漏水あるが、滴下量が少なく、水質も問題ない ・覆工，リングに漏水がある場合，施設の整備に影響を及ぼす恐れがあるため３点とする
27	特に諸設備に対しての建築限界外余裕量	建築限界車測定，光波測距儀	−	−
28	排水設備の状況(排水溝のつまり等)	位置・程度：目視，写真撮影	−	−
29	建築限界外余裕量(巡回・点検における待避用の空間)	建築限界車測定，目視検査	−	−
30	維持管理段階では評価されない	−	−	−
31	周辺地下水位の変動	水位計測	−	−
32	周辺地下水質	水質調査	−	−
33	トンネル内漏水状況調査	目視、写真撮影	−	−
34	周辺地表面の変位量	地表面変位：地割れ，沈下観察，変位量測定	−	−
35	漏水発生状況	漏水量：目視，写真撮影，漏水（湧水）量測定	−	−
36	近接物件の変位量・ひび割れ等の発生有無	変位量：変位量測定 ひび割れ：ひび割れ幅などひび割れ調査	−	−
37	地表面・周辺建物での振動・騒音レベル	振動・騒音レベル：振動・騒音測定	−	−

表 5-2　性能評価基準(鉄道シールドトンネル)

番号	性能評価基準 配点 ： 5 詳細調査・評価が必（A2）	配点 ： 7 適切な時期での対策が望ましい（A1）	配点 ： 15 直ちに対策が必要（AA）
1	－	－	－
2	－	－	－
3	・走行安全を脅かす範囲に剥落の危険性はないが、 ・変状に進行性がある・変状の進行性の有無が確認されていない リング ・前回の点検では確認されていないひび割れが多く発生している 二次覆工 剥落危険範囲に ・３つ以上のひび割れが重なっている場合 ・亀甲状のひび割れ模様であるがひび割れは閉合していない		・安全走行を脅かす範囲に剥落の危険性がある リング ・リブ，セグメントの過度などにひび割れがあり，剥落が予想される 二次覆工 剥落危険範囲に ・ポップアップ，ポップアウトが確認できる ・ひび割れが閉合しているため剥落の危険が高い
4	・軌道への漏水かかり量が一定以上で、軌道が湿潤しており、電食発生のおそれがある	・軌道への漏水かかり量が一定以上で、軽微な電食欠損が発生しはじめている	・軌道への漏水かかり量が一定以上で塩分等を含んでおり、著しい電食欠損が発生している
5	－	－	－
6			・利用者に安全を脅かす範囲に剥落の危険性がある リング ・リブ，セグメントの過度などにひび割れがあり，剥落が予想される 二次覆工 剥落危険範囲に ・ポップアップ，ポップアウトが確認できる ・ひび割れが閉合しているため剥落の危険が高い
7	・利用者に安全を脅かす範囲（ホーム・コンコース天井等）に軽微な漏水が発生している ・軌道上（剥落危険範囲）に漏水がある		－
8	－	－	－
9	－	－	－
10			
11	－	－	－
12	・構造的に問題となるようなひび割れ・損傷が確認され、現段階では進行性は見られない（収束している） リング ・つなぎ目にひび割れがあることで，リブにゆるみなどが生じるおそれがある 二次覆工 ・覆工の1/3以上が大幅亀裂で囲まれているにひび割れがある	・明らかに構造的な安定性を損なうひび割れ・損傷が確認され、将来の進行可能性が高い リング ・何リングにも連続して(前後数リング)ひび割れが発生している 二次覆工 ・覆工の1/3以上にひび割れがあり，横断でひび割れがある	・明らかに構造的な安定性を損なうひび割れ・損傷が確認され、かつ顕著な進行が見られる ・0.3ミリを超えるひび割れがある一内部鉄筋腐食によって構造安定が脅かされる恐れがあるため リング ・リングは評価を行わない，最高点７点とする 二次覆工 ・覆工の1/3以上ににひび割れがあり，縦断，斜めにひび割れが混じっている
13	－	－	－
14	－	－	－
15	－	－	－
16	－	－	－
17	－	－	－
18	鉄筋腐食が原因のひび割れ、浮き等が一定規模以上に発生しており、進行性が認められる リング ・亀甲，枝状のひび割れがある 二次覆工 ・亀甲または枝状のひび割れがある 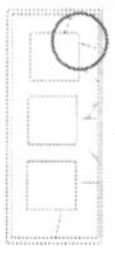	・鉄筋腐食が原因のひび割れ、浮き等が一定規模以上に発生して剥落も見られ、明らかに進行性がある 0.3ミリを超えるもの，0.2ミリ程度でリングを連続するひび割れがあるポップアップ，ポップアウトがある リング ・覆工に1/3以上のひび割れがある ・何リングにも連続して(前後数リング)ひび割れが発生している 二次覆工 ・覆工に1/3以上のひび割れがある・閉合亀裂がある 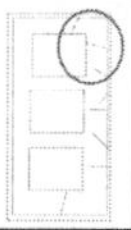	・鉄筋腐食が原因のひび割れ、浮き・剥落等広範囲に発生し、コンクリートと鉄筋の一体性が損なわれ、構造安定性能に影響している可能性がある ・0.3ミリを超えるもの，0.2ミリ程度でリングを連続するひび割れがある ・ポップアップ，ポップアウトがある リング ・覆工に1/3以上のひび割れがある ・何リングにも連続して(前後数リング)ひび割れが発生している 二次覆工 ・覆工に1/3以上のひび割れがある ・閉合亀裂がある
19	・孔食あるいは鋼材全周の浮き・軽微な断面欠損が見られ、進行性も認められる ・鉄筋露出がある	・鋼材の断面欠損が著しく、進行性も早く、構造用鋼材としての機能が損なわれている ・漏水＋鉄筋露出がある	－
20	・かぶりが極端に薄く（10mm程度以下）そもそも鉄筋の腐食保護が期待できていない。 ・かぶりが一定以上あり、中性化深さが鋼材発生限界以上となっており、かつ、漏水・滞水・乾湿繰り返しなどが見られる。 （中性化：深さ限界以上、高含水率または乾湿繰り返し） ・かぶりが一定以上あり、塩化物濃度が鋼材腐食限界以上になっているが、飛来塩分・塩分含有漏水等は見られない。 （塩害：限界濃度以上、塩分供給なし）	・かぶりが一定以上あり、塩化物濃度が鋼材腐食限界以上で、飛来塩分・塩分含有漏水等が見られる。（塩害：限界濃度以上、塩分供給なし）あり	・かぶりが極端に薄く、塩化物濃度が鋼材腐食限界以上で、飛来塩分・塩分含有漏水等が見られる。（塩害：かぶり薄、限界濃度以上、塩分供給あり）
21	－	－	－
22	・漏水が見られ、ひび割れ・浮き等他の変状と複合している。 ・漏水が見られ、他の変状との複合はないが、水質に問題がある可能性がある（沿岸、河川交差、工場近接等）または水質が悪い ・漏水が流下することでひび割れにかかる位置に漏水が発生している，または，後がある ・剥落危険範囲(アーチ上部)から漏水があり，ひび割れが生じることでひび割れと漏水が複合するおそれがあるため５点とする	・漏水が見られ、他の変状との複合しており、水質に問題がある可能性がある（沿岸、河川交差、工場近接等）または水質が悪い ・漏水がひび割れや鉄筋腐食と複合している	－
23	－	－	－
24			・列車運行に関わる諸設備に影響する範囲に剥落の危険性がある
25			・列車運行に関わる諸設備に影響する範囲の鋼材腐食が著しい
26			・列車運行に関わる諸設備に影響する範囲への漏水かかり量が一定以上で、塩分等を含んでおあり、諸設備が痛んで見れる
27	－	－	－
28	－	－	－
29	－	－	－
30	－	－	－
31	－	－	－
32	－	－	－
33	－	－	－
34	－	－	－
35	－	－	－
36	－	－	－
37	－	－	－

表 6　重み係数(鉄道シールドトンネル)

大項目		中項目		小項目	
A利用者の安全性能	0.317 (0.125)	A1利用者が安全に走行できる	0.152 (0.222)	A11走行安全性能を支障するようなトンネル変形が生じない	0.052 (0.128)
				A12線形が適切で走行安全性能を支障するようなトンネル変化が生じない	0.050 (0.148)
				A13走行安全性能を支障するようなはく落・漏水が生じない	0.050 (0.210)
		A2利用者の安全を直接脅かさない	0.092 (0.197)		
		A3非常時に防災設備が確実に機能できる	0.073 (0.191)		
B利用者の使用性能	0.124 (0.075)	B1乗り心地がよい	0.079 (0.235)		
		B2利用者に不快感・不安感を与えない	0.045 (0.235)		
C構造安定性能	0.211 (0.093)	C1常時作用する加荷重に対して安定している	0.088 (0.146)		
		C2必要な耐震性能を有している	0.039 (0.099)		
		C3想定される荷重の変化に対して安定している	0.047 (0.088)		
		C4想定される荷重の変化に対して安定している	0.037 (0.134)		
D耐久性能	0.128 (0.085)	D1鋼材の防食性がよい	0.041 (0.162)		
		D2コンクリートが劣化しない	0.037 (0.160)		
		D3止水性がよい	0.049 (0.209)		
E管理者の使用性能	0.037 (0.017)	E1必要な需要を満足できる	0.011 (0.188)		
		E2列車が安定的に(定時に)運行できる	0.015 (0.199)		
		E3列車運行のための諸設備が確実に稼動できる	0.010 (0.162)	E31列車運行に関わる諸設備を適切に配置・使用できる	0.005 (0.235)
				E32トンネル内の水が適切に排水され諸設備に影響しない	0.005 (0.235)
F維持管理性能	0.056 (0.037)	F1安全・安易に点検できる	0.031 (0.213)		
		F2安全・容易に点検ができる	0.025 (0.213)		
G周辺への影響度	0.127 (0.077)	G1地下水への影響が少ない	0.027 (0.152)		
		G2地表面への影響が少ない	0.027 (0.120)		
		G3周辺の物件への影響が少ない	0.036 (0.162)		
		G4周辺での振動・騒動が少ない	0.037 (0.178)		
合計	1.000		1.000		1.000

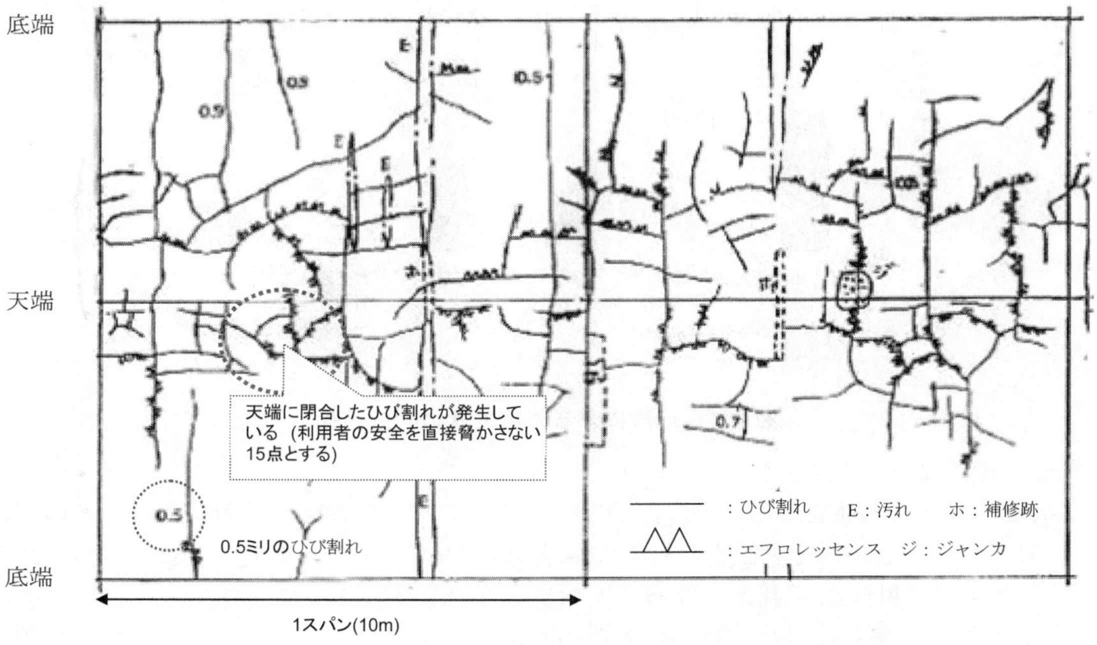

図 1　地下鉄シールドトンネル覆工展開図(二次覆工)

現行の点検評価では，主にひび割れ，漏水および材料劣化を変状要因の指標として評価している．現行の点検評価結果と保有性能評価結果の整合性を分析するため，健全度判定結果の区分(A,B,C,S)ごとに求めた *TPI* の集団を各判定区分の母集団ととらえ，母集団ごとに *TPI* の確率分布を求めた．なお，性能評価基準が無記入の項目は他の性能項目に影響しないように 1 点を与えて評価した．

4 保有性能評価結果およびその分析

(1) 現行法の判定結果と保有性能評価結果の関係

図 2 および図 3 は現行法による健全度判定区分ごとに，*TPI* の分布を示したものである．*TPI* は現行法の判定結果をほぼ表現しており，現行法の健全度判定区分ごとに *TPI* の母集団が分かれている．また健全度の低下が大きいほどボラティリティが大きくなっている．図 4 は現行法の点検判定結果の変状要因を整理したものである．

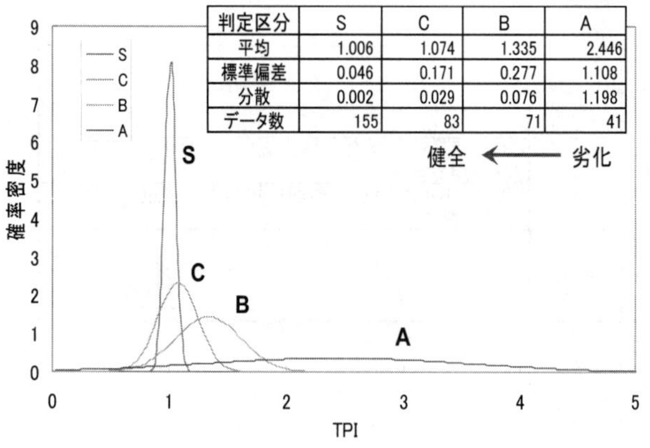

図 2 TPI の評価結果(中子形セグメントリング)

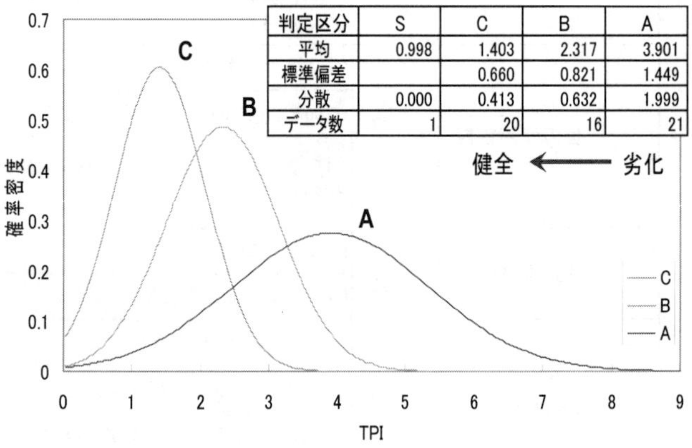

図 3 TPI の評価結果(二次覆工区間)

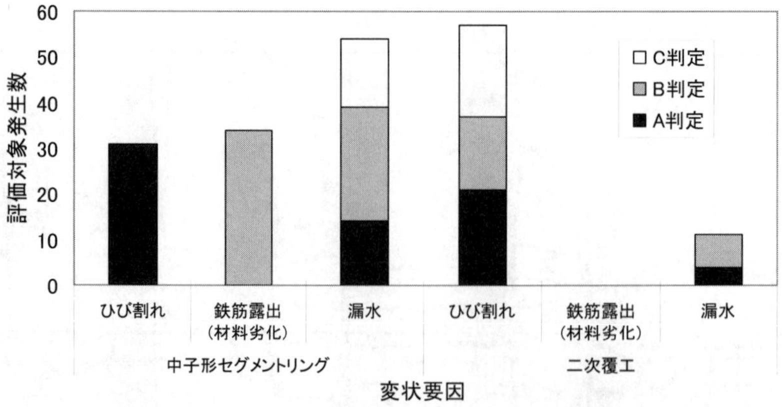

図 4 現行法による路線変状の判定結果

(2) 保有性能評価とその主要因

TPI を決定づけた要求性能大項目，要求性能中項目および要求性能小項目ごとに，どの要求性能項目が *TPI* に影響しているか，その要因を分析して保有性能評価の有効性を検討した．図 5～図 7 は中子形セグメントリングの現行法 A 判定となったリングの主要因を示したものである．図 8～図 10 は二次覆工区間の現行法 A 判定となったスパンの主要因を示したものである．なお，要求性能中項目および要求性能小項目の分布は最も影響している 6 つの要求性能項目を抽出している．

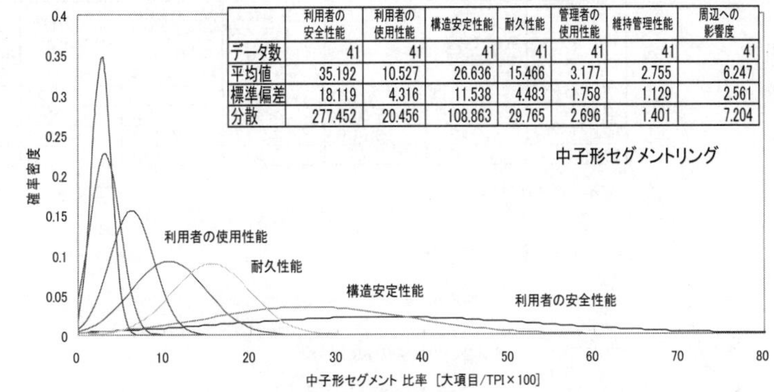

	利用者の安全性能	利用者の使用性能	構造安定性能	耐久性能	管理者の使用性能	維持管理性能	周辺への影響度
データ数	41	41	41	41	41	41	41
平均値	35.192	10.527	26.636	15.466	3.177	2.755	6.247
標準偏差	18.119	4.316	11.538	4.483	1.758	1.129	2.561
分散	277.452	20.456	108.863	29.765	2.696	1.401	7.204

図 5　要求性能大項目の主要因

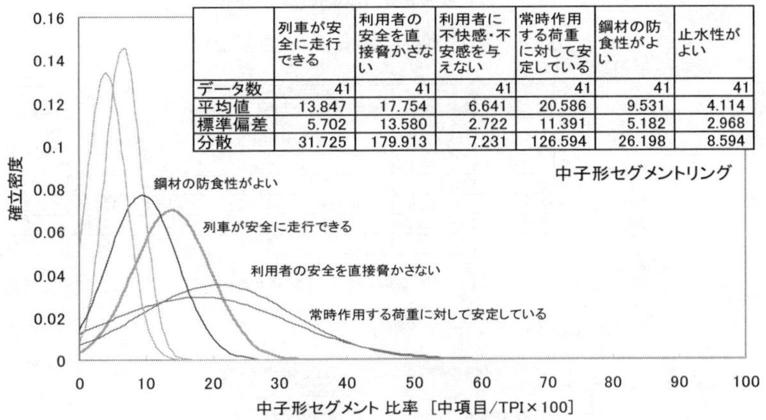

	列車が安全に走行できる	利用者の安全を直接脅かさない	利用者に不快感・不安感を与えない	常時作用する荷重に対して安定している	鋼材の防食性がよい	止水性がよい
データ数	41	41	41	41	41	41
平均値	13.847	17.754	6.641	20.586	9.531	4.114
標準偏差	5.702	13.580	2.722	11.391	5.182	2.968
分散	31.725	179.913	7.231	126.594	26.198	8.594

図 6　要求性能中項目の主要因

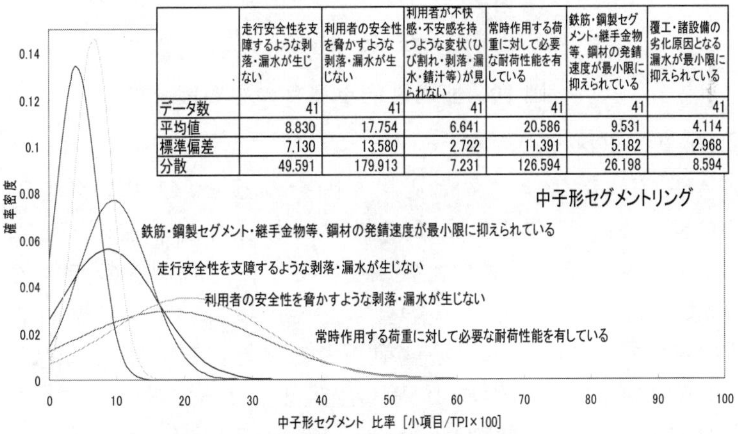

	走行安全性を支障するような剥落・漏水が生じない	利用者の安全性を脅かすような剥落・漏水が生じない	利用者が不快感・不安感を持つような変状(ひび割れ・剥落・漏水・錆汁等)が見られない	常時作用する荷重に対して必要な耐荷性能を有している	鉄筋・鋼製セグメント・継手金物等、鋼材の発錆速度が最小限に抑えられている	覆工・諸設備の劣化原因となる漏水が最小限に抑えられている
データ数	41	41	41	41	41	41
平均値	8.830	17.754	6.641	20.586	9.531	4.114
標準偏差	7.130	13.580	2.722	11.391	5.182	2.968
分散	49.591	179.913	7.231	126.594	26.198	8.594

図 7　要求性能小項目の主要因

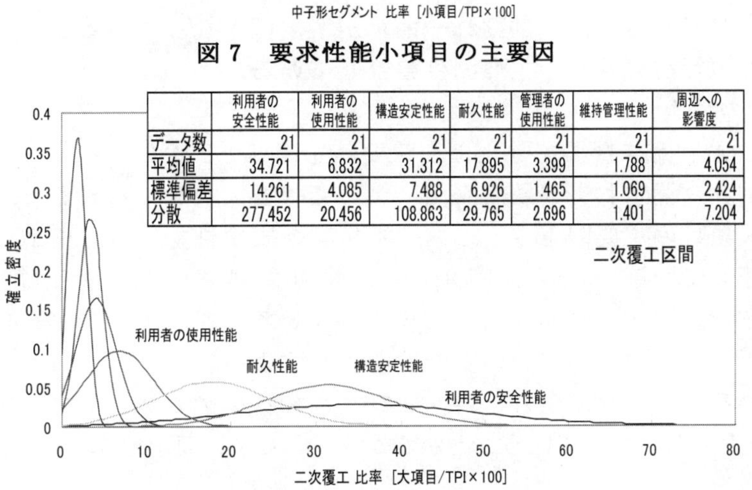

	利用者の安全性能	利用者の使用性能	構造安定性能	耐久性能	管理者の使用性能	維持管理性能	周辺への影響度
データ数	21	21	21	21	21	21	21
平均値	34.721	6.832	31.312	17.895	3.399	1.788	4.054
標準偏差	14.261	4.085	7.488	6.926	1.465	1.069	2.424
分散	277.452	20.456	108.863	29.765	2.696	1.401	7.204

図 8　要求性能大項目の主要因

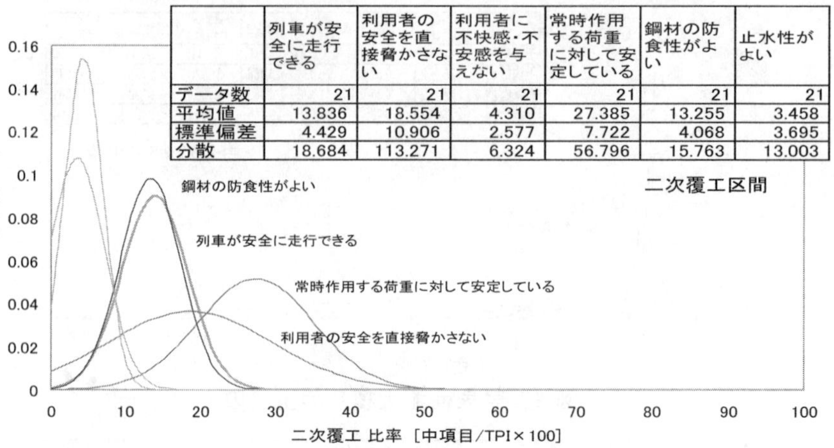

	列車が安全に走行できる	利用者の安全を直接脅かさない	利用者に不快感・不安感を与えない	常時作用する荷重に対して安定している	鋼材の防食性がよい	止水性がよい
データ数	21	21	21	21	21	21
平均値	13.836	18.554	4.310	27.385	13.255	3.458
標準偏差	4.429	10.906	2.577	7.722	4.068	3.695
分散	18.684	113.271	6.324	56.796	15.763	13.003

図 9　要求性能中項目の主要因

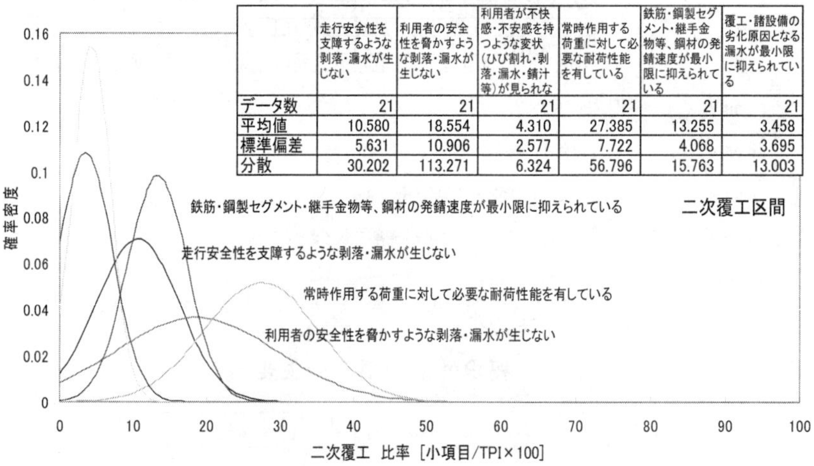

	走行安全性を支障するような剥落・漏水が生じない	利用者の安全性を脅かすような剥落・漏水が生じない	利用者が不快感・不安感を持つような変状(ひび割れ・剥落・漏水・錆汁等)が見られな	常時作用する荷重に対して必要な耐荷性能を有している	鉄筋・鋼製セグメント・継手金物等、鋼材の発錆速度が最小限に抑えられている	覆工・諸設備の劣化原因となる漏水が最小限に抑えられている
データ数	21	21	21	21	21	21
平均値	10.580	18.554	4.310	27.385	13.255	3.458
標準偏差	5.631	10.906	2.577	7.722	4.068	3.695
分散	30.202	113.271	6.324	56.796	15.763	13.003

図 10　要求性能小項目の主要因

(a)　中子形セグメントリング区間の考察

図 4 に示す現行法 A 判定に影響を与えた変状要因をみると, 41 リング中 31 リングにひび割れの変状を確認しており, ひび割れおよび漏水による変状要因が現行法の主要因となっている. 一方, 図 5 に示す中子形セグメントの要求性能大項目の主要因をみると, “利用者の安全性能”や“構造安定性能”が *TPI* に影響している. また, 図 6 および図 7 の要求性能中項目および要求性能小項目の主要因をみると, “常時作用する荷重に対して安定している”, “利用者の安全を直接脅かさない”や“利用者の安全性を脅かすようなはく落, 漏水が生じない”の性能項目が主要因となっている. この性能項目と表 5-1 のモニタリング項目とをあわせてみると, ひび割れや漏水が主要因となっていることがわかる. よって, 要求性能項目の主要因と現行法の判定の主要因は整合している.

(b) 二次覆工区間の考察

図 4 に示す現行法 A 判定に影響を与えた変状要因をみると, 21 スパンすべてにひび割れの変状を確認しており, ひび割れ, 漏水および鉄筋露出による変状要因が挙げられる. 一方, 図 8 に示す二次覆工区間の要求性能大項目の主要因をみると, “利用者の安全性能”, “構造安定性能”および“耐久性能”が *TPI* に影響している. また, 図 9 および図 10 の要求性能中項目および要求性能小項目の主要因をみると, “常時作用する荷重に対して安定している”, “利用者の安全を直接脅かさない”, “鋼材の防食性がよい”および“利用者の安全性を脅かすようなはく落, 漏水が生じない”の性能項目が主要因となっている. この性能項目と表 5-1 のモニタリング項目とをあわせてみると, ひび割れ, 漏水および材料劣化が主要因となっていることがわかる. よって, 要求性能項目の主要因と現行法の判定の主要因は整合している.

5 まとめ

本研究は既存の地下鉄シールドトンネルの保有性能評価を検討した．その結果，階層分析法(AHP)を用いることで，地下鉄シールドトンネルの総合的な保有性能を *TPI* で定量的に評価する有効性が示された．また，*TPI* を決定づけた主要因と現行法による主要因が整合することを確認した．

今後は多くの路線や区間を数量化とした分析を行い，より精度の高い保有性能評価手法を検討する予定である．

参考文献（References）：

[1] 土木学会　包括設計コード策定基礎調査委員会：包括設計コード(案)　性能設計概念に基づいた構造物設計コード作成のための原則・指針と用語　第 1 版，2003.2.

[2] 例えば，財団法人　鉄道総合技術研究所：鉄道構造物維持管理標準・同解説(構造物編)トンネル，pp16,55~57，2007.1.

[3] 木村定雄，山本努：日本におけるシールドトンネルの設計法の変遷と性能規定の提言，第 5 回日中シールド技術交流会，2009.9.

[4] 土木学会：性能規定に基づくトンネルの設計とマネジメント，トンネルライブラリー21，2009.10(発刊予定)

[5] ISO13822:Bases for design of structures – Assessment of existing structures,2001.12.

[6] 社団法人土木学会：トンネル・ライブラリー14　トンネルの維持管理，p3,185，2005.7.

[7] 木下栄蔵：入門 AHP－決断と合意形成のテクニック，p２，2006.4.

[8] 木下栄蔵：AHP 手法と応用技術，1993.8.

[9] 地下空間委員会・トンネル工学委員会 :地下構造物のライフサイクルデザイン/マネジメント一時代に求められる良質な地下構造物のつくり方とつかい方のトレンドー, 土木学会全国大会, 研究討議会資料, p.18, 2007.9.

[10] 東京地下鉄株式会社：建造物検査規則，2004.4.

[11] 安田亨，畑生浩司　内藤幸弘，野田賢治：トンネルのデザインとマネジメント(9)　トンネルの性能照査型マネジメント手法の検討，土木学会第 62 回年次学術講演会概要集，6-174，p347，2007.9.

著者紹介（Bio-data）：

横山　正浩　金沢工業大学大学院

Masahiro YOKOYAMA　Kanazawa Institute of Technology Graduate School

木村　定雄　教授　博士(工学)　技術士(建設)　トンネル工学・建設マネジメント

Sadao KIMURA　Professor Dr. Eng. P.E.(Japan)　Tunnel Engineering and Management

s.kimura@neptune.kanazawa-it.ac.jp

Tel. +81 76-274-7704　Fax. +81 76-274-7102

山本努　東京地下鉄株式会社　工務部

YAMAMOTO Tsutomu　Tokyo Metro Co., Ltd.　Infrastructure Maintenance Dept.

E-mail:t.yamamoto@tokyometro.jp

テールシールがセグメントリングの断面力に与える影響に関する研究

鈴木雄士　高橋正朗　小泉 淳
早稲田大学 理工学術院　社会環境工学科，東京　169-8555

シールドトンネルの主体構造物であるセグメントは，組立てから裏込め注入圧が作用するまでの施工過程において，様々な施工荷重を受ける．また，最近ではシールド工事の大深度化にともない，大きな土水圧が作用する．このような状況下においても経済的な施工を可能にするためには，施工後のセグメントに土水圧のみが作用するような状況を作りだすことが望ましい．しかし，大深度地下では，大きなテール部の接触圧がセグメントに作用し，この影響が長期にわたって残留するケースが多く見られるようになってきた．本研究はテールシールによって発生する施工時荷重のセグメントに与える影響を検討したものである．まず，テール部をモデル化した実験を行い，その変形特性やセグメントとの接触圧を推定した．つぎに，変形特性や接触圧を用いて，セグメントの断面力にそれらがどの程度の影響を与えるかを算定した．
キーワード：シールドトンネル；テールクリアランス；シール材；覆工断面力；大深度地下

EFFECT OF SEALING MATERIAL AT THE TAIL OF SHIELD MACHINE ON THE SEGMENTAL LINING

Takeshi SUZUKI，Masaaki TAKAHASHI，Atsushi KOIZUMI
Department. of Civil and Environmental Engineering, Faculty of Science and Engineering, Waseda University, Tokyo 169-8555, Japan

Abstract: Segmental lining is the main structure of shield-driven tunnel. Many kinds of loads are acted on it during its construction. When shield is driving in deep underground, large earth pressure and water pressure act on the lining. In this condition, shield-jacking pressure has to enlarge to resist these large external pressures. With this fact, the segmental lining suffers with many kinds of effect due to assembly of the segment and driving of the shield machine. Among these effects, one of the serious problems is the contact pressure that acts on the segment at the tail of shield machine. The stress occurred in the segment due to this effect may remain for long time after construction of shield tunnel. In this paper, the contact pressure between the segment and tail seal is verified through model tests and *in-situ* measurements, and the stress occurred in segmental lining is discussed.
Key words: shield tunnel; tail-clearance; sealing material; lining stress; deep underground

1　はじめに

シールドトンネルの覆工部材であるセグメントは，トンネルの主体となる構造部材でありながら，その組立て後にジャッキ推力やテールシールの接触圧，裏込め注入圧などの施工時荷重を受ける特殊な部材である．従来から，最大の施工荷重であるジャッキ推力の影響については多くの研究がなされ[例えば1)]，セグメントの検討とあわせて，ジャッキ推力の大きさ，作用位置，および作用方向などの評価が行われてきた[2)]．

近年，シールド工事の大深度化が進み，大きな土水圧に対応するため，テールシール圧やジャッキ推力が増大し，とくに，蛇行修正時や曲線施工時には，ジャッキ推力の偏心によってテールシールの接触圧がセグメントに偏って作用することから，セグメントとテールシールとの接触圧が原因と考えられるセグメントの損傷が増加する傾向にある．これらの傾向は定性的には確認されているが[2)]，その定量的な評価やそれが長期にわたってセグメントに与える影響などは未解明の状況にある．

大深度地下におけるシールド工事では，施工時荷重の影響が長期にわたって残留することが多くなるものと予想されている．経済的で品質のよいシールドトンネルを構築するためには，施工時荷重をよ精度よく評価する必要性が強く指摘されている．

本研究は，セグメントとテールシールとの接触圧に着目して，まず，テールブラシの模型実験を行い，その変形特性やセグメントとの接触圧を推定し，つぎに，実際の現場における計測結果を用いて，テールシールがセグメントリングの断面力に与える影響を検討したものである．

2　模型実験

2.1　実験の概要

実験は図-1 に示すように，テールシールを部分的に取り出し，シールドテール内の状況をモデル化した実験治具を用いて行った．実験治具は外枠と内枠とからなり，内枠の底面にテールブラシをボルトにより固定した．内枠が鉛直方向に 130 mm 変位したとき，外枠の底面に内枠の底面が接触するように設計されている．

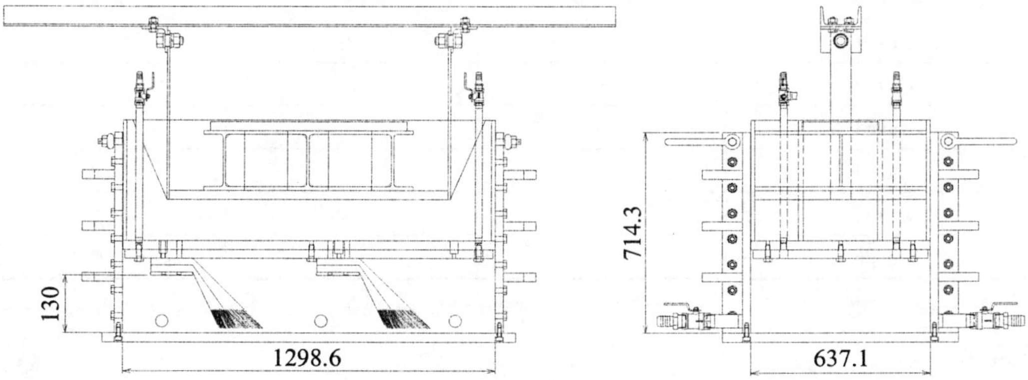

図-1　実験治具（単位：mm）

テールブラシは東京メトロ１３号線の高田Ａ線工区で実際に用いたブラシと同じもの(図-2)を４枚使用している．

2.2　実験の方法

図-3 は実験に用いた載荷装置を示したものであり，これによりテールブラシおよびテールグリスに一軸圧縮荷重を作用させた．

圧力変換器と変位計は，図-4 に示すように設置し，試験装置全体に作用する荷重と相対変位との関係，テールブラシの押付けにともなうテールグリスの圧力を計測している．

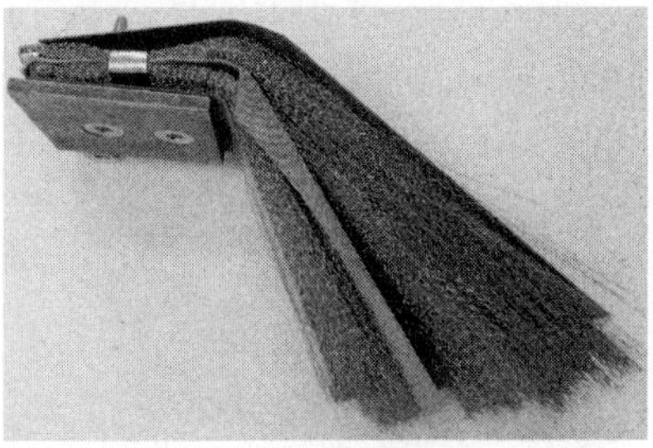

図 2　テールブラシ

荷重の載荷ピッチは，テールブラシのみを用いた予備試験結果にもとづいて，適切な荷重－変位曲線が得られるように設定した．テールブラシの自重によるつぶれ量は，予備試験で把握し，必要に応じてその影響を除去した．

表-1 は実施した実験のケースを示したものである．Case1 はテールブラシのみの場合，Case2 はグリスのみの場合であり，Case3 はテールブラシにグリスを入れた場合，Case4 はテールブラシに裏込め材を入れた場合，Case5 はテールブラシにグリスと裏込め材を入れた場合，Case6 は，これに加えて裏込め注入材の塊(440×265×50mm)を治具内の中央に入れた場合をそれぞれ表している．グリスを入れたケースでは，外枠の下部に設置した管から適宜テールグリスを抜くことで，圧力 0.30MPa を保持しながら載荷した．また，Case4，5，6 は裏込め材がテールシールに流入して固化した状況を想定したものであり，テールブラシにあらかじめ裏込め材を詰めて固化させてから実験を行ったケースである．裏込め注入材の材齢は実状を考慮して２日とした．

図-3　載荷実験の状況

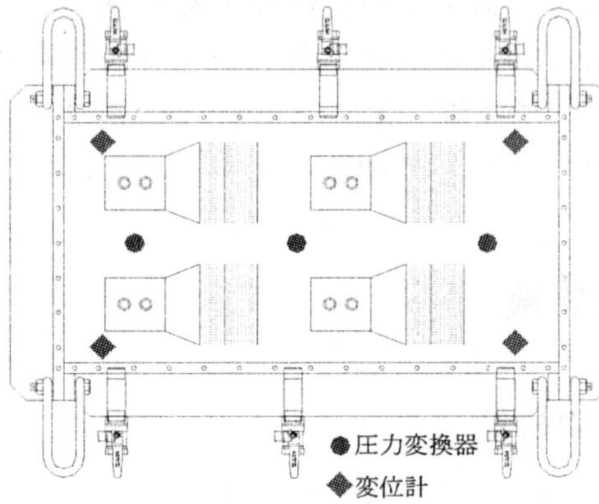

図-4　計測器の配置

表-1　実験のケース

実験ケース	ブラシ	グリス	裏込め材
Case1	○	×	×
Case2	×	○	×
Case3	○	○	×
Case4	○	×	○
Case5	○	○	○
Case6	○	○	○（塊）

2.3　実験結果

図-5 は載荷荷重と鉛直変位量との関係を示したものである．Case3,5,6 では，テールグリスの影響

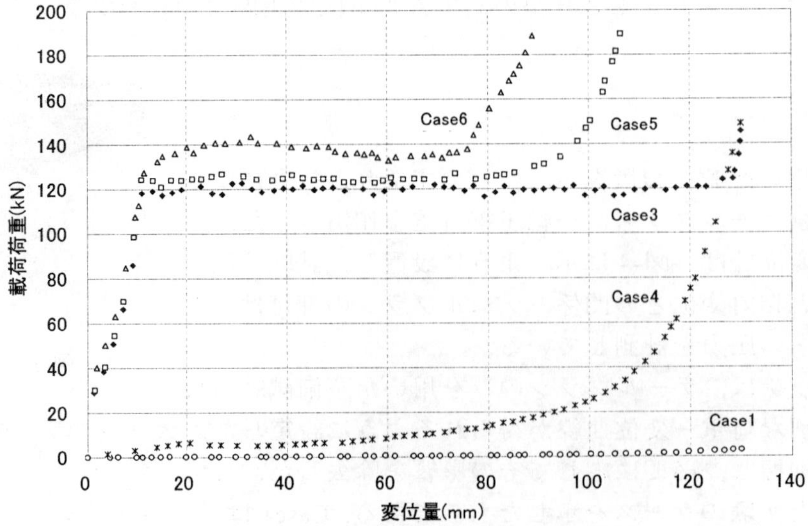

図-5　実験結果

により載荷の初期に鉛直上向きの変位が発生したので，内枠と外枠が接触するときを 130 mm として補正した．Case2 は，Case3 と同様な関係を示したので省略する．

Case1 からテールブラシのみでは荷重が無視できるほど小さいことがわかる．また，Case4 についても，内枠と外枠が接触する直前では 150 kN の荷重が作用しているが，クリアランスが十分ある場合には Case1 と同様に無視できると思われる．これらのことから，テールグリス圧がテールシール接触圧にもっとも大きな影響を与えることがわかる．

Case3,5,6 を比較すると，裏込め注入材とその塊により立ち上がり位置が早まっていることがわかる．内枠と外枠の距離は Case5 では 30 mm，Case6 では 50 mm となっている．これは，実際の現場のテールクリアランスとしては標準的な大きさであり，テールクリアランスが比較的大きくても，セグメントに損傷を与えうる程の大きな接触圧が作用する可能性があることを示している．

図-5 から，テールシール部のばね（以下，シールばねと呼ぶ）のばね定数を算出するにあたり，安全側を考慮して最初の立ち上がり部分を採用することにした．テールクリアランスが大きいときは Case3(変位量 3.2 mm から 11.0 mm)，テールクリアランスが小さいときは Case5(7.2 mm から 10.8 mm) の傾きからばね定数を算出した．その結果，以下の値が得られた．

$$k_1=12\ 057\ (\mathrm{kN/m^3})$$

$$k_2=13\ 172\ (\mathrm{kN/m^3})$$

3　現場計測

3.1　計測の概要

検証の対象とした断面は，副都心線の千駄ヶ谷工区の３断面であり，断面①は発進から３０リング目（直線部），断面②は８８リング目（直線部），断面③は３５６リング目（曲線部 R=253 m）である．各計測断面の周辺地盤は N 値 50 以上の安定した洪積世以前の土層であり，長期的にトンネルに作用する土圧はあまり大きくないものと推測されることから，施工荷重の影響を確認しやすい条件であると考えられた[3)]．

図-6　副都心線路線図

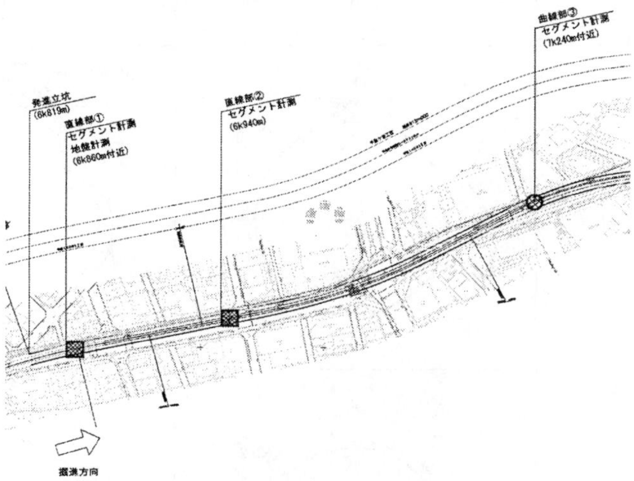

図-7　計測位置の平面図

断面①，②のセグメントはセグメント幅が B=1 600 mm，厚さが h=400 mm，断面③はセグメント幅が B=1 200 mm，厚さが h=400 mm のＲＣ平板形セグメントである．セグメント継手にはスライドロック継手を，リング継手には TA-SRING 継手を用いている．図-8 に示すように，周方向鉄筋計，軸方向鉄筋計，土圧計，テールクリアランス計をそれぞれ配置して計測が行われた．

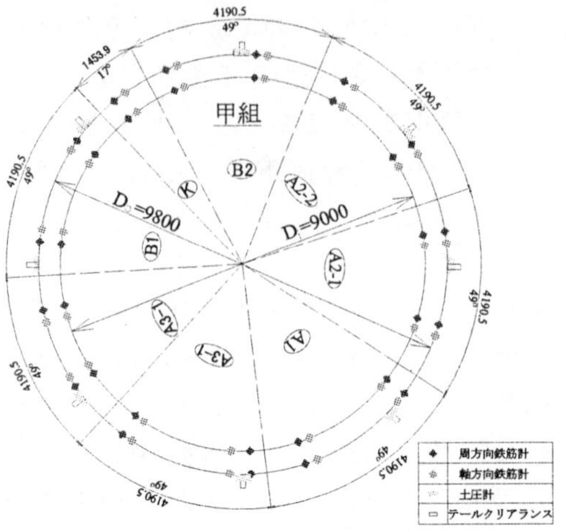

図-8 セグメントの計測位置

3.2 計測結果

図-9は各断面において，土圧計が最大値を示した時刻におけるテールクリアランス，テールシールの接触圧（以下接触圧と略称する），曲げモーメント，軸力の計測結果を示した図である．図中の角度はトンネルの頂部を0°として時計回りを正にして示している．

	荷重分布/(kPa) テールクリアランス(mm)	曲げモーメント/ (kN·m/ring)	軸力/ (kN/ring)
断面① 直線	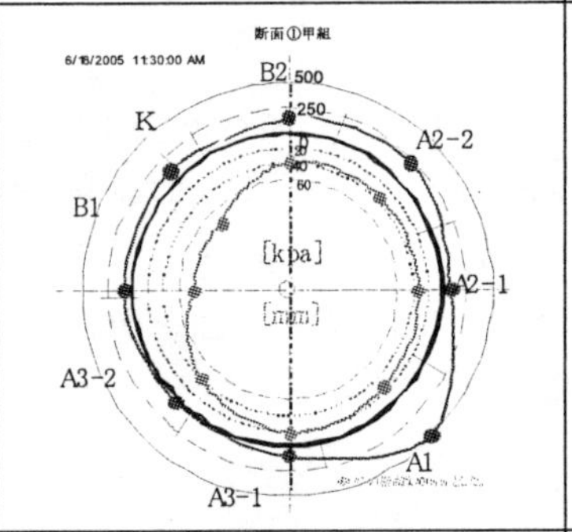	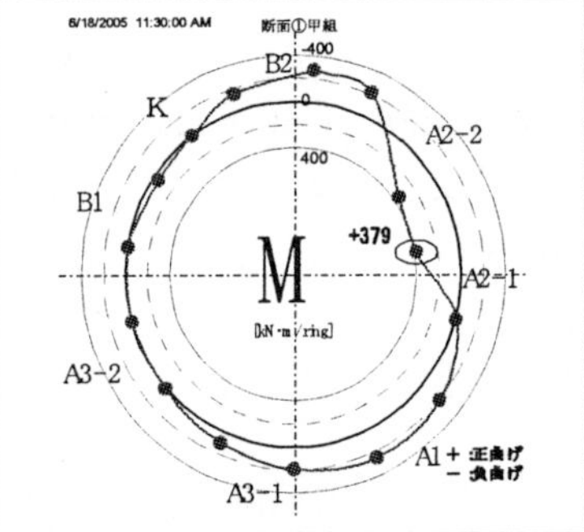	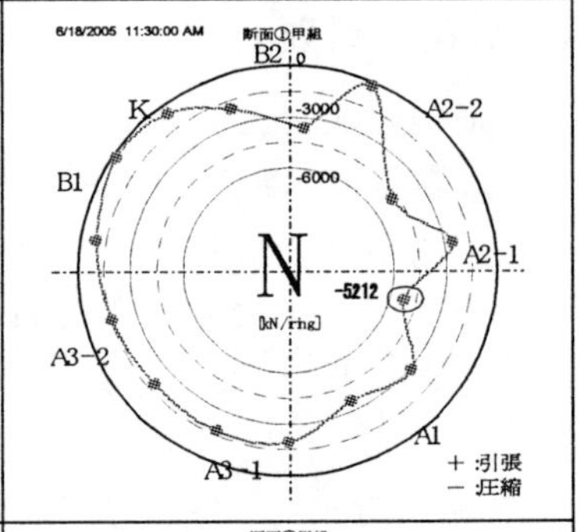
断面② 直線	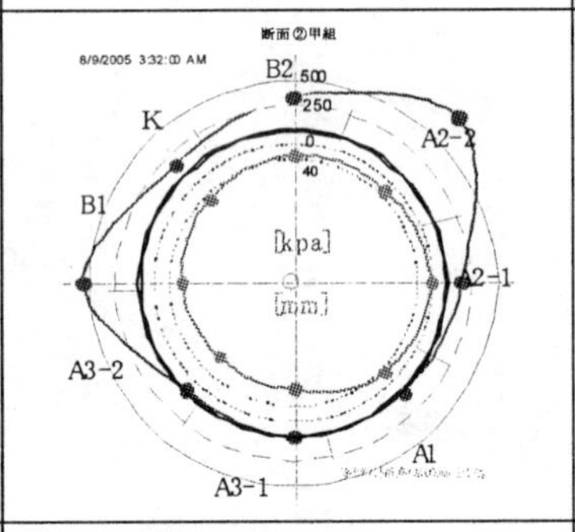	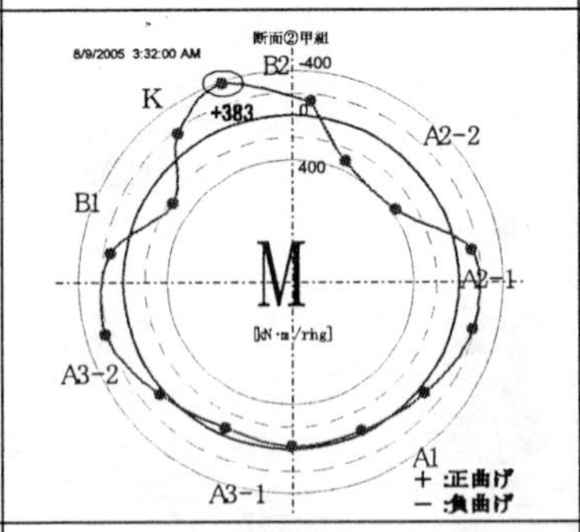	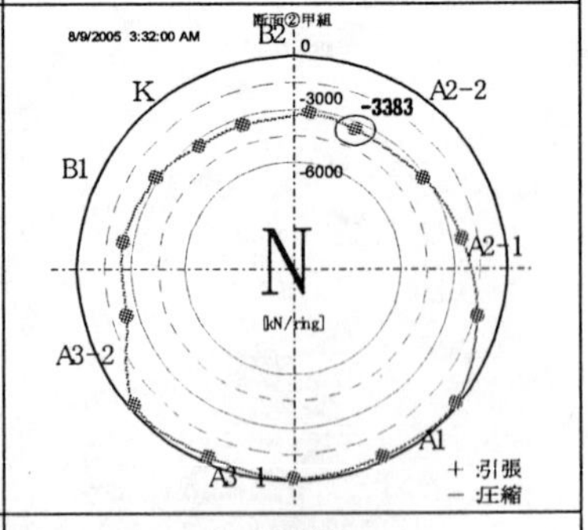
断面③ 曲線	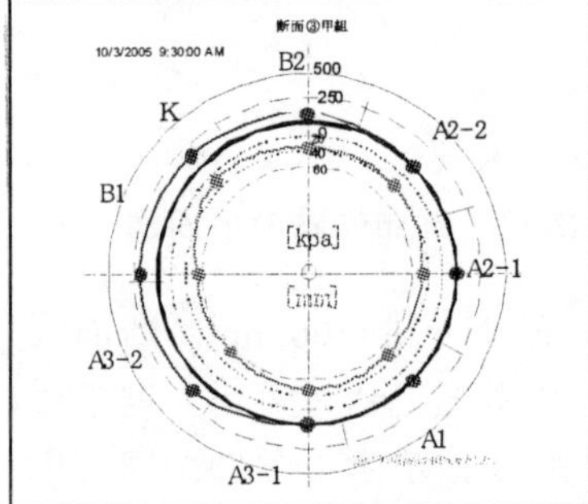	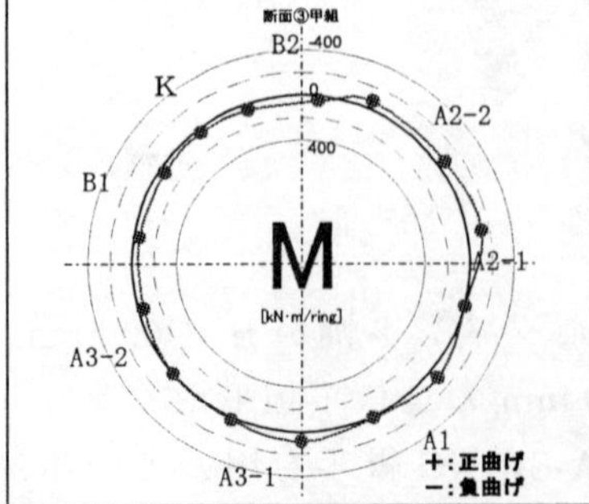	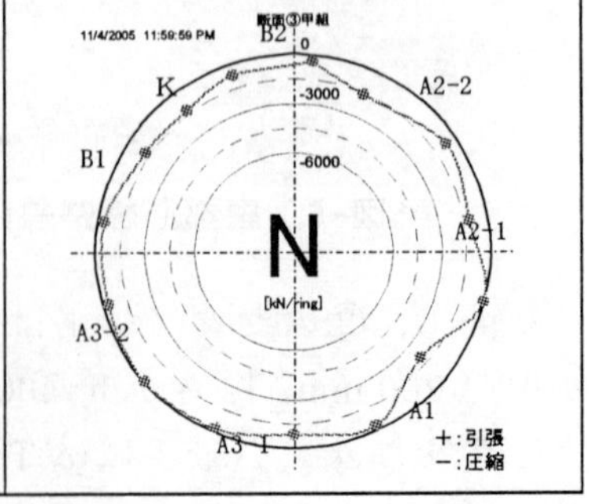

図-9 テールシールの接触時の計測結果

接触圧とテールクリアランスとの関係をみると，テールクリアランスが小さい計測点では，接触圧が大きく作用していることが確認でき，テールクリアランスの大小が接触圧の大きさに影響を与えていることがわかる．しかし，他の計測点に比べて，断面①の 135°の計測点と断面②の 45°と 270°の計測点では非常に大きな接触圧が計測された．これは，裏込め注入材がテールブラシに浸入して固化したためと思われる．

一方，接触圧と発生した断面力との関係をみると，接触圧が大きい計測点では，正の曲げモーメントが発生していることがわかる．また，比較的接触圧が小さい計測点では，負の曲げモーメントが発生し，軸力が大きくなる傾向が確認できる．これらのことから，テールシールの接触圧はセグメントに発生する断面力に大きな影響を与えることがわかる．

4　数値解析

4.1　数値解析の概要

解析には「シェルーばねモデル解析ソフト，MOLEMAN-i」を用いた．これは「はりーばね構造モデル」のはりにあたる部分をシェルに置き換える以外は，「はりーばね構造モデル」と同様な考え方で，セグメントリングを解析するソフトである．この解析ソフトに，テールシールの実験から得られたシールばねを組み込んで解析を行った．解析の対象リングは切羽側から 5 リングまでとした．

4.2　解析条件

表-2 はＲＣセグメントの諸元を，表-3 および表-4 はそれぞれセグメント継手とリング継手のばね定数を示したものである．セグメント継手およびリング継手の圧縮方向の軸ばねのばね定数は，それらの実状を考慮して数値解析上無限大とした．また，セグメント継手およびリング継手の回転ばね定数は，小泉らの提案式[4),5),6),7)]から算出した．なお，セグメント継手の無次元した回転ばね定数は $k^*=0.5$ である．

表-2　セグメント諸元

半径(m)	4.7
ヤング率(kN/m^3)	4.05×10^7
ポアソン比	0.2
単位体積重量(kN/m^3)	26.5
セグメント高さ(m)	0.4

表-3　セグメント継手のばね定数

軸ばね	圧縮(kN/m)	∞
	引張(kN/m)	1.55×10^6
せん断ばね	(kN/m)	∞
回転ばね	(kN/m)	3.62×10^4

シールばねのばね定数は，表-5 に示すように，セグメントリングがテールシール部を通過するとき，裏込め注入時，地盤に出た後を区分して用いた．このうち，テールシール部を通過するときは，接触部のテールクリアランスが 30 mm 以上の場合は Case3 のばね定数を，30 mm 未満のときは Case5 のばね定数を用いている．また，裏込め注入時のばね定数は Case6 から算出した安全側の値を用いた．なお，表-5 にはトンネル周辺地山の地盤ばねのばね定数も併せて示してある．また，表-6 はシールばねのばね定数をテールクリアランスの減少量との関係で示したものである．

表-4　リング継手のばね定数

軸ばね	圧縮 (kN/m)	∞
	引張 (kN/m)	8.5×10^7
せん断ばね	(kN/m)	1.83×10^5
回転ばね	(kN/m)	4.4×10^5

表-6　シールのばねのばね定数

テールクリアランスの減少量	ばね定数(kN/m^3)
10mm 以下	12057
10mm 以上	13172

表-5　シールばねおよび地盤ばねのばね定数

		圧縮	引張
Case3	法線	1.21×10^4	6.05×10^3
	接線	4.03×10^3	4.03×10^3
Case5	法線	1.32×10^4	6.59×10^3
	接線	4.39×10^3	4.39×10^3
Case6	法線	1.77×10^4	8.89×10^3
	接線	5.92×10^3	5.92×10^3
地盤	法線	7.00×10^4	3.50×10^4
	接線	2.33×10^4	2.33×10^4

現場計測結果を参考にして，セグメントリングにジャッキ推力，テールシールの接触圧，裏込め注入圧，土水圧を施工過程に応じて作用させた．すなわち，テールシールの接触圧は切羽側の１リング目の中間から２リング目の中間までにわたって作用させ，裏込め注入圧は２リング目の中間から３リング目の中間まで作用させた．また，ジャッキ推力による偏心荷重として，テールクリアランス量に応じたモーメントを作用させている．なお，５リング目の坑口側の境界条件は完全固定とした．

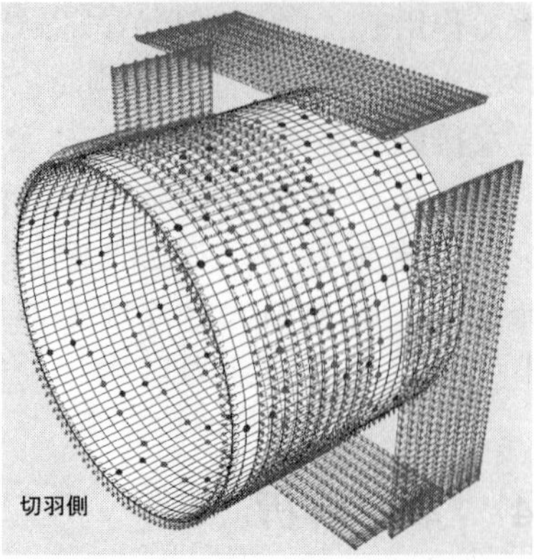

図-10　解析モデルと荷重

4.3　解析結果

図-11 は「シェルーばねモデル」によって得られた断面②の曲げモーメント図を示したものであり，図-12 はその解析結果と現場計測結果とを比較して示したものである．図-12 に示す断面力は，テールシールの影響がもっとも大きく現れると思われる 1 リング目の結果である．

図-11 から，切羽側から 1 リング目と 2 リング目に大きな曲げモーメントが発生していることがわかる．とくに,リング間の境界付近に曲げモーメントが集中していることがわかる．

図-12 をみると, 曲げモーメントは 0°から 225°の位置において,解析結果が現場計測結果によく符合していることがわかる．300°の位置では多少の誤差があるが，この位置にはテールグリスのポンプが存在するため,ポンプからの突出圧によって局所的に大きな荷重が作用したのではないかと考えられる．軸力の解析結果は，トンネルの頂部付近で大きく，下部付近で小さくなっており，計測結果の軸力分布形状と概ね一致していることがわかった．

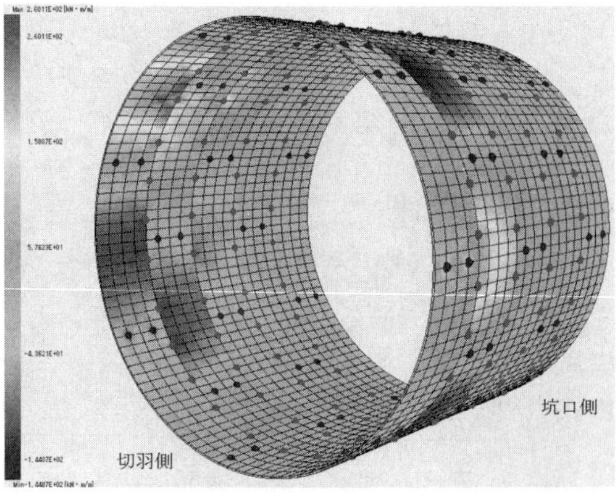

図-11　曲げモーメントのコンター図

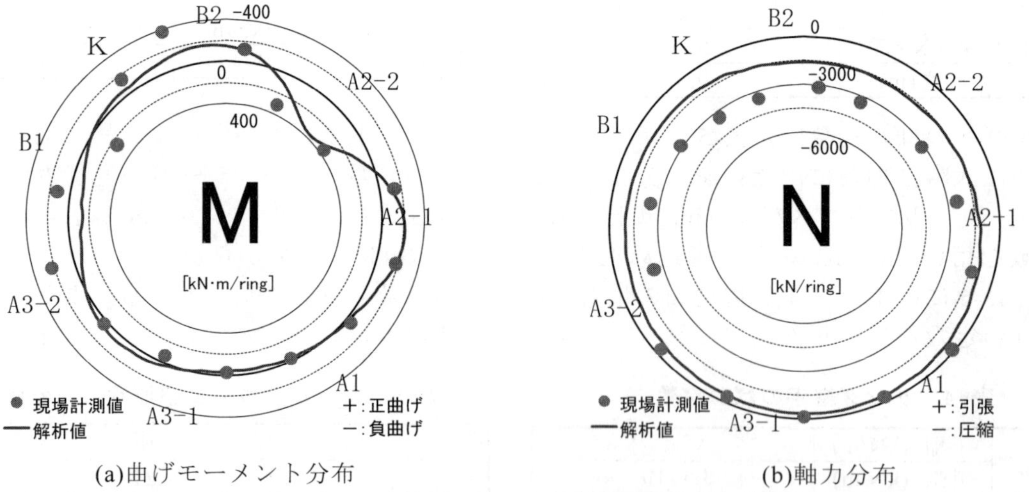

図-12　現場計測結果と解析結果との比較

5　結論

テールシールの模型実験および現場計測の数値解析から以下の知見が得られた．

(1) テールシールとセグメントとの間の接触圧のうち，テールブラシの反発力のみによる接触圧は無視できるほど小さく，テールグリス圧の影響が大きいことがわかった．しかし，裏込め注入材がテールブラシの内側で固化すると，テールクリアランスが十分大きくてもセグメントに多大な影響を与えるほどの接触圧が発生することがわかった．このことは，ジャッキ推力などの施工時荷重と同様に,テールシール部の接触圧をセグメントの設計段階において検討する必要があることを示している．

(2) 現場計測結果と数値解析結果との比較から，シールばねを用いて，「シェルーばねモデル」により解析を行うことは有効であることがわかった．

(3) シールばねのばね定数に，設計テールクリアランス量からテールクリアランスの減少量を乗じることで，テールシールの接触圧が容易に算定できる．

今後は，複数の工区で得られた現場計測結果を用いて，本研究で提案した「シェルーばねモデル」による解析の妥当性を検証する予定である．また，FEMを使った数値解析も実施して，シールばねのばね定数や接触圧の推定法の検討も進めていく予定にしている．

謝辞

本研究を進めるにあたり，東京地下鉄株式会社と日本シビックコンサルタント株式会社には，貴重な現場データをご提供いただき，また，実験に際してもいろいろとお世話をいただいた．関係各位に深甚の感謝の意を表する次第である．

参考文献（References）：

[1] 鈴木哲太郎，張穏軍，小泉淳：ジャッキ推力による鋼製セグメントの座屈挙動に関する研究，トンネル工学報告書，vol16，pp319-324.

[2] 土木学会，トンネル工学委員会：トンネル標準示方書[シールド工法]・同説，pp48-49.

[3] 矢萩秀一，荻野竹敏，沼澤憲二郎，深井直光，斉藤正幸：シールドトンネルの施工時荷重の影響に関する現場計測結果と考察，トンネル工学論文集，vol17，pp63-74.

[4] 小泉淳，村上博智，岡村光政，大塚一雄：セグメント継手の合理的な設計法に関する研究（1），早稲田大学理工学研究所報告 82 輯.

[5] 小泉淳，村上博智，当麻純一，菊田征勇：セグメント継手の合理的な設計法に関する研究（2），早稲田大学理工学研究所報告 88 輯.

[6] 小泉淳，村上博智，新延泰生，日比野悦久：セグメント継手の合理的な設計法に関する研究（3），早稲田大学理工学研究所報告 101 輯.

[7] 小泉淳，上原精治，三上博，石田智朗：シールドトンネルの軸方向剛性確認実験，土木学会論文集 No.418/Ⅲ－13.

著者紹介（Bio-data）：

鈴木　雄士

早稲田大学　理工学術院　創造理工学研究科　建設工学専攻　修士課程２年

研究内容：テールシールがセグメントリングの断面力に与える影響に関する研究

施工時荷重による鋼製セグメントの継手に発生する目開きのメカニズムに関する研究

Takeshi SUZUKI, 2nd-year master's degree student at Dept. of Civil and Environmental Engineering, Faculty of Science and Engineering, Waseda University .

Studies: The Effect on the Segmental Lining by Sealing Material at the Tail of Shield Machine

The Deflection Behavior for Joint Plates of Steel Segment in Construction.

E-mail: sky-dream@toki.waseda.jp

PART TWO

EQUIPMENT AND CONSTRUCTION

设备与施工

小覆土水底隧道盾构掘进泥水压力研究

袁大军[1] 黄清飞[1] 尹凡[1] 王胤[1] 王华伟[2]
[1]北京交通大学 隧道及地下工程教育部工程中心，北京 100044
[2]中铁十四局集团有限公司，山东 济南 250014

【摘 要】 在我国过江跨海软土隧道中，泥水盾构成为了应用最多的工法。泥水盾构的最大特点是以泥水压力维持开挖面稳定。一般条件下，泥水压力的设定以及泥水特性的选择有较成熟的方法安全设定，是没有问题的。但在水底隧道高水压小覆土的条件下，如何设定泥水压力以及选择泥水特性，用以防止由于泥水劈裂地层发生泥水喷发或开挖面坍塌事故的发生是工程成败的关键。本论文在充分讨论小覆土水底泥水盾构掘进时，根据地形及覆土的不同，为确保开挖面稳定以及防止泥水劈裂地层，如何考虑泥水压力设定和可能存在的风险的基础上，以南京长江隧道高水压小覆土特别是地形突变段为研究对象，针对江中冲槽段地形突变，覆土急剧变浅后以较陡的坡度增加，使得既要以较大的泥水压力维持开挖面的稳定，又要防止泥水压力过大劈裂地层发生泥水喷发现象等难题展开研究。在总结室内试验及现场试验成果，具体分析劈裂可能发生位置及土水压力和泥水压力的基础上，研究分析该危险区段的合理泥水压力设定方法。提出了具体的泥水压力以及泥水特性的设定值以及掘进参数为工程所用。使工程在未采用任何加固方法的条件下，顺利通过该危险区域。为今后的类似工程积累了宝贵经验。

【关键词】 小覆土；冲槽；高水压；泥水盾构；泥水压力；开挖面稳定；劈裂；掘进速度

STUDY ON SLURRY PRESSURE DURING SHIELD TUNNELING IN SHALLOW COVER AND UNDERWATER GROUND

Dajun YUAN[1], Qingfei HUANG[1], Fan YIN[1], Yin WANG[1], Huawei WANG[2]
[1]Research Center of Tunneling and Underground Works, Beijingjiaotong University, Beijing 100044, China;
[2]CRCC 14th Bureau Group Co., Ltd. Jinan 250014, Shandong, China

Abstract: Slurry shield operation is the most widely used construction method in river-crossing and undersea tunnel in soft ground engineering in China. The key feature of shield tunnel is depending on slurry pressure to maintain cutting face stability. Generally, there is well-established method to set slurry pressure and to choose different slurry based on the performance. However, when consider the high water pressure and shallow cover condition in underwater tunnel, it is crucial to set slurry pressure and make choice on different slurry performance, which could prevent accidents of slurry gushing and cutting face collapse caused by hydraulic fracture. Based on how to consider setting slurry pressure and possible risks to ensure cutting face stability and prevent slurry hydraulic fracturing during slurry shield tunneling in shallow cover and different terrain and cover thickness, this paper focuses on the section of Yangtze River tunnel with high water pressure, shallow cover, and especially discontinuous terrain. The underwater terrain is discontinuous suddenly, and the cover soil becomes shin rapidly with the slope increasing. The tough conditions require the engineer to not only consider the large enough slurry pressure to maintain cutting face, but also prevent the pressure too high to cause accidents. Based on results of indoor test and field test, especially the specific analysis of the position where hydraulic fracturing may happened to, the paper analyze the rational setting method of slurry pressure in the risk area, provides specific slurry pressure, and set value of slurry performance and tunneling parameter for project, which made shield pass through the risk area without any reinforced method. This study also accumulates precious experiences to later similar project.

Key words: shallow cover; stamping notches; high water pressure; slurry shield; slurry pressure; cutting face stability; hydraulic fracture; tunneling speed

1 引 言

泥水盾构是现代盾构法中重要分支，在世界范围内得到了广泛的应用。特别是在过江海湖等水底软土隧道工程中，泥水盾构成为了应用最多的工法[1]。在我国在建或将建的大型跨江海软土隧道几乎都采用了泥水盾构工法[2]。泥水盾构在软土隧道施工时，为了保证施工的质量和工程安全，最重要的问题之一就是如何以泥水压力平衡开挖面土水压力来保证开挖面的稳定 2)。特别是盾构在江海中段掘进时，由于覆土厚度一般较小，水压较大，开挖面稳定难以控制，如有不慎，就有可能发生泥水劈裂地层，从而产生塌陷和江水倒灌等重大事故。泥水盾构的最大特点是以泥水压力维持开挖面稳定。一般条件下，泥水压力的设定以及泥水特性的选择有较成熟的方法安全设定，是没有问题的。但在水底隧道高水压小覆土的条件下，如何设定泥水压力以及选择泥水特性，用以防止由于泥水劈裂地层发生泥水喷发或开挖面坍塌事故的发生是工程成败的关键。对南京长江隧道南京长江隧道高水压小覆土特别是地形突变段进行了分析研究。特别是针对江中冲槽段地形突变，覆土急剧变浅后以较陡的坡度增加，使得既要以较大的泥水压力维持开挖面的稳定,又要防止泥水压力过大劈裂地层发生泥水喷发现象等难题进行了具体分析。在总结室内试验及现场试验成果，具体分析劈裂可能发生位置及土水压力和泥水压力的基础上，研究分析该危险区段的合理泥水压力设定方法。提出了具体的泥水压力以及泥水特性的设定值以及掘进参数为工程所用。使工程在未采用任何加固方法的条件下，顺利通过该危险区域。为今后的类似工程积累了宝贵经验。

2 高水压小覆土开挖面稳定及泥水劈裂问题

2.1 开挖面稳定

以泥水压力来平衡土水压力，保证开挖面的稳定是泥水盾构的基本原理。在平坦地形体条件下，由相应的经验及理论计算，一般以平面问题考虑该处的土水压力，基本没有问题。但在特殊条件下，如地层突变以及冲槽地段，应考虑地层滑移趋势，进行合理的开挖面稳定计算，如设定不好，就有失稳，造成开挖面稳定无法控制。图 1 是泥水盾构泥水压力平衡土水压力一般原理图。

2.2 泥水劈裂

关于泥水式盾构的劈裂研究，是从日本的东京湾海底公路隧道开始的。栗原（Kurihara）[3, 4]用盾构模型机对泥水盾构施工中可能产生的泥水劈裂喷发现象进行了研究。其结论是在砂土层，除了覆盖层过薄这一特殊条件以外，几乎没有发生泥水喷发的可能；而在软黏土层中，劈裂喷发发生的泥水压力与维持切削面稳定所需的泥水压力相近，文献给出了一个劈裂喷发的经验公式。但因为当时试验所用的加压液体是水，即没有考虑浆液黏性的影响。另外，因为是小型的模型试验，没有考虑

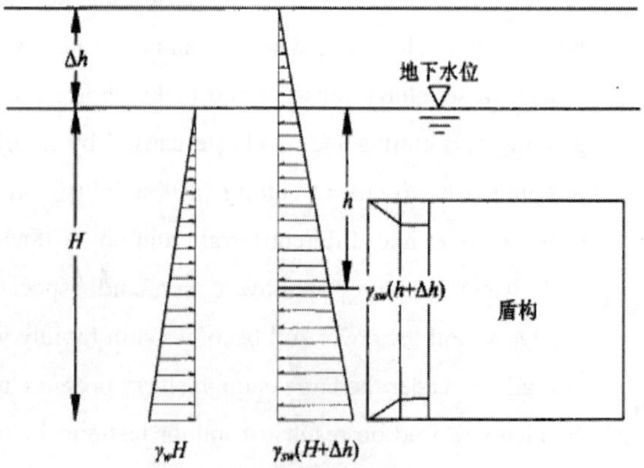

图 1 泥水盾构泥水压力作用原理

劈裂伸展的影响，难以评价工程中的劈裂喷发现象。森麟（A Mori）[5]对盾尾注浆时的劈裂现象进行了室内实验研究，并对各种黏性的浆液对劈裂压力的影响进行了研究，得出了劈裂压力与泥水的黏性和土层强度的关系（式 1）。并指出系数 α 是与泥水黏性等相关的系数。

$$P_f = \sigma_3 + \alpha q_u \tag{1}$$

式中 σ_3——小主应力；

q_u——无侧限抗压強度；

α——系数。

3 小覆土水底隧道泥水压力设定特征

水底隧道或江底隧道，一般，水底面呈 U 字型或 V 字型，应考虑具体地形条件，设定泥水压力以及泥水特性以确保开挖面稳定及工程安全。在高水压小覆土条件下，存在如图 2 所示的几种盾构掘进及土层特征，为了方便说明，把地表平坦盾构水平掘进叫做一般掘进；地表下坡盾构也下坡叫做前期掘进；地表上坡盾构也上坡叫做后期掘进。其中为了维持开挖面稳定及防止劈裂现象的发生，在泥水压力设定以及泥水特性选择时，应给与注意：

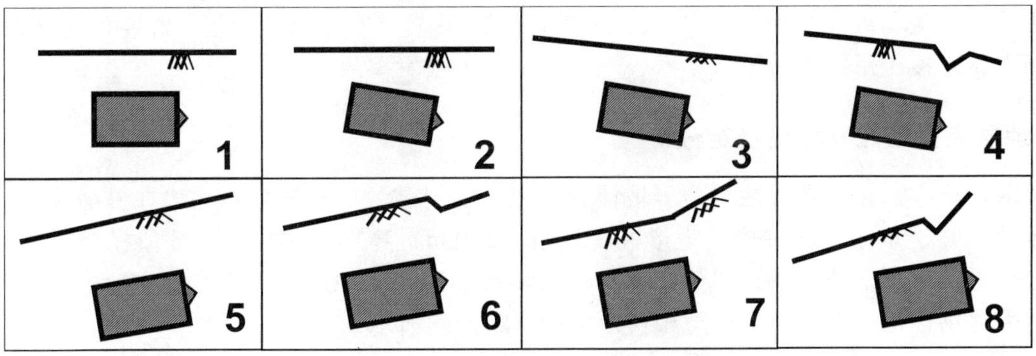

图 2 水底泥水盾构掘进特征

（1）地表（江底面）较平坦，盾构机掘进水平，一般掘进形式。江中段覆土小，水压大，地层稳定性差，需对泥水压力审慎设定及控制，对泥水特性有要求。

（2）地表较平坦，盾构机掘进朝下方向，初始掘进模式。在初始掘进段属于该种情况。从小覆土条件讲是相对安全地段，但需注意的是，泥水压力按盾构切口位置设置，在盾构中部或尾部，覆土厚度小，劈裂有可能在盾构中部或尾部发生。需对泥水压力审慎设定及控制，对泥水特性有要求。

（3）地表向下倾斜，盾构机掘进朝下方向，前期水中初始掘进模式。在盾构进入水中后属于该种情况。从小覆土条件讲是相对安全地段，但需注意的是，水压增高，需对泥水压力审慎设定及控制，对泥水特性有要求。

（4）地表向下倾斜，盾构机掘进朝下方向，前期水中初始掘进模式（有浅槽）。在盾构进入水中后属于该种情况，与（3）基本相同。但有小的浅槽出现，水压力大，需注意对泥水压力的设定及控制，防止劈裂的发生，对泥水特性有要求。

（5）地表向上倾斜，盾构机掘进朝上方向，后期水中初始掘进形式。在盾构进从江底改变掘进方向后属于该种情况。水压虽然渐渐减小，但覆土厚度也在较小的范围内，且开挖面稳定难以控制。需注意对泥水压力的设定及控制，防止劈裂的发生，对泥水特性有要求。

（6）地表向上倾斜，盾构机掘进朝上方向，有冲槽存在，冲槽过后，坡度不变。在盾构进从江底改变掘进方向后属于该种情况。水压虽然渐渐减小，但覆土厚度也在较小的范围内，且开挖面稳定难以控制。需注意对泥水压力的设定及控制，防止劈裂的发生，对泥水特性有要求。

（7）江底面呈上坡，盾构机掘进上坡；但坡度变陡，随掘进的深入，覆土厚度变大。属后期掘进时的一种情况。在该区域掘进，由于盾构前方土层变厚，开挖面稳定需较大的泥水压力，但盾尾部覆土厚度较薄，可能会出现泥水劈裂地层现象，对泥水特性有要求。

（8）江底面呈上坡，盾构机掘进上坡；且有冲槽存在，冲槽过后，坡度变陡，盾构由覆土小地段向突变覆土大地段掘进，是最大风险区域。泥水压力难以设定。必须同时满足小覆土劈裂及高覆土开挖面稳。施工难度大，地层稳定性差，需对掘进参数及泥水压力、泥水特性。南京长江隧道最危险区段就属于该类最大风险区域。

4 南京长江隧道小覆土高水压冲槽地形突变段安全泥水压力设定分析

南京长江隧道地质条件复杂，盾构掘进通过的地层以粉细砂为主，但江中地段数百米长度为粉细砂、砾砂和卵石混合地层，土质缺乏黏性，呈松散、流塑状态，稳定性很差，易坍方冒顶、造成严重后果；水压高，盾构机工作压力约 6.5bar，在同等直径及更大直径泥水盾构项目中是世界最大的。地层透水性强，长江南京河段的江中地层主要为松散、稍密～中密的粉细砂地层，以及部分砾砂、卵石层，透水系数是黏土土质的千倍以上，达到 $10^{-3}\sim10^{-4}$ cm/s。在如此条件下盾构推进具有很高的风险，尤其是江南冲槽段覆土厚度小（0.7D），而且冲槽段过后，地形坡度突然增大，开挖面稳定很难控制，稍有不慎，就有可能发生开挖面失稳或泥水劈裂地层、江水倒灌事故。因此，在此地段附近，既要保证开挖面的稳定，又要保证高水压小覆土条件下的泥水不劈裂地层发生泥水喷发事故。

4.1 冲槽地层突变区域开挖面稳定分析

采用数值计算方法和经典算法确定斜坡段水土压力的斜坡效应；经典算法已在其他论文中阐述，在此省略。数值方法选取小覆土冲槽及地形突变地段（200 m）建立地层与隧道数值模型，并对冲槽段盾构开挖面稳定进行分析，找出满足稳定要求的最大和最小泥水支护压力，为工程实际中泥水压力设定，防止地层劈裂提供理论参考。地层模型和初始水压分布如图所示：

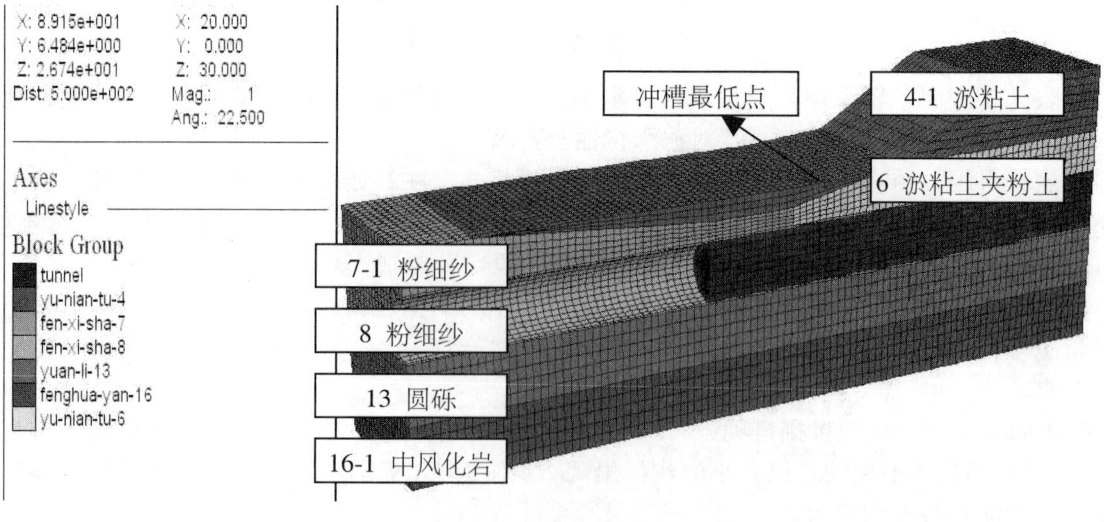

图 3 计算模型图

试算结果表明：当泥水仓中心支护压力达到 4.1bar 时，开挖面发生主动破坏，开挖面发生被动破坏的压力非常大。图 4 是泥水仓中心支护压力和开挖面水平位移的关系。

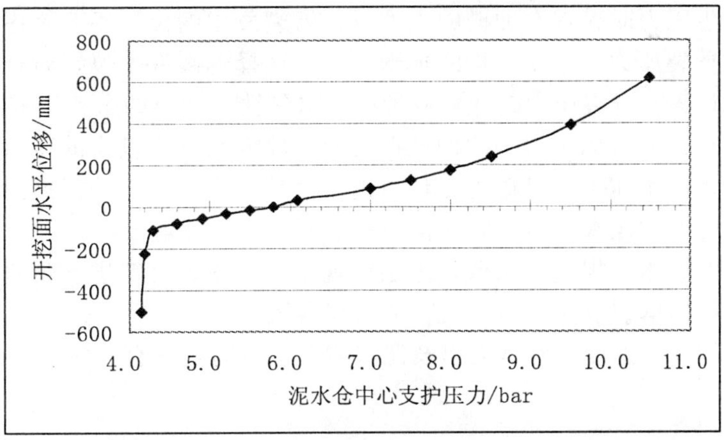

图 4 泥水仓中心支护压力和开挖面水平位移的关系曲线

4.2 冲槽地层突变区域劈裂压力

劈裂压力的计算，充分考虑盾构机切口所在位置及斜坡效应，特别是考虑切口处与盾尾处泥水压力连通的特点，即切口位置在覆土厚度较大处，而劈裂发生位置在盾尾处最小覆土处位置，如图 5 所示。根据公式(1)计算出相应位置的劈裂发生压力，其中，系数 α 根据经验及现场试验结果取 1.8。由于篇幅的原因，其计算结果及分析在此省略。

图 5 考虑斜坡效应的泥水压力及劈裂发生位置示意图

4.3 安全泥水压力的设定方法及应用

根据开挖面稳定及劈裂发生压力的计算结果，选取其中即能维持开挖面稳定的泥水压力（处于静止土压力与主动土压力之间），又能不使小覆土区域产生劈裂的泥水压力。特别注意覆土较大处的开挖面稳定的同时，其压力是否满足覆土较小处（盾尾处）的劈裂发生压力。在充分考虑泥水压力设定基准的条件下，适当考虑泥水黏性的影响，在危险区域适当增大泥水黏性。在掘进参数设定上，考虑快速掘进等方法。在穿越该地段的盾构掘进过程中，泥水压力的设定严格按照事前计算的结果设定，其误差值也严格要求。现在，南京长江隧道左线及右线均已安全通过危险区。现场检测结果证明本泥水压力设定方法是基本合理的。

5 结论及建议

本论文在分析了高水压小覆土水底泥水盾构开挖面稳定及劈裂发生压力设定方法的基础上，根据水底盾构隧道地形特征，分析研究了水底盾构隧道在冲槽存在且地层突变的条件下，泥水压力的设定必须同时考虑前方开挖面稳定及盾尾（覆土较小处）泥水劈裂地层发生泥水喷发的危险。通过对南京长江隧道具体案例的分析研究，得出了南京长江隧道高水压小覆土冲槽地形突变段的安全泥水压力设定方法，为工程所用，使工程安全顺利完成。

（1）在高水压小覆土条件下，泥水压力的设定必须同时满足开挖面稳定及不产生泥水劈裂为基本条件。

（2）在冲槽及地形突变升高地段，开挖面稳定应充分考虑地形的变化及滑动趋势计算保持开挖面稳定所需的泥水压力。在现已有经典理论计算分析的前提下，配合有限元分析计算，根据开挖面变形趋势寻求静止土压力及主动土压力。

（3）在计算劈裂发生压力时，在有冲槽的上坡段，劈裂发生的位置不应考虑切口位置，应考虑计算覆土较小的盾尾位置的劈裂压力。无论怎样的地形条件，选择劈裂发生位置时，都应选择盾构机切口至盾尾之间覆土最小位置计算；劈裂压力的计算应考虑泥水黏性等性质的影响选取 α 系数。

（4）南京长江隧道在充分考虑小覆土冲槽地形突变地段泥水压力设定的特点，在应用经典理论及有限元计算开挖面稳定所需泥水压力的基础上，计算出了劈裂发生压力，并根据同时保证开挖面稳定及不发生劈裂的原则，确定合理的泥水压力，使工程顺利地通过了危险地段。

（5）对于如何适当的泥水，规避泥水劈裂地层的现象的发生，有待进一步研究，但有一点可以肯定是泥水黏性的加大，可以使劈裂发生压力增大，适当规避风险。

（6）适当的加大盾构推进速度，对劈裂以及泥水喷发现象的发生有一定积极的作用。

参考文献（Referenles）：

[1] 孙钧. 海底隧道工程设计施工若干关键技术的商榷[J]. 岩石力学与工程学报，2006，25(8): 1513-1521.

[2] 袁大军，黄清飞等. 水底盾构掘进泥水喷发现象研究[J]. 岩石力学与工程学报，2007，26(11)：2296-2301.

[3] Akira Mori, Masahito Tamura: Hydrofracturing pressure of cohesive soils, Soils and Foundations, Vol.No.1 pp.14-22, 1987.

[4] 栗原　和夫，森　麟，田村　昌仁：泥水式シールドのブロー現象に関する実験的研究，土木学会論文集，No.397, pp.95-104, 1988.

[5] Akira Mori, Masahito Tamura, Fukui Yoshihiro: Fracturing pressure of soil ground by viscous materials, Soils and Foundations, Vol.30, No.3, pp.129-136, 1990.

作者简介（Bio-data）：

袁大军，男，1961 年 7 月生，早稻田大学博士，北京交通大学教授，博士生导师，隧道中心副主任，主要从事盾构隧道方面的教学与研究工作。

Dajun YUAN (1961—), male, graduated from Waseda University with doctor’s degree, professor and Ph.D. Supervisor of Beijing Jiaotong University, vice-director of Research Center of Tunneling and Underground Works. Now is mainly employed in the research work of shield tunneling technologies.

E-mail: yuandj603@163.com

超长距离超大直径盾构隧道若干关键施工技术研究及应用

杨国祥　林家祥　王吉云
上海隧道工程股份有限公司，上海　200082

【摘　要】 本文以上海长江隧道为工程背景，针对超长距离超大直径盾构法隧道施工难度大、风险高、工期短的特点，重点开展了高水压复杂地层条件下泥水盾构开挖面稳定、隧道施工期抗浮稳定性、超长距离快速施工新技术、联络通道施工风险控制等关键施工技术的研究，并通过工程示范应用证实了其有效性，各项研究成果可为今后同类隧道施工提供借鉴。
【关键词】 盾构隧道；同步注浆；隧道抗浮；施工技术

RESEARCH AND APPLICATION OF SOME KEY CONSTRUCTION TECHNIQUES FOR SHIELD TUNNEL WITH SUPER-LARGE DIAMETER AND SUPER-LONG DISTANCE

Guoxiang YANG，Jiaxiang LIN，Jiyun WANG
Shanghai Tunnel Engineering Co., Ltd, Shanghai 200082, China

Abstract: Based on Yangtze riverbed crossing tunnel as project background, study on some critical technical issues with salient features of high difficulties and risks, tight progress were conducted. These issues included excavation face stability under high water pressure and complex ground conditions, anti-floating stability of tunnel at construction stage, high speed mining for super long distance tunnel, risk control of cross passage construction etc. The effectiveness of research results were proved by the demonstration project, and can provide references for other similar tunnel constructions in future.
Key words: TBM mining tunnel; simultaneous grout; tunnel anti flotation; construction technology

1 引　言

近年来，随着我国市政基础设施建设的全面展开，地下空间开发和利用得到更广泛的发展，地下工程的施工技术水平有了大幅度的提高。在隧道施工方面，盾构法隧道施工技术以其独特的优势广泛应用于上海、广州、北京、深圳、南京、武汉等城市市政建设，尤其在城市道路交通网络、公路交通网络和高速公路交通网络的构建规划中。据不完全统计，至 2010 年，全国计划新建大型越江公路隧道约 30 条，累计掘进长度 66 km。过河、越江和跨海的水底隧道建设任务越来越多，建设规模越来越大。随着城市建设的迅速发展，城市的公路隧道呈现超大直径、超长距离，隧道结构功能多样化发展趋势。

国际上，代表当前超大直径泥水平衡盾构施工的隧道已有数条。荷兰“绿心隧道”采用直径为 14.87 m 泥水平衡盾构掘进施工，一次性推进 2 km 后进入工作井进行盾构检修。日本东京湾双线公路隧道单线全长近 10 km，采用 4 台直径为 14.14 m 的超大型泥水平衡盾构采用地下对接技术施工，一次性推进距离约 2.5 km；德国易北河第四隧道采用了直径为 14.2 m 德国海瑞克公司制造的混合式盾构掘进机进行施工。

在国内，上海已建成的有上中路隧道（直径为 14.87 m，一次推进 1.27 km），正在建设中的有上海长江隧道（直径为 15.43 m，一次推进 7.5 km）和上海磁悬浮隧道（直径为 14.88 m，一次推进 2.18 km）；杭州规划建造的钱江隧道（直径为 15.43 m）。针对诸多超大直径盾构隧道的建设，尤其是上海长江隧道盾构直径和一次性掘进距离均为世界之最，施工难度大、风险高、工期短的特点，开展了一系列超前施工技术的研究，并通过实际工程的应用证实是富有成效的。

上海长江隧道工程位于长江口，穿越长江南港，工程建设规模为双向双管 6 车道公路隧道，圆隧道外径 15 m，内径 13.7 m，衬砌环宽 2 m，采用ϕ15.43 m 泥水平衡盾构掘进机，掘进距离达 7.5 km。图 1 为上海长江隧道工程纵断面图。

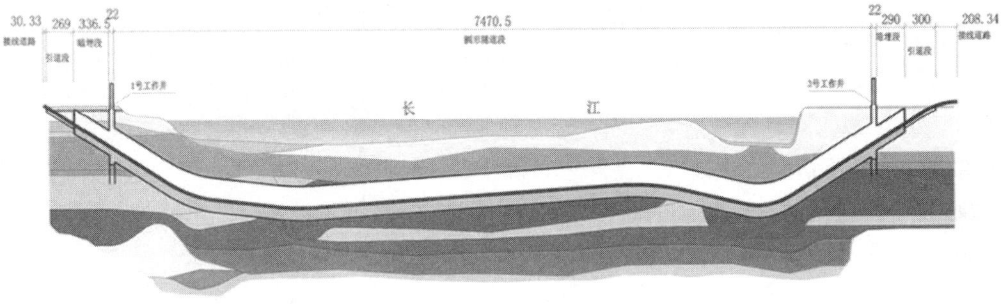

图 1　上海长江隧道工程纵断面图

2　高水压复杂地层条件下泥水盾构开挖面稳定施工新技术

2.1　盾构进出洞施工新技术

超大断面泥水平衡盾构在进出洞区域隧道的上部覆土厚度仅为隧道直径的 0.6～0.8 倍，属浅覆土施工。由于上海地区浅层土均为含水量高，空隙率高的软土地层，在松软的浅覆土层内如何确保盾构推进时切口处土体的稳定，建立有效的泥水循环，并保证洞圈密封性是超大直径盾构进出洞段的施工的关键。一旦洞口周边土体受到扰动和破坏，被扰动后的土体将难以达到良好的泥膜止水效果，无法建立正常泥水循环，并将导致泥水冒溢至地面，泥水平衡体系就会被打破。为确保出洞段土体的稳定，通常对盾构正面土体进行加固。在常规的多种加固方法的比选与试验论证后，选择了冻结法和水泥土搅拌加固两种方式(见图 2)。这两种方法分别在上海上中路隧道(盾构直径 14.87 m)和上海长江隧道(盾构直径 15.43 m)得到了应用，并取得了良好的效果。

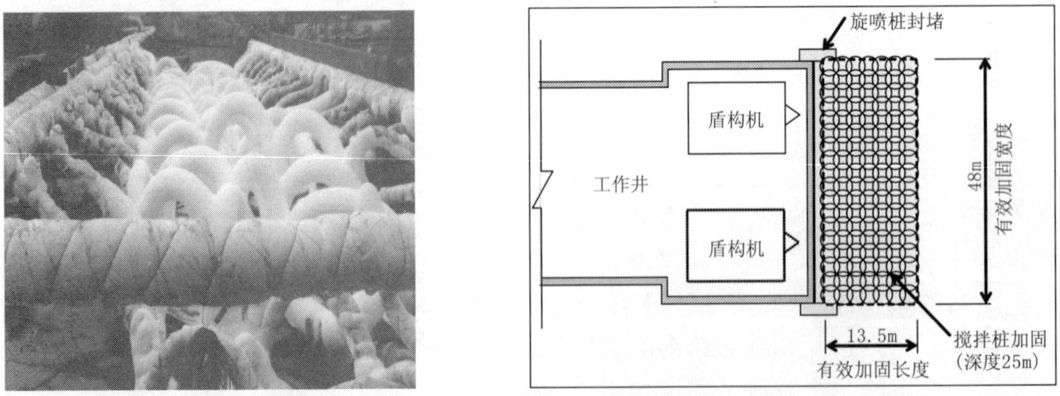

（a）冻结法加固　　　　（b）搅拌加固

图 2　盾构出洞加固方法

洞圈的止水是盾构进出洞又一施工关键技术，只有在确保盾构正面土体稳定，并且保证洞圈完全止水或内外压力平衡的情况下，盾构机正面泥水压力方能建立，泥水正常的循环才能保证。上海长江隧道和上中路隧道的盾构出洞洞圈密封均采用了如图 3 所示的止水装置。其密封的主要原理是由 2 道帘布橡胶、2 道钢丝刷以及气囊等组成。盾构出洞后，通过注浆孔对止水箱体进行注浆，同时可添加堵漏剂等辅助材料，实际应用结果表明其止水效果良好，为盾构顺利出洞建立泥水平衡提供了有利的保障。

对于含承压水的高水压条件下，复杂土层中的盾构进洞也可选用向工作井中灌水平衡的水中进洞的方法。该方法巧妙地利用了工作井外水压力平衡的原理，可减少盾构进洞区域加固范围，并可取消承压水降水引起对周边环境不利影响，是一种减小盾构进洞风险，保护周边环境的行之有效的盾构进洞的施工方法。上海长江隧道在国内首次采用了水中进洞的方法施工，并取得了成功。图 4 为盾构水中进洞的实况照片。

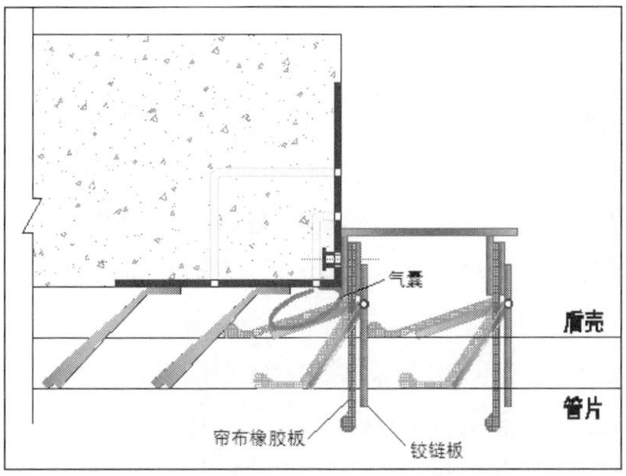

图 3 盾构出洞洞圈止水装置

图 4 盾构水中进洞

2.2 开挖面稳定施工新技术

超大直径隧道法隧道施工中，盾构开挖面的稳定性直接关系到工程的成败。确保盾构开挖面稳定是降低施工风险、提高施工安全、确保施工质量的关键施工技术。盾构机自身具备的良好的性能无疑是保证开挖面稳定的基础。上海上中路隧道和上海长江隧道采用的是泥水气平衡式盾构机，它运用了泥水压力和空气压力的双通道联合控制模式，具有压力可控制范围大，调节精度高（0.001 MPa）等特点。然而，根据施工现场的土质情况，研发一套与盾构机基本性能相适应的施工工艺和施工技术则是确保盾构开挖面稳定的关键。

为此，首次在工程实施前采用泥水盾构相似模型试验、数值模拟分析和施工三维可视化仿真技术相结合的方法，进行超大断面泥水盾构开挖面稳定、施工参数匹配的研究。通过模拟在高水压浅覆土条件下泥水盾构的推进试验（见图 5），并结合二维和三维数值静态模拟分析开挖面受力机理、变化特征和极限破坏形式，以及采用超级计算机进行全三维的准动态和动态相结合的数值仿真（见图 7），进行超大直径长距离掘进施工的开挖面稳定的预测仿真分析。形成了一套盾构施工控制开挖面稳定的施工工艺和施工技术，总结出了一套不同施工条件下以及对周边环境保护的盾构掘进施工参数匹配优化方法。表 1 为盾构施工关键施工技术参数控制表。

图 5 大型泥水盾构模拟试验水装置

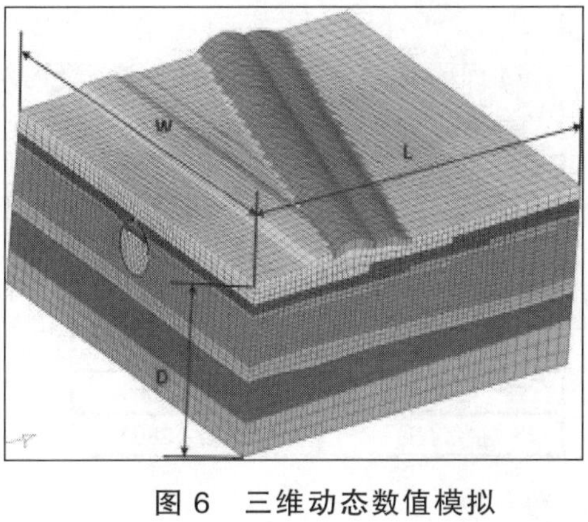

图 6 三维动态数值模拟

表 1 盾构施工相关技术参数控制表

序号	项 目	参 数 要 求
1	切口水压	根据不同覆土深度、不同地质条件设定
2	压力波动	$-0.2\sim+0.2$ kg/cm^2
3	掘进速度	2～4.5 cm/min 遇障碍物或周边有建构筑物需要保护时应低于 1 cm/min
4	泥水指标	比重 1.08～1.25　黏度 18～25 s
5	同步注浆	根据地表变形监测数据设定、调整

3 隧道施工期抗浮稳定性施工新技术

盾构法隧道被开挖土体重量与取而代之的隧道衬砌的重量相比，前者比后者大得多，尤其是超大断面隧道衬砌的重量比同排开水的重量要小。因此，在富地下水的土层中隧道总体呈上浮趋势。施工期引起隧道上浮的原因大致可分为两个方面，其一是由于盾构上部覆土较浅加上盾构开挖面一定程度受到扰动后，使土层与隧道及盾壳周边的握裹力减弱，盾构正面泥水沿盾壳流向已建成隧道，沿通道形成压力泥浆后穿，导致隧道上浮。另一方面由于管片脱出盾尾后的隧道被同步注浆浆液所包裹，同步注浆的自身质量因素，被注出衬砌外的浆液不能形成环箍，起不到有效阻止泥浆渗流和隔绝管片与泥浆及地下水之间的水力联系，从而导致隧道上浮。此外，盾构的推进速度和多点同步注浆压力设定不当，浆液充填不均匀也会引起隧道上浮。因此，同步注浆体的质量以及盾构推进施工时注浆压力的合理设定是确保超大直径隧道稳定的关键。

3.1 新型同步浆液的研制和施工工艺的研究

以往上海地区同步注浆大多采用双液浆，双液浆需要两种不同浆液混合后才能产生强度。就该浆液材料而言：一方面控制凝结时间不易掌握；另一方面浆液析水量大，凝固后填充后体积收缩大，压注量需加大。双液浆压注系统复杂，泵送性能差，管口处经常发生浆液堵管，影响施工进度和施工质量的现象时有发生。针对以往的浆液泵送性能差，早期强度低且强度增长发展速度慢的不足，通过反复对比试验，创新研制出具有自主知识产权的高重度、高稠度、抗剪型、抗液化的新型同步注浆浆液，以及与浆液材料相适应的一套施工工艺。

新型浆液选用水泥、石灰以及粉煤灰中的一种或几种组合作为胶凝材料，并结合细砂、膨润土以及外加剂混合配制而成。该新型浆液基本性能指标如表 2 所示，强度随时间增长曲线如图 6 所示。通过室内性能试验和现场使用结果表明，该新型浆液在充填到建筑空隙后并不会很快结硬，限制管片上浮的能力依靠自身的重度（19 kN/m^3）和抗剪切强度。浆液本身不具有流动性，拌制成的注浆材料呈牙膏状见图 8、图 9，在注浆泵的压力作用下，注浆材料呈现很好的流动性，具有较高的坍落度（12～14 cm）。

新型浆液的注浆工艺主要针对浆液的拌制设备、浆液的储运等进行了研究。在盾构推进过程中，盾构本体同步注浆系统 6 个注浆点对盾尾后管片外部建筑空隙实施同步注浆。各个注浆点压力的设定是根据后述“3.2 同步注浆压力设定与实物大管片整环加载试验研究”的试验结果严格控制。同时根据实际盾构推进施工过程中地表变形和环境监测反馈结果及时进行优化和调整。

表 2 新型浆液基本性能指标

指标名称	性能指标
渗透性	5×10^{-5} cm/s
初凝值	30h
重度	19kN /m^3
坍落度	12～14 cm
屈服值	800kPa（20h）
抗压强度	0.5MPa（28d）

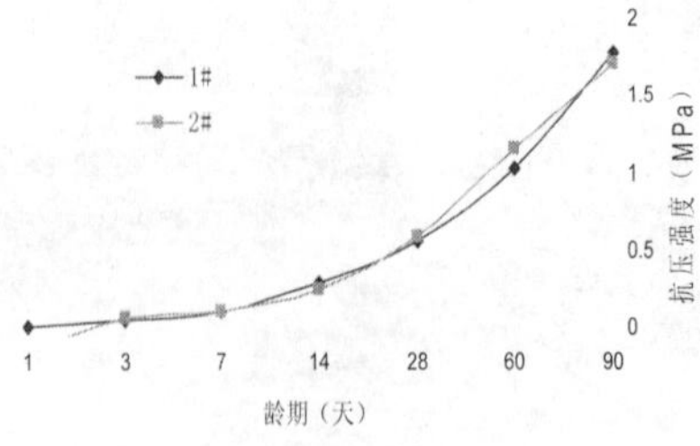

图 7 浆液强度增长曲线

图 8　新型浆液坍落度试验

图 9　新型浆液泵送试验

3.2　同步注浆压力设定与管片整环加载试验研究

超大断面盾构法隧道在盾构机本体上设置的多点同步注浆孔，使压注浆液均匀充填，以确保施工期及隧道后期的稳定性。因此，各同步注浆点压力的合理设定是控制隧道上浮确保隧道质量的关键。注浆压力过大或各注浆点压力设定不均衡，不仅会引起隧道变形，导致注浆孔周围管片过大的残余应力，同时也会导致地表隆起。而注浆压力过小建筑空隙未能得到有效充填，导致隧道上浮，而且地表会产生过大的沉降。

为验证超大断面盾构法隧道注浆压力对管片的影响，以上海长江隧道管片为对象进行了 1∶1 整环加载试验。图 10 为整环加载试验装置及试验场景的实物照片，图 11 为同步注浆注浆孔周围附加压力示意图。

试验结果及理论分析结果表明，为减小同步注浆压力对管片的影响，原则上多点注浆孔应同时均匀注浆；当注浆孔位置接近管片顶部附近时，位于管片顶部附近注浆孔的注浆压力应控制在其他注浆孔压力的 2/3 以下；同步注浆压力应根据隧道的覆土深度、管片周围土体的土层特性以及同步注浆浆液的性能合理设定注浆压力，单孔附加注浆压力控制在 0.6 MPa 以下，特殊情况需进一步增大注浆压力时，应另作管片结构验算。

图 10　管片整环加载试验装置及试验场景

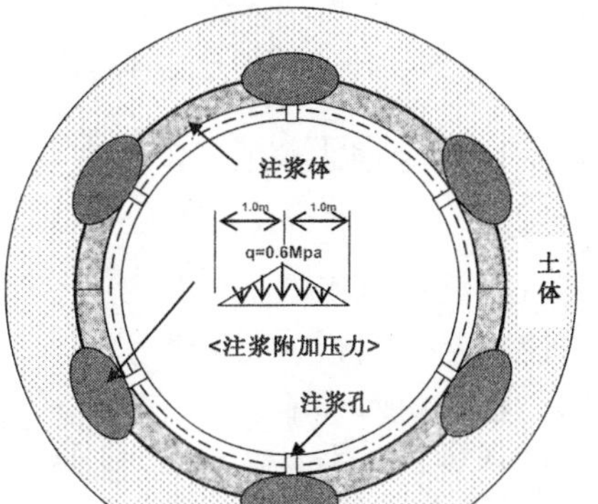

图 11　同步注浆管片附加应力示意图

3.3　模型隧道上浮试验研究

一般来说，被隧道置换出的土体重量均要大于隧道自身的重量，因此，在同步注浆浆液达到一定的龄期之前，由于浆液的抗浮力较小，隧道的自重不足于抵抗作用在隧道上的浮力，因此，隧道总体趋势是上浮的。施工期隧道在同步注浆浆液中的受力情况可分为，隧道自身的重力、浮力以及抵抗隧道上浮的黏结力和侧向摩擦阻力、垂直水土压力和侧向水土压力。其中，作用在隧道上的黏结力和侧向摩擦阻力随浆液龄期的增长而增大，浮力则减小。而黏结力和侧向摩擦阻力与作用在隧道周围的水土压力有关。由于同步注浆体从开始的注入盾尾建筑空隙时的塑性体，随着时间的推移向半塑性体和固体状发展，只有浆液达到一定的强度以后才能完全阻止隧道上浮，隧道处于抗浮稳定状态。因此，注浆材料这种复杂的体态变化过程要从理论上去推导一个理论解是非常困难的。为此，以上海长江隧道为对象，进行了 1:40 的模型隧道抗浮试验，以验证施工期隧道在同步注浆浆液中时间增长和浮力之间的关系，通过抗浮实测数据分析，找到隧道抗浮稳定的临界状态。图 12 为隧道模型抗浮试验原理图，模型隧道在浆液不同龄期下的临界浮力是通过排出模型隧道内的水后剩余水与模型隧道自重之和来定义的。

图 13 为作用在隧道上的广义浮力重度随时间增长的曲线。这里，将浆液在不同龄期的抗浮临界状态时的模型隧道和隧道内水的重量之和定义为广义浮力，该广义浮力和模型隧道的外形体积之比定义为广义浮力重度。图中可知，地铁隧道当采用新型浆液时，隧道达到抗浮极限平衡状态需要 109 h（约 4.5 d），上海长江隧道则需要 186 h（约 7.8 d）。

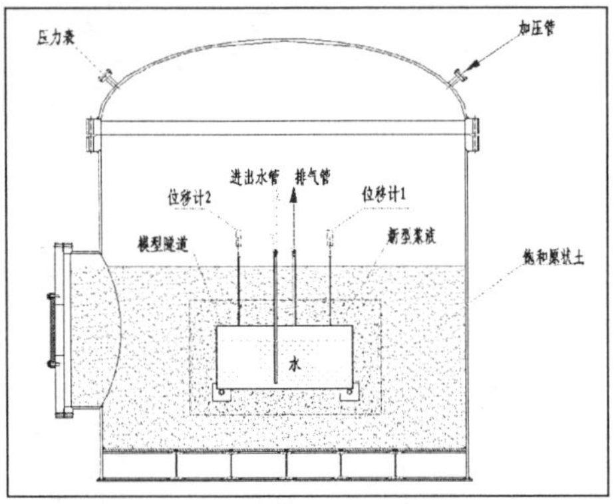

图 12　模型隧道抗浮试验原理

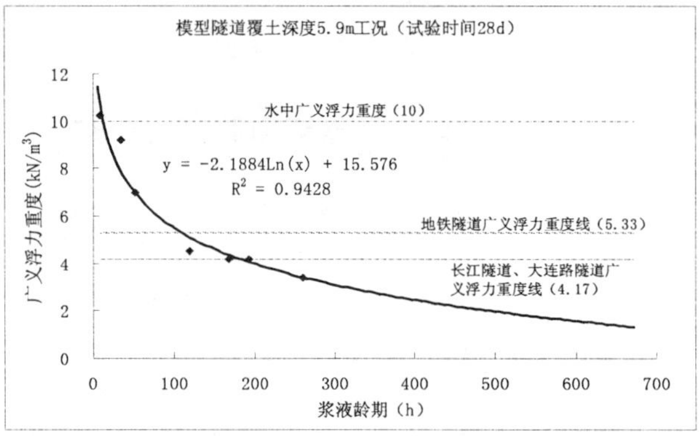

图 13　模型隧道广义浮力重度曲线

3.4　上海长江隧道实际使用效果

上海长江隧道应用本项目研制的新型同步注浆浆液以及相应的施工工艺，应用结果表明，隧道推进施工地表沉降控制在＋10 mm～－40 mm 以内，沿线穿越民房、厂房、防汛墙和地下管线均保护良好。隧道的轴线控制、管片的成环质量、渗水和碎裂控制均超过设计标准；隧道施工对周边环境影响小，地表沉降控制和建（构）筑物保护较为成功；隧道后期稳定性控制良好。

4　超长距离快速施工新技术

长距离盾构隧道施工的运输是影响工程进度的因素之一，以往长距离隧道施工的物流大多采用双轨运输方案或设置活动岔道，提高牵引车运输效率，压缩材料的运输时间。但考虑到超长距离隧道掘进工程如果采用全程电机车运输，对于隧道的工期影响极大。为了进一步加快施工进度，在道路结构的同步施工中，随盾构掘进在盾构与车架同步架设中间“口”字形预制构件，作为运输通道，隧道内水平运输则可以使用专用卡车来完成，它不但消除了大坡度隧道中电机车易出轨等安全隐患，同时还大大提高了运输能力，进一步确保了工程的安全、实现高效运输（见图 14、图 15、图 16）。

图 14　道路同步施工口字件安装

图 15　双头无轨运输车辆

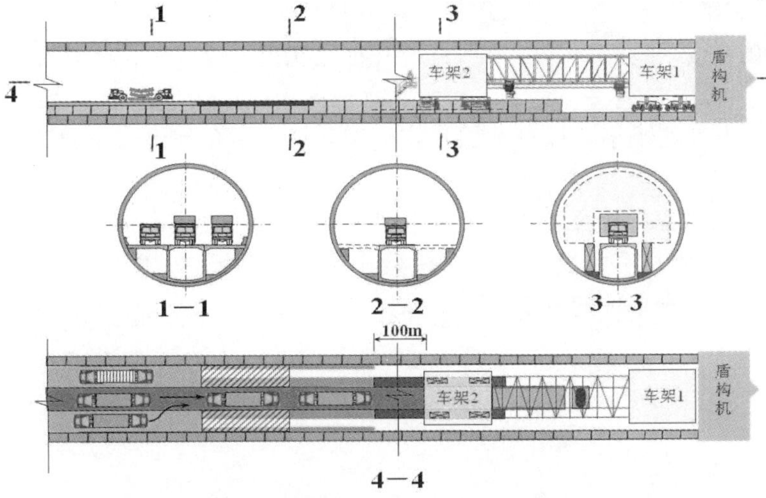

图 16　超长距离隧道施工高效物流运输的布置

5　联络通道施工风险控制技术

上海长江隧道需在长江底下水压力高达 0.6 MPa 的条件下施工 8 条联络通道，施工难度大、风险极高。经充分论证比选后决定采用冰冻法施工。冻结法施工的主要施工流程为：采用水平冻结方法冻结土体，以实现土体自立，有足够强度支撑外部荷载，并形成可靠的止水帷幕，然后人工开挖，随挖随撑，施作临时支护，喷射混凝土，提供可靠的结构施工空间，并施工外防水。由于整个衬砌结构为全封闭状态，人员无法进入结构振捣混凝土，无法用肉眼观察混凝土的浇捣状况，由此针对性采取自密实混凝土施工，即采用具有高工作性能（高流动性、高抗离析性、高间隙通过性和高填充性）的自密实混凝土，通过浇筑孔泵送至预留排气孔的封闭模板结构内，混凝土在自重和泵送压力作用下无需振捣，自行填充模板的空间，形成均匀密实的混凝土结构。联络通道结构施工完成后对隧道外的冻土采取强制解冻，并进行融沉注浆（详见图 17、图 18、图 19）。

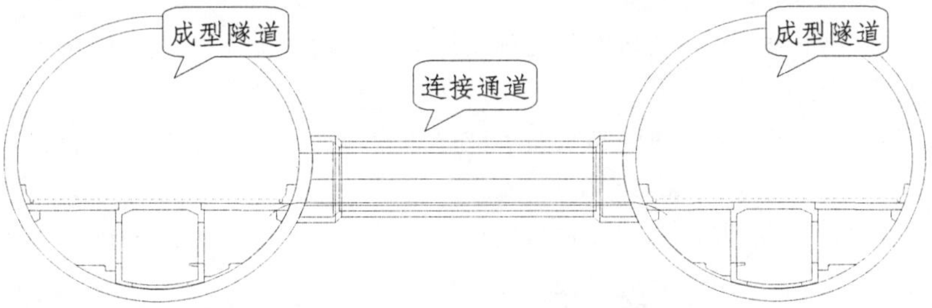

图 17　上海长江隧道联络通道

图 18　联络通道支护结构

图 19　联络通道防护门

为确保联络通道的施工安全，施工中采取以下技术措施：

① 采用在隧道两侧打孔、喇叭口部分采用双排孔冻结措施，以确保冻土帷幕的厚度、强度以及与管片的良好胶结；

② 冻结孔开孔前，先打若干小孔探测地层稳定情况。每个钻孔都设有密封装置，以防钻进时大量出砂、出水；

③ 在冻结过程和开挖过程中加强监测，布置测温孔和压力释放与观测孔，全面监测冻土帷幕的形成过程，开挖施工时如遇冻土帷幕有明显变形及时调整开挖构筑工艺；

④ 设置安全门，防止突发事件的发生。

6 结 语

上海长江隧道采用国际上直径最大的ϕ15.43 m 泥水气压平衡盾构进行施工，一次推进距离 7.5 km。在工程实施前进行了上述的一系列超前技术研究，通过 2 条隧道累计 14 km 的推进施工，工程质量优良。盾构施工参数配置合理，开挖面泥膜效果良好，盾构推进速度达到 3～4 cm/min，使工期提前 1 年完成；采用创新的同步注浆材料和同步单液注浆施工方法，很好地控制了隧道稳定，管片最大上浮量仅为 1cm，相临管片的环高差控制在 6 mm；采用即时同步施工方式，确保了管片脱出盾尾后隧道纵向稳定，预制构件安装与管片拼装同步，实现了隧道快速施工。

在经济全球化趋势的推动下，各国以及各城市间都将建立更为密切的合作关系，越江隧道和海峡隧道具有广泛的建设前景，为提高使用效率，隧道建设向大直径、长距离发展是必然的趋势。掌握超大型盾构掘进机的施工技术能极大地提高市场竞争力，是走向世界，与国际接轨的重要步骤，以使我国的盾构技术跻身于世界盾构技术的先进行列之中。

参考文献（Referenles）：

[1] J.X.Lin,F.Q.Yang,T.P.Shang&B.Xie, Study on tunnel stability against uplift of super-large diameter shield tunneling[J].THE SHANGHAI YANGTZE RIVER TUNNEL THEORY, DESIGN AND CONSTRUCTION. 2008:267-274.

[2] 杨国祥，林家祥，杨方勤. 超大直径盾构法隧道施工期衬砌结构安全性研究[M]. 地下工程施工与风险防范技术，上海：同济大学出版社，2007.

[3] 余暄平、沈永东、凌宇峰，等. 超大直径超长距离隧道盾构施工技术初探[M]. 大直径隧道与城市轨道交通工程技术，上海：同济大学出版社，2005.

[4] 杨国祥，吴惠明，林家祥，等. 长距离超大直径盾构隧道关键施工技术探讨[M]. 中国土木工程学会第十二届年会暨隧道及地下工程分会第十四届年会，2006.

作者简介（Bio-data）：

杨国祥，1949 年出生，毕业于同济大学，教授级高级工程师，隧道股份总工程师，上海建设科技委评审专家，上海土木工程学会地下工程专业委员会副主任。长期以来，杨国祥同志一直从事隧道和地下工程的技术管理和科技管理工作，先后负责和参与了上海地铁多条线路车站和区间隧道工程、上海长江隧道等多条大型越江隧道工程的建设，获得十余项省部级科技进步奖，发表论文数十篇。

杨国祥同志还负责了隧道股份承担的国家 863 计划四个课题的总体协调和技术攻关，是其中的“盾构装备相关技术标准研究”项目的负责人。

Guoxiang YANG, Chief Engineer of Shanghai Tunnel Engineering Co. Ltd (STEC), was born in 1949. Mr. Yang graduated from Tongji University and possessed Professor Senior Engineer certificate. Mr. Yang is member of Shanghai Technical Commission Review Board, and deputy director of Under Ground Branch of Shanghai Civil Society Association. Mr. Yang engaged technical management of underground construction for many years, and was in charge or involved construction of a number of stations and tunnel sections for several Shanghai metro lines. As a team leader, he set up and completed a string of research topics focused on critical technical issues of large diameter riverbed crossing tunnels. As part of research results, more than ten provincial level awards were issued to him and dozens of paper were published. Meanwhile, Mr. Yang was a general coordinator of four research topics which financed by National 863 Research Plan and also was team leader for one of aforementioned research topics under title of Study on Relevant Technical and Standards for TBM Equipments.

E-mail: zgs@stec.net

大伙房输水工程特长隧洞施工方法优化与TBM选型研究

梅志荣[1] 张军伟[1,2] 唐 与[3] 章元爱[1]
[1]中铁西南科学研究院，四川 成都 610031
[2]中国铁道科学研究院，北京 100081
[3]辽宁润中供水责任有限公司 辽宁 沈阳 110000

【摘 要】 限于工程地质条件，技术经济和环境指标，以及TBM、钻爆法的自身特点等因素，决定在大伙房输水工程特长隧洞采用以TBM为主、钻爆法为辅的施工方法，为了更好地发挥TBM的效率，洞内出碴采用了连续皮带机出碴技术，施工效率大大提高，特别是使用锚喷支护+模筑混凝土复合衬砌结构代替管片衬砌结构，不仅节约了资金，而且保证了工程质量。工程实践表明，这些技术已经取得了较好的经济、社会和环境效益，希望能为同类工程提供参考。
【关键词】 水利工程；特长隧洞；TBM；钻爆法；皮带机；全环整体模筑衬砌

STUDY ON OPTIMIZATION OF CONSTRUCTION METHOD AND TBM LECTOTYPE TECHNOLOGY OF SUPER-LONG TUNNEL

zhirong MEI[1], Junwei ZHANG[1,2], Yu TANG[3], Yuanai ZHANG[1]
[1]China Railway Southwest Research Institute, Chengdu 610031, Sichuan, China;
[2]China Academy of Railway Sciences, Beijing 100081, China;
[3]Liaoning Runzhong Water-supply Ltd, Shenyang 110000, Liaoning, China

Abstract: According to characteristics of TBM, drilling and blasting method of its own, engineering geological conditions, as well as economic and environmental indexes, it has been decided that TBM were mainly used that drill and blast construction method were supplemented. In order to improve the efficiency of open-style TBM, a continuous belt conveyer technology has been used to deliver ballast. Particularly concrete segment lining structure replaced by both anchor bolting and full-circular monolithic lining has not only saved money, but also ensured construction quality of tunnel. It is hoped to provide a reference for similar projects in the future.
Keywords: hydraulic engineering; super-long tunnel; TBM; drilling and blasting method; belt conveyer; full-circular monolithic lining

1 引 言

大伙房输水工程特长隧洞全长85.32 km，开挖洞径8.03 m，属大断面特长隧洞，是我国隧洞建设史上具有里程碑意义的宏大工程，也是目前世界上隧洞连续开挖和TBM单机掘进距离最长的地下工程之一，其工程规模和技术难度在国内外极为罕见。

隧洞工程进水口端前24.58 km为钻爆法施工标段，出水口端后60.84 km为TBM法施工标段，主要采用 3 台 TBM 施工，其中，TBM1 标段长 20.748 5 km，为顺坡掘进；TBM2 标段长 19.539 2 km，为逆坡掘进；TBM3 标段长 18.594 2 km，为逆坡掘进。本工程主洞线穿越两大向斜构造、29 条断层、50 座山峰和 51 条河流谷地。河谷段总长约 10 km，大部分为季节性河流，其中六河为工程区内最大的常年性河流，多年平均径流量为 1.89 亿 · m^3。围岩主要为硬岩，饱和抗压强度一般为 19～60 MPa，其中石英砂岩的饱和抗压强度为 85～115 MPa。在如此困难条件下修建特长隧洞，工程特别艰巨，技术难度极大。在设计施工以及运营过程中有一系列的难点问题需要逐一研究、解决。本工程主洞采用以 TBM 掘进为主、钻爆法为辅的联合施工方法，TBM 单机连续掘进长度设计要求达到 20 km，如何优化选用适宜的 TBM 进行施工？设计、制造和施工都存在很大风险。因此，施工方法的优化，TBM 的选型、主要技术参数确定、相关设备的配置，是首当其冲需要解决的关键问题。

2 钻爆法还是 TBM

本工程在工程伊始对于采用 TMB 施工还是钻爆法施工一直争论不休，最终选择以 TBM 为主、钻爆法为辅的联合施工方式主要由以下因素决定的，第一就是 TBM、钻爆法工法自身的特点，第二就是工程地质条件，第三就是经济和环境指标。

2.1 TBM 的特点

（1）TBM 的优点：

① 掘进速度快；

② 施工安全；

③ 污染小、施工环境条件好，利于环境保护；

④ 大大节省劳动力；

⑤ 成洞质量高；

⑥ 综合经济和社会效益高。

（2）TBM 的缺点：

① 对地层变化和不良地质的适应能力差；

② 洞径变化不灵活。

③ 设计制造需要一定的周期；

④ TBM 运输及安装需要条件；

⑤ 一次性投资成本较高。

2.2 钻爆法的特点

钻爆法与 TBM 比较，虽不具有快速、优质、安全等优势，但是它的特点也很突出：

（1）钻爆法对施工人员的素质要求较低，使用人工较多，在我国劳动力低廉，又能解决大量就业人口，适宜我国国情；

（2）钻爆法前期准备时间少，使用灵活；

（3）钻爆法对地质条件变化适应能力强，并且隧道断面可以多样性变化；

（4）钻爆法前期投入相对 TBM 大为减少；

（5）钻爆法在地质复杂时有较强的持续生产能力，而 TBM，尤其是双护盾式 TBM，遇到不稳定地质条件往往被卡住，一筹莫展，不得不借助钻爆法通过不良地质。

2.3 工程地质条件

在进水口端前 24.58 km 地段，该段地层岩性复杂，地质构造问题较多，区内共有 29 条断层，而本段就占了 13 条，特别是 5 条影响最大的断层破碎带中有 4 条分布于本段，Ⅴ类围岩总长 490 m，占全洞线Ⅴ类围岩总长的 68%，并且最大的涌水地段和岩石强度最高的地层也分布于本段中。而且在桩号 58+676.86～60+676.86 m 之间围岩比较破碎，并且 F41 大断层从此穿过，由于 TBM 工法在处理断层和涌水没有有效的办法，因此，在此段采用钻爆法施工可以灵活地处理各种不利的地质问题。在出水口端后 60.84 km 地段，除修建扩大洞室地段使用钻爆法施工外，其他地段围岩以Ⅱ、Ⅲ类为主，岩石强度中等，沿线的工程地质及水文地质条件相对比较单一，岩体完整性较好，适用于 TBM 施工。

2.4 经济和环境指标

在确定采用钻爆法还是 TBM 法施工时，考虑到经济和环境两个因素，分别对全部采用钻爆法或者 TBM 与钻爆法联合施工两种方案的经济和环境指标进行了比较。

（1）经济比较

全部钻爆法：根据规范要求和国内钻爆法施工的经验，结合本工程的地形特点，至少需要布置 33 条施工支洞，总长到达 24.1 km。

联合施工法：根据 TBM 施工经验，布置 14 条施工支洞，总长 14.4 km，其中 TBM 段布置 7 条支洞。上游约 24.58 km 采用钻爆法施工，其余主洞段采用 3 台 TBM 施工，每台 TBM 施工段长约 20 km，经济比较情况见表 1。

表 1 全部钻爆法、TBM 与钻爆法联合施工经济比较情况 （单位：万元）

工程或费用名称	钻爆法	联合法
建筑工程	267 731.25	352 697.22
机电设备及安装工程	8 362.80	328.79
金属结构及安装工程	197.67	189.30
临时工程	67 813.64	37 527.85
其他费用	47 029.27	40 528.53
小 计	391 134.63	431 271.69
总投资	430 248.10	474 398.86

从表 1 不难看出，采用联合施工方案的投资略高于钻爆法方案，但是，若工期提前 10 个月，本工程年引水量 17.86 亿 m^3，以每立方米水量按 0.6 元计，则提前增加收益为 9 亿元左右，其经济效益是十分显著的。

（2）环境比较

① 采用钻爆法施工辅助支洞数量增多、施工作业面多而且分散、临时便道大量增多、施工弃碴占地面积增大、天然植被破坏严重等等，这些对生态环境和自然景观影响很大，各类补偿也相对多；而 TBM 法施工则这些影响相对较小。

② 采用钻爆法施工，永久占地的征地面积较大，以工程为例，钻爆法施工占地 10 809 亩，其中永久占地 4 798 亩，施工临时占地 6 011 亩；而联合施工法（TBM+钻爆法）施工占地共计 2 289 亩，其中永久占地 867 亩，其他施工临时占地 1 020 亩，道路占地 402 亩。钻爆法施工弃碴场地为 41 处，TBM 施工弃碴场地为 14 处。TBM 法施工影响相对较小，但弃碴运输工作量较大；

③ 采用钻爆法施工，爆破和作业分散使施工期噪声、粉尘对环境的污染加剧，持续时间也较长，TBM 法施工则影响小，持续时间也较短。

可以看出，对于复杂山区特长隧洞来说，TBM 联合施工方法要优于钻爆法。联合方法综合利用两者的优势，形成优势互补，即提高了隧洞修建速度，也避免了只采用一种方法将造成的浪费，充分体现了特长隧洞采用联合施工方法的优越性。

3 开敞式 TBM 还是双护盾 TBM

3.1 TBM 选型依据及原则

根据以往的 TBM 施工情况分析来看，TBM 选型依据按其重要性排列如下：地质条件；断面大小；环境因素；支护类型；走向及坡度；工期造价；安全要求；辅助工法和配套条件；人员素养要求等等。

从国内外 TBM 施工情况来看，常用的 TBM 有三种机型，分别为开敞式、单护盾和双护盾 TBM，这三种 TBM 特点比较见表 2。

表 2 不同 TBM 的特点情况

项目	开敞式	单护盾	双护盾
适用岩石类别	硬岩	软岩	硬岩～软岩
对围岩完整性要求	完整	可破碎	完整、破碎均可
开挖速度	快	较慢	较快
连续作业	只更换撑靴时停止开挖	安装完管片后才能开挖	硬岩时同开敞式，极软岩时单护盾，一般软岩时同开敞式
初期支护要求	锚杆、喷射砼	管片	管片
处理塌方	较易	较难	难
设备价格比	1	1.2～1.3	1.4～1.5

从表 2 内容可以看出，比较适合大伙房输水工程的 TBM 是开敞式 TBM（见图 1）和双护盾 TBM（见图 2）。

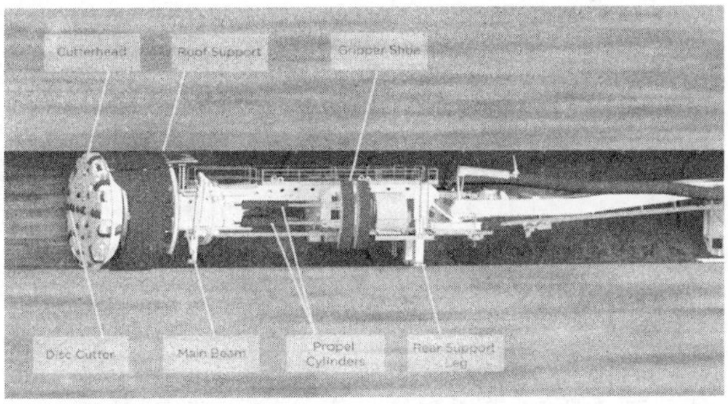

图 1 开敞式 TBM（也称支撑式 TBM，Main Beam TBMs）

图 2 双护盾式 TBM（Double Shield TBMs）

3.2 开敞式 TBM、双护盾 TBM 对地质条件适应性的比较

（1）软弱、破碎地层

在软弱、破碎地层中掘进，岩体胶结性能差、围岩破碎、开挖面自稳时间短。双护盾式 TBM 可利用已安装的管片来提供推力完成掘进。而开敞式 TBM 在通过软弱、破碎地层时，不但初期支护需花费较长时间，围岩也不能为撑靴提供足够的支撑反力推进机器掘进，可以看出双护盾式 TBM 对软岩的适应能力强。同开敞式 TBM 比较，双护盾式 TBM 的作业人员，处于一个由盾壳和管片保护的封闭空间，无论是掘进还是管片安装，作业环境好，安全感更强。

（2）中、硬岩地层

在中、硬岩地层中掘进，岩体相对完整，围岩自稳能力强。开敞式 TBM 以其盾壳短、岩面暴露早、可尽早对已开挖隧洞做地质描述和分类，从而有的放矢地简化了对暴露围岩的支护。同时较完整的围岩也为强大的支撑系统提供了足够的支撑反力，推进刀盘掘进。

虽然双护盾式 TBM 在后盾上也设置了支撑靴，也具备了在中、硬岩地层中的掘进能力。但它只能依靠判断岩碴和掘进参数的变化，才能间接地了解刀盘前方掌子面围岩变化，来指导使用不同配筋率的管片安装，其随意性比较大。同开敞式 TBM 的换步行程长（行程 1.8 m～1.9 m），以及在中、硬岩中可不支护或少支护相比较，双护盾式 TBM 换步行程短，管片安装用时长、辅助工序复杂的不足也就显现出来。

3.3 开敞式 TBM、双护盾 TBM 对不良地质洞段处理方式的比较

（1）涌（渗）水

采用钻爆法开挖隧洞，即使涌（渗）水达到 2.5 m^3/min～3.5 m^3/min 的数量，也很容易得到处理。但对于采用 TBM 法开挖隧洞来说，开挖工作面只要有大于 0.5 m^3/min 的渗水量，就会产生比较大的问题。

若采用这两种 TBM 机型施工，当地质勘察或超前地质预报探明前方可能出现较大规模的涌（渗）水时，解决此问题的最有效方式，就是用最少的钻孔，对刀盘前方做全环封闭栓塞式的超前预灌浆处理。而双护盾式 TBM 由于其盾壳长，无效钻孔距离长，不仅钻孔成本高、角度大，机器内部也无布置钻机设备的位置，无法做到全环封闭式的超前预灌浆。而开敞式 TBM 则不然，仅有的顶、侧护盾只有 3 m～4.5 m 长，如工程需要，完全可以加长主梁，配备 1～2 台液压凿岩钻机来满足预灌浆孔的钻孔要求。

（2）松散、挤压性围岩

松散、挤压性围岩，是由岩层的脆性和塑性变形所产生的断裂、坍塌、挤压等围岩收敛现象。虽然均归属于比较极端的地层条件，但在长隧洞的开挖施工中遭遇的几率仍很大。施工中由于盾壳周围岩体的变形，导致侵占开挖断面和盾壳被卡住的现象，或多或少在使用过 TBM 的工程上都曾有过发生。

卡住的后果，无论是对开敞式还是双护盾式，仅依靠加大油缸推力都不能使 TBM 前移，因为变形的围岩和管片的强度都不足以提供足够的支撑反力，刀盘顶不住掌子面，将使前方的坍塌面无法控制。

TBM 脱困的处理方式：通常是采用在顶护盾上方扩挖上导洞，再按由顶到边；由前到后的施工处理顺序进行脱困。开敞式 TBM 与双护盾式 TBM 相比较，在处理方式上有下列优势：

① 开敞式 TBM 的顶、侧护盾较短，只有双护盾式 TBM 护盾长度的 1/3～1/4，只要拆除保护作业安全的指型护盾，就可以开挖上导洞做相应的超前处理。

② 开敞式 TBM 的边护盾，除了用油缸控制盾壳伸缩外，大都装有楔块锁紧装置，使护盾在受到岩体挤压后，不至于进一步缩小开挖半径。而仅依靠油缸控制盾壳伸缩的双护盾式 TBM，在受到岩体挤压后，油缸的自保护措施使得压力一旦超限，油缸就会自动回油，使有效开挖洞径进一步缩小。

③ 对那些超出有效开挖洞径的拱顶和边墙的岩体变形，开敞式 TBM 只要在二次砼衬砌之前，都容易对其进行处理。但双护盾式 TBM 的管片衬砌，会由于管片和隧洞开挖洞壁间隙的缩小，使细砾石无法充填、回填灌浆无法实现。

3.4 开敞式 TBM、双护盾 TBM 占地和环境影响的比较

（1）占地面积

双护盾式 TBM 采用预制砼管片衬砌。预制混凝土管片需要占用大片的土地来建设生产厂房、存放管片、储存水泥钢筋材料、建蒸气养生设施等。以本工程为例，如采用三台双护盾式 TBM，经粗略估算，三个 TBM 施工标段总计需要预制砼管片 39.5×104 m^3。各支洞口单独设置砼管片预制厂和管片存放场的占地面积分别为：TBM1 标段占地 35 600 m^2；TBM2 标段占地 35 600 m^2；TBM3 标段占地 30 200 m^2。

当采用三台开敞式 TBM，砼衬砌改为复合式衬砌时。三个 TBM 施工标段各支洞口实际设置的混凝土生产系统、钢筋加工系统、材料存储库、部分骨料临时堆放场等，占地面积只有：TBM1 标段占地 4 000 m^2；TBM2 标段占地 4 300 m^2；TBM3 标段占地 4 300 m^2，占地面积大大减少。

（2）环境影响

采用双护盾式 TBM，由于管片的生产和存放造成占地面积大量成倍的增加，对环境的影响是显而易见。除此还有加大的料源开采占地，施工场地的占地等，这些都进一步加剧土壤侵蚀，增大了水土流失面积。

本工程决定采用开敞式 TBM 进行隧洞施工，并且将预制混凝土管片衬砌改为锚喷支护+模筑混凝土衬砌支护方案。促成这一重大决策变化的是下列主要因素：

① 工程地质条件。从本工程 TBM 施工段的地质条件来看，无论是采用双护盾 TBM 还是开敞式 TBM 从技术上都是可行的。但是，本段的围岩类别以Ⅱ、Ⅲ类为主，岩石强度中等，沿线的工程地质及水文地质条件相对比较单一，岩体完整性较好，适合采用开敞式 TBM 施工。

② 节约资金。通过设备造价、施工占地、围岩条件以及支护衬砌经济性等方面的综合比较。双护盾式 TBM 改为开敞式 TBM、预制混凝土管片衬砌改为锚喷支护+模筑混凝土衬砌后，单从投资造价上分别对 3 台 TBM 施工段的投资指标进行分析，后者比前者综合造价可节约 4.6 亿元左右，占 TBM 施工段总造价的 19.21%，折合到每延米的隧洞造价，可节省 7 800 元左右，达到了节约投资的目的。

③ 保证工期。采用开敞式 TBM，能够充分发挥的 TBM 开挖的高效性和临时支护的灵活性，保证 TBM 迅速通过不良地质洞段。采用开敞式 TBM，与钻爆法联合作业，施工方法互相转换更加灵活。TBM 法与钻爆法的锚喷支护+模筑混凝土衬砌实现了统一，衬砌与开挖互不干扰。

4 合理出碴运输方式的选择

TBM 施工的最大优点就是快速高效，一般速度为常规钻爆法的 3～5 倍，甚至更高。掘进速度快，单位断面出碴量大，运距长是特长隧洞施工的特点，出碴效率的高低，直接影响本工程进度。如何选择一套高效的出碴系统与 TBM 施工配套，成为本工程需要解决的关键技术之一。

目前国内外 TBM 施工中普遍采用的出碴方式有三种：有轨运输、无轨运输及皮带机运输，皮带机运输包括固定式皮带机和连续式皮带机。

比较适用于复杂山区特长隧洞出碴施工的有两种方式，一种是有轨低污染的内燃机车牵引机车的运输方式，一种是连续皮带机运输方式。下面针对两种出碴方式进行分析：

（1）轨道机车出碴方案

循环进尺 1.8 m，开挖面积 50.27 m^2。循环时间 100 min，共需机车编组 6 组，行车速度 12 km/h，每列车由 1 辆 29 t 机车、11 节 15 m^3 侧卸机车、1 节混凝土车及 1 节人员车组成。设置 43 kg/m 双轨，需设工字钢 H25a 横梁以满足铺轨的需要。在主支洞交汇处设置转碴坑尺寸 5 m×27 m×7 m，由转载皮带与支洞出碴系统连接。

（2）连续皮带出碴方案

由于设置了中间施工支洞，因此连续皮带机最大长度按 10 km 考虑，宽度 900 mm，出碴效率 800 t/h。材料运输编组 3 组，每列车由 1 辆 8 t 机车、1 节混凝土车及 1 节人员车组成。设置 43 kg/m 单轨。

两种出碴方案的技术和经济比较详见表 5 和表 6。可以看出，TBM 处于正常掘进状态下，掘进循环时间受地质状况的影响较大，一般情况下，Ⅲ、Ⅳ类围岩掘进效率最高，平均每循环时间约 40 min，出碴量为 153.8 m^3。列车配备能满足施工生产的需要的情况下，每列车由 11 节 15 m^3 侧卸机车组成，出碴量为 165 m^3，一次运完碴。行车速度 12 km/h，在洞内运输超过 10 km 的条件下，平均每列车循环时间约 170 min，因此共需机车编组 6 组，其中一组作为备用，5 组投入使用。机车出碴效率为 54.29 m^3/h；连续皮带出碴效率为 454.55 m^3/h，与机车出碴效率比提高值为 400.26 m^3/h。

表 5　轨道机车与皮带机出碴方案技术对比

运输方式	皮带输送机	轨道机车
运输过程	TBM 皮带机⇨隧洞皮带机⇨斜井皮带机⇨自卸汽车	TBM 皮带机⇨机车⇨洞内转运⇨斜井皮带机⇨自卸汽车
运输能力	高、连续输送	较低、间断输送
TBM 后配套	短	要求有较长的装碴长度，后配套较长
洞内转运	简单	复杂
轨道系统	只进行材料的运输供应，可以采用单线轨道。轴重小，轨道要求低	需要进行出碴和材料的运输供应，采用双线轨道。轴重大，轨道要求高
维护性	除对轨道系统设备进行维护外，还要对皮带系统的维护要求高	除对轨道系统设备进行维护，还需要对转碴设备、支洞皮带机进行维护
运输管理	需要进行皮带的延伸，管理较简单	需要进行列车编组管理，管理复杂
施工安全性	好	差
设备可靠性	要求高	要求高

从对表 5 两种方案比较看，连续皮带运输系统相对机车牵引机车系统有以下优点：由于无需等待碴车，可以使 TBM 获得较高的利用率，连续输送能力强；减少施工人员数量和降低工人的劳动强度；对环境不产生污染，通风费用低；运输管理简单，施工安全性好；可以使 TBM 后配套系统设计更轻、更短。出碴线与材料运输线分离，干扰小。连续皮带出碴效率远远高于轨道机车出碴效率。缺点是初次设备投入大。通过反复比较，本工程出碴方式采用连续皮带出碴方式。

表 6　轨道机车与连续皮带机出碴方案投资对比

方　案	名　称	单位	数量	单价（元）	合价（元）
轨道机车方案	机车 29 t	辆	6	3 045 000	18 270 000
	矿车 15 m^3	辆	66	168 000	11 088 000
	人员车	辆	6	52 500	315 000
	混凝土(砂浆)车	辆	6	210 000	1 260 000
	道岔	个	10	47 250	472 500
	轨道双轨 43 kg	km	41.2	258 000	10 629 600
	道床 0.8mH25aL=4.6 m，38.105 kg/m	t	2 629	4 800	12 619 200
	转碴坑 2 个 5*27*7	m^3	1 890	250	472 500
	转料斗 20 m^3	套	4	150 000	600 000
	喂料机 50 t/h7.5kw	台	4	200 000	800 000
	转载皮带 50 m30kw	m	50	3 000	150 000
	变压器	台	8	200 000	1 600 000
	劳务费	人.班	78 400	50	3 920 000
	电费	kw·h	14 672 000	0.8	11 737 600
	燃料费	kg	725 760	3.5	2 540 160
	合计 A	元			76 474 560

续表 6

方　案	名　称	单位	数量	单价（元）	合价（元）
连续皮带方案	连续皮带 B=900 mmL=10 km	km	10	4 275 489	42 754 890
	机车 8t	辆	3	840 000	2 520 000
	人员车	辆	3	52 500	157 500
	混凝土(砂浆)车	辆	3	210 000	630 000
	道岔	个	7	47 250	330 750
	轨道单轨 43 kg	km	20.4	322 500	6 579 000
	变压器	台	4	200 000	800 000
	劳务费	人.班	54 600	50	2 730 000
	电费	kwh	17 472 000	0.8	13 977 600
	燃料费	kg	127 080	3.5	444 780
	合计 B	元			70 924 520
分析	差值 C=A－B	元			5 550 040

5　TBM 隧洞支护系统优化

TBM 隧道的支护结构形式一般为两种，即锚喷+模筑混凝土复合衬砌和装配式预制管片衬砌（图 3）。采用 TBM 进行施工的隧道断面多为圆形，围岩条件较好，采用装配式预制管片结构形式可以实现隧道一条龙施工。同时，预制管片采用工厂式生产模式制作，精度高，质量容易保证，对结构受力也很有利。而对于锚喷支护复合衬砌来说，它灵活性好，对围岩条件变化的适应性较强。

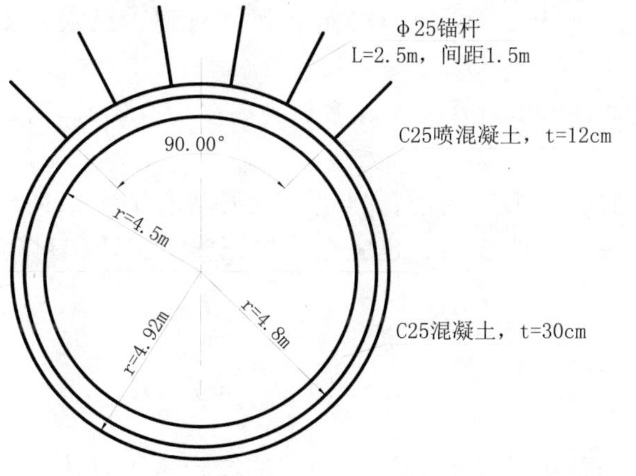

（a）锚喷支护复合衬砌

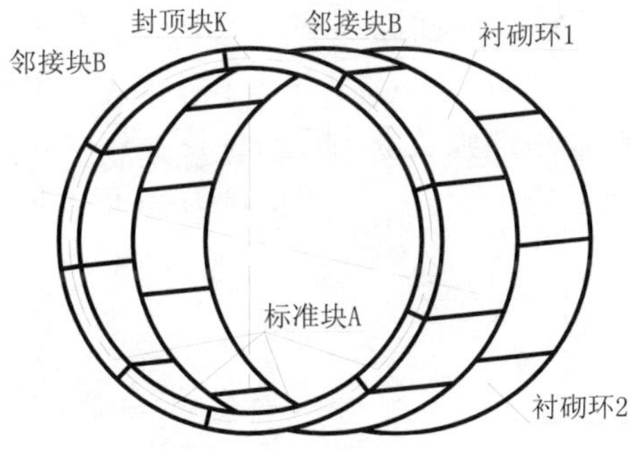

（b）装配式衬砌

图 3　TBM 隧道的支护结构形式

根据工程实际情况，本工程采用开敞式 TBM 进行施工，支护衬砌形式由原来的管片衬砌调整为锚喷支护衬砌。工程实践表明：

（1）对于复杂山区硬岩特长隧洞来说，锚喷支护加二次模筑混凝土复合衬砌分期施作支护，更加符合 NATM 的基本原则；采用管片衬砌对于较好的围岩，支护刚度、强度不匹配，设置时间不合理，并且大大增加了衬砌费用。

（2）锚喷支护的基础上，增设二次模筑混凝土，主要是提高结构的安全系数，起到了安全储备的作用。施工时采用全圆式模板台车，使Ⅲ～Ⅴ类围岩的衬砌内径保持一致，更能减小水流的局部水头损失（图 4）。

图 4 TBM 隧道不同支护结构形式洞内情况

（3）管片衬砌止水是目前施工及维护管理中的难题（图 5）。而采用锚喷支护+二次模筑混凝土衬砌，其止水与排水设计技术比较成熟。

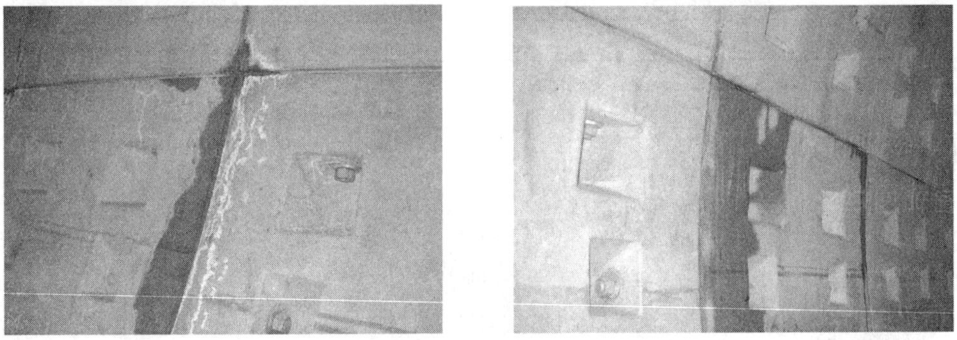

图 5 管片接头的漏水情况

（4）管片生产大量占地会对区域的生态环境造成破坏。而锚喷+模筑混凝土衬砌，只须在支洞口设置普通的混凝土拌合站即可，无需大面积占地。

（5）从衬砌表面的糙率系数来看，两者相差不多，由于管片接头较多，国内多取 0.015，略高于模筑衬砌。

（6）采用锚喷支护+模筑混凝土衬砌，尽管施工速度相对稍慢，但是，只要精心组织，采用先进的衬砌混凝土施工模式，包括，全环台车，仰拱台车等，实践表明，也完全能保证施工工期和衬砌质量。

6 结 论

工程实践表明，大伙房输水工程特长隧洞采用 TBM 为主、钻爆法为辅的联合施工方法；选择连续皮带机出碴技术；按照 NATM 理论采用锚喷支护+模筑混凝土复合衬砌结构代替管片衬砌结构等重大技术措施是科学合理的，并且直接节约投资约 4.6 亿元人民币，占 TBM 施工段总造价的 19.21%，折合到每延米的隧洞造价 7 800 元左右，产生了明显的经济效益，对大伙房输水工程特长隧洞高速度、高标准、高质量的建成发挥了重要的保证作用，对我国 TBM 的技术引进和消化吸收再创新具有重要的借鉴和推动作用。

参考文献（Referenles）：

[1] 谢明等. 双护盾隧道掘进机（TBM）技术浅谈，现代隧道技术〔J〕. 2006（5）：23-30.

[2] 中国水利学会施工专业委员会. TBM 掘进技术在中国的应用与发展. 盾构 TBM 隧道技术网，2007-4.

[3] 钱七虎等. 全断面掘进机在中国地下工程中的应用现状及前景展望〔J〕. 建筑机械，2002（05）.

[4] 张镜剑等. 长大隧道掘进机的运用及其主要岩石力学问题的处理，中国岩石力学与工程世纪成就

〔M〕. 2004:582-597.
[5] 王梦恕等. 岩石隧道掘进机（TBM）施工及工程实例〔M〕. 2004:5-16.
[6] 刘风华. 岩石掘进机（TBM）技术探析〔M〕. 软土隧道及地下工程技术文集，2000:135-41.
[7] ITA Working Group. Recommendations and Guidelines for Tunnel Boring Machine，2000..
[8] 张晓伟等. 输水长隧洞 TBM 的类型选择. 水利水电技术，2006(3)：12-15.
[9] 陈馈. TBM 在铁路隧道施工中的应用前景. 建筑机械，2006（08）.
[10] 李建斌. 双护盾 TBM 的地质适应性及相关计算〔J〕. 隧道建设，2006(02).
[11] 中国铁道建筑总公司. 隧道掘进机施工技术〔M〕. 2005:1～6.
[12] 张镜剑等. 隧道掘进机在我国应用的进展. 岩石力学与工程学报〔J〕. 2007(2)：226-238.
[13] 王梦恕. 开敞式 TBM 在铁路长隧道特硬岩、软岩地层的施工技术. 土木工程学报，2005(5)：54-58.
[14] 铁道部工程管理中心. 西安-安康铁路秦岭隧道 TBM 掘进施工技术总结〔M〕，2004.
[15] 中铁西南科学研究院. 大伙房输水工程特长隧洞 TBM 施工关键技术研究报告，2009.
[16] 中铁西南科学研究院. 全环内通式衬砌模板台车与 TBM 联合作业的研究与应用研究报告，2008.

作者简介（Bio-data）：

梅志荣，男，汉族，院长，研究员，博导，1953 年 8 月出生，大学毕业，长期从事隧道及地下工程应用基础理论研究工作，取得了多项科技成果和专利，国内外发表学术论文 30 余篇。为四川省有突出贡献优秀专家，四川省学术和技术带头人。并兼任中国岩石力学与工程学会常务理事、隧道及地下工程学会副理事长、岩土锚固工程协会副理事长等职务。

Zhirong MEI, (1953.8—), a civil engineer in the field of transport, he is one of the famous experts in China on the design and construction of underground works, the president and doctoral advisor of China Railway Southwest Research Institute Co.,Ltd. He has been engaged in the application of basic theory research tunnels and underground works and made a number of scientific and technological achievements and patents since graduation. The author of more than 130 publications he has held more than 30 national and international conferences on the subjects of tunneling.

He has filled many institutional roles including executive director of Chinese Society for Rock Mechanics and Engineering, vice chairman of the tunnels and underground engineering, vice chairman of Chinese Society for Anchorage Geotechnical Engineering. He is also one of outstanding experts who have made outstanding contributions of Sichuan Province, and Academic leaders of Sichuan Province.

E-mail: meizhirong@vip.163.com

扰动地层塌陷隧道原位修复综合技术

余暄平 朱卫杰
上海隧道工程股份有限公司，上海 200082

【摘 要】 上海轨道交通四号线修复工程经综合比选采用了原位修复的总体方案，针对修复工程中的综合方案必选、超深地下连续墙、深层障碍物清理、超深地基加固、承压水降水及环境控制、大断面冻结暗挖、超深基坑施工等主要难点，开展综合研究。项目研究采用模型试验、有限元分析和现场实施相结合的方法，取得了一批超深地下空间开发施工技术，为今后更大规模的地下空间开发利用提供了借鉴。

【关键词】 扰动地层；塌陷隧道；原位修复；超深基坑；综合技术

THE COMPREHENSIVE REPAIRING TECHNOLOGY FOR COLLAPSED TUNNEL IN DISTURBED SOILS IN ITS ORIGINAL SITE

Xuanping YU，Weijie ZHU
Shanghai Tunnel Engineering Co., Ltd, Shanghai 200082, China

Abstract: Through comprehensive comparison, the repairing project for Shanghai Rail Transit line 4 has adopted repairing method in the original site as the general program. Aiming at the main difficulties such as comprehensive comparison for suitable repairing program, ultra-deep diaphragm wall, deep-seated obstacles clearing, ultra-deep foundation strengthening, dewatering of confined water and controlling of environmental, mining the freezing of large-section, ultra-deep foundation pit construction, comprehensive study has been carried out for the overall program. With a combination of site construction, model test and finite element analysis, the study has obtained a group of construction technology for ultra-deep underground space development, providing a reference for future large-scale development and utilization of underground space.

Key words: disturbed soils; collapsed tunnel; repairing in original site; ultra-deep pit; comprehensive technology

1 引 言

随着城市建设发展，地下空间得到开发利用。近年来，国内各大城市建造了以地铁为主的大量地下工程。地下工程施工环境复杂，风险大，国内外地下工程事故时有发生，如何尽快修复成为地下工程界关注的焦点。隧道股份结合上海地铁 4 号线修复工程，研究了一套以超深地下空间设计施工技术为主的扰动地层塌陷隧道原位综合技术，为超深软土地下空间开发提供技术指导和示范。

2 主要研究技术

项目结合上海轨道交通 4 号线修复工程，在广泛调研和科学分析论证的基础上，通过大量理论和计算分析、设计优化、现场和物理实验，结合现场施工应用等手段，对本项目总体方案和各专项技术难题进行了研究和攻克。

2.1 总体方案比选

上海轨道交通 4 号线修复工程根据事故和抢险后对隧道顶标高的反复探摸和研判，基本确定了隧道坍塌破坏范围：由事故点向东延伸约 111 m，伸入了黄浦江约 50 m；向西延伸约 153 m，平面上与南浦大桥匝道非常接近；坍塌范围以外为完好隧道，其内部在抢险过程中被充满水以平衡内外水土压力。同时探摸表明隧道最大沉降量达 9.17 m。地面塌陷区域周边主要有近 90 m 的高层建筑和 3 栋 5 层砖混建筑等。

根据广泛调研和对比国内外类似工程案例，提出了原位修复和搭桥修复两种总体技术方案。原位方案即为在隧道坍塌破坏的位置进行修复重建，修复后的线路线型与原线型基本相同；搭桥方案又称改线或绕线方案，即对线路局部进行调整，调整后的线路避开隧道损坏区域并与两侧完好隧道连接。

经过全面科学综合分析和客观论证，扰动地层中塌陷隧道重建创新的采用了国内外尚无先例的原位修复总体技术方案（见图 1）。原位修复方案涉及诸多关键技术难题，必须逐一进行研究和攻克。

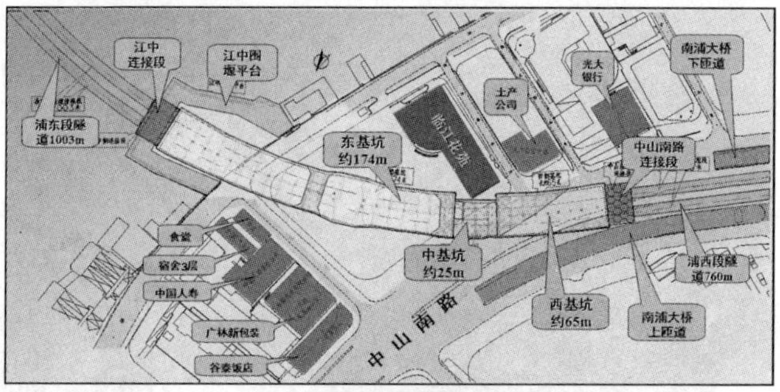

图 1　总体方案平面图

2.2 扰动土层中 40 m 基坑支护体系结构设计优化研究

本工程的基坑开挖深度达到 41 m，创软土地基国内之最。由于地层经过了沉陷、坍塌等严重扰动，土层中埋入坍塌隧道等大量复杂障碍物，邻近高层建筑的保护要求和临江施工的特殊要求等极大的增加了工程技术难度。根据工程地质和环境条件，进行了广泛的现场勘察和原位试验，对修复主体部分确定采用地下连续墙围护明挖法、钢筋混凝土支撑并辅之以深层降水及适度地基加固的技术方案。

江中段基坑外侧需要设置围堰形成陆地施工条件。为此项目组采用空间有限元仿真计算对围堰结构与下部完好隧道和基坑开挖过程中围护结构相互影响进行分析，经设计优化摒弃了传统重力式围堰，选用了钢管桩平台结合钢板桩挡水的轻型围堰结构，也为基坑施工提供科学依据，见图 2。

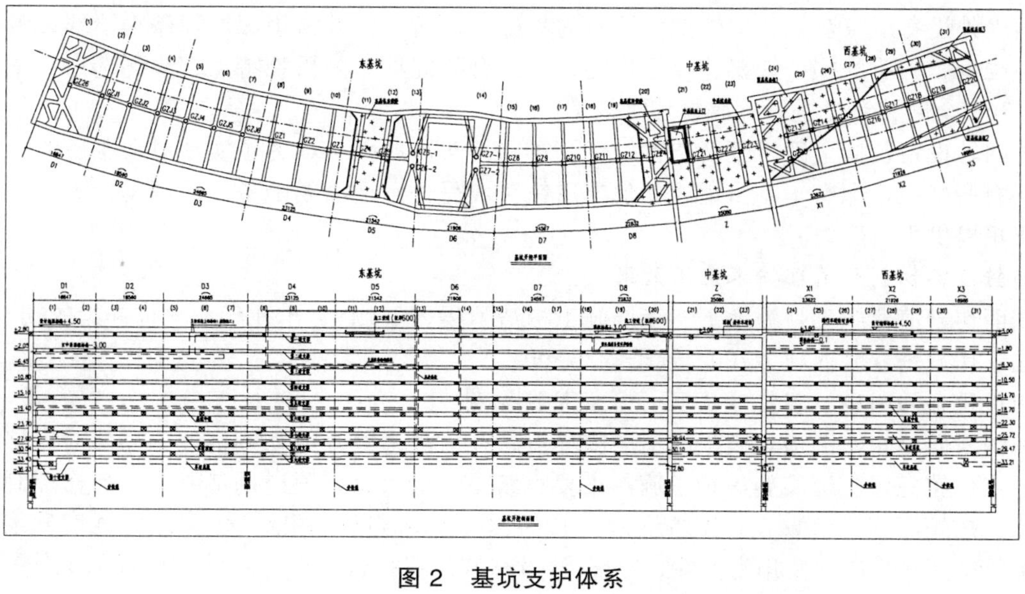

图 2　基坑支护体系

2.3 大面积深层地下障碍物清理技术研究

本项目在原先隧道发生破坏和地层产生塌陷的位置进行工程修复，不可避免的需要对塌陷和抢险作业产生的众多复杂障碍物进行清除，其中研究重点为地下 30～40 m 深度范围内钢筋混凝土等各种障碍物的清理。

2.3.1 深层障碍物分布

深层障碍物主要埋在地表以下 30～40 m 范围内，根据抢险后的统计资料主要有：塌陷的隧道管片（C50 的高强钢筋混凝土和高强螺栓），隧道内原联络通道冻结施工时的 2 套冷冻机组，盾构推进时使用的部分轨枕、轨道以及大量ϕ40 钢管。

通常对于地下 5 m 以上的障碍物采用开挖清理，浅层的桩基直接从地面拔除处理。对于在 30～40 m 深度如此复杂的障碍物，根据广泛调研资料，国内外尚无直接在地面进行切割清理的工程案例，必须采取深层切割专业设备和相应技术进行清理（详见图 3）。

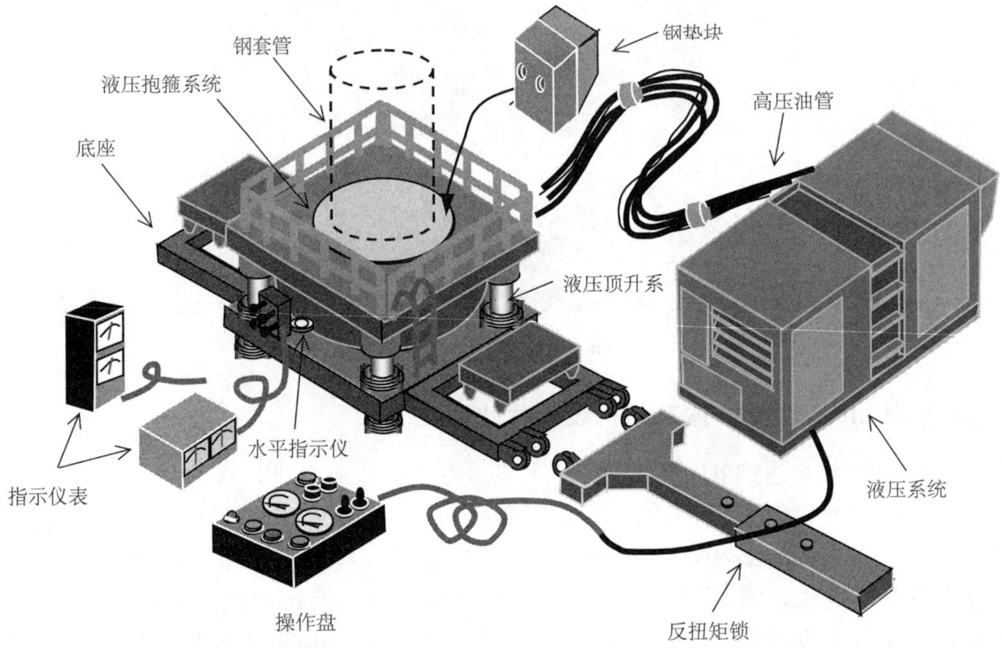

图 3 清障设备示意图

2.3.2 设备比选

在对国内外设备厂家及施工单位充分调研的基础上，对比国外常用深层障碍物清理设备垂直度、刀头受力均匀程度、刀头磨损、切割速度等性能，并结合研究项目障碍物特点，最终选用日本车辆生产的 RT260H 型 360º全回转钻机进行障碍物切割清理。

整套全回转设备包括全回转驱动装置、钢套管、刀头、冲抓斗，为了实现对切割后的大体积混凝土进行破碎，有些情况还配有十字重锤或其他专用钻头。另外，还需要配备专用吊车，进行冲抓斗的使用并为套筒扭矩提供平衡反力。

2.3.3 全回转设备切割和清理技术应用效果

基坑端面切割清理施工是为地下连续墙施工扫清障碍，通过叠交布孔形成一个连续的切割清理断面。统计情况显示切割垂直度达到 1/700，最低为 1/500。

2.3.4 全回转设备切割和清理特殊技术——保护性切割

由于两侧断面为完好隧道与破损隧道的临界点，在对隧道管片的切割清理中需要对完好隧道实施保护。对临界点位置完好隧道实施保护措施的主要思路是：增大完好隧道局部刚度；严格控制切割施工中套筒下压力、扭矩等施工参数。具体措施为：① 对隧道顶部进行钻孔；② 采用低强度砂浆对隧道内部充填，确保砂浆良好的自立性和密实性；③ 在隧道充填位置打设垂直冻结孔实施局部冻结，形成一个刚度较大的冻结塞体，见图 4。

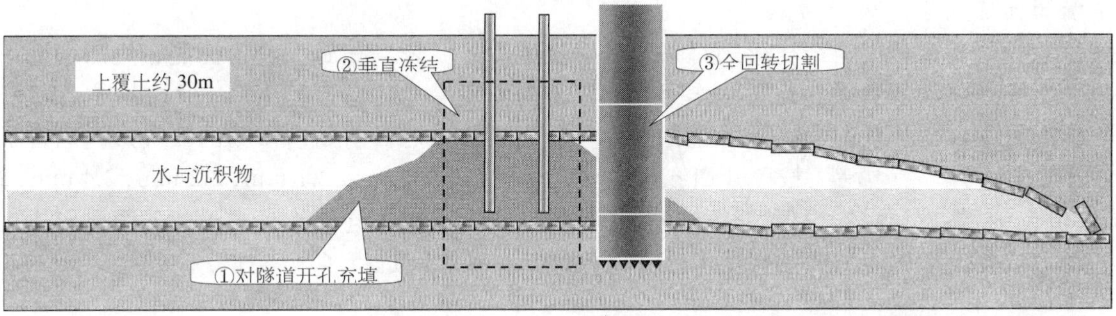

图 4 保护性切割示意图

冻结体的平均温度保持在－10°C 以下，冻结体的抗压强度为 4.5 MPa 以上。由于临近冻结体，切割钻进过程需要保证良好的连续性，避免套管长时间静止于低温地层中被冻结。

通过上述保护性切割措施，地下 36 m 深完好隧道与损坏隧道结合部位的管片得到了成功清除，完好隧道内抽水清理后管片未有任何损坏状况，测量表明完全符合地铁隧道使用标准。这也为地下环境保护要求严格的深层障碍物清理提供了借鉴。

2.4 超深地基加固技术研究

我国目前在该领域内的代表水平为普通三重管旋喷工艺，最大加固深度达到 37 m，设计桩径为 1.5 m，代表工程为上海外环沉管隧道浦西基坑工程，在该技术领域我国与国外还存在较大差距。项目组在对各种地基加固工艺充分调研和比较的基础上，结合目前国内技术现状“三重管双高压旋喷工艺”作为研发对象。

2.4.1 旋喷设备选型与参数匹配

本项目在设备选择上坚持两条原则：① 立足于国内市场；② 立足于在普通三重管的基础上进行改进。为了获得在上述设备体系条件下的最佳施工参数匹配，并根据施工反馈对设备选型进一步优化，先后在 4 号线修复现场和上海长江隧道试验段基坑工程进行了现场试验。

表 1 双高压（RJP）法施工工艺参数

名　称	项　目	参数值
高压水	压力（Mpa）	35～38
	流量（l/min）	75
压缩空气	压力（Mpa）	0.7～1.0
	流量（m^3/min）	2×1.5
浆　液	压力（Mpa）	30
	流量（l/min）	70～75
	水灰比（强加固区）	1：1
注浆管提升	提升速度（cm/min）	4
	旋转速度（r/min）	5～7
注浆材料为 32.5 级普通硅酸盐水泥。		

在 4 号线修复工程现场进行了浅层喷射的试验，内容包括：① 对比普通三管法、RJP 工法和 SJS 工法的旋喷加固效果；② 对比施工中间断提升和连续提升方式对桩径的影响；③ RJP 工法施工中现有机具的配套及其可靠性。在长江隧道试验段基坑工程现场共布置两根旋喷试验桩，桩深度地面以下 2.1～23.0 m，桩间距 2 600 mm。随着基坑开挖逐层暴露深达 17 m 的试验桩，桩径在 2 000 mm 以上，强度值

均在 1.4 MPa 以上。

2.4.2 喷嘴的优选试验

相关研究成果表明喷嘴的结构形式对高压喷射效果影响显著，在施工设备性能相近的情况下，喷嘴的结构尺寸对喷射能量的衰减起到关键作用。目前,国内的喷嘴为各家自己生产，形式各异，无统一标准。鉴于此，本项目首次对喷嘴的几何形状进行了优化研究。首先对目前国内市场的喷嘴形式进行了全面地调查与收集，选用了 13 个喷嘴，按照开口孔径共分 7 个系列：2.0 mm，2.1 mm，2.2 mm，2.4 mm，2.6 mm，2.8 mm，3.0 mm；然后运用物理模型试验与数值模拟两种手段对不同结构形式喷嘴的喷射效果进行了全面分析；最后推荐出最优的喷嘴结构形式，并就各尺寸因素影响进行了敏感性分析。

2.4.3 三重管双高压旋喷技术的工程应用

"三重管双高压旋喷技术"在上海市长江隧道工程及 4 号线修复工程中得到成功应用。其中前者在直径 15.43m 盾构出洞加固区，采用一排共 32 根旋喷桩作为止水帷幕，设计桩径 1 800 mm，桩深 28.0 m，盾构出洞过程中无渗漏情况，取芯检验加固强度符合设计要求。

4 号线修复工程中设计采用旋喷桩作为坑内"裙边"地基加固和坑外地下连续墙接缝止水帷幕，最大的加固深度 50 m，桩径 1 800 mm，为目前国内深度最深、直径最大的旋喷桩。此外施工范围障碍物异常复杂，成孔难度较大，接缝止水帷幕对成孔的垂直度要高。

整个修复工程合计施工坑内桩为 827 根，地下墙接缝止水桩合计 265 根。通过对 77 个试件强度值的统计分析，结果表明：取样强度值均超过了设计值；不同土层加固强度差异较大；随着深度加大及土层变化，强度分布的离散性加大，见图 5。

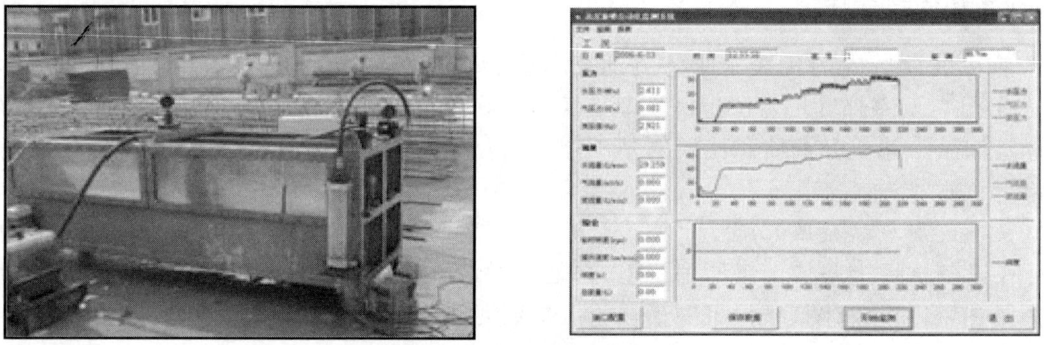

图 5 喷嘴试验装置及数据采集

2.5 复杂地层条件下 65 m 地下连续墙施工技术研究

本项目地下连续墙深度达到 65.5 m，涉及的关键技术难点有：地下连续墙接缝止水性能控制、扰动地层下槽段稳定性控制、超深土层的成槽效率、超长钢筋笼起吊安全等。

2.5.1 接头形式优选

由于修复工程基坑开挖深度为 38.5～41 m，从 30 m 开始进入⑦$_1$、⑦$_2$层粉砂层，降水后基坑内外水头差达到 30 多米，一旦发生围护接缝渗漏水，将对基坑安全和周边环境带来致命影响。综合考虑目前国内外地下连续墙接头形式并进行比选，最终选用"增长型十字钢板止水接头"。止水钢板伸出接头 50 cm，与钢筋笼整体焊接固定，有利于钢筋笼的沉放，并防止后续反力箱起拔的风险。

2.5.2 超深地下连续墙成槽技术

在现场实验阶段，先行幅和填仓幅间隔咬合的工艺顺序暴露了地下连续墙端头协调余地小、4 根反力箱同时起拔对设备和人员要求极高以及先行幅混凝土浇灌后向相邻先行幅反力箱孔位穿孔的问题，经分析主要原因为：① 场区内土层经过严重扰动，浅层土体极易塌方从而形成空洞；② 地下连续墙超深，分幅长度不能过长，填仓幅在扣除先期反力箱位置后，剩余墙体宽度有限，更容易造成浅层塌方和混凝土绕管问题。因此，在后续施工中采用了以顺幅为主的成槽工艺流程，实际施工证明该措施对施工质量和过程有利。

2.5.3 刷壁、扫孔工艺

超深地下连续墙施工中的另一个控制重点就是十字钢板接头清理工作。常规地下连续墙只进行刷壁→扫孔一次循环。而超深地下连续墙由于成槽时间很长，泥浆比重变得很大，十字钢板上附着劣化泥浆很厚，超声波探测结果显示，有些槽段达到 40 cm 以上，刷壁工作因此变得难度很高。项目研究中依据实际施工试验不断改进，形成了一套较为成熟的刷壁工艺。刷壁工艺包括了改进的十字钢板刷壁机、新设计的液压抓斗刷壁器以及冲击型尖头反力箱相结合方法，有针对性的根据超声波探测的接头情况进行清理，取得了较好的效果。

2.5.4 清孔技术

清除槽底沉渣有沉淀法扫孔和置换法两种。沉淀法针对槽底沉渣较厚的情况，置换法针对的是泥浆比重超标的情况。本项目根据试验幅的情况，沉渣厚度和泥浆比重均有超标现象，在清孔工艺的确定上采用了置换法和沉淀扫孔法结合的工艺，其流程为：成槽结束静置 3 小时→第一次扫孔→第一次清孔→下放钢筋笼→第二次清孔。并使用特制清孔管，配制 10 m^3 大功率的空压机，在清孔性能和效率方面进行了改进。

2.5.5 超长钢筋笼制作、起吊、对接

围护结构承受的主动区水土压力极大，为加强围护结构刚度，同时降低钢筋笼重量，直径ϕ28 以上主筋和主筋加密筋均采用三级钢。再综合考虑了以往工程经验，最终确定将十字钢板固定于钢筋笼上的制作方案，有十字钢板的一侧均设置吊点。根据现场配备的 280 t 和 150 t 吊车拔杆长度、角度和起吊能力进行演算，64.45 m 长钢筋笼整幅起吊风险极大，采用了分节吊装拼接方法。连接主筋采用单面焊错位连接，然后整幅起吊入槽，见图 6。

图 6 超长钢笼起吊

2.5.6 超深地下连续墙施工泥浆的比选

该项目配置了新型的复合钠基膨润土泥浆，该泥浆的具备以下特点：① 固相含量。膨润土添加量只有 3%～4%；② 具有一定选择性絮凝作用。使分散较细土粒（非造浆土）更多、更快沉降清除；③ 泥浆化学稳定性强，携渣能力强；④ 低密、低切力。密度一般在 1.02～1.03 g/cm^3，容易净化，混凝土受泥浆的危害减小；⑤ 配制简单，快速。

经过实际工程应用检验，新型泥浆配制简单，护壁能力强，稳定性高，携渣能力强，尤其适合于土质较差和超深地下连续墙施工。

2.6 超深承压水降水和环境变形控制技术研究

目前国内外基坑工程降水设计，趋向于采用数值解法来设计基坑降水方案，并将地下水渗流模型和土体应力一应变模型耦合起来，力争在预测基坑降水引起地下水渗流场变化时，对降水引起的地面沉降进行同步预测，以实现对基坑降水引起的地面沉降进行最优化控制的目的。但迄今仍未形成一套完整、成熟的可用于指导实践的理论和方法。

本项目采用了理论研究、室内和现场试验、数值模拟分析、软件研制、设计优化和施工应用分析等多种手段进行了研究，创新建立了三维非稳定渗流模型、三维渗流-应力全耦合模型，研制开发了专业可视化软件，并最终成功解决了 41 m 超深基坑承压水降水和环境变形控制问题。降水方案见图 7。

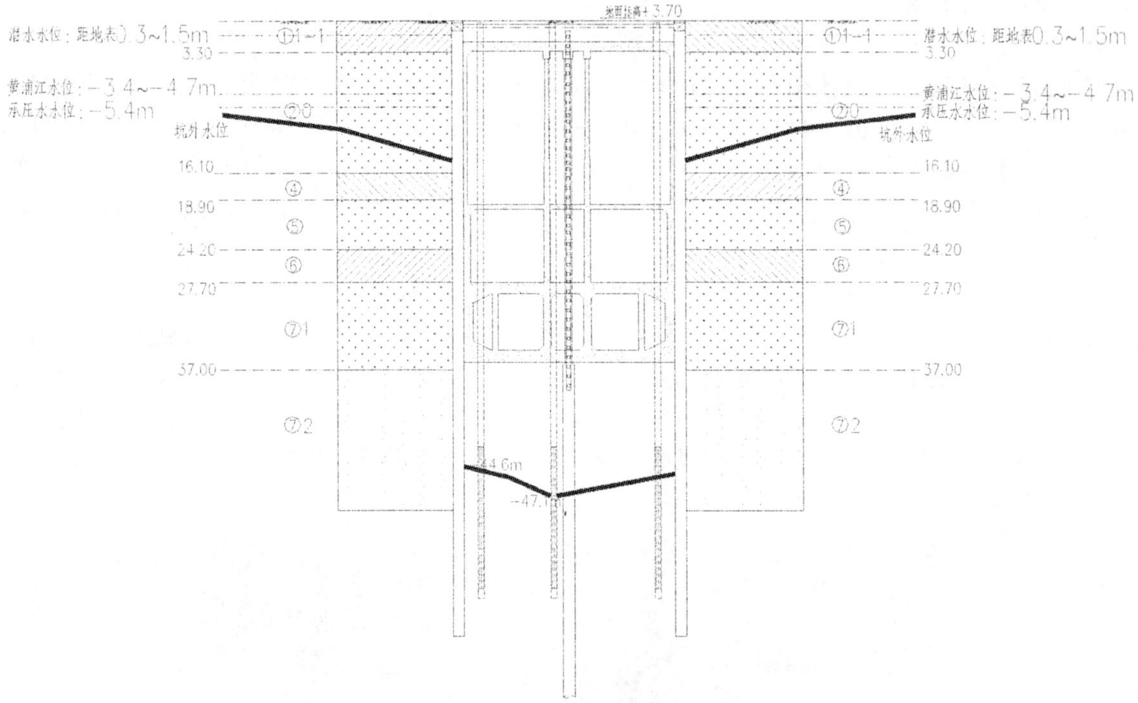

图 7　降水方案示意图

2.6.1　三维非稳定渗流模型

基坑降水渗流是具有自由面的非稳定渗流，属复杂的非线性问题，常用的数值解法是有限差分法和有限单元法，并采用迭代法来求解代数方程，其解的稳定性一直是模型求解的难点。针对目前计算模型的不足，本项目通过研究建立了三维非稳定渗流模型。

2.6.2　三维渗流-应力全耦合模型

基坑降水过程实际是渗流场和应力场相互影响、相互作用的过程。全耦合模型由于可一次性同时求出渗流场和应力场，从而自然地考虑了渗流场与应力场之间的耦合效应。但目前大多数模型并未考虑土体的变形参数和渗透性质随土体中应力场改变的动态变化，实际上随着土体应力场的改变，土体的变形参数和孔隙率以及渗透性也必然发生改变，因此在预测由深基坑降水引起的地面沉降时，不仅要考虑土体变形参数随有效应力状态的变化，还要考虑渗透性的相应动态变化。

2.6.3　可视化计算机软件（GWS）的研制

在建立了地下水三维非稳定渗流模型和三维渗流-应力全耦合模型的基础上，为了使编制的相应三维有限元计算机程序 3DF 和 FSC-3D 对计算结果有较好的表达效果，具有更强的可操作性及更好的推广应用价值，在 Microsoft Windows XP 操作系统环境下，使用 Microsoft VisualBasic6.0 语言研制了可视化的计算机软件 GWS。

2.7　扰动软土地基 40 m 超深基坑施工技术

2.7.1　基坑开挖过程模拟计算与反馈分析及安全度分析评价

本项目对基坑开挖施工进行了全面和全过程的监测，对数据进行了反馈分析，并以此为依据进行信息化施工。同时，采用 FLAC 软件实现了基坑开挖过程的弹塑性数值模拟，综合考虑各种影响因素，真实地模拟了基坑开挖的全过程，分析了基坑开挖各工况对地连墙水平位移、垂直位移的影响，支撑轴力的大小，立柱上抬的规律及地表沉降等。创新建立起了一套基坑安全度性状评价体系，该体系可以有效地指导工程施工，并能较好地反映基坑所处的安全性状，为超深基坑的风险管理提供了实时监控、数据分析、应急措施决策的平台。

（1）基坑监测

本项目监测内容主要包括：① 基坑围护体系的安全与稳定监测；② 江中围堰的安全与稳定监测；③ 基坑开挖过程中的降水监测；④ 周围环境的安全与稳定监测。

（2）基于实测数据的数值模拟分析

模拟分析步骤：① 根据实际工况建立三维模型；② 初始地应力模拟，得到初始应力场；③ 消除初始应力场所对应的位移场；④ 根据实际施工工况进行开挖施工的模拟分析。根据模拟分析了基坑开挖各工况对地连墙水平位移、垂直位移的影响，支撑轴力的大小，立柱上抬及地表沉降规律等。

通过数值模拟分析真实再现了基坑施工的全过程，提供了更加直观深入认识超深基施工规律的新途径，也为其他相似工程提供了借鉴参考。

2.7.2 基坑开挖施工技术难点与工艺

在基坑围护结构变形控制方面，主要体现在对“时空效应”理论的应用上，提高挖土效率、限时完成支撑、减少基坑暴露时间是围护结构变形控制关键技术所在。而本项目开挖深度超深、土体垂直运输困难，大量地下障碍物存在、挖土困难，均成为制约开挖效率因素。采用的主要施工技术：① 严格执行“分层、分块、逐层开挖”的挖土原则，将挖土、支撑和降水三者有机地结合起来，同时针对浅层和深层土体的不同特性，调整开挖流程，即上部浅层土体以分层为主、分块为辅，避免出现大范围放坡，进入第 6 号土层后，调整为分块为主，尽可能快的抢筑底板；② 限制混凝土支撑制作时间，确保 72 小时、力争 48 小时内浇筑围檩支撑，并适当提高支撑体系混凝土标号，并在支撑混凝土中适当添加早强剂，使支撑体系尽早达到设计强度；③ 根据监测结果，变形速率过大或趋向超标，必要时制作支撑前先浇筑 40 cm 厚，3～4 m 宽高标号混凝土垫层，并掺加早强剂，在 24 小时内达到一定强度，起到预支撑作用，更好的控制围护变形，详见表 2。

表 2 基坑开挖变形控制值及实测值

编号	项　目	变形控制标准	开挖完成变形最大值
1	地墙水平位移	7.6 cm	4.80 cm
2	临江花苑大厦	控制倾斜 1.6‰ 累计沉降 6 cm	倾斜 0.19‰ 累计沉降 3.44 cm （开挖后沉降 1.24 cm）
3	防汛墙	累计沉降 4 cm	累计沉降 1.79 cm

2.8 4 号线修复工程冻结法技术研究

本研究项目依托轨道交通 4 号线修复工程，其超深基坑与两侧完好隧道连接段采用冻结暗挖的方式进行开挖并形成贯通。特点为：① 修复工程的江中段，在破损隧道与完好隧道的临界点处要实施两次冻融循环，即先进行垂直冻结，完成隧道切割和浦东侧完好隧道清理后解冻，然后进行水平冻结（见图 8），在暗挖对接贯通后再次解冻。文献资料检索表明，在如此复杂条件下进行反复冻结在国内外尚属首次。② 中山南路段冻结分为三期垂直冻结，一期冻结为浦西侧完好隧道试排水和隧道切割创造条件，二期冻结为浦西侧完好隧道清理创造条件，三期冻结为暗挖对接提供地基加固帷幕。

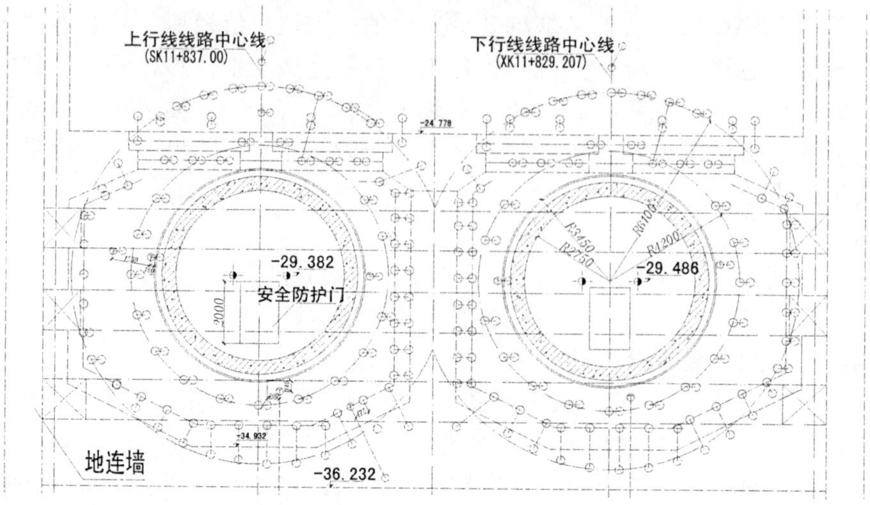

图 8 江中段水平冻结示意图

2.8.1 土层二次循环冻融试验

对冻结暗挖涉及的⑥、⑦$_1$、⑦$_2$三层土体进行了二次循环冻融试验，研究二次冻结和融化过程对土体性能的影响，为冻结暗挖提供设计参数。

2.8.2 4 号线修复工程冻结法设计

修复工程冻结法设计总体上可分为江中段和中山南路段两部分，按性质可分为冻结塞体和冻结暗挖帷幕。冻结塞体作用为：① 嵌固完好隧道管片，在全回转设备切割破损隧道时对完好隧道起到保护作用；② 抵抗完好隧道抽水清理后两侧不平衡压力。

在面临诸多新课题情况下，修复工程冻结设计充分利用了土层二次循环冻融试验、现场解冻试验和数值分析、物理模型试验研究的各项成果，对垂直冻结塞体、水平和垂直冻结暗挖帷幕设计进行了多方案技术经济比选，同时采用传统力学结合三维有限元数值分析对冻结暗挖过程进行模拟和设计优化。优化后冻结塞体在两个工程部位均采用垂直冻结；暗挖冻结帷幕在江中段和中山南路段分别采用水平和垂直冻结。

在损坏隧道临界点处施工垂直冻结塞体，在国、内外尚无工程先例和施工经验，经过反复研究创新的采用了隧道顶部开孔、隧道内充填水泥砂浆、充填区打设垂直冻结孔实施冻结的方案。充填材料选用了低冻胀率、适当流动性和自立性的低强度水泥砂浆。

3 主要技术创新点

扰动地层塌陷隧道原位修复综合技术是软土地下工程领域的重大技术突破，代表了国内外同类技术最高水平。项目结合上海轨道交通 4 号线修复工程，以详细的调研、现场和物理模型试验、理论分析和有限元计算为基础，结合现场应用进行综合研究，形成了以下创新点：

(1) 首次研究并创新性地优选了深埋地铁隧道塌陷区原位修复总体方案，开创了世界深埋隧道修复史的先河；

(2) 首次在中国内地地铁基坑中采用了 1.2 m 地下连续墙和全钢筋混凝土支撑、辅之以深层降水及适度地基加固的超深基坑总体设计方案；

(3) 通过物理模型试验和数值分析优选了喷嘴结构形式，开发了一套大深度、大直径高压旋喷工法；

(4) 研究了大面积超深地下复杂障碍物清理技术，开发了一套全回转钻机地下超深障碍物清除工艺；

(5) 国内首次对软土地层 65 m 地下连续墙技术进行综合研究，开发了一套超深地下连续墙施工工艺；

(6) 建立了多层松散含水层组地下水三维渗流数值模型及渗流与土体变形耦合模型，有效地解决了 40 m 以上承压水降水和环境变形问题；

（7）选用了新型轻型钢结构围堰设计方案，有效控制了对下部完好隧道及邻近超深基坑的影响；

（8）进行了二次循环冻融试验和江底新老隧道对接物理模型试验，系统研究了冻结温度场、冻结壁的强度和稳定性、不同解冻条件下地层融沉变化规律，并首次研究了冻结暗挖对既有隧道的影响。

4 结 论

上海市轨道交通 4 号线于 2003 年 7 月 1 日发生事故，经过半年多的调研、试验、论证和比选确定了原位修复的总体技术路线，2003 年 8 月完成了初步设计和施工大纲的编制并通过市建委科技委的评审。修复工程于 2003 年 8 月底正式开工，历经 34 个月，2007 年 6 月底攻克了所有的技术难关，圆满实现了修复工程的结构贯通。

（1）上海市轨道交通 4 号线修复工程为国际工程事故修复提供了一个范例。修复工程的成功实施表明，类似的市政隧道事故，采用合理的施工方案和相应的施工技术，采用原位修复是可行的。

（2）本修复工程取得成功的关键在于施工方案是在充分的调研、现场试验的基础上，经专家反复研讨后确定，关键的方案和工艺选定具有较高的科学性、可行性和合理性。

（3）修复施工过程，对关键的隧道破损点判断、选用基坑明挖为主的修复方案等是准确和适当的，为今后类似工程提供了可借鉴的经验。

（4）本工程中的一些突破性创新工艺和技术如超深地下连续墙施工、超深地下障碍物清理、超深双高压旋喷加固、超深承压水降水、连接段冻结暗挖施工等，大大提升了国内软土地下工程的施工技术水平，为今后上海乃至全国大规模地下空间开发奠定了技术基础。

（5）目前修复工程已经竣工通车近两年。但是还需密切关注修复段长期稳定性问题，尤其是明挖基坑和隧道连接段采用了冻结暗挖方式，其后期沉降和跟踪注浆是我们今后关注的重点。

参考文献（Referenles）：

[1] 余暄平，朱卫杰. 上海轨道交通四号线修复工程综述. 第三届上海国际隧道工程研讨会论文集，2007.

[2] 朱卫杰，肖晓春等. 深层障碍物切割清理施工技术及其应用研究. 地下空间与工程学报，2006.8

作者简介（Bio-data）：

余暄平（1966—），男，浙江诸暨人，学士，教授级高工，上海隧道工程股份有限公司副总经理。主要从事岩土工程、隧道与地下空间工程施工与科研工作。曾经主持了国内第一条桩基沉管法隧道－宁波常洪隧道、上海市大连路隧道、上海轨道交通四号线修复工程以及上海长江隧道工程等项目的建设和技术研究工作。本项目获得 2008 年上海市科技进步二等奖。

Xuanping YU（1966—）, male, born in Zhuji, Zhejiang, Bachelor, senior engineer (professorship), Deputy general manager of Shanghai Tunnel Engineering Co., Ltd. He has mainly engaged in construction and scientific research in geotechnical engineering, tunnel and underground space engineering. He presided over the construction and research work for the domestic first immersed tube tunnel-Ningbo Changhong tunnel, Dalian road tunnel in Shanghai, Shanghai Rail Transit Line 4th restoration works and the Shanghai Yangtze River Tunnel, etc. In 2008 the project of Shanghai Yangtze River Tunnel won the first prize of scientific and technological progress of Shanghai.

E-mail: yxp@stec.net

朱卫杰（1974—），男，江苏海门人，学士，高级工程师，上海隧道工程股份有限公司副总工程师。主要从事软土地下工程施工和科研工作。曾经参与和主持了上海地铁二号线、宁波常洪沉管隧道、上海市大连路隧道以及上海轨道交通四号线修复工程等建设和科研工作。

Weijie ZHU(1974—), male, born in Haimen,Jiangsu, Bachelor , Senior engineers, Deputy chief engineer of Shanghai Tunnel Engineering Co., Ltd. He mainly engaged in construction and research for underground engineering in soft soil. He has taken part in and presided over the construction and research work for the Ningbo-Changhong tunnel, Shanghai, Dalian Road Tunnel and Shanghai Rail Transit Line 4th restoration works.

E-mail: zhuweijie@stec.net

成都地区富水砂卵石地层盾构机选型及其适应性探讨

张 延 肖中平

成都地铁有限责任公司，四川 成都 61003

【摘 要】 本文通过成都地铁 1 号线盾构工程的实践，探讨了针对成都地铁富水砂卵石地层，两种不同类型泥水平衡与土压平衡盾构的适应性，可供类似工程参考。

【关键词】 富水砂卵石地层；泥水平衡盾构；土压平衡盾构；适应性

STUDY ON SHIELD MACHINE TYPE SELECTION AND APPLICABILITY IN WATER-RICH COBBLE GROUND CHENGDU AREA

Yan ZHANG，Zhongping XIAO

ChengDu Metro Co.,Ltd., Chengdu 610031，Sichuan，China

Abstract: Based on the practice of the shield construction in Chengdu Metro Line 1, this article discusses the applicability of slurry shield technique and EPB shield technique in the special stratum of water-rich cobble ground. And it provides references for similar projects.

Key Words: water-rich cobble ground; slurry shield; EPB shield; applicability

1 引 言

成都地铁 1 号线为南北走向，北至新都大丰镇，南至华阳，全长 31.6 km，其中一期工程盾构施工区间北起红花堰，南止于火车南站，全长 18.601 km。成都地铁 1 号线一期工程盾构区间隧道穿越地层基本为全断面的砂卵石层，地表建筑物和管线非常复杂，盾构在该条件下的施工在国内目前属首次。在砂卵石地层中采用盾构法施工，卵石含量、粒径、强度和充填物的性质对盾构机选型和施工起决定性作用，盾构隧道的上覆地层、地下水情况和地表建（构）筑物分布状况也对盾构机选型和施工有一定影响。

2 工程地质与水文地质

区间隧道主要在含水量丰富、补给充足的强透水的砂卵石土中通过。隧道结构底板埋深约为 14.0～21.0 m。其埋深位于地下水位以下，地下水水压力对隧道施工及衬砌结构有较大影响。隧道穿越地层卵石含量约占 55%～80%。含少量大粒径漂石，一般含量为 5%～10%，前期勘测阶段发现漂石最大粒径为 670 mm，施工中发现的漂石最大粒径为 600 mm。充填物以细砂、中砂为主，含量约 10%～35%。

该区段卵石含水层渗透性较强，富水性较好，含水较丰富，渗透系数一般在 20 m/d。根据四川省地矿厅环境地质监测总站对成都市地下水动态长期观测资料，区间地下水水位埋深浅，一般在 4.1～8.75 m 左右。实际施工中观测，水位在 8～11 m。

3 盾构机的选型

3.1 泥水平衡盾构机方案

根据欧美和日本的施工经验，两种不同类型盾构能够适应的地层渗水系数范围如图 1 所示。由图 1 可以看出，当地层的透水系数大于 10^{-4} m/s 时，宜选用泥水盾构；当地层的透水系数小于 10^{-7} m/s 时，可以选用土压平衡盾构；当地层的渗水系数在 10^{-7} m/s 和 10^{-4} m/s 之间时，既可以选用土压平衡盾构也可以选用泥水式盾构。

本工程隧道穿越地层的渗透系数为 1.736×10^{-4} m/s，大于 10^{-4} m/s，采用泥水盾构施工是可行的。泥水盾构利用泥浆作为支护材料，开挖面的稳定是利用泥浆的渗透形成不透水的泥膜，通过泥水压力来平衡作用于掌子面的土压力和水压力。本工程隧道洞身范围内含大量卵石和水，细颗粒含量少，采用泥水盾构施工有利于地表沉降的控制；另一方面长距离卵石的存在，泥水盾构所形成的泥膜能更好地稳定掌子面，采用泥水盾构可更好保证施工安全。

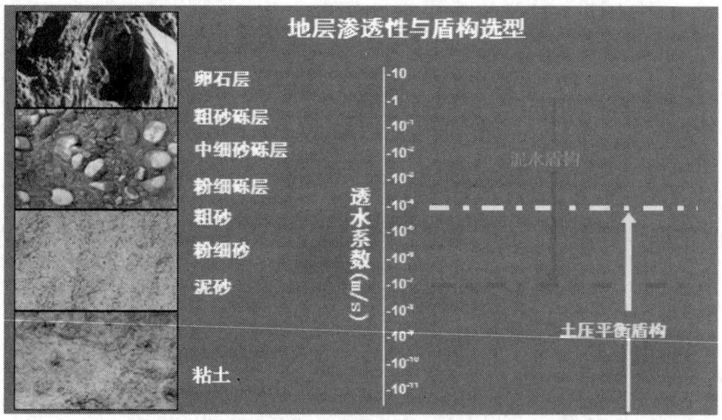

图 1 地层渗透系数与盾构选型关系示意图

3.2 土压平衡盾构机方案

土压平衡盾构能够适应较大的地质范围与地质条件，既能用于黏结性、非黏结性、有水或无水的软土、硬岩或卵石土层等多种复杂的地层；同时又具有土压平衡盾构的功能，施工速度较高，能有效的控制地表沉降。经过采取适当的辅助措施如加泥（膨润土）、加泡沫、聚合物等，可以在松散的砂、卵地层中很好地稳定开挖面，增强不透水性，从而可靠安全地掘进；特别是双螺旋的采用，即使土仓内的碴土处于液态状态，仍能连续出碴而不会发生喷涌，保证含水较高地层施工的安全可靠。另外土压平衡盾构机先进的带压作业设备人员仓加压系统、碴土报警系统及盾构机良好的密闭性能也为工程提供了可靠的保障。

3.3 盾构型式的确定

根据对工程地质水文特点的分析，综合国内外盾构生产厂家对本地质特点的盾构机选型的参考意见，鉴于成都地铁工程首次采用盾构法施工，为了摸索和总结不同类型盾构机对成都地层的适应性，为后续工程提供借鉴和参考，决定在盾构 4 标试验段（火车南站～省体育馆站区间）的右线隧道采用泥水平衡盾构机施工，其余盾构区间隧道采用土压平衡盾构机施工。

4 泥水平衡盾构机的不适应性分析

4.1 排碴易堵塞

根据泥水平衡盾构的循环理论，砂卵石地层中泥水盾构施工，泥浆管路中的泥浆流速，必须保持在临界值以上，低于临界值时，泥浆中的卵石和沙粒就会产生沉淀而堵塞管路，造成出碴不畅。其临界流速可按杜郎德公式计算如下：

$$V_L = F_L \cdot \sqrt{2gd(\rho/\rho_0 - 1)}$$

式中 V_L ——临界流速(m/s)；

F_L ——流速系数(根据颗粒直径和泥水浓度而定)，当颗粒直径大于 1 mm，F_L=1.34；

g ——9.8(m/s^2)；

ρ_0 ——母液泥水比重，一般 ρ_0=1.05～1.25；

ρ ——固体比重；

d ——管子内直径(m)。

$$V_L = 1.34\times\sqrt{2\times9.8\times0.325\times(2.3\div1.15-1)} = 1.34\times2.52 = 3.38\ \text{m/s}$$

采用管径为ϕ325 的泥浆管，其流量为：

$$Q_{\phi325} = 3.38\times\frac{1}{4}\times3.14\times(0.325)^2\times3\,600 = 1\,009\ \text{m}^3/\text{h}$$

实际施工中泥浆流量能达到 1 200 m^3/h，表明在砂卵石地层中采用泥浆输送系统是可以保证泥浆顺畅排出的。但由于隧道范围内的卵石含量大、大粒径卵石多，排碴过程中在泥水仓、气压仓、碎石机、泥浆泵等部位易发生堵塞（如图 2）。

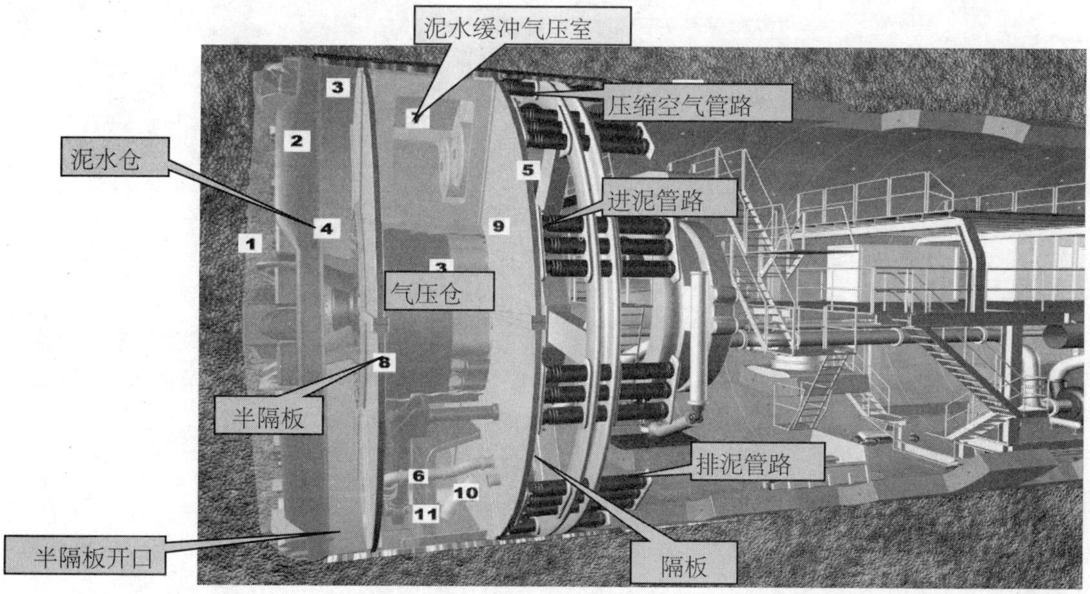

图 2 泥水盾构结构示意图

（1）泥水仓：进浆流量中的一半进入泥水仓，由于泥浆门口的面积，该流量不足以将泥水仓的卵石携带到气垫仓，卵石在泥水仓底部堆积形成自然堆积坡度后才能进入气垫仓，即使刀盘搅拌棒也不能有效改善这种状况。堆积极容易造成仓门堵塞并增大刀盘扭矩；

（2）气压仓：进入气垫仓的卵石不容易被两根主冲刷管喷浆翻起，经常在气压仓底部堆积大块的卵石，详见图 3；

（3）破碎机：进入破碎机鳄口的卵石，不管大小均要被鳄口挤压，造成破碎机长期的重载，破碎机有效工作寿命大大缩短，破碎频率降低，反过来又影响到该处的排碴。由于破碎机的通过流量减少，又使卵石在气压仓内堆积，如图 3 所示。气压仓堆积的卵石又干扰破碎机的摆动部件及油管，造成损坏；

（4）泥浆泵：长条形的卵石卡住叶轮，造成泵前管路堵塞，如图 4 所示。

泥水平衡盾构在富水砂卵石地层中掘进，排碴不畅的是影响掘进进尺的最大问题。

图 3 气压仓堵塞的砂卵石

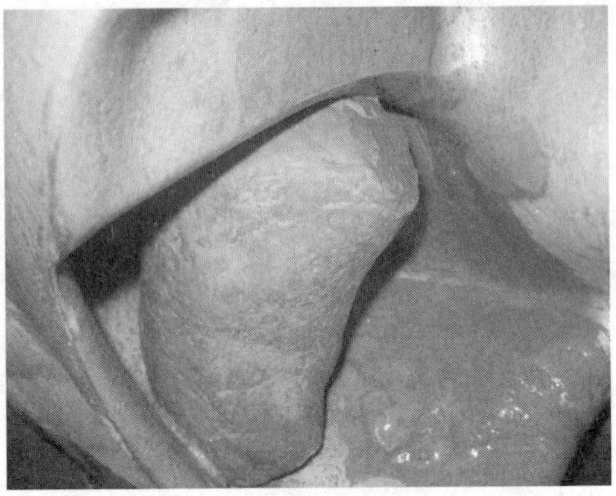

图 4 泥浆泵处堵塞的砂卵石

4.2 局部地段穿透冒浆

选择泥水平衡盾构机主要是考虑通过膨润土泥浆在开挖面形成的泥膜与泥浆压力，在细颗粒少、富水的卵石地层里可有效保持泥水仓压力，防止坍塌。泥水盾构施工过程中把进浆比重调到 1.2 以上，泥浆黏度调整到 30 s，除了希望能够增强携碴能力外，还希望能够堵塞地层空隙形成泥膜，但仍不能解决局部地段穿透冒浆问题。由于仅能保持水头压力避免冒浆，泥水仓压力不足以抵抗地层压力而引起坍塌，地表沉降严重，如图 5 所示。

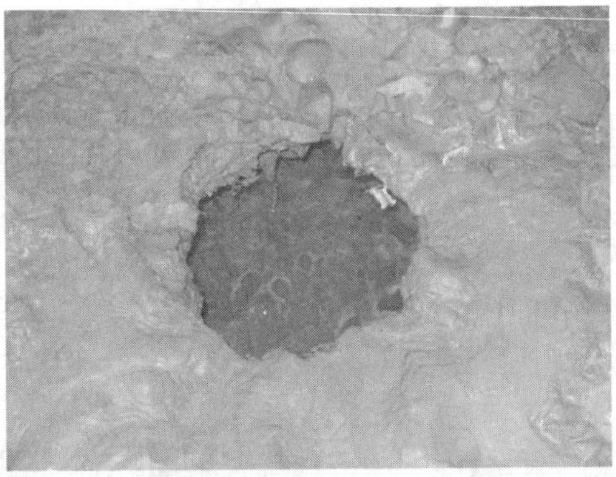

图 5 冒浆引起的地面坍塌

4.3 卵石对设备过度磨损问题

成都地质对盾构设备的磨损也超出了当初的估计，表现在刀盘刀具的磨损，破碎机的磨损，泵的磨损，以及由于过度磨损带来的设备高故障率，如图 6、图 7 所示。

图 6 刀具磨损严重

图 7 碎石机鳄板磨损严重

4.4 过度的坍塌处理和堵塞清理

由于泥膜问题导致的地层坍塌处理，特别是卵石堵塞，包含加固地层进行刀盘泥水仓气压仓的卵石清理，堵管堵泵的清理，占据了大量有效的掘进时间，使得泥水盾构的日历月进度极低，见图 8、图 9。

图 8　泥水仓堵塞的卵石

图 9　刀盘切口的卵石

4.5 泥浆循环耗费的电能

泥水输送系统的总功率相当于盾构主机的功率，由于输碴系统的堵塞，当出浆泵进口出现负压时，不得不停止掘进进行长时间的清仓循环，每次刀盘启动和停止之后也要进行长时间的清仓循环，额外的泥浆循环时间耗费了大量电能。

5 土压平衡盾构机的适应性分析

5.1 掘进模式的选择

土压平衡盾构机具有三种工作模式，即土压平衡模式（EPB）、敞开式（OPEN）和半敞开式（SEMI-OPEN）。

土压平衡式就是在盾构开挖时，利用土仓内的土压或加注辅助材料产生的压力来平衡开挖面的土压及地下水压力，以避免掌子面坍塌或地层失水过多而引起地表下沉的一种盾构掘进模式。在富水砂卵石地层中，地层稳定性较差，地下水丰富，因此采用土压平衡模式进行掘进，如图 10 所示。

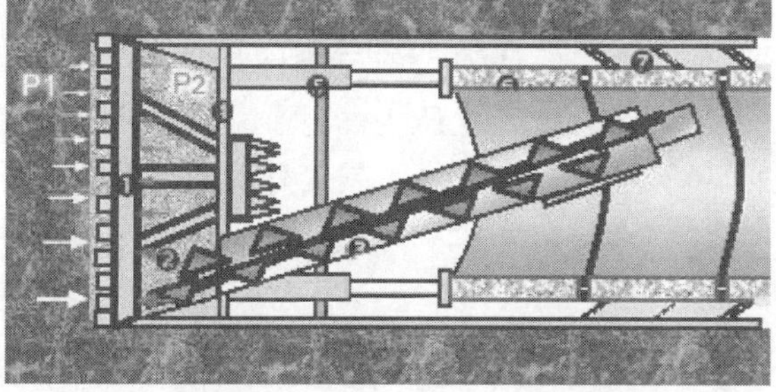

图 10　土压平衡模式示意图

5.2 碴土改良技术

碴土改良的目的是：降低碴土的内摩擦角，降低刀盘的扭矩，增加碴土的流动性、渗透性，从而达到堵水、减磨、降扭及保压的效果。

在工程施工中，盾构机配有两套碴土改良系统：泡沫系统、膨润土（泥浆）系统。两者共用一套输送管路，所有管路经旋转接头均可到达刀盘面板。其工作原理如图 11 所示。

（1）泡沫系统

泡沫系统主要由泡沫泵、水泵、电磁流量阀、泡沫发生器、压力传感器和管路组成。

泡沫系统在刀盘和螺旋输送机共设置14路泡沫孔，其中刀盘面八路、土仓隔板预留四路、螺旋输送机设置2路。土仓隔板预留四路泡沫孔又兼作膨润土等的注入孔。

（2）膨润土（泥浆）系统

将膨润土（泥浆）输送管道打开，通过膨润土（泥浆）输送泵将泥浆或者膨润土压入刀盘、土仓和螺旋输送机内，压入膨润土（泥浆）的量为出碴量的10%～20%左右，达到进一步改良碴土的目的。

通过泡沫、膨润土系统同时对碴土进行改良，系统性能良好，完全能够满足该地层条件下碴土改良的需要。

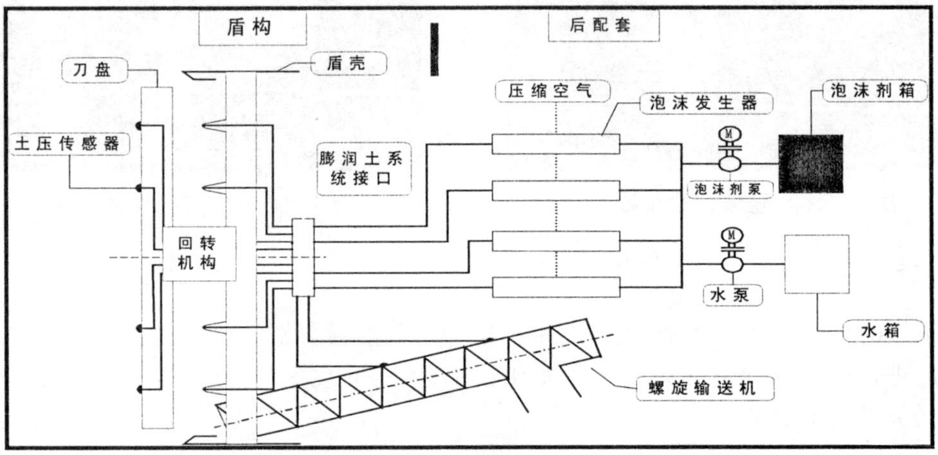

图11　泡沫及膨润土系统示意图

5.3　换刀方案的选择

就成都特有的富水砂卵石地层而言，换刀相当频繁。在该地层换刀，可采用常压换刀和带压换刀两种方式。

（1）常压换刀方式

在富水砂卵石地层开仓换刀，掌子面土体稳定性差，砂卵石地层遇水易坍塌。在该地质条件下，采用常压进仓方式必须对换刀位置进行降水并辅以注浆、旋喷、人工挖孔桩或灌注桩等加固措施，否则难以保证换刀处掌子面的稳定。

（2）带压换刀方式

经过对刀盘前方地层进行处理后，在保证刀盘前方周围地层和土仓满足气密性要求的条件下，通过在土仓建立合理的气压来平衡刀盘前方的水、土压力，达到稳定掌子面和防止地下水渗入的目的，为在土仓内进行刀盘刀具检查和更换刀具创造工作条件。其工作原理如图12所示。

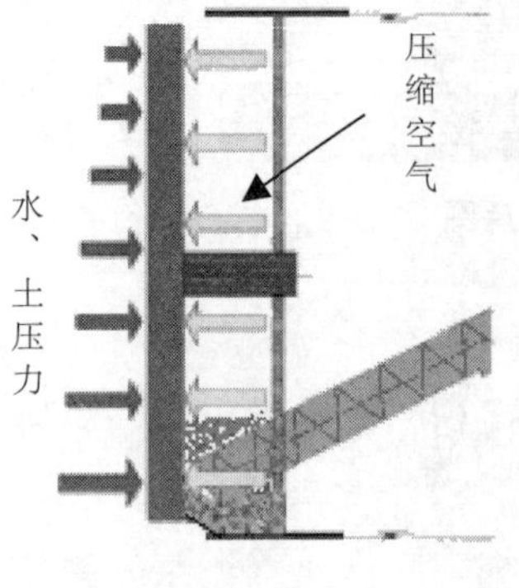

图12　带压作业原理示意图

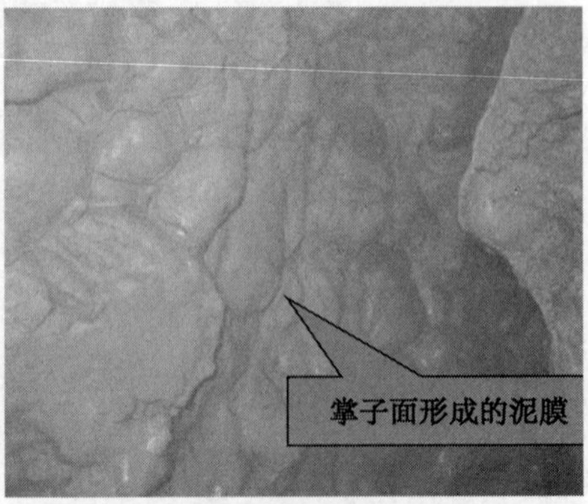

图13　掌子面形成的泥膜图

富水砂卵石地层孔隙率大，带压过程中气体易逃逸，导致压力难以保持，进而影响施工安全。为有效填充地层孔隙，防止气体逃逸，在带压进仓换刀过程中,首先通过膨润土注入系统向土仓内注入优质的膨润土泥浆置换原有仓内的碴土，在掌子面形成良好的泥膜。当压力保持稳定后，进行带压进仓换刀。通过采取上述措施后，成功实现了富水砂卵石地层带压进仓作业，掌子面形成的泥膜如图 13 所示。

由于成都地铁沿线基本都处于繁华的都市内，地面建（构）筑物、管线密布，采用常压换刀方式需占用地面场地进行加固施工，对地面环境影响大；而采用带压进仓方式基本不影响地面环境，因此在换刀方式的选择上应首选带压进仓方式而尽量避免采用加固后常压进仓方式。

5.4 螺旋输送机问题

成都地铁一号线盾构工程区间隧道穿越的地层基本为全断面富水砂卵石，为防止喷涌，土压平衡盾构机采用了双级螺旋输送机，如图 14 所示。但从实际施工情况看，盾构施工时由于建立了合适的土压力、碴土改良效果也较好，地下水虽然比较丰富，但尚未达到喷涌的程度。而且砂卵石地层中螺旋输送机磨损严重，螺旋输送机拆除修复极为困难。因此，建议采用单级螺旋进行出碴，以减小施工难度、降低工程成本。

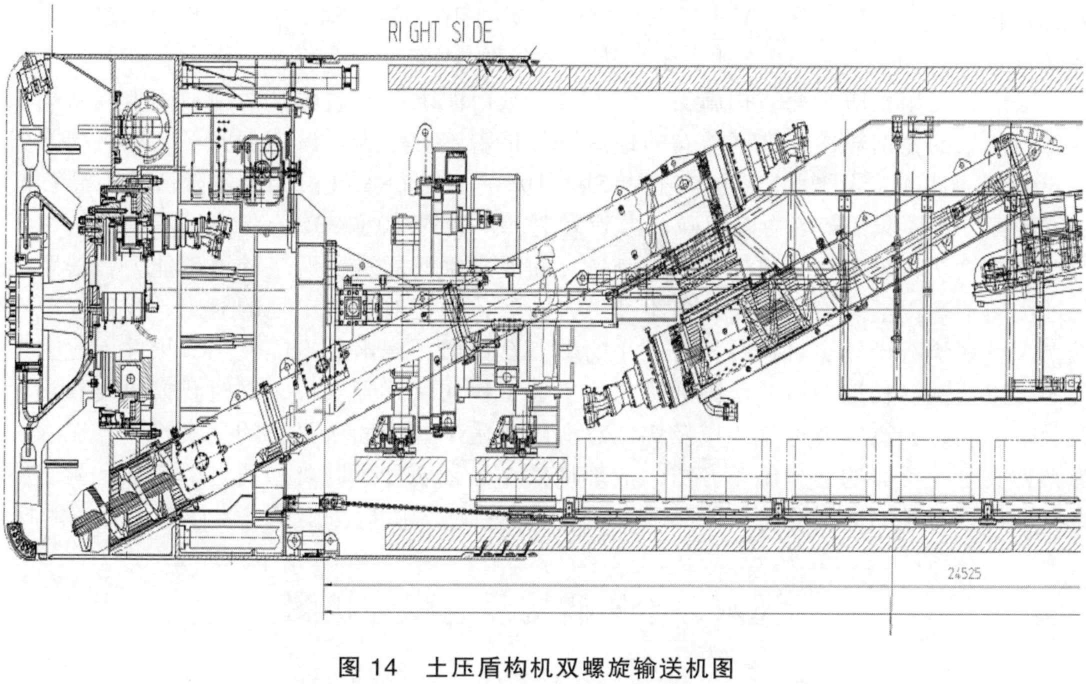

图 14　土压盾构机双螺旋输送机图

5.5 地表沉降相对较大

盾构在富水砂卵石地层掘进，其地表沉降槽曲线基本沿隧道中线呈正态分布，一般在轴线处的沉降值最大，在隧道洞径范围是其沉降的主要范围，离隧道中线 5 m 处的沉降值基本占峰值的 65%左右；轴线 5～10 m 为次要沉降区，距隧道中线 10 m 处的沉降值占峰值的 10%～15%左右，其单线沉降槽宽度为 20 m 左右(约三倍洞径)，如图 15 所示。

从沉降量看，土压盾构施工引起的地表最大沉降量一般为 12～15 mm（图中左线隧道中线处)，而泥水盾构施工引起的地表最大沉降量一般只有 8～11 mm 左右（图中右线隧道中线处）。两者均能满足规范要求，但土压盾构施工引起的地表最大沉降量明显要大于泥水盾构施工引起的地表沉降量，特别是隧道埋深较浅时土压盾构施工的地表沉降控制相对困难。

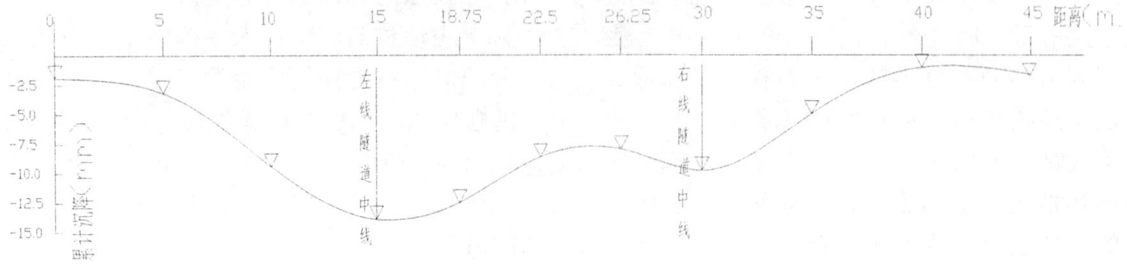

图 15 地表沉降槽曲线图

6 结论和建议

采用盾构法进行成都地区富水砂卵石地层施工，在全国尚属首次。从成都地铁 1 号线两种不同类型盾构机的试用情况看，采用泥水盾构施工其施工难度大、施工进度慢（平均月进度仅 79.2 m）、施工成本高（仅施工用电量就比土压盾构高 1 倍以上），而采用土压平衡盾构其施工难度相对较小、施工进度快（月平均进度达到 237 m，见图 16 泥水、土压进度柱状图）、施工成本可控。因此，在成都地区特有的富水砂卵石地层适宜采用土压平衡盾构施工，而不适宜采用泥水平衡盾构。两种不同类型盾构机在成都地铁 1 号线使用效果的差别与成都地区特有的地质情况是密不可分的，该地层卵石含量极高（卵石含量约占 55%～80%）、大粒径漂石含量高（含量为 5%～10%）且粒径大（前期勘测阶段发现漂石最大粒径为 670 mm）、充填物含量少（充填物以细砂、中砂为主，含量约 10%～35%），土压平衡盾构由于采用刀具破碎卵石、螺旋输送机出碴能有效破解以上难题，而泥水平衡盾构受泥浆的携碴能力、长距离卵石输送以及设备过度磨损等因素的制约使用效果不理想。当然，通过对类似工程的对比，我们发现在卵石含量相对较低，大粒径漂石含量少且粒径相对较小的砂卵石地层，泥水盾构的使用效果并不比土压盾构差，这一点我们可以从武汉长江隧道、沈阳地铁二号线等工程实例得到实证；同时我们也要看到泥水平衡盾构在地表沉降控制、大直径隧道施工以及穿江越海隧道施工等方面所具有的巨大优势，泥水平衡盾构仍然不失为一种安全、可靠的盾构施工方法。成都地铁 1 号线两种不同类型盾构的成功试验，对摸索和总结不同类型盾构机对成都地层的适应性、深入理解砂卵石地层盾构法施工技术做出了有益的探索。

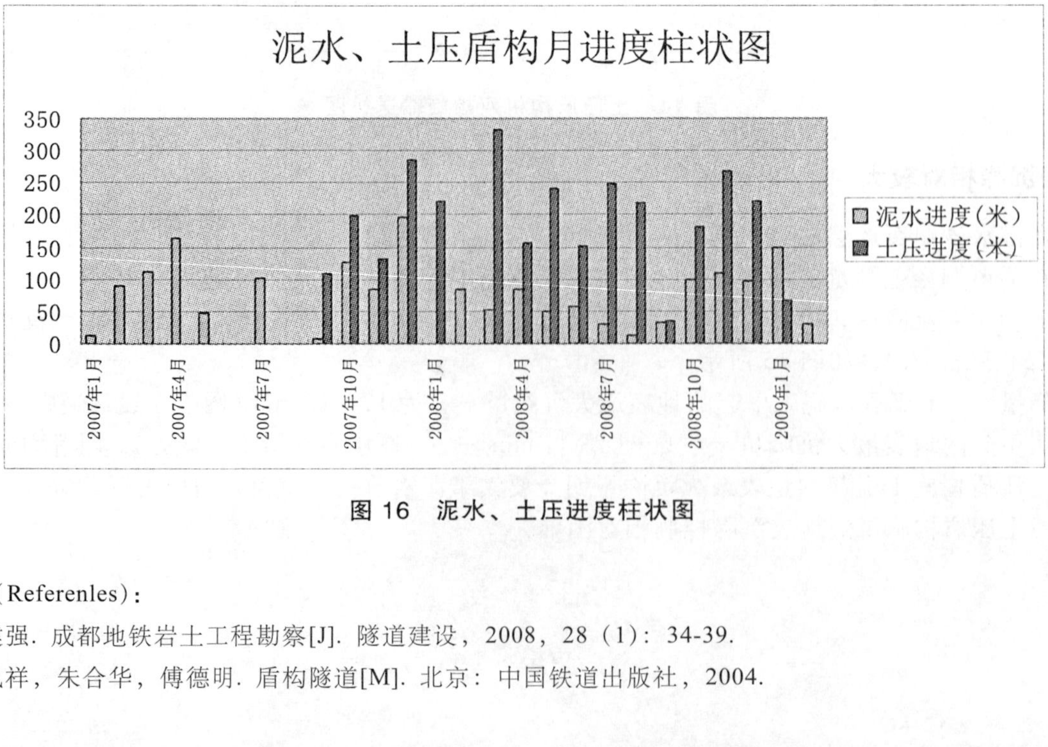

图 16 泥水、土压进度柱状图

参考文献（Referenles）:

[1] 李建强. 成都地铁岩土工程勘察[J]. 隧道建设，2008，28（1）：34-39.

[2] 张凤祥，朱合华，傅德明. 盾构隧道[M]. 北京：中国铁道出版社，2004.

[3] 王梦恕. 不同地层条件下的盾构与 TBM 选型[J]. 隧道建设，2006，26（2）：1-3，8.
[4] 唐健，陈溃. 成都地铁试验段盾构选型探讨[J]. 建筑机械化，2006，27（6）：43-46.
[5] 项兆池，楼如岳，傅德明. 最新泥水盾构技术[M]. 上海隧道工程股份有限公司施工技术研究所科技情报室，2001.
[6] 晏启祥，耿萍，何川. 地铁砂卵石地层采用加泥式土压平衡盾构机的设备配置及顶推力检算[J]. 建筑机械化，2007，27（6）：19-21.
[7] 何其平. 土压平衡盾构刀盘结构探讨 [J]. 工程机械，2003（11）：10-16.
[8] 宋云，张君，张立宇. 成都地铁施工中盾构机的应用[J]. 桥隧机械&施工技术，2008（01）：68-71.
[9] 徐润泽，宋天田. 成都地铁土压平衡盾构隧道工程风险识别与评价[J]. 隧道建设，2007，27（6）：89-93.
[10] 刘树山. 砂卵石地层盾构隧道刀具更换方案研究[J]. 隧道建设，2008，28（3）：268-270，276.

作者简介（Bio-data）：

张延，1972年10月男，成都地铁有限责任公司，高级工程师，工学硕士，主要从事地下工程建设管理。

Yan ZHANG, Male, Manager, Senior Engineer, Chengdu Metro Co., Ltd. Engaged in management of underground engineering construction

E-mail: cametrozhyan@126.com

肖中平，男，成都地铁有限责任公司，副总经理，西南交通大学兼职教授。

Zhongping XIAO，Male，Vice General Manager，Chengdu Metro Co., Ltd. Part-time Professor

富水砂卵石地层土压平衡盾构施工关键技术

李 林
中铁二局股份有限公司城通公司，上海 200336

【摘 要】 本文以成都地铁 1 号线省体育馆至天府广场区间盾构工程为例，针对成都富水砂卵石地层特点，以理论分析和现场试验为基本手段，从盾构施工的几各个主要方面进行了详细分析和深入研究，阐述了成都富水砂卵石地层土压平衡盾构施工的关键技术，特别是用试验的方法解决了高透气性地层带压换刀施工工艺，对于改进和完善盾构设备的适应性、减少盾构施工对周围环境影响，找到了有效的探索途径，为以后类似工程盾构施工提供了大量有参考价值的经验和数据。
【关键词】 富水砂卵石地层；土压平衡盾构机；关键技术

STUDY ON DRIVING OF EARTH-PRESSURE BALANCED SHIELD MACHINE IN WATER-RICH COBBLE GROUND

Lin LI
Engineering Department of Chengtong Branch, China railway NO.2 Engineering Group Co., Ltd., Shanghai 200336, China

Abstract: The interzone between Stadium to Tianfu Square of Chengdu subway line No.1 is located in complicated water-rich cobble strata. The tubes will be constructed by earth-pressure balanced shield machines. Theoretical analysis and field tests are conducted to study the key techniques for the construction of the tunnel under the particular circumstances in details. Especially, the paper illustrates the technique of changing cutter with pressure in highly ventilated strata based on the field tests. The effective exploration way has been found to improve the suitability of shield machines and reduced its effect on circumstance of shield construction. The findings of this study would be beneficial to the construction of shield machines for similar projects.
Key words: water-rich cobble ground; earth-pressure balance shield machine; key techniques

1 工程概况

成都地铁 1 号线一期工程天府广场站—省体育馆站盾构区间隧道工程包括省体育馆站—小天竺站区间、小天竺站—锦江宾馆站区间、锦江宾馆站～天府广场站共 3 个区间；隧道为外径ϕ6 000 mm 的单圆盾构隧道，隧道全长 4 078.347 m，采用两台ϕ6 250 mm 海瑞克土压平衡盾构掘进；区间段内线路隧道最大埋深为 13.8 m，最小埋深 8.1 m，最小坡度 2‰，最大坡度 26.1‰，左右线间距 11～13 m。

盾构由省体育馆站始发，沿人民南路由南向北掘进，先后经过小天竺站和锦江宾馆站，最后到达天府广场站，在天府广场站吊出。

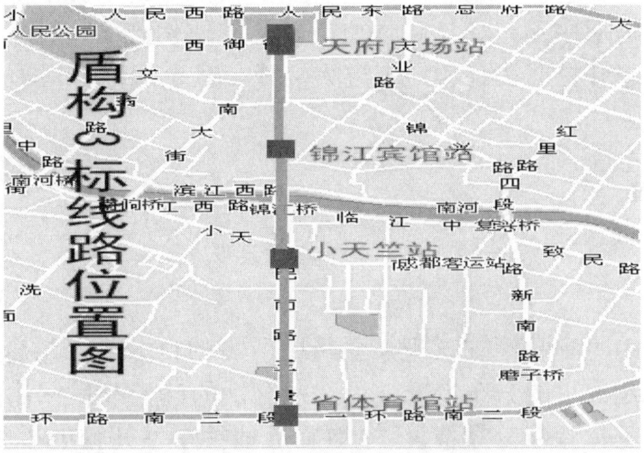

图 1　盾构 3 标线路位置图

区间隧道主要在<3-7>、<4-4>卵石土层中穿过，局部穿越<2-8>粉质黏土层、<4-4>卵石土层、<3-4>细砂层，在隧道线路的局下部主要为<5-2>强风化泥岩层和<5-3>中等风化泥岩。

隧道穿过的地质断面主要有三种形式：全断面的砂卵石地层、上半断面为砂卵石和下半断面为泥岩的复合地层、全断面的粉细砂层。

隧道上部含有对盾构掘进不利的<2-5>细砂层和<2-6>中砂、粗砂层，下部为强风化泥岩。

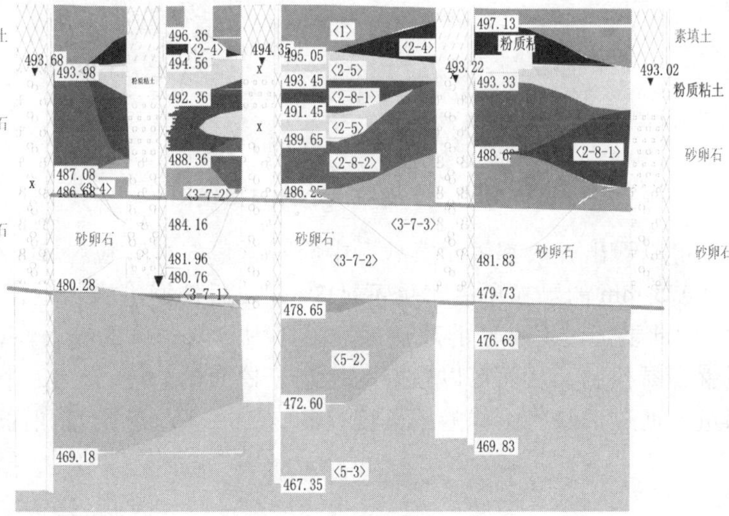

图 2　地层剖面图

工程位于成都市中心，道路两侧高楼林立，人口密集，交通繁忙，属于繁华的商业区。在盾构隧道施工影响范围内的建（构）筑物主要有开行大厦、锦江大桥、滨江路下穿隧道。另外，沿线地下管线众多，主要有电力管线、污水管道、通信光缆、雨水管线、上水管、煤气等多种市政管线。

2　富水砂卵石地层的特点

卵石含量高：卵石土层中卵石含量达 55%以上，为成都地层的骨架成分；

漂石粒径大：1 号线区间探井揭示漂石最大粒径为 350 mm，天府广场站开挖揭示漂石最大粒径为 670 mm，含量为 5%～10%，随机性分布。

卵石和漂石强度高：卵石和漂石单轴抗压强度达 90 MPa 以上，最高强度高达 200 MPa。

地下水位高：地下水位埋深约 3.9～8.9 m，补给丰富。

地层透水性强：卵石土层渗透系数为 12～27 m/d，透水性强。

盾构主要在富水砂卵石地层中通过，这种地质条件下的盾构施工，开挖面容易产生涌水、涌砂，造成细颗粒物质大量流失，引起开挖面失稳和地表过大沉降、甚至塌陷，对盾构掘进要求高。

3 关键因素分析和试验

3.1 地层土体分析

颗粒大小分析是测定土中各种粒组在该土总质量中所占的百分数。结合成都砂卵石地层的特点进行筛分试验，了解这种地层颗粒大小的分布情况，为选择合适的碴土改良方法提供重要的依据。

为了了解盾构拟穿越的土体颗粒分布情况，选取临近地铁车站开挖的砂卵石土进行了 6 组筛分试验，试验结果如图 3 所示。

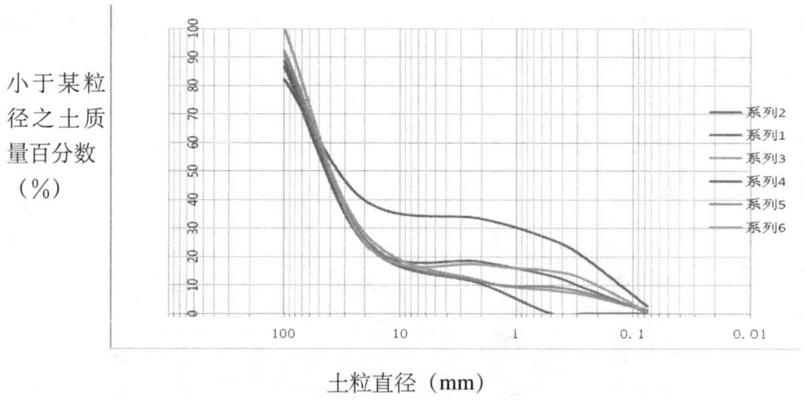

图 3 土颗粒大小分布曲线图

通过筛分试验结果可以看出，成都砂卵石地层中卵石含量较高，粒径 20～200 mm 的颗粒所占比重达到 65%以上，小于 0.075 mm 的颗粒所占比重不足 3%，在盾构掘进施工时，容易因碴土的流动性差而导致堵塞现象的发生。因此要通过对碴土的改良来提高压力舱内土体的流动性，如果土体的流动性较好，螺旋排土器的排土量就容易控制，从而可以较好的控制开挖面的稳定。一般对于土仓内土体的流动性可以用坍落度试验来衡量，通过试验将土体的坍落度控制在 10～15 cm 的范围内，其状态满足塑性流动状态的要求。

3.2 透气性研究

由于成都富水砂卵石地层地质条件特殊，全世界范围内找不到具有对比和借鉴意义的地层漏气资料和参考工程案例，国内也没有相应规范。为获得这种地层自然条件下的透气和用膨润土浆液改良后的保气特征，在 2007 年 10 月采用变水头法进行了压气试验，为此后空压机的选配和带压作业提供指导作用。

压气试验所得结论如下：

（1）对于成都地层天然土体，从 0.6 bar 加压到 1.0 bar，再卸压至 0.6 bar，其空气损失率见表 1。

表 1 天然土体工况的空气损失率

状 态	压力（bar）	空气损失率（m^3/h）
1	（加压至）0.6	13.0
2	（加压至）0.8	16.5
3	（加压至）1.0	52.0
4	（卸压至）0.8	44.0
5	（卸压至）0.6	39.0

（2）采用膨润土泥浆改良后，从 0.6 bar 加压到 1.0 bar，再卸压至 0.6 bar，其空气损失率见表 2。

表 2　加入膨润土后空气损失率

状　态	压力（bar）	空气损失（m^3/h）
1	（加压至）0.6	11.5
2	（加压至）0.8	13.0
3	（加压至）1.0	14.0
4	（卸压至）0.8	14.0
5	（卸压至）0.6	11.0

（3）试验表明加入膨润土后气体渗透性明显下降：在 1.0 bar 的压力下，加入膨润土后气体损失是未加前的 27%。

估算出钻孔的气压损失面积约为 1.2 m^2。实际盾构土仓加入压缩空气的气压损失面积是 35.2 m^2（开挖仓内有半仓碴土，盾构机周围膨润土泥浆 100%有效）至 129.6 m^2（开挖仓清空，盾构机周围膨润土泥浆 50%有效）。

压气试验结果表明在土仓加 1.0 bar 压缩空气时的气体损失量如下：

当土仓半空时，膨润土泥浆注入效果良好：漏气量为 400 m^3/h。

当土仓清空时，膨润土泥浆注入效果一般：漏气量为 1 500 m^3/h。

3.3　刀具磨损分析

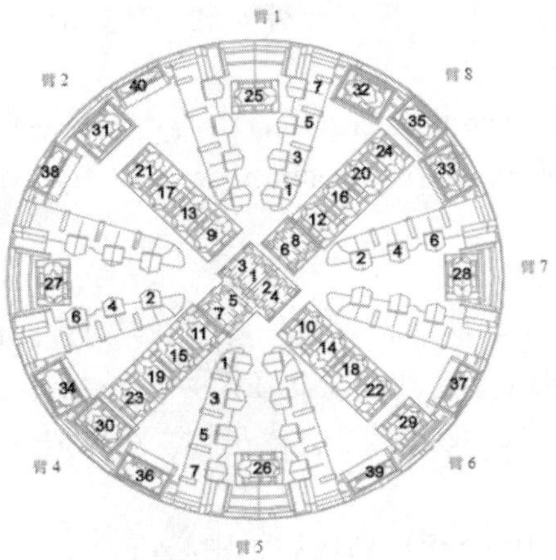

图 4　刀具布置图

（1）第一次刀具配置

第一次刀具配置采用双刃滚刀和单刃滚刀相结合的配置方式。即：中心刀 1#~8#为中心滚刀，9#~25#、40#共 18 把单刃滚刀，26#~39#共 14 把双刃滚刀。在完成 35 环隧道掘进后，带压换刀对刀具进行检查和更换。

图 5　单刃滚刀，多边偏磨

经检查发现，在仅仅完成 35 环（52.5 m）掘进后，大部分单刃滚刀发生了严重偏磨现象，除 19#~25#外，其余 10 把单刃滚刀均出现不同程度的多边偏磨，其中 13#刀最大偏磨量达到了 45 mm。其中靠近刀盘中心的单刃滚刀（9#~18#）偏磨比较严重，靠近刀盘外侧的双刃滚刀属于正常磨损。

造成内侧单刃滚刀磨损的原因主要是内部滚刀线速度小、开挖面不能为单刃滚刀提供足够的转动力矩，从而使得内部滚刀发生严重偏磨。因此，可以认为刀盘内侧不适合采用单刃滚刀。

在这种刀具配置条件下，盾构在砂卵石地层下掘进速度缓慢，平均约 12 mm/min。

（2）第二次刀具配置

第二次配置刀具时，我们将 1#~8#中心滚刀更换为 4 把中心双刃羊角刀，9#~24#、26#~31#共 21 把更换为正齿刀，25#安装为双刃滚刀，32#~40#共 9 把安装为单刃滚刀。在完成 161 环隧道掘进后，带压换刀对刀具进行检查和更换。

经检查发现，在完成 161 环（241.5 m）掘进后，中心齿刀 5#~7#均匀磨损，磨损值 40 mm，其余中心齿刀刀磨损量不超过 30 mm；单刃齿刀磨损量随刀具的旋转半径增大而增大，26#~31#单刃齿刀磨损非常严重；32#~40#的单刃滚刀中，除 38#~40#正常磨损约 15~20 mm 外，其余严重偏磨。

齿刀在内侧基本适用，但在刀盘外侧由于线速度较大因而磨损较大；单刃滚刀在外侧偏磨现象严重，单独安装不适合成都的砂卵石地层，而双刃滚刀基本不偏磨。在刀盘中部滚刀替换为齿刀后，掘进速度有了显著的提高，平均约 25 mm/min。

（3）第三次刀具配置

在第三次安装刀具采用如下布置：1#~8#为 4 把中心双刃齿刀，9#~12#、16#共 5 把齿刀，17#~23#、25#～27#、29#、31#、33#、37#、40#共 15 把单刃滚刀，其余 13#～15#、24#、28#、30#、32#、34~36#、38#、39#共 12 把双刃滚刀，即将刀盘外侧单、双刃滚刀交替安装。在完成 132 环隧道掘进后，带压换刀对刀具进行检查和更换。

经检查发现，在完成 132 环（198 m）掘进后，中心齿刀 1#~3#、2#~4#、5#~7#、6#~8#均匀磨损，磨损量大；9#~12#、16#单刃齿刀磨损从内侧的 80 mm 逐步扩大为外侧的 116 mm；双刃滚刀和单刃滚刀无偏磨，磨损基本正常。

（4）第四次刀具配置

第四次刀具配置如下：1#~8#为 4 把中心双刃齿刀刀，9#~12#、16#共 5 把齿刀，17#~23#、25#~27#、29#、31#、33#、37#、40#共 15 把单刃滚刀，其余 13#～15#、24#、28#、30#、32#、34#~36#、38#、39#共 12 把双刃滚刀，即在刀盘外圈将单、双刃滚刀交替安装。在完成 73 环隧道掘进后，带压换刀对刀具进行检查和更换。

经检查发现，在完成 73 环（109.5 m）掘进后，中心齿刀由于实际掘进长度短，磨损不大，而其余刀具实际掘进距离为 205 环（307.5 m），由于掘进距离较长，因此刀具磨损普遍偏严重，但均表现为均匀磨损，未发生偏磨现象，掘进寿命有了大幅度的提高。

盾构掘进速度也保持了较高的水平，平均速度约 48 mm/min，最高速度达到 61 mm/min。

（5）第五次刀具配置

第五次安装刀具布置如下：1#~8#为 4 把中心双刃齿刀，9#~10#，12#~14#，16#~22#，共 12 齿刀，其余刀具为双刃滚刀，即将刀盘外侧全部配置为双刃滚刀。在完成 183 环隧道掘进后，带压换刀对刀具进行检查和更换。

经检查发现，在完成 183 环（273 m）掘进后，1#～8#中心齿刀磨损严重；单刃齿刀均匀磨损；部分双刃滚刀偏磨。

这次刀具布置表明，除盾构中心齿刀磨损严重外，其余刀具磨损基本正常。因此，在隧道贯通前，盾构需要破除混凝土洞门，中心刀具不宜采用中心齿刀，刀盘应主要配置为滚刀。

通过对不同的刀具配置进行磨损分析，可以得出以下盾构刀具的磨损规律：

（1）整体来说，刀具的磨损随其旋转半径增大而增大。

（2）单刃滚刀主要表现为单边、多边弦偏磨，部分单刃滚刀由于未及时更换而发生刀圈和轴承磨损，位于刀盘中心部位的单刃滚刀磨损更为严重。单刃滚刀偏磨的主要原因是由于内部滚刀线速度小、开挖面不能为单刃滚刀提供足够的转动力矩，从而使得内部滚刀发生严重偏磨。另外，刀盘中心位置碴土流通不畅，有时候会发生结泥饼现象，也是造成单刃滚刀偏磨的原因之一。

（3）双刃滚刀主要表现为均匀磨损，双刃滚刀耐磨性能较好。

（4）齿刀磨损主要表现为刃偏磨，刀刃靠刀盘旋转径向方向内侧磨损较外侧大，位于刀盘外侧的齿刀由于磨损量过大而容易导致轴承磨损。

（5）单个刮刀的磨损形式主要表现为两侧磨损量大，中间小。同一号位置的刮刀的磨损量基本一样。随着号数增大，刮刀的磨损量也越严重。刮刀的磨损随刀具的行程有关，行程越大磨损量也越大。刮刀耐磨性能基本满足掘进要求。

（6）刀盘内侧不适合单刃滚刀，刀盘外侧不适合齿刀。刀盘内侧刀具（9#～20#）应配置齿刀，外侧刀具（21#～40#）应配置双刃滚刀。

（7）在全盘使用滚刀的过程中，开挖出的卵石完全被滚刀所破损，而刀盘部分使用齿刀时，由于砂卵石地层的特殊性，即卵石和砂的组合固结体，整体性差，因此仅需齿刀破坏组合固结体的整体性，将砂和卵石剥离开，就能实现掘进的目的，而不需要将卵石破坏，避免无谓的能耗浪费。

（8）在隧道线路竖线曲线最低部，隧道下部为强风化和中等风化泥岩，具有一定的强度，整体性能好，必须使用滚刀破除。

（9）在隧道贯通前，盾构需要破除洞门围护桩（墙）混凝土，因此，中心位置不适应布置齿刀，而应采用破除硬岩能力强的滚刀。

（10）中部单刃滚刀调整为齿刀后，刀盘扭矩明显增大，盾构掘进速度也显著增大。

3.4 膨润土泥浆试验

膨润土泥浆对土层的改良效果在带压换刀过程中有着举足轻重的作用。膨润土泥浆的技术指标包括：膨润土配比；发酵时间；制备流程。根据现场施工经验，不同地区的膨润土原料具有很大差异。为了使泥浆改良效果达到带压换刀施工的需要（黏性太大，不宜注入砂卵石孔隙；黏性太小，开挖面不宜形成泥饼），对其配比和黏稠度关系进行室内试验，得出了一些有益的结论：

（1）膨润土泥浆黏性与发酵时间关系密切。试验发现，随着发酵时间增长，膨润土泥浆的黏性明显提高（以 24 小时为宜，建议不要超过 72 小时，否则黏性反而下降，乃至膨润土泥浆失效），且提高的速度与温度和搅拌质量有关。温度越高，黏性提高越快；搅拌质量越好，黏性提高越快。

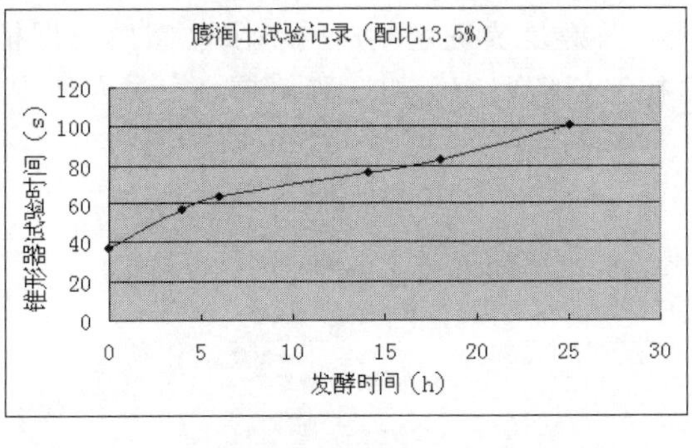

图 6 膨润土泥浆黏性与发酵时间关系

（2）制备过程直接影响膨润土泥浆效果。在前几次的带压换刀尝试中,将室内试验应用于实际时，由于忽略了膨润土泥浆搅拌制备过程，而以失败告终。而后改用高速竖向旋转搅拌器，膨润土粉末与水充分反应，在将膨润土泥浆从竖向搅拌器转移至水平搅拌罐后，保持水平搅拌罐 24 小时旋转，以防止沉淀发生。终于首次成功实现富水砂卵石地层带压换刀操作。

（3）根据室内试验确定的配比和黏性关系，结合实际带压换刀尝试的失败与成功经验，建议膨润土质量配比（膨润土粉末：水）取 10.5%，相应的锥形漏斗稠度仪计量值（发酵 24 小时后）为 35 s 左右。

3.5 碴土改良试验

通过对右线第 15 环至 90 环掘进过程中分别使用 A、B、C 三种泡沫实验室配比进行现场试验与应用，盾构在掘进第 15 环至第 19 环过程中多次停机，存在推力大、扭矩大、进尺小、刀盘被卡死、出碴量不易控制、姿态偏差过大、地表沉降控制相当困难等问题。在掘进至第 19 环时，盾构机最大推力达到 1 627.3 t，最大扭矩达到 4.59 MN · m，推进平均速度仅 4 mm/min，从螺旋输送机排出的碴土温度达到 56 摄氏度，不得不停机，开仓检查后发现刀盘开口被泥饼封住，土舱内的卵石土潮湿，有结球现象。刀盘上的泥饼固结坚硬，附着在刀盘上需用风镐清除，内有卵石及小岩粒，完全结成泥饼，放置后硬度变低，粉细砂、卵石土混合形成，泥质含量高。经过分析认为，刀盘在破除混凝土桩的时候，破除下来的干燥混凝土粉末与水结合，在刀盘旋转时产生高温的条件下，在刀盘开口位置形成了具有一定强度的“低标号混凝土”。

在保持掘进过程中土舱压力一定的情况下，通过向开挖面注入泡沫后，盾构掘进参数得到明显的改善，加入国产 A 型泡沫后，使得在掘进第 33 环至第 37 环过程中的平均掘进速度达到 44 mm/min，且千斤顶总推力降低约 22.4%，刀盘扭矩降低约 18.3%；加入进口 B 型泡沫后，使得在掘进第 51 环至第 55 环过程中的平均掘进速度达到 47 mm/min，且千斤顶总推力降低约 21.7%，刀盘扭矩降低约 12.1%；加入国产 C 型泡沫后，使得在掘进第 69 环至第 73 环过程中的平均掘进速度达到 35 mm/min，且千斤顶总推力降低约 13.8%，刀盘扭矩降低约 9.3%；在掘进过程中加入三种泡沫后，从土舱内排出的碴土均呈流塑状态，盾构掘进正常，且地表沉降得到有效控制。

综合现场试掘进过程中盾构的掘进参数并结合室内试验结果，最终确定选用国产 A 型泡沫。在盾构施工中按照泡沫原液与水的体积比进行配制泡沫液，试验结果表明该泡沫液体在 0.03 MPa 的压力下发泡倍率达到 15 倍，在砂卵石土层中的最大注入率达到 60%。

3.6 地层水压试验

“洞内同步测水压”技术，即将管片中心吊装孔（二次注浆预留孔）用钢钎打穿，安装带球阀的注浆头，在注浆头上安装水压力传感器，现场读取换刀前盾构机位置实际水压值。

地下水位随着季节的变化而变化，且与盾构施工或周边工程施工密切相关，所以每次带压换刀前有必要对盾构机位置的水头进行现场测试，以求获得准确水压力。“洞内同步测水压”技术大大方便了现场测试实际水压值。

3.7 气压值的确定

带压换刀所需气压值的确定，关键是要确定气压的下限，然后根据相关规范规定的工人可承受气压值，以及考虑一定的安全系数，按较低值取用。加压幅值越小，对人体生理健康越有利，劳动效率越高，单班持续工作时间可延长。

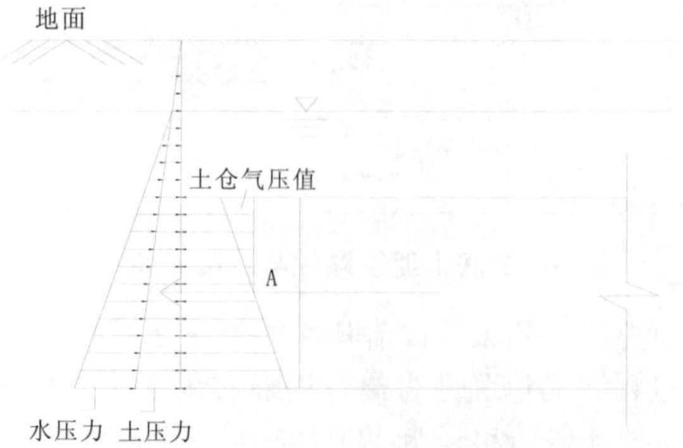

图 7　带压换刀气压值的选择

带压换刀所需气压值，因覆土厚度、地层渗透性、隧道直径、地下水埋深而异。理论上，如上图所示，土仓气压值应根据空仓底部（即图中 A 点，一般为半空状态）的水土压力值来确定。针对成都富水砂卵石地层，以水土分算为宜，因此本项目研究所得经验公式仅适用于水土分算的透水性地层，不适合水土合算的黏土地层。

对于一般透水性地层（采用水土分算时），带压换刀气压值可按下式计算：

$$p_{下限}=K\cdot Max\{\gamma_{水}h_{水},\ e_{侧}\}$$

式中 $p_{下限}$ ——气压下限值；

K ——安全系数，一般 $K>1$；

$\gamma_{水}h_{水}$ ——空仓底部水压；

$e_{侧}$ ——空仓底部土层侧压力，若处于水位以下时按浮容重计。

对于成都富水砂卵石地层，从本工程多次成功带压换刀经验来看，可按以下经验公式计算带压换刀所需气压值：

$$p_{下限}=k\cdot\gamma_{水}h_{水}$$

式中 k ——气压的取值系数，可小于 1（首次实现），按下表取值；

其他符号意义同前。

k 的取值见表 3。

表 3

膨润土浆液的注浆效果	好	中	差
k 的建议取值	0.9	1.0	1.1

4 盾构推进关键技术

4.1 带压换刀技术

盾构机到达预定换刀地点前的操作流程如图 8 所示。

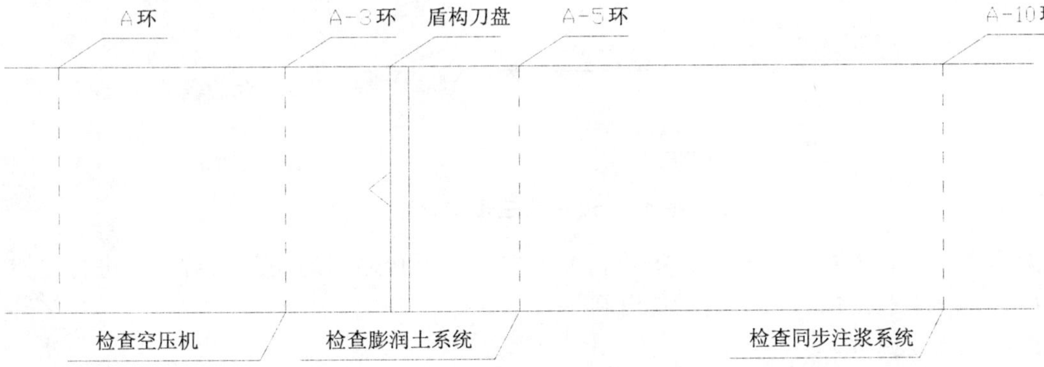

图 8 盾构机到达预定换刀地点前的操作流程示意图（A 环为预定换刀地点）

到达 A 环的前五环，在盾构周边注入膨润土，并且要保证发酵时间。此时盾构机掘进速度调整为 30～50 mm/min，刀盘转速调整为 1～2 rpm。持续掘进速度和转速到达距 A 点前一环（1.5 m）处，盾构掘进速度调整为 25 mm/min，刀盘转速调整为 0.8～1.5 rpm，最多不能超过 1.5 rpm。并同时用盾构刀盘前方八个注浆孔中位于盾体上方的四个注浆孔注入膨润土泥浆，设定压力 1.1 倍开挖面的压力。在到达 A 点前注入 25 m^3 泥浆在开挖面上形成泥膜。

盾构机到达预定换刀点（A 点），盾构停止掘进，但是继续转动刀盘和注入膨润土泥浆。持续上述操作 5 min 后停止刀盘转动。随后向土仓内加压缩空气，进行气压和土压置换。

带压换刀的人闸加减压及人员进、出仓流程如图 9 至图 11 所示。

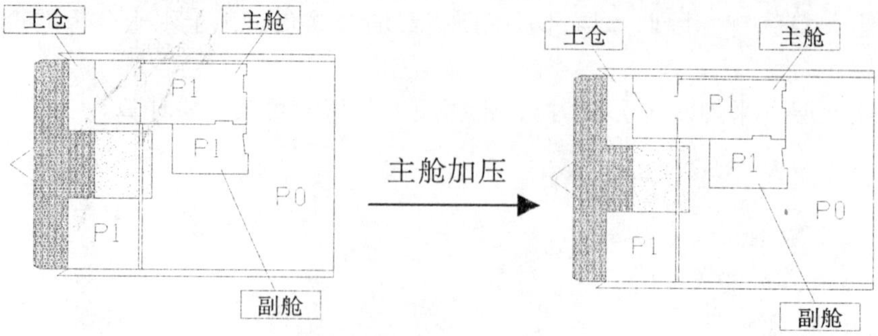

图 9　流程第一步示意图

（1）关闭主舱闸门，打开通风球阀，对主舱进行加压,直至土仓与主舱实现气压平衡，停止加压，开启土仓闸门，人员进入土仓。

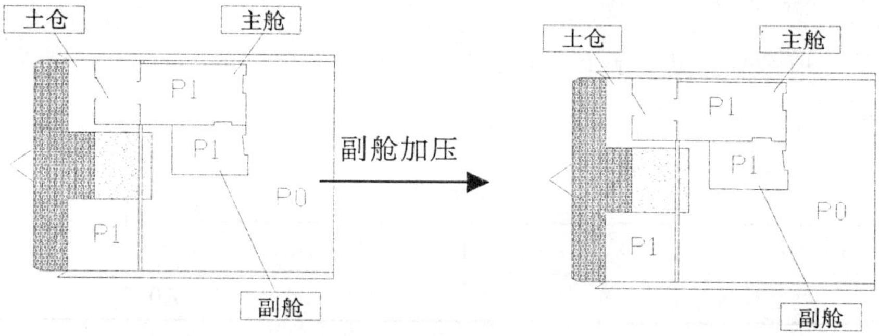

图 10　流程第二步示意图

（2）主舱和土仓继续保持畅通，关闭副舱闸门，打开通风球阀，对副舱进行加压，直至副舱与主舱实现气压平衡，停止加压，开启主、副舱间闸门，人员、材料、工具进入主舱和土仓进行检查和换刀作业。

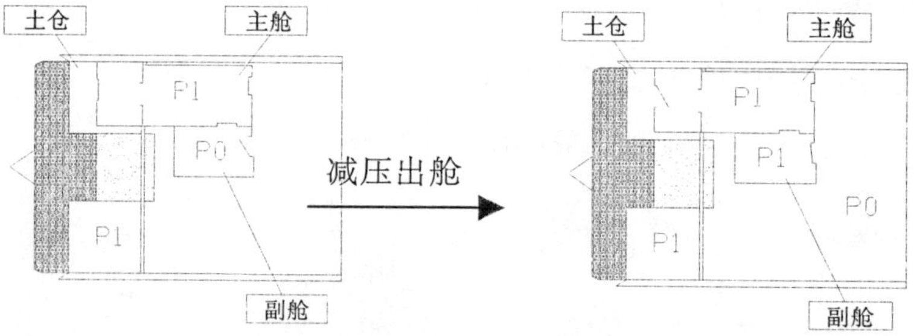

图 11　流程第三步示意图

（3）换刀作业完成，人员、工具进到主舱，关闭主舱与土仓之间的闸门，对主舱进行缓慢减压，直接减为大气压，打开主舱闸门，人员、工具出闸。

换刀结束后的恢复掘进:

换刀结束后，待人员与设备撤出土仓和人闸后，启动刀盘，恢复掘进（暂时不出土）。通过压力传感器可以看到土仓内压力变化，此时通过土仓内排气阀排出一部分气体保持恒定的支撑压力，重复以上动作至满仓，重新建立土压平衡，进入正常掘进施工。

由于恢复掘进地点、地质条件的差别，恢复掘进采用不同的模式:

（1）砂卵石地层恢复掘进:

由于砂卵石土层有一定的稳定性，因此，采用加气推进的模式。即更换刀具结束后，启动刀盘与千斤顶恢复盾构掘进，同时保持土仓内气压值暂不出土，逐渐恢复土仓内存土量，增加土压，同步逐渐减小气压，最终实现土压完全代替气压平衡。

（2）砂层恢复掘进:

由于砂层稳定性差，在砂层中恢复掘进时，采用回填土仓的方式来实现土压代替气压，即在换刀结束后，盾构暂不恢复掘进，而是往土仓内注入膨润土，用膨润土回填土仓，同步逐渐减小气压，当土压完全代替气压后，启动刀盘与千斤顶恢复盾构掘进。

4.2 刀具磨损控制技术

成都富水砂卵石地层的卵石主要成分为砂岩与石英岩，中粗砂颗粒主要成分为石英，它们对刀具、刀盘造成非常严重的磨损。此外，由于大粒径的卵石致使刀具切削的不均匀性和冲击破坏，容易使刀具产生异常损坏。

因此，如何提高刀具的耐磨性，以及根据不同刀具的开挖机理摸索适合成都地层的刀具选型和布置，从而延长刀具、刀盘使用寿命，直接关系到生产成本、进度效益、安全风险。

通过多次不同的刀具类型、布置形式进行掘进磨损分析，总结出了在富水砂卵石地层条件下刀具的磨损规律，及适合砂卵石地层的刀具选型和配置。

刀具的磨损随其旋转半径增大而增大。

单刃滚刀主要表现为单边、多边弦偏磨。单刃滚刀发生偏磨的主要原因是由于内部滚刀线速度小、开挖面不能为单刃滚刀提供足够的转动力矩。

双刃滚刀主要表现为均匀磨损，双刃滚刀耐磨性能较好。

齿刀磨损主要表现为刃偏磨。

单个刮刀的磨损形式主要表现为两侧磨损量大，中间小，刮刀耐磨性能基本满足掘进要求。

刀盘内侧不适合单刃滚刀，刀盘外侧不适合齿刀；刀盘内侧刀具应配置齿刀，外侧刀具应配置双刃滚刀。

由于砂卵石地层的特殊性，即卵石和砂的组合固结体，整体性差，因此仅需齿刀破坏组合固结体的整体性，将砂和卵石剥离开，卵石研磨程度低，而不需要将卵石破坏，避免了无谓的能耗浪费。

在隧道线路竖线曲线最低部，隧道下部为强风化和中等风化泥岩，具有一定的强度，整体性能好，必须使用滚刀破除。

在隧道贯通前，盾构需要破除洞门围护桩（墙）混凝土，因此，中心位置不适应布置齿刀，而应采用破除硬岩能力强的滚刀。

中部单刃滚刀调整为齿刀后，刀盘扭矩明显增大，盾构掘进速度也显著增大。

5 结束语

通过对成都富水砂卵石地层的带压换刀尝试，提出了适用于成都富水砂卵石地层带压换刀的气压值经验计算公式，总结出了“到达预定换刀地点前”、“到达预定换刀地点时”、“换刀完成后的恢复掘进”三阶段控制的施工工艺，以及摸索出了改良地层透气性的膨润土泥浆配比。

通过对富水砂卵石地层土压平衡盾构刀具、刀盘磨损规律的研究，摸索出了不同刀具类型和布置对该地层的适应性，并在本工程进行了改进运用，取得了较好的掘进效果和经济效益。

作者简介（Bio-data）：

李林，男，1965年6月出生，教授级高级工程师，研究生学历，中铁二局城通公司总工程师。从事铁路、公路、水电站等工程施工技术管理；近五年主要从事城市轨道交通及地下工程施工技术管理。

Lin LI, (1965—) male, Professor of Engineering with post-graduate education, is a chief engineer in China Railway Erju Group Co.,ltd ChengTong Branch. He Engages in the construction management of railway, highway, and hydropower station. In the recent five years he has been mainly in charge of the management of urban rail transport system and underground engineering technology.

E-mail: lilin413@sina.com

素混凝土连续墙在盾构始发端头加固施工中的应用

易 觉 姜自明 王家星
广东华隧建设股份有限公司，广东 广州 510635

【摘 要】 通过选用素混凝土连续墙进行加固，并配以搅拌桩或单管旋喷桩，成功解决了富含水软弱地层中盾构出洞所遇到的难题，这对于泥水盾构还是土压盾构，在类似地质条件下端头加固具有指导和借鉴意义。
【关键词】 素混凝土；连续墙；始发；端头加固；盾构

THE APPLICATION OF PLAIN CONCRETE DIAPHRAGM WALL IN THE SHIELD LAUNCHING SOIL REINFORCEMENT

Jue YI，Ziming JIANG，Jiaxing WANG
China Tunnel Construction Co., LTD., Guangdong 510635, Guangzhou, China

Abstract: By using the plain concrete diaphragm wall and with the mixed pile or jet grouting pile reinforce soil; the problem in the weak geologic strata was successfully solved. It provided guidance and reference to slurry shield and EPB shield in the similar geologic strata.
Key words: plain concrete；diaphragm wall；launching；soil reinforcement；shield

1 引 言

随着社会的发展，地下工程越来越多，尤其在能源、通讯及城市市政工程建设方面非开挖施工技术的应用越来越广泛，而盾构施工技术又是非开挖施工中的前沿技术，在地铁施工中被广泛应用。目前深圳地区的地铁施工中，地质复杂多变，尤其是填海区，地层相当软弱且含水丰富，稍有扰动，即会造成严重后果。

借鉴国内盾构工程施工经验教训，盾构工程在始发阶段出现问题的概率较高，尤其是加固体未能达到理想效果或加固失效时，极容易发生安全事故，轻则地面产生较大沉降，重则危及设备、人员安全，导致重大安全事故。根据加固地段地质特性，采用素连续墙为主，搅拌桩配合的加固模式，确保了加固体的有效性，确保了盾构始发安全。

本工程四次盾构始发均获成功，在富含水软弱地层中，可以认为素连续墙是非常有效的加固方法之一。因此，研究如何有效的使用素连续墙进行端头加固，确保盾构施工安全，是十分必要的。

2 工程概况

深圳地铁 2 号线是深圳市优先发展的轨道交通线路，是连接城市中心区与蛇口、南头半岛的纽带，也是特区内东西向交通走廊内的第二条轨道客运干线，沿途将经过蛇口、后海开发区、南山商业文化中心和深圳湾填海区，串联了上述片区主要的居住区和商业文化密集区，满足了南山与福田、罗湖二级客运走廊的客运需求。地铁 2 号线建成后在深圳世界之窗站与 1 号线换乘，将直接为 300 万以上的市民提供安全便捷的交通服务，能有效缓解南山区的交通压力。深圳地铁 2 号线线路经过新近填海区，地质较为软弱。某标段土压盾构机从后海站向南北两个方向掘进，区间左、右线隧道平面最大曲线半径为 1 000 m，最小曲线半径为 400 m，左、右线线间距 13.2～14.2 m，区间隧道最大线路纵坡为 28‰，最小纵坡为 2‰，竖曲线半径最大为 5 000 m，最小为 3 000 m，隧道拱顶埋深为 8～15 m。

3 地层分布特点和岩层特性分析

该标段始发端头隧道拱顶及洞身主要为①1 填土、①2 填石、①3 填砂、③2 淤泥、⑤2 砾砂、⑥2 淤泥质黏土、⑧2、⑧3 砂质黏性土。各土层土性如下：①1 素填土：褐黄、褐红、灰黑等色，主要由黏性土混少量砂砾组成，局部夹有碎块石；①2 填石：灰白、褐灰等色，主要由花岗岩块石组成，块石直径 20～150 cm，其余为碎石、角砾及黏性土充填；①3 填砂：褐灰色，主要由中砂组成；③3 淤泥：灰黑色，含有机质，可见贝壳及蚝壳，具腥臭味，饱和，软～流塑状；⑤2 砾砂：灰白色、浅黄等色，主要成分为石英质，混黏性土；⑥2 淤泥质黏土：灰黑色，局部混砂及腐木，局部以淤泥质砂为主，软塑～可塑状；⑧2、⑧3 砾（砂）质黏土：褐红、灰黄夹灰白等色，由下伏粗粒花岗岩风化残积而成，原岩结构可辨，局部硬塑状。水位在地面下 1.0～1.5 m，属富含水软弱地层，覆土厚度仅为 8 m。淤泥、砂层较厚，地下水丰富、稳定性差，若土体不能进行有效加固，存在涌砂、坍塌危险。地下水与海水有水力联系，地下水水位随海水涨落潮起伏变化。地下水是盾构始发主要隐患之一，如果能够有效隔绝地下水对掌子面的侵蚀，即可确保掌子面稳定。结合地质情况，在端头加固中采用素混凝土连续墙，并以搅拌桩辅助，可以有效隔绝地下水确保加固体无明显渗漏水，从而确保盾构始发安全。

4 加固方式

4.1 端头加固形式

深圳市地铁 2 号线工程土建 2203 标登～后区间和后～科区间共 2 个始发端头，在始发端头围护结构外紧贴围护结构施工一排素连续墙，然后进行搅拌桩的施工，在搅拌桩外侧再施工“U”型素混凝土墙，该“U”型素混凝土墙与搅拌桩搭接 30～50 cm，确保有效止水。始发后盾构机钻进素混凝土包裹的加固体内，依靠素连续墙的有效支档，可以提前破除洞门，加快施工进度，确保盾构始发顺利安全，节省工期。加固顺序为先施工搅拌桩，后施工素混凝土墙。素混凝土墙宽度为 0.8 m，纵向加固长度为 8.5 m，加固体上下左右外包隧道 3 m，搅拌桩和“U”型素混凝土墙上部为空桩，加固示意图如下。

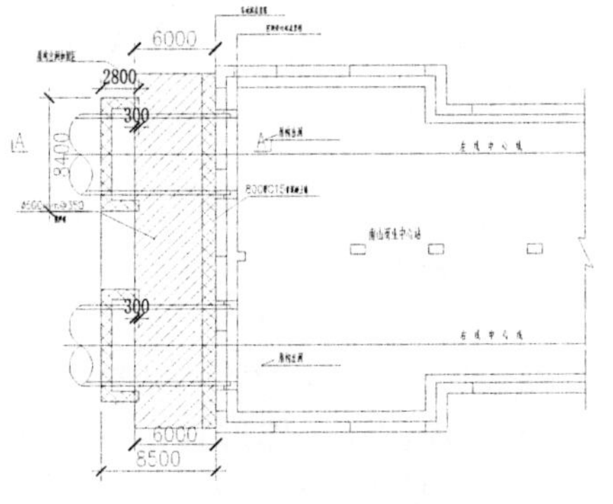

图 1 始发端头加固平面示意图

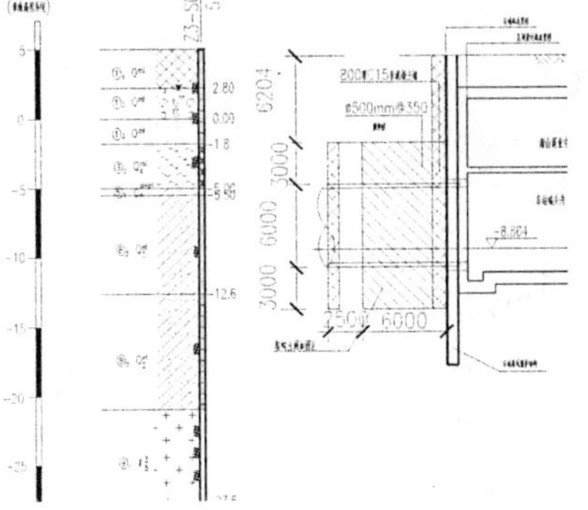

图 2 始发端头加固剖面示意图

4.2 加固特点

在端头加固中采用素混凝土连续墙，可以在洞门原围护结构连续墙破除后，继续维持洞门后土体的平衡，从而保证端头地层土体的稳定性。素连续墙因其自身强度比较高，能够承受扰动或振动产生的较大水土压力，在洞门原连续墙破除后，素连续墙抗弯能力足以满足要求。同时传统的搅拌桩或旋喷桩加固，其防水效果无法满足富含水软弱地层盾构始发需要，在始发过程中容易产生较大安全隐患。素连续墙防水效果明显比搅拌桩或旋喷桩强，加固完成后，可以有效隔绝地下水，为盾构始发提供有利的条件。

加固采用素连续墙施工质量要求比围护结构连续墙低，接头位置的防水要求不高，无需专门制作接头；因素混凝土墙数量不多，施工时现场若无抓斗成槽，成槽时可直接用冲桩机连续冲孔即可，简化了连续墙施工工艺。素连续墙一般采用 C15 水下混凝土，为避免素混凝土强度过高，磨损刀具，水下混凝土浇注之前可适度往混凝土搅拌车内掺入 1～2 m^3 泥浆，在确保素连续墙防水效果的前提下，尽量降低混凝土强度，以便盾构顺利始发掘进并保护刀具、刀盘。采用素连续墙加固后，加固范围明显减小，特别适用于施工场地小、地下管线密集、地面交通繁忙、距离地面建筑物基础比较近的工程场地，加固周期短，达到强度所需龄期短，整个端头加固的造价相对较低。

4.3 素混凝土强度分析

素连续墙支撑土体的最不利工况为洞门处素连续墙，此时围护结构连续墙已经全部破除，土体压力全部由素连续墙支撑，只要洞门处素连续墙强度满足要求，即可认为素连续墙满足盾构始发要求。素连续墙安全检算主要为强度验算，即在破除围护结构连续墙后，在盾构刀盘切割期间要保证素混凝土连续墙能够承受足够的侧向水土压力，最大拉应力要满足设计强度要求。采用有限元分析计算，混凝土采用 C15，弹性模量 E=3.15×10MPa，泊松比 μ=0.2，厚度 t=0.8 m。

（1）水土压力

根据钻孔资料显示，加固范围内拱顶地层主要为⑧2、⑧3 砂质黏性土层，容重 T=19 kN/m^3，黏聚力 c=23 kPa，内摩擦角φ=24°，参数取自区间详勘阶段岩土工程勘察报告，地下水位高程取地面以下 1.0 m，地面超载 q=20 kPa。现场经搅拌桩加固后的土体 c、φ值增大，为简化计算，取原状土进行计算，相当于增大了安全系数。

计算采用水土分算，盾构底部处水土压力：

$$P_{K1}=r_{水}h'+(q+r'h)\tan^2\left(45-\frac{\varphi}{2}\right)-2c\cdot\tan\left(45-\frac{\varphi}{2}\right)=285\ \text{kN/m}$$

盾构顶部处水土压力：

$$P_{k2}=r_{水}h^{l}+(q+r^{l}h)\tan^2\left(45-\frac{\varphi}{2}\right)-2c\cdot\tan\left(45-\frac{\varphi}{2}\right)=202\ \text{kN/m}$$

（2）素混凝土墙强度验算

按照以上计算结果建立模型，素混凝土连续墙采用固体单元模拟，6.6 m 盾构机直径范围以外按全部支撑约束，直径范围内为自由面。素混凝土墙上部考虑按固端约束，其余各边为自由约束 [1]。计算的最大拉应力满足 C15 混凝土的抗拉设计强度限值，强度验算合格。

5 关键技术

（1）素连续墙划分槽段时，刀盘切削范围内，设置整幅连续墙，避免连续墙接头漏水影响盾构施工；

（2）因素连续墙需刀盘直接切削，需适度降低混凝土标号，以保护刀具，若混凝土标号较高，可往每车混凝土搅拌车内注入 1～2 m^3 泥浆，降低混凝土强度，保护刀具；

（3）素混凝土连续墙作为与围护结构连续墙叠合的墙[1]，其结合面最好密实，在冲孔时要多冲刷几次,确保尽量不要存在夹层，破除围护结构连续墙后，素混凝土墙暴露时间要短，如若出现裂纹、渗水现象，盾构刀盘要尽早顶在素混凝土墙上，保证墙体稳定。

6 结 论

此项素连续墙在盾构施工中的应用技术在深圳市地铁 2 号线工程某标段的应用效果良好。始发加固达到了强度的要求，且不会发生渗水流砂现象，满足了盾构施工的需要。此项技术有利于提高工程质量，加速施工进度，同时节约施工成本有助于相关工程施工高质、高效、经济、文明地进行。该技术应用效果明显，应用前景广泛，值得在地铁工程中推广运用。

参考文献（Referenles）：

[1] 王琪，番茜，李宵辉. 盾构端头素混凝土连续墙加固技术. 都市快轨交通，2008（5）.

作者简介（Bio-data）：

第一作者：易觉，1965 年 2 月，男，高级工程师，硕士研究生，副总经理兼总工程师，目前主要从事地铁盾构施工。

Jue YI (1965—), male, senior engineer, candidate for master's degree, General Engineer and, vice-general manager, mainly engaged in the subway shield construction.

E-mail: yijue-001@163.com

第二作者：姜自明，1981 年 12 月，男，助理工程师，硕士研究生，技术负责人，主要从事地铁盾构施工。

E-mail: Ezimingjiang@sohu.com

第三作者：王家星，1984 年 12 月，男，助理工程师，大学本科，技术人员，主要从事地铁盾构施工技术管理。

E-mail: jsbwang@126.com

富水砂卵石地层土压平衡盾构带压换刀研究

刘向阳　陈　强
中铁二局股份有限公司城通公司，上海　200336

【摘　要】 土压平衡盾构在成都砂卵石地层掘进刀具的磨耗非常严重，须进行带压作业检查和更换刀具。针对砂卵石土夹透镜体砂层，土体松散，且地层富水，自稳能力差的特点，通过砂卵石地层进气量和气体损失量的确定、膨润土泥浆配比、机械配套及机械改造和现场试验研究分析，提出了合理的带压换刀方法。
【关键词】 富水砂卵石地层；土压平衡盾构；带压换刀

THE RESEARCH OF CHANGING CUTTER TOOLS UNDER AIR PRESURE FOR EPB EXCAVATING IN WATER SAND AND GRAVEL STARATUM

Xiangyang LIU，Qiang CHEN
Engineering Department of Chengtong Branch, China railway NO.2 Engineering Group Co., Ltd., Shanghai 200336, China

Abstract: Cutter tools of earth pressure balance shield excavating in water-rich sand and gravel stratum in Chengdu wears seriously, and it needs carrying out hyperbaric inspection and changing cutter tools under air pressure. Water-rich sand and gravel stratum is characterized by sand lens layer content, loose soil, rich water content and poor stability. Based on the methods of obtaining air input and air loss in sand and gravel stratum, bentonite/water ratio, mechanical equipment improvement and on-site test study, suitable method to change cutter tools working under air pressure is given.
Key words: water-rich gravel stratum; earth pressure balance shield; cutter changing under air pressure

1 引　言

成都地区地层卵石含量高、粒径大、强度高、局部含有漂石。成都地铁 1 号线的 4 个标段掘进表明，在砂卵石地层中开挖刀具的磨耗非常严重，须及时进行刀具检查，掘进平均 120～150 m 全面更换一次刀具。而该地层为砂卵石土夹透镜体砂层，松散土体，且地层富水，自稳能力差。因此，如何采用行之有效的加固措施保证安全、快速、顺利的进行刀具更换是成都富水砂卵石地层地铁施工的一个难题。先行标段的实践表明，地面降水、加固等措施不但会造成地面干扰、而且安全风险很大，施工成本很大，所以采取气压作业是解决刀具更换的最佳办法。

国内外对气压换刀都进行了多次成功运用，以往带压换刀案例均未在成都富水砂卵石地层实施，成都地铁 1 号线的其他标段进行的多次土压平衡盾构带压换刀尝试均以失败告终，曾经一度使人们认为土压平衡盾构不可能在成都富水砂卵石地层中进行带压换刀作业。这足以说明在成都富水砂卵石地层进行土压平衡盾构气压换刀作业是一个公认的技术难题。

2 前期基础研究

2.1 气压值的确定

带压换刀所需气压值的确定，关键是要确定气压的下限，然后根据相关规范规定的工人可承受气压值，以及考虑一定的安全系数，按较低值取用，加压幅值越小，对人体生理健康越有利，劳动效率越高，单班持续工作时间可延长。

选择压气压力的方法，因覆土厚度、地层渗透性、隧道直径、地下水埋深而异。理论上，如下图所示，土仓气压值应根据空仓底部（即图 1 中 A 点，一般为半空状态）的水土压力值来确定。成都富水砂卵石地层以水土分算为宜，因此本经验公式仅适用于水土分算的透水性地层，不适合水土合算的黏土地层。

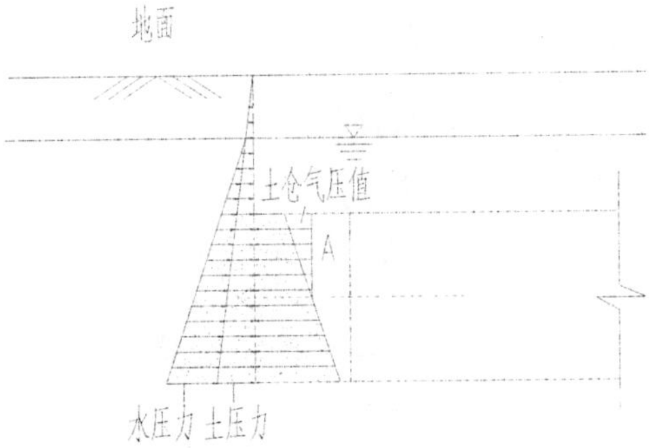

图 1 压气压力的选择

对于水土分算的透水性地层，根据孔隙率的概念，实际上是有土压的地方没有水压，有水压的地方没有土压，气压所需要平衡的仅是空仓底部的水压力和土体侧压力的较大值，在此基础上，考虑一定的安全系数。

本研究对所有带压换刀位置进行了水压实测试验，采用洞内同步测水压技术：将管片中心吊装孔（二次注浆预留孔）用钢钎打穿，插入带球阀的注浆头，在注浆头上安装压力传感器，现场读取换刀前盾构机位置实际水压值，与气压值进行对比分析。

实际气压换刀时的气压值出现了小于空仓底部（即图中 A 点）的水压值（气压需平衡水压和土压的较大值，因此不应该出现小于其中任何一个值），且从每次持续一周的带压换刀过程来看，实际采用的气压值是稳定和安全的。根据实际反馈于理论，分析气压平衡水土压的受力细节，进而寻求一个适合于成都富水砂卵石地层的实用公式。

（1）开挖面土层脱水和较小的刀盘开口率可使开挖面前方土体自稳性提高

土仓内的气体压力一方面可以阻止地下水涌入土仓，同时也使得位于工作面的土层由于脱水而稳定性提高。加上刀盘的八根辐条，辐条起到了挡土作用，辐条与辐条之间间距很小，易形成土拱。从几次带压换刀的经验来看，在成都富水砂卵石地层，利用土压平衡盾构进行带压换刀可以不考虑土压作用。

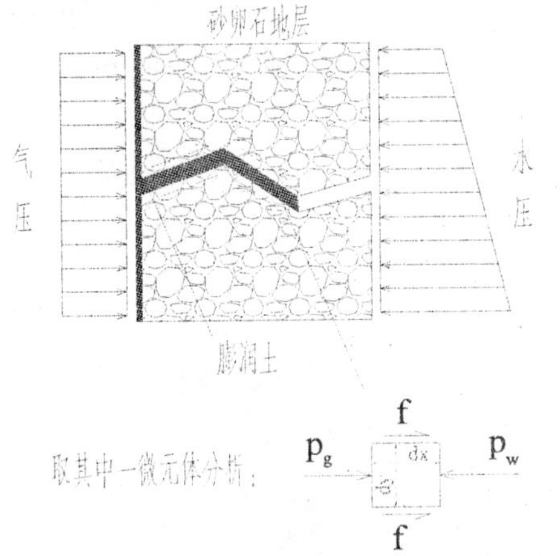

图 2 膨润土浆液的泥塞作用

（2）膨润土浆液的泥塞作用

为减小土层的渗透性，需向盾构壳体周边和开挖面前方注入膨润土浆液。浆液涂在土层表面形成泥膜外，还可以渗入孔隙通道一定深度，堵塞水的通路，如图 2 所示。因此，水要进入土仓，除了水压要大于气压外，还需克服膨润土泥塞作用（摩擦力的积分）。这样，气压的大小与膨润土浆液注入效果密切相关。这一点也是被实践所证实的，实际气压值表现出大于水压值，也表现小于水压值的现象，大体趋势是实际气压值在实测水压值的上下波动。

综合以上各因素，推导成都富水砂卵石地层土压平衡盾构带压换刀所需气压值经验公式如下：

$$p_g \times dy + f \times dx \geqslant p_w \times dy$$

一般透水性地层（采用水土分算时）带压换刀气压值可按下式计算：

$$p_{下限} = K \cdot Max\{\gamma_{水} h_{水},\ e_{侧}\}$$

式中 $p_{下限}$ ——气压下限值；

K ——安全系数，一般 $K>1$；

$\gamma_{水}h_{水}$ ——空仓底部水压；

$e_{侧}$ ——空仓底部土层侧压力，若处于水位以下时按浮容重计。

在保证安全前提下，气压值越小越好。从本研究多次成功带压换刀经验来看，由于开挖面地层脱水和较小的刀盘开口率，加之泥浆护壁作用使其前方土体自稳性提高，侧土压力可以不考虑，当然由于气压是均一的，在气压止水的同时也挡土，这也提高了开挖面土体这部分的安全性；此外由于膨润土浆液的泥塞作用，气压可以做到小于水压。因此，成都富水砂卵石地层土压平衡盾构带压换刀可按以下经验公式计算所需气压值：

$$p_{下限}=k\cdot\gamma_{水}h_{水}$$

式中 k ——气压的取值系数，可小于 1；其他符号意义同前。

根据几次成功带压换刀经验，k 可取值 0.9～1.1。

2.2 进气量和气体损失量的确定

由于成都富水砂卵石地层地质条件特殊，国内外找不到具有对比和借鉴意义的地层漏气资料和参考工程案例，国内也没有相应的规范。为获得该地层自然条件下和加入膨润土浆液后的透气和保气特征，进行了压气试验，为今后空压机的选配和带压作业提供指导作用。压气试验流程如下：

（1）首先，用直径 94 mm 钻头钻孔（实际出孔 100 mm）至 15 m 深，钻孔过程中放入套管（钻孔与下套管同时进行，以保持孔壁稳定）。

（2）钻孔达到 15 m 后，停止向下延伸套管，继续往下钻 3 m 深度，提出钻机。从孔底向上 3 m 范围内填充砾石以保持孔壁稳定。其中，卵石要求磨圆度好，且冲洗干净。

（3）在 15m 位置即卵石上方加入带圆形钢板的 PVC 管，此管从钢板中心穿过，与钢板密封焊死，长度 15m。管和圆型钢板放好后，在管与钻孔之间的空间注浆，充分密实。

（4）第一次压气试验,分别使用三种空气压力。第一次空压机输出压力，通过 PVC 管向下压气，压力达到 1.0 bar 后持续时间不少于 15 min，然后每分钟记录一次空气压力、流量、时间。第二次，压力达到 1.5 bar 后持续时间不少于 15 min，然后每分钟记录一次空气压力，流量，时间。第三次将压力加大到 2.0 bar，重复上述步骤。

（5）加入 0.4 m^3（400L）的膨润土（配方：60 kg/1 000L，6%膨胀土粉末，94%水）至孔顶，此时孔底压力约为 1.5～1.8 bar，与实际开挖面前方压力大致相同，因此，在加入膨润土泥浆时稍微加压力（不大于 3 bar）即可。

（6）进行第二次压气试验，分别使用三种空气压力。第一次空压机输出压力，通过 PVC 管向下压气，压力达到 1.0 bar 后持续时间不少于 15 min，然后每分钟记录一次空气压力、流量、时间。第二次，压力达到 1.5 bar 后持续时间不少于 15 min，然后每分钟记录一次空气压力、流量、时间。第三次将压力加大到 2.0 bar，重复上述步骤。

（7）压气试验结束，整理数据，计算隧道上部地层的空气在压力条件下的损失率。

① 天然土体（见表 1）。

表 1 天然情况下空气损失表

状　态	压力（bar）	空气损失（m^3/h）
1	0.6	13.0
2	0.8	16.5
3	1.0	52.0
4	0.8	44.0
5	0.6	39.0

② 加入膨润土后（见表 2）。

表 2　加入膨润土后空气损失表

状态	压力（bar）	空气损失（m^3/h）
1	0.6	11.5
2	0.8	13.0
3	1.0	14.0
4	0.8	14.0
5	0.6	11.0

③ 结论：

试验表明加入膨润土后气体渗透性明显下降：在 1.0 bar 的压力下，加入膨润土后气体损失是未加前的 27%。估算出钻孔的气压损失面积大概为 1.2 m^2。开挖面加入压缩空气的气压损失面积是 35.2 m^2（开挖仓内有半仓碴土，盾构机周围膨润土泥浆 100%有效）至 129.6 m^2（开挖仓清空，盾构机周围膨润土泥浆 50%有效）。

根据这些数值，可以估算出在开挖面上加 1.0 bar 压力的压缩空气时的气体损失量变化如下：

膨润土泥浆注入效果良好：开挖仓内有半仓碴土时，进气量/漏气量为 400 m^3/h。

膨润土泥浆注入效果一般：开挖仓被清空时，进气量/漏气量为 1 500 m^3/h。

2.3　膨润土泥浆配比及制备

膨润土泥浆在带压换刀过程中控制气压和漏气量起到极其重要的作用，为了使泥浆的效果达到施工需要，在带压换刀前应对其配比和效果进行试验。

膨润土泥浆的技术指标包括：膨润土配比；发酵时间；制备流程。

根据现场施工经验，不同地区的膨润土原料具有很大差异。因此，为了使膨润土泥浆符合施工需要，对其不同配比做了多次试验，最终给出了推荐制备方案。

首先，计算出各配比下所需膨润土原料质量，并分别量取；然后，将膨润土粉末与配比所需水充分混合，并持续搅拌一段时间；搅拌好后放置于常温条件下发酵（20Co）。再次，每隔 4 个小时，将发酵的膨润土泥浆提取少量样品，并用锥形漏斗稠度仪测量时间，并记录当次已发酵时间。最后，处理数据并提出膨润土泥浆效果评估，如不符合要求，调整配比并重新试验至满足要求为止。

试验成果：

（1）膨润土泥浆性能与发酵时间关系密切。试验发现，随着发酵时间增长，膨润土泥浆的黏性明显提高。提高的速度与温度和搅拌质量有关：温度越高，黏性提高越快；搅拌质量越好，黏性提高越快。

（2）根据成都地层特点和带压换刀工作需要，建议使用 10.5%配比膨润土。

根据室内试验确定的配比和黏性关系，结合实际带压换刀尝试的失败与成功经验，建议膨润土质量配比（膨润土粉末：水）取 10.5%，相应的锥形漏斗稠度仪计量值（发酵 24 小时后）为 35 s 左右。

（3）制备过程直接影响膨润土泥浆效果。在前几次的带压换刀尝试中,将室内试验应用于实际时，由于忽略了膨润土泥浆搅拌制备过程，而已失败告终。而后改用高速竖向旋转搅拌器，膨润土粉末与水充分反应，在将膨润土泥浆从竖向搅拌器转移至水平搅拌罐后，保持水平搅拌罐 24 小时旋转，以防止沉淀发生。终于首次成功实现富水砂卵石地层带压换刀操作。

2.4　机械配套及机械改造

德国海瑞克公司设计生产的 EPB6250 型 S-394/S-395 号盾构机在带压换刀作业实施过程中某些设备不能完全符合要求，为了更好地实施换刀作业，必须对部分机械设备进行调整和改造。

（1）机械改装

① 增加空压机

在带压换刀过程中，气压须由足够的压缩气源来保证，经过多次加压实践，证明海瑞克盾构机原本配套两台 9.6 m^3/min 空压机难以满足带压换刀工作，因此新增加了一台 12.6 m^3/min、一台 15.6 m^3/min 空压机。

② 排水装置

在带压状态下，从人闸外面承压墙的通道上放水或者放气，很难控制土仓压力。因此，在带压状态下，利用土仓内与外界的气压差，通过管道把水压到人闸底部，由外界的人员打开或者关闭人闸底部的连通球阀，即可把土仓内的水放出。

③ 注浆设备、膨润土注入方式

为保证带压换刀的保压效果，向周边注入膨润土是非常必要的，盾构机往土仓、刀盘前面这两个方位注入的同时，为了防止盾体后面的水涌进、防止过多的气体从开挖面与盾体之间的间隙流出，还须往盾体周边注入膨润土。而盾构机原带的膨润土泵、原带的膨润土系统只能往土仓、刀盘前面注入，已经不能够满足同时往这三个方位注入膨润土，因此须增加一台浆液注入泵。同时，为了避免盾尾后部注浆量不足而空隙过大，采用双液注浆泵在盾尾后面 5 环增加浆液注入，以填满空隙，防止过多的气体往盾体空隙流动。

④ 管路设计

增加膨润土注入方位，则需要增加一定的管道进行注入，

压力表可以监测注入到盾体周边膨润土的压力，采用同一个出口的注入分布方式，可以达到所注入的所有点位的压力是一致的。

⑤ 膨润土搅拌系统

原有膨润土搅拌系统只包含一个低速水平搅拌罐，现场发现，大量膨润土粉末黏滞在旋转轴和搅拌罐内壁，不能完全与水融合和发生水化反应，造成膨润土浪费和膨润土浆液达不到使用要求。为解决这个问题，采用自行设计的膨润土搅拌系统进行搅拌，之后直接输送到浆液运输车，再进入到盾构机的膨润土罐。膨润土改造系统原理如下图：

（2）供气量与供气能力配备

每台盾构机带压作业所具备的压缩气源有：两台 9.6 m^3/min 空压机，新增加一台 12.6 m^3/min 空压机和一台 15.6 m^3/min 空压机；

成都地铁地层主要是以砂卵石、强风化泥岩为主，局部位置主要以砂层为主。经过多次带压换刀试验，在泥岩中只要 1~2 台 9.6 m^3/min 空压机即可；在砂卵石地层则采用两台 9.6 m^3/min 空压机，一台 12.6 m^3/min 空压机备用；在砂层中，采用两台 9.6 m^3/min 空压机，一台 12.6 m^3/min 空压机和一台 15.6 m^3/min 空压机备用，而在砂层中，每台盾构机所配备的空压机不一定就可以满足土仓内气体的流失，因此，需要另外租赁一定供气量的空压机进行备用。所以，尽可能避免在砂层中作带压换刀施工。理论上通过多加空压机，选用大型空压机的办法加大进气量能够保持土压仓内压力稳定，方法简单。但这种方法往往造成仓内换气速度加快，对换刀人员健康造成不良影响，换刀效率也将下降。

（3）安全风险防范所需相关设备

① 应急电源

为了以免随时停电，备用 200 kW 发电机一台，随时提供给两台或者以上的电源，以免在带压过程中忽然停电而导致的停气。

② 应急气源

在忽然停电或者电力空压机忽然出现故障的情况下，备用 12.6 m^3/min 的柴油空压机及时供气，以保证土仓内的气源能满足人员安全离开土仓。

③ 挡板、气囊

在换刀过程中，如果土仓内忽然出现涌水、坍塌情况，挡板和气囊的临时防护的必要设备。

如果涌水、坍塌情况不严重，而且是局部情况，则可以采用挡板挡住开口的地方，临时封堵，待换刀人员出土仓后，再迅速拆除。

如果涌水、坍塌情况，则采用气囊，把整个刀盘开口区域完全堵塞，待换刀人员离开土仓后，气囊放气，迅速取回气囊，之后关土仓门；如果不能及时取回气囊，则让气囊遗留在土仓内，通过螺旋输送机把之输送出。

3 现场试验研究

为实现带压换刀，在 18 环、20 环、25 环的时候进行了三次土仓保压试验，压力保持时间均低于 6 h，难以达到换刀作业要求。

为了更好地做好准备工作，详细分析了所有可能影响带压换刀压力不恒定的主要原因。主要原因如下：

（1）地层部分形成泥膜或根本没有形成泥膜。

（2）膨润土质量差和没有正确的配置膨润土浆液。

（3）同步注浆浆液稠度低：若盾体与周边土体之间空隙不能很好的封闭，就会发生气体沿着盾壳跑气的现象。

（4）压缩空气系统没有正常的工作：SAMSON 压缩气体自动补偿系统没有很好的工作，空气压缩机的每小时供气量可能不够。

（5）刀盘中央形成泥饼：硬泥饼的存在可能在土仓上下部之间形成泥拱，导致不能通过出土确定土仓中碴土的位置，从而也不能确定空气散射表面。

第三次土仓保压试验后，根据土仓保压失败的原因进行了以下方面的改进和完善：

（1）膨润土浆液的配置：用高速旋转的搅拌器搅拌膨润土浆液（保证膨润土粉末和水的充分融合），保证膨润土浆液具有高抗剪能力。根据现场试验结果，膨润土的百分率取为 10.5%。

（2）膨润土粉末的水化最小时间控制在 24 h，将其存储在泥浆罐中并不断的搅拌。在膨润土泥浆被使用之前，用马氏漏斗黏度计测试浆液黏度，以检查泥浆的最终黏性是否满足要求（测试结果应在 32 到 35 s 之间，以确保泥浆有合适的黏度特性）。如果因为膨润土的质量不合格或没有正确的配置，导致最后出现絮凝现象，添加带有分散功能的添加剂。

（3）同步注浆浆液配合比的改进：为了检查浆液的稠度，从而检查浆液是否能够很好的充满管片背后的空隙。进行塌落度（锥入度）试验。为了达到良好稠度的结果，适当添加水泥。确保 TBM 盾壳周围所有的空隙被完全填充对于最终目的（保压）来说是非常重要的，否则不可能长时间保持气压。

（4）避开前几次试验（18 环、20 环、25 环）地层扰动过的区域，至少向前掘进 10 环以上再进行带压换刀试验。在掘进盾构机停机之前的 5 环范围内，避免土仓压力降到警告值（顶部 1 号传感器的警告值为 0.8 bar）以下，以主动、连续地支撑开挖面，保持开挖面前方土体处于弹性状态，从而更适合于建压。

第 35 环位置的带压换刀试验，由以下几个步骤组成：

根据隧道掘进计划提供（PAT）的 1 号传感器参考值 1 bar，按此参数开始第 35 环的掘进。在这个过程中，继续向开挖面加泡沫：泡沫系统按半自动方式进行操作（泡沫特性参数：Cf=2%，FER=8%～10%，实际泡沫注入量 150 l/min，相应的 FIR 值约为 90%）。与此同时，在 TBM 掘进时保持同步注浆系统正常工作。

根据隧道掘进计划（PAT）提供的参考值保持同步注浆的压力，以保证管片背后环向空隙被充分填满。

在开始第 35 环掘进之前，通过超前探孔向盾壳周围注入膨润土。

在第 35 环开挖的最后 15 cm，用膨润土浆液代替泡沫，通过泡沫注入系统往开挖面注入膨润土浆液，保持 1 号传感器压力值高于 1 bar。注入膨润土浆液的具体参数见下表。

在开挖完第 35 环后，刀盘仍然要保持以 1 rpm 的速度旋转 10 min；同是，以 2 bar 的注浆压力往开挖面注入膨润土泥浆，保持 1 号传感器的压力值在 1.4～1.5 bar 左右。

通过螺旋输送机慢慢出碴，同时将压缩空气注入到土仓内，保持 1 号土压传感器的压力值在 0.6 bar 左右。这个过程输出两箱碴土，即 12 m^3 碴土。

带压作业人员在 0.6 bar 的气压下开仓进入土仓，检查土仓中碴土顶面位置（土仓的充满程度）。碴土表面在人闸门以上，离盾壳顶只有 20 cm，刀盘中心存在泥饼，破除困难。

为了降低土仓碴土顶面位置，往土仓内加 1 m^3 膨润土和水 1.5 m^3，在加膨润土加水的同时旋转刀盘 20 min。在这个过程中，螺旋输送机输送出来 9 m^3 的碴土（碴土为水、膨润土浆液和泥饼的混合物）。

随后作业人员在 0.6 bar 气压下进入土仓再次检查碴土表面位置：碴土表面降到了人闸底板以下约 1 m 处，在土仓边墙位置降到了刀盘的水平轴线以下。

在这个操作期间，土仓中的压力传感器气压降低了 0.05～0.08 bar，检查周围环境发现隧道开挖面附近降水井发生漏气。

为了解决这个问题，我们将较浓的膨润土浆液（20%）填充降水井，然后将降水井连同周围部分地面用黏土封住。但无论采用什么样的方法，总是存在着一些漏气的裂缝。

因此，在盾构机再安装一台空气压缩机（总共达到 3 台），以便为空气压缩系统提供足够的进气量。

4 关键施工技术

带压换刀关键技术包括“到达预定换刀点前的施工技术”、“到达预定换刀点时的施工技术”和“恢复掘进技术”三步曲。

4.1 到达预定换刀点前的施工技术

（1）设备检查和浆液准备

① 注浆系统的检查

在掘进到 A－10 环时检查同步注浆系统，主要是四个注浆管路是否运转正常。如果有管路不通；浆泵无力；冲程数与实际泵送放量差距较大等情况，进行管路疏通和浆泵的全面清洗，使整个注浆系统各本分处于优良的工作状态。

在掘进第 A－5 环时对整个膨润土系统进行检查，包括刀盘前方和盾体周围两个方向的膨润土管路和膨润土泵的运转情况。整个系统的各部分检查就绪后进行试注浆。试注浆过程中主要是观察各管路的压力是否正常，如果压力过大或者过小都必须对系统进行调试。

② 空气系统的完善和检查

在掘进至 A－3 环时检查空压机运行状况，达到良好的使用效果。根据前几次带压换刀的经验，必须有三台空压机处于工作状态，一台柴油空压机处于待机状态。柴油空压机的管路必须连接到位并处于待机状态。

同时进行向土仓内供气的呼吸系统调试，一二号呼吸器进行调试必须同时处于良好的工作状态。人闸系统要进行加减压测试，通过测试观察各种压力表、温度表以及各种阀门是否工作正常。在检查的同时把人闸各个气管特别是进气管全部打开，使其排气 30 min 尽可能地把气管里的油和水排出，以免影响作业人员的健康。

在螺旋输送机下方安装工业气体输入气管并且加装限压阀压力值调为 1.0 bar。

③ 浆液的准备工作

通过膨润土浆液稠度试验确定膨润土浆液的配比。带压换刀对膨润土稠度的要求是 35 s 左右，通过膨润土稠度仪进行测试。在确定膨润土浆液的配比后根据盾构机推进情况，在盾构推进第 A 环 24 h 之前拌制膨润土，具体拌制量由现场协调人员控制。

同步注浆浆液的配比由现场试验结果确定，浆液的锥入度控制在 11～13 cm 之间，初凝时间控制在 6 h 左右。每环的注浆量为 6.5 m^3，同步注浆压力控制在 2.0 bar 左右。从 A－2 环开始,同步注浆应连续不中断，每环掘进至最后一车碴土后停止，并且要尽量保证掘进的连续性以保证注浆的连续与饱满。

④ 设备检查与维护

通过压力表，检查前仓、主仓、作业仓的密闭性能。对空气压缩机和储气罐进行检查观察其工作压力是否正常。在加压前，检查压缩空气系统的封签和功能。进仓作业所需各种起重工具和切割工具要进行进仓前的检查，避免工作时所需工具不能正常使用，导致作业人员工作时间延长和压缩空气的计划外使用。

- 膨润土注入系统；
- 仪表显示系统；
- 压缩空气系统（管路、闸阀）；
- 通信系统；
- 换刀工具。

（2）到达预定换刀点前的掘进关键工艺

到达 A 点前五环，在盾构周边注入膨润土，并且要保证发酵时间。此时盾构机掘进速度调整为 30～50 mm/min,刀盘转速调整为 1～2 rpm。持续掘进速度和转速到达距 A 点前一环（1.5 m）处，盾构掘进速度调整为 25 mm/min，刀盘转速调整为 0.8～1.5 rpm，最多不能超过 1.5 rpm。并同时用盾构刀盘前方 8 个注浆孔中位于盾体上方的 4 个注浆孔注入膨润土泥浆，设定压力 1.1 倍开挖面的压力,泥水配合比不变。在到达 A 点前要求注入 25 m^3 泥浆在开挖面上形成泥膜。

4.2 到达预定换刀点时的施工技术

盾构机到达 A 点后，盾构停止掘进，但是继续转动刀盘和注入膨润土泥浆。持续以上操作 5 min 后停止转动刀盘。随后向土仓内加压，进行气压和土压置换。加压过程采用分阶段排土、分阶段加压的方式进行，出土量按照所换刀具位置确定。

将土仓中的碴土输出约 1/3，观察土仓压力值的变化，同时安排人员观察地表上漏气是否严重，若土仓压力无法保持，则重新恢复注浆或重新推进。

若土仓压力保持 2 h 没有变化，则继续出土至 1/2 略偏下处，观察土仓压力值的变化，若土仓压力保持 2h 没有变化或不发生大的波动时（压力变化值＜0.05 bar），则表明土仓压力保持情况合格。

（1）加减压和人员进仓

① 正常条件下：

- 原始位置：P1 > P0（P0：大气压力，P1：支撑压力），原始状态时，主仓与副仓压力为大气压力。
- 主仓的加压：P1 > P2 > P0（P0：大气压力，P1：支撑压力，P2：主仓压力，介于 P1 和 P0 之间），关闭主仓闸门后，打开通风球阀，对主仓进行加压。
- 土仓与主仓压力平衡：P1＝P2，土仓与主仓实现气压平衡，停止加压。此时，可以开启土仓闸门，进入土仓。副仓始终保持不加压。

② 后续入闸（通过副仓入闸）：

在正常条件下，出闸仅仅在主仓进行；同时，副仓总是不加压。因为在紧急情况下，急救人员任何时候可能通过副仓入闸。如果通过前仓入闸的过程与主仓操作类似。

- 原始位置：P1>P0（P0：大气压力，P1：支撑压力，主仓压力），原始状态时，土仓压力等于主仓压力，均为 P1，副仓压力为大气压 P0。
- 副仓加压：P1>P2>P0，（P0：大气压力，P1：支撑压力，P2：主仓压力，介于 P1 和 P0 之间）。关闭副仓闸门后，打开通风球阀，对副仓进行加压。
- 土仓与主仓压力平衡：P1＝P2，副仓与主仓、土仓实现气压平衡，停止加压。此时，可以开启主、副仓间闸门，进入主仓和土仓。

③ 减压过程

- 初始条件：P1>P0（P0：大气压力，P1：支撑压力）
- 主仓减压：P1>P2>P0（P0：大气压力，P1：支撑压力，P2:主仓压力）
- 主仓与外界气压平衡：P1>P1＝P0，主仓压力同大气压平衡，打开主仓闸门，人员出闸。

（2）自动加气系统的使用与参数调整

自动加气系统控制目标是保持土仓压力恒定，同时要求系统对扰动的抑制能力较高，因此没有采用微分控制，仅采用 PI(比例积分)控制方式。调节器参数调整，是指在控制规律已经确定为 PI 形式时，通过调整 PI 调节器的参数，使得控制回路的动态特性满足期望的指标要求，达到理想的控制目标。

可以使用试凑法调定 PI 参数。根据经验公式和自动加气系统的特性对参数实行下述先比例后积分的调定步骤。

首先调定比例部分，即先将积分时间 Tn 设为最大（20 min），然后由小变大逐步改变比例系数 Kp，同时观察调节器输出信号和被调整参数的变化情况。如果调节过程是衰减振荡的，则应使 Kp 续减小;如果调节过程是增幅振荡的，则应使 Kp 增大，这样调整直至调节过程成为等幅振荡为止。由于此时系统仍有静差，且静差仍在一个较大的范围内，所以单用比例调节器还不能达到控制目的，应进入下一步积分调节。

调定积分系统。首先设置 Tn 为一个较小的值，并将第一步调整得到的 Kp 略微缩小，如缩小为原值的 0.8 倍。然后逐步增大 Tn，观察系统响应曲线，使系统在保持良好动态性能的情况下，静差得到消除。在此过程中，可根据响应曲线的好坏反复改变 Kp 和 Tn，以期得到反应快、超调小的响应曲线。

（3）刀具检查和更换

① 刀具检查

盾构刀具磨损的标准是:中间滚刀磨损量为 20 mm,周边滚刀磨损量为 10 mm,刮刀磨损量为 10 mm,齿刀磨损量为 6 cm。这个指标的确定和刀具耐磨层厚度有很大关系。

② 刀具更换

刀具更换的原则是先易后难，螺栓拆除采用风动扳手，螺栓紧固采用扭矩扳手，确保刀具安装质量。更换刀具步骤如下：

- 每次更换时，工作人员先将刀具周围的泥土清掉，保证留有一定的工作空间。
- 由刀盘外侧向内逐个检查刀具的磨损情况，确定需要更换时，用相应标号的刀具进行替换。
- 用套筒及加力杆卸下固定螺栓，将拆下的螺栓及附件放入随身携带的工具袋内，以防丢失。
- 将换下的刀具递到人闸内，同时将固定螺栓和固定座用水清洗干净，并检查一下是否有裂纹，如有裂纹必须更换新螺栓，以确保新装刀具有足够的固定强度。
- 将新的刀具按原来的位置安装好，并将固定螺栓拧紧。
- 每次带一批刀具和螺栓进仓，每批刀具换完后，把废刀具和没有安装的新刀放进料闸内。
- 同时操作手转动刀盘。工作人员通过料闸把下一批刀具送入土仓内，再继续更换下一组刀具。
- 每换完一批刀具后，由值班机械工程师检查一遍安装质量，并检查是否有漏掉的或者没有固定好的。机械工程师确认无误后方可继续作业。
- 更换速度按实际情况定，必须以保证安装质量为前提。
- 换刀过程中当遇到断螺栓时，一般采用以下两种处理方案：若断口在螺孔之外，则直接拆除；若断口在螺孔里面，则要用风动手钻打孔，用取丝器取出断螺栓，严禁采用电动工具。

4.3 恢复掘进技术

换刀作业结束后，待人员与设备撤出土仓和人闸后，启动刀盘，恢复掘进（暂时不出土）。通过压力传感器可以看到土仓内压力变化，此时通过土仓内排气阀排出一部分气体保持恒定的支撑压力，重复以上动作至满仓，重新建立土压平衡，进入正常掘进施工。

刀具更换完毕后，待人员与设备撤出土仓和人闸，封闭土仓闸门后，就要立即恢复正常掘进，这个恢复过程也就是由气压平衡转换到土压平衡的一个过程，如果这个转化过程控制不当，也将会导致开挖面土层失稳，甚至引起地表坍塌。

由于恢复掘进地点地质条件的差别，恢复掘进就有不同的模式。

（1）砂卵石地层恢复掘进

由于砂卵石土层有一定的稳定性，因此采用加气推进的模式。即更换刀具结束后，启动刀盘与千斤顶恢复盾构掘进，持续往土仓内加入压缩空气，但严格控制出土量，逐渐恢复土仓内存土量，增加土压，同步逐渐减小气压，最终实现土压完全代替气压平衡。

（2）砂层恢复掘进

由于砂层稳定性差，在砂层中恢复掘进时，必须采用回填土仓的方式来实现土压代替气压。即在换刀结束后，盾构暂不恢复掘进，而是往土仓内逐渐注入膨润土，用膨润土回填土仓，同步逐渐减小气压，当土压完全代替气压后，启动刀盘与千斤顶恢复盾构掘进。

5 结 论

成都地铁 1 号线盾构 3 标成功进行了 19 次带压换刀和多次带压检查刀具的作业。而且，带压作业过程中地面沉降小，进仓人员身体无不良反应，换刀效率高。

实践证明，在成都浅埋隧道特有的砂卵石地层（卵石含量高、粒径大，地下水位高、地层透水性强，卵石和漂石强度高）中实现带压检查和更换刀具、进行刀盘维护等作业是完全可行的。带压换刀是一种安全、高效、经济的换刀方式。

带压换刀技术避免了由于地表加固而造成地面交通拥堵，降低了换刀成本，确保了隧道上方道路的畅通和既有管线和建（构）筑物的安全和正常使用，未对环境造成对危害，维护了城市的良好形象，环境效益良好。可应用于富水砂卵石及类似地层带压换刀，具有重要的推广意义，已经被成都地铁公司在成都地铁 1 号线所有盾构工程中推广应用，为成都地铁 1 号线的顺利完工提供了坚实的技术保障。

成都地铁土压平衡盾构带压换刀技术的试验成功是一项重大技术突破，取得了显著的经济效益和社会效益，为富水砂卵石地层地铁工程提供了成功的范例。伴随着成都地铁 2~7 号线线网总长共计 275 km 区间隧道大规模建设的进行，项目研究所取得的一系列成套技术和相关理论必将在越来越多的工程中得到应用，为带压换刀技术的推广应用提供有力指导，推动地下工程技术进步。可保障即将施工的成都地铁 2~7 号线线网总长共计 275 km 区间隧道的安全、优质、快速掘进。

参考文献（Referenles）：

[1] 《空气潜水减压技术要求》(国家标准编号：GB-12521-90).

[2] 《异常气压危害标准》中国台湾标准.

[3] AS4774.1－2003, Australian Standard TM Work compressed air and hyperbaric facilities－Work in tunnels, shafts and caissons.

[4] 周文波. 盾构法隧道施工技术及应用[M]. 北京:中国建筑工业出版社,2004.

[5] 国际隧道协会. 隧道风险管理指南（Guidelines for Tunneling Risk Management)，2004.

[6] 中国土木工程学会等. 地铁及地下工程建设风险管理指南，2007.

[7] 意大利 GEODATA 公司. 深埋长隧道风险评估方法建议书，2007.

[8] GB/T 16180—2006 职工工伤与职业病致残程度鉴定标准.

[9] 地铁及地下工程建设风险管理指南，2007.

作者简介（Bio-data）：

刘向阳，男，1965年3月出生，工程师，大学本科，西南交通大学在职研究生，中铁二局股份有限公司城通公司总经理。从事过铁路、公路、桥梁等工程施工管理，近五年主要从事城市地下工程施工项目管理及施工企业管理。

Xiangyang LIU, male, born on March,1965,Engineer,bachelor degree, incumbency graduate education in Southwest Jiaotong University, Chief manager of Chengtong Branch, China railway NO.2 Engineering Group Co., Ltd. He majors in construction management of railway, road and bridge and mainly in city underground project construction management and company management.

Email: r413@263.com

陈强，男，1973年12月出生，高级工程师，西南交通大学土木工程本科，中铁二局股份有限公司城通公司工程部长，主要从事地下铁道工程的施工管理和科研工作。

Qiang CHEN, male, born on DEC,1973, senior engineer, graduated from Civil Engineering College of Southwest Jiaotong University, engineering manager of Engineering Department of Chengtong Branch, China railway NO.2 Engineering Group Co., Ltd, majors in construction management and scientific research of metro project.

Email: shchenqiang@126.com

卵石地层盾构掘进机刀盘刀具适应性分析及对策

彭健成 吴惠明 阮关荣
上海隧道工程股份有限公司 盾构工程分公司，上海 200023

【摘 要】 针对成都独特富水砂卵石地层下盾构隧道施工的刀具管理，通过分析地质条件对盾构工法带来的困难，从刀具摸索的一般理念出发，详细介绍了施工实例中刀具应用的不断改进，提出了根据刀具在平面、空间位置的不同作用，对刀具结构、刀具种类进行完善的方法。
【关键词】 砂卵石地层；盾构隧道；刀具管理

CUTTER ADAPTABILITY ANALYSIS AND COUNTERMEASURES FOR SHIELD MACHINE IN GRAVEL STRATUM

Jiancheng PENG，Huiming WU，Guanrong RUAN
Shanghai Tunnel Engineering Co., Ltd.,Shanghai 200082 ,China

Abstract: In the light of tool management for shield tunnel engineering in the unique water-rich stratum of sand and gravel of Chengdu, through the analysis of the difficulties caused by geological conditions, proceeding from the general ideas of tool exploration, this paper gives a detailed introduction about continuous improvement of tool application in construction living examples. Then a method is proposed for improving the structure and type of the cutters, by means of analyzing the different roles of cutters in the flat position and spatial location.
Key words: gravel stratum; shield tunnel; cutter management

1 引 言

成都市在城乡一体统筹的大背景下，也展开了地铁 1 号线的建设。盾构法能适应各种复杂的地质条件，对环境的影响、施工安全性、质量、工程进度等方面也具有优势，成都地铁主城区地下隧道工程的施工，最终选用了盾构法。

成都地质是典型的富水砂卵石地层，卵石含量高，漂石粒径大，卵石强度高，地下水丰富，透水性好，地层条件相当独特，盾构工法的应用同样面临重重困难。刀具的选用上既要考虑大粒径卵石的破碎，同时刀具的高度组合、刀具类型都需要考虑渣土流动性等影响掘进效率的因素。成都地铁 1 号线刚开始的掘进中，刀具的失效速度和更换频率远超预想，掘进约 100～200 m 即需更换一次刀具，这给地面环境保护、工程造价控制带来相当不利的影响。

由此可见，刀盘刀具设计，是盾构机功能实现的重要部分，刀具的布置和刀具类型的选择直接影响盾构的切削效果和掘进速度，也是工程安全、经济性的重要保障。

2 盾构掘进机掘削机理

2.1 盾构选型

2.1.1 成都地层特点

成都地铁 1 号线地下隧道盾构掘进主要集中在<3-7>砂卵石（局部<3-4>粉细砂透镜体分部）这一层，底埋深约 10～25 m，该地层具有以下特点：

（1）卵石含量高：卵石土地层中卵石含量 55%以上，为该地层的骨架成分；

（2）砂含量高：砂卵石中砂含量高，含量约 10%～35%，呈透镜体分布；

（3）颗粒间胶结物：胶结物广泛分布于砂卵石中；

（4）漂石粒径大：区间探井揭示漂石最大粒径为 350 mm，天府广场揭示漂石最大粒径为 550 mm，含量为 5%～10%，随机性分布。

（5）地下水位：由于沿线车站等基坑降水作用，区内地下水位埋深约 8～13 m；

（6）地层透水性：卵石土地层渗透系数高达 12.5～27.4 m/d，透水性强。

（7）卵石和漂石强度高：卵石和漂石单轴抗压强度达 86～98 MPa。

从盾构工法三个最基本的功能单元——支护、切削、排渣来看，存在以下困难：

（1）受砂卵石土层和较大渗透率的影响，不易形成不透水塑流性的碴土而不能建立土压平衡机理，或土仓压力不稳定，容易造成地表发生沉降。

（2）刀盘、刀具由于卵石致使切削的不均匀性和冲击，容易产生异常损坏；以及砂的摩擦作用，刀盘、刀具和螺旋输送机磨损都会较严重。

（3）石头粒径较大且强度高，部分较大粒径无法通过刀盘开口和排碴装置，极易造成刀盘、刀具的异常磨损。

（4）隧道穿越卵石土夹透镜体砂层或局部穿越粉砂层，均匀性差，软硬夹杂，容易造成地面沉降、超挖、偏离线路方向，该地层下纠偏相对困难。

（5）由于卵石土中存在胶结物，对于刀盘中心流动性较小的部位容易产生泥饼现象，并黏结限制该处滚刀的转动而偏磨，以及造成前方土体无法入仓。

（6）需要开仓对刀盘刀具进行处理，由于地下水、岩层的不稳定性，需要采取辅助手段对地层进行降水加固。地面降水措施的效果时好时坏，特别对于粉细砂和下部基岩上部卵石土两种地层，降水效果不明显。

2.1.2 泥水盾构与土压盾构比选

为了适应成都地铁 1 号线工程特殊的地质条件，建设施工单位对盾构机类型进行了选型研究。普通的泥水平衡盾构机，在粒径大于 30 mm、卵石含量约为 60%～70%、渗透系数大的＜2-8＞、＜3-7＞和＜4-4＞卵石土层中掘进，在泥水输送前需进行大量的块石破碎，很难满足推进速度的需要，况且一般的泥水平衡盾构机所需的总功率配备高，对施工场地也有较高要求，施工成本较高。

而土压平衡盾构机采用螺旋输送机出土，可输送较大粒径的石块，对成都砂卵石地质条件的适应性更好。因此最终选用了德国海瑞克生产的复合式土压平衡盾构机来进行成都地铁 1 号线一期工程大部分标段的隧道掘进施工。

一般土压盾构的功能配置如下：

（1）盾构壳体	（2）刀盘装置（刀盘、刀盘驱动）	（3）推进装置
（4）铰接装置	（5）人行闸	（6）双螺旋输送机出土系统
（7）管片运送装置	（8）管片拼装机	（9）液压系统
（10）集中润滑系统	（11）加泥系统	（12）注浆系统
（13）盾尾密封系统	（14）冷却系统	（15）电气系统
（16）数据采集系统	（17）警报、互锁系统	（18）隧道导向系统

（19）可选配的保压泵碴装置　　（20）车架

2.2 掘削原理

土压盾构采用土压平衡模式施工。开挖时，碴土通过刀盘开口进入土舱，再经过双螺旋输送机从土舱底部排出，由皮带输送机运送排入土箱，然后由土箱车送至地面。

土舱里充满了碴土、天然水和高浓度泥浆或泡沫等添加剂的混合物，该混合物具有良好的流塑性。在开挖过程中，通过调节螺旋输送机的转速以平衡进土（碴土+水+高浓度泥浆）与排土量，使土舱内的土体（混合物）保持在设定的土压力值上。土舱里的土压值在开挖过程中始终受到控制并保持。在开挖过程中，螺旋输送机的转速随着土压力传感器的指示会作相应的调整。

3 海瑞克盾构机刀盘刀具对地层的适应性考虑

德国海瑞克作为成熟的盾构机设计制造厂商，针对成都卵石地层，在刀盘刀具对地层适应性方面，其总体设计理念偏安全考虑，在刀盘开口率、刀具的布置、掘进效果评估上都充分考虑到成都独特地层下应用盾构工法的安全性。但是，这种偏安全考虑的设计，在加强正面支护的同时，牺牲了掘进效率，导致了刀具磨损严重、换刀频繁、掘进效率低、成本高等不利影响。

3.1 刀盘设计形式对地层的适应性

（1）刀盘具有适宜的开口率（装有滚刀的刀盘开口率是 26%；安装齿刀时，开口率为 28%），刀盘开口设计限制大于约 520 mm × 240 mm 的块石进入，进入土舱的块石可以通过螺旋输送机运送出去。

（2）面板式刀盘对开挖面进行机械支撑，采用重型刀盘设计（前板厚 50 mm），连接到刀盘驱动装置的牢固连接臂（厚壁梁）保证了刀盘良好的稳定性。刀盘的设计可降低刀具磨损。

（3）4 个辐条的设计以使每个旋转方向都有 4 个进土开口，进土通道的具有专门的几何设计使开挖舱的进土更加容易，角度渐变能够防止碴土沉积。具有大尺寸的物料通道从刀盘外缘通到刀盘中心区域，便于将挖掘的碴土运输到土舱。

（4）刀盘背面设有搅拌棒及刀盘正反向运转有利于对螺旋机进行喂料。

（5）刀盘前面 4 条独立的注入管用于碴土改良以降低磨损保证出土顺畅。

（6）刀具/刀盘配有专门磨损保护（例如刀盘面上焊有 hardox 板，外圈上有耐磨格条）。

详见图 1。

	刀盘结构	面板形结构	面板形结构	面板形结构	面板形结构	辐条式面板结构
刀盘设计	刀盘直径	6250mm	6280mm	6280mm	6280mm	6280mm
刀盘设计	刀具组合（数量，配置，布置）	12 把周边滚刀，20 把羊角刀，28 把刮刀，4把中心双刃羊角刀和8铲刀	4 把中心双刃滚刀、32 把单刃滚刀、28 把强力刮刀和8铲刀	4 把中心双刃滚刀、32 把单刃滚刀、28 把强力刮刀和8铲刀	4 把中心双刃滚刀、32 把单刃滚刀、28 把强力刮刀和8铲刀	4 把中心双刃滚刀、32 把单刃滚刀、28 把强力刮刀和8铲刀
刀盘设计	刀盘转速 r/min	0~4.5 r/min	0~4.5 r/min	0~4.56 r/min	0~4.5 r/min	0~5 r/min
刀盘设计	开口率	28%~30%	25%	28%	25%~28%	35%
刀盘设计	示意图		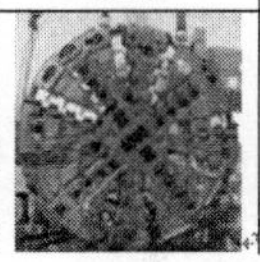		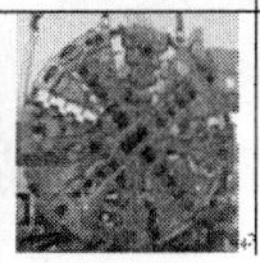	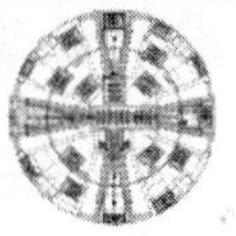

图 1

3.2 刀具布置对地层的适应性

3.2.1 刀具的种类及用途

海瑞克盾构机共配备 32 把单刃滚刀、4 把中心双刃滚刀、28 把正面方刮刀、16 把周边刮刀。刀具布置具有对称性。具有如下特点。

（1）主要刀具类型为双刃滚刀、单刃滚刀、刮刀和铲刀，所有滚刀都可以替换成软土刀具（齿刀）以适应地质的变化。

（2）所有的刀具都可以在刀盘背后换装，从而保证安全、高效地更换刀具。

（3）刮刀为专门设计、制造用于砂砾地层切削的形式，刮刀通过 4 个水平安装的螺栓连接在刀盘上，宽 250 mm，露出刀盘的距离较短。这些设计特点使刮刀更加坚硬稳定、能够承受更高的撞击力，从而更加耐受磨损。由于刀盘能正反旋转，因此刮刀也是正反方向布置。为了提高刮刀的使用寿命和可靠性，在每个轨迹上至少布置 2 把，刮刀的刀具材料具有高耐磨性。

（4）针对卵石地层，特别选用了 17#专用滚刀，滚刀在卵石等较硬地层中有更高的切削效率。中心部位布置 4 把双刃滚刀，其余 32 把单刃滚刀布置在盘面各个位置，刀具切割轨迹覆盖整个断面，滚刀具有高度耐磨的切削刀刃，17#单刃滚刀具有在 150 MPa 的岩石中掘进的能力。滚刀结构见图 2。

（5）刀盘周边圆角处正反方向布置 8 把铲刀，这样均可以大大延长周边刀具的寿命，保证开挖直径。

（6）考虑到刀盘的受力均匀性，刀具布置具有对称性。

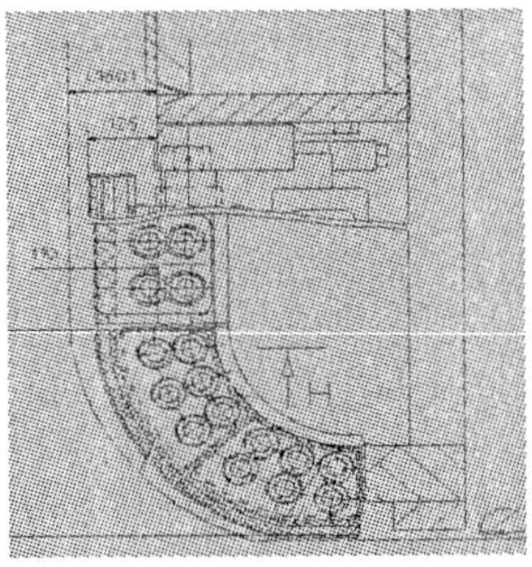

图 2

3.2.2 刀具配置

刀具的布置方式充分考虑了成都工程地质情况，进行了针对性设计，以获得良好的切削效果和掘进速度。刀具配置主要考虑各种刀具种类、刀具数量、刀具高度和刀具高度差。

海瑞克原始的段差设计中，滚刀高度 160 mm，滚刀切削破碎为主。正面方和周边刮刀高度 110 mm，将渣土刮削进土仓。

3.3 海瑞克刀盘适应性分析

原海瑞克盾构刀盘为面板式盾构，开口率为 26%。对于在粒径较大的砂卵地层，刀盘的开口率过低，不利于盾构的切削掘进以及正面土体的稳定。在盾构掘进过程中，正面的块状卵石在刀具无法切削的情况下，也无法通过刀盘开口部分直接进入土仓内，而是仍在盾构正面，这势必将严重影响盾构的开挖掘进。

另外此盾构刀盘的中心区域为封闭式的，当刀盘正面切削时，中心区域的块状卵石在切割后无法进入土仓内而是堆积在刀盘正面，随着盾构的推进，中心区域的块石将越积越多，这样也势必影响到盾构的掘进。

根据以上分析我们认为：在粒径较大的砂卵地层中施工，盾构刀盘的开口率应适当增大，通过较大的刀盘开口率使卵石直接进入到密闭舱，既能有利于维持开挖面土体稳定，又能避免刀具的过渡切削磨损。

另外在砂卵地层中施工，刀盘必须具备耐磨性措施，尤其在刀盘结构几个比较易磨损的部位必须要有保护措施，可在刀盘每个进渣口的周圈进行硬化处理并堆焊耐磨材料，可在刀盘的中心和外缘进行硬化处理并堆焊耐磨材料，亦可在刀盘外圈设有保护刀具。

3.4 海瑞克刀具配置适应性分析

综合分析海瑞克盾构机配置刀具的特性，结合工程实践，其刀具适应性如下：

（1）单刃滚刀

单刃滚刀多用于破碎单轴抗压强度较高（UCS>70 MPa）的硬岩，是掘进破碎岩石的关键部件（见

图 3)。作为硬岩切削的主要刀具，比较适合在岩石地层中掘进。以往的实践经验证明单刃滚刀的破岩效果最佳，且适应于较软的中硬岩到硬岩（岩石单轴抗压强度30～350 MPa）。隧道围岩为 III～VI 类围岩则使用盘形滚刀效果较好。

图 3

在成都砂卵石地层，卵石属松散体，地层对卵石缺少约束力，且由于卵石的抗压强度较高，滚刀只能部分破碎卵石，不能对卵石进行有效破碎。而从实际推进过程中可以看到：滚刀存在严重的偏磨现象，甚至出现了滚刀磨至刀轴，整把刀报废以及刀圈脱落等现象。

滚刀发生偏磨主要原因为：滚刀自身的启动扭矩较高，在刀盘转动的同时滚刀的轴承未发生转动，从而造成滚刀在开挖面上不能滚动，使刀圈呈单边受力磨损。如果发现不及时，不但会加速这把刀的磨损，并且会造成相邻滚刀过载失效，从而迅速向外部扩张，直到整个刀盘上的滚刀全部磨损。

因此，全部采用盘形滚刀在类似成都的砂卵地层中施工是不适宜的，极易发生部分盘刀被松散的卵石卡住，从而使滚刀不能产生自转而严重偏磨。如采用滚刀与其他刀具组合，对滚刀采取保护措施，可发挥滚刀破碎大粒径漂石的作用。

（2）双刃滚刀

双刃滚刀作为中心滚刀安装在刀盘的中间部分（见图 4）。中心滚刀由于靠近刀盘中心，转动半径小，刀圈在转动的同时也有滑动，易发生刀圈偏磨现象。同时由于靠近刀盘中心，渣土排除不畅，易造成渣土对中心滚刀的刀圈、刀体的重复磨损。

图 4

（3）羊角刀

羊角刀适宜切削强度较低的岩石（见图 5），一般应用于隧道围岩为 I、II 类地层，通常超前切刀布置，先行切削地层，先对卵石进行冲击和撕裂，对卵石进行部分破碎并解除地层对卵石的约束力，然后由超前量较小的切刀切削剩余部分。

在软土地层中的掘进效率比滚刀高，但对硬岩地层比较敏感，对地层的适应性不强，在遇到岩石的冲击下，易造成合金块的崩裂甚至脱落，进而失去切削功能。在实际施工中先期安装的羊角刀，磨损十分严重，其强度和刚度不能满足刀盘的切削功能。因此对于成都特殊的地质情况，若要选用羊角刀，必须选用加强型羊角刀，选用的合金块具有好的耐磨性及抗冲击韧性，与刀体的焊接可靠，不易发生合金崩裂及脱落现象。

图 5

（4）刮刀

刮刀安装在刀盘排渣口的两侧，主要是通过刀盘转动产生的刮削作用将被滚刀碾压过的岩面修整平，减小滚刀下次碾压时因不平引起的冲击。一般选用优质合金块通过焊接镶嵌在刀体中，不易发生合金块的崩裂与脱落，使用寿命长。

边刮刀安装在刀盘的边缘部分（见图 6），主要作用是刮削被滚刀或齿刀切削下来的渣土顺利进入土仓，同时也有将被隧道壁修整成圆形的辅助作用。边刮刀的母体一般应该通过锻压成型，球齿合金通过压力压入母体，与母体过盈配合。

图 6

4 盾构刀具磨损形式和改进

在海瑞克目前盾构配置情况下，刀盘开口率较低、螺旋输送机直径较小等限制了卵石的入仓，同时也加大了刀盘刀具磨损。直接导致了以下几个掘进困难：

① 地层塌陷；② 刀盘及刀具磨损；③ 掘进效率低、代价昂贵

从掘进看，配置的硬岩刀具组合，滚刀未能充分发挥作用，对较大粒径的卵石有部分破碎作用，而对稍小粒径的土体作用不是很明显，反而滚刀基本上属于侧面磨损失效（只是保护了刀盘受损）；其实对于大多数较小粒径的土体而言无须破碎，可直接进仓，但开口率受限，致使砂卵石在前方加剧磨损刀盘。因此有必要进一步探索刀具配置（甚至包括刀盘等）的合理性。

碴土改良是土仓建压、减少磨损、防止泥饼等的最重要措施。碴土改良的好坏决定于改良剂类型的选择、添加量的确定、添加的时机等。借鉴类似工程施工经验，对改良剂的科学分析及实践，完善现有盾构配置的改良系统，探索出最有效方式。

4.1 刀具磨损形式及原因分析

（1）滚刀正常磨损：卵石中滚刀刀刃的磨损主要表现在宽度上的“尖状”磨损，与硬岩中滚刀的端面高度磨损不同。

（2）滚刀偏磨：启动力矩大，导致滚刀接触土体后不转动，刀刃单边偏磨，滚刀偶尔转动一次，刀刃尖状偏磨。尤其在粉细砂层中容易发生偏磨，另外，中心刀转动半径小，容易偏磨。掘进过程中刀具出现偏磨而未及时发现是非常危险的，一把刀由于偏磨而失效会造成相邻刀具过载而失效，从而迅速向外扩展，直至整个刀盘上的刀具全部失效。

（3）滚刀刀圈断裂：卵石碰撞或脱落的刀盘部件(如齿刀等)，会导致刀圈局部过载而使刀圈应力集中、发生断裂。或由于滚刀偏磨，一段刀圈逐渐磨损殆尽，亦会发生断裂。

（4）滚刀轴承损坏：卵石撞击下轴承过载、渣土发热致密封失效继而进泥、安装误差、端盖磨损、刀具漏油都会造成刀具轴承损坏，轴承损坏将导致刀具出现偏磨甚至整把磨损报废。

（5）滚刀漏油：发热、过载、装配不良等情况都有可能导致密封受损，刀具漏油。

（6）刀具螺栓松、脱、断及掉刀等：随着换刀次数的增加，刀具螺栓松、脱、断甚至掉刀的现象(统称为螺栓问题)也会逐渐严重。

（7）刮刀磨损：由于刮刀切削部分材料时刻经受卵石的碰撞和摩擦，经过 200 m 左右切削时磨损。

（8）耐磨环磨损：刀盘旋转部分在盾构本体切口环处不断与卵石摩擦，导致耐磨环磨损。

（9）螺旋机磨损：纵观刀具磨损的原因，有一些是卵石地层中不可避免的磨损问题，需要在刀具材料等方面加以改进，有一些非正常磨损则是由于刀具的切削作用与刀具结构、段差设计之间没有良好匹配引起的。

4.2 刀具材质的改进

切削刀具一般按照切削体（俗称刀头）、安装体、连接体三个部位来划分，其中切削体是直接与切削对象接触的，其材质根据切削对象不同，要求也不一样。岩层掘进时，刀头需要挤压破碎正面岩体，其承受的载荷包括挤压、弯曲、扭转、冲击、摩擦等，十分复杂。卵石地层中掘削，卵石对刀头的碰撞和摩擦，要求材料能抵抗冲击、同时具有适当的韧性，因此，合金材料得到了广泛的应用。刀具的连接体、安装体主要作用是将刀头的载荷传递至刀盘本体，因此其材料要求有良好的强度和韧性，高强度合金钢在可加工性、强度等方面都满足。

合金材料的利用，主要是以下四种（见图 7）：

耐磨环的镶嵌合金以后，掘进距离从原本的 200 m 可以提高至 1 000 m 以上

采用镶嵌合金的贝壳刀，综合考虑合金块大小、安装高度、硬度，可耐磨损

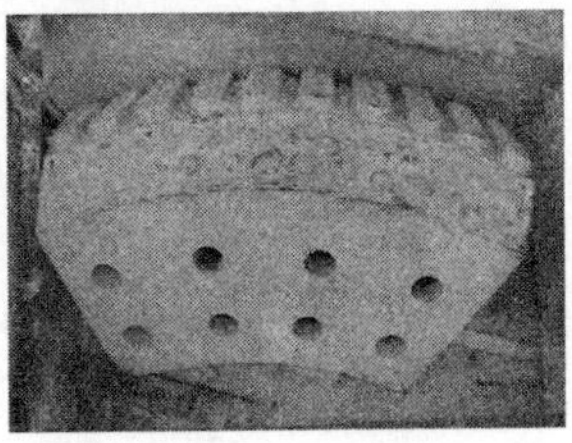

刮刀镶嵌合金以后，掘进距离从原本的 200 m 可以提高至 500 m 以上。

滚刀刀毂上镶嵌合金，可以有效增强刀毂的耐磨性能，提高滚刀的综合耐磨性能。

图 7

4.3 刀具特性的改进

刀具的特性按照切削刃的活动性划分，可以分为活动刃和固定刃 2 种，固定刃刀具主要包括刮刀、羊角刀、贝壳刀等，其形式较为简单，对前方土体有一个固定的切削角，承受的载荷比较单一，在刀盘扭矩计算等方面更容易简化，成本亦比较低廉；活动刃刀具主要是指滚刀（单双刃等），其切削刃端头与土体间主要的作用为挤压，刃体的两侧部位受土体的摩擦作用，因其刃体会滚动，可以降低破岩、时刀盘的扭矩，其结构亦十分复杂，成本较高。

按照刀具在刀盘面上的位置划分，可以分为周边刀、正面刀、中心刀等。周边刀切削轨迹半径较大，磨损较快，因此，可重点增强刀刃的耐磨性，以适应不同地层的变化。中心刀具切削轨迹半径较小，易结泥饼导致偏磨，因此让其充分转动或是增强固定刃的耐磨性，是刀具改进的重点。刀盘正面的刀具，需要全面考虑卵石破碎、刮削效率、刀盘保护等问题。

按照刀具在刀盘空间上的关系划分，可以分为先行刀、刮刀等。卵石地层中，先行刀的先行量必须考虑卵石粒径，保证其充分的流动性，同时，先行量对于刀盘扭矩的变化，亦必须进行充分的考虑，避免扭矩过大。

4.3.1 *活动刃刀具的改进*

根据滚刀磨损的规律，卵石地层中刀具的磨损主要发生在刀刃，因此将周边能转动的单刃滚刀改为双刃滚刀，加强其耐磨性能。

4.3.2 *固定刃刀具的改进*（见图 8）

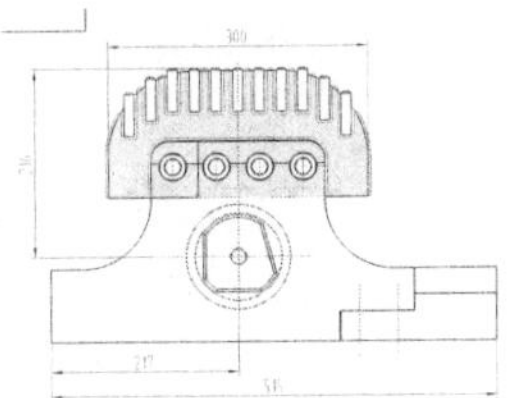

细齿贝壳刀，切削合金分布成弧形，合金剖面为阶梯状，端面平，优点是扭矩小。缺点是磨损较快。

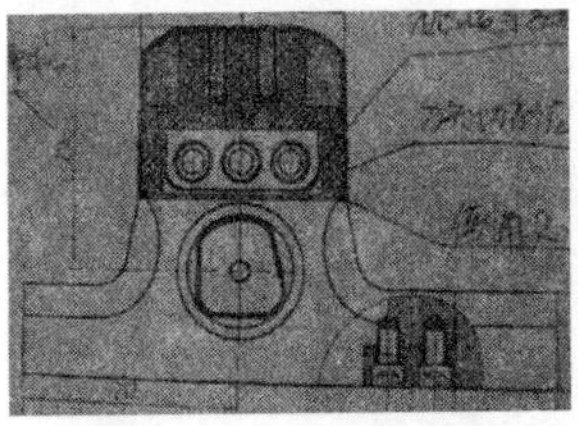

粗齿贝壳刀，侧向与安装面齐平，合金块较大，脆性大，易崩落。

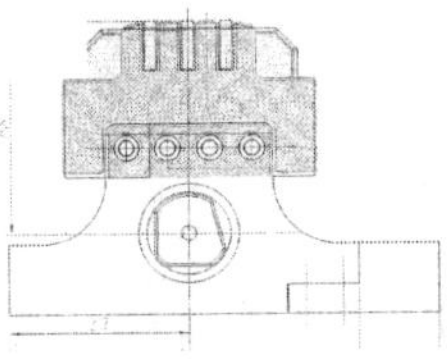

改良贝壳刀，两侧合金块高度适当降低，从侧向安装面内缩，受到保护，硬度合适，不易崩落，耐磨损。

中心先行刀，先行量达 275 mm，磨损严重。

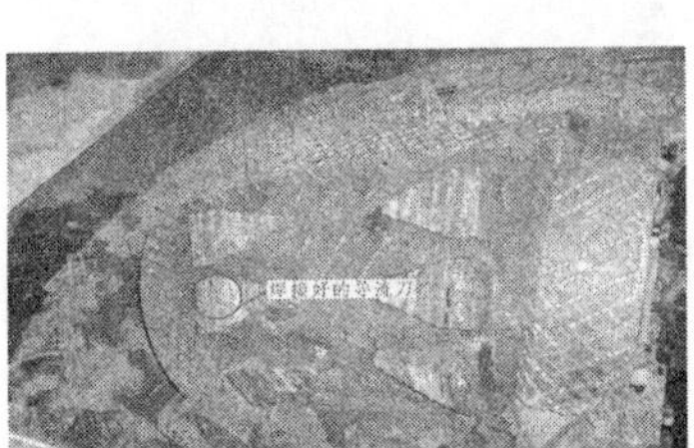

导流刀，焊接在周边刮刀两侧，对周边刮刀形成保护，效果良好。

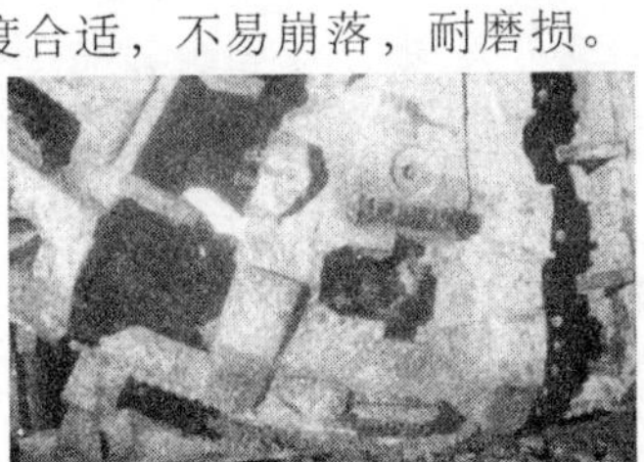

焊接贝壳刀，焊接在滚刀轨迹线上，对滚刀形成保护，效果良好。

图 8

4.4 刀具平面位置改进的效果

周边切削轨迹半径较大，磨损较快，进行了双刃滚刀、单刃滚刀、贝壳刀的试验摸索，3 种刀具可混合使用或单独使用，以适应不同地层的变化。

刀盘正面的刀具，试验使用了全滚刀、全羊角刀、正面滚刀＋羊角刀、正面滚刀＋贝壳刀等不同组合方式。羊角刀的磨损严重，滚刀＋贝壳刀的组合可满足快速掘进的需要

中心刀具切削轨迹半径较小，易结泥饼导致偏磨，试验使用了中心双刃滚刀、中心贝壳刀、中心先行刀等刀具。流动性保证情况下，中心双刃滚刀磨损小。

4.5 刀具空间位置改进的效果

突出刀盘的先导刀具试验了 125 mm 的羊角刀，160 mm 的单（双）刃滚刀，160 mm、180 mm、200 mm 的贝壳刀，中心先行贝壳刀。

周边刮刀、正面方刮刀突出刀盘 110 mm。未做调整。

综合适用效果看，突出刀盘 200 mm 的贝壳刀结合滚刀使用，效果良好。

4.6 刀具摸索的技术要点

4.6.1 刀具的磨损检测

使用测量工具，对每把换下来的刀具进行磨损量的测量，分析预测刀具磨损状况，及时换刀，降低施工风险。详见图 9。

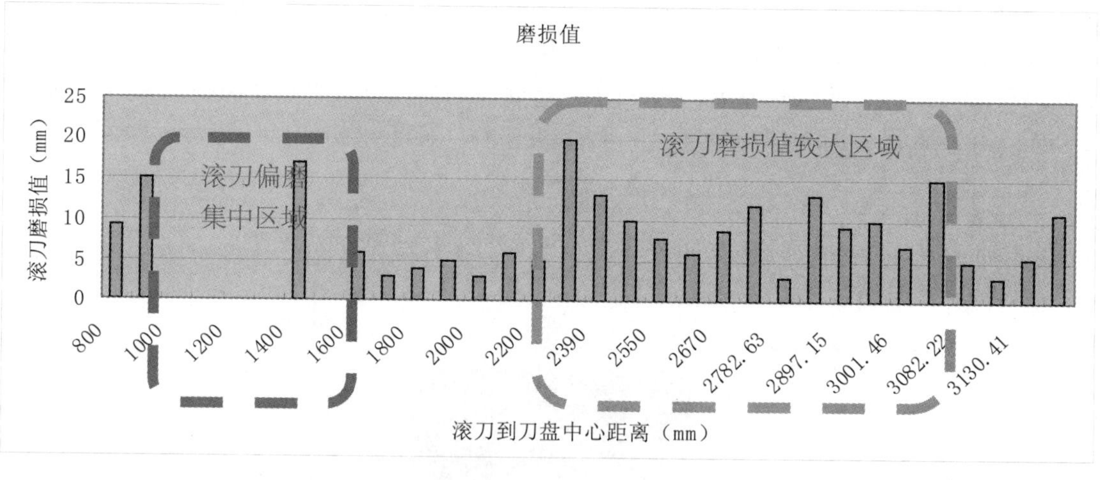

图 9

4.6.2 刀具、刀盘本体的耐磨

切削体（俗称刀头）、安装体、连接体等各部位的耐磨性能须全面加强，相互匹配，综合提高刀具配置的施工效果。

4.6.3 滚刀启动力矩合理设置，避免偏磨

启动力矩 30～50 N · m，朝低限设置。

4.6.4 掘进过程中设法增大渣土流动性，减少磨损

渣土流动性是砂卵石地层中盾构掘进的关键控制因素，应试验不同的土体改良方式、掘进模式，在掘进效率和刀具磨损中寻找最佳平衡。

4.6.5 提早分析地层条件，针对性调整刀具配置形式

<3-4>粉细砂层中掘进，发生过掘进困难，多出土导致地面塌陷、刀具及刀盘非正常磨损的情况。

5 刀具更换及维修技术

5.1 刀具更换

成都地铁通过的地层具有稳定性差、透气性大、地下水丰富、水位高、水压大等特点。砂卵石地层中，选择地面加固措施效果不明显或难以实施，在换刀时如采取有压换刀、地面注浆加固地层，将增加换刀的安全风险；采取旋喷桩或挖孔桩加固掌子可能存在时间、环境上的不便。成都砂卵石地层在降水条件下稳定性较好，可以均衡安全风险和施工成本，在降水条件下开仓换刀。

一般地铁线路均位于城市的主要交通干道和繁华地段，降水井的位置难以选择，因此应根据现场情况确定降水井施作的地点，降水井深度应超过隧道底部 5～7 m，位置在选定的换刀地点横向轴线附近且距隧道边界 1～2 m 为宜。

如需在带压条件下开仓换刀，加气前为防止砂卵石地层透气性大，难以保压，可以在清仓前向土仓中注入膨润土、聚合物，同时转动刀盘先行对碴土进行改良，然后再向土舱中加气以实现在掌子面上形成渗透性泥膜来保住压力的目标。

5.2 刀具维修技术

破损刀具的维修对于刀具残值的利用、降低工程成本都是十分必要的。

滚刀分为主轴、轴承、轮毂、刀圈等部分，针对各个部件的损毁情况，相应进行更换、维修处理，修复利用。并统计各部件损毁的规律，针对性加强处理。

刮刀、贝壳刀主要采取堆焊修补的方式修复利用。

6 结 语

成都独特富水砂卵石地层下盾构隧道施工的刀具管理，必须适应其独特地质条件，本文从刀具摸索的一般理念出发，分析了刀具材质、刀具特性在卵石地层中的适应性，详细介绍了施工实例中刀具应用的不断改进，提出了根据刀具在平面、空间位置的不同作用，对刀具结构、刀具种类进行完善的方法。

应用此刀具摸索改进的方法，在刀盘刀具配置上找到了适合成都地层的方式，工程取得了 250 m 不停机换刀穿越住宅小区、连续 220 m 不换刀穿越运营中的成都客站 11 股铁路股道、不换刀一次掘进距离最长至 580.6 m 等多项成功。

作者简介（Bio-data）：

彭健成，男，1980 年 2 月出生，工程师，上海东华大学机电一体化专业本科毕业，目前任职上海隧道工程股份有限公司盾构分公司副总工程师，主要从事盾构隧道施工技术研究。

Jiancheng PENG, male，born Feb.1980, Engineer，graduated from Shanghai Donghua University of Mechanical Electrical Department.

present position: deputy chief engineer of TBM Branch Company of STEC, mainly engaged in technology research of Shield tunnel construction。

E-mail: ctupjc19800201@126.com

富水砂卵石地层土压平衡盾构关键施工技术

王明胜[1] 章龙管[2]
[1]中铁隧道集团有限公司，河南 洛阳 471009
[2]中铁隧道股份有限公司，河南 郑州 450001

【摘 要】 成都地铁 1 号线试验段某区间盾构法隧道沿成都市交通主干道人民南路下穿行，隧道洞身地层为全断面砂卵石层,且沿线建（构）筑物众多，管线密集，埋深 9～15 m，盾构在该条件下的施工在国内目前尚属首次。具有相当大的技术难度。本文就解决盾构选型、盾构掘进参数与地层匹配,碴土改良和同步注浆等关键施工技术进行了深入的探讨,为以后国内类似工程提供经验和参考。
【关键词】 地铁；盾构选型；砂卵石地层；掘进；参数

KEY TECHNOLOGY FOR EPB SHIELD BORING IN WATER-RICH SAND/GRAVEL GROUND

Mingsheng WANG[1], Longguan ZHANG[2]
[1]China Railway Tunnel Group Co., Ltd., Luoyang 471009, Henan, China;
[2]China Railway Tunnel Stock Co., Ltd., Zhengzhou 450001, Henan, China

Abstract: A shield-bored running tunnel of trial section of Line 1 of Chengdu Metro goes underneath along South Renmin Road, which is a trunk traffic corridor in Chengdu. The full cross-section of the tunnel is located in sand/gravel ground. There are numerous buildings and structures, as well as densely-distributed utility lines, along the tunnel alignment. The hidden tunnel ranges from 9m to 15m under the earth. It is the first time in China that an EPB shield machine is used to bore tunnels in such geological conditions; therefore there exist great difficulties in the shield tunneling. In the paper, discussion is made on such key construction technologies as shield type selection, shield tunneling parameters adaptable to the ground conditions, ground conditioning and simultaneous grouting, which can provide reference for similar works in the future.
Key words: metro; shield type selection; sand/gravel ground; tunneling; parameter

1 引 言

盾构施工以其安全、快速、高效在国内外地下工程，尤其是城市地下铁道建设中得到越来越广泛的应用。在使用盾构法进行城市地铁隧道修建中，不可避免的要对线路沿线地面建（构）筑物造成一定程度的影响，要求在盾构施工时既要保证盾构施工隧道本身的安全，还要解决好盾构穿越地层时对邻近既有建（构）筑物的影响问题。

成都地铁一号线盾构法隧道自 2006 年试验段开工以来，由于成都地区地质的特殊性，采用盾构法施工富水砂卵石地层在国内目前没有成熟的经验。本文主要结合成都地区特殊地层，来探讨成都地铁富水砂卵石盾构法施工技术。

2 工程概述

成都地铁 1 号线盾构某工程起于省体育馆站南端，止于火车南站北端。隧道总长 4 900.43 单线延米，其中左线隧道长 2 328.2 单线延米，右线隧道长 2 572.23 单线延米，线路基本沿人民南路中部敷设，分省体育馆路—倪家桥站区间、倪家桥站—桐梓林站区间、桐梓林站—火车南站站区间三个区间。

3 工程地质及水文地质

成都地铁试验段盾构隧道穿越的地层主要为粉质黏土、卵石土夹砂层，围岩级别为Ⅱ类（Ⅴ级）。根据初勘报告资料显示，在盾构穿越中会遇到大漂石和有害气体。盾构试验段穿越的典型地层：

（1）粉质黏土岩，层厚 2.3～2.8 m。天然快剪黏聚力 39.6 kPa；内摩擦角 18.9°。具弱膨胀性，渗透系数 K＝0.001 m/d，为弱透水层。

（2）卵石土夹砂层，广泛分布于基岩顶面，厚度 15～22.5 m；卵石含量 60%～70%，粒径以 30～70 mm 为主。

（3）通过地层中漂石占 0～22.3%（重量比），大粒径砾石含量较高且局部富集成群。

（4）有害气体，遗漏和产生的污水渗入地下，危及隧道施工。

区间分布的卵石土及所夹透镜状砂层为地下水主要含水层，综合含水层厚 15.00～22.50 m，地下水以潜水赋存其间，渗透性较强。地下水主要受大气降水及地表水补给。雨洪期地下水位埋深建议按 2 m 考虑，隧道顶板埋深 3～15 m，隧道底板埋深 10～22 m，故隧道洞身范围的地下水压力为 10～200 kPa。

4 盾构法隧道结构形式

采用管片拼装式衬砌，管片外径 6 000 mm，厚 300 mm，环宽 1.5 m，采用错缝拼装，弯曲螺栓连接。管片与围岩之间的环形间隙采用水泥砂浆同步注浆回填。

5 盾构选型

盾构选型是工程成功的关键因素之一，应从对地质的适应性、安全性、可靠性、经济性等方面综合考虑，所选择的机型要能尽量减少辅助施工并能确保施工安全可靠。不同类型的盾构适应的地质范围不同，盾构选型主要依据土质、岩性、水文条件等，要确保所选择的盾构能适应地质条件，施工中能够保持开挖面的稳定（详见表 1）。

表 1　泥水平衡盾构和土压平衡盾构对地质的适应性

比较项目	土压平衡盾构		泥水平衡盾构	
	简要说明	评价	简要说明	评价
稳定开挖面	保持切削土舱压力支持开挖面土体稳定	良	有压泥水使开挖面地层保持稳定	优
地质条件适应性	在砂性土等透水性地层中要有特殊的措施	良	泥膜有效的阻隔和压力各处均匀的传递，使之适用于大多数地层	优
抵抗水压	靠土舱压力及泥土的不透水性能抵抗水压	良	靠泥水在开挖面形成的泥膜和泥水压力抵抗水压	优
控制地表沉降	保持土舱压力、控制推进速度、维持切削量与出土量相等	良	控制泥浆质量、压力及推进速度、保持进、排泥量的动态平衡	优
碴土处理	直接外运	简单	进行泥水分离处理	复杂
施工场地	占用施工场地较小	良	要有较大的泥水处理场地	差
工程成本	减少了泥水处理设备	低	增加泥水分离设备，费用高	高

5.1 盾构类型与水压、渗透性关系

地层渗透系数是盾构选型的重要因素。根据欧美和日本的施工经验，两种盾构能够适应的地层渗透系数范围如图 1 所示。当地层的渗透系数小于 10^{-7} cm/s 时，可以选用土压平衡盾构；当地层的渗透系数在 10^{-7} cm/s 和 10^{-4} cm/s 之间时，既可以选用土压平衡盾构也可以选用泥水盾构；当地层的渗透系数大于 10^{-4} cm/s 时，宜选用泥水盾构。

成都地铁卵石土层渗透系数 k＝（1.5～3.2）×10^{-5} cm/s，可采用泥水平衡盾构或土压平衡盾构。

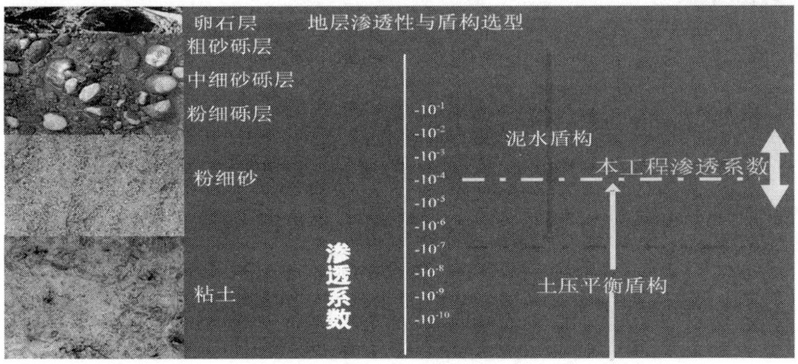

图 1 地层渗透系数与盾构选型关系示意图

5.2 土压平衡盾构施工可行性

根据试验段施工结果表明，成都地区土压平衡盾构明显优于泥水盾构。

6 土压平衡盾构施工关键技术

6.1 施工掘进及参数

（1）盾构在完成试掘进后，将对掘进参数进行必要的调整，为后续的正常掘进提供条件。主要包括：

① 根据地质条件和试掘进过程中的监测结果进一步优化掘进参数。

② 正常推进阶段采用 90 m 试掘进阶段掌握的最佳施工参数。通过加强施工监测，不断地完善施工工艺，控制地面沉降。

③ 推进过程中，严格控制好推进速度，不断将人工测量结果地电子测量系统的数据进行比较，发现问题及时调整，将偏差控制在误差范围内。

④ 根据技术交底设定的参数推进，推进出土与衬砌背后注浆同步进行。不断完善施工工艺，控制施工后地表最大变形量在+10～－30 mm 之内。

⑤ 掘进过程中平稳调整盾构姿态，隧道轴线和折角变化控制在 0.4%范围内。

⑥ 盾构掘进施工过程中严格受控，根据地质变化、隧道埋深、地面荷载、地表沉降、盾构姿态、刀盘扭矩、千斤顶推力等各种勘探、测量数据信息，并及时跟踪调整。

⑦ 盾构掘进初始出现的小偏差应及时纠正，应尽量避免盾构机走“蛇”形，盾构机一次纠偏量不宜过大，以减少对地层的扰动。

（2）盾构掘进参数见表 2。

表 2 盾构掘进主要参数表

掘进施工参数					工程地质
土仓压力（bar）	刀盘转速（rpm）	推力（t）	掘进速度 (mm/m)	刀具贯入量 (mm/r)	
0.9～1.3	1.0～1.2	1 200～1 500 t	40～60	40～50	砂卵石、粉细砂原状地层

6.2 砂卵石地层土压平衡盾构碴土改良和开挖面稳定技术

(1) 碴土改良

碴土改良主要是降低碴土的内摩擦角，降低刀盘的扭矩，增加碴土的流动性、渗透性、和易性，从而达到堵水、减磨、降扭及保压的效果。本工程根据需要在盾构上配备两套碴土改良系统：泡沫系统、膨润土（泥浆）系统。两者共用一套输送管路，所有管路经旋转接头均可到达刀盘面板。

① 泡沫系统

泡沫系统在刀盘和螺旋输送机共设置 14 路泡沫孔，其中刀盘面八路、土仓隔板预留四路、螺旋输送机设置两路。土仓隔板预留四路泡沫孔又兼作膨润土等的注入孔。工作原理见图 2。

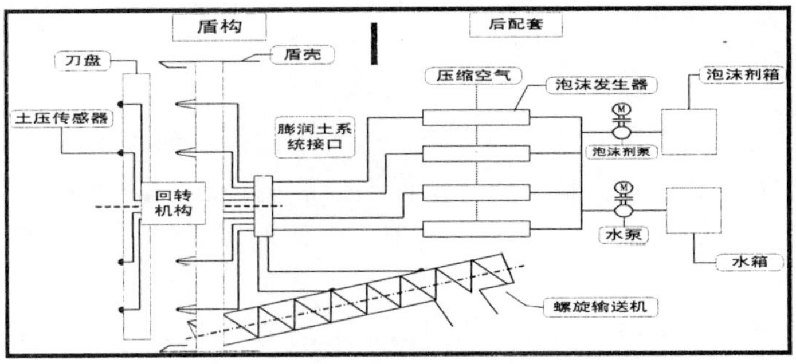

图 2 泡沫及膨润土系统示意图

② 膨润土（泥浆）系统

在确定不使用泡沫剂的情况下，关闭泡沫输送管道，同时将膨润土（泥浆）输送管道打开，通过膨润土（泥浆）输送泵将泥浆或者膨润土压入刀盘、土仓和螺旋输送机内，达到改良碴土地目的，通过泡沫、膨润土系统同时对碴土进行改良，系统性能良好，完全能够满足本工程的需要。

(2) 开挖面稳定技术

针对成都地区特有的富水砂卵石地层，盾构做出了如下针对性设计：

① 加入约 10%的膨润土以及黏土组成的泥浆用以改良碴土。

② 在螺旋机入口的两侧备有纯聚合物溶液注入口，胶化稀碴以进一步加强“土塞”作用，防止喷涌。

③ 旋转接头有各自独立的膨润土和泡沫通路，并均能注入刀盘前面，保证与碴土的充分混合和搅拌，形成非渗透性和塑流性的碴土。

④ 主轴承芯部的隔板是固定的并有搅拌棒，以加强土仓内的整体搅拌效果。

⑤ 螺旋输送机采用双螺旋。

经过采取如加泥（膨润土）、加泡沫、聚合物等措施，可以在松散的砂、卵地层中很好地稳定开挖面，增强不透水性，从而可靠安全地掘进；特别是双螺旋的采用，即使土仓内的碴土处于液态状态，仍能连续出碴而不会发生喷涌，保证含水较高地层施工的安全可靠。

合理的刀盘及出碴系统等设计，同时加注辅助材料如泡沫、膨润土、聚合物等进行碴土改良，有效地控制了开挖面及地表稳定。

6.3 同步注浆浆液配制及施工技术

(1) 浆液配制

注浆配合比,由于盾构隧道穿越卵石地层，同步注浆采用水泥砂浆，浆液的配合见表 3。

表 3 同步注浆材料配比表

水泥（kg）	粉煤灰（kg）	膨润土（kg）	砂（kg）	水（kg）	黄黏土（kg）	外加剂
126	180	72	720	480	216	据试验加入

浆液主要性能指标,胶凝时间一般为 3～10 h，根据地层条件和掘进速度，通过现场试验加入促凝剂

及变更配比来调整胶凝时间。固结体强度一天不小于 0.2 MPa，28 天不小于 2.5 MPa。浆液结石率>95%，即固结收缩率<5%。浆液稠度 8～12 cm，浆液稳定性倾析率（静置沉淀后上浮水体积与总体积之比）小于 5%。

（2）施工技术

同步注浆采用设备配置两台双活塞注浆泵在盾尾分四路同时注入。

① 注浆模式

注浆可根据需要采用自动控制或手动控制方式，自动控制方式即预先设定注浆压力，由控制程序自动调整注浆速度，当注浆压力达到设定值时，自行停止注浆。手动控制方式则由人工根据掘进情况随时调整注浆流量，以防注浆速度过快，而影响注浆效果。一般不从预留注浆孔注浆，以大大降低从管片渗漏水的可能。

② 主要参数

• 注浆压力：同步注浆时要求在地层中的浆液压力大于该点的静止水压及土压力之和，做到尽量填补而不劈裂。注浆压力过大，隧道将会被浆液扰动而造成后期地层沉降及隧道本身的沉降，并易造成跑浆；注浆压力过小，浆液填充速度过慢，填充不充足，会使地表变形增大。同步注浆压力设定为 0.2～0.4 MPa，并根据量测结果作适当调整。

• 注浆量：在富水砂卵石地层中，同步注浆量为建筑间隙的 150%～180%，即为 6.1 m^3～7.3 m^3/环。

• 注浆时间及速度：盾构掘进的同时，进行同步注浆，同步注浆的速度与盾构推进速度相匹配。

• 注浆顺序：采用 4 个注浆孔同时压注，在每个注浆孔出口设置压力检测器，以便对各注浆孔的注浆压力和注浆量进行检测与控制，从而实现对管片背后的对称均匀压注。

• 注浆结束标准和注浆效果检查，采用双指标标准，即注浆压力达到设计压力或注浆压力未达到设计压力，但注浆量达到设计注浆量，即可停止注入。

• 注浆效果检查主要采用分析法，即根据 P-Q-t 曲线，结合掘进速度及衬砌、地表与周围建筑物变形量测结果进行综合分析判断。必要时采用无损探测法进行效果检查。

（3）刀具更换

① 刀具磨损

滚刀包括中心双刃滚刀和单刃正滚刀，本工程滚刀的磨损主要是滚刀支架磨损造成刀具漏油、进砂、弦磨等，从检修情况来看主要是支架的材料硬度不够高，为了防止此类情况的发生需在新刀与修理的刀具支架及滚刀刀体上都堆焊了耐磨层，这种防护措施能有效延长刀具支架的使用寿命。

② 换刀作业

就成都地区特有的富水砂卵石地层而言，换刀相当频繁。在该地层换刀，可采用常压换刀和带压换刀两种方式。

• 常压换刀方式：

在富水砂卵石地层开仓换刀，掌子面土体稳定性差，砂卵石地层遇水易坍塌。在该地质条件下，采用常压进仓方式必须对换刀位置进行降水并辅以注浆、旋喷、人工挖孔桩或灌注桩等加固措施，否则难以保证换刀处掌子面的稳定。

• 带压换刀方式：

经过对刀盘前方地层进行处理后，在保证刀盘前方周围地层和土仓满足气密性要求的条件下，通过在土仓建立合理的气压来平衡刀盘前方的水、土压力，达到稳定掌子面和防止地下水渗入的目的，为在土仓内进行刀盘刀具检查和更换刀具创造工作条件。其工作原理见图 3。

富水砂卵石地层孔隙率大，带压过程中气体易逃逸，导致压力难以保持，进而影响施工安全。为有效填充地层孔隙，防止气体逃逸，在带压进仓换刀过程中,首先通过膨润土注入系统向土仓内注入优质的膨润土泥浆置换原有仓内的碴土，在掌子面形成良好的泥膜。当压力保持稳定后，进行带压进仓换刀。通过采取上述措施后，成功实现了富水砂卵石地层带压进仓作业，掌子面形成的泥膜见图 4。

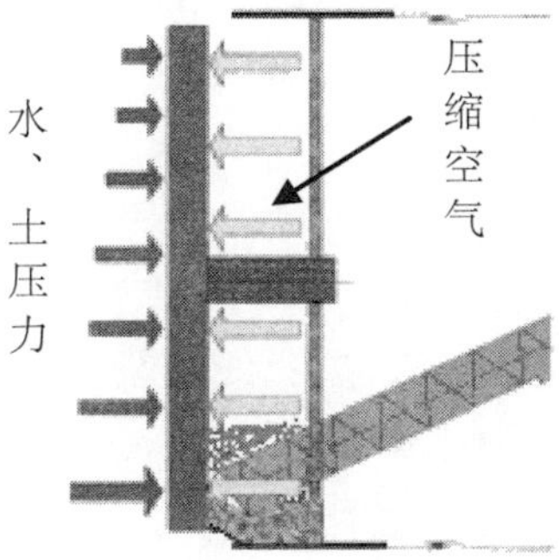

图 3　带压作业原理示意图

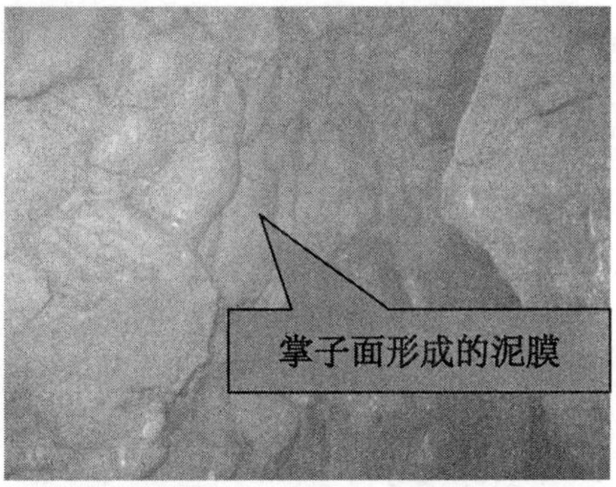

图 4　掌子面形成的泥膜图

鉴于地铁沿线基本都处于繁华的都市内，地面建（构）筑物、管线密布，采用常压换刀方式需占用地面场地进行加固施工，对地面环境影响大；而采用带压进仓方式基本不影响地面环境，因此在换刀方式的选择上应首选带压进仓方式而尽量避免采用加固后常压进仓方式。

7　施工中出现问题的及时处理

7.1　土压力不稳定且不易保持

由于成都地层的特殊性，富水砂卵石地层由大中粒径卵石、砾石及小微粒径沙砾组成，成分具有不均一性，在盾构土压力仓内不能形成均一的流塑体，因此盾构在该地层中掘进时表现出土压力不稳定且不易保持，时常发生波动。

主要通过从碴土改良出发，加入泡沫剂、膨润土等改变碴土的性状，增强其流塑性，达到稳定土压力保持掌子面稳定的目的,盾构掘进中以总推力为指导，作为与掌子面平衡的一项参考指标，来保证开挖面的土压力平衡。

7.2　出碴量不易控制

成都特有富对砂卵石地层，在富水饱和条件下是极不稳定的。盾构掘进时，若碴土改良存在问题，掌子面极易发生坍塌，使得出碴量不易有效控制，造成超挖，严重时发生地表塌陷,主要通过加强碴土改良，使出碴量可控，防止发生掌子面坍塌,盾构不连续掘进时，掌子面易发生坍塌，造成超挖塌陷。加强掘进控制，尽量减小由于机械故障等原因引起的停机，提高掘进的连续性。

7.3　刀盘、刀具磨损严重

成都地层砂卵石中石英含量高，硬度大，在该地层中掘进，刀盘、刀具磨损严重。主要通过对刀盘耐磨处理，在刀盘每个进碴口的周圈进行硬化处理并堆焊耐磨材料；在刀盘的中心和外缘进行硬化处理并堆焊耐磨材料；在刀盘外圈设有保护刀具。盾构刀盘的周边焊有两道耐磨条，刀盘的面板用进口焊条焊接有格栅状的耐磨材料，充分保证刀盘在岩层掘进时的耐磨性能,从碴土改良入手，在盾构掘进中，适量加入泡沫剂、膨润土等，可有效降低刀盘、刀具的磨损，延长使用时间。

8　效益分析

8.1　社会效益

盾构法施工消除了对城市交通的严重影响，施工产生的振动、噪音、粉尘等公害也得到了最大限度的降低。工程建设时，周围的居民及企事业单位能正常生活及工作。地表建（构）筑物、管线均未受到破坏损伤，为以后城市地下工程在类似情况下的规划建设提供了可靠的决策依据和技术指标，新颖的工法技术将促进城市地下工程施工技术进步，社会效益和环境效益明显。

8.2 经济效益

确保周围既有建（构）筑物完好无损，确保居民生命、财产安全，避免线路绕行和居民临时迁移，节约了大量工程拆迁、地面场地占用等费用，同时，在施工进度、材料消耗、机械零部件消耗、水电消耗等作业成本上较泥水盾构有较大优势，形成了良好的经济效益。

土压平衡盾构左线全线平均日进度 7.9 m/天，月平均进度 237 m/月。日最高推进为 22.5 m（15 环）；月最高进度为 357 m（2008 年 3 月），创造了在成都富水砂卵石地层施工中的盾构掘进月进度的新纪录。

9 监测与评价

施工过程中对沿线建（构）筑物、管线的安全稳定，及时监测了施工各阶段引起的沉降动态数值，地表沉降监测结果显示，地表最大沉降量为－20.2 mm，发生在隧道中线位置，隧道发生沉降最大发生在管片脱离盾尾时，该部分沉降占总沉降量约为 70%。施工全过程处于安全、稳定、快速、优质的可控状态。建筑物基础沉降监测结果显示，最大沉降值为 4.9 mm，平均沉降为 2.7 mm，房屋倾斜率 0.4‰，建筑物安全。得到了各方的好评。

参考文献（Referenles）：

[1] 竺维彬，鞠世健. 复合地层盾构施工技术[M]. 北京：中国科学技术出版社，2006.

[2] 水利部科技推广中心. 全断面岩掘进机[M]. 北京：石油工业出版社，2005.8

[3] 竺维彬. 广州地铁三号线盾构隧道工程施工技术研究. 厦门：暨南大学出版社，2007.

[4] 龚维明. 地下结构工程. 南京：东南大学出版社，2002.

[5] 张凤祥，朱合华，傅德明. 盾构隧道. 北京：人民交通出版社，2004.

[6] 盾构标准规范（盾构篇）及解说. [日]土木学会编，朱伟译. 北京：中国建筑工业出版社，2001.

[7] 伊旅超，朱振宏，李玉珍，等. 日本隧道盾构新技术仁[M]. 武汉：华中理工大学出版社，1999.

作者简介（Bio-data）：

王明胜，男，1976 年 1 月出生，工程师，本科学历，科长，主要从事地下工程科研，工法、知识产权开发工作。

Mingsheng WANG (1976—), male, bachelor, engineer, section chief. He specializes in the scientific research, construction method development and intellectual property development in the field of underground works.

E-mail: jdwms@126.com

北京地区砂卵石地层盾构掘进参数分析

郭玉海[1,2] 李兴高[1] 袁大军[1]

[1]北京交通大学隧道及地下工程教育部工程研究中心，北京 100044

[2]北京市政集团四处，北京 100055

【摘 要】 砂卵石地层中减少盾构刀具磨损，其中一个重要的措施就是采用合理的盾构掘进参数。因此，有必要了解盾构掘进参数之间的关系。基于北京地铁 4 号线某典型工程，采用数理统计方法和神经网络方法，全面研究了现场推进速度、土仓压力等掘进参数之间的关系。绘制了能够清晰展示掘进参数分布特征的直方图。数理统计表明，在盾构推进速度、刀盘转速等参数近似呈正态分布的前提下，盾机刀盘扭矩和推力也近似呈正态分布，并给出了砂卵石地层盾构掘进参数的合理范围。其次，考虑到现场实际数据之间并不存在明显的规律性，借助于人工神经网络建立起盾构掘进参数之间的定量关系，并介绍了盾构掘进参数计算模型在实际工程中的应用。研究结论有助于类似地层条件下的盾构掘进参数选取。

【关键词】 盾构施工；掘进参数；砂卵石地层；刀具磨损；数理统计；BP 神经网络

ANALYSIS OF SHIELD TUNNELING PARAMETERS IN SANFY COBBLE GROUND IN BEIJING AREA

Yuhai GUO[1,2], Xinggao LI[1], Dajun YUAN[1]

[1] *Engineering Research Center of Tunnel and Underground Engineering, Beijing Jiaotong University, Ministry of Education, Beijing 100044, China;*

[2] *Fourth construction division of Beijing municipal group, Beijing 100055, China*

Abstract: To reduce shield cutter wear in sandy cobble ground, one of the important measures is to adopt the rational shield tunneling parameters. Therefore, it is necessary to grasp relations of shield tunneling parameters. Based on a certain typical project in Line 4 of Beijing Metro, the in-situ shield tunneling parameters including the advance speed, the chamber pressure and etc., are overall studied by means of mathematical statistics and nerve network method. The histograms of shield tunneling parameter are plotted, which can clearly exhibit the distribution characteristics of the parameters. The mathematical statistics show under the prerequisite of the advance speed, the rotation speed and etc. approximately in Gaussian distribution, the torque and the thrust of the shield are also approximately in Gaussian distribution, and the valid ranges of shield tunneling parameters in sandy cobble ground are put forward. Considering the fact that the in-situ data represents no obvious law, the quantitative relations among shield tunneling parameters are set up by using the artificial nerve network method, and the application in engineering of the computation model of shield tunneling parameters is explained. The research conclusion is helpful for shield tunneling parameter selection in similar conditions.

Key words: shield tunneling; tunneling parameters; sandy cobble ground; cutter wear ; mathematical statistics; BP nerve network

1 引 言

近年来，随着北京地铁工程的快速发展，盾构施工技术得到了广泛的应用。在推广应用过程中，盾构在砂卵石地层中盾构刀具磨损等技术难题也随之而来。北京新线建设中盾构法隧道的比例更大，且大部分隧道全断面或部分断面位于砂卵石地层中。盾构在砂卵石地层中施工，刀具磨耗严重，容易破损、脱落。掘进中一旦出现这类情况，将导致刀盘扭矩上升，盾构推进困难，甚至无法施工，被迫开舱换刀，容易引起开挖面坍塌，给整个工程的工期、造价带来严重的影响，甚至威胁施工人员的安全。为实现砂卵石地层快速掘进，必须研究砂卵石地层中的盾构掘进参数的优化问题，以降低盾构机刀具磨损，以充分发挥盾构工法所具有的安全可靠、快速高效且对周围环境影响小等优点。目前，对于盾构掘进参数之间的关系研究已经不少[1][2]，但对于砂卵石地层盾构掘进参数的分析还比较少。有鉴于此，本文结合北京地铁 4 号线白石桥站~动物园站区间工程的盾构实际掘进参数，进行系统分析研究。通过工程中刀具磨损的测试分析可知，采取掘进参数优化控制和有效施工措施，在全断面砂卵石地层中，盾构刀具磨损系数可分别控制在 0.033 3 mm/km 和 0.031 7 mm/km 左右[3]。按上述磨损系数可以进一步推算出砂卵石地层盾构不换刀最长掘进距离。最终，长达 1 339.8 m 的白石桥站～动物园站区间未开仓换刀持续掘进完成。因而，依据本工程得到的实际掘进参数开展相关研究具有现实意义，可为以后类似工程施工提供有益的实践经验。

2 工程概况

北京地铁 4 号线是一条贯穿南北的轨道交通线，其中白石桥站~动物园站区间总长 1 339.8 m，该区间隧道水平方向大致呈“C”型，设计最小曲线半径为 350 m，曲线长度约占区间全长的 85%左右。由于要与地铁 2 号线西直门站相接，该区间段自白石桥站向动物园站一路下扎，落差近 7.5 m，竖曲线最小半径为 5 000 m，竖曲线同平曲线叠加构成了一条立体空间的长距离急曲线地铁隧道。

根据工程地质勘察报告，盾构主要穿越的地层为卵石圆砾层，杂色，密实，湿～饱和，重型动力触探 N63.5 为 33～90，剪切波速 Vs 为 294.1～475.6 m/s，属低压缩性土，最大粒径 280 mm，一般粒径 10～30 mm，粒径大于 20 mm 颗粒含量约为总质量 14%（现场砂石筛分试验结果），中粗砂充填，母岩成份为辉绿岩，仅局部夹砂或黏性土透镜体。图 1 为白石桥站~动物园站区间地层断面。

工程使用的盾构机是日本 IHI 生产的ϕ6.14 m 加泥式土压平衡盾构机，盾构机刀盘的结构形式为辐条式，开口率大，适合在砂卵石地层中（尤其是可能含有大粒径卵石地层）施工。铰接装置的水平张角为±2°，垂直张角为±1°，设计最小曲线施工半径为 150 m。

为严格控制超挖量，启用了盾构铰接及仿形刀装置，预先推出弧线。首先根据设计曲线半径计算出所需用的铰接角度，使盾构机前盾与后端的张角与设计曲线近似吻合，经现场试验及建模模拟后确定水平张角为 0.5°，竖直张角为 0.1°，然后根据铰接张角计算出需超挖的范围及超挖量，因该区间为左转，故确定仿形刀超挖范围为左侧 180°，超挖量为 20 mm 左右。

针对无水砂卵石地层中盾构掘进时的推进阻力比较大的情况，增加了盾构壁外加泥的措施，即配制高浓度膨润土泥浆，通过盾构壳体预留的泥浆注入口将泥浆注入到盾构壳体与土层的间隙中，在盾构壳体与土体之间形成一层黏稠、润滑效果良好的泥膜，减少了盾构壳体与土体之间的直接接触面积，使得盾构推进阻力由 3 700 t 降至 1 600～2 000 t 之间，一方面增加了推进千斤顶编组选择的空间，另一方面使得推进速度大大提高了，可以达到 70 mm/min。根据现场的实际数据，泥浆的浓度为 9%，黏度为 18 s，比重 1.07。图 2 为加泥后盾构机出土情况。

尽管采取了多种措施，白石桥—动物园区间未开仓换刀持续掘进完成，但工程完工后，刀具的磨损还是很严重的，有的切削刀已经完全磨损掉。

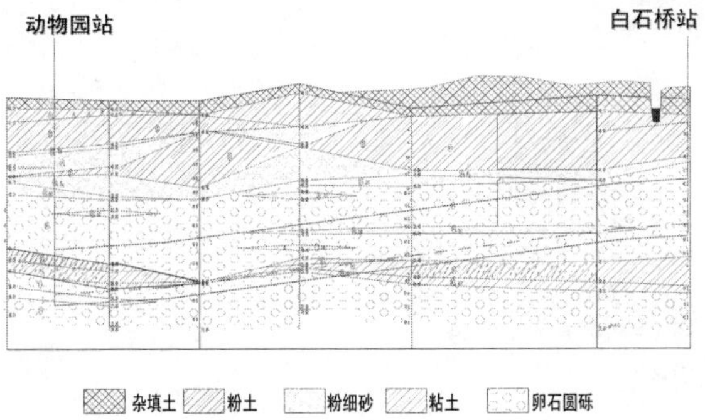

图 1　白石桥站—动物园站区间地层断面

图 2　加泥后盾构机出土情况

3　掘进参数统计分析

掘进参数的采集主要依靠内嵌于盾构机内的数据采集系统实时采集。每环主要采集的掘进参数有推进速度、刀盘转速、刀盘扭矩、盾构机总推力、土仓内土压、螺旋机回转速度、注浆 A 液流量、注浆 B 液流量、No1 加泥流量、No2 加泥流量、No1 泡沫流量、No2 泡沫流量、实际挖掘时间等。篇幅所限，并考虑工程实际条件，本文选取了白石桥～动物园区间左线的 319 环到 418 环的数据作为分析对象，将各参数按照数理统计方法进行处理，绘制出各参数的直方图，见图 3。需要说明的是，为简化分析，图 3 中的参数注浆总量为每环的注浆量、加泥量和加泡沫量之和。

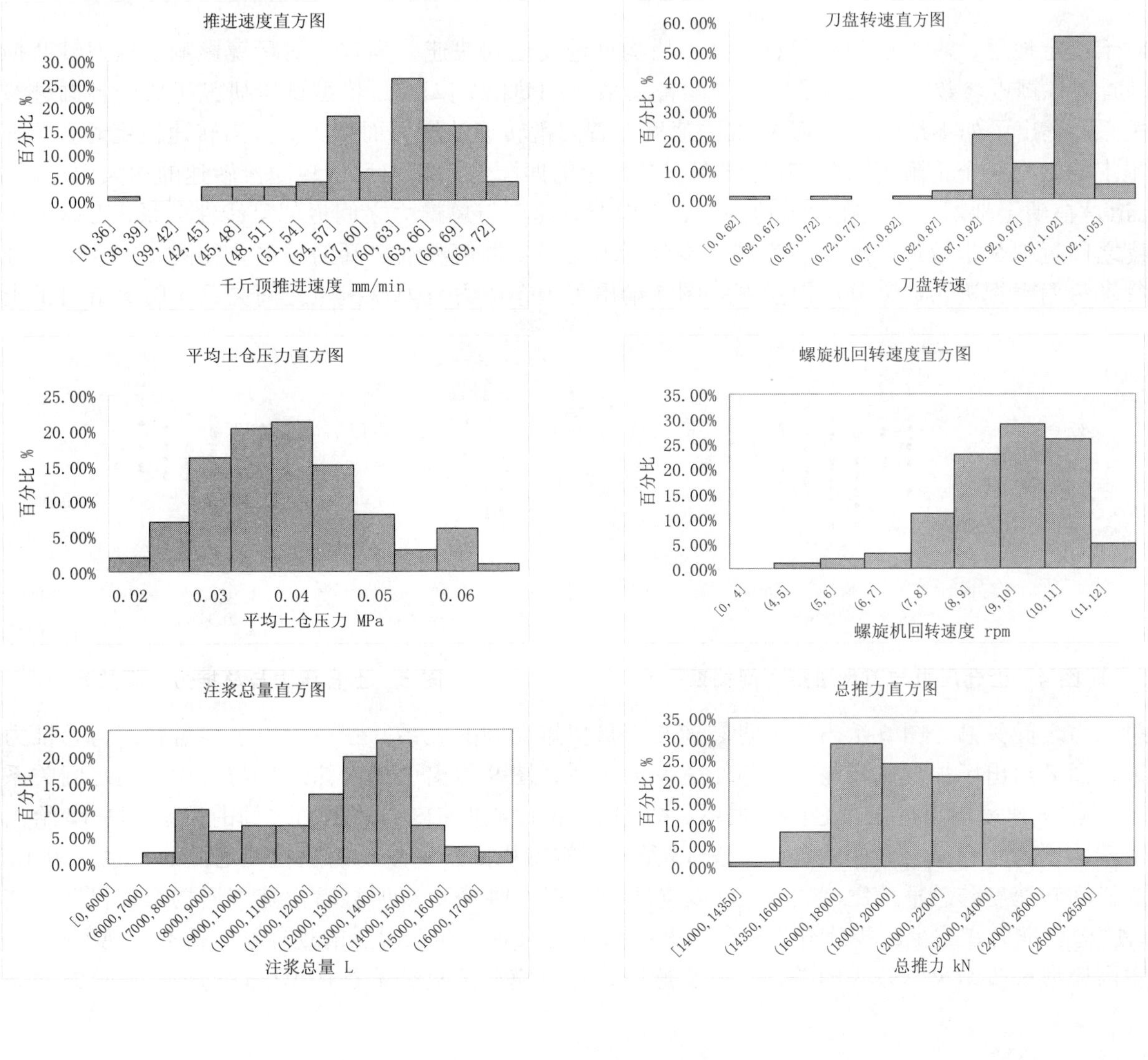

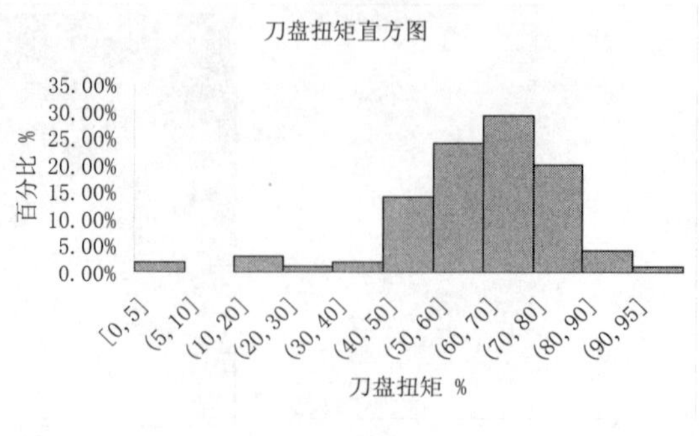

图 3 掘进参数直方图

由图 3 可以发现，盾构推进速度大致在 5～7 cm/min，平均约为 6 cm/min，基本维持在较高的掘进速度；盾构刀盘转速大致在 0.87～1.05 rpm，平均约为 1.0 rpm；土仓压力取土仓内上、左、右 3 个压力盒的平均值，基本维持在 0.03～0.05 MPa 之间，平均值约为 0.04 MPa；螺旋机转速大致维持在 8～11 rpm 之间；注浆总量大致维持在 7 000～16 000 L 之间；总推力大致在 16 000～26 000 kN 之间；刀盘扭矩大致为额定最大扭矩的 40%～80%之间，有些环甚至达到了额定最大扭矩的 95%。对于各掘进参数的分布特征，由图 3 可以发现，在盾构推进速度、刀盘转速、土仓压力、螺旋机转速、注浆量基本成正态分布的前提下，盾构机总推力、刀盘扭矩也可以近似认为服从正态分布。

4 掘进参数相关性分析

对于特定地层，本工程为砂卵石地层，盾构掘进要达到快速、高效、对环境影响小且刀具磨损小的目标，盾构各掘进参数之间须满足一定的配备关系。文[1]和文[2]通过模型试验研究了盾构各掘进参数之间的关系，得出了如下结论：① 盾构推进速度随着刀盘转速的增大而增大，且当转速恒定时，推进速度也基本上稳定在某个值附近，即二者之间存在参数上的匹配性；② 刀盘扭矩随着转速的加大而逐渐增大；③ 无论是在硬土地层，还是在软土地层中，盾构推进速度与总推力之间近似呈线性关系；刀盘扭矩与推进速度之间近似呈指数形式增加。为进一步分析本工程各掘进参数之间的关系，在图 4～14 中，分别绘制了每环每两个掘进参数之间的散点图。图 4 给出了土仓压力与刀盘扭矩之间关系，图 5 给出了土仓压力与总推力之间关系，图 6 给出了刀盘转速与刀盘扭矩之间的关系，图 7 给出了刀盘转速与总推力之间的关系，图 8 给出了加泥总量与刀盘扭矩之间的关系，图 9 给出了加泡沫总量与刀盘扭矩之间关系，图 10 给出了推进速度与刀盘扭矩之间的关系，图 11 给出了推进速度与总推力之间的关系，图 12 给出了螺旋机回转速度与土仓压力之间的关系，图 13 给出了螺旋机回转速度与刀盘扭矩之间的关系，图 14 给出了螺旋机回转速度与总推力之间关系。可以发现，除在图 14 中可以明显看出随着盾构螺旋机回转速度的增加，盾构总推力在减少的规律外，其余各掘进参数之间并不存在明显的规律性，基本呈现无规则分布，这与室内模型试验结果有较大的差别。究其原因，室内模型试验结果是在单一理想地层环境条件条件下

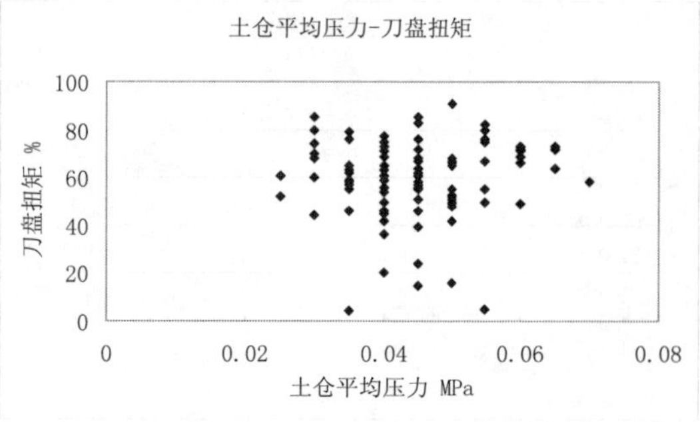

图 4 土仓压力与刀盘扭矩之间关系

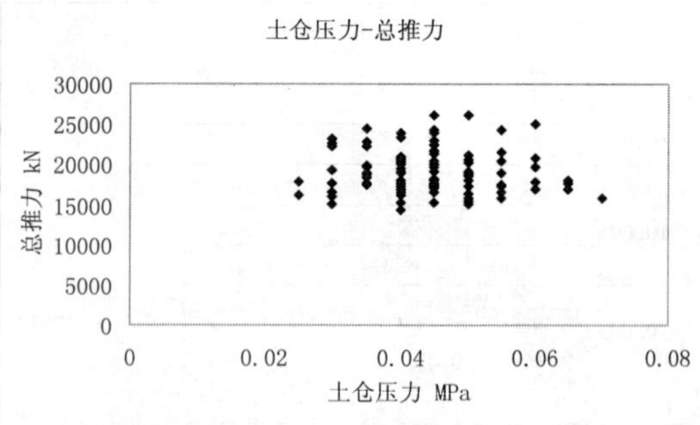

图 5 土仓压力与总推力之间关系

得出的；而工程实际数据受到复杂地层条件和人工操作条件等多种不确定因素的影响，每两个掘进参数之间表面上很难呈现出明显的规律性，而且每一掘进参数都与其余多个掘进参数之间存在关联性。要想进一步搞清每环推进速度、刀盘扭矩、盾构机总推力等参数之间的关系，必须借助于更加科学的方法。

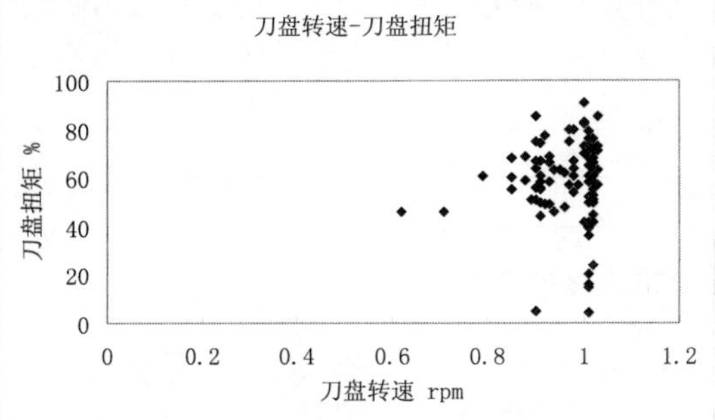

图 6　刀盘转速与刀盘之扭矩间关系

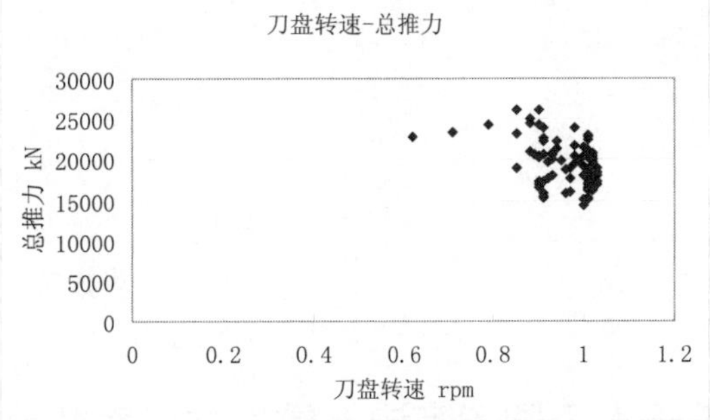

图 7　刀盘转速与总推力之间关系

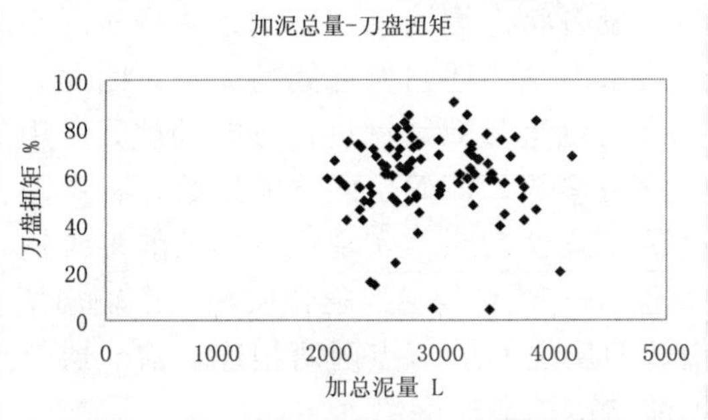

图 8　加泥总量与刀盘扭矩之间关系图

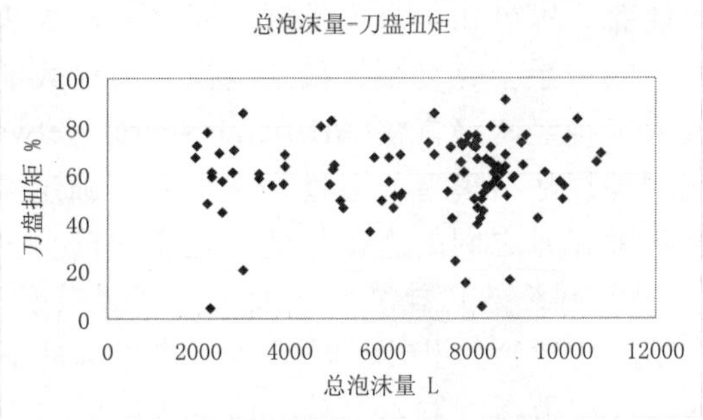

图 9　总泡沫量与刀盘扭矩之间关系

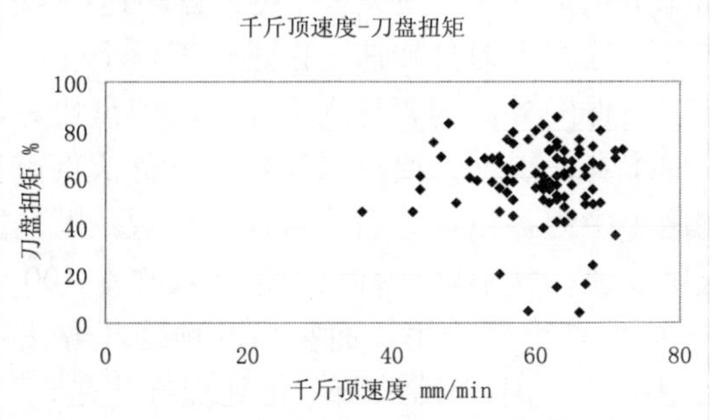

图 10　推进速度与出刀盘扭矩之间关系

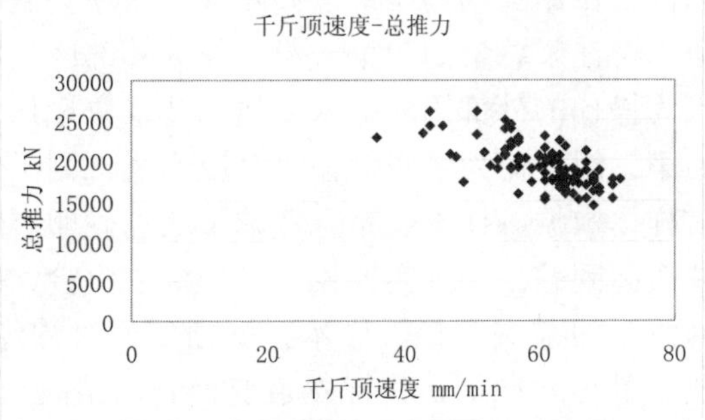

图 11　推进速度与总推力之间关系

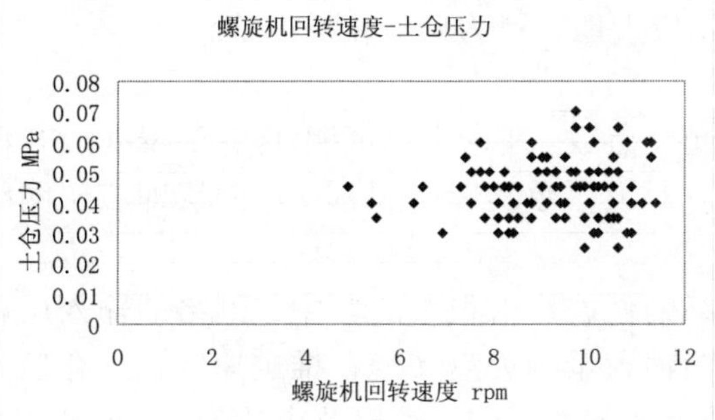

图 12　螺旋机回转速度与土仓压力之间关系

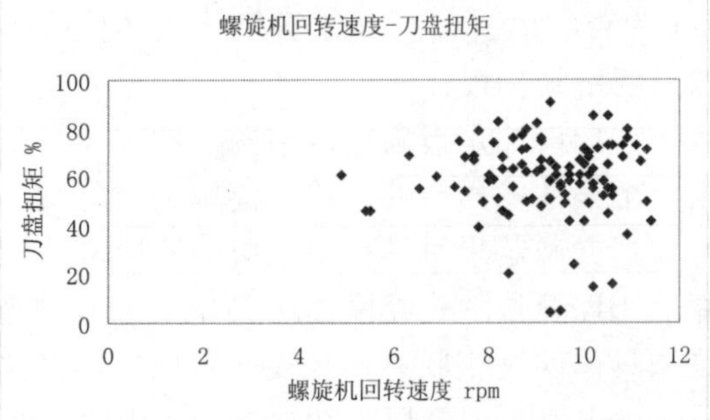

图 13　螺旋机回转速度与刀盘扭矩之间关系

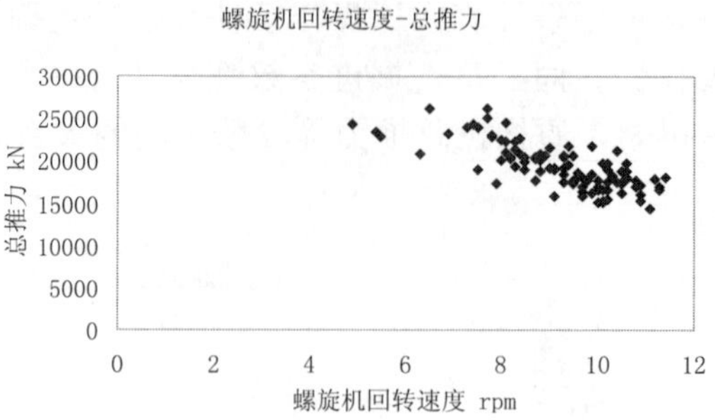

图 14　螺旋机回转速度与总推力之间关系

5　基于人工智能方法的盾构掘进参数分析

由前面分析可知，由于受到地质条件、人为操作水平、设备状态等因素的影响，盾构实际施工掘进参数之间的关系十分复杂，很难给出一个显式的数学表达式来准确描述它们之间的关系。因此，本文试图引入人工神经网络方法(Artificial Neural Networks-ANN)来对掘进参数数据进行分析处理。应用具有人工智能的神经网络模型，通过样本学习，确定网络结构和学习参数，即确定网络的层数、各层的神经元数以及各神经元之间的连接权值，建立起输入输出变量间的非线性关系，实现掘进参数的多维输入和多维输出。BP 网络的拓扑结构一般由三部分组成：输入层、包含一层或多层的隐含层和一个输出层；每层由多个节点(神经元)组成，同层之间的节点互不相连，相邻两层之间的节点两两相连，前一层节点的输出即为后一层节点的输入，输入信号在层层递进的基础上前向传播通过网络。

（1）掘进参数数据预处理

以白石桥站～动物园站区间左线的 319 环到 418 环的掘进数据作为研究对象。将刀盘转速、推进速度、土仓压力、注浆总量划为第一组，作为外部因素的输入变量，其中，刀盘转速、推进速度、土仓压力作为反映人为操作的外部因素输入变量，注浆总量作为反映地层条件的外部因素输入变量；将刀盘扭矩、总推力划为第二组，作为系统的输出响应变量。为了保证参数样本有代表性，要对采集样本进行认真审核，剔除异常样本数据。样本点充分考虑了北京砂卵石地层盾构施工中刀盘扭矩、盾构机推力设置范围，能很好地反映实际问题。经过实地校对、分析和检验，并作均一化处理，共采集到有效掘进参数样本 100 个。

网络学习前掘进参数样本数据预处理对神经网络的训练具有重要作用。而常用的预处理方法是归一化方法，其根本原则是将样本值变换到网络收敛最快的范围内。文中采用的归一化处理方法是：

$$x^* = (x - x_{\min})/(x_{\max} - x_{\min}) \tag{1}$$

式中，x 为真实值，$x_{\min}$、$x_{\max}$ 分别为真实值中的最小值和最大值，x^*为归一化后的值。

（2）网络结构设计

网络结构设计是指确定网络的层数以及各层的神经元节点数。理论上已证明:具有至少一个 S 型隐含层加上一个线性输出层的网络，能够逼近任何有理函数。对大多数实际问题，一层隐层即三层网络已经足够。故本文确定采用具有单隐层的三层网络结构。

基于 BP 算法的神经网络中各层节点数的选择对网络的性能影响很大。其中，网络的输入层和输出层都是和具体问题相联系，代表一定的实际意义。文中的输入量为刀盘转速、推进速度、土仓压力和注浆总量，输出量为刀盘扭矩和总推力。因此，网络输入节点数确定为 4，输出节点数为 2。另外，本文采用反复试验的方法确定隐含层单元数。当网络结构为 4-11-2 时，已收敛到指定误差 0.05；同时，4-11-2 结构网络收敛速度很快。故本文采用隐层神经元数目为 11，结构为 4-11-2 的 BP 神经网络。

（3）神经网络的训练

现有的神经网络的训练方法主要于侧重试验，在实验中不断改进，直到选取一个满意方案为止。传递函数的选择是整个网络训练过程中重要的一项。传递函数代表了处理单元输入与输出之间的关系。网络的输入层的节点只起到缓冲器的作用，不具有传递函数的功能。隐层节点的 S 型传递函数包括对数函数 logsig 和双曲正切 S 型传递函 tansig，对应的表达式如下：

$$\log sig(x)=1/(1+e^{-x}) \tag{2}$$

$$\tan sig(x)=(1-e^{-x})/(1+e^{-x}) \tag{3}$$

BP 网络传递函数是取 logsig 还是 tansig，应视具体问题情况而定。在本研究中，经过归一化处理的掘进参数值都在（0，1）间，故隐含层与输出层间传递函数只能为 logsig 函数，同时，采取对比的方法确定输入层与隐含层间传递函数。比较两种函数组合，tansig-logsig 组合较 logsig-logsig 组合在网络收敛速度上有明显优势。因此，在本研究中，输入层与隐含层间的传递函数为 tansig，隐含层与输出层间的传递函数为 logsig。

由于人工神经网络系统是非线性的，初始值的取值对于网络的学习是否能够达到局部最小、是否能够收敛以及训练时间的长短有着很大的关系。一般取初始权值取在（−1，1）之间的随机数。

（4）神经网络的预测仿真

典型 BP 神经网络的应用不仅需要一个训练样本集，而且还需要一个评价网络泛化能力的测试样本集。如果通过测试样本集中的样本测试网络，结果较为理想，那么说明该网络的泛化能力较强。将完成预处理的 100 个样本分为两组：其中前 94 个样本作为神经网络的训练样本集，完成对网络学习训练；后 6 个样本作为神经网络的测试样本集，对网络的泛化能力进行测试，并将预测结果代入式（4），并求得预测数据实际量值及绝对相对误差，结果见表 1。

$$x=x^{*}(x_{\max}-x_{\min})+x_{\min} \tag{4}$$

表 1　网络预测结果与原始数据对比

环号	原始数据		预测数据		绝对误差		相对误差	
	盾构机扭矩	盾构机推力	盾构机扭矩	盾构机推力	盾构机扭矩	盾构机推力	盾构机扭矩	盾构机推力
413	59	24 423	56.6	24 112	2.4	311	4.1%	1.3%
414	44	22 657	41.9	23 412	2.1	755	4.7%	3.3%
415	63	18 356	64.5	17 899	1.5	457	2.3%	2.5%
416	77	17 674	78.2	16 454	1.2	1 220	1.6%	6.9%
417	57	17 744	53.4	16 926	3.6	818	6.3%	4.6%
418	61	16 123	63.2	16 217	2.2	203	3.6%	0.6%

由表 1 中的预测结果可知，盾构机扭矩及推力的预测精度比较高，最大相对误差为 6.9%，最小相对误差仅为 0.6%，完全能够满足实际工程要求。可见，该 BP 神经网络的泛化能力是很强的。因而，应用 BP 神经网络对盾构掘进参数之间关系进行定量表达是完全可行的。特别是对于砂卵石地层条件下的盾构掘进，BP 神经网络可对部分掘进参数进行有效预测，有助于实现盾构机的安全控制，减少刀具磨损。

6　结　论

通过前面的分析，得出结论如下：

（1）由于白石桥站—动物园站区间通过盾构掘进参数控制和加泥、加泡沫等措施的采取，未开仓换刀持续掘进完成，本工程掘进参数的取值对于北京地区砂卵石地层盾构掘进参数选取有较高的参考价值。

（2）统计分析表明，在刀盘转速、推进速度等掘进参数基本成正态分布的前提下，盾构机扭矩、推力也可以近似认为服从正态分布。

（3）与模型试验测试结果不同，工程实测数据由于受地层条件、人为控制等多种因素的影响，各掘进参数之间并不存在明显的规律性，基本呈现无规则分布，很难以一定的显式表达式加以描述。

（4）应用 BP 神经网络对盾构掘进参数之间关系进行定量表达是完全可行的。对于砂卵石地层条件下的盾构掘进，BP 神经网络可对部分掘进参数进行有效预测，有助于实现盾构机的安全控制，减少刀具磨损。

参考文献（Referenles）：

[1] 袁大军，胡显鹏，李兴高，孙立．砂卵石地层盾构刀具磨损测试分析[J]．城市轨道交通研究，2009，12(5): 48-51.

[2] 王洪新，傅德明．土压平衡盾构掘进的数学物理模型及各参数间关系研究．土木工程学报, 2006, 39(9): 86-90.

[3] 朱合华，徐前卫，廖少明，傅德明，于宁．土压平衡盾构法施工参数的模型试验研究．岩土工程学报，2006，28(5): 553-557.

作者简介（Bio-data）：

郭玉海，男，1972 年 11 月出生，高级工程师，北京市政集团第四工程处项目经理，北京交通大学博士生，主要从事盾构施工技术方面的研究工作。

Yuhai GUO, male, born in December 1972, senior engineer, project manager of the fourth construction division of Beijing municipal group, doctor student of Beijing Jiaotong University, is mainly employed in the research work of shield tunneling technologies.

E-mail: yuhai1120@126.com

地铁盾构隧道扩挖车站方案初探

罗世培

中铁二院工程集团有限责任公司，四川　成都　610031

【摘　要】 本文对地铁盾构隧道扩挖车站采用的结构型式及其关键技术、措施进行了探讨，提出的扩挖车站方法，可为今后类似工程提供借鉴。

【关键词】 地铁；盾构；隧道；扩挖；车站

EXPLORATORY STUDY ON SCHEME FOR ENLARGEMENT OF STATION IN METRO SHIELD TUNNEL

Shipei LUO

China Railway Eryuan Group Co., Ltd., Chengdu 610031, Sichuan, China

Abstract: A discussion has been done on structure type and its key technique used for the enlargement of station in the metro shield tunnel, and the method for enlargement of station presented may be supplied for reference for similar engineering in the future in this paper.

Key words: metro; shield; tunnel; enlargement; station

1　概　述

常规地铁工程施工，一般要求地铁车站先行施工来为盾构隧道工程施工提供场地条件。但由于车站体量较大，在城市老城区施工时，往往受建筑物拆迁、道路交通疏解的影响无法按期动工，从而给盾构隧道施工及项目总工期造成影响。为此，中国内地地铁发展较快的城市，如广州、北京等，都欲尝试盾构隧道先行而后再扩挖形成车站的全新施筑方法。本文结合笔者前期参与的广州地铁五号线站隧逆序施工可行性研究，对地铁盾构隧道扩挖车站方案进行初步探讨，以期为类似工程提供借鉴。

2　盾构隧道扩挖车站结构形式

前苏联列宁格勒地铁工程最早采用了区间隧道通过后再扩挖车站的工法，其后日本、英国、美国等地铁工程也先后采用了类似工法，扩挖的方法主要包括矿山法和明挖法。

2.1　大断面盾构基础上扩挖车站

该方案在两到三条大断面盾构隧道基础上扩挖。

① 伦敦地铁车站扩挖采用 2 台盾构并行施工，而后扩挖修筑车站顶部。见图 1。

② 莫斯科地铁用 2 台盾构并行开挖两侧隧道，而后用半盾构修筑车站顶部的方法。见图 2。

③ 基辅地铁用 3 台盾构机先修建平行的盾构隧道，然后再进行扩挖，最后修建成地铁车站。见图 3。

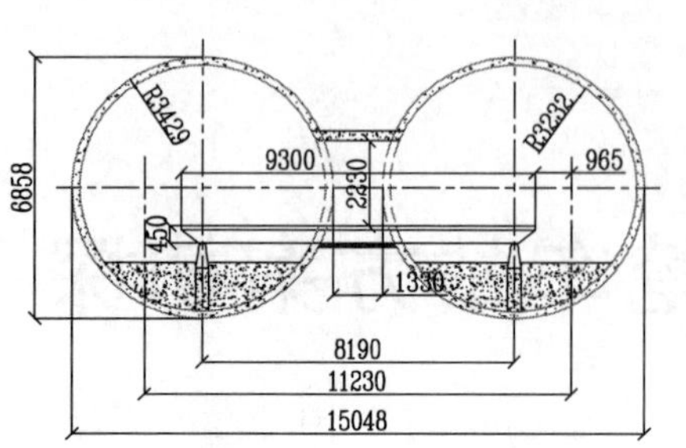

图 1 伦敦地铁车站结构断面图

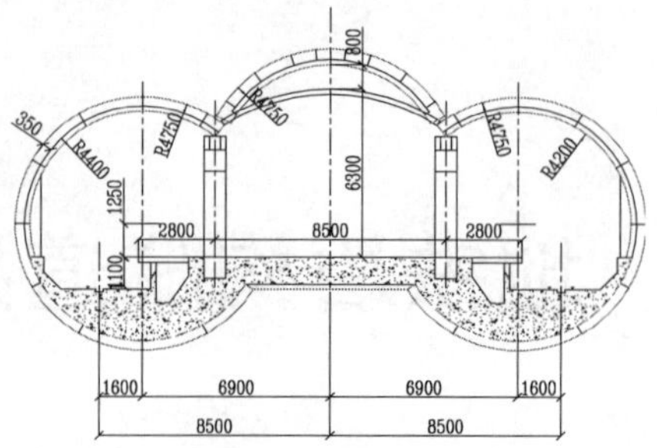

图 2 莫斯科地铁车站结构断面图

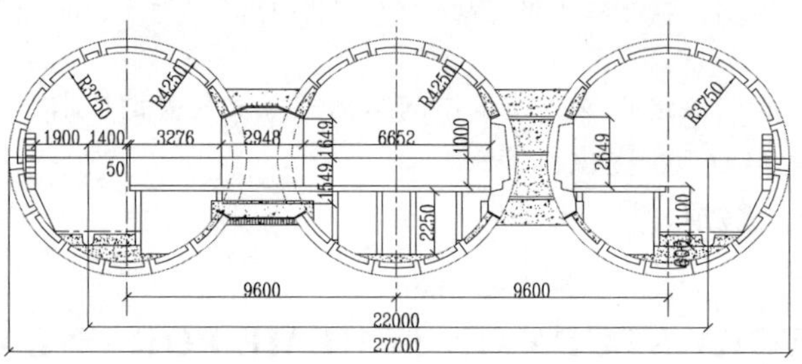

图 3 基辅地铁车站结构断面图

该方案的特点为：

① 采用通道连接扩挖时类似于地铁区间联络通道采用矿山法施作，开孔部位管片需作特殊处理。

② 采用三联拱断面扩挖时可采用类似于双侧壁导坑（眼镜法）矿法施作，管片需作特殊处理。

③ 先在开孔四周施筑钢筋混凝土框架，管片内架设型钢支撑架，而后逐环拆除管片。

2.2 矿山法扩挖车站

（1）暗挖双通道或三通道扩挖车站

该方案为废弃已经修建好的盾构隧道，采用浅埋暗挖法扩挖地铁车站。根据车站客流需求可扩挖为暗挖双通道或三通道车站（采用直径 5 400 mm 标准盾构区间断面时见图 4，当采用站台隧道圆形盾构时，同大断面盾构隧道）。

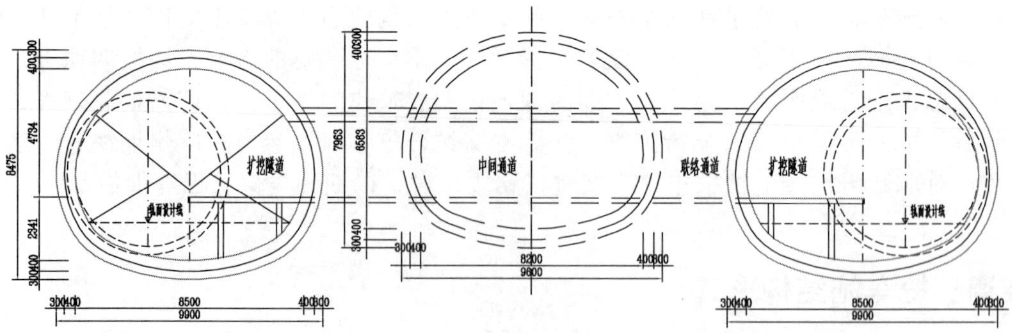

图 4 暗挖双（三）通道隧道扩挖车站断面图

该方案的特点为：

① 可根据车站的客流量选择车站设置为三通道式或双通道式车站。

② 两端的站厅、通道、设备管理房可根据交通疏解情况采用明挖、盖挖或暗挖等施工方法，建筑布置组合灵活。

（2）大跨度扩挖车站

前苏联列宁格勒地铁胜利公园站：在相对稳定的寒武纪泥岩、泥灰岩岩层中采用“土盾构”掘进、简易设备拼装铸铁管片，采用矿山法扩挖形成车站，见图 5。

列宁格勒地铁体育馆站为大跨度单拱双层换乘站，采用先导隧道空间回填混凝土形成大拱拱脚，支撑中间的大拱，扩挖形成车站，见图 6。

该方案的特点为：

① 宜在地质条件较好、围岩较稳定、线路埋深相对较深的地段采用。

② 由盾构隧道扩挖成大跨度站台，建筑空间宽阔，布置简单；乘客搭乘、疏导条件好。

③ 原盾构隧道基本废弃，废弃工程量较大；站台规模较大。

④ 结构处理较容易，可避免连拱的复杂受力，相对提高防水效果。

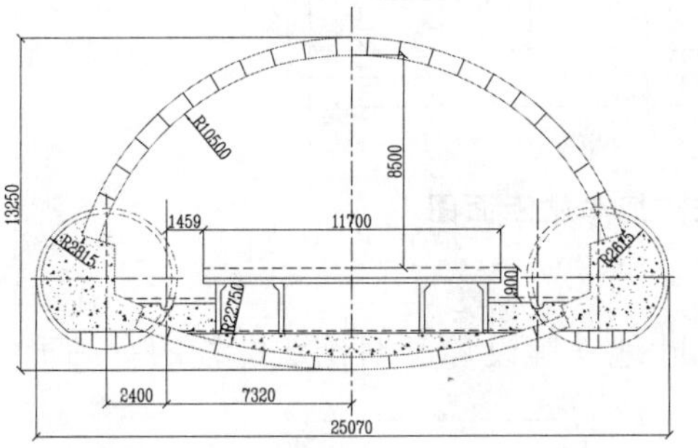

图 5 列宁格勒胜利公园站车站断面

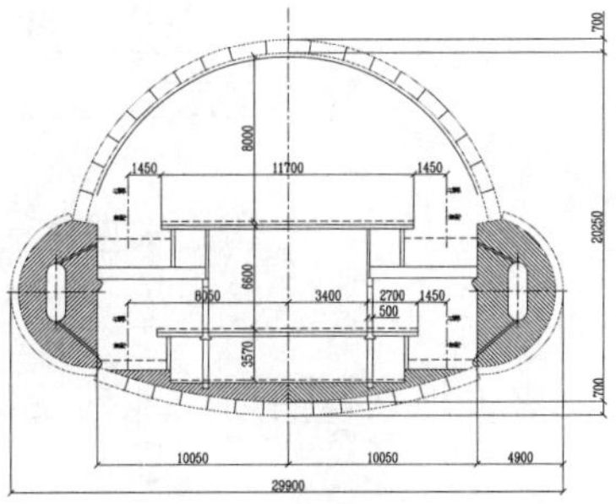

图 6 列宁格勒体育馆站结构断面图

2.3 明挖法扩挖车站

(1) 外置明挖法（盾构隧道置于明挖结构外）

该方案为利用已经修建好的盾构隧道的行车空间，采用标准明挖法或盖挖法扩挖车站，见图 7。

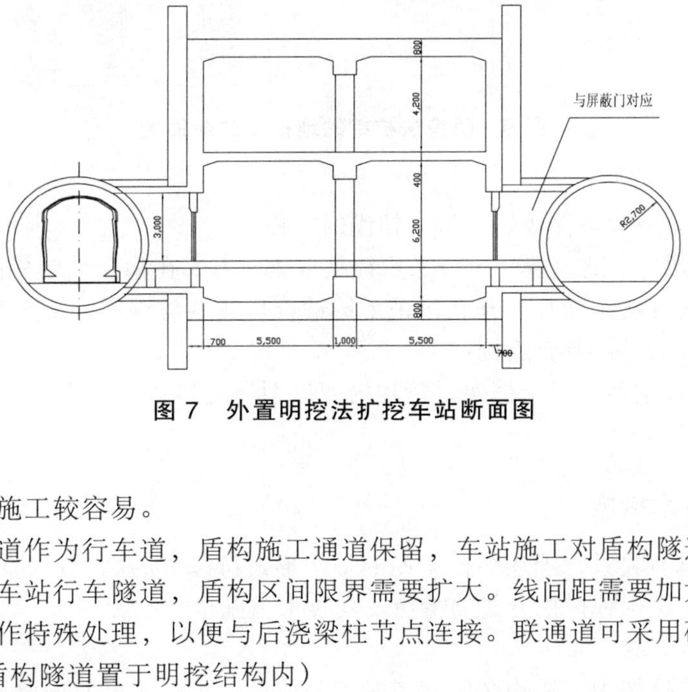

图 7 外置明挖法扩挖车站断面图

该方案的特点为：

① 建筑布置简单，施工较容易。

② 利用盾构区间隧道作为行车道，盾构施工通道保留，车站施工对盾构隧道施工影响小。

③ 利用盾构隧道作车站行车隧道，盾构区间限界需要扩大。线间距需要加大。

④ 开孔部位管片需作特殊处理，以便与后浇梁柱节点连接。联通道可采用矿山法施作。

(2) 内置明挖法（盾构隧道置于明挖结构内）

该方案为废弃已经修建好的盾构隧道，采用标准明挖法或盖挖法扩挖车站，见图 8。

该方案特点为：

① 建筑布置简单，内支撑配合盾构隧道内桁架支撑开挖，施工较容易。

② 车站外包盾构管片，车站宽度较常规大；需要待盾构隧道贯通后才能施工站台层并拆除管片，施工影响大。

③ 车站端墙围护结构宜先于盾构通过前施工。

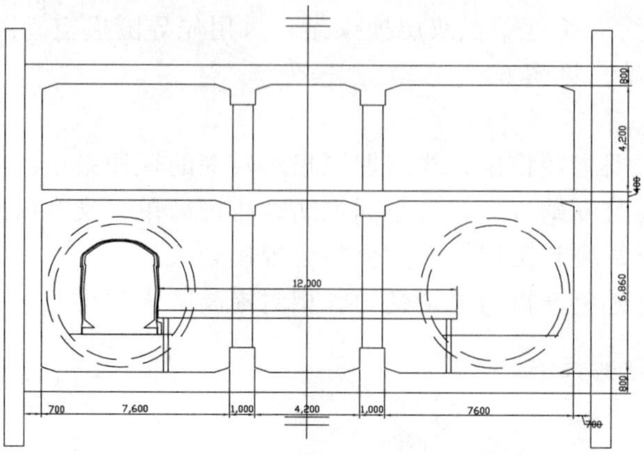

图 8　内置明挖法扩挖车站断面图

(3) 垂直明挖法

前苏联古比雪夫地铁、明斯克地铁及日本东京京叶地铁等设计了明挖法扩挖的车站形式，见图 9。

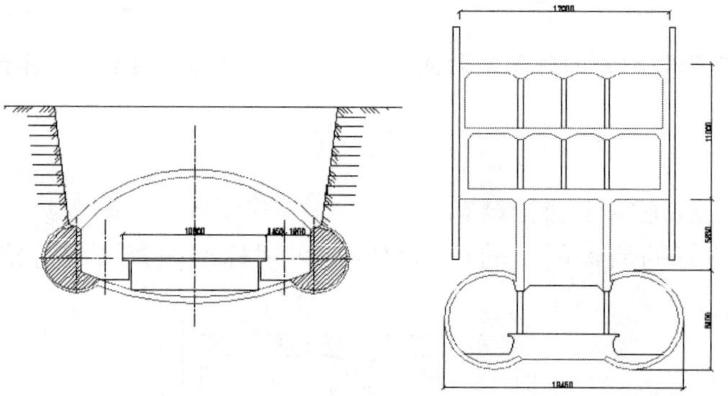

图 9　明挖法扩挖的地铁车站断面图

该方案的特点为：

① 适宜于地质及水文地质条件较好，基岩较浅的工程。

② 在稳定性较差地层中，隧道管片一般采用铸铁或钢管片；在稳定性较好的地层中，盾构管片在非开孔段可采用高强度钢筋混凝土管片，开孔段采用铸铁管片或钢与钢筋混凝土组合管片；开孔部位管片需作特殊处理，以便与后浇梁柱节点连接。

③ 先在开孔四周施筑钢筋混凝土框架，管片内架设型钢支撑架，而后逐环破除洞口顶、底部管片，安装钢梁形成整体结构。

2.4　扩挖车站的关键技术措施

按照与已建盾构隧道的关系，上述扩挖车站的结构形式可以分为利用已建盾构隧道扩挖和废弃已建盾构隧道扩挖两种方式，这两种扩挖方式的特点及其技术措施也不尽相同。

2.4.1　利用已建盾构隧道扩挖

利用已建盾构隧道扩挖即为：盾构区间隧道施工完成后，扩挖车站时破除部分管片，与其他工法施工的车站部分连接，形成整个车站结构。如“外置明挖法”。

该扩挖车站方法需要解决好：

(1) 行车区间盾构限界应满足车站使用功能

以地铁 B 型车为例，当车站客流较大，利用的盾构行车空间需要布置测式站台时，圆形盾构隧道建筑限界直径约为 6 700 mm，比常规圆形盾构区间隧道建筑限界直径 5 400 mm 需增加 1 300 mm，见图 10。当车站客流较小，盾构行车空间布置为小站台，采用通道与车站集散空间连接时，圆形盾构隧道建筑限界直径约直径 6 000 mm，，比常规圆形盾构区间隧道建筑限界直径 5 400 mm 仅需增加 600 mm，见图 11。

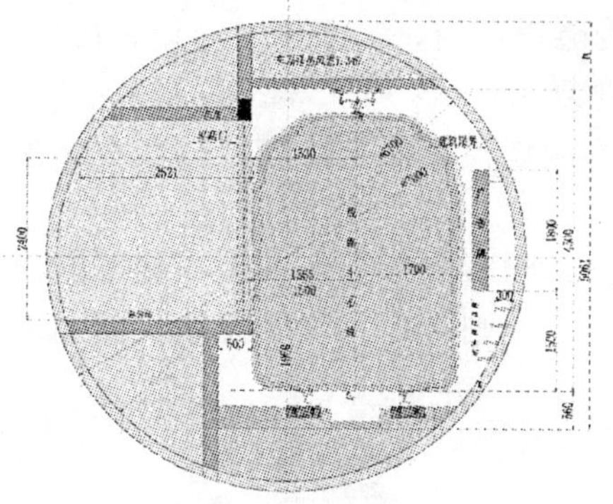

图 10 侧式站台盾构隧道限界图

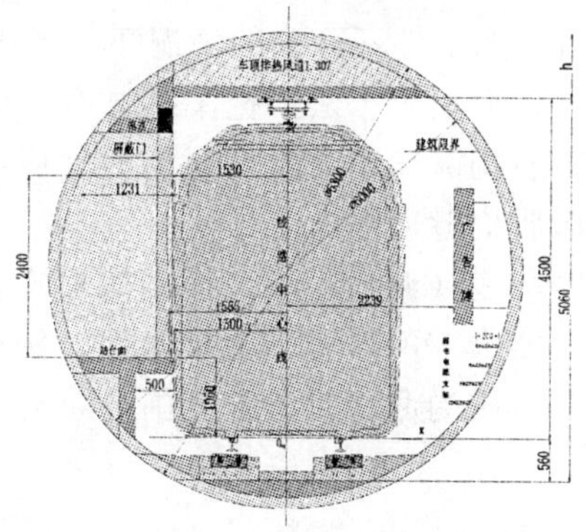

图 11 小站台盾构隧道限界图

（2）确保已建隧道拆除时的结构稳定性

在已建成的隧道中，盾构预制管环承受着四周的水土压力，当扩建车站时、无论采取明挖或暗挖，均会产生不对称的卸载，使管环产生形变、严重时甚至会使管环松脱脱扣。因此，需采取措施保证管环间的结构稳定性。可采用如下措施：

① 盾构隧道内可架设桁架支撑或修筑支撑墙体，分步拆除管片，施工连接结构；

② 盾构隧道内可在隧道的管环内向外施作注浆锚杆形成树根桩，使管片锁定在周边围岩；

③ 可对需破除的盾构管片结构连接点作特殊处理，以利结构连接。

（3）保证防水效果

扩挖车站的防水薄弱环节除扩挖施工时可能导致的管片松动外，管片与扩挖结构的连接部位的防水效果如何保证是难点。可采用以下措施：

① 加强临时支护和辅助工程措施，控制围岩的变形；

② 通过地层预注浆和补充注浆，封闭围岩裂隙；

③ 采用特殊异型管片，简化扩挖施工时连接构件的施工工艺；

④ 在连接节点部位预留截水槽，有序疏导渗透水等。

2.4.2 *废弃已建盾构隧道扩挖*

废弃已建盾构隧道扩挖即为：盾构区间隧道施工完成后，采用明挖法或矿山法施工车站，此时车站范围内的盾构隧道管片全部拆除。如“内置明挖法”。

该扩挖车站需要解决好：

（1）隧道过站前先完成车站两端墙的围护结构

先施工车站两端头的围护结构，盾构按正常的进站方式掘进，穿切已施工的两端头墙（围护结构墙），车站扩挖后再做接口处理。

（2）确保车站端墙附近区间隧道的稳定性

① 利用车站端墙作盾构隧道的定位、锁定的基体，从隧道的管环内向外施工锚杆，使管环能锁定在作为基体的端头墙上。

② 临近车站端墙段，通过盾构隧道对较软弱的土层、破碎的岩层进行注浆加固止水。

（3）盾构隧道内可架设桁架支撑，分步开挖、拆除管片，既保证残余的管环结构保持稳定，又保证车站扩挖作业的安全。保证扩挖时管片的稳定性。

3 结 语

以上扩挖车站方案提出了几种盾构隧道扩挖车站的基本形式，这些方案还可以结合环境条件、地质条件进一步组合。综合比较，不难看出：

（1）在车站后期具备明挖条件的情况下，采用内置明挖法（废除管片）扩挖车站实施难度较小。

（2）在车站明挖条件不具备的情况下，采用站台盾构隧道扩挖，工序相对简单；在地层条件较好时，也可采用三（二）通道矿山法扩挖车站方案，但工序相对复杂。

（3）当利用盾构隧道作为站台隧道时，应结合车站客流规模，综合比较区间、车站扩挖的经济性，确定适宜的圆形盾构隧道限界。

（4）鉴于停车线（渡线）隧道的结构形式多为不同跨径的隧道段分级扩大，由于断面类型多，洞室跨度大，在自稳能力差的软弱围岩中修建，施工难度较大，原则上停车线（渡线）隧道采用矿山法、明挖法施工完成后，盾构通过后再继续掘进。

参考文献（Referenles）：

[1] 广州地铁总公司，铁道第二勘察设计院. 广州市轨道交通五号线工程站隧逆序施工可行性论证报告[R].

作者简介（Bio-data）：

罗世培，男，汉族，1968年3月出生，工学学士，高级工程师。1990年毕业于同济大学地下建筑与工程系，现任中铁二院工程有限责任公司地下铁道设计研究院总工程师。主要从事城市轨道交通工程与地下结构、隧道工程方面的设计和科研工作。

Shipei LUO, male, the Han Nationality, born in March, 1968, bachelor of engineering, senior engineer, graduated from the Department of Geotechnical Engineering of TongJi University in 1990. Now he works in China Railway Eryuan Engineering Group Co.Ltd, serving as chief engineer of Metro Design and Research Institute of CREEC, mainly engaging in the design and research work in the field of urban rail transit engineering and underground& tunnel engineering.

盾构先行条件下拓展地铁车站的施工过程风险分析

路美丽 [1,2]　刘维宁 [1]　张新金 [1]
[1] 北京交通大学土建学院，北京　100044
[2] 中铁第五勘察设计院集团有限公司，北京　102600

【摘　要】 在对国外相关工程实例资料进行调研分析的基础上，结合国内目前的经济和技术水平，提出了盾构先行条件下拓展地铁车站的新型建造技术；借鉴相关工程经验、课题前期研究成果和大量相关专家的意见，对明挖拓展的立柱式车站和暗挖拓展的塔柱式车站两种结构方案，进行了车站施工过程特殊风险源的分析和相应对策的建议；在此基础上提出了合理可行的施工工艺。
【关键词】 盾构法；明挖法；浅埋暗挖法；地铁车站；施工过程；风险分析

CONSTRUCTION RISK ANALYSIS OF THE EXPANDED METRO STATION UNDER SHIELD RUNNING TUNNEL

Meili LU [1,2], Weining LIU [1], Xinjin ZHANG [1]
[1] *School of Civil Engineering and Architecture, Beijing Jiaotong University, Beijing 100044, China;*
[2] *The Fifth Survey and Design Institute(Group) CO., LTD. of CRCC, Beijing 102600, China*

Abstract: A new-style station construction method has been brought forward in this paper based on large numbers of overseas project examples and domestic economy and technology level. The new-style station construction method is that A station will be constructed by shield method and tunneling method (or cut and cover method) under the condition of shield running tunnel. By adopting analogous engineering experience and study achievement and advices of pertinent experts, especial construction risks have identified and countermeasure to answer these risks have been also brought forward for the vertical shaft station and the pylon shaft station. In conclusion the feasible construction techniques was commended.
Key words: shield method; cut and cover method; tunneling method; metro station; construction process; risk analysis

1 引　言

为解决目前中国内地地铁区间盾构施工和车站施工工期矛盾的问题，寻求盾构法在我国地铁工程中大规模应用的突破口，在对国外相关资料和工程实例大量查阅和整理分析的基础上，结合国内目前的经济和技术水平，提出了盾构先行条件下拓展地铁车站的思路[1]：利用国内目前现有的 6 m 外径的区间盾构机直接贯通车站的行车隧道部分，在保留大部分管片的基础上拆除部分管片，采用明挖法或浅埋暗挖法拓展建造地铁车站。

作为一种新型的车站建造方法，为确保施工工艺的可行性和经济性，降低施工中的危险性，必须要充分了解施工过程中可能存在的主要风险源，并提前进行相应对策的研究。也只有建立在风险分析基础上的施工方案比较，才是业主进行方案综合评估的首选方式[2]。因此本文在前期对盾构先行条件下明挖拓展的立柱式车站和暗挖拓展的塔柱式车站结构形式研究的基础上[3]，进行了车站施工过程中存在的特殊风险源的分析，并提出了相应的对策。最后提出了合理可行的施工步序。

2 明挖拓展的立柱式车站风险分析

图 1 为北京地铁十号线三元桥车站 18.6 m 试验段的车站结构形式。根据实际的工程地质和水文条件，设计采用盾构先行贯通车站行车隧道部分结构后，采用明挖法拓展建造地铁车站。设计线间距为 15 m，站台宽度为 12 m，侧站台宽 2.5 m，上部基坑采用土钉墙围护结构形式。

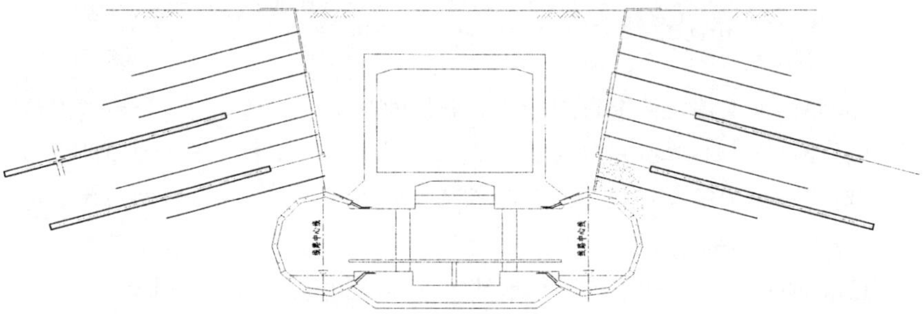

图 1 明挖拓展的立柱式车站

如图所示，车站结构的施工过程主要包括盾构隧道的开挖支护、上部基坑的开挖、盾构隧道间土体的开挖和盾构管片的拆除四部分。其中盾构隧道施工过程中的风险不属于本新型车站施工过程中的特殊风险，也即这一步不存在特殊的风险源；随着上部基坑的开挖和土体的卸载，可能会引起盾构隧道向内侧移动，同时由于上部基坑采用的土钉墙围护结构没有入土深度，在墙脚与盾构隧道管片间可能存在向内侧转动的趋势；接着的盾构隧道间土体的开挖，会进一步加剧盾构隧道向内侧移动的趋势；而部分盾构管片的拆除使得原来由整环管片受力的隧道结构变成了一个开口状的非稳定结构，这不仅会加剧管片向内侧移动的趋势，还可能会引起管片在环向和纵向上的松弛以及剩余管片环内力的突变。因此施工步骤的设计必须考虑这些主要的风险因素。

依据上述分析，图 2 给出了明挖拓展的立柱式车站可行的施工步序，以下详细分析各施工步中存在

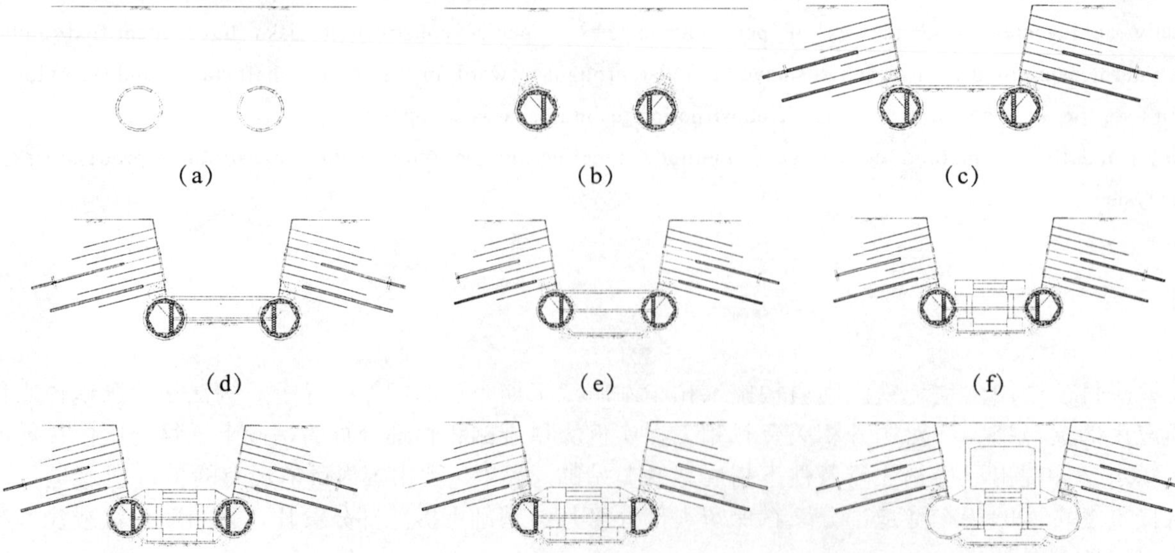

图 2 明挖拓展的立柱式车站施工步骤

的具体风险源，并提出相应的应对措施。依此说明可行的施工步序拟定时所考虑的因素。

（1）盾构隧道开挖和支护。这一步不存在特殊的风险源。

（2）在盾构隧道内架设临时支撑，从地面上对土钉墙坡脚地层进行搅拌桩加固，并在管片纵向上施加预应力钢索。这一步主要是进行加固措施，不存在特殊的风险源。

（3）降水、施做土钉墙，跳槽开挖至第一道支撑底，待架设第一道钢支撑后方可开挖槽间土体。这一步存在的风险源主要在于，随着基坑的开挖，盾构隧道原有的平衡状态被打破，盾构隧道有向内侧移动的趋势，由于土钉墙没有入土深度，可能会导致土钉墙底部与盾构管片不能够按设计接触；因此应该在基坑开挖前，从地面上对土钉墙坡脚地层进行注浆加固，并在盾构过站后架设隧道内临时支撑，同时在下一步基坑开挖前，确保第一道钢横撑与管片按设计连接。

（4）跳槽开挖至第二道钢支撑底，在管片上局部钻孔，待架设第二道钢支撑后方可挖除槽间土体。这一步中第二道钢支撑是经过在管片上局部钻孔后架设到隧道内支撑上的，目的在于避免管片拆除过程中支撑体系的多次转换。

（5）左右线底部注浆加固地层，开挖地下二层基坑，并施做底部临时混凝土支撑。这一步存在的风险源在于：随着地下二层基坑的开挖，盾构隧道管片底部土体被挖空，施做底部临时混凝土支撑前，盾构隧道有绕着管片底部向车站内转动的趋势；因此待第二道钢横撑架设后，继续向下开挖前，应首先注浆加固底梁处地层，同时确保隧道内支撑和隧道间两道横撑的作用。

（6）施作车站底板、梁柱，拆除第一道钢横撑，施作中楼板及楼板间的横撑。这一步存在的主要风险源在于：盾构隧道顶部的第一道临时钢横撑作用取消后，盾构管片有绕着上部管片与土钉墙坡脚连接点内移的趋势。因此在拆除该道支撑前，必须确保隧道内支撑和隧道间第二道横撑及底板支撑共同组成整体受力体系，并确保土钉墙坡脚地层的加固作用，以控制结构的水平变形。

（7）施作上部节点的型钢支撑。这一步存在的主要风险源在于：第一道钢横撑拆除后，原来由隧道间三道横撑与隧道内支撑体系共同形成的强有力的受力框架体系变成了隧道间两道横撑的作用，在之后的管片切割后，可能会造成盾构管片沿上部土钉墙坡脚向内转动的趋势。因此在管片切割前，应利用上部管片内预埋的钢板，首先施作从预埋钢板位置向车站顶纵梁的型钢支撑，每环管片上设置两根型钢支撑，以确保管片切割前的受力框架和变形控制框架体系。也即这一施工步是为了下一步管片切割时结构的稳定性作准备的。

（8）分段拆除盾构管片，施作管片节点。这一步是本新型车站施工工法中最为关键和最为不利的工况。存在的风险源主要在于：拆除管片过程中，盾构隧道由一个整环管片受力的结构变成了一个开口状的非稳定结构。这不仅会加剧管片向内侧移动的趋势，还可能会引起管片环向和纵向的松弛，且剩余管片上的内力也会发生突变。这些都极大地增加了车站结构的施工危险性，也关系到本工法的成败。因此为确保管片拆除过程中剩余管片的内力和变形处于允许的范围内及隧道结构的稳定，设计要求在盾构过站后架设隧道内支撑、管片纵向上施加预应力到设计值、同时在拆除第一道钢横撑后、拆除部分管片前，首先施做上部节点的型钢支撑，确保隧道间有三道横撑作用，这三道横撑与隧道内支撑及管片纵向上的预应力钢索共同形成一个坚固的受力框架体系。

（9）浇筑上层结构，回填覆土，拆除支撑，施工完成。这一步已经是完成了主体结构的施工，不存在特殊的风险源。

3 暗挖拓展的塔柱式车站风险分析

图 3 为北京某地铁车站的结构方案，根据实际的工程地质和水文条件，设计采用盾构先行贯通车站行车隧道的条件下，浅埋暗挖法扩挖两行车隧道之间的土体，形成塔柱式的车站结构形式。如图所示，站台层采用三个单洞暗挖的结构形式，其中两侧内径 5.4 m 的盾构隧道作为行车隧道，中间为开挖宽度 14.2 m，高度 10.4 m，开挖断面积 147.68 m^2 的大断面隧道，三者之间以每侧 12 条宽为 6.680 m 的横通

道相连，形成了复杂的群洞体系。设计车站的线间距为 23 m，站台宽度在塔柱部位为 12 m，通道部位为 20 m。适用于客流量较大、线间距较大的情况。

如图所示，该车站施工包括盾构隧道的开挖支护、中间站厅隧道的开挖支护、横通道的开挖和管片切割四个主要部分。其中盾构隧道的开挖不存在特殊的风险源；随着盾构隧道间大断面站厅隧道和横通道的开挖支护，盾构隧道间土体的卸载会引起盾构隧道向站厅隧道内侧移动，从而可能引起盾构隧道线路中心线与设计的偏差；之后的管片切割不但加剧了这种趋势的发展，还会因为管片环变成开口状而引起剩余管片环在纵向和横向的松弛和张开以及内力的突变，危及车站的施工安全和运营安全。基于这些分析，图 4 给出了可行的施工工艺。

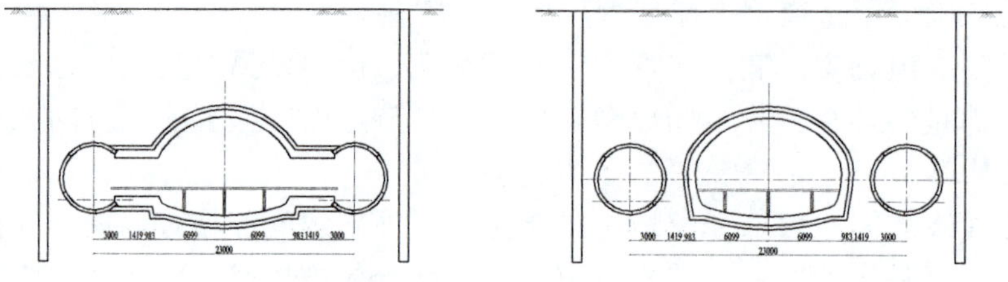

（a）横通道部位　　（b）塔柱部位

图 3　浅埋暗挖法拓展的塔柱式车站

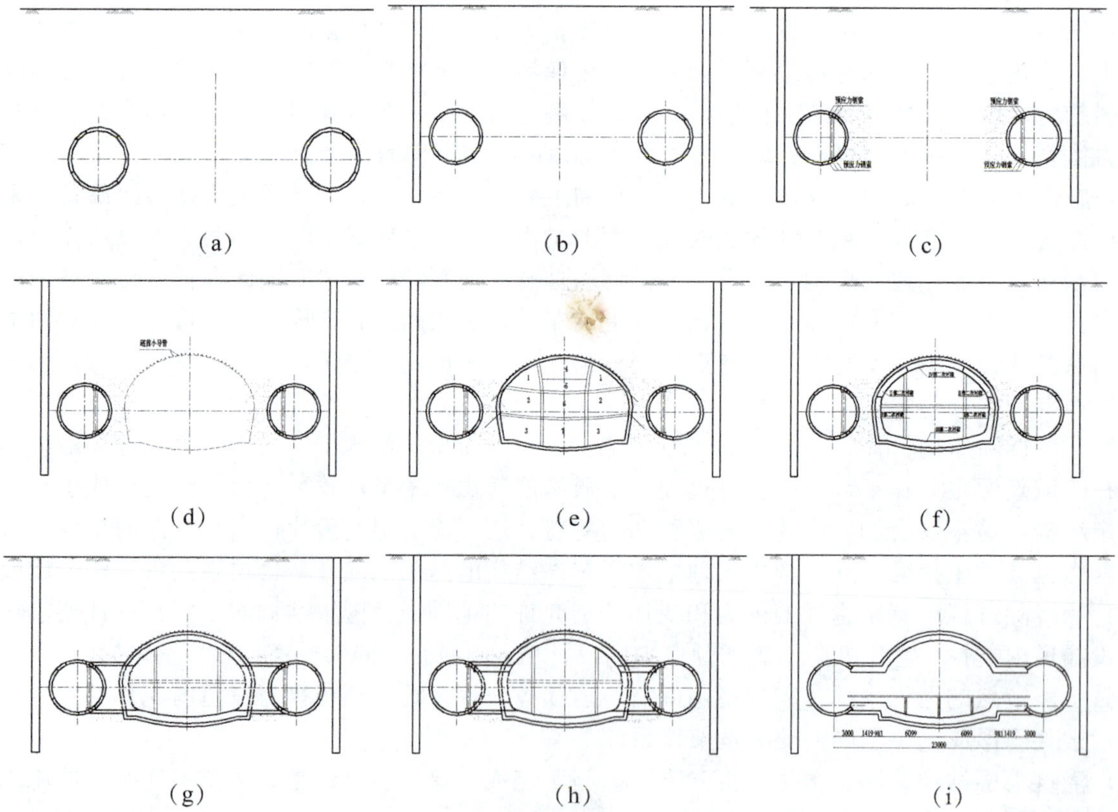

（a）　（b）　（c）

（d）　（e）　（f）

（g）　（h）　（i）

图 4　浅埋暗挖法拓展的塔柱式车站施工步骤

以下从风险源分析的角度出发，对上述各施工步骤进行了详细的施工过程特殊风险源分析，依此解释施工步骤拟定的合理性和可行性。

（1）盾构过站。这一步属于目前已经成熟的技术，不存在特殊的风险源。

（2）在盾构隧道外侧施作挡土隔离桩。

（3）在盾构隧道内向中间土体注浆加固，注浆范围进入站厅隧道开挖轮廓线 0.5 m，以增加站厅隧道开挖时中间土柱的承载力，同时在管片纵向上施加预应力、隧道内架设临时钢管柱支撑。

（4）在暗挖站厅隧道拱部 120°范围内超前小导管注浆加固。这三步都属于施工过程中的加固措施，因此不存在特殊的风险源。

（5）CRD 侧洞法开挖站厅隧道 1，2，3，4，5，6，7 部土体，架设钢格栅和临时仰拱，挂网喷射 C20 混凝土，形成闭合环。大断面站厅隧道的开挖在国内目前已有成功的经验，但在两盾构隧道间进行大断面隧道的开挖还未有相关的经验。由于站厅隧道和两侧盾构隧道之间的土柱厚度不大，属于小间距施工问题，站厅隧道的开挖对其周围地层扰动较大，研究表明，站厅隧道开挖引起的洞周地层变位和管片结构变形在整个施工过程中都是最大的。因此设计中的应对措施是在盾构过站后从隧道内向其中间土体注浆加固，确保中间土柱的稳定；调整优化站厅隧道的开挖顺序和辅助工法，以控制地表沉降达到规定要求；隧道外侧的挡土隔离桩和隧道内架设的临时钢管柱支撑及管片纵向上的预应力共同控制结构在外侧土压力作用下的变形和内力突变。

（6）分段拆除中隔壁和临时仰拱支撑，架设临时倒换支撑，施做Ⅰ，Ⅱ，Ⅲ和Ⅳ部二次衬砌。这一步的风险源在于站厅隧道由于开挖断面较大，二衬施作时引起的地表沉降和结构变形也比较大。因此设计中采用分段浇注二衬混凝土的方式来应对。

（7）CD 法跳槽开挖横通道，施做横通道初期支护和临时中隔壁支撑。这一步的风险源在于开挖通道土体时，盾构隧道靠近站厅隧道一侧土体的大幅度卸载会引起盾构隧道有向站厅隧道内移动和发生较大变形的趋势，内移和变形过大会使盾构隧道线路中心线偏离设计值。因此设计中在盾构隧道内架设临时钢管柱支撑，隧道外侧打设挡土隔离桩以降低外侧土压力的作用，开挖横通道时采取跳槽分块施作，并确保横通道初支能够及时形成一个封闭的受力门框体系。

（8）分段拆除横通道部位处的管片，施做横通道二衬结构。这一步同样属于该新型车站施工中最为不利的工况。主要的风险源在于拆除部分管片过程中，原来由整环管片受力的结构变为开口状的管片受力，此时管片内力变化较大，有可能超出其承载能力；同时管片向车站内侧移动的趋势加大；管片在外侧土压力作用下在纵向上会出现较大的拉力，可能会造成管片纵向上的松弛，进而导致结构不稳定和漏水现象发生。针对这些风险，相应的对策有：管片设计时应选择施工中最不利工况进行配筋设计，同时确保管片拆除前横通道封闭门框体系已经形成，能够起到及时转换内力的目的；另外还需在管片纵向上施加预应力钢索，以增加管片纵向上的整体性，并与隧道内钢管柱支撑形成临时的梁柱受力体系。

（9）拆除盾构隧道内的临时钢管柱支撑，施做车站站台板，完成车站结构施工。这一步车站主体结构已经施做完毕，不存在特殊的风险源。

4 结 论

盾构先行条件下拓展地铁车站为解决目前国内区间盾构施工和车站施工工期矛盾提出了一种新的模式，同时为盾构法在我国的大规模应用找到了突破口。在课题前期对采用该新型工法建造的地铁车站结构方案设计研究的基础上，本文从风险分析的角度，对该新型车站施工过程进行了特殊风险源的分析和相应对策的研究，进一步诠释了本文拟定的新型车站施工工艺的合理性和可行性。

（1）明挖拓展的立柱式车站已被北京地铁十号线三元桥车站试验段采纳并已完成施工图的设计[3]，不过由于三元桥工期问题，最后未能得以实施。

（2）暗挖拓展的塔柱式车站已通过 1∶10 大比尺模型试验和数值模拟进行了实施和验证[4]，证明了本文提出的施工工艺是可行的。

（3）本文提出的新型车站施工方法不需要额外的盾构设备和难度很高的技术，在现有的技术和经济条件下是可以实现的。

参考文献（Referenles）：

[1] 路美丽，刘维宁，孙晓静. 盾构法、暗挖法结合修建地铁车站在我国的应用前景[J]. 都市快轨交通，2004，17(2):30-33，38.

[2] 路美丽，刘维宁，罗富荣，李兴高. 隧道与地下工程风险评估方法研究进展[J]. 工程地质学报，2006，14(4):462-469.

[3] 北京市轨道交通建设管理有限公司，北京交通大学，北京城建设计研究总院有限责任公司，中铁二十局集团10号线10标项目部，住总集团10号线11标项目部. 盾构法与浅埋暗挖法结合建造地铁车站综合技术研究阶段报告[R]. 2006.5.

[4] 路美丽，盾构先行条件下拓展地铁车站的方案研究及风险分析[博士论文]. 北京：北京交通大学，2007.11.

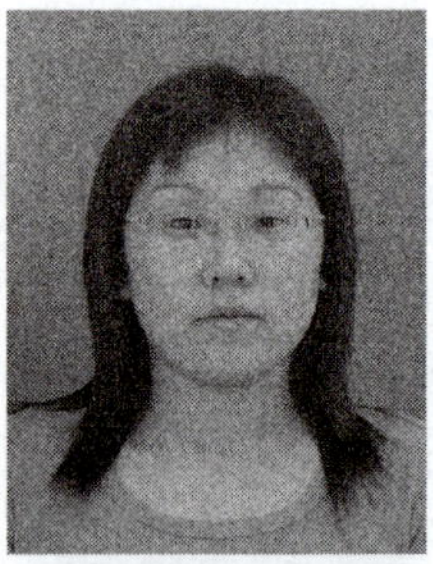

作者简介（Bio-data）:

路美丽，女，1976.3，工程师，博士，主要从事隧道及地下工程结构设计及施工技术研究。

Meili LU, (1973—), female, Engineer, Doctor, Major in structural design of tunnel and underground engineering and research on construction technonlogy.

E-mail: lu_meili@126.com

刘维宁，男，1960.4，博士，教授，博士生导师，国际隧协(ITA)执委，主要从事地下铁道施工方法及运营坏境影响方面的教学与研究工作。

Weining LIU, (1960.4—), male, Professor, Doctor, PHD supervisor, a member of international tunnel association, Major in teaching and research on construction method and operation environment of underground railway.

E-mail: wnliu@bjtu.njtu.edu.cn

砂卵石地层盾构刀盘选型、刀具组合配置设计研究

黄清飞　袁大军　王梦恕　肖衡
北京交通大学隧道及地下工程研究中心，北京　100044

【摘　要】　总结国内砂卵石地层盾构刀盘刀具选型配置不良及成功案例，全面分析比较不同刀盘结构形式、不同刀具组合配置优缺点，在此基础上指出砂卵石地层盾构刀盘结构选型相比刀具设计配置更具首要意义，辐条式刀盘+Φ800 带式螺旋输送机是适应砂卵石地层的合理选择；刀具配置采用“切削刀（小刮刀）、先行刀、鱼尾刀、盘圈贝型刀”组合具显著优势，其中先行刀和鱼尾刀是掘进关键，且尤以先行刀最为重要，切削刀只起辅助剥落作用，建议其刀刃采用嵌入式且不做主副刀高差设计；先行刀可采用主副刀高差设计，延长掘进距离；论文最后提出改进型辐条式刀盘设计方案，可实现先行刀、切削刀及特殊情况下滚刀的快速便捷更换，进一步延长掘进距离并增强刀盘对地质的适应能力，对砂卵石地层盾构设计施工具有重要意义。

【关键词】　盾构隧道；砂卵石地层；刀盘选型；刀具组合配置

STUDY ON SHIELD CUTTING WHEEL TYPE SELECTION AND CUTTING TOOL COMBINATION DISPOSITION IN SANDY COBBLE STRATUM

Qingfei HUANG, Dajun YUAN, Mengshu WANG, Heng XIAO
Research Center of Tunnel and Underground Engineering, Beijing Jiaotong University, Beijing 100044, China

Abstract: Based on successful and unsuccessful cases of shield cutting wheel type selection and cutting tool combination disposition in sandy cobble stratum, and complete analysis of advantage and disadvantage of different cutting wheel structural style and tool disposition, the study showed that cutting wheel type selection is more significant than cutting tool design and disposition. Spoke type wheel and belt screw conveyor with O.D. 800mm is reasonable choice for sandy cobble stratum; The cutting tool disposition of “cutter bits, pre cutting bits, fish tail bits, trim shell bits” has obvious advantage, in which pre cutting bits and fish tail bits are key point of shield driving, especially the pre cutting bits is most important. The cutter bits just plays an auxiliary role to strip cobble, and suggesting of which the carbide adopting inlaid type and design without height difference between primary and assistant bits; pre cutting bits may adopt design of height difference between primary and assistant bits, to extent the driving distance. At last the study put forward a design plan of improved spoke type cutter wheel, which may make easy change of pre cutting bits, cutter bits and disk cutter in particular cases, extent the driving distance and enforce geological suitability of cutter wheel further, which is significant for design and tunneling of shield machine in sandy cobble stratum.

Key words: shield tunnel; sandy cobble stratum; cutter wheel type selection; cutting tool combination disposition

1 引　言

目前，盾构在我国隧道工程的建设中得到了越来越广泛的使用，盾构的广泛使用在促进隧道工程优

质、快速、安全建设的同时，也暴露出了很多问题，砂卵石地层盾构掘进刀盘刀具严重磨损，导致频繁换刀即为突出问题之一，这直接影响了工程工期和工程经济性；而如何优选刀盘结构形式及刀具配置，实现长距离掘进以充分发挥盾构优势亦成为当前急需解决的重大工程难题。

目前国内相关学者对特定地区砂卵石地层盾构刀盘刀具选型配置已经进行了较深入探讨研究，文献[1]～[4]根据北京地铁盾构隧道施工经验总结，建议北京砂卵石地层采用辐条式刀盘，对刀具配置也提出了见解，认为相对于面板式刀盘，辐条式刀盘土压平衡更易于控制，可保证较好的掘进性能；文献[5]、[6]针对成都地铁盾构施工经验总结，认为面板式复合刀盘适合于成都砂卵石地层，建议配置滚刀破除特大粒径卵石。

总结相关文献可以看见，国内学者对砂卵石地层盾构刀盘选型配置意见并不统一，均局限于特定地区特定工程施工经验进行比较，未对国内不同地区不同工程施工经验进行综合比较，导致已有研究认识难免偏颇。笔者对国内典型砂卵石地层盾构刀盘刀具选型配置成功案例和失败案例进行横向和纵向比较分析，提出自己的看法，以期对业内有所启发。

2 砂卵石地层特点和盾构施工中主要问题[7,8]

2.1 砂卵石地层特点

不同地区砂卵石地层有各自特征，但总体而言，性质及特点相差不大，总结如下：

(1) 卵砾石含量多、粒径大、强度高：卵砾石含量约占 30%～70%，通常粒径为 30～200 mm，最大粒径可超过 500 mm，卵石最高强度可达 180 MPa 以上；

(2) 地层属易扰动不稳定地层，流动性及透气性差，盾构掘进时土压平衡不易控制，易造成开挖面局部失稳；

(3) 地层胶结较少，黏聚力小，掘进中控制不当易造成地表坍塌。

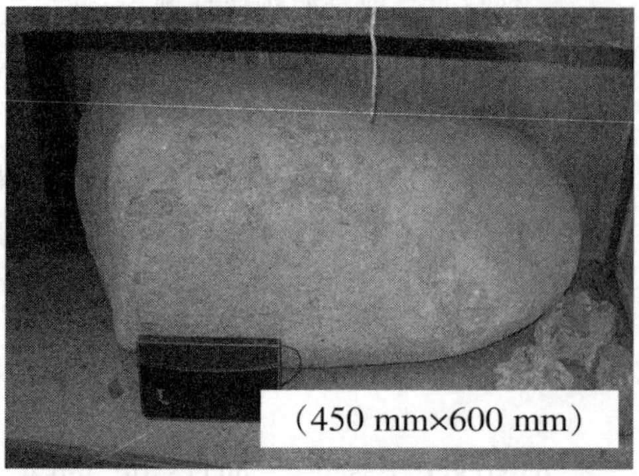

图 1 北京地下铁路直径线工程特大漂石

2.2 砂卵石地层盾构施工中主要问题

(1) 地层自然磨损系数大，易造成刀盘、刀具及螺旋输送机严重磨损，且刀具硬质合金易受卵石冲击崩裂破坏，导致刀具正常磨损和非正常失效均非常严重，给硬质合金性能参数选择带来矛盾；

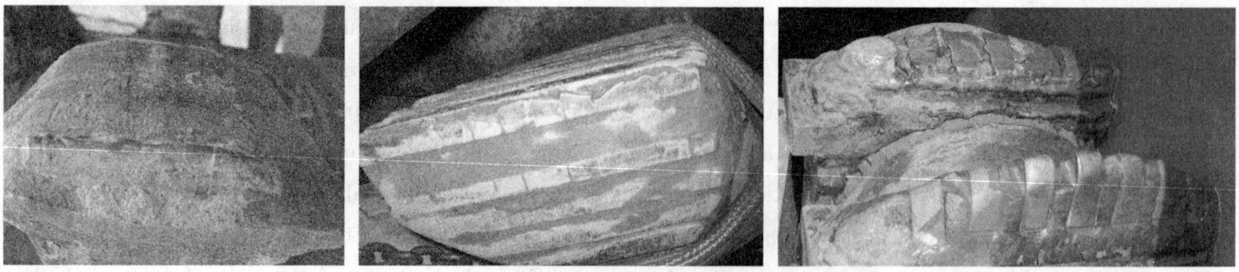

图 2 刀具硬质合金崩裂示意

(2) 砂卵石地层通常为中粗砂填充，黏土颗粒少，渣土流塑性差，改良要求高；

(3) 掘进控制有一定难度，对施工水平和经验要求高，合理的刀盘选型与成熟的施工技术相结合可达到绝佳的施工效果，否则掘进速度慢，掘进参数不协调，进尺不稳定；

(4) 富水砂卵石地层需防止喷水涌砂；

(5) 地层保气性差，盾构开舱换刀作业困难，风险高。

3 砂卵石地层合理刀盘结构选型工程案例分析及合理选型建议

3.1 辐条式刀盘和面板式刀盘优缺点分析

目前国内砂卵石地层所选面板式刀盘通常配置滚刀，为复合式刀盘结构，用其破除特大孤石。结合已有文献和笔者个人看法总结两种刀盘结构形式优缺点论述见表 1[3,8]。

表 1 辐条式刀盘与面板式刀盘优缺点对比

	面板式	辐条式
开挖面压力控制	土仓压力与开挖面压力不能直接传递，控制有一定难度（缺点）	土仓压力等于开挖面压力，压力易于控制（优点）
渣土流畅性	受面板影响，渣土进入土仓不顺畅，易黏结，易堵塞。（缺点）	开口率非常大，渣土流动顺畅，不易堵塞（优点）
刀盘扭矩	刀盘扭矩阻力大，需增加设备能力，造价高（缺点）	刀盘扭矩阻力小，设备造价低（优点）
刀盘刀具磨损	受面板挤压，磨损相对严重（缺点）	无面板挤压，磨损相对轻微（优点）
大粒径卵石适应性	将大卵石阻挡在面板外，可滚刀破除（优点）	超大粒径卵石无法输出时，需人工处理（缺点）
开仓换刀安全性	面板辅助开挖面稳定，安全性高（优点）	开口率过大，安全性低（缺点）
盾构操作 技术水平要求	要求相对低（优点）	要求相对高（缺点）

从上表可以看出，两种刀盘结构各有优缺点，砂卵石地层合理刀盘结构选型需经过工程案例及理论综合分析得出。

3.2 砂卵石地层盾构刀盘刀具选型配置不良案例分析

3.2.1 北京地铁五号线某标

北京地铁五号线某标段，采用面板式土压平衡盾构机掘进。盾构掘进约 346 m 后出现推进缓慢、扭矩激增等异常现象，经开舱检查，发现刀盘外侧的 4 对周边刮刀已完全磨损，正面切削刀大面积严重磨损，刀盘本体也严重磨损，最后补焊修复刀盘，全部重新安装周边刀，更换 68 把正面切削刀恢复掘进，刀盘结构形式、磨损区域及磨损局部特写见图 3。

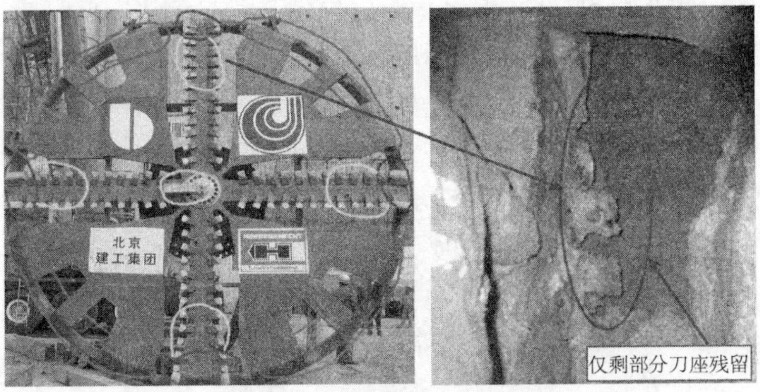

图 3 北京地铁五号线某标盾构刀盘磨损示意

刀盘刀具选型配置不足浅析：刀盘开口率过小，不足 30%；采用四辐条设计，切削刀数量不足；未布置先行刀和鱼尾刀，掘进时地层没有预先松动效应，切削刀受力过大。

3.2.2 北京地铁四号线某标

北京地铁四号线某标采用复合式盾构，在经历多次更换滚刀后，实现区间贯通，贯通后发现刀盘刀具损毁严重，刀盘中心区外首层面板全部磨损脱落，仅剩腹板和地板，空腔泥土充填，中心区外切削刀和周边刮刀全部脱落。

刀盘刀具选型配置不足浅析：刀盘开口率过小，约 25%；滚刀难以取得足够反力，偏磨严重；无先行刀和鱼尾刀，滚刀在该工程意义等同先行刀，但效果较差，卵石在面板和地层之间受挤压造成严重二次磨损，导致切削刀和面板异常损毁。

3.2.3 成都地铁二号线某标

成都地铁二号线某标采用两台ϕ6.24 m 复合式盾构施工，刀盘开口率约 20%，未配置先行刀，刀盘结构见图 5。由于地层卵石含量高、粒径大，滚刀偏磨严重（见图 6），换刀频繁，换刀距离为 50～100 m。施工单位联系国内厂家对刀具进行改进，改变切削刀和周边刮刀合金形式和工艺，部分滚刀刀箱安装羊角刀（相当于一对切削刀），同时在面板上加焊加强型先行刀，改造后换刀距离提高到 300 m 以上。

图 4 北京地铁四号线某标刀盘磨损照片

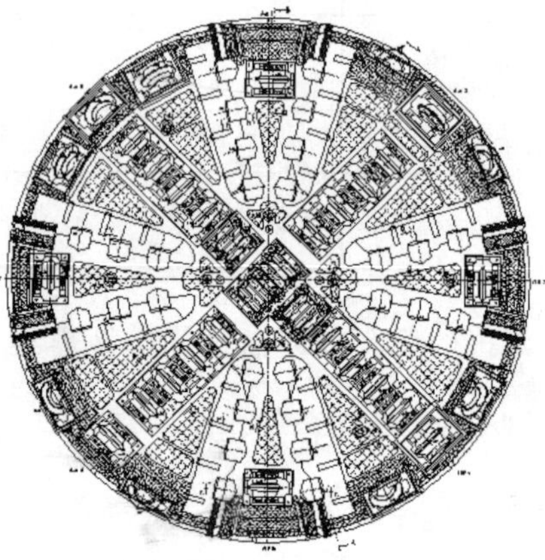

图 5 成都地铁 2 号线某标刀盘

图 6 成都地铁 2 号线某标刀盘

刀盘刀具选型配置不足浅析：刀盘开口率过小，仅约 20%，刀具配置不尽合理，导致换刀频繁，尽管通过改进刀具提高了换刀距离，但由于刀盘结构无法改进，难以进一步提高刀具寿命。

3.2.4 北京地下铁路直径线

北京地下铁路直径线工程采用ϕ11.9 m 泥水平衡盾构施工，刀盘结构见图 7，刀盘由 6 根主辐条和 6 块副面板组成，开口率略大于 20%，刀具由主切削刀、先行刀、周边刮刀等组成。盾构始发掘进了约 60 m 后出现推进缓慢、扭矩激增等异常现象，经带压开舱检查，发现切削刀硬质合金大面积崩裂脱落（见图 8），周边刮刀严重磨损（见图 9）。解决方案：在盾构前方挖临时竖井对刀盘结构进行改造，同时联系国内厂家重新设计刀具。

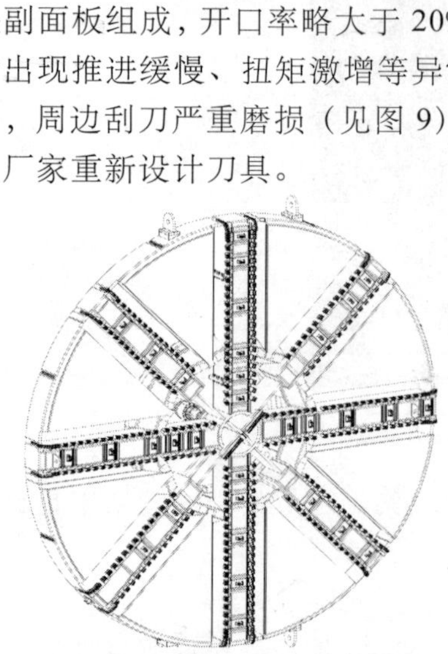

图 7 北京地下铁路直径线盾构刀盘

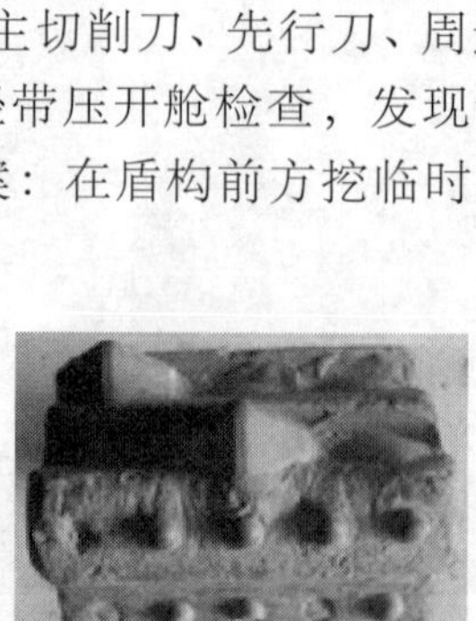

图 8 切削刀合金脱落后新旧对比

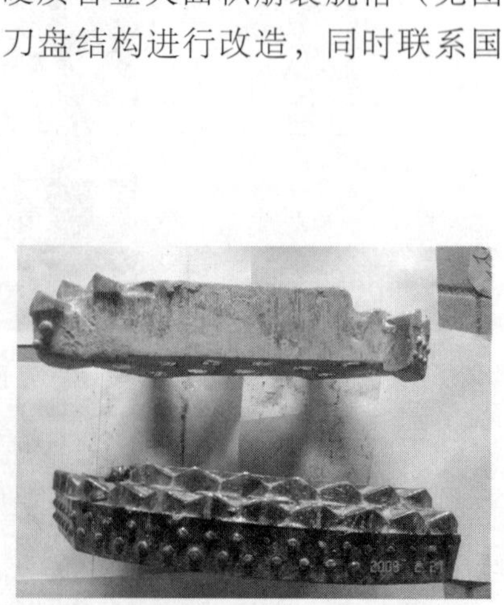

图 9 周边刮刀磨损后新旧对比

刀盘刀具选型配置不足浅析：刀盘开口率过小，略大于 20%；刀具设计不良不适应砂卵石地层，导致短距离掘进后硬质合金大面积崩裂脱落，过早失效。

3.2.5 南京长江隧道

南京长江隧道选用两台ϕ14.93 m 泥水加压平衡盾构施工，刀盘结构见图 10，开口率约 35%，刀具由固定切削刀、常压可更换切削刀、先行刀及周边刮刀等组成。

图 10 南京长江隧道盾构刀盘

南京长江隧道总长约 3 km，其中有约 1 km 为砾砂地层，卵石含量 35%左右，盾构设备供应商承诺一次掘进中途不换刀，但现行始发的右线盾构在掘进至 655 环（共约 1 310 m，进入砾砂层不足 400 m）时出现推进缓慢、扭矩激增等异常现象，强行试推几环后停机检查发现刀具过度磨损，根据刀具磨损程度可判断刀盘外圈亦出现了严重磨损。解决方案：带压开仓修补刀盘、补焊周边刮刀并重新设计可更换切削刀，整个修复过程历时半年。

刀盘刀具选型配置不足浅析：刀盘结构良好（江底砾砂地层超大直径盾构采用 35%开口率较合理），刀具配置也基本合理，但切削刀设计过于简单粗糙，硬质合金尺寸偏小，焊接工艺太差，导致盾构进入砾砂层后切削刀硬质合金大面积整体脱落，先行刀设计不良，过早失效，无法继续推进。

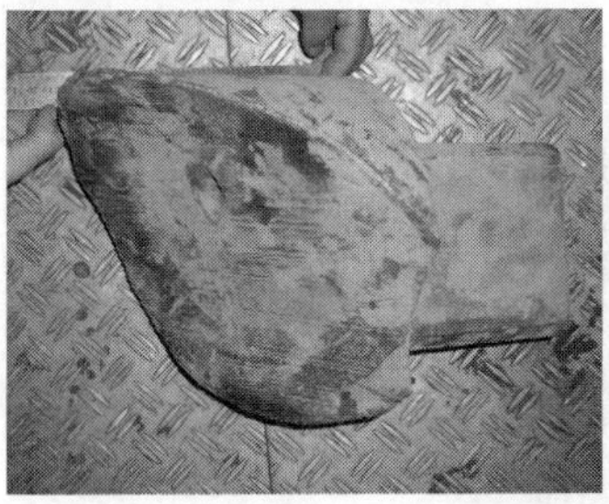

图 11 边缘可更换刀异常磨损

图 12 合金整体脱落及在刀槽内翻转

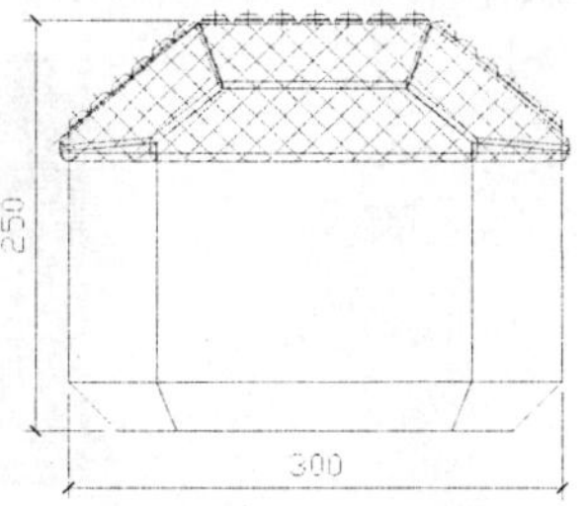

图 13 先行刀结构

3.3 砂卵石地层盾构刀刀盘选型配置优良案例分析

3.3.1 北京地铁四号线十四标（北京市政施工）

北京地铁四号线十四标，总工程包括两站三区间及双榆树站得一部分，三区间分别为双榆树站－学院南路站区间、学院南路站－白石桥站区间、白石桥站－动物园站区间，区间长度分别为 0.82 km、1.47 km 及 1.33 km，采用盾构法施工。

双榆树站－学院南路站区间隧道断面内大部分都附存黏土层、粉细砂层、中粗砂层、卵石圆砾层，其中黏土层、砂层和卵石层所占比例较均匀。学院南路站－白石桥站区间隧道断面内基本为全断面卵石圆砾层。白石桥站－动物园站区间隧道断面内大部分为卵石圆砾层，部分地段夹少量的其他砂层。

工程所用盾构采用 6 圆柱辐条设计，刀具配置由主、副切削刀（高差 20 mm）、先行刀、盘圈贝型刀、中心鱼尾刀及仿形刀组成，刀具采用焊接方式与辐条相连，如图 14 所示。第一个区间（0.82 km 混合地层）贯通后刀具磨损非常小，如图 15 所示，对部分刀具堆焊处理后继续推进第二个区间，在经历 1.47 km 全断面砂卵石地层切削刀崩裂磨损严重，先行刀边角崩裂磨损，如图 16 所示，但掘进贯通过程顺利，未有任何异常。

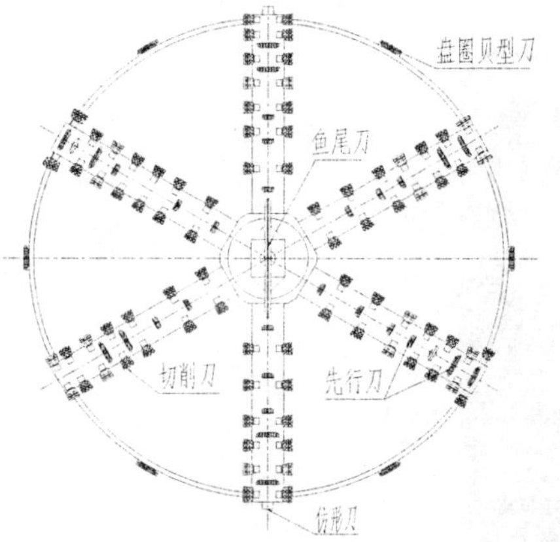

图 14　北京地铁四号线十四标盾构刀盘

图 15　0.82km 混合地层贯通后刀具

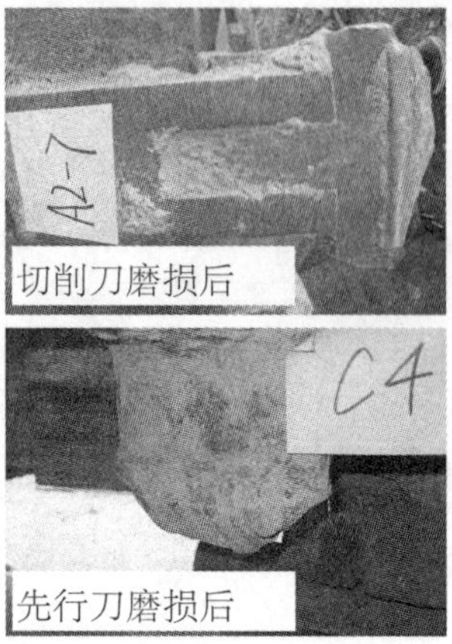

图 16　1.47km 砂卵石地层贯通后刀具

3.3.2　北京地铁 10 号线 11 标[9]（北京市政施工）

北京地铁 l0 号线 11 标区间隧道包括麦子店西路站～亮马河站区间及亮马河站～农展馆站区间，长度分别为 2.1 km 及 0.7 km。隧道区间全断面处于砾砂-砂卵石地层中，根据地质勘探资料，粒径 15 mm 以上的砾石占总体积的 45%，标贯 N 值为 60～65，工程采用 3.3.1 中完全同型号盾构施工，如图 14 所示。

实际施工中，盾构在完成第一个区间约 2.1 km 砾砂-砂卵石地层后，经观察刀盘刀具磨损大大低于理论计算值，仅约 2～3 mm，对刀具进行堆焊处理后，不换刀又继续开始了第二区间的掘进施工。

3.3.3　北京地铁 5 号线 18 标（北京市政施工）

北京地铁 5 号线 18 标东四站—张自忠路站区间长约 0.82 km，区间地质以粉细砂层、圆砾层及粘质粉土、砂质粉土为主，圆砾层约占 40%，采用盾构形式与图 14 相同，掘进过程中未换刀，贯通对刀具进行磨损测量，切削刀和先行刀均正常磨损，形态良好，如图 17 所示。

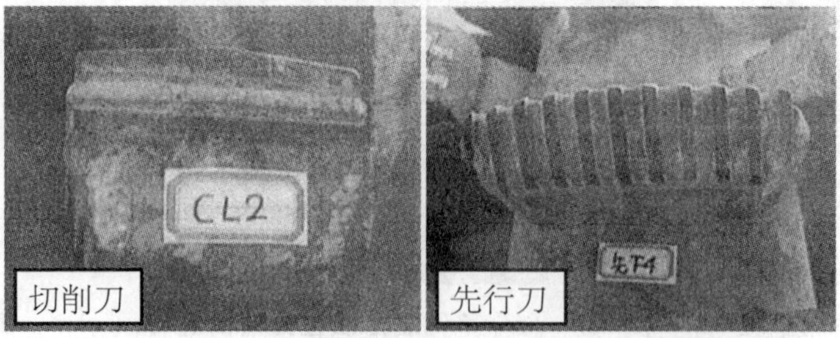

图 17　北京地铁四号线 18 标贯通后盾构刀具

3.3.4　沈阳地铁一号线 9 标（中建一局施工）

沈阳地铁一号线 9 标南京街站—南市站区间长约 1.02 km，采用辐条式盾构施工，盾构刀盘形式同图 14(同一厂家生产)，区间主要通过圆砾层，卵、砾石含量 50%～60%，一般粒径 2～20 mm，最大 100 mm，亚圆形，中、粗砂充填，饱和，中密，密实。该层局部夹砾砂及中、粗砂层。右线于 2009 年 4 月 5 日贯通，掘进期间未换刀。贯通后刀盘及大部分刀具磨损不太严重，仅个别齿刀磨损较严重，进行了更换，其余齿刀进行了耐磨堆焊，在原有盘圈贝型刀存在的情况下，增加了相同数量的盘圈贝型刀，刀盘及刀具贯通后如图 18 所示。

图 18 沈阳地铁一号线 9 标刀盘

3.3.5 沈阳地铁一号线 13 标（中隧集团与北京市政联合施工）

沈阳地铁一号线 13 标怀远门站～中街站区间长约 1.17 km，采用辐条式盾构施工，盾构刀盘形式同图 14（同一厂家生产），洞身穿越地层主要为粉质黏土、中粗砂、，砾砂及圆砾，圆砾层占 46%，一般粒径 2～20 mm，含大于 20 mm 颗粒占总重的 20%～30%，钻探过程中所见最大粒径 110 mm。目前右线已经贯通，掘进期间未换刀，贯通后切削刀崩裂严重，鱼尾刀崩裂一角，说明刀具受卵石冲击严重，先行刀边缘崩裂，形态较好，尚未失效。

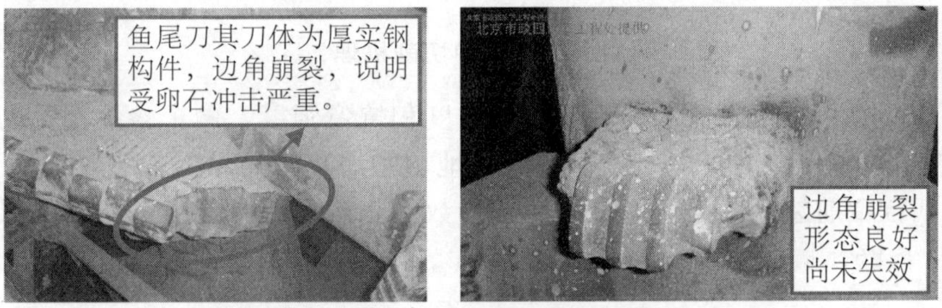

图 19 沈阳地铁一号线 13 标贯通后鱼尾刀和先行刀形态

3.4 小 结

通过以上工程案例可以看出，图 14 所示辐条式刀盘在北京和沈阳砂卵石地层地铁隧道所有标段施工中均表现优异，中途从未换刀。地质条件十分不利时（长距离全断面卵石地层），刀具崩裂磨损严重，但依然实现一次掘进顺利贯通；地质条件相对一般时（粗砂、卵石混合地层），贯通后刀具磨损轻微。反观刀盘刀具选型配置不良案例，无一例外均采用面板式刀盘，刀具设计配置也不合理，一方面大大加剧刀具磨损，另一方面刀具磨损后即出现掘进异常，二者相互制约。这些案例表明砂卵石地层盾构刀盘结构选型比刀具设计配置更具重要意义，采用辐条式刀盘，一方面是对刀具的最有力保护，另一方面即使刀具磨损较严重，对掘进影响也较小，可在最大程度上实现长距离掘进，二者相互促进。辐条式刀盘结合合理的刀具组合配置，是砂卵石地层盾构选型的正确选择。

4 砂卵石地层合理刀具设计及组合配置探讨

当前砂卵石地层刀具组合配置通常有两种方案：方案一：切削刀（小刮刀）、周边刮刀、正面滚刀、边缘滚刀、仿形刀（滚刀形式）；方案二：切削刀（小刮刀）、先行刀、鱼尾刀、盘圈贝型刀、仿形刀（圆柱刀头）。笔者倾向性认为第二种方案更合理，结合不同工程刀具磨损现状对刀具设计及组合配置等问题分述如下。

4.1 切削刀设计

4.1.1 前后角参数确定及硬质合金性能参数确定

切削刀前后角参数定义如图 20 所示，盾构刀具前后角通常取 5°～20°，根据地质的不同确定具体值。砂卵石地层刀背面二次磨损严重，为延缓这一趋势，后角不可过小，建议取 15°；根据地层性质、刀具参数（前、后角）、切削厚度等不同，有关学者盾构刀具切削概况为四种[10,11]：① 流水型切削；② 剪切型切削；③ 断裂型切削；④ 剥落型切削，砂卵石地层对应为剥落型切削，为达到最优切削效果，减小刀具硬质合金崩裂破坏，切削刀前角不可过大，建议取 5°～10°。

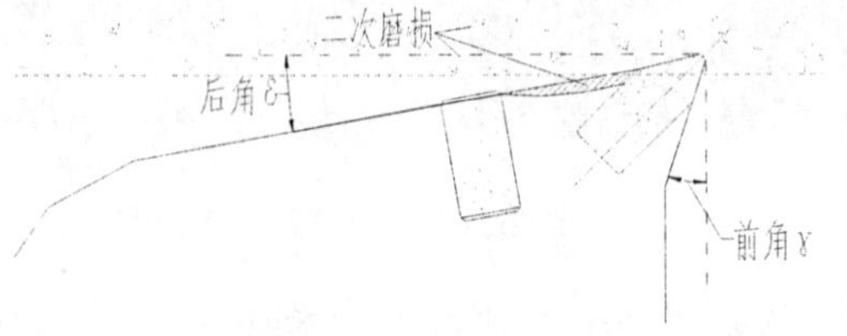

图 20　切削刀参数定义及二次磨损示意

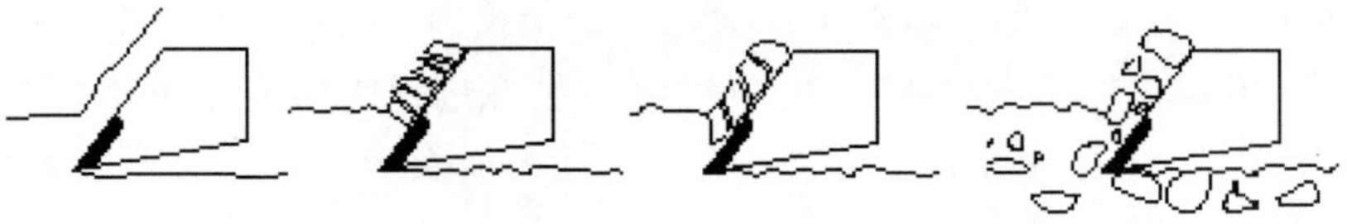

(a) 流水型切削　(b)剪切型切削　(c) 断裂型切削　(d) 剥落型切削

图 21　四种切削机理

刀具硬质合金（刀刃）有两个性能评价参数，硬度和抗弯强度，两个参数相互制约，提高硬度有利于耐磨，但抗弯强度将降低，抗冲击性能差，砂卵石地层中盾构刀具易发生合金崩裂，故适当牺牲硬度，提高抗弯强度，降低合金崩裂概率是选择合金性能参数的正确思路。建议砂卵石地层刀具硬质合金硬度取洛氏硬度 HRA 大于 86，抗弯强度大于 2 000 N/mm^2，与日本 E5 材料标准相对应。

表 2　砂卵石地层切削刀参数建议值

前角（°）	后角（°）	合金硬度（洛氏 HRA）	合金抗弯强度(N/mm^2)
5～10	15	>86	>2 000

4.1.2　*硬质合金与刀体结合方式选择、截面尺寸及刀刃倒角半径确定*

切削刀硬质合金与刀体通常有两种结合方式，面贴式和嵌入式，如图 22 所示，二者各有优缺点，具体陈述见表 3，砂卵石地层中切削刀最主要的问题是防止合金崩裂，地层为剥落型破坏，对其切削功能要求相对不高，故建议砂卵石地层硬质合金与刀体结合方式采用嵌入式。

硬质合金截面尺寸宽×高（b×h）定义如图 22 所示，当采用面贴式结合方式时，宽度过小将导致抗冲击能力弱，高度过小将导致掘进中硬质合金全部进入地层，加剧合金底部刀体磨损，导致合金脱落；当采用嵌入式结合方式时，合金宽度取常规值（≥15 mm）即可，但高度不可过小，否则合金两侧刀体稍有磨损即导致嵌固深度不足（图 20），发生合金脱落，南京长江隧道盾构原装刀具普遍出现合金脱落（见图 23），除焊接质量问题外，合金高度不足(仅 35 mm)、嵌固深度过浅也是主要原因，合金截面尺寸建议值见表 3。

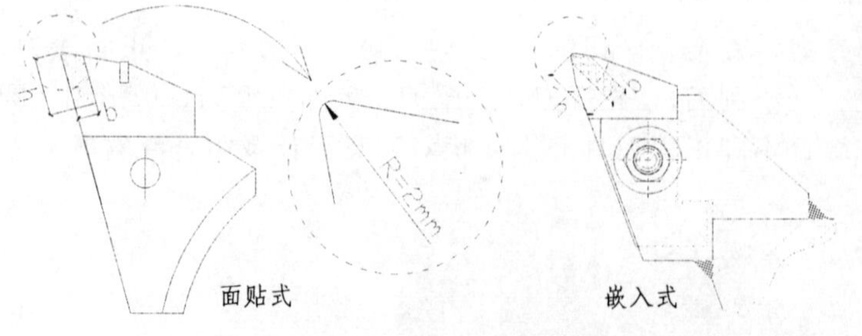

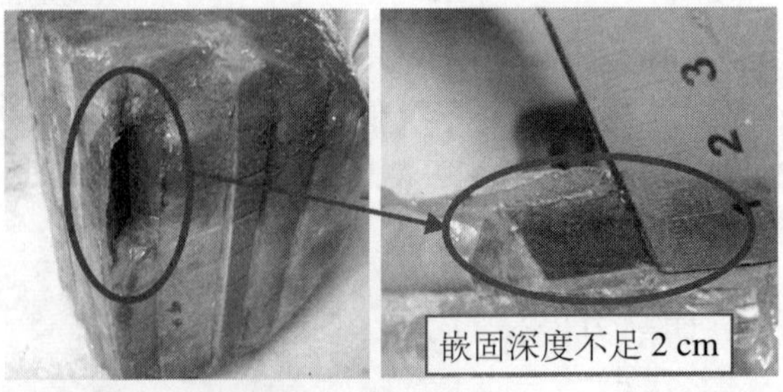

图 22　合金与刀体两种结合方式及刀刃半径示意　　图 23　合金高度不足，嵌固深度过浅，合金脱落

刀刃倒角半径 R 反映的是刀具的锐利程度，通常盾构刀具取 R＝2 mm，见图 22。一般而言增大刀刃

半径将导致刀具变钝，降低切削能力，但在实际工程中，砂卵石地层按常规设计的刀具其刀刃（硬质合金部分）往往在初始掘进中就发生崩裂（见图 24），且如上文所述，砂卵石地层为剥落型破坏，对切削功能要求不高，实际工程中南京长江隧道和北京直径线新改进切削刀其刀刃倒角半径达到 10 mm（见图 25），工程应用效果良好（见图 26），故建议砂卵石地层切削刀其刀刃倒角半径 R=5～10 mm，区间含黏土类地层时取低值。

图 24　刀刃崩裂

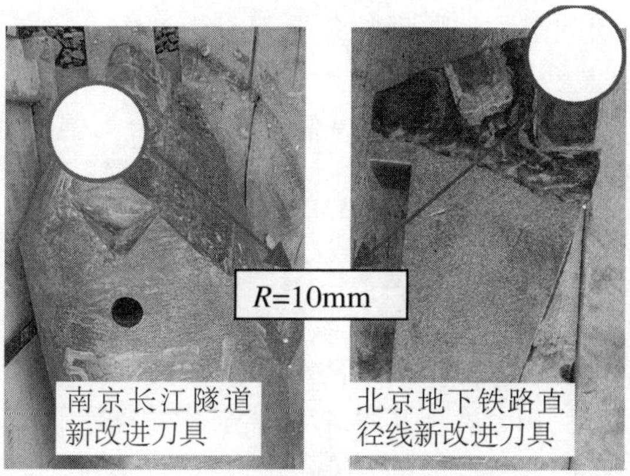

图 25　工程中“钝刀”设计实例

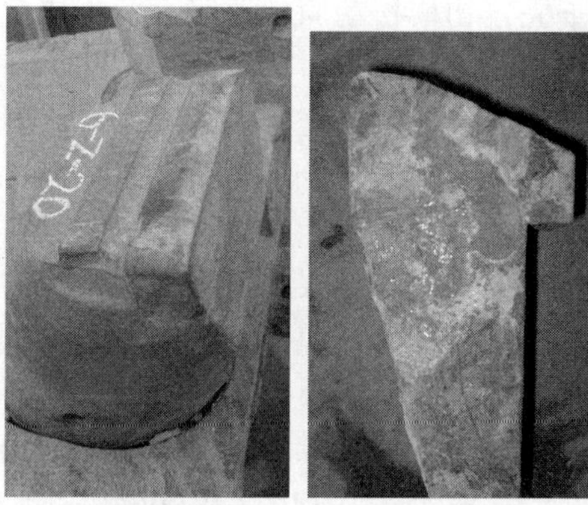

图 26　“钝刀”应用后效果

表 3　合金与刀体两种结合方式优缺点分析及硬质合金形式参数确定

	优　点	缺　点	截面尺寸建议值（$b \times h$）	刀刃倒角半径建议值（mm）
面贴式	焊接工艺相对简单，切削能力强，前、后角设计不受限制	合金易崩裂，要求较大截面宽度要求，否则抗冲击能力差，截面高度设计残留值大，否则磨损合金根部刀体	≥25 × 55	5 ~ 10 mm
嵌入式	合金受刀体保护，抗冲击能力强，不易崩裂，要求合金截面尺寸小，利用程度高。	焊接工艺复杂，切削能力稍弱，前后角设计需保证合金前后有足够刀体保护层厚度	≥15 × 50	

4.1.3　切削刀高差设计合理性探讨

为达到整体延长刀具寿命，提高一次掘进距离的目的，有相关学者建议砂卵石地层切削刀配置时设主副切削刀，二者高差取 20 mm 左右[9]，见图 27，其设计思路为：主切削刀磨损后副刀接替工作，有效增大刀具允许磨损量。但在实际掘进过程中，刀具采用面贴式结合方式时，合金极易受卵石冲击崩裂，很可能副刀尚未工作但其合金已经损毁。实际工程中北京地下铁路直径线盾构初装切削刀采用双层刀刃设计，其设计思路类似主副刀配置，但掘进 60 m 后查看发现大部分刀具高刃和低刃均崩裂，见图 28。且考虑到盾构掘进时贯入度（每转切深）因素，主刀正常工作时，副刀刀尖几乎表现为在卵石表面摩擦掠过，对副刀合金保护非常不利（两种结合方式均存在此问题），难以起到应有效果，故建议盾构切削刀不作高差设计。

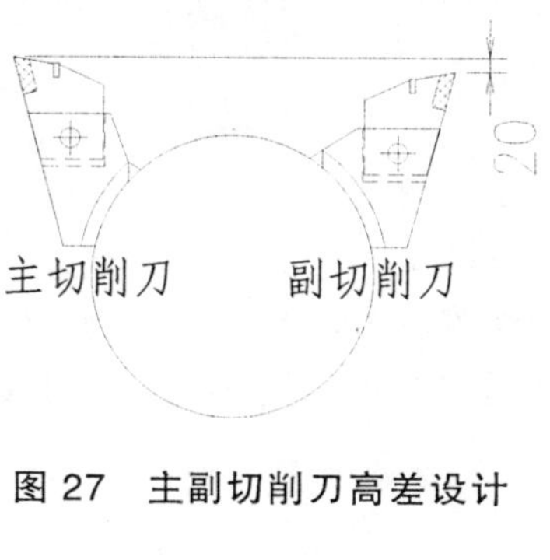

图 27　主副切削刀高差设计

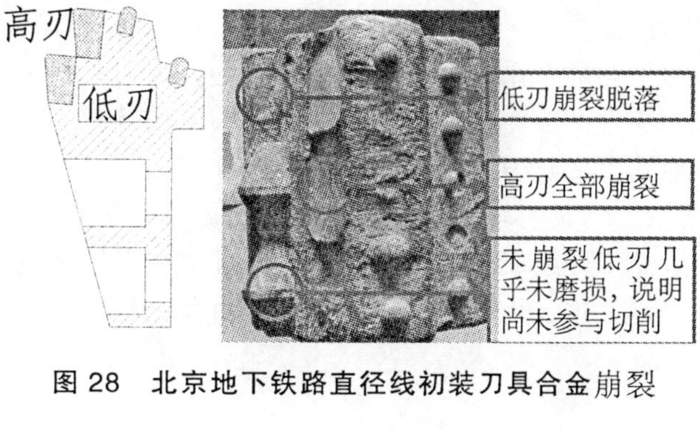

图 28　北京地下铁路直径线初装刀具合金崩裂

4.2 鱼尾刀、先行刀工作原理及与滚刀优劣势分析

4.2.1 鱼尾刀、先行刀工作原理

鱼尾刀安装在盾构刀盘中心，尺寸大、强度高，一般长 1 200～1 500 mm，高 400～500 mm，高出普通切削刀 200～300 mm，盾构掘进时首先在刀盘中心掘出小圆，松动地层，大大减小其他刀具掘削阻力，降低磨损。先行刀布置在切削刀切削轨迹之间，通常比切削刀高 40～50 mm，不起直接切削作用，用于先行切槽松动原始地层，减小切削刀切削阻力，原理与鱼尾刀有相通性，鱼尾刀和先行刀作用原理见图 29、图 30。

砂卵石地层是一种咬合不稳定地层，粒径大，致密，内摩擦角大，咬合力强，常规切削有很大难度，但受扰动后极易自行崩塌，在鱼尾刀和先行刀的扰动作用下，切削刀只需辅助剥落即可完成掘进切削过程。

对于砂卵石地层，鱼尾刀和先行刀的意义和重要性远大于切削刀，其中又因先行刀可实现满盘灵活布置的优势使其比鱼尾刀更加不可或缺。在刀盘结构选型合理、渣土流动顺畅的前提下，只要保证鱼尾刀和先行刀发挥作用，就基本可保证掘进的顺利进行，以下两个工程实例可证明这一点。

北京地铁四号线 14 标盾构刀盘见前文图 14，在经历 1.47 km 全断面砂卵石后，统计切削刀失效率达 73%，但先行刀失效率仅 30%，如前面图 16 所示，切削刀其刀体前端仅有部分残余，先行刀边角崩裂磨损但未失效，掘进贯通过程中没有任何异常。

北京地下铁路直径线工程停机后刀盘改造为复合式结构，安装有滚刀和切削刀，掘进 88 m 试验段后检查刀具，滚刀正常磨损，切削刀几乎没有任何磨损痕迹（见图 31），由于滚刀在该工程中起类似先行刀作用（无岩石，无需破岩，与切削刀高差达 30 mm，类似先行刀，但寿命太短，是其最大弊端），说明切削刀几乎未参与工作的前提下靠滚刀完成掘进，当然将滚刀换成先行刀工程效果更佳。

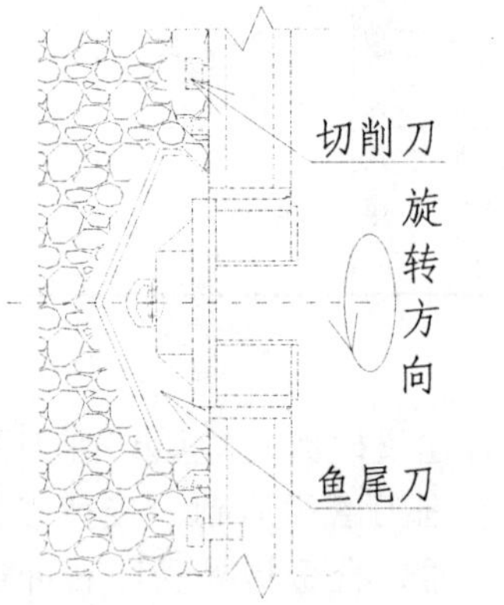

图 29 鱼尾刀工作原理

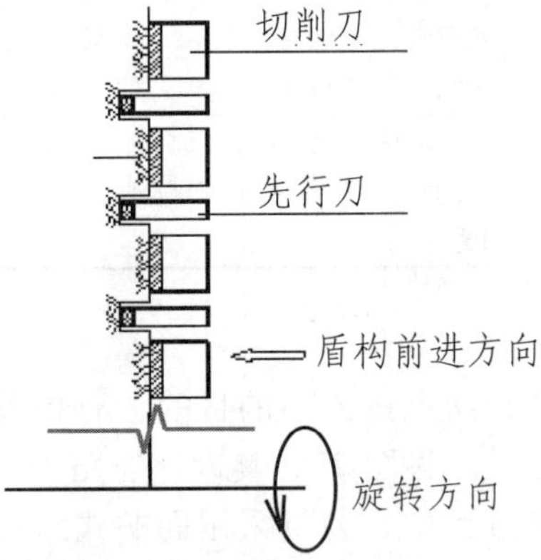

图 30 先行刀工作原理

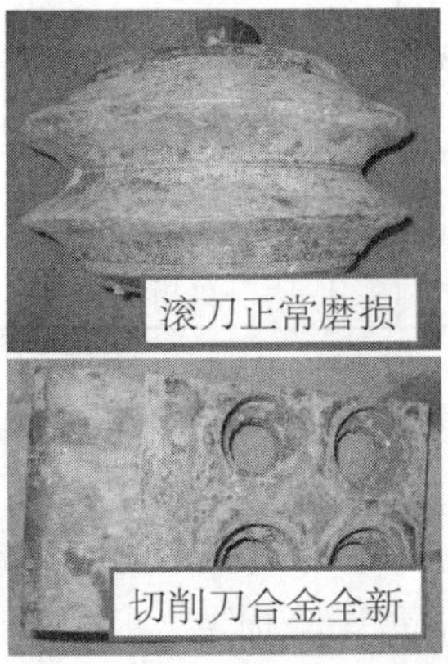

图 31 北京地下铁路直径线滚刀切削刀磨损对比

4.2.2 先行刀与滚刀优劣势分析

先行刀优势分析：

（1）寿命长：根据国内工程相关统计及我们在北京地下铁路直径线工程测量计算得滚刀在砂卵石地层正常磨损系数为 70×10^{-3}～100×10^{-3} mm/km，根据北京地铁四号线 14 标和北京地铁五号线 18 标测量计算得先行刀平均磨损系数为 33×10^{-3} mm/km，滚刀允许磨损量一般取为 20 mm，先行刀允许磨损量可超过 40 mm，综合而言，先行刀寿命可达滚刀寿命 5 倍以上。

成都地铁上海隧道股份项目部利用强化先行刀代替滚刀，掘进 274 环（1.5 m/环，共 411 m）后检查如图 32 所示，刀具有轻微磨损，堆焊后完成整个区间推进，超过 1 000 m。

成都地铁 1 号线 4 标中铁隧道集团项目部利用强化先行刀代替滚刀，掘进 280 环（1.5 m/环，共 420 m）后刀体有一定磨损，堆焊后继续使用，项目部主管人员认为成都地质完全可利用先行刀代替滚刀。

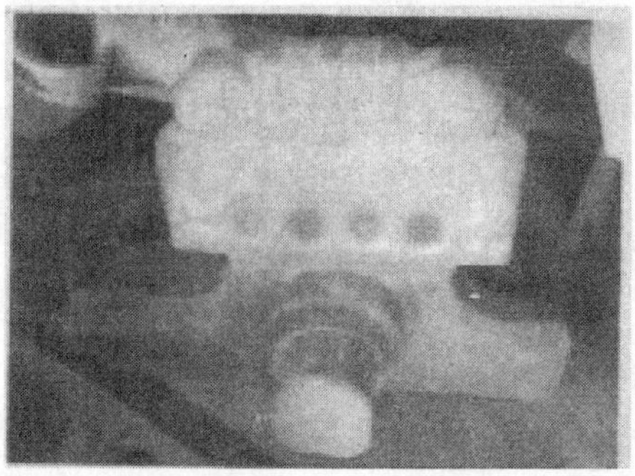

图 32 成都地铁盾构采用先行刀代替滚刀

（2）价格便宜

目前国内单刃滚刀大约为 2.3 万元至 2.5 万元一把，图 32 所示先行刀 0.9 万元至 1.0 万元一把，不含底座普通先行刀 0.3 万元至 0.5 万元一把，砂卵石地层中滚刀掘进距离约 200 m，先行刀掘进距离在 1 000 m 以上，综合比较经济效益明显。

滚刀优势分析：

对于砂卵石地层，采用复合式刀盘安装滚刀是为了利用滚刀破除大漂石，达到顺利出渣的目的，这是滚刀相对于先行刀的唯一优势，滚刀同时也起到先行松动地层保护切削刀的作用，类似先行刀。但在实际工程中，滚刀破除大漂石虽有成功案例[6]，但通常效果非常较差，原因在于漂石不易固定，滚刀难以取得破除反力。北京地铁四号线 20 标北宫门—龙背村站区间采用复合式盾构施工，区间大卵石采取从地面挖小导洞方式取出（图 33）；广州地铁某标段对复合地层中未风化大岩核采取进仓微型爆破方式解决，这均说明滚刀破除孤石有很大的局限性。且现在砂卵石地层盾构通常选配ϕ800 带式螺旋输送机，最大出渣粒径达到 600～730 mm。笔者通过调研，广州及深圳复合地层地铁区间出现过粒径大于此粒径未风化岩核，北京、成都、沈阳等地砂卵石地层地铁区间到目前为止尚未出现。故滚刀破除大漂石这一优势实际意义不大，采取辐条式刀盘+ϕ800 带式螺旋输送机基本可满足当前所有砂卵石地层，假如出现超预期大孤石，可采用参照广州案例采取进仓微型爆破的方式解决。

图 33 盾构隧道开挖导洞取出大卵石

4.3 盘圈贝型刀与周边刮刀优劣势对比

盘圈贝型刀与周边刮刀均为保护刀盘边缘不被磨损而设置，周边刮刀还兼备将渣土刮入土仓的作用。盘圈贝型刀用于垂直边缘刀盘，周边刮刀用于弧形或折角边缘刀盘。

盘圈贝型刀优势分析：盘圈贝型刀受力方式同先行刀，合金有刀体保护，不易崩裂，在砂卵石地层中掘进其寿命也在 1 km 以上，如图 34 所示；周边刮刀受力方式类似切削刀，合金极易受损，如图 35 所示。

图 34 盘圈贝型刀受力方式示意

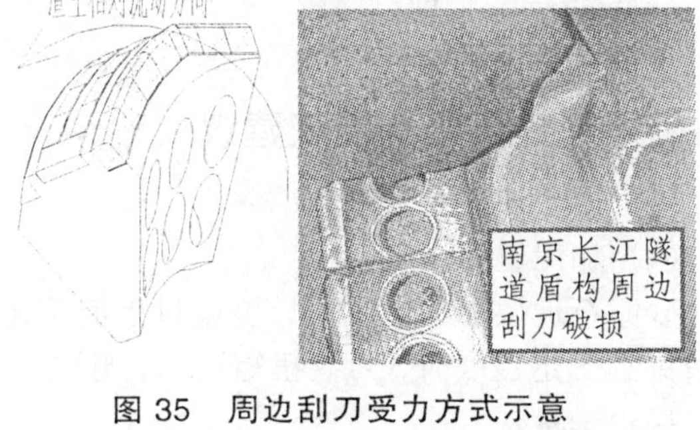

图 35 周边刮刀受力方式示意

周边刮刀仅因适应刀盘采用弧形或折角型边缘形式而设，相对于盘圈贝型刀几乎没有其他优势。

4.4 小 结

通过以上分析可得出，砂卵石地层刀具组合采用“切削刀（小刮刀)、先行刀、鱼尾刀、盘圈贝型刀”合理可行，相比“切削刀（小刮刀)、周边刮刀、正面滚刀、边缘滚刀”组合具压倒性优势。组合配置中切削刀只起辅助剥落作用，鱼尾刀和先行刀是盾构掘进的关键，其中又以先行刀最为重要，其设计和布置是整个刀具配置的关键。

5 砂卵石地层合理刀盘刀具选型配置建议

建议砂卵石地层盾构选型采取辐条式刀盘+ϕ800 mm 带式螺旋输送机方案，刀具组合采用“切削刀、先行刀、鱼尾刀、盘圈贝型刀”，基本可满足中国内地地铁区间砂卵石地层出渣要求。

根据目前中国内地施工案例，区间长度在 1.5 km 以内普通砂卵石地层采用图 14 所示辐条式刀盘结构、刀具形式及配置，配合良好的辅助施工技术（主要表现为砂卵石地层加泥加泡沫减磨降矩技术)，可保证一次掘进不换刀。

为进一步增强辐条式刀盘对地层的适应性并延长掘进距离，建议辐条式刀盘可借鉴复合刀盘形式，设计矩形辐条，内置刀箱，刀箱内可选配羊角刀（对称切削刀)、先行刀及滚刀，实现三者快速便捷更换，如图 36、图 37 所示。

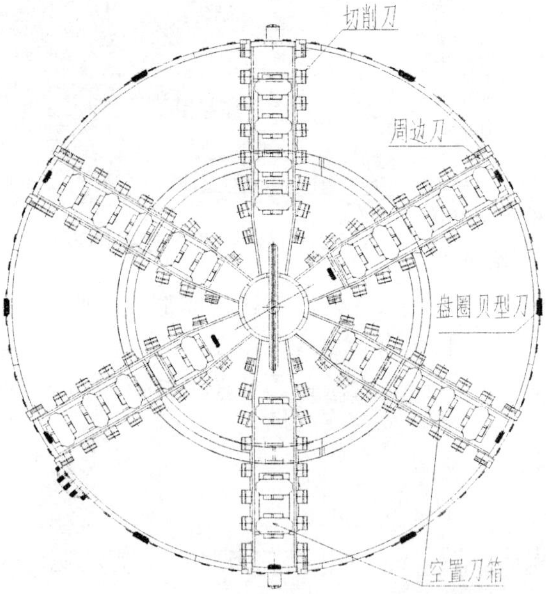

图 36 改进辐条式刀盘

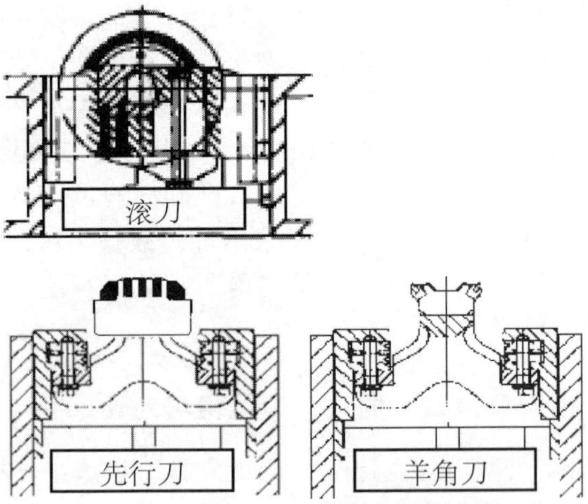

图 37 各种可更换刀头形式

另外，在无水或水位较低卵石、漂石地层，漂石过多粒径过大以致刀盘或螺旋输送机难以适应或工程经济性太差时，可考虑采用开敞式盾构、机械手挖掘，如图 34 所示。

6 砂卵石地层盾构施工建议

（1）加泥量不可过大

砂卵石地层加泥量过大，渣土过于流塑化会导致卵石离析沉积，螺旋输送机无法及时将卵石排出，当聚集到一定程度时，刀盘扭矩过高，导致推进速度减慢，并进一步加剧卵石离析，如此形成恶性循环，导致掘进异常。

（2）土压控制不可过严

受砂卵石地层特性影响，盾构掘进时土仓中土压波动幅度较大，难以做到严格控制，强行要求将导致掘进参数设定极其不稳定，严重影响施工操作。砂卵石地层盾构施工土压的控制要求应根据出渣情况及地表沉降数据分析反馈结果而定。

（3）泡沫质量确保合格

砂卵石地层中加泡沫可起增强渣土流塑性、降低刀盘扭矩和刀具磨损的作用，与加泥作用类似，其意义在于降低加泥量，提高工程经济性，但必须保证泡沫质量，否则还会起反作用。

（4）推进速度、加泥加泡沫量保证稳定

掘进时将推进速度稳定控制在合理范围内，并保证螺旋输送机的转速与推进速度相匹配，以此尽可能保证土仓内土压稳定，同时稳定控制每环的加泥量和泡沫量，不因一时出土的稀稠情况而大幅度调整总量及流量。在停机或推进停止一段时间后，泥浆和泡沫会渗透到土层中，所以盾构启动前提前加一点泥浆和泡沫，刚推进时，不可因刀盘的油压低而加大推进速度，应该按照上一环的参数推进，并随时根据出土的情况对各种参数进行控制调整。

图 38　开敞式盾构

7 结　论

（1）砂卵石地层盾构刀盘结构选型相比刀具配置设计更具重要意义，ϕ800 带式螺旋输送机可满足国内砂卵石地层目前已知最大卵石粒径的出渣要求，辐条式刀盘+ϕ800 带式螺旋输送机是适应砂卵石地层的合理选择。

（2）刀具组合配置采用“切削刀（小刮刀）、先行刀、鱼尾刀、盘圈贝型刀”在砂卵石地层具压倒性优势，滚刀不是破除大粒径卵石的良好选择，超预期粒径卵石可采取进仓微型爆破方式解决；刀具配置中切削刀只起辅助剥落作用，鱼尾刀和先行刀是盾构掘进的关键，其中又以先行刀最为重要。

（3）砂卵石地层切削刀设计的关键在于硬质合金的保护与抗冲击，故建议硬质合金与刀体采用嵌入式结合方式，合金性能参数选取遵循“高抗弯强度、适当低硬度”原则，可取日本 E5 材料对应参数标准；考虑到砂卵石地层特性和刀具切削原理，建议切削刀不做主副刀高差设计。

（4）砂卵石地层先行刀可考虑主副刀高差设计，接替工作，延长掘进距离。

（5）超长距离砂卵石地层盾构隧道施工建议采用改进型辐条式刀盘结构，辐条内设置刀箱，并设计配套同底座先行刀及切削刀，实现先行刀、切削刀及特殊情况下滚刀的快速便捷更换。

（6）特殊卵石漂石地层，闭胸式盾构难以适应或工程经济性太差时，可考虑采用开敞式盾构，机械手挖掘。

参考文献（Referenles）：

[1] 邹积波. 盾构刀具磨损原因探析[J]. 建筑机械化，2003，24(11)：57-58.
[2] 宋克志，朱建德，王梦恕，等. 无水砂卵石地层盾构机的选型[J]. 铁道标准设计，2004(11)：51-54.
[3] 张国京. 北京地区土压式盾构刀具的适应性分析[J]. 市政技术，2005，23(1)：9-13.
[4] 李建斌. 浅谈盾构刀盘的设计与应用[J]. 建筑机械化，2006，27(3)：31-35.
[5] 刘高峰，宋天田. 成都地铁盾构刀具磨损分析研究[J]. 隧道建设，2007，27(6)：89-93.
[6] 李海峰. 卵石含量高、粒径大的富水砂卵石地层中盾构机选型研究[J]. 现代隧道技术，2009，46(1)：57-63.
[7] 胡显鹏. 砂卵石地层土压平衡盾构掘进刀具磨损研究(硕士学位论文)[M]. 北京交通大学, 2007.
[8] 张明富. 土压平衡盾构掘进刀具动态磨损研究(硕士学位论文)[M]. 北京交通大学, 2008.
[9] 彭少杰. 提高土压式盾构在砂砾石地层中掘进刀具耐用性的对策[J]. 城市道桥与防洪，2006，6：126-129.

[10] 矢野信太郎. 盾构工法[M]. (日)鹿岛研究所出版会, 1980.
[11] 富昭治郎. 建设机械学[M]. (日)鹿岛研究所出版会, 2001.

作者简介（Bio-data）:

黄清飞（1983.7—），男，北京交通大学博士研究生，从事盾构刀盘刀具选型设计相关研究工作。

Qingfei HUANG (1983.7—), male, Ph.D. candidate of Beijing Jiaotong University, engaged in relevant research work of cutting wheel type selection and cutting tool design.

Email: af1639@sohu.com

盾构隧道数字化远程监控系统的研究与实现

袁 钊[1] 李晓军[1] 高小庆[2] 杨文威[2] 陆晓龙[2]
[1]同济大学 地下建筑与工程系，岩土及地下工程教育部重点实验室，上海 200092
[2]上海市电力公司电网建设公司，上海 200002

【摘 要】 从保护周边建筑物及地下管线的安全的角度出发，本文应用数字化远程监控系统，在施工的过程中，对盾构隧道施工进行实时监控；并实现监控信息及时共享、分析与可视化。首先介绍系统用到的几项关键技术：Web 服务技术、虚拟现实技术、SVG 技术，然后以上海电力电缆隧道为例，重点介绍了该系统的实现和应用。

【关键词】 盾构隧道；数字化；远程监控

RESEARCH AND IMPLEMENTATION OF SHIELD TUNNEL DIGITAL REMOTE MONITORING SYSTEM

Zhao YUAN[1], Xiaojun LI[1], Xiaoqing GAO[2], Wenwei YANG[2], Xiaolong LU[2]
[1] Department of Geotechnical Engineering, Key Laboratory of Geotechnical Engineering, Tongji University, Shanghai 200092, China;
[2] Shanghai Municipal Electric Power Company power network construction Company, Shanghai 200002, China

Abstract: From the perspectives of protecting the surrounding buildings and underground pipeline, the digital monitoring system was applied to carry out the real-time monitoring on shield tunnel construction. And the timely sharing, analysis and visualization of monitoring information were achieved. At first, the key technologies used in this system were introduced: Web services technology, virtual reality technology, SVG technology, then the realization of the system and engineering application was further studied based on the Shanghai electricity cable tunnel project.

Key words: shield tunnel; digital; remote monitoring

1 引 言

目前，隧道工程领域的信息化、数字化施工研究蓬勃发展。美国 Marte Gutierrez（2006）基于 IT 技术，针对岩石隧道的规划、设计、施工开发了 AMADEUS (Adaptive Real-Time Geologic Mapping, Analysis and Design of Underground Space)系统[4]；韩国 Yoo Chungsik 等（2006）基于地理信息系统软 ArcGIS 开发了一个隧道风险管理系统，用于对隧道施工中周围环境受到的影响进行评估[2]；意大利 Andrea Toninil（2008）利用 GIS 技术和 CAD 技术对隧道工程环境及施工进行了三维可视化模拟[1]；韩国 Yosoon Choi（2009）基于 ArcScene 三维 GIS 软件开发了隧道分析模块，用于隧道围岩分类和施工中破坏区域分析[3]。与此同时，中国国内仅在盾构隧道领域，张庆贺、胡向东等（2003）对盾构隧道掘进监控数据库及变形控制系统进行了研究[7]；周文波（2004）开发了面向盾构隧道信息化施工的智能管理系统[10]；朱合华、李晓军等先后提出了数字地层（1998）、地下工程数字化（2006）、数字地下空间与工程（2007）的概念[9]，在这一系列的概念中，体现了信息化技术在岩土及地下工程的研究现状与趋势。其中数字化隧道的理念[6]是数字地下空间与工程的一个重要组织部分和研究重心，本文主要介绍数字化隧道在城市盾构隧道施工远程监控中的应用。

2 技术背景

2.1 Web 服务技术[8]

将 Web 技术应用到盾构隧道施工监控中，可以及时整理分析监测数据，生成监测数据变化曲线和监测报表，必要时可以自动预警，通过网络实现监测信息的无障碍沟通，不仅提高隧道监测的工作效率和准确度，节省大量人力物力，而且有关各方可以及时了解隧道监测工作情况和监测成果，针对现场情况及时采取适当措施，为隧道安全顺利施工做好服务。此处主要介绍要应用的 Web 服务的一些基本概念。Web 服务是一种 Web 应用程序，它没有传统 Web 应用程序的用户界面，与传统 Web 应用程序不同，它不是为终端用户设计，而是向其他应用程序提供服务。Web 服务通过向外界提供 API 函数完成网络间的各种操作。在实际应用中，有了 Web 服务，只要在客户端程序中通过访问某个服务（如查询监测曲线）的 URL 地址，得到一个 XML 描述，并使用这个描述文件产生一个接口文件，通过这个接口文件来访问服务。

2.2 虚拟现实技术

虚拟现实（Virtual Reality）融合了数字图像处理、计算机图形学、多媒体技术、传感器技术、人工智能技术等多个信息技术分支，具有沉浸性，交互性，多感知性和自主性的特征。它通过生成一个虚拟环境，实现人机交互、互相交流的操作环境及身临其境的感觉，使人产生强烈的真实感、参与感、操作感，从而更直观的认识了解事物。本文以 Multigen Creator 和 Vega 作为虚拟现实开发包，在 Creator 的“所见即所得”建模环境中，建立所期望的、优化的三维盾构隧道施工、监控环境；Vega 软件提供完整的 C++语言应用程序接口，即 OpenFlight API 接口，通过该接口操作虚拟模型文件，在此基础上开发可视化控件，直接嵌入到 Internet Explorer 浏览器中，在客户端实现 Web 服务。

2.3 SVG 技术

一个隧道工程涉及大量的图纸，为使图纸在网络平台上可视化，本文采用 SVG 技术实现二维图像的网络发布。SVG(Scalable Vector Graphics，可缩放矢量图像)是互联网联盟(W3C)推荐的标准[5]。它是一种描述二维图像的语言平台，主要包括两部分：基于 XML 的文件格式和面向应用的图形开发接口。SVG 支持 3 种形式的图像对象，矢量图形、文本和光栅图像。SVG 是一个开放的标准，被多数软件和硬件厂家认可，在信息共享和发布方面有着极强的应用价值。SVG 的特性主要有：图像自由缩放，文本独立，文件较小，超强的图像和颜色显示效果，支持 XML 标准，可以与 Web 标准进行良好的互操作。

3 系统实现与应用实例

本研究以上海市电力电缆隧道工程为应用实例。该隧道线路全长约 15.05 km，其中盾构法隧道长约 8.83 km，顶管法隧道长约 6.22 km，共设 14 座工作井。该工程穿越闹市区、黄浦江防汛墙；横向交叉穿越轨道交通线 12 次，最大距离 4.7 m，最小距离仅 1.5 m；与高架道路近距离并行约 3.6 km，与高架桥桥墩最小净距离 2 m 左右。

3.1 数字化监控平台

该隧道施工监控现场包括 14 个一般段施工监控区间、微扰动穿越南浦大桥桥墩自动监控和微扰动穿越民房群自动监控；监控数据的存储、管理和分析以及各种服务功能都由服务器端提供；在客户端管理方、施工方、监理方、设计方和监测方通过不同权限的账户分配到不同的服务功能。数据的传输和各种服务功能都通过网络进行传递。

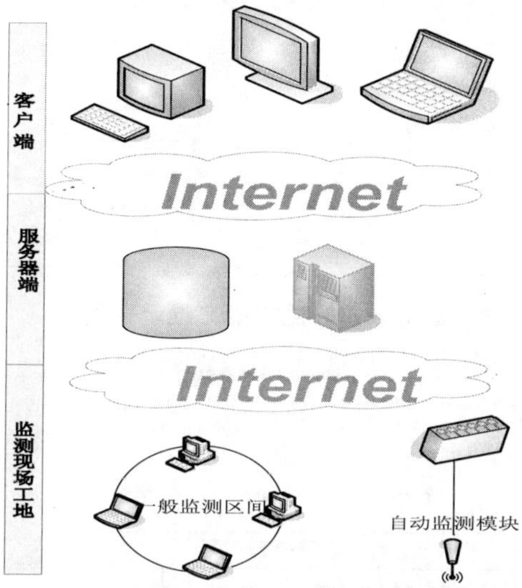

图 1 数字化监控平台结构图

3.2 数据的传输

在电力隧道 0#～14#的 14 条区间段的施工中进行了一般区间的施工监控。监测项目主要包括：轴线地表沉降、建筑物沉降、人行天桥沉降、燃气管线沉降、上水管线沉降、雨水管线沉降、污水管线沉降、电力管线沉降和高架桥桥墩沉降等等。监测数据的远程输入提供两种输入方法给施工单位和监测单位。一是在网页上面进行单次输入，通过网络传送到数据库备份、存储。另一种是通过固定的标准化格式在 excel 里面整理后，在通过网络平台进行批量传送提交（图 2）。在两个自动化监测断面，数据由传感器监测后通过网络直接传送到数据库服务平台。数据亦可以在客户端通过网络进行下载。

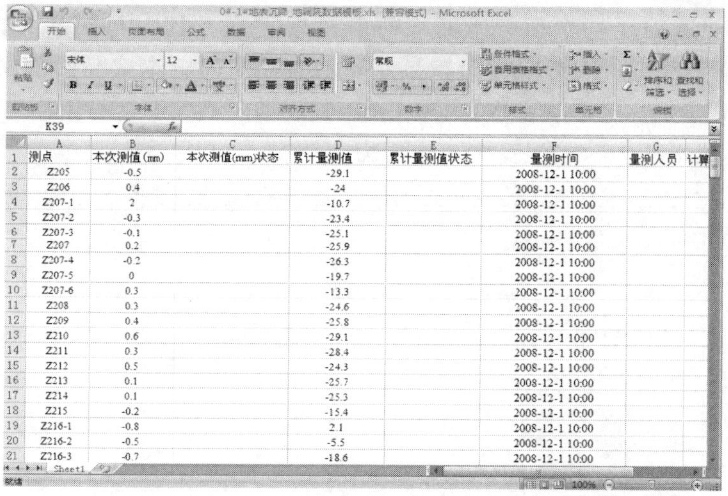

测点	本次测值(mm)	本次测值(mm)状态	累计量测值	累计量测值状态	量测时间	量测人员	计算
Z205	-0.5		-29.1		2008-12-1 10:00		
Z206	0.4		-24		2008-12-1 10:00		
Z207-1	2		-10.7		2008-12-1 10:00		
Z207-2	-0.3		-23.4		2008-12-1 10:00		
Z207-3	-0.1		-25.1		2008-12-1 10:00		
Z207	0.2		-25.9		2008-12-1 10:00		
Z207-4	-0.2		-26.3		2008-12-1 10:00		
Z207-5	0		-19.7		2008-12-1 10:00		
Z207-6	0.3		-13.3		2008-12-1 10:00		
Z208	0.3		-24.6		2008-12-1 10:00		
Z209	0.4		-25.8		2008-12-1 10:00		
Z210	0.6		-29.1		2008-12-1 10:00		
Z211	0.3		-28.4		2008-12-1 10:00		
Z212	0.5		-24.3		2008-12-1 10:00		
Z213	0.1		-25.7		2008-12-1 10:00		
Z214	0.1		-25.3		2008-12-1 10:00		
Z215	-0.2		-15.4		2008-12-1 10:00		
Z216-1	-0.8		2.1		2008-12-1 10:00		
Z216-2	-0.5		-5.5		2008-12-1 10:00		
Z216-3	-0.7		-18.6		2008-12-1 10:00		

图 2 监测数据 excel 模板

3.3 数据的查询与可视化

图 3 中的测点布置图、施工环境二维底图、隧道施工进度模拟图，图 4 中的监测查询分析曲线是通过 SVG 技术实现。在图上可以对测点点击，通过 web 服务与远程数据库进行操作查询，实现图与数据库的交互查询，可以得到各种实时的监测曲线。

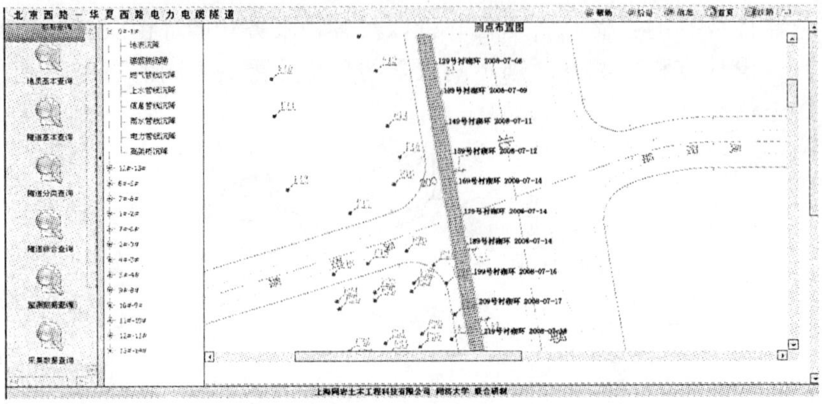

图 3 一般监控段二维示意图

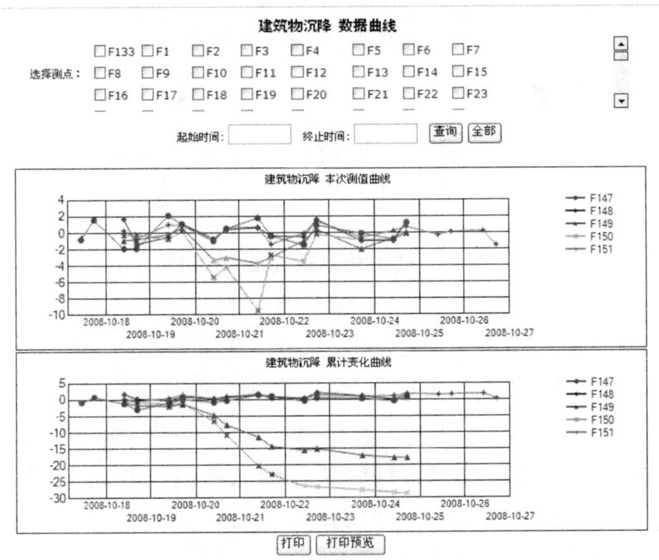

图 4 监测数据曲线查询

此隧道 9#～8#段隧道轴线基本都与南浦大桥引桥相平行，其中与南浦大桥引桥桥墩最近距离为 2.9 m，为了掌握隧道施工对大桥的影响，布置了此自动监控断面。本次断面剖面如图 5，隧道顶部埋深约 14 m，中心线埋深 17.2 m，隧道底部埋深 20.4 m。共设置 4 排 20 个钻孔，具体监测项目为：分层沉降、分层水平沉降、孔隙水压力，水位变化、土压力。

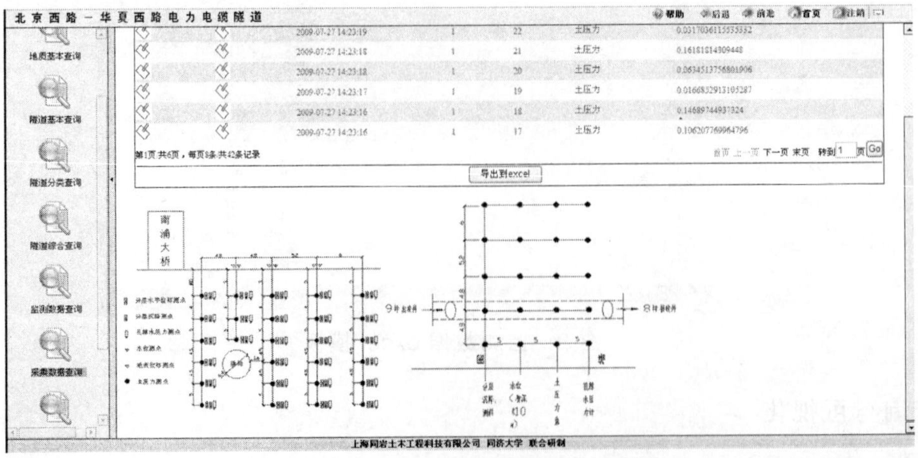

图 5 自动监控剖面图与平面图

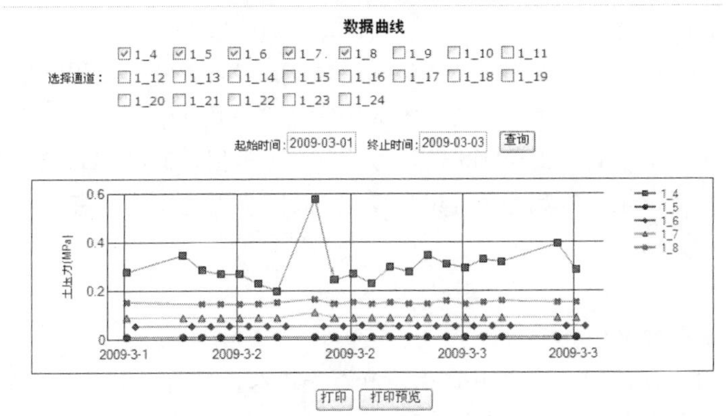

图 6 自动监控土压力实时曲线

在此系统中，通过虚拟现实技术，对整条隧道线路的周边环境进行了三维可视化，主要包括地质地层、周边建筑物、地下管线、轨道交通、隧道工作井，在隧道的推进过程中，对施工进行了可视化模拟，使有关人员能够实时了解整条隧道的施工状况。图 7 显示的是穿越南浦大桥时的三维监控环境。

图 7 微扰动三维监控环境

4 结 论

施工信息化是隧道工程建设和发展的必然趋势，本文在已有的研究基础之上，介绍了该系统在网络化、虚拟化方面的研究成果。通过 web 服务平台，相关人员可以实时了解施工监控信息，通过监测曲线分析，根据具体情况提出决策措施，为安全施工提供了方便；在虚拟施工环境，身临其境感受现场情况，实现室内办公现场化。该系统在预警报警、空间分析、控制决策等方面还需大量的研究工作。

参考文献（Referenles）：

[1] Andrea Toninil. 3D geo-mapping based on surface data for preliminary study of underground works: A case study in Val Topina (Central Italy) [J]. Engineering Geology, 2008, 99:61-69.

[2] Chungsik Yoo, Young-Woo Jeon. IT-based tunnelling risk management system (IT-TURISK) – development and implementation [J]. Tunnelling and Underground Space Technology, 2006, 21(2):190-202.

[3] Choi Yosoon, Yoon Seo-Youn. Tunneling Analyst: A 3D GIS extension for rock mass classification and fault zone analysis in tunnelling[J]. Computers and Geosciences, 2009, 35(6):1322-1333.

[4] Marte Gutierrez, Doug Bowman, An IT-based system for planning, designing and constructing tunnels in rocks [J].Tunnelling and Underground Space Technology, 2006, 21:221.

[5] Scalable Vector Graphics (SVG).http://www.w3.org/TR/1998/REC-XML-19980210, 1998.

[6] Xiaojun Li, Hehua Zhu. Digital Tunnel and Its Application in an Undersea Tunnel[J]. Electronic Journal of

Geotechnical Engineering. 2007, v12B.
[7] 胡向东，张庆贺. 盾构推进监控数据库及动态显示系统[J]. 岩石力学与工程学报，2003，11(5): 834-837.
[8] 王长虹. 数字地下空间与工程数据管理核心技术的研究及其应用[D]. 上海：同济大学，2008.
[9] 朱合华，李晓军. 数字地下空间与工程[J]. 岩石力学与工程学报，2007 (11): 2277-2288.
[10] 周文波. 盾构隧道信息化施工智能管理系统设计及应用[J]. 岩石力学与工程学报，2004(7): 5122-5127.

作者简介（Bio-data）:

袁钊，男，1983 年 2 月出生，河南许昌人，现为同济大学地下建筑与工程系硕士研究生，研究方向为盾构隧道施工信息化与数字化。

Zhao YUAN (1983—), male, postgraduate of Dept. of Geotechnical Engineering, Tongji University. Research fields: geo-digital shield tunnel information and geo-digital engineering.

E-mail: yuanzhao401@163.com

土压平衡式盾构壁后注浆量的影响因素分析

刘泉维[2, 3] 钟小春[1] 左 佳[1] 闵凡路[1] 韩月旺[1]

[1]河海大学 土木工程学院，江苏 南京 210098

[2]中铁十四局集团南京长江隧道工程指挥部，江苏 南京 211800

[3]北京交通大学 隧道及地下工程教育部工程研究中心，北京 100044

【摘 要】 盾构技术在我国地铁建设中得到广泛的应用，能有效地控制地层沉降是其重要优点之一。壁后注浆作为主动控制地层沉降的重要工序正得到越来越多重视，一般通过控制注浆量和注浆压力这两个参数来控制壁后注浆，使得实际注入量往往达到理论注浆量的 150%～200%。为什么远远超出了理论注浆量？目前无法解释这种现象，也没有注相应的理论依据。通常认为是由于姿态控制不当引起的超挖或者劈裂注浆引起的。论文从工程实例出发，从开挖面变形引起超挖、姿态控制不当超挖、注浆压力顶起等角度研究了对壁后注浆量的影响。认为开挖面变形引起的超挖量最大，能够达到理论超挖量的 25%～66%，姿态控制和注浆压力分别达到 13%左右，总的超挖率达到 150%以上，与工程实际情况吻合较好。

【关键词】 盾构；壁后注浆；开挖面变形；姿态控制；注浆量；注浆压力

STUDY ON THE FACTORS INFLUENCING ON BACKFILL GROUTING QUANTITY OF EPB SHIELD

Quanwei LIU[2,3], Xiaochun ZHONG[1], Jia ZUO[1], Fanlu Min[1], Yuewang Han[1]

[1]College of Civil Engineering, Hohai University, Nanjing 210098, Jiangsu, China;

[2]Nanjing Yangtze River Tunnel Engineering Headquarters,China Fourteenth China Railway, Group Corporation Nanjing 211800, Jiangsu, China;

[3]Tunnel and Underground Engineering Research Center of Ministry of Education, Beijing Jiaotong University, Beijing 100044, China

Abstract: The Shield tunneling method has become a major method applied in city subway construction in China, with one of the advantages that the stratum displacement can be actively controlled. For backfill grouting is a necessary and key procedure which can control settlements, it should get more attention. Usually, it is complied by two parameters: injection volume and grouting pressure, which always make the actual injection volume of grouting reach 150%~200% comparing to the theoretical value. It is hard to explain the above result in some related theory. Generally, it is considered that the phenomenon may be caused by two reason: i) the improper behavior control of the Shield tunneling machine leads to over-excavation; ii) the stratum layers are spitted by over grouting pressure. This thesis aims at the case project by analyzing the influencing factors to the grouting injection volume from three cases: i) Over-excavation caused by face deformation; ii) Over-excavation caused by the improper behavior control of the Shield tunneling machine; iii) Spitted by over grouting pressure. The results agree well with shield tunnelling engineering practice, and show that the first case takes the greatest impact, which accounts for 25%~66% of the theoretical over-excavation value, while the others account for about 13% each.

Key words: shield; backfill grouting; face deformation; behavior control; grouting volume; grouting pressure

1 引 言

盾构隧道施工由于具有良好的可较好地控制地层变形，在国内外地铁建设中得到了广泛地使用。为了便于在盾构机尾部拼装管片环和便于将管片环推出盾尾，管片环的直径必然小于盾构机直径，其中的间隙即为盾尾空隙[1]，如图 1 所示。为了主动控制土体的变形、及时稳定管片环，必须同步或及时进行空隙注浆。

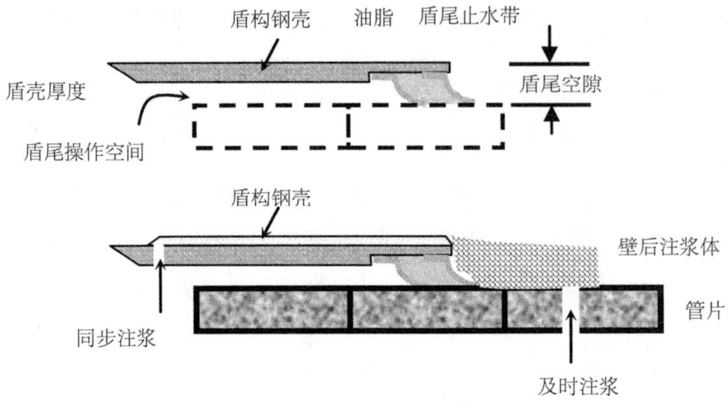

图 1 盾尾空隙及壁后注浆

根据空隙大小可以直接得到理论应注入浆液量。但实际工程中，实际注入的量远大于理论注入量。根据日本地盘工学会的调查，日本标准区间（不利用辅助工法的区间）的注浆率的实际利用情况[2]，如图 2 所示，平均为 143%。我国盾构工程界也有类似的规律[3-5]。

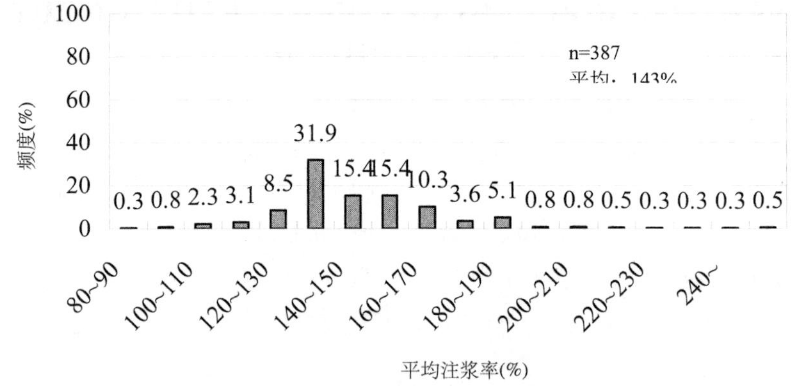

图 2 标准区间的平均注浆率

这就使得工程实践中如何有效地控制壁后注浆缺乏统一标准，一般由各家施工方经过多次摸索得到适合该地、该段的注浆参数，有时也通过注浆压力来联合控制壁后注浆。这给工程施工带来了一定地风险。

为什么实际注浆量远超过理论注浆量的壁后注浆？这就很值得开展研究工作，以明确哪些因素对注浆量有较大的影响以及影响程度如何，以便更好地指导工程实践。

2 壁后注浆机理分析

在盾构机掘进的同时，注浆材料注入盾尾空隙。在注浆压力的作用下，浆液在盾尾空隙中的扩散如图 3 所示。扩散方向包括隧道环向扩散和隧道纵向扩散。当土体性质较为软弱，在较高压力作用下浆液有可能发生劈裂注浆，浆液扩散到周围地层中，甚至流出地面，造成较大的浪费和工程危害。劈裂压主要和注浆材料的黏性、覆土压力、覆土高度与盾构直径之比有关。森等人曾经通过室内试验对黏性土的劈裂压问题进行了研究[6]，其试验公式如下所示：

$$p_f = \gamma_t h + \alpha q_u \tag{1}$$

式中，p_f 为劈裂压，γ_t 为土体湿容重，h 为隧道上覆土厚度，q_u 为土体无侧限抗压强度，系数 α 是与浆液黏性等相关的系数，一般情况下大于 1.0。从以上分析可以看出，由于软弱地层其强度较低，可能发生劈裂注浆造成浆液的流失。但大多数地层中，目前盾构施工中还没有明显证据证明存在大量的劈裂注浆现象，地质雷达现场监测数据[7]也证实这一点。

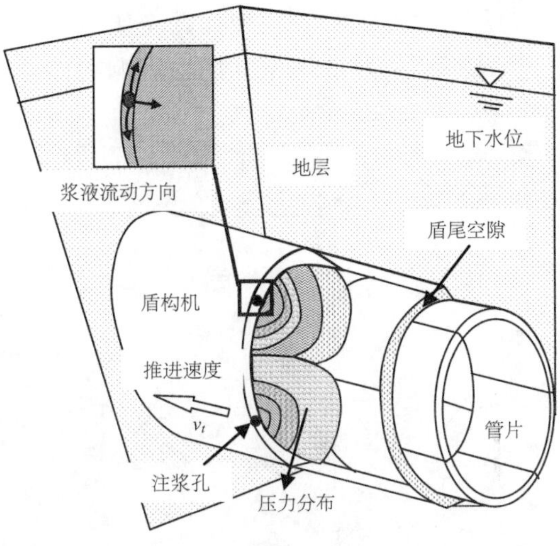

图 3 壁后注浆在盾尾空隙中的运动

壁后注浆在地层压力的作用下，在浆液初凝前部分游离水发生向地层渗透，这个可以从注浆体收缩试验中得到证明[8]。在这样的情况下，当已注入的浆液还未凝固前，新注入的浆液可能对此进行补充。这部分补充的浆液应在 5%～10%左右。

在较为坚硬的地层掘进时，盾构施工往往采用欠土压开挖。这样就形成了从盾尾空隙到开挖面的压力差，当浆液配制没有达到标准时，可能发生浆液流向开挖面，进入压力舱内。这在现场有时可从出土中看到较多的水泥浆，得到证明。

当盾构姿态控制上对设计线路存在的偏差，为了修正掘进线路，必然要进行超挖，超挖部分的体积必然由壁后注浆来填充。

3 工程实例及计算模型

某盾构区间穿越地层贯入阻力和典型剖面如图 5 和图 6 所示。主要地层大致可以分为三层，第一层为填土层，第二层为粉质夹砂粉质黏土层，属于较好地地层，常用作该地区的浅基础持力层，第三层为淤泥质粉质黏土层，地质条件较为软弱。

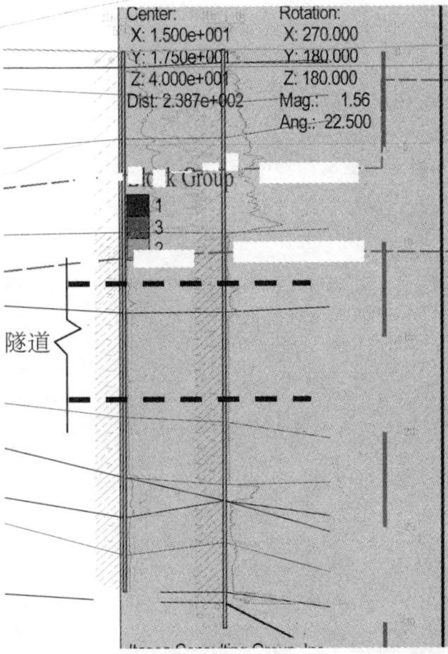

图 5 典型地层贯入阻力测试曲线

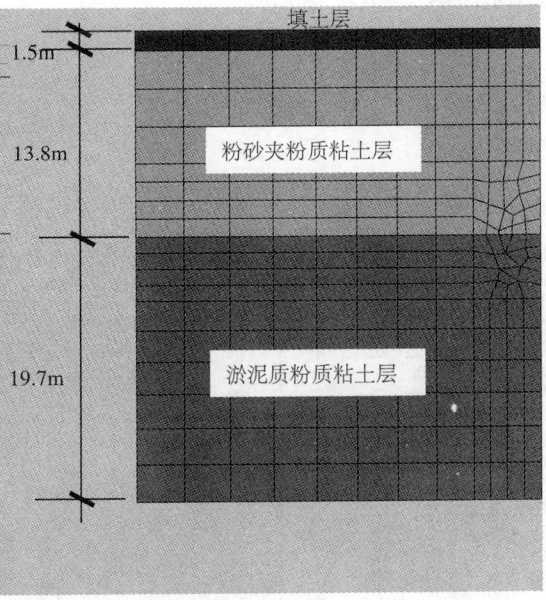

图 6 典型土层分布示意图

开挖面变形计算模型如图 7 所示，除顶部外，其他各边界均固定。

注浆压力对盾尾空隙扩大影响的计算模型如图 8 所示，除顶部外，其他各边界均固定。

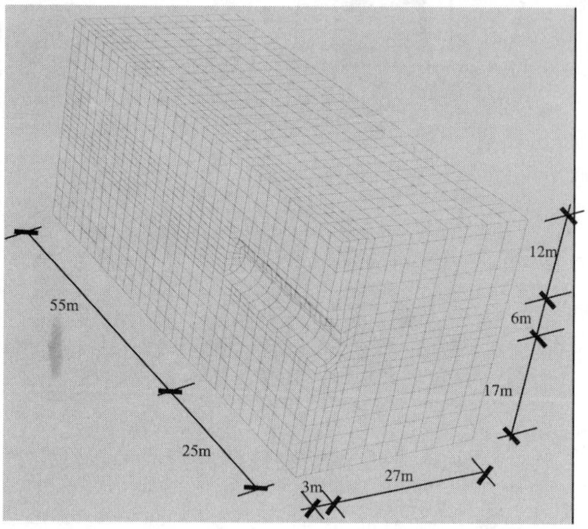

图 7 盾构开挖对地层变形影响的 $Flac^{3D}$ 计算模型

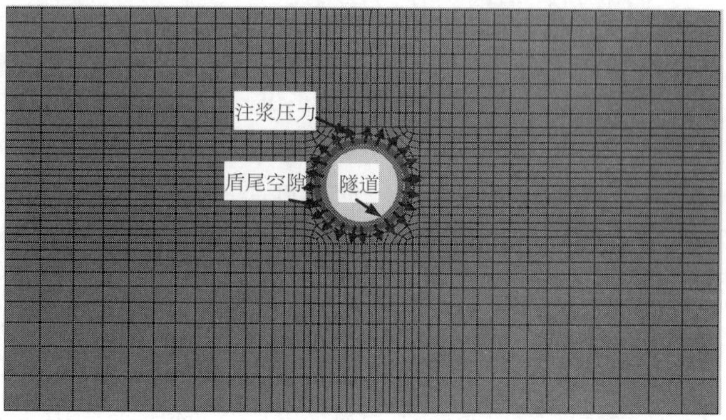

图 8 注浆压力对盾尾空隙扩大影响的 $Flac^{3D}$ 计算模型

以上两个计算模型中，土体采用摩尔-库仑模型模拟，隧道结构采用弹性模型模拟，相关参数如表 1 所示。

表 1 某区间隧道计算参数表

地层名称	天然密度（kg/m^3）	压缩模量（Mpa）	摩擦角（°）	黏聚力（kPa）	泊松比	侧压力系数
填土层	1 700	5.0	20	10	0.3	0.5
粉砂夹粉质黏土层	1 890	7.5	28	8	0.3	0.5
淤泥质粉质黏土层	1 740	6.0*	10	14	0.3	0.7
盾构隧道	2 450	3450	—	—	0.17	—

4 注浆量影响因素分析

4.1 注浆压力

为了更好地控制地层变形，通常情况下注浆压力等于或者约大于地层上覆土自重应力，这样的话必然对地层有一定的顶起作用，如图 9 所示。通常情况下其变形扩大模式可假定为半个椭圆形。

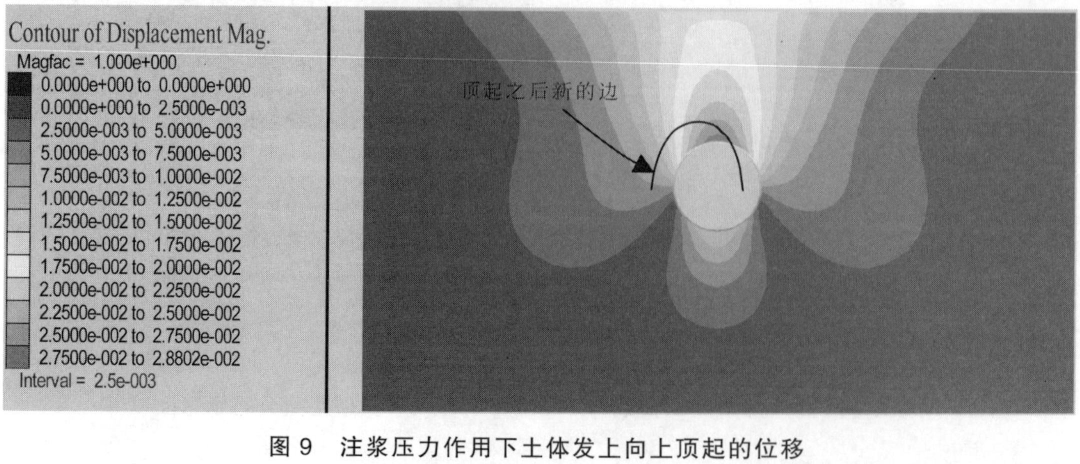

图 9 注浆压力作用下土体发上向上顶起的位移

盾构注浆压力对盾尾空隙扩大的影响如图 10 所示。从中可以看出，随着注浆压力的增大，上覆土体被顶起的位移越大，产生更大的盾尾空隙。目前盾构施工中较为常用的注浆压力为 0.25～0.3 MPa，盾尾空隙扩大率大约在 11%～13%左右，需要增加不少的注浆量，当然也更有效地控制地层沉降。

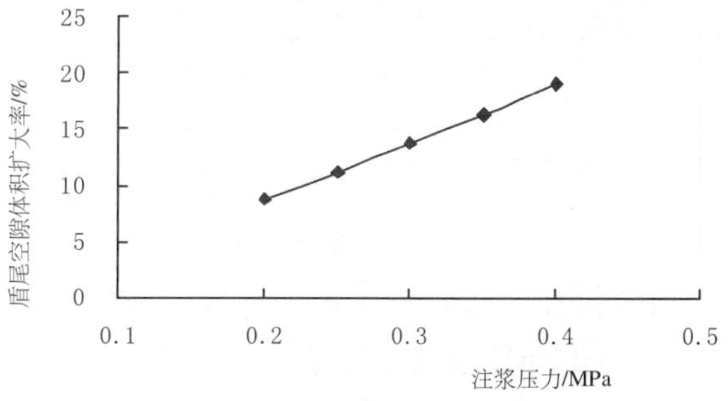

图 10　壁后注浆压力对盾尾空隙扩大的影响

4.2　支护压力不足引起的开挖面变形

随着盾构开挖面支护应力比的降低，即开挖面控制压力在降低，地层变形也在逐步增加，当支护应力比超过 0.7 以后，变形加速。这也可以从开挖面中心点的水平位移看出。地面变形曲线大约可以分为三个阶段，一是线弹性变化阶段，地层变形随着支护压力的降低缓慢线性增大；二是快速发展阶段，地层变形随着支护压力的降低快速增大；三是开挖面坍塌阶段，当位移增加到一定程度时，开挖面土体出现坍塌，并影响到地面，如图 11、图 12 和图 13 所示。从图 13 中可以看出其变形为整体向压力舱内移动，保守计算时，可以认为超挖量为盾构截面面积乘以开挖面中心点的水平位移，计算成果如表 2 所示。从中可以看出，盾构支护压力降低对盾构开挖面变形的影响较大。从现场开挖面支护压力监测值来看，支护压力略低于初始地压力，为了避免开挖面过大变形，支护应力比应控制在 0.8 以上，与理论注浆量相比的超挖率 25%～66%。

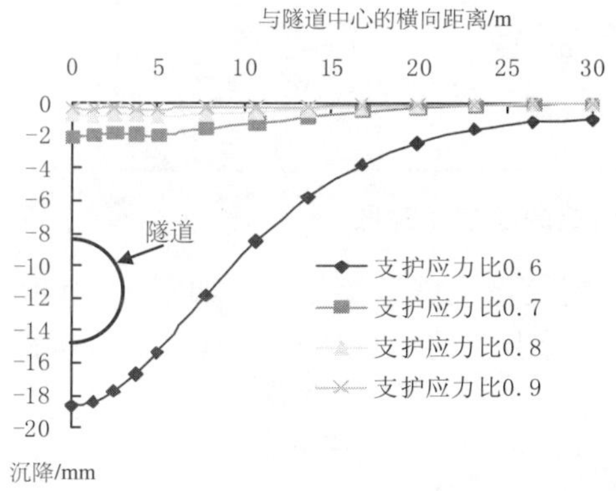

图 11　盾构开挖面上方地表沉降槽

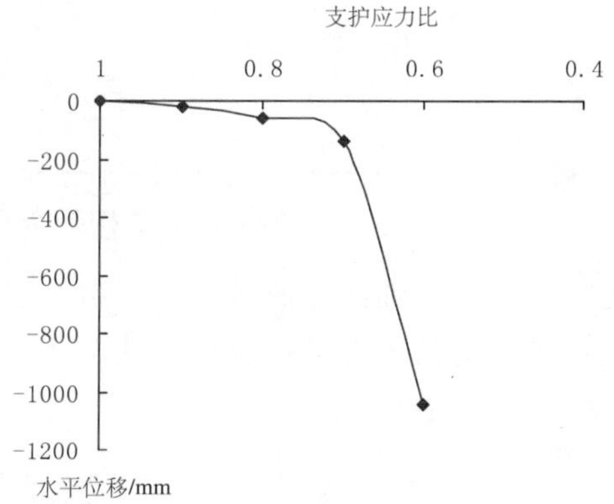

图 12　开挖面中心点随着支护应力比变化的水平位移

图 13　支护压力减少引起的位移云图

表 2 支护压力降低引起的超挖量与壁后注浆的关系

支护压力比	开挖面发生的水平位移（mm）	开挖面超挖量（m^3）	理论注浆量（m^3/m）	超挖量与理论注浆量的比值（%）
0.9	－21.7	0.66	2.69	25
0.8	－57.8	1.75		66
0.7	－137.5	4.15		157

4.3 姿态控制不当引起的超挖

盾构姿态控制不好，为了保持与设计轴线基本一致，必然需要超挖，以纠正盾构姿态。盾构姿态不良引起的超挖量如图 14 所示。超挖量的计算公式如下所示：

$$\Delta V = \xi\pi\left(D_1^2 - D^2\right)B/4 \tag{2}$$

式中，D_1 为超挖后的开挖截面直径，$D_1=D+L\cdot\tan\alpha$，D 为盾构机直径，L 为盾构机长度，B 为管片环宽度，α 为盾构机偏离设计轴线角度，ξ 为超挖范围影响系数，一般情况下为半圆超挖，系数可取 0.5～0.7。

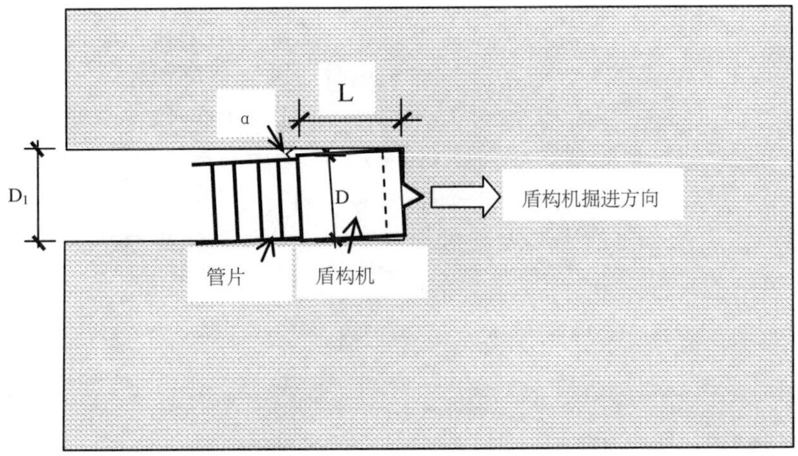

图 14 盾构姿态不良引起的超挖示意图

随着盾构机偏离设计轴线距离的增大，由此引起的超挖量也就逐渐增大，如图 15 所示。一般情况下盾构机偏离设计轴线的角度在 0.4°以下，从图 15 中可以看出超挖部分体积占盾尾空隙体积的 12.5%，不容忽略。

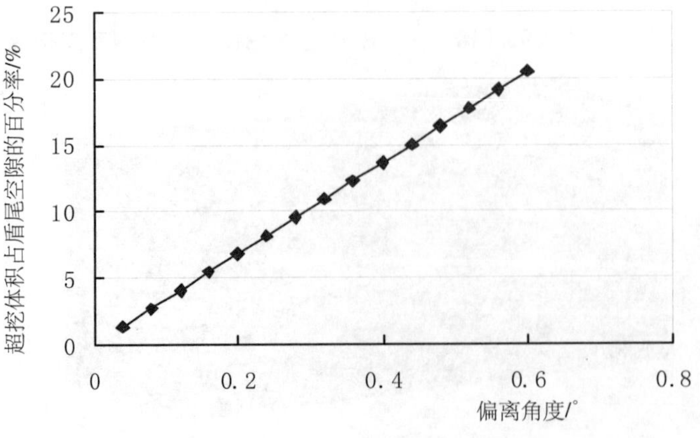

图 15 盾构超挖对盾尾空隙扩大的影响

5 结 论

通过以上分析，可以看出，盾构隧道壁后注浆量受到较多因素的控制，论文对各个影响进行了定量分析，得到了如下结论：

（1）由于开挖面支护压力不足引起的开挖面变形，必然导致盾构机超挖，而且其超挖量不可忽略。这种超挖必然被紧接其后的盾尾壁后注浆所充填，这应该是壁后注浆实际注入量超过理论注浆量的主要影响因素，达到 25%～66%以上。

（2）注浆压力一般略超过地层初始地应力，这有利于较好地控制地层变形。超过地层初始地应力的注浆压力对地层顶起引起盾尾空隙扩大效应大约 13%左右。

（3）盾构姿态控制不当，必然引起盾构机超挖，在不超过规范规定的最大偏离距离时，超挖引起的盾尾空隙扩大效应在 12.5%以内。

（4）考虑开挖面支护压力不足、注浆压力、盾构姿态不当引起的超挖，再加上浆液凝固前在地层压力的作用下发生的固结、导致浆液中的部分游离水渗透地层中的损失 5%～10%左右，盾尾壁后注浆将达到 150%～200%，与目前我国盾构工程实践较为吻合。

参考文献（Referenles）：

[1] 朱伟，陈仁俊. 盾构隧道施工技术现状及展望（第 1 讲）——盾构隧道基本原理及在我国的使用情况[J]. 岩土工程界，2001, 4(11): 19-21.

[2] 牛清山，陈凤英，徐华，译. 盾构法的调查 · 设计 · 施工[M]. 北京：中国建筑工业出版社，2008.

[3] 赵书银. 盾构隧道惰性浆液同步注浆技术应用[J]. 铁道标准设计, 2003(12): 20-22.

[4] 张凤祥，朱合华，傅德明. 盾构隧道[M]. 北京:人民交通出版社, 2004.

[5] 周文波. 盾构法隧道施工技术及应用[M]. 北京:中国建筑工业出版, 2004.

[6] 森. シールドトンネル裹込め注入および切羽泥水压よわ黏性土地盘の劈裂现象[J]. トンネル地下，土木工学会, 1991: 30-34.

[7] 田海洋. 越江公路盾构隧道壁后注浆探地雷达探测试验及应用研究[D]. 同济大学硕士学位论文，2008.

[8] 韩月旺，梁精华，袁小会. 盾构隧道壁后注浆体变形模型及土体位移分析[J]. 岩石力学与工程学报，2007, 26(2): 3646-3652.

作者简介（Bio-data）：

刘泉维（1977 年—），男，2007 年毕业于中国海洋大学岩土工程专业，获工学硕士学位，北京交通大学隧道及地下工程专业在读博士研究生，目前在南京长江隧道工程从事超大直径盾构隧道科研及管理工作。

Personal Introduction:

Chinese Name: Quanwei LIU

Sex: Male

Born: 1977

University: Graduated from Ocean University of China in 2007, Master Degree

Major: Geotechnical Engineering

Direction: Undertaking Study and Management of Shield Tunnel

E-mail: Liuquanwei@tom.com

软土盾构隧道工程综合效益评估

尹 玫[1] 芮 易[1] 闫治国[2]
[1]同济大学 土木工程学院地下建筑与工程系，上海 200092
[2]同济大学 岩土工程重点实验室，上海 200092

【摘 要】 为研究软土盾构隧道工程的综合效益，分析各因素指标，并采用改进的层次分析法区分不同指标的权重差异。综合考虑各影响因素，提出一具有科学性，合理性，可操作性的模糊综合评价方法。
【关键词】 模糊综合评价；层次分析；指标因素；权重

COMPREHENSIVE BENEFIT EVALUATION ON SHIELD TUNNEL ENGINEERING IN SOFT SOIL

Mei YIN[1], Yi RUI[1], Zhiguo YAN[2]
[1]Department of Geotechnical Engineering, Tongji University, Shanghai 200092, China;
[2]Key Laboratory of Geotechnical and Underground Engineering of Ministry of Education, Tongji University, Shanghai 200092, China

Abstract: In order to study comprehensive benefit of shield tunnel engineering in soft soil, all relevant fact indicators were analyzed. The improved AHP method was applied to distinguish the weight difference between different indicators. Considering the impact of various factors, a scientific, reasonable and feasible method of fuzzy synthetic evaluation was introduced.
Key words: fuzzy synthetic evaluation; AHP; indicators of factors; weight

1 引 言

目前软土盾构隧道设计方案决策，仅考虑建设成本的投入，很少考虑到维护成本、社会成本和环境成本，因而有较大的缺陷和局限性。这直接导致了盾构隧道维护成本、建设期交通堵塞成本及环境成本过高，社会负面影响大的问题。因此，软土盾构隧道工程综合效益评估正是针对这一问题。要解决这一问题，必须要首先建立起软土盾构隧道工程的科学的综合的评价体系，而不只是像以往的评价那样只侧重于某些方面，要对示范工程的经济效益、社会效益和环境效益进行综合的评估。相比于经济效益，工程的社会效益和环境效益是难以定量评价的，但是对于诸如盾构隧道的地下工程来说，社会效益和环境效益往往比经济效益更能体现出工程和技术的优越性，也能跟好的反映工程的综合效益和“以人为本”的思想。

软土盾构隧道工程的综合效益评价是一个层次复杂、因素较多的多变量系统，在我国，尚未建立一套标准的软土盾构隧道工程综合效益评价体系，主要原因在于，地下空间的发展在我国还处于起步阶段，因此，对其综合评价体系的研究极具现实意义。

2 软土盾构隧道工程综合效益评估方法

由于盾构隧道工程十分复杂，其效益反映在诸多方面。因此，在对盾构隧道工程进行评价时应该综合考虑多重因素的影响。为此，按照研究综合评价问题的一般原理和步骤需要对软土盾构隧道工程的综合效益进行研究。以盾构隧道工程综合效益的评价结果为目标，先对影响因素进行深入分析，确定地下盾构隧道工程的评价指标，以此为基础，合理构造盾构隧道工程综合评价指标体系，使待解决问题层次化；然后根据组成指标体系的各评价指标的特性，建立各因素指标的判定标准，以实现对个指标的判定；再根据盾构隧道工程综合效益评价的特点，采用一定的方法，确定各指标的权重；最后根据上述层次化的指标体系[1,2]和指标判定标准，采用一定的评价模型，以实现对软土盾构隧道工程综合效益的评价。

2.1 确定综合评价指标体系

软土盾构隧道工程的综合效益评价应从工程质量、经济效益、社会效益、环境效益等方面来考虑，每一方面又可以用一些因素指标来反映，并建立相应的评分标准，具体见图 1 所示：

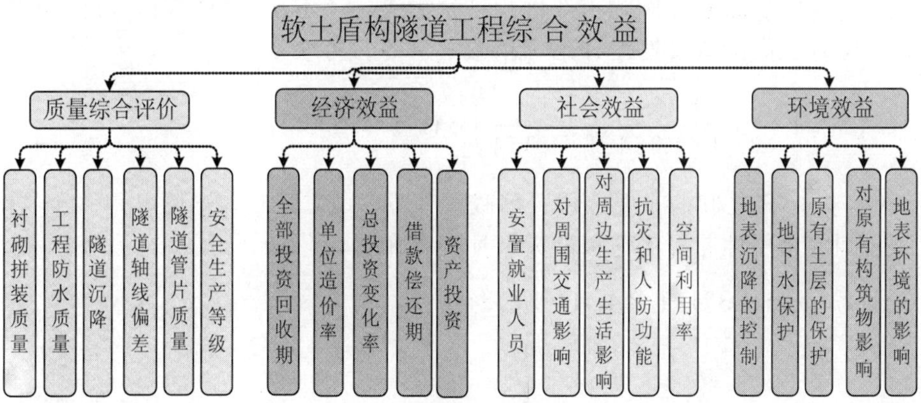

图 1 软土盾构隧道综合效益体系图

仅以经济效益中的投资回收期和质量综合评价中的工程防水质量为例，对其判定标准做一介绍。

图 1 中全部投资回收期是隧道工程经济效益的重要指标，它是指使累计的经济效益等于最初的投资费用所需的时间，计算公式为：投资回收期（Pt）=[累计净现金流量出现正值年数]-1+[上年累计净现金流量绝对值/当年净现金流量]。将项目评价求出的投资回收期(Pt)与部门或行业基准投资回收期(Pc)比较，当 Pt<0.6 Pc 时，应认为项目在这项指标评定等级为优。当 Pt<0.6 Pc 时，应认为项目在这项指标评定等级为优；当 0.6 Pc<Pt<0.8 Pc 时，认为项目在这项指标评定等级为良；当 0.8 Pc<Pt<1.0 Pc 时，认为项目在这项指标评定等级为中；当 1.0 Pc<Pt<1.2 Pc 时，认为项目在这项指标评定等级为合格；当 Pt>1.2 Pc 时，认为项目在这项指标评定等级为不合格。

工程防水质量是隧道工程质量综合评价的一个重要指标。本研究将工程防水质量分为五级。优：不允许渗水，结构表面无湿渍；良：不允许漏水，结构表面可有少量湿渍（湿渍总面积不大于总防水面积的 1%，单个湿渍面积不大于 0.1 m^2）；中：有少量漏水点，不得有线漏和漏泥沙（单个湿渍面不大于 0.3 m^2，单个漏水点的漏水量不大于 2.5 L/d，任意 100 m^2 漏水点不超过 7 处）；合格：有漏水点，不得有线流和漏泥砂（整个工程平均漏水量不大于 2 L/m^2 · d，任意 100 m^2 防水面积的平均漏水量不大于 4 L/m^2 · d）；不合格：有漏水点，出现线流或漏泥沙。

2.2 指标体系的权重分析

本文采用层次分析法，来对工程的综合效益进行评价，采用一种改进的标度法——乘积标度法[1,2,3]。乘积标度法的思路是，在诊断指标重要性的两两比较时，不先划分过多的等级，而只是设置两个等级，即评价指标 A 和评价指标 B 的重要性“相同”或“稍微大”，然后以此作为基础进行乘积分析。这样可以使确定方法具有更大的灵活性。

在对指标 A 和指标 B 进行两两比较时，对“相同”和“稍微大”一般有如下数量上的大体概念，即：认为“相同”是允许指标 A 和指标 B 之间存在微小的差别（绝对的“相同”是不存在的），通常在做工程计算时允许误差为 10%。本文参考常用的 9/9~9/1 标度法[1]、10/10~18/2 标度法[1]、指数标度法标度方法[1]，取后 3 种标度法中“稍微大”的标度值的平均值作为标度，即

$$\omega_A : \omega_B = \frac{1.286 + 1.500 + 1.277}{3} : 1 = 1.354 : 1 \tag{1}$$

并确定简单二层评价系统指标权重的乘积标度法的基本步骤为：

（1）根据经验或实测资料，对 m 个指标定性地进行重要性排序。

（2）对评价指标进行两两对比，确定指标 A 和指标 B 之间的重要性差异属于“相同”或“稍微大”。当指标 A 和指标 B 之间的重要性“相同”时，取权重为

$$(\omega_A, \omega_B) = (0.5, 0.5) \tag{2}$$

当指标 A 的重要性和指标 B 之间的重要性用“稍微大”还不足以反映时，可以用多个“稍微大”来反映。如当认为 A 与 B 之间的重要性差异比“稍微大”时，可取

$$(\omega_A, \omega_B) = \left(\frac{1.354}{1+1.354}, \frac{1}{1+1.354}\right) = (0.575, 0.425) \tag{3}$$

（3）当指标 A 与指标 B 之间的重要性用“稍微大”还不足以反映时，可以用多个“稍微大”来反映。如当认为 A 和 B 之间的重要性差异比“稍微大”还要“稍微大”时，可取

$$\omega_A : \omega_B = (1.354 \times 1.354) : 1 = 1.833 : 1 \tag{4}$$

依次类推。

（4）将同曾 m 个评价指标两两比较的结果进行综合，并满足归一化条件，即 $\sum_{i}^{m} \omega_i = 1$，最终得到下一层各指标对相领上层研究对象的层次单排序权重。

2.3 模糊综合评判

由于软土盾构隧道工程综合效益是一个外延不太明确而内涵丰富的概念，效益的好坏是模糊的。而且其涉及的因素也比较复杂，一方面，有些指标不能用精确的数量来描述，只能是模糊概念；另一方面，各种因素的变化与综合效益之间不存在一一对应的函数关系，不可能建立精确的数学模型来求解。因此，引入模糊理论来对软土盾构隧道工程综合效益进行评价。模糊综合评价的基本步骤：

（1）确定评价指标集，根据评价对象的特点，确定评价指标集 $C = \{c_1, c_2, \cdots, c_m\}$。

（2）确定评语等级集合，根据评价对象的特点，将评价指标划分为若干等级，制定相应的等级判定准则，从而将定性指标转化为定量指标。假设评语有 n 个，评语等级集合为：$V = \{v_1, v_2, \cdots, v_n\}$。同时将评语等级进行数值化。

（3）确定评价指标的权重向量，一般情况下，各评价指标对被评价对象并非是同等重要的，各个指标对总体表现的影响是不同的，因此在模糊合成之前要确定权重向量 $\omega = \{\omega_1, \omega_2, \cdots, \omega_m\}$。

（4）利用隶属函数进行单因素模糊评价，建立模糊关系隶属矩阵 R。

（5）进行复合运算得到综合评价结果向量，$X \cdot R^T = (z_1, z_2, \cdots, z_m) \overset{\Delta}{=} Z$。式中：$z_j$ 表示评价对象中第 j 个评价指标的综合评价结果。

（6）对评价目标进行模糊综合分析 $F = f(\omega, Z)$。

3 工程实例

3.1 工程简介

本工程为上海长江隧道工程，工程自浦东五号沟，接上海市郊区环线，以隧道方式穿越长江南港水域，经长兴岛，以桥梁方式跨越长江北港水域止于崇明岛陈家镇，连接陈海公路。工程全长 25.5 km，其中南港隧道长 8.95 km，长江北港桥梁长 10.3 km，陆域接线长 6.25 km。隧道外径 15.0 m，内径 13.7 m。

3.2 权重分析

上海长江隧道工程综合效益评价采用上面介绍的改进的层次分析法研究，首先建立递阶层次结构图如图 1 所示通过乘积标度法[3]，得出在单一准则下的相对权重（即单排序）后，在此基础上进行递阶层次结构总排序，即得出总准则下底层元素的组合权重，见表 1。

表 1 递阶层次结构总排序

指标层 C1~C21	目标层 A				结构层次总排序（组合权重）
	准则层 B1 0.261	准则层 B2 0.353	准则层 B3 0.193	准则层 B4 0.193	
C1	0.164				0.042
C2	0.222				0.058
C3	0.164				0.042
C4	0.164				0.042
C5	0.164				0.042
C6	0.121				0.032
C7		0.258			0.091
C8		0.258			0.091
C9		0.179			0.063
C10		0.125			0.044
C11		0.179			0.063
C12			0.217		0.042
C13			0.312		0.060
C14			0.217		0.042
C15			0.151		0.053
C16			0.105		0.020
C17				0.161	0.031
C18				0.112	0.022
C19				0.232	0.045
C20				0.334	0.064
C21				0.161	0.031

表格中，A 表示软土盾构隧道工程综合效益、B1 表示质量综合评价、B2 表示经济效益、B3 表示环境效益、B4 表示社会效益、C1 表示衬砌拼装质量、C2 表示工程防水质量、C3 表示隧道沉降、C4 表示隧道轴线偏差、C5 表示隧道管片质量、C6 表示安全生产等级、C7 表示全部投资回收期、C8 表示单位造价变化率、C9 表示总投资变化率、C10 表示借贷偿还期、C11 表示资产投资、C12 表示安置就业人员、C13 表示对周围交通影响、C14 表示对周边生产生活影响、C15 表示抗灾和人防功能、C16 表示空间利用率、C17 表示地表沉降的控制、C18 表示地下水保护、C19 表示原有土层的保护、C20 表示对原有构筑物影响、C21 表示地表环境的影响。

3.3 模糊综合评价

在进行模糊评价，除了以上建立的指标体系和指标权重计算外，还有一个关键步骤就是在前面判定标准的基础上，建立各个指标的评语等级的隶属函数，而不是简单的评判优良中差。目前还无法用理论来证明对隶属函数选择效果的好坏，主要是根据实践经验来选取。对于定性指标和隶属度为明集(非模糊集合)的单值选择问题，由于其描述多为语言变量进行数字赋值，为方便起见，可采用单值型。对于定量指标，本研究采用 Cauchy 分布，其主要类型有三种，见图 2。

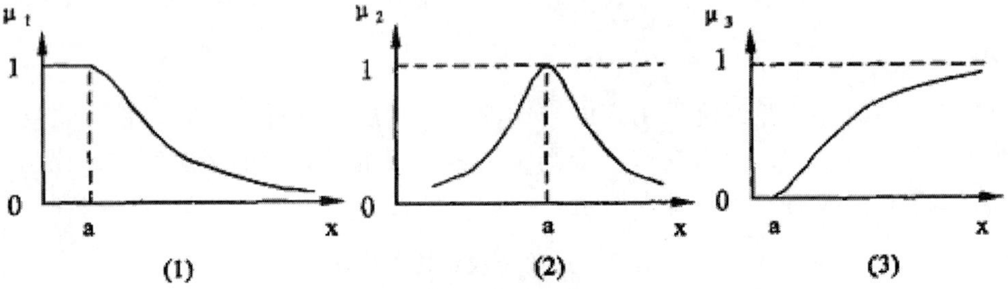

图 2 Cauchy 分布隶属函数

针对本文研究的软土盾构隧道工程综合效益，在这里对经济效益中全部投资回收期这一指标作详细说明。其隶属函数可以如下表示：

$$\mu_1(Pc)=\begin{cases}1 & ;Pc\leqslant 0.6Pt\\ \dfrac{1}{1+0.2(Pc-0.6Pt)^2} & ;Pc>0.6Pt\end{cases} \tag{5}$$

$$\mu_2(Pc)=\frac{1}{1+0.6(Pc-0.7Pt)^2} \tag{6}$$

$$\mu_3(Pc)=\frac{1}{1+0.6(Pc-0.9Pt)^2} \tag{7}$$

$$\mu_4(Pc)=\frac{1}{1+0.6(Pc-1.1Pt)^2} \tag{8}$$

$$\mu_5(Pc)=\begin{cases}\dfrac{1}{1+0.2(Pc-1.2Pt)^2} & ;Pc\leqslant 1.2Pt\\ 1 & ;Pc>1.2Pt\end{cases} \tag{9}$$

式 5、式 6 分别是评价等级优、良、中、合格、不合格的隶属函数，其中 Pt 为投资回收期，Pc 为部门或行业基准投资回收期。通过隶属度概念的引入，对全部投资回收期这一指标的判定不再是一个简单的数字，而是一个通过隶属函数求得的模糊评价向量。

最终通过上述的步骤得到上海长江隧道综合评价体系中每个指标的模糊评价向量，乘上权值相加便可以得到软土盾构隧道综合效益的一级模糊评价结果。其中质量综合评价 B1：R1=（0.496，0.431，0.043，0.017，0.013）经济综合评价 B2：R2=（0.258，0.603，0.103，0.024，0.012）环境综合评价 B3：R3=（0.321，0.577，0.086，0.009，0.007）社会综合评价 B4：R4=（0.159，0.467，0.254，0.076，0.044）。

在一级模糊评判的基础上，并根据准则层权重可以进一步得到二级模糊评判的最终评价向量

$$Z=\omega_a\times(R_1,R_2,R_3,R_4,R_5)$$

$$Z=(0.313,0.527,0.113,0.029,0.025)$$

分别给评语等级优、良、中、差、合格、不合格赋以值 95 分、85 分、75 分、65 分、55 分，就可以得到单值化的上海长江隧道综合效益评价结果 86.265 分。

4 结 语

（1）建立软土盾构隧道工程综合评价的指标体系，利用层次分析法，对工程进行综合评价，该方法实用性强，可加少人为因素的影响，增强了决策的客观性和科学性。

（2）对层次分析法中单一准则下的相对权重，采用改进的乘积法计算，使得所得权重更具客观、合理性。

（3）模糊评判方法理论性强、使用性好并具可操作性，评价结果客观合理，并且利于软土盾构隧道的综合效益评判的定量化。

（4）为完善该评价体系，结合具体实践，今将在后续研究中逐步解决软土盾构隧道工程评价方法和完善评价涉及等问题,以便进一步提高该评价方法的实用性和可靠性。

参考文献（Referenles）：

[1] 侯岳衡，沈德家．指数标度及其与几种标度的比较．系统工程理论与实践，1995，15(10)：43-46.

[2] 吕厚伟，马成松．建筑工程评标中模糊层次分析法的应用[J]．水利与建筑工程学报，2007，5（2）：61-65.

[3] 赵焕臣．层次分析法[M]．北京：科学出版社，1986.9.

作者简介（Bio-data）：

尹玫，女，1984年9月出生，2007年毕业于安徽理工大学土木工程学院工业与民用建筑系，获得学士学位，现为同济大学土木工程学院地下建筑与工程系硕士。主要从事专业及研究方向：地下工程综合效益评估方法研究，基于人工神经网的模糊评估系统研究。

Mei YIN, female, born Sep 15th, 1984, graduated fromAn Hui university of science & technology Civil Engineering.Now she is studying inTongji University Geotechnical Engineering for Master Degree.Major and Research Fields: The method of comprehensive assessment for Underground engineering and Fuzzy assessment system based on artificial neural network.

E-mail: enid_915@sina.com

南京长江隧道冲槽段大直径泥水盾构开挖面稳定研究

王 胤[1] 袁大军[1] 肖 衡[1] 黄清飞[1] 刘泉维[2]
[1]北京交通大学 隧道及地下工程教育部工程中心，北京 100044
[2]中铁十四局集团有限公司，山东 济南 250014

【摘 要】 泥水式盾构工法几乎是水底隧道特别是过江跨海软土隧道施工的必选工法，而在施工过程中的一个关键问题就是如何控制开挖面稳定。南京长江隧道直径大、水压高，特别是江中冲槽地段覆土较小且地形突变，如何以泥水压力维持开挖面稳定称为工程成败的关键。以往的研究和经验都以平坦地面考虑泥水压力及泥水特性的设定来维持开挖面稳定，而在冲槽和地形突变的地段没有很好的理论和经验。本研究用已有的土压力计算方法对南京长江隧道小覆土，特别是冲槽和地形突变施工风险极大地段进行理论分析和计算，得出了保持开挖面稳定所需要的泥水压力的上下限值为工程所用，使得盾构安全顺利通过该地段，也为以后类似的工程设计施工提供了宝贵经验。

【关键词】 泥水盾构；开挖面稳定；泥水压力；小覆土；高水压；冲槽

STUDY ON CUTTING FACE STABILITY OF YANGTZE RIVER TUNNEL DURING LARGE DIAMETRE SLURRY SHIELD TUNNELING IN STAMPING NOTCHES

Yin WANG[1], Dajun YUAN[1], Heng XIAO[1], Qingfei HUANG[1], Quanwei LIU[2]
[1]Research Center of Tunneling and Underground Works, Beijingjiaotong University, Beijing 100044, China;
[2]CRCC 14th Bureau Group Co., Ltd. Jinan 250014, Shandong China

Abstract: The slurry shield operation is the required constructive measure in underwater tunnel, especially in the cohesive soil ground across river or sea. The key point in construction is to keep cutting face stable by controlling slurry pressure. The large diameter of Yangtze River Tunnel, the high water pressure, the thin soil and especially the sharply discontinuous terrain in the stamping notches all make threats to the project. How to maintain the cutting face stability is the key point to the success of passing through. The previous studies and experiences of slurry pressure are all based on even and flat terrain and slurry characteristics to maintain cutting face stability. However, there is no related theory and experience which can be well applied in the section of stamping notches, where the terrain is discontinuous. This study applies previous earth pressure calculating method to analyze and calculate the slurry pressure in the dangerous terrain, and the calculation results provide the upper and lower limitations of slurry pressure, which makes shield pass through the terrain securely and successfully and also offer precious experience to later similar construction design.

Key words: slurry shield; cutting face stability; slurry pressure; shallow cover; high water pressure; stamping notches

1 引 言

相对于盾构施工技术的不断发展，对其施工中引起的开挖面稳定相关方面的分析方法及理论也在不断发展。在一些盾构法工程应用较多的国家如英国、日本、德国等，其关于开挖面稳定相关理论研究已经取得不少研究成果，与之相比，国内盾构施工技术刚刚起步，相关研究还处于初始阶段。根据目前研究的泥水盾构施工中土体的应力变化，分析可能引起开挖面发生失稳的主要原因是：盾构开挖面泥水压力不能有效的平衡前方土压力和孔隙水压的共同作用，或泥浆系统不能有效的保持泥水压力作用，泥水压力的过小或过大，造成了泥水盾构施工开挖面的失稳。

因此，开挖面支护压力的确定是泥水盾构在开挖过程中的一个重要问题，是工程中的关键。在现有国内外关于泥水盾构开挖面的稳定研究中，大多理论都是基于一般的地形条件和掘进状态，即：开挖面前方覆土厚度变化不大，地面平坦，盾构机基本处于水平掘进状态，地层条件对盾构影响较小。在这种条件下，国内外学者在分析开挖面失稳破坏模式的基础上提出了许多计算模型。根据开挖面失稳破坏机理，开挖面极限支护压力的计算模型主要包括微细观分析模型和宏观力学分析模型，其中宏观力学分析模型大体又分为塑性极限理论分析方法及基于仓筒理论的楔形体力学分析模型。

（1）微观破坏分析模型。该模型主要分析泥水盾构法在无黏性或低黏性地层中开挖面土体单个颗粒由于重力作用失去稳定脱离整个土体，而相邻颗粒随后继续失去稳定，逐渐发展最终导致局部或整个开挖面破坏。

（2）塑性极限分析理论。塑性极限分析理论通过假设开挖面前方滑动块的形状，利用上、下限定理来计算开挖面支护力的最大最小值。Broms-Bennermark（1967）最早提出了黏土中不排水开挖条件下的开挖面稳定系数法，如下式表示：

$$N = (\sigma_s - \gamma H - \sigma_t)/S_u \tag{1}$$

（3）楔形体模型。楔形体理论模型是通过假定开挖面前方滑动区域为棱柱体形状，通过力的平衡来求解最小支护压力，模型有采用二维对数螺旋线滑移面计算方法、二维直线滑移面计算方法和三维筒仓计算理论。

三维筒仓模型能够反应开挖面前方土体失稳变形的三维问题，在极限压力研究中得到较为广泛的应用，其假定开挖面前方土体滑动区域由位于开挖面前方的楔型块和上方的棱柱体两部分组成（图 1 所示），开挖面前方的楔型块受到的作用力为：① 土体自重；② 沿着滑动面 ADE, BCF 和 ABFE 周围土体作用的正应力及剪应力；③ 作用于面 ABCD 上的开挖面支护作用力；④ 开挖面顶部至地表面松动棱柱体作用于面 DEFC 的竖向作用力。通过滑动块上力的平衡可以得出面 ABCD 上作用力的大小，通过假定开挖面前方楔型块不同楔型量（值大小），可以得到不同值对应面 ABCD 作用力大小，则最大值即为保证开挖面稳定的极限支护压力值。

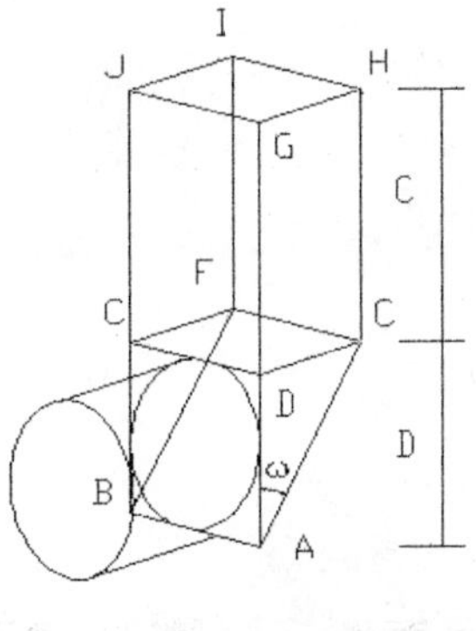

图 1 三维筒仓理论模型

2 小覆土高水压的南京长江隧道

南京长江隧道的情况极为复杂，如图 2 所示，① 该隧道是当今世界上盾构直径第二大的超大盾构隧道，盾构隧道直径达到 14.50 m；② 隧道在江底穿越的最小覆土厚度 10.2 m；③ 隧道内线路最大纵坡 4.5%，最大坡长 1 130 m；最小竖曲线半径 $R=7\ 500$ m；④ 在江中段盾构机工作压力约 6.5 bar，在同等直径及更大直径泥水盾构项目中是世界最大的；⑤ 并且在穿越时经过冲槽地形突变地段，施工风险极大。

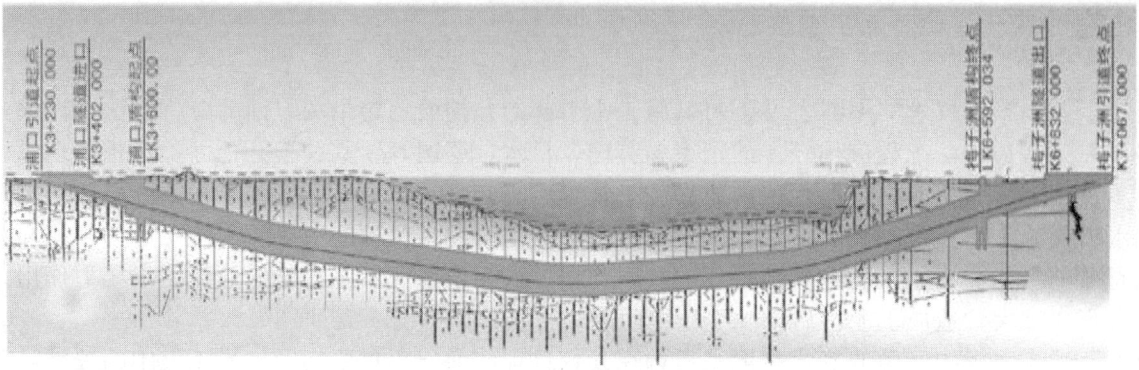

图 2 南京长江隧道工程纵断面图

这种复杂的情况一方面使得开挖面的稳定控制显得尤为重要，另一方面又对泥水压力的计算造成极大困难。首先在高水压和小覆土这种情况下，为防止事故发生必须严格控制开挖面稳定。其次，因为隧道路线有坡度，而且受冲槽段地形突变的影响，使得在计算泥水压力时，不能按照以往的理论研究和经验公式，只考虑开挖面土体的厚度，必须考虑开挖面前方覆土厚度对开挖面滑动土体的作用和松动区的超载影响（如图 3 中箭头所示）。而考虑不同范围的前方土体和超载又会使计算结果有很大差别，如图 3 中①、②部分所示，只考虑土体①和同时考虑土体①②，后者得出的结果肯定远大于前者，过度的考虑这种影响又会造成泥水劈裂、冒浆的事故。因此，为尽量得出准确水压力，必须解决好上述问题。

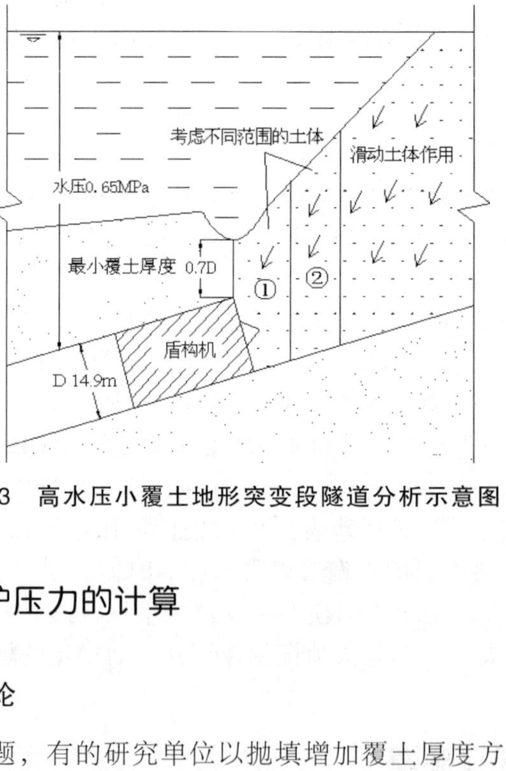

图 3 高水压小覆土地形突变段隧道分析示意图

3 南京长江隧道开挖面支护压力的计算

3.1 开挖面支护压力的计算理论

针对南京长江隧道的这些问题，有的研究单位以抛填增加覆土厚度方案来解决。而本文考虑用朗肯土法和二维法村山公式计算泥水压力。

朗肯土压力法：首先采用国内普遍使用的朗肯主动土压力公式及静止土压力公式计算盾构中心泥水支护压力的下限值和上限值，并在此基础上，加上一个泥水平衡盾构的浮动压力（20 kPa）作为安全余度。这种压力设定方法在一般的实际工程中已经得到了很好的验证。

$$P_a = P_1 + P_2 + P_3 = \gamma_W \times h + K_a \times (\gamma - \gamma_W) \times H - 2 \times C \times \sqrt{K_a} + 20 \quad (2)$$

$$P_0 = P_1 + P_2 + P_3 = \gamma_W \times h + K_0 \times (\gamma - \gamma_W) \times H + 20 \quad (3)$$

二维对数螺旋线滑移面计算模型：为了考虑前土体对滑动面的影响，本文采用了村山氏等学者根据二维试验及施工时的塌方状况提出了二维法村山公式。村山公式的基本原理如图 4 前方土体的平衡,作为滑动力有开挖面前方的滑动土块重量(W_f)和它上部的松动土压(Q)；作为阻力有泥水过剩压力(在顶部的泥水压和地下水压的压差△P_f)，将以上三个力对滑动中心点 O 点的力矩平衡。根据设定的开挖面稳定的安全系数 F_s 可以求出泥水过剩压力。并最终求得极限泥水支护压力。

$$F_s = \frac{M}{M_w + M_Q} = \frac{M}{W_f \cdot l_w + Q \cdot l_a} \tag{4}$$

其中 M——泥水压力产生的阻力力矩；

M_w——开挖面前方滑动土体自重产生的力矩；

M_Q——松动土压产生的力矩。

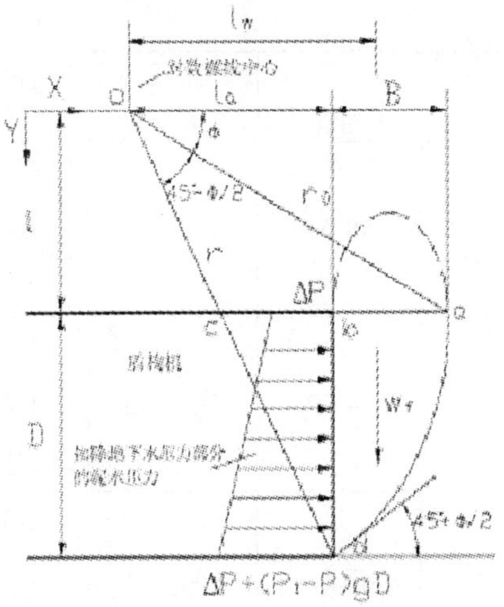

图 4 村山公式基本原理

3.2 计算断面选取

在具体计算过程中，由于是否考虑前方土体和取不同范围的前方土体会对泥水压力的计算结果产生影响，为考虑这种影响，得出准确的泥水压力值，本文根据南京长江隧道实际工程情况，对江中粉细砂段和风险最大的冲槽地段进行仔细分析，选取了开挖面稳定难度最大盾构线路中心附近的变坡点和位于冲槽段水压最大，覆土最浅和冲槽段凹点的 8 个断面，并分别在开挖面前 1/3 直径，1/2 直径，2/3 直径长度处取值考虑 1/3、1/2、2/3 不同坡长松动区超载的影响，进行泥水压力的比较判定。

8 个断面，如图 5 示。其中，盾构线路中心里程附近的选取 3 个断面，分别为 K5+90，K5+100，K5+110；在位于冲槽段水压最大，覆土最浅和冲槽凹点处选取 5 个断面，分别为 K6+60，K6+73.1，K6+96.2，K6+110，K6+120。并且取滑动体厚度分别在开挖面前 1/3 直径，1/2 直径，2/3 直径长度处取值；分别记为滑动体厚度 1、滑动体厚度 2、滑动体厚度 3。

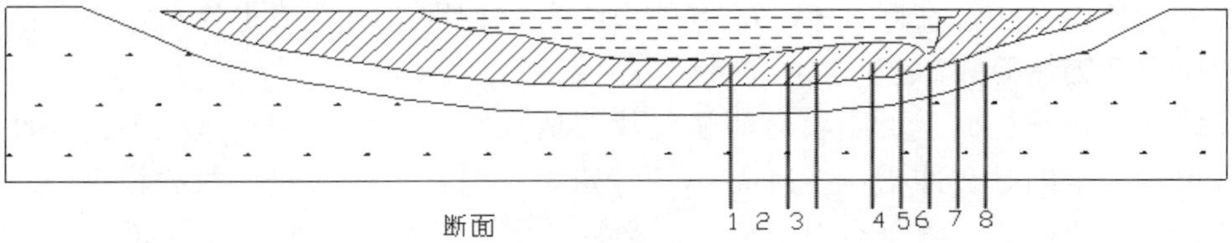

图 5 计算断面的选取

3.3 计算结果

根据前文提到的朗肯土压力和村山公式计算 8 个断面的泥水支护压力的上下限值和支护极限压力值，计算结果见表 1。

表 1 泥水支护压力计算结果

断面	主动压力（kPa）	静止压力（kPa）	村山公式（1/3）D 处压力值（kPa）	村山公式（1/2）D 处压力值（kPa）	村山公式（2/3）D 处压力值（kPa）
1	573.722	617.529	552.407	552.245	552.079
2	574.205	617.953	552.338	552.178	552.021
3	574.217	617.723	552.207	552.064	551.924
4	460.375	497.782	452.222	452.245	452.228
5	457.853	496.362	447.23	447.21	447.169

续表 1

断面	主动压力（kPa）	静止压力（kPa）	村山公式（1/3）D 处压力值（kPa）		村山公式（1/2）D 处压力值（kPa）		村山公式（2/3）D 处压力值（kPa）	
6	458.093	500.111	1/3 坡长	565.264	1/3 坡长	565.269	1/3 坡长	565.334
			1/2 坡长	571.67	1/2 坡长	571.677	1/2 坡长	571.743
			2/3 坡长	575.801	2/3 坡长	575.809	2/3 坡长	575.876
7	464.278	510.463	1/3 坡长	513.062	1/3 坡长	513.328	1/3 坡长	513.265
			1/2 坡长	516.125	1/2 坡长	516.392	1/2 坡长	516.33
			2/3 坡长	518.485	2/3 坡长	518.752	2/3 坡长	518.691
8	487.537	544.681	1/3 坡长	458.05	1/3 坡长	458.329	1/3 坡长	458.695
			1/2 坡长	457.785	1/2 坡长	458.063	1/2 坡长	458.429
			2/3 坡长	457.81	2/3 坡长	458.088	2/3 坡长	458.455

注：1/3 坡长指按开挖面前 1/3 坡长处高度计算超载，1/3 坡长与 2/3 坡长同理。

3.4 计算结果分析及结论

（1）江底中心附近即 1、2、3 断面的主动土压与静止土压值几乎相等。在冲槽段除覆土最浅处断面 5 外主动与静止压力均随着覆土厚度的增加而逐渐增大，土压力的浮动范围变大，有利于其对盾构机的控制。

（2）在江底中心附近和冲槽段无论是取 1/3D、1/2D、2/3D 处土层参数作为滑动面计算参数，计算出的盾构中心泥水支护压力值，基本相同，这是由于土层参数变化不大。

（3）在断面 1、2、3、4、5、8 处，即江底较为平坦不用考虑开挖面前方土体作用的区域，由村山公式计算出的数据均略小于主动土压力计算出的数据。而在 6、7 断面，由于前方坡度较陡，二维对数螺旋线滑动模型必须考虑开挖面前方土体作用，所以其村山公式计算出的值大于由主动土压力计算出的值。

（4）断面 4、5 处，由于覆土厚度减小，松动区土体厚度减少，土层松动区加权内摩擦角减小所以导致盾构中心泥水支护压力减小。在断面 6、7、8 处由于有盾构推进前方覆土作用于松动区的超载所以盾构中心泥水支护压力又突然变大。

（5）通过计算得出在开挖面上覆土没有明显起伏的情况下使用朗肯主动土压力公式计算盾构中心泥水支护压力下限值是安全的，在冲槽段（断面 6、7）如果用朗肯土压公式计算盾构中心支护压力作为下限值则不能维持开挖面的稳定，甚至有坍塌危险，必须考虑前方覆土厚度对开挖面滑动土体的作用。

4 结 语

本文利用二维对数螺旋线模型和朗肯土压力公式对盾构中心泥水支护压力的计算分析，求出盾构开挖面的极限支护压力和上下限值。通过对计算结果的分析得出，在南京长江隧道高水压、小覆土、冲槽地形突变段需要考虑前方滑动土体对泥水压力的影响。研究结果也在实际工程中得到了证实，通过设定泥水压力，调整泥水特性，快速平稳推进等措施下，盾构机已安全顺利地通过该危险地段。

然而本文的研究主要是考虑开挖面极限支护压力的确定(主要为欠压情况)，而泥水压力过大导致劈裂地层发生事故的研究并没有涉及，有关这方面的研究也不是很多，有待进一步完善。

参考文献（Referenles）:

[1] 张凤祥，朱合华等. 盾构隧道. 北京：人民交通出版社，2004.

[2] 韦良文，张庆贺等. 大型泥水盾构隧道开挖面稳定机理与应用研究地下空间与工程学报. 2001，3 (1)：87-91.

[3] 汪成兵，刘丰军等. 大直径泥水盾构浅覆土掘进隧道稳定性分析. 路. 2007，(9)：216-219.
[4] 袁大军，黄清飞等. 水底盾构掘进泥水喷发现象研究[J]. 岩石力学与工程学报，2007，26(11)：2296-2301.
[5] 秦建设，尤爱菊. 盾构隧道开挖面稳定数值模拟研究. 矿山压力与顶板管理. 2005（1)：27-30.
[6] 韦良文，张庆贺等. 盾构隧道开挖面稳定研究进展. 重庆交通大学学报（自然科学版）2007，26（6)：67-72.
[7] 秦建设. 盾构隧道施工中开挖面失稳事故分析. 浙江建筑.2005，22（增刊)：48-50，54.
[8] 肖广良. 盾构在软土地层穿越既有铁路施工技术. 隧道建设.2008，28（3)：324-329.
[9] 徐静文，李梅. 南京长江隧道盾构工作井降水技术. 建筑施工.2008，30（5)：397-398.
[10] 龚金全. 南京长江隧道浦口盾构始发井地下连续墙施工技术. 山东交通科技，2008，(2)：28-31.
[11] 李昀，张子新. 泥浆渗透对盾构开挖面稳定性的影响研究. 地下空间与工程学报，2007，3（4)：720-725，750.
[12] 叶慷慨. 沈阳地铁过河隧道盾构施工技术. 隧道建设，2007，27（6)：3942.
[13] 裴洪军，孙树林等. 隧道盾构法施工开挖面定性研究方法评析. 地下空间与工程学报，2005，1（1)：117-119.
[14] 秦建设. 盾构施工开挖变形与破坏机理研究[D]. 河海大学博士学位论文，2005，5.

作者简介（Bio-data)：

王胤，男，1985 年 4 月出生，硕士，2006 年毕业于同济大学土木工程专业，现在北京交通大学读硕士，主要研究方向是盾构隧道。

Yin WANG (1985—), male, graduated from Tongji University. Now he is pursuing the master's degree in Beijing Jiaotong University, majoring in shield tunneling technologies.

E-mail: ryan.wangyin@gmail.com

ＩＨＩ　シールド最新技術

団野　均

㈱ＩＨＩ　社会基盤セクター　油機・シールド部　シールド設計Ｇ　，愛知，478-8650

大断面シールドの需要が今後全世界的に高まりを見せる．日本においては，外郭環状道路向け，中央リニア新幹線向け，海外では，道路トンネル向けのφ15mクラスのシールド工事が予定されている．これらの大型プロジェクトで必要とされる技術要素として，高水圧対応，長距離対応，高速施工対応などの取り組みや工夫を，実績工事を踏まえて説明する．

併せて，近年の納入実績として，用途や各種条件に応じたシールド機の紹介と，ＩＨＩが得意としている特殊シールドに関して，紹介を行なう．

キーワード：大口径シールド；高水圧；長距離；特殊シールド

THE LATEST IHI SHIELD TECHNOLOGY

Hitoshi DANNO

Tunnel Boring Machine Design Group, Hydraulic Machinery & Tunnel Boring Machine Engineering Dept., Infrastructure Operations, IHI Corporation, Aichi478-8650, Japan

Abstract: Recently many projects of super large diameter tunnel are planning. For example Tokyo Outer Ring Road and Central Linear High Speed Express in Japan and for road tunnel project 15m diameter tunnel overseas. These super large tunnel projects will need updated shield machine technologies. This paper will introduce the high water pressure, long distance excavation and high speed excavation technologies, and the delivery records.

IHI has supplied various types of shield machines, in accordance with usage or conditions.

Also, machine manufactured records of various shield machines for special construction conditions will be introduced.

Key words: large-diameter-shield; high-pressure; long-distance-excavation; special-shield

1　はじめに

IHIは1960年（昭和35年），名古屋市地下鉄工事用としてシールドを納入して以来，大口径から小口径に至るまで各種のシールドを製作している．その中でも密閉型シールドについては，豊富な実績と経験を蓄積し，特殊シールドについても実績を積み重ねている．

本論文では，シールド機に要求される技術的，条件的な制約や顧客要望に対して，どのように反映しているかの一例を紹介すると共に，IHIの用途別の納入実績や得意としている異形断面や分岐などの特殊シールド最新技術を紹介する．

2　シールド機に求められる技術要素

日本における用途別のシールド機に求められる技術要素をまとめると下表の如くと考える．

実際の工事では，地質条件や各種施工条件，制約条件などを総合的に加味し，シールド機の装備仕様や機能を選定し，条件に適合した機械を設計，製作してゆく．近年の傾向としては，長距離施工の工事が多く行なわれており，それに伴い，高速施工，ビットの寿命向上や交換などの要素に，高い技術力が要求されている．また，分岐，接合技術も同様の背景で増えてきており，IHI の独自技術を各分野に応用することにより，厳しい条件に対応している．

表-1　シールド機に求められる技術要素

用途		口径別					技術要素					
		≤φ3m	φ3～φ5 m	φ5～φ7 m	φ7～φ10 m	≥φ10 m	長距離	急曲線	急勾配	高水圧	高速施工	地中分岐接合
上下水道	枝管	◎	○	△			○	◎				
	本管		○	○	△		○	○				○
共同溝			○	◎	△		○		○			
ガス		◎	○				◎	○	○			○
電力			○	○	△		○	○	◎			
鉄道	単線			◎			△			○		
	複線				○	○	△			○		
道路						◎	◎	△	△	◎	◎	○
特殊要素							◎	◎	◎	◎	◎	◎

写真 1　φ6.14 m 泥土圧シールド（中国地下鉄向け）

3　大断面シールドの技術要素

今後見込まれる工事（大型プロジェクト含む）は，以下の条件で計画が進められている．

表-2　大型プロジェクトの設計条件（推測）

	掘削距離	水　　圧	高速施工
東京外郭環状道路	8 km*	0.6 MPa*	500 m/月以上*
中央リニア新幹線	10 km*		

（*：想定数値含む）

IHIとして，これらの項目への懸念事項・配慮点をまとめると下表のごとくとなる．

表-3　大断面シールド機　計画時の配慮点

配慮項目	懸念事項	備考
高水圧（大深度）	• 推力の増大	1 500 kN/m^2 以上
	• シール性（止水性）	耐圧 1.0MPa 以上
	• 外圧に対するマシン強度	水圧の考慮
	• その他	
超長距離	• 機器の耐久性（信頼性）	寿命設計/汎用品の交換
	• ビット摩耗	目的別新型ビットの開発
	• シール類の長寿命化と交換技術	ｶｯﾀｼｰﾙ・ﾃｰﾙｼｰﾙ
	• 排土機構（掘削土砂の効率的搬出）	
	• その他	
高速施工（工期短縮）	• 装備仕様の不足	標準の 1.5 倍以上
	• 装備カッタトルク・回転数の不足	高トルク・高回転
	• セグメント組立時間短縮	自動化技術の導入
	• 同時掘進の必要性	
	• その他	

これらの技術要素に関して，詳細な検討を加え，具体的な装備・仕様の検討を現在進めている．なお，現在，IHIにて製作中の大口径マシンは下記である．

・『都市計画道路　大和川線　シールド工事』向け

(大鉄工業·吉田組·森組·紙谷工務店 JV 施工) φ12.54 m 泥土圧シールド

・『中央環状品川線シールドトンネル工事-2』向け

(大成·大豊·錢高 JV 施工) φ12.53 m 泥土圧シールド

写真 2　φ12.94 m 泥水式シールド

首都高速道路公団向け『中央環状新宿線 SJ11 工区(1·2)SJ13 工区トンネル工事』

（清水·鴻池·東亜 JV 施工）

4　用途別シールド機の紹介

用途や顧客ごとに口径は異なるが，ここでは(1)上下水道用；(2)電力用；(3)鉄道用について記載する．これらの用途に使用されるシールドは，φ2 m～φ7 m クラスの小口径～中口径機種で日本では主流である．

4.1　上下水道用シールド

上下水道用のシールドは φ2 m～φ4 m の口径が主流であり，限られた条件下（民地境界条件等）の掘削となるため，急カーブ施工を有するものが多い．

写真 3 は，φ3.94 m 泥土圧シールドである．名古屋市上下水道局（愛知県）向けの『南野雨水幹線下水道築造工事』（岩田地崎·中部土木·丸彦渡辺 JV 施工）で，施工条件は下記である．

掘削距離：1994.5 m，最小カーブ：15 mR，掘削対象土質：黏性土・砂質土・礫質土

最大想定礫径：φ19 mm，N 値：6～50 以上，土被り：9.2～11.2 m

セグメント：RC（半径方向挿入式）外径 φ3.8 m

シールド機の特長は，下記である．

① 15 mR 施工へ対応するために最大 10.5°の中折れ機構（X 中折れ）を装備

② 約 2 km の長距離掘削に対応するため先行ビットの多条配置

③ ワイヤブラシ間へのテールシーラ自動充填機構の装備

4.2　電力用シールド

電力用のシールドは φ4 m～φ6 m の口径が主流であり，上下水道用と同様に限られた条件下（民地境界条件等）の掘削となり，高土被り，急曲線，急勾配かつ都心部での工事となる場合が多い．

写真 4 は，φ5.325 m 泥土圧シールドである．台湾電力向けの『高港～五甲～高雄 345 kV 地下電線線路　中華路段潜盾洞道統包工程』（春原·岩田地崎 JV 施工）で，台湾の南部・高雄へ納入したものであり，施工条件（3 工区施工のうちの 1 工区のみを抜粋）は下記である．

掘削距離：2 411.2 m，最小カーブ：35 mR，掘削対象土質：シルト質砂・黏土

N 値：17，土被り：最大 35.43 m，勾配：上り 1.8%・下り 1.228%

セグメント：RC（軸方向挿入式）外径 φ5.175 m

シールド機の特長は，下記である．

① 35 mR 施工へ対応するために最大 6.5°の中折れ機構（V 中折れ）を装備

② 長距離層掘削対応として，先行ビットの多条配置，ワイヤブラシ 3 段装備

③ ワイヤブラシ間へのテールシーラ自動充填機構（外面突起無）の装備

④ 台湾島内輸送制限を考慮した大型分割の採用

写真 3　φ3.94 m 泥土圧シールド

写真 4　φ5.325 m 泥土圧シールド

4.3 鉄道用シールド

鉄道用のシールドはφ5 m～φ7 mの口径（単線の場合）が主流である.

写真 5 は，φ6.85 m 泥土圧シールドである．京王電鉄株式会社向け『調布駅付近連続立体交差工事（土木）第 4 工区』（清水·京王·間 JV 施工）で，施工条件は下記である.

掘削距離：1 606 m（379 m+424 m+424 m+379 m：U ターン施工 3 回），最小カーブ：160 mR

掘削対象土質：立川礫層砂礫・上総層群砂質土・上総層群砂黏土互層

最大想定礫径：φ600 mm（確認 φ300～350 mm 程度）N 値：50 以上

土被り：4.3～15.333 m，勾配：上り・下り 3.5%

セグメント：RC（軸方向挿入式）外径 φ6.7 m

シールド機の特長は，下記である.

① 礫層掘削対応として強化型先行ビットの多条・段差配置および大型スクリュコンベア装備

② 低土被り施工への配慮として土圧計の多数配置，ジャッキ式地山探査装置の装備，注入口の多数配置

③ カッタインバータ駆動の採用（低土被り施工および礫層への配慮）

④ 160 mR 施工へ対応するために最大 1.6°の中折れ機構（X 中折れ）を装備

⑤ ワイヤブラシ間へのテールシーラ自動充填機構（外面突起無）の装備

写真 5 φ6.85 m 泥土圧シールド

5 特殊シールドの紹介

IHI は特殊シールドの開発・設計・製作を得意としている．今回はその一部として，異形シールドと分岐シールドに関し，近年の実績を紹介する.

- 特殊シールド
  - 異形シールド
    - DOTシールド
    - 扁平シールド・矩形シールド
  - 分岐シールド
    - 縦向き分岐シールド
    - 横向き分岐シールド

5.1 DOTシールド

写真 6 は，φ6.42×W11.62 mDOT シールドである．台北市政府捷運工程局北區工程處向け『台灣桃園國際機場聯外捷運系統 CA450A 標工程』（達欣工程·清水建設 JV 施工）のために使用されるものである．

5.2 扁平シールド

写真 7 は，H8.66 m×W9.96 m 複合円形泥土圧シールドである．東京地下鉄株式会社向け『13 号線神宮前工区土木工事』（鹿島·大豊·東急 JV 施工）のために使用されたものである．

写真 6　φ6.42 m×W11.62 mDOTシールド

写真 7　H8.66 m×W9.96 m 複合円形泥土圧シールド

5.3 矩形シールド

写真 8 は，H3.99 m×W3.465 m 矩形シールドであり，西大阪高速鉄道株式会社向け『西大阪延伸線建設工事のうち土木工事（第 3 工区）』（大成·前田·五洋 JV 施工），写真 9 は，H3.98 m×W3.83 m 矩形シールドであり，国土交通省関東地方整備局向け『国道 1 号線原宿交差点立体工事』(大成建設施工)，のために使用されたものである．

写真 8　H3.99 m×W3.465 m 矩形シールド

写真 9　H3.98 m×W3.83 m 矩形シールド

5.4　上向きシールド（縦向き分岐シールド）

上向きシールド工法は，地下トンネル内から地上へ上向きにシールド掘削して立坑を構築する技術であり，地上より施工する従来工法でのリスクを軽減できることが最大の特徴である．地上部での作業は，簡易な到達立坑や路面覆工などの準備工事と，シールド回収のためのクレーン工事のみで，大半が地中での施工となるため，地上作業における施工条件に左右されることが少なく，大幅な工期短縮が可能である．

上向きシールドは，従来トンネルの掘削とは異なり，地山の自重に逆らう施工のため泥土圧式とし，常にチャンバ内を加泥材と混練りされた改良土砂で充填することで，切羽地山の圧密を防ぐようにしている．また，複数の立坑にシールドを転用することから，輸送・揚重・坑内運搬・マシン組みばらしなどを考慮して，フランジ・ボルト構造の分割可能構造としている．

写真 10 は，φ3.11 m 上向きシールドである．名古屋市上水道局向け『名駅南雨水幹線下水道築造工事（その 3)』(大成･鹿島･大豊 JV 施工）のために使用されたものである．

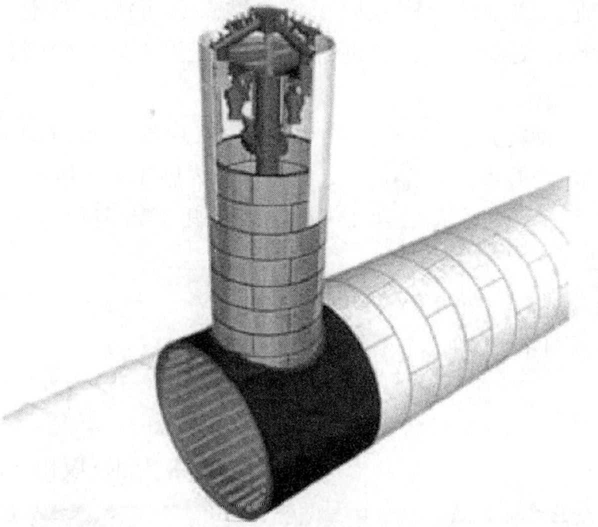

図-1　上向きシールド工法の概要

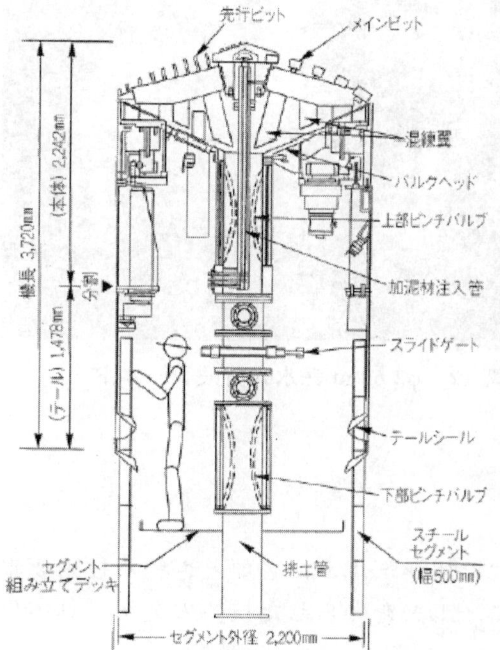

図-2　上向きシールド構造図

写真 10　φ3.11 m 上向きシールド

5.5　横向き分岐シールド

シールドトンネルの分岐・接合は，長期間地上を占有する開削立坑から施工するか，トンネル内から施工する場合には特殊なシールド機や大規模な地盤改良工事を必要としていたが，ＪＵＣ（Joints in Underground Conveniently）工法などは，あらかじめ分岐・接合用の開口補強構造およびシールドによる直接切削が可能な覆工材料で構成した専用セグメントを組み立てておくことで，トンネル内部からのシールド発進，外部からのシールド到達を容易に行うことができる．

分岐シールドには以下のような特徴がある．

① 立坑が不要なため，開削や地下埋設物の切り回しなどの地上環境への影響がない．

② 地上の用地に関係なく，分岐・接合箇所を任意の位置に設置できる．

③ 特殊セグメントを直接切削することで，地山開放がなく安全に施工できる（施工条件により補助工法を併用）

シールドの形式は，泥水式，泥土圧式いずれの型式も可能である．カッタヘッドは，面板形・スポーク形のいずれも採用可能であるが，発進部の特殊セグメント切削にあわせた形状とする必要がある．

写真 11 は，φ2.13 m 泥水式分岐シールドであり，東京都下水道局向け『杉並区堀ノ内一，二丁目付近枝線その 2 及び二次覆工工事』（三井住友・鴻池 JV 施工），写真 12 は，φ2.68 m 泥水式分岐シールドであり，東大阪市上下水道局向け『平成 16 年度公共下水道第 5 工区菅きょ築造工事』（大林組施工），のために使用されたものである．

なお，現在製作中の分岐シールドは下記である．

・『木戸排水区雨水貯留施設築造工事』向け

(飛島・鴻池・ﾉﾊﾞｯｸ・坂詰 JV 施工)φ2.93 m 泥土圧シールド

・『墨田区八広一，四丁目付近再構築工事』向け

(竹中土木・坂田 JV 施工)φ2.25 m 泥土圧シールド

写真 11　φ2.13 m 泥水式分岐シールド

写真 12　φ2.68 m 泥水式分岐シールド

6　おわりに

本編では，用途別に求められる技術要素，今後の大口径シールドに必要とされる技術要素についての考え，および実績の紹介を行った．これらをもとに，工夫を凝らした技術の提案・具体化を進めていく所存である．

著者紹介（Bio-data）：

著　　者：団野　均

所　　属：㈱ＩＨＩ　社会基盤セクター　油機・シールド部

シールド設計Ｇ　課長

業　　務：シールド機の設計

Hitoshi DANNO

Tunnel Boring Machine Design Group, Hydraulic Machinery & Tunnel Boring Machine Engineering Dept. Infrastructure Operations IHI Corporation.

Design of Shield Machine.

E-mail: hitoshi_danno@ihi.co.jp

伸縮カッターを用いた大断面複合円形シールドの掘進管理実績と評価

大塚　努　沼田　敦

東京地下鉄株式会社　鉄道本部　改良建設部，東京　110-8614　日本

東京メトロ神宮前工区は，明治神宮前から渋谷間のシールドトンネル工事であり，伸縮カッターにより複合円形トンネルを採用した．これは複線シールドトンネルとして断面最適化したもので，トンネル断面積を従来の円形断面に比べ約１０%縮小し，不要空間に打設するインバート材を約４０%減少したもので，環境負荷低減と地下空間の有効利用を可能とした．

本稿は、複合円形シールド工法の概要と施工結果について報告するものである．

キーワード：シールドトンネル；伸縮カッター

RESULTS AND EVALUATION OF THE CONTROL OVER DRIVING THE SHIELD MACHINE WITH A LARGE FLAT CIRCLE SECTION BY EXCAVATION METHOD OF ADJUSTABLE CUTTER

Tsutomu OOTSUKA，Atsushi NUMATA

Renovation and Construction Department Design Section, Tokyo Metro Co., Ltd, Tokyo 110-8614, Japan

Abstract: Jinguumae public work by Tokyo Metro Co., Ltd is construction of shield tunnel between Meijijinguu-mae and Shibuya with a large flat circle section by excavation method of adjustable cutter. It becomes possible to decrease an area of a tunnel section about 10% rather than a Circular shield. And invert material was reduced 40%. For this reason, environmental impact reduction and effective use of underground space were enabled.

Key words: shield tunnel; adjustable cutter

1　はじめに

東京メトロ副都心線は，既に営業している志木～和光市間の東武東上線，和光市～池袋間の有楽町線の延伸工事として池袋～渋谷間の 8.9 kmを新たに建設したものであり，2012 年には渋谷駅では東急東横線との相互直通運転を行う予定である．これにより，埼玉県南西部方面から都心を経由し横浜方面に至る広域的な鉄道軸が完成し，利用者の利便性の向上と慢性的な道路交通渋滞の混雑緩和が期待されている．

本報告では，このうちの神宮前工区において採用した写真 1 に示す伸縮カッターを用いた大断面複合円形シールド工法の概要と施工実績・評価について紹介する．

写真１　シールドマシン

2　神宮前工区の概要

神宮前工区は，明治神宮前～渋谷間を結ぶ延長 738.5 m(458 リング)にトンネル外径高さ 8.4 m，横幅 9.7 mの複合円形断面（非円形断面）のシールドトンネルを施工するものである．複線シールドトンネルとして断面最適化した複合円形断面により，トンネルの断面積を従来の円形断面に比べ約 10%縮小し，不要空間に打設するインバート材料を円形断面に比べて約 40%減少した．このため，シールド掘進による発生土量の抑制，シールド機製作・セグメント製作による建設資機材の減量が可能となり，環境負荷の低減に寄与するとともに，地下空間の有効利用が可能となる[1)]

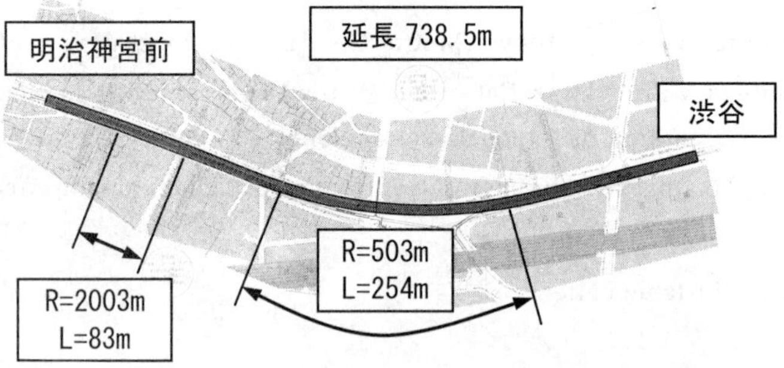

図１　平面線形図

2.1　線形概要

明治神宮前～渋谷間の延長 738.5 mについて，明治神宮前を発進側，渋谷を到達側として，明治通りの下に建設するものである．平面線形図を図 1 に示す．全線に渡って概ね曲線となっており，発進側から直線区間 71.8 mの後，曲線半径 2 003 mの右曲線が 83m，曲線半径 503 mの左曲線が 254 mと続き，到達側で再び直線となる．

縦断勾配は，発進側から 3.0‰の一定の下り勾配となっており，到達側約 100 mで 10.0‰の下り勾配に変化する．

また，東京電力渋谷神宮前洞道及び城南河川清流復活導水管路がほぼ全区間にわたり近接している．

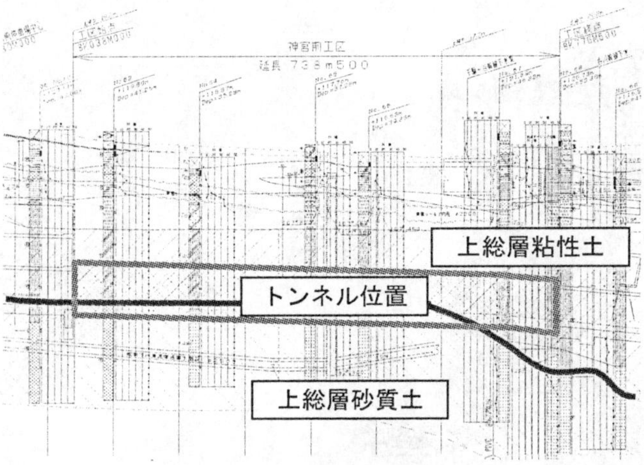

図２　地質縦断図

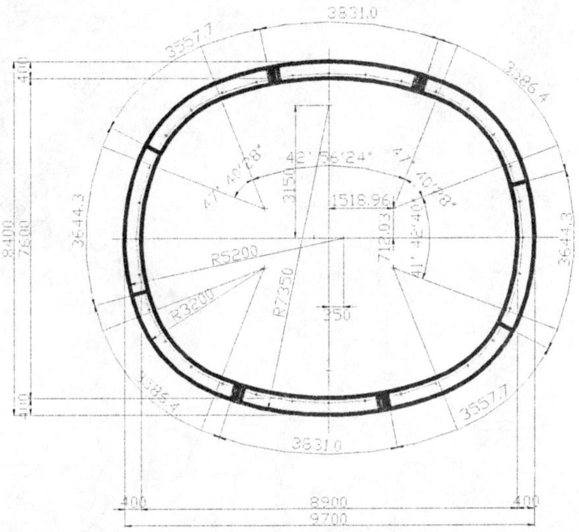

図３　セグメント

2.2　地質概要

本工区における掘進部（土被り約 18 m）の土質は，全般に N 値 50 以上の安定した上総層黏性土層であるが，発進側から到達部手前約 100 m までは上総層砂層地盤も介在しており，非常に高い被圧地下水を有している．透水係数は 10^{-5}～10^{-4} cm/sec 程度である．工事地点の地質縦断図を図２に示す．

2.3　覆工構造

本セグメントは，複合円形トンネルであることから，図３に示す３つの曲線半径を有する形状とし，K 型セグメントを除いて各ピース２つの曲線半径を有するセグメントとなっている．セグメントは全てコンクリート製セグメントとしている．セグメント幅は,リング継手の削減の観点から，これまでの実績では最大となる 1,600 mm とした．分割数は，テーパーリングの転用や道路輸送・現場内の搬送の制約条件から８分割とした．セグメント１ピースの重量は約６ｔで，形状は最大で 3,831 mm×1,600 mm×400 mm（K 型）である。また，セグメント製作費の抑制を図るため，トンネル上下に K 型セグメントを配置する構造とした．

なお，継手にはいずれもインサートタイプの継手となる高剛性継手（セグメント間継手）と DUET 継手（リング間継手）を採用した．

3　施工計画

3.1　複合円形シールド

（1）掘削機構

シールド工法は，土質条件等から図４及び表１に示す泥土圧式複合円形シールド工法とし，掘削機構には伸縮カッター方式を採用した．本伸縮カッターは，矩形シールド断面で多数の実績のある WAC(Wagging Cutter Shield)工法[2)] の基礎技術を応用して，シールド機のカッターを回転に応じて伸縮させることにより，複合円形状の掘削を可能としている．また，伸縮カッターの伸縮に伴うチャンバー内容積の変動により，切羽土圧が変動しないように，２箇所に土圧変動抑制装置を装備した．

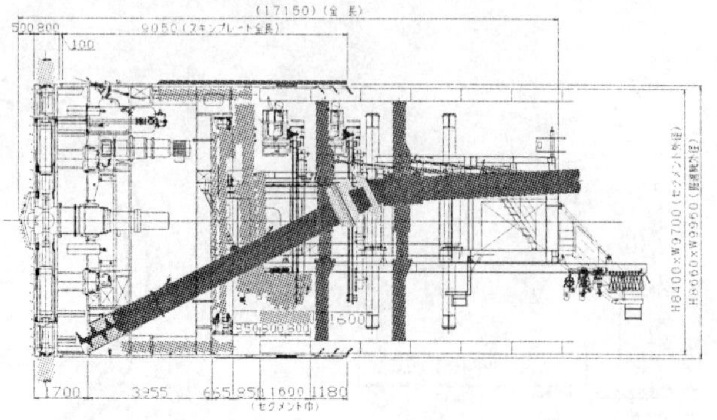

(a)側面図

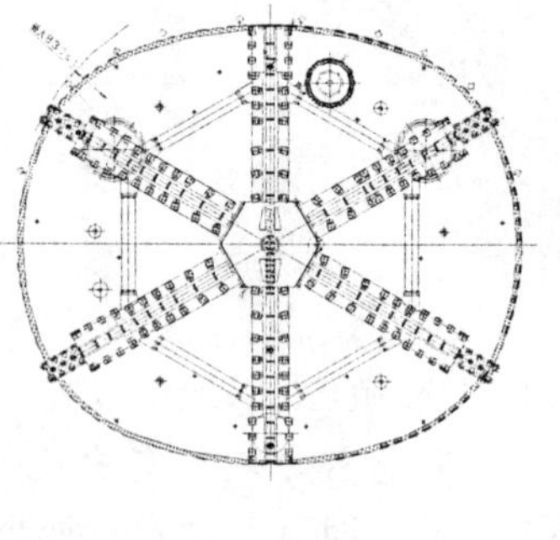

(b)正面図

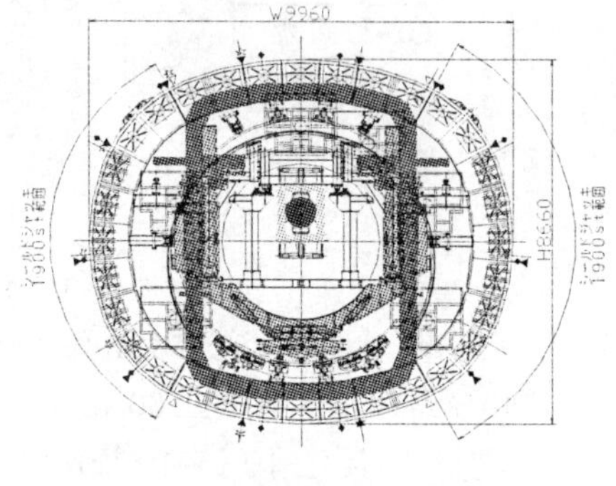

(c)背面図

図4　シールドマシン構造図

表1　シールドマシン仕様一覧

シールド本体	形式	泥土圧式複合円形シールド(EX-MAC工法)
	外形寸法	高さH8,660mm×幅W9,960mm×機長L9,050mm
	推進装置	総推力80,000ｋN(=2,500kN×32本) ジャッキ伸長速度55mm/min
カッター	構造形式	面板部：開放スポーク形 支持部：中間支持方式
	駆動部	電動駆動 最大トルク時：28,113kNm (トルク係数長径α=19.0) 常用時：18,742kNm (トルク係数長径α=28.5)
	伸縮カッター	490kN×20.6MPa×830mm×4本
スクリューコンベア	形式と形状	油圧駆動, シャフト型：径Φ700mm×ピッチp510mm 排土量：257m^3/h
	回転トルク×回転速度	1次：43kNm×24.2rpm 2次：67kNm×24.2rpm
エレクタ	旋回部	リングギヤ式 回転数：0～0.9rpm，回転角度：±200°
	ヘッド部	押付け，摺動，引込み，傾き
形状保持装置		エアバッグ式×1列，上下拡張式×２列
同時裏込め注入装置		油圧ジャッキ開閉式 (注入圧検知用土圧計付) A,B液先端混合方式 4基(上部左右2箇所,1箇所当たり2本)

(2) 形状保持装置

形状保持装置は，空気圧によりセグメント外部から圧力をかけてセグメントを安定させるテール内形状保持装置×１基，裏込注入等によるセグメントの変形を抑えるために，セグメント内部からセグメントを支える門型形状保持装置×２基を設置した．テール内形状保持装置は，本セグメントが1.6 m の幅広セグメントで，楕円形のトンネル形状であるため，無拘束状態での変形が大きいことが予想されることから，これを防止するために設置を行っている．配置されるエアバッグはジャッキ本数と同数の 32 個とし，使用圧力は組立時 0.7MPa，掘進時 0.5MPa としている．

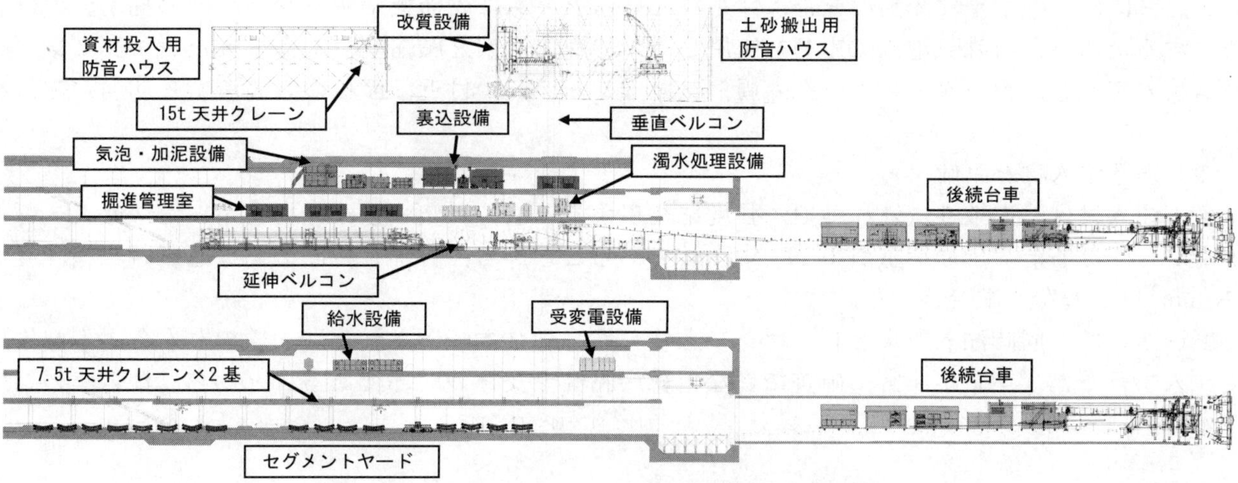

図５　シールド設備配置図

3.2　シールド設備計画

発進立坑がある明治神宮前停車場は，原宿の中心街に位置し，交通量が約 3 万台/日と非常に多い明治通りの下にある．このため，シールド設備は資材投入用の防音設備と土砂搬出用の防音設備を除いて全て新設駅構内に設置を行った．また，防音設備についても，車線幅及び車両限界を確保するため，下部の幅を狭めた形状としている．主要シールド設備配置を図５に示す．また，主要シールド設備一覧を表２に示す．

表２　主要シールド設備一覧

使用場所	設備名	機械名	仕様	台数
地上設備	揚重設備	天井クレーン	15.0 t	1台
	土砂貯留設備	土砂ピット	$280m^3$	1基
	土砂搬出設備	垂直コンベアー	$150m^3/h$	1台
		No1搬出ベルコン	$224m^3/h$	1台
		No２搬出ベルコン	$274m^3/h$	1台
	改質設備	パドルミキサー（連続処理型）	$150m^3/h$	1基
		固化材ｻｲﾛ	30 t	1基
		固化材ｻｲﾛ	15 t	1基
		固化材ﾌｨｰﾀﾞ		1基
		助剤（高分子）タンク	$1m^3$	1基
		助剤添加装置		1基
	防音ハウス	ﾀｲﾌﾟC		2棟
構築内設備	揚重設備	天井クレーン	7.5 t	2台
	土砂搬出設備	垂直コンベア	$150m^3/h$	1台
	濁水処理設備		$40m^3/h$	1式
	排水処理設備	ﾊﾞｷｭｰﾑ設備		1式
	裏込設備	自動作液プラント		1式
	添加材設備（分散材）	自動作液プラント		1式
	添加材設備（起泡材）	自動作液プラント		1式
	変電設備			1式
	給水設備			1式
	土砂搬出設備	連続ベルトコンベアー	$149m^3/h$	1台
	揚重設備	揚重クレーン	20.0 t	1台
	土砂搬出設備	ベルト延長設備	テイルユニット	1式
	軌条設備	サーボロコ	12 t	1台
換気・環境測定設備	構内換気設備	コントラファン	$\phi 1100$	1式
	ガス検知設備	定置及び移動式検知器		1式

(1) 残土搬出設備

マシンで掘削された土砂は，トンネル坑内を延伸ベルコンで運搬し，垂直ベルコンにより地下約 30 m から地上に揚土後，パドルミキサーで改良して地上の土砂搬出設備内の土砂ピットに堆積する．堆積した土砂は，路上から約 5 m に設置したトラバーサー上のバックホウにより，ダンプトラックに積込まれて，場外に搬送を行う．

（2）加泥材と設備

加泥材には，掘削土に流動性と止水性を持たせるとともに，面板やチャンバー内の掘削土の付着を防止するために，特殊気泡剤(OK-1)を使用した．特殊気泡剤と圧縮空気で作られたシェービングクリーム状の気泡を，カッタースポーク外周，フィッシュテール付近，面板の３箇所から切羽に注入を行った．

（3）裏込注入材と設備

裏込注入材は，充填性に優れ早期に強度を発現する二液性可塑状型注入材を用いた．セグメントが地山から受ける計算上の荷重が 0.297 N/mm^2 であることから，材齢３時間における三軸圧縮強度が 0.3 N/mm^2 以上となる配合とした．

裏込注入は，同時注入方式とし，マシン上部左右に各２本配置された注入管の左右各１本を使用して注入を行った．土質が非常に硬質で密な上総層黏性土及び砂層部であることから，注入率の初期値は 120%とした．

3.3 計測管理

シールド掘進に伴った周辺地盤の影響及び土水圧の載荷状況とトンネルの安全性を確認するために，地盤挙動計測及びセグメント挙動計測を行った．計測位置は，切羽から約 65m に位置する直線部の 41R，42R とした．地盤挙動計測の計測位置図を図６に，セグメント計測位置図を図７に示す．

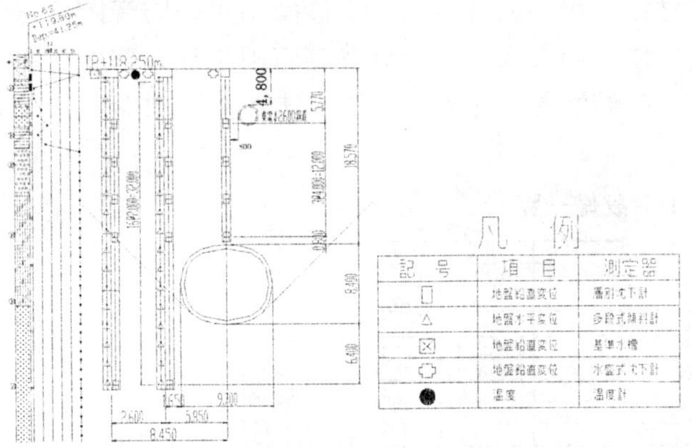

図６　地盤挙動計測位置図(42R)

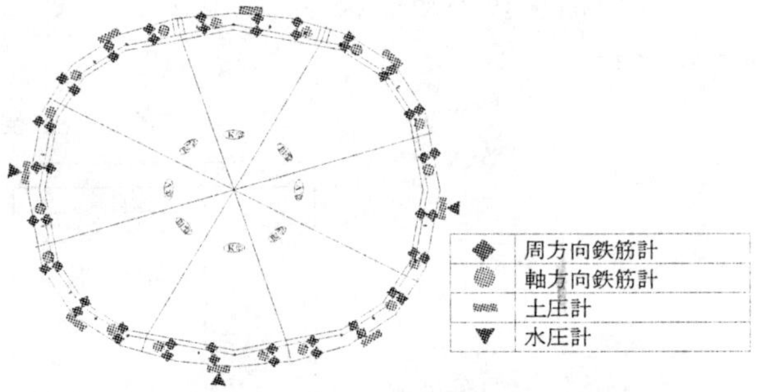

図７　セグメント計測位置図

4 施工実績

4.1 掘進実績

日進量は，初期掘進時で段取り替えなどを除いて４リング/日(6.4 m)，本掘進時で８リング/日(12.8 m)を達成した．これにより，月進量は最大で 320 m/月を確保した．

4.2 切羽土圧管理

計画時の管理土圧は，上総層黏性土層の自立性が高いことを考えて最小土圧を間隙水圧＋予備圧(20 kN/m^2)とし，最大土圧を主働土圧＋間隙水圧＋予備圧として，この範囲で管理を実施するものとした．しかしながら，実際の土圧計によるマシン停止時の計測値は，図８に示すようにボーリングデータから算出した間隙水圧よりも小さな値を示した．このため，切羽の自立性が高く，地下水の影響が小さい地盤と判断して，過圧密及び地盤変状抑制を考慮して，図９に示すように管理土圧の最小土圧側で切羽土圧の管理を行った．

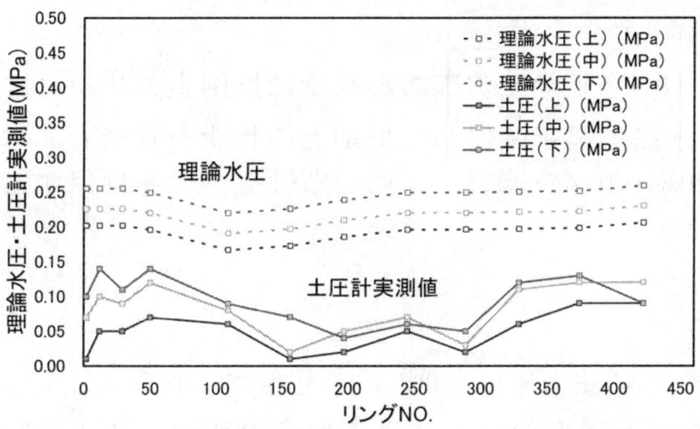

図 8　マシン停止時の土圧計実測値

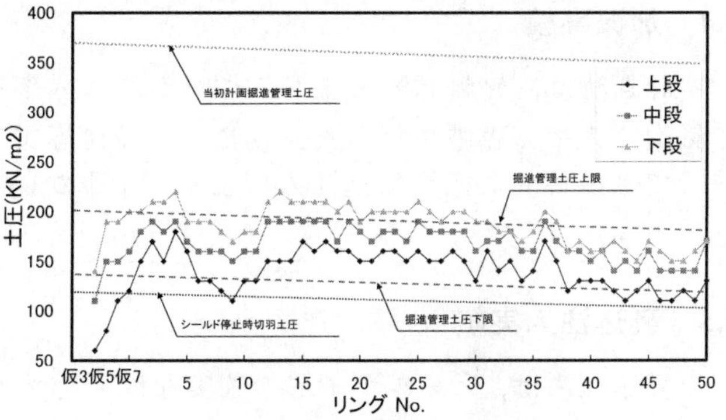

図 9　土圧管理結果

また，切羽土圧の管理は，掘進速度・カッタートルク・1 次スクリューの回転速度をバランス良く制御し，土質の性状に合わせて気泡注入率をリアルタイムに調整することにより，十分可能であった．

4.3　排土管理

チャンバー内土圧の管理のみでは，予期せぬ崩壊土層に対応できないことから，土量管理についてはレーザースキャナーによる容積計測，ベルトスケール及びダンプスケールによる重量計測の３つの方法を用いて入念な管理を行った．施工への迅速なフィードバックを行うためにレーザースキャナー及びベルトスケールを，正確な重量確認を行うためにダンプスケールを利用した．各リングの排土量計測結果を図 10 に，ダンプスケールの初期掘進時の理論排土量との比較を表３に示す．レーザースキャナーは理論排土量に対して若干のばらつきがあるものの，ベルトスケールはほぼ一致することが確認できた．また，理論排土量に対してダンプスケールは一致することも確認できることから，重量管理を主体として排土管理を行った．

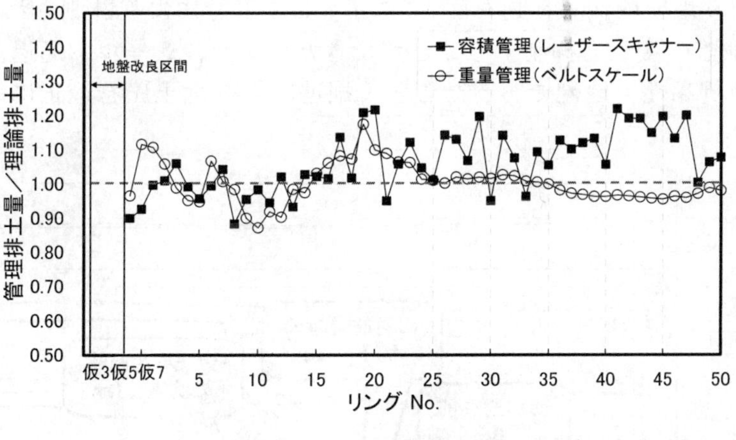

図 10　各リングの排土量

表 3　ダンプスケールと理論排土量の比較

	排土量（t）	実測値/理論値	備考
理論排土量	10993.8	−	排土量×平均比重+改質材添加量
重量管理型ダンプスケール	10877.6	0.99	

4.4 加泥実績

計画時は，材料試験結果から標準気泡注入率を 30%とした．実際の掘削では掘削土の状況に応じて気泡注入率の調整を行った．初期掘進時は標準気泡注入率を確保して掘削土の状態を確認し，本掘進時では最終的に標準気泡注入率より若干少ない 20%～30%の範囲で適切な塑性流動性を確保することができた．

4.5 裏込注入実績

裏込注入は，テールボイドの確実な注入を図るために注入率(=120%以上)を主体に管理し，上限圧力(=間隙水圧+100 kN/m^2)を設定して確実な裏込の充填と過度な圧力による地盤の変状の防止を図った．裏込注入率と注入圧力を図 11 に示す．

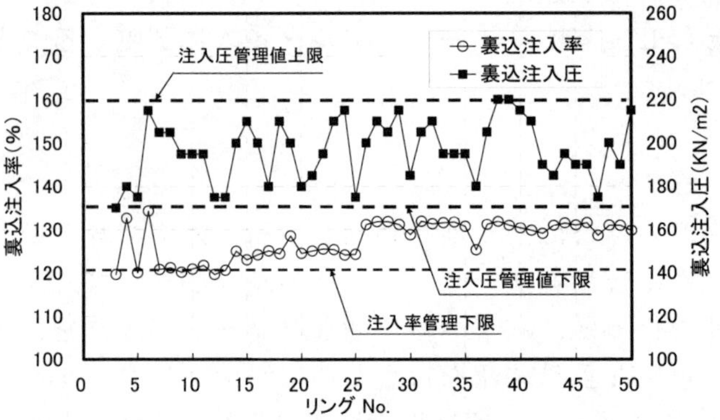

図 11 裏込注入実績(初期掘進時)

4.6 地盤変状結果

シールド通過に伴う地盤の沈下挙動を図 12 に示す．沈下計により計測された沈下量は，路面部で 1.1 mm 程度であり，地盤の変状を抑制することができた．また，シールド通過前の地盤の隆起は生じなかった．これは，硬質黏性土地盤であったこと，掘進時の管理土圧を適正に制御できたことによるものと考えられる．

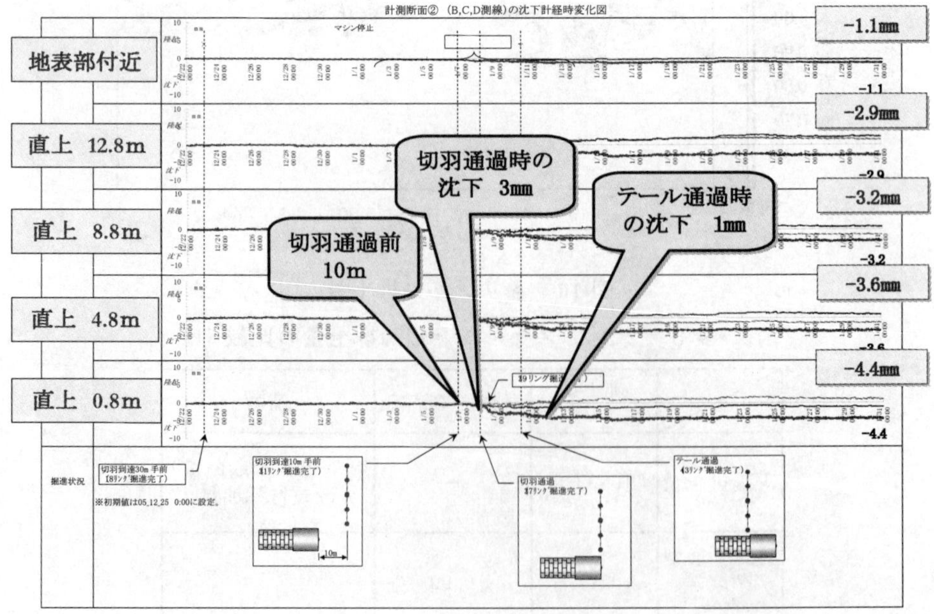

図 12 地盤沈下挙動計測

4.7 セグメントの発生応力

マシンのテールを通過して地山内で安定状態になった時の鉄筋応力計から算出した発生断面力を図 13 に示す．軸力は設計値と概ね同じ値となった．曲げモーメントについては，設計と同様のモーメント分布となったが，計測値と設計に差が生じた箇所もあった．これは，計測値が局所的な値であること，実際の土圧分布，裏込め注入圧等の複合的な影響よるものと考えられる．

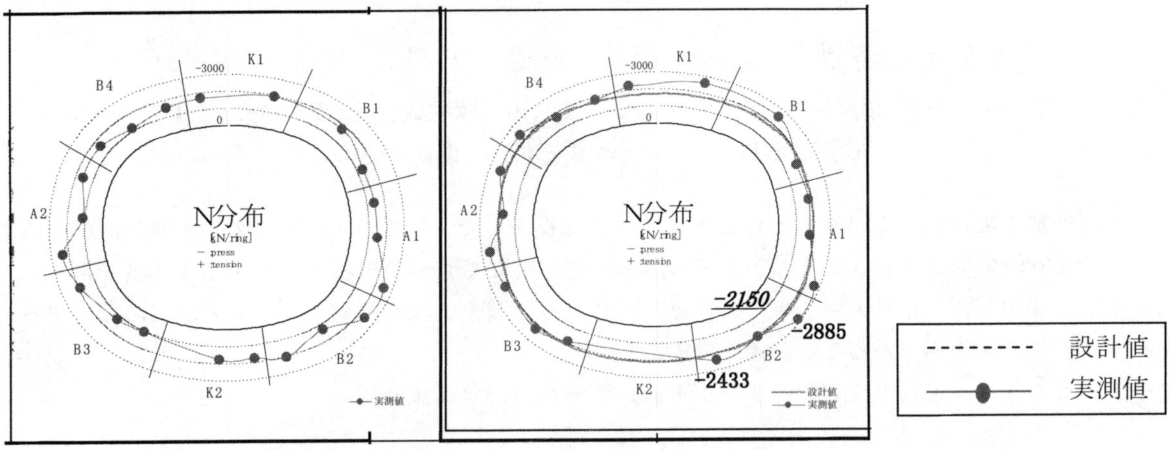

図 13　セグメント発生断面力

5　まとめ

東京メトロ副都心線の神宮前工区における伸縮カッターを用いた大断面複合円形シールド工法の計画と掘進管理実績について述べた．今後は，さらに各種データをとりまとめて詳細な分析を行うとともに，従来の円形断面にかわる特殊形状断面シールドの設計および施工に，有効に活用をしていきたいと考えている．

参考文献（References）:

［1］ 矢萩秀一，藤木育雄，入江健二，大塚努：環境負荷低減を考慮した複合円形シールドトンネルの設計，第 59 回年次学術講演会，pp.73-74，平成 16 年 9 月．

［2］ 中村浩，久保田敏和，古川衛，中尾努：大断面矩形シールドで渡り線部と一般線路部を施工，トンネルと地下，第 33 巻 8 号，pp.27-33，2002.

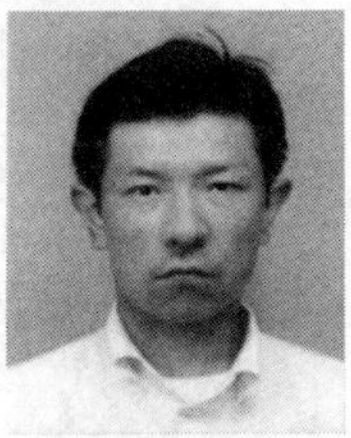

著者紹介（Bio-data）:

大塚　努　　技術基準担当課長

Tsutomu OOTSUKA, supervisor in charge of technical standards

E-mail address: tsu.ootsuka@tokyometro.jp

沼田　敦　　改良建設部設計課　課長補佐

Atsushi NUMATA, associate supervisor of design section ,in renovation and construction department .

E-mail address: a.numata@tokyometro.jp

シールドテール内形状保持装置（TKS）の効果

藤木　育雄[1]　大塚　努[2]　吉成　寿男[3]　守山　亨[3]

[1]メトロ開発株式会社 技術部，東京 103-0001；[2]東京地下鉄株式会社 改良建設部 東京 110-8614;
[3]佐藤工業株式会社 土木事業本部，東京 103-8639

東京メトロの副都心線に鉄道で最大幅となるセグメントを採用した．セグメントリングの大型化に伴い自重が増加し，組立て直後の変形が予想されることなどの理由から，組立て直後の形状を拘束するＴＫＳを開発し，シールド工事全線に採用した．セグメントリングの変形に対する計測を実施した結果，セグメントに発生する応力の変化を制御することが可能であることが確認できた．

キーワード：セグメント形状保持装置；シールド機；テール内形状保持装置

EFFICACY OF POSITION RETAINING SYSTEM FOR SHIELD TUNNEL SEGMENT

Ikuo FUJIKI [1], Tsutomu OOTSUKA [2], Hisao YOSHINARI [3], Toru MORIYAMA [3]

[1]METRO DEVELOPMENT CORPORATION 103-0001, Japan ;[2] Renovation & Construction Department., TOKYO METRO CO., LTD. 110-8614, Japan ; [3]Civil Engineering Department., SATOKOGYO CO., LTD 103-8639, Japan

Abstract: In the shield tunnel project of Fukutoshin subway line of Tokyo Metro, segment with the maximum width that never used before was adopted. Because of the big size and heavy weight of the segment ring, large deformation of the segment ring was considered to occur immediately after assembly. To solve this problem, a position retaining system for shield tunnel segment named as TKS was developed and adopted in this whole project. According to the measurement results of the segment deformation, it is confirmed that the stress of the segment ring during construction can be effectively controlled by using the developed TKS system.

Key words: retaining segment position system; shield machine; TKS

1　はじめに

近年，シールドトンネルの継手面の減少による品質確保やコスト縮減のためにセグメント幅を拡大する傾向にある．継手面の減少は，漏水の原因となる箇所を減少させることになりトンネルの品質確保につながる．セグメント幅の拡大化は，セグメントの製作リング数の削減，継手間の止水用のシール材の削減およびセグメントの総組立て時間の削減による各種の損料，機器の供用日数の減少などのコストの縮減になる．

一方，セグメント幅とセグメント厚さの研究も進められ，セグメント幅とセグメント厚さの比が５以上の場合は継手付近の曲げ応力の集中を考慮してセグメント端部の鉄筋の配置を増やすなどの工夫が必要とされている．[1)]

シールド断面の大型化やセグメント幅を広くすることによってセグメントの自重は大きくなる傾向にある．それにともなって組立て直後のセグメントリングには大きな変形が生じ，また，発生する曲げモーメントも大きくなる．セグメントリングが地山に出ると，トンネル周辺の地山によってその自重が支えられるものと想定されることから，組立て直後にこの自重を支持してリングの変形を抑制すれば，セグメント継手面の割れや欠けを防止でき，また自重による発生曲げモーメントを低減できることから経済的なセグメントの設計が可能になると考えられる．

テール内形状保持装置（以後，ＴＫＳと呼ぶ）は，セグメントリングの組立て完了時からシールド掘進の途中までの間，それを外側から拘束して，その変形を抑制しＲＣ断面を軸圧縮状態に近づけることを目的として新たに開発した装置である[2]．

本稿は，東京メトロ副都心の建設において，シールド工事の全線で実施したセグメントに対する計測管理の結果から，ＴＫＳの効果の概要について報告するものである．

2　ＴＫＳの概要

2.1　概　要

ＴＫＳの最大の特徴は，シールド機のテール内に取り付けた膨張および縮小が可能な袋状の膨張体を膨らませて，セグメントの組立て完了直後からシールドの掘進の途中までの間，セグメントリングをその外側から拘束して自重による変形を抑制するという点にある．ＴＫＳの概要図を図１に示す．写真１はＴＫＳの取り付け状況，写真２はセグメントの組立て状況を示す．

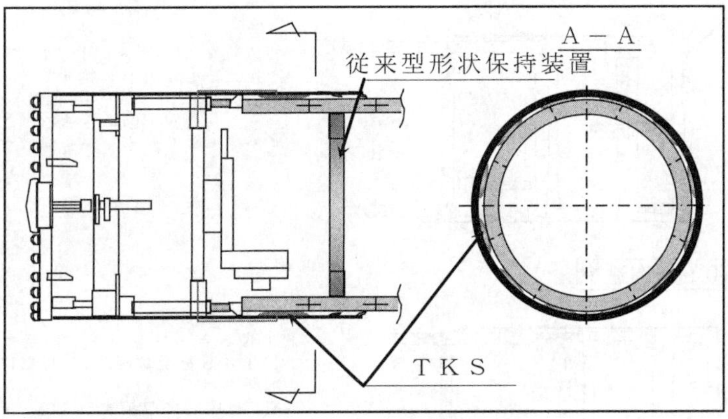

図１　ＴＫＳの概要

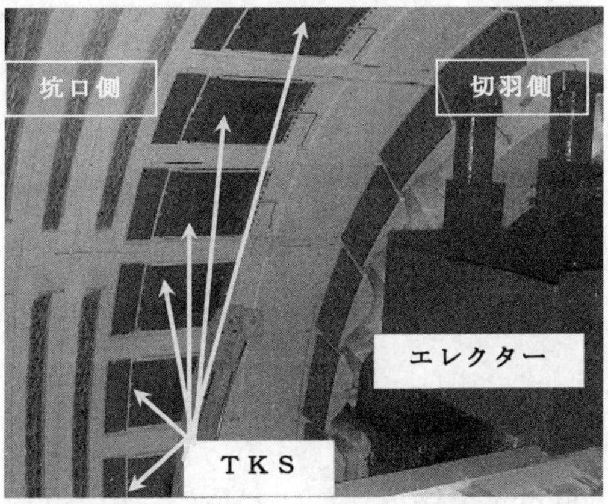

写真１　ＴＫＳの取り付け状況

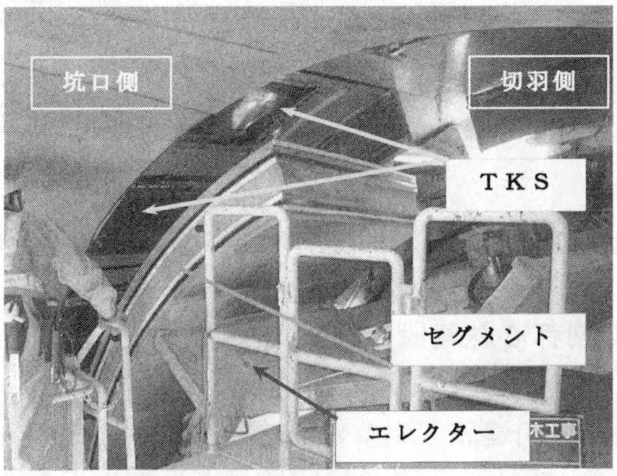

写真２　セグメントの組立て状況

2.2　施工順序

ＴＫＳはセグメントリングを支持する膨張体とそれを制御する空気圧の制御装置からなる．図**2**に施工順序を示す．膨張体は圧縮空気により膨張させ，また，強制排気により収縮させることができるもので，シールド機内のテール部に格納されている．空気圧の制御装置は膨張体への圧縮空気の送気と膨張体からの強制排気を制御する装置である．

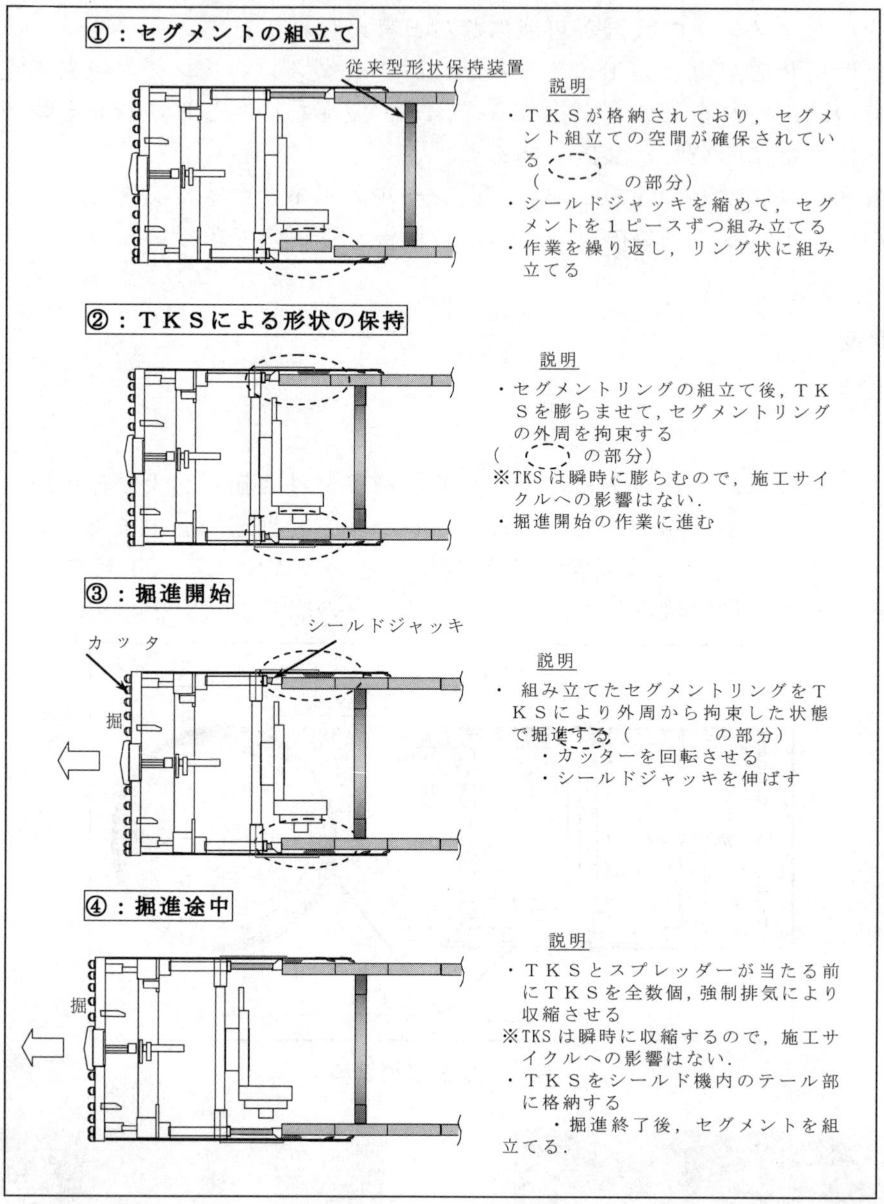

図 2　ＴＫＳによる施工順序

3　東京メトロ副都心線におけるセグメント計測

3.1　副都心線建設の概要

副都心線は和光市～渋谷間 20.2 km の路線で，和光市～新線池袋間は 1994 年までに部分開業している．今回建設区間は新線池袋～渋谷間 8.9 km で，7 駅を新設した．駅間および 2 駅はシールド工法である．今回，セグメント幅を国内鉄道で最大となる 1 600 mm を採用したことから，10 機のシールド機すべてに TKS を装備した．

3.2　セグメント計測の概要

(1) セグメントリングの内空

セグメントリングの内空測定は，表 1 に示すトンネルで実施した．測定器はレーザープロファイラーと呼ばれるノンプリズム方式のレーザー測距器を用いた．測定方法は，作業デッキなどにより横断面を直接見通せないことから，図3に示すように1断面あたりで2箇所からセグメントの内空断面の形状を測定し，その測定位置を後方の不動点から計測して横断面の形状に補正して求めた．

表-1　トンネルの概要

No.	工区名	セグメント外径（m）	セグメント幅（m）	セグメント高さ（m）	シールド工法
①	南池袋B	6.6	1.4	0.32	泥　水
②	高田A	6.6	1.6	0.32	泥土圧
③	高田B	6.6	1.6	0.32	泥土圧
④	西早稲田	8.0	1.6	0.35	泥土圧
⑤	新宿	6.6	1.6	0.32	泥　水
⑥	新宿御苑	9.8	1.6	0.40	泥　水
⑦	千駄ヶ谷	9.8	1.6	0.40	泥土圧
⑧	神宮前	9.7×8.4	1.6	0.40	泥土圧

(2) セグメントリングの発生応力

セグメントリングの発生応力の測定は鉄筋計を用いて実施した．鉄筋計の配置を図4に示す．

(3) セグメント継手の目開き

セグメント継手の目開きの測定は継手間を渡るように変位計を設置した．本稿で結果を報告する測定位置を図4に示す．

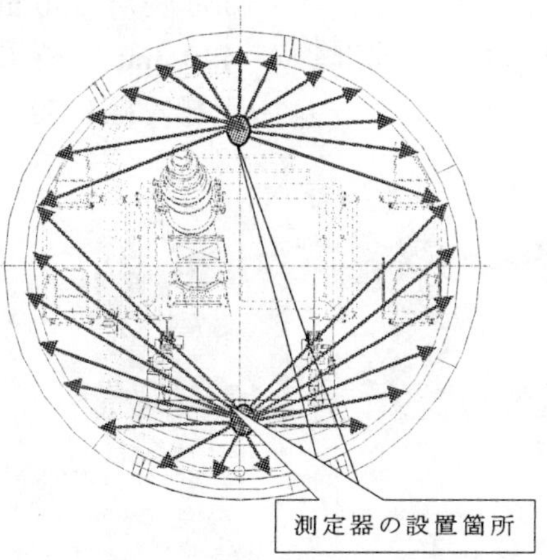

図3　内空の測定方法

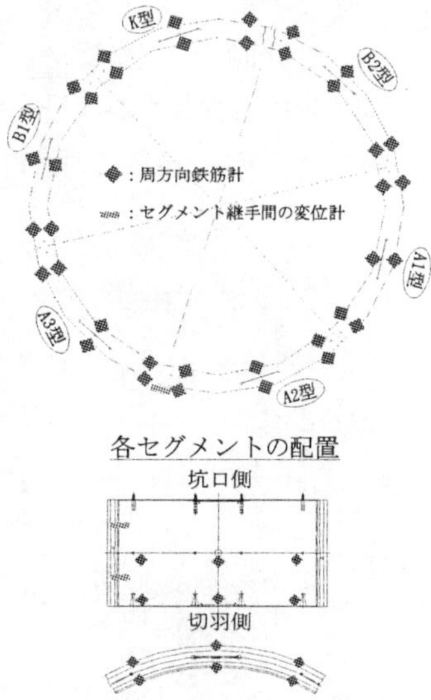

図4　鉄筋計・目開き変位計の配置

4　計測結果

4.1　セグメントリングの内空

計測は，ＴＫＳを作動させる前後で実施した．図5は，8工区の水平方向および鉛直方向の内空変化量の測定結果を示した図である．1ヶ所あたりＴＫＳを作用させる前を△，作用させた後を○で表示した．この図をみると全測定点8ヶ所のうち矢印を付けた6ヶ所で内空変位量が原点を通る水平・鉛直軸の方向に移動した．このことは，組立て誤差が小さくなったことを示している．ＴＫＳにより組立て直後のセグメントリングの形状が設計断面に近づく方向に矯正されたと考えられる．

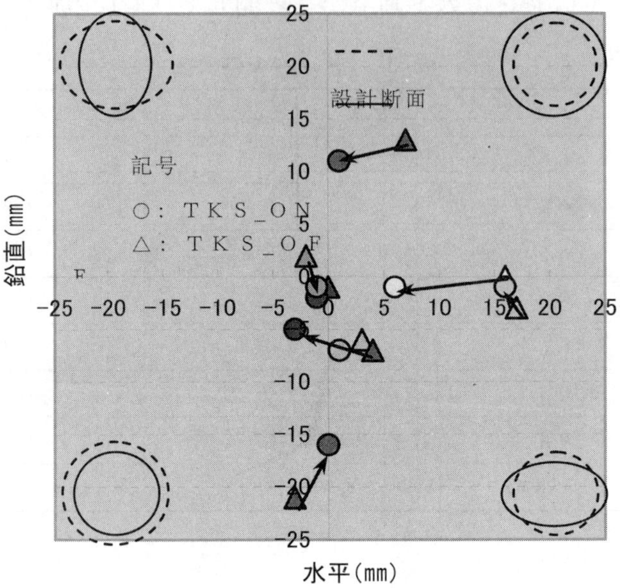

図 5　内空の測定結果

4.2　セグメントリングに発生する断面力

図 6 は新宿工区で計測されたセグメントリングの上下左右における発生応力を，横軸に掘進距離をとり示したものである．ＴＫＳを使用した掘進と使用しなかった掘進を隣接して実施した．計測は鉄筋計により行い，計測開始はセグメントリングの組立て完了直後とした．掘進長が 330 mm の時点でセグメントリングは 1 段目のテールシール(S1)の影響を受けた．掘進長が 440 mm の時点でＴＫＳを収縮して格納した．その後，2 段目(S2)および 3 段目(S3)のテールシールの影響を順に受けて

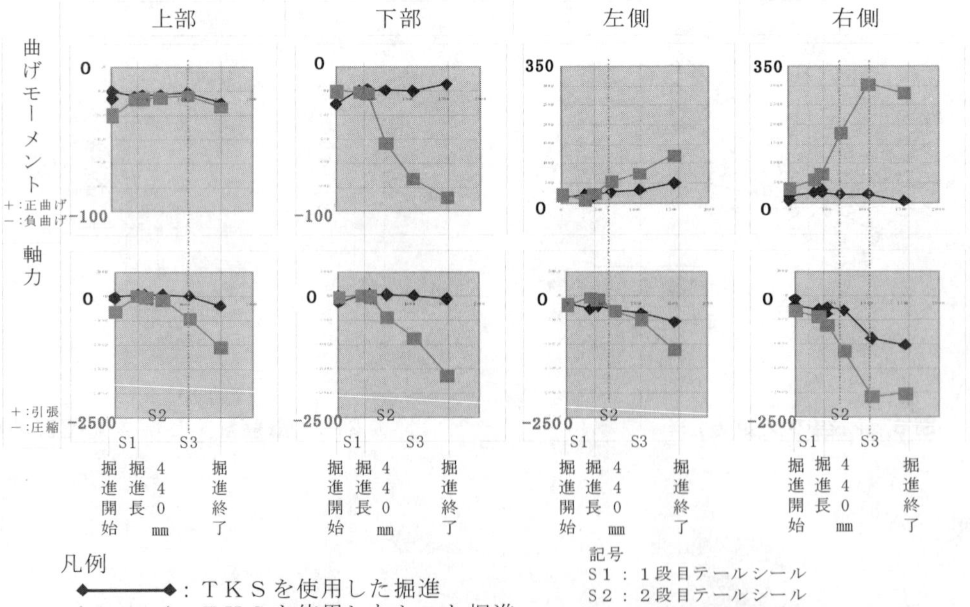

図 6　掘進中のセグメントリングの発生応力の比較

掘進を終了した．掘進中，ＴＫＳを使用した掘進は，使用しなかった掘進に比べて発生応力の変化が小さいことがわかった．とくに，2 段目および 3 段目のテールシールの影響を受ける時点では，

大きな差が現れた．これは，ＴＫＳによりセグメントリングの形状が設計断面近づき，セグメント外周からの作用力に対して影響が小さかったものと考えられる．

4.3　セグメント継手の変位

掘進前のセグメントリングにＴＫＳを作動させ，その後解放してセグメント間の目開き量を計測した．その結果，ＴＫＳを解放させると切羽側で約 5 mm の目開きが発生し，坑口側で約 1 mm であった．ＴＫＳを作動させると元にもどった（図 7 参照）．切羽側と坑口側で目開き量の差が生じたのは，セグメントリング両側の拘束状態の違いによると考えられる．ＴＫＳでセグメントリングの継手の変位を抑制できることを確認した．

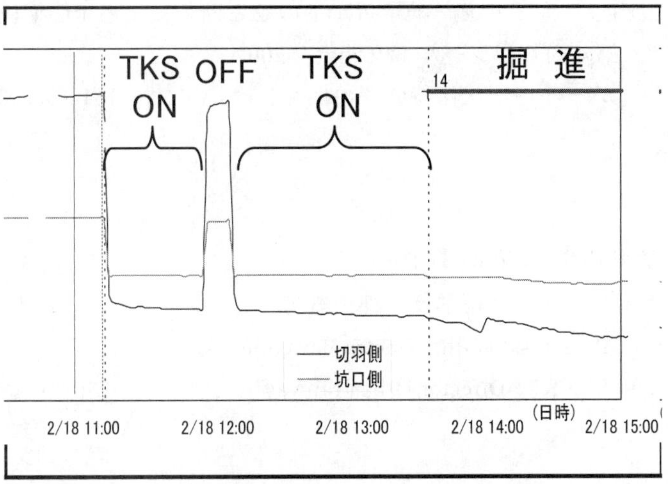

図 7　掘進中の目開きの計測結果

5　ＴＫＳの効果

これらの計測結果から，ＴＫＳはセグメントリング組立て時の形状を設計断面に近づく方向に矯正すること，セグメントリングの変形を抑制し，掘進中は発生応力の大きな変化を抑制することが分かった．

ＴＫＳの効果はつぎのとおりである．

① 組立て直後のセグメント継手の目開きなど，施工にともなう初期不良を矯正できるので，セグメントの割れや欠けなどの潜在化する損傷のリスクを低減できる．

② 組立て直後のセグメントリングを外周から拘束できるので，セグメントリングの切羽側が拡がる傾向の変形も抑制可能となり，割れや欠けなどの損傷のリスクを低減できる．

③ セグメントリングを設計断面に近い方向に矯正し，セグメントリングを外周から拘束することは，このリングに軸力が導入されることにつながり，発生する応力状態はコンクリート構造に有利となる．このため，セグメント幅を広くすることが可能となる．

④ 組立て，掘進に伴う施工誤差やテールシールによる影響など設計に見込めない荷重に対して，ＴＫＳはその影響を抑制することができる．ＴＫＳを使用することは，施工時荷重の影響を抑制し，設計断面に近い形状を確保するなど，設計どおりのシールドトンネルを構築できる．

6　おわりに

ＴＫＳによりセグメントリングの形状を矯正すること，セグメントリングに発生する応力の変化を抑制できることを確認した．今回の施工では，1 段目のテールシールの拘束によりＴＫＳと同様にセグメントリングの外周から形状を保持する効果を期待して，スプレッダーとＴＫＳが接触する直前から掘進完了までＴＫＳを作動させないこととした．しかし，計測結果から，テールシールの影響が相当に大きいことが分かった．このため，セグメントリングの組立て完了から掘進終了までセグメントリングの形状を保持可能な装置も開発済みである．

最後にＴＫＳの研究に際し，共同開発者である早稲田大学理工学術院理工学部の小泉淳教授（東京地下鉄㈱：シールドトンネル調査委員会委員）に深く感謝申し上げます．

参考文献（References）：

[1] 官　林星，藤沼　愛，小泉　淳：リング継手ボルトのせん断力によるRC平板形セグメントの応力分布に関する研究，pp.71-77，第4回日中シールド交流会，2007.

[2] 藤木　育雄，守山　亨：テール内形状保持装置の開発について，pp.151-158，第4回日中シールド交流会，2007.

著者紹介（Bio-data）：

藤木　育雄　技術部長　都市鉄道
E-mail address：fujiki@metro-dev.co.jp
Ikuo FUJIKI：Director Urban railway

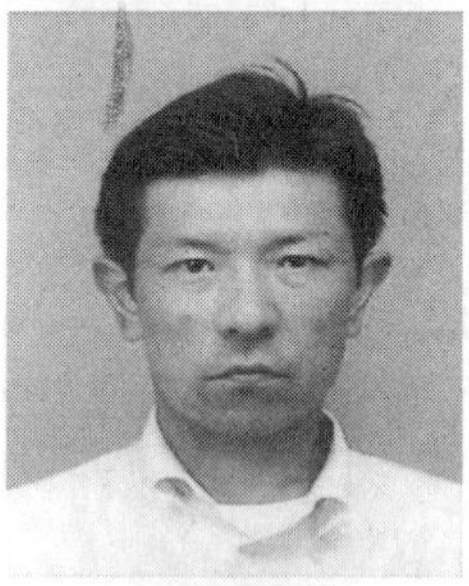

大塚　努　技術基準担当課長
E-mail address：tsu.ootsuka@tokyometro.jp
Tsutomu OOTSUKA：Manager in charge of technical standards

吉成　寿男　土木事業本部　副本部長
E-mail address：Yoshinari@satokogyo.co.jp
Hisao YOSHINARI：Deputy Chief of Civil Division

守山　亨　担当部長　シールド分野
E-mail address：t.moriyama@satokogyo.co.jp
Toru MORIYAMA：General Manager Shield Method

日立造船におけるシールド掘進機の新技術・新製品

花岡　泰治[1]　富木　広志[2]

[1]日立造船(株)産業機械事業部　開発生産技術部，大阪　592-8331

[2]同　設計部

当社は 1967 年にシールド掘進機の製作を開始し，シールド技術の発展とともに現在まで様々な技術と製品を開発してきた．本稿では当社のこれまでの実績と最新の製品及び技術の一部を紹介する．

キーワード：シールド掘進機；シールドマシン；特殊断面；特殊形状；新技術

NEW TECHNOLOGIES AND PRODUCTS OF HITACHI ZOSEN SHIELD TUNNELING MACHINES

Yasuharu HANAOKA[1], Hiroshi TOMIKI[2]

[1]Development & Production Engineering Department, Industrial Machinery Division, Hitachi Zosen Corporation, Osaka 592-8331, Japan; [2]Design Department, the same

Abstract: The shield tunneling machines have been produced since 1967. Until now, various technologies and products have been developed with the development of the shield technology. The past achievements and the latest products and technologies are expounded in this paper.

Key words: shield tunnelling machine; shield machine; special section; special shape; new technology

1　はじめに

シールド掘進機は 1818 年に考案されたが，急速に発展を遂げたのは，当社(日立造船株式会社)がシールド業界に参入した 1967 年頃からの約 40 年間である．当初は開放型の人力掘削の機械であったが，その後密閉型の機械が開発されて急速に技術が向上した．今日では日本のシールド技術は世界トップレベルであり，大型化・大深度化・長距離化・自動化・ハイテク化・異形断面化へと様々な発展を遂げてきた．

本稿では当社のこれまでの実績と最新の製品及び技術の一部を紹介する．

2　シールド掘進機の実績

当社のシールド掘進機の製造実績は，2009 年 3 月末現在で 1 160 台を超え，そのなかで特徴的な機械を年代別に表したのが図 1 である．1977 年に初めて密閉型泥水式シールド機を製作，1992 年には当時世界最大径の東京湾横断道路用ϕ14.14 m 泥水式シールドを製作した．巨礫地盤用として初めてリボンスクリューを採用し，礫地盤へのシールドの適用拡大に貢献，大型，長距離，急曲線，自動化，親子・複円・矩形・機械式接合シールドなどにおいても種々の特徴ある機械を送りだしてきた．泥土圧式シールドの最大径はϕ13.6 m，岩盤対応型シールドの最大径としてはϕ10.82 m の実績(図 2)がある．図 3 は駅舎用の 3 連複円形泥水シールド（MF シールド）で，図 4 はセグメントの自動組立装置の写真である。

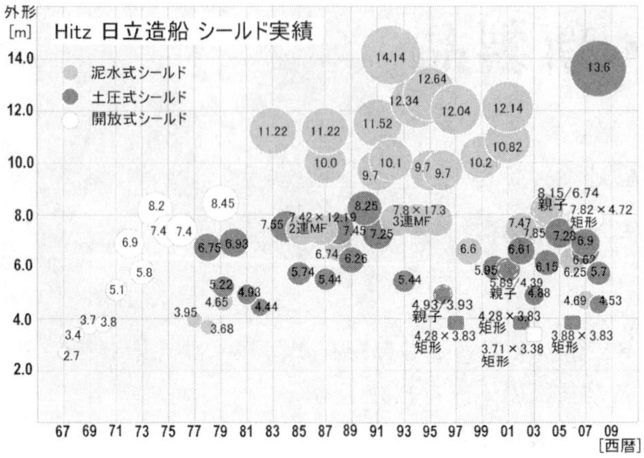

図 1　シールド掘進機の実績

図 2　ϕ10.82 m 岩盤対応泥水シールド

図 3　ϕ7.8 m×17.3 m 3 連複円泥水シールド

図 4　セグメント自動組立装置

3　海外シールドの実績

海外シールドは 1983 年に初めてシンガポールに半機械掘りシールドを納入後，中国の台湾 40 台，シンガポール 16 台，タイ 7 台，韓国 2 台，中国内陸 2 台，中国の香港 1 台，アメリカ 7 台，トルコ 4 台の実績があり，特に中国の台湾ではトップのシェアを確保している．国内市場の縮小もあり，当社では現在海外向けの比重が高くなっている状況にある．海外工事では後続のセグメント搬送，加泥，裏込め設備等もマシンメーカーの所掌となる例が多く，システム全体を取りまとめるエンジニアリング力が要求される．図 5 は昨年掘進を終えたボストン雨水トンネル用の高速仕様 EPB シールド掘進機であ

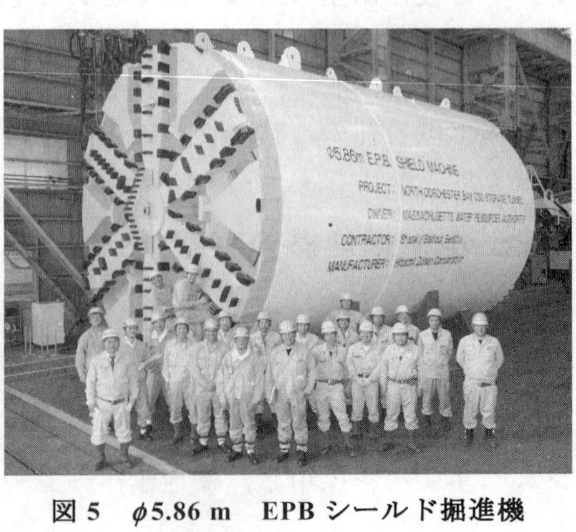

図 5　ϕ5.86 m　EPB シールド掘進機

る．トンネル延長約 3 300 m を約 10 ヶ月で掘進，掘進速度は平均 80 mm/min，最大 100 mm/min，最大月進 630 m，最大日進 35 m を記録した．

中国市場については，2008 年 5 月に中国メーカーと協業を開始し，当社から技術支援と設計・部品供給を行っている．

4 側面ドッキングシールド

側面ドッキングシールド工法は，すでに完成しているトンネルに新たに掘削したトンネルを接合する工法で，ここで紹介するシールド機は，そのうちの T-BOSS 工法に用いられるものである．機械に内蔵された特殊な切削ビットを配置した切削リングで既設トンネル壁を直接切削するもので，下記のような特徴を有している．

(1) 切削ビットは鋼製及び RC セグメントとも切削可能．

(2) 切削リングが接合時の山留めと止水の機能を有するため，地盤改良が大幅に削減できる．

(3) 機械的な接合方法であり，安全に効率よく接合を行なうことができる．

図 6 T-BOSS 工法 接合イメージ

図 6 に本工法の接合イメージを示す．

図 7 は切削に用いられるリングとビットの写真である．この特殊なビットは自生刃ビットと呼ばれ，棒状の超硬チップを多数埋め込んだ構造で，ビットが磨耗すれば新たに鋭利な刃先が生まれ切削性を維持するように考えられている．このリングを高速で回転させながら押し出し，既設トンネル壁を切削する．

図 8 は，飛鳥山幹線工事に用いられた外径 ϕ2.89 m の地中接合シールド機である．切削する既設トンネルは外径 4.3 m の鋼製セグメントであったが，大きなトラブルもなく，切削作業は切込速度 1 mm/min，約 17 時間でほぼ予定通り完了した．

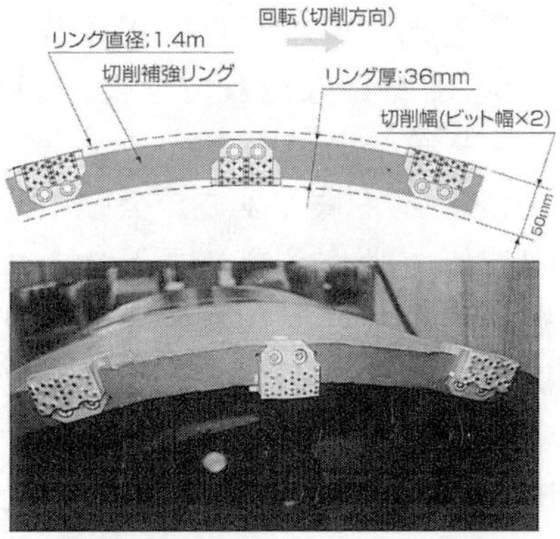

図 7 特殊切削ビット(自生刃ビット)

図 8 ϕ2.89 m 泥水式側面ドッキングシールド

5 分岐シールド

分岐シールド工法には，シールド機本体内から子機を発進させるものと，構築されたセグメント壁から発進させるものがあるが，ここで紹介するのは前者の工法のもので，大井給水所工事に採用された．この機械は分岐胴と言われる中間の部分にゲート及び子機発進エントランスを設けた構造で下記の特徴を有している．

（1）子機発進孔には旋回式のゲートが設けてあり，発進部の地盤改良が不要なため短期間に発進可能で，工期及び工費を縮減できる．

（2）ゲートの可動範囲及び子機のエントランスは水密構造となっており，ゲートを開放する前にこの水密室を泥水によって外部と同圧にすることで，ゲートの動作を軽負荷で行なえるとともに，開放時の切羽の安定を図っている．

（3）アーチ形状のゲートであるので，空間効率が高く，大きな土水圧に耐えることができる．

図 9 は子機の発進ゲートを開放した状態の写真である．子機が本体側面より直角方向に発進する．親機は正面異径ドッキング(MSD 接合)を行なう構造にもなっており，この親機の正面に別の小径のシールド機が MSD 接合を行なう．図 10 は，ゲートを閉じた状態で，工場内耐圧試験を行った時の写真である．本機は分岐・MSD 接合とも順調に施工を終えた．

図 9　ϕ4.5/2.396 m 泥水式分岐シールド

図 10　分岐胴

6　特殊断面シールド

特殊断面シールドは，主に掘削断面の高さ制限や掘削断面の最適化の要求から採用され，円形連結形状の MF シールドや DOT シールド，矩形や楕円状のシールド等の開発がなされてきた．当社では，世界で初めて円形 2 連の MF シールドを開発，その後も種々の製品を送り出してきた．

図 11 は，特殊かつ合理的な機構によって矩形断面を掘削するシールド機である．公転ドラムに所定量偏心した位置に自転カッタ軸が設けられ，お互いを所定の回転比で動作させることにより，カッタヘッドの先端は矩形断面を描いて回転する．他の矩形掘削機構と異なり，シンプルな回転運動であるので，効率がよく混練性が高いのが特徴である．また，この機械は回転比をひとつの駆動源で機構的に実現しているため，所定の掘削断面を精度よく得ることができる．

この特徴を生かし，アンダーパス工事用に開発されたのが図 12 の URUP 工法である．この工法では，従来考えられなかった地上発進，地上到達を実現している．この工法では，上記の矩形シールドを配列して大断面に対応しており，個々の矩形シールド単位できめ細かく土圧管理をすることによって低土被りでの施工を可能としている．また，開削工事と比較し工期が短く騒音も少ない．最適断面とすることができ掘削土砂量の低減が図れ，掘削後の転用も容易であるので環境負荷が非常に少ない工法である．

図 13 に実験施工の状況を示す．矩形シールドを 2 連にしたもので，所定の断面を精度よく掘削することが可能で，土圧管理に優れる機構・構造であり低土被りでの施工に十分対応できることが立証された．

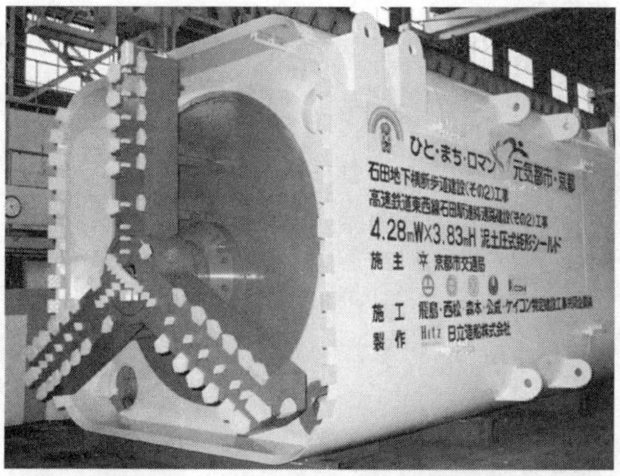

図 11 ϕ4.28×3.83 m 矩形泥土圧シールド

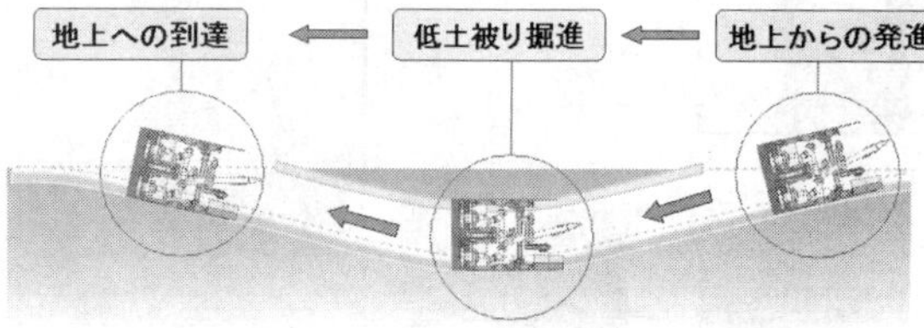

図 12 アンダーパスシールド(URUP 工法)
「資料提供 大林組」

図 13 URUP 工法実験施工シールド機「資料提供 大林組」

7 ビット交換技術

シールド工事は種々の施工条件やコスト縮減の要求から長距離化の傾向にある．1 台のシールド機で連続して掘削する距離を伸ばすためには，機械式のカッタビット交換技術がもっとも重要な課題となる．大型の機械では，気密に構成されたカッタヘッド内部へ作業者が直接入って交換する技術が実用化されている．この技術は中・小口径では適用が難しく，カッタヘッドが大型化し掘削性そのものへの影響が少なからず存在する．

そこで当社では，カッタヘッド形状への影響が少なく掘削性能を損なわない交換技術として，「押出式」のビット交換装置を開発，土槽での実証実験を行った．図 14 は装置のイメージを示したもので，掘削寿命を主に左右する先行ビットの交換に対応し，前面にビットを設けたブロックを，ガイドに沿って中心部から外周に向かって押出す方式である．

図 15 に交換フローを示す．機内側サプライゲートから新しいビットブロックを投入し，先端に送りこむ．その後最外周ビットブロックを後方に引抜・回収後，中心部からビットブロックを押出す．最も磨耗の激しい最外周ビットをひとつ手前の内側のビットに順次置き換えることになるが，一度の作業で 1 個でも全数でも交換可能である．最外周のビットが確認できることで磨耗状況を確実に把握することができる．図 16 は土槽実験の状況で，確認のため土槽上部を開放している．

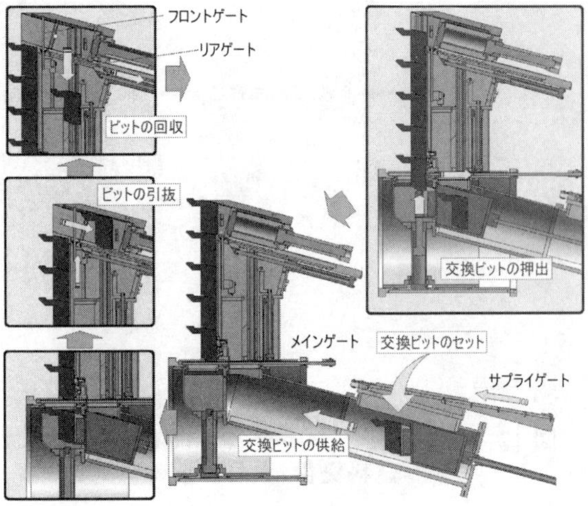

図 15 押出式ビット交換装置のフロー

図 16 土槽実験状況

この技術は，外径ϕ3.5 m のシールド機から適用可能であるが，回収機構を省略し地山への押出方式とすればより小径のシールド機にも適用可能である.

図 17 は，別タイプの簡易式ビット交換装置である．ビットが設置されたプレートをガイドにセットした状態で掘削し，交換時はこのガイドを傾動させプレートを引抜いて中央部に設置したボックスに回収する．チャンバー内をある程度空洞にする必要があるため軽微な地盤改良を必要とするが，作業の工期短縮，安全性の向上に有利な技術である.

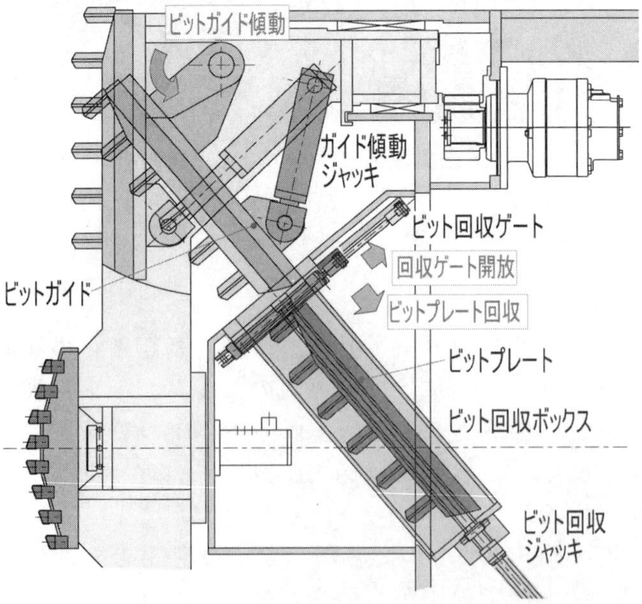

図 17 ガイド傾動回収式ビット交換装置

8 まとめ

当社のこれまでの実績と最新の製品及び技術の一部について紹介した．最近のシールド技術は施工サイドからの要求に対して技術的課題を順次解決し，あらゆる対応が可能になってきた．日本では公共工事は縮減傾向にあるが，地球環境を考慮すると地下の社会資本整備は今後も重要な分野である．世界的な需要は十分にあり，またより高い技術力を求められる工事が増えると考えられ，当社の技術が役立つことができるよう，今後とも技術革新に努力していきたい．

著者紹介（Bio-data）：

著者名：花岡　泰治

職位：日立造船株式会社　機械・インフラ本部　産業機械事業部　開発生産技術部　部長

最終学位・資格：修士(機械)，技術士(機械部門)

職務：産業機械及び建設機械の開発設計・基本設計，生産技術管理

Name: Yasuharu HANAOKA

Official Position: General manager of Development & Production Department, Industrial Machinery Division, Machinery & Infrastructures Headquarters, Hitachi Zosen Corporation

Degree: Master of engineering, Professional Engineer JP(Mechanical Engineering)

Official Job: Development and design for industrial and construction machinery, Management of production engineering

E-mail: hanaoka_y@hitachizosen.co.jp

シールドマシーンの後退と岩盤掘進対応型マシーンへの地中における改造

金野　正一
大成建設株式会社　名古屋支店，静岡県静岡市　420-0859，日本

静岡県静岡市内において，泥土加圧式シールド工事（ϕ3.53 m）にて，当初想定していない中硬岩からなる岩盤を掘進する必要が発生した．しかし，粘性土，砂礫土層等の一般土質掘進用に設計されたシールドマシーンでは，泥岩，砂岩の互層からなる岩盤層の掘進はできなかった．また，最重要交通路である国道 1 号直下であり，営業線近接および病院の直近でもあり，対策用の立坑設置ができない場所であった．そこで，岩盤掘進対応型のシールドマシーンに改造すべく，シールドマシーンを 1.2 m 後退させた．また，カッタービットを交換可能な構造のシールドマシーンに地中において改造した．その結果，中硬岩層の掘進は，2.4 m/d の進捗があり，岩盤部約 131 m を約 4 ヶ月間で無事掘進できた．これにより，新規のシールドマシーン製作，新規立坑築造等の余分な施工をすることなしに，最小の工事費，最短の期間で安全に施工できた．今後，このような事例があれば，応用できる技術であると考える．

キーワード： シールドトンネル；岩盤掘進；シールドマシーン改造

SHIELD MACHINE SHIFT BACK AND UNDERGROUND REMODELLING FOR THE EXCAVATION OF ROCK GROUND

Shouichi KONNO
Nagoya Branch, Taisei Co., Ltd., Shizuoka 420-0859, Japan

Abstract: In a EPB shield tunnel construction site (ϕ = 3.53 m) in Shizuoka, Japan, there is necessity to drive the shield passing through D class rock ground which was not expected in the design stage. The shield machine that was designed for regular clay and sandy gravel layer unables to excavate the rock ground which is composed of mud and sandy rock. Furthermore, the site is under important traffic line—State Route 1, and also adjacent to live railway line and hospital, there is no space to construct a vertical shaft for remodelling the shield machine. Therefore, the shield machine was shifted back 1.2m, and remodelled underground as that the cutter bit can be changed for the excavation of rock ground. As a result, the remodelled shield machine can excavate 2.4 m per day, and finished the 131 m rock ground driving at around 4 months. Due to no needs for building new machine and the construction of vertical shaft, the remodelling leads to the safe tunnel construction at the least cost, shortest time. This technology also can be applied in the future similar construction case.

Key words: shield tunnel; rock ground excavation; remodeling of shield machine

1　はじめに

2005 年 4 月に政令指定都市となった静岡県静岡市においては，21 世紀における豊かな暮らしを支

える都市基盤整備の一環として，共同溝整備事業を進めている．写真 1 に現在の静岡市駅前の状況を示す．この国道部分の下に，共同溝を築造する．

写真 1 ：発展を続ける静岡市静岡駅前

共同溝の築造方法として必要内空は，ϕ3.53 m であり，40 000 台/日の交通量の多い国道 1 号直下での施工となることから，シールド工法により施工することとしている．また，当該地域は，透水係数が高い砂礫地盤（玉石層）であり，井戸による地下水利用がなされていること，最大礫径ϕ360 mm の玉石に.

対して破砕することなく機内に取り込むため，ビットの磨耗が少なく，ビット交換の回数も少なくできる点を考え，泥土加圧式シールド工法を採用した．

今回シールド工法で施工するトンネル部分の延長は約 3 400 m あり，その間には，約 200 m 間隔程度でボーリングにより地質構成が想定されている．シールドマシーンによる掘削を中断した位置は，静岡層群の泥岩，砂岩の互層からなる岩盤層の中であり，一軸圧縮強度 qu＝35 MN/m^2 が確認されている．地上には，入院病床のある病院，静岡鉄道営業線が近接しているところであった．中硬岩盤層の掘進を約 130 m 残していることが地質調査の結果判明した．開削工法，山岳工法によるトンネル掘削，立坑を築造し新規製作したシールドマシーンを投入組立し掘進するなどの対策工法を検討した．

図-1 にシールドマシーン設計製作段階の地質想定断面図を示す．地質想定図の右側（西側）に安

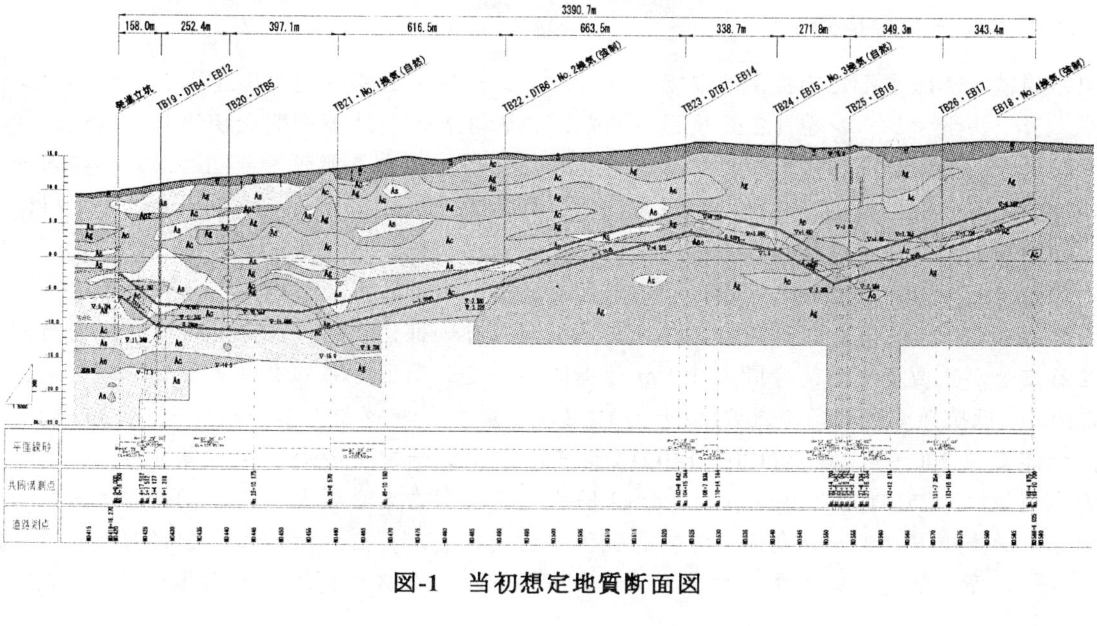

図-1　当初想定地質断面図

倍川が流れており，全体地形は，河川堆積物からなる扇状地を呈している．シールドマシーンは，図面左側（東側）から掘削を開始し，右側（西側）に到達する．トンネル延長 3.4 km の内，掘削する土質は，約 1.4 km が沖積層からなる粘性土が主体，後半約 2.0 km が玉石を主体とする砂礫層である．

図-2 に追加ボーリング調査を実施した後の，地質想定断面図を示す．当初は，粘性土主体と想定していた範囲に，静岡層群からなる泥岩，砂岩の互層が埋没していた．シールド掘削する位置では，岩盤の延長は約 250 m あった．

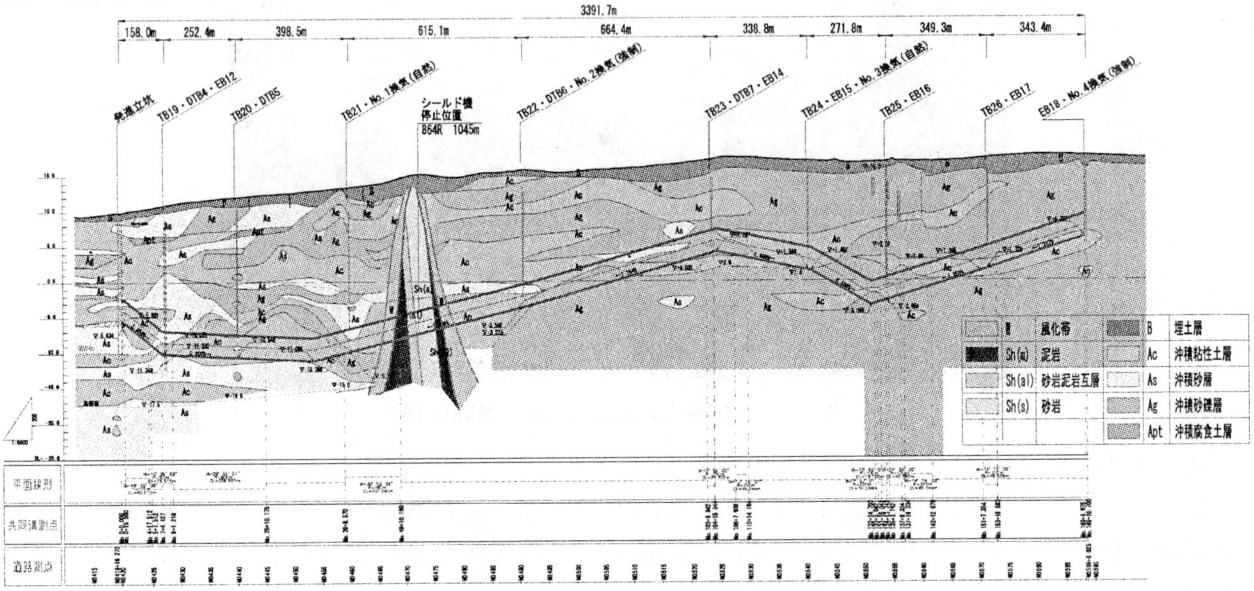

図-2　岩盤調査後地質断面図

その結果，地中において一般土質対応用のシールドマシーンを岩盤掘進対応型に改造し，掘進する工法に決定した．当該位置に立坑を設置し，地上からの材料投入，作業員の出入りを実施する施工法は，国道 1 号線を夜間車線規制を実施すること，夜間工事に伴う騒音，振動が想定されること，岩盤部を地上から掘ることになるため，施工日数の増大となり，工事期間の延長が想定された．開削工法となるため地下水位の低下も考えられた．

2 シールドマシーンの改造

2.1 シールドマシーンの後退

上記の問題を克服するために，地中でシールドマシーンを岩盤掘進対応型のシールドマシーンに改造すべく，シールドマシーンを 1.2 m 後退させた．この 1.2 m の地下空間を使用して改造を行った．シールドマシーンの後退方法については，まとめられた資料があまり無い．今回は，岩盤内という特殊条件においてシールド機を後退させた．後退方法は，センターホールジャッキを 4 台と牽引材にＰＣ鋼棒を用いてシールドマシーンを後方に牽引する方法である．シールドマシーンの後退に於いて，注意すべき点は，左右，上下のストローク管理をすることである．すでに円形に組立てられたセグメントに沿って後退させるが，シールドマシーンとセグメントが競らない様に，テールクリアランスを計測しながら後退させることが重要である．今回の 1.2 m 後退において，上下左右のクリアランス値を変更無く牽引できたことが，抵抗無く牽引できた要因の一つである．最大ジャッキ 1 本あたり 300～350 kN（30～35 t）程度で，全体で 1 200～1 400 kN(120～140 t)でシールドマシーンを後退させる事が出来た．シールドマシーンの全重量は，75.3 t であり自重の 1.5～2 倍程度の牽引力を必要とした．切羽，チャンバー内に清水を充填し，シールドマシーン全体に浮力を発生させているが，これだけの力を必要とした．図-3 にシールドマシーン牽引状況図を示す．セグメントのボルトボックスを利用し反力体を組立てた．その端部にセンターホールジャッキを配置した．写真 2 に牽引時の状況写真を示す．セグメントよりシールドマシーンを撮影したものである．奥に見えるのがシールドマシーンである．

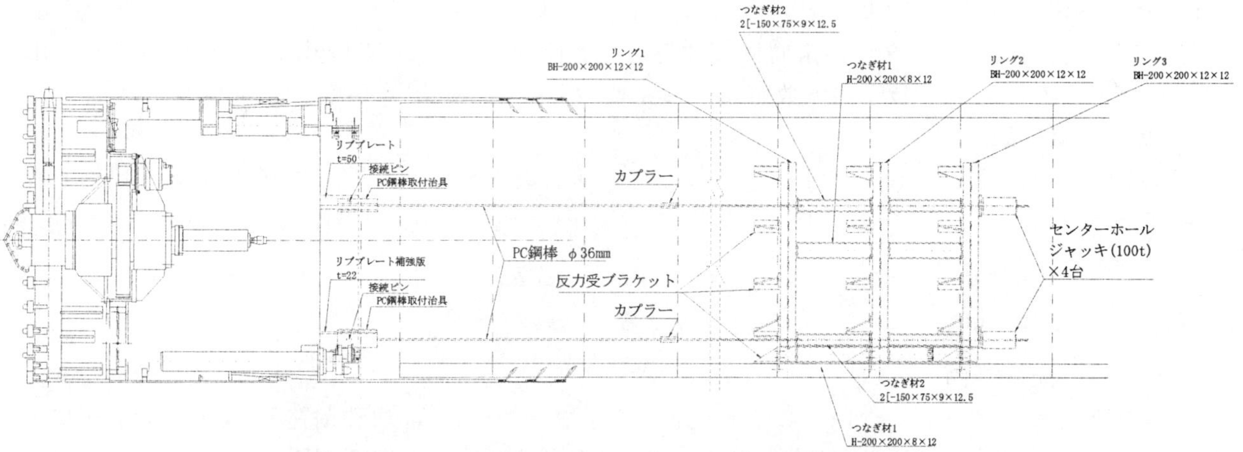

図-3　シールドマシーン牽引図

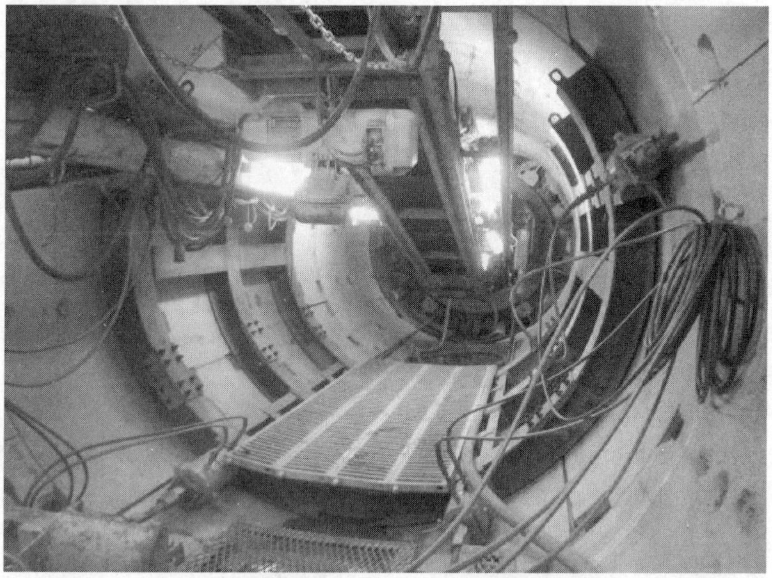

写真 2　シールドマシーン牽引状況

2.2　カッタービットについて

岩盤掘進対応型シールドマシーンの改造の基本は，地中で施工可能の範囲であり，シールドマシーンベアリング等の基本構造を変更できないことである．そのため，岩盤掘削への基本対応は，カッタービットの変更が基本となった．

（1）ビットの基本条件

カッタービットの選定に当っては，一軸圧縮強度 qu=35 MN/m^2　程度の岩盤に対して，理論上で貫入が可能であること．岩盤やコンクリート等の硬質なものを切削した実績があることと，入手が困難でないことを基本条件に選定した．シールドマシーンでの使用実績がないものも検討した結果，鋼管杭先端に取り付け，岩盤の掘削をするケーシングビットを採用した．

（2）岩盤に対して貫入

ビットは，岩盤に対して貫入可能の必要があるため，岩盤に対して貫入の可否を判定するための計算方法を示す．

a）カッタートルクの設定

地山切削に可能な抵抗トルクは，シールドマシンの常時使用状態であることと，カッター回転速度が一定値を守れることを考え設定した．この値は，スポーク撹拌抵抗トルク，練混ぜ翼撹拌抵抗トルク及びカッター外周摩擦トルクを控除する必要がある．

b）ビット総押付け可能力の算出

総押付け力(F)は，カッターが常時回転することが必要であり，押し付け力×摩擦係数＝地山切削可能トルクとなる．岩盤への摩擦係数値は，２を使用した．

c）ビット貫入圧の算出

ビット貫入圧は，ビット１個当りの貫入力をビット貫入断面積で除した値とする．ビット貫入可否の判定方法としては，ビット貫入圧pと岩盤の一軸圧縮強度quの大小関係から下式により判定する．

$p \geqq qu$	貫入可能
$p < qu$	貫入不能

（3）ビット配置計画

前項で選定したビットについてビット配置を検討した．ここに岩盤対応用のケーシングビットのパス間隔は50 mm以下をとした．これにより，ビット純間隔（ビット内面間隔）は30mm以下となる．ケーシングビットで岩盤面を切削し，削り残し部分をメインビットで剥離させるために，30mm 程度が最適であると判断した．

フィッシュテールは，岩盤層の切削において大きな抵抗が恐れがあることから，突出長を短くし，カッタートルク低減を図った．

最外周の先行ビットは，摺動距離が最も長いことから，ビットの割欠けが発生した場合の安全代を考慮し，パス数を増加させ，複数パス配置とした．最外周および最外周から５パス程度内周側について，小型シェルビットを設置した．写真3に小型シェルビット，写真4にケーシングビットを示す．

（4）ビット交換頻度の推定

限界摺動距離は限界磨耗量から求める．岩盤における磨耗係数は，施工業者の実績値として0.07 mm/km を採用し，計算を行った．また，ケーシングビットの限界磨耗量を3 mmと設定した．NOMST のような硬質なものを掘削するときの実績から設定した．カッター回転速度（Nc＝1.58 rpm），掘進速度（V＝1 mm/min）より限界掘進距離を算定した結果は，最外周部で2.4 m毎のビット交換が必要となる計算結果であった．

写真3　小型シェルビット

写真4　ケーシングビット

3　掘進結果

シールドマシーン改造完了後，岩盤部分の掘進を再開した．シールド掘進速度は，1～3 mm/分で順調に掘進可能であった．カッタートルクについても，管理目標値　常用トルクの60%以内で掘進ができた．シールド総推力も全装備推進力の 50% 以下での掘進ができた．掘進管理値以下での掘進を継続することができ，当初想定していた 2.4 m 毎のビット交換も行うことなく改造後 56.4 m 掘進し，シールドマシーンの点検を実施した．ビットの磨耗がビット母材に達する物（磨耗寮 6 mm 以上）は全て交換し，残りの岩盤掘進中に母材まで磨耗が達すると想定される物（磨耗量 4～5 mm）も全て交換．磨耗量が微量な物は（磨耗量 1～3 mm），内側の磨耗していないビットと交換を行った．この時点での磨耗係数を計算したところ磨耗係数 0.046 mm/km（想定磨耗係数 0.07 mm/km）であった．

写真 5 に，掘進前後のケーシングビットを示す．掘進後のケーシングビットは，56 m 掘削した時に，最外周に配置した，ビットである．超鋼チップの磨耗が進み，背面の母材（ＳＳ材）の座滅が進んでいるのがわかる．

写真 5　掘進前後のケーシングビット

4　結　論

一般土質掘進用シールドマシーンを岩盤対応に変更し，無事岩盤部分を掘進できた．岩盤対応シールドマシーン，TBM 用シールドマシーンに装備されているようなデスクカッターの装備，ベアリングの変更などの主要構造部材を変更することなく，岩盤掘進を完了できた．岩盤掘進における地表面における影響も無く，地下水位低下も発生しない．また，地上交通にあたえる影響もなかった．今後，複雑な土質構成の地中をシールドマシーンで掘進する際に応用できる技術であると考える．

著者紹介（Bio-data）：

金野　正一

大成建設株式会社静清共同溝工事作業所所長

1986 年　早稲田大学理工学部土木工学科学部卒業

職務：都市土木工事指揮監督

Shouichi KONNO(1963—), graduated form the Waseda University in 1986. He works for Taisei Corporation, the Project Manager of Seisinkyoudoukou Project Office.

E-mail: s-konno@ce.taisei.co.jp

泥水式シールドによる複合地盤の掘削

田中　善広[1]　野村　朝雄[2]　三野　秀作[2]　山内　健二[2]

[1]株式会社大林組 土木本部生産技術本部シールド技術部，東京　108-8502，日本

[2]株式会社大林組 ピッツバーグ工事事務所，Pittsburgh　15212，USA

アメリカのピッツバーグにおいて，アルゲニー川を横断する地下鉄単線併設トンネルを，1台の泥水式シールドマシンのUターン施工により構築する工事を担当した．アメリカでは泥水式シールド工法の採用例は少なく，また，本工事の施工条件は小土被り，玉石砂礫層，トンネル離隔の小さな併設施工，築100年以上のビルとの近接施工等と厳しいものであった．

本稿では上記の施工条件下において，地盤変状を抑制し，ビルへの影響を最小限に抑制するためのシールド機および掘進管理方法の概要および施工結果について述べる．

キーワード：Mixシールド；泥水式；砂礫層；切羽圧力

APPLICATION OF SLURRY PRESSURE BALANCE (SPB) TUNNELING METHOD UNDER CHALLENGING PROJECT CONDITIONS

Yoshihiro TANAKA[1], Asao NOMURA[2], Shusaku MINO[2], Kenji YAMAUCHI[2]

[1]Shield Tunnel Engineering Department, Civil Engineering Technology Division, Obayashi Corporation, Tokyo 108-8502, Japan;

[2]Northshore Constructors OBYASHI TRUMBULL JV, Obayashi Corporation, Pittsburgh PA 15212, USA

Abstract: The North Shore Connector Project is the extension of the existing Pittsburgh light rail transit system in Western Pennsylvania, which ultimately connects the downtown business district located on the South Shore of the Allegheny River and residential/recreational district located on the North Shore of the River. A single Slurry Pressure Balance (SPB) Tunnel Boring Machine was used to drive both tunnels underneath the river utilizing a TBM U-turn method at the receiving pit located in historical downtown area. Under some challenging conditions, acute planning and construction management were required to minimize the ground settlement.

This paper describes the construction techniques and methods including the execution of controlled excavation to minimize the ground settlement under mixed face ground conditions.

Key words: mix shield; slurry shield: sand and gravel; slurry pressure

1　はじめに

ノースショアコネクタープロジェクトは，アメリカのピッツバーグにおいてライトレール地下鉄の既設線を延伸し，アルゲニー川南岸のダウンタウン地区と北岸の住宅地・レクレーション地区を結ぶプロジェクトである．OBAYASHI-TRUMBULL JV（NSC-003/006）はアルゲニー川を横断する地下鉄トンネルとレクレーション地区に設置する駅を構築する工区を担当した．この工事のうち，アルゲニー川を横断する地下鉄トンネル工事（NSC-003）は1台のシールドマシンのUターン施工により，

単線併設トンネルを構築する工事であった．

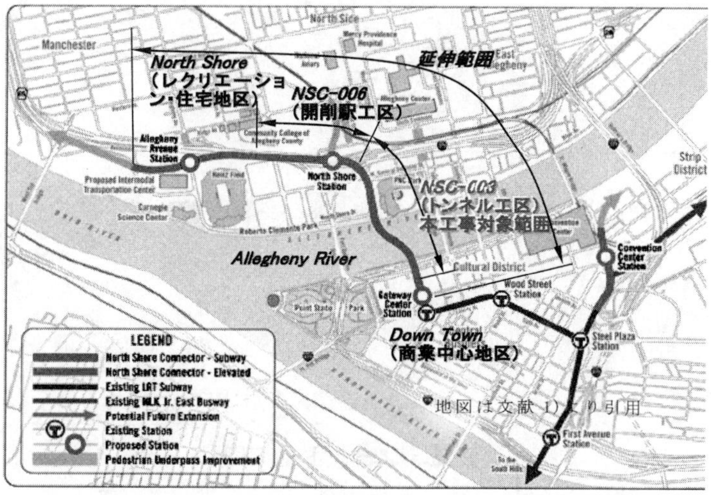

図-1　工事位置

本工事では泥水式シールド工法を採用し，Herrenknecht 社製の Mix シールドを使用した．アメリカでは泥水式シールド工法の採用例は少なく，当現場で 3 事例目であった．本工事の施工条件を以下に示す．

① DownTown 地区（回転立坑付近）では土被りが小さい（0.6D，D：掘削外径）

② 併設するトンネルの離隔が小さい（0.1D）

③ ベタ基礎構造のビルとの離隔が小さい

④ 掘削対象である洪積砂礫層は透水係数が大きく，径 φ600 mm 以上の転石を含む

その他の施工条件として，掘削対象土質は洪積砂礫層だけでなく，川底直下では岩盤層となり，移行部を含めた複合地盤に対応する必要があった．

2　工事概要

表-1 に工事概要を，図-2 にシールド平面図を，図-3 に地質縦断図を示す．シールドは野球場（PNC

表-1　工事概要

工事名称		North Shore Connector North Side Tunnels & Station Shell Contract No.NSC-003/006
発注者		Port Authority of Allegeheny County
工期		2006.10～2010.2
工事内容	シールド機径	6 920 mm
	トンネル延長	Left Tunnel 681.3 m，Right Tunnel 684.1 m 合計 1 365.4 m
	掘削土量	52 000 m^3
	トンネル線形	平面線形：最小曲率半径 R=183m（左，右カーブとも） 縦断線形：i=7.45%（上り最急勾配） i=－8.13%（下り最急勾配）
	掘削工法	泥水式シールド工法（Mix シールド）
	一次覆工	RC セグメント：1 121 リング 外径 φ6 655 mm，桁高 279 mm，幅 1 219 mm
	発進・到達方法	グラスファイバービームを使用した土留壁を直接切削
	土質	砂礫，石灰岩，頁岩，石炭，粘土岩，シルト岩，砂岩
	土被り	4.4～18.3 m（0.6D～2.7D）

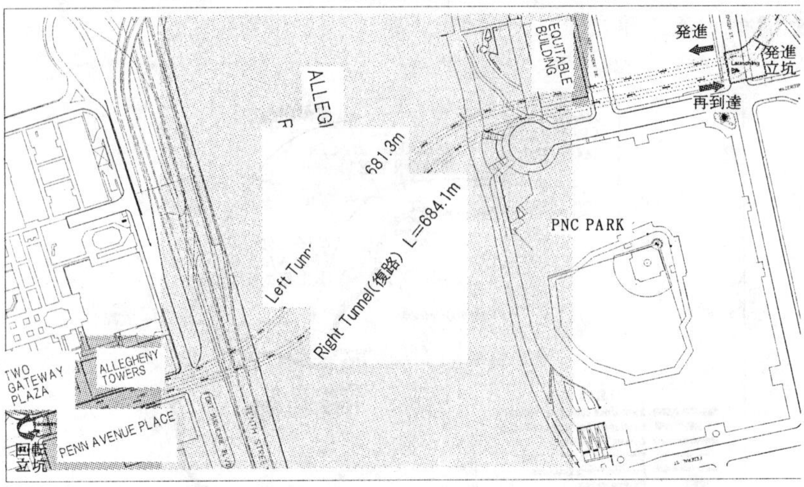

図-2　シールド平面図

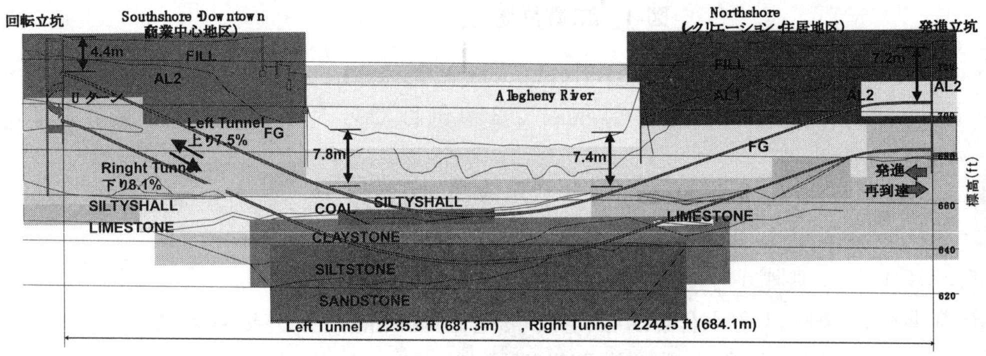

記号	層種類	一軸圧縮強度(N/mm²)
AL1	シルト質砂	N=2～14
AL2	シルト質粘土	N=2～5
FG	玉石混じり砂礫	N=30～50 以上
LIME STONE	石灰岩	19～68
SILTY SHALL	頁岩	37～81
COAL	石炭	6～14
CLAY STONE	粘土岩	2～33
SILT STONE	シルト岩	41～83
SAND STONE	砂岩	32～173

図-3　地質縦断面図

PARK）の横に設置された発進立坑から Left Tunnel 側を発進し，既設ビルの杭基礎の間を通過し，河川部を横断した後，対岸の既設建物基礎に近接しながら掘進し，回転立坑へ到達した．次に，回転立坑内でシールドＵターンを施工した後に，Right Tunnel 側を発進立坑まで再掘削した．

掘削対象地盤は全断面砂礫層から始まり移行区間を経て，河川横断部では頁岩，石灰岩，粘土岩，シルト岩および砂岩層となる複合地盤である．砂礫層は透水係数が 10^{-2}～10^{-4}(cm/min)であり，所々にϕ600 mm 程度の転石が出現する．転石の一軸圧縮強度は 48～207（N/mm²）である．また，河川横断部は比較的軟らかい岩から硬い岩まで出現し，一軸圧縮強度は 2～173（N/mm²）と変化に富む岩盤である(図-3).

3　施工方法

3.1　シールド機

泥土圧シールド工法の場合，砂礫層から変化に富む岩盤層への移行区間において，必要な切羽土圧を保ちながら，掘削土砂の塑性流動性を確保することが難しいことが予想された．またアメリカでは出現地盤に臨機応変に対応するために，様々な添加材をすぐに入手することが困難であったことから，泥水式シールド工法を選定した．

今回の泥水式シールド機はドイツの Herrenknecht 社製の Mix シールド機であり，切羽泥水圧の制御方法および礫への対応が日本で一般に使用される泥水式シールドとは異なる特徴を持つ．

(1) 切羽泥水圧制御

切羽泥水圧は，日本式のように送泥ポンプと排泥ポンプの流量を制御することによって一定に保つのではなく，掘削用チャンバーの背面に圧気用チャンバーを設け，圧力調整弁により圧気圧を一定に保ち，掘削チャンバー内の切羽泥水と排泥口の間の圧気チャンバー内の泥水圧を制御する．よって，図-4 に示すとおり，掘削チャンバー内の泥水圧（以下，切羽泥水圧とする）は圧気チャンバー内の圧気圧と泥水高さ（以下，圧気圧と泥水高さとする）で決定される．送排泥ポンプの回転数制御は，泥水高さの変動がシールド中心に対して±0.1～0.15 m となるように，シールド運転手が手動運転で行うのみで，複雑な自動制御運転は必要がない．

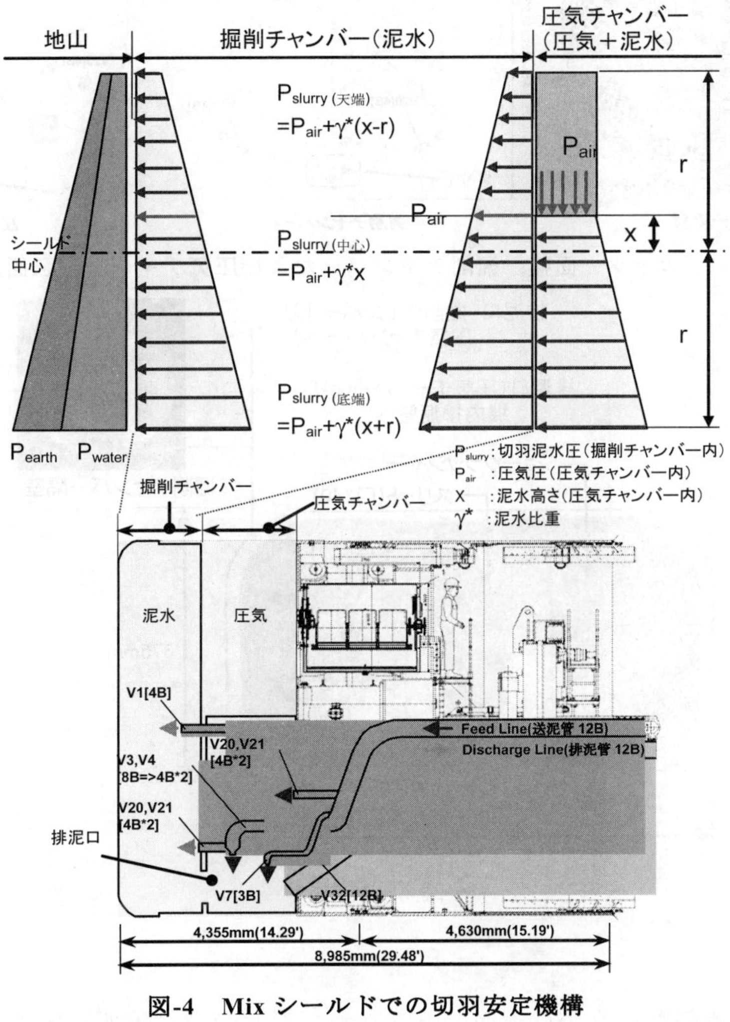

図-4　Mix シールドでの切羽安定機構

切羽泥水圧の設定は静止土圧＋水圧＋変動圧を基本として行い，地盤変状量を監視しながら調整を行った．Mix シールドにおける切羽泥水圧の指示は，泥水高さをシールド中心に調整することを前提として，圧気圧により行った．

（2）礫への対応

掘削土砂に含まれる礫は，カッター面盤に設置されたローラーカッターと圧気チャンバー内の排泥口手前に設置されたジョークラッシャーにより，破砕される（図-6 参照）．排泥管へ取り込む礫の寸法は，排泥口手前に設置されたスリットにより制限される．ジョークラッシャーおよびスリットには閉塞を防止するため，図-4，5 に示すように送泥水を噴き付ける洗浄ラインが設けられている．圧気チャンバーへの洗浄ラインの設置に伴い，地上からの送泥水は機内で掘削チャンバーおよび圧気チャンバーへの配管へ分配されるが，掘削チャンバーの泥水循環を確保するためには，大量の送泥流量が必要となる．日本の泥水式シールドのように，すべての泥水を掘削チャンバー上部から送り込み，チャンバー内の泥水循環とともに掘削土砂を下部から取り込むように配慮する設計思想と比較すると，今回のマシンでは掘削チャンバー内の泥水循環が弱く，排泥口において閉塞が度々発生した．そのため，シールド機内に循環用ポンプを増設し，チャンバー内への送泥量が多くなるように改造した．また，掘削チャンバー下部に掘削土砂が滞留しないように，攪伴棒と固定棒を増設した．

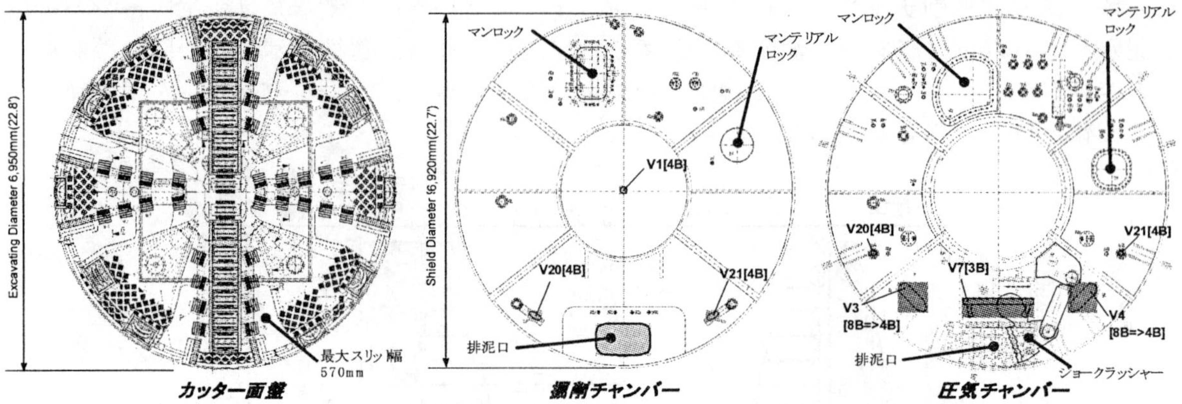

図-5　カッター面盤，掘削チャンバーおよび圧気チャンバー正面図

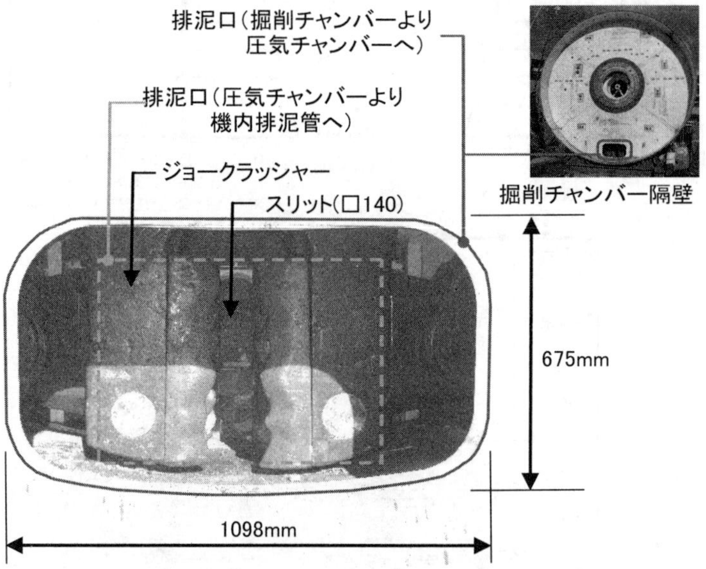

図-6　排泥口

3.2　泥水性状管理

掘削対象地盤が透水係数の高い砂礫層であるため，泥水管理は重要管理項目のひとつであった．泥水は通常，有効泥水圧（切羽泥水圧のうち，地下水圧よりも大きい分）によって地盤に浸透する．地盤の間隙が小さい（透水係数が低い）場合には，掘削面のごく近傍において泥水中の土粒子によって地盤の間隙が目詰めされ，泥水膜が形成されて，浸透は止まる．一方，本工事のように透水係数が高い（間隙が大きい）場合には，泥水中の土粒子では目詰めされにくいので，泥水浸透による損失圧力と有効泥水圧が等しくなる地点まで泥水が浸透し，泥水浸透によるゾーンとして切羽を安定させる．損失圧力の勾配に関係するのは降伏値であるため，通常の泥水管理項目であるファンネル粘性ではなく，降伏値に着目して，泥水品質調整を行った．表-2 に砂礫層掘削時における管理基準値を示す．補給泥水は日本では通常，ベントナイト，一般粘土，添加材で配合するが，アメリカでは一般粘土が入手困難であったた

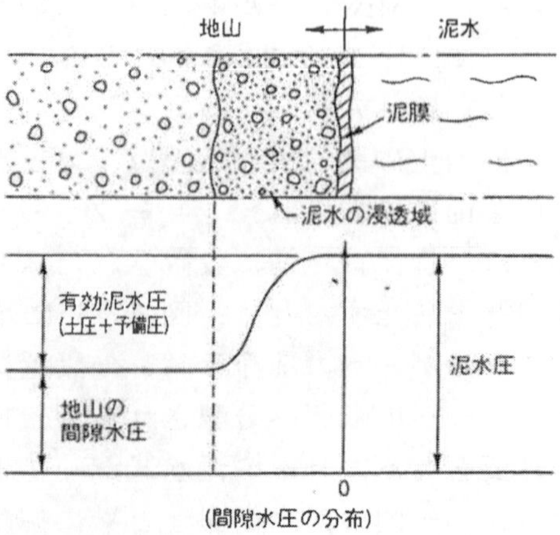

図-7　切羽付近の状況模式図

め，ベントナイトと添加材で配合した．砂礫層掘削時の泥水性状は，セグメント組立中の地山への逸泥量を監視しながら，管理値が適正であるか，確認した．

表-2　泥水の品質管理値（砂礫層掘削時）

測定・管理項目		試験方法	管理値	測定頻度
造壁性(脱水量)		API 規格加圧ろ過試験器(7 kgf/cm^2，30 分)	50 ml 以下	各リング毎 ・掘削開始前 ・掘削完了後
流動特性	降伏値	Fann VG メータ	60～150 dyn/cm^2	
	粘性	API 規格ファンネル粘度計(946/1 500 ml)	－ （測定のみ）	
比　重		API 規格マッドバランス	1.03～1.25	
砂分率		API 規格砂分計	10%以下	
pH		ガラス電極法	－	

岩盤層掘削時には循環泥水中に掘削土砂の一次処理設備で分離できない細粒分が残留し，比重が上がっていったため，掘削開始前に，比重が掘削前に 1.20 以下となるように，水道水による希釈で泥水調整を行った．

4　施工結果

4.1　切羽泥水圧制御

図-8 に砂礫層掘削時のシールド中心高さでの切羽泥水圧，圧気圧と泥水高さを示す．切羽泥水圧の変動は，砂礫層掘削に伴う切羽泥水圧の直接的な変動，泥水高さの変動および圧気圧の変動に起因するが，すべてを含めて±0.005 MPa の範囲内に収まっている．砂礫層において掘削状態が安定している場合，切羽泥水圧は手動運転による泥水高さの変動に伴って緩やかな振幅と，その振幅に対して砂礫層掘削による変動に伴う微動の振幅を示す．その微動の振幅は，圧気チャンバーが圧力変動を吸収することで±0.001 MPa 程度に収まっている．

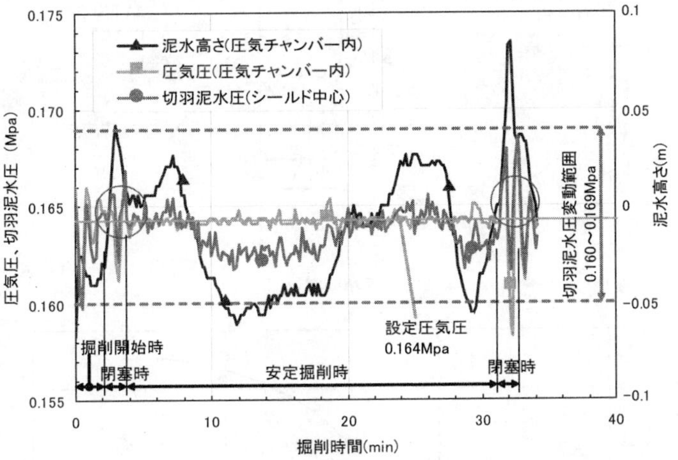

図-8　砂礫層掘削時の切羽泥水圧，圧気圧および泥水高さ

また，排泥口スリット部で礫が閉塞した場合には，泥水高さはまず急上昇し，ジョークラッシャーがスリット部の閉塞を解除した後に，泥水高さは急降下している．この閉塞時においても，圧気圧の自動制御により，掘削チャンバー圧力の変動は±0.005 MPa の範囲に収まっていることがわかる．これは，泥水式シールド工法によって砂礫層を掘削した場合に変動圧が±0.01 MPa 程度であることと比較すると，非常に小さな変動である．

4.2 地表面沈下量

図-9 に Downtown 地区（回転立坑付近）の平面図を示す．Downtown 地区ではトンネル両側のビルと近接しながら掘削し，回転立坑に向かって，土被りが急激に小さくなり，回転立坑では 4.4 m となる．近接する建物は築 100 年以上と古い建物であり，特に PENN AVENUE PLACE はベタ基礎構造であるため，建物への影響は最小限に抑制する必要があった．そのため，事前検討を行い，建物の健全性が確保できる範囲まで Right Tunnel 側に CJG 工法による近接防護を実施した．

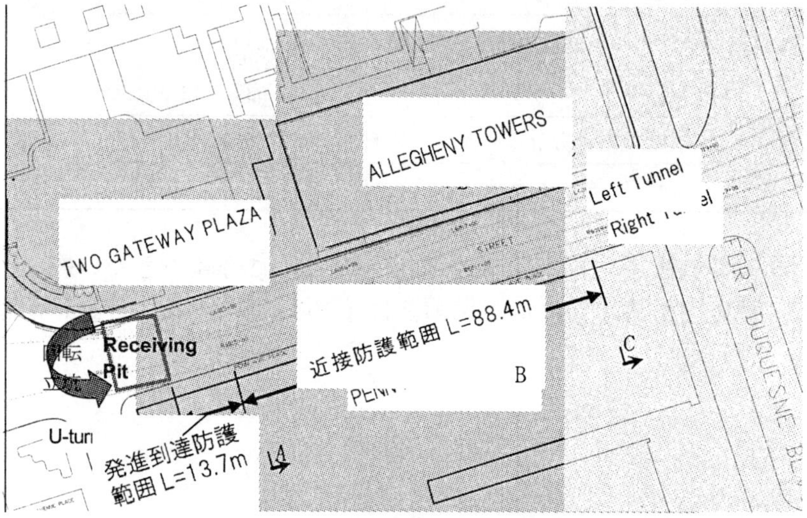

図-9 回転立坑付近平面図

図-10～12 に Downtown 地区における地表面沈下量について，FEM 解析値と実測値の比較を示す．比較断面として，①発進到達防護区間と近接防護区間の境界（A 断面），②近接防護区間の代表断面（B 断面），③近接防護区間と一般区間の境界（C 断面）を選定した．FEM 解析は弾性 2 次元有限要素法を用い，地盤要素は平面ひずみ要素，セグメントおよび内部支保工要素は梁要素とし，応力解放率は 5%とした．

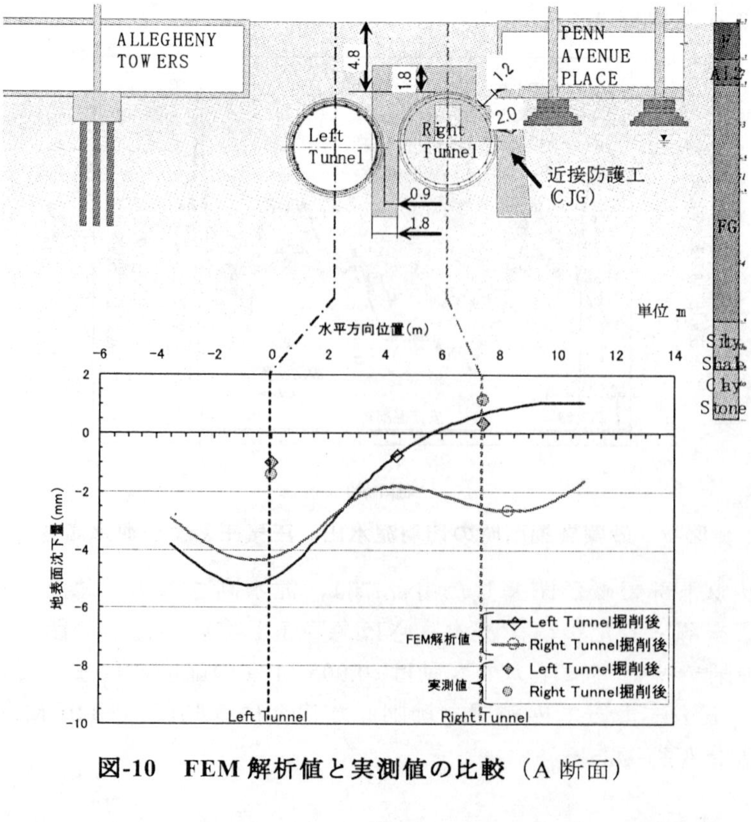

図-10 FEM 解析値と実測値の比較（A 断面）

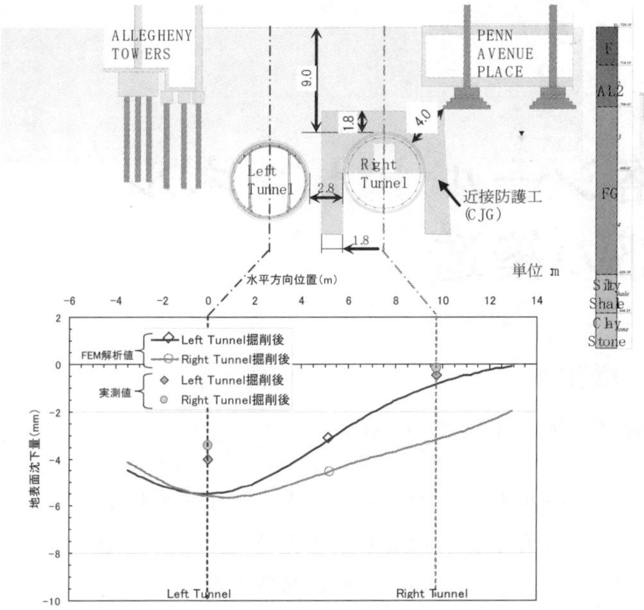

図-11 FEM 解析値と実測値の比較（B 断面）

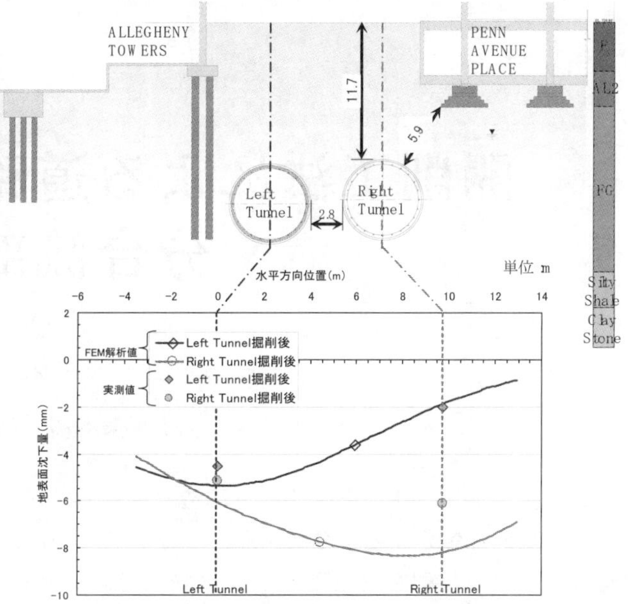

図-12 FEM 解析値と実測値の比較（C 断面）

FEM 解析値と実測値はおおむね一致しており，FEM 解析により地盤変状をシミュレートできていると考えられる．応力解放率は最近の日本の実績では 5%～15%に設定しており，今回の結果では応力解放率 5%の解析値と実測値がほぼ同じであったことから，Mix シールドの切羽安定性が高く，また，掘進管理が適正であったと言える．

5 結 論

今回，Mix シールドを用いて砂礫層を掘削した結果，通常の泥水式シールドよりも切羽圧力の変動が小さいことがわかった．ベタ基礎構造のビルへの近接施工時にも，構造物の変位はほとんど見られなかった．圧気チャンバー内の泥水高さを監視しながら，泥水ポンプを自動制御できるようになれば，切羽圧力の変動はさらに小さくできると考えられる．また，この Mix シールドは圧気設備を常時配置していること，圧気作業時には圧気チャンバーを圧気作業室として使用できることから，ローラーカッターの交換を効率的に行える．したがって，今回のような複合地盤の掘削に効果を発揮すると考えられる．

参考文献（References）：

[1] Port Authority of Allegheny County ホームページ： http://www.portauthority.org/

著者紹介（Bio-data）：

田中 善広 株式会社大林組土木本部生産技術本部シールド技術部 課長

最終学位：大阪市立大学大学院修士課程 専門分野：シールド工法

職務：シールド工法に関する施工技術検討および技術開発

Yoshihiro TANAKA, Supervisor, Shield Tunnel Engineering Department, Civil Engineering Technology Division, Obayashi Corporation The final degree: Master's degree in Osaka City University Graduate school of engineering .Specialized field: Shield Tunnel Engineering.

E-mail: tanaka.yoshihiro@obayashi.co.jp

開削工法による道路シールドトンネル分合流部の築造

三木　章生

ハザマ　土木事業本部 技術第一部，東京　105-8479

道路シールドトンネルの分合流部を築造するため，併設したシールドトンネルを開削工法によって切開き工法を実施した事例を報告する．切開き施工に対して、土留壁の安定対策や止水対策として先行地中梁や土留壁背面の地盤改良，二次土留を実施し,シールド安定対策に対しては、逆巻き工法，シールド内部支保工，トンネル間支保工，開削幅の広い区間においては中間土留壁などを施工した．

キーワード：シールドトンネル；分合流部；切拡げ；開削工法；逆巻き工法

CONSTRUCTION OF ENLARGING ROAD SHIELD TUNNEL FOR THE OPEN-CUT METHOD

Akio MIKI

First Engineering Department, Civil Engineering Division, HAZAMA　Corporation, Tokyo 105-8479, Japan

Abstract: This paper describes the construction of the cut and open of a part of steel segments installed in two-parallel large dimensional shield tunnels using the open-cut method. The construction method is the open-cut method, which is using ground improvement, top-down construction method, timbering and wall of second.

Key words: shield tunneling; branch and connection; space enlargement; open cut method; top-down construction method

1　はじめに

大都市部を中心に道路トンネルでシールド工法の採用が増えている．とくに出入口など分合流部に対しては，シールドトンネル側部を掘削し，セグメントを部分的に撤去し，地中に大きな空間を設ける切開き施工が採用されている．首都高中央環状新宿線においては，シールド工法を主体とした地下道路トンネルであり，出入口や連結路の分合流部の構築方法としてこの切開き工法を最初に採用した道路である．その施工方法としては，分合流部躯体を地上から施工する開削工法，もしくは地中から地山を支保しながらシールドトンネル上部に地中空間を設け，そこからトンネル間地山を掘削して躯体を構築する非開削工法がある．ここでは，開削工法によって施工した事例を報告する．中央環状新宿線は，すでに北側の 4 号～5 号に至る区間は平成 19 年 12 月に開通済みであり，本工区は 4 号よりも南側に位置する工区である．本工区の位置図を図-1 に示す．

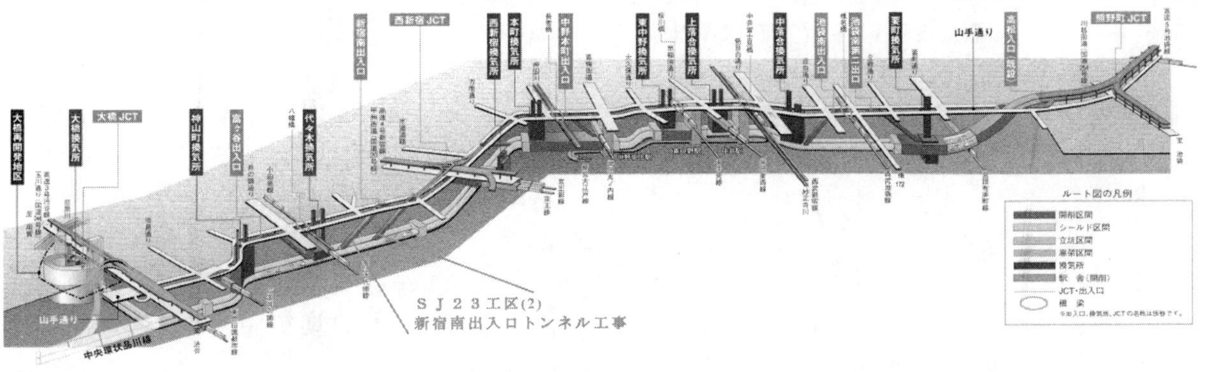

図-1　中央環状新宿線・路線図

2　開削切開き工事の概要

2.1　工事概要

本工区は，首都高速中央環状新宿線と高架構造の４号線を結ぶ新宿南連結路および新宿南出入口２つの分合流が接近した区間であり，本線シールドトンネル（ϕ12.83 m）を延長 190 m にわたり開削工法による切開き工法によって施工する工事である．当工事における縦断図，平面図および標準断面図を図-2～図-3 に示す．以下に工事概要を示す．

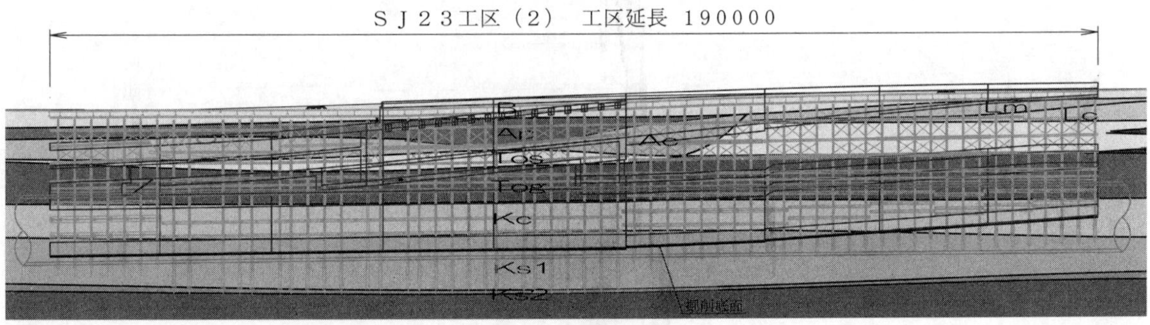

図-2　土層縦断図

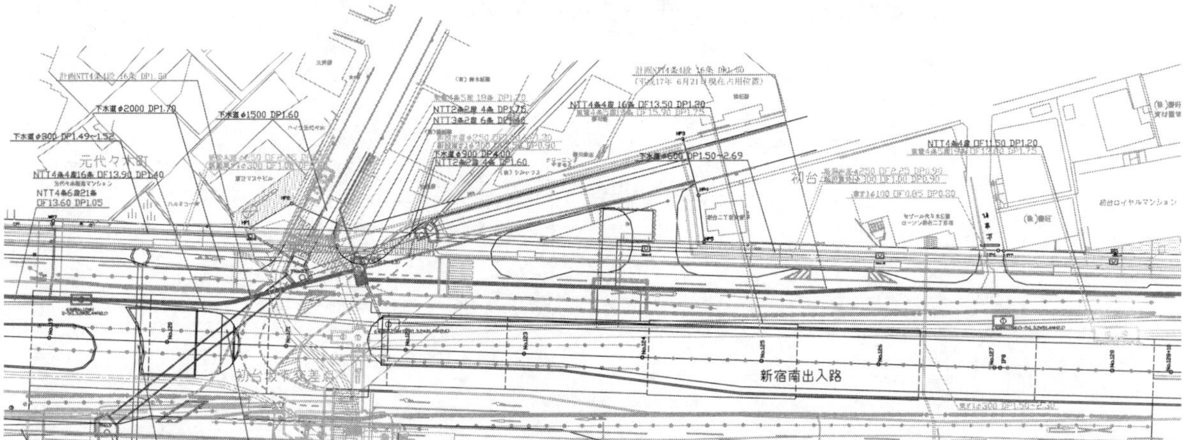

図-3　平面図

工事名称：① (高負)SJ23 工区(2)新宿南出入口トンネル工事

② (高負)SJ23 工区(2)新宿南出入口トンネル（その２）工事

施工者：ハザマ・東鉄・大木(高負)SJ23（2）新宿南出入口トンネル特定建設工事共同企業体

施工場所：東京都渋谷区元代々木町、初台二丁目

工　期：① 平成 14 年 3 月～平成 17 年 3 月

② 平成 17 年 3 月～平成 21 年 12 月（予定）

切開き対象：シールドトンネルϕ12.38 m(外径)×2 本（他ＪＶ施工），延長 190 m

代表工種：地中連続壁工(5 400 m^2)，高圧噴射攪拌工（3 300m^2），切梁腹起工(3 300 t)，掘削工（71 000 m^3），躯体工（25 000 m^3）

2.2 本工区における切開き工事の特徴

本工区における切開き工事の特徴は次に示すとおりである．

① 上部の出入口トンネルと切開き施工の対象となる連結路トンネルのダブルデッキ構造となっている(図-4 参照).

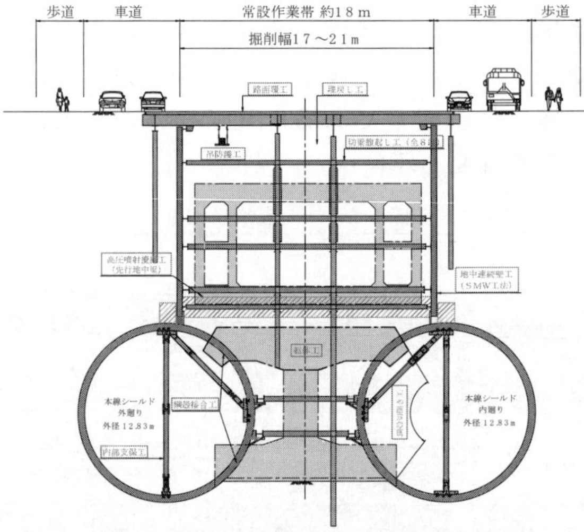

図-4　代表的な切開き断面図の概要

② 延長が長く，躯体構造が２本柱，１本柱，ボックス構造と連続的縦断的に変化する(図-5，図-6 参照).

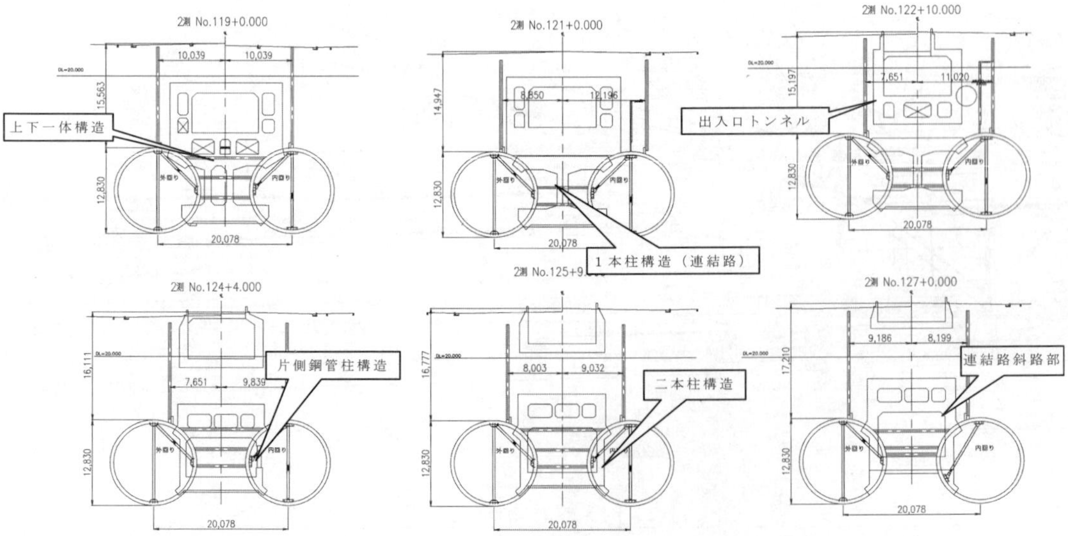

図-5　部の構造断面図

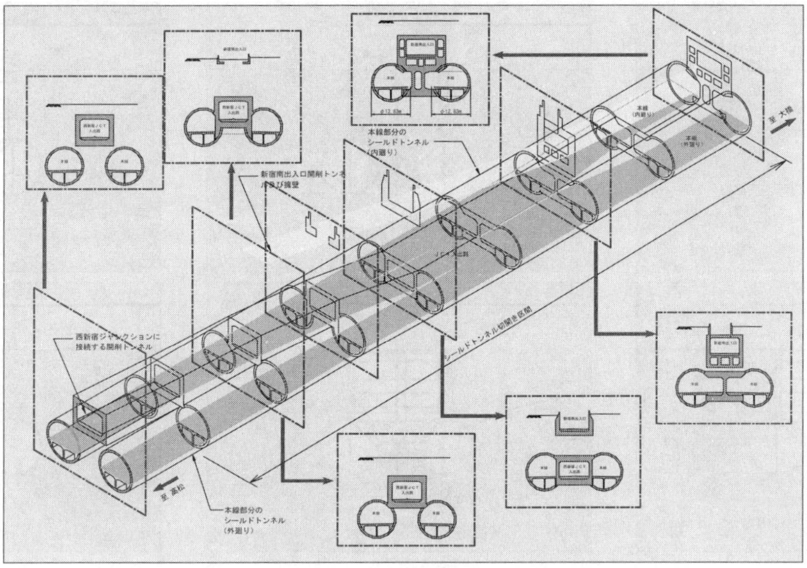

図-6　分合流部における鳥瞰図

③ 地下埋設物等により左右の土留め位置や鋼殻剛性が左右対称でない断面が数多く存在する．さらに同時に施工する電力洞道の推進工事により開削幅が広い区間があることから，逆巻き施工，鉛直荷重を確保する二次土留め，地下水制御などによるトンネル安定対策を併用している（図-7 参照）．

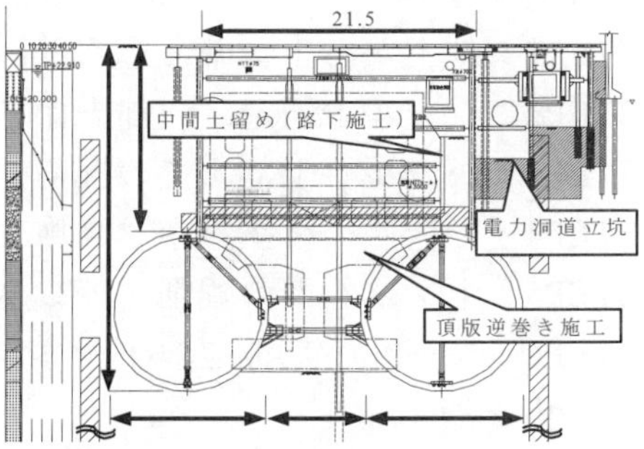

図-7　掘削幅が広い断面

2.3　開削切開き工事の課題

開削切開き工事では，上部の土留構造において根入れがなくなること，掘削に伴い上下・左右の荷重バランスが崩れセグメントに大きな断面力が生じること，トンネル上部掘削によりシールドの浮き上がりや変形が大きくなることなどが課題として挙げられる．対策として，上部土留壁に対して先行地中梁の設置や土留壁下端部への対策などを実施した。また，セグメント躯体接合部は大きな断面力に耐えうる構造を採用した．主な課題と対策方法については，参考文献 1)にて報告されている．

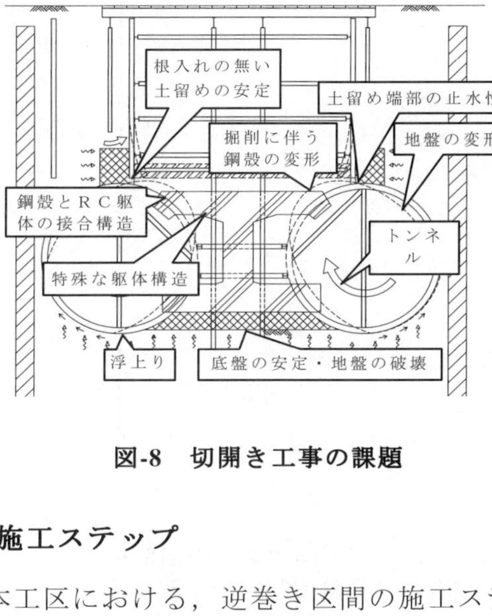

図-8　切開き工事の課題

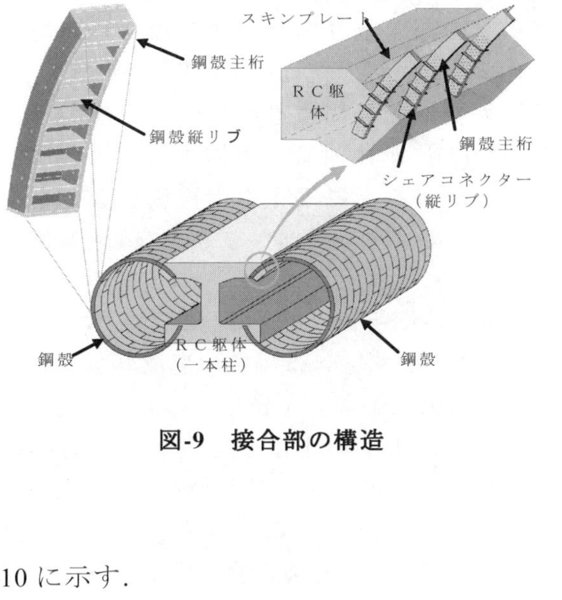

図-9　接合部の構造

2.4　施工ステップ

本工区における，逆巻き区間の施工ステップを図-10 に示す．

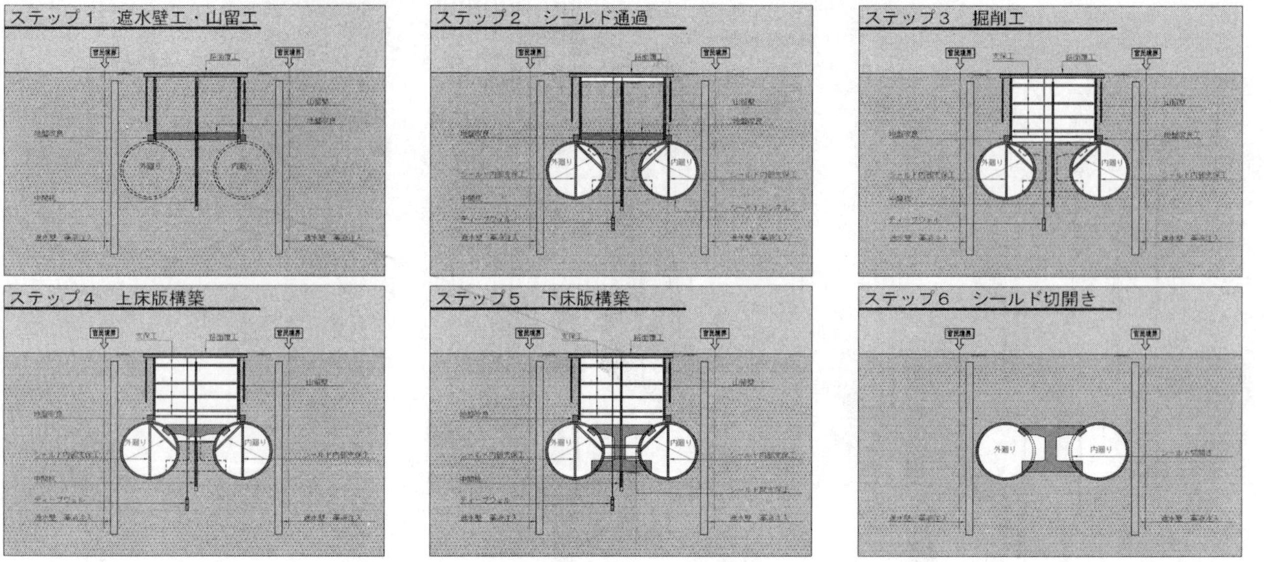

図-10 逆巻き区間の施工ステップ図

主な施工手順は下記のとおり.

STEP1：地上から土留壁，遮水壁，先行地中梁，路面覆工までを施工

STEP2：シールド通過，内部支保工の施工（他 JV 施工）

STEP3：シールド上部までの掘削，土留支保工の設置

STEP4：上床版の構築（逆巻き施工）

STEP5：トンネル間の掘削，トンネル間支保工設置，躯体構築

STEP6：シールド切開き（トンネル間支保工撤去，セグメント撤去，内部支保工撤去），埋戻し，トンネル内床版の施工

3 施工状況

切開き工事の課題に対する対策工を中心に，代表的な施工状況を紹介する.

（1）上部掘削工

シールド上部掘削時には，土留壁の変形やシールドの浮き上り等を計測しながら実施した．土留壁下端部の先行地中梁撤去時には，下端の過大変形などによる出水の危険性があったため，(2)に示す対策を実施すると共に，事前に計測結果を元に実際の土質状況などもとに土留変位のフィッティングを実施し，変位予測解析を行った.

変位予測解析結果を図-11 に示す．撤去後の変位量は予測結果とほぼ同等の変位となった.

（2）根入れのない土留壁への対策と施工

シールド上部の土留壁はトンネル間の掘削により根入れがない土留となるため，土留壁安定と土留壁下端部の止水対策として先行地中梁・土留壁背面の地盤改良，土留壁下端の二

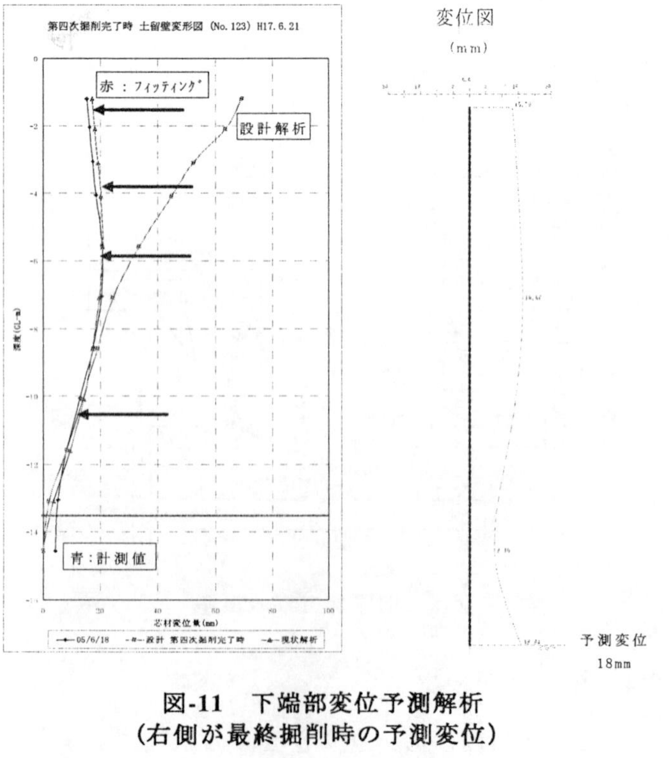

図-11 下端部変位予測解析
(右側が最終掘削時の予測変位)

次土留工を施工した．二次土留工は，セグメントと二次土留鋼材の間は，トンネル間掘削時のシールドの変形に追従できるよう弾力性のある材料を用いて接続した．図-12 に土留下端部の構造を，写真-1 に二次土留の施工状況を示す．

(3) トンネル間掘削

トンネル間は最小約 7 m 程度と狭隘で，特に 1 本柱区間では中間杭が 2 列施工となっており掘削重機の施工性や効率の低下が懸念された．特に逆巻きスラブ下の掘削では，掘削残土の搬出等を考慮して，低空頭掘削機械にカッターローダ（写真-2）を使用して施工を行った．

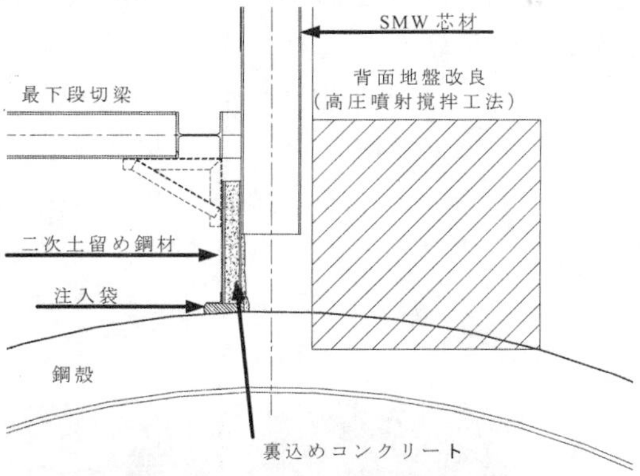

図-12　土留下端部の構造

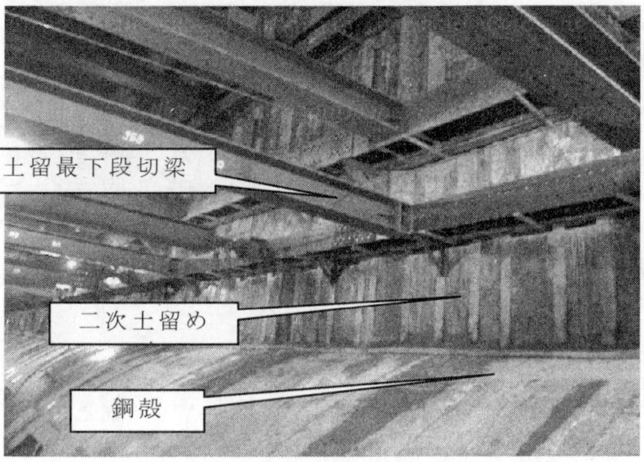

写真-1　二次土留め

写真-2　カッターローダー

(4) トンネル間支保工

トンネル間掘削時および躯体構築時のシールド変形抑制のため，トンネル間支保工を設置した．支保工とセグメントの接続部はシールド主桁部に確実に力を伝達でき，円形のトンネルに腹起し・切梁を設置するために，接続治具を主桁に溶接しそれに腹起しを接続する構造とした（図-13，写真-3）．

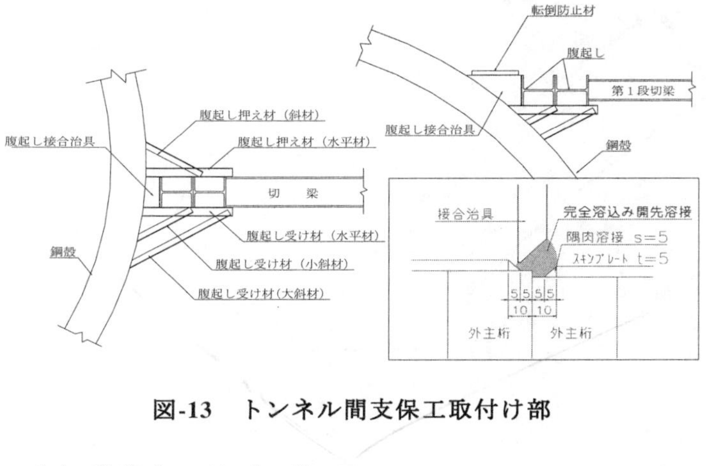

図-13　トンネル間支保工取付け部

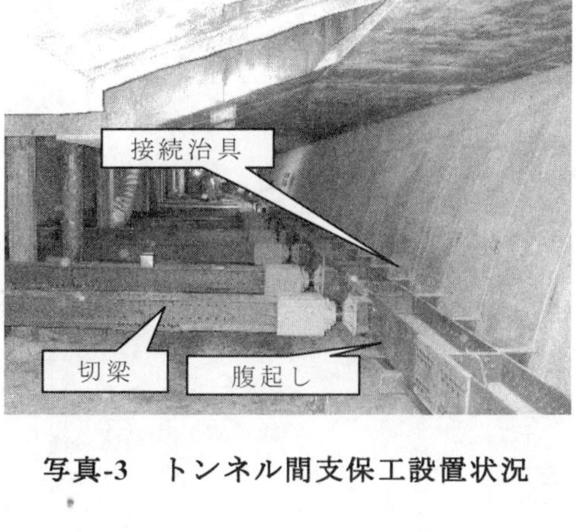

写真-3　トンネル間支保工設置状況

(5) 逆巻きスラブの施工

シールドトンネルの安定のため，躯体形状が 1 本柱区間においては，逆巻き工法を採用した．トンネル間掘削時に剛性の高いスラブを先行施工することにより，シールドの安定を確保できる構造である．

逆巻きスラブは，トンネル間掘削時の変形を抑制するため，出来るだけ先掘りを小さくできる地下受け方式で施工を行った．躯体設計上，柱接続部のハンチが大型化していたため底型枠の施工精度確保に，軽量盛土材を使用した（写真-4）.

（6）セグメント躯体接合部の施工

接合部は図 2-8 に示すように，主桁を躯体コンクリートに巻き込むことで一体化を図っており，セグメントの縦リブを一部残してシェアコネクタの役割を持たせた構造となっている．主桁と主桁の間には，躯体構造としての主筋が配筋されるとともに，主桁周囲に補強鉄筋が配置され，過密配筋になることが予想された．そのため，事前に接合部の実大モデルを作成して施工性を確認した．現場での配筋状況を写真-5 に示す.

写真-4 逆巻きスラブの底型枠（この上に型枠材を設置した）

写真-5 鋼殻・躯体接合部配筋

（7）接合部の防水

セグメント切断部やセグメント周囲からの漏水防止のため，それぞれの水みちに対して二重の防水仕様とした.

防水仕様は下記のとおりである(図-14).

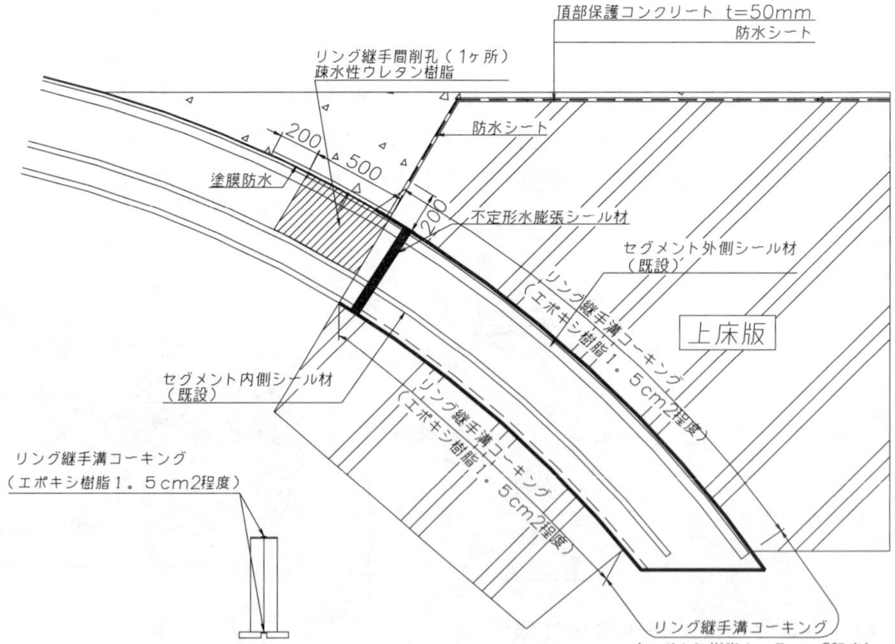

図-14 接合部の止水方法

① 主桁間はウレタン樹脂の注入
② セグメント外側の躯体との接続箇所は，継手防水として吹付け塗膜防水を採用
③ 躯体内および切断面の主桁目地部はコーキングを実施
④ 主桁周りに不定形型水膨張シール材を設置

（8）セグメント切断撤去および内部支保工の撤去

セグメントの切断撤去は，主桁を除くスキンプレートと縦リブは躯体構築前に撤去を行い，主桁の撤去は躯体構築後に撤去した．主桁や内部支保工撤去時には，シールドの変形や主桁残留応力の解放によりシールドの安定が損なわれる危険性があったため，計測によって軸力増加などを見ながら施工を行った．計測の結果は，内部支保工に多少軸力増加が見られたものの主桁応力はほとんど変化しなかった．写真-6，-7にセグメント撤去状況，写真-8に内部支保工の撤去状況，写真-9に撤去完了後の状況を示す．

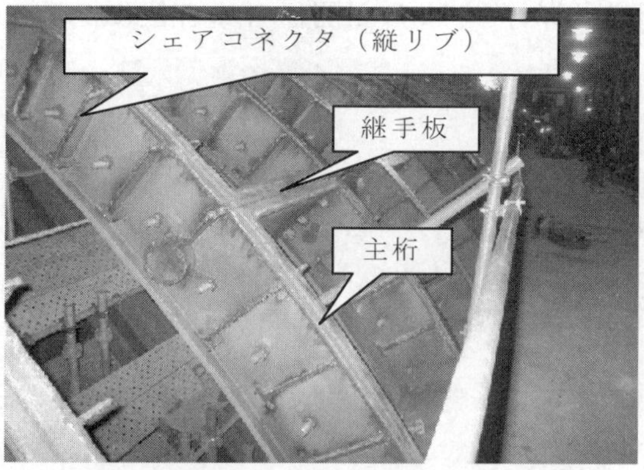

写真-6　鋼殻撤去状況

写真-7　主桁切断状況

写真-8　内部支保工撤去状況

写真-9　撤去完了後

（9）シールド内床版施工

シールド内床版は躯体構築が終了した後に施工するため，資材の搬入経路が限られることや，シールド内での使用重機の大きさに制限があることなどから出来るだけ軽く工程の短縮できる合成床版を採用した．これにより，4.9 t クラスのミニクレーンで施工が可能となった．

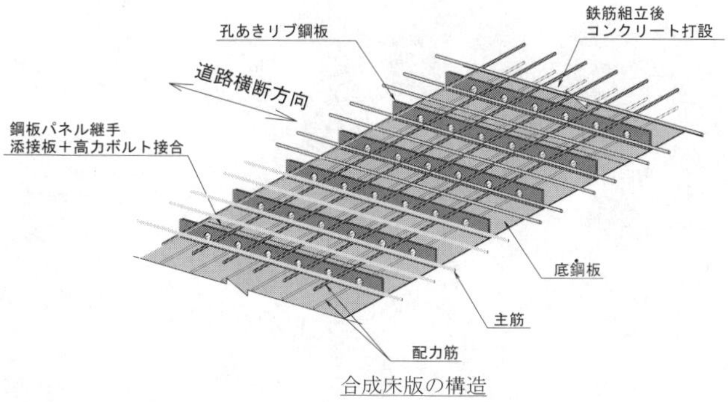

図-15　合成床版の構造

写真-10　鋼板の設置状況

4 おわりに

本工事は，前例がなく，きわめて難易度が高い工事であった．開削切開き工事の設計施工に関しては，企業者である首都高速株式会社とともに，設計手法・設計の妥当性・施工方法に至るまで共に考え，協議しながら実施していった．

現在（平成21年8月）の施工状況は，切開き躯体，上部の出入口躯体および埋戻しが完了し，内装工事を施工している段階であり，本年度中の開通に向けて鋭意施工を進めている．

最後に本報告をまとめるにあたり，ご指導，ご協力をいただきました関係者の各位に誌面を借りて心から感謝申し上げるものである．

参考文献（References）：

[1] 名倉：2種類の大断面・併設シールドの切拡げ施工，第3回日中シールド技術交流会，2005.8.

[2] 土橋・名倉・宮脇・三木：道路分合流部における大断面・併設シールドの切開き施工，第50回「シールドトンネル工法施工技術」講習会，日本プロジェクトリサーチ.

著者紹介（Bio-data）：

三木　章生
所属・役職：株式会社間組　土木事業本部　技術第一部　主任
専門分野：シールドトンネル
Akio MIKI
Chief, First Engineering Department, Civil Engineering Division, HAZAMA Corporation.
Specialized field: Shield Tunnel Engineering
E-mail: amiki@hazama.co.jp

FFU 横矢板を用いたシールド機の直接発進到達

竹中　計行[1]　深田　和志[1]　中川　達也[2]
[1]株式会社　錢高組　技術本部　技術研究所，東京　163-1011
[2]株式会社　錢高組　大阪支社　土木部，大阪　550-0005

シールド直接発進到達（SEW）工法は，シールド機が通過する土留め壁に新素材（FFU）を組み込んだものであり，シールド機が直接土留め壁を切削して発進到達することが可能な技術である．SEW 工法はこれまで約 150 件の施工実績があり，その施工性・安全性・確実性を確認してきた．これまで，シールド発進部や到達部に埋設管による土留め欠損がある場合は，鋼製の横矢板が設置されるためシールド直接発進到達工法の適用が困難であった．そこで，筆者らはシールド機で切削可能な FFU 横矢板を欠損部に設置して土留め掘削時の土砂の押し抜きを防止し，その後シールド機で直接切削する方法を開発した．本報告では，土留め欠損部に初めて FFU 横矢板を設置してシールド機の直接発進到達を行ったので，その開発結果とその施工結果について述べる．
キーワード：FFU；横矢板；土留め壁；シールド

DEPARTING AND ARRIVING DIRECTLY OF SHILD MACHINE WITH FFU HORIZONTAL LAGGING

Kazuyuki TAKENAKA[1]，Kazuyuki FUKADA[1]，Tatsuya NAKAGAWA[2]
[1]The Zenitaka Corporation , Tokyo 163-1011, Japan; [2]The Zenitaka Corporation , Osaka 550-0005, Japan

Abstract: SEW method is the technique which allows drilling directly a earth retaining wall that shield passes with newly developed material called FFU. There were about 150 results with the SEW method and were confirmed with its workability, safety, certainty. In previous method, it was difficult to apply SEW method when there is in earth retaining wall loss part for a underground pipe because unbreakable steel lagging was use to support the wall. Therefore a method have been developed to support the earth retaining wall loss part with the material FFU horizontal lagging which can be drilled though directly with shield and can be resisted of pressure of soil. This is the report providing construction result and developed result in the first situation where FFU horizontal lagging was used at Earth retaining wall loss part.
Key words: FFU; horizontal lagging; earth retaining wall; shield

1　はじめに

中之島新線建設工事は，堂島川と土佐堀川に囲まれた大阪市の中心に位置する中之島地区で，2008 年 10 月 19 日に開業した中之島線を建設する工事であった．中之島地区は関西における国際・文化・情報ゾーンとして注目を集めており，今後，再開発の進展に伴い発生する交通需要に対応するため，玉江橋駅から京阪本線天満橋駅に至る約 2.9 km 間に中之島新線が計画された．

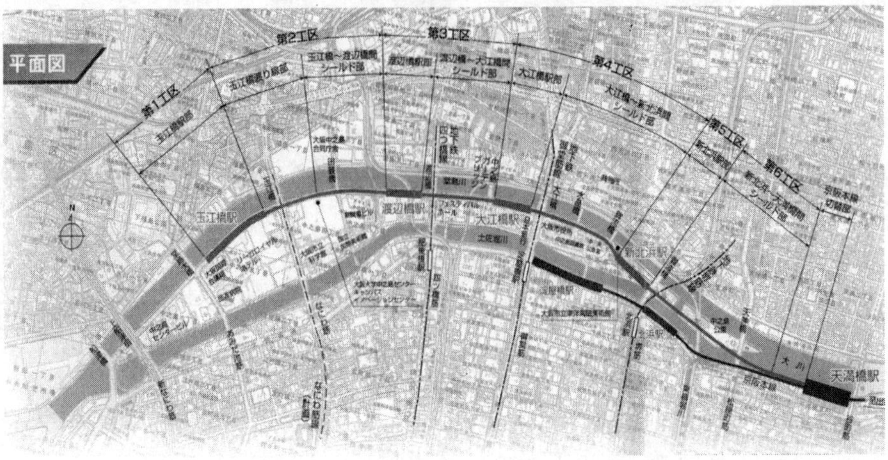

図-1 中之島新線建設工事

中之島新線建設工事（第２工区）（以降，本工事と呼ぶ）のシールド発進到達部には構造物や河川が近接していたため，シールド発進到達時に周辺環境に影響を与えないシールド直接発進到達(SEW)工法を検討した．しかし，大阪市中心部の施工のため，埋設管による土留め欠損が多く見られ，その欠損位置がシールド発進および到達部にも存在していた．よって，鋼製の横矢板では，シールド切削の障害となるため，従来の SEW 工法では欠損部の適用は不可能であった．そこで，筆者らは欠損部に鋼製の横矢板ではなく，シールド機で切削可能な FFU 横矢板を設置して掘削時の土砂の押し抜きを防止し，その後シールド機で直接切削する方法を開発し，本工事に採用した．ここで FFU とは，硬質発泡ウレタンをガラス長繊維で強化した合成材（FFU:Fiber reinforced Foamd Urethane）を接着剤（エポキシ樹脂）で圧着積層したものである．

2 FFU 横矢板の開発

FFU 横矢板の開発は，これまでの SEW 工法の開発 1)から FFU 部材の強度は把握していたので，FFU 横矢板の接合部の仕様を決定することを目的として行った．なお，FFU 横矢板の接合部に求められる機能は，①土水圧に抵抗できる耐力を有する，②シールド機で切削時に障害にならない，である．

2.1 FFU 横矢板の設計

FFU 横矢板を設置する土留め壁の種類は，日本においてシールド機の発進部や到達部に最も多く施工されている柱列式連続壁(SMW)を設定した．FFU 横矢板の配置例を図-2 に示す．

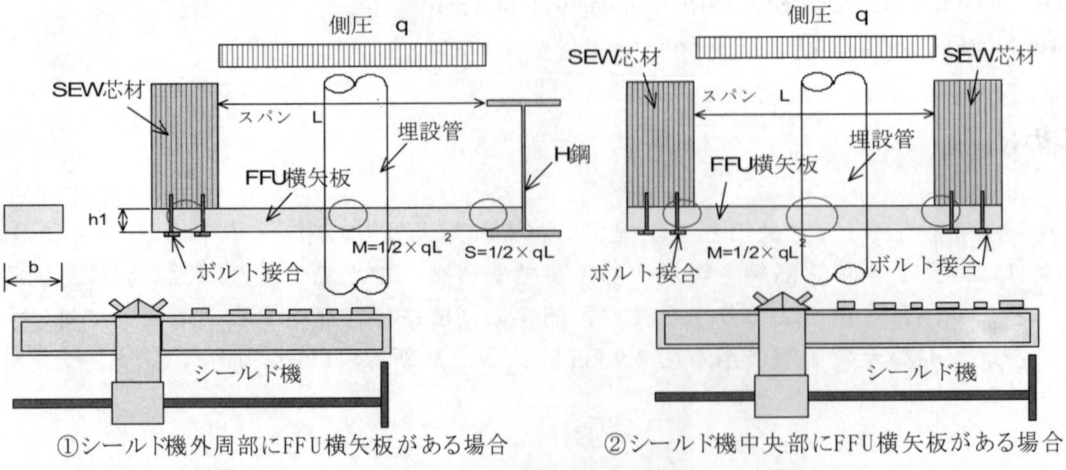

図-2 FFU 横矢板の配置

FFU 横矢板の設計は，通常の親杭横矢板と同様に親杭で支持された単純梁として曲げおよびせん断の断面照査を行い，サイズを決定する．

FFU 横矢板の配置は，埋設管やシールド機の位置によって異なり，①シールド機の外周部に設置される場合と，②シールド機の中央部に設置される場合の２通りある．①の場合は，図-2(左)に示すように，H 鋼と FFU 横矢板の固定となり，これは通常の矢板と同様にフランジ内に FFU 横矢板を挿入して固定する．この時の押抜き検討は FFU のせん断強さで照査する．もう一方は SEW 芯材と FFU 横矢板を固定することになるが，現場での FFU 横矢板の施工性及びシールド機での切削性を考慮し，SEW 芯材と FFU 横矢板をボルトで固定する方法とした．②の場合は，図-2(右)に示すように，両端とも SEW 芯材と FFU 横矢板の固定となる．

FFU の物性値を表-1 に示す．FFU は繊維方向と繊維直角方向で強度特性が異なる異方性材料であり，繊維方向は高圧縮強さ，高引張強さを有している．

表-1　FFU の物性値 [1)]

項　目		単位	FFU74
比　重			0.74
曲げ強さ	繊維方向	N/mm^2	72
弾性係数	繊維方向	N/mm^2	1.0×10^3
圧縮強さ	繊維方向	N/mm^2	56.9
	繊維直角方向	N/mm^2	13.2
引張強さ	繊維方向	N/mm^2	127
せん断強さ	繊維方向	N/mm^2	9.1
	繊維直角方向	N/mm^2	6.2

2.2　ボルト引抜き実験

FFU とボルトの引抜き実験は，枕木などで使用する鋼製ボルトでは実施していたが，現場で短時間に固定でき，かつシールド機で切削可能な FRP ボルト（FRP : Fiber Reinforced Plastic）での引抜き耐力は把握していなかった．そこで，FFU 横矢板に使用するボルトの引抜き耐力を把握するため実験を行った．

（1）実験方法

実験方法は，図-3 に示すように，ボルト頭部を掴んで上方に引抜く試験方法で，FFU のボルト周囲は動かないように固定した．FFU の大きさは，埋込み長さを考慮して□200 mm×200 mm とした．

（2）実験ケース

実験ケースは，表-2 に示すように，ボルトの固定方法とボルトのネジ径をパラメータとして 5 種類で実施した．なお，④のケミカルアンカー樹脂で固定する方法では実施工を想定してボルトを FRP ボルトとした．

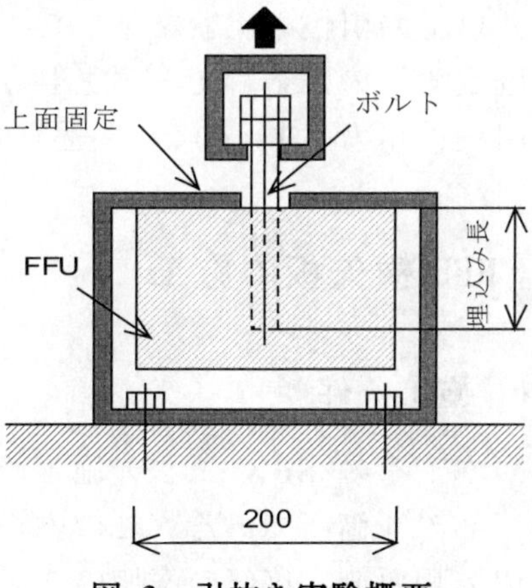

図-3　引抜き実験概要

（3）実験結果

実験結果を表-2，実験状況を写真-1 に示す．⑤金属拡張アンカーは，小さい引張力（5～10 kN）で抜け始めた．FFU にボルトを直付けする方法は，②ボルトをねじ込み接着剤で固定する方が，①ボルトをねじ込むだけに比べて約２倍の引抜き耐力があることがわかった．しかし，FFU にタップ（雌ネジ切り）を立てることは熟練した作業員でないと安定した引抜き耐力を確保できないので，現場作業では不向きである．③と④は，予めボルト径より大きな穴をあけて，ボルト周囲を樹脂で固定させる方法であり，高い引抜き耐力結果が得られた．④は，FRP ボルトであるが，鋼製ボルトと同等程度の引抜き力を発揮し，写真-1 に示すように，荷重 69 kN で FRP ボルト(M20)が破断する結果が得られた．

表-2 ボルト引抜き実験一覧表

番号	方法の種類		ネジ径	下穴	ネジ長	引抜き力
①	FFU にタップ立て　鋼製ボルト ネジ込み固定のみ	FFU にボルトを直付け	M20	ϕ17	80	荷重 25 kN でボルト引抜け
			M24	ϕ20.5	120	荷重 30 kN でボルト引抜け
②	FFU にタップ立て　鋼製ボルト 接着剤で固定		M20	ϕ17	80	荷重 42 kN でボルト引抜け
			M24	ϕ20.5	120	荷重 68 kN でボルト引抜け
③	FFU にタップなし　鋼製ボルト ポリエステル樹脂で固定		M20	ϕ21	80	荷重 40 kN でボルト引抜け
			M24	ϕ25	120	荷重 74 kN でボルト引抜け
④	FFU にタップなし　FRP ボルト ケミカルアンカーで固定		M20	ϕ22	170	荷重 69 kN でボルト破断
⑤	プラグアンカー　鋼製ボルト	金属拡張アンカー	M20	ϕ27	80	荷重 5 kN で引抜け始め最大 15 kN
			M24	ϕ33	110	荷重 10 kN で引抜け始め最大 20 kN

④ケミカルアンカー（打込み式）は，穴にカプセルを入れボルトをたたき込むだけで固定できる方法であり，③に比べて現場作業に優れた方法である．写真-2 に，ケミカルアンカーの施工道具を示す．

写真-1　引抜き実験概要

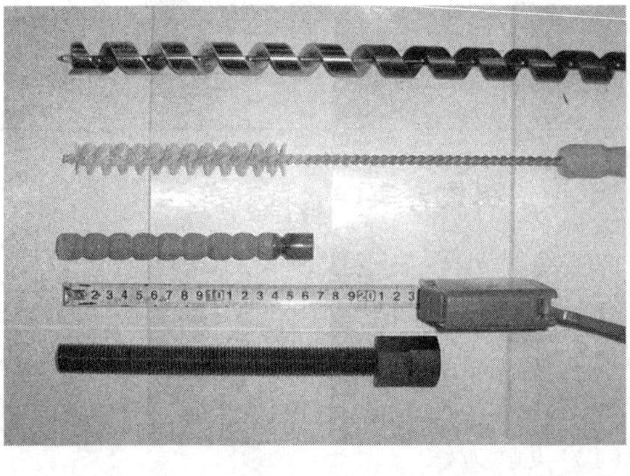

写真-2　④ケミカルアンカー

以上の引抜き実験結果から，FFU 横矢板は，FRP ボルトを使用してケミカルアンカー（打込み式）で固定するのが最適であると判断し，その後④について追加実験を実施した．その結果，1 本あたりの引抜き耐力が P＝60 kN 以上有していること確認し，定着部の引抜き設計値とした．

3　FFU 横矢板の施工

3.1　施工条件

本工事の SEW 工法の施工箇所は，中之島渡り線部東側の発進・到達部と渡辺橋駅西側の発進・到達部の 4 箇所である．この内，土留め欠損となっていた箇所は中之島渡り線部東側立坑部の南側と渡辺橋駅西側立坑部の南側の 2 箇所であった．

渡辺橋駅西側立坑部の土留め壁は柱列式連続壁で，掘削深さは 23～27 m であり，ビルや高速道路等に非常に近接した状態での施工であった．

写真-3　中ノ島新線建設工事（第２工区）**の全景**

本箇所において，掘進してきたシールドマシン（外径；Φ6 950，泥土圧式，土被り 15 m）は北側で到達し，立坑内で回転した後再発進する U ターン施工となっていた．渡辺橋駅西側立坑南側は，図-4 に示すように，電気・下水等の埋設管が輻輳しており，シールド発進位置に土留め欠損が２箇所存在した．欠損幅は 2.5 m と 3 m で，欠損防護工として高圧噴射撹拌工法と薬液注入工法を併用する形で施工を行なった．

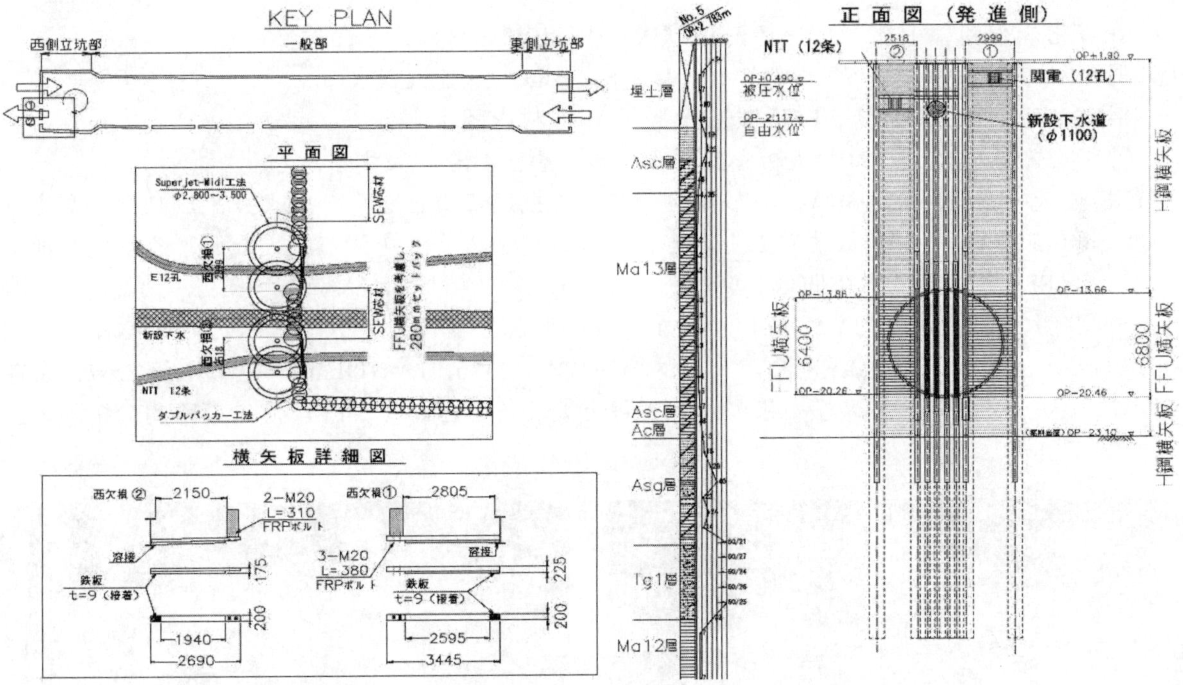

図-4　土留め欠損部平面・断面図（（仮称）渡辺駅 西側立坑部）

3.2　地盤及び施工条件

地盤は深度 10.0 m までは埋土層･沖積上部層の砂質土層であり，その下位には沖積粘性土層（Ma13 層：N 値 1～5）が層厚 14.0 m 程度と厚く存在し，シールドマシンはこの粘性土層を掘進する．その下層は Asc 層（砂質土優勢層）Ac 層（粘性土層）の互層となり，床付面下端からは Asg 層（砂質土層）となる．洪積層（Tg1 層：天満砂礫層，Ma12 層：洪積粘性土層）は，深度 28 m 以深に層厚がほぼ水平に分布している．尚，地下水位は，自由水が GL-4.0m 付近で，Asg 層・Tg1 層の被圧水は GL-1.5 m 付近に存在している．

3.3 FFU 横矢板の施工

欠損部は，２箇所ともシールドマシンの外周付近に位置しており，FFU 横矢板の端部支持は H 鋼芯材と SEW 芯材の両方となる．特に H 鋼芯材側の FFU 横矢板は本体躯体の構築箇所となるため，本体躯体との離隔（250 mm）を確保する必要があった．そこで FFU 横矢板が通常の土留め壁面に収まるように，両端部の固定方法の違いを考慮して，土留め壁造成時に，該当する SEW 芯材を通常の土留め面より 280 mm（FFU 横矢板厚+α）セットバックして施工した．

FFU 横矢板の施工は，写真-4 に示すように通常の H 鋼横矢板と同様に掘削に伴って 1.0 m 毎に FFU 横矢板（５段分）を下段から設置した．最大重量は約 150 kg であり，H 鋼材（H-200）とほぼ同程度であった．

写真-4 FFU 横矢板設置状況

欠損幅は，SEW 芯材の建込み精度により異なるので，立坑掘削を進めるとともに欠損幅を予測して FFU 横矢板の長さを決めた．SEW 芯材側の FFU 横矢板の支持は，渡辺橋駅西側立坑の発進側では FRP ボルトを，中之島渡り線部東側立坑の到達側では鋼製ボルトを用いて固定した．

FFU 横矢板の設置手順は以下の通りである．

① 掘削完了後，最下段の FFU 横矢板を位置決めする．

② H 鋼側は，FFU 横矢板端部に接着固定した鉄板と H 鋼を溶接して固定する．

③ SEW 芯材側は，削孔ドリルで FFU 横矢板と SEW 芯材に穴を開ける．

④ 削孔穴にケミカルアンカーをセットし，FRP ボルトを叩きこむ．

⑤ 平座金とナットにより，FFU 横矢板と SEW 芯材を固定する．

⑥ ①～⑤を繰り返し FFU 横矢板を設置完了後，裏込材を打設する．

FFU 横矢板の背面側裏込材は，シールドマシンの掘進障害とならないように流動化処理土（一軸圧縮強度 qu=0.5 N/mm^2）を打設することとし，背面地盤との密着を図った．なお，流動化処理土の漏出防止として FFU 横矢板間の隙間はシリコーン系シーリング材で目詰めを行った．

シールド切削範囲は，写真-5，6 に示すように，腹起し受けブラケットを FFU 部材に直接取付ける必要があり，所定の下孔（ϕ16）にコーチボルト２本（M20，L＝100 mm）をねじ込む方法を採用した．以上により，通常の鋼製の横矢板の設置工程と変わることなく，FFU 横矢板区間の掘削・土留め支保工を施工できた．

写真-5 FFU 横矢板設置詳細

写真-6 FFU 横矢板設置全景

4　シールド掘進

4.1 シールド機

シールド機は，図-5 に示すように，泥土圧式シールド機でマシン外径ϕ6 950 mm である．シールド機のカッタビットは粘性土を切削することからティースビットを主体とした形状であり，SEW 芯材を切削するために特別なビットは装備していない．排土機構は，チャンバーからϕ700 mm の軸付きスクリューで，パイプライン方式（土砂圧送）により土砂を地上へ排土する方式である．シールド機には同時注入管が装備されていたが，その部分の SEW 芯材の切削はコピーカッタによって実施した．コピーカッタの前面と上部にビット取付け，コンピューター制御によって同時注入管位置でコピーの出し入れをすることで SEW 芯材を切削した．

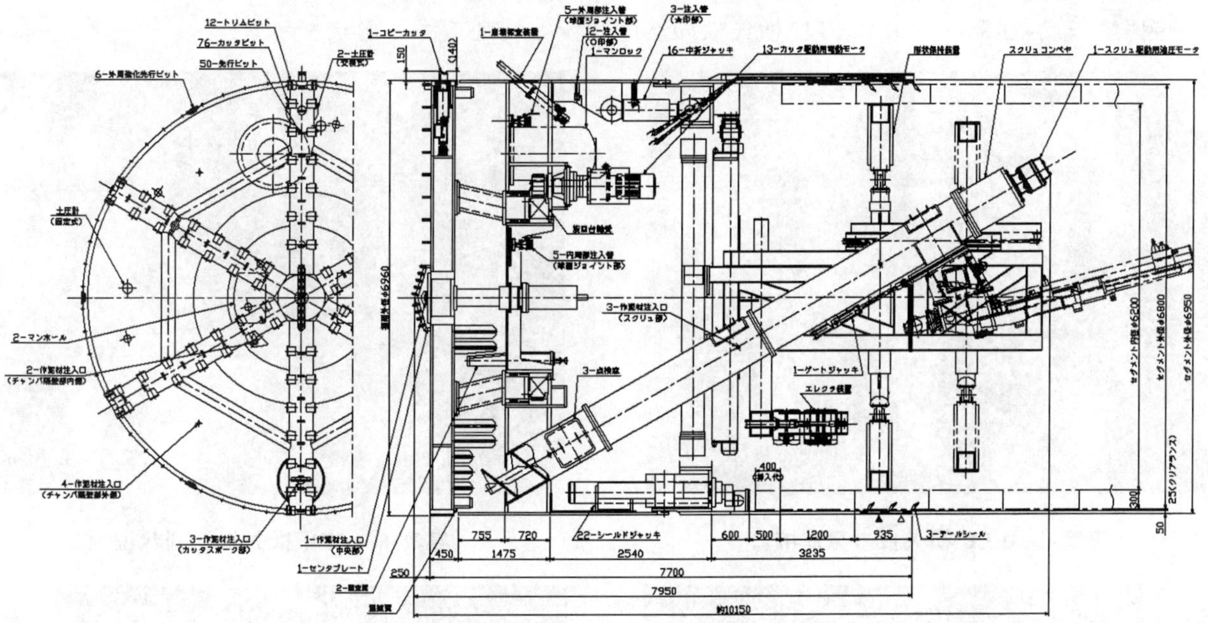

図-5　泥土圧シールド機

4.2 シールド発進

（1）発進準備

発進準備として，切削時の FFU 横矢板の移動を拘束しカッタビットの片当りを防止するため，FFU 横矢板間の SEW 芯材との段差を流動化処理土(σ= 0.5 N/mm^2)にて間詰めを行った．写真-7 に FFU 横矢板の発進坑口の状況を示す．SEW 工法を用いたシールド発進では，予めチャンバー内を土砂等にて充填する必要がある．その理由は，①SEW 芯材切削開始とともに切羽圧と土水圧をバランスさせる，②FFU 切削くずをチャンバー内に大量に溜め込まずに確実に排出する，である．FFU 横矢板はシールド機で FRP ボルトのナットを切削した後に拘束力が弱くなるので，切削時の FFU 横矢板の倒れこみを防止するため切削前にチャンバー及びスクリュー内は充填材でほぼ満杯とした．充填材は，表-3 に示す配合のクレーショックとし，その粘性により FFU 切削くずとソイルモルタルを絡めて塑性流動性を確保した．

表-3 クレーショックの配合(1 m^3 当り)

A 液		B 液
特殊ｸﾚｰｻﾝﾄﾞ	水	塑強剤
TAC-β II	清水	TAC-3S
420 kg(50 kg)	839 L(100 L)	50 L

（2）シールド発進

発進部の SEW 芯材を 2007 年 2 月 22 日 9：00 より切削を開始し約 12 時間で SEW 芯材及び FFU 横矢板の切削が完了した．

発進時のジャッキ推力は，SEW 芯材切削時は 7 000 kN，地盤切削時は 8 000 kN であった．単位面積当りのジャッキ推力は，SEW 芯材切削時は 150～200 kN/m^2，地盤切削時は 200 kN/m^2 と微少な推力であり，装備推力の 1/5 程度であった．掘進速度は，SEW 芯材の区間で 2 mm/min，地盤で 8～20 mm/min とした．カッタトルクは，SEW 芯材切削時に 2 800 kN·m，地盤切削時は 1 300 kN·m であった．トルク係数で比較すると，SEW 芯材切削時の α 値で 8，地盤切削時は α 値で 4 と微少であり，SEW 芯材切削時は装備トルク（常用）の半分程度であった．SEW 芯材切削時のカッタトルクは，SEW 芯材の掘進速度が 2 mm/min と遅いにもかかわらず地盤切削の約 2 倍程度大きくなった．これは，SEW 芯材のガラス繊維の直角方向の圧縮強度（σ =15 N/mm^2）が地盤（qu=0.05 N/mm^2）に比べて大きいことが原因である．写真-8～10 に FFU 横矢板の切削状況と切削くずの形状を示す．

写真-7　FFU 横矢板の発進坑口

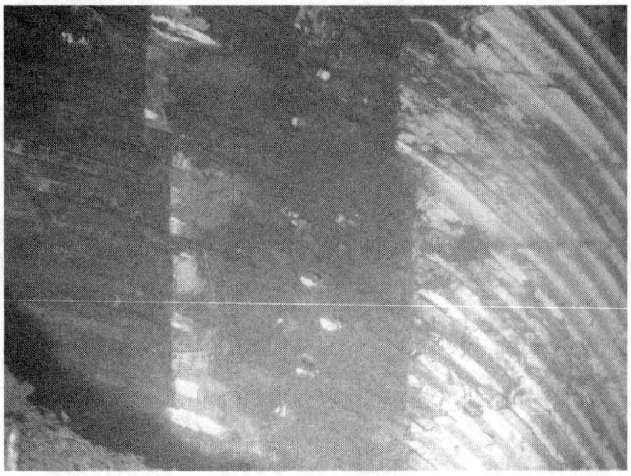

写真-8　FFU 横矢板切削状況

写真-9　FFU 切削くず

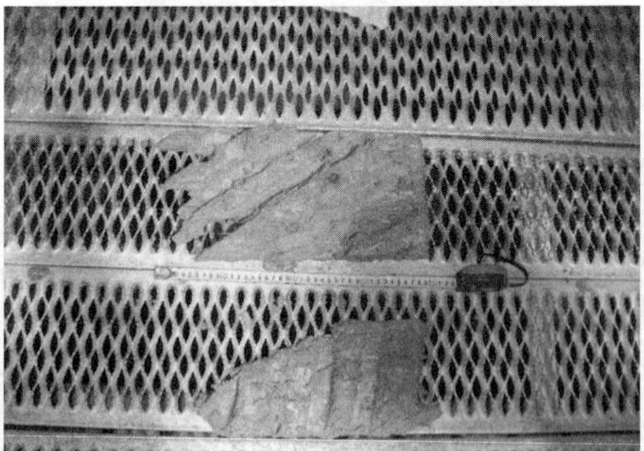

写真-10　FFU 横矢板切削くず

FFU 切削くずは長さ 200 mm 程度のものが多く，土砂と共に圧送によって立坑外へ排出された．また，FFU 切削くずの形状は，概ねカッタービットの幅及び先行ビットの間隔と同等程度であった．SEW 芯材と FFU 横矢板を固定する FRP ボルトは，良好に切削されて排出された．

FFU 切削時には，何度か圧送装置に設置したスクリーン部で閉塞が見られたが，FFU 横矢板を採用した箇所が特に多いわけでもなく，SEW 芯材のみの切削と大差はなかった．

FFU 切削時は，エントランスパッキンおよび坑口からの出水はなく，無事に発進を完了することができた．

5 おわりに

中之島新線建設工事（第２工区）の発進・到達部において，初めてFFU横矢板を用いたSEW工法を施工した．その結果，FFU横矢板は，土留め掘削時は構造部材として性能を有すること，そして発進到達時はシールド機で容易に切削可能であることを確認した．今後は，FFU横矢板の実績を増やすとともに，更なる改良を進めていく所存である．

最後になりましたが，FFU 横矢板の開発や施工にあたり，中之島高速鉄道(株)の関係者に多大なご指導とご協力をいただきました．ここに感謝の意を表します．

参考文献（References）：

[1] 深田，竹中他：新素材を複合させた土留め壁（SEW）工法の開発 土木学会第53回年次学術講演会VI 1998.9.
[2] 定藤，天野，中川：ＦＦＵ横矢板を用いた土留欠損防護工 基礎工 2008 Vol.36,No.2.

著者紹介（Bio-data）：

竹中　計行
所属：錢高組　技術研究所
最終学歴：九州工業大学工学部
職務：立坑及びシールド技術の開発
Kazuyuki TAKENAKA
Affiliation: ZENITAKA Corporation
The final degree:Kyushu Institute of Technology
Occupation: Technological development of shaft and shield
E-mail: takkenaka_kazuyuki@zenitaka.co.jp

PART THREE

EXPERIMENT AND MONITORING

试验与监测

青草沙水源地原水工程输水隧道衬砌管片接头试验

朱合华[1,2] 顾 赟[3] 丁文其[1,2] 闫治国[1,2]

[1]同济大学 土木工程学院地下建筑与工程系，上海 200092

[2]同济大学 岩土及地下工程教育部重点实验室，上海 200092

[3]上海青草沙投资建设发展有限公司，上海 201206

【摘 要】 本文主要介绍青草沙水源地原水工程输水隧道衬砌管片接头试验的基本情况，其中包括工程背景、试验目的、试验系统的构成、试件的结构形式、试验工况、测点类型及布置，以期让读者对本次试验的基本情况有所了解。最后介绍部分已取得的试验成果以及总结试验过程中所得到的一些经验，为今后开展类似的试验提供参考和帮助。

【关键词】 盾构隧道；管片；接头；原型试验

INTRODUCE TO THE JOINT TEST OF THE SHIELD TUNNEL'S LINING STRUCTURE IN QINGCAOSHA WATER CONVEYANCE PROJECT

Hehua ZHU[1,2], Yun GU[3], Wenqi DING[1,2], Zhiguo YAN[1,2]

[1]*Department of Geotechnical Engineering, Tongji University, Shanghai 200092, China;*

[2]*Key Laboratory of Geotechnical and Underground Engineering of Ministry of Education, Tongji University, Shanghai 200092, China;*

[3]*Shanghai Qing Cao Sha Raw Water Engineering Co., Ltd., Shanghai 201206, China*

Abstract: This paper mainly introduced the basic situation of the joint test of the shield tunnel's lining structure in Qingcaosha water conveyance project. The description of several aspects, such as engineering background, test purpose, components of the test, structure of the specimens, test conditions, types and layout of measuring points, made readers to understand the basic situation of the test. Finally, it showed some test results and concluded some experience from the test in order to provide reference and assistance for the future similar studies.

Key words: shield tunnel; segment; joint; prototype test

1 引 言

改革开放三十年来，中国经济的迅猛发展和城市化进程的不断加剧使得越来越多的城市对于公共交通提出了越来越高的要求。因此近十几年来一些城市开始大量兴建地铁工程和越江隧道工程。由于城市环境的日益复杂和人们对于环境要求的日益提高，在已兴建的地铁工程和越江隧道工程中主要采用盾构法。并且在可以预见的将来，盾构法隧道在国内将拥有更为广阔的发展前景。

在国内大量的工程实践促进了对盾构隧道衬砌结构力学行为研究的发展。不少学者在前人研究的基础上，通过理论分析、数值模拟和模型试验等手段就管片构造、接头形式和拼装方式对于衬砌结构力学

基金项目：国家自然科学基金项目（No.50878149）；"十一五"国家科技支撑计划项目（2006BAJ27B05）；上海市重点学科建设项目（B308）

行为的影响进行深入分析研究。如朱合华等通过对管片接头部位的力学分析，提出了梁-接头不连续模型[1]；何川等通过室内模型试验方法对超大断面单层装配式管片衬砌在高水压条件下的力学行为特征、结构与周围土体的相互作用关系进行研究[2]；朱伟等通过研究分析得到了管片接头弯曲刚度与接头内力的非线性关系，建立了实用的管片接头弯曲刚度双直线模型[3]；陈俊生等通过数值模拟的方法研究了盾构隧道衬砌管片在施工阶段各种荷载作用下应力分布与变化[4]。

近些年来由于试验条件的改善和工程实践的要求，国内开始结合具体工程开展 1：1 的盾构隧道衬砌管片力学试验。如结合南水北调中线穿黄隧洞工程开展的管片接头荷载试验，该试验就接头受力、变形和破坏过程、接头各部分强度进行研究[5]。又如结合上海长江隧道工程开展的衬砌水平整环试验，该试验就衬砌管片的承载能力、稳定性及施工荷载作用下结构的受力和变形进行研究。以及本文将要介绍的在同济大学进行的结合上海青草沙水源地原水工程开展的盾构隧道衬砌结构接头试验。本试验就盾构隧道衬砌结构接头的力学特性、各工况荷载作用下衬砌结构各部分的内力分布情况、通过模拟实际工程中错缝拼装方式研究其对于衬砌结构内力的影响以及对管片接头的破坏形式进行分析研究。本文将对该试验的各个方面进行介绍，以期让读者对于本次试验基本情况有所了解，并为其他类似试验提供参考和帮助。

2 工程背景

青草沙水源地原水工程于 2007 年 6 月开始全面启动，计划于 2010 年投入运营。其目的是在建成后为上海提供占总规模 50%以上的原水供应。青草沙水源地原水工程由青草沙水库及取输水泵闸工程(含中央沙圈围工程)、长江原水过江管工程、岛域陆域输水管线及增压泵站工程三个主体工程组成。该工程的输水系统分为长兴岛域输水管道工程、长江原水过江管工程和陆域输水管线及增压泵站工程。

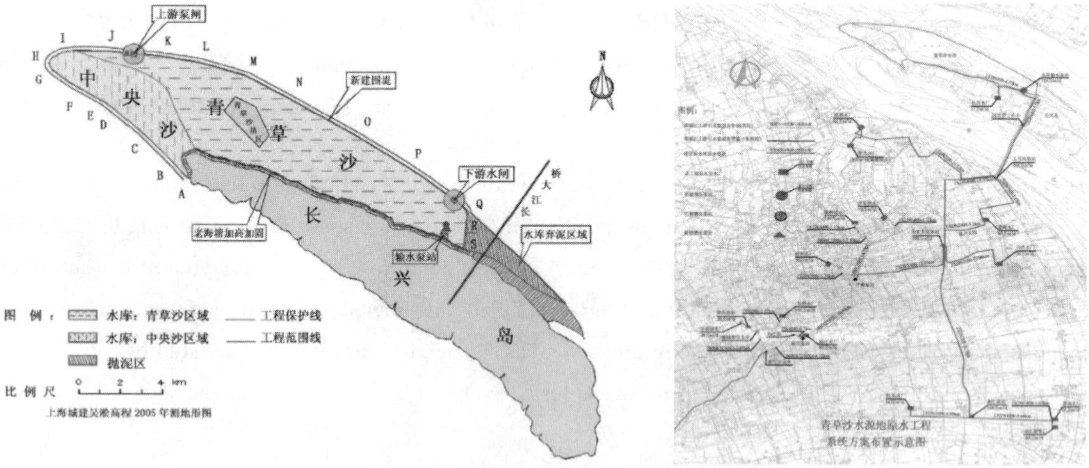

图 1 青草沙水源地原水工程

3 试验目的

青草沙水源地原水工程输水隧道是我国首次采用盾构法修建的单层衬砌输水管道工程，与一般的盾构法公路隧道不同，输水隧道不仅承受外部水土压力，而且在营运时还需承受内部水压作用。另外由于输水隧道在建成后需经历营运及检修状态的交替，因此必须考虑内部水压反复加、卸载对于隧道衬砌结构的影响。为了确保输水隧道单层衬砌结构在外部水土压力和内水压的作用下能够满足承载能力和水密性的要求，使工程取得更好的技术、经济效益，需开展 1：1 的错缝夹片和直接头试验。试验主要目的是研究盾构隧道衬砌结构接头在不同荷载形式作用下的力学特性以及拼装方式对于接头力学性能的影响，其中包括错缝拼装时管片间的弯矩传递分配情况、径向剪切刚度、切向剪切刚度以及块间径向剪切刚度、纵缝承受正、负弯矩的受力特性，即纵缝张角随弯矩变化规律及转角刚度值。

4 试验系统构成

整个试验系统是一个复杂的体系。它由多个相互联系的部分组成，主要包括控制系统、加载系统、数据采集系统和数据记录分析系统。其相互关系如图所示。其基本流程为：试验人员通过控制系统控制整个试验进程，包括选择加、卸载方式，控制加、卸载速度和目标值等。控制系统将控制指令发送至加载系统。加载系统根据指令完成加、卸载过程。同时试件对于荷载变化的反应由布设在试件上的测点传送至数据采集系统。数据采集系统将测点信号转化为试验数据并传输至数据记录与处理系统。数据记录与处理系统将试验数据记录并实时显示，供试验人员随时掌握试件情况并及时处理异常情况。

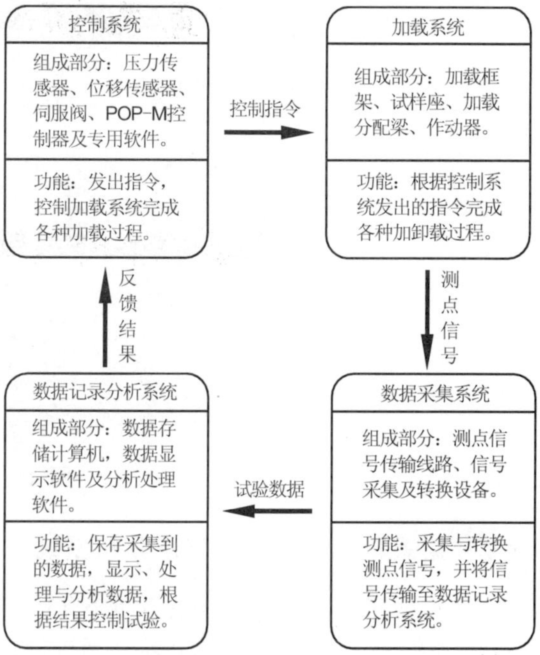

图 2 试验系统各组成部分关系图

4.1 控制系统与加载系统

由于实际工程中盾构隧道衬砌管片的受力状态较为复杂，主要包括沿隧道轴线方向的纵向力、沿衬砌管片环向的轴力和弯矩，因此在试验中需通过三种不同方向的加载方式来模拟上述三种荷载，以达到尽可能按盾构隧道衬砌管片实际受力状态施加荷载的要求。经过精心构思和巧妙设计，同济大学设计研制的 TJ-GPJ2000 管片接头加载系统能达到上述要求。整个加载框架的加载作动器主要分为三类，即垂向作动器、横向作动器与纵向作动器。通过不同的加载组合满足事先制订的各种工况的加载要求，较好地模拟了盾构隧道衬砌管片在实际状态下的受力情况。经已完成的试验证明，本加载系统所采用的加载方式切实可行且便捷高效。

图 3 加载系统实景图

加载系统的整个加、卸载过程均由控制系统控制。控制系统由压力传感器、位移传感器、伺服阀、POP-M 控制器及专用软件构成。压力传感器和位移传感器实时反馈加载系统的作动器的压力和位移情况。伺服阀根据控制器发出的电信号控制作动器的液压状态来实现加、卸载过程。专用软件用以控制整个加载过程。并且实时反馈荷载与位移情况，有利于试验人员掌握这个试验情况。

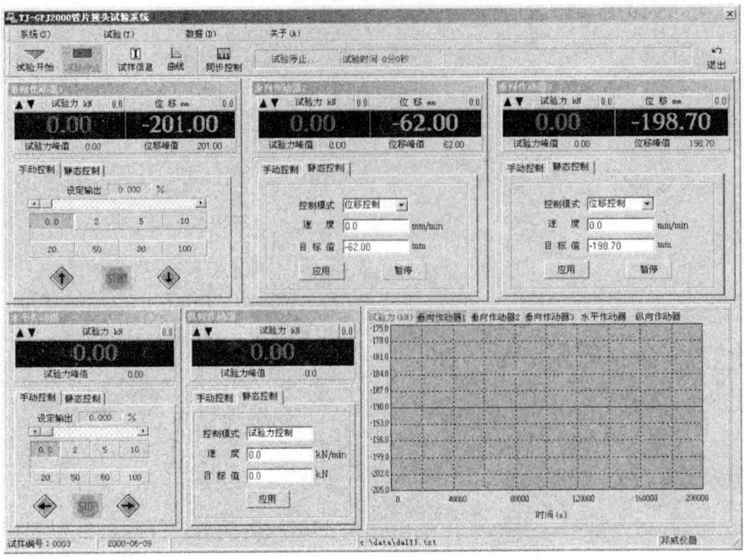

图 4 控制系统操作软件界面

4.2 数据采集系统与数据记录分析系统

数据的采集与处理由数据采集系统和数据记录分析系统完成。数据的采集与处理不是在正式试验时开始进行，而是在试件安装就位后就开始进行，用以检查所有测点的状态，评价螺栓预紧前后的内力变化等。

数据的采集主要由信号采集与转换设备完成。其按照试验人员设定的时间间隔同步采集所有测点的数据并完成转换工作，然后将数据传输至数据记录分析系统。信号采集与转换设备可以对不同类型的传感器进行同步信号采集，因此简便试验数据采集工作同时能反映某一时刻试件所有测点的状态，对于今后进行数据对比、分析与判断大为有利。数据记录分析系统主要功能是将由数据采集系统采集到的数据记录保存并实时显示，供试验人员监控整个试验过程。并可通过对试验数据的初步分析判断试验状态并及时做出合理的决策。

5 试验内容

5.1 试件结构形式

因此本次试验主要采用两种试件结构形式，即直接头形式和错缝夹片形式。直接头形式主要是为了得到接头承受压、拉力情况下块间径向剪切刚度以及纵缝承受正、负弯矩的受力特性；错缝夹片形式主要是为了得到径向、切向剪切刚度以及确定弯矩传递分配情况。

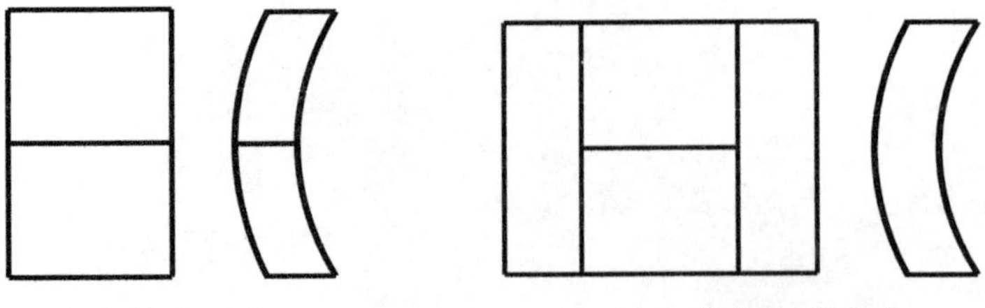

（a）直接头形式　　（b）错缝夹片形式

图 5 两种试件的结构形式

5.2 试验工况

由于本次试验拟研究的内容较多，因此设计的试验工况数量较多，为后期试验结果的对比分析提供了丰富的原始资料。试验工况主要分为两个大类，即直接头试验和错缝夹片试验。

直接头试验主要包括：块间径向剪切试验、转角刚度试验。其中块间径向剪切试验包括接头承受压力和拉力两种情况。转角刚度试验包括施加不同压力以及拉力时，接头在正、负弯矩作用下的力学行为。

错缝夹片试验主要包括：环间径向剪切试验、环间切向剪切试验和弯矩传递试验。环间径向剪切试验主要研究不同纵向力情况下环间径向剪切刚度。环间切向剪切试验主要研究不同纵向力情况下环间切向剪切刚度。弯矩传递试验主要研究施加不同纵向力与正、负弯矩情况下衬砌管片接头的力学性能。其具体目的详见表 1。

表 1　试验工况

工况名称		备　　注
直接头	块间径向剪切试验	研究接头承受压力或拉力情况下，接头径向剪切刚度
	转角刚度试验	研究接头承受压、拉力与正、负弯矩情况下的力学特性
错缝夹片	环间径向剪切试验	研究在环向力一定情况下，不同纵向力与环间径向剪切刚度的关系
	环间切向剪切试验	研究在环向力一定情况下，不同纵向力与环间切向剪切刚度的关系
	弯矩传递试验	研究不同纵向力、不同环向力以及正、负弯矩作用下，接头的力学性能

5.3　测点类型及布置

为了尽可能得到详尽的试验数据，在本次试验中布置了多种类型的测点，主要测试混凝土应力、钢筋应力、接头张角、试件挠度与错动量、铸铁面板应力、环向与纵向螺栓内力等。采用的传感器类型也不尽相同，主要有多种类型的应变片、振弦式应变计、振弦式钢筋计与位移计。测点名称、传感器类型与各试验布置情况详见表 2。

表 2　测点名称、传感器类型与布置情况

名　　称	传感器类型	直接头试验	错缝夹片试验
纵缝张角测点	位移计	√	√
挠度变形测点	位移计	√	√
环间径向错动量测点	位移计		√
环间切向错动量测点	位移计		√
块间径向错动量测点	位移计	√	
铸铁面板应力测点	应变片	√	√
纵向螺栓应力测点	应变片		√
环向螺栓应力测点	应变片	√	√
混凝土应力测点	应变片	√	√
接头主筋应力测点	振弦式应变计	√	√
跨中主筋应力测点	振弦式钢筋计	√	√
锚筋应力测点	振弦式应变计	√	√
箍筋应力测点	振弦式应变计		√

6　结　语

在撰写本文时，本试验尚未结束。但就已取得的试验结果进行初步分析后发现，试验结果规律性强，能较好反映盾构隧道衬砌管片在各种工况下的力学行为特性。至于具体的规律特性有待于全部试验完成以后，对所有试验结果做深入分析总结后方能得出。

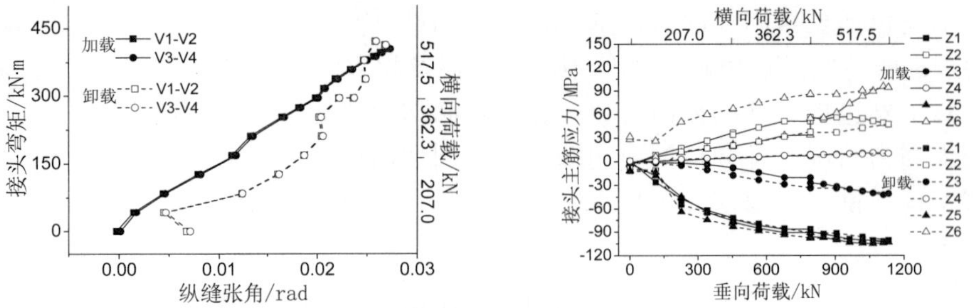

图 6　部分试验数据图

就试验过程而言，亦有诸多可总结的经验。首先，原型试验试件体积、重量较大且一般试验室往往没有专业的拼装设备，因此管片拼装的难度较高。然而从已进行的试验发现拼装质量对于试验结果的影响较为明显。因此能否高质量地完成试件拼装是能否取得可靠试验结果的前提条件。

另外，试件的制作质量对于试验结果的影响也较大，可采用与实际管片相同的制作工艺和流程制作，以保证试件与原型的一致性。另外，为方便拼装与试验过程的顺利进行，需对试件部分构造进行设计，如增加吊装环方便试件拼装，在试件与支座接触处加设承压钢板防止试验时混凝土局部受压破坏。

还有，试验的加载方式对于试验结果的影响较大。如在进行直接头试验时，环向轴力与接头弯矩的加、卸载过程对于试验结果的影响较大。一般说来，如果先加载轴力至最大值，然后加载接头弯矩至最大值时，接头的张开量较两者同步加载至相同最大值时小。

最后，螺栓的预紧力大小、安放试件的支座位置与间距、荷载作用位置等诸多方面也会对试验结果有不同程度的影响。这些方面都是在试验时需特别注意的。

由于国内在开展 1∶1 盾构隧道衬砌管片试验方面起步较晚，试验手段、试验设备、试验经验等诸多方面并不成熟，然而原型试验往往较其他试验在对试验设备的要求、试件的制作、测点布置、试件的拼装与安装、试验过程的控制等诸多方面的要求更为严苛。因此笔者通过对已进行的试验进行经验总结，为相关人员提供参考和帮助，有利于今后类似试验的顺利开展。

参考文献（Reference）：

[1] 朱合华，杨林德，桥本正. 盾构隧道管片接头衬砌系统得两种受力设计模型[J]. 工程力学，1996（增刊）：395-399.

[2] 何川，封坤，杨雄. 南京长江隧道超大断面管片衬砌结构体的相似模型试验研究[J]. 岩石力学与工程学报，2007，26（11）：2260-2269.

[3] 朱伟，钟小春，秦建设. 盾构衬砌管片接头力学分析及双直线刚度模型研究[J]. 岩土力学，2006，27(12)：2154-2158.

[4] CHEN Jun-sheng. MO Hai-hong. Mechanical Behavior of Segment Rebar of Shield Tunnel in Construction Stage [J]. Journal of Zhejiang University SCIENCE A，2008，9(7): 888-899.

[5] 张厚美，傅德明，过迟. 盾构隧道管片接头荷载试验研究[J]. 现代隧道技术，2002，39(6)：28-33.

作者简介（Bio-data）：

姓名：朱合华

出生年月：1962 年 10 月

最终学历：博士

职称：教授、博士生导师、国家注册土木（岩土）工程师

职务：同济大学土木工程学院院长

主要研究方向：

1. 隧道及地下工程设计理论
2. 岩土力学数值方法与应用
3. 数字地下空间与工程
4. 地下空间防灾减灾

Name: Hehua ZHU
Date of Birth: Oct.1962
Max. Degree: Doctor
Qualification: Professor, Doctoral Supervisor, National Registry of Civil (Geotechnical) Engineer
Official Duty: Director of College of Civil Engineering, Tongji University

Main Research Directions:

1. Design Theory of Tunnel and Underground Engineering
2. Research and Application of Numerical Methods in Rock and Soil Mechanics
3. Digital Underground Space and Engineering
4. Disaster Prevention and Reduction in Underground Space

E-mail: zhuhehua@tongji.edu.cn, geofba2d@263.net

水压条件对水下盾构隧道结构内力影响的模型试验

封 坤 何 川 夏松林 邹育麟
西南交通大学地下工程系，四川 成都 610031

【摘 要】 以南京长江隧道为工程背景，将自行研制的水压装置应用于南京长江隧道管片衬砌主体结构的相似模型实验研究中，并采用相似模型试验的研究手段，对于不同水压条件下水下盾构隧道管片主体结构的力学行为进行了系统研究，并针对高水压条件、均匀与非均匀水压条件对于管片衬砌主体结构受力的影响进行了分析，研究结论可为类似工程的设计、施工和研究提供借鉴。
【关键词】 盾构隧道；管片结构；模型试验；水压装置

MODEL TEST ON THE IMPACT OF WATER PRESSURE ON MECHANICAL CHARACTERISTICS OF UNDERWATER SHIELD TUNNEL

Kun FENG，Chuan HE，Songlin XIA，Yulin ZOU
Department of Underground Engineering, Southwest Jiaotong University, Chengdu 610031, Sichuan, China

Abstract: Based on the Nanjing Yangtze River tunnel project, the water pressure device is used in the model test of the main structure of the tunnel. The model test is carried out to study on the mechanical behavior of the main structure under different water pressure, and it focus on the impact of high-pressure conditions, non-uniform and uniform water pressure condition. The experiences and conclusions presented can be adopted in the design，construction and research of similar projects.
Key words: shield tunnel; segmental structure; model test; water pressure device

1 引 言

随着国家经济的快速发展，盾构法逐渐成为修建水下隧道的主要工法[1]。水下盾构隧道场体环境复杂，隧道主体结构受力难以明确[2-3]，加之目前水下盾构隧道断面的大型化，水压对于结构的影响愈来愈重要，鉴于此，研究水压对于隧道主体结构的作用也愈发重要[4-5]。

水下盾构隧道在外静水压力作用下，水压的分布形态为顶部小底部大的“灯泡”形状。在施工和运营期间，隧道承受的水压变化非常大，加之隧道断面激增，水下盾构隧道在施工期和运营期承受的非均匀水压不可忽略，如何精确模拟真实水压的作用进而研究真实水压条件下管片衬砌力学行为特征成为当前水下隧道研究的重要问题。

2 管片衬砌结构形式

文章所研究的南京长江隧道是我国目前开工建设的穿越长江的大型隧道工程，是一座世界级的水下

基金项目：国家自然科学基金（50778154）；863 计划（2006AA11Z116）

公路隧道。隧道将穿越软硬程度差异极大的地层，隧道顶部与长江最高水位差约 60 m，主要穿越砂卵石透水地层。隧道主体结构采用单层装配式钢筋混凝土管片衬砌，原型管片外直径 14.5 m，内直径 13.3 m，管片厚度 0.6 m，采用通用环形式平均幅宽为 2 m。衬砌环分 10 块，封顶块圆心角 12°51′25.71″，两邻接块圆心角 38°34′17.14″，七块标准块的圆心角 38°34′17.14″。管片衬砌在纵向按通缝式和错缝式拼装，纵向螺栓 42 颗，按 4°27′和 10°37′55.71″的角度交替布置，如图 1 所示。

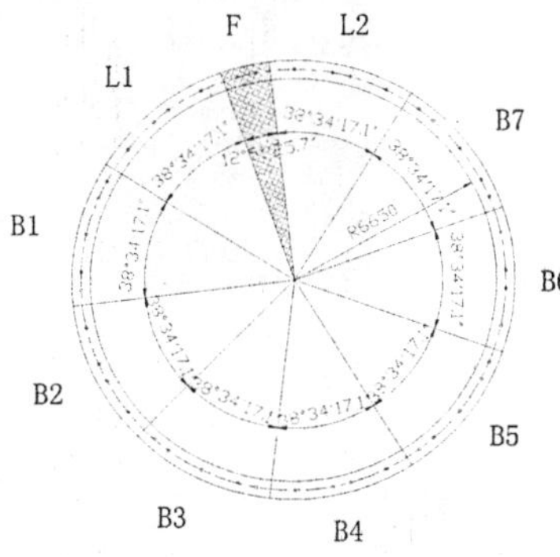

图 1　管片衬砌分块图

共有 7 种拼装方式，其中第 1 种为通逢拼装方式，第 2～6 种为设计拼装方式，第 7 种为可能出现的最不利拼装方式，具体如下：① 通缝拼装，前后环都是封顶块管片中心轴相对竖向轴左偏 12°51′25.71″；② CF1，以两环一组，第一环起始位置为封顶块管片中心轴相对竖向轴左偏 12°51′25.71″，第二环相对第一环右偏转 25°42′51.4″；③ CF2，以两环一组，第一环起始位置同上，第二环相对第一环右偏转 102°51′25.7″；④ CF3，以两环一组，第一环起始位置同上，第二环相对第一环偏转 180°；⑤ CF4，以两环一组，第一环起始位置同上，第二环相对第一环偏转 257°8′34.3″；⑥ CF5，以两环一组，第一环起始位置同上，第二环相对第一环偏转 334°17′8.6″；⑦ CF6，第一环起始位置为封顶块管片中心轴相对竖向轴左偏 37°34′17.13″，第二环相对第一环右偏转 25°42′51.4″。

3　水压装置

隧道通过水位较高的透水地层时，隧道衬砌结构将承受较大的径向水压作用，尤其对于越江盾构隧道，通常承受高水压进行工作，此时水压力对结构内力影响很大，而由于断面增大，底部的不均匀部分也愈发明显。为了在试验中真实模拟水压力对管片结构作用的影响，将“灯泡形”水压分解为均匀水压与非均匀水压两部分相叠加，见图 2。

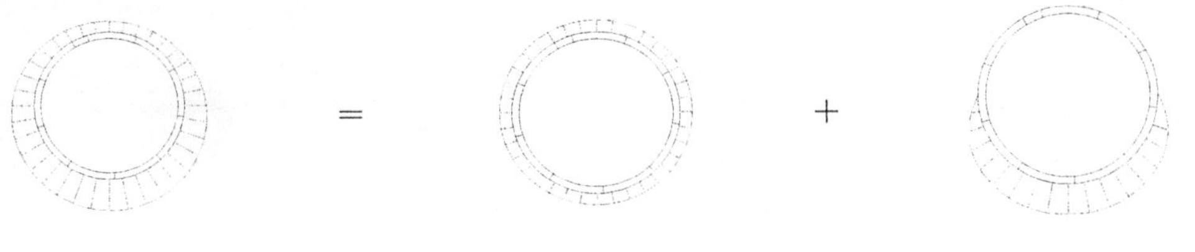

（a）实际水压　　（b）均匀水压　　（c）非均匀水压

图 2　水压模拟原理图

3.1　均匀水压装置

当圆形盾构管片结构处于透水地层时，水压将对结构直接产生径向压力。故采用旋转式装置加载（见图 4 至图 5）能够实现不同直径、多种幅宽的盾构隧道管片环模型的环向均布力加载，并且其加载能力能够达到管片环模型（石膏材料）的破坏强度。

该水压的模拟主要通过钢绞线箍紧管片环来实现。钢绞线沿管片环纵向均匀分布，用于环箍加载从而模拟均布压力。为保证钢绞线受力一致，钢绞线中部设置了测试段，能够测试钢绞线的应力和应变，并且在钢绞线端头设置了可以调节其拉伸程度的锚具。

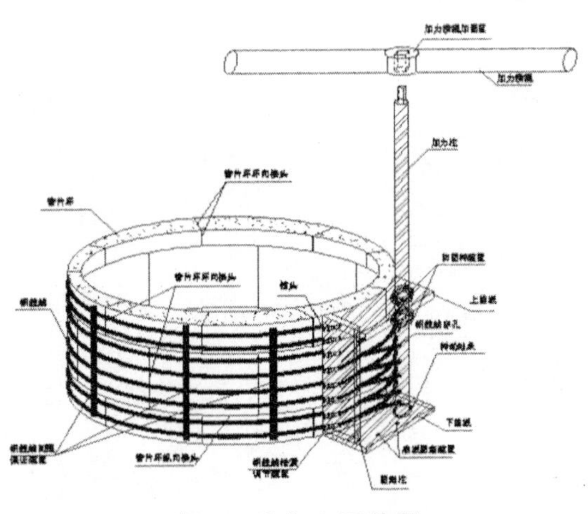

图 3　均匀水压装置

图 4 水压装置工作总体图

图 5 均匀水压装置安置图

3.2 非均匀水压装置

当隧道外径较小、水位较高时隧道外径高度的非均匀水压产生的弯矩值较小，在模型试验中一般没有考虑其非均匀水压的影响。而对于断面较大的水下盾构隧道衬砌结构，非均匀水压的影响不能忽略。

故采用非均匀水压装置考虑此影响，装置的加载示意见图 6，装置工作时需先预埋施力钢绞线、钢绞线网兜及钢绞线套筒在。施力钢绞线作用是导入张拉力；钢绞线网兜是为把张拉力均分到管片上；钢绞线套筒消除钢绞线与试验土体的摩擦力。通过反力支座、加载吊篮、加载砝码来施加张拉力，见图 7。

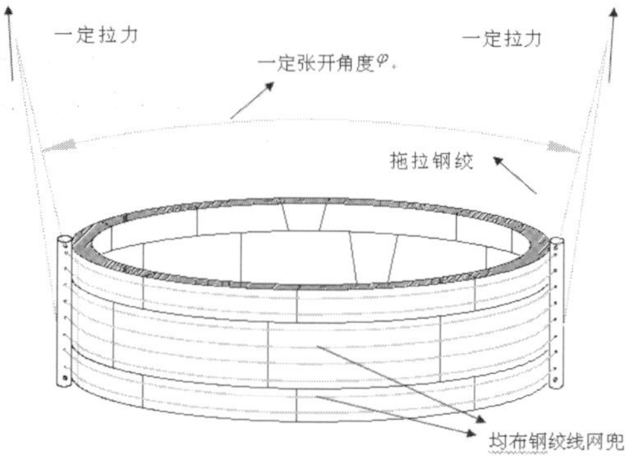

图 6 非均匀水压加载示意图

图 7 非均匀水压加载图

4 相似模型试验

4.1 相似关系

以 1/25 的几何相似比和 1/1 的容重相似比为基础相似比[6]，在弹性范围控制各物理力学参数完全相似性。根据相似理论，推得泊松比、应变、摩擦角相似比：$C_\mu = C_\varepsilon = C_\varphi = 1$，强度、应力、凝聚力、弹性模量相似比：$C_R = C_\sigma = C_C = C_E = 25$。

4.2 相似材料

根据工程地质勘测报告，南京长江隧道江中段主要穿越中密粉细砂、粉细砂、砾砂软土地层。隧道穿过土体的力学参数变化范围如下：$c = 5 \sim 6$ kPa，$\phi = 31.9° \sim 34°$，$E_s = 18.7 \sim 56.1$ MPa，$\gamma = 19 \sim 20.1$ kN/m^3。土体材料采用特定比例的重晶石粉、石英砂、河砂、松香、机油的混合物模拟。土体模型和原型物理力学参数见表 1。

表 1 土体材料物理力学参数

参数名称		地层参数取值
凝聚力 C/MPa	原型	5 ~ 6
	模型	0.22
内摩擦角 ϕ	原型	31.9 ~ 34.0
	模型	30
弹性模量 E/MPa	原型	18.7 ~ 56.1
	模型	1.542
容重 γ/(kN/m^3)	原型	19 ~ 20.1
	模型	20
	对应原型值	20

管片衬砌材料。管片混凝土为 C60 钢筋混凝土，采用水:石膏：硅藻土为 1：1.33：0.1 的复合材料通过预制加工的方法模拟。

管片混凝土环向主筋。采用直径为 1.2 mm 的铁质材料对称配筋进行模拟。

5 试验系列及量测内容

根据实际工程情况，采用 7 套管片环，包括一种通缝拼装和六种错缝拼装方式，对 20 m 土压，10 m 至 50 m 均匀及非均匀水压等不同情况进行试验分析。

主要量测内容有：

（1）管片衬砌的径向位移。从拱顶开始，在管片环内侧沿顺时针方向每 30 度布设 0.001 mm 精度差动变压器式位移传感器进行量测，一环共布置 8 个测点。

（2）管片衬砌结构内力。以 10 度为单位在环结构内、外侧对称布设环向电阻应变片，测试内外侧应变值，以此获得内外侧的应变后计算出管片环结构截面内力。单个管片环共布置 72 个测点。

（3）管片衬砌与土体间的接触压力。从拱顶以 30 度为单位在环外侧周边位置布置测点，用精密土压力盒进行量测。一环布设 12 个测点，如图 8 所示。

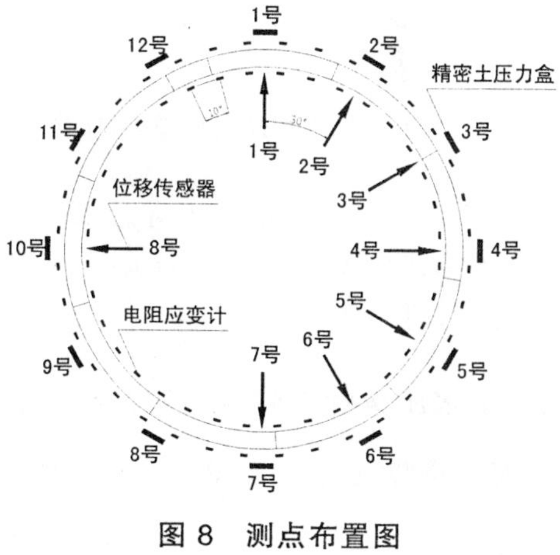

图 8 测点布置图

6 试验结果分析

6.1 不同水压条件下管片衬砌的力学特征

采用 CF1 拼装方式为例，当土压力不变时，随着水压力从 10 m 加大到 20 m 时，管片衬砌结构的最大正弯矩值从 1 002.12 kN · m 急剧降至 648.29 kN · m，水压力从 20 m 加大到 50 m 时，正弯矩又缓慢增大，见图 9。水压力从 10 米加大到 50 米时，最大负弯矩从 619.49 kN · m 减至变到 72.03 kN · m 又平缓增大，相应的平均轴力水平从 5 840 kN 迅速增大到 9 770 kN，见图 10。从试验看随水压力增大，弯矩、轴力沿圆周分布图形状基本不变。水土分算的情况下，水压力增大使管片衬砌结构的偏心矩水平明显减小，在结构受力允许的范围内对结构是有利的。

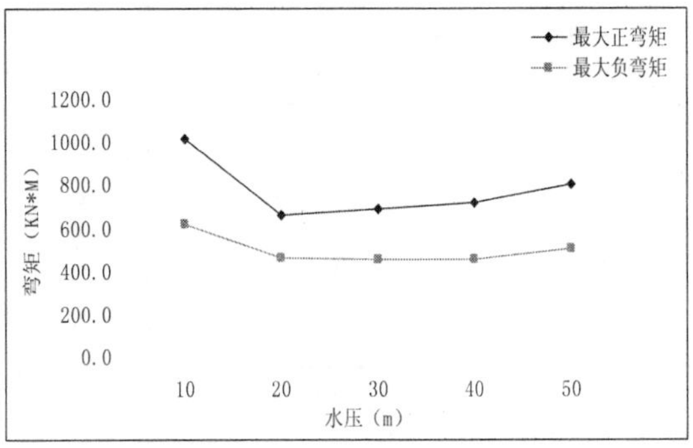

图 9 CF1 拼装方式弯矩-水压力关系曲线

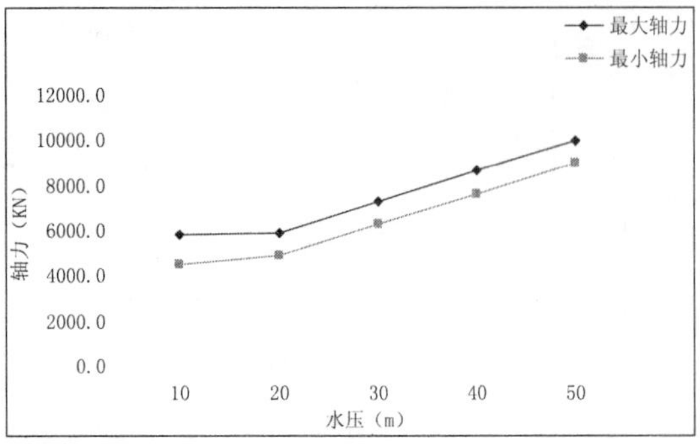

图 10 CF1 拼装方式轴力-水压力关系曲线

分析衬砌结构变形情况。由图 11 可见随着水压力不断增大，衬砌结构的变形量从 8.45 mm 缓慢变化到 6.96 mm。变形量先减后增，但变化不大。

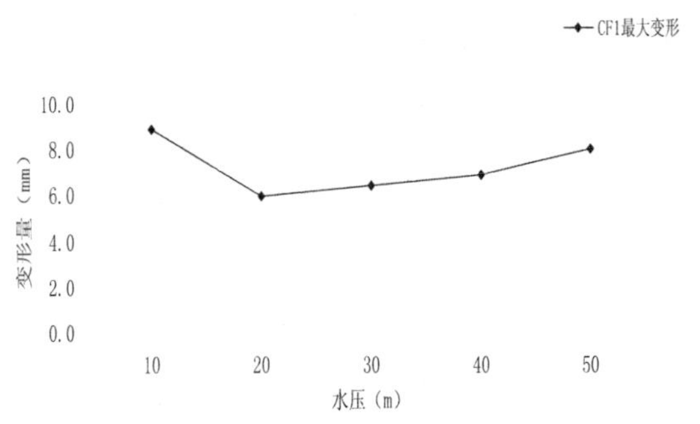

图 11 CF1 拼装方式变形量-水压力关系曲线

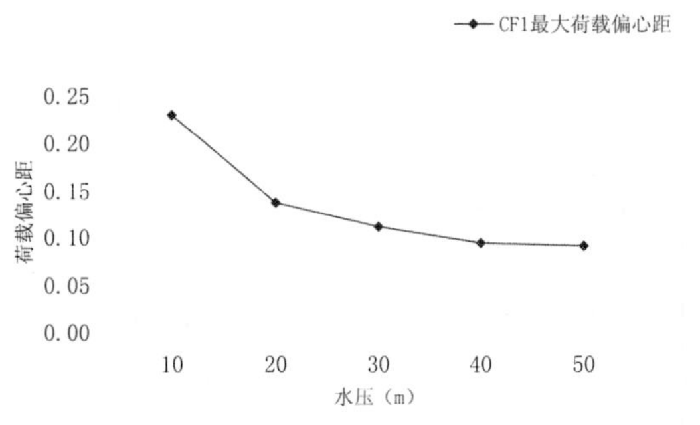

图 12 CF1 拼装方式荷载偏心矩-水压力关系曲线

由此表明，在以砂性土等透水性土质条件下，水压力的增大，加大了轴力总体水平，降低了偏心距水平，详见图 12，有利于结构配筋和防水部位变形控制。为安全考虑，对于水土分算的情况，应取最低水位进行计算。

6.2 高水压条件下管片衬砌的力学特征

对各拼装方式进行 20 m 土压无水压与 20 m 土压 50 m 高水压水土分算对比试验，试验结果列于表 2。

表 2 高水压及无水压条件下各拼装方式结果

拼装方式	无水压				高水压			
	最大正弯矩 / kN·m	最大负弯矩 / kN·m	最大轴力 / kN	最小轴力 / kN	最大正弯矩 / kN·m	最大负弯矩 / kN·m	最大轴力 / kN	最小轴力 / kN
TF	479.35	−64.24	5 600	4 240	316.35	−267.35	9 890	9 050
CF1	1 611.56	−45.19	5 730	3 580	695.81	−440.05	9 980	8 890
CF2	1 776.98	−27.22	5 760	3 600	628.67	−302.97	9 970	8 890
CF3	1 380.13	−07.05	5 630	3 540	641.85	−396.74	9 940	8 840
CF4	1 392.58	−15.08	5 740	3 580	590.04	−365.43	9 900	8 870
CF5	1 557.06	−75.18	5 570	3 590	602.67	−357.21	9 960	8 880

由表 2 比较可知，从内力量值上分析，高水压条件下管片错缝拼装方式与通缝拼装方式最大弯矩比值增大，而各错缝拼装间相对变化很小，50 m 高水压使各拼装方式管片平均轴力水平增大大约 4 500 kN；从内力分布分析，高水压条件下管片拱底正弯矩较拱顶正弯矩小很多，拱腰以下的正负弯矩都较小；从变形上分析，管片错缝拼装方式相对通缝拼装方式最大变形量量值上小很多，说明在高水压错缝拼装比通缝拼装具有更好的变形抵抗能力；从荷载偏心距上分析，高水压条件下管片的荷载偏心距大幅度降低，当水压很大时所有拼装方式的最大荷载偏心接近一定值。

总之，高水压相对水压较低的情况，管片结构具有弯矩小、变形小、荷载偏心距小、轴力大的特点，在轴力容许的范围内对结构受力有利。

6.3 均匀水压与非均匀水压加载下管片衬砌的力学特征

考虑到管片结构尺寸大，管片外径高度的 14.5 m 非均匀水压不能忽略，故采用非均匀水压装置，引入 14.5 m 非均匀水压的影响。

从 CF1 拼装方式的非均匀水压加载、均匀水压加载对比曲线图 13 至图 14 可知，最大正弯矩、最大负弯矩、最大变形量的变化曲线走向大体一致。均匀水压加载相对非均匀水压加载在试验结果上前者比后者最大变形量大 2～2.6 mm，最大正弯矩大 300 kN · m 左右，最大负弯矩小 200 kN · m 左右，最小轴力小 200 kN 左右，最大轴力小 50 kN 左右，同时荷载偏心矩减小。综上可知，非均匀水压使管片衬砌结构受力更趋于均匀。

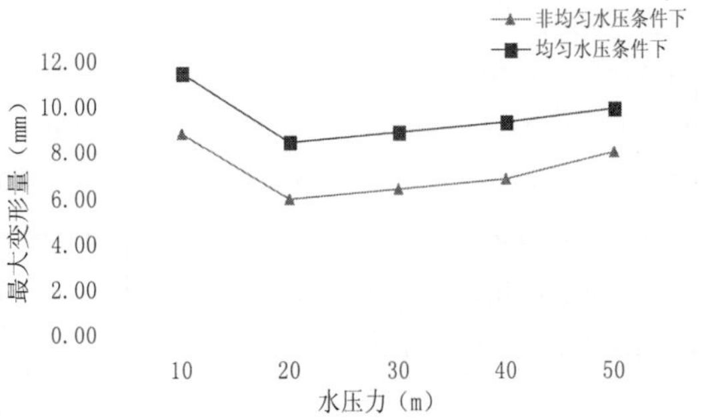

图 13 非均匀、均匀水压加载最大变形量对比曲线

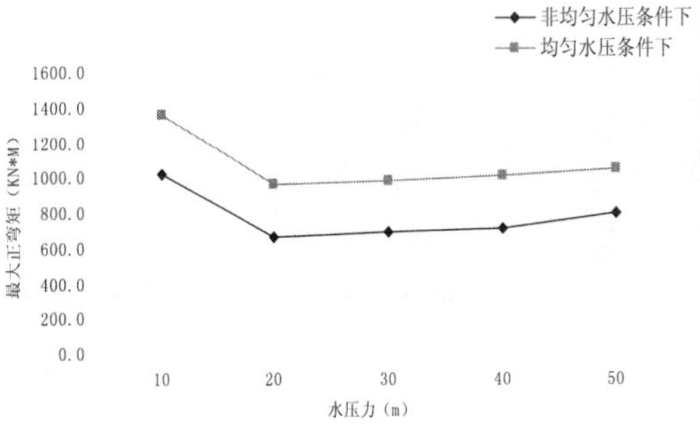

图 14 非均匀、均匀水压加载最大正弯矩对比曲线

7 结 论

通过研发可精确模拟真实水压的水压装置，并以南京长江隧道为背景，应用于相似模型试验，对水下隧道管片衬砌结构力学特征进行了分析，得出以下有益结论：

（1）对于砂性土等透水性土质条件下，水压力的增大有利于结构配筋和防水部位变形控制，为安全考虑，应取最低水位进行计算。

（2）高水压相对水压较低的情况，管片结构具有弯矩小、变形小、荷载偏心距小、轴力大的特点，在轴力容许的范围内对结构受力有利。

（3）对于水下隧道，非均匀水压的作用不可忽略，在一般情况下，非均匀水压对结构受力有利。

（4）试验中水压试验装置加载将均匀水压与非均匀水压分别控制，真正实现了水压模拟控制，为水下隧道结构的受力特征研究方法提供了试验手段。

参考文献（References）：

[1] 何川，曾东洋. 盾构隧道结构设计及施工对环境的影响[M]. 成都：西南交大出版社，2004.

[2] KOYAMA Y.Present status and technology of shield tunneling method in Japan[J]. Tunneling and Underground Space Technology，2003，18（2-3）：145-159.

[3] 苏宗贤，何川．荷载-结构模式的壳-弹簧-接触模型[J]．西南交通大学学报，2007，42（3）：288-292.

[4] 周俊英．装配式圆形衬砌计算浅论[J]．地下工程与隧道.1988（4）：2-6.

[5] 朱合华，崔茂玉，杨金松．盾构衬砌管片的设计模型与荷载分布的研究[J]．岩土工程学报，2000（3）：190-194.

[6] 唐志成，何川，林刚．地铁盾构隧道管片结构力学行为模型试验研究[J]．岩土工程学报，2005，27(1)：85-89.

作者简介（Bio-data）：

封坤（1983.3.9—），男，博士研究生，主要从事现代盾构隧道技术与设计理论方面的研究工作。

Kun FENG(1983.3.9—)，male，candidate of Ph.D. degree，majored in theory of modern shield tunnel technology and design.

E-mail: windfeng813@163.com

何川，1964年生，工学博士（早稻田大学）。西南交通大学地下工程系主任、博士生导师、教育部长江学者特聘教授。长期从事隧道与地下工程的教学与科研工作。主要研究领域为：现代盾构法隧道设计理论、地下铁道结构设计、特殊隧道结构施工控制、高速公路隧道运营控制。

Chuan HE was born in June 1964 and obtained the Dr. Eng. in the Waseda University. Currently, Dr. HE is the director of Department of Underground Engineering in Southwest Jiaotong University, the doctor supervisor, the professor of Changjiang Scholar Programm, Ministry of Education of PRC. He has been engaging in the teaching and research of tunnel engineering for many years. He specializes in design theory of modern shield tunnel, structural design of subway, construction technique of tunnel under complicated condition, tunnel ventilation control system.

Tel: +86-28-87601932

E-mail: chuanhe21@163.com

地下工程预制化结构接头力学特性试验研究

王明年　魏龙海　李志业　刘惠敏　贾永刚
西南交通大学　土木工程学院，四川　成都　610031

【摘　要】 在地下工程预制化结构技术中，接头构造及其设置位置不仅要考虑结构合理的受力状态，更要考虑构件的制造和安装的可行性，并要求减少构件的类型便于实现规模化生产。通过模型试验，对地下工程预制化结构接头的力学特性进行了研究，并建立了接头抗弯刚度模型。
【关键词】 预制化结构；接头模型试验；力学特性

STUDY ON THE JOINT MECHANICS CHARACTERS OF THE PREFABRICATED STRUCTURE BY MODEL TEST

Mingnian WANG, Longhai WEI, Zhiye LI, Huimin LIU, Yonggang JIA
Department of Underground Engineering, Southwest Jiaotong University, Chengdu 610031, Sichuan, China

Abstract: When the joints structure is been building and its position is been setting, it need consider not only the stress state of the whole structure, but also the feasibility of the fabrieation and installation of the components. What's more, it should reduce types of the components in order to produce the components on a large scale. The joint mechanics characters of the prefabricated structure were studied by model test, and established the joint bending stiffness model.
Key words: prefabrieated structure; joint model test; mechanical characteristics

1 引　言

地下工程预制化结构的重要特征是接头的存在，接头的性能对结构的受力和变形有很大影响，这是设计中必须考虑的因素。表征接头性能的最主要参数是接头抗弯刚度，它定义为接头产生单位转角所需的弯矩。目前，接头抗弯刚度的取值尚无现成的公式或图表可循，工程上一般根据接头试验确定，以便为计算结构内力和改进接头构造提供依据。

2 试验模型及方法

2.1 试验目的及研究内容

试验研究的内容包括：接缝的受力、变形和破坏过程的研究；接头抗弯刚度的定量评价；研究轴力、弯矩、偏心矩等因素对接头抗弯刚度的影响规律。

2.2 试验设备及方法

（1）加载设备与方法

试验衬砌块放入试验坑中进行卧式加载，加载方式按图 1 进行，轴向采用一台 1 500 kN 的液压式千斤顶，侧向采用两台 700 kN 的千斤顶，即图 1 中的 N 和 P1、P2 所示。它们分别为可独立控制的轴向荷载和侧向荷载。

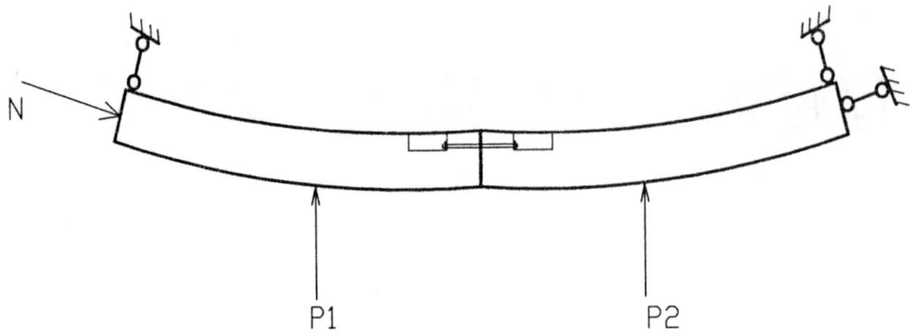

图 1　加载图示

（2）试件构件

采用 1∶1 的钢筋混凝土衬砌接头进行试验，使接头处产生与设计相等的弯矩和轴力，通过试验结果可以了解接头的抗弯能力和抗弯刚度系数。试件的外径为 10.9 m，单块管片的扇形夹角为 6.67°，厚度 30 cm，高度 75 cm，每个手孔在环向开有一个 ϕ40 mm 的螺栓孔，螺栓直径为 ϕ30 mm，材料为 45 号钢，管片混凝土标号为 C30。

（3）测试方法及内容

试验中直接测量的数据包括：混凝土应变、螺栓拉力、接缝位移、裂缝宽度和方向，通过这些参数可以求得接缝转角、接头抗弯刚度的试验值。

管片位移主要包括接头的径向位移和接缝两侧的相对位移，使用位移传感器进行测量，具体测点布置见图 2。内、外弧面各布置 6 支，其中 A3、A4、B3、B4 用来测量接头径向位移，其余测量接缝两侧管片的相对位移。

（4）加载等级设计

通过调整轴向千斤顶作用力 N 和侧向千斤顶作用力 P，可以进行多种接头内力组合，见图 3。

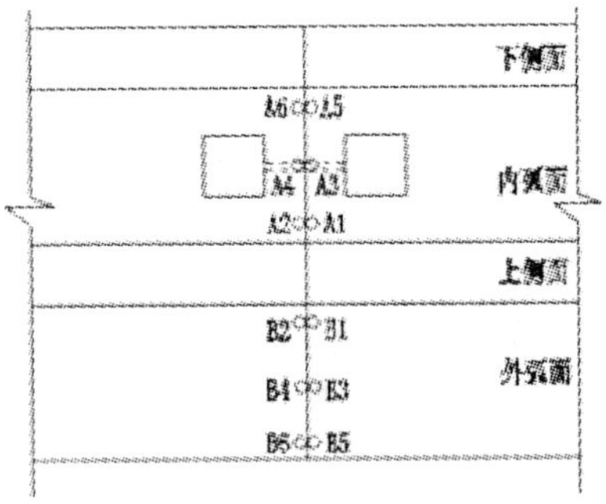

图 2　位移计位置

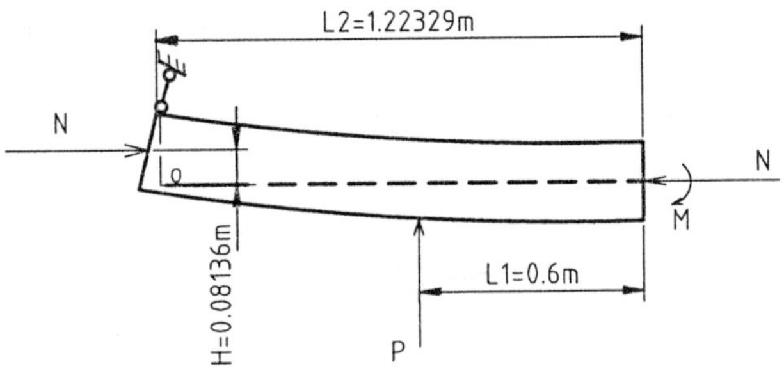

图 3　接头受力简图

为了保证试验的顺利进行，按偏心矩进行试验分组，共进行了 6 种偏心矩的试验，即 $e=0.15$ m、$e=0.13$ m、$e=0.12$ m、$e=0.10$ m、$e=0.03$ m、$e=0.01$ m。在每一个偏心矩下，进行了分级加载试验，由于分级加载过程中涉及轴向千斤顶作用力 N 和侧向千斤顶作用力 P，因此，为了保证加载过程中偏心矩保持不变，则必须保证轴向千斤顶作用力 N 和侧向千斤顶作用力 P 维持一定的关系。

接头试验的荷载一般是按偏心距分组进行设计。接缝偏心距定义为接缝弯矩与接缝轴力之比。习惯上约定：使衬砌内侧面受拉的弯矩为正弯矩，对应的偏心距为正偏心距，反之为负偏心距。偏心距应事先确定，每组试验的偏心距保持不变，增大荷载过程中保证偏心距不变的实质是使接缝处的弯矩和轴力按同一比例增加。

（5）试验组数

本次共进行了 6 组试验，具体情况见表 1。

表 1　试验组数

<table>
<tr><th rowspan="2">轴向力（kN）</th><th colspan="6">偏心距（m）</th></tr>
<tr><th>1</th><th>2</th><th>3</th><th>4</th><th>5</th><th>6</th></tr>
<tr><td>50</td><td rowspan="8">0.15</td><td rowspan="7">0.13</td><td rowspan="7">0.12</td><td rowspan="7">0.10</td><td rowspan="9">0.03</td><td rowspan="9">0.01</td></tr>
<tr><td>100</td></tr>
<tr><td>200</td></tr>
<tr><td>300</td></tr>
<tr><td>400</td></tr>
<tr><td>500</td></tr>
<tr><td>600</td></tr>
<tr><td>700</td><td></td><td></td><td></td></tr>
<tr><td>800</td><td></td><td></td><td></td><td></td></tr>
</table>

3　试验结果分析

3.1　接头转角位移和径向位移的变化规律

接头转角与偏心距的关系见图 4，接头径向位移与偏心距的关系见图 5。

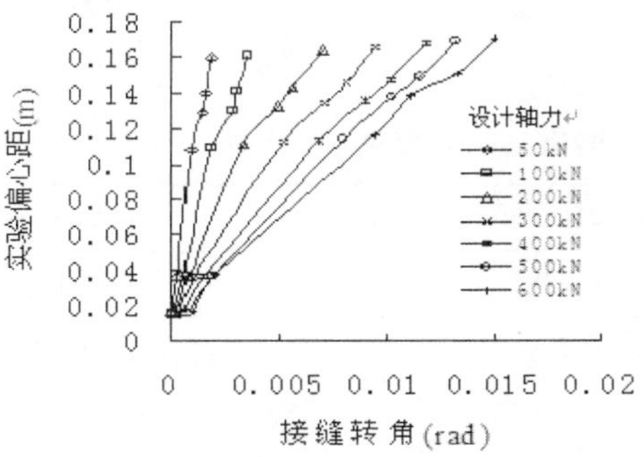

图 4　接头转角与偏心距的关系

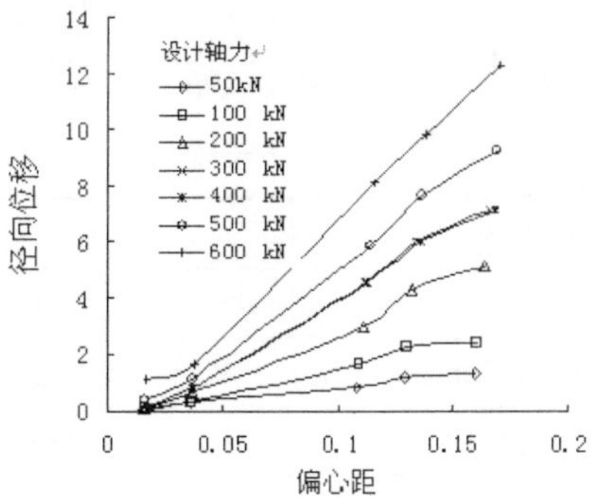

图 5　接头径向位移与偏心距的关系

由图 4 和图 5 可以看出：

（1）在偏心矩 $e<0.04$ m 时，在不同的轴力作用下，接头转角和接头径向位移与偏心矩成非线性关系，轴力越大，非线性关系越强。

（2）在偏心矩 $0.04\ \text{m}\leqslant e\leqslant 0.11$ m 时，在不同的轴力作用下，接头转角和接头径向位移与偏心矩成线性关系，表明此时的垫层成弹性。

（3）在偏心矩 $e>0.11$ m 时，在不同的轴力作用下，接头转角和接头径向位移与偏心矩成非线性关系，表明此时的垫层已经进入塑性，其中接头转角的非线性相对强一些，接头径向位移非线性要弱一些。

总的来说，在不同的轴力作用下，接头转角和接头径向位移与偏心矩表现的非线性关系不强，可用线性关系来表达，由此可以推出，接头转角和接头径向位移与接头内力可用线性关系来表达。

3.2　接头弯矩与接头转角的关系

接头弯矩与接头转角的关系见图 6。

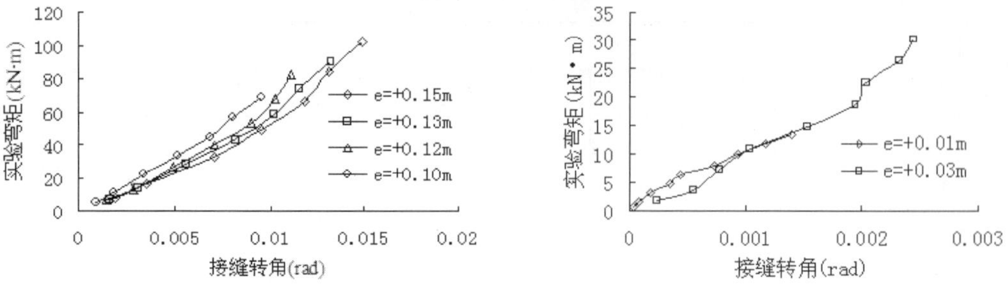

(a) (b)

图 6 接头弯矩与接头转角的关系

由图 6 可以看出：

(1) 在偏心矩 e 较大时，在弯矩较小的情况下，接头弯矩与接头转角成线性关系，在弯矩较大的情况下，这种关系表现出一定的非线性。

(2) 在偏心矩 e 较小时，在弯矩较小的情况下，接头弯矩与接头转角成非线性关系，以后随着弯矩的增大，接头弯矩与接头转角表现为线性关系，当弯矩较大时，这种关系又表现出一定的非线性。

(3) 总的来说，无论是偏心矩较大或较小，接头弯矩与接头转角之间的关系表现的非线性都不强，因此，接头弯矩与接头转角之间的关系可以用线性关系来表达。

3.3 接头抗弯刚度试验公式

由上分析可以看出，接头转角与接头弯矩可用线性关系来表达。所以，采用直线方程对不同偏心距接头转角与接头弯矩的试验数据加以拟合。其结果见表 2。

表 2 不同偏心距下接头抗弯刚度试验数据拟合结果

偏心距	k_θ /(kN·m/rad)	M_0 /(kN·m)	相关系数
$e=+0.15$ m	6 898.4	−10.641	0.971 4
$e=+0.13$ m	6 921.5	−7.819 6	0.982 8
$e=+0.12$ m	7 433.3	−8.192 5	0.974 9
$e=+0.10$ m	7 328.8	−2.584 6	0.995 8
$e=+0.03$ m	1 2293	−2.441 8	0.974 2
$e=+0.01$ m	9 048.1	1.270 4	0.985 5

为便于分析，将线性关系式用通式表达：

$$M = k_\theta \theta + M_0 \tag{1}$$

式中 M——接头弯矩（kN·m）;

θ——接头转角（rad）;

k_θ、M_0——拟合系数，单位分别为 kN·m/rad，kN·m。

根据抗弯刚度的定义，切线刚度可用接头弯矩对接头转角的一阶导数表示，对式（1）求一阶导数得：

$$k_\theta = \frac{dM}{d\theta} \tag{2}$$

由表 2 可以看出，偏心距不同，其接头的抗弯刚度也不相同，基本规律是：

(1) 偏心矩 e 较大时，接头抗弯刚度在 6 800～7 500 kN · m/rad;

(2) 偏心矩 e 较小时，接头抗弯刚度在 9 000～12 500 kN · m/rad。

3.4 接头径向位移与接头内力的关系

接头径向位移与接头内力关系见图 7。

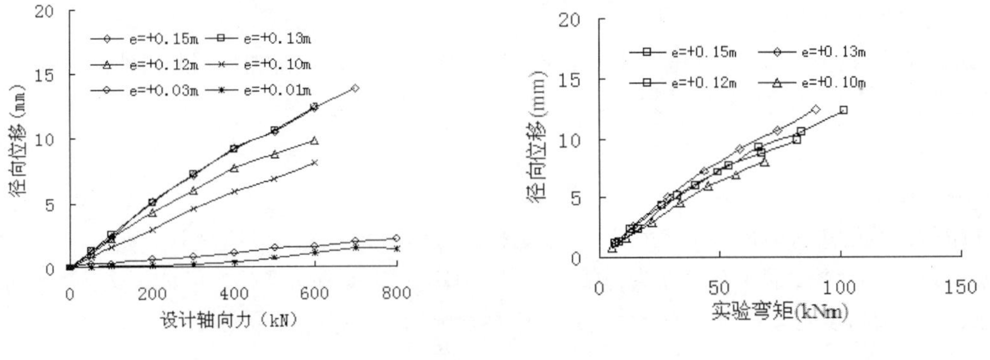

（a）　　　　　　　　（b）

图 7　接头径向位移与接头内力关系

由图 7 可以看出：

（1）在内力较小的情况下，接头的径向位移与接头内力基本上成线性关系；

（2）在内力较大的情况下，接头的径向位移与接头内力成非线性关系；

（3）总的来说，接头的径向位移与接头内力之间的非线性关系不强，因此，接头的径向位移与接头内力之间的关系可以用线性关系来表达。

3.5 衬砌块混凝土的应变变化规律

衬砌块混凝土的应变规律见图 8。

由图 8 可知，衬砌块内弧面受拉，外弧面受压，中心线处应变接近 0，应变沿中线呈反对称分布。

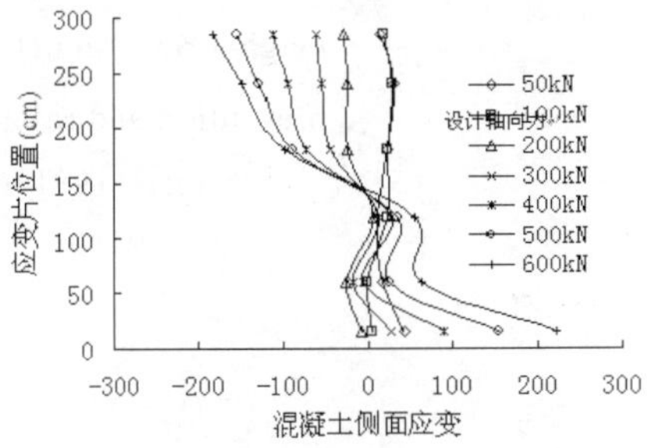

图 8　$e=+0.12$ m 侧面混凝土应变变化规律

3.6 接头的破坏特征

由试验过程可以看出，接头破坏多以受压区边缘混凝土局部剪切剥落破坏为主，而衬砌块本体却完好无损，说明接头强度小于衬砌块本体的强度，提高接头强度，对整体强度的提高有很大的促进作用。

4 结　论

本文通过试验，对地下工程预制化结构力学特性进行了探讨，得出结论如下：

（1）接头转角位移和径向位移的变化规律

在偏心矩 $e<0.04$ m 时，接头转角和接头径向位移与偏心矩成非线性关系，轴力越大，非线性关系越强。在偏心矩 0.04 m $\leqslant e \leqslant$ 0.11 m 时，接头转角和接头径向位移与偏心矩成线性关系。在偏心矩 $e>0.11$ m 时，接头转角和接头径向位移与偏心矩成非线性关系，其中接头转角的非线性相对强一些，接头径向位移非线性要弱一些。

（2）接头弯矩与接头转角的关系

在偏心矩 e 较大时，在弯矩较小的情况下，接头弯矩与接头转角成线性关系，在弯矩较大的情况下，这种关系表现出一定的非线性。在偏心矩 e 较小时，在弯矩较小的情况下，接头弯矩与接头转角成非线性关系，以后随着弯矩的增大，接头弯矩与接头转角表现为线性关系，当弯矩较大时，这种关系又表现出一定的非线性。

（3）接头径向位移与接头内力的关系

在内力较小的情况下，接头的径向位移与接头内力基本上成线性关系。在内力较大的情况下，接头的径向位移与接头内力成非线性关系。

（4）衬砌块混凝土的应变变化规律

衬砌块内弧面受拉，外弧面受压，中心线处应变接近 0，应变沿中线呈反对称分布；接头破坏多以受压区边缘混凝土局部剪切剥落破坏为主，而衬砌块本体却完好无损。

参考文献（References）：

[1] 新建铁路隧道装配式衬砌技术的应用研究. 试验报告，西南交通大学，2004.10.

[2] 刘惠敏.地下铁道明挖区间装配式衬砌力学特性研究[D]. 西南交通大学硕士学位论文，2004.02.

[3] 贾永刚. 铁路隧道装配式衬砌力学特性研究[D]. 西南交通大学硕士学位论文，2003.07.

作者简介（Bio-data）：

王明年（1965—），男，博士，1988 年毕业于西南交通大学桥梁与隧道工程专业，现任教授、博士生导师。主要研究领域及方向：隧道施工力学，隧道结构动力学，复杂隧道结构设计理论，邻近隧道施工技术，隧道智能通风技术，隧道防灾救援技术，隧道机电控制技术。

Mingnian WANG（1965—），Male，professor and PhD supervisor，Ph.D.，main study areas：Mechanics tunnel，tunnel structural dynamics，structural design theory of the complex tunnel，the neighboring tunnel construction technology，intelligent tunnel ventilation technology，disaster prevention and rescue techniques tunnel.

E-mail: 19910622@163.com

管片背后注浆效果无损检测试验研究

曹大明　黄　亮　温佐彪
成都畅达通地下工程科技发展有限公司，四川　成都　610041

【摘　要】 盾构隧道管片注浆效果检测是一个新型研究课题，对于测定和评价同步注浆、及时注浆或二次注浆效果，进而控制地层沉降，保护盾构隧道周边建构筑物安全，具有重要意义。本文通过实例介绍了采用地质雷达对管片注浆效果进行无损检测的方法，说明了其适用性和有效性。并对进一步检测研究提出了建议。
【关键词】 无损检测；地质雷达；管片注浆效果；盾构隧道；地层沉降

THE STUDY ON NONDESTRUCTIVE TESTING EXPERIMENT OF THE EFFECT OF GROUTING BEHIND SHIELD TUNNEL SEGMENT

Daming CAO, Liang HUANG, Zuobiao WEN
Chengdu Chang Da Tong underground engineering science & technology development Co .LTD, Chengdu 610041, Sichuan, China

Abstract: The effect testing of The Shield Tunnel Segment grouting is a new research topic that is of great significance in the field of determination and evaluation of the effect of synchronous grouting, grouting timely or secondary, the control of ground settlement, and the protection of the security of the structure that around the shield tunnel. This article introduced the method by use the Ground Penetrating Radar to carry on the effect of the segment grouting, illustrates the applicability and effectiveness of this method and gives suggestion for the further testing.
Key word: nondestructive testing; ground penetrating radar; effect of the segment grouting; shield tunnel; ground settlement

1 引　言

盾构隧道在软土和砂卵石地层中施工引起的地表沉降常常导致周围地层发生过大变形，甚至地层塌陷，亦影响到了线路周边建构筑物安全。沉降主要根源在于开挖引起的水土流失和对原状地层的扰动，导致隧道附近土体沉降、变形的发展，进而导致周邻建（构）筑物产生沉降、倾斜、开裂等等不良影响问题，甚至安全问题。盾构通过时的地表沉降占总沉降量的20%～100%，盾构在软土层产生的地表沉降影响要大于硬质土层和岩层，是影响地表沉降的最主要因素。产生的原因是由于盾构机的外径大于管片外径，盾尾过后，留下来的空隙就需及时充填，往往因盾尾壁后注浆没能及时填充盾尾空隙，或是注浆不当，造成浆液厚度环向分布不均（拱部薄），充填不实。盾顶土层在不能形成有效承载拱情况下就充填盾尾空隙，引起上部土层应力释放，地表下沉[1]。因此及时进行盾尾注浆是控制地表沉降一个重要施工工序。

同步注浆是在盾尾间隙形成同时注入浆液，能够最及时、有效地阻止地层土体位移。在盾后数环后，才对盾尾间隙进行注浆，称之为及时注浆，相对不利于地层位移控制。常用的注浆材料由水泥、砂、水、外掺剂等拌和组成，由于水泥活性材料存在，称为硬性浆液。由于浆液的流动性、泌水性、渗透性、稳定性等，以及隧道所处地层的特性，导致浆液在管片背后的分布形态不均匀，盾尾未能被有效充填，因此对管片背后注浆效果进行检测是必要的。我公司先后对成都地铁、广州地铁项目开展管片背后注浆效果进行无损检测试验研究，主要以地质雷达作为主要检测设备进行了多次检测试验。本文结合上述检测试验介绍检测方法和效果并提出盾构管片背后注浆效果检测的建议。

2 可探性分析

地质雷达具有分辨率高、无损、速度快、操作简便等优点，而且相对探测深度范围大，现已运用于工程检测领域，并取得了良好效果。因而作为管片背后注浆效果检测手段被优先考虑。

地质雷达（Ground Penetrating Radar，简称 GPR）方法是一种用于确定地下介质分布的广谱电磁波技术。在检测范围无大量铁磁性物体干扰的情况下，可采用地质雷达理进行探测。地质雷达利用天线向地中发射电磁脉冲，并接收由地中不同介质界面的反射波。电磁波在介质中传播时，其路径、电磁场强度与波形将随所通过介质的电性质（如介电常数 ε_r）及几何形态的变化而变化。根据接收到的回波时间、幅度和波形等信息，可判定地下介质的结构与埋藏体的位置与形态[2]。其测试原理如图 1 所示。

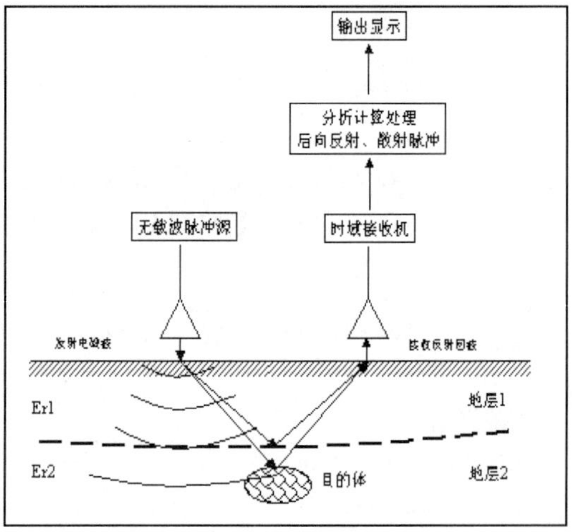

图 1 地质雷达测试原理图

脉冲波的走时为:

$$t=\sqrt{4h^2+x^2}/v \tag{1}$$

式中 t——脉冲波走时（ns）;

h——目标深度（m）;

x——发射天线与接收天线的距离（m）;

v——电磁波波速（m/ns）。

常见的介质为非磁介质，在探地雷达的频率范围内，因此介质的电磁波速度为:

$$v=\frac{c}{\sqrt{\varepsilon_r}} \tag{2}$$

式中 $c=0.3$ m/ns （光速）;

ε_r——介质相对介电常数。

地质雷达检测成功与否与检测对象和其存在环境直接有关[3]，首先要求探测目标体与周围介质有明显电性差异，其次雷达波目标体所处深度应在雷达探测深度范围内，再次检测区域干扰要少。探测注浆体距离探测接触面在 50 cm 内，龄期 28 d 后为水泥砂浆凝固体，与管片、围岩层（砂卵石层、粉质砂岩）介电常数差异较大，故雷达信号在界面存在较强反射，以此来探测注浆体厚度分布和注浆缺陷情况是可行的。但由于探测区为圈闭空间，且存在金属器件、电线，需要滤除和压制杂波。

3 检测试验实例

以成都地铁 1 号线盾构Ⅳ标火车南站至桐梓林区间 1～135 环（管片幅宽 1.5 m）和广州地铁 6 号线海珠广场至北京路站盾构区间部分探测试验结果为例进行说明。考虑到注浆管、盾壳刮土、盾构纠偏以及盾构蛇行等因素影响，实际的壁后存在的空隙量应为 0.14～0.20 m 左右。

（1）探测方法

采用瑞典 RAMAC 雷达及 500 MHz 屏蔽天线，剖面法进行探测。探测结果采用时间剖面图像表示，其横坐标记录了天线在地表（或衬砌面）的位置，纵坐标为反射波双程走时，表示雷达脉冲从发射天线出发经过地下界面反射回到接收天线所需要的时间。这种记录能够准确描述测线下方地下各反射界面的形态。由于地下介质对电磁波的吸收，来自地下深处界面的反射波会由于信噪比过小而不易识别，这时可应用不同天线距的发射～接收天线在同一测线上进行重复测试，然后将测试记录中相同位置的记录进行叠加，以增强对地下深部介质的分辨率。

对所选区段主要进行纵向探测。探测布置测线 7 条（由于 e 测线处有施工供电高压线未能进行探测，实探 6 条。）每条测线长度为 200 m，测线布置如图 2 所示：

探测前进行了同配比、自然养护条件下 28 d 后的浆液凝固体的介电常数测定和雷达波速标定。本次探测参数设置如下：采样时窗：48 ns；采样道数：3600；采样点数：1024；叠加次数：4；触发方式：时间采集。

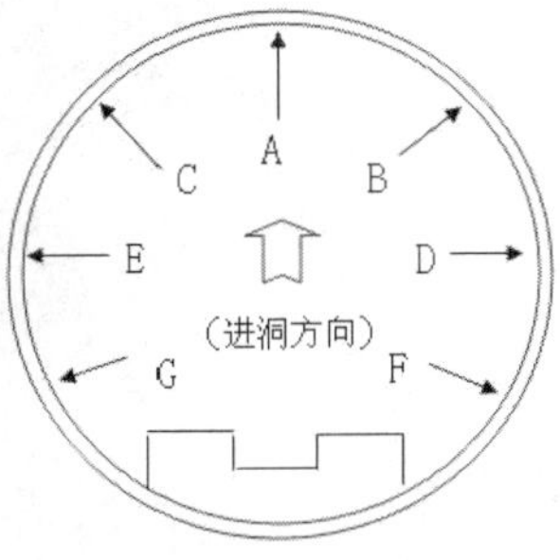

图 2 成都地铁 1 号线管片注浆效果检测试验雷达测线布置图

（2）数据处理

雷达数据处理的目的是压制随机的和规则的干扰波，最大限度地提高雷达剖面的信噪比，提取电磁回波各种有用参数，用来解释不同介质的物理特征。正因为存在螺栓、管片钢筋、动力线等干扰，所以对本检测试验来说，数据处理是技术重点。数据处理中应用了各种反褶积技术，确定性反演滤波、递归滤波、最小平方滤波、小波变换和子波处理等。

（3）数据分析和解释

①注浆厚度

将现场所采集数据（截取 a 测线 3～15 环的一段数据）处理所得剖面图（图 3）作为示例。从图中可以看出，通过数据处理后得到的雷达图像能很清楚地识别出隧道壁后注浆体的分布，第四道反射波即为浆液的界面位置。从图上看，隧道管片与注浆体的界面，注浆体与围岩的界面都非常清楚。以层速度分析时，取电磁波在管片（钢筋混凝土）中的传播速度为 0.12 m/ns，第 3 道反射波即为管片外表面与注浆体之间的界面，深度坐标显示其深度为 0.30，与管片实际厚度一致。从所截取图像上看，隧道壁后注浆还是比较均匀的，最大注浆厚度约为 0.21 m，最小注浆厚度约为 0.12 m 。

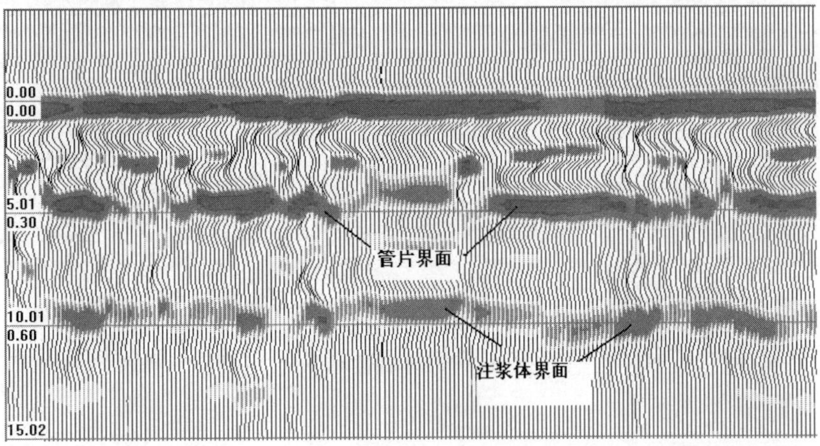

图 3 成都地铁 1 号线管片注浆效果检测试验 a 测线截取段雷达时间剖面图

实际探测中由于天线晃动以及隧道内的干扰信号等因素，导致所得图像波形同相轴会出现扭曲断裂等现象，但仍可以看出两者波形特征基本一致，反射层信号清晰，能清楚看出注浆厚度变化趋势，由此可以说采用地质雷达进行管片注浆厚度检测是可行的。

②注浆层缺陷

根据雷达信号的反射特征，如若注浆层中存在注浆空洞，其反射特征应是从管片层下开始，在空洞位置出现强反射能量，有较明显的双曲线反射，同相轴出现错断，并有明显的三相位反射特点，可以结合振幅谱、能量谱分析。

检测试验中我们注意到管片联结螺栓和管片钢筋对雷达波发射信号干扰很大，需要对照现场仔细识别。图 4 是广州地铁检测试验中截取 a 测线 1-3 环数据的时间剖面图，从图上可以清楚地看出 2 处明显的反射异常区（画圈处），其反射特征有较明显的双曲线反射，从表面一直延伸至注浆层下，虽然其反射特征与介质中圆形空洞的反射极为相似，但我们根据其时窗范围分布与现场实际情况相对应，推测其应为管片表面的金属螺栓干扰所引起，而不是注浆层存在注浆缺陷所导致。

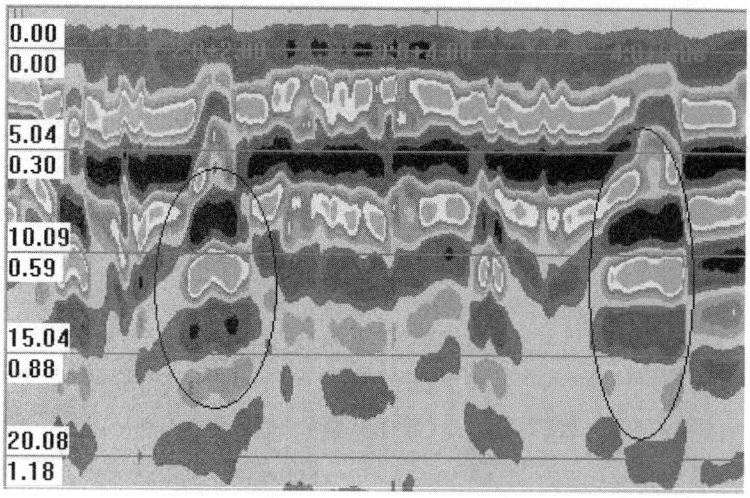

图 4 广州地铁 6 号线管片注浆效果检测试验 a 测线截取段雷达时间剖面图

（4）探测结果

通过北京矿大雷达处理软件得到雷达探测时间-深度剖面图（以测线 c 示例，图 5），并将最终数据按道输出（每道对应一个厚度数据），并将其与里程相对应即得到各条测线注浆厚度值，输出各测线上的注浆厚度表，此处不再列出。将各测线厚度数据表利用 EXCEL 作出厚度分布图（图 6），此处仅列出测线 c 的厚度分布图示例说明。并利用 SURFER 软件做整体注浆等值线图（图 7）。

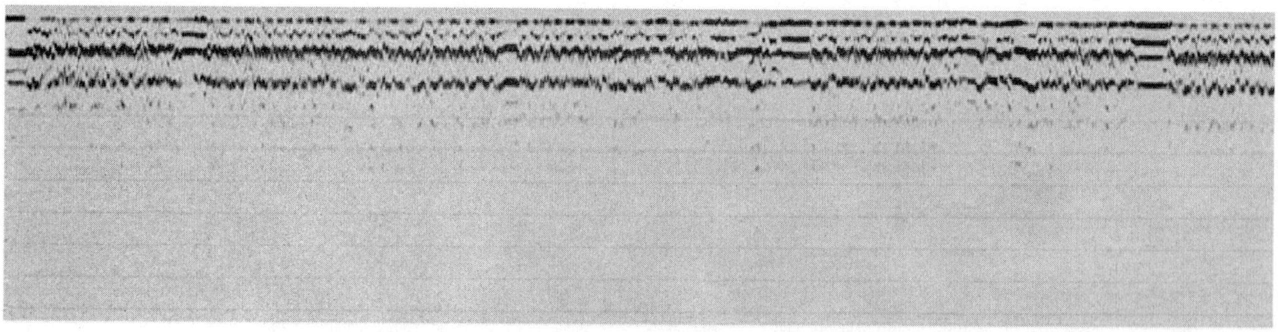

图 5 成都地铁 1 号线管片注浆效果检测试验 c 测线雷达时间剖面图

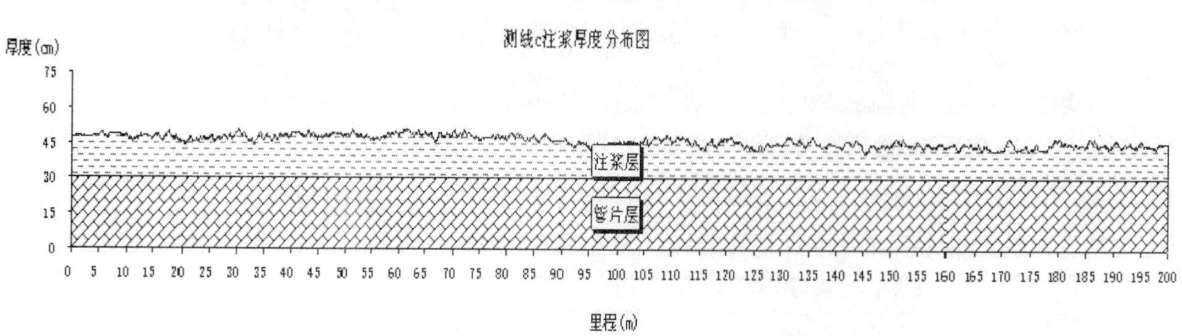

图 6 成都地铁 1 号线管片注浆效果检测试验 c 测线注浆厚度分布图

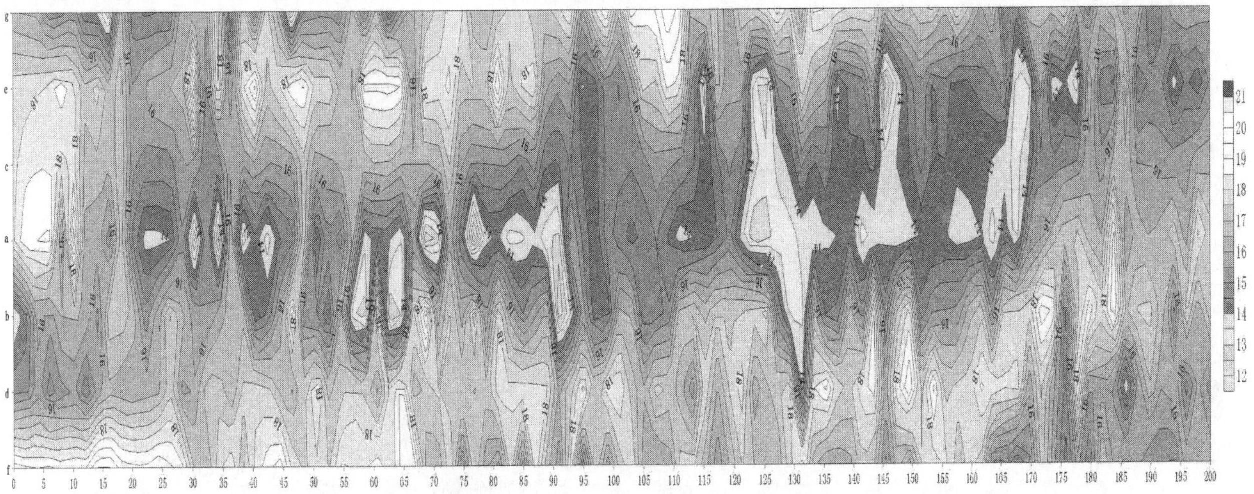

图 7 成都地铁 1 号线管片注浆效果检测试验各测线注浆厚度等值线图

4 结论与建议

通过在成都地铁、广州地铁盾构管片注浆效果检测试验，从实践上说明地质雷达的适用性和有效性，通过对地质雷达实测图像进行分析处理，可较为准确地确定注浆体分布、缺陷及其厚度。注浆凝固体与围岩介电常数差异大小，对雷达图像解释和检测结果有重要影响，在成都地铁砂卵石层围岩检测效果要优于广州地铁泥岩效果，为提高雷达反射信号强度，可考虑改变注浆体介电常数。从控制地层沉降角度考虑，要求检测及时，最好能对同步注浆效果检测，仍需开展无损检测试验相关研究。由于注浆液有不同的配比，且有不同外掺剂，检测前需要测定相应介电常数，并做雷达波速标定。另外由于盾构隧道干扰源较多，在探测过程中尽量减少周围干扰源对雷达信号的影响，在后期数据处理中应提高信号的信噪比，才能取得满意的效果。

参考文献（References）：

[1] 刘建航等. 盾构法隧道. 中国铁道出版社，1991.
[2] 李大心. 探地雷达方法与应用. 地质出版社，1994.12.
[3] 夏才初，李永盛. 地下工程测试理论与监测技术. 同济大学出版社，1999.

作者简介（Bio-data）:

曹大明（1962.5—），男，高级工程师，博士学历，成都畅达通地下工程科技发展有限公司总经理，主要从事隧道及地下工程监测、检测及超前地质预报方面的研究。

DaMing CAO（1962—），male，Senior Engineer，Dr. qualifications，the General Manager of the Chengdu Chang Da Tong underground engineering science & technology development Co .LTD，Mainly engaged in the tunnel and underground engineering monitoring，testing and forecasting geological research.

E-mail: caodam@sina.com

盾构隧道管片土体之间接触应力测试分析

李兴高[1] 袁大军[1] 吴晓军[2]
[1]北京交通大学 隧道及地下工程教育部工程研究中心，北京 100044
[2]北京城建工程研究院工程检测中心，北京 100081

【摘 要】 为掌握盾构隧道管片背后的荷载分布，在北京地铁 5 号线试验段，根据不同的地质情况选择 3 个断面进行了地层与管片接触应力的测试工作。测试工作表明，每个测点的应力变化曲线都存在加速段、减速段和匀速段，管片周边应力一般情况下在推出后 24 h 基本稳定，后续变化较小。注浆和地层类型对管片与土体的接触压力发展有直接影响。对于黏土地层，管片脱离尾板保护前后，环周应力值变化较大，上部 45°、315°和下部 180°位置处应力值较大。对于砂土层、卵石层及其与黏土层组成的复合地层，管片在脱离尾板保护前后，环周应力值变化不大，管片环周应力分布与注浆郊果关系密切。

【关键词】 盾构隧道；管片周边接触应力；测试分析

MEASUREMENT AND ANALYSIS OF CONTACT STRESS BETWEEN SHIELD TUNNEL SEGMENT AND SOIL

Xinggao LI [1], Dajun YUAN [1], Xiaojun WU [2]
[1]*Engineering Research Center of Tunnel and Underground Engineering, Beijing Jiaotong University, Ministry of Education, Beijing 100044, China;*
[2]*Engineering Measurement and Inspection Center Beijing Urban Construction Group Co. Ltd. , Beijing 100081, China*

Abstract: In order to master the load distribution on segments of shield tunnel, three sections are chosen according to different geological conditions to measure the contact stress between soil and segment. Measurements show the stress development curve of each point including acceleration part, deceleration part and uniform speed part. And in most cases segment circumference stress reaches the steady state 24 hours after looping, and changes little thereafter. Grouting and ground type have direct influences on the contact stress development between segment and soil. To the clayey soil, the segment circumference stress changes much out of tailgate, and the stresses at positions of 45°, 315° and 180° have large values. To the composite ground made of sand, pebble and clay soil, the segment circumference stress changes little out of tailgate, and its distribution has much to do with the grouting effect.

Key words: shield tunnel; segment circumference contact stress; measurement and analysis

1 引 言

北京地铁 5 号线在本地区首次采用盾构法施工。为掌握盾构隧道在施工中及施工后管片与土体之间的接触应力，同时也为盾构隧道设计参数进一步优化提供依据，应根据不同的地质情况进行了地层与管片接触应力的测试工作[1]-[4]。地铁 5 号线试验段工程为北新桥站—雍和宫站左线区间隧道，全长 1 688 m，隧道顶埋深 9.68～15.26 m，主要穿越的地层为粉细砂层、中粗砂层、黏土层，地下水位埋深约为 14.5 m。

试验段施工采用德国海瑞克生产的直径 6.2 m 土压平衡盾构。盾构隧道采用圆形装配式管片单层衬砌，内径为 5 400 mm，外径为 6 000 mm，管片厚度 300 mm。管片环宽为 1 200 mm，环向分为 6 块，环向、环间采用螺栓连接，错缝拼装。此次测试工作时间为 2001 年 10 月 13 日至 2002 年 5 月 22 日，第一组和第二组测试工作在 2001 年完成，第三组测试工作在 2002 年完成[5]。通过对施工过程中管片与土体之间接触应力的测试，及时掌握了管片的荷载状态，为完善施工工艺及改进设计提供了宝贵的基础数据，亦可为今后类似工程提供很好的参考和借鉴。

2 测试方案

管片与土体之间接触应力测试采用具有分辨率高、反应灵敏、可靠、稳定等优点的振弦式土压力盒。根据试验段的地质状况，选择典型地层布设了 3 个测试断面，见图 1 所示。与每一测试断面相对应，测试项目设三个测试组，每一测试组由 A、B 两环组成，测试里程及状况见表 1 所示。测点的布设选择典型和有代表性的位置，同时，考虑到测试结果相关性，也为避免偶然误差和个别测点损坏导致数据断续，布设相邻测试环为校正环。在具体测量时间上，选择能体现施工各阶段的变化工况。在每一环 8 等分处布设压力计，见图 2 所示。A 环布设 8 个，分别为 T-0，T-45，T-90，T-135，T-180，T-225，T-270，T-315，分别表示了在 0°、45°、90°、135°、180°、225°、270°、315°位置处布设了压力计；B 环为校核环，压力计布设 4 个分别为 T-0，T-90，T-180，T-270，分别表示了在 0°、90°、180°、270°位置处布设了压力计。同时考虑到 A、B 两环的的相互作用问题，测试采用 A、B 和 B、A 交换布置，以进行相关对比。根据以上原则，本次测试布置土压力计 36 个。

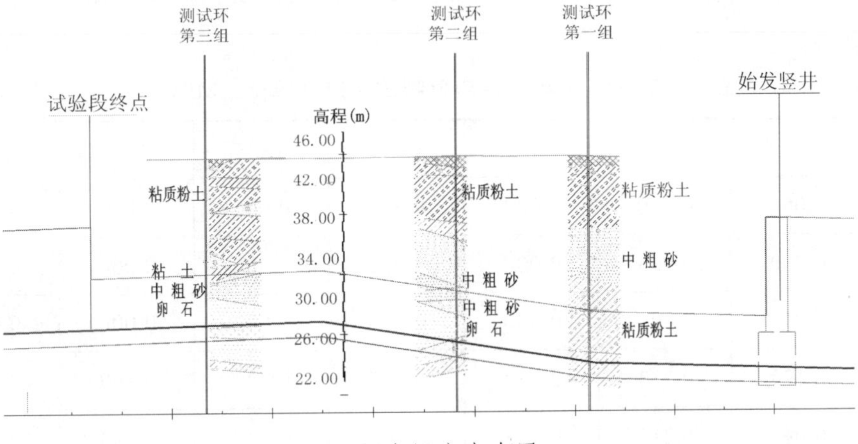

A 环土压应力布置

图 1 地层剖面及测试组位置

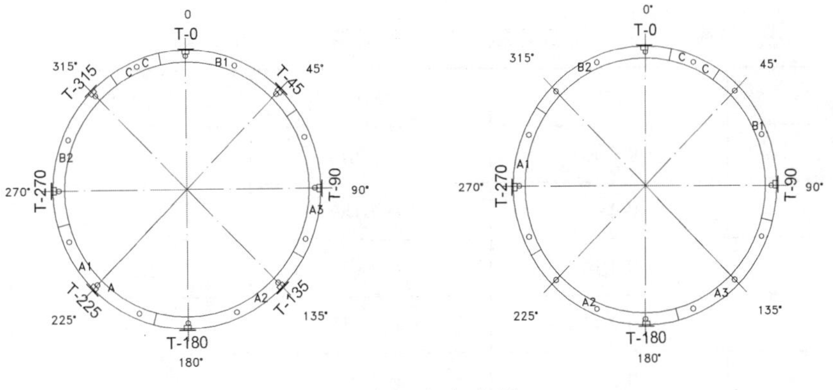

B 环土压应力布置

图 2 接触应力测点环向布置图

表 1 不同测试组情况

测试组	测试环名称	里程（km）	施工环号	埋深（m）	所处地层
第一组	B 环	K12 + 014.82	143	21.79	黏质粉土
	A 环	K12 + 013.60	144		
第二组	A 环	K11 + 882.68	253	19.62	砂土层 卵石层
	B 环	K11 + 881.50	254		
第三组	B 环	K11 + 635.08	459	17.90	黏土层 砂土层 卵石层
	A 环	K11 + 633.84	460		

3 测试结果分析

3.1 测试结果

第一组 A 环测点随盾构向前推进不同位置时的测试结果见表 2 所示，测试结果随时间变化曲线见图 3 所示。第一组 B 环测试结果见表 3 所示。第二组 A 环测点随盾构向前推进不同位置时的测试结果见表 4 所示，测试结果随时间变化曲线见图 4 所示。第二组 B 环测试结果见表 5 所示。第三组 A 环测点随盾构向前推进不同位置时的测试结果见表 6 所示，测试结果随时间变化曲线见图 5 所示。第三组 B 环测试结果见表 7 所示。

表 2 第一组 A 环接触应力测试结果（单位：MPa）

测点位置	0°	45°	90°	135°	180°	225°	270°	315°
首 值	0.000	0.000	0.000	0.000	0.000	0.000	0.000	0.000
过一环	0.000	0.003	0.000	0.002	0.000	0.000	0.000	0.010
过二环	0.000	0.007	0.000	0.005	0.002	0.000	0.000	0.023
过三环	0.123	0.233	0.168	0.115	0.240	0.169	0.167	0.232
过四环	0.093	0.213	0.123	0.107	0.237	0.153	0.134	0.222
距测试环 60 m	0.089	0.215	0.107	0.095	0.234	0.138	0.124	0.219

表 3 第一组 B 环接触应力测试结果（单位：MPa）

测点位置	45°	180°	225°	315°
首值	0.000	0.000	0.000	0.000
过一环	0.190	0.401	0.282	0.201
过二环	0.150	0.388	0.319	0.135
过三环	0.202	0.317	0.206	0.247
过四环	0.177	0.289	0.083	0.358
距测试环 60 m	0.164	0.292	0.077	0.316

表 4 第二组 A 环接触应力测试结果（单位：MPa）

测点位置	0°	45°	90°	135°	180°	225°	270°	315°
首值	0.000	0.000	0.000	0.000	0.000	0.000	0.000	0.000
过一环	0.104	0.041	0.098	0.106	0.205	0.059	0.597	0.374
过二环	0.108	0.043	0.090	0.104	0.207	0.063	0.587	0.375
过三环	0.109	0.044	0.094	0.108	0.211	0.068	0.589	0.373
过四环	0.109	0.046	0.102	0.102	0.210	0.067	0.591	0.372
距测试环 60 m	0.117	0.061	0.099	0.118	0.219	0.084	0.575	0.363

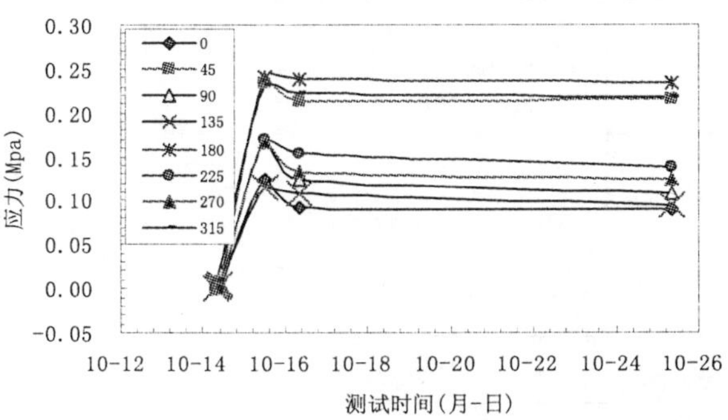

图 3 第一组 A 环接触应力测试结果随时间变化曲线

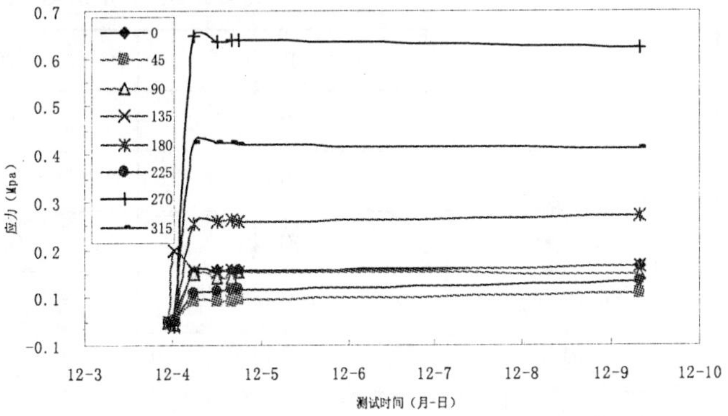

图 4 第二组 A 环接触应力测试结果随时间变化曲线

表 5 第二组 B 环接触应力测试结果（单位：MPa）

测点位置	0°	90°	180°	270°
首值	0.000	测点损坏	0.000	0.000
过一环	0.002		0.017	0.019
过二环	0.009		0.051	0.058
过三环	0.013		0.065	0.065
过四环	0.014		0.064	0.064
距测试环 60 m	0.015		0.064	0.065

表 6 第三组 A 环接触应力测试结果（单位：MPa）

度数	0°	45°	90°	135°	180°	225°	270°	315°
首值	0.000	0.000	0.000	测点损坏	0.000	0.000	0.000	0.000
过一环	0.092	0.046	0.070		0.084	0.087	0.100	0.065
过二环	0.117	0.045	0.083		0.107	0.082	0.127	0.073
过三环	0.101	0.047	0.083		0.101	0.096	0.110	0.067
过四环	0.103	0.047	0.083		0.078	0.082	0.112	0.065
距测试环 60 m	0.090	0.047	0.082			0.077	0.098	0.060

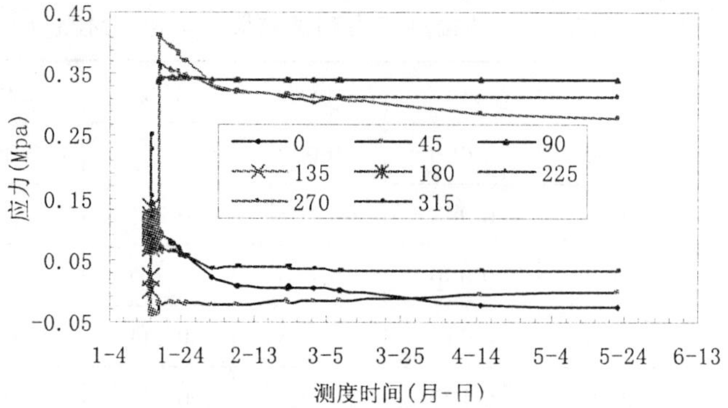

图 5　第三组 A 环接触应力测试结果随时间变化曲线

表 7　第三组 B 环接触应力测试结果（单位：MPa）

测点位置	0	90	180	270
首值	0.000	0.000	0.000	0.000
过一环	0.060	0.054	0.093	0.145
过二环	0.054	0.052	0.084	0.110
过三环	0.054	测点损坏	0.089	0.105
过四环	0.052		0.076	0.086
距测试环 60 m	0.107		0.018	0.067

3.2　测试结果分析

由表 2 可以看出，在安装相邻的一、第二非测试环时，测试环仍在尾板保护范围之内，应力变化不大，应力值最大为 0.02 MPa；在安装下一非测试时（即相邻第三环时），数值明显变化，两环管片总长为 2.4 m，这与所知尾板长度相符，管片已基本脱离尾板的保护，此时土体和填充液已对管片起到作用。可以看出 180°位置处数值较大，应力值为 0.24 MPa 左右；处于顶部的 0°位应力值较小，仅为 0.123 MPa；由于竖向力远远大于水平方向力，处于 90°、270°位置处数值也比较小，最大数值为 0.168 MPa；底部应力值最大为 0.24 MPa；当距测试环 60 m 后，由于外界土层基本稳定及测试环内力重新分配基本完成，此后的应力变化幅度都在 0.01 MPa 左右。在整个变化过程中，不难看出上部 45°、315°和下部 180°压力值最大，管片环周应力基本呈对称分布。

由表 4 可以看出，测试环除了 270°、315°位置处应力值较大外，其他应力变化不大，而且在脱离尾板的保护后，应力值也无太大变化。分析原因，应力分布与地层类型有关，由于此测试环上半部为砂土层，下半部分为卵石层。即使管片在尾板的保护范围内，由于土体孔隙率较大，注浆效果较好，浆液已对管片起到了作用，管片与土体之间孔隙填充密实，管片周围应力始终保持较为稳定的状态，已与测试环的位置关系不大，管片环周应力为非对称分布。

由表 6 可以看出，测试环应力总体变化不大，即使在脱离尾板的保护后，应力值也无大的变化。分析原因，可能与地层类型有关，由于此测试环处于组成断面为黏土层、砂土层、卵石层的土体。即使管片在尾板的保护范围内，由于注浆效果较好，已将管片与土体之间孔隙填充密实，管片周围应力始终保持较为稳定的状态，已与测试环的位置关系不大。在脱离尾板的保护后，两侧应力值较大，整环管片受力为非对称分布。

由表 3、表 5 和表 7 可知，B 环测点测试结果规律性与 A 环一致。

由图 3、图 4 和图 5 应力-时间变化曲线可以看出，各测点的变化具有相同的规律，即每个测点的变化曲线都存在加速段、减速段和匀速段。当管片拼装完毕形成整环后，在尾板保护范围之内时，管片自身进行内力平衡，一般变化不大。当管片脱离尾板的保护，或土体和填充液对管片起到了作用时，管片外部压应力骤然加大，即为加速段，这时的变化速率最大，是整个受力过程的关键所在，也是出现峰值的地方。随着管片外部注浆的压力值恒定后，外部的压力保持平衡，此时压应力慢慢缓和，结构调节自身平衡，进行内力重分布，使应力值出现小幅回落，形成了减速段。待外部填充液慢慢凝固后，外部土体与填充液形成整体，直接作用于管片上，压力值基本保持恒定，形成匀速段。

4 结 论

通过对测试结果的分析，可以得到以下结论：

（1）从已有结果来看，管片土体之间应力稳定后，最大值约为 0.3～0.4 MPa，最小值仅为 0.06 MPa 左右，变化幅度较大。

（2）管片环周应力变化存在加速段、减速段和匀速段。当管片脱离尾板保护或填充液对管片起到作用时，管片外压应力骤然加大，这时为加速段，是整个受力过程的关键所在，应当密切关注。

（2）管片环周与土体接触应力分布与地层类型、注浆施工有着密切的关系，不存在统一的管片环周接触应力分布模式。

（3）在实际工程设计中，管片土体之间的作用通常按照对称荷载处理，在实际工程施工中应通过调节注浆效果保持管片均匀受力，使管片土体之间的作用与管片结构内力计算模式尽可能一致。

参考文献（References）：

[1] Fathalla El-Nahhas，Farouk El-Kadi，Ali Ahmed . Interaction of tunnel linings and soft ground[J]. Tunnelling and Underground Space Technology，1992，7（1），33-43.

[2] S. Bernat，B. Cambou. Soil-structure interaction in shield tunnelling in soft soil[J]. Computers and Geotechnics，1998，22（3-4），221-242.

[3] Toshi Nomoto，Shinichiro Imamura，Toshiyuki Hagiwara，Osamu Kusakabe and Nariaki Fujii. Shield Tunnel Construction in Centrifuge[J]. Journal of Geotechnical and Geoenvironmental Engineering. 1999，125（4），289-300.

[4] H.J. Kim，Z. Eisenstein. Prediction of tunnel lining loads using correction factors[J]. Engineering Geology，2006，859（3-4），302-312.

[5] 北京城市建设工程研究院工程检测中心. 北京地铁 5#线试验段盾构法施工监测方案[R]. 2001.

作者简介（Bio-data）：

李兴高，男，1971 年 9 月生，副教授，博士，现主要从事地铁施工环境影响方面的研究工作。

Xinggao LI（1971—），male，associate professor of Beijing Jiaotong University，doctor，is mainly employed in the research work of metro construction-induced effects on environments.

E-mail: lxg_njtu@163.com

地铁施工过程自动安全监测系统的应用及展望

曹大明　段　强

成都畅达通地下工程科技发展有限公司，四川　成都　610041

【摘　要】 针对地铁工程施工过程，集成了自动安全监测系统，该系统精度高、稳定性好，并在成都地铁北站盾构 1 号线施工中进行了成功应用。该系统可进行后期功能扩展，有望用于地铁工程决策层对施工现场安全状态的动态监管，实现现场安全状态的实时掌控，为地铁工程安全管理提供强有力的支持。

【关键词】 地铁；自动化采集；监测系统

THE APPLICATION AND PROSPECT OF THE AUTOMATIC SAFETY MONITORING SYSTEM IN SUBWAY CONSTRUCTION PROCESS

Daming CAO, Qiang DUAN

ChengDu ChangDaTong Underground Engineering Science & Technology Development Co.,LTD, Chengdu 610041, Sichuan, China

Abstract: The construction process for the subway project has integrated automatic security monitoring system. This system is of high-precision and stability; it's successfully applied in the shield line 1 of Chengdu Metro north station. The system can be extended function to the later stage，expected to achieve dynamic supervision in the security state of construction site for the subway engineering decision-making. And it would ensure the safety of the scene in real-time control，and provided strong support for the subway management.

Key words: subway; automatic collection; monitoring system

1　问题的提出

地铁工程建设大多位于交通繁忙、人口密集的大城市，其周边通常有重要的建（构）筑物或地下管网，地铁施工过程中对周边土体的影响有可能使建筑物产生沉降、倾斜、变形，使地下管网扭曲、变形甚至破坏，有可能造成严重的工程事故。通过施工现场监测数据的采集分析，可以及时掌握地铁施工时支护结构变位情况和周围环境条件的变化，反馈信息以指导施工。因此，现场监测数据的及时分析和保存在地铁施工过程中具有重要的意义。然而，现场监测数据的管理也存在许多问题，主要表现在现场监测数据大多还停留在文件管理模式下。监测数据的计算由人工完成，监测数据用 word、excel 等保存，导致数据不能共享，查询困难，降低了工作效率和管理分析水平，而且由于施工现场的设施简单，环境较差，监测数据的保存缺乏安全性和可靠性。

随着各种传感器、微电子技术和网络通信技术的发展，各种自动化监测系统在大坝、提防、高边坡等重大工程和环境工程中得到了广泛的应用，并且监测的项目如变形、渗流、渗压、温度、应力、应变等技术也日趋成熟，自动化监测具有实时、数据准确、监测频率大而且人工工作量小等特点。在城市轨道交通建设中，施工的安全受到了越来越多的重视，传统的人工监测系统已无法满足安全施工的要求，因此，地铁施工过程自动化监测系统具有广泛的应用前景。

本文结合我公司集成和开发的地铁施工过程自动安全监测系统在成都地铁 1 号线的应用实例重点介绍该系统的构成，同时展望其在业主决策动态监管方面的应用前景。

2 自动安全监测系统集成

2.1 自动数据采集设备集成

自动数据采集设备集成包括硬件和数据采集软件两部分，硬件部分包含自动采集仪、振弦分析模块、数据接收存储设备、连接电缆、元器件等，单套自动数据采集设备集成的主要框图如下。

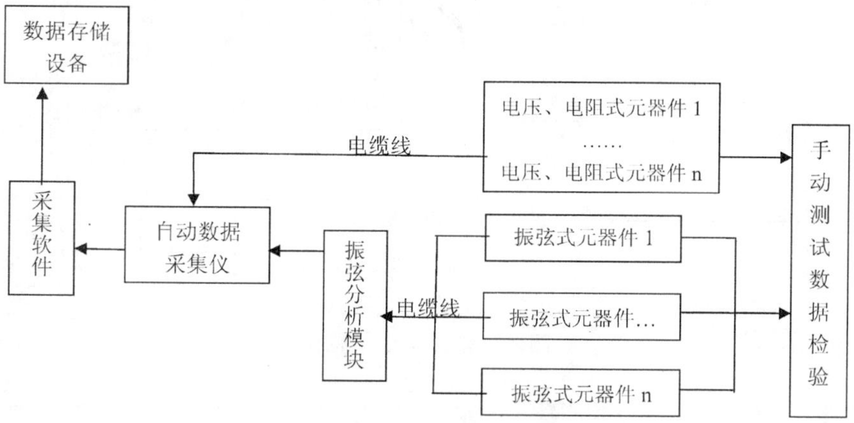

图 1 自动数据采集设备集成结构图

在已应用的几个项目中我们集成了自动数据采集设备，其中选用了美国 CAMPBELL 工公司研制生产的 CR1000（CR800）自动化数据采集仪同先进的两通道振弦分析模块 AVW200 结合，数据的采集和实时监控等功能都是由 LoggerNet 软件来实现，实现自动化数据采集，遇险情前兆时，可 24 h 不间断监测。

该集成设备能在恶劣环境下工作，即可在系统的网络监测站遥控下完成对传感器的激励、监测、数据寄存等工作，也可在未联网情况下，作为现场数据自动化记录仪使用。其主要功能包括：实时监控、数据采集、数据记录到磁盘、数据下载与支持编程文件等。

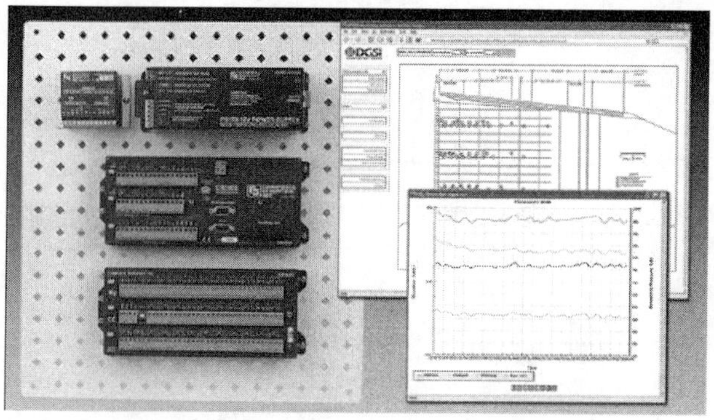

图 2 数据采集器与采集软件

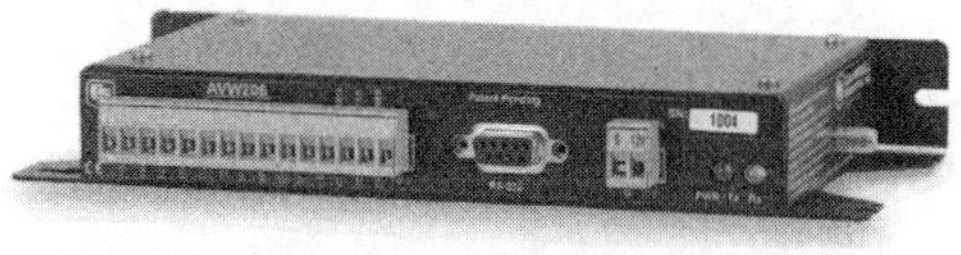

图 3 AVW200 振弦测量模块

2.2 软件集成

采用 LoggerNet 数据采集软件采集数据，利用自主研发的《土木工程监测处理软件系统》专业监测软件，对监测数据进行统一管理及分析，从而提高监测效率，确保监测的及时性。整套软件集成后的主要功能框图如下。

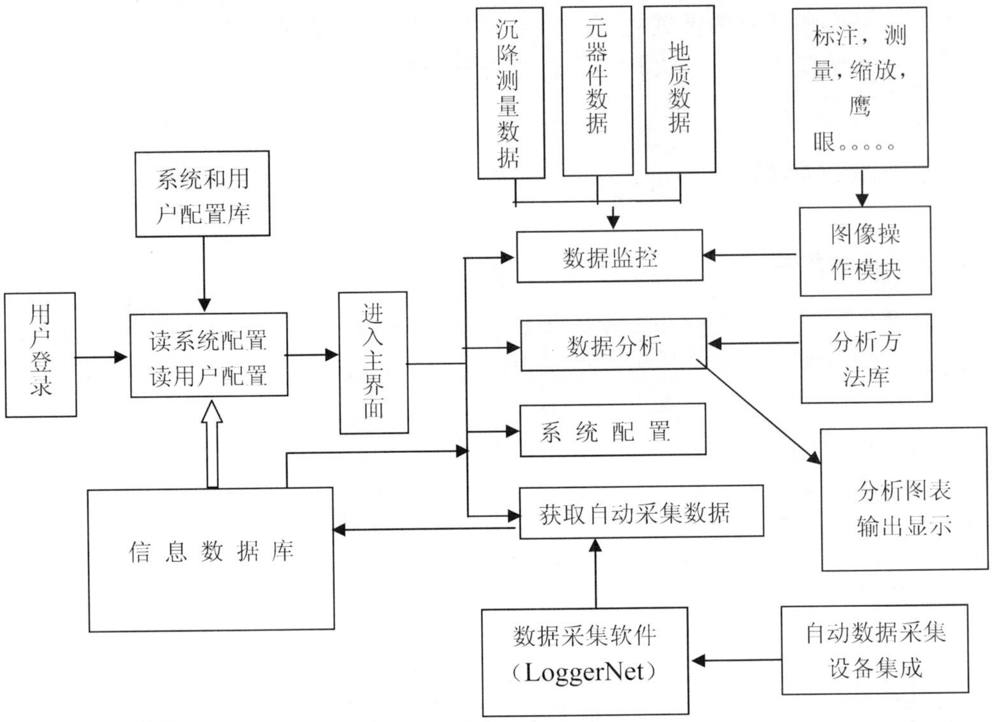

图 4　软件集成结构图

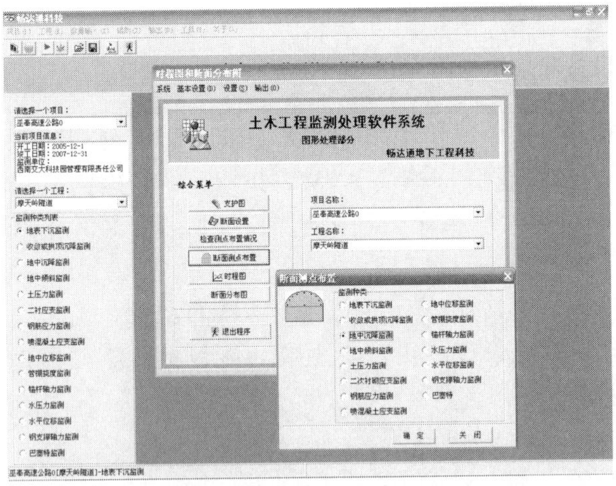

图 5　软件系统界面

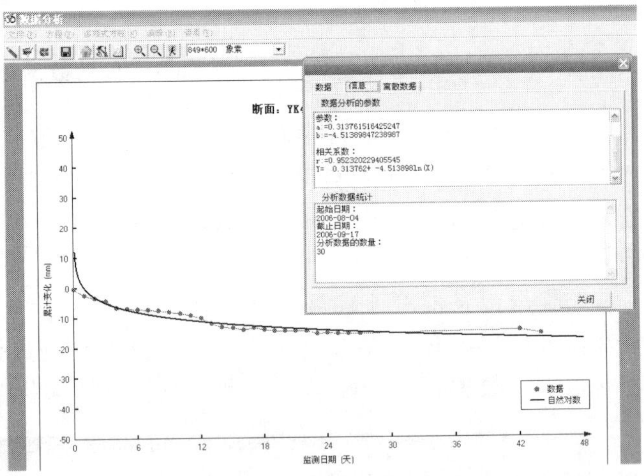

图 6　数据分析示意图

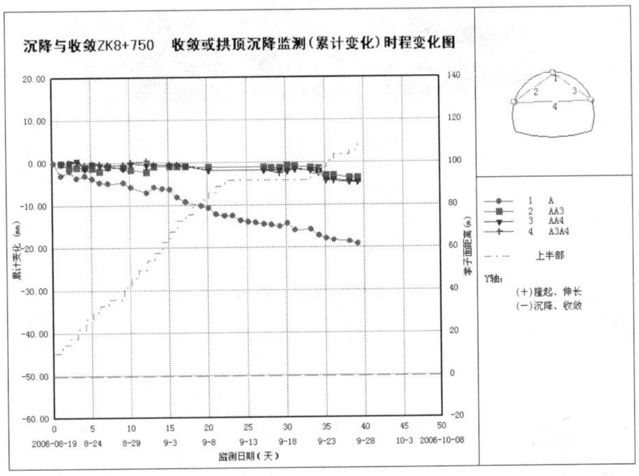

图 7　时程图

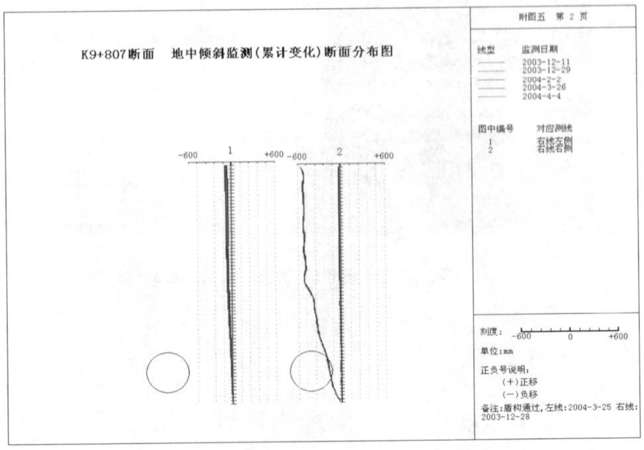

图 8　断面分布图

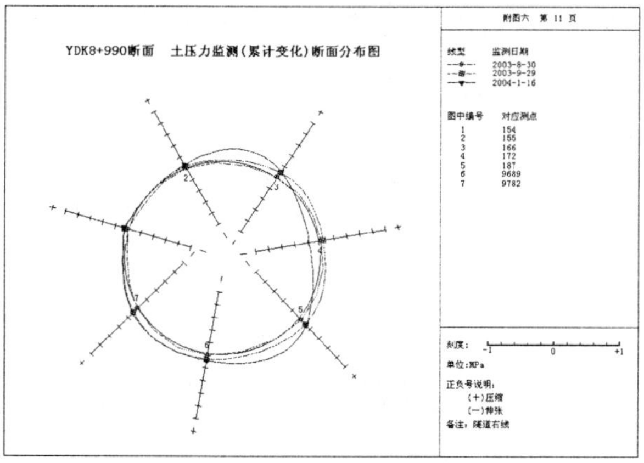

图 9 土压力累计变化断面分布图

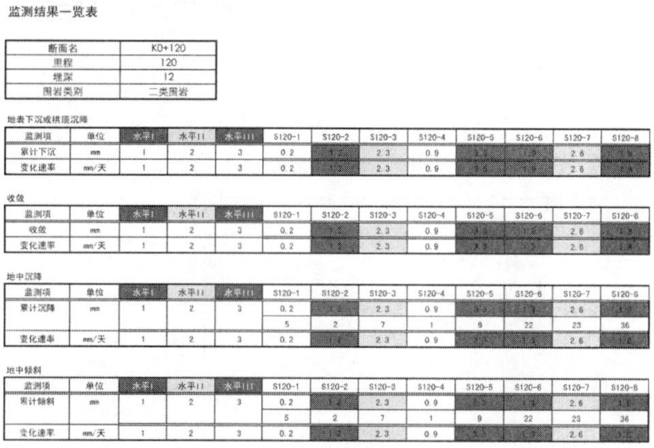

监测结果一览表

断面名	K0+120
里程	120
埋深	12
围岩类别	二类围岩

地表下沉或拱顶沉降

监测项	单位	水平I	水平II	水平III	S120-1	S120-2	S120-3	S120-4	S120-5	S120-6	S120-7	S120-8
累计下沉	mm	1	2	3	0.2	[illegible]	2.3	0.9	[illegible]	[illegible]	2.6	[illegible]
变化速率	mm/天	1	2	3	0.2	[illegible]	2.3	0.9	[illegible]	[illegible]	2.6	[illegible]

收敛

监测项	单位	水平I	水平II	水平III	S120-1	S120-2	S120-3	S120-4	S120-5	S120-6	S120-7	S120-8
收敛	mm	1	2	3	0.2	[illegible]	2.3	0.9	[illegible]	[illegible]	2.6	[illegible]
变化速率	mm/天	1	2	3	0.2	[illegible]	2.3	0.9	[illegible]	[illegible]	2.6	[illegible]

地中沉降

监测项	单位	水平I	水平II	水平III	S120-1	S120-2	S120-3	S120-4	S120-5	S120-6	S120-7	S120-8
累计沉降	mm	1	2	3	0.2	[illegible]	2.3	0.9	[illegible]	[illegible]	2.6	[illegible]
					5	2	7	1	9	22	23	36
变化速率	mm/天	1	2	3	0.2	[illegible]	2.3	0.9	[illegible]	[illegible]	2.6	[illegible]

地中倾斜

监测项	单位	水平I	水平II	水平III	S120-1	S120-2	S120-3	S120-4	S120-5	S120-6	S120-7	S120-8
累计倾斜	mm	1	2	3	0.2	[illegible]	2.3	0.9	[illegible]	[illegible]	2.6	[illegible]
					5	2	7	1	9	22	23	36
变化速率	mm/天	1	2	3	0.2	[illegible]	2.3	0.9	[illegible]	[illegible]	2.6	[illegible]

图 10 “三色”数据简报示意图

数据处理系统可以自动读取安全监测系统数据进，对于实时监测的数据进行过滤、分析和统一管理。

2.3 自动安全监测系统

综上所述，整套自动安全系统由硬件集成和软件集成两部分组成，整套体统包括了元器件信号识别、转换、数据采集、数据监控、数据传输、数据存储、数据分析处理、预警处理等各个方面。硬件系统布设完成后，使用 LoggerNet 数据采集软件从采集设备中获取监测数据，在土木工程监测处理软件系统中将 LoggerNet 获取的数据导入信息数据库中，对监测数据进行统一管理及分析，从而提高监测效率，确保监测的及时性。

3 应用成果

在成都地铁一号线盾构项目中，为研究成都砂卵石地层盾构施工土体扰动影响，在部分区段采用安全自动化监测系统进行了数据采集和分析。

成都的地质条件为中砂和砾石、中密～密实卵石土，最大漂石粒径 $\phi = 210$ mm，特有的成都粘土，其天然含水量 w 和天然孔隙比 e 较小，压缩系数 a 值小而抗剪强度较高，属于卵石复合地层。

监测项目主要包括原位水土压力及孔隙水压力测试，以双膜水土压力盒量测土体原位压力。以孔隙水压力计记录盾构周围孔隙水压力的变化；并在盾构开挖正前方放置土压力计，监测盾构切口到达前土压力的实际分布，为盾构掘进土压力的设定提供依据。

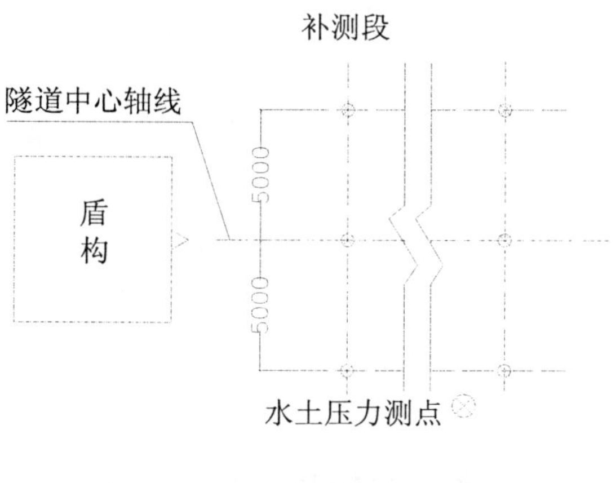

图 11 水土压力测点布置总平面图

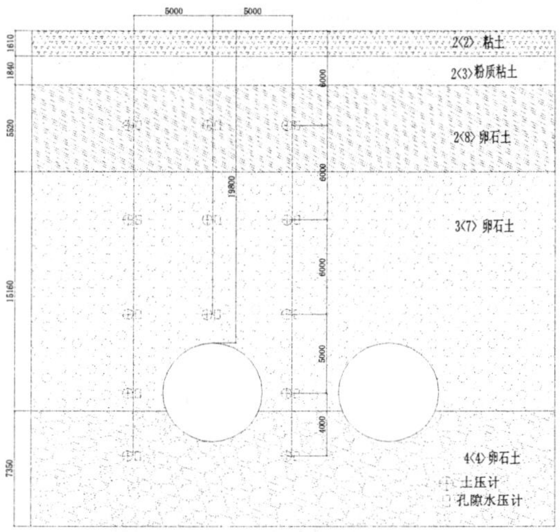

图 12 水土压力测点布置图

实际监测中水压力和土压力时程变化见图及断面分布图见图 13 至图 20，自动数据监测时间间隔为 10 min/次。

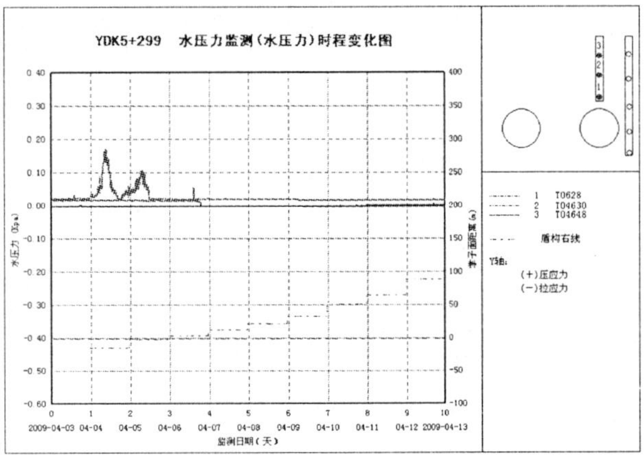

图 13 盾构顶部水压力时程图

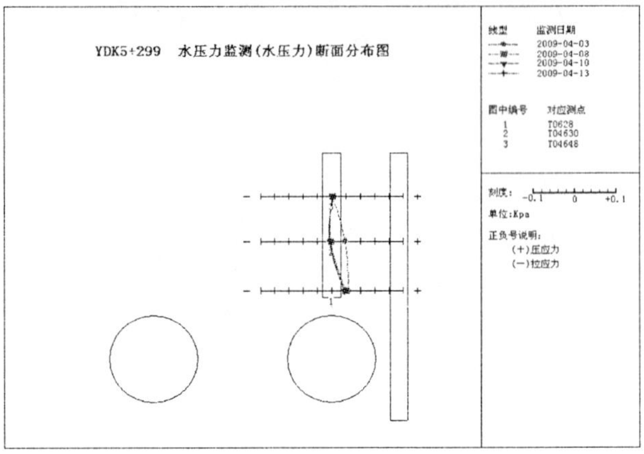

图 14 盾构顶部水压力断面分布图

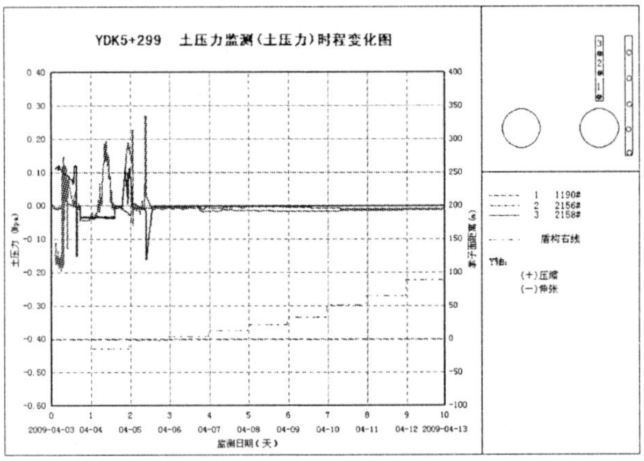

图 15 盾构顶部土压力时程图

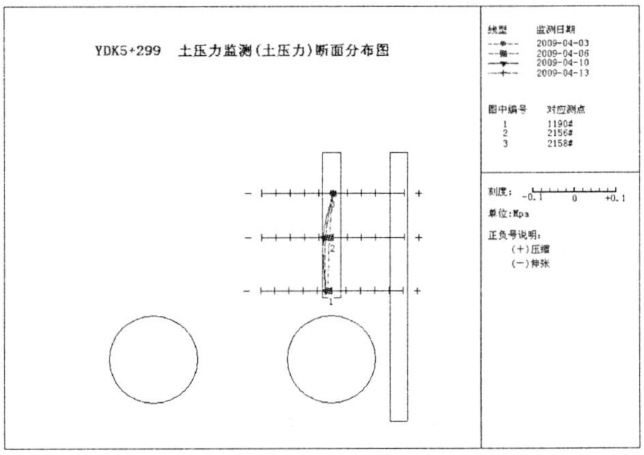

图 16 盾构顶部土压力断面分布图

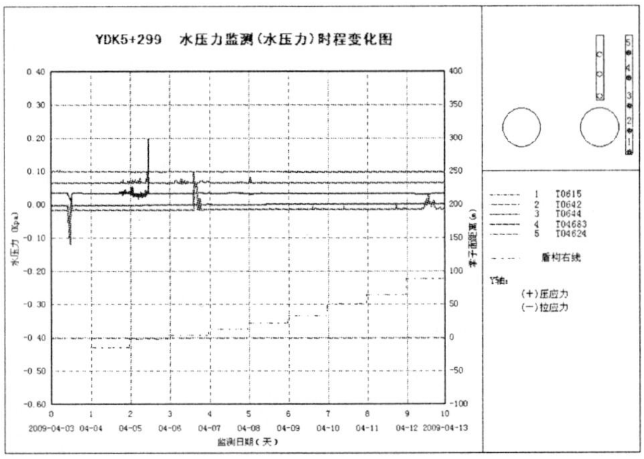

图 17 盾构右侧水压力时程图

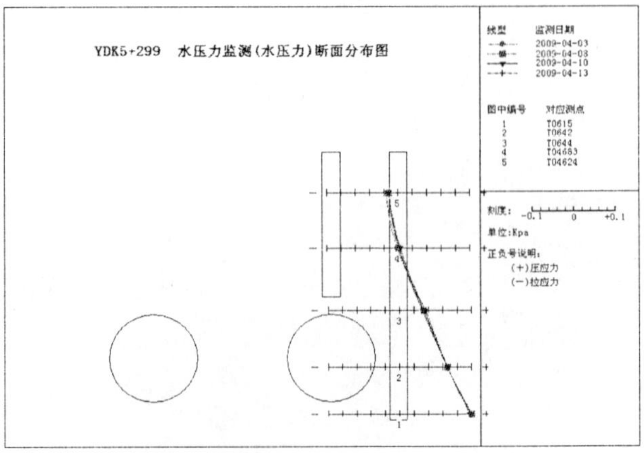

图 18 盾构右侧水压力断面分布图

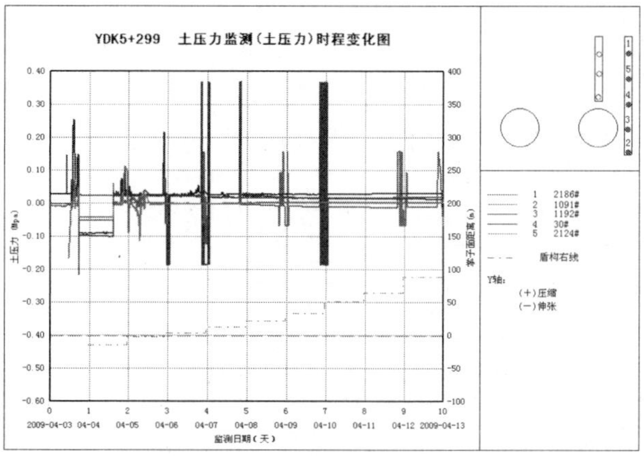

图 19 盾构右侧土压力时程图

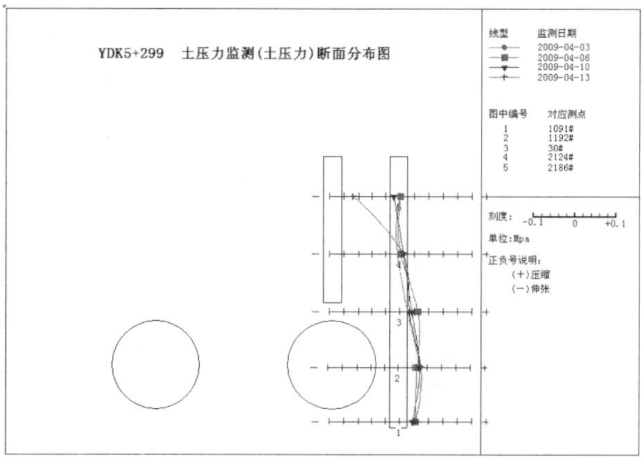

图 20 盾构右侧土压力断面分布图

在上图的水压力和土压力时程图曲线和盾构掘进曲线中，2009 年 4 月 3 日前的数据为人工手动监测获取的压力计算值，其后时间土压力监测设置在 2009 年 4 月 3 日至 5 日期间，为验证不同振弦分析模块测试精度和稳定性，测试整个监测系统最优化配置，中间频繁调整硬件配置和参数配置，验证 AVW200 监测模块的测试稳定性和精度，造成其间数据测试的波动。

从时程曲线图中我们可以看出，自动监测相对于手工监测的优点在于能长时间不间断监测，反映出盾构推进过程中每个阶段土体受力和水压变化情况，相对手工监测而言，自动化监测所采集的数据更准确，更能体现盾构推进中各阶段土体受力状况，为研究盾构推进时土体受力分布，优化盾构推进参数，指导盾构施工提供了详实的数据。

值得关注的是，通常自动化监测设备对于仪器的接地要求都比较高，而且通常施工用电的电缆中不包含地线的情况比较多，在这种情况下自动化监测设备一般均会针单独采取接地措施，实验结果表面，部分自动化采集振弦类元器件的测量模块对系统的接地要求比较严格，在没有良好的接地措施的情况下，测量数据的信号干扰比较大；而此次采用的两通道弦振分析模块 AVW200 采用了新技术光谱插入方法来测量传感器的共振频率率，在此次试验中接地情况不太好或者不接地的情况下，中短期测试的数据结果基本与手工测试频率一致，说明新的测量方法对仪器的适应范围更广，同时在测试中还发现，进口元器件在不接地情况下，测试结果稳定性和信号干扰普遍要高于国内生产的元器件。系统调试完成后，整个系统运行期间测值精度好，稳定性较高，和人工监测数据一致，真实反映出在盾构穿越过程中，土体的实际受力情况。

4 决策动态监管功能设计

地铁自动安全监测系统除了实时采集数据，分析处理数据功能外，还有一个重要的功能就是提供了为决策层动态监管提供了一个信息管理服务平台，一个为地铁决策层和主管、工点单位（第三方监测、施工、工点设计单位）、地铁总体设计单位之间互动的施工监测信息与预警信息处理平台。

整个系统基于广域网来开发，通过网络来管理、传递、和共享信息，适应网络化信息化的趋势。

系统总体架构如下图所示。

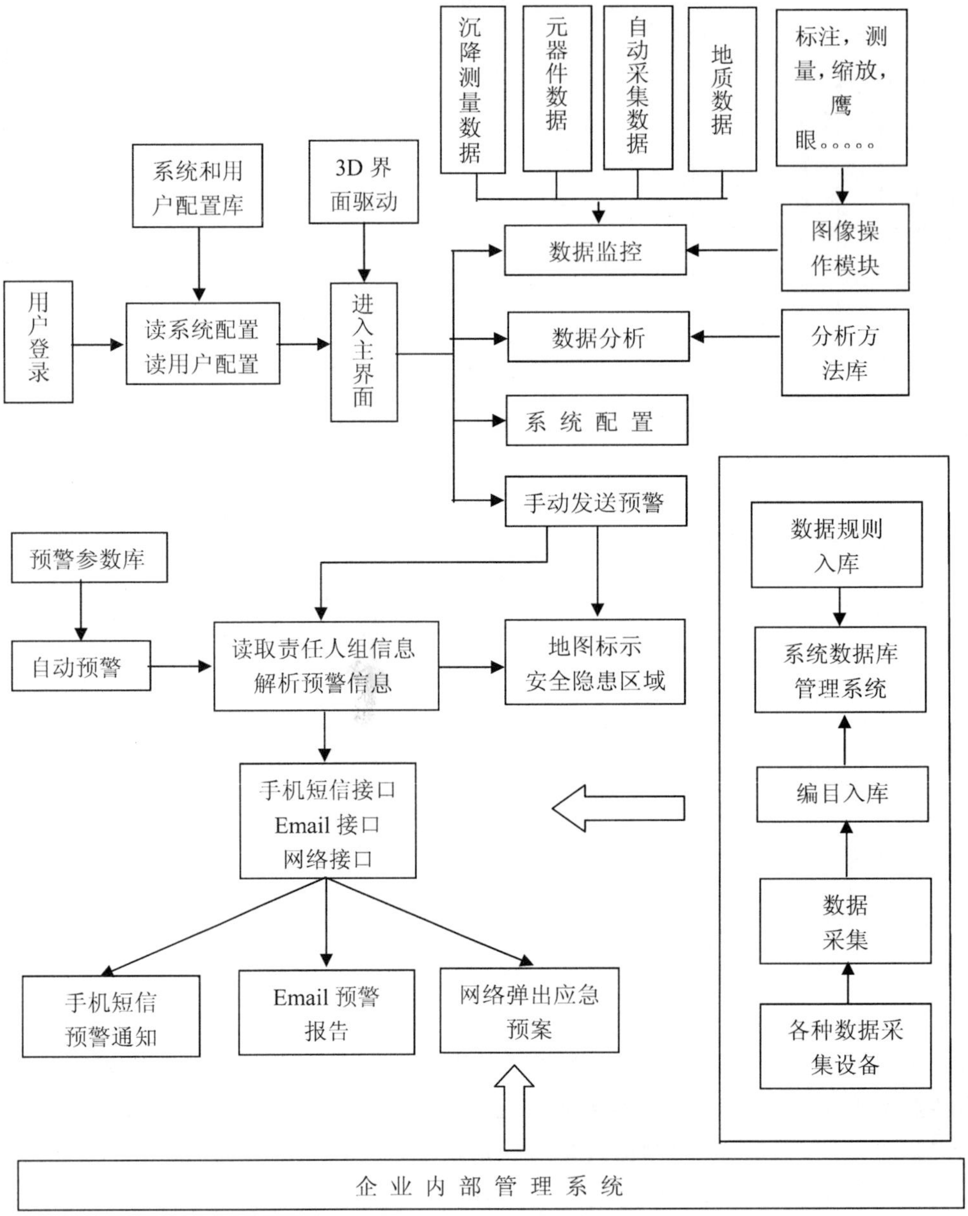

图 21 自动安全监测系统总体结构图

5 结 论

随着科技的发展，计算机网络的大面积普及，各种传感器技术日趋成熟，在各类工程的大量应用检验。自动化监测设备在地铁工程中的应用条件已经成熟，而对于地铁的决策层而言，一个高效、快速获取施工各工点监测信息，分析数据，及时提出预警信息，并能快速有效使地铁施工参与的各单位共享信息，与各单位互动的信息管理平台无疑会对地铁的有效管理，事故的预防等方面产生巨大的作用。

参考文献（References）：

[1] 刘朝明，文志云. 远程监控管理技术及在轨道交通建设中的应用[J]. 上海建设科技，2005（5）：11-12.

[2] 王建宇. 隧道施工监测技术和信息化设计[J]. 中国铁道科学，1987，8（2）：50-57.

[3] 王浩，葛修润，邓建辉，等. 隧道施工期监测信息管理系统的研制[J]. 岩石力学与工程学报，2001，20（增刊 1）：1684-1686.

[4] 孙玉国. 隧道工程信息化管理与施工系统研究[J]. 铁道工程学报，2004，9（3）.
[5] 周文波. 盾构隧道信息化施工智能管理系 bbre 统设计及应用[J]. 岩石力学与工程学报，2004，23（增 2）.

作者简介（Bio-data）：

曹大明（1962.5—），男，高级工程师，博士学历，成都畅达通地下工程科技发展有限公司总经理，主要从事隧道及地下工程监测、检测及超前地质预报方面的研究。

Daming CAO （1962.5—），male，Senior Engineer，Dr. qualifications，the General Manager of the Chengdu Chang Da Tong underground engineering science & technology development Co .LTD，Mainly engaged in the tunnel and underground engineering monitoring，testing and forecasting geological research.

E-mail: caodam@sina.com

砂卵石地层盾构法施工地面滞后塌陷成因初探

张治国 曹大明 黄 亮
成都畅达通地下工程科技发展有限公司，四川 成都 610041

【摘 要】 针对成都地铁盾构法施工区间数次出现地面滞后塌陷现象，在分析其成因的基础上，采用地质雷达探测手段对已推进区段进行了探测实验。通过对地质雷达探测资料的对比分析，确定采用洞内外跟踪注浆的措施，实现控制地面滞后塌陷的目的，确保因盾构推进引起的地面塌陷在可控范围内。

【关键词】 盾构法；滞后塌陷；地质雷达；跟踪注浆

EXPLORATION OF THE CAUSES OF LAGGING SUBSIDENCE IN SANDY COBBLE STRATUM BY SHIELD METHOD

Zhiguo ZHANG，DaMing CAO，Liang HUANG
Chengdu Chang Da Tong underground engineering science & technology development Co .LTD, Chengdu 610041, Sichuan, China

Abstract: For the land lagging subsidence happened several times when construction is taken in the Chengdu Metro by shield method, based on the cause analysis, it was taken the use of ground penetrating radar to detect sections that have been advanced. By comparison analysis of the data taken by the Ground Penetrating Radar, it was determined to use the measure by tracking grouting both inside the cave and outside that could achieve the purpose of control the settlement lagging. Then the land subsidence which caused by the shield advance was under control.

Keyword: shield tunneling method; lagging subsidence; ground penetrating radar; tracking grouting

1 引 言

盾构法（shield tunneling method）施工技术经历了近两百年的发展，已经是一项相当成熟的施工技术，目前已经成为在软土（饱和软黏土、淤泥质软土、粉质黏土，甚至饱和沙质粉土、粉质沙土等）中施工隧道的一种主要手段。但是在软土和砂卵石地层中施工引起的后期沉降控制常常导致周围地层发生过大变形，甚至地层塌陷，亦影响到了线路周边建构筑物安全。尤其是在大城市进行这样大规模的地铁以及地下隧道的建设，势必要求其在施工以及运营过程中保证其结构的安全性，同时最大限度地减小因施工而产生的对周围环境的影响[1]。

成都地铁盾构隧道埋深较浅（9.0～17.0 m 左右），洞身主要位于砂卵石地层中，盾构过后路面时常发生滞后塌陷，为保证路面交通安全，需要查明盾顶地层中有无形成空洞或存在不密实区（主要指较大孔隙），进而有针对性地进行加固处理。地质雷达以其分辨率高、速度快、无损作业等优点，因而在空洞或松散层探测中被优先选取。

2 滞后塌陷成因分析

要对目标体进行探测，首先要了解目标体的形成机理。以下为盾构通过后，地层空洞或孔隙变大形成机理的初步分析：

通常认为盾构推进中，盾顶部分、换刀位置、车站端头位置，地层受扰程度大，刀盘切削可能带走盾顶较多的土体，尤其是分布于卵石层中粒径较小的粉细砂颗粒，土体变松，力学性质降低（尤其是抗剪强度），反映到施工中就是出渣量加大。砂卵石土中的内聚力是很小的，但由于土体颗粒间存在的内摩擦，卵石颗粒起到骨架作用，在盾顶及两腰位置形成承载拱，这种整体性和抗剪强度都差的承载拱只能是临时性的，在路面上振动荷载和地下水渗流作用下，可能发生突发性解体，导致路面上形成与盾构施工同步发生的塌陷。另一方面，路面下粉细砂层在地下水及震动荷载作用下不断充填盾顶扰动空隙，致使路面粉砂层（或填土层）中空隙不断扩大，在盾后较长一段时间后，即在路面下形成空洞，从而在路面荷载频繁作用下，导致路面发生突发性滞后塌陷。

3 地质雷达探测原理

地质雷达（Ground Penetrating Radar，简称 GPR）方法是一种用于确定地下介质分布的广谱电磁波技术。其利用天线向地下发射电磁脉冲，并接收由地下不同介质界面的反射波。电磁波在介质中传播时，其路径、电磁场强度与波形将随所通过介质的电性质（如介电常数 ε_r）及几何形态的变化而变化。根据接收到的回波时间、幅度和波形等信息，可判定地下介质的结构与埋藏体的位置与形态[2]。

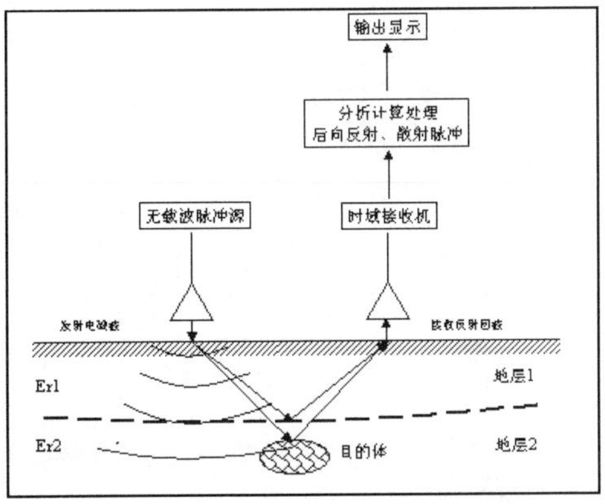

图 1 地质雷达探测原理

$$t = \sqrt{4h^2 + x^2} / v \tag{1}$$

式中 t——脉冲波走时（ns）；

h——目标深度（m）；

x——发射天线与接收天线的距离（m）；

v——电磁波波速（m/ns）。

常见的介质为非磁介质，在探地雷达的频率范围内，因此介质的电磁波速度为：

$$v = \frac{c}{\sqrt{\varepsilon_r}} \tag{2}$$

式中 $c = 0.3$ m/ns（光速）；

ε_r——介质相对介电常数。

4 探测实例

4.1 地铁 1 号线某小区探测

（1）工作概况

地铁一号线所穿越的某小区地形平坦，临近多小区及公共设施。根据现场钻探揭露，场区砂卵石地层透水性好。进入雨季后，盾构已穿越的小区出现两次较大塌陷，并且小区居民反映房屋附近很多地方变形严重。为了配合施工单位的抢险工作，我们对小区及附近进行了雷达探测，主要目的包括：

① 了解小区内（包括有条件的房屋）混凝土路面下部是否因为盾构施工存在空洞、不密实区域，是否存在安全隐患，并推测其大小及位置；

② 探测小区外附近的房屋、广场、公路下方是否存在因为地铁施工而造成的空洞、不密实区域，并推测其大小及位置。

（2）现场工作方法

① 设备及参数选取

探测采用瑞典生产的 RAMAC/GPR 型地质雷达系统，采集参数根据对现场同一条剖面进行多次试验来确定，如下：

天线频率：100 MHz 屏蔽天线；采样点数：512；时间窗：400 ns；迭加次数：16

触发方式：时间触发。

② 测线布置

由于小区内地形较为复杂，测线根据实际现场情况进行确定，探测时沿测线以一定速度拖动天线得到雷达剖面图。

（3）数据处理及解释

通过采集得到原始数据后，通过中国矿业大学（北京）研发的 GR 雷达处理分析系统进行数据的进一步处理从而得到最终的雷达剖面图。图 2 为该小区 2 栋 2 单元的楼梯出口处的雷达探测剖面图，为本次探测的重点地段之一，从图中可以看出，雷达浅部信号反射均一，同相轴连续，应为混凝土路面层，而深部信号反射杂乱，同相轴连续性较差，推测为地下土层受地铁施工扰动而变得松散。

图 3、图 4 为两次对同一坍塌地段的雷达探测剖面图。图 3 为灌浆加固前的探测图像，从图中可以看出，雷达探测比实际坍塌范围大，其周围一定范围都存在安全隐患，而且有向房屋延伸的可能。通过灌浆加固后（图 4），从图上可以看出雷达信号反射均一，坍塌位置出现明显界面反射，其应为灌浆而形成的混凝土层，表明塌陷位置的加固效果较好。

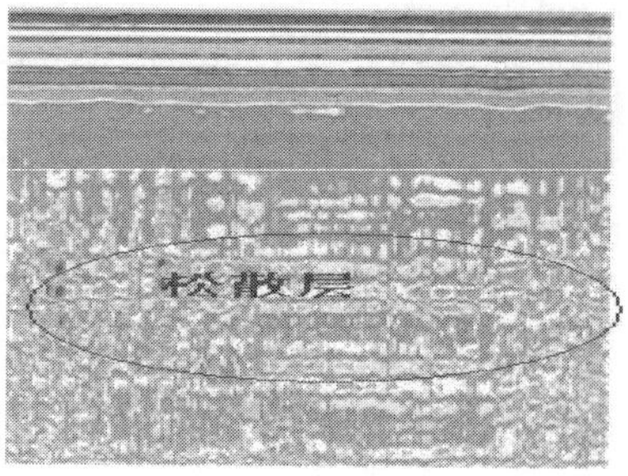

图 2　雷达探测剖面图

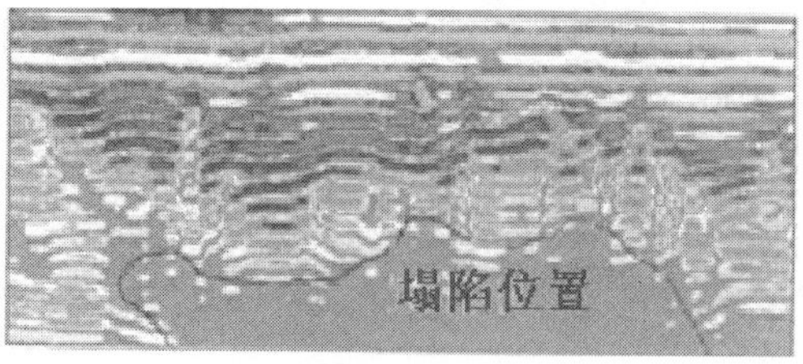

图 3　灌浆前雷达剖面图

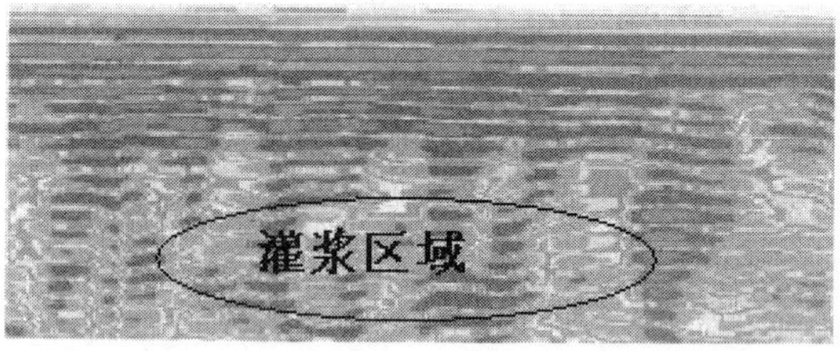

图 4 灌浆后雷达剖面图

4.2　地铁 1 号线某区间探测实例

（1）工作概况

成都地铁 1 号线盾构通过后，路面多次发生塌陷，给城市交通带来极大安全隐患，为保证路面交通安全，查明盾顶地层中空洞或不密实区（主要指较大孔隙），进而有针对性地进行加固处理，我们利用地质雷达对已推进区段进行了探测，现以其中某段区间为例进行说明。

（2）现场工作方法

① 设备及参数选取

探测采用拉脱维亚 Zond-12e 型地质雷达，采集参数根据现场试验确定如下：

天线频率：150 MHz 非屏蔽天线；采样点数：512；时间窗：200 ns；迭加次数：16

触发方式：时间触发。

② 测线布置

鉴于探测空洞位置大小、形状未知，现场布置测线呈方格探测网。通常盾顶部分、换刀位置等处地层受扰程度较大，因此在布网时应更注重这些薄弱地段位置的测线布置：(a) 沿盾构纵向，左右线分别布设一条测线；(b) 换刀位置从中心至两边布设 3 条横向测线，间距 5.0 m。区间纵横向测线布置如图 5 所示，探测时沿测线以一定速度拖动天线得到雷达剖面图。

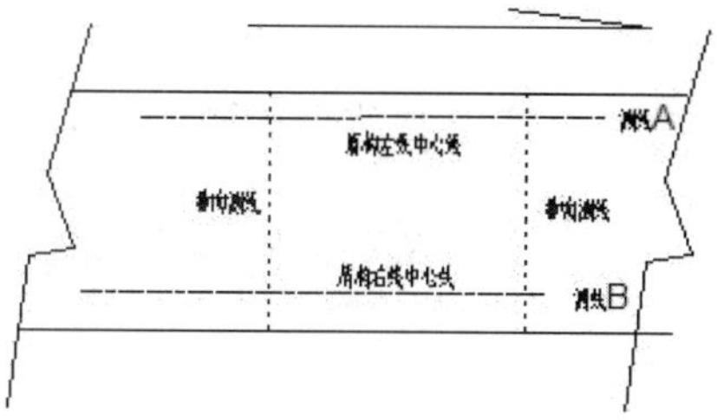

图 5 测线布置图

(3) 数据处理及解释

室内工作主要采用矿大软件对采集的数据进行处理、分析，最终得到各测线的成果图。图 6 为纵测线上某区段的雷达剖面图，从图中可以看出，画框处雷达反射信号杂乱，能量强弱变化大，同相轴连续性较差，从深度上看，其多处于人工填土层范围内，判断其是由盾构施工扰动所引起。经现场施工方后期注浆验证，雷达探测所指位置确为地层松散区域。

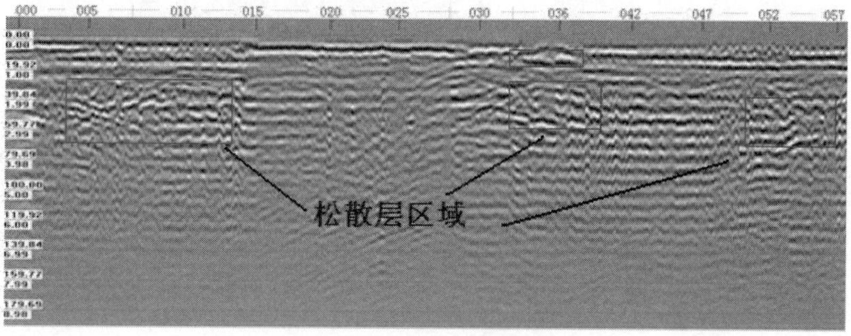

图 6 实测雷达剖面图

5 结论与建议

通过在成都地铁工程的应用结果一方面说明了利用探地雷达进行盾构隧道上方地层扰动、空洞探测是较为准确可行的，其能及时发现盾构施工中地层的扰动变化情况并为其后的注浆控制提供依据。另一方面，由于测区地处城市，电线、电缆、地下管网等都会对雷达产生较多干扰，再加上黏土层及地下水影响，地质雷达信号对深部地层情况的反映较为薄弱，这也是其局限与不足之处。

参考文献 (References)：

[1] 刘建航等. 盾构法隧道. 中国铁道出版社，1991.

[2] 李大心. 探地雷达方法与应用. 地质出版社，1994.12.

作者简介 (Bio-data)：

张治国（1978.9—），男，工程师，学士，成都畅达通地下工程科技发展有限公司技术部长，主要从事隧道及地下工程监测、检测及超前地质预报方面的研究。

Zhiguo ZHANG（1978.9—）, male, Senior Engineer, bachelor, the minister of technology of the Chengdu Chang Da Tong Underground Engineering Science & Technology Development Co .LTD, Mainly engaged in the tunnel and underground engineering monitoring, testing and forecasting geological research.

E-mail: zhangcdut@yahoo.com.cn

某地铁岩溶注浆浆液配比试验研究

杨秀竹[1] 赵国旭[2] 孙成伟[2] 雷金山[1]

[1]中南大学土木建筑学院，湖南 长沙 410075

[2]广州市地下铁道总公司，广东 广州 510380

【摘 要】 采用正交试验方法，对某地铁岩溶注浆浆液进行了配比试验研究。浆液由红黏土、水泥和水玻璃制成。在对浆液结石体无侧限抗压强度进行极差分析的基础上，得出红黏土固化浆液的最佳配比。

【关键词】 岩溶注浆；红黏土固化浆液；无侧限抗压强度；最佳配比

EXPERIMENTAL STUDY ON MIXTURE RATIO OF GROUT FOR FILLING SOLUTION CAVITY AND SOIL CAVE UNDER ONE SUBWAY

Xiuzhu YANG[1], Guoxu ZHAO[2], Chengwei SUN [2], Jinshan LEI[1]

[1]Civil Architectural Engineering College, Central South University, Changsha 410075, Hunan, China;

[2]Guangzhou Metro Corporation, Guangzhou 510380, Guangdong, China

Abstract: Orthogonal method was adopted to study the grout ratio which would be used to fill solution cavity and soil cave under one subway. The grout was made from red clay, cement and water glass. Extreme difference of the grout concretion unconfined compressive strength was analyzed. On these bases, best ratio of red clay-hardening grout was obtained.

Key words: grouting of solution cavity and soil cave; red clay-hardening grout; unconfined compressive strength; best ratio

1 引 言

随着城市地面交通的日趋紧张，地铁对缓解城市地面交通压力的作用也日显重要，但随着工程地质复杂程度的提高，地铁建设的难度也随之增加。以我国南方及西南地区部分城市为例，有些地铁线路正好经过岩溶区，一旦处理不好，就会引发盾构机塌陷、掘进面涌水涌砂、地面塌陷等问题。因此需要对岩溶土洞进行加固。考虑到水泥浆充填溶洞的成本太高，所以我们拟采用黏土固化浆液。目前为止已有不少学者对黏土固化浆液进行了研究[1-6]，但制浆所采用的黏土主要为高岭土、蒙脱石等，对在我国南方地区广泛分布的红土是否可以制浆以及浆液结石体的力学性能等方面的研究没有看到相关报导。本文主要对这种红黏土固化浆液结石体强度进行研究，并以此为指标得出浆液的最佳配比。

2 工程背景

某地铁隧道通过地层自上而下是人工填土层、粉细砂层、中粗砂层、冲积—洪积土层，河湖相淤泥

基金项目：湖南省自然科学基金资助项目（07JJ3104）；广州市地下铁道总公司科技经费资助项目（09A003）

质土层、可塑状残积土层、硬状残积土层、灰岩中风化层、灰岩弱风化层。其中灰岩地层岩溶发育强烈，以岩层上部的浅层溶洞发育为主要特点，其分部规律性差，形态规模各异，岩溶洞体充填不好，部分呈未充填、半充填状。洞内充填物工程性质软弱，易被水流冲蚀，局部洞体充填物夹灰岩，为近期坍落物，多属于不稳定洞体，对结构稳定性不利，可能造成地面沉陷、突水等工程事故。

3 注浆材料的选取及浆液的制备

3.1 注浆材料的选取

（1）黏土的选取

在现场选取两种代表性的土样，作为实验的样本，标号分别为 A 和 B，装入保湿袋中，带回实验室。然后将土样从保湿袋中取出，初步观察分析：A 袋土为红色土，黏性较大，无异常气味，土中没有夹杂物，颗粒分布不太均匀，颗粒较小；B 袋土为黄色土，黏性大，亦无异常气味，土中无异常夹杂物。表 1 为红土和黄土的基本物理力学指标，表 2 和表 3 分别为红土和黄土的粒度分布。从粒度分布来看，红土的细颗粒土含量较多，另外，从现场取土情况来看，该层土样成色均匀，原料充足，符合就地取材的条件。因此，选用红土作为制备粘土浆的原料。

表 1　红土和黄土基本物理力学指标对比

	含水量（%）	比重	液限（%）	塑限（%）
红　土	3.11	2.71	37.48	15.57
黄　土	4.94	2.71	31.96	15.05

表 2　红土粒度分布

粒　径	0.050	0.024	0.010	0.005	0.002
小于某粒径土的质量百分比（%）	93.1	70.0	43.8	28.9	19.1

表 3　黄土粒度分布

粒　径	0.052	0.025	0.011	0.006	0.002
小于某粒径土的质量百分比（%）	81.6	50.3	27.3	16.5	9.2

（2）水玻璃

试验采用娄底五环化工有限公司下属的长沙水玻璃厂生产的水玻璃，二氧化硅含量为 27.32%，氧化钠含量为 8.82%。模数为 3.26，波美度为 32，使用时稀释为 25 波美度。

（3）水泥

水泥采用 $325^{\#}$ 普通硅酸盐水泥。

3.2 浆液的制备

制浆时先将黏土在水中浸泡并搅拌均匀，测黏土浆的漏斗黏度值达到设计要求，然后向黏土浆中加入水泥，搅拌均匀，最后加入水玻璃，搅拌均匀。最后将配置好的浆液倒入试模中，脱模后放入水中养护。浆液结石体的尺寸是 40 mm×40 mm×40 mm。浆液黏度测试如图 1 所示，图 2 为结石体水中养护的情况。

图 1 泥浆黏度测定

图 2 浆液结石体水中养护

3 浆液配比试验

进行浆液配比实验时，我们采用正交实验法。正交实验法根据实验目的和数据的分析来选择试验点，不仅使每一个试验点获得的数据含有最大的信息量，而且大大减少试验次数，从而使得统计分析具有较好的性质。考虑到影响黏土固化浆液强度的主要因素有泥浆黏度、水泥含量、水玻璃含量，因此实验设计为三因素三水平正交试验，各水平具体取值见表 4。表 5 列出了 7 d、14 d、28 d 无侧限抗压强度。

表 4 泥浆黏度，水泥掺量、水玻璃影响因素及影响水平

	1 水平	2 水平	3 水平
黏土浆黏度/s	20	25	30
水泥含量/（g/100 ml）	20	10	15
水玻璃含量/（ml/100 ml）	1	3	5

注：100 ml 为黏土原浆的体积.

表 5 无侧限抗压强度

试验编号	泥浆黏度（S）	水泥（g/100 ml）	水玻璃（ml/100 ml）	7 d/kPa	14 d/kPa	28 d/kPa
1	20	20	1	73.08	113.49	145.74
2	20	10	3	34.25	56.00	86.57
3	20	15	5	52.50	87.02	122.35
4	25	20	3	65.08	103.79	150.71
5	25	10	5	99.29	109.11	153.73
6	25	15	1	26.84	60.09	111.56
7	30	20	5	157.71	246.05	354.67
8	30	10	1	27.00	43.73	79.21
9	30	15	3	51.32	92.37	158.42

4 试验结果分析

表 6 对 7 d、14 d、28 d 无侧限抗压强度进行极差分析，发现对 7 d 无侧限抗压影响最大的是水玻璃含量，其次是水泥含量，影响最小的是泥浆黏度；对 14 d 和 28 d 无侧限抗压的影响，水泥含量居于首

位，其次是水玻璃含量，影响最小的是泥浆黏度。

根据实验数据处理的结果，我们得到室内试验最佳配比为：黏土浆粘度 30 s，水泥含量 20 g/100 ml，水玻璃含量 5 ml/100 ml，对于这个比例我们也做了测试试验，测试其 28 d 无侧限抗压强度大于 300 kPa，满足工程要求。

表 6 无侧限抗压强度极差分析表

项目	编号	同水平累计			平均值及极差			结论
		A	B	C	A	B	C	
7 天	K1	159.83	295.87	126.92	53.28	98.62	42.31	影响因素次序 C>B>A 最优组合 C3B1A3
	K2	191.21	160.54	150.65	63.74	53.51	50.22	
	K3	236.03	130.66	309.50	78.68	43.55	103.17	
	$\bar{R}$				25.4	55.07	60.86	
14 天	K1	256.51	463.33	217.31	85.50	154.44	72.44	影响因素次序 B>C>A 最优组合 B1C3A3
	K2	272.99	208.84	252.16	91.00	69.61	84.05	
	K3	382.15	239.48	442.18	127.38	79.83	147.39	
	$\bar{R}$				41.88	84.83	74.95	
28 天	K1	354.66	651.12	336.51	118.22	217.04	112.17	影响因素 B>C>A 最优组合 B1C3A3
	K2	416.00	319.51	395.7	138.67	106.50	131.90	
	K3	592.30	392.33	630.75	197.43	130.78	210.25	
	$\bar{R}$				79.21	110.54	98.08	

注：表中 A 代表粘土浆粘度，B 代表水泥含量，C 代表水玻璃含量。

5 结 论

（1）采用正交试验方法，对 7 d、14 d、28 d 无侧限抗压强度进行测试，发现对 7 d 无侧限抗压影响最大的是水玻璃含量，其次是水泥含量，影响最小的是泥浆黏度；对 14 d 和 28 d 无侧限抗压的影响，水泥含量居于首位，其次是水玻璃含量，影响最小的是泥浆黏度。

（2）通过对无侧限抗压强度进行极差分析，得出红粘土固化浆液的最佳配比为：黏土浆黏度 30 s，水泥含量 20 g/100 ml，水玻璃含量 5 ml/100 ml。

（3）在实际施工中，对红黏土固化浆液配比的选择上，还要考虑具体的施工目的以及浆液的可注性。

（4）在地铁隧道施工中，无论是采用盾构法还是矿山法，上述研究成果均具有一定的适用性。

参考文献（References）：

[1] 王星华. 黏土固化浆液在地工程中的应用[M]. 北京：中国铁道出版社，1998.

[2] 王星华. 黏土固化浆液在广州地铁杨体区间隧道含水砂层中防水固砂注浆的应用[A]，中国岩石力学与工程学会第五次学术年会论文集[C]. 北京：科学出版社，1998，521-526.

[3] 杨秀竹，王星华，倪宏革，雷金山. 铁路岩溶路基加固的一种新方法. 岩土力学，2004，25（6）：988-990.

[4] 张可能，邹银生. 黏土固化注浆技术在垃圾填埋场防渗中的应用. 湖南大学学报（自然科学版），1999，26（5）：76-80.

[5] Xinghua Wang，Hailin Zhou. An improved hyperbola rheological model for fresh cement–clay grouts. Tunnelling

and Underground Space Technology, Volume 16, Issue 4, October 2001, Pages: 353-357.

[6] Wang Xinghua, Gao Quqing. Study of a new cheap grouting material: clay-hardening grout.Tunnelling and Underground Space Technology, Volume 12, Issue 4, October-December 1997, Pages 497-502.

作者简介（Bio-data）:

杨秀竹，1972年8月生，女，副教授，博士，从事岩土与地下工程的研究，主要研究方向：岩土与地下工程地基处理与加固，土动力学，岩土与地下工程结构静动力响应分析。

Xiuzhu YANG (1972—), associate professor. She took the doctor's degree in bridge and tunnel field in 2005 and now engages in the study of geotechnical engineering and underground construction. Study direction mainly: Subsoil treatment of geotechnical engineering and underground construction,Soil dynamics, Static and dynamic analysis of geotechnical engineering and underground construction.

E-mail: xzyang1661@126.com

盾构隧道近距离穿越地下管线施工监测分析

王荣劲　曹大明
成都畅达通地下工程科技发展有限公司，四川　成都　610041

【摘　要】 地铁盾构隧道在通过不良地质条件地段施工过程中会对地层产生扰动，可能引起地表及周边建筑物变形或沉降，尤其是隧道穿过地下管道时，可能引起地下管线的变形造成地下管线渗漏或断裂，因此必须进行监测。本文通过成都地铁盾构隧道小角度穿越地下污水管区段的施工监测成果分析，论述施工监测的作用和意义，以资今后类似工程参考。
【关键词】 成都地铁；盾构隧道；地下管线；监测

THE MONITORING ANALYSIS ON THE CONSTRUCTION OF SHIELD TUNNEL CROSSING UNDERGROUND PIPILINE IN SHORT DISTANCE

Rongjin WANG, Daming CAO
ChengDu ChangDaTong Underground Engineering Science & Technology Development Co.,LTD,
Chengdu 610041, Sichuan, China

Abstract: Metro shield tunnel across the area of adverse geological conditions would distribute strata in the process of construction, it may cause deformation and settlement of the surface and the surround buildings particularly bring about leakage or rupture of the underground pipeline, so it must be monitored. This paper analyzed the monitoring result of the construction when Chengdu Metro shield tunnel crossing the area of the underground sewage pipe, and discussed the effect and significance of construction monitoring in the expectation of providing references for similar construction.
Key word: Chengdu Metro; shield tunnel; underground pipeline; monitoring

1　引 言

城市地铁线路大多沿主要干道布设，而这些主要干道下多布设有城市地下管网。地铁施工时不可避免地会近距离穿越这些地下管线。当隧道在地下管线附近进行施工时，由于地层损失、地层原始应力状态的改变、土体受扰动后重新固结等原因造成周边地层的变形及位移，从而引起地下管线的变形造成地下管线渗漏或断裂。为掌握地铁施工对地下管线的影响，在地铁施工过程中必须对地下管线进行监测[1]。本文通过对成都地铁盾构隧道近距离穿越地下管线监测分析，为今后相似工程提供参考。

2　成都地铁 1 号线穿越污水管监测实例

成都地铁 1 号线倪家桥站—省体育馆站区间在 YDK12＋144～YDK12＋070 处盾构穿越污水管线，隧道与污水管小角度斜交，污水管受地铁施工影响区段较长。盾构穿越的管线为成都市主要排污管，管径 ϕ1 200 mm，排污量 10 万方/d。该区段盾构隧道隧顶埋深约 8.5 m，污水管底至盾构顶垂直距离 1.6 m

左右。地表至洞顶地层为：杂填土，粉质黏土，卵石土。

2.1 施工概况

为确保盾构掘进中污水管的安全，减少通过污水管区段的时间，保证掘进的连续性，在盾构到达前，施工单位对设备进行了维护且制订了应急预案，并在管线两侧从地面预埋了注浆管，提前采取措施结合实际监测数据进行适时跟踪注浆。

2.2 施工监测

结合现场施工情况进行了如下监测项目：

（1）地表沉降监测：沿隧道轴线共布设 11 个地表中线监测点，同时在盾构到达污水管位置前及盾构隧道与污水管交叉位置布设了 2 个地表监测沉降槽。

（2）污水管道地表监测：沿污水管道共布设 15 个监测点，其中 WSG-1、-15 距隧道轴线大于 3 m，WSG-2、-3、-14 距隧道轴线在 2～3 m 之间，其余测点在距轴线 2 m 范围内。

（3）地层垂直位移监测：共布设 3 个测孔

（4）水位监测：共测试 3 个污水检查井

同时对以上项目在盾构穿越污水管过程中进行了间隔 4 小时的加密监测。测点布置示意如图 1、图 2 所示。

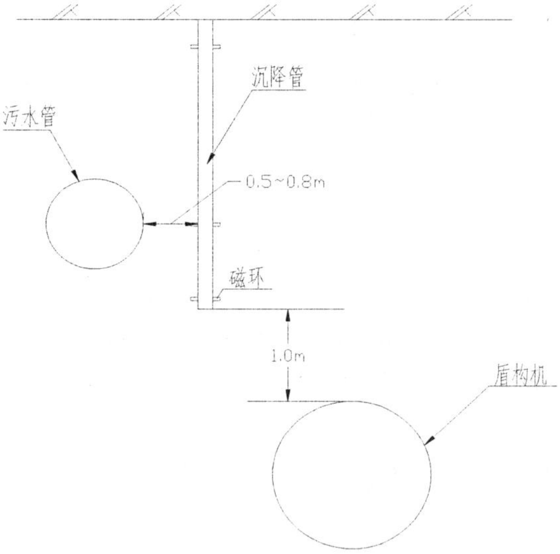

图 1　地中垂直位移监测埋设示意图

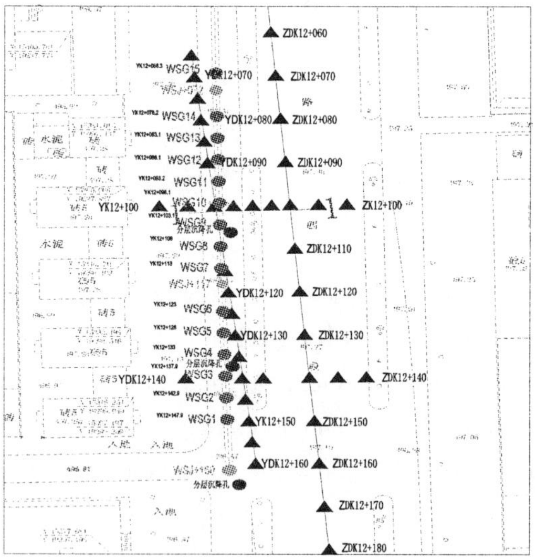

图 2　测点平面布置示意图

3 监测成果与分析

3.1 地表沉降监测

从 2008 年 11 月 5 日到 2008 年 11 月 12 日对 YDK12＋145 至 YDK12＋070 区段线路中线地表沉降点；污水管道顶地表沉降点进行了沉降监测。

从监测结果来看，线路中线地表沉降累计最大为－17.64 mm（YDK12＋135 监测点），污水管道地表沉降累计最大为－14.4 mm（WSG-4 监测点），部分测点在进行地表注浆后有一定的隆起，但均在控制范围内。所有地表沉降点均是在盾构到达后 2～3 天内沉降较明显，3 天后趋于稳定。由于同时采取了地中注浆加固，沉降槽较平缓，影响范围在 2 倍洞径范围。

以上特点从以下监测成果图（图 3 至图 5）可明显看出。

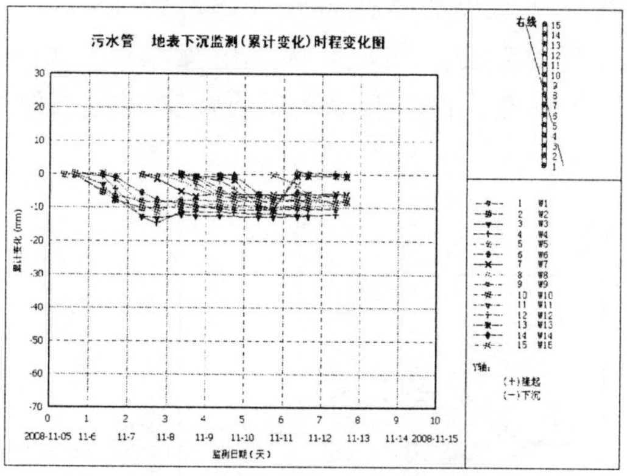

图 3　污水管顶地表累计沉降时程变化图

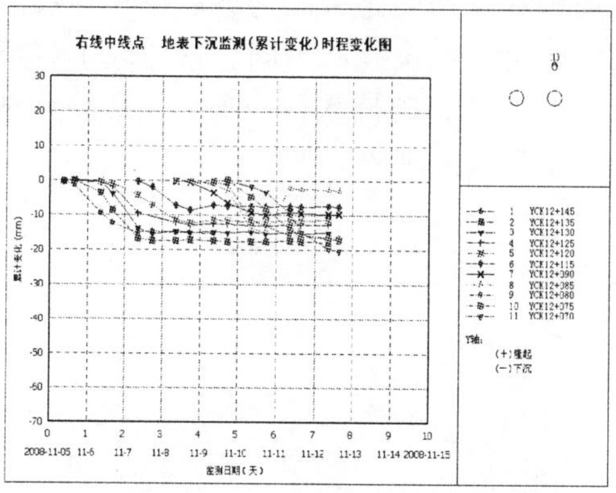

图 4　线路中线地表沉降时程变化图

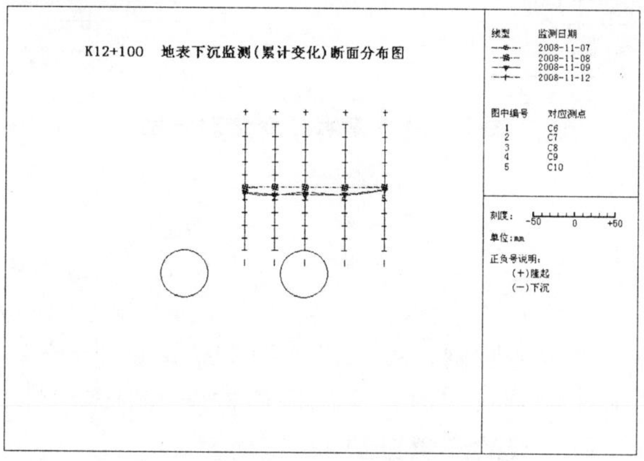

图 5　地表沉陷槽断面分布图

3.2　地层垂直位移监测

通过对 K12＋162、K12＋136、K12＋105 三个地层垂直位移测孔监测，可看出在盾构接近测孔时，深层土体有少量变形，盾构经过及盾尾脱出变形较大，直至盾构通过后 20 m 左右，变形趋于稳定。最大变形为－22.22 mm（K12＋136 测孔）。通过对深层土体不同深度测点与地表沉降测点沉降数据比较，同一测孔内不同深度测点及对应的地表沉降量大致相当,表明盾构所通过地段上方地层变形为整体沉降。地层垂直位移监测成果如图 6 所示。

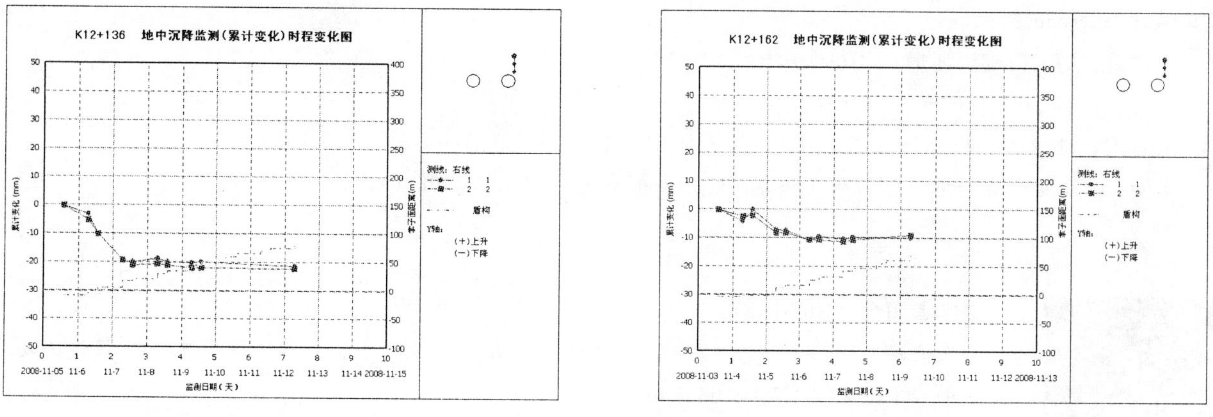

图 6　地层垂直位移时程变化图

3.3　水位监测

在盾构穿越污水管期间，在盾构影响范围内对三个污水检查井井内水位进行了连续监测，以确认污水管在盾构穿越期间是否因为地层位移导致污水管发生渗漏。从监测污水检查井井内水位来看，同一天不同时段内管内水位有所不同，这体现了每天排污高峰及低谷的变化，而每一天水位变化高度均是一致的，而仅 11 月 5 日晚间水位有所异常因降雨所致。通过图 7 水位变化图可确认，在盾构穿越污水管期间，污水管未发生渗漏现象。

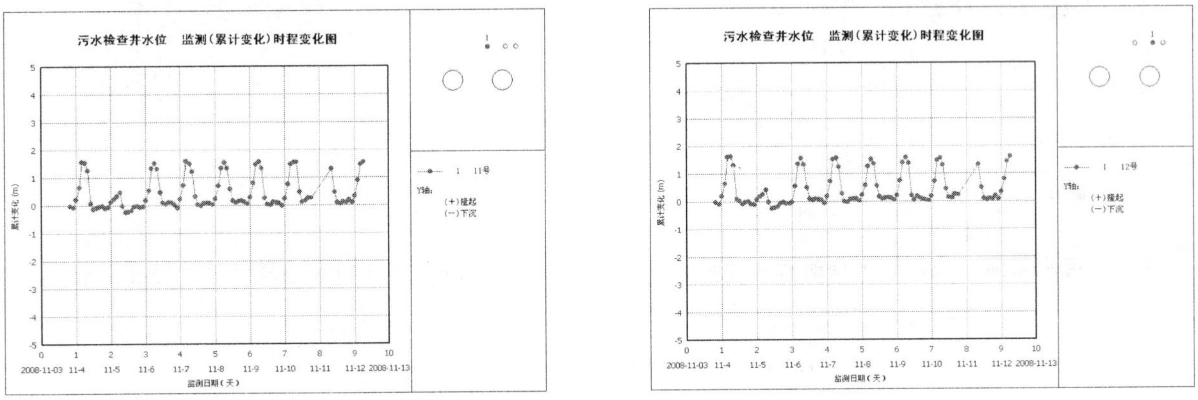

图 7 污水管水位变化时程图

4 结 语

通过对盾构近距离穿越污水管过程监测，可以得出如下结论：

（1）在砂卵石地层中盾构施工穿越管线时，应确保盾构施工的连续性，控制盾构掘进速度，避免盾构在穿越过程中停机。并提前做好管线的应急保护工作。

（2）盾构对砂卵石地层的扰动，影响范围约 2 倍洞径范围内。地层从扰动到趋缓从时间上来看约 2～3 天；从距离上来看盾构通过约 20 m 后变形趋缓，砂卵石地层土体固结速度较快。

（3）砂卵石地层在受扰动后，不同深度沉降量有所不同，深层沉降稍大（约 2～3 mm），但总体来看深层与浅层及地表的沉降量大体一致，地层体现为整体沉降。

（4）在砂卵石地层盾构近距离穿越地下管线施工过程中，通过提前在管线位置从地表埋设注浆管，盾构通过时根据监测成果有针对性地从地表进行适时、适量注浆可较好地控制地下管线周围地层的变形及位移，从而达到对地下管线的保护。

参考文献（References）：

[1] 刘建航，等. 盾构法隧道. 中国铁道出版社，1991.

[2] 吴为义，孙宇坤，张土乔. 盾构隧道施工对邻近地下管线影响分析. 中国铁道科学，2008（3）.

[3] 王启耀，郑永来，杨林德，凌宇峰. 挤压式盾构施工对邻近隧道的影响分析. 2003（5）.

[4] 李刚. 盾构隧道穿越地下管线施工技术. 科技情报开发与经济，2008（12）.

作者简介（Bio-data）：

王荣劲（1973.12—），男，高级工程师，在读工程硕士，成都畅达通地下工程科技发展有限公司。邮箱 wangrj73@163.com

Rongjing WANG (1973.12—), male, Senior Engineer, Master candidate of Engineering, working in the Chengdu Chang Da Tong underground engineering science & technology development Co .LTD.

E-mail: wangrj73@163.com

大直径盾构隧道壁后注浆无损探测技术研究

刘 浩
中铁第四勘察设计院集团有限公司

【摘 要】 阐述了应用地质雷达对大直径盾构隧道壁后注浆无损检测的技术，介绍了探地雷达的基本原理和方法以及该新技术在工程应用中的技术方法，并分析了异常情况在雷达图像上的反映，得到了对南京长江隧道盾构壁后注浆的结论及建议，从而为进一步推广探地雷达在大直径盾构壁后注浆检测中的应用提供了依据。
【关键词】 探地雷达；盾构隧道；注浆检测

STUDY ON NON-DESTRUCTIVE DETECTION OF BACKFILL GROUTING IN LARGE-DIAMETER SHIELD TUNNEL

Hao LIU
China Railway Siyuan Survey and Design Group CO., LTD， Wuhan 430063, Hubei, China

Abstract: this paper explained the non-destructive detection of backfill grouting in large-diameter shield tunnel by employing the geological radar. By introducing the basic principles of ground penetrating radar and the application of this new technique in practical engineering, and analyzing the inflection of abnormal situation on radar image, the conclusion and suggestion of Nanjing Yangtze Shield Tunnel after backfill grouting had been got. It provided the basis for extending the application of ground penetrating radar in the backfill grouting examination of large-diameter shield.
Key words: ground penetrating radar; shield tunnel; grouting examination

1 引 言

随着工程建设的需要，在盾构法隧道施工中大直径的盾构隧道机也在国内出现了，而且对其施工和运营中出现的沿隧道纵向不均匀沉降的控制手段和措施更是相对缺少确定的依据。当前在我国的地铁隧道的施工中，仅仅依靠施工中的控制手段，包括注浆时间，注浆压力，注浆量等，结合地面沉降观测、隧道本身的沉降变形监测进行质量控制。由于没有相对成熟的注浆检测手段，在盾构隧道施工过程中，往往会出现很多问题。因此，研究合适的注浆工艺，开发和利用盾构隧道的无损探测技术，使盾构隧道壁后浆液可视化，进而实现盾构隧道施工和沉降控制的科学化、合理化，提高盾构隧道工程施工的安全性、施工质量以及施工效率等均具有重要的意义。

2 工程概况及地质条件

本文所依托工程为南京长江隧道左线盾构隧道壁后注浆情况得无损探测。该工程左汊盾构隧道采用双管单层的结构形式，隧道分为东西两线，自浦口工作井始发。盾构隧道采用德国海瑞克公司生产的

ϕ14.93 m 的泥水混合式盾构机，盾构管片环外径 14.5 m，内径 13.3 m，壁厚 0.6 m，环宽 2 m，混凝土强度等级 C60，抗渗等级 S12。

3 探地雷达基本原理与盾构壁后注浆检测可行性分析

3.1 基本原理

探地雷达方法是根据高频（偶极子）电磁波在地下介质传播的理论，利用发射天线将高频电磁波（50～2 000 MHz）以宽频带短脉冲形式送入介质内部，经目标体反射后回到表面，再由接收天线接受回波信号。电磁波在介质中传播时，其路径、电磁场强度及波形随所通过的介质的电性性质及几何形态而变化，根据接收到反射回波的双程走时、幅度、相位等物理信息，可对介质的内部结构进行判释。

雷达图像剖面图常以脉冲反射波的形式记录。波形以彩色剖面形式表示，等色线可形象地表征出地下反射面或目的体．另外在波形记录图上．各测点的水平位置以测线的铅垂方向记录波形，构成雷达成像剖面。根据雷达剖面图像，可判断反射界面或目的体，而且快速、直观、无损伤。

用 LTD-2100 探地雷达进行隧道质量检测时，数据处理采用电波所配备的 IDSP 处理软件进行数据处理。其流程如图 1 所示。

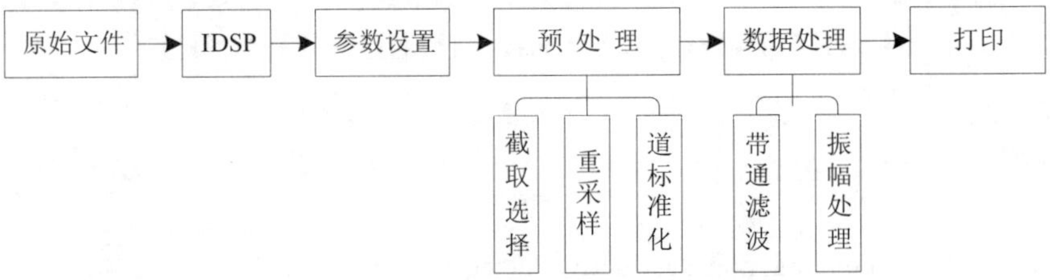

图 1 LTD-2100 探地雷达数据处理流程

根据电磁波理论，电磁波以一定角度入射到第一电磁界面时，就会产生电磁波的反射和折射（见图 2a），形成反射波和折射波。对于第二电磁界面，可把第一界面的折射波作为第二界面的入射波看待，则在第二电磁界面又形成反射波和入射波。如此可以在各个电磁分界面上继续分下去。雷达工作时，以位于地面上的接收天线在接收到地下回波后，直接传输到接收机，信号在接收机经过整形和放大等处理后，经电缆传输到雷达主机，经处理后传输到微机，就会形成如图 2b 所示的雷达信号。

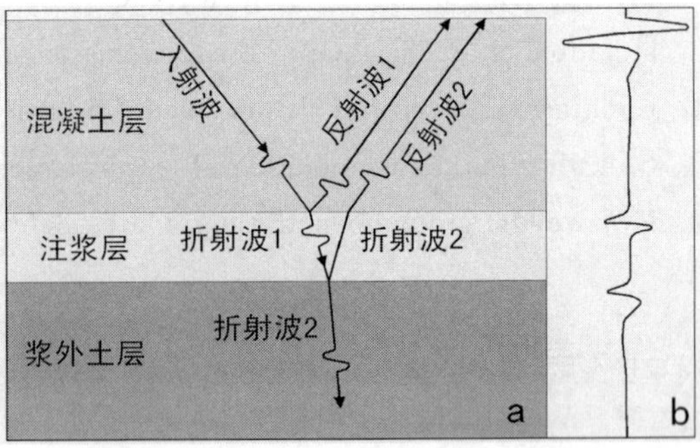

（a. 模型示意图 b. 雷达信号示意图）

图 2 电磁波传播示意图

3.2 雷达探测盾构壁后注浆可行性分析

由于电磁波产生反射的基础是介质存在电磁性质存在差异，因此在对盾构壁后注浆分布探测前需要对混凝土层、注浆层及注浆层外土层的电磁性质进行测试分析以确定用雷达探测盾构壁后注浆分布可行性。一般情况下，混凝土层的介电常数 6.4，注浆层介电常数随着注浆龄期的增加而减小，在此取 20，浆外饱和土层的介电常数取 30。根据反射系数的定义：

$$R=\frac{A_{入射}}{A_{反射}}=\frac{\sqrt{\varepsilon_1}-\sqrt{\varepsilon_2}}{\sqrt{\varepsilon_1}+\sqrt{\varepsilon_2}} \tag{1}$$

其中：ε_1 和 ε_2 分别为入射层和反射层的介电常数。

把上述介电常数代入公式 1 可以求得混凝土层和注浆层的反射系数分别为－0.25 和－0.13，其平方值均大于 0.01，说明介质之间的电性差异有足够的发射或散射能量被雷达系统所识别。

由于电磁波在介质中的传播速度与介质的介电常数有关[5]，如公式（2）所示，如果对注浆厚度实施比较准确的测量需要准确测出介质的介电常数。

$$v = \frac{c}{\sqrt{\varepsilon}} \tag{2}$$

其中：c 为光速；ε 注浆介电常数。

由以上的分析可以得出，探地雷达用于盾构壁后注浆分布是完全可行的。

3.3 隧道中雷达波相识别

公式（1）中隧道衬砌与结构层位雷达反射系数的正负，决定反射波振幅正负，雷达波在隧道盾构壁后注浆检测中的主要反射有：

空气-管片内表面：负反射，差异大，反射强；

管片外-注浆内壁：负反射，差异小，反射弱；

注浆外壁-注浆外土层：负反射，差异小，反射弱。

通常根据反射波的振幅与方向、反射波的频谱特性及反射波同相轴形态特征进行综合判断、分析、识别。

4 现场工作的开展

4.1 雷达介电常数检测试验

为了定量检测盾构隧道壁后注浆的厚度和分布情况，必须在检测前确定浆液的介电常数。由于电磁波在介质中的传播速度与介质的介电常数有关，如果对注浆厚度实施比较准确的测量需要准确测出介质的介电常数。

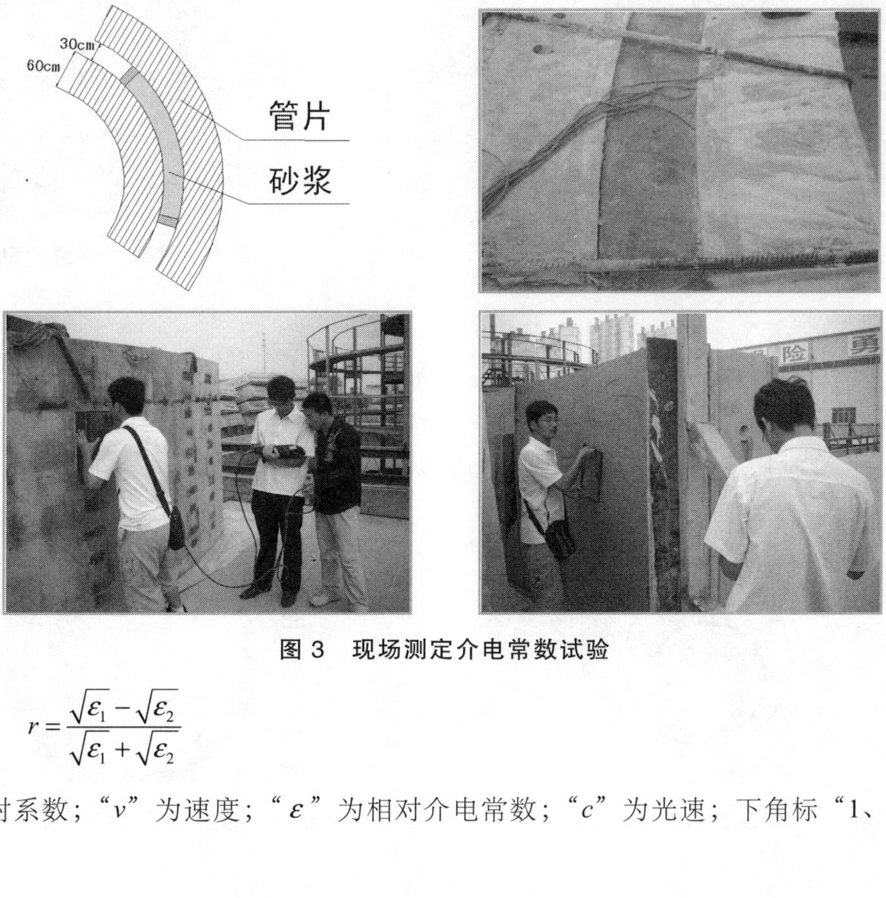

图 3 现场测定介电常数试验

$$r = \frac{\sqrt{\varepsilon_1} - \sqrt{\varepsilon_2}}{\sqrt{\varepsilon_1} + \sqrt{\varepsilon_2}} \tag{3}$$

式中，“r”为反射系数；“v”为速度；“ε”为相对介电常数；“c”为光速；下角标“1、2”分别表示上、下介质。空气的相对介电常数为 1，最小；水的相对介电常数为 81，最大。电磁波由空气进入水泥板，会出现强反射（对应地面，并且由于空气中电磁波传播速度较快，这时的地面对应的是负相位）；同样，当电磁波由水泥板层传播至水稳层时，由于两者的电性特征差异，亦会出现强反射轴（速度也是由高到低，它对应的也是负相位），这两个强反射之间对应的就是水泥板层，由此可得到实际水泥板的厚度；另外，如果水泥板下面存在裂隙或空洞，由于混凝土的介电常数为 6，与空气的有较大差别，这时雷达系统接收到的回波幅度会明显变强，在雷达剖面上将出现明显异常。当电磁波穿过水稳层进入原始土层时，在其交界处亦会出现与电磁波穿过水泥板下界面时类似的反映，我们由此可以追踪其厚度和查找存在的缺陷。

电磁波在管片中传播双程走时为 11.8 ns（厚度为 0.6 m），在砂浆层传播双程走时为 9.5（厚度为 0.3 m），根据波速公式：

$$v = \frac{2d}{\Delta t} \tag{4}$$

其中 Δt 为双程走时，得到电磁波在管片和砂浆层中的传播速度分别为 0.10 m/ns 和 0.063 m/ns。根据公式：

$$v = \frac{c}{\sqrt{\varepsilon}} \tag{5}$$

得到管片和砂浆层的介电常数分别为 8.7 和 22.6. 本次测得的注浆的相对介电常数是浆龄为 3 天，由于注浆层的相对介电常数随着浆龄增加而减小，因此在实际测试过程中仍然取相对介电常数为 13。由公式 3 得到注浆层的中电磁波的传播速度为 0.075 m/ns。

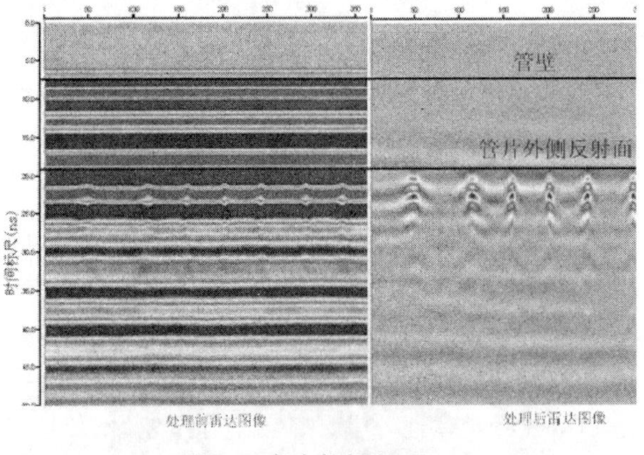

图 4 试验数据处理

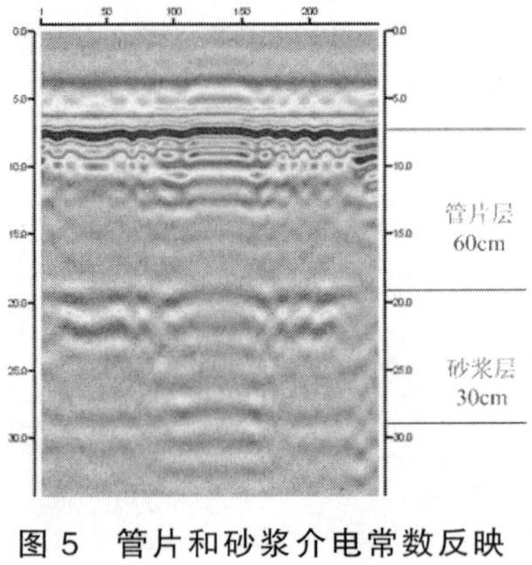

图 5 管片和砂浆介电常数反映

4.2 测线布置

由于现场施工条件的限制，加之隧道直径较大，现有设备无法对整个隧道所有管片进行探测，现场根据条件选取有代表性的测线和环向进行探测。本次探测共选取了两条纵向测线（一条在隧道顶部，一条在隧道左侧）和十环管片进行检测，具体测线布置见图 6 至图 7。

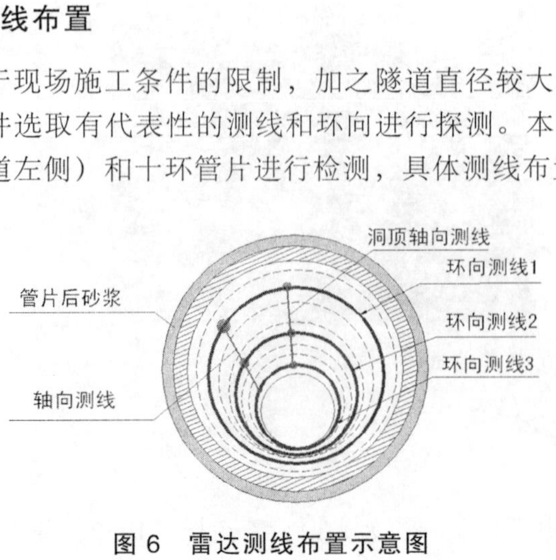

图 6 雷达测线布置示意图

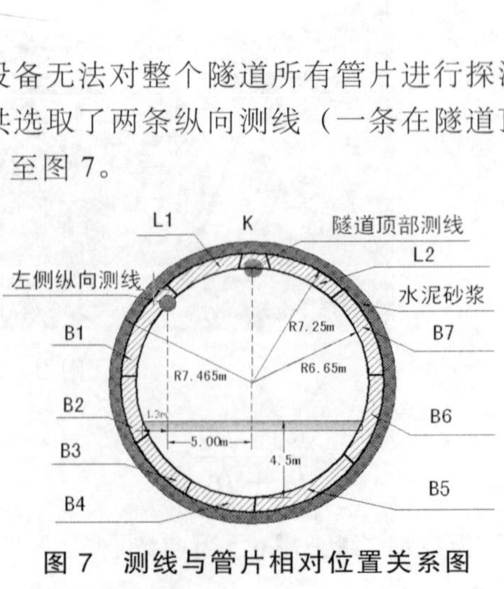

图 7 测线与管片相对位置关系图

4.3 配套设备

为了本次检测的顺利开展，我方对雷达检测作业设备进行了专项研究和调研，对隧道顶部纵向测线、左侧纵向测线和环向测线分别采用了三种不同的作业方式，并取得了成功，为今后大直径盾构隧道雷达探测做了有益的尝试。具体操作方式如图示：

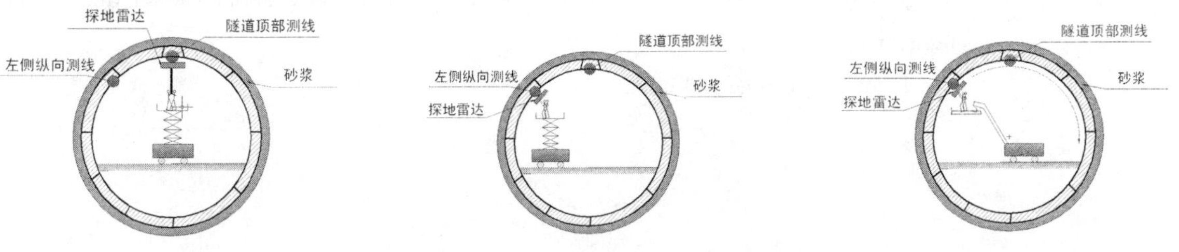

图 8　隧道环向测线作业示意图

5　数据处理结果

对现场测试得到的探地雷达原始数据进行进一步的处理，得到了南京长江隧道左右两线的探地雷达的探测结果。根据实验结果，电磁波在混凝土与注浆层之间形成比较明显的反射，在雷达图上的位置约为 19.5 ns，而注浆层与浆外土层的形成的反射界面大部分处于 28 ns 左右，按照 0.75 cm/ns 的速度计算，注浆层的厚度大部分均在 21 cm 左右。纵观 10 个环向管片雷达成果图，注浆层厚度平均在 19～22 cm。从两条轴向测线图中可以看出，大部分测线上雷达注浆层发射较为均匀，厚度约为 18～23 cm，说明盾构注浆层的分布比较均匀。本次探测了隧道顶部和隧道测线各一道测线以及测了 10 个环向剖面，通过数据处理可知在注浆过程中有少量位置存在注浆不均匀的现象。总的来说异常区位置主要聚集在隧洞的顶部位置，可能由于重力等因素出现顶部注浆量少。

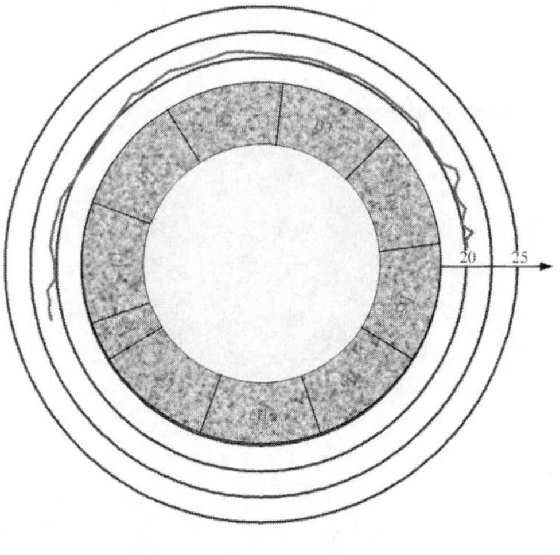

图 9　158 环管片成果图

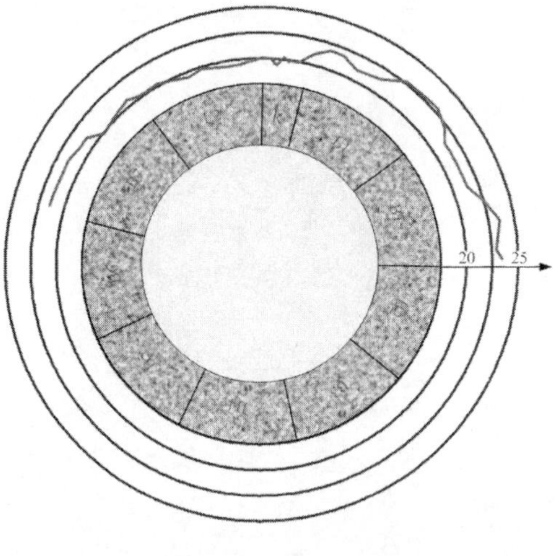

图 10　1100 环管片成果图

6　结　论

由上述雷达探测结果可以看出，在本工程中采用地质雷达手段对盾构隧道管片壁后注浆密实性及注浆层分布情况进行探测是完全可行的，倘若具备一定的现场条件，采取一些辅助措施能够对盾构隧道环向进行全断面的雷达扫描，则必将获得有更大参考价值的信息，从而为盾构施工过程中某些技术参数的调整和实施提供重要的参考与验证。

作者简介（Bio-data）：

刘浩，1980 年 2 月生，男，工程师，工学硕士学位，工作单位是中铁第四勘察设计院集团有限公司，主要从事隧道及地下工程的设计和研究工作。

Hao LIU, (1980—), Male, Master Degree, Served in China Railway SIYUAN Survey And Design Group CO.,LTD. Engaged in the design and study about tunnel and underground engineering.

E-mail: boraliu@163.com

泥水盾构开舱时泥浆配制及泥膜形成试验研究

闵凡路[1] 朱 伟[1,2] 王守慧[3] 钟小春[4]

[1]河海大学岩土工程科学研究所，江苏 南京 210098;
[2]河海大学环境学院，江苏 南京 210098;
[3]中铁十四局集团 长江隧道工程指挥部，江苏 南京 210098;
[4]河海大学土木工程学院，江苏 南京 210098

【摘 要】 目前国内外在修建过江过河隧道时常使用泥水盾构施工，而且一次掘进距离比较长，施工中有时会需要开舱检修机器设备。以怎样的泥浆形成什么样的泥膜对开挖面稳定更有利，如何保持并增强开挖面的稳定性，成为开舱时亟待解决的难题。本文结合南京长江隧道工程在砾砂地层中开舱检修机器设备，对开舱时泥浆特性的调整进行理论分析和实验研究，提出了确保开挖面稳定的泥浆调整方案，成功地保证了开舱作业的安全的进行，对今后泥水盾构开舱作业有着重要的指导意义。

【关键词】 泥水盾构；开舱；泥膜；调整

STUDY ON ADJUSTING SLURRY PROPERTY WHEN OPENING THE PRESSURE CABIN OF SLURRY SHIELD

Fanlu MIN[1], Wei ZHU[1, 2], Shouhui WANG[3], Xiaochun ZHONG[4]

[1]*Geotechnical Research Institute, Hohai University, Nanjing 210098, Jiangsu, China;*

[2]*College of Environmental Science and Technology, Hohai University, Nanjing 210098, Jiangsu, China;*

[3]*Nanjing Yangtze River Tunnel Engineering Headquarters China Railway Fourteenth Group Corporation, Nanjing 211800, Jiangsu, China;*

[4]*College of Civil Engineering, Hohai University,Nanjing 210098, Jiangsu, China*

Abstract: For tunnel projects across the river, slurry shields are widely used nowadays. During a relatively long distance tunneling, it is inevitable to open the pressure cabin for examining and repairing the equipments. There are also some urgent problems need to be solved, such as how to build up a dense filter-cake and maintain and enhance the stability of the excavation face. In this paper, for opening the pressure cabin of the Nanjing Yangtze River Tunnel project in gravel sand strata, a lot of theoretical analysis and experimental studies were made to adjust the slurry property. An adjustment program of slurry property was made which ensured the stability of the excavation face and the success of opening the pressure cabin. The successful adjustment of slurry property is also a suggestion for the similar projects.

Key words: slurry shield; opening of the pressure cabin; filter-cake; adjustment

1 引 言

随着社会经济不断发展的需要，国内外掀起的修建大型过江过河隧道的热潮[1]。过江过河及海底隧道一般掘进距离都比较长，而且由于其穿越的地质条件及水文条件比较复杂，因此有时会需要对盾构机进行开舱检查。一般开舱时盾构机多处于江河底部，水压力很大，同时为确保进舱人员安全，会下调泥浆压力的设定值，因此研究开舱时如何有效的利用泥浆保证开挖面的稳定性非常重要。

泥水盾构以压力泥浆支护开挖面，泥膜的形成对开挖面稳定非常重要[2]。大量工程和试验结果表明，根据不同的地层条件和泥水特性，泥浆在开挖面上的渗透形态可以分为三种：① 只有泥浆中的水流入地层，泥浆中的土颗粒几乎完全不向地层中渗透；② 泥浆中的部分细粒成分向地层间隙渗透、填充，形成一段渗透带；③ 全部泥浆在压力作用下从地层间隙流走。根据泥浆渗透形态的不同，泥膜也可以分为三种：泥皮型泥膜、渗透带型泥膜和泥皮-渗透带型泥膜[3][4]。

目前国内外学者在开挖面稳定性理论研究上，常采用“薄膜模型”，即不考虑泥浆的渗透作用对开挖面稳定性的影响，认为形成的泥膜完全不透水，泥浆压力全部用来支护地层土压力和水压力。但是在实际工程中，特别是在砂砾地层中，泥浆中的水及细粒成分会穿过泥膜渗透到地层中一定的距离，造成泥浆的失水或损失，减小了有效泥浆压力，影响了开挖面的稳定性。

Anagnostou 和 Kovari 在 1994 年提出了考虑泥浆渗透的楔形体“渗透模型”[5]，并提出在砂性土中，掘进时盾构所需提供的支护力可以采用“薄膜模型”进行计算，而在盾构停止开挖的静止状态泥浆渗透将会大大影响开挖面的稳定性。李昀等在 2007 年考虑泥浆的渗透区域与滑动面之间的几何关系，对村山公式进行化简计算有效泥浆压力的修正系数，得到了泥浆渗透模型的开挖面稳定性安全系数[6]。

胡欣雨等在 2009 年采用真三轴实验定量研究一般应力状态下泥浆渗入对泥水盾构开挖面土体剪切强度的影响，研究表明泥浆的入渗增大了剪切滑移中的粒间接触面积，同时增大了土体颗粒间的咬合作用，宏观表现即为内聚力的增大[7]。

已有研究表明泥浆渗透对开挖面稳定性主要有两方面的影响：一方面造成了泥浆的失水或损失，减小了有效泥浆压力，对开挖面的稳定不利；另一方面泥浆中的土颗粒渗入地层，增大了地层的黏聚力，利于开挖面的稳定。这些研究成果对开舱时泥浆调整方案的提出有很大的参考意义。本文以南京长江隧道工程为背景，结合在江底复杂的砂砾复合地层中开舱，提出了开舱时保证开挖面稳定的泥浆调整方案和泥膜形态，并以自制的泥浆渗透装置开展泥浆特性的调整试验及泥浆成膜试验，以期对工程起到一定的指导作用。

2 工程概况及开舱泥浆特性调整方案的提出

2.1 工程概况

南京长江隧道是目前世界上最大的过江隧道之一，设计为双管盾构隧道，采用两台泥水平衡盾构同向施工。工程采用“左汊盾构隧道+右汊桥梁”的方案，隧道段长 3.905 m，其中左线盾构段长 3 022.17 m，右线盾构段长 3 015.06 m；盾构开挖直径为 14.93 m。

隧道主要穿越第四系和白垩系地层，隧道场地通过部位不存在断裂或破碎带。盾构穿越主要地层为④号淤泥质粉质黏土、⑥号淤泥质粉质黏土夹粉土、⑧号粉细砂、⑩号砾砂以及⑬号圆砾。如图 1 所示，盾构机停机位置位于江面下约 60 m，其中覆土约 25 m，水压最高值达 0.6 MPa。其所处断面上

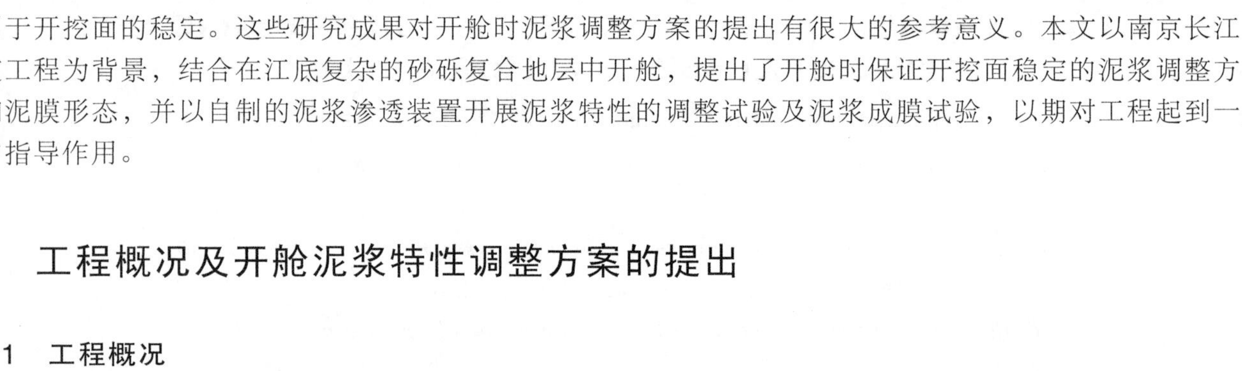

图 1 盾构机在江中的位置示意图

部约 1/4 为⑧号粉细砂地层，其渗透系数约为 6×10^{-3} cm/s；下部约 3/4 为⑩号砾砂地层，其渗透系数约为 3×10^{-2} cm/s。在这样高水压高渗透性的地层中开舱，如何调整泥浆以保证开挖面的稳定性成为是工程中十分关注的问题。

2.2 开舱泥浆特性调整方案的提出

盾构机停机前的掘进施工中，由于盾构机已经进入透水性强且水压力大的砾砂地层，采用的是比重、黏度都较大的聚合物泥浆，在实验室内的泥浆成膜试验显示，泥浆滤失较少，形成的泥膜多为泥皮型泥膜。但是聚合物泥浆在长时间停机时不够稳定，泥浆容易出现老化等质量变差的现象。因此，在开舱时采用稳定性好的膨润土泥浆。

根据泥浆渗透对开挖面稳定两方面的影响，并结合现场泥浆特性，对开舱泥浆特性的调整分两步：① 在保证泥浆可以形成泥膜的前提下，先在压力舱中以比重比较小、黏度较低的纯膨润土泥浆，使其在开挖面地层中渗透一定距离，形成含有渗透带的泥膜。这一步调整是为了增加地层的黏聚力，但同时泥浆损失也较多。② 在压力舱泥浆已经形成渗透带的基础上，再提高泥浆的黏度和比重，再使其在开挖面上形成致密的泥皮型泥膜。这一步是为了减少泥浆损失，提高有效泥浆压力。在开舱之前，先在实验室内进泥浆成膜试验，以验证上述方案的可行性。

3 泥浆特性调整及泥浆成膜实验

3.1 纯膨润土泥浆渗透成膜试验

为了使泥浆在地层中渗透一定的距离，提高开挖面土体的黏聚力，采用的 Na 级膨润土，分别按浓度 3%、5%、8%、12% 进行膨化，膨化 24 小时，泥浆比重、黏度值见表 1。

本次试验选用对成膜最不利的砾砂层作为试验地层，该地层大于 2 mm 的粗颗粒占整个地层含量的 40%左右，试验中地层的渗透系数约为 3.95×10^{-2} cm/s，与实际工程中砾砂地层的渗透系数 3×10^{-2} cm/s 基本相符。

试验仪器与试验方法如图 2、图 3 所示，一次性加压 0.3 MPa，测泥浆渗透稳定、泥膜形成时的滤水量和成膜时间，作为泥膜质量好坏的评价指标[3][8]；并观察形成泥膜的形态。滤水量越小，成膜时间越短，形成泥膜越致密，泥膜质量也越好。

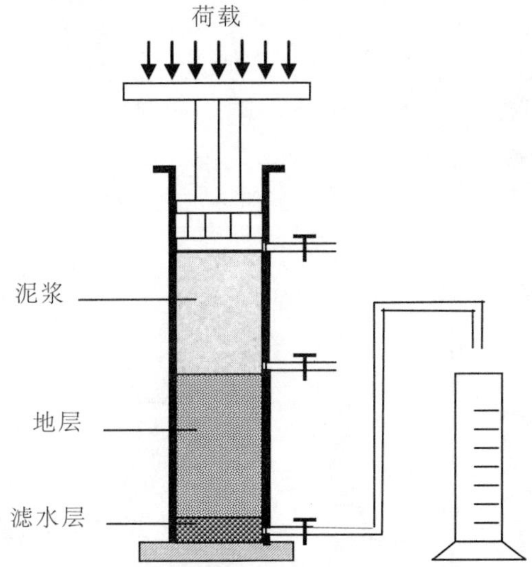

图 2 泥浆成膜装置示意图

图 3 泥浆成膜试验

四种泥浆的基本性质及在⑩地层中成膜试验结果见表 1。

表 1 四组膨润土泥浆的基本性质及成膜试验结果汇总

泥浆浓度	比重	漏斗黏度（s）	是否形成泥皮	是否形成渗透带	泥膜形成时间
3%	1.03	17.6	否	形成 10 cm 渗透带	15 s
5%	1.04	18.9	否	形成 8 cm 渗透带	约 10 s 形成泥膜
8%	1.06	21.3	形成 2 mm 泥皮	形成 3 cm 渗透带	约 2 s 形成泥膜
12%	1.08	23.8	形成 1 mm 泥皮	形成 2 cm 渗透带	约 2 s 形成泥膜

由表 1 可知，浓度 3%～5%的膨润土泥浆粘度较低，比重低于 1.05，可以在⑩地层中形成渗透带型泥膜，但是泥浆损失量比较大，成膜时间较长；浓度 8%～12%的膨润土泥浆粘度在 20 s 以上，泥浆向地层中渗透一定距离后，迅速稳定下来，泥浆损失也比较少，形成泥皮-渗透带型泥膜（如图 4 所示），且成膜时间很短。

图 4 浓度 12%的膨润土泥浆成膜情况

3.2 提高比重和黏度的泥浆成膜试验

在开挖面上形成泥皮-渗透带型泥膜后，将泥浆比重提高至 1.15 至 1.20 之间、黏度 25 s 以上 [0]，开展泥浆成膜试验。

由于纯膨润土泥浆的比重一般不大，若用纯膨润土将泥浆比重调到 1.15 至 1.20 之间，则其黏度会很大，难以满足泵送要求。因此，考虑以较高黏度的低比重膨润土泥浆和天然黏土泥浆（盾构机穿越淤泥质粉质黏土地层时储存的多余的泥浆）混合，配置比重在 1.15 至 1.20 之间、黏度 25 s 以上的物理稳定性高的泥浆。

（1）测试泥浆物理稳定性。以 24 h 泥浆的析水率表示。泥浆析水率越小，其物理稳定性越好。将泥浆装入容量为 100 ml 的量筒，24 h 后的析水体积 1 ml，即 24 h 析水率为 1%，泥浆物理稳定性很好。

（2）泥浆成膜试验。本次试验在⑩地层中进行的，试验方法和步骤与上述泥膜试验相同，只是本次试验是分级加压，绘制泥浆滤水量的变化曲线。泥浆形成泥皮型泥膜（如图 5 所示），滤水量和时间及泥浆压力的关系如图 6 所示。

图 5 泥皮型泥膜

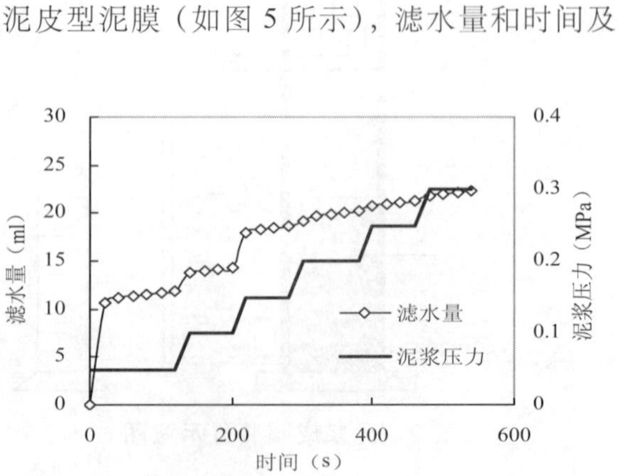

图 6 滤水量变化曲线

由图 8 可以看出，在每级压力作用下，泥浆的滤水量很小，每分钟的滤水量约为 0.6 ml，换算到真实的开挖面上滤失水量约为每 2 小时 3 m^3（满足滤失水量经验值：每两小时 10～20 m^3）。

以上实验的结果显示，浓度 8%～12%左右的膨润土泥浆可以在开挖面上快速形成含有渗透带的泥膜；比重 1.15 至 1.20 之间、黏度 25 s 以上的膨润土与天然黏土的混合泥浆性质良好，物理稳定性较高，可以在开挖面上快速形成微透水的泥皮型泥膜。

4 成功开舱

置换原泥浆舱的泥浆，分两步进行泥浆调整，开舱。开舱时，将泥浆舱的泥浆液位降低一些，只以气压来支护开挖面，以便于人员观察。从现场气压及泥浆压力的变化情况和拍摄照片（图 7）显示，开挖面上形成了质量良好的泥膜，而且泥膜密闭性较好，没有出现漏气的现象，气压有效的作用在开挖面上，维持了开挖面的稳定。

图 7 开舱泥膜照片

5 结 论

（1）泥水盾构开舱时一般位于江河底部，水压力很大，且会下调泥浆压力设定值，因此有必要通过泥浆特性调整来增强开挖面的稳定性；

（2）先以较稀的泥浆向开挖面渗透一段距离，再以质量较高泥浆在开挖面上形成致密的泥皮型泥膜的泥浆调整方案，是在无黏性地层开舱时保持开挖面稳定的一种可行的方案；

（3）南京长江隧道在砾砂地层开舱时，可以先浓度 8%～12%左右的膨润土泥浆作为渗透泥浆，使开挖面地层中形成一定距离的渗透带，增加地层的黏聚力；再以比重 1.15～1.20 之间、黏度 25 s 以上的泥浆在开挖面上形成泥皮型微透水的泥膜，减少泥浆压力的损失。

参考文献（References）：

[1] 项兆池，楼如岳，傅德明. 最新泥水盾构技术[M]. 上海：上海隧道工程股份有限公司施工技术研究所科技情报室，2001.

[2] 朱伟译. 隧道标准规范（盾构篇）及解说[M]. 北京：中国建筑工业出版社，2001.

[3] 张凤祥，朱合华，傅德明. 盾构隧道篇[M]. 北京：人民交通出版社，2004.

[4] 韩晓瑞. 基于泥浆与地层匹配性的泥水盾构泥膜形成规律研究[D]. 南京：河海大学，2009.

[5] ANAGNOSTOU G, KOVARI K. The face stability of slurry-shield-driven tunnels[J]. Tunneling and Underground Space Technology. 1994, 9(2):165-174.

[6] 李昀，张子新. 泥浆渗透对盾构开挖面稳定性的影响研究[J]. 地下空间与工程学报，2007，3(4): 720-725.

[7] 胡雨欣，张子新. 一般应力状态下泥浆渗入对泥水盾构开挖面土体剪切强度影响分析[J]. 岩石力学与工程学报，2009，28(5): 1027-1036.

[8] 韩晓瑞，朱伟，刘泉维等. 泥浆性质对泥水盾构开挖面泥膜形成质量影响[J]. 岩土力学，2008，29(SUPP): 288-292.

作者简介（Bio-data）：

闵凡路（1985 年 8 月—），男，现为河海大学博士研究生，主要从事盾构隧道工程方面的研究工作。

Fanlu MIN, Male，born Oct.85, Pursuing a doctor's degree of Geotechnical Engineering in Hohai University, backfill grouting during shield tunneling engineering.

E-mail: minfanlu@126.com

盾构壁后注浆浆体收缩规律及对间隙参数的影响

左 佳[1] 钟小春[2] 王华伟[3] 朱 伟[1,4]
[1]河海大学岩土工程科学研究所，江苏 南京 210098
[2]河海大学土木工程学院，江苏 南京 210098
[3]中铁十四局集团南京长江隧道工程指挥部，江苏 南京 210098
[4]河海大学环境学院，江苏 南京 210098

【摘 要】 盾构法施工中，壁后注浆工序必不可少，是控制地层变形和地表沉降的关键环节。当前关于盾尾空隙壁后注浆的研究主要集中在数值分析方面，为了更为准确地预测地表位移，需要对盾尾空隙进行合理的模拟，国内外许多学者引入间隙参数的概念模拟盾尾空隙。在注浆完成后，注入的浆液在初始阶段会发生较大的变形，从而影响盾尾空隙的闭合，因此间隙参数需要作出修正。而其中对间隙参数的选取过分依赖于人为的经验和统计规律，对于壁后注浆体在硬化的过程中受注浆压力作用下的变形规律认识仍不明确。通过室内模型实验对硬性浆在不同配合比、不同注浆压力下的体积收缩规律进行研究，提出了能够反映浆体随时间的变形规律的计算模型。利用浆体变形模型可以更为准确地确定壁后注浆完成后的盾尾间隙参数。

【关键词】 壁后注浆；盾尾空隙；间隙参数；浆体体积收缩模型

ANALYSIS ON THE IMPACT OF GAP PARAMETERS FOR GROUT DEFORMATION PROPERTIES OF SHIELD TUNNEL

Jia ZUO [1], Xiaochun ZHONG [2], Huawei WANG [3], Wei ZHU [1,4]
[1]*Geotechnical Research Institute, Hohai University, Nanjing 210098, Jiansu, China;*
[2]*College of Civil Engineering, Hohai University, Nanjing 210098, Jiansu, China;*
[3]*Nanjing Yangtze River Tunnel Engineering Headquarters, China Railway Fourteenth Group Corporation, Nanjing 211800, Jiansu, China;*
[4]*College of Environmental Science and Technology, Hohai University, Nanjing 210098, Jiansu, China*

Abstract: During shield tunnel construction, backfill grouting is a necessary and key procedure, which can actively control stratum displacement and ground settlements by filling the shield tail void. Current studies, focus mainly on the numerical simulation of backfill grouting. For a reasonable prediction of shield tunneling-induced ground movements by numeric modeling, it is important to simulate the shield tail void, and the concept of gap parameter are introduced in many domestic and foreign research. However, with the liquid loss after backfill process being completed, the grout volumes shrinkage leads to the closure of shield tail void, and gap parameter should be reclaimed. But the deciding of parameters excessively relied on construction experience and statistical data, therefore it is still unclear about the deformation law of hardening grout under grouting pressure. Utilizing the element model devices of backfill grouting, the change laws of hard grout deformation are studied under different grout material mixtures, different grouting pressure in sandy soil. Then a mathematical model is proposed to simulate grout deformation at any time, which could make gap parameters more exactly when predicting ground movement.

Key words: backfill grouting; shield tail void; gap parameters; grout deformation model

1 引 言

近年来，盾构法以其独特的施工方法和经济、影响小的特点在地铁、铁路、公路、市政、水电等隧道工程中得到广泛应用。然而无论盾构法施工隧道技术已经发展得多么成熟，技术多么改进，都不可避免地产生对周围土体的扰动，从而引起不同程度的地层位移和地层变形[1]。盾构施工中引起地层位移的因素较多，其中最主要的是压力舱支护压力与地层土、水压力不平衡导致开挖面前方土体的移动，以及盾尾空隙的闭合引起周围地层移动。而壁后注浆正是对盾尾空隙进行注浆回填，主动控制围岩应力释放和地层位移的重要手段。

为了最大限度地降低施工对邻近建（构）筑物的影响，往往需要对地层变形进行及时准确的预测，以对受影响的建（构）筑物采取合理地保护措施。预测地层变形方法有许多，主要包括室内模型实验、现场监测和数值模拟。而目前采用数值模拟，为了提高计算精度，往往需要对盾尾空隙进行合理有效的模拟。对于盾尾空隙和壁后注浆作用的模拟，主要有以下四种模拟方法，应力加载模拟盾尾空隙闭合，位移加载模拟盾尾空隙闭合，应力释放系数的模拟方法以及间隙参数模拟盾尾空隙。

其中间隙参数是 Rowe 和 Lo（1983）[2]应用弹塑性有限单元程序分析研究地层损失（包含环状盾尾空隙）及壁后注浆等因素对隧道施工引起的地基沉降的影响时提出的概念，其大小决定于盾构机直径与衬砌直径的差以及施工的质量。

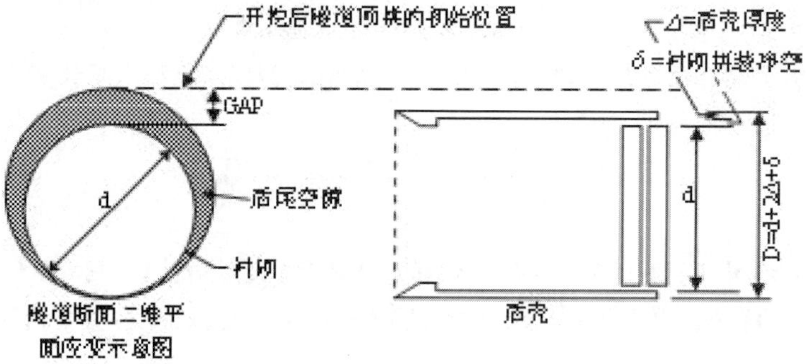

图 1 间隙参数的定义

Lee 等人（1992）[3] 进一步定义间隙参数 GAP（参见式 1），由于衬砌环片脱离盾壳后因重力将沉到盾构开挖面的最底端，因此盾尾空隙闭合量并非均匀分布。所采用的盾尾空隙分布如图 1 所示为如下弦月的分布，闭合量在顶拱为最大，在仰拱为零。

$$\mathrm{GAP} = G_p + u_{3D}^{*} + \omega \tag{1}$$

其中 $G_p = 2\Delta + \delta$ 代表盾构机与衬砌直径大小在几何上所形成的孔隙，包含两倍的盾壳厚度（Δ）及拼装衬砌所需的净空（δ），考虑壁后注浆的作用需要对 G_p 进行适当修正。u_{3D}^{*} 为开挖面的等效三维弹塑性变形量。ω 则考虑施工不当而超挖所造成的额外地层损失量。

若由公式(1)确定了间隙参数，便可以利用弹塑性有限单元程序分析盾尾空隙闭合引致的地表沉降。Rowe 和 Kack（1983）[4]、Ng（1986）[5]、Lee（1992a）[6] 等人及 Loganathan 和 Poulos（1998）[7]将此分析方法应用于各个隧道施工案例分析上，将预测的地基变形和实测数据比较，都能获得良好的结果。

在实际工程中，由于壁后注浆的作用，盾尾空隙首先被浆液充填满，然后注浆材料逐步趋硬，浆液中水分逐步渗出，浆体发生变形，因此隧道周围土体也随之发生位移，G_p 实际上是随浆体变形而变化的。在以上的研究中考虑壁后注浆的作用，对间隙参数的修正一般是通过人为经验来确定的，认为黏土中壁后注浆消除 G_p 达 60%～80%，在砂土中可以达到 70%～90%。因此，有必要进行实时测量浆体体积变化过程的试验，以更真实的反映注浆体注入盾尾空隙后的变化，对间隙参数进行合理修正，以更加准确的预测地表沉降。

韩月旺（2007）[8]通过室内单元模型试验对浆体在不同配方下的体积变形规律进行了探讨，认为注浆材料的配比对浆体的变形影响较大，浆液性能较优时其变形曲线较为平缓，在变形达到稳定时，可保证胶凝材料水化作用充分，提高浆体的最终强度。但是没有明确浆液配比的各个因素对变形的影响。本文在此基础上运用文献中的试验装置，研究了砂土地层下不同浆液配合比、不同注浆压力下浆体体积收缩变化规律，分析了配合比中单因素对浆体变形的影响，可以对浆液的配方调整提供一定参考，建立的浆体收缩计算模型可以确定间隙参数的取值。

2 浆体收缩试验及结果分析

2.1 试验装置

盾尾脱出管片后，在围岩土体与管片外壁之间形成一定厚度的环形盾尾空隙，对盾尾空隙进行壁后注浆回填后，在土体–浆体–管片共同作用下，浆体水分流失，浆体逐渐收缩硬化。

本试验的目的重在考察浆液硬化过程中浆体的变形，因而假定浆体压力在此过程中不发生变化，采用的试验装置如图 2 所示。圆柱筒内最下方是饱和土体，土体按所需模拟隧道周围地层进行配置，饱和土体上方是浆液，浆体压力的模拟依靠活塞上方的砝码堆载施加。因为浆液体积收缩主要是由于水分的渗出引起，因此，将渗出的水分用置于电子天平上的烧杯收集，将电子天平与计算机连接，就可实时读取渗出的水分量，即为体积收缩量，而浆液的体积收缩率定义为收缩量与浆液初始高度之比。

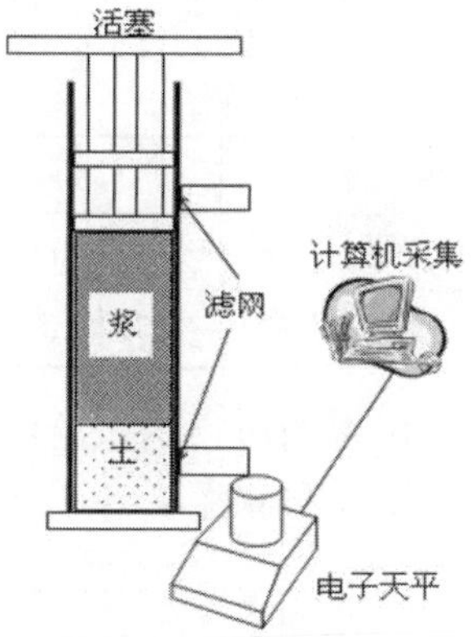

图 2 浆液体积收缩试验装置

2.2 不同壁后注浆液配合比下的浆体收缩试验

2.2.1 试验方案设计

根据对目前工程上常用注浆材料的分析，单液硬性浆的影响因子可分为 5 个，他们分别是：水胶比、胶砂比、膨水比、减水剂、粉灰比。其中，水胶比是水与胶结材料（水泥和粉煤灰）的质量比，膨水比为膨润土与水的含量之比，减水剂为减水剂含量所占胶凝材料的百分数，粉灰比为粉煤灰与水泥的含量之比。

根据统计，常用水胶比范围在 0.6～0.8 之间，胶砂比范围在 0.5～0.7 之间，膨水比为 0～0.2 之间，减水剂为胶凝材料的 0%～1%之间，粉灰比为 1.0～2.0 之间。为了分析各影响因子对浆液体积收缩的影响，利用上述试验装置，均在 0.18 MPa 的压力下选定一个基本配方，变化其中一个因子，并在其取值范围内发生变化，而其他因子保持不变进行试验。实验设计如表 1 所示。试验中所配砂土用于模拟南水北调穿黄隧道中细砂密实地层，具体材料参数见表 2，颗粒分析曲线如图 3 所示。

表 1 单液硬性浆试验设计表

因素	水胶比	胶砂比	膨水比	减水剂	粉灰比
基本配方	0.65	0.5	0.05	0.85%	2
试验水平	0.6	0.5	0	0.0%	1
	0.7	0.6	0.1	0.5%	1.5
	0.8	0.7	0.2	1.0%	2

表 2 砂土材料物理力学参数

土体	γ（kN/m^3）	c（kPa）	ϕ（°）	v	k（cm/s）
砂土	19.4	11.4	33.1	0.25	1.16e-3

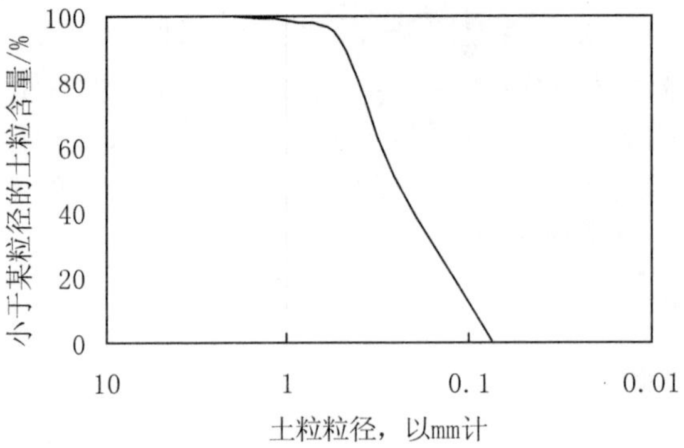

图 3　地层颗粒分析试验曲线

2.2.2　试验结果分析

根据前面阐述的试验设计方法，得出浆体收缩的试验成果见表 3。

表 3　单液硬性浆体积收缩试验结果

因　素	水胶比			胶砂比			膨水比			减水剂			粉灰比		
试验水平	0.6	0.7	0.8	0.5	0.6	0.7	0	0.1	0.2	0%	0.50%	1.00%	1	1.5	2
浆体收缩率（%）	8.5	10.0	11.6	9.5	9.2	9.0	10.8	8.0	4.6	7.9	8.2	10.0	8.2	9.0	9.4

利用上面所得的试验结果，进行注浆材料各影响因子与浆液体积收缩率的单因素影响分析，可得如下系列变化关系图。

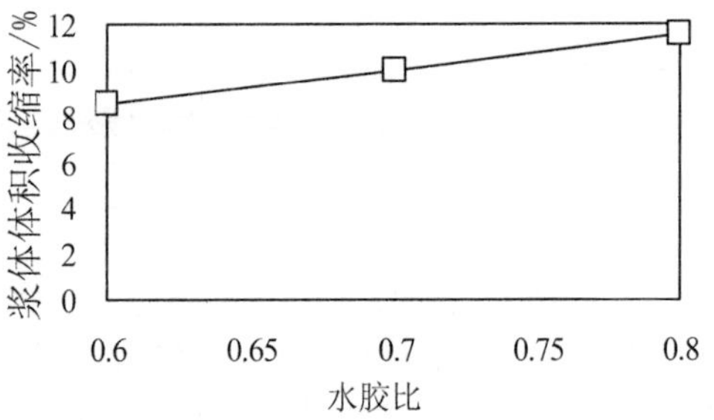

图 4　硬性浆体积收缩率与水胶比的关系

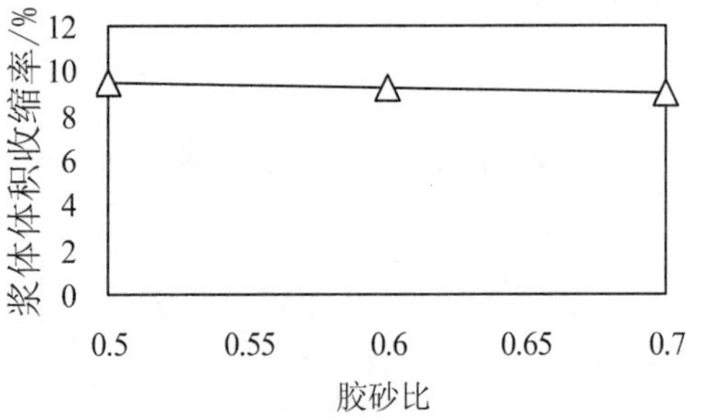

图 5　硬性浆体积收缩率与胶砂比的关系

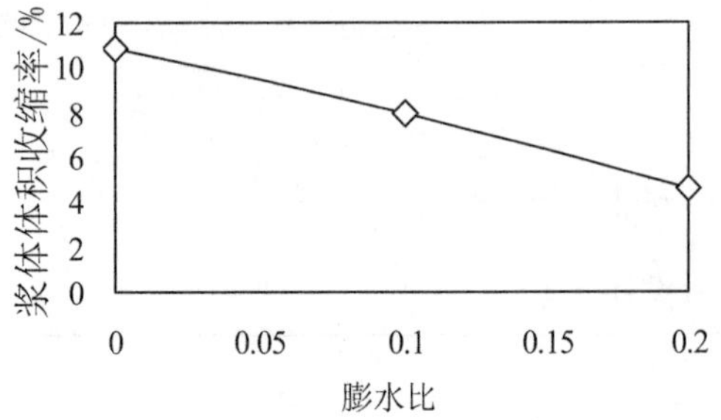

图 6　硬性浆体积收缩率与膨水比的关系

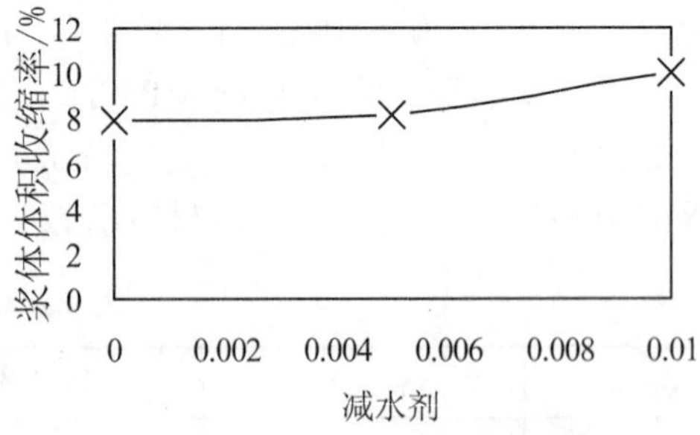

图 7　硬性浆体积收缩率与减水剂的关系

由图 4 至图 8 可知：体积收缩率受水胶比、膨水比、减水剂的影响显著，体积收缩率随着水胶比和减水剂增大而增大，在水胶比的变化范围内体积收缩率变化达到 4% 左右；但在减水剂含量较少时，这种变化并不明显，当减水剂含量超过胶凝材料的 0.5%时，这种变化趋势越来越大，体积收缩率变化接近 2%；而随膨水比的增大显著减少，在膨水比的变化范围内体积收缩率达到几乎 7%。

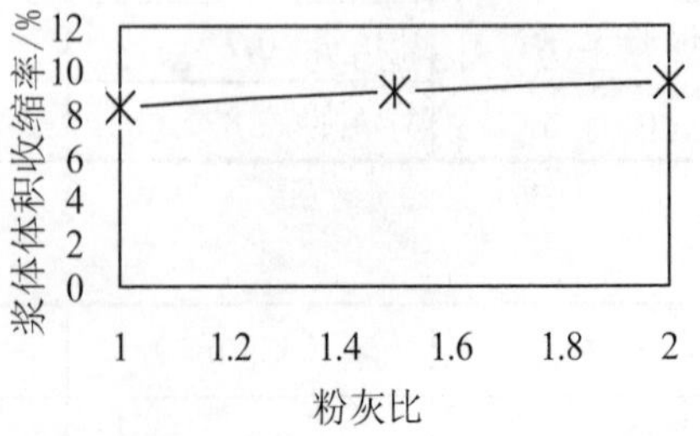

图 8　硬性浆体积收缩率与粉灰比的关系

浆体从凝胶开始到固结前，由于压力作用，致使浆液脱水压密，浆液中自由水分含量越高，浆体体积收缩率就会越大。用水量以及减水剂含量的增加，都会使得浆液中的自由水分增加，膨润土则相反使得浆液中的自由水分显著减少，粉煤灰的反应活性低于水泥，会使浆液中的结合水量减少，也会导致自由水分增加，从而随水胶比、减水剂含量、粉灰比的增大，体积收缩率随之增大，但随粉灰比变化的幅度不大。

2.3 不同注浆压力下的浆体收缩试验

2.3.1 试验方案设计

利用前述的试验装置，进行了不同注浆压力的浆体体积收缩试验。

注浆压力的施加通过在活塞上方堆放砝码实现，分别加载 60 kg，80 kg，100 kg，经换算即为 144.4 kPa，192.6 kPa，240.7 kPa。

注浆材料选用一种工程性能良好的单液硬性浆，其配比见表 4。试验中所配砂土同样用于模拟南水北调穿黄隧道中细砂密实地层，具体材料参数见表 2，颗粒分析曲线如图 3 所示。

表 4 试验所用浆液配比

因　素	水胶比	胶砂比	膨水比	减水剂	粉灰比
各组分配比	0.75	0.65	0.10	0.01	1.67

2.3.2 试验结果分析

图 9 为选定的硬性浆在模拟地层中不同注浆压力作用下的浆液体积收缩率变化曲线。从中可以看出：

（1）不同注浆压力下浆液体积随着时间的延长均逐渐收缩，而注浆压力越大时趋于稳定的时间越短。如注浆压力为 240.7 kPa 时，8 小时后基本上趋于稳定，而其他两组 8 小时后浆液体积还有增加趋势。

（2）浆液体积收缩速率呈非线性变化，初始时浆液压力越大的浆液收缩速率越快，随后收缩速率逐渐减慢并趋于一致，单位时间的收缩量均减小。

（3）在同一时刻，体积收缩率并不随注浆压力线性增长，增加相同的注浆压力（如 $t=2$ h），注浆压力较小时，浆液收缩量较大，注浆压力较大时，浆液收缩量较小；而当浆液收缩趋于稳定时（如 $t=8$ h），注浆压力较大时，随着注浆压力的增大浆液基本不再收缩。

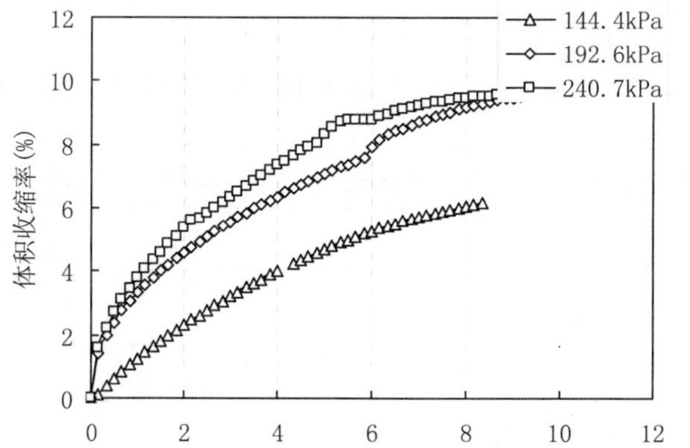

图 9 硬性浆在不同注浆压力作用下的体积收缩变化曲线

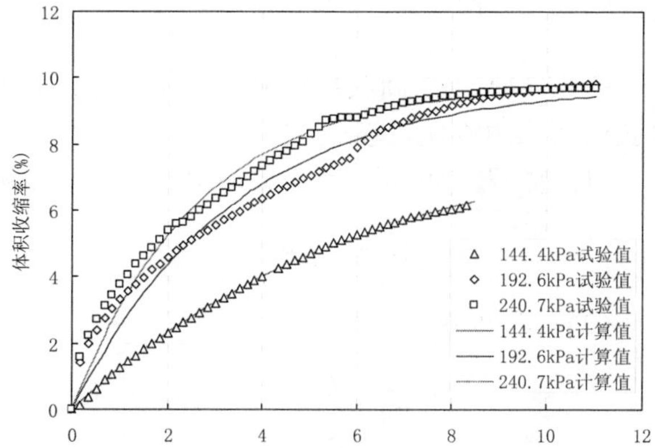

图 10 浆体体积收缩模型计算值与试验结果的比较

壁后注浆施工中，根据隧道所处地质条件以及注浆材料本身的性质，选择合适的注浆压力非常重要。

在盾构机完成壁后注浆的初始阶段，浆液在一定注浆压力作用下发生压密脱水。当注浆压力较小时，浆体体积收缩的速率相对较慢，趋向于稳定体积收缩率的时间亦越长，这样在达到最大体积收缩率以前就可获得较高的早期强度，有利于减少周围地层损失和地表沉降，但同时注浆压力过小也会导致注浆充填盾尾空隙不满而造成大的地层位移和地表沉降。

2.4 浆体体积收缩模型

浆体随时间的变形曲线较符合 Kelvin 流变模型，故利用该模型描述浆体的变形特性。

浆体变形可表示为

$$\varepsilon=\varepsilon_c\left(1-e^{-\frac{E}{K}\cdot t}\right) \tag{2}$$

$$E_c=\sigma/\varepsilon_c \tag{3}$$

式中：ε 为模型任意对应时刻的应变；ε_c 为最后稳定应变状态时的应变；E_c 为浆体达稳定状态时的割线模量，与浆体所受的应力水平有关；K 为浆体的粘滞系数；t 为时间。

具体参数的求解过程：

（1）首先，根据浆体体积收缩曲线得出稳态变形的应变值 ε_c；

（2）然后，根据浆体变形试验数据进行数据拟合得出 E_c 和粘滞系数 K 的取值，求解过程采用最小二乘法求解。

利用上述模型对图 9 中硬性浆在 144.4 kPa、192.6 kPa、240.7 kPa 压力作用下的试验数据进行拟合，即可得出 144.4 kPa 压力作用下的参数 $\varepsilon_c=8.35\%$，$E_c=1.7$ MPa，$K=10.5$ MPa · h；192.6 kPa 压力作用下的参数 $\varepsilon_c=9.81\%$，$E_c=2.0$ MPa，$K=6.7$ MPa · h；240.7 kPa 压力作用下的参数 $\varepsilon_c=9.82\%$，$E_c=2.5$ MPa，$K=6.5$ MPa · h，方程分别为：

$$\varepsilon=8.35\%\times(1-\mathrm{e}^{-0.163\,9t}) \tag{4}$$

$$\varepsilon=9.81\%\times(1-\mathrm{e}^{-0.297t}) \tag{5}$$

$$\varepsilon=9.82\%\times(1-\mathrm{e}^{-0.384t}) \tag{6}$$

用所建立上述三种压力作用下的浆体体积收缩模型对硬性浆的试验数据进行检验，图 10 中计算结果表明，上述模型计算得到的数据与试验得到的数据比较吻合，说明上述建立的浆体体积收缩模型是合理的。

3 浆体体积收缩对间隙参数的修正

公式（1）中，间隙参数由三部分构成，本试验可以通过测定浆体的变形来确定间隙参数，同时可以得到随时间的变化过程：

（1）对 G_p 的修正：考虑浆液对盾尾物理空隙的填充，当其收缩率为 ε 时，实际的物理空隙则为：

$$G_p^*=G_p\cdot\varepsilon \tag{7}$$

（2）u_{3D}^* 的确定：

$$u_{3D}^*=\frac{k_l}{2}\delta x \tag{8}$$

其中系数 k_l 代表支护压力与地层土、水压力不平衡导致开挖面前方土体发生的往压力舱的涌进位移受到盾构机盾尾的拖曳呈现出的不均匀分布，大约在 0.7～0.9，在工程应用上可保守地令 $k_l=1$，即开挖面涌进位移量为均匀大小的分布。在土压平衡式盾构中，正常掘进过程，一般认为 $\delta x=0$，即 u_{3D}^* 为零。

（3）考虑施工质量的 ω 参数的确定：

$$\omega=\min\left(0.6G_p^*,\frac{1}{3}u_i\right) \tag{9}$$

其中，u_i 为平面应变顶拱的弹塑性位移量，与土体的材料性质以及隧道稳定比有关。

其中稳定比 N 定义如下：

$$N = \frac{\sigma_{v0} - P_i}{c_u} \tag{10}$$

σ_{v0} 为隧道中心垂直覆土压力，c_u 为土体不排水剪切强度。

在弹塑性情况下（$N > 1$ 时），顶拱径向位移 u_i 可为：

$$\frac{u_i}{R} = 1 - \left\{1 + \frac{2(1+v_u)c_u}{E_u}\left[\exp\left(\frac{\text{N-1}}{2}\right)^2\right]\right\}^{-1/2} \tag{11}$$

其中 R 为盾壳半径，E_u 及 v_u 分别为土体不排水情况下的弹性模量和泊松比。

通过以上分析，结合公式（7）、公式（8）和公式（9），即可得到修正间隙参数 GAP 的表达式：

$$g = G_p\varepsilon + \frac{1}{2}k_l\delta_x + \min\left(0.6G_p\varepsilon, \frac{1}{3}u_i\right) \tag{12}$$

即建立了间隙参数与浆液体积收缩率 ε 的定量关系。由公式（12）获得的间隙参数，结合相应的数值解法便可更为合理地预测隧道周围的变形情况。

4 结 论

（1）本文通过室内模型实验对不同浆液配合比下浆液的体积收缩规律进行了研究，分析了配合比中单因素对浆体变形的影响，发现体积收缩率受水胶比、膨水比和减水剂的影响显著，体积收缩率随着水胶比、减水剂和粉灰比的增大而增大，而随膨水比的增大显著减少，对浆液的配方进行调整时需要注意对这些材料的配比进行合理控制，保证体积收缩率不致过大。

（2）通过对不同注浆压力下的体积收缩试验，发现注浆压力过大会造成更大的浆体脱水压密，引起地层更大的沉降。注浆压力较小时，浆体体积收缩的速率相对较慢，在达到最大体积收缩率以前就可获得较高的早期强度，有利于减少周围地层损失和地表沉降。

（3）提出了浆体随时间的变形曲线较符合 Kelvin 流变模型，并利用该模型描述了浆体的变形特性，建立了三种不同注浆压力下的浆体体积收缩模型，通过试验对比验证了该模型的合理性。

（4）考虑浆体的体积收缩的影响对间隙参数进行了修正，建立了间隙参数与浆液体积收缩率 ε 的定量关系，可以更为合理地对隧道周围的变形情况进行预测。

参考文献（References）：

[1] 张冬梅，黄宏伟，王箭明. 盾构推进引起地面沉降的黏弹性分析[J]. 岩土力学. 2001, 22（3）.

[2] Rowe, R.K. and Lo, K.Y.. A method of estimating surface settlement above tunnels constructed in soft ground [J]. Canadian Geotechnical Journal, 1983, 20: 11-22.

[3] Lee, K.M., Keery, R., and Lo, K.Y.. Subsidence owing to tunneling I estimating the gap parameter[J]. Canadian Geotechnical Journal, 1992, 29: 929-940.

[4] Rowe, R.K. and Kack, G.J.. A theoretical examination of the settlements induced by tunnelling: four case histories[J]. Canadian Geotechnical Journal, 1983, 20: 299-314.

[5] Ng, M.C., Lo, K.Y., and Rowe, R.K.. Analysis of field performance—the Thunder Bay tunnel[J]. Canadian Geotechnical Journal, 1986, 23: 30-50.

[6] Rowe, R.K. and Lee, K.M.. Subsidence owing to tunnelling. II. Evaluation of a prediction technique[J]. Canadian Geotechnical Journal, 1992, 29: 941-954.

[7] Loganathan, N., and Poulos, H.G . Analytical prediction for tunneling-induced ground movements in clay[J].

Journal of Geotechnical and Geoenvironmental Engineering, ASCE, 1998, 124(9): 846-856.
[8] 韩月旺，钟小春，虞兴福. 盾构壁后注浆体变形及压力消散特性试验研究[J].地下空间与工程学报. 2007, 3(6).

作者简介（Bio-data）:

左佳，男，1985 年 11 月出生，2008 年毕业于河海大学土木工程学院，现为河海大学硕士研究生，主要从事盾构隧道工程方面的研究工作。

Jia ZUO, male, born Nov.1985, graduated at College of Civil Engineering from Hohai University in 2008.Now he is pursuing a master's degree of Geotechnical Engineering ,majored in backfill grouting during shield tunneling engineering.

E-mail: zuoj408@163.com

北京砂卵石地层泥水盾构泥浆特性试验研究

于 娇[1] 袁大军[1] 叶旭洪[1] 黄清飞[1] 李建华[2]
[1]北京交通大学 土建学院隧道中心，北京 100044
[2]中铁隧道集团有限公司洛阳科学技术研究所，河南 洛阳 471009

【摘 要】 泥浆特性对于泥水盾构施工稳定开挖面有着十分重要的影响。结合北京铁路地下直径线泥水盾构隧道工程，进行了砂卵石地层泥浆特性试验研究，分组进行泥浆配比试验及渗透试验，得出了满足工程要求的泥浆参数及配比，并总结了泥浆性能影响因素及相关变化规律。研究结果表明：在膨润土百分含量相同的情况下，化学添加剂对于泥浆的黏度和状态有显著的影响；在泥膜的形成过程中，土体的孔隙水压、渗流量随着时间的变化呈现三个明显的阶段，分别为突变段、缓冲段和稳定段，论文最后通过土的有效应力原理对该现象进行了合理解释。
【关键词】 砂卵石地层；泥水盾构；泥浆特性；配比试验；渗透试验

TESTS STUDY ON MUD FLUID PROPERTIES OF SLURRY SHIELD IN BEIJING SANDY COBBLE STRATUM

Jiao YU[1], Dajun YUAN[1], Xuhong YE[1], Qingfei HUANG[1], Jianhua LI[2]
[1]Research Center of Tunneling and Underground Works, Beijing Jiaotong University, Beijing 100044, China;
[2]Luoyang Research Institute of Science and Technology, China Railway Tunnel Group Co.Ltd., Luoyan 471009, Henan, China

Abstract: The properties of mud fluid have important effect on the safety of excavation face in slurry shield construction. Based on the slurry shield tunnel construction of Beijing Underground Zhijing Line under the situation of sandy cobble stratum, some tests on mud fluid properties have been done. According to the formation sampling, mud proportioning tests and permeability tests were carried out. Then the parameters of mud fluid which met the needs of construction situation were got, and the influence factors of the mud qualities and related change laws were summarized. The results showed that in the same percentage content of bentonite, chemical additives had significant effect on the viscosity and state of mud. It was also found that in the formation process of filter-cake, the change of pore water pressure and seepage presented three stages with time, that sudden change stage, slow change stage and stable stage. At the end of this paper, the explanations of the change phenomenon of pore water pressure and seepage were given according to the effective stress principle of soil.
Key words: sandy cobble stratum; slurry shield; mud fluid properties; mud proportioning tests; mud permeability tests

1 引 言

泥水盾构工法以其施工质量好、效率高、技术先进、安全可靠等优点，近年来已经得到了广泛的应用。对于大直径泥水盾构施工，最主要的是保持开挖面的稳定，而泥浆的特性是影响开挖面稳定的重要因素之一，因此，对泥浆特性的研究就显得尤为重要。

北京地下铁路直径线全长 9.16 km，隧道长 7.23 km，其中 5 245 m 采用了 ϕ11.97 m 膨润土-气垫式泥水加压盾构机施工。盾构掘进区间 95%以上的地层以卵石土、圆砾土为主，另加中砂、粗砂、粉质黏土和粉土，并长距离穿越富水地带，地层的最大渗透系数为 1.74×10^{-3} m/s，最大水土压力为 0.3 MPa。粒径在 0.08 mm 以下的仅为 2.4%，大于 20 mm 的颗粒含量约占总重的 60%，最大粒径为 550 mm，亚圆形，中粗砂充填[1]。

本文结合北京地下直径线泥水盾构隧道工程，进行了砂卵石地层泥浆特性试验研究，主要包括泥浆配比试验和泥浆渗透试验两部分。通过对试验数据的分析，确定了优质泥浆的配比、总结了泥浆性能影响因素及相关变化规律，并可作为今后试验的重要参考。

2 泥浆配比试验

2.1 泥浆特性参数及试验步骤

2.1.1 泥浆特性参数

泥浆的作用是形成泥膜以稳定开挖面和运送排放掘削土砂，而泥浆的特性参数以及泥浆状态对其有着十分重要的影响。

泥浆特性参数主要包括物理及化学稳定性、黏性、比重、滤水量、渗透成膜状态等[2]。论文[3]指出，在泥浆黏度一定的条件下，比重越大，泥膜形成时泥浆的渗流量越小、形成泥膜的隔离效果越好；黏度最重要的作用是保证泥浆中细颗粒能够悬浮，利于地层中黏土的利用。因此，在砂卵石这种典型的力学不稳定地层中采用泥水盾构工法施工，应选用黏度和比重均较大、滤水量较小[4]的泥浆以高效地稳定开挖面。

结合工程条件，需要的泥浆特性参数如下：物理稳定性好、黏度（30～35 s）、送泥浆比重（1.05～1.07）、滤水量（＜20 ml）、细分散泥浆。通过对泥水系统参数的校核以及参考砂砾石地层泥水盾构掘进实例，证明了上述泥浆参数的选择是合理的[5]。

2.1.2 泥浆制备材料及试验步骤

泥浆制备材料：黏土：现场提供的烘干原土，粒径 $d<0.075$ mm，主要用于提高泥浆比重；膨润土：现场提供的两种改性钠膨润土，根据颜色不同分别定义为 BPRT 和 HPRT；化学添加剂：PAA（聚丙烯酰胺）、LV-CMC（羧甲基纤维素钠）、正电胶干粉[6]、xy-27 降黏剂以及中小分子聚合物等。

试验前先配制一定百分含量的膨润土纯浆，保证其充分水化后（＞24 h），再向其中加入化学添加剂以及黏土，通过常规的试验仪器（1006 型漏斗黏度计、NB-1 型泥浆比重计、精密电子秤、滤水量测定仪等）测定各项参数值并进行分析。

2.2 试验结果及分析

2.2.1 添加剂对泥浆特性的影响

通过大量的对比试验，得出了三种主要的化学添加剂与质量分数为 4%的 HPRT 泥浆黏度、比重间的关系，[0]见图 1 至图 3，由此可知添加剂对于泥浆的黏度和状态有明显的影响，而对比重则没有太大的影响。

经对比发现，三种主要的增黏剂各有优缺点：PAA 的增黏效果最强，正电胶干粉次之，LV-CMC 最弱；浆液中加入正电胶后，泥浆状态由细分散状态变为不分散状态[7]（类似于果冻状的胶态），因此从泥浆能够悬浮小粒径土砂以提高其比重的角度看，只选用正电胶干粉作为增黏剂不合适；当 PAA 百分含量超过 0.007 5%时，浆液开始絮凝，滤水量加大，不利于稳定开挖面；LV-CMC 虽然不会改变泥浆的细分散状态，泥浆的质量也不会随着时间的延长发生较大的变化，但由于其造价偏高，从经济性角度考虑，不建议只选用 LV-CMC 作为添加剂。通过上述对比，建议泥浆的添加剂采用组合的形式，如 PAA+正电胶，PAA+正电胶+LV-CMC，PAA +正电胶+xy-27 降黏剂等。

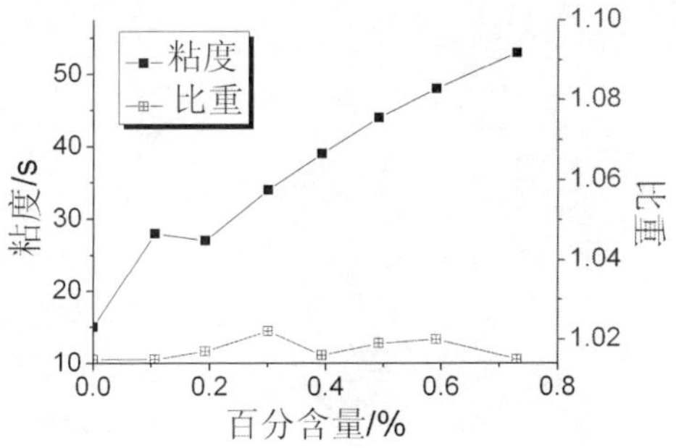

图 1　正电胶与泥浆黏度、比重的关系

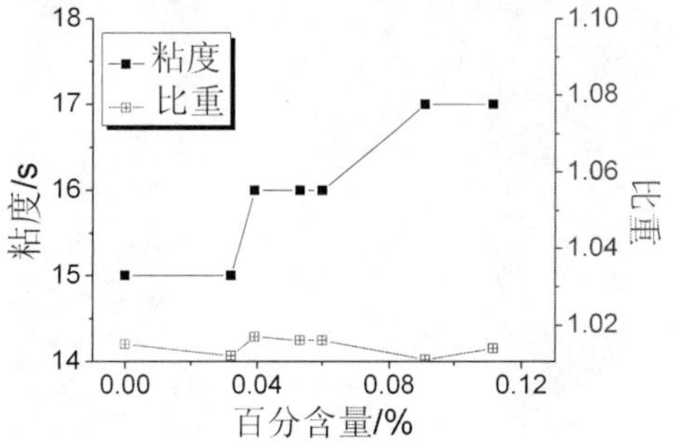

图 2　CMC 与泥浆黏度、比重的关系

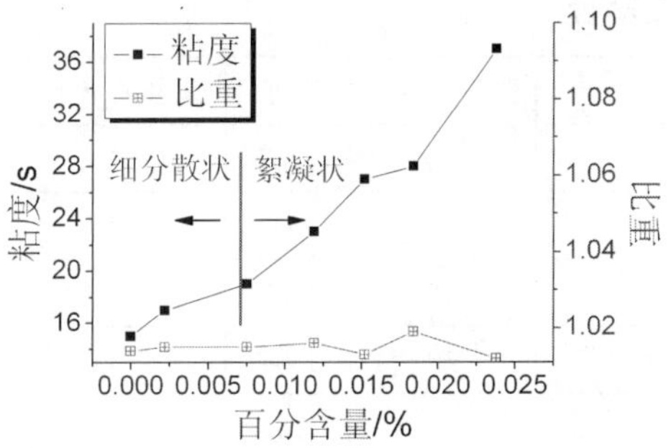

图 3　PAA 与泥浆黏度、比重的关系

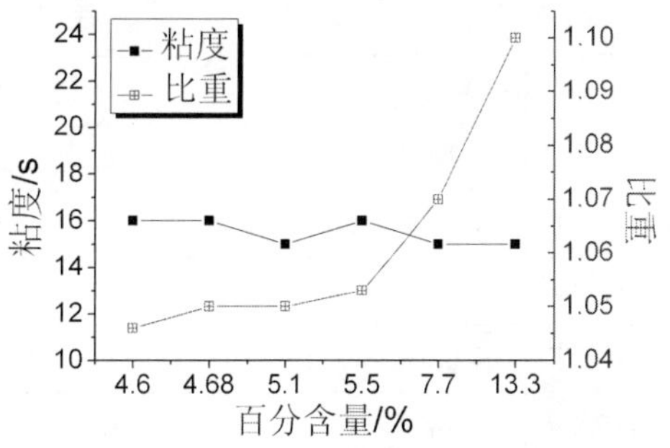

图 4　现场黏土与泥浆黏度、比重的关系

2.2.2　现场黏土对泥浆特性的影响

试验得出了现场黏土与泥浆黏度、比重关系线，见图 4，可知黏土仅对泥浆的比重有影响，对黏度无影响。

当分别使用 CMC、PAA 作为增黏剂时，黏土与泥浆黏度、比重的关系见表 1，发现黏土对泥浆的黏度几乎无影响，故可认为 CMC、PAA 与黏土之间无相互作用。

表 1　现场黏土与泥浆黏度、比重关系

CMC/ g	黏土	黏度（s）	PAA（g）	黏土	黏度（s）
0.2	5.10%	18	0.02	4.68%	17
	0	18		0	18
0.3	5.10%	18	0.02	7.90%	18
	0	17		0	19
0.5	5.10%	19	0.02	13.30%	18
	0	19		0	18
			0.05	7.70%	19
				0	20

注：表中黏土的百分数均表示质量分数。

2.2.3　泥浆状态对比

图 5、图 6 分别为两组不同状态的试验泥浆照片，前者为细分散泥浆，颗粒级配均匀，滤水量小；后者为粗分散泥浆，黏土粒子处于适度絮凝的粗分散状态、滤水量较大。由于北京地下直径线工程长距离穿越富水地层，应采用低渗透性泥浆以降低其滤水量，因此图 5 的泥浆在状态上是满足要求的。

2.2.4　优质泥浆

通过试验，对比优选了 6 组优质的泥浆，参数分别如表 2 所示。

图 5 细分散泥浆样本

图 6 粗分散泥浆样本

表 2 优质泥浆参数

泥浆编号	膨润土	黏土	化学添加剂	黏度（s）	比重	滤水量（ml）	状态
①	8%BPRT	2.34%	PAA + 正电胶 + xy-27	34	1.07	14	细分散
②	6%BPRT	4.65%	PAA + 正电胶	29	1.07	17	粗分散
③	6%BPRT	4.96%	PAA + LV-CMC	35	1.07	13	细分散
④	6%BPRT	4.63%	PAA + 正电胶 + LV-CMC + xy-27	28	1.07	14	细分散
⑤	4%HPRT	5.94%	PAA + 正电胶	30	1.08	18	细分散
⑥	4%HPRT	5.94%	PHP（阴离子聚丙烯酰胺，增粘剂）	25	1.08	19	细分散

注：表中膨润土、黏土的百分数均表示质量分数。

3 泥浆渗透试验

进行泥浆渗透试验是为了衡量泥浆对土层的渗透特性以及成膜效果，试验模拟的是静态泥膜形成，即拼装管片和停机的时候的状态。

试验主要分析在恒定压力下泥膜的形成过程、土体的渗流量和孔隙水压力随时间的变化关系、泥膜形成后土的渗透系数等。

3.1 试验仪器

试验采用独立设计的泥浆渗透仪器，制造原则是既能模拟实际情况，又便于操作，同时能够承受 30 m 水头的压力，如图 7、图 8 所示。试样圆筒的尺寸为 400 mm（内径）×500 mm（高度），从而可以模拟最大粒径为 80 mm 的砂卵石地层的泥浆渗透情况[8]。

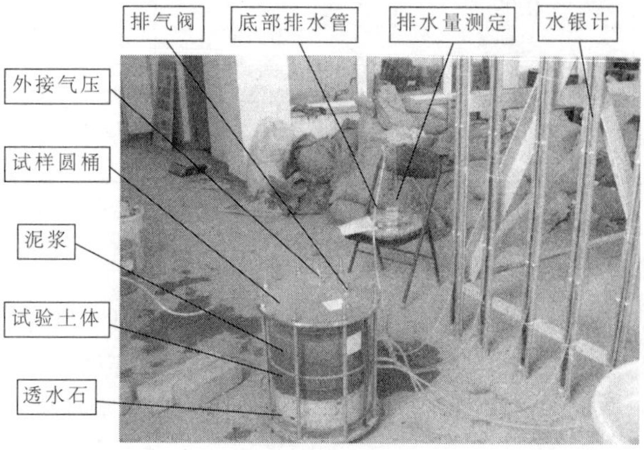

图 7 泥浆渗透试验仪

图 8 渗透仪孔隙水压测定管

3.2 土样制备及试验步骤

3.2.1 土样制备

试验的土样均为现场土体，根据土工试验规程中粗颗粒的试样制备要求以及地勘资料中的砂卵石土筛分试验，制备了渗透试验所需的砂卵石土样，参数如下表所示。在土层条件基本一致的前提下，比较并得出不同泥浆在土层中的渗透规律。

表 3 土层参数均值表

土层厚度/cm	总重（kg）	重度（t/m^3）	比重	含水率	孔隙比
17.83	40.76	2.11	2.72	1.20%	29.50%

3.2.2 试验步骤

试验前向试样圆桶中自下而上分别装入透水石、纱布、铁丝网后，将制备好的土样分成 5 等份，分份往试样筒中装，并进行振捣，最后通过底部排水孔自下而上对土体试样缓慢注水，使其饱和，静置 12 小时。

试验正式开始前，记录量筒内水的体积、底部排水孔高度以及 6 个孔隙水压管的液面高度，关闭排气阀并打开调压阀，调整气压至预定值，然后按一定的时间间隔记录排水量、孔隙水压管液面高度。

当单位时间内泥浆渗流量很小且稳定时，泥膜已形成。关闭调压阀，打开排气阀，松开连接螺栓，将上部未渗入土体的泥浆移去，观测泥膜厚度及泥膜质量，估算泥膜形成后土体的渗透系数。

3.3 试验结果及分析

3.3.1 ⑤号泥浆渗透试验

由于每组泥浆的试验步骤、测量数据均相同，故选取⑤号泥浆的渗透试验作为案例进行详细介绍。

（1）试验数据

0.05 MPa 下孔隙水压、渗流量与时间的变化关系以及单位时间内渗流量变化曲线分别如下图所示。

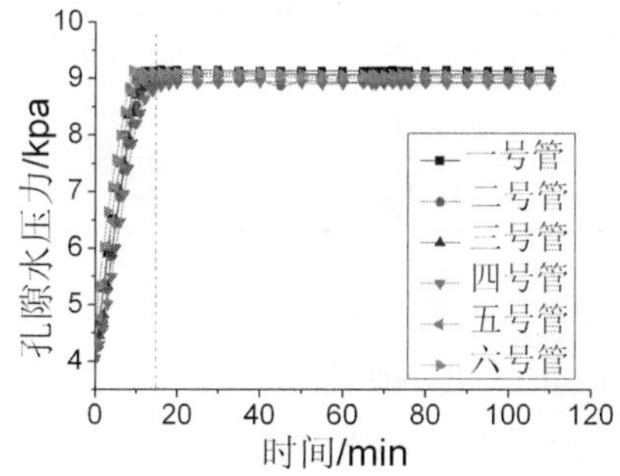

图 9 孔隙水压-时间关系曲线

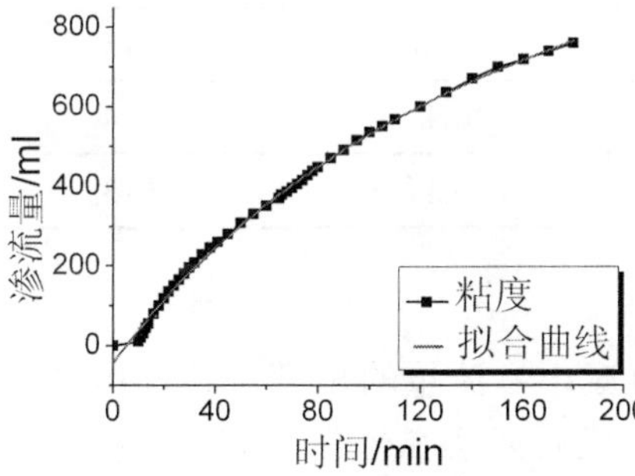

图 10 渗流量-时间关系曲线

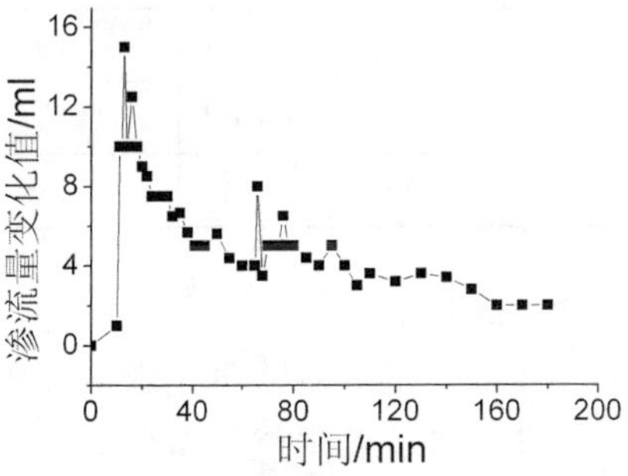

图 11 单位时间内渗流量变化曲线

通过孔隙水压力曲线和渗流量变化曲线可以看出泥膜约在 16 min 形成，而且单位时间内的渗流量较小。说明泥水中细颗粒的分散状态较好，能够充分的吸附聚集在掘削面表层，在短时间内有效地形成泥膜，减小了渗流量。

（2）渗流曲线的拟合

采用公式（1）[9]进行渗流曲线的拟合，而且各参数也有较为明确的物理意义。

$$y = A_1 e^{-x/t_1} + A_2 e^{-x/t_2} + y_0 \tag{1}$$

当 $x = 0$ 时，$y \approx 0$；y_0 是泥浆渗透的极限流量。

⑤号渗流曲线拟合公式为：

$$y = -1\,46.89 \times e^{-x/53.28} - 1\,049.43 \times e^{-x/178.85} + 1\,152.91 \tag{2}$$

极限渗流量为 1 152.91 ml。

（4）泥膜形成后土的渗透系数

由于试样圆筒直径较大，且渗流量较小，因此可以将此渗透试验作为常水头试验来处理，根据土工试验规范，用公式（3）来估算成膜后土体的渗透系数：

$$k = \frac{Ql}{Aht} \tag{3}$$

式中 k——土体的渗透系数；

Q——形成泥膜后渗透试验的渗透量；

l——土层的厚度；

A——土层的截面积（与土样的截面积一致）；

t——渗透时间；

h——水头损失。

试验发现，泥水渗透距离一般在 1.5～3 cm，均没有超过 3 号孔隙水压管位置，因此在计算泥膜形成后土体的渗透系数时，只计算了 1～2 和 1～3 管之间土的渗透系数，取平均值。

经计算，⑤号泥浆在泥膜形成后的渗透系数为 2.58×10^{-9}m/s，与原土样相比，渗透系数有了明显的降低。

3.3.2 其他泥浆试验结果

其他泥浆试验结果如表 4 所示，从极限渗流量和快速形成泥膜两个方面综合考虑，较好的泥浆为③号泥浆和⑤号泥浆。

表 4 泥浆渗透试验结果

泥浆号	黏度（s）	比重	滤水量（ml）	泥浆压力（MPa）	成膜时间（min）	极限渗流量（ml）	渗透系数（m/s）
②	35	1.07	13	0.05	10	4 482.64	—
⑤	30	1.08	18	0.05	16	1 152.91	2.58×10^{-9}
⑥	25	1.08	19	0.05	15	1 976.09	1.02×10^{-9}
③	35	1.07	13	0.1	14	1 420.24	—
④	28	1.07	13	0.1	13	3 301.48	—

3.3.3 试验小结

（1）从泥浆能够迅速形成泥膜以减小渗流量的角度看，选用黏度和比重均大的泥浆效果好。

（2）通过多组渗透试验，总结了优质泥浆在恒压状态下孔隙水压力变化曲线形状以及单位时间内渗流量变化曲线形状，分别如下图所示。

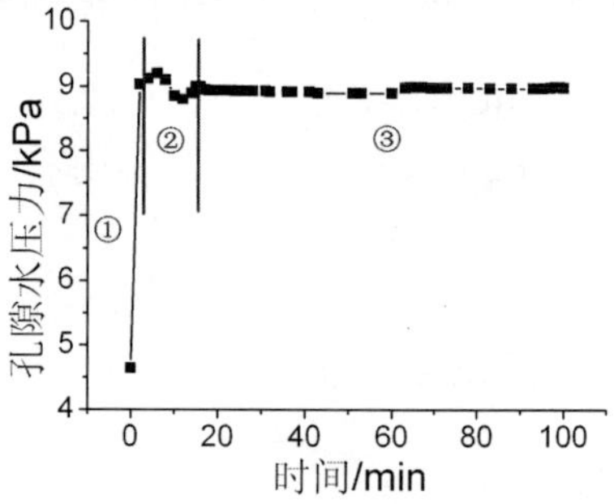

图 12 恒压状态下孔隙水压力变化曲线

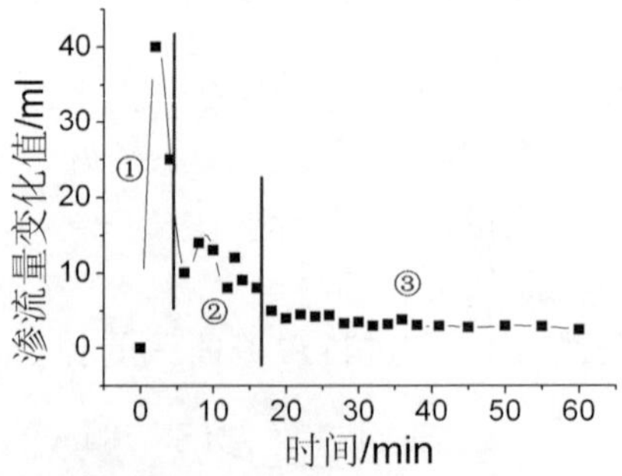

图 13 恒压状态下单位时间内渗流量变化曲线

根据土的有效应力原理和太沙基一维固结理论[10]解释如下：

① 阶段——突变段：在外界压力施加的瞬时，土体原有的平衡状态被打破，依据土的有效应力原理，

压力由孔隙水承担，故孔隙水压值会有明显的上升，同时单位时间内的渗流量会瞬时变大。

② 阶段——缓冲段：随着时间的变化，孔隙水继续渗透流失，部分压力由土的有效应力承担，故孔隙水压会降低、渗流量会减少。但同时泥浆中的水和细颗粒向土体中渗透，逐渐形成泥膜，将土体与外界压力隔离，使得孔隙水压逐渐稳定而不会有明显的回落，单位时间内的渗流量开始减小并会有一定波动，但趋势是逐渐减小。

③ 阶段——稳定段：泥膜形成，孔隙水压不变，单位时间内的渗流量趋于定值。

4 结 论

（1）自行设计了一套能够模拟泥浆在地层中渗透的试验仪器，可以模拟最大粒径为 80 mm 的砂卵石地层泥浆的渗透。

（2）对于北京这种粗颗粒居多的砂卵石地层，泥浆特性参数为：比重 1.05～1.07，黏度 30～35 s，滤水量＜20 ml。

（3）在膨润土百分含量相同的情况下，化学添加剂只对泥浆的黏度和状态有显著的影响；通过对泥浆状态、黏度及稳定性的分析，建议添加剂采用组合的形式。

（4）在泥膜的形成过程中，土体的孔隙水压、单位时间内的渗流量随着时间的变化呈现三个明显的阶段，分别为突变段、缓冲段和稳定段。

（5）从极限渗流量和快速形成泥膜两方面考虑，较好的泥浆为③号泥浆和⑤号泥浆。

参考文献（References）：

[1] 叶慷慨．北京铁路直径线大断面地下隧道盾构机选型研究[J]．隧道建设，2006（6）：20-23.

[2] 张凤祥，朱合华．盾构隧道[M]．北京：人民交通出版社，2004.1.

[3] 袁大军，李兴高，叶旭洪，等．砂卵石地层泥水盾构泥浆渗透试验分析[J]．都市快轨交通，2009，22（3）：32-35.

[4] 韩晓瑞，朱伟，刘泉维，等．泥浆性质对泥水盾构开挖面泥膜形成质量影响[J]．岩土力学，2008，29（Supp.）：288-292.

[5] 袁大军，李兴高，李建华，等．北京地下直径线泥水盾构泥浆特性参数确定[J]．建筑技术，2009，40（3）：279-282.

[6] 张春光，徐同台．正电胶钻井液[M]．北京：石油工业出版社，2000.2.

[7] 韦良文等．用于泥水盾构隧道的聚合物正电胶泥浆研究[J]．建筑材料学报，2007，10（1）：66-70.

[8] 叶旭洪．砂卵石地层泥水盾构泥浆特性及对开挖面稳定性影响研究（硕士学位论文）[M]．北京交通大学，2008.

[9] 杨扶银．粗粒土泥浆渗透特性及泥皮抗渗性研究（硕士学位论文）[M]．西安理工大学，2007.

[10] 赵成刚，白冰等．土力学原理[M]．北京：清华大学出版社，北京交通大学出版社，2006.2.

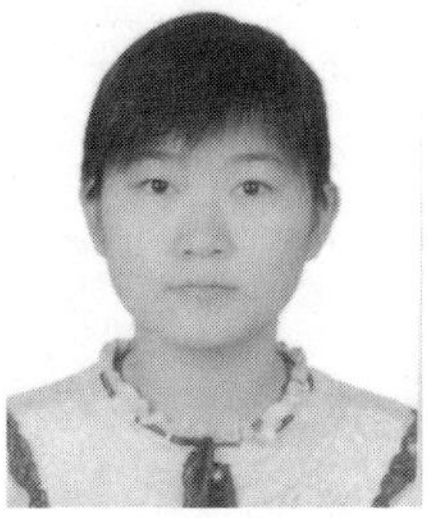

作者简介（Bio-data）：

于娇，女，1986 年 5 月生，于 2008 年 9 月入北京交通大学土木建筑工程学院隧道工程专业攻读硕士学位，研究方向为盾构隧道。

Jiao YU, female, born in May, 1986, now is a graduate student majoring in shield tunnel in Beijing Jiaotong University.

E-mail: is jerryyujiao@163.com

通信用シールドとう道の補修に関する実験的な研究

官　林星[1]　入江　浩志[2]　島田　徹[2]　小泉　淳[1]

[1]早稲田大学　理工学術院　社会環境工学科

(〒169-8555 東京都新宿区大久保 3-4-1)

[2]日本電信電話株式会社アクセスサービスシステム研究所

(〒305-0805 茨城県つくば市花畑 1-7-1)

既設の通信用シールドとう道において，二次覆工である無筋コンクリートに未充填の箇所が確認されており，状況によっては，一次覆工の漏水によって二次覆工に水圧がかかり，二次覆工の崩落の危険性が懸念される．異常出水による事故などを未然に防止するために，二次覆工のクラウン部に空洞がある場合の二次覆工の健全度を評価することは，重要な事項である．

本研究は実際のとう道模型を用いて，一次覆工と二次覆工のクラウン部の空洞に水圧をかける実験を行い，その結果と模型実験の数値解析結果とを比較して，二次覆工の挙動と解析モデルの合理性について検討を行ったものである．

キーワード：シールドトンネル；セグメント；二次覆工；数値解析；維持管理

EXPERIMENTAL TEST ON COMMUNICATION CABLE TUNNEL CONSTRUCTED BY SHIELD TUNNELING METHOD FOR MAINTENANCE

Linxing GUAN[1], Hiroshi IRIE[2], Toru SHMADA[2], Atsushi KOIZUMI[1]

[1]*Department of Civil and Environment Engineering, Faculty of Science and Engineering, Waseda University*

(3-4-1 Ohkubo, Shinjuku-ku, Tokyo 169-8555, Japan);

[2]*Access Network Service Systems Laboratories, Nippon Telegraph and Telephone Corporation*

(1-7-1 Hanabatake, Tsukuba-city, Ibaraki 305-805, Japan)

Abstract: Cavities between the primary lining and secondary lining have been conformed in the communication cable shield tunnels in operation. The secondary lining of concrete is loaded by water pressure due to the leakage from the primary lining. The managers of tunnels are concerned with the collapse probability of the secondary lining. It is essential to evaluate the health of secondary lining with cavities, for the prevention of accident due to the leakage.

In this paper, the two prototype cable tunnel models were used and the cavities between the secondary lining and the first lining were man-made. The models were tested by loading the water pressure in the cavities. The strains of central section of secondary lining are recorded. The models are analyzed by using three dimensional finite element method and the results are compared with the experimental result. The behavior of secondary lining and the rationality of numerical model are discussed.

Key words: shield tunnel; segment; secondary lining; numerical analysis; maintenance

1 はじめに

通信用のケーブルを収容するシールドトンネルは，直径 2～6 m 程度であり，光ケーブルへの移動にともない小口径化する傾向にあった．そのため，一次覆工には鋼製セグメントが用いられ，その内側に無筋コンクリートの二次覆工を打設して構築されたトンネルが多い．図-1 はそのような通信シールドトンネルの断面を示したものである．二次覆工は蛇行修正や防水・防食などの目的で施工されており，外水圧および型枠の脱型時の二次覆工自身の自重に対して設計した例があるが，二次覆工に発生する断面力や応力度の計算を行わない場合がほとんどである[1,2]．シールド工法で造られた通信用とう道の中には建設後 40 年以上も経過したものもあり，それらの健全性を適切に評価することは，それらを維持・管理していく上で重要な課題である．

最近の点検検査によると，トンネルのクラウン部分に二次覆工コンクリートが十分に充填されていないものが多く確認されている．このようなケースでは，空洞部分に地下水が充満して二次覆工の無筋コンクリートには水圧が作用しているものと思われる．現況を適正に評価し，必要に応じて補修したり補強したりして，とう道の安全性を確保しなければならない．図-2 は実際の空洞状況を示したものである．

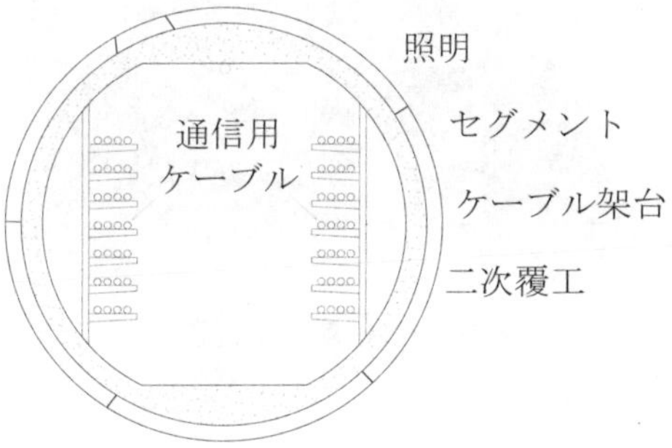

図-1 通信トンネル断面

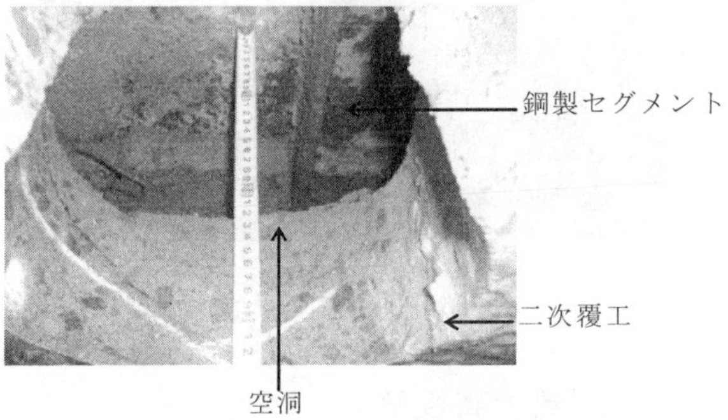

図-2 通信用トンネルの空洞

本論文は，まず，二次覆工部に空洞を作ったとう道模型を用いて，この空洞部に水圧を作用させる実験を行い，作用水圧とひずみ値を測定し，つぎに，三次元 FEM による解析を実施し，それらの結果を検討するとともに，二次覆工の安全性を評価する方法について提言を行うものである．

2 実験の概要

2.1 実験モデル

模型実験は，一次覆工である鋼製セグメントの内側に無筋コンクリートの二次覆工を打設して，図-3 に示すように人為的に空洞を作り，この空洞に水圧を作用させて，二次覆工コンクリートに発生するひずみを計測するものである．鋼製セグメントは 2 つ用いて半円型に組まれている．図-4 は実験に用いた鋼製セグメントを示したもので，スキンプレート厚さは 3 mm，主桁は 125 mm×14 mm，セグメント幅は 1 000 mm である．表-1 は人為的に造った空洞の大きさと二次覆工の寸法とを示したものである．供試体はその両側を水が漏れないように鋼板で押さえて，高圧洗浄機で水圧を加圧した．図-5 は供試体の状況を，また，図-6 は実験装置を組み立てた状況を示したものである．

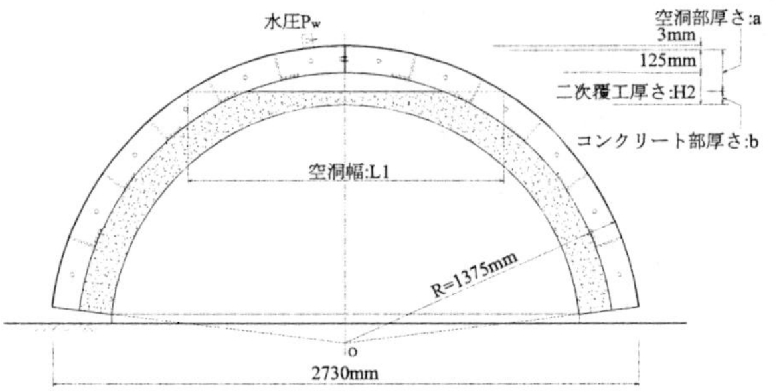

図-3　実験供試体の概要

図-4　鋼製セグメント

表-1　空洞の大きさと二次覆工の寸法

供試体 ID	空洞厚さ *a*（mm）	ｺﾝｸﾘｰﾄ厚さ *b*（mm）	二次覆工厚さ H2（mm）	空洞長さ L1（mm）
No.1	179	93	147	1 355
No.2	340	100	150	1 376

図-5　供試体の状況

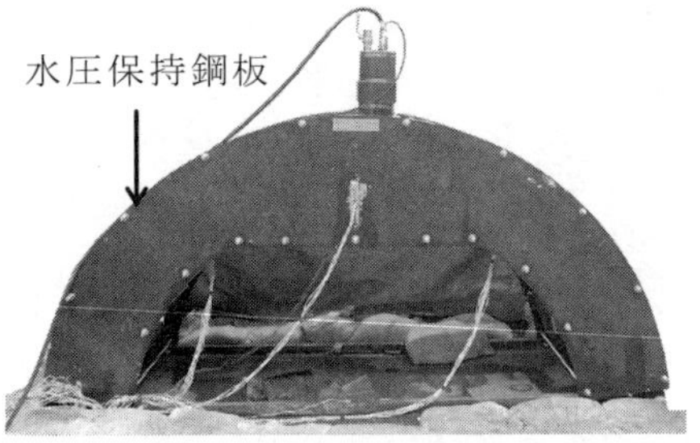

図-6 実験の状況

2.2　使用材料の特性値

二次覆工コンクリートには早強ポルトランドセメントを用いた．最大スランプは 12 cm，最大粗骨材寸法は 20 mm である．コンクリートの圧縮強度は 34.0 kN/mm^2 で，引張強度は 3.08 kN/mm^2 であり，コンクリートのヤング係数は 27.3 kN/mm^2 であった．これらはテストピースの実験結果か求めたものである．また，鋼製セグメントの鋼材のヤング係数は 210 kN/mm^2 とした．

2.3　計測方法と計測位置

ひずみゲージは，図-7 に示すように，二次覆工の幅中央断面の内面側に，円周方向に貼付した．また，断面に発生する軸圧縮力を計測する目的で，供試体下部の拡がり防止用の等辺山形鋼にもひずみゲージを貼付してある．

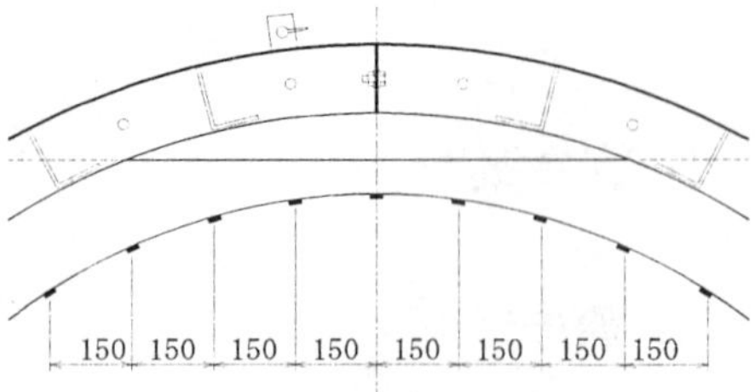

図-7　二次覆工のひずみ測定位置
(中央断面)

3　解析の概要

3.1　解析モデルの概要

有限要素法による解析では，供試体の形状，セグメントの組立ておよび載荷状況を再現できるように可能な限り忠実にモデル化を行った．二次覆工はソリッド要素で，一次覆工のスキンプレートと主桁はシェル要素で，それぞれ評価した[3]．図-8 は解析モデルを示したものである．一次覆工と二次覆工の間は，連結ばねで評価した[4,5]．図-9は一次覆工と二次覆工間の連結ばねを示した図である．この連結ばねのばね定数は，セグメントと二次覆工が離れるときにはゼロにし，セグメントと二次覆工が近づくときには無限大にした．

図-8 解析モデル

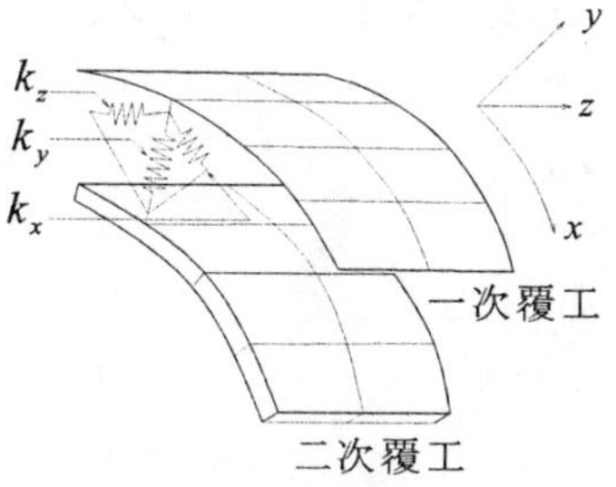

図-9 一次覆工と二次覆工間のばね

3.2 境界条件

供試体下部の拡がり防止用の4本の等辺山形鋼は，ばねにモデル化した．そのばね定数は式(1)で計算した．結果として，このばね定数kは192.08 kN/mmとなった．

$$k_b = \frac{4A_sE_s}{l} \tag{1}$$

ここに，k_b：ばね定数，A_s：1本あたりの等辺山形鋼の断面積，E_s：鋼材の弾性係数，l：鋼材の長さである．

ひずみゲージは円周方向のひずみを測定しているので，有限要素法による計算結果は式(2)によりその方向のひずみに変換した．図-11はそのひずみの計算方法を示したものである．

$$\varepsilon_\alpha = \frac{1}{E}(\sigma_x \cos^2\alpha + \sigma_y \sin^2\alpha - 2\tau_{xy}\cos\alpha\sin\alpha) \tag{2}$$

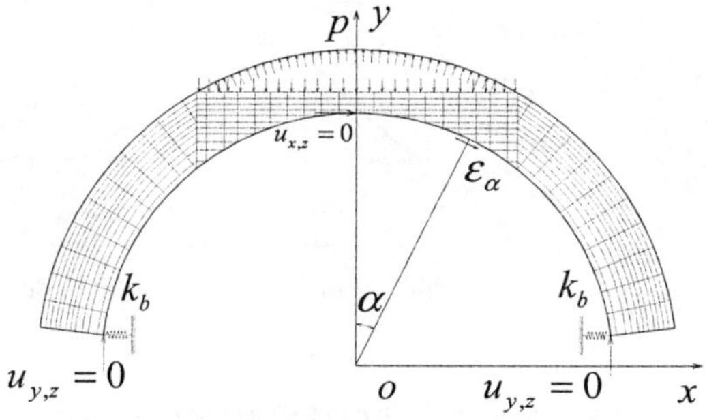

図-10 境界条件

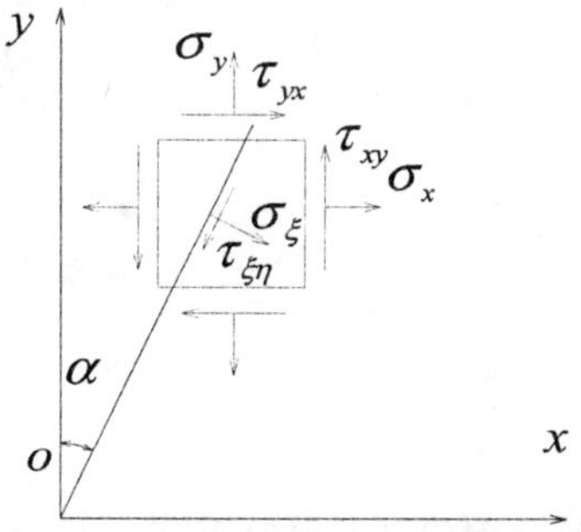

図-11 円周方向のひずみ計算方法

4 実験結果と解析結果との比較および考察

4.1 荷重とひずみの関係

図-12と図-13はそれぞれ，供試体No.1,No.2の荷重とひずみとの関係の実験値を示したものである．図中の凡例はクラウンからの距離を表す．ひずみの実験値は測定位置の対称性を考えて平均してある．これらの図を見ると，いずれの供試体も最大ひずみはクラウンに発生し，クラウン部を離れると圧縮ひずみが発生している．クラウンのひずみは非線性を示した．供試体No.1, No.2の同じ荷重時のひずみを比較すると，空洞部の二次覆工コンクリートが薄い供試体No.2の方が大きいひずみを示した．なお，供試体は水圧保持鋼板で覆われているため，破壊まで水圧をあげることはできなかった．

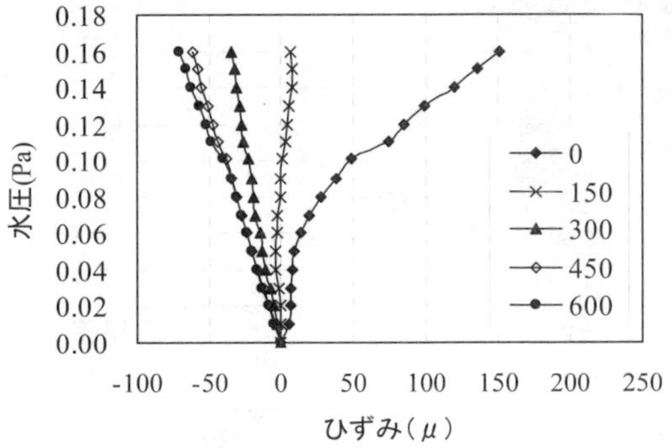

図-12　供試体 No.1 クラウン部のひび分布

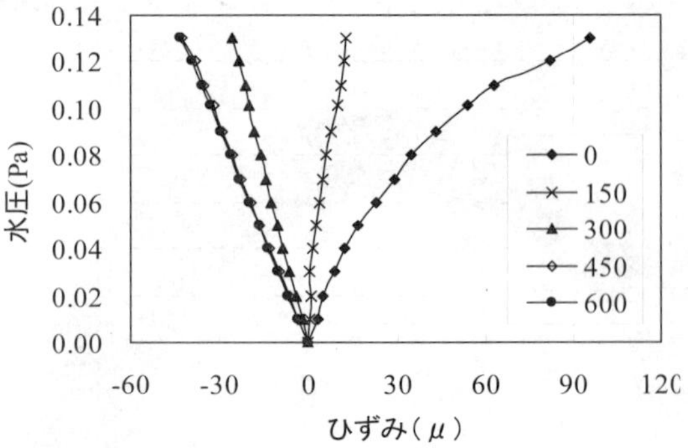

図-13　供試体 No.2 クラウン部のひび分布

4.2　クラウン部のひずみ分布

図-14 と図-15 はそれぞれ供試体 No.1 の水圧が 0.05 MPa 時および 0.1 MPa 時のクラウンのひずみ分布をしめしたものである．図-16 と図-17 は供試体 No.2 の同様なひずみ分布である．これらは対称性を考えて平均し，片側のみを示した．また，これらの図中には解析結果も示してある．解析結果と実験結果はともに，引張ひずみはクラウン部近傍で発生し，クラウン部を離れると圧縮ひずみは発生することがわかる．解析結果によれば，中心部から 200 mm のところで，ひずみは引張から圧縮に変化する．実験結果では，中心部から 450 mm，600 mm の位置のひずみはほぼ同じ値となっている．全体的にみると，解析結果と実験結果とはその傾向が一致していることがわかる．水圧が 0.1 MPa のとき，供試体 No.1 と No.2 の最大引張ひずみの実験結果と解析結果との差はそれぞれ，4%と 21%であった．

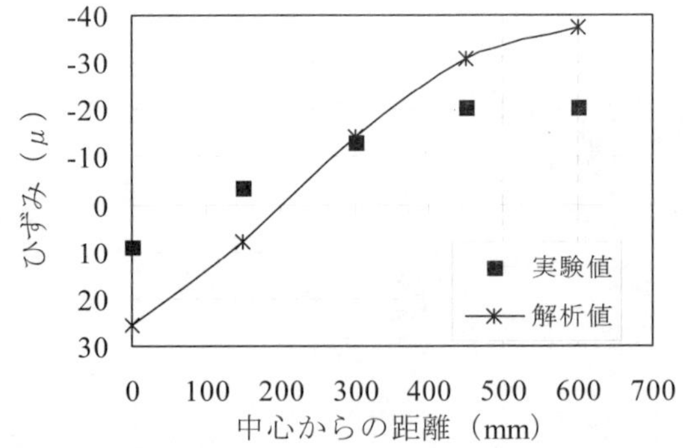

図-14　クラウン部のひずみ分布(No.1 P＝0.05 MPa)

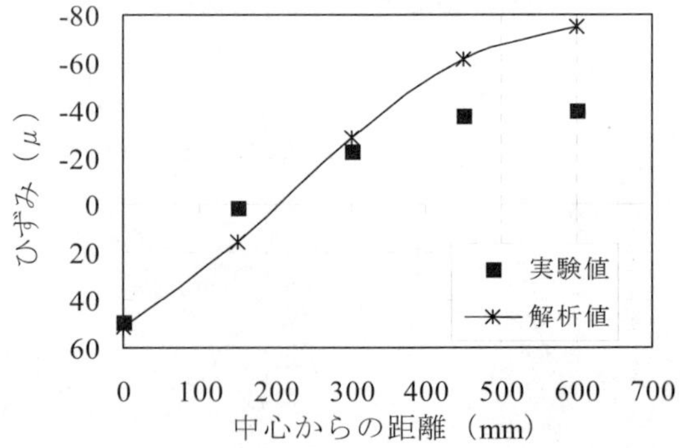

図-15　クラウン部のひずみ分布(No.1 P＝0.1 MPa)

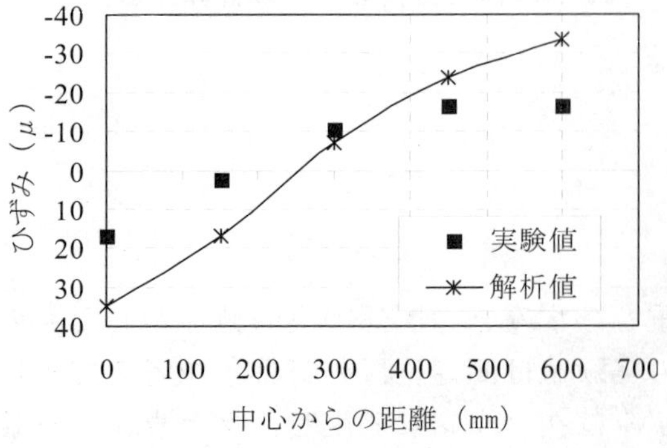

図-16　ラウン部のひずみ分布(No.2 P＝0.05 MPa)

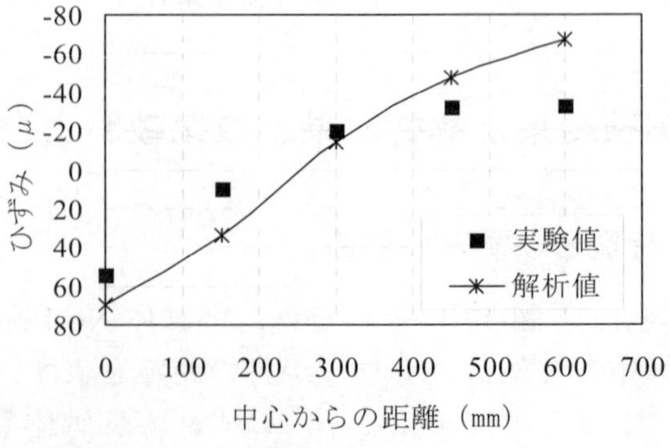

図-17　ラウン部のひずみ分布(No.2 P＝0.1 MPa)

5 結　論

以上の検討の結果から得られた結論は以下のとおりである.

(1) 二次覆工のひずみは，クラウンで最大の引張ひずみが発生し，クラウンから離れると圧縮ひずみに変わる.

(2) クラウンの中心部から 200 mm のところで，下縁のひずみが引張から圧縮に変化していることか，空洞部の端部には負の曲げモーメントが発生しているものと推定される.

(3) 一次覆工をシェルで，二次覆工をソリッドで，また，両覆工間の力のやりとりを連結ばねで評価するのは合理的と思われる.

本実験では荷重として，水を直接用いたため漏水が生じて大きな水圧を載荷することができなかった．また，供試体の両側からの水圧保持鋼板が実験結果に影響を与えたことも考えられる．基本的な性状は把握できたと思われるので，今後はゴムチューブを用いて水圧を作用させる実験を検討している.

参考文献（Refernces）:

[1] 土木学会：トンネル標準示方書・シールド工法，pp. 74~82, 2006.

[2] International Tunnelling Association (ITA), (2000). “Guidelines for the design of shield tunnel lining.” Tunnelling and Underground Space Technology, 15, 541-542.

[3] MSC.Marc theory and user information manual, version 2005. (2005). MSC.Software corporation.

[4] 佐久間彰三，石田智明，上原精治，小泉　淳：一次覆工・二次覆工間のせん断特性を考慮したシールドトンネルの軸剛性評価．土木学会論文集，Vol.424, III-14,pp. 251~259, 1990.

[5] 高松伸行，村上博智，小泉淳：二次覆工されたシールドトンネル軸方向曲げ特性のモデル化について．土木学会論文集，Vol.481, III-25,pp. 97~106, 1993.

著者紹介（Bio-data）:

官　林星

早稲田大学理工学術院　社会環境工学科　助手

研究内容：

シールド工法によって構築された通信とう道の補強・補修に関する研究

平板形鉄筋コンクリートセグメントのセグメント幅に関する研究

Linxing GUAN, Research Associate, Dept. of Civil and Environmental Engineering, Faculty of Sciennce and Engineering, Waseda University. Study on Communication Cable Tunnel Constructed by Shield Tunneling Method for Maintenance, the behavior of flat-type reinforced concrete segment with widened width.

E-mail: guanlinxing@aoni.waseda.jp

補剛リブを設けた大深度地下水道管の外水圧による座屈挙動に関する実験的研究

天野　裕基　王　剣宏　小泉　淳

早稲田大学　理工学術院　社会環境工学科，東京　169-8555

日本の大都市圏では，その中浅深度地下の利用がすでに飽和状態にある．限りある地下のスペースをより有効的に利用

するための一つの手段として，地下 40 m 以深の大深度地下に水道管網のようなインフラ施設の建設することが有効である．大深度地下では，中浅深度の地下に比べ水圧が卓越するため，トンネルの長期の供用により発生する漏水により，水道管には大きな外水圧が作用する可能性がある．そのため，水道管の外水圧による座屈を防ぎ，安定的な水供給を維持するために，その座屈挙動を明らかにする必要がある．本研究は補剛リブを設けた鋼管の外水圧による座屈実験を行い，すでに提案されている二段階座屈計算法の妥当性について検討したものである．

キーワード：大深度地下；水道管；外水圧；座屈；二段階座屈計算法

EXPERIMENTAL STUDY ON BUCKLING OF STIFFED STEEL PIPE UNDER EXTERNAL WATER PRESSURE FOR DEEP WATER SUPPLY TUNNEL

Yuki AMANO，Jianhong WANG，Atsush KOIZUMI

Department of Civil and Environmental Engineering, Faculty of Science and Engineering, Waseda University, Tokyo 169-8555*, Japan*

Abstract: In large cities of Japan, the shallow underground is being extremely congested nowadays. In order to use underground space more effectively, new underground infra-structures in a great depth larger than 40m need to be constructed. Water pipelines are not exceptional. In deep underground the static hydraulic water pressure exceeds, extremely high external water pressure will act on water pipelines. In these cases, the buckling of steel pipes may occur. To prevent the buckling, it is necessary to study the mechanism of its buckling behavior for the design of such pipelines. In this paper, considering the balance of safety and cost of pipelines, the buckling behavior of steel pipes stiffed by ring ribs are presented. From the model test results, the adequacy of our proposed method for estimating the buckling behavior, “two-stage calculation method” is validated.

Key words: deep underground; water pipeline; external water pressure; buckling; two-stage calculation method

1　はじめに

現在，日本の大都市圏では，その地下利用が飽和状態にあり，都市機能の向上やライフラインのネットワーク機能の強化のための有効な手段の一つとして，大深度地下空間の利用が期待されている．大

深度地下水道管路網は，大都市圏の地下 50～100 m に設置した送水管路や給水管路により複数の浄水場や配水基地を有機的に連結し，安定した源水の確保，貯留や水供給を行うための水道施設である．

水道管路の敷設には，開削工法，シールド工法，推進工法などが用いられるが，本研究では，大深度地下に構築される水道管を検討の対象とするため，シールド工法による導水施設を想定した．シールド工法による水道管路の建設は，一般に，一次覆工のみによるシールドトンネルを構築した後に，その内側に鋼管を挿入し，管とセグメントの間をモルタルで充填する内挿管方式が多く採用されている．この方法は実績も多く，施工性もよいが，水道管として必要な断面以上の掘削が必要となり，また，トンネルの完成した後に，内挿管を敷設するため，工期が長くなるという問題がある．これを解決する目的で，財団法人水道技術研究センター，神戸市水道局，および大深度地下水道布設技術研究会の三者は共同で『大深度水道管のコスト縮減に関する研究』[1] をテーマとした研究グループを組織し，水道管の敷設に関する新しい方法を検討してきた．その結果として，２つのタイプの構造が提案された．一方がセグメント一体型と呼ばれるものであり，もう一方がセグメント分離型と呼ばれるものである．前者はシールドトンネルのセグメントに改良を加え，それ自体を水道管として用いようとするものである．後者は，シールドトンネルの中に鋼管などを敷設する内挿管方式のものであるが，シールドトンネルの断面をできるだけ小さくするため，トンネルと内挿管の間に間詰めを行わないものである．両者の概略検討の結果，想定した 1.6 MPa 程度の大きな内水圧にも十分に適応できるセグメント分離型を基本として，詳細な検討が進められた．この構造を採用することによって，従来に比べて小さな掘削断面で済むことはもちろんのこと，シールドの掘進と同時に，内挿管を構成する鋼板の搬入や溶接を行うことができるので，工期の短縮が図れる．さらに，鋼管に補鋼リブを設置して，肉薄化を図ることができれば，コストの縮減も可能である．また，一次覆工のセグメントと鋼管とが分離しているので，土水圧によるトンネル覆工の変形を鋼管に伝達しないというメリットもあり，鋼管の板圧を低減できる可能性がある．

一方，シールドトンネルの止水性は，現在ではかなり改善されているものの，長期にわたっての漏水を完全に止めることはできないと考えられ，その場合には，鋼管に外水圧が作用する．とくに，水道管内の清掃や補修が必要になったときには，内水圧を除去する必要があり，薄肉シェル構造である水道管[2] が座屈する危険性がある．

本研究はこのような状況を想定したものであり，鋼管の模型供試体を用いて，これに外水圧を作用させ座屈実験を行い，その座屈圧力や座屈形状の実験結果を，すでに筆者らによって提案された「二段階座屈解析法」による結果と比較することで，その妥当性を検証するとともに，より安全で経済的な水道管の設計方法を検討したものである．

2　模型実験

2.1　実験装置

図 - 1は本実験に用いた実験装置の概要を示したものである．実験装置本体は,高圧配管用炭素鋼管

STS を用いており，10 気圧の内水圧に耐えられるように設計されている．また，本体両側の蓋の内側には２つの溝を設け，２種類の径に対して実験が行えるようにしてある．実験装置の内部には厚さ 120 mm の木製の板を設けることで，様々な長さの供試体に対して実験が行えるようにした．また，蓋の溝と木製の板には支持ゴムを設置して，その止水性を高めている．供試体を実験装置内の溝にセットした後，蓋を閉め，外側の６つのナットで締めることにより，供試体内に水が浸入することを防ぐ．また，供試体に偏圧がかからないように，ナットは少しずつ締めている．装置内を水で満たしたあと，手動ポンプを用いて装置内に水を送り，徐々に水圧を上げる．この実験装置では，供試体に外水圧だけではなく,木製の板が供試体に押し付けられることで発生する軸力を考慮する必要がある.図 - ２は実験装置の外観を示したものであり，図 - ３は蓋の断面図である．

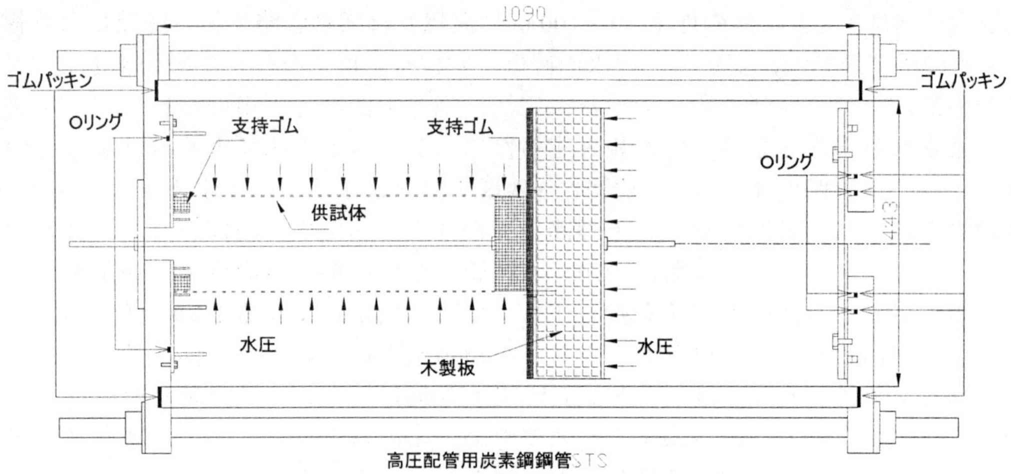

図-1　実験装置の概略図

図-2　実験装置の外観

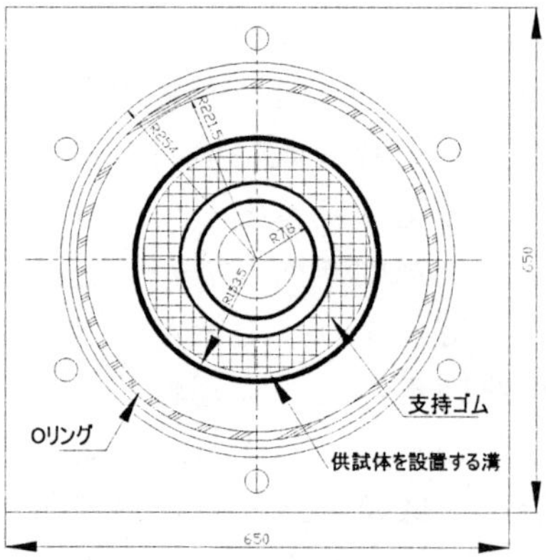

図-3　蓋の断面図

2.2　実験供試体

(1) 供試体の寸法

補剛リブがない鋼管（以下，円筒管と呼ぶ）と補鋼リブをもつ鋼管（以下，補剛円筒管と呼ぶ）にそれぞれ外水圧を作用させ，補剛リブの有無やその形状，間隔によって座屈荷重や座屈形態にどのような影響がでるかを検討する．供試体には熱間圧延軟鋼 SPHC（JIS G 3131）を用いて，ロールにより円筒形状の鋼管を製作し，焼きなましを行っている．表 - 1は供試体の仕様を示したものであり，図 - 4は供試体の種類を表わしたものである．

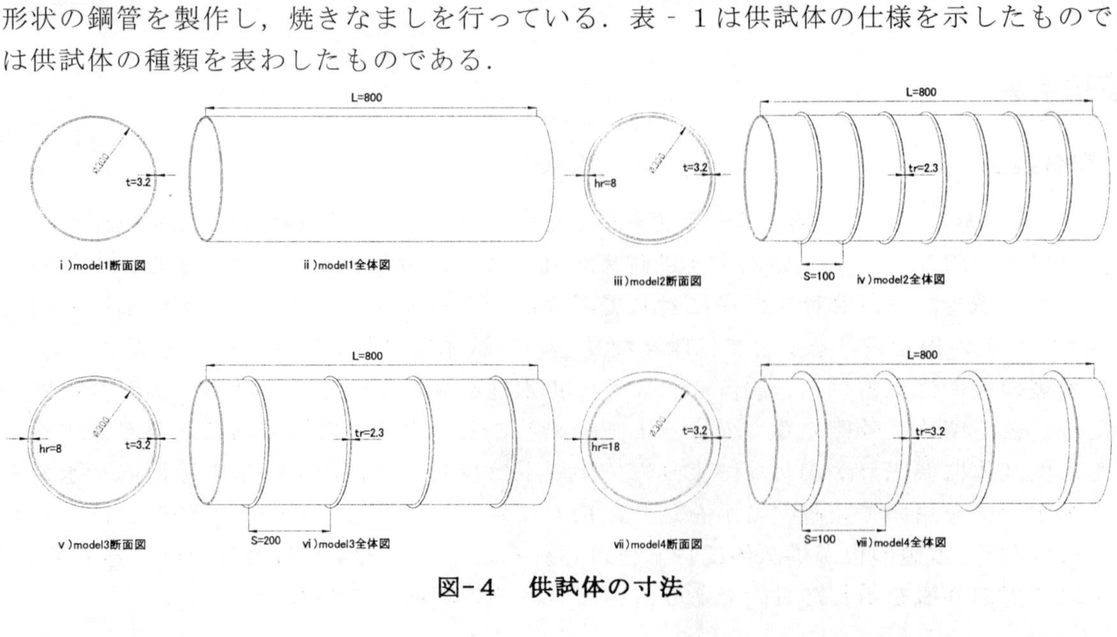

図-4　供試体の寸法

(2) 供試体の物性値

解析を行う際に供試体の物性値が必要となる．そこで，供試体に用いたものと同じ材料で，５号試験片

（JIS Z 2201）を４枚用意して引張試験を行った．表－２は引張試験の結果を示したものである．

2.3　実験結果およびその考察

表－３は実験で得られた各供試体の座屈圧力を，また，図－５は実験後の供試体の状況を示したものである．円筒管の model1 に比べて補剛円筒管である model3，4 は座屈圧力が大きく，補剛材による補剛効果を確認できる．model2 の座屈圧力は円筒管より小さい結果となった．これは，その補剛間隔や初期不整，端部の支持条件が鋼管の座屈に大きな影響を与えたためであると考えられる．

表－１　供試体の種類

Model	鋼管部分			補剛リブ		
	外径 φ (mm)	長さ L (mm)	厚さ t (mm)	補剛間隔 S (mm)	高さ hr (mm)	厚さ tr (mm)
model1	300	800	3.2	-	-	-
model2	300	800	3.2	100	8	2.3
model3	300	800	3.2	200	8	2.3
model4	300	800	3.2	200	18	3.2

表－２　引張試験の結果

弾性係数(N/mm^2)	2.12E+05
降伏点(N/mm^2)	316.1
引張強さ(N/mm^2)	372.9
伸び率〈%〉	35.2

表－３　座屈圧力

	座屈圧力(N/mm2)
model1	1.71
model2	1.67
model3	2.31
model4	4.16

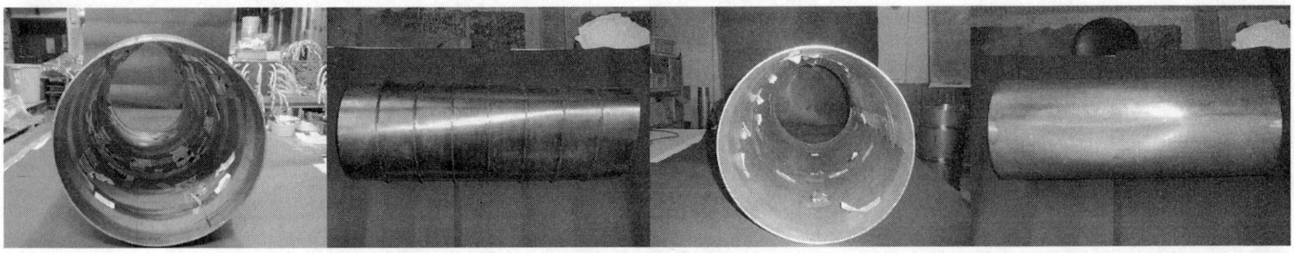

ｉ）実験後 model1 断面図　ⅱ）実験後 model1 全体図　ⅲ）実験後 model2 断面図　ⅳ）実験後 model2 全体図

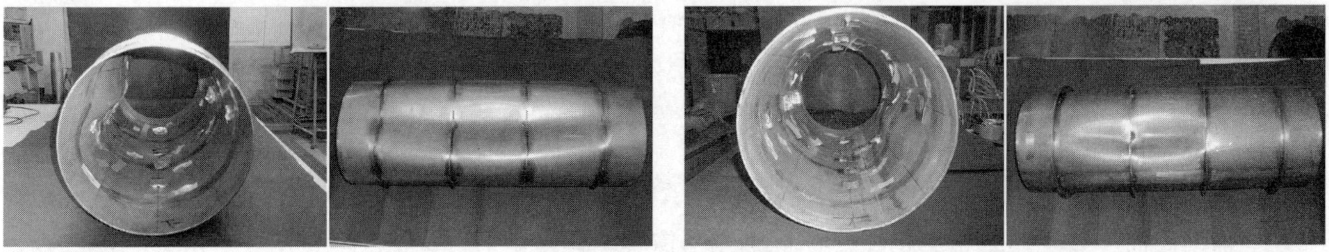

ｖ）実験後 model3 断面図　ⅵ）実験後 model3 全体図　ⅶ）実験後 model4 断面図　ⅷ）実験後 model4 全体図

図－５　実験後の供試体

3 三次元 FEM を用いた座屈解析

(1) 解析概要

本研究では，三次元 FEM プログラム，Marc の四辺形薄肉線形シェル要素[3)]を用いて実験供試体のモ

デル化を行い，座屈解析を実施した．前述したとおり，実験では，供試体に外水圧を作用させた際に軸方向の軸力が発生するため，解析でも供試体に作用する軸力を考慮した．また，実験前に供試体の断面の周長を測定したところ，溶接付近などで初期たわみを確認した．この幾何学的初期不整は，円形断面において，その影響を無視できない．そのため，最大内径と最小内径の許容差は，基準内径の１%以下という条件[4)]のもとで，初期たわみを確認した点に直径の 0.5%の初期不整を与えた．

(2) 解析条件

表 - 4は解析で用いた端部の境界条件を示したものである．X，Y，Z はそれぞれ管の半径方向，円周方向および軸方向の変位を表し，Rx，Ry，Rz はその回転変位量を表す．表中のばね固定とは，実験において供試体の端部の支持にゴムを用いたため，供試体の端部の変形によるゴムの反発力をばねで表現したものである．解析に使用したばね定数値 K は実験で求めたゴムの軸方向変位から算出した．また，材料特性は，引張試験で求めた表 - ２と同じものを使用した．

表-4 解析に用いた支持条件

X	Y	Z	Rx	Ry	Rz
ばね固定	固定	片端	自由	自由	自由

4 実験結果とＦＥＭによる解析結果，二段階座屈計算法による計算結果の比較およびその考察

4.1 二段階座屈計算法の概要[5)]

補剛円筒管の座屈形態は，補剛リブが鋼管と同じ座屈波数で座屈する全体座屈と補剛リブと鋼管の座屈

波数が異なる，もしくは，鋼管部分のみが座屈する局部座屈に分けられる．座屈形態は補剛剛性の増加により，局部座屈から全体座屈に変わる．水道管の安全性と経済性の両方を満足するためには，局部座屈から全体座屈に座屈形態が変化するような補剛剛性が最適であると考えられる．そのため，最適な座屈設計を行うためには，座屈形態の照査が欠かせないものと考えられる．

二段階座屈計算法は，一つの供試体に対し，全体座屈および局部座屈それぞれの座屈理論式を用いて

理論値を求め，その二つの値を比較することで座屈形態を判断し，座屈応力を求める計算法である．図－6は二段階座屈計算法の計算フローを示したものである．図中の $P_{cr}{}^{G}$ は全体座屈圧力を，$P_{cr}{}^{L}$ は局部座屈圧力を表している．

4.2 座屈理論式[5)]

(1) 全体座屈の理論式

補剛円筒管の全体座屈が起こる場合,補剛円筒管全体のポテンシャルエネルギーが最小になるときの外

圧が座屈圧力となる．式（１）は補剛円筒管の全体座屈圧力を示したものである．

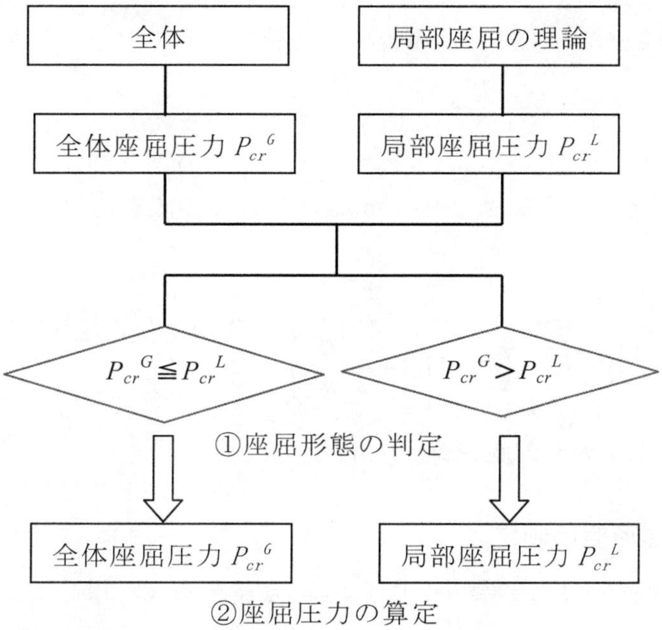

図-6　二段階座屈計算法の計算フロー

$$P_{cr}{}^G = \frac{Et}{(n^2-1)R}\left[\frac{t^2(\alpha^2+n^2-1)^2}{12(1-\mu^2)R^2} + \frac{I_r(n^2-1)^2}{ltR^2} + \frac{\alpha^4}{\left(\alpha^2+n^2\right)^2}\right] \tag{1}$$

ここに，$P_{cr}{}^G$：補剛円筒管の全体座屈荷重(N/mm^2)

R：鋼管の半径（mm）

t：厚さ（mm）

μ：ポアソン比

n：座屈時の円周方向波形数

l：補剛間隔（mm）

L：支持間隔（mm）

I_r:有効二次曲げモーメント（mm^4）

I：補剛リブの剛性断面の中心軸に対する二次曲げモーメント（mm^4）

である．また，波形数 n は次のように表わされる．

$$n = \sqrt[8]{\frac{3\alpha^4}{K}}$$

ここに，$K = \dfrac{t^2}{12(1-\mu^2)R^2} + \dfrac{I_r}{ltR^2}$，　$\alpha = \dfrac{\pi R}{L}$　である．

また，水道管は一般的に，無限長管として考えられ，無限長管の全体座屈は，次のようになる．

$$\alpha = \frac{\pi R}{L} \approx 0\ ,\ n = 2 \tag{2}$$

式（2）を式（1）に代入すると無限長管の全体座屈圧力 $p_{cr}{}^{G\infty}$ は式（3）になる．

$$P_{cr}{}^{G\infty} = \frac{Et^3}{4(1-\upsilon^2)R^3} + \frac{3EI}{LR^3} \tag{3}$$

(2) 局部座屈の理論式

式（4）は両端で変位が拘束される場合の円筒管の座屈圧力を示したものである[6]．補剛円筒管の局部座屈

は補鋼材がほぼ真円の形状をしているため，補剛材を支持とみなし，補剛材間のみを対象とすれば，円筒管と同じ考え方で処理されるとされている[7]．このことから，補剛円筒管の局部座屈には式（4）を用いることができる．円筒管である model1 にはこの式を適用する．

$$\frac{p_{cr}{}^{L}\left(1-\mu^{2}\right)R}{Et}=\frac{1-\mu^{2}}{\left(n^{2}-1\right)\left(1+\dfrac{n^{2}L^{2}}{\pi^{2}R^{2}}\right)^{2}}+\frac{t^{2}}{12R^{2}}\left\{\left(n^{2}-1\right)+\frac{2n^{2}-1-\mu}{1+\dfrac{n^{2}L^{2}}{\pi^{2}R^{2}}}\right\} \tag{4}$$

ここに，$p_{cr}{}^{L}$ ：局部座屈時の座屈荷重(N/mm^2) である．

4.3 各モデルの座屈形態の判定

上記の二段階座屈計算法および式（1），（4）の座屈理論式を用いて，補鋼円筒管である model2～model4

に関して，座屈形態の判定を行った結果は表－5に示すとおりである．実験後の供試体の変形から各モデルの座屈形態を判断すると，model2 と model3 は補剛リブが鋼管本体と一緒に変形したため，全体座屈が発生したと考えられ，model4 は補鋼リブと鋼管が一体となって変形せず，補剛リブ間での部分的な変形を生じたため，局部座屈を起こしたものと考えられる．表－5をみると，その座屈形態は一致しているため，補剛円筒管の二段階座屈計算法を用いた座屈形態の判定は有効であると考えられる．

表－5　座屈形態

供試体	全体座屈圧力 P_{cr}^{G} (N/mm^2)	局部座屈圧力 P_{cr}^{L} (N/mm^2)	座屈形態	理論座屈圧力 (N/mm^2)
model2	5.19	27.74	全体	5.19
model2	3.82	11.34	全体	3.82
model4	14.42	11.34	局部	11.34

4.4 座屈圧力の比較およびその考察

表－6は座屈圧力の実験値，ＦＥＭによる解析値，および二段階座屈計算法による計算値を示したものである．まず，実験値と解析値との比較を行う．本研究の解析では，モデルに初期不整を与え，端部の円周方向の支持条件をばね固定にすることで，より実験に近い条件を表現した．実験値と解析値とはほぼ一致しており，三次元 FEM を用いた座屈解析が有効であることがわかる．

表－6　座屈圧力の比較

供試体	実験値 E（N/mm^2）	解析値 A（N/mm^2）	計算値 C（N/mm^2）	E/C
model1	1.71	1.79	2.45	0.70
model2	1.67	2.26	5.19	0.32
model3	2.31	2.47	3.82	0.60
model4	4.16	4.43	11.34	0.37

次に，実験値と二段階座屈計算法による計算値との比較を行う．表 - 6をみると，両者には大きな差があることがわかる．とくにmodel2とmodel4では誤差が大きかった．model2では，その座屈位置は他の供試体と異なり，端部での座屈が確認された．model2は，補剛リブの補剛間隔を100 mmの等間隔としたため，端部の剛性が弱くなったことが原因であると考えられる．対称性を考えて供試体長さを倍の1600mmとして計算し直すと，表－7に示すように座屈荷重は1.79 N/mm^{2}となり，実験値に近づくことがわかる．また，model4は，実験中に溶接部がはがれて強度が低下した．model4の補剛間隔を200mmから倍の400mmに変えて計算し直すと，座屈荷重は5.34 N/mm^{2}と実験値に近づく．

表-7　実験で得られた座屈長さを用いた計算値

供試体	実験値 E（N/mm^2）	計算値 C（N/mm^2）	E/C
model2'	1.67	1.79	0.93
model4'	4.16	5.34	0.78

また，補剛円筒管であるmodel2とmodel3は全体座屈をしているので，無限長管の全体座屈圧力式（3）を用いて計算すると，座屈圧力は表 - 8のようになる．表 - 8から，model2は，実験値と理論値がほぼ一致し，model3は，実験値が理論値の約2倍の値となった．

最後に，鋼管の外水圧による座屈に対して，設計で用いられる安全係数の妥当性について検討する．

表-8　全体座屈圧力（無限長）

供試体	実験値(N/mm^2)	計算値 C (N/mm^2)	E/C
model2∞	1.67	1.74	0.96
model3∞	2.31	1.17	1.97

現在の設計では，鋼管に作用すると想定される1.5倍の外水圧に対して安全が確保されるよう安全係数が設定されている[8)]．表 - 6，7，8に示した計算値を安全係数1.5で除し，実験値と比較したものが表 - 9である．表 - 9中のA値をみると，補剛円筒管であるmodel2～4はともに危険側となっている．しかし，実際の座屈長さに合わせて再計算を行った結果（model2'とmodel4‘）を見ると，これらは安全側となった．また，model2，3をそれぞれ無限長管として

再計算した結果（model2∞とmodel4∞）は，E/(T/1.5)

が1.0を大きく超えていることから，現状の安全係数1.5は過剰である可能性がある．

水道管の座屈形態や座屈長さによって安全係数を変えることができれば，その低減が図れるものと思われるが，現状では実験データの数が少なすぎる．初期不整や支持条件の影響をより明確にするため，今後さらに実験を行い，多くのデータを収集することが必要と考えている．

表-9　安全係数を考慮した値

供試体	実験値 E (N/mm^2)	計算値 C (N/mm^2)	A=E (C/1.5)
model1	1.71	2.45	1.05
model2	1.67	5.19	0.48
model3	2.31	3.82	0.91
model4	4.16	11.34	0.55
model2'	1.67	1.79	1.40
model4'	4.16	5.34	1.17
model2∞	1.67	1.74	1.44
model3∞	2.31	1.17	2.96

5 おわりに

本研究で得られた知見は以下に示すとおりである.

1) 円筒管に補鋼材を設けることで座屈圧力は増加するが，補剛円筒管の補剛間隔や初期不整，支持条件などがその座屈圧力に大きな影響を与え，場合によっては円筒管の座屈圧力よりも小さくなる.

2) 初期不整や支持条件をできるだけ忠実に表現した三次元 FEM は, 鋼管の外水圧による座屈現象に対して有効である.

3) 二段階座屈計算法を用いることで，補剛円筒管の座屈形態を判断することができる.

4) 想定したとおりの座屈が発生する場合，現在用いられている鋼管の外圧による座屈に対しての安全係数 1.5 は，おおよそ妥当であると思われる．しかし，実験では，初期不整や支持条件の影響により危険側となるケースも確認できた．また，水道管を無限長管としてその全体座屈圧力を算出した場合，1.5 という安全係数は過剰であることが確認できた．このことから，設計する水道管の形状や座屈形態によっては安全係数を低減できる可能性がある.

ただし，実験データが少なく，合理的な安全係数を定めるためには，今後さらに実験を重ねて，検討を加えていく必要がある.

参考文献（References）：

[1] 財団法人　水道技術研究センター：『大深度水道管のコスト縮減に関する研究報告書』，2004.3.

[2] 社団法人　日本機械学会：『シェルの振動と座屈ハンドブック』，pp3-5，2003.1.

[3] Marc Analysis Research Corp.：MSC.Marc2003，Volume B，pp3-339，2003.

[4] 社団法人　水門鉄管協会：『水門鉄管技術基準　水圧鉄管・鉄鋼構造物編』pp118-119，2001.8.

[5] 王　剣宏, 小泉淳『大深度地下水道管の外水圧による座屈に関する理論的研究』, 土木学会論文集 A, Vol64, No3，pp588-602.

[6] チモシェンコ・ギアー：『弾性安定の理論　下』pp451-458，1974.10.

[7] 社団法人　水門鉄管協会：『水門鉄管技術基準　水圧鉄管・鉄鋼構造物編』pp60-65，2001.8.

[8] 社団法人　水門鉄管協会：『水門鉄管技術基準　水圧鉄管・鉄鋼構造物編』pp40，2001.8.

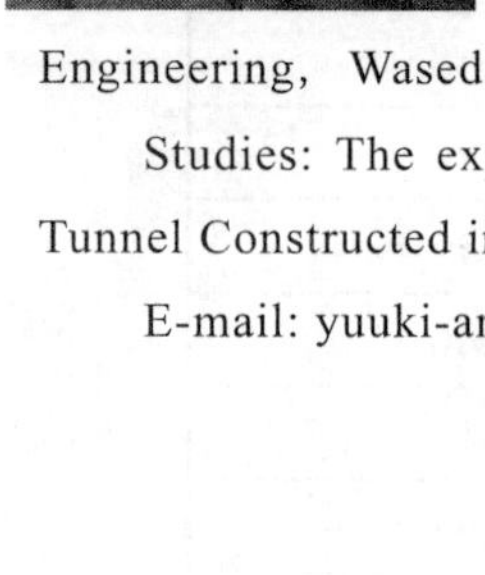

著者紹介（Bio-data）：

天野　裕基

早稲田大学　理工学術院　創造理工学研究科　建設工学専攻　修士課程２年

研究内容：大深度地下水道管の外水圧による座屈挙動に関する実験的研究

東京都新宿区大久保３−４−１

Yuki　AMANO

Graduate Student, Dept. of Civil and Environmental Engineering, Faculty of Science and Engineering，Waseda University

Studies: The experimental study of Buckling of Steel Pipe under External High Water Pressure for Water Supply Tunnel Constructed in Deep Underground

E-mail: yuuki-amano@asagi. waseda. jp

PART FOUR

ENGINEERING CASE

工程案例

杭州庆春路过江隧道工程设计

肖明清　焦齐柱　张 迪　孙文昊

中铁第四勘察设计院集团有限公司，湖北　武汉　430063

【摘　要】 在建的杭州市庆春路过江隧道是下穿钱塘江的第一条交通隧道工程，隧址工程地质条件及河段水文条件复杂，隧道过江段采用盾构法施工，南北岸边段采用明挖法施工。本文介绍了庆春路过江隧道工程的建设环境和建设标准，并从隧道平面布置、纵断面及横断面设计方面对总体设计方案进行了介绍。结合该工程特点，对大直径盾构结构设计方案、高承压水作用下深基坑设计方案以及水底隧道防灾系统设计等方面进行了较详细的介绍。

【关键词】 过江隧道；总体设计；盾构；深基坑

DESIGN OF QINGCHUN RODE RIVE-CROSSING TUNNEL IN HANGZHOU

Mingqing XIAO，Qizhu JIAO，Di ZHANG，Wenhao SUN

China Railway Siyuan Survey and Design Group CO., LTD, Wuhan 430063, Hubei, China

Abstract: Qingchun Road River-crossing Tunnel under construction in Hangzhou is the first traffic tunnel under passing Qiantangjiang River. The geological condition and hydrological condition of tunnel site are complex. The River-crossing section is constructed in shield method, while the bank side section in open excavation method. The construction environment and the construction standard of Qingchun Road River-crossing Tunnel project are introduced, and the overall design is presented from three aspects: tunnel layout design, longitudinal section design and cross section design. Finally, the structure design of large diameter tunnel shield, deep foundation pit design under high pressure water and design of disaster prevention system of river-crossing tunnel are presented in detail according to the construction characteristics.

Key words: river-crossing tunnel; overall design; shield method; deep foundation pit

1　工程概况

庆春路过江隧道位于杭州市的中心位置，它北接下城区庆春路，南连萧山区市心路，整条通道贯穿钱江新城与规划钱江世纪城的中心地带（隧道地理位置如图 1 所示）。根据城市总体规划和综合交通规划，庆春路越江通道的性质为大城市主干道，其功能应定位为沟通钱江两岸两个中央商务区的联系通道，并兼有服务主城与江南副城间的功能。

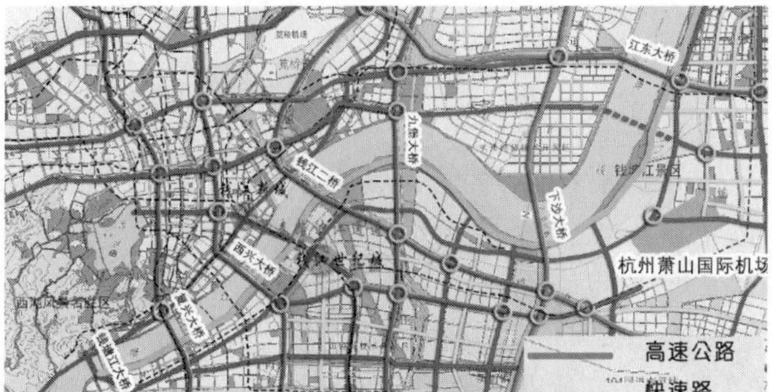

图 1　庆春路过江隧道地理位置图

1.1　交通流量及建设规模

采用 EMME/2 软件对杭州市过江交通总量和

基金项目：863 计划（2006AA11Z116）；铁道部课题（2007G036、2006G007B）

庆春路过江隧道交通量进行了流量分析，结果如表 1 所示。根据交通流量预测结果，本工程设计采用双向四车道的建设规模。

表 1 各目标年过江交通总量及隧道交通量（单位：pcu/h）

年份	过江交通总量	庆春路隧道交通量	占总量比例	增长率
2010 年	46 871	4 307	9.19%	
2020 年	71 654	5 459	7.62%	2.4%
2030 年	89 881	5 970	6.65%	0.9%

1.2 主要技术标准

（1）道路等级：大城市主干道

（2）计算行车速度：主线 60 km/h，匝道 40 km/h

（3）车道宽度：3.75 m＋3.5m

（4）车道净高：4.5 m

（5）路缘带宽度：0.5 m

（6）侧向净宽：0.75 m

（7）道路最小平曲线半径：600 m

（8）最大纵坡：主线不超过 4.5%，匝道不超过 6%

（9）设计使用年限：100 年

（10）设计洪水位：按百年一遇设计，按三百年一遇校核

（11）人防等级：六级

2 工程建设条件

2.1 地形地貌

沿线场地地貌主要为钱塘江河床及两岸的钱塘江河口冲海积平原，地形一般开阔平坦。北岸为钱江新城，已建成庆春路，道路两侧以绿化带为主，南岸以苗木、鱼塘为主，因人工渔塘开挖影响，微地貌有一定起伏。拟建隧道与钱塘江垂直，该段河面宽度约为 1 200 m 左右，河床面标高一般为－2.30～0.85 m，局部地段受航道及主流线冲刷作用，水深达 10～13 m。

2.2 工程地质与水文地质

2.2.1 工程地质

隧道沿线两岸主要层土层为②层、③层，属粉土、粉砂类，其物理力学性质为一般～较好，厚度及分布相对较稳定，其渗透性相对较好。其中②-2 层、③-2 层、③-3 夹层内夹少量淤泥质土薄层、微层理，性质略差。盾构段主要开挖土层为③、④、⑤黏性土层以及⑧-1 圆砾层，其中⑧-1 层卵石含量约占 25%，圆砾占 50% 以上，一般砾径以 1～2 cm 为主，最大砾径达 5 cm 以上。

2.2.2 水文地质

勘察期间实测场地上部孔隙潜水水位埋深埋深 0.60～2.15 m，相对于标高为 4.55～6.12 m，平均水位标高为 5.44 m，变化不大；根据施工期间现场抽水试验结果，承压水含水层静止水头绝对标高为－2.5 左右。水质对混凝土无腐蚀性，对混凝土中钢筋无腐蚀性，对钢结构有中腐蚀性。

2.3 隧址河段水文

2.3.1 河段潮汐特征

庆春路隧道工程的位置处于动力条件较为复杂的河口段的上段。钱塘江河口为强潮河口，其潮汐为非正规半日浅海潮，一日两涨两落。河口段河床冲淤剧烈，自然条件下，主槽平面摆动频繁，摆幅较大。

隧址处平均高潮位 4.45 m，平均低潮位 3.86 m，平均潮差 0.59 m，最大潮差 3.96 m。

隧址断面百年一遇高水位 8.36 m，三百年一遇高水位 8.81 m。

2.3.2 河床冲刷深度

采用实测资料分析、动床数学模型计算、动床比尺模型试验等研究结果表明：隧道断面百年、三百年一遇的设计条件下河床最低冲刷高程分别为−17.2 m、−17.7 m。同时根据断面历史地形资料分析和水槽模型冲刷试验等得到河床的上、下包络线及设计条件下的工程断面冲刷线。

3 工程总体设计

3.1 隧道平面设计

隧道工程起点自江干区庆春东路—新塘路交叉口，向东略偏南直至江边，过江后接江南萧山区市心路。隧道在江北布置一对与主线并行的匝道。根据原城市规划，隧道主线在江南（萧山侧）于滨江一路交叉口北侧终止，预留与规划的钱江世纪城综合地下空间开发系统的接口，且地铁 2 号线进入市心北路后布置在两主线隧道之间；江南通过东西线匝道接规划公园东路、公园西路，近期承担主线进出口功能，隧道平面示意见图 2。为了满足规划条件，江南工作井处左右线间距约 64 m。根据规划及景观要求，隧道管理用房设在江南且采用半地下结构，故左右线江南工作井合建，中间部分作为隧道管理用房。

后来根据城市发展需要，钱江世纪城规划及地铁 2 号线线位均做了调整，庆春路隧道不考虑与钱江世纪城地下空间的结合，主线隧道从原设计终点向南延伸，下穿钱江二路后出地面与市心路相接，取消了与规划公园东路、公园西路相接的两条匝道。由于江北及江南工作井主体结构已经施工，故线路平面、纵断面调整较为困难，调整后的线路平面如图 3 所示。

调整后的隧道建筑长度 3 765 m，隧道长度约 3 395 m，其中下穿钱塘江段约 1 766 m 采用盾构法施工，其余均采用明挖法施工。

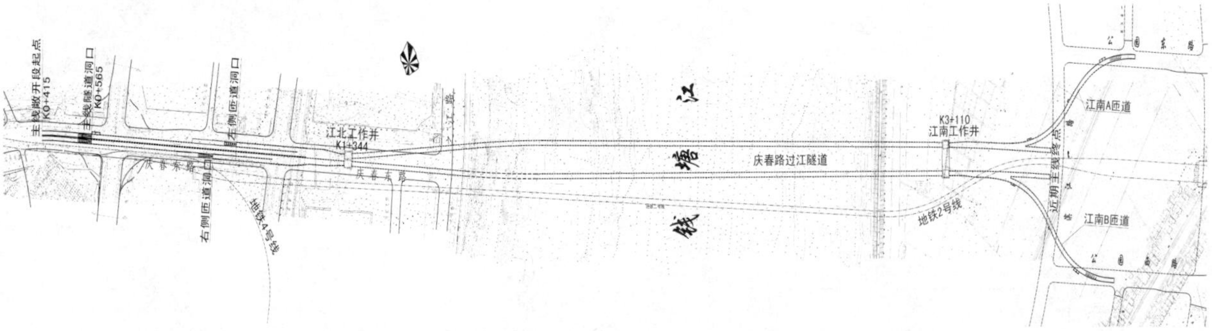

图 2 原规划隧道平面图

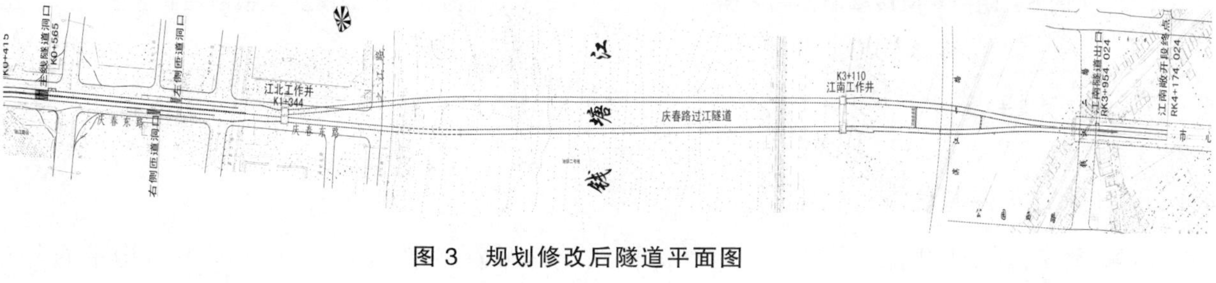

图 3 规划修改后隧道平面图

3.2 隧道纵断面设计

纵断面设计时，考虑在满足三百年一遇冲刷线摆动范围下运营期抗浮安全系数不小于 1.1 的要求以及施工安全需要的覆土厚度条件下，尽量减小隧道覆土厚度，改善行车条件，并尽可能避开⑧-2 卵石层，减小盾构掘进难度。隧道设计纵断面（西线）如图 4 所示，西线最大纵坡 4.25%，东线最大纵坡 4.0%。

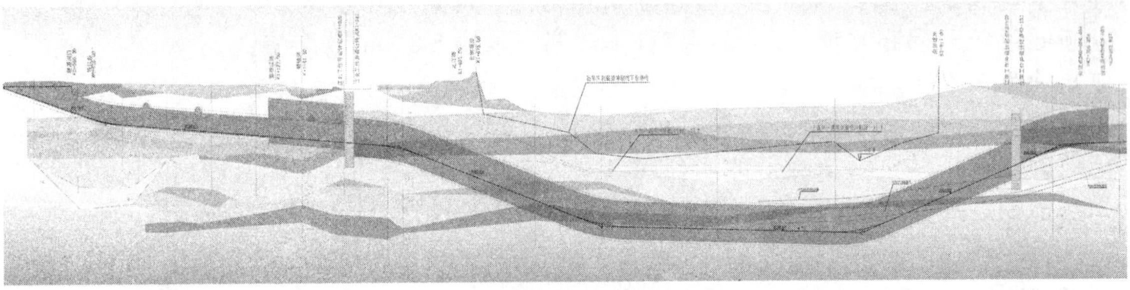

图 4 隧道纵断面图

3.3 隧道横断面布置

江北覆土较浅明挖暗埋段采用双孔一管廊的矩形横断面形式，中间设置设备管廊及安全疏散通道；江北岸边覆土较深的明挖暗埋段以及江南主线及匝道均采用双层结构，隧道标准横断面如图 5 所示；江中盾构段采用圆形断面（如图 6 所示），车道板下方设置逃生通道及电缆廊道。

3.4 附属工程布置

本隧道在江北主线隧道以及左、右匝道洞口各设雨水泵房一座，在江南洞口设雨水泵房一座；在每条隧道最低点以及两岸工作井内各设置废水泵房一座；在江北洞口、江南洞口各设降压变电所一座；结合盾构法施工需要及隧道通风、防灾的需要，在两岸各设一个工作井和风塔。

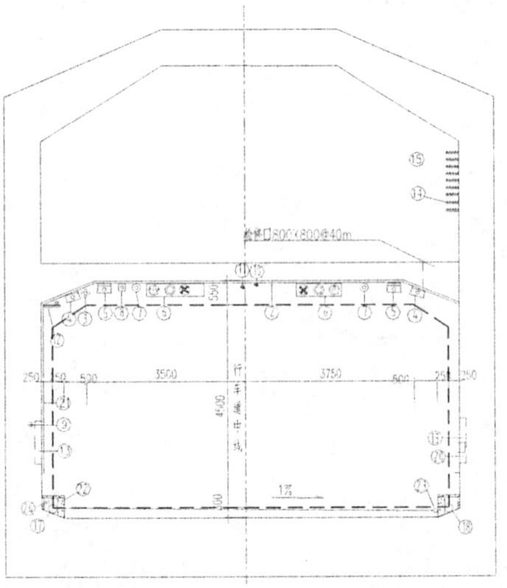

图 5 明挖双层段横断面布置图

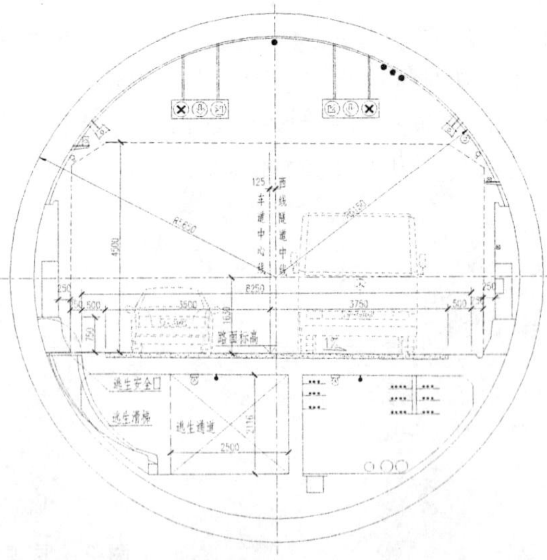

图 6 盾构段典型横断面布置图

4 工程设计特点

4.1 承压水地层深基坑

本隧道江南工作井深约 30 m，为目前杭州地区最深的基坑。工作井围护结构平面外包尺寸

25.2 m×86.8 m。围护结构采用壁厚 1.2 m 地下连续墙，明挖逆作法施工，竖向设 5 道钢筋混凝土支撑和 1 道钢支撑。

根据水文地质资料，第四系孔隙承压水主要赋存于下部砂土和圆砾、卵石层内，上覆粘性土相对隔水层构成了含水层的承压顶板。实测承压水头 25.3 m，经计算，基坑开挖时必须降低承压水头 18.4 m,才能满足防突涌要求。设计中对纯降水方案和隔渗帷幕结合减压降水方案进行了经济、技术比较，最终选用了在工作井外围做 0.8 m 厚素混凝土地下连续墙作为隔渗帷幕，井内布置少量减压降水井的方案。目前江南工作井施工已经顺利结束，隔渗降水效果良好。

4.2 大直径盾构隧道

江中盾构段隧道外径 11.3 m，内径 10.3 m，采用通用楔形管片。每环由 9 块管片组成，管片厚度 0.5 m，幅宽 2.0 m，采用 C50 钢筋混凝土平板型管片，抗渗等级 S12。管片环与环之间采用 36 条 M30 斜螺栓连接，块与块间通过 2 条环向 M36 斜螺栓连接，衬砌环结构三维模型如图 7 所示。根据隧道纵向分析结果，在局部地段增设了剪力销，并设置了多条变形缝。

本隧道江中最深处位于强透水地层，最大水压 0.43 MPa，因此防水设计是设计的一个重点。管片接缝防水采用双道防水，外侧为 EPDM 弹性橡胶密封垫，紧靠其内侧为聚醚聚氨酯遇水膨胀止水条。为了降低隧道内烟雾对密封防水材料的腐蚀，加强防水效果，管片内侧留有嵌缝槽，对外露接缝进行嵌缝处理。

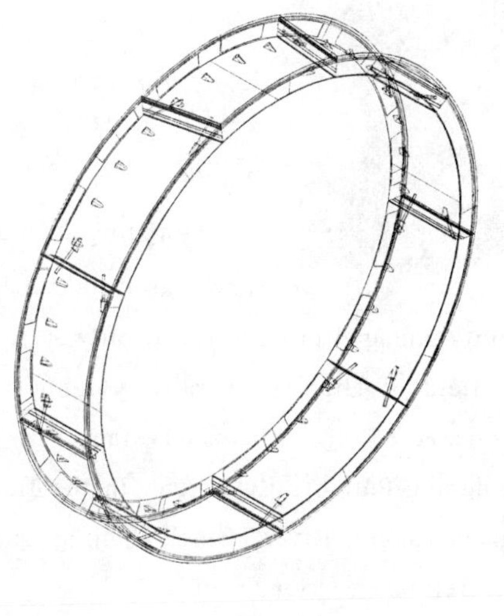

图 7 盾构衬砌环三维模型图

4.3 防灾系统

在设计过程中，对本隧道的防灾系统进行了多项专题研究，形成了较为完善的防灾系统设计，主要体现在如下几个方面：

(1) 盾构隧道段在车道限界上部设置专门的排烟道，沿隧道纵向每隔 80 m 设置安全逃生滑梯，从逃生滑梯可进入车道板下方的纵向疏散通道。两岸明挖段每隔 250 m 左右设置 1 条横通道。

(2) 确保火灾事故工况通风系统具有足够的排烟功能，尽可能控制烟雾和热量扩散，并为逗留在隧道内的乘用人员、消防人员提供一定的新风量，以利于人员疏散和灭火扑救。

(3) 在隧道中采用消火栓系统、泡沫－水雾联动灭火系统、灭火器系统、火灾自动报警系统。

(4) 监控系统能够迅速检测隧道内可能发生的诸如火灾、车祸等各种灾情；对于隧道灾害时能实时判断和报警，并自动联动相应设备、抵御灾害、把损失降至最低。

(5) 在隧道管理中心内考虑设急救、检修等特种车辆，并与消防、交警等联动，当灾情发生时，能迅速进入隧道进行救援、维修作业。

5 结 语

庆春路过江隧道是一项大型的综合性市政工程项目，也是下穿钱塘江的第一条水底隧道，盾构隧道直径以及工作井基坑深度目前均为杭州地区之最。该工程设计中涉及到的各个专业的关键技术、难点问题较多，设计中始终贯穿技术先进、科学创新的原则和以人为本、环境和谐的设计理念，力争将其设计为一项精品工程。该工程于 2006 年 7 月开工建设，计划于 2010 年 7 月建成通车。该过江隧道的建成对杭州市实现南北互动、平衡发展，促进以钱塘江为轴线的跨江、沿江发展格局，从而使杭州市的建设从“西湖时代”快速走向“钱塘江时代”有着重要意义。

参考文献（References）：

[1] 董天乐，张 迪，朱丹. 庆春路过江隧道江南工作井降水设计与施工. 岩土工程界，2007(7).

[2] 董天乐，张 迪，焦齐柱. 庆春路过江隧道公铁分合建方式分析. 隧道建设，2007(4).

作者简介（Bio-data）：

肖明清，1970年生，男，教授级高工，博士研究生，现任中铁第四勘察设计院集团有限公司副总工程师。主要从事高速铁路隧道及越江隧道工程的理论研究与设计。在越江隧道领域：主持了武汉长江隧道、南京长江隧道、狮子洋隧道等多条水下隧道的研究和设计；在高速铁路领域：主持了武广客运专线、郑西客运专线、杭长客运专线、向蒲铁路等多条铁路的设计及科研工作。

Mingqing XIAO (1970—), candidate for doctor's degree, senior engineer (professorship) , Served as Deputy Chief Engineer of China Railway Siyuan Survey and Design Group CO., LTD., mainly engaged in High-speed railway tunnel and River-crossing tunnel engineering design and theoretical research. In the field of High-speed railway tunnel, he presided over the design and research of Wuhan-Guangzhou Passenger Dedicated Line, Zhenzhou-Xian Passenger Dedicated Line, Hangzhou-Changsha Passenger Dedicated Line, Xiangtang-Putian railway, etc. In the field of River-crossing tunnel, he presided over the design and research of the Wuhan Yangtze River Tunnel, Nanjing Yangtze River Tunnel, and Shiziyang tunnel, etc.

Tel: 027-51156624 (office)

E-mail: tsyxmq@vip.163.com

台湾超高压地下电缆隧道潜盾施工案例探讨

李文权[1] 吴福祥[2] 张达德[3] 王义夫[4] 陈聪海[5]

[1]李文权 / 台湾伟盟工业股份有限公司，工务部总经理
[2]吴福祥 / 台湾中华大学建筑规划学院，院长 教授
[3]张达德 / 台湾中原大学土木系 教授 / 中国铁科院铁建所，顾问
[4]王义夫 / 台湾建丰工程股份有限公司，项目经理
[5]陈聪海 / 台湾世曦工程顾问股份有限公司，设计副理

【摘 要】 台湾社会经济高度发展，生活素质不断提高，电力建设为满足都市化及现代化的需求，超高压电缆隧道地下化为当前建设趋势。潜盾工法因具有安全性高、免地面开挖、不影响地面交通、不阻碍地下水流及降低对生态环境影响等优点，近年来已成为都会区地下化工法的主流。

本文系以台湾电力公司「高港—五甲—高雄 345 kV 地下电缆线路凤林路段潜盾隧道统包工程」为例，针对高地下水位、砂质土壤及砾石地层之工址地质特性，分别就发进直井深开挖施工安全考虑、潜盾隧道正上方设置分歧井设计、大口径潜盾隧道急曲线施工、联络横坑推进施工等经验进行介绍。

【关键词】 电缆隧道；潜盾工法；直井；急曲线

CONSTRUCTION CASE STUDY ON THE SHIELD TUNNEL FOR 345KV POWER CABLES IN TAIWAN

Wenchuan LEE[1], Fuhsiang WU[2], Tathechang DAVE[3], Yihfu WANG[4], Tsunghai CHEN[5]

[1]*(Taiwan) General Manager, Wei Mon Industry Co., Ltd.;*

[2]*(Taiwan) Dean & Professor of General Affairs and Institute of Construction Management, Chung Hua University;*

[3]*(Taiwan) Professor of Civil Engineering Department, Chung Yuan Christian University Consultant, China Academy of Railway Sciences;*

[4]*(Taiwan) Project Manager, Chian Feng Engineering Co., Ltd.;*

[5]*Design Assistant Manager, CECI Engineering Consultants, Inc., Taiwan.*

Abstract: To meet the requirement of the high living quality in the urban area of Taiwan, it is unavoidable that the 345kV power cables have to be built in the underground. Shield tunnel construction possesses the characteristic of safe, free from excavation underneath the road, having no impaction on transportation, and ecological environmental condition, etc. It has become the major method to be adopted for ground water tunneling in urban area.

This paper, focus on a care study of the Turnkey project for 345kV power cable connecting works, which handled by Taiwan Power Company. This study provides the safety construction experience in the deep excavation of starting shaft, cross passage, the sharp curve of large diameter shield tunnel, and the design of branch shaft right on the shield tunnel.

Key words: power cable tunnel; shield method; shaft; sharp curve

1 前 言

台湾电力公司为配合新增电源及负载成长之需要，并解决目前输变电设备利用率偏高及特高压用户无法

核供之困境,办理第六输变电计划,以提升输变电系统供电能力及优良之电力质量;高港—五甲—高雄 345 kV 地下电缆线路凤林路段潜盾洞道暨高港(丙)冷却机房统包工程属「第六输变电计划」之一部分。

工程范围所在之高雄县大寮乡凤林二路交通流量大，路面下方密布重要民生管线，加以工址地盘属砂性地层，地下水位高，对于地下工程极具潜在施工风险性。本工程关键课题包括:

(1) 高地下水位、砂质及砾石地层之地质条件，工作井开挖工程难度高，潜盾发进与到达作业之风险高。

(2) 长距离潜盾掘进，地质变异大，潜盾机设计须特别考虑。

(3) 分歧井设置于潜盾隧道正上方，接头设计与施工极为复杂与困难，台湾输电工程无相关实绩案例可供参考。

(4) 到达工作井已由他标施工完成，囿于路权及线形规划，潜盾隧道需以 R＝50 公尺之急曲线施工，衔接既设工作井。

(5) 潜盾隧道上方民生管线密集、穿越在莱大排、邻近台 88 高架道路，结构物保护难度高；紧急逃生孔及分歧井施工困难。

本工程统包团队于备标时，就本工程邀标文件进行设计理论与工法研析，搜集相关计划就技术、管理、环境、安全加以统整分类，并进行可行性方案评估及执行策略探讨。本文就实际执行内容予以归纳整理，分别于第 3 章介绍设计成果与工法分析，第 4 章介绍施工管理与执行成效，最后第 5 章为个案分析与成果应用，提供工程界参考与指正。

2 工程概述

2.1 工程概况

本工程考虑工区之交通、民情、道路管理单位要求等因素，设计采用潜盾工法施筑电缆洞道，以减少对当地交通、环境之冲击，工程范围自高港(丙)变电所旁#1 直井起，穿越在莱大排、沿凤林二路北上，迄凤林二路与台 88 线路口，工程内容包括内径 5.2 公尺潜盾隧道 1.56 公里，#1 直井（发进工作井）、直径 3.5 公尺紧急逃生孔、直径 3 公尺分歧井各一座；衔接既有电缆涵洞采明挖覆盖工法为 2.2×2.5 公尺单孔电缆涵洞及 2.8×3.6 公尺双孔电缆涵洞各一段（全长约 53 公尺）；冷却机房一栋为地上二层、地下一层等，为土木设计与施工合并发包之统包工程。本工程位置及现况如图 1 及图 2 所示。

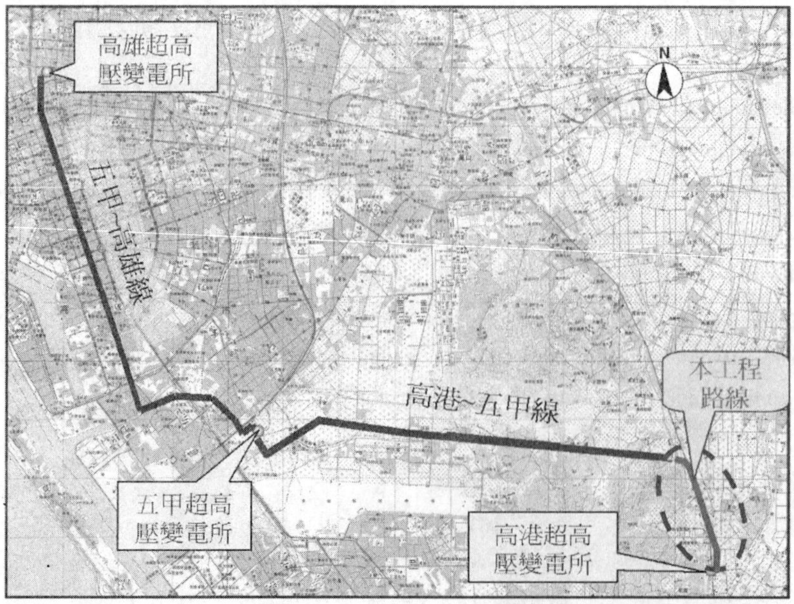

图 1 高港—五甲—高雄 345 kV 地下电缆线路凤林路段平面位置图

图 2 凤林路段工程位置鸟瞰图

2.2 地质概况

本工程位于高雄县大寮乡，潜盾隧道通过之地层均属第四纪地层，屏东平原为全新世冲积层，以砂、粉砂、黏土及砾石所组成，地下水位约位于 GL.-2～GL.-5 公尺间，区域地质如图 3 所示[1]。另依本工程钻探数据整理之地质纵剖面图[2]（如图 4 所示），隧道覆土厚度介于 12～18 公尺间。

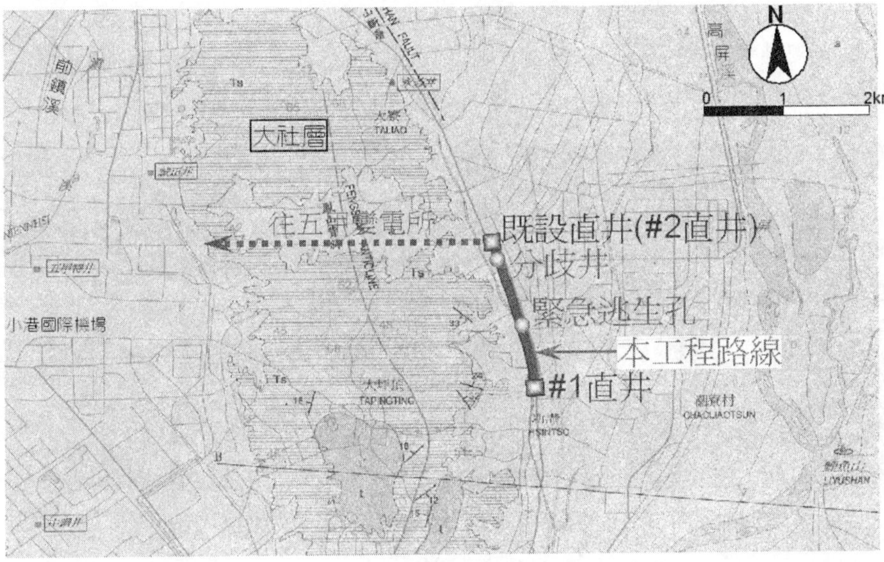

图 3 区域地质图

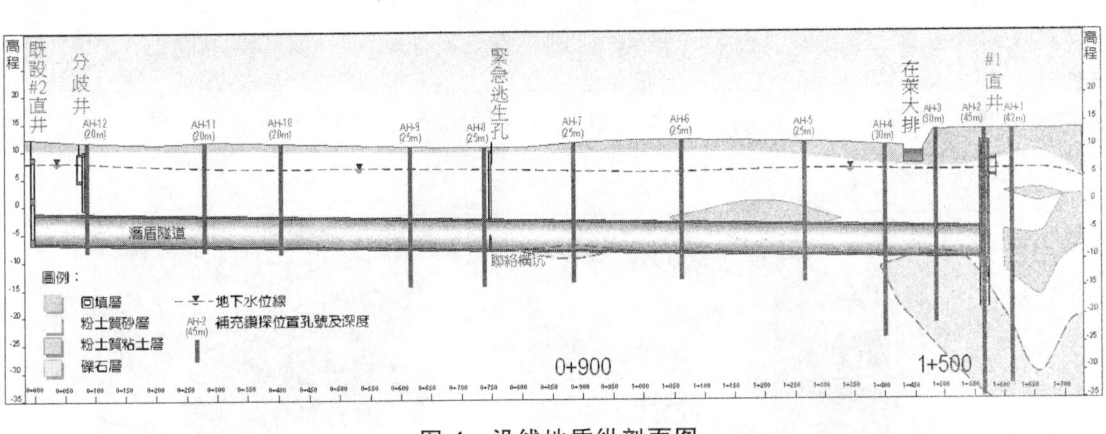

图 4 沿线地质纵剖面图

3 设计成果与工法分析

确保本工程之施工安全与达成业主需求，统包团队展现了设计与施工慎密完整的结合，克服了高雄地区地下水位高、深层粉土质砂土对潜盾施工潜在风险。以下分别说明具体成效包括:① 发进工作井开挖安全工法选择与监测;② 潜盾破镜采 FRP（玻璃纤维棒）可切削工法；③ 分歧井设于潜盾隧道正上方之布置与工法；④ 潜盾线形重新调整；⑤ 大口径潜盾急曲线关键施工对策；⑥ 建物安全保护措施与灾害预防管理等。

#1 直井支撑系统

3.1 发进工作井开挖安全工法选择与监测

#1 直井为本工程潜盾隧道之发进工作井，设置于高港（丙）变电所与在莱大排间。直井开挖深度 24 公尺；设计劲度高、止水性良好之连续壁（厚度 1.2 公尺，深度 42 公尺）作为挡土壁，内支撑系统共有 8 层，以符合安全需求。

针对工址地质特性及参考高雄地区深开挖工程经验，为确保连续壁质量及止水性，相关对策如下:

(1) 连续壁槽沟挖掘时，增加稳定液黏滞性及液面与地下水位之液差，确保沟壁稳定性[3]。

(2) 于连续壁内埋设 PVC 管[4]，并于连续壁混凝土达强度需求后进行超音波检测，以确认连续壁质量（如图 5 所示)。

(3) 对于超音波检测结果，经分析有包泥疑虑或可能造成工作井开挖时漏水漏砂范围，开挖前于连续壁外侧进行补强及止漏作业。

图 5 连续壁内 PVC 检测管及超音波检测

3.2 潜盾破镜采 FRP（玻璃纤维棒）可切削工法

潜盾破镜为潜盾施工过程中，最重要的作业项目，也是发生意外事故几率最高的工项之一。考虑发进工作井紧邻在莱大排，为确保施工安全及避免传统破镜工法可能发生之砂涌意外，本工程于潜盾机破镜范围以 FRP 取代传统钢筋（详图 6)，因潜盾机可直接切削 FRP 及连续壁掘进，除可缩短工期外，并大幅提升潜盾破镜之安全性[5]。

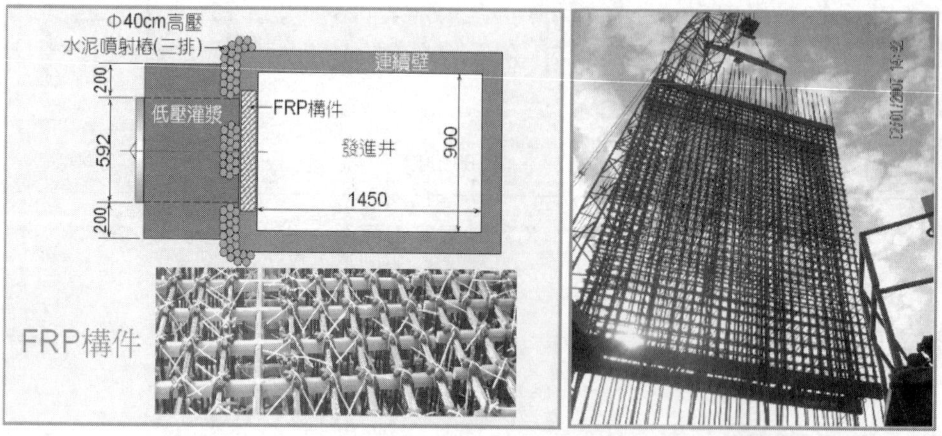

图 6 FRP 可切削工法

3.3 分歧井设于潜盾隧道正上方之布置与工法

于隧道正上方设置分歧井，并采内径 2.4 公尺、高度 1.85 公尺之可挠性伸缩接头与潜盾隧道连接（如图 7 所示），可确保接头部之安全性并提高结构耐震性能，也可避免传统分歧井需设置隧道横坑(联络通道)，易造成横坑施工砂涌意外及发生不均匀沉陷之缺点。

分歧井开挖采全套管工法施工，配合设计地盘改良灌浆[6]、潜盾隧道内设置密闭隔舱及临时支撑系统，可确保接合部之稳定及安全。为确保可挠性伸缩管之功能，施工过程中分歧井侧墙重量需借由锚定钢筋传递至钢套管，以避免分歧井自重造成可挠伸缩管变形；此外，分歧井侧墙上方设置水平翼版，利用翼版承载力支撑分歧井结构体重量，避免分歧井对隧道产生集中荷重，影响隧道结构之安全。

图 7　可挠伸缩管施工示意图

3.4 潜盾线形重新调整

原规划电缆隧道路线于在莱大排段转向，以连接高港（丙）变电所与凤林二路隧道，线形采一段转弯半径 75 公尺及一段转弯半径 100 公尺之曲线相连接（如图 8 所示），因未规划至少潜盾机一倍机身长度之缓冲段，施工时需进行扩挖，将不利于潜盾掘进及在莱大排之保护，且因转弯半径仅 75 公尺，需采用钢环片衬砌施工，工期长且工程经费较高。

经检讨将该区段线形调整为两段转弯半径 120 公尺之曲线，并以 68 公尺长直线段相连接。线形调整后，除可减化曲线形式、异型环片种类及加速工程进度外，因转弯半径较大，可改采钢筋混凝土环片衬砌施工，因环片较宽、施工速度快，并且降低工程费用。

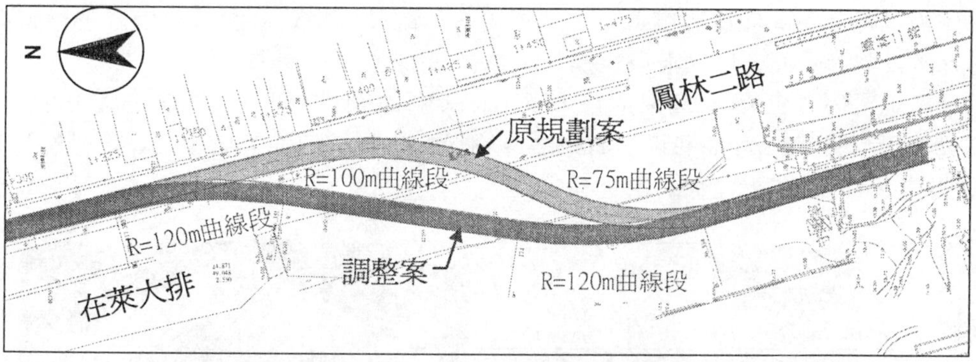

图 8　调整前后在莱大排段潜盾路线线形比较

3.5 大口径潜盾急曲线关键施工对策

因工址地下既有管线密集，无法设置转向工作井，且受限于道路宽度及到达工作井已施工完成，故需采急曲线潜盾施工，工址情况如图 9 所示。本工程首创国内 5.93 公尺大口径潜盾隧道急曲线施工（R＝50 公尺）之案例，为顺利达成线形需求，采取对策如下[7]：

(1) 潜盾机设计球面中折及配置超挖刃设备，中折角度可达 4.7°以上。

(2) 隧道结构采钢环片设计，标准钢环片宽度 50 公分；异型钢环片起拱处最大宽度 50 公分、最小宽度 39 公分，偏差量 11 公分，以符合线形需求。

(3) 施工中利用全测站掘进操控数据管理（图 10），进行潜盾线形蛇行修正与控制。

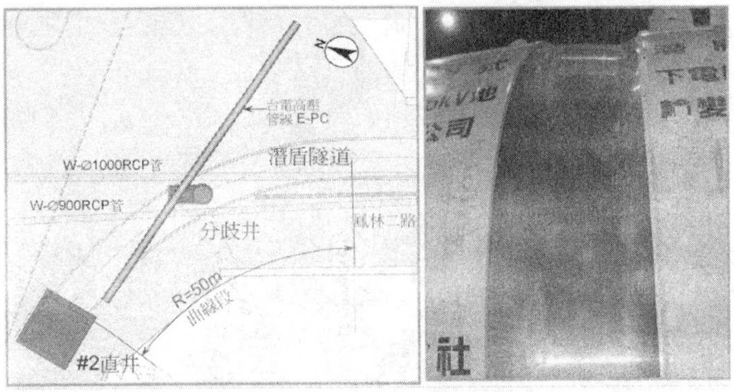

图 9 地下管线分布及中折潜盾机

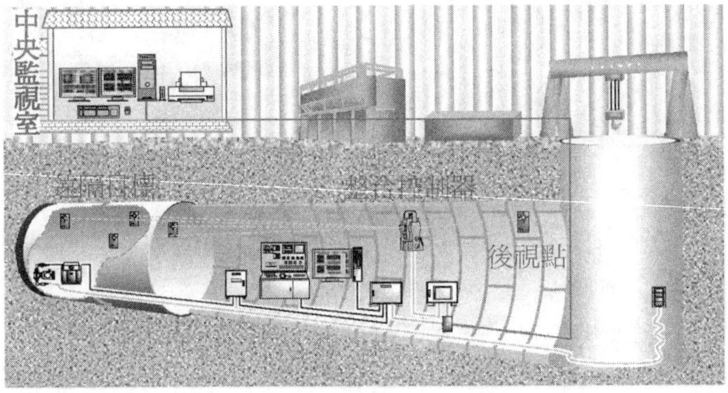

图 10 全测站掘进操控管理示意图

3.6 建物安全保护措施与灾害预防管理

本工程潜盾隧道穿越在莱大排，沟底至潜盾顶部约 11 公尺，加以凤林二路埋设大口径民生管线及邻近建物，潜盾到达端急曲线段由台 88 线高架道路旁通过等情况，大排、建物、桥梁保护相当重要。经研拟本工程建物保护策略首在降低潜盾施工之土壤漏失率，故设计完整监测系统借以进行施工管控，并于重要结构物前方布设监测断面，以供潜盾机操作手选择最佳之施工参数。

为避免潜盾施工对邻近台 88 线高架道路产生不良影响，设计时配合采专业之 ANSYS 程式进行三维有限元素法模拟分析详图 11 所示，并设计有效之建物保护措施－加强背填灌浆、微型桩及监测管理，另于施工前聘请技师公会进行邻近建物之现况鉴定。

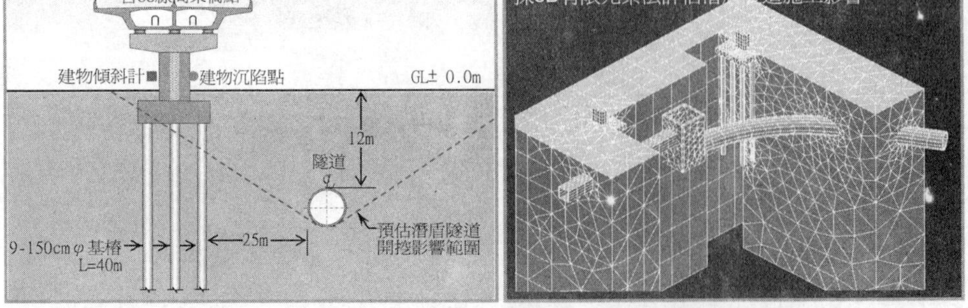

图 11 台 88 线高架桥建物保护及三维模拟

4 施工管理与执行成效

本工程自 2006 年 3 月 27 日开工，于 2008 年 6 月 24 日顺利完成潜盾隧道掘进作业，潜盾机于到达井地盘改良区弃壳、拆解、后送经由#1 直井运出。本章介绍：① 发进工作井连续壁特殊工法；② 分歧井及紧急逃生孔全套管挖掘工法；③ 潜盾掘进施工管理；④ 潜盾机组与急曲线施工；⑤ 联络横坑推进施工等，具体施工管理与执行成效分别叙述如下：

4.1 发进工作井连续壁特殊工法

本工程发进工作井连续壁共分 12 单元施工，施工过程中除确保稳定液液差外，经由钢筋笼内预埋 PVC 管，并于混凝土浇置 7 日后进行超音波检测，检测成果显示连续壁质量良好，壁体无包泥现象，开挖过程亦证明连续壁无漏水情形[8]。

FRP 为高强度、低韧性之材料，其材料特性可供潜盾机直接切削掘进，为降低潜盾切刃盘之磨耗，特别增设 38 个 FRP 专用切削刀，其高度较一般切削刀外凸 2.5 公分，以达到先行掘削 FRP 连续壁之目的。潜盾机安全发进破镜施工如图 12 所示。

图 12 潜盾机安全发进破镜施工

4.2 分歧井及紧急逃生孔全套管挖掘工法

潜盾隧道于凤林二路上设置紧急逃生孔一处，以利维修人员使用，紧急逃生孔直径 3.5 公尺、深度 21.4 公尺，直井与潜盾隧道仅相距约 60 公分；另外，潜盾隧道于凤林二路与台 88 线路口设有分歧井一处，以满足未来电缆引接需求，分歧井直径 3.0 公尺、深度 12 公尺与潜盾隧道相衔接。因凤林二路交通流量大且道路下方密布大口径民生管线，紧急逃生孔及分歧井必须在有限空间施工，为确保施工精度及直井两侧自来水管（管径 900 mm 及 1 000 mm DIP）之安全，采全套管摇入沉设工法进行挡土开挖施工，配合于连接处之地盘改良及于隧道开口处附近使用钢环片、临时钢支保支撑、密闭隔舱等措施，可确保施工安全，相关施工情况如图 13 所示。

图 13 紧急逃生孔钢管压入施工

4.3 潜盾掘进施工管理

本工程电缆隧道全长约 1.56 公里，位于交通繁忙之凤林二路下方，采免地面开挖之潜盾工法施工，施工方式如图 14 所示。因电缆隧道邻近建物、重要民生管线、在莱大排及台 88 高架桥等结构物，潜盾施工过程中需进行妥适的施工管理，除要确保潜盾隧道施工安全外，尚须尽可能降低潜盾施工造成之土壤沉陷量，俾确保邻近结构物之安全，相关管理项目、目的及方法如表 1 所示。

潜盾隧道施工将造成上方地表呈凹槽状沉陷，沉陷量随着与隧道中心之距离增加而减少，沉陷槽断面积与隧道断面积之比值称为土壤漏失率，为评估潜盾施工引致地表沉陷及对邻近结构物影响的重要指标。潜盾隧道施工前于工程沿线布设监测仪器，并设置监测断面，以提供施工作业人员调整潜盾掘进参数之参考。

本工程依循施工前预测、施工中监测管理及施工后回馈分析之步骤，进行动态监测管理。依监测成果进行回馈分析，本工程潜盾隧道施工造成土壤漏失率约 0.5%～0.8%，低于一般捷运工程 0.5%～2.0%（平均 1.3%）土壤漏失率，显示本工程潜盾施工相当严谨，并确实依管理程序执行作业。

表 1　潜盾掘进施工管理项目、目的及方法一览表

<table>
<tr><th colspan="2">管理项目</th><th>管理目的</th><th>管理方法</th></tr>
<tr><td colspan="2">潜盾机掘进控制</td><td>潜盾机运转操作时，控制其螺运机之扭力值、千斤顶之推力、土压值、潜盾机旋转角度及高程显示计</td><td>视地质情况调整掘进速度及排土速度，控制潜盾机之操作数值在容许范围内。切削扭力 400A～600A；千斤顶推力 5 000 kPa～8 000 kPa</td></tr>
<tr><td colspan="2">土压管理</td><td>(1) 不得超过潜盾机之设计安全值；
(2) 土压舱内之土压不超出或低于自然地盘之水压加土压太多，以免造成地面下陷或隆起</td><td>计算挖掘面自然地盘之水压及土压值作为土压管理之依据；
土舱压力 260 kPa～280 kPa</td></tr>
<tr><td colspan="2">作泥材注入管理</td><td>减低螺运机及切削盘之扭力并防止土舱内土壤之固化，增加掘削土之塑性流动及不透水性，使掘削土容易排出防止地下水喷发</td><td>视排土情况注入高浓度之作泥材，并适当调整注入量</td></tr>
<tr><td colspan="2">出土量管理</td><td>潜盾掘进时之掘进土量与排出土量约略相等，以避免地面下陷或隆起</td><td>以运土台车土桶装载之土量容积与潜盾机掘削断面乘以掘进长度所产生之土量(含松方及作泥材)相较作为管理，每环（m）出土量 27 m^3～28 m^3</td></tr>
<tr><td colspan="2">背填灌浆管理</td><td>防止环片接缝漏水及地面下陷</td><td>当环片组立完成推离潜盾机盾尾后立即由环片灌浆孔实施背填灌浆，背填灌浆压力在 2.5 kg/cm^2～3 kg/cm^2，灌浆量约 2 200 公升～2 600 公升，必要时实施二次灌浆以防止环片漏水</td></tr>
<tr><td colspan="2">盾尾油注入管理</td><td>防止盾尾漏水</td><td>采用三层式盾尾钢刷，并装置盾尾油自动注入泵随时补充盾尾油</td></tr>
<tr><td rowspan="3">施工测量管理</td><td>导线及基准点测量</td><td>导线测量：潜盾洞道设计中心定线之基准；
水平基点测量：潜盾洞道高程测量之基准</td><td>利用光波经纬仪于潜盾路线上布设导线坐标点，并作成测量纪录；
依据甲方提供之水平基点，引测于潜盾路线上，并设置水平基点作成测量纪录</td></tr>
<tr><td>掘进施工测量</td><td>(1) 作为潜盾掘进时高程、方向修正之依据；
(2) 作为标准与修正环片组装选用之依据</td><td>(1) 工作井设置坐标及高程基准点，作为潜盾机掘进时方向、高程修正之依据；
(2) 潜盾隧道内，每隔 50 公尺设置坐标基点一处；
(3) 每环环片组装后，量测环片外缘与潜盾盾尾之间隙及环片之真圆度</td></tr>
<tr><td>潜盾隧道贯通之测量</td><td>作为调整隧道底部高程之依据，提供步道仰拱厚度调整之用</td><td>隧道贯通后实施环片底部高程测量，并作成纪录</td></tr>
</table>

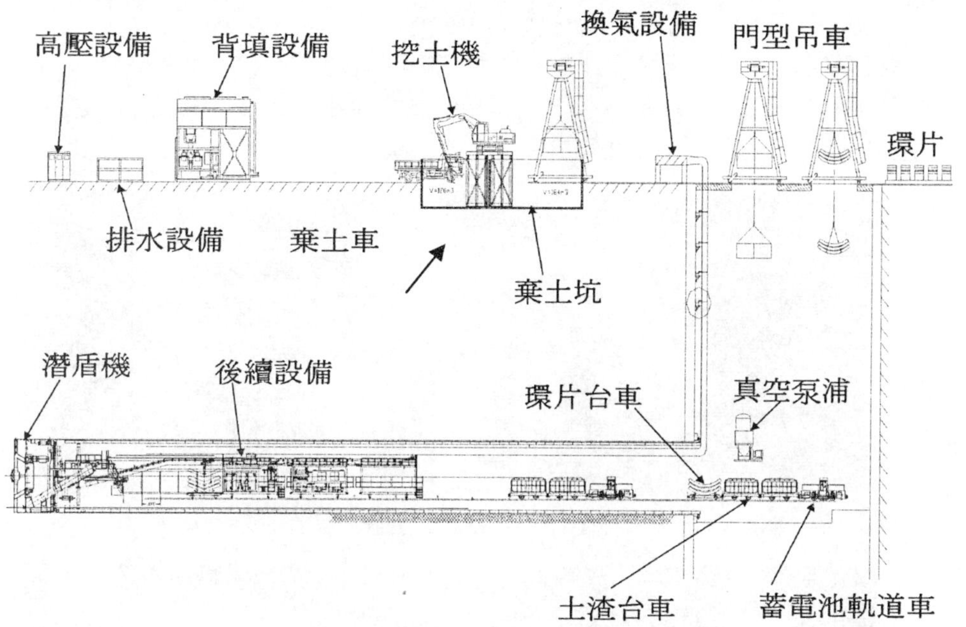

图 14 潜盾隧道施工示意图

4.4 潜盾机组与急曲线施工

因应潜盾机将通过砂土、黏土、砾石等地层，经评估采土压平衡式潜盾机，面盘采六支轮辐状、开口率约 65%，以达快速取土兼具挡土之效能。因本工程属长距离潜盾施工且直接切削连续壁发进，为避免中途更换切刃延误工期及增加施工风险，特别增加切削刃数量及硬度（E5 提升为 E3）；此外，考虑部分路段通过砾石地层，订制前端无中轴之螺运机及闸门设备，可顺利排除砾石及障碍物。

本工程潜盾机外径 5.93 公尺，机身长度 8.84 公尺，由土舱部、环梁部及盾尾部等三部分组合而成，为因应到达端 R＝50 公尺急曲线转弯之需求，潜盾机需具备球面中折机构并设置超挖刃设备，潜盾机结构大样如图 15 所示。

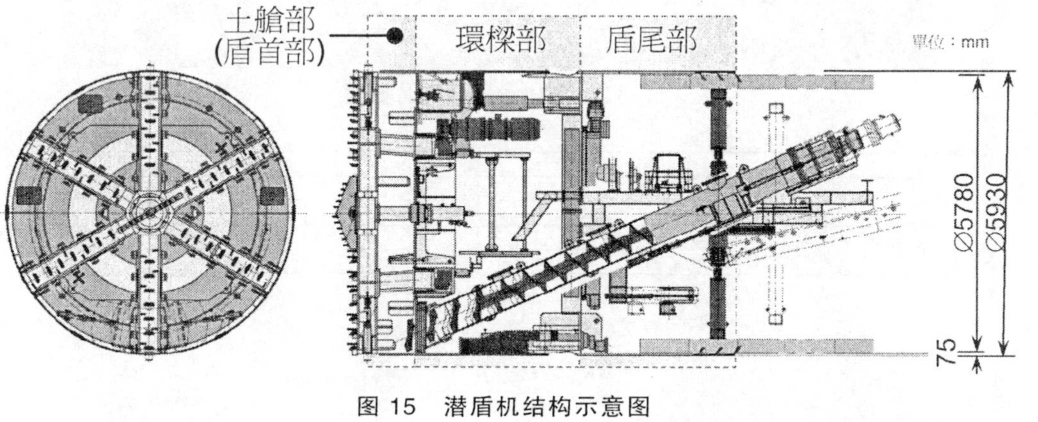

图 15 潜盾机结构示意图

因应到达端急曲线施工，相关施工步骤简述如下：

(1) 配合急曲线曲率半径，设计异型钢环片之异型量。

(2) 施工前于施工图上套绘环片布置，计算每一环片之坐标，并将环片坐标数据输入全测站监测掘进管理系统。

(3) 潜盾机掘进施工时，操作手依据全测站监测掘进系统显示之掘进偏差量（图 16），适时调整潜盾中折角度、超挖量及超挖范围，以修正潜盾机方位。

(4) 每一环环片装设完成后，测量各方向之环片与盾壳间隙量，视需要采用修正环片，并加强曲线段背填灌浆。

(5) 每工班换班时，以人工测量方式进行线形复测。

本工程急曲线段钢环片完工照片如图 17 所示，施工偏差量统计成果如图 18 所示，水平平均偏差量 1.4 公分，垂直平均偏差量 5 公分，最大偏差量 8.9 公分均小于规范值（10 公分），到达端垂直偏差量 3.2 公分、水平偏差量 1 公分，顺利衔接#2 直井。

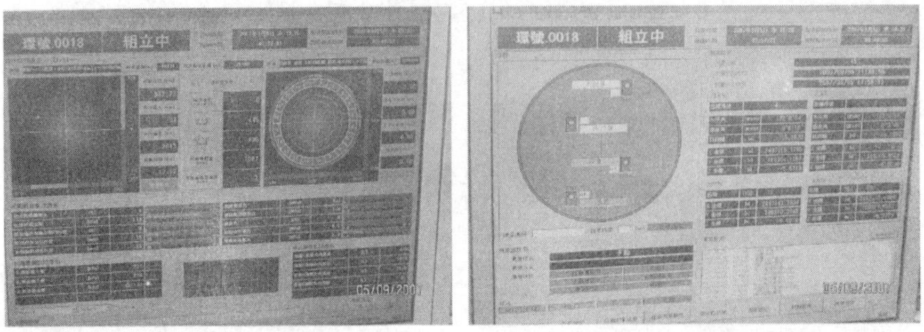

图 16 中央监视室监控屏幕

图 17 急曲线段钢环片隧道

潛盾隧道掘進偏差統計表						到達偏差
隧道段	全長	水平平均偏差	水平最大偏差量	水平最大偏差量環號	規範值	水平最大偏差量
		-13.9 mm	右 84 mm	位於 75 R	±100mm	右 10 mm
鳳林路段	共 1599 環	垂直平均偏差	垂直最大偏差量	垂直最大偏差量環號	規範值	垂直最大偏差量
		50.4 mm	下 89 mm	位於 49 R	±100mm	上 32 mm

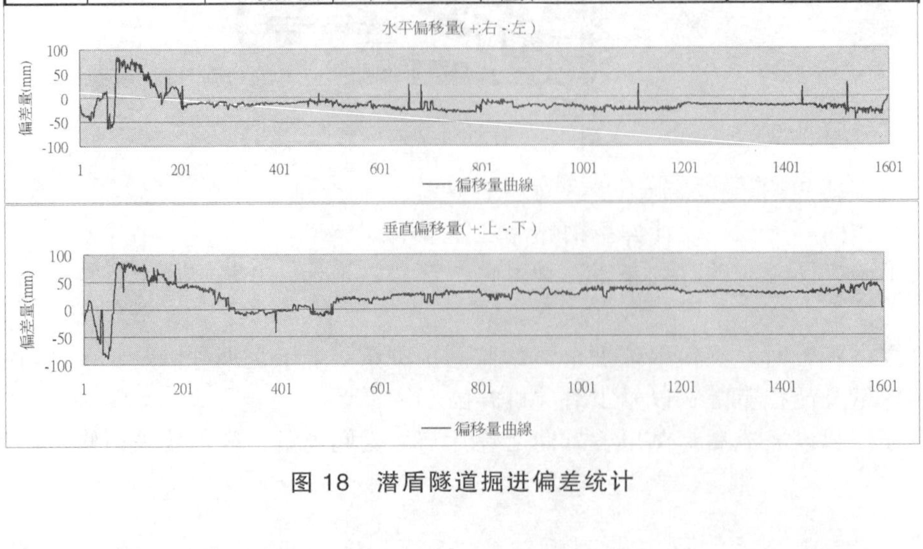

图 18 潜盾隧道掘进偏差统计

4.5 联络横坑推进施工

潜盾隧道以联络横坑与紧急逃生孔连接，联络横坑通道采刃口式马蹄形钢环推进施工，配合地盘改良灌浆、潜盾隧道内设置密闭隔舱及临时支撑系统，可确保接合部施工之稳定及安全。另外，于钢环刃口处加装一道安全门，以备于挖掘面有发生漏水情况时，可立即关闭安全门并撤离施工人员，于补充灌浆并确认完全止水后再进行钢环推进施工，钢环推进完成后将刃口与隧道钢环片焊接，确保横坑之止水性。联络横坑结构体、隧道内架设临时支撑及隧道钢环片补强作业施工完成后，再进行隧道钢环片切除破镜作业，相关施工情况如图 19 所示。

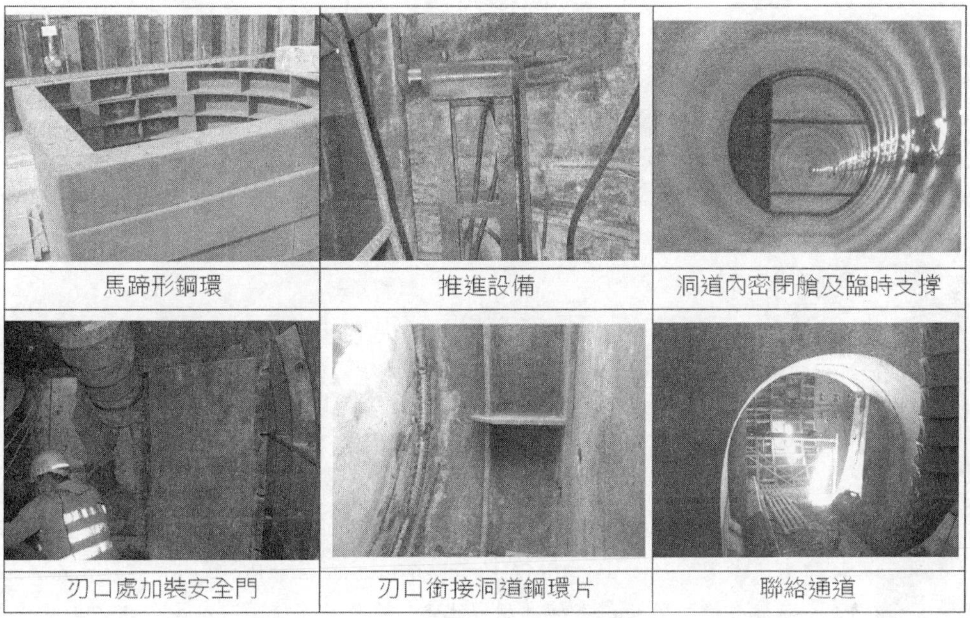

图 19　联络横坑施工

5　个案分析与成果应用

(1) 本工程采用提高稳定液黏滞性及其液面与地下水位之液差，确保连续壁槽沟稳定；连续壁内埋设 PVC 管，并于连续壁混凝土达强度需求后进行超音波检测，确认连续壁质量，确保后续开挖之安全。

(2) 潜盾机破镜范围以 FRP 取代传统钢筋，提高潜盾破镜之安全性，顺利完成深开挖及潜盾发进作业。本工法虽增加潜盾机设备费及 FRP 材料费，但减少发进端地盘改良数量，并大幅提高潜盾破镜施工安全性，破镜施工时无涌砂、涌水情况，本工程施工经验可提供类似地质情况或高风险作业之参考。

(3) 本工程为台湾首创 5.93 公尺大口径潜盾急曲线施工（R＝50 公尺）之案例，潜盾机设计球面中折及配置超挖刃设备，中折角度可达 4.7° 以上，配合设计钢环片衬砌，施工中利用全测站掘进操控数据管理系统，已准确地到达既有之#2 直井。由于#2 直井已由他标先行施工完成，其结构尺寸及方位除影响本工程潜盾到达施工方式外，亦限制潜盾线形布设－潜盾机无法与工作井正交、无法规划直线到达线形，不但施工难度提高亦增加工程风险，经限制开挖面范围、采止水钢板补强及密集加强线形测量，顺利完成急曲线施工。

(4) 紧急逃生孔、分歧井采全套管工法施工，配合设计接合部之地盘改良灌浆、潜盾隧道内设置密闭舱及临时支撑系统，可确保接合部施工安全。囿于施工时程安排，潜盾隧道及破镜处之地盘改良作业需于潜盾机通过前先行施工，造成后续紧急逃生孔及分歧井钢套管压入施工困难，经辅以钻机预钻孔，总算顺利完成任务。由本案施工经验，尔后类似工程应再检讨施工流程或分阶段进行地盘改良作业，以利钢套管沉设施工。

(5) 联络横坑采用马蹄形钢管推进工法，配合地盘改良作业进行施工，因工作井作业空间受限，加以紧急逃生孔、联络横坑、潜盾隧道均为圆弧形结构，均增加钢管推进之困难性，在施工团队锲而不舍的努力下，终于克服挑战顺利完成任务。

参考文献（References）：

[1] 台湾世曦工程顾问股份有限公司. 设计成果报告，2007.

[2] 广记营造股份有限公司. 地质钻探报告书，2007.

[3] 何泰源，陈聪海. 连续壁施工管理要点与工程案例探讨. 第十一届大地工程学术研讨会暨国科会成果发表会，2005.

[4] 广记营造股份有限公司. #1 直井连续壁施工计划书，2007.

[5] 软土潜盾隧道工程设计与实例手册. 科技图书.

[6] 地盘改良设计施工及案例. 科技图书.

[7] 潜盾隧道施工技术规范之研订. 科技图书.

[8] 广记营造股份有限公司. #1 直井连续壁完整性试验报告书，2007.

作者简介（Biao-data）：

李文权，男，1950年12月出生。1972迄今36年余主要工程经历（1）以潜盾施工工法为主包括台电潜盾洞道、自来水大型输水管线、科学园区污水管线排放，（2）以综合营建管理为主工程包括污水处理厂兴建、捷运机厂兴建、都市污染改善河廊环境营造工程。2004年起担任伟盟工业公司工务部总经理。2009年8月完成中华大学营建管理研究所两年课业，获营建、专案管理硕士、IPMA Level D(International Project Management Associate)认证。经济部标准检检验局国家标准制定土木、建筑技术委员。本文介绍之工程于案例执行及研究所修课期间，感谢中华大学指导教授吴福祥博士、中原大学教授张达德博士、台湾日商清水建设阿部优所长等担任咨询顾问，协助统包商完成任务。

E-mail: leo@weimon.com.tw

Wenchuan LEE, Born in 1950, Male. 36 years working experience majorly in the areas of:

(1) Shield tunnel construction for power cables, water supply lining and others.

(2) Construction management on the projects of the water treatment plant, MRT maintenance Factory yard, and environmental renew project on urbane water canal system.

Since 2004, he has being in charged the G.M. position for the Constriction division of Weimon Group. During this period, he also completed his Mater degree in Chung Hua University. And earned IPMA Level D (International Project Management Associate) Certification. He also involves the building and Civil Engineering related Committee members for the National Standard Bureau.

E-mail: leo@weimon.com.tw

土压平衡盾构近距离穿越污水管施工技术

杨书江

中铁隧道股份有限公司，河南　郑州　450000

【摘　要】　成都地铁一号线盾构4标三次近距离穿越主城污水管，施工难度和风险极大，被列为全线头号重大危险源。施工中根据“盾构掘进控制为主、地面辅助注浆为辅”的总体思路，采取了相应的技术及组织管理措施，确保了污水管的运行安全。其施工工艺在地铁一、二号线得到推广。

【关键词】　盾构；砂卵石地层；污水管；掘进；危险源

SHORT-DISTANCE ACROSS SEWAGE PIPE CONSTRUCTION TECHNIQUE OF EPB SHIELD

Shujiang YANG

China Railway Tunnel Stock Co., Ltd., Zhengzhou 450000, Henan, China

Abstract: The shield lot 4 of Chengdu Metro Line 1 has been carried out short-distance across main city sewage pipe for three times. Due to the big construction difficulty and risk, it is considered as number one major hazard sources among all the lines. According to the general approach of “putting boring control first, supplemented by ground-assisted grouting”, the corresponding technical and organizational management measures are adopted so as to ensure the safe operation of the sewage pipe. The construction technology is extended into Metro Line 1 and 2.

Key words: shield; sandy cobble stratum; sewage pipe; tunneling; hazard sources

1　引　言

成都地铁一号线一期工程盾构4标全长4 900 m，隧道主要穿越〈3-7〉卵石土层，部分地段穿越〈4-4〉卵石土层，卵石含量高达55%～80%，卵石成分主要为中等风化的岩浆岩与变质岩，单轴抗压强度65.5～184 MPa，最大值为206 MPa。卵石粒径以30～70 mm为主，局部80～120 mm，地层中粒径大于200 mm的漂石含量占0%～22.3%（重量比），全线已发现最大漂石粒径达670 mm，大粒径卵石含量较高且局部富集成群。地下孔隙水主要赋存于砂卵石土层中，含水层总厚度18.2～23.8 m，为强透水层，渗透系数12.53～27.4 m/d，枯水期地下水位埋深3～5 m，丰水期2～4 m。采用盾构法施工全断面富水砂卵石地层，施工难度和风险极大。

盾构掘进过程中三次近距离穿越污水干管，成都市主城中心区及城区南部的大部分污水汇集到此污水干管后排往三瓦窑污水处理厂，此干管污水流量大，管内污水水流速度快，水位较高，最高日流量40～50万立方米，埋在深度约为8.5 m的地下。如果施工控制不力造成污水干管破裂，后果不堪设想。盾构穿越污水干管施工被列为成都地铁一号线工程头号重大危险源，如何确保盾构顺利穿越污水干管成为施工中的难题。

2　污水干管形式

施工前对沿线的污水管进行了补充调查。通过对污水管的高程及检查井的现场实测，判断出污水管的埋深、走向以及与隧道的空间关系等，同时到相关部门进行了调查走访，获取了污水管的管壁厚度、接口形式、基础厚度等详细资料。

2.1 平口相接带形基础

【桐梓林站—倪家桥站区间】ZDK12＋605～ZDK12＋655（共 50 m）、【倪家桥站—省体育馆站区间】YDK12＋069.51～YDK12＋144.09 段（共 74.58 m）污水管与隧道斜交，污水管管底埋深为 6.8～8.3 m，污水管管底距离隧道顶部距离约为 1.6 m。污水管管径为 1 200 mm，每节管道的壁厚为 100 mm，长度为 2 000 mm，其接口形式为平口相接，接口采用水泥砂浆封堵，砂浆内埋入 20＃10×10 镀锌铁丝网，铁丝网埋入封堵砂浆内的深度为 150 mm。污水管线基础形式为钢筋砼带形基础，如图 1 所示。

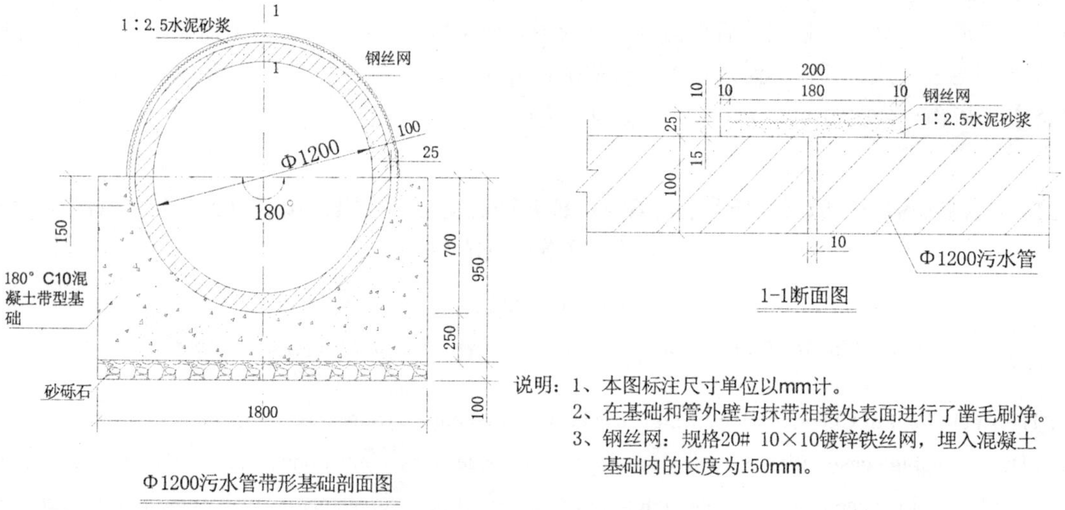

图 1 ϕ1 200 mm 污水管基础图

2.2 平口相接无基础

【倪家桥站—省体育馆站区间】YDK11＋874.42～＋634.31 段（长 240.11 m）污水管原位于左、右线隧道之间，在省体育馆站车站施工时改移至右线隧道上方，改移后污水管走向基本与盾构隧道平行，管底距离隧道顶部垂直距离为 1.28～1.81 m，极大的增加了盾构掘进风险。后经协调，在不恶化线路条件和行车安全的前提下，对线路进行了调整，污水管全部调整至隧道结构线外约 400～500 mm。

该段污水管直径为 1 000 mm，每节管道的长度为 2 000 mm，接口形式为平口相接，采用 50 mm 宽 200 mm 长工字形钢板卡槽连接，详见图 2。

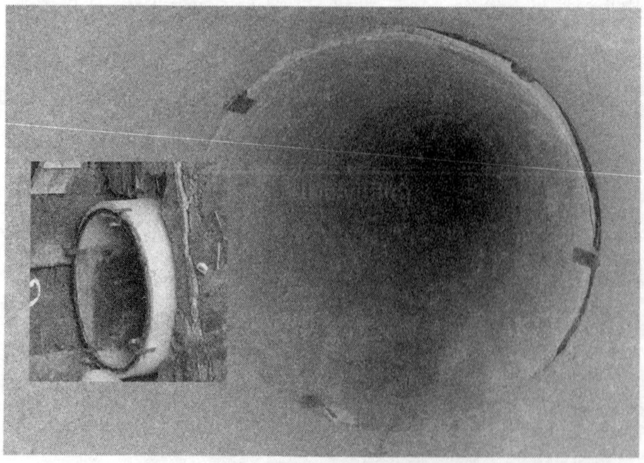

图 2 ϕ1 000 mm 污水管照片

3 施工技术措施

为保证盾构顺利通过污水管，项目部分别于2007年1月6日、2007年3月30日及2008年10月17日邀请成都市质监站、安监站、成都地铁有限责任公司、西南交通大学、中铁二院、成都水务局、四川省建筑科学研究院、中铁西南科学研究院、中煤重庆设计研究院、中铁十三局等单位的专家召开了三次专家论证会，确定了以盾构掘进控制为主、地面跟踪注浆为辅的总体施工思路。

3.1 加强盾构维修保养，避免故障停机

在到达污水管前对盾构机及其配套设备进行全面的维修保养，在掘进通过污水管段时将维修保养工作穿插到施工当中去，保证盾构机连续快速掘进。维修保养项目如下：

（1）盾构机

做好液压系统、泡沫系统、膨润土系统、空气系统、循环冷却水系统、砂浆系统、润滑及密封油脂系统的维护，确保在掘进过程中不出现故障。

（2）配套设备

重点做好水平运输系统（电瓶车等）、垂直运输系统（16T门吊、45T门吊）、砂浆拌和系统等的维护，确保施工的连续性。

穿越污水管期间掘进速度大部分控制在了50～60 mm/min，没有因设备故障造成停机，以快速、平稳的速度通过污水管，减少了对地层的扰动时间。

3.2 有计划地检查更换刀具

有计划地进行刀盘、刀具检查，进行刀具磨损分析、制定刀具维修与更换方案，确保设备完好率，提高施工效率。在YDK12＋685、YDK12＋175和YDK11＋893处（盾构到达污水管前约20～30 m）进行带压进仓更换刀具。

YDK12＋685处刀具更换数量和磨损情况见表1。

表1 YDK12＋685处刀具更换表

序号	刀具号码	刀具类型	磨损量（mm）	备注
1	1#	双刃滚刀	14	刀体磨损严重
	3#		11.4	刀体磨损严重
2	2#	双刃滚刀	刀圈偏磨	刀体磨损严重
	4#		9.8	刀体磨损严重
3	5#	双刃滚刀	17.2	刀体少量磨损
	7#		10.8	刀体少量磨损
4	6#	双刃滚刀	17	刀体、隔环磨损严重
	8#		11	刀体、隔环磨损严重

3.3 做好掘进控制，减少地层扰动

3.3.1 严格控制掘进参数，尽量减小对地层的扰动

（1）降低刀盘转速，减轻与卵石的碰撞冲击，减少对土体的扰动，刀盘转速控制在1.0～1.1r/min左右，避免大的波动。

（2）采用相对较小的推力，推力控制在1 200 T左右，避免波动幅度过大。

（3）土仓内上部压力保持在0.06～0.07 MPa，严格控制压力波动，调整掘进速度和螺旋输送机的转速，保证土仓压力的稳定。

3.3.2 加强碴土改良，严格控制出碴量

通过向刀盘前方加入适量的泡沫剂、膨润土泥浆和水进行碴土改良，每环泡沫剂用量在 40 Kg 左右，膨润土泥浆约 6 m^3，碴土改良效果较好。

盾构下穿污水管施工期间，通过体积和重量两个指标严格控制出碴量，每环出碴量控制在 58～60 m^3，120 t 左右。

3.3.3 确保同步注浆质量，必要时进行洞内二次补充注浆

在掘进过程中做好同步注浆，及时填充管片背后的环形间隙，控制地表沉降。每环注浆量至少 6 m^3 砂浆，个别地段注浆量在 10 m^3 以上，采用注浆压力控制，注浆压力≥2.5 bar。

地表沉降异常时，及时利用管片上预留的注浆孔进行二次补充注浆，浆液采用水泥－水玻璃双液浆，水泥浆、水玻璃体积比为 1:1，水泥采用 P.O32.5 普通硅酸盐水泥，水泥浆水灰比为 1:1，注浆压力不低于 3 bar。

3.3.4 加强盾构姿态调整与控制

掘进过程中做好盾构姿态的控制，减少盾构姿态的调整。姿态调整时遵循“勤调、多调、量小”的原则，每环调整量控制在 10 mm 以内。

3.4 地表预埋跟踪注浆管，必要时进行注浆填充

对 YDK12＋069.51～144.09、ZDK12＋605～655 段与隧道斜交的污水管，沿污水管走向在污水管与盾构隧道间，提前预埋跟踪注浆管。YDK11＋874.42～YDK11＋634.31 段，污水管与隧道走向基本平行，根据沉降监测情况，必要时打孔注浆填充。

预埋跟踪注浆管每隔 5 m 布置一根，共设 27 个孔，YDK12＋069.51～144.09 段布设 16 个跟踪注浆孔、ZDK12＋605～655 段布置 11 个跟踪注浆孔，注浆孔孔深约 7 m，注浆孔位置距离污水管净距离 1 m，注浆管采用ϕ42 钢管，为防止地面冒浆，地面以下 2 m 范围钢管采用实管，2 m 以下管体上预留泻浆孔，环向间距 65 mm，径向间距 150 mm，呈梅花型布置，管尾封口。

盾尾通过预留注浆管后，采用水泥-水玻璃双液浆进行跟踪注浆。水泥浆水灰比 0.8：1～1.2：1，水泥-水玻璃体积比 1：1，水玻璃波美度 20～30Be′，注浆压力注 0.6～1.0 Mpa。

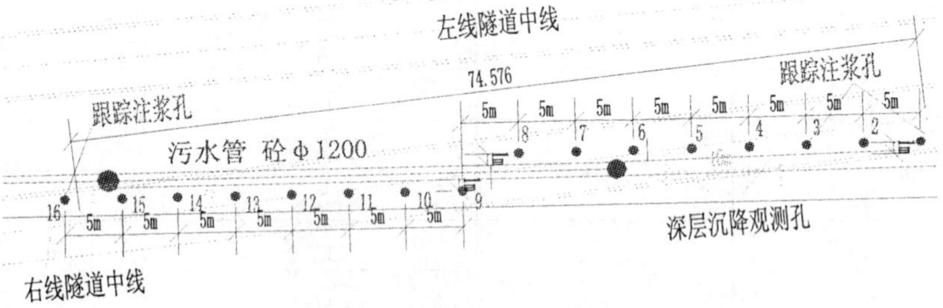

图 3 跟踪注浆孔平面布置图

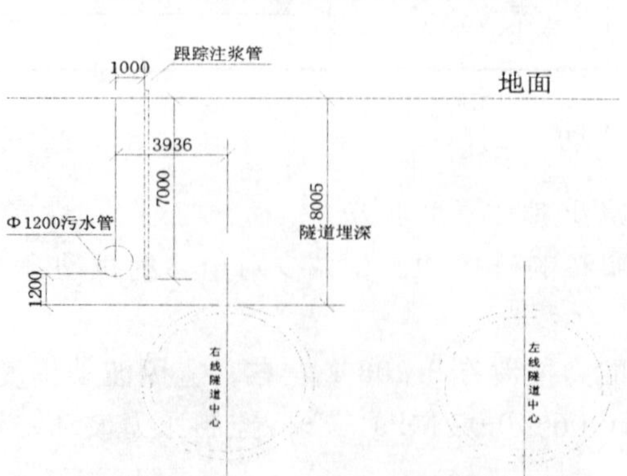

图 4 跟踪注浆孔布置剖面图

4 施工管理措施

没有严格的执行力，再好的方案也只能流于形式，施工中主要采取了以下组织管理措施。

(1) 根据前期调查，污水管运行基本正常，没有发生泄露现象。在盾构通过前后分别进行地质雷达探测，对比分析两次探测结果，发行异常及时采取措施处理。

图 5 污水管内水位监测

(2) 在盾构通过前半年时间里，通过检查井对污水管内水位进行了长期监测，了解不同时段的流量情况。

(3) 加强施工管理，严肃施工纪律

① 项目经理、副经理、总工程师实行 24 小时轮流值班，总体协调施工生产，妥善处理施工过程中出现的各种问题。

② 根据总体施工方案，制定详细可行的技术交底，组织所有施工人员进行学习，做到每位施工人员清楚自己的工作职责和作业要求，确保工序衔接到位。

③ 维修电工、盾构保养工跟班作业，设备故障时确保尽快恢复，避免盾构长时间停机。

(4) 安排专人进行不间断地面巡视，每小时对检查井水位监测一次，密切关注水位变化情况。

(5) 准备好应急人员和物资，出现险情时立即启动应急预案。

5 监控量测

监控量测已经成为盾构法隧道信息化施工的重要一环，监测信息及时反馈指导施工。

5.1 监测内容及结果

(1) 地表沉降

地表沉降测点布置分别在污水管中线地表和隧道中线地表，按间距 5.0 m 布置。

从监测结果看，一般沉降值在 7～12 mm，隧道中线地表累计沉降最大为－17.64 mm，污水管地表累计沉降最大为－14.4 mm，均未超出控制值，后期受地表注浆影响，部分测点隆起。

土体从扰动到趋缓从时间上来看约两天，以后变形量较小，表明砂卵石地层土体固结速度较快；特别是在地面跟踪注浆后 1 天内土体基本稳定。从产生的沉降槽来看，主要沉降区域集中在二倍洞径范围。

(2) 土体垂直位移

沿污水管走向轮廓外 0.6 m，在靠近盾构隧道一侧，每隔 10.0 m 布置一个土体分层沉降孔，孔底距离隧道结构顶约 1.0 m。

在盾构接近测孔时，深层土体有少量变形，盾构经过及盾尾脱出时变形较大，直至盾构通过后20 m左右，变形趋于稳定。最大变形为－22.22 mm。

（3）污水管流量、水位观测

利用检修井进行污水流量、水位观测，观测频率1 h/次，异常情况下加大观测频率。

从水位监测成果可看出，相同时段井内水位基本一致，表明盾构掘进未对管道造成破坏，引起管道内水流失或地下水涌入。

5.2 监测频率

按管理等级确定监测频率，当监测值小于预警值时，监测频率按2次/d；当监测值在预警值和控制值之间时，3～4次/d；当监测值大于控制值，应暂停施工，采取加固措施，4～6次/d。

6 结束语

在掘进时建立合理的土仓压力，严格控制出碴量、保证同步注浆回填饱满，及时进行跟踪注浆填充地层中的空隙，完全可以确保污水管的安全。

对富水砂卵石地层，待盾构机通过后地层受扰动变得松散时再注浆是非常有效的，可以有效地填充地层中的空隙，确保地层的密实性。注浆一般在盾尾脱出管片2～3 m时进行，过早注浆，浆液可能固结盾尾密封刷，也可能固结住盾体，增大推进阻力；注浆过晚，土体松散速率过快，可能造成地面沉降过大，影响污水管的安全。

作者简介（Bio-data）：

杨书江，1973年3月，男，高级工程师，工学硕士，公司副总工程师兼成都地铁二号线土建11标项目经理，中国土木工程学会隧道掘进机（盾构、TBM）专业委员会委员，主要从事隧道及地下工程施工管理。

Shujiang YANG (1973—), Male, Senior Engineer, Master of Engineering, Vice Chief Engineer of China Railway Tunnel Stock Co., Ltd., Project manager of civil work lot 11 in Chengdu Metro Line 2, One tunnel boring machine (Shield, TBM) professional committee member of China Civil Engineering Society, mainly engaged in tunnels and underground engineering construction management.

E-mail: ysj0321@163.com

土压平衡复合型盾构双级螺旋输送机对喷涌的控制技术

雷金山[1,3] 刘德智[2] 杨秀竹[1]
[1]中南大学土木建筑学院，湖南 长沙 410075
[2]广州市地下铁道总公司建设总部，广东 广州 5103802
[3]长沙持尔岩土工程技术有限公司，湖南 长沙 410004

【摘 要】 广州地铁六号线盾构区间部分在全断面淤泥质粉细砂层中掘进，该砂层密实性差、富水性和渗透性强、承载力较低，盾构机在掘进过程中，易产生喷涌现象，造成地表沉降，必须进行有效控制。本文结合六号线盾构“大一黄”区间工程实例，探讨盾构机在采用双级螺旋输送机后，通过控制密封仓内土压力，可有效控制变形，避免发生地面塌陷。总结了土压平衡盾构穿越富水砂层时的主要施工技术和措施。

【关键词】 土压平衡盾构；富水砂层；喷涌；掘进控制
中图分类号：TU 文献标识码：A

CONTROL TECHNIQUES OF SPEWING BY TWO-STAGE SCREW CONVEYOR IN EPB COMPOSITE SHIELD

Jinshan LEI[1,3], Dezhi LIU[2], Xiuzhu YANG[1]
[1]*Civil Architectural Engineering College, Central South University, Changsha 410075, Hunan, China;*
[2]*Guangzhou Metro Corporation, Guangzhou 510380, Guangdong, China;*
[3]*Changsha Cheer Geotechnical Engineering Technique Co.Ltd, Changsha 410004, Hunan, China*

Abstract: The shield section of Guangzhou Metro Line 6 is partially tunneled in full section stratum of silty soil, which is incompact, rich in water, and has strong permeability and low bearing capability. Spewing phenomenon emerges easily, which leading to settlement of ground surface; so, the tunneling process must be controlled effectively. Based on the construction example of the section from Datansha to Ruyifang in of Guangzhou Metro Line 6, this paper talks the avoidance of settlement after applying two-stage screw conveyor by means of controlling the pressure of soil in sealed cabin. At last, the main construction techniques and measurement of EPB shield crossing water-rich soil stratum has been summarized

Key words: EPB shield; water-rich soil stratum; spewing; tunneling control

1 引 言

盾构机是一种广泛应用于地下隧道工程的技术密集型重大工程设备，而土压平衡复合型盾构机以其施工安全、施工进度快、对环境影响小等优点，尤其适合于下穿江河海湖等土质地层中的隧道施工。螺旋输送机是土压平衡复合式盾构机的重要组成部分，它主要用来从盾构密封仓内将刀盘切削下来的泥土排出盾体，同时保持密封仓内土压力，维持开挖面土体的稳定。由于受不良地质的影响，螺旋输送机在

基金项目：湖南省自然科学基金资助项目（07JJ3104）

出土过程中，容易产生喷涌现象，导致土仓内压力急剧下降，引起开挖面土体失稳，从而发生地面塌陷事故。本文结合广州地铁六号线盾构二标（大—黄区间）工程实例，探讨盾构机在采用双级螺旋输送机后，如何有效地控制密封仓内土压力，避免发生地面塌陷事故。

2 概 况

2.1 工程概况

广州市轨道交通六号线盾构二标盾构隧道全长 5 115.5 单线延米，设计为双孔圆形隧道。沿线地处珠江海陆冲积平原，地势较为平坦，微向河流流向倾斜，线路经过江心洲并穿越珠江，然后基本与珠江平行延伸，地面标高 5.16～8.50 m。穿越地区主要为珠江、道路和建筑物。左右线始发时线路中线间距为 9 m，始发端头覆土厚度仅为 6.5 m。

2.2 工程地质及水文地质

根据线路地质勘探资料，左线 ZCK5＋211～ZCK5＋350 和右线 YCK5＋213～YCK5＋326 为全断面<2-2>、〈3-1〉、<3-2>砂层，左线 ZCK5＋350～ZCK5＋553 和 YCK5＋326～YCK5＋543.5 上部为<3-2>砂层下部〈5〉、<6>、<7>地层的上软下硬地层。砂层密实性差、富水性和渗透性强、承载力较低，特别是淤泥质砂层，强度低，容易产生变形。其中不良地质地层为:

<2-2>为淤泥质粉细砂层平均地层厚度为 7.24 m，深灰、灰、灰黑等色，呈饱和，松散～稍密状态，组成物为粉砂、细砂，局部为中粗砂，含淤泥质及少量有机质，局部有贝壳碎片；

<3-2>为中粗砂层平均地层厚度为 2.7 m，灰白、浅黄、灰等色，呈饱和，稍密～密实状，组成物主要为中砂、粗砂、砾砂，含少量粘粒。

盾构始发段砂层位于珠江江心岛——大坦沙岛上，四面环水，砂层中地下水与珠江存在水力联系，水量极为丰富，且补给及时。盾构隧道前约 300 m 为全断面＜2-2＞、＜3-2＞砂层以及上＜3-2＞、＜9C-2＞软下硬地层，透水性极好，如图 1 所示。

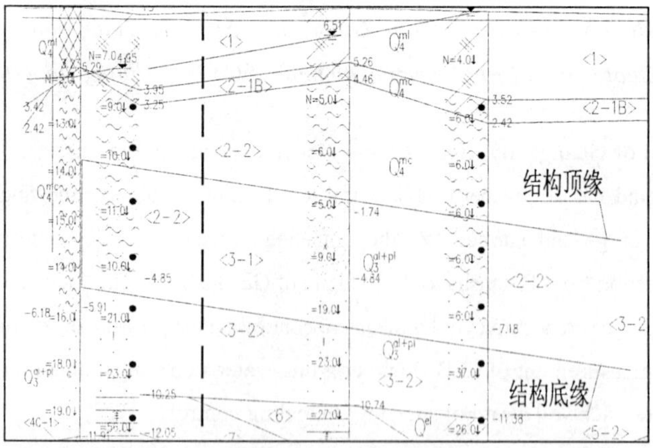

图 1 广州地铁六号线右线 YDK5＋199～YDK5＋329 地质纵剖面图

3 砂层盾构灾害及其发生机理

3.1 工程风险与灾害

广州市轨道交通六号线盾构二标（大—黄区间），由于在全断面（2-2）淤泥质粉细砂层等不良地质中掘进，隧道处于高水头不良地质条件，掘进中的突发性风险(塌方、喷涌、突泥等)较大。螺旋输送机在出土过程中，容易产生喷涌现象，必须进行有效控制。

现代盾构施工控制地表沉降最基本的方法是土压平衡技术，要求根据工作面实际压力的变化及时调整排土量，以调整和保证工作面有合适的支撑压力。目前通常用的方法是通过预先设定土仓内压力值，在施工中根据地表沉降情况再进行调整来稳定地层，是一种“滞后式”的土压纠正。由于开挖面上土层的原始应力非常复杂，这种预先设定与滞后调整的结果会使地面产生较大隆起或塌陷，地层的稳定和地表沉降控制的效果在很大程度上取决于施工人员的经验，施工质量难以保证。因此，如何根据工作面土压或地表变形实时调整螺旋输送机是关系到土压平衡盾构可靠掘进的关键技术问题，也是一个技术难点问题

3.2 盾构喷涌发生机理

土压平衡式盾构法施工是盾构机通过一定开口率的前方刀盘的切削，使开挖面土体进入压力舱，搅拌后形成渣土，利用千斤顶的推进及压力舱内隔板的作用，使切削下来的渣土对开挖面产生支护力，同时通过螺旋排土器不断排出渣土，达到开挖隧道的目的，如图 2 所示。

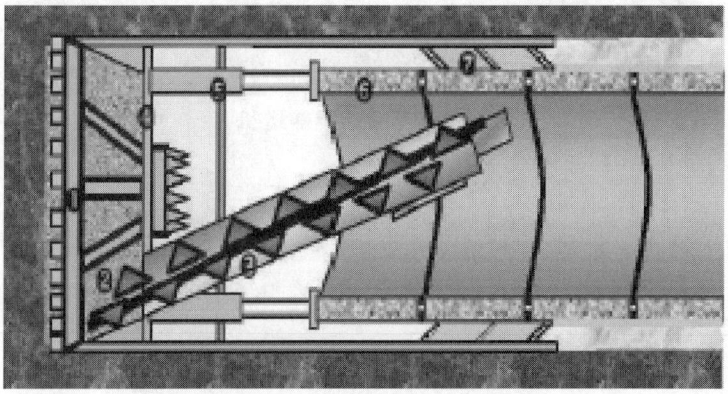

图 2 土压平衡式盾构机掘进示意图

土压平衡式盾构在富水砂层掘进过程中，由于开挖面存在高水头，导致盾构机内渣土存在压力水头，是喷涌发生的前提条件；同时，由于在砂层中，由于没有足够多的黏土物质，地下水与进入密封土舱内的固体物质不能糅合成一体，在密封场内形成“水是水”，“渣是渣”的状态。此事，此时进入密封土舱中的水流量要大于渣土量，这样，螺旋输送器变成具有一定压力的液流管道，而不是流塑或软塑状固体通道，一旦打开螺旋输送器闸门，就会有高压水夹带泥砂喷射出来，形成喷涌。

4 富水砂层喷涌控制技术

4.1 双极螺旋输送机的采用

螺旋输送机是土压平衡盾构的重要组成部分，它主要由圆筒状机壳和中心螺旋杆组成。其主要功能有：① 从有压力的密封土仓内将开挖下的泥土排出盾构；② 泥土在螺旋输送机内形成密封土塞，阻止土仓中的水流出，保持密封土仓土压平稳；③ 改变螺旋输送机转速，调节排土量，即调节密封土仓内土压力值，使其与开挖面水土压力保持动态平衡。

工作时，螺旋杆旋转，泥土充满机壳，由于泥土重量和泥土与机壳之间产生的摩擦阻力，机体内的泥土就像不旋转的螺母一样沿螺旋杆轴线平移输送。为了保持密封仓内的土压力平稳，一个重要因素是密切保持土仓内的进土量与排土量相匹配。通常采取两种控制模式，一种是控制进土量的推进速度控制土仓进土量，即通过土压检测，改变推进速度控制进土量，此时螺旋输送机转速事先设定；另一种是控制排土量的排土控制模式，即通过土压检测，改变螺旋输送机的转速控制排土量，此时盾构推进速度事先设定。

为了适应始发段的不良地质情况，该段选用了德国海瑞克生产的复合式土压平衡复合型盾构机，并对盾构机进行了相应技术改进，将原单级螺旋输送器改为双级螺旋输送器，转速为 0～22 rpm，在此转速范围内可以无级调速，从而可以实现在土压平衡模式下出碴量的控制，如图 3 所示。通过单独控制二级螺旋输送机的转速和起停，可有效地防止喷涌。

图 3 双级螺旋输送机

4.2 渣土改良技术

本段盾构机采用第二种排土控制模式，根据对地层条件的分析，对可能的喷涌根据施工向螺旋输送机内注入膨润土，高分子聚合物，改善渣土的和易性、增加渣土的黏度，形成有效的土塞，达到堵水和防止喷涌发生的效果。

通过试验室对（2-2）淤泥质粉细砂、（3-2）中粗砂进行各种改良试验探寻最佳的渣土改良添加剂和添加量。将砂土含水量控制在与实际情况相符的条件下，将各种改良材料（泡沫剂、高分子聚合物、膨润土等）。按照比例单独或相互混合掺入一定体积的砂土中，然后测试改良后渣土的流动性、渗透性等参数。

通过对试验室的试验结果进行分析，选取了能够有效降低砂土渗透性、改善砂土流动性且使用成本较低的泡沫剂作为此次盾构机穿越长距离全断面浅埋富水砂层的渣土改良剂。泡沫剂通过盾构机配备的泡沫泵与空气混合发泡后再通过土仓壁及刀盘面板上的泡沫注入管道注入。

采用泡沫剂改良砂层的要点在于降低砂土的渗透性、提高流动性和保水性，而泡沫剂的发泡率和掺入量对这些性能的影响非常的大，因此在采用泡沫剂改良渣土时应着重控制泡沫的发泡率、体积掺入量两个参数，使泡沫发泡后细腻，掺入砂土后仍能维持较长时间而不破裂。经过泡沫剂的改良后，刀盘前方及土仓内砂土的渗透性明显降低、保水性和流动性明显提高，基本不发生喷涌现象。

图 4 实际掘进渣土改良后的状态

4.3 喷涌控制施工要点

土压平衡盾构机在砂层中掘进最为关键的在于建立良好的土压平衡关系，本段始发段砂层位于珠江江心岛——大坦沙岛上，四面环水，砂层中地下水与珠江存在水力联系，水量极为丰富，且补给及时。盾构隧道所处砂层大部分为<3-2>砂层，为透水性极好的中粗砂。一旦发生喷涌，掌子面的砂层将会迅速流动、坍塌。在盾构机工作时应注意如下两点：

4.3.1 土仓压力的设定

对于本区段如何保持土仓压力与刀盘前方水土压力平衡，防止喷涌等是该段的施工关键。重点需要解决的问题是如何准确计算刀盘前方水土压力，为土仓压力设定提供理论依据。

根据朗金土压力理论，对于透水性较大砂层，采取水土分算的方法进行土压力计算。通常按照朗金主动土压力和被动土压力计算，计算时地下水位以下的土的重度采用浮重度。

（1）主动土压力

$$P_a = \sum \gamma_i Z tg^2\left(45^\circ - \frac{\varphi_i}{2}\right) \tag{1}$$

$$\sigma_a = P_a \cdot K_0 \tag{2}$$

（2）被动土压力：

$$P_p = \sum \gamma_i Z tg^2\left(45^\circ + \frac{\varphi_i}{2}\right) \tag{3}$$

$$\sigma_p = P_p \cdot K_0 \tag{4}$$

（3）水压力：

$$\sigma s = H\gamma s \tag{5}$$

土仓压力取值为主动土压力和被动土压力范围之间：

$$P=(\sigma_a+\sigma_s) \sim (\sigma_p+\sigma_s) \tag{6}$$

由上述公式即可计算出大如区间盾构隧道前 100 环的主动土压力理论值和被动土压力理论值，在实际盾构掘进施工中，土仓压力设定时为避免土压太大难以推进，取主动土压力理论值再增加 0.2 bar 左右作为土仓压力设定值。

4.3.2 双级螺旋输送机调控

在此类砂层中掘进，虽然采取了以上的各种改良渣土的措施，但是仍然难以保证渣土改良的效果，一旦螺旋输送机出渣口发生喷涌，就会造成土舱内压力骤减，使土压平衡破坏，开挖面土体失稳而造成坍塌。对此，可以通过双级螺旋输送机进行有效控制。

一旦发生了喷涌，立即利用盾构机所特有的双级螺旋输送器进行调节。

（1）首先关闭 1、2 级螺旋输送器的出渣口，使水、砂不再涌出，并向土仓及螺旋输送器前端注入高分子聚合物或膨润土等材料改善其渣土保水性，保持土仓压力不会减小；

（2）打开 2 级螺旋输送器后端的排水口慢慢将 2 级螺旋输送器内积水排除，再打开 2 级螺旋输送器将输送器内渣土排出后，再关闭出碴闸门；

（3）打开 1 级螺旋输送器的出碴口将土舱内渣土排出；a～c 循环进行直到土舱内渣土正常。

充分利用盾构机双级螺旋输送器的设备优势，经过上述步骤操作即可在发生喷涌后立即制止喷涌的继续进行，并可继续掘进而不造成土仓压力变化导致地表沉降。

5 结 语

土压平衡复合型盾构机采用双级螺旋输送机，是从机械设备上添加功能，在各种渣土该良措施均无明显效果时，可迅速起到止喷的作用，保持密封仓内土压力，避免发生地表塌陷。在地表有重要设施和建筑物时，是一种必要的安全保障措施。但不能从根本上该良渣土，在施工中还须针对各种不良地质，添加泡沫剂、膨润土、化学聚合物等材料，有效改良渣土。只有两者相辅相成，才能确保盾构施工的安全。

参考文献（References）：

[1] 竺维彬，鞠世健. 广州地铁 2 号线旧盾构穿越珠江的工程难题及对策[J]. 土木工程学报, 2004, 1(28).

[2] 华波，徐卫亚，吴来明. 砂层地段土压平衡盾构施工技术探讨[J]. 人民珠江，2006, 4.

[3] 江招胜，郭广才，黄威然. 水砂层中土压平衡盾构施工的技术措施[J]. 城市轨道交通研究，2006, 7.

[4] 朱伟，秦建设，魏康林. 土压平衡盾构喷涌发生机理研究[J]. 岩土工程学报，2004, 9(26).

[5] 刘德智，雷金山，杨秀竹. 广州地铁淤砂层明挖区间围护工程涌水涌砂分析与处治技术[J].长沙铁道学院学报，2009, 2.

[6] 秦建设，朱伟. 土压式盾构施工中地下水出渗机理研究[J]. 岩土力学，2004, 10(25).

[7] 竺维彬，鞠世健等. 复合地层中的盾构施工技术[M]. 北京：中国科学技术出版社，2006.

作者简介（Bio-data）：

雷金山，1973 年 6 月生，男，高级工程师，博士研究生，中南大学土木建筑学院岩土及地下工程系，长期从事岩土与地下工程的研究。主要研究方向：岩土与地下工程灾害防治，软弱地基处理与加固，岩土边坡稳定分析与加固。

Jinshan LEI (1973—), senior engineer, doctoral candidate engaged in the study of geotechnical engineering and underground construction. Main study direction: Subsoil treatment of geotechnical engineering and underground construction, stability analysis and reinforcement of slope.

E-mail: jslei8522@126.com

刘德智，1972 年 12 月生，男，工程师，广州市地下铁道总公司建设事业总部，从事盾构隧道建设管理工作。

大直径泥水盾构在中硬岩地层中的施工难点及对策

刘广钧　姚永勤　常　鑫　王冬胜
中铁十二局集团有限公司

【摘　要】文章系统总结了狮子洋盾构隧道在中硬岩地层中施工时遇到的碎石机故障和刀具磨损更换的两大技术难题，并通过在施工实践中不断的总结完善优化，提出了针对性的技术对策，供借鉴。

【关键词】 大直径；泥水盾构；中硬岩；施工难点

CONSRUCTION DIFFICULTY AND COUNTERMEASURE OF MAJOR DIAMETER SLURRY SHIELD IN MEDIUM-HARD ROCK CONDITION

Guangjun LIU，Yongqin YAO，Xin CHANG，Dongsheng WANG
China Railway 12 Bureau Group Co.Ltd

Abstract: The article summarizes the two major technical difficulties in the construction about crusher failure and tool wear replacement of the Shiziyang TBM in medium-hard rock. Through the improvement and the optimization during the practical construction, technical measures are put forward as reference.

Key words: large diameter; slurry shield; medium-hard rock; construction difficulty

1　概　况

1.1　工程概况

狮子洋隧道位于广深港客运专线东涌站—虎门站区间，全长 10.8 km，采用单洞单线结构形式，速度目标值为 350 km/h，盾构开挖直径为 11.2 m，采用 4 台 NFM-沈重生产的泥水平衡盾构机“双向施工，地中对接”。隧道在现状河床下覆盖厚度最大 45 m，最小 10 m。隧道最大水压力 67 m，为目前国内水压力最大的盾构隧道。

1.2　工程、水文地质

盾构隧道穿越地层为淤泥质土、粉质黏土、粉细砂、中粗砂、全风化-弱风化泥质粉砂岩、粉砂岩、细砂岩、砂砾岩。盾构穿越弱风化基岩、半岩半土、第四系覆盖物地层的长度分别占掘进长度的 73.3%，13.3%，13.4%。基岩的最大单轴抗压强度为 82.8 MPa，基岩层的渗透系数达 6.4×10^{-4} m/s，基岩的石英含量最高达 55.2%，岩石地层的粘粉粒（≤75 μm）含量为 26.1%～55.3%。岩石强度分布见表一。

表 1 岩石抗压强度分布情况表

试验状态	抗压强度			
	<5MPa	5 ~ 20MPa	20 ~ 50MPa	>50MPa
弱风化天然状态	0%	30%	60%	10%
弱风化饱和状态	2% ~ 3%	约 30%	60%	7% ~ 8%

2 碎石机的合理运用及优化

2.1 碎石机设计简介

碎石机用于破碎隧道盾构机挖掘的岩石，盾构机通过刀盘旋转切削掌子面的土体，使土体岩面的切削碎块通过开口率自然脱落至开挖仓内底部位置，岩石被大流量泥浆冲刷带至碎石机前进行“颚式”运动破碎后，达到管路可载动的粒径范围，由泥浆带出仓内至泥水站分离形成出渣。主要由碎石机壳体、工具支架和油缸三部分组成。

碎石机壳体由尾部和前部组成。尾部由焊接件组成（尾部墙，壳体底部及上部），前部通过螺栓进行密封。通过螺栓连接这两部分。尾部墙带一个隔栅，该隔栅限制了所运输通过的岩石的尺寸，保证岩块粒径大小。配有碎石机钢板的工具支架和油缸旋转座是通过螺栓和铰接轴承安装的。

工具支架（左、右）由焊接件制成，安装在旋转轴承中，通过螺栓和在碎石机壳体上的铰接轴承进行安装。碎石机钢板嵌入到每个工具支架腔中，通过螺栓进行紧固。根据使用不同的碎石机钢板件，碎石机钢板末梢均匀分布。安装在工具支架中铰接轴承上的螺栓固定碎石机油缸。此外，工具支架尾墙配有搅拌冲洗装置，用于清扫尾墙的隔栅间隙。

碎石机油缸通过法兰连接在油缸转轴上，油缸转轴固定在碎石机壳体上。碎石机产生的破碎力由油缸液压单元能力决定。

2.2 施工中遇到的主要问题

(1) 螺栓断裂

油缸法兰与破碎机耳轴采用 14 颗 M24×120（10.9 级）螺栓连接，使用中频繁断裂见图 1。

图 1 连接螺栓断裂

(2) 油管连接处漏油

油缸连接处经常性的漏油，密封圈损坏，见图 2。

(3) 活塞杆锈蚀、划伤

在长时间的使用过程中，油缸活塞杆不同程度地出现锈蚀、划伤等现象，见图 3。

图 2　密封圈损坏漏油

图 3　活塞缸锈蚀、划伤

2.3　碎石机故障原因分析

在中硬岩地层中掘金时,碎石机已成为制约正常掘进的主要故障之一,维修时间占到了总时间的 20% 左右，为提高其使用寿命，对碎石机进行了分析，故障的主要原因有：① 碎石机使用工况恶劣。按照碎石机的设计，每分钟动作 4 次，在中硬岩地层掘进时，尤其是遇到节理、裂隙较发育的地层，碎石机需一直工作，按照每环（2 m）掘进 2.5 h 计算，每环碎石机需开合 600 次，全隧 2 442 环大约需开合 146 万次，工况恶劣；② 油缸法兰与碎石机耳轴连接螺栓属动态不稳定型受力，波动性大，易产生脉冲受力，螺栓长时间运行下易产生疲劳而破坏；③ 油缸法兰与耳轴连接处采用单向螺栓受力方式连接，加大了螺栓的疲劳损坏的程度；④ 油缸活塞杆运行时浸泡在泥水及渣土中，甚至是与石块接触，导致活塞杆已锈蚀、划伤；⑤活塞杆密封受活塞杆的锈蚀、划伤影响而泄漏；⑥ 油管由于处于泥水中且随时摆动，导致易磨损和泄漏；⑦ 耳轴处螺栓的选型（强度）对受力有影响；⑧ 耳轴的运动状态对缸体与耳轴连接处的螺栓受力也有一定影响。

2.4　碎石机改造优化

依据现场的实际情况及故障原因分析，优化方案主要为：① 废除原油缸底部位置的耳轴设计，在油缸顶部位置重新设立一个“耳轴”，此耳轴设计为一个销轴型固定于油缸顶部位置，销轴两侧固定于碎石机侧板上，并在侧板顶部加焊一个直角三角形的压板固定销轴；② 销轴孔处增加一个小轴承，减小刚体机械磨损；③ EP2 润滑油脂管路改造至销轴端部；④ 原油缸顶部的进油口改至油缸侧面位置；⑤ 油缸活塞杆采用质量好、防腐蚀、防划伤的材质进行制造，密封采用进口密封件。

对碎石机改造好，其使用寿命明显延长，但修理的时间仍占到 10% 左右，需要进一步分析、优化。

2.5　辅助技术对策

(1) 碎石机在工作时出现异常情况，特别是在行程达不到标准值时，应及时进行开仓检查，避免螺栓折断后长时间动作对缸体、活塞杆及耳轴带来更大损坏；

(2) 在环流系统出渣畅通情况下（速度在 15～18 mm/min），尽量试着不用碎石机，能不用及时停止使用,或进行时用时停方式运行破碎机，由操作手时时注意环流出渣状况而定，需逐步摸索；

(3) 依据岩层的强度、硬度，对油压适当降低，提高其使用寿命；

(4) 辅助泵站每日应观察油质、油位情况，发现异常应及时检查并报告相应管理人员，每月对油质进行检验；

(5) 勤检查刀具情况，尽量保证刀具磨损在标准范围内（正面滚刀磨损量 15 mm，边缘滚刀磨损量 8mm），确保刀具的有效切屑，从而对环流出渣有益。

3 刀具磨损及更换

3.1 盾构刀具配置

狮子洋隧道选用的盾构机刀盘由 8 块辐条及和相应的幅板所组成的面板式刀盘，刀盘结构和驱动装置之间通过 8 个梁来连接，这 8 个梁位于刀盘面板横梁和用螺栓连接于驱动部分的重型环圈之间。主要参数见表 2。

表 2 刀盘主要技术参数

刀盘结构形式	8 个辐条 + 面板
分块数量	3
开挖直径	11 200 mm
开口率	32%
先行撕裂刀数量	无
切刀数量	278 把
切刀型式	双层碳钨合金刀齿、背部装有双排碳钨合金柱齿
切刀最大磨损量	2×32 = 64 mm
周边刮刀数量	16 把
周边刮刀型式	装有一排连续碳钨合金齿和双排碳钨合金柱齿
周边刮刀最大磨损量	32 mm
仿形刀数量	1 把
扩挖刀行程	75 mm
周边保护刀	16 把
17″ 滚刀	50 把单刃滚刀 + 10 把中心滚刀
换刀方式	背装式（可从刀盘后部拆卸、安装刀具）
搅拌臂数量	4 个
刀盘防磨保护	硬化处理并堆焊耐磨材料

3.2 刀具使用中存在的主要问题

在中硬岩地层中掘进时，刀具的使用与更换是最重要的问题之一，据统计，刀具更换的时间已占到总时间的 27% 左右。在硬岩地层中掘金，刀具方面遇到的主要问题有：① 刀具磨损快，更换频繁。按照刀具设计，边滚刀磨损限值为 20 mm，正滚刀磨损限值为 25 mm，超过磨损限值的需及时更换，据统计数据分析，刀具正常磨损一般在 80～100 环，需更换一次。② 刀具异常磨损多。刀具异常磨损包括刀具偏磨、刀轴磨损，刀圈断裂等，刀具异常磨损的原因有很多，不同的磨损形式也对应不同的原因，但最主要的原因是由于地层节理、裂隙不同程度的发育。据统计数据分析，在岩层完整性较差的地段，刀具没 30 环左右，将产生非正常的磨损，需对刀具进行更换。③ 刀具固定不牢固，掉刀频繁。在裂隙异常发育的地层，由于刀具在刀盘旋转中受力不均，刀座和楔快在不均匀受力下变形，容易使固定刀具的螺栓破换，或者大块岩层掉落，对刀具的固定造成严重影响，从而使得刀具掉入土仓。

3.3 主要技术对策

（1）定期开仓，对刀具进行检查、紧固。在施工中每 30～50 环定期开仓对刀具进行检查并更换磨损严重的刀具。经开仓统计，边滚刀和正滚刀的使用寿命一般在 80 到 100 环，边滚刀对盾构机的开挖直径、保护刀盘和刀盘扭矩方面有重要影响，同时考虑部分刀座的变形和楔块的脱落对刀具的影响，通常每 30～50 环就开仓一次，目前看效果还不错。

（2）加强对地质的预判和出渣情况的分析，实时修正掘进参数，避免刀具的过度使用。尤其对于岩层裂隙发育的地段，更应及时检查、更换刀具。

（3）细化掘进餐宿，减少刀具磨损，如在裂隙发育地段，采用降低刀盘转速、减小贯入度、降低掘进速度等方法保护刀具。

（4）细化进仓方案，形成进仓的标准化作业程序。将进仓作为盾构施工不可或缺的正常施工工序来管理，着力加快进仓的作业安排，缩短进仓的作业时间，提高进仓作业的效率。

4 结 语

狮子洋隧道施工中面临的大直径泥水盾构长距离在岩层中掘进技术在国内尚属首次，无类似的经验可供借鉴。在施工实践中通过不断总结经验和教训，丰富和发展了类似地层的盾构施工技术，初步取得了较好的效果，可供类似工程借鉴。

作者简介（Bio-data）：

刘广钧，男，出生于1970年7月，大学本科毕业，高级工程师，现为中铁十二局集团第二工程有限公司副总经理、广深港客运专线狮子洋隧道 SDⅡ标项目部经理。一直从事施工技术和管理工作，先后参建了京九铁路、湖南资兴过船轮水电站、深圳盐坝高速、深圳地铁等多项国家和地方重点工程的建设。

Guangjun LIU (1970—), male, bachelor, Senior Engineer. He is currently the general deputy manager in the Second Engineering Co., Ltd. the Group of China Railway 12 Bureau, and the project manager of the Guangzhou-Shenzhen-Hong Kong Passenger Line Shiziyang Tunnel SD Ⅱ project. He has been always engaged in construction technology and management .He has worked in a number of national and local key projects, such as the Beijing-Kowloon Railway, Hunan Zixing hydroelectric station, Yanba express highway in Shenzhen and the Shenzhen Metro.

大型盾构输水隧洞技术应用研究

张 弢 王 雷 杨文明

北京市水利规划设计研究院，北京 100048

【摘 要】 盾构以其机械化程度高、推进速度快、对环境适应性强、工程拆迁量小等优点广泛的应用在城市交通隧洞工程中。北京市南水北调配套工程团城湖至第九水厂输水工程隧洞采用盾构管片内衬钢筋砼的结构形式，开创了北京市大型盾构输水隧洞的先例，为盾构技术在水利工程中的应用奠定了基础。团城湖至第九水厂输水工程（一期）输水隧洞全长 8.23 km，其中盾构全长约 7 km，工程主要位于清河北岸，工程地质和水文地质条件复杂，地下水位平均位于洞顶以上 2～3 m。隧洞沿线穿越多处住宅区、河道、立交桥区、高速公路和多条铁路。盾构机采用土压平衡盾构机，设计盾构直径为 6 m，成洞直径为 4.7 m。本文以南水北调工程为背景，结合水利工程的特点，在盾构管片和内衬混凝土结构连接形式、隔离层兼防排水、空气阀井的设置、盾构端头和排气井连接等方面进行了研究和工程应用。通过监测数据和实践证明，盾构和钢筋混凝土复合衬砌结构模型及相关构造要求是合理可行的，为以后类似工程提供技术参考。

【关键词】 南水北调；盾构输水隧洞；结构形式；隔离层；防排水设置；端头连接

APPLLIED RESEARCH ON WATER DELIVERY TUNNEL OF LARGE SCALE SHIELD

Tao ZHANG, Lei WANG, Wenming YANG

Beijing Institute of China, Beijing 100048, China

Abstracts: Shield machine is extensively used in the city tunnel project for its advantages of high level of mechanization, fast speed, easily adjustment to the environment and less work of the removal, etc. The structural style of Concrete precast pipe element and the reinforced concrete inside it is adopted in the tunnel water delivery project from Tuancheng Lake to the Ninth Water Factory of South-to-North Water Diversion Auxiliary Project of Beijing, which created a precedent in such kind of project in Beijing and laid a foundation in the application of the hydraulic engineering. The water delivery tunnel of the first-stage construction is 8.23km long; whose shield tunnel length is about 7km.The project is mainly located in the North of Qing River in the north of Beijing. Engineering and hydrologic geology are complicated, and the water table is averagely 2 to 3 meters above the tunnel. The tunnel passes through several residential areas, watercourses, flyover areas, free ways and two or more railways. Earth Pressure Balance Shield Machine is used with 6m in designed shield diameter and the last diameter of the tunnel is 4.7m. Taking it as the background of South-to-North Water Diversion Project and according to the characteristics of the water conservancy project, A study and application in engineering have been done in this paper in terms of the following aspects, the link form of the Concrete precast pipe element and the inner reinforced concrete, isolation layer and water-proof and drainage, the installation of the well of exhaust valve and the joint between the Concrete precast pipe element and the well of exhaust valve. This compound structure has been proved reasonable and feasible by monitoring data and practice, which give technical reference in the similar project.

Key ways: South-to-North water diversion; large water delivery tunnel; the form of structure; isolation layer; the intercalation of water-proof and drainage; front-end joint

1 引 言

盾构施工法是在地面下暗挖隧洞的一种施工方法，它使用盾构机在地下掘进，在防止软基开挖面崩塌或保持开挖面稳定的同时，在机内安全地进行隧洞的开挖和衬砌作业。其施工过程需先在隧洞某段的一端开挖竖井或基坑，将盾构机吊入安装，盾构机从竖井或基坑的墙壁开孔处开始掘进并沿设计洞线推进直至到达洞线中的另一竖井或隧洞的端点。

团城湖至第九水厂输水工程（一期）为北京市南水北调配套工程，新建输水隧洞 8.23 km。输水隧洞采用盾构管片内衬钢筋混凝土的结构形式，圆形断面，外层衬砌为外径 6 m，厚 0.3 m 拼装预制钢筋混凝土管片；内层衬砌为厚 0.35 m，内径为 4.7 m 现浇混凝土结构。最大内水压力为 30 m 水头，输水隧洞平均覆土厚度为 12 m 左右，最大厚度为 18 m，所处地层以中细砂、圆砾和粉质黏土为主。地下水位高于洞顶高程 3～7 m 左右。盾构管片内衬钢筋混凝土的结构形式为北京地区压力输水隧洞首次采用。

2 盾构输水隧洞结构分析

盾构隧洞通常用于市政工程中，主要应用于铁路和公路行业，盾构隧洞通常用拼装完成的管片结构作为隧洞的主要结构，主要承担外部水土等荷载。对于输水隧洞，由于隧洞承受内压，北京目前市场上生产的盾构用管片多数以弯螺栓连接为主，这种管片主要是压弯构件，所以一旦直接承担内部水压力，将使管片间承受拉力，管片间接缝的开张度超过限制值将发生渗漏现象，同时影响结构的整体强度。团城湖至第九水厂输水工程隧洞既要考虑充分利用盾构施工的优点同时应满足输水隧洞承受内水压力的特点。工程采用盾构管片内衬钢筋混凝土的结构形式。隧洞不但要依靠外衬管片承受外部荷载，还要依靠内衬钢筋混凝土承担内部水压力。盾构管片与内衬钢筋混凝土的受力分担和相互作用及双层间接合面处理是复合衬砌盾构输水隧洞关键技术。根据双层衬砌受力特性和接合面结构处理方式的不同，有 5 种相互作用模型，具体见图 1。

形式一：

盾构管片、内衬钢筋混凝土衬砌共同组成隧洞的主要结构，把盾构管片和内衬钢筋混凝土之间用突出物等连成一体，使其成为承担外压和内水压结构。施工期盾构管片单独承受外围土压力、外水压力和施工荷载，运行期盾构管片和内衬钢筋混凝土共同承担内水压力、外水压力和地面荷载变化等附加荷载。内衬混凝土甚至钢筋伸入外管片手孔等凹槽中，这些部位能传递压力、剪力及弯矩。可设置为刚接杆，其余部位设置为不抗拉压缩弹簧。但是这个模型难以分析在盾构管片和内衬钢筋混凝土一体化时管片已发生的应力并难以选用一体化后的荷载的评价方法。

形式二：

盾构管片衬砌作为隧洞的主要结构，内衬 40 mm 钢丝网水泥砂浆，主要起着减少过水断面糙率和对外衬管片补强、防水等维护作用。施工期盾构管片单独承受外围土压力、外水压力和施工荷载，运行期仍是盾构管片承受内水压力、外水压力、土压力和地面荷载变化引起的附加荷载。内衬施工前将外管片内表面的螺栓手孔、注浆孔、起吊孔等凹槽用水泥充填抹平。内衬 40 mm 钢丝网水泥砂浆。由于内衬钢丝水泥砂浆仅起到减小断面糙率，所以结构计算模型上不考虑，在承担内水压力时，主要受力结构仍然是外衬管片。依据北京市现有的管片生产情况，管片间采用弯螺栓连接，当直接承受内水压力时将增大管片间张开量，影响隧洞的结构安全和防水效果。

形式三：

盾构管片、内衬钢筋混凝土衬砌共同组成隧洞的主要结构。施工期盾构管片单独承受外围土压力、外水压力和施工荷载，运行期盾构管片和内衬钢筋混凝土共同承担内水压力、外水压力和地面荷载变化等附加荷载。浇筑内衬前抹平外管片内表面较大的凹槽，其余部位凿毛或不作处理。此时内外层之间能传递压力及部分剪力，双层之间的作用以沿接合面均布的抗压抗剪组合弹簧模拟。由于内外层间结合的不规则性，所以很难确定剪切弹簧的刚度和分布情况。

形式四：

盾构管片、内衬钢筋混凝土衬砌均为隧洞的主体结构，采用单纯荷重分担模式。这种模式需外衬和内衬之间有充分的间隔。盾构管片、内衬钢筋混凝土衬砌相互独立工作，即：盾构管片承受外围土压力、外水压力和地面荷载变化引起的附加荷载；而内水压力则由内层衬砌来承担。盾构管片与内衬钢筋混凝土间下半拱 90°范围内采用抗压弹簧模拟。此种结构计算模型要求，管片与内衬钢筋混凝土间的间隙足够大，这样会导致结构的过水断面减小。

形式五：

盾构管片、内衬钢筋混凝土衬砌均为隧洞的主体结构，其间由弹性垫层分隔，使盾构管片和内衬钢筋混凝土分离的作用，该结构形式鉴于形式四和形式一、三之间。盾构管片主要承受外围土压力、外水压力和地面荷载变化引起的附加荷载，内水压力主要由内衬钢筋混凝土承担，当内衬变形到一定范围，将通过弹性垫层将部分压力传递到管片。内衬施工前将外管片内表面的螺栓手孔、注浆孔、起吊孔等凹槽用水泥充填抹平。此时可假定内外层之间只传递压力而没有剪力和弯矩，双层之间的作用以沿周向均布的不抗拉压缩弹簧模拟。

通过上面的分析，形式四需要双层衬砌间有足够的间隔，应完全变形，计算模型如图 1 所示。形式三由于没有隔离层，虽然在内衬混凝土浇注完后，由于混凝土的收缩作用，在内外衬之间将产生间隙，可是由于间歇非常小，在考虑管片有符合要求的错台及施工中内衬与外衬不同心的影响作用。所以当承担内水压力后，外衬管片对内衬的变位将起到很大的制约作用。势必导致剪力和压力的传递。采用形式五，即可以起到形式四的作用有可以避免形式三和一传递剪力及弯矩的作用，考虑到现有的厂家制造管片的情况（大多为弯曲螺栓），工程工期的紧迫性，施工技术难易性，过水断面的不减小。采用形式五隔离层连接形式受力明确，工期较短，投资合理。

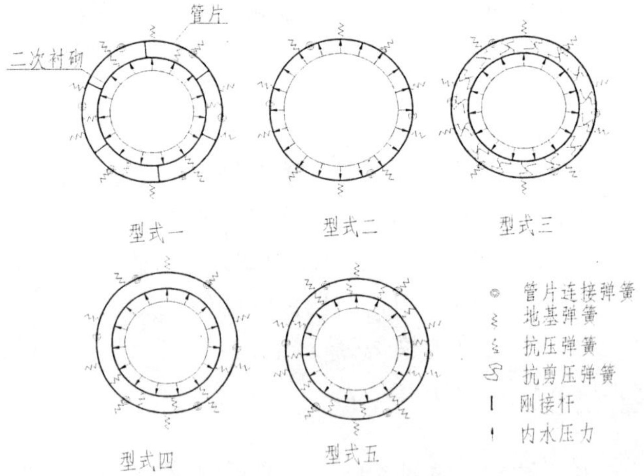

图 1　双层衬砌连接模型图

采用盾构管片和内衬钢筋混凝土之间设置隔离层的形式五，在输水隧洞布置有安全监测仪器，如：钢筋计、应变计、混凝土应力计等监测复合衬砌隧洞在不同工况条件下的受力状况。安全监测仪器断面图如图 2 所示：

从图 2 中可以看出在隧洞 0°、90°、180°、270°、360°分别在二衬混凝土结构上布置有监测应力和应变的仪器。现根据不同工况条件下有代表性的监测到的数据折算成弯矩和轴力表 1 进行分析。

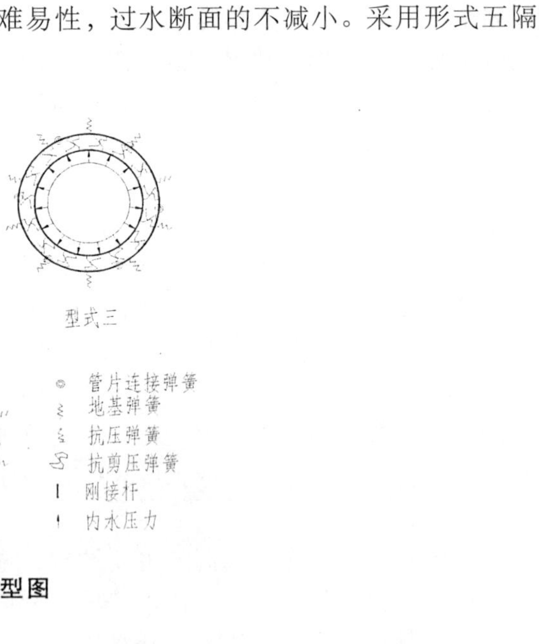

图 2　盾构输水隧洞监测仪器布置断面图

表 1　弯矩轴力表

工　况	结构形式	弯矩（kN.m）	轴力(kN)	备　注
隧洞施工完建	内衬结构(90°)	−10	5	自重产生
	内衬结构(0°，180°)	7	−4.5	自重产生
	内衬结构(270°)	−12	−5.5	自重产生
通水运行	内衬结构(90°)	−50	643	内水压力产生
	内衬结构(0°，180°)	58	636	内水压力产生
	内衬结构(270°)	−62	657	内水压力产生

注：表中轴力拉为正，压为负；弯矩内侧拉为负，外侧拉为正。

从表中数据可以看出，在隧洞施工完建后，外衬管片变形已基本稳定，外部荷载没有传递到二衬结构，二衬结构产生弯矩和轴力主要是自重产生。通水运行阶段，二衬由于受内水压力比较大，有一部分力传递到一衬管片但大部内水压力由二衬承担。从表 1 可以看出结构受力状态比较吻合盾构管片和内衬钢筋混凝土之间设置隔离层的形式五模型假定。

3　隔离层设置及防排水研究应用

在确定的盾构和钢筋混凝土复合衬砌结构基础上，关键是如何确定结构间隔离层的设置，隔离层应即起到隔离衬砌间弯矩和剪力的传递，同时应起到排水和防水的作用。隔离层采用复合土工布和防水板结合的形式，双层衬砌间设排水管网，外包裹复合土工布。复合土工布紧贴盾构管片铺设与管片用单组分氯丁-酚醛胶黏剂黏接，防水板靠紧二衬混凝土铺设。防水板主要作用起到防水作用，排水管网主要起到排除缝间积水，总的起到内防外排的作用。

4　空气阀井设置研究

对于有压输水隧洞避免气囊运动和水锤压力的不利影响，按照规范要求，在拐点高处和一定距离设置空气阀，团城湖至第九水厂输水工程工程，采用复合衬砌的结构形式，在复合衬砌的盾构管片和钢筋混凝土上设置空气阀，将对结构强度和隧洞的防排水产生不利影响。

根据隧洞所处地质条件及沿线局部穿越建筑物的具体情况，最终确定盾构区间长度控制在 2 km 左右。结合现场场地条件，共布置了 5 座盾构工作井，其中单始发井 1 座、始发兼接收井 1 座、双始发井 1 座，接收井 2 座。将盾构隧洞划分成了 4 个盾构区间，区间长度为 1.7～2.1 km 不等。隧洞平面布置上受地表条件限制设转弯 10 处，最小转弯半径 400 m。纵段上设拐点 1 处，转弯半径 5 000 m，最大纵坡 0.67%。

盾构机在掘进 1 km 左右需要检查刀盘。结合施工特点，在沿线 4 个盾构区间分别依区间长度和场地条件布置了 1～2 座竖井，共 7 处竖井，竖井主要作用为临时用作盾构机检查井和二衬材料设备的进出口，永久作为空气阀井。及大的节约投资和加快施工进度。

竖井内采用现浇钢筋混凝土结构， 现浇钢筋混凝土隧洞顶预埋设钢管，钢管上安装空气阀。竖井与两侧的复合衬砌采用止水带连接。

5　端头井构造连接研究

盾构管片为 C50W10 的高强度预制钢筋混凝土管片。以下为团城湖至第九水厂输水工程采用的盾构管片形式。管片厚度为 300 mm，隧道管片衬砌外管片环宽 1 200 mm，环向分 6 块，即 3 块标准块（中心角 67.5°），2 块邻接块（中心角 67.5°），一块封顶块（中心角 22.5°）。管片之间采用弯螺栓连接（螺栓直径 24 mm），环向有纵缝 6 个，每接缝有环向螺栓 2 个；纵向端面共设纵向螺栓 16 个封顶块 1 个，其他管片端面 3 个。管片环与环之间采用错缝拼装方式。管片端面采用平面式，仅在设置防水胶条处留有沟槽。管片有 3 种类型，即标准环、左转弯环和右转弯环。

盾构预制管片及钢筋混凝土二衬和沿线的竖井如何连接将直接影响结构强度和全线工程的防排水问题。

团城湖至第九水厂输水工程中，采用如图 3 的连接形式。

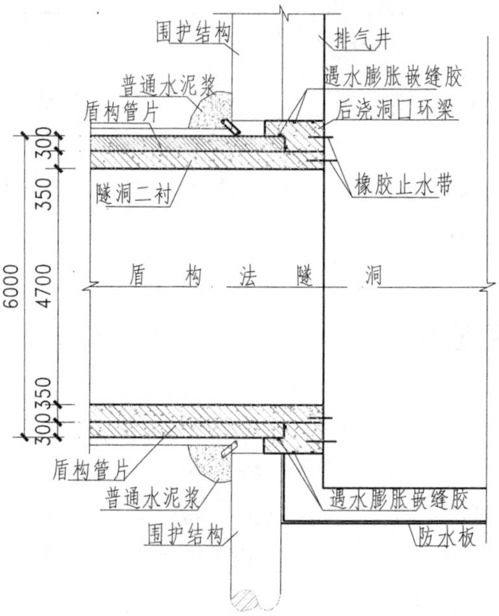

图 3 端头结构连接防水构造图

图 3 中盾构管片在竖井位置通过后浇环梁与排气阀井连接。管片预制中，进出洞环管片迎竖井端面预埋钢板，拼装管片完成后，预埋钢板上焊接钢筋锚固到后浇环梁中。后浇环梁和管片及竖井洞口处共粘贴 4 道遇水缓膨胀嵌缝胶。在管片与竖井围护结构间预埋设注浆管，在管片拼装后，根据隧洞的防水情况对其进行灌浆处理。后浇环梁和隧洞二衬分别通过橡胶止水带和排气井中现浇隧洞结构相连。隧洞中排水系统跨越两道止水带入排气井的积水坑。供运行管理人员根据积水情况进行抽排。

6 结 论

盾构输水隧洞在南水北调配套工程中的应用，为输水隧洞工程开辟了新的施工工法和结构形式。在工程的实施过程中，在盾构管片和内衬混凝土结构连接形式、隔离层及防排水设置、空气阀井的布设、盾构管片端头和排气井连接等方面进行了研究和应用。为以后类似输水隧洞工程提供技术参考。

参考文献（References）：

[1] 张弢等. 盾构管片内衬钢筋混凝土大型输水隧洞结构研究. 水利水电技术, 2009（7）.

[2] 杨秀仁. 北京地铁盾构隧道设计施工要点. 都市快轨交通, 2004（6）.

[3] 张厚美，过迟，吕国梁. 盾构压力隧洞双层衬砌的力学模型研究. 水利学报，2001（4）：28-33.

[4] 周文波. 盾构法隧道施工技术及应用. 中国建筑工业出版社，2004（11）.

[5] 张凤祥等. 盾构隧道. 人民交通出版社，2004（9）.

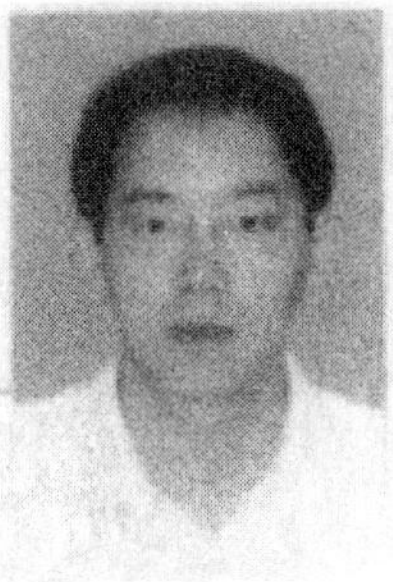

作者简介（Bio-data）：

张弢，1977 年出生，男，工程师，大学本科，北京市水利规划设计研究院设总，从事水利水电工程设计。

Tao ZHANG, (1977—), male, engineer, bachelor degree, Beijing Institute of Water, the general design engineer, engaging in engineering design of water resources and hydropower.

Telephone number: 13693511690;

Email: ztao1977@163.com

盾构采用辅助工法通过硬岩段施工技术的研究与应用

王家祥 贾 科

中铁二局股份有限公司城通公司，上海 200336

【摘 要】 随着城市地铁的快速发展，采用盾构法修建城市地铁隧道的情形越来越多，在软硬不均或软硬交互且岩石强度差异很大的复合地层采用盾构法修建地铁隧道就越来越复杂，本文通过深圳地铁5号线盾构工程的实例介绍盾构采用辅助工法通过硬岩段施工技术的研究与应用，意在为以后类似工程提供借鉴。

【关键词】 盾构；辅助工法；硬岩段；施工技术；应用

THE STUDY AND APPLICATION OF SHIELD METHOD IN COMPOSITE FORMATION USING AUXILIARY CONSTRUCTION TECHNOLOGY THROUGH HARD ROCK ABOVE

Jiaxiang WANG，Ke JIA

China Railway Erju Co.Ltd, Shanghai 200336, China

Abstract: With the rapid development of Metro, the subway shield tunnel construction of the city where more and more uneven in the soft and hard or soft and hard rock strength interaction and different strata of the composite used to build metro tunnel shield on the more complex. Based on the Shenzhen Metro Line No. 5 examples, this paper introduced the study and application of shield method in composite formation using auxiliary construction technology through hard rock above, it is aimed to provide future references for similar projects.

Key words: shield; support engineering; hard rock above; construction technology; applications

1 引 言

1.1 中国内地地铁的发展趋势

首次获批修建地铁的城市有北京、上海、广州、天津、南京、深圳、武汉、西安、重庆、成都、哈尔滨、长春、沈阳、杭州、苏州、宁波等；正在规划报批地铁的城市有南宁、无锡、大连、东莞、昆明、郑州、长沙、福州、贵阳等；正在筹备建设地铁的城市有合肥、青岛、济南、厦门、太原、大同、兰州等。这些城市地域跨度大，地质条件迥异，目前中国内地地铁施工水平正处在高速发展的阶段，要在全国范围内优质、高效的修建地铁，必须探索新工艺、新工法。

1.2 深圳地铁5号线的特点

深圳地铁5号线贯穿深圳城市建设的第一、二圈层，连接城市总体规划的西、中、东三条发展轴，是深圳市轨道交通网络中“南北贯通、西联东拓”、“扩大内陆腹地对外交通”的骨干线，地铁5号线的建设对形成深圳轨道网络基本骨架至关重要。深圳地铁 5 号线采用 BT 模式建设，是目前国内最大的地铁 BT 项目，地铁 5 号线之所以采用 BT 模式修建，其最直接的好处，是能最大程度地加快施工进度，缩短工期，以保证为将于 2011 年在深圳举办的世界大学生运动会提供良好的城市轨道交通条件。深圳地铁 5 号线也是深圳市目前最长、地质最复杂的一条地铁线，综合施工难度巨大，在这种条件下，要想把深圳地铁 5 号线建成绿色、环保、节约型人文地铁，要想缩短工期、节省投资，我们必须要深入研究新的工法。

2 辅助工法方案设定及评估分析

2.1 盾构区间工程概况

深圳地铁 5 号线 5305 标两个盾构区间分别为长龙站—布吉站区间及布吉站—百鸽笼站盾构区间。线路整体成南北走向，最小曲线半径 $R=400$ m，最大曲线半径 $R=450$ m，区间隧道设计施工工法如图 1 所示。

图 1 区间隧道设计施工工法图

2.2 方案分析和设定

盾构机在长距离硬岩地层中掘进，应根据盾构机的破岩能力、刀盘结构布置及盾构机的其他性能，评估盾构机在硬岩段掘进的适应性，辨识和分析各种施工风险，考虑采用辅助工法的可行性，并进行进度和技术经济比较，选择在硬岩段施工中合理的施工方法。

（1）本工程区间隧道根据地质初勘、详勘、补勘,准确地判定硬岩段连续掘进距离长，最长地段连续掘进长度达 700 m，岩石强度 160～215.2 MPa 之间，高于盾构机设计破岩能力 15 MPa，目前在广深地区，盾构机对岩石单轴抗压强度低于 80 MPa 的硬岩地层施工是基本适应的，但盾构机在 100 MPa 以上硬岩段连续掘进长度超过 100 m 的工程实例基本没有，但根据海瑞克经验和评估，盾构机在 100 MPa 以上硬岩段掘进工效很低，且本工程硬岩段连续掘进距离长，最长地段连续长度达 700 m，掘进风险极高。

（2）根据调查及了解，国内通常在岩石单轴抗压强度达到 80 MPa 且连续长度达到 100 m 以上时，采用矿山法先行开挖及施作初支，盾构机拼装管片通过的方式来通过硬岩段。

（3）盾构机在局部硬岩地层中掘进易造成刀具意外破坏和非正常磨损，不仅增加直接成本，且由于掘进速度慢，其他辅助工作费用也增大，将造成施工成本增加。

（4）盾构机拼装管片通过已开挖硬岩段的速度比盾构法在一般较硬岩层地段的掘进速度快，经比较，能够提前工期，节约工程成本。

2.3 总体施工方案

本区段（暗挖盾构空推段）在盾构机空推前，首先进行盾构与暗挖段分界端头墙、混凝土导台、暗挖段堆碎石等的施工；然后在空推掘进过程中，进行同步注浆，并采用管片固定螺杆对已拼装好的管片加固；最后在空推通过后，对空推段进行二次补充注浆固结整环管片。

3 主要施工工法和技术要求

3.1 总体施工流程

暗挖盾构空推段总体施工流程图如图 2 所示：

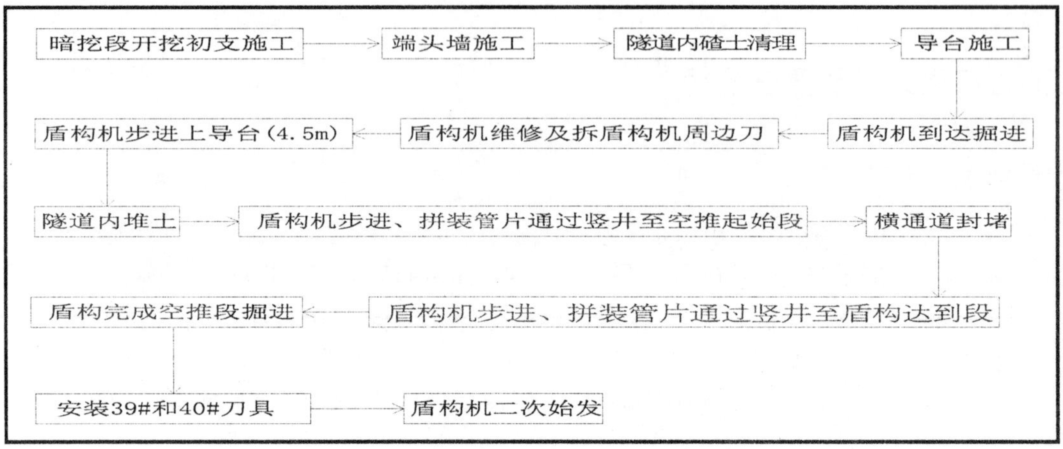

图 2 暗挖空推段总体施工流程图

3.2 主要施工方法和工艺

3.2.1 *矿山法暗挖段导台施工*

矿山法隧道开挖完成初期支护后，在隧道底部 60°范围内施工钢筋砼导台，钢筋砼导台的内径 $R=$ 3 150 mm，外径 $R=$3 300 mm；钢筋砼导台的中心线与隧道中心线重合，且钢筋砼导台对称于隧道中心线。

3.2.2 *矿山法暗挖空推段堆填碎石施工*

盾构机导台施工完成并达到设计强度的 80% 之后，暗挖空推段隧道 25 m 范围内首先要进行碎石回填，25 m 以后要在半断面内进行碎石回填。

（1）碎石回填目的

① 给盾构机提供足够反力，推进千斤顶顶推管片使管片三元乙丙橡胶止水条挤压密贴，达到良好止水效果。

② 在刀盘前方形成密闭堆载体，让盾构机形成正常推进的土压平衡模式。

（2）碎石回填施工

导台施工完成后，待砼强度达到设计强度的 80% 后，方可在隧道内进行碎石回填施工，碎石粒径宜采用 10～30 mm，所需碎石从区间竖井向下投放至竖井底，通过汽车运输到预定施工地段，采用 ZLC40 装渣机进行堆填，从盾构与暗挖分界点开始往竖井方向回填。盾构推进前，刀盘前方依次全断面填碎石长度 15 m，然后放坡填碎石长度 10 m，隧道碎石回填示意图如图 3 所示。

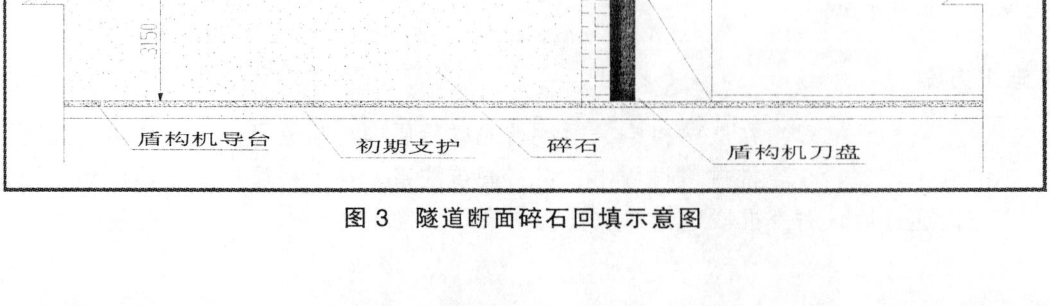

图 3 隧道断面碎石回填示意图

（3）碎石回填后对盾构机的提供的反作用力计算

① 推进时砼导台对盾构机的摩擦阻力

$F_1 = \mu_{摩} \cdot W_g = 0.3 \times 3\ 430 = 1\ 029$ kN

W_g——盾构及附属物总重＝3 430 kN

$\mu_{摩}$——摩擦系数取 0.3

② 回填碎石受到的摩擦阻力

$F_1 = \mu_{摩} \cdot (\pi D2/4) \cdot L \cdot \gamma_{石} \cdot K = 0.3 \times (3.14 \times 6.252/4) \times 22.5 \times 1.87 \times 9.8 \times 0.83 = 3\ 148.32$ kN

L——回填碎石的长度，全断面 15 m，放坡 10 m，故折算成全断面共 22.5 m

K——碎石的松散系数

$\gamma_{石}$取 1.87 t/m^3

③ 盾构支撑碎石所受的轴向阻力

$F_2 = S_{盾构面积} \cdot P_{盾构中心土压} = (\pi D2/4) \cdot L \cdot \gamma_{石} \cdot K_g = (3.14 \times 6.252/4) \times 1.87 \times 6.25/2 \times 9.8 \times 0.39 = 684.88$ kN

K_g——碎石的侧压力系数

④ 盾尾刷与管片之间的摩擦阻力（以 2 环管片计算）

$F_3 = \mu_{磨} \cdot 2W_{管} = 0.5 \times 2 \times 200 = 200$ kN

每环管片 W 管取 200 kN

⑤ 后部拖车的牵引阻力

$F_4 = \mu_{磨} \cdot W_{拖} = 0.5 \times 1\ 700 = 850$ kN

因此，盾构机掘进时堆碎石后所提供盾构反作用力总计为：

$F = F_1 + F_2 + F_3 + F_4 + F_5 = 1\ 029 + 3\ 148.32 + 684.88 + 200 + 850 = 5\ 912.2$ kN

（4）管片止水条需要挤压力计算

管片三元乙丙橡胶止水条挤压性能如下图所示，单条管片橡胶止水条挤压量达到 12 mm 时的挤压力 50 kN/m,一环管片橡胶止水条总长约 18.84 m，则挤压一环管片橡胶止水条需要的推力为 $F_1 = 50*18.84 = 942$ kN，相领管片橡胶止水条为 2 道，则总挤压力 $F = F_1*2*1.5$(安全系数)＝2 826 kN。盾构机前方堆填碎石后的总推力计算为 5 912.2 kN＞止水条挤压力 2 826 kN，故盾构机推进产生的推力满足管片止水条挤压力的要求。

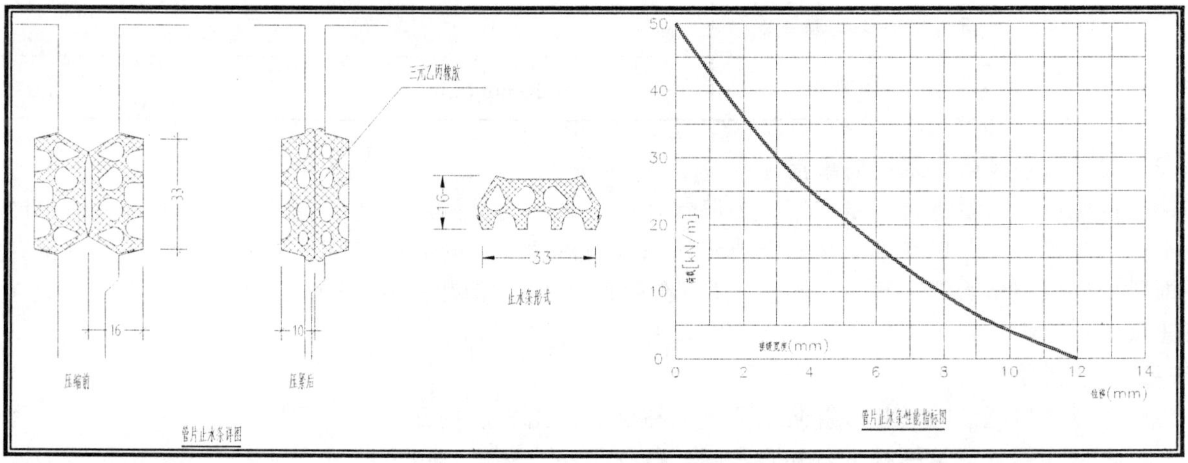

图 4　管片止水条性能指标图

3.2.3　盾构到达段施工

（1）拆除刀具

暗挖空推段钢筋砼导台半径为 3.15 m，故在盾构上导台之前应拆除 2 把铲刀、2 把刮刀。为确保盾构顺利通过分界墙，准确步入导台，在拼装完实推最后一环时，开仓将 2 把铲刀及 2 把周边滚刀（39# 及 40#）拆除。

（2）盾构掘进

根据到达段的工程地质及水文地质条件和到达段对掘进施工的特殊要求，在到达段盾构掘进采用敞开式模式进行掘进。盾构机进入到达段时，首先逐步减小推力、降低推进速度，加强每一环掘进的出土量的监控频次。其掘进施工参数见表 1。

表 1　掘进参数表一

编号	项　目	参数	备注
1	土仓压力	敞开式	
2	刀盘转速	1.7 ~ 1.9 r/min	
3	推　力	≤800T	
4	盾构姿态水平偏差	0	
5	盾构姿态垂直偏差	+ 10 mm	
6	推进速度	≤35 mm/min	

在贯通前的最后 3 环，要进一步减小推力、降低推进速度。盾构机采用小推力、低速度掘进完到达段，进入盾构接收段。其掘进施工参数见表 2。

表 2　掘进参数表二

编号	项　目	参　数	备注
1	土仓压力	敞开式	
2	刀盘转速	1.6 ~ 1.8 r/min	
3	推　力	≤600T	
4	盾构姿态水平偏差	0	
5	盾构姿态垂直偏差	+ 10	
4	推进速度	≤20 mm/min	

（3）管片注浆及防止浆液前窜措施

每环按照设计方量进行同步注浆，为确保在盾构到达空推段后，纯盾构段隧道地下水及同步注浆的浆液不往空推段涌入，以切断后续水源或浆液涌入刀盘位置，同时提高管片抗浮能力，在掘进拼装完成至空推段分界里程倒数第三环后，停止掘进，在倒数第 10 至倒数第 6 环进行二次注浆，确保连续 5 环全断面注满。

（4）管片拼装

为确保隧道贯通后的管片接缝防水要求，在到达矿山与盾构分界里程后开始，安装每一片管片时，先用人工将每片管片连接螺栓进行初步紧固；待安装完一环后，用风动扳手对螺栓进行进一步的紧固；待管片出盾尾之后，重新用风动扳手进行紧固。

3.2.4　盾构机步入导台施工

碎石回填密封刀盘前方断面，碎石充填盾体与暗挖初期支护间的间隙，同步注浆正常开启，管片止水条密封良好，此条件下的两种工况示意如下：

（1）工况一

盾构机到达碎石回填断面，未向前推进，见图 5。

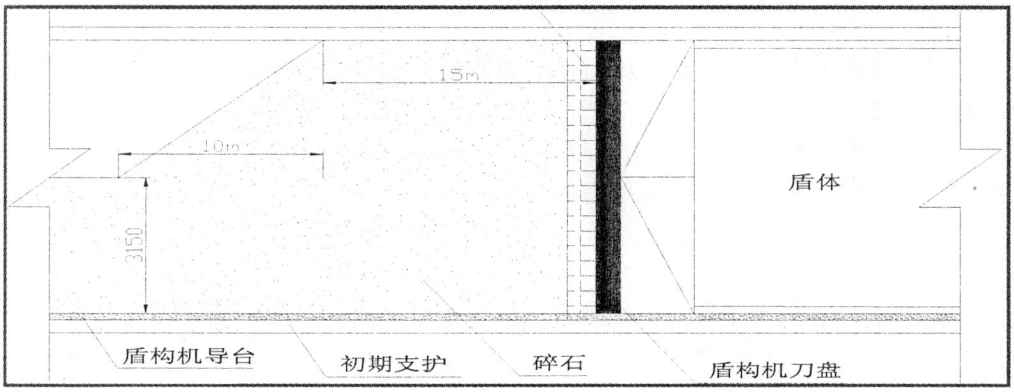

图 5　工况一示意图

（2）工况二

盾构机向前推进，管片拼装和同步注浆与正常段掘进时一样，见图 6。

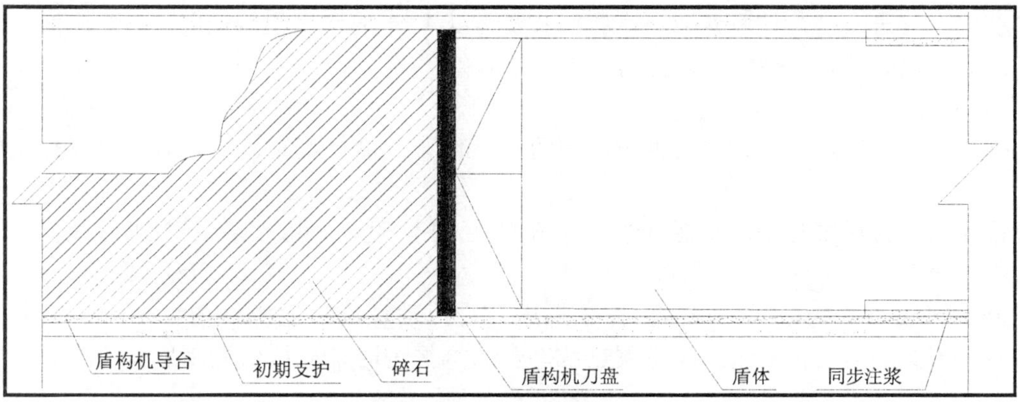

图 6　工况二示意图

3.2.5　*盾构空推段施工*

当盾构机进入导台后，启动盾构机往前掘进，根据刀盘与导向平台之间的关系，调整各组推进油缸的行程，使盾构姿态沿线路方向进行推进。然后开始进行管片拼装、管片背衬回填工作。推进时，推进速度不能过快，控制在 35 mm/min 之间，同时启动同步注浆工作。盾构机向前推进，见图 7。

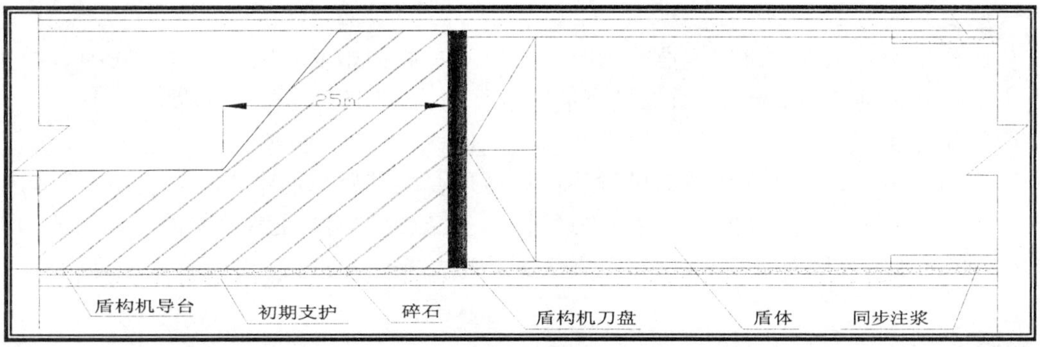

图 7　盾构机推进示意图

管片与已开挖成型隧道间由回填小碎石充填，同时开启同步注浆加水玻璃进行填充，当土仓内土压（1 号位置达到 0.8 bar）或推力达到 800 t，开启螺旋输送机进行出土。

（1）盾构掘进

盾构掘进模式采用不建压模式，掘进推力控制在 800 t 以内（主要以掘进速度控制在 30 mm/min 来控制推力大小），当掘进推力大于 800 t 以上，可启动螺旋输送机出渣，但要控制出渣量，掘进过程中，土仓内不加气压和泡沫。

（2）拼装管片

盾构在推进时，保持上下推进油缸油压相等，使盾构机在导台的导向下往前推进。在轴线高程中推进。通过控制盾构盾尾与管片外围间隙的控制，控制管片符合设计轴线要求。管片拼装工艺与正常掘进时的工艺相同，管片选型时要根据盾尾间隙与油缸行程差结合盾构姿态选择合适的管片。

在安装每一片管片时，先用人工将每片管片连接螺栓进行初步紧固；待安装完一环后，用风动扳手对螺栓进行进一步的紧固；待管片出盾尾之后，重新用风动扳手进行紧固。

（3）管片固定

盾构掘进过程中启动了同步注浆，并且隧道内目前从掌子面上有较大的水在涌入隧道，为防止管片上浮，待管片拖出盾尾后及时在顶部（9 点至 3 点以上位置）将管片进行固定，管片固定采用从吊装头上安装螺杆进行固定，每隔 2 环固定一环。

（4）管片背衬回填

① 空推掘进阶段

当盾构机开推后启动同步注浆系统。运用特制三通，利用盾构机自身的同步注浆系统由盾尾压注水泥砂浆和水玻璃同时进入进行注浆作业。砂浆和水玻璃以 4：1 的比例混合同时进入，以期达到快速凝固来使管片与初支及地层间紧密接触，以提高支护效果。

② 空推完成后

空推段掘进完成后停止掘进，对空推段所有管片拱顶背后进行填充，同时对所有管片螺栓进行再次复紧。

空推段管片拱顶背后填充采用水泥砂浆作为填充料，注浆设备采用砂浆泵，注浆压力控制在 0.5Mpa。

3.2.6 盾构二次始发

盾构机到达矿山与盾构分界里程后，停止掘进，将启动螺旋输送机将土仓内土全部出完，将原拆除的 39#和 40#刀具安装就位后进入正常掘进状态。盾构掘进时，应严格控制盾构机姿态，避免出现大的突变。

4 辅助工法方案实施效果

4.1 施工进度

（1）掘进速度方面

盾构机从盾构始发井始发后进行实推，同时在布吉站—盾构始发井区间竖井，对硬岩段实施矿山法开挖。矿山法平均开挖进度为 2 m/d，盾构机空推进度平均为 15 环/d（即 24 m/d）。

（2）工期风险方面

在硬岩段采用矿山法开挖初支后盾构机拼装管片通过，能够避免途中岩石强度超出盾构机破岩能力不能掘进而停机后，等待矿山法初支，然后空推通过，大大拖延工期。更为严重的是如果盾构卡在途中硬岩段，盾构硬岩实推掘进段地面有建筑物群，无施工矿山竖井采用辅助工法的条件，拖延的工期将会更长。

4.2 管片姿态

空推施工完成后对盾构姿态进行了测定，相邻管片允许高差≤4 mm，相邻环的环面间隙≤1 mm，纵缝相邻块块间间隙≤1 mm，衬砌成环后（刚出盾尾时）直径允许偏差：2% D（D 为隧道竖向外径）。衬砌环椭圆度≤20 mm，隧道水平轴旋转角度≤0.6°。

4.3 盾构机的使用寿命和性能方面

盾构实推段也存在局部硬岩，在硬岩段掘进时换刀频率高，刀具磨损较大，已掘进硬岩段刀具磨损情况如图 8 所示。

图 8　刀具磨损图

对区间硬岩段采用矿山法爆破开挖初支后采用盾构空推拼装管片通过，避免了盾构在硬岩段实推掘进时，出现刀具严重偏磨后，盾构通过的净空不够，盾体被卡；避免了盾构机在硬岩段掘进时，岩石强度太高，损坏盾构机刀盘和驱动设备。

5　结论与建议

由于目前城市地铁施工普遍面临工期紧、任务重的特点，采用辅助工法提高施工效率是非常必要的。辅助工法是由地质、工期、环境等因素共同决定的。考虑到城市地铁施工特殊的施工环境，在类似地质条件下，应该尽量减少纯矿山法隧道的施工，发展盾构法及其辅助工法施工技术，一方面可以减少隧道施工对城市环境的影响；另一方面盾构施工可以减少城市隧道施工的安全、工期以及成本风险。

参考文献（References）:

[1]　吴全中. 盾构隧道长距离硬岩地层钻爆法开挖管片衬砌施工技术.

[2]　周文波. 盾构法隧道施工技术及应用.

[3]　白云，丁志诚. 隧道掘进机施工技术.

作者简介（Bio-data）:

王家祥，男，1979 年 10 月出生，大学本科，工程师，现任中铁二局股份有限公司城通公司深圳地铁 5 号线 5305 标项目经理部总工程师。自大学毕业后一直从事城市地铁盾构隧道工程施工技术管理，对地铁隧道盾构施工有较深的认识。

Jiaxiang WANG, male, born in October 1979, undergraduates, engineer, the current position is the Chief Engineer which is of the China Railway Erju Co.Ltd's section 5305 ChengTong Project Manager of the Shenzhen Metro Line No. 5.After graduating from the University has been engaged in the management of subway tunnel using shield technology, have gained a better understanding on the subway tunnel using shield.

E-mail: wjx756221@163.com

贾科，男，1973 年 11 月出生，硕士学位，高级工程师，现任中铁二局股份有限公司城通公司深圳地铁 5 号线 5305 标项目经理部项目经理。

Ke JIA, male,born in November 1973,master's degree,senior engineer, working as a project manager of section 5305 projects of Shenzhen Metro Line No. 5 of ChengTong company of China Railway Erju Co.Ltd.

新建盾构隧道下穿运营隧道的相互影响研究

夏炜洋 何 川 汪 洋 汪 波 晏启祥
西南交通大学 地下工程系，四川 成都 610031

【摘 要】 新建地铁隧道下穿既有运营隧道时，隧道的施工和运营会相互产生影响。以深圳地铁 3 号线下穿运营 1 号线为工程背景，采用数值模拟方法，分析了 3 号线下穿施工对 1 号线轨道位移的影响，计算了列车运行产生的荷载，并对 3 号线产生的内力影响进行了研究。

【关键词】 盾构隧道；数值模拟；施工；运营

INTERACTION INFLUENCE BETWEEN RUNNING TUNNEL AND NEW SHIELD TUNNEL IN STAGE OF CONSTRUCTION AND OPERATION

Weiyang XIA, Chuan HE, Yang WANG, Bo WANG, Qixiang YAN
Department of Underground Engineering, Southwest Jiaotong University, Chengdu 610031, Sichuan, China

Abstract: The interaction influence between shield tunnel in the stage of construction and operation when new bulding tunnel crossing running tunnel. Based on the LINE 3 project crossing LINE 1 in SHENGZHENG METRO, analysis of track displacement of LINE 1 caused by construction of LINE 3 has been analyzed by means of numerical simulation, and then, the vibration loads of train in LINE 1would be got. Finally, this paper studies tunnel internal force of LINE 3 caused by train vibration of LINE 1.

Key words: shield tunnel; numerical simulate; construction; operation

1 引 言

拟建深圳市地铁 3 号线购物公园站—福田站区间呈南北走向，区间隧道为两条并行的单线隧道，采用盾构法施工。出购物公园站北端约 30 m，3 号线区间隧道下穿既有深圳市地铁 1 号线（已运营）购物公园站—香蜜湖站区间隧道，1 号线区间隧道大致呈东西走向，区间隧道为两条并行的单线隧道，采用盾构法施工，两条隧道在平面上大致正交，隧底之间净距约 1.2 m，具体位置关系见图 1。

图 1 地铁 3 号线与 1 号线位置关系图

基金项目：863 计划（2006AA11Z116）；铁道部课题（2007G036、2006G007B）

近距离隧道下穿既有隧道施工，会对既有隧道的结构和运营带来影响，对近接施工这一地下工程问题，已引起大家的广泛重视和研究[1, 2]。同时，地铁列车运营也给周边环境带来了新的问题，包括噪音和周边建筑物的结构问题[3, 4]。因此，深圳地铁 3 号线盾构的施工对 1 号线隧道的营运必然会造成较大影响，同时 1 号线隧道在运营过程中也会对 1 号线隧道产生结构上的影响，为了量化该相互影响，需对两隧道的施工运营进行结构分析，以保证隧道施工及结构安全。

2 下穿施工对运营轨道的影响

2.1 计算模型

根据深圳地铁地勘报告和相关资料确定计算模型的物理力学参数见表 1。管片、道床、轨道三者的相互关系如图 2 示，由于轨道依附于道床近似固接，在计算中可利用道床上的纵向节点建立梁单元来模拟轨道，轨道尺寸由梁单元截面控制，本区间钢轨拟采用 60 kg/m 耐磨普通热轧钢轨，钢轨横截面近似为工字形截面，左右轨距 1.435 m，线路中心线处的轨面至界限圆底部的高度为 0.74 m，隧道与轨道的细部模型如图 3，整体计算模型见图 4。

表 1　地层与结构材料物理力学参数

材料	黏聚力/kPa	内摩擦角/°	变形模量/MPa	泊松比
素填土	18	14	3	0.39
粉质黏土	22	15	20	0.3
砾质黏土	24	21	40	0.28
全风化花岗岩	25	24	60	0.26
强风化花岗岩	26	24	80	0.25
管片衬砌	/	/	27600	0.2

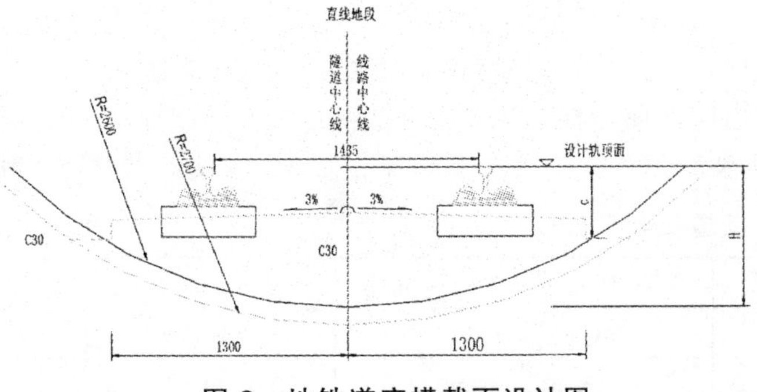

图 2　地铁道床横截面设计图

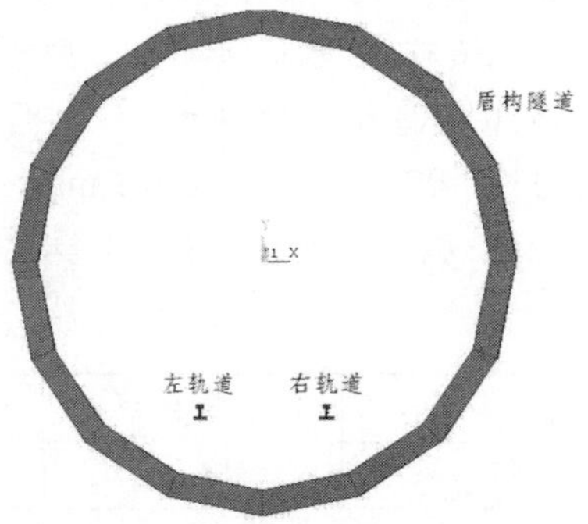

图 3　地铁轨道与盾构隧道相互关系图

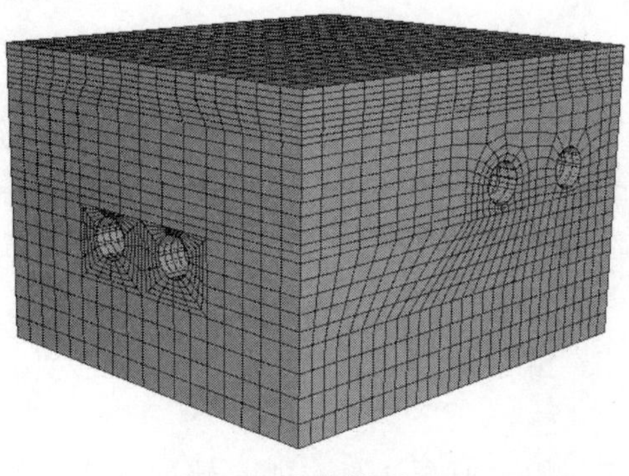
图 4　计算模型图

2.1 计算结果分析

根据运营线路轨道静态尺寸的监测控制指标，轨道的监测包括4大方面：轨道竖向变形、两轨道横向高差、水平及水平三角坑高低差、轨距变化。通过数值模拟得出了相应的结果如图5、图6所示。

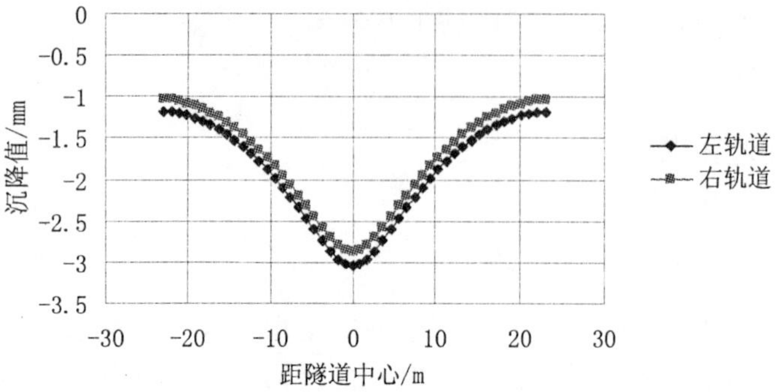

图5 地铁轨道竖向变形图

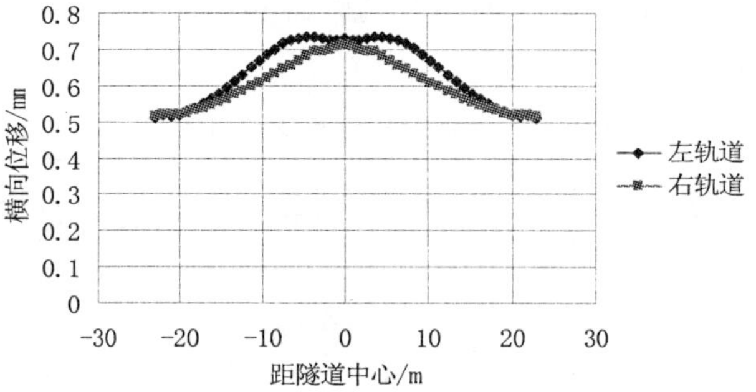

图6 地铁轨道横向变形图

从图5中很明显地看出，由于拟建隧道施工使轨道产生了竖向变形，最大值在拟建隧道中心部位上方约为 3 mm；同时由于左右轨道的不均匀竖向位移使两轨道产生了横向高差，通过分析其最值约为 0.17 mm；在两股钢轨顶面产生了水平三角坑高低差，其值约为 2 mm/46 m。

从图6中很明显地看出，由于拟建隧道施工轨道沿盾构掘进方向产生了横向变形，最大值在拟建隧道中心部位上方不到 1 mm；同时由于左右轨道的不均匀横向位移使轨距发生了变化，通过分析其变化范围为+0.07 mm，−0.0012 mm(“+”为两轨道向两侧分离，“−”为两轨道向中心靠拢)。经过计算，由表2可以看出由于3号线下穿1号线正交施工使轨道产生的变形在控制指标内，轨道本身是安全的。

表2 轨道安全评定表

指　标	轨道竖向变形	两轨道横向高差	水平及水平三角坑高低差	轨距变化
控制指标	±4 mm	<4 mm	<4 mm/10m	+6 mm，−2mm
数值模拟结果	约−3 mm	约−0.17 mm	2 mm/46 m	+0.07 mm，−0.001 2 mm

3 一号线运营对三号线结构的影响

地铁列车在运行过程中产生的振动会对周边地层和建筑物产生影响。车辆和轨道是一个耦合系统，该系统产生的振动传递给道床，经过衰减后作用于地层。因此在考察车辆运营时需先求解车辆——轨道耦合模型的荷载问题。

3.1 模型建立

目前在用的求解列车运行时荷载的主要方法是车辆—轨道耦合系统模型[5]，图7为该模型示意图。

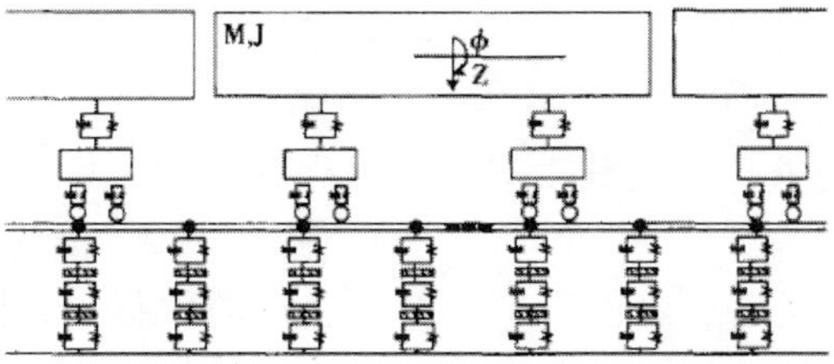

图 7 车辆——轨道耦合动力学模型

地铁中车辆的运行速度一般在 100 km/h 左右，考虑到适用性，取 100 km/h，地铁车辆的编组为 6 节，车长 25 m，质量为 40 t。在计算机上进行动力学模拟，可以得到某时刻作用于道床底部的列车荷载，见图 8。

列车的振动是通过列车底部的轮对对轨枕施加影响的，而一般认为该动力响应的影响范围为前后 6 个轨枕距离。考虑对称性，建模研究 1 号线列车经过 3 号线右线正上方时对隧道的结果影响。

3.2 计算结果分析

图 9 为 1 号线列车通过过程中 3 号线隧道的竖向位移等值线图，可以看出 3 号线隧道的位移在 1 号线下方较大，两边程减小趋势，其值在 E-4 量值上。通过位于 1 号线下方的点 477 的位移时程曲线，看出在列车行驶过程中，点 477 位移逐渐向下，在 2 s 时达到最大位移值，为 0.22 mm，随后位移逐渐减小，见图 10。

从图 11 看出，弯矩随列车行驶过程而变化，在列车通过隧道正上方时其值最大，为 800 N · m。3 号线隧道的轴力分布类似于弯矩分布，1 号线下方影响较大，两端影响较小。

1 号线运营过程中对 3 号线隧道产生的最大位移为 0.22 mm，远小于隧道施工过程中产生的最大沉降；运营引起的最大附加弯矩为 800 N · m，最大附加轴力为 30 KN，一般管片衬砌能承担 10^2 KN · m 量级的弯矩和 10^3 KN 量级的轴力。因此可以得出在该工况下，既有 1 号线的运营，会对 3 号线的隧道结构产生一定的影响，但影响可不作为控制设计和施工的考虑。

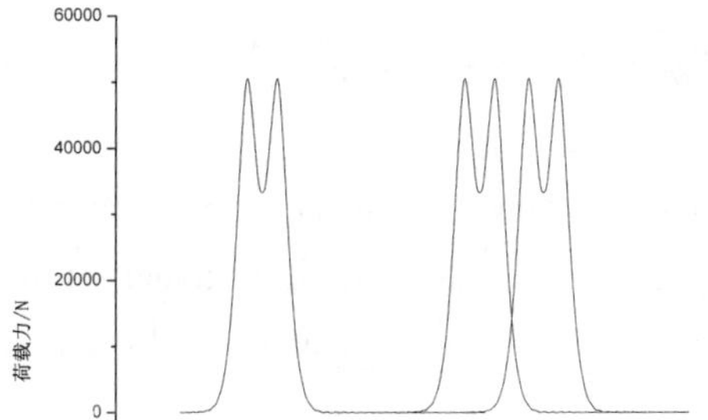

图 8 列车荷载曲线图

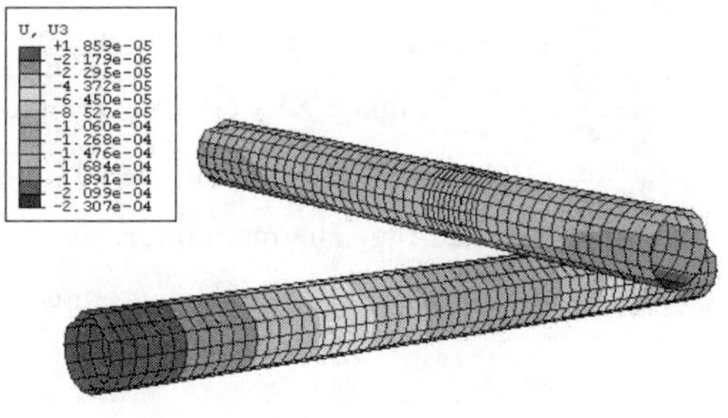

图 9 隧道竖向位移等值线图

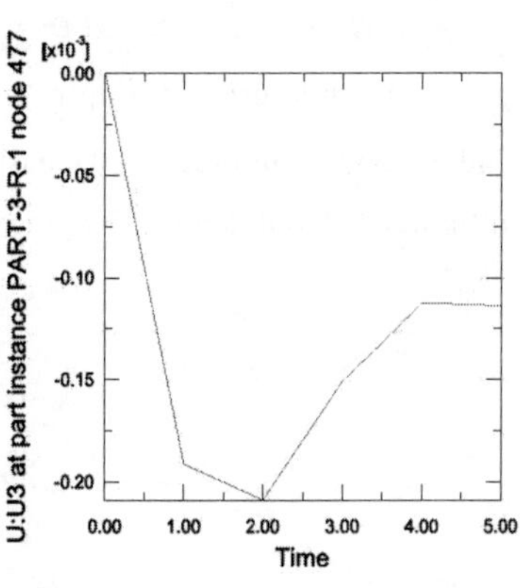

图 10 点 477 位移时程曲线

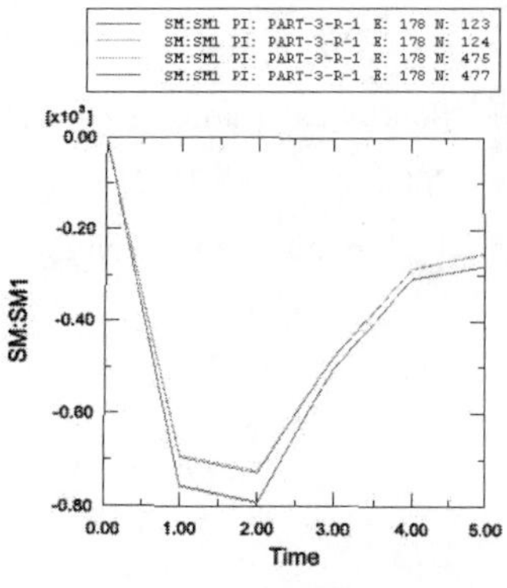

图 11 单元 178 弯矩时程曲线

4 结 论

本文采用数值模拟对深圳地铁 3 号线施工对 1 号线运营的相互影响进行了分析，通过计算，得出如下结论：

（1）3 号线施工对于 1 号线运营产生的影响主要在轨道的位移上，因 3 号线施工而产生的最大轨道竖向位移为 3 mm，接近控制指标，但仍是安全的，在施工过程中应加强监控量测。其他位移远小于控制指标。

（2）1 号线运营对 3 号线隧道的影响主要是由于列车振动而引起的动力响应，其产生的荷载是双峰值曲线形式，3 号线隧道在荷载峰值经过时产生最大的内力值。

（3）1 号线在运营过程中对下方 3 号线管片产生的最大位移为 0.22 mm；运营引起的最大附加弯矩为 800 N · m，最大附加轴力为 30 KN，均远小于管片的内力设计值，因此 1 号线运营不会对 3 号线施工产生较大影响。

参考文献（References）：

[1] 张志强，何川. 南京地铁区间盾构隧道“下穿”玄武湖公路隧道施工的关键技术研究[J]. 岩土力学，2005，26(11)：1711-1716.

[2] 邵华，张子新. 盾构近距离穿越施工对已运营隧道的扰动影响分析[J]. 岩土力学，2004，25(supp.2)：545-549.

[3] 王祥秋，杨林德，周治国. 列车振动荷载作用下隧道衬动力响应特性分析[J]. 岩石力学与工程学报，2006，25(7)：1337-1342.

[4] 张 贵，王 建，贾颖绚. 新线隧道列车运营对既有地铁结构振动影响的研究[J]. 铁道建筑，2008, 5：46-49.

[5] 翟婉明. 车辆-轨道耦合动力学[M]. 北京：中国铁道出版社, 2002.

作者简介（Bio-data）：

夏炜洋，1975.1，男，1996 年毕业于西南交通大学工程力学系，现为地下工程系博士研究生，主要从事地下结构及隧道工程研究。

Weiyang XIA (1975—), male, gradated from Department of Mechanic Engineering, Southwest Jiaotong University in 1996. He is now the Ph.D. candidate in department of underground enjineering. The main interests are covered in undergrond engineering and tunnel engineering.

E-mail: wyxia2002@tom.com

汪波，1976.10，男，西南交通大学地下工程系讲师，2008 年毕业于西南交通大学地下工程系，获工学博士学位，主要从事隧道结构及岩土工程方面的研究、教学工作。

Bo WANG (1976—), male, lecturer, worked in Underground Engineering Department of Southwest Jiaotong University, gradated from Underground Engineering Department of SWJTU in 2008, obtained D.E. Main interests are covered in tunnel & Geotechnical Engineering.

E-mail: ahbowang@163.com

配合盾构法修建三条平行隧道地铁车站横向通道时车站结构力学行为研究

张海波[1,2]　何　川[1]
[1]西南交通大学，四川　成都　610031
[2]上海市城市建设设计研究院，上海　200125

【摘　要】　结合广州地铁三号线林和西路站，进行了在区间盾构隧道的基础上修建三条平行隧道地铁车站的施工方案研究。就修建横向通道时盾构隧道管片结构、中间站台隧道结构以及横向通道结构本身的力学行为进行了数值模拟。同时就施工对地面环境的影响范围进行了分析，以及隧道衬砌结构的安全性作出了评价。
【关键词】　地铁车站；盾构法；横向通道；数值模拟

STUDY ON MECHANICAL BEHAVE OF THREE PARALLEL TUNNELS METRO STATION CROSS PASSAGE BASED ON SHIELD TUNNEL WITH NATM

Haibo ZHANG[1,2], Chuan HE[1]
[1]Southwest Jiaotong University, Chengdu 610031, Sichuan, China;
[2]Shanghai Urban Construction Design& Research Institute, Shanghai 200125, China

Abstract: Combined with the construction of Linhe Xilu Station of Guangzhou Metro Line 3, Station construction Scheme with three parallel tunnels is studied on the base of conducting running shield tunnel. Numerical simulation of mechanical behaviors has been carried out by the analysis of TBM tunnel structure, platform tunnel structure and cross passage structure. Also, the influence on all the structure and Stratum deflection from different scheme which includes different excavation is analyzed.
Key words: metro station; shield driven method; cross passage; numerical simulation;

1 前　言

目前，在我国城市地下铁道建设中，区间隧道多采用盾构法修建，如上海、广州和南京等，盾构法具有良好的防渗漏水性、安全快速和对环境影响小等优点。这样就要求先修建地铁车站，然后将车站的端头井作为盾构施工的始发与到达井，而车站所占的土建费用又昂贵，故导致工期增长、造价增加。如果采用在盾构隧道的基础上扩建地铁车站这一施工思路，可有效地提高盾构机的掘进长度，同时无需先修车站，这样可缩短建设周期，从而从总体上降低工程造价，还可避免明挖法对交通要道的占用、影响车辆通行等弱点[1]。在国外配合盾构法修建地铁车站得到了大量采用，如日本在盾构隧道的基础上，采用托梁法或半盾构法扩挖建成地铁车站，如日本采用托梁法建成了营团地铁 8 号线的永田町站[2]；而前苏联，以小盾构隧道为拱座，修建单拱结构车站，如俄罗斯彼得保勇敢广场站[3]。

基金项目：铁道部课题（2007G036、2006G007B）

本文结合广州地铁三号线林和西路站，作者在国内首次对在区间盾构隧道的基础上修建地铁车站的方案进行了研究，提出了三条平行隧道岛式站台车站方案。就三天隧道间横向通道结构的修建进行研究，得出其修建时对盾构管片结构、中间站台结构及其对本身结构的力学影响。同时，就施工对地面环境的影响范围和隧道衬砌结构的安全性进行分析。

2 工程概要

林和西路站位于天河北路与林和西路交叉口，呈南北向，周围超高层的地域标志性建筑物较多,为该地区主要城市景观结点之一。该车站的主要特点：车站所在的林和西路现状道路较窄，交通繁忙；站两侧建筑物距离较近，站位东、西向调整幅度非常有限；站位所处位置两旁建筑物的地下室已超出道路规划红线，造成出入口及风亭的布置困难；客流量较大；地下管线都很密集。该站地层从上到下为人工填土，冲积黏土层，残积土层，岩石强、中等风化带，岩石风化带和岩石微风化带。该段地层主要为部分地段砂层孔隙水，及中风化岩裂隙水，稳定地下水位埋深 1.90～5.70 m。场地为珠江一级堆积阶地，第四系覆盖层以人工堆积、冲积、洪积、残积为主，厚 5.1～14.5 m，局部可见透镜体状淤泥质土和细砂，地质构造简单，未发现有断层通过。

林和西路站拟采用盾构过站后扩挖建成三条平行隧道岛式站台车站的施工方案。即在两条已经建成的区间盾构隧道中间，再单独采用暗挖法修建一条结构独立的隧道作为站台，用联络通道的方式将该隧道与盾构隧道联结，站厅设在地面或两端地下，按照三级车站的标准设计的断面如图 1 所示。

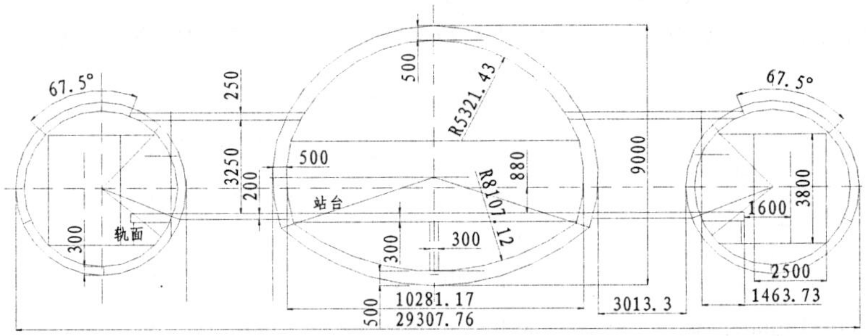

图 1 车站断面图（单位：mm）

3 施工方案设计

中间站台隧道采用全断面开挖，考虑到冻结法加固方案的施工技术要求高、加固施工的时间长以及较高的加固费用，本章节采用水平搅拌桩的方案进行地层加固。根据中国内地地下铁道列车车门的布置情况，同时综合考虑横行通道开挖的最小影响范围、客流量大小以及方便乘客上下车，车站内部沿线路方向布置联络通道如图 2 所示。根据国内外施作联络通道的成功经验以及客流量的大小，选择如图 3 所示的联络通道结构断面形式。

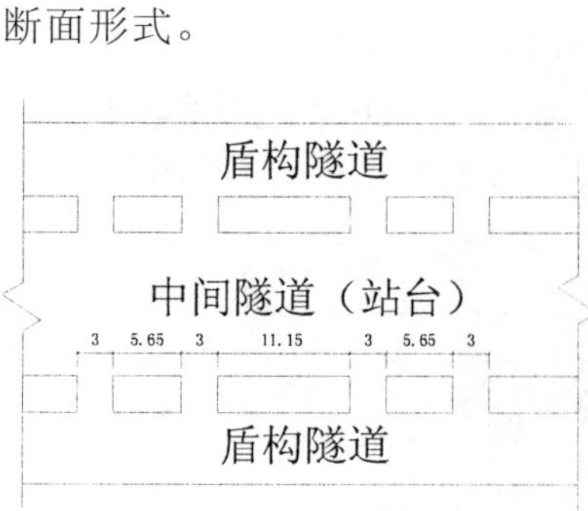

图 2 联络通道的纵向分布

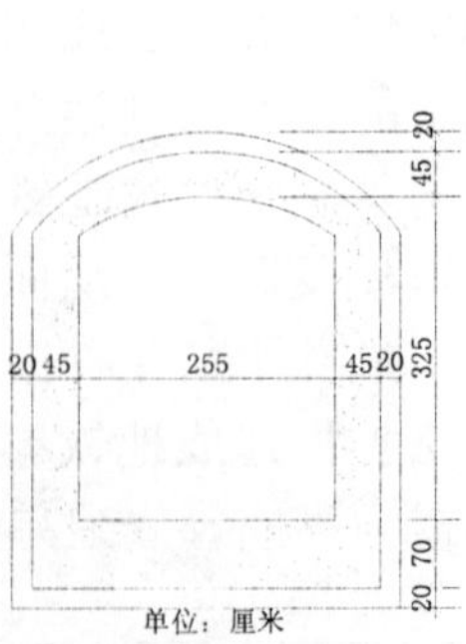

图 3 联络通道结构断面图

4 数值模拟

4.1 建 模

根据车站的实际情况以及联络通道的空间位置关系的重复性，采用三维模型计算，并简化模型尺寸分别为：沿线路方向 51.15 m，垂直于线路方向为 70 m，竖直方向为 40 m。周围土体采用实体单元模拟，盾构管片结构、中间隧道结构、联络通道结构采用壳体单元模拟。联络通道与盾构隧道管片、联络通道与中间站台隧道连接部位，采用弱化刚度的方法进行模拟。根据国内外修建联络通道成功的经验，采用通道部分两侧至少 5.5 m 的加固范围，根据本车站横向联络通道分布情况，在车站内部采用全加固的方案。车站内部开挖情况及加固区范围如图 4 所示。

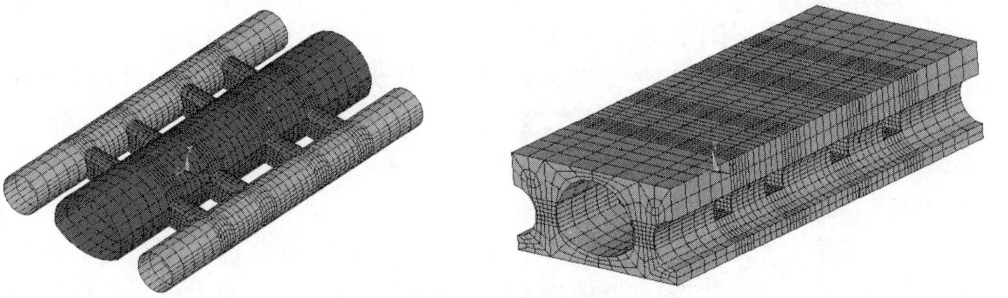

图 4 结构计算模型

4.2 计算结果分析

本章节主要分析盾构隧道管片结构、中间隧道衬砌结构在联络通道逐步修建过程中结构的变形、应力的变化情况；分析联络通道衬砌结构在相邻联络通道修建过程中附近应力的变化情况；分析众多联络通道开挖引起的地表地中位移的变化情况；分析地层在联络通道开挖过程中的应力变化情况。

4.2.1 盾构隧道管片结构内力及变形分析

（1）盾构隧道管片结构主应力分析

联络通道开挖后，其第一主应力分步情况如图 5（a）所示。盾构隧道管片结构大部分结构受到的第一主应力较小，一般为－0.2 MPa～－0.21 MPa(受压状态)，可见整个结构处于较小的拉应力情况下，大部分结构处于受压状态。但是局部位置出现了较大的拉应力值，出现部位为盾构隧道内侧与联络通道连接部位的两侧。最大值达到了 12.8 MPa，如图 6 可知，随着联络通道的逐步开挖，结构的主应力有所变化，但是变化趋势较平缓。同时最大拉应力的出现部位随着联络通道的逐步开挖而逐步蔓延，但都分布在与联络通道交接处的两侧。

盾构隧道管片结构大部分结构受到比较理想状态的第三主应力，如图 5（b）所示，其最大值为 4.7 MPa。随着开挖，其位置也发生了变化，开挖前最大值出现在管片腰部内侧，联络通道修建完成后，改部位出现在盾构隧道顶部和底部内侧。其量值也有所减小，变化趋势如图 7 所示。

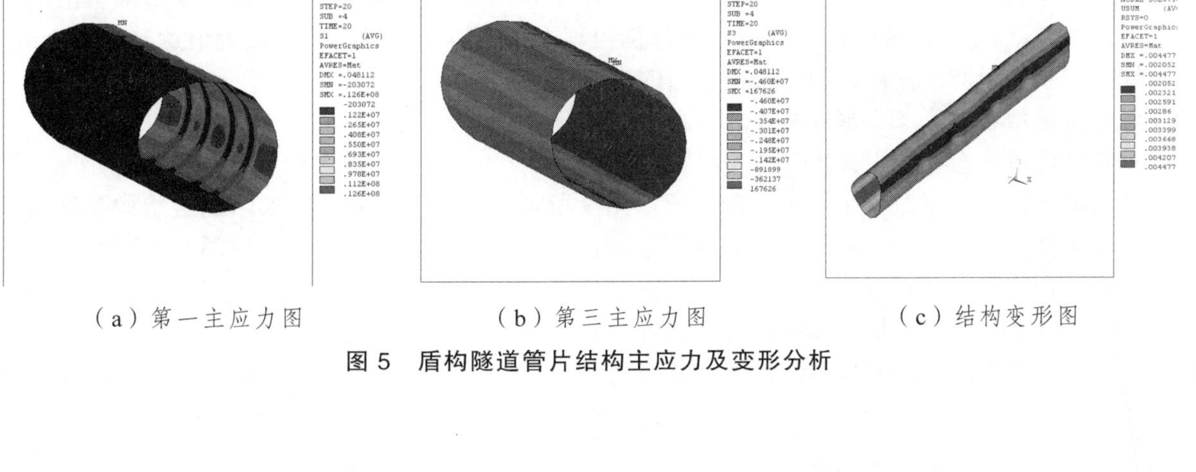

（a）第一主应力图　　（b）第三主应力图　　（c）结构变形图

图 5 盾构隧道管片结构主应力及变形分析

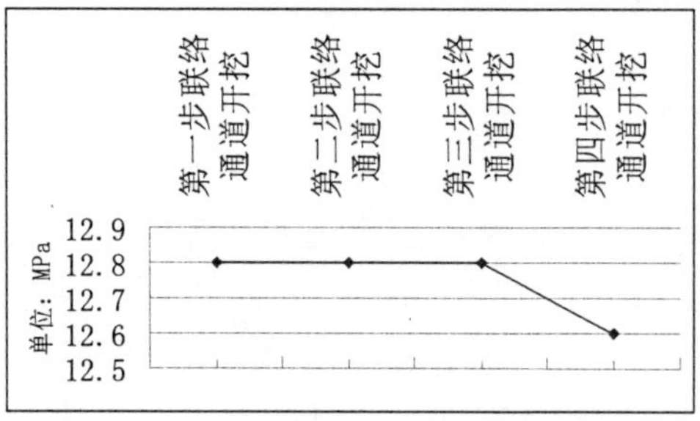

图 6 第一主应力随开挖过程极值变化图

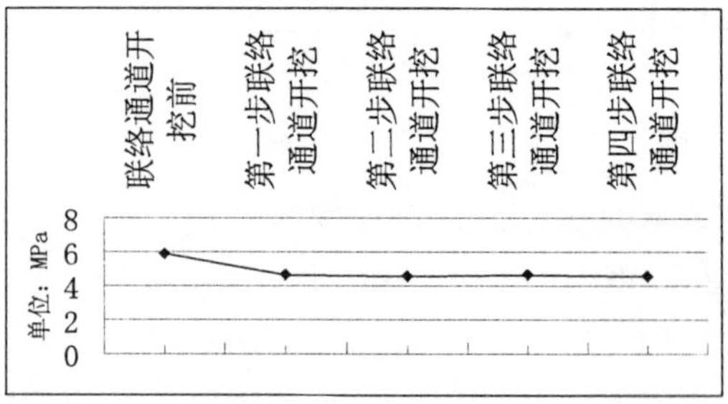

图 7 第三主应力随开挖过程最大值变化图

（2）盾构隧道管片结构变形分析

盾构管片结构的变形见图 5（c），可以看出由于联络通道的开挖以及中间隧道的限制，盾构隧道靠中间站台隧道侧的变形较小，远离中间隧道侧变形则较大，变形最大部位出现在盾构隧道底部远离中间隧道侧，最大值达到 4.633 mm，根据相关规范，直径变形值为 0.2%。本例盾构直径为 6 m，允许的变形值为 12 mm。显然联络通道开挖后，盾构隧道的变形满足要求。

4.2.2 中间站台隧道结构内力及变形分析

（1）中间站台隧道结构第应力分析

联络通道开挖后，其第一主应力分步情况如图 8（a）所示。中间隧道衬砌结构大部分结构受到的第一主应力一般小于 9.39 MPa (受拉状态)，但是局部位置出现了较大的拉应力值，出现部位为中间隧道衬砌内侧与联络通道连接部位，分布区域很小，最大值达到了 18.2 MPa，最大拉应力的出现部位随着联络通道的逐步开挖而逐步蔓延，但都分布在与联络通道交接处周围很小的范围内，其最大值变化很小。

联络通道开挖前后，其第三主应力分步情况如图 8（b）所示。由图可以看出，中间隧道衬砌结构大部分受到比较理想状态的第三主应力，其最大值为 3.97 MPa (受压)，最大值出现在联络通道与中间隧道交接部位的下侧。随着联络通道的开挖，其量值变化较小。

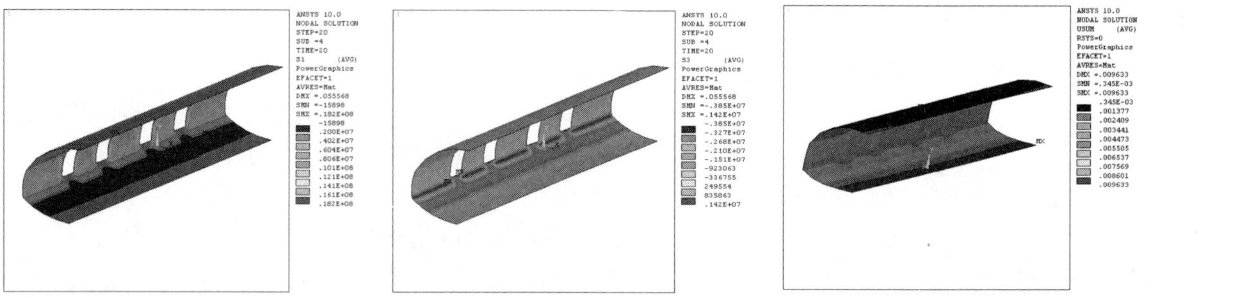

（a）第一主应力图 （b）第三主应力 （c）结构变形图

图 8 中间站台隧道结构主应力及变形图

（2）中间站台隧道结构变形分析

中间站台隧道结构的变形见图 8（c），由图可以看出由于联络通道的开挖以及边界约束条件的限制，中间站台隧道靠盾构隧道侧的变形相对较小，分布在 2.409 mm～5.550 5 mm。最小变形部位出现在中间站台隧道拱顶部位，为 0.345 mm。变形最大部位出现在中间隧道仰拱部位，最大值达到 9.633 mm，根据相关规范，联络通道开挖后，中间站台隧道的变形满足这要求。

4.2.3 联络通道结构内力及变形分析

（1）联络通道结构主应力分析

联络通道开挖后，其第一主应力分步情况如图 9 所示。由图可以看出，联络通道结构受到的第一主应力一般小于 0.67 MPa (受压状态)，但是局部位置出现了较大的拉应力值，出现部位为联络通道结构的仰拱与拱墙结合部位以及拱墙和底板结合部位，该处截面均发生突变，故产生了较大的应力集中，最大值达到了 5.62 MPa。同时，随着联络通道的逐步开挖，结构的主应力有所变化程减小趋势，但是变化趋势较平缓。同时最大拉应力的出现部位随着联络通道的逐步开挖而逐步分不在各联络通道截面突变处。

联络通道开挖前后，其第三主应力分步情况如图 10 所示。由图可以看出，联络通道衬砌结构大部分结构受到比较理想状态的第三主应力，其最大值为 13.3 MPa (受压) (满足 C30 混凝土的设计抗压强度 15 MPa)。最大值出现在联络通道边墙与底板交接部位的内侧。随着联络通道的开挖，其量值变化较小。

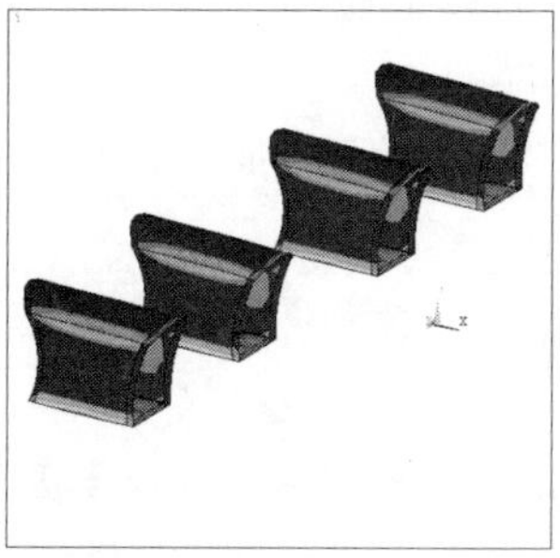

图 9　联络通道结构第一主应力图

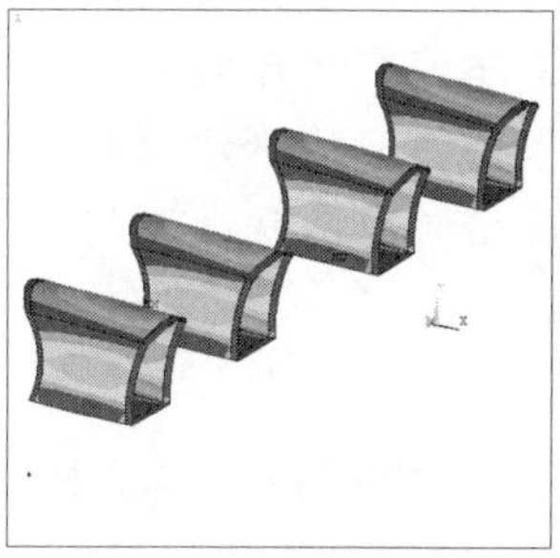

图 10　联络通道结构第三主应力图

（2）联络通道结构变形分析

联络通道结构变形见图 11，由图可以看出由于联络通道的开挖以及边界约束条件的限制，大部分结构变形分布在 3.564 mm。最小变形部位出现在与中间站台隧道交接处联络通道拱顶部位，为 0.345 mm。变形最大部位出现在与中间隧道交接处联络通道地板部位，最大值达到 4.447 mm。根据相关规范，联络通道开挖后，联络通道结构变形满足要求。

4.2.4　*地层变形分析*

如图 12 所示，在联络通道开挖后，由于上覆土的作用，中间站台隧道拱顶部位出现了最大向下的位移，最大位移值为 2.254 mm。同时由于底部土的作用，在中间站台隧道的仰拱部位出现了最大竖直向上的位移，位移值达 9.656 mm。同时可以看出，在联络通道下部的土体也出席了较大的竖直向下的位移。其原因是因为开挖联络通道前，土体进行加固，重量等发生变化，故产生较大的向下位移。在地表，产生的竖向位移呈漏斗装分布，越偏离中部越小，在中间站台隧道正上方偏联络通道部位，其值最大，为 7.009 mm，满足地表沉降要求。

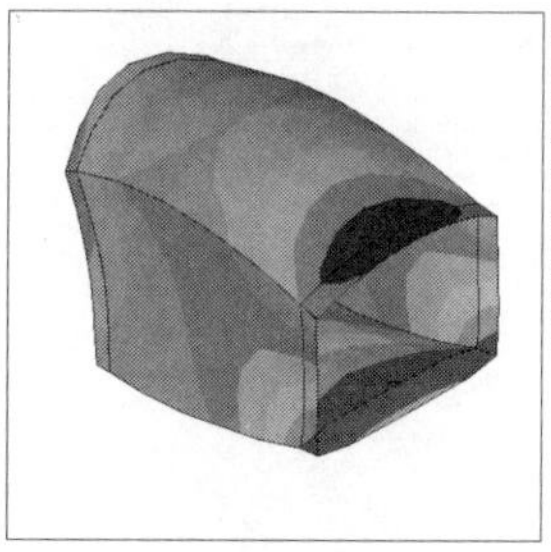

图 11　管片结构变形图

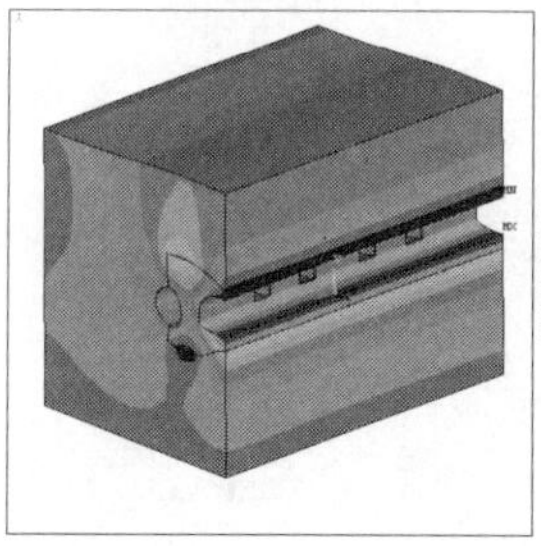

图 12　地层在 Y 方向的位移

5　结　论

用三维数值模拟计算了盾构隧道一次性掘进，中间站台隧道一次性全断面开挖，联络通道间隧道对称逐步一次性开挖，并分析了在不同开挖步下结构的内力变化情况、地层的应力变化情况、结构的位移变化情况、地层的位移变化情况等。通过分析，可以得出以下结论和建议:

（1）联络通道的修建，对盾构管片结构的拉压力区域产出了重新分布，其中在联络通道附近的管片结构处于较大的受拉状态，在设计中应予足够的重视。为了满足受拉要求，建议在该部位采用钢管片，同时采用柔性的连接方式来降低甚至消除这不利影响。

（2）联络通道的修建，对中间隧道的连接部位产生了较大的拉力作用，为了减少拉力作用，满足裂缝要求，建议对接头部位采用特殊处理，采用更柔性的连接方式等来降低甚至消除这不利影响。

（3）对于联络通道结构，在其边墙部位底部出现较大的压应力和最大位移。同时在拱顶和边墙连接部位以及底板和边墙连接部位截面突变处出现了应力集中。建议在设计施工中尽力不要采用直角来处理该部位，最好用仰拱来代替较厚的底板。

（4）联络通道的逐步修建，对其他已建联络通道的影响无论在位移上还是在应力大小及其分布规律上影响均很小。可见在该加固方案下，联络通道的修建是相互独立的。

（5）整个三条平行隧道的修建，对地层位移产生了影响。但是采用相应的加固措施，地表的最大位移在 10mm 左右。满足城市地铁修建的位移要求。

参考文献（References）：

[1] 李围，何川等. 地铁车站盾构法综合技术在我国的应用前景探讨[A]. 见：地下铁道专业委员会第十四届年会论文集. 北京：中国科学技术出版社，2001.

[2] (日)シールド工法の调查·设计から施工まで编辑委员会编. シールド工法の调查·设计から施工まで[M]. 东京：地盘工学会，1997.

[3] 钱七虎院士及戚承志博士译校. 俄罗斯地下铁道建设精要[M]. 北京：中国铁道出版社，2002.

作者简介（Bio-data）：

张海波，男，1981 年 4 月生于江苏泰兴。2007 年毕业于西南交通大学地下工程系并获得硕士研究生学位。毕业后一直在上海市城市建设设计研究院从事地下铁道结构的设计与研究工作，主要设计并配合施工完成了印度新德里地铁机场快线工程 C5 标的盾构区间、明挖区间及工作井等工作。

Haibo ZHANG (1981—), Male, born in Taixing county Jiangsu province, Graduated & got master degree from Southwest Jiaotong University in 2007. Now he is engaged in the design & research work on metro structure in Shanghai Urban Construction Design & Research Institute.

上海世博电力隧道盾构下穿地铁 1 号线施工控制分析

付昱凯 [1, 2] 丁文其 [1, 2] 高小庆 [3]

[1]同济大学 土木工程学院地下建筑与工程系，上海 200092
[2]同济大学 岩土及地下工程教育部重点实验室，上海 200092
[3]上海市电力公司电网建设公司，上海 200025

【摘 要】 本文针对上海世博电力隧道盾构下穿越运营地铁 1 号线工程，分析了下穿越施工过程中的盾构施工控制要素并提出了主要施工参数的范围。然后对实际下穿越的施工参数及 1 号线变形监测数据进行分析，分析结果表明盾构的土压力、同步注浆量及注浆压力是影响 1 号线隧道变形的主要施工控制参数。

【关键词】 盾构隧道；下穿越；地铁 1 号线；土压力；注浆压力；注浆量；推进速度

STUDY ON CONSTRUCTION CONTROL OF SHANGHAI WORLD EXPO POWER TUNNEL UNDER-PASSING THROUGH METRO LINE 1

Yukai FU[1, 2], Wenqi DING[1, 2], Xiaoqing GAO[3]

[1]*Department of Geotechnical Engineering, Tongji University, Shanghai 200092, China;*

[2]*Key Laboratory of Geotechnical and Underground Engineering of Ministry of Education, Tongji University, Shanghai 200092, China;*

[3]*Shanghai Municipal Electric Power Company, Shanghai 200025, China*

Abstract: Regarding to the construction control of Shanghai World Expo power tunnel under-passing through metro line 1, the control factors have been analyzed with determination of the span of the major construction parameters. Then the practical construction parameters and the deformation monitoring data of metro line 1 have been analyzed. The analysis result indicates that the value of earth chamber pressure, the amount and the pressure value of synchronous injecting are the critical factors.

Key words: shield tunnelling; under-passing; metro line 1; earth pressure; injecting pressure; injecting amount; driving velocity

1 引 言

近年来，在城市基础设施建设中，出现了大量新建隧道穿越城市交通、电力、市政管线等已运营隧道的工程。其中新建隧道穿越已运营地铁隧道时，由于施工条件复杂，安全责任重大，对运营地铁变形控制严格，因此施工控制难度大。国内许多学者从不同的角度对盾构下穿越已运营地铁隧道施工进行了研究。邵华[1]通过实测数据对盾构近距离穿越扰动影响问题进行了定量分析，并指出盾构穿越对已建地

基金项目：教育部新世纪优秀人才支持计划（No.NCET-08-0402）；上海市重点学科建设项目（No.B308）

铁隧道的扰动影响主要以隧道的竖向位移为主。胡群芳[2]通过对上海地铁 4 号线近距离下穿越已运营地铁 2 号线工程施工过程的监测，近距离下穿越施工的过程和特点，讨论了 2 号线周围地层土体的沉降变形和规律。

本文针对上海北京西路～华夏西路世博电力隧道工程一标 1#～2#工作井区间隧道下穿越运营地铁1#线，分析了下穿越施工过程中的盾构施工控制要素及并提出了主要施工参数的范围，并结合穿越期间地铁 1 号线的变形监测数据进行了验证。

2 穿越工程特点及变形控制要求

2.1 穿越工程特点

本次穿越位于电力隧道一标 1#～2#工作井区间，该区间电力隧道为土压平衡盾构法施工，隧道管片外直径 6.2 m，内径 5.2 m。运营中的地铁 1 号线是上海的第一条地铁，亦为上海轨道交通最为繁忙、最重要的大动脉，因此其安全运营显得尤为重要。电力隧道盾构先穿越地铁 1 号线下行线，后穿越 1 号线上行线。地铁 1 号线下、上行线轴线距离约 10.5 m，穿越范围宽度约 17.92 m。穿越段电力隧道与地铁 1 号线成 89.2°角，近乎正交，该段电力隧道轴线标高埋深－18.493 m～－18.711 m 左右，地铁 1 号线标高埋深 13.1 m 左右。穿越段电力隧道与地铁 1 号线净间距 3.0 m～3.2 m。穿越段电力隧道与地铁 1 号线隧道位置关系及地层情况如图 1 所示。

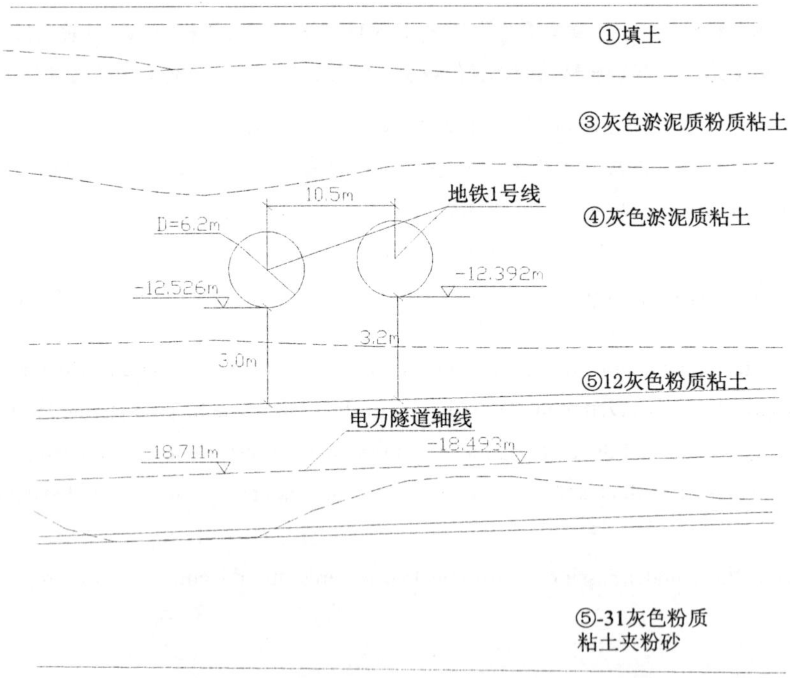

图 1 电力隧道下穿越段地铁 1 号线剖面示意图

穿越段的电力隧道位于灰色粉质粘土⑤$_{12}$层，地铁 1 号线隧道位于灰色淤泥质黏土④层，这两层土为饱和、软塑-流塑，属中-高压缩性土，施工易受扰动，扰动后沉降大，穿越施工控制难度大。

2.2 地铁变形控制标准

盾构穿越正在运营的地铁隧道，必须确保 1 号线地铁列车的运行安全，穿越施工时的保护标准要求很高。根据上海地区运营地铁保护的相关文件[3]，运营地铁保护要求见表 2，其中监测值超过总变形量 1/2 时报警，并采取应急措施。

表 2 运营地铁保护要求

运营地铁保护等级	一级
线路安全正常运营要求	隧道内两轨道横向高差≤2 mm 轨向偏差和高低差<2 mm/10 m （即横向差异沉降<1.4‰）
结构变形控制要求	隧道结构纵向沉降与隆起≤±5 mm 隧道结构纵向水平位移≤±5 mm 隧道收敛值<20 mm

3 盾构下穿越施工控制因素分析

3.1 盾构土压力的设定

（1）土压力理论值

电力隧道处在第⑤灰色粉质黏土层内，所在土层的渗透系数较小，土压力的计算采用水土合算法，盾构常规施工阶段土压力理论值按下式计算

$$P_0 = k_0 \gamma H \tag{1}$$

其中：$k_0 = 1 - \sin\varphi'$，φ'是土的有效摩擦角；H为开挖面中心处深度；γ为土的饱和重度。

（2）下穿越盾构土压力控制原则

盾构推进土压力的理论值为开挖面处的静止土压力，但由于掘进过程中因盾构开挖面超挖、盾尾注浆不足等难免会产生地层损失，加之盾构通过后受扰动土体的固结、蠕变，从而 不可避免的引起地层沉降，因此，在土压平衡盾构接近穿越段的过程中，使开挖面土压力略微大与计算的静止土压力值，引起轻微的挤土效应，以减小后期沉降。另外，由于穿越段上部隧道内部土体被淘空以及上部建构筑物存在一定的刚度，盾构到达上部隧道下方时，开挖面实际的土压力值比静止土压力小，必须考虑土压力的损失[4][5]。

综合考虑以上两点，对穿越段进行了分区，如图 2 所示。因此，电力隧道盾构下穿越地铁 1 号线的盾构开挖面土压力的设定值根据图 3 所示的不同穿越阶段的特点，按照先减小、后增大、再减小、再增大的趋势变化调整。穿越段土仓压力取值按照（2）式考虑。

$$P = kP_0 \tag{2}$$

P_0按照式(1) 带入土层参数计算可得，为 0.213 MPa，k为考虑隆起的土压力增加与考虑上部已建隧道刚度及土体掏空效应的土压力调整系数。各分区土压力计算的k值建议值如表 2 所示，将土压力值控制在 1.5～1.8 倍的静止土压力，略小于被动土压力，带入表 2 计算参数，可得各区段土压力设定建议值如表 3 所示。

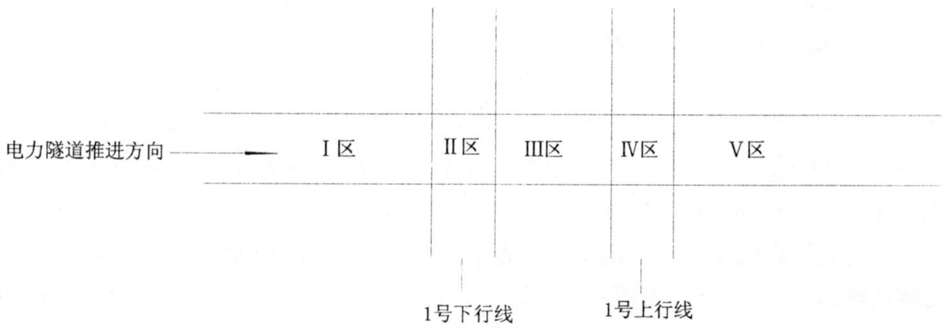

图 2 穿越阶段分区示意图

表 3 数值模拟土仓压力分区取值表

穿越分区	I 区	II 区	III 区	IV 区	V 区
土仓压力计算系数 K	1.8	1.5	1.5 ~ 1.8 ~ 1.5	1.5	1.8
土仓压力值 P（MPa）	0.38	0.32	0.32 ~ 0.38 ~ 0.32	0.32	0.38

由于盾构开挖面实际土压力受地层条件、周边环境变化等多种不确定性因素的影响，设定精确的静止压力往往比较困难。因此，在穿越过程中，土压力设定应在以上基础上，结合地铁 1 号线的变形监测数据的分析、反馈，及时调整。

3.2 注浆措施

（1）同步注浆

通过同步注浆及时填充盾尾建筑空隙及由于超挖引起的地层损失，减少施工过程中土体的变形。同步注浆由注浆压力和注浆量控制，实践证明，注浆压力应控制在注浆孔位置的地层压力值附近，注浆量控制在盾尾间隙的 140%～180% 范围内效果最佳，盾构每环注浆量 Q 可由公式（3）确定。

$$Q = a\pi\eta\ (R^2 - r^2) \tag{3}$$

其中：a 为管片环宽；η 为注浆率（注浆量/理论开挖空隙），考虑下穿越特殊情况，η 值控制在 140%～180% 之间；R 为盾构开挖面直径；r 为隧道管片外径。计算可得本穿越次注浆量控制范围为 2.3～3.0 m^3/环，盾尾推进至既有线正下方时，适当增大注浆量，以保证间隙填充率。

（2）二次注浆

进行管片壁后的二次注浆是控制上部隧道沉降变形的有效辅助手段。二次注浆材料一般选用可控制凝结时间的双液浆体。双液浆体通过注浆管注入土层后立即凝固，对盾构推进过后的扰动土体起到加固作用，可有效控制地层沉降，弥补同步注浆的不足。二次注浆施工时，为避免对盾构周围土体及地铁 1 号线隧道产生过于骤然的作用，减少对土体的进一步扰动，注浆过程一般分多次进行[6]。

3.3 盾构推进速度

盾构切口离开运营隧道下方到尾脱出的过程中，缺少控制其变形的手段，因此，在保证地铁 1 号线变形满足控制标准的前提下应适当缓慢的提高施工速度，使壁后注浆尽早对隧道起作用[7]。在盾构下穿运营地铁隧道越施工时应即时调整掘进速度，以保证盾构机均匀、慢速地通过影响区。根据以往地铁实时监控数据及相关资料，掘进速度建议值一般情况下为 8～10 mm/min；监测变形量数据较大时为：6～8 mm/min。

4 下穿越实际施工参数及监测数据分析

实际穿越工程中，1 号线隧道的变形以隆起为主，少数测点出现沉降变形；上、下行线最大变形均小于 5mm，满足对运营地铁隧道结构变形的控制要求，达到了成功穿越的目的。本文对穿越期间各施工参数控制及其变化趋势进行分析总结，为以后类似的穿越工程积累相关经验。

4.1 土仓压力

穿越期间，各区段土压力平均值随盾构切口距 1 号线两隧道间距中点距离变化的趋势如图 3 所示。图中横坐标＋5.65 m、－5.65 m 处分别为盾构切口位于 1 号线下、上行线隧道轴线正下方。可以看出，进入穿越范围时土压力值逐渐减小；盾构推出穿越范围后土压力值开始增大至正常推进阶段数值。在 1 号线下、上行线隧道轴线正下方土压力值最小。整个穿越阶段土压力值控制在 0.38 MPa～0.42 MPa 之间，比建议值 0.319 MPa～0.383 MPa 大，各区段土仓压力平均值依次为：Ⅰ区 0.403 MPa、Ⅱ区 0.393 MPa、

Ⅲ区 0.398 MPa、Ⅳ区 0.388 MPa、Ⅴ区 0.392 MPa，变化趋势同表 3 的建议值一致，即在下、上行线正下方时均有所减小。由于穿越下行线时隧道隆起较大，在穿越上行线时根据监测信息反馈施工控制，调整土压力值，因此土压力在穿越上行线及穿越完成后有所减小。

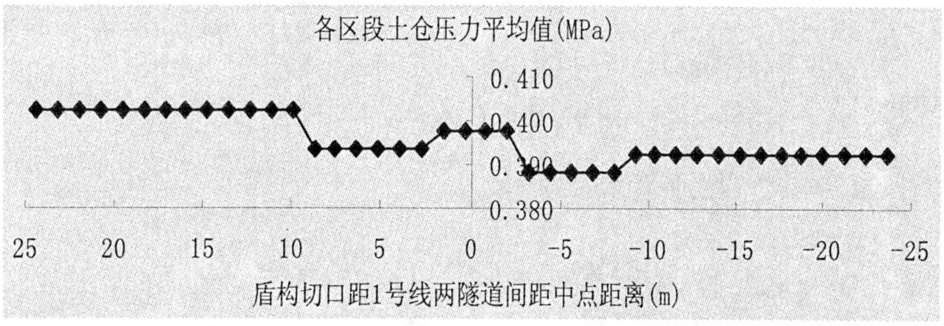

图 3 穿越段各区段土仓压力平均值变化趋势

4.2 同步注浆量

盾尾同步注浆压量变化趋势如图 4 所示，图中横坐标 +5.65 m、−5.65 m 处分别为盾尾位于 1 号线下、上行线隧道轴线正下方。可以看出：穿越段同步注浆量控制在 2.0～3.2 m^3/环之间，平均值为 2.6 m^3/环，与建议值 2.3～3.0 m^3/环基本一致。从穿越试验段到 1 号线下行线穿越完成时，同步注浆量均维持在 2.7 m^3/环左右；1 号线下行线穿越完成后，盾尾进入下、上行线之间区段时，同步注浆量减小到 2.2 m^3/环左右；盾尾到达 1 号线上行线下方时同步注浆量又增加至 2.6 m^3/环；盾尾通过地铁 1 号线隧道后同步注浆量回落至 2.3 m^3/环左右。

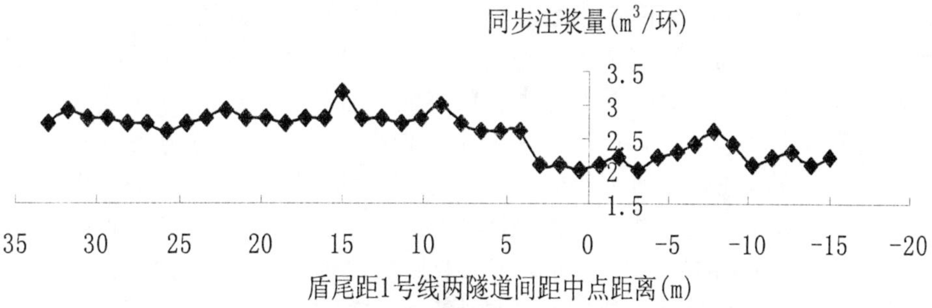

图 4 穿越段盾构同步注浆量变化曲线

4.3 推进速度

穿越段盾构推进速度随盾构切口距 1 号线两隧道间距中点距离的变化时程如图 5。穿越段推进速度变化时程曲线呈下凹型，盾构切口到达 1 号线隧道之前及通过 1 号线隧道之后推进速度均维持在较大值 30 mm/min 左右；盾构到达 1 号线隧道下方范围内时推进速度减小至 20 mm/min 左右，整个穿越段平均推进速度为 23.8 mm/min。

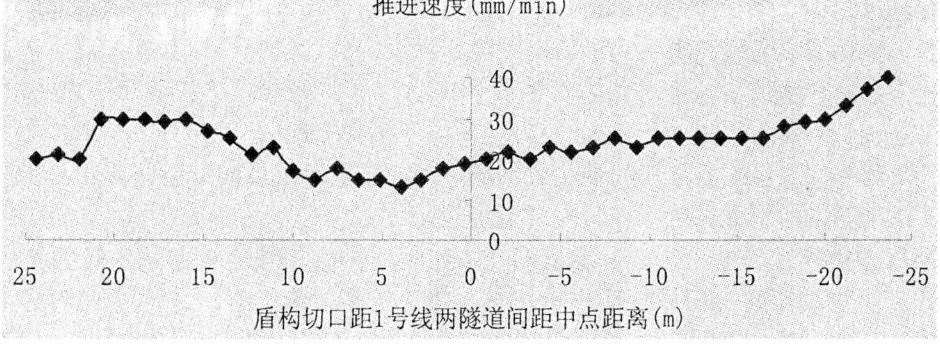

图 5 穿越段盾构机推进速度变化曲线

4.4 地铁 1 号线变形分析

由穿越段 1 号线隧道变形监测数据可知，穿越期间下行线最大沉降变形值为－0.056 mm，最大隆起变形值为 3.678 mm；上行线最大沉降变形值为－0.159 mm，最大隆起变形值为 2.434 mm。由于本次穿越过程中 1 号线隧道各变形监测点主要表现为隆起变形，并且隆起变形最大值一般均出现在电力隧道轴线正上方测点处。因此主要对其隆起变形最大值进行分析，穿越期间 1 号线下、上行线的最大隆起变形值随盾构切口距 1 号线下、上行线隧道轴线距离变化的时程曲线分别如图 6 所示。

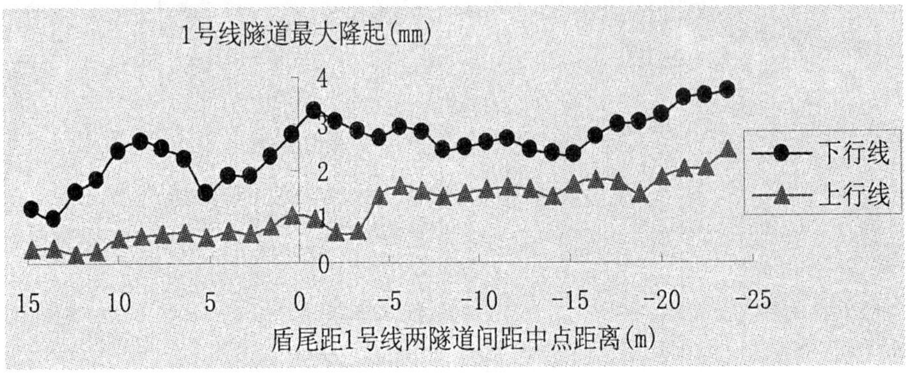

图 6 地铁 1 号线下行线的最大隆起变形值变化时程曲线

1 号线下行线隧道最大隆起值在盾构切口到达前、后均维持在较大值，即 2.5 mm 以上。并且，在盾构切口到达时，最大隆起值出现下跌，对比土压力和注浆参数变化趋势曲线的分析可知，这是由于盾构机土压力值的下降（由 0.4 MPa 减小到 0.38 MPa）引起的；切口到达下行线隧道正下方时最大隆起值跌落到 2.0 mm 以下；切口通过 1 号线下行线隧道 7 m 左右时下行线隧道隆起最大值增至 3.2 mm，此时正好盾尾通过下行线隧道，结合同步注浆压力及注浆量的变化曲线可知，此处盾尾注浆压力及注浆量均增至较大值，因此此处隧道隆起最大值的增大是由于盾尾注浆引起的。

1 号线上行线隧道最大隆起值在切口到达前较小，切口到达上行线隧道正下方时最大隆起值开始增大，直到切口通过后一直维持在较大值 1.8 mm 左右，并有逐渐增大的趋势。1 号线上行线隧道最大隆起值的变化时程曲线趋势与施工参数的变化相关性不太明显，但还是可以看出在盾构切口及盾尾到达时，1 号线上行线最大隆起值均有小的峰值，盾构土压力及盾尾注浆对既有隧道的变形有较大的影响。

由上述分析可知，盾构下穿越既有隧道时盾构土压力、同步注浆压力及注浆量是影响既有隧道变形的主要施工因素，在以后类似的穿越工程应注意调整盾构土压力、盾尾同步注浆压力、注浆量。特别是盾构切口、盾尾到达既有隧道正下方时应根据既有隧道的实时变形监测数据，适当降低盾构土压力值及减小注浆量、注浆压力，进一步减小既有隧道隆起变形量，使列车运行更加安全。

5 结 论

（1）本次穿越过程中 1 号线隧道变形满足《上海市轨道交通管理条例》对地铁隧道结构变形的控制要求。穿越过程中 1 号线隧道变形以隆起变形为主，随着盾构的通过隆起变形有逐渐增大的趋势；但穿越完成后随着盾构施工期间产生的超孔隙水压力的消散、扰动土体的固结，以后长期隆起变形会有所减小。

（2）盾构的土压力、同步注浆量及注浆压力是影响 1 号线隧道变形的主要施工控制参数，1 号线隧道变形对土压力、同步注浆量及注浆量的变化较敏感。因此在以后类似的穿越工程中应加强对盾构的土压力、同步注浆量及注浆量的施工控制；并且对穿越段进行区段划分，各施工参数实行分区段的动态控制。

（3）虽然盾构推进速度的变化对既有隧道的变形影响不大，但还应引起足够重视，为了便于穿越期间的盾构姿态控制，穿越期间尽量保持盾构机均匀、慢速的通过影响区，以减少对周围土层的扰动，减小地层及既有隧道后期的长期沉降。

参考文献（References）：

[1] 邵　华，张子新. 盾构近距离穿越施工对已运营隧道的扰动影响分析[J]. 岩土力学，2004，25(S)：545－549.

[2] 胡群芳，黄宏伟. 盾构下穿越已运营隧道施工监测与技术分析[J]. 岩土工程学报，2006，28(1)：42－47.

[3] 上海市城市交通管理局. 上海市轨道交通管理条例. 2002.

[4] 廖少明，杨俊龙，奚程磊，等. 盾构近距离穿越施工的工作面土压力研究[J]. 岩土力学，2005，26(11)：1727－1730.

[5] 周学领，王益群. 软土地层盾构超近距离穿越运营地铁隧道的风险与施工控制[J]. 上海建设科技，2008，(1)：45－48.

[6] 白廷辉，尤旭东，李文勇. 盾构超近距离穿越地铁运营隧道的保护技术[J]. 地下空间，1999，19(4)：311－316.

[7] 杨俊龙，范垚垚. 大直径泥水盾构近距离穿越运营地铁隧道的施工控制技术[J]. 地下工程与隧道，2008，(4)：26－30.

[8] 孙钧，刘洪洲. 交叠隧道盾构法施工土体变形的三维数值模拟[J]. 同济大学学报，2002，30(4)：379－385.

[9] 上海市政工程研究总院. 北京西路—华夏西路电力电缆工程岩土工程详细勘察报告[R]. 2008.

作者简介（Bio-data）：

付昱凯（1983.1—），男，陕西杨凌人，最终学历硕士，同济大学隧道及地下建筑专业在读博士生，主要从事盾构隧道及岩土力学方面的研究。

Resume of the first author

Name: Yukai FU

Gender: Male

Date of Birth: 01/17/1983

Native Place: Yangling, Shanxi province, Acquired educational qualification: Master, Institute: Department of Geotechnical Engineering, College of Civil Engineering, Tongji University, Shanghai, P.R.China.Major Research field: shield tunnel and geotechnical mechanics.

E-mail: fw1278@126.com

黄土地区修建地铁区间平行盾构隧道数值模拟分析

高云龙　何 川　方 勇　汪 洋

西南交通大学　地下工程系，四川　成都　610031

【摘　要】 本文以西安地铁某区间盾构法隧道为例，运用二维数值模拟方法模拟了平行盾构隧道开挖过程，分析了平行隧道净距、地层条件以及应力释放系数等参数对地表沉降、塑性区以及管片结构内力的影响，详细论述了由于这些参数的变化所引起的地表沉降、塑性区范围及管片结构内力变化的原因。最后得出了上述参数变化时地表沉降、塑性区范围及管片结构内力的变化规律。本文结论对于西安地铁盾构法隧道的设计与施工具有参考价值。

【关键词】 黄土地层；盾构隧道；数值模拟

NUMERICAL SIMULATION ANALYSIS OF SUBWAY INTERZONE PARALLEL SHIELD TUNNEL CONSTRUCTION IN LOESS AREA

Yunlong GAO, Chuan HE, Yong FANG, Yang WANG

Department of Underground Engineering, Southwest Jiaotong University, Chengdu 610031, Sichuan, China

Abstract: Two-dimensional numerical simulation method is done in the paper based on some interzone of Xi'an subway shield tunnel to simulate the construction of parallel shield tunnel. This paper analyzes the impact on surface settlement, plastic zone and inner forces of the lining which is caused by the parameters such as clear distance of parallel tunnel, ground conditions and load release factor. Then, the detailed explanation of the reasons , that changes in these parameters cause corresponding changes in surface settlement, plastic zone and inner forces of the lining, has been made. Finally, the changing regularities of the surface settlement, plastic zone and inner forces of the lining with the variation of parameters, have been concluded. The conclusion has referential value for the design and construction of Xi'an Metro shield tunnel.

Key words: loess; shield tunnel; numerical simulation

1 引 言

目前，在黄土地区城市地铁工程中，做了许多比较各种施工方法方面的研究，如倪玉山等（2006）进行了黄土隧道施工方案的数值分析[1]；翁效林等（2007）通过离心模型试验，评价了黄土地区不同施工方法对城市地铁开挖引起地表沉降的影响[2]。但是相对而言，黄土地区盾构隧道中平行隧道净距、地层条件及应力释放系数等参数对地表沉降、塑性区及衬砌内力影响等方面的研究相对较少。本文以西安地铁某区间盾构法隧道为例，运用二维数值模拟方法模拟了平行盾构隧道开挖过程，分析了平行隧道净距、地层条件以及应力释放系数等参数对地表沉降、塑性区以及管片结构内力的影响，详细论述了由于

基金项目：863 计划（2006AA11Z116）；铁道部课题（2007G036、2006G007B）

这些参数的变化所引起的地表沉降、塑性区范围及管片结构内力变化的原因。最后得出了上述参数变化时地表沉降、塑性区范围及管片结构内力的变化规律。

西安地铁区间隧道主要修筑于第四系全新统、上中更新统风积及冲积地层中，沿线主要地层为黄土、古壤土、砂性土，且大部分为黄土层地段，对区间隧道影响较大的地质问题有饱和软黄土、湿陷性黄土等，需要对其着重进行分析，以保证施工顺利进行。

2 建 模

模型示意图如图 1 所示，两洞圆心到模型相应侧边界距离为 4.5D，到模型底部边界距离为 5D，净距与埋深需根据具体情况进行调节，不再赘述。本次计算采用了两种单元：用于模拟围岩的二维实体单元，用于模拟衬砌结构的梁单元，其中二维实体单元处理为平面应变问题。土体及结构材料物理力学参数如表 1 所示。管片衬砌在计算中按等价圆环作刚度折减处理，折减系数取定为 0.8[3]。

表 1 土体及材料物理力学参数表

围岩及结构	变形模量 E	泊松比 μ	天然重度 γ (kN/m^3)	粘聚力 C (kPa)	内摩擦角 ϕ (°)
填土	6 MPa	0.35	17.3	18	11
新黄土	6 MPa	0.32	17.7	30	15
饱和软黄土	5 MPa	0.36	18.7	20	12
老黄土	10 MPa	0.30	20.1	30	16
粉质黏土	12 MPa	0.30	20.1	40	16
管片衬砌	27.6 GPa	0.2	26	–	–

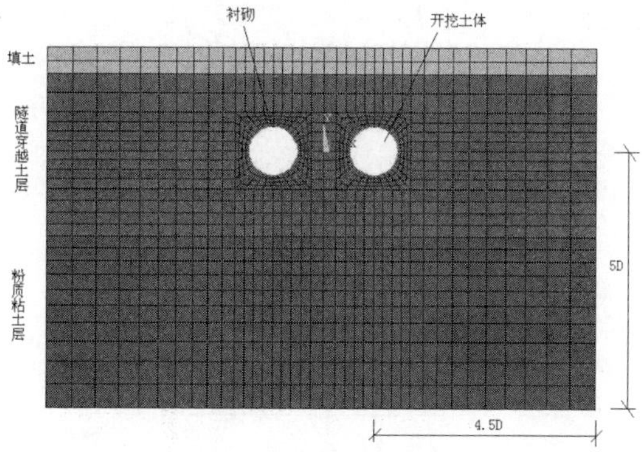

图 1 模型示意图

计算采用生死单元法[4]进行盾构隧道开挖过程的模拟，即通过单元的“杀死”来模拟隧道核心土体的开挖，通过施加径向节点反力来模拟荷载释放，通过单元的“激活”来模拟盾构隧道管片支护的形成。具体计算步骤为：① 求解自重应力场；②“杀死”右洞核心土体单元，模拟核心土体的开挖；③ 右洞洞周施加径向作用力，模拟荷载释放；④“激活”右洞管片单元；⑤ 按照②～④步的顺序继续开挖左洞。

3 结果分析

3.1 不同净距下结果分析

（1）不同净距下地表沉降槽分析

埋深 2D 情况下不同净距下的地表沉降槽曲线如图 2 所示。净距越小，对两洞中间处地层的沉降影响就越大，两洞中间处地表的沉降值越大，但是净距对左洞左侧和右洞右侧的地层沉降几乎没有影响，可以认为在这两侧沉降槽仍与单洞开挖时的相同，故净距越大，沉降槽曲线开口范围越大。当净距较小时，地表最大沉降发生在两洞中间处的地表，随着净距增大地表最大沉降发生的位置逐渐移动到隧道正上方的地表。

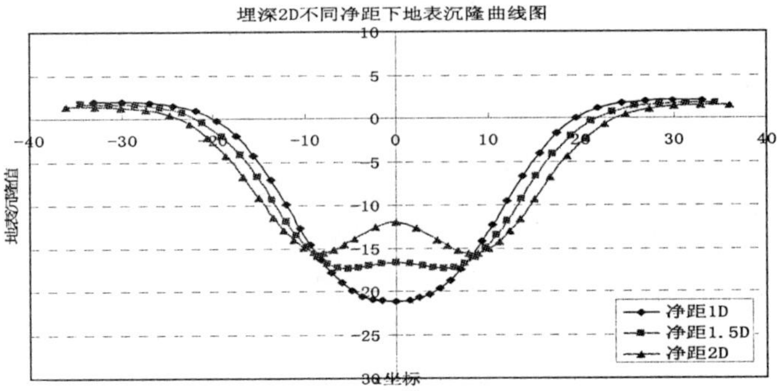

图 2 埋深 2D 时不同净距下地表沉降槽曲线

（2）不同净距下塑性区的比较

埋深 2D 时不同净距下塑性区等值线图如图 3 所示。在隧道埋深较浅但围岩强度较低时，隧道开挖形成的弹性二次应力状态可能超过围岩的抗压强度，在坑道附近围岩内形成塑性应力区域[5]。塑性区只会在一定范围之内产生，当平行隧道净距较小时，两洞中间地层塑性区重合的区域就会增多，这样就会使两洞相邻侧的塑性应变增加，并且两洞相邻侧的地层在单洞开挖时不会出现塑性应变的区域也产生了塑性应变，但是本次模拟中，单洞开挖所形成的塑性区范围较小，净距只会影响两洞相邻侧的塑性区，左洞左侧及右洞右侧的地层不会受净距影响，从图 3 中可以很明显地看出，随着净距的增大，两洞中间地层的塑性区域越来越小，而左洞左侧及右洞右侧的塑性区范围几乎不变。

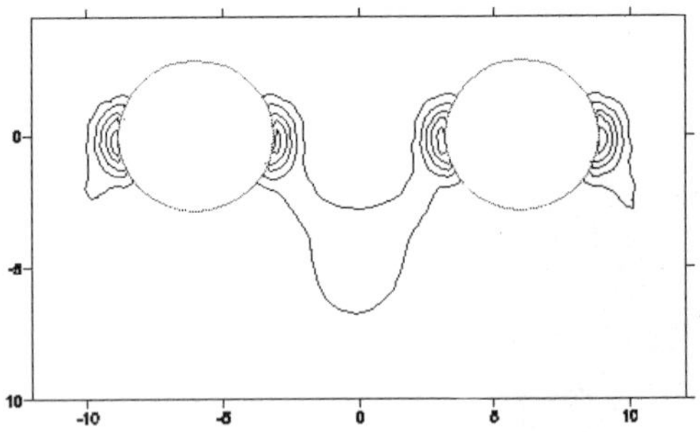

（a）净距 1D 时塑性区图

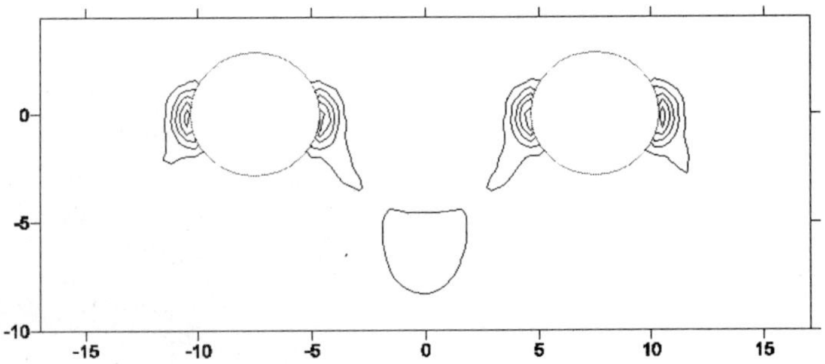

（b）净距 1.5D 时塑性区图

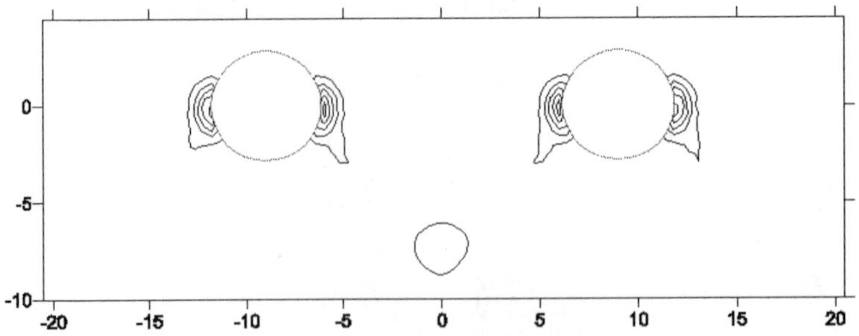

（c）净距 2D 时塑性区图

图 3 埋深 2D 时不同净距下塑性区等值线图

（3）不同净距下衬砌内力比较

为了使结果便于比较，现规定所有内力结果中角度方向定义如图 4 所示，其中左洞以拱顶 A_1 点开始，顺时针方向旋转为正，右洞以拱顶 A_2 为 0°，逆时针旋转为正。

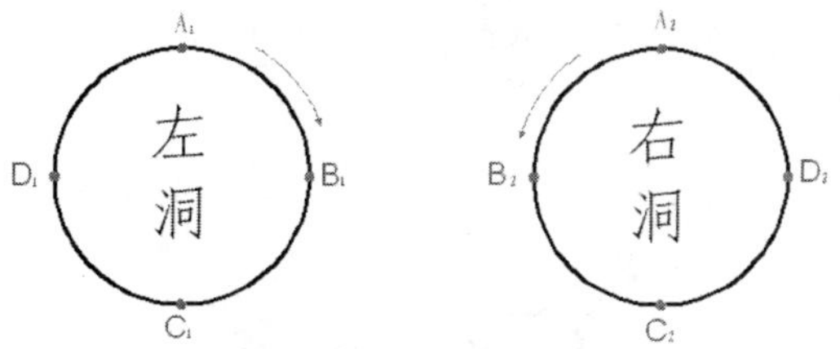

图 4　角度方向定义图

不同净距下衬砌轴力如图 5 所示。右洞衬砌施作后，右洞周围围岩与支护结构共同工作形成三次应力状态[6]。当左洞修建后，对右洞周围的应力状态造成一定影响，从位移来看，左洞修建好后，比起右洞修建完成时，右洞左侧拱腰处的点位移方向为 x 轴正方向，相当于增大了侧向土压力，净距越小影响就越大，从图 5 中可以明显地看出，右洞左侧的点即 B_2 点，轴力明显变化，随着净距增大轴力有所减小，右洞其他点处及左洞各点处也有较小的减小。左洞和右洞弯矩和剪力也略有减小，仅列出右洞部分轴力和弯矩值如表 2 所示。总体来说，增大净距可以降低衬砌上的内力。

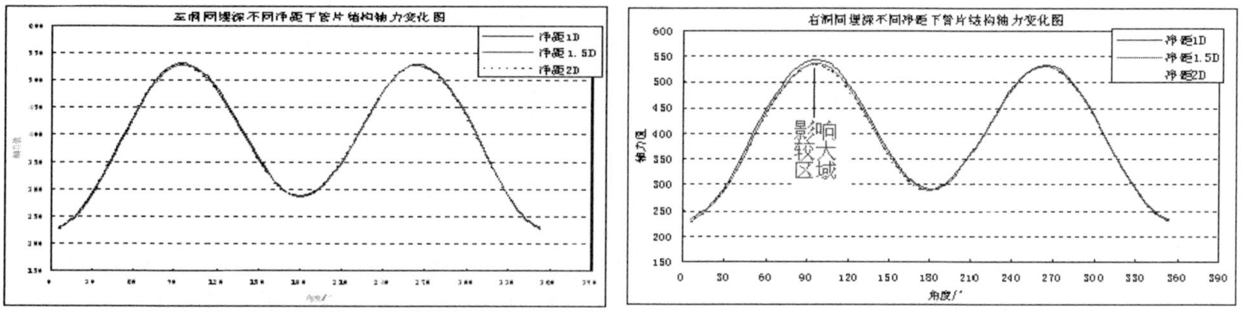

（a）左洞衬砌轴力图　　　　（b）右洞衬砌轴力图

图 5　不同净距下衬砌轴力图

表 2　右洞部分弯矩和剪力值

右洞剪力值				右洞弯矩值			
角度(°) ＼ 净距	1D	1.5D	2D	角度(°) ＼ 净距	1D	1.5D	2D
45	− 121.8	− 120.8	− 120.3	0	164.8	163.4	162.6
135	133.6	132.8	131.8	90	− 176.3	− 175.3	− 174.4
225	− 132.8	− 132.0	− 131.4	180	178.4	177.4	176.5
315	122.2	121.1	120.6	270	− 176.5	− 175.2	− 174.4

3.2　不同土质下结果分析

（1）不同土质下地表沉降槽分析

不同土质下地表沉降图如图 6 所示。从表 1 来看，老黄土与新黄土的黏聚力相同并且大于饱和软黄土的黏聚力，老黄土的内摩擦角要大于新黄土的内摩擦角，这就决定了图 8 中在同样埋深同样净距的条件下，同一 x 坐标处老黄土的地表沉降值要小于新黄土的地表沉降值，饱和软黄土的地表沉降值要大于新黄土的地表沉降值，并且老黄土产生地表沉降的范围最小，新黄土其次，饱和软黄土产生地表沉降范围最大。

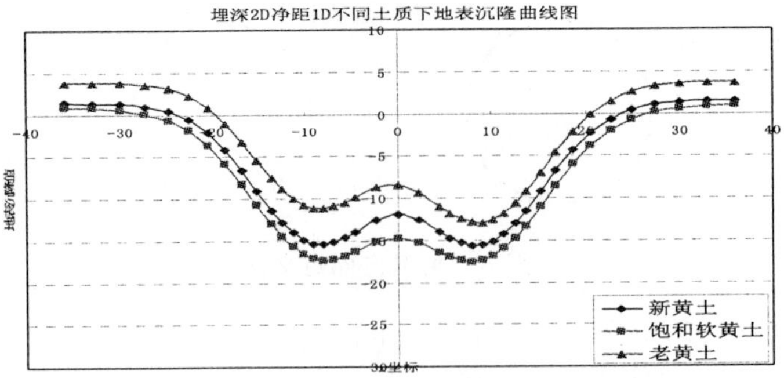

图 6 埋深 2D 净距 2D 时不同土质下地表沉降图

（2）不同土质下塑性区分析

同埋深同净距不同土质下塑性区等值线图如图 7 所示。老黄土与新黄土的黏聚力相同并且大于饱和软黄土的黏聚力，老黄土的内摩擦角要大于新黄土的内摩擦角，这就使得隧道开挖之后形成的塑性区范围不同，其中老黄土的最小，新黄土次之，饱和软黄土的最大。

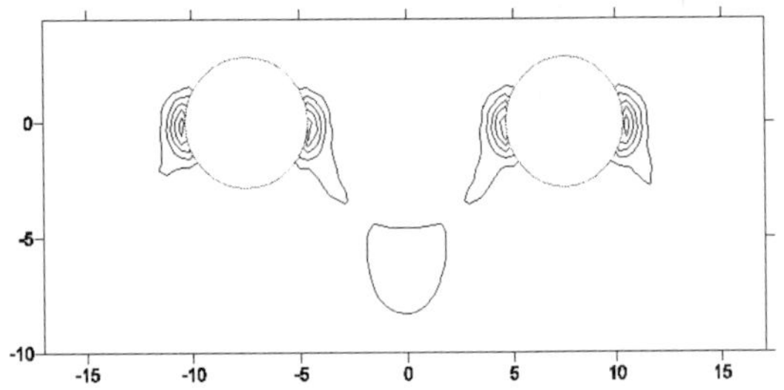

（a）埋深 2D 净距 1.5D 时新黄土塑性区图

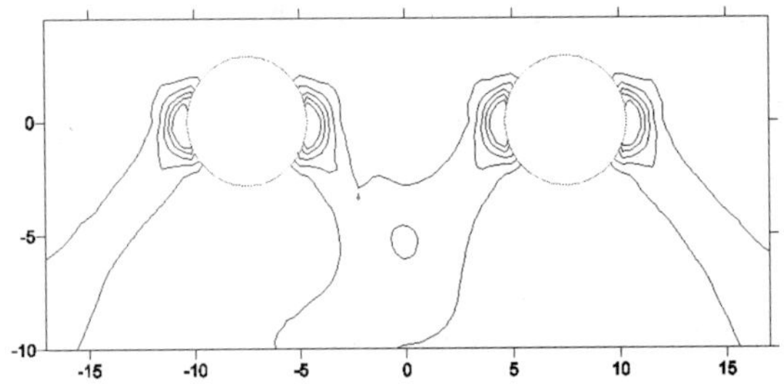

（b）埋深 2D 净距 1.5D 时饱和软黄土塑性区图

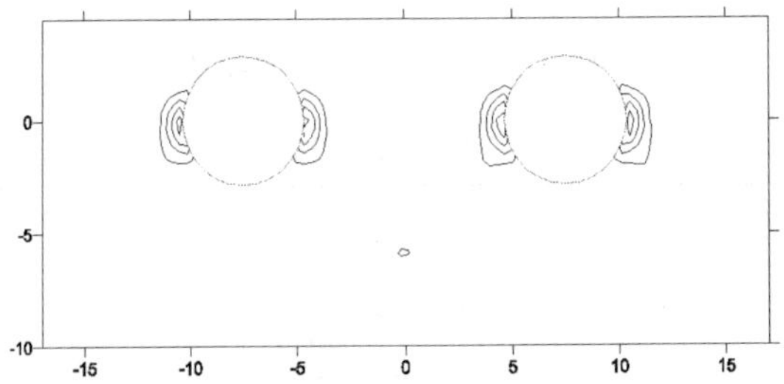

（c）埋深 2D 净距 1.5D 时老黄土塑性区图

图 7 不同土质下塑性区等值线图

（3）不同土质下衬砌内力分析

为了便于结果分析，首先明确荷载结构模型中作用在衬砌上的荷载。衬砌设计时所要考虑的各种荷载，应根据不同的条件和设计方法进行假定，并根据隧道的用途，组合这些荷载[7]。本次计算没有考虑地下水，将弹性抗力按修正惯用法思路以一定值直接施加在结构体，根据相关的管片所受荷载示意图及荷载计算方法，将作用在结构上的土压力简化如图 8 所示。各种荷载计算结果如表 3 所示。

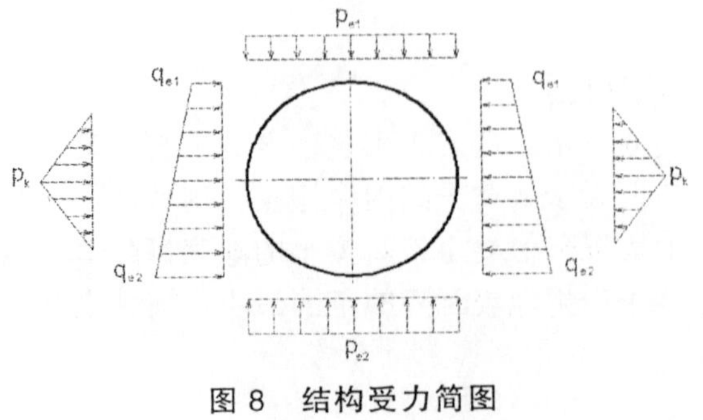

图 8 结构受力简图

表 3　作用在衬砌上的荷载值表

荷载项 / 土质名	p_{e1} /kPa	q_{e1} /kPa	q_{e2} /kPa	p_k /kPa
新黄土	211.2	100.6	148.1	10.4
饱和软黄土	220.2	125.4	185.4	7.0
老黄土	232.8	101.1	150.2	20.0

从表 3 中可以明显地看出，作用在衬砌上的上覆土压力大于侧向土压力。在上覆土压力的作用下，拱顶和拱底相对向内变形，拱腰相对向外变形，侧向土压力的作用刚好和上覆土压力作用相反，它限制了拱腰向外的相对变形。一般而言，在拱顶和拱底附近产生最大正弯矩，在拱腰附近产生最大负弯矩，侧向土压力越大，上覆土压力越小，衬砌上的弯矩绝对值越小。在比较轴力时主要看作用在衬砌上的径向压力值，该值越大，衬砌的收缩变形就越大，那么衬砌的轴力就越大。

在不同土质下，左右洞内力变化规律相似，仅以右洞进行分析如图 9 所示。从表 3 中可以看出，当地层为新黄土时作用在衬砌径向上的土压力值最小，故新黄土地层中，衬砌结构的轴力最小，老黄土和饱和软黄土地层中，衬砌结构所受的上覆土压力相差不大，但饱和软黄土地层中，侧向压力值很大，相对来说，在饱和软黄土地层中衬砌结构上的径向土压力要大一些，这样轴力值比较结果如图 9（a）所示，在新黄土地层中的值最小，在饱和软黄土地层中的值最大。

三种土质下弯矩图如图 9（c）所示。在 0°、90°、180°及 270°处弯矩出现极值，在这些区域，对于老黄土和新黄土而言，两种地层中衬砌结构上的侧向土压力相差不大，但老黄土的上覆土压力值要大，故老黄土地层衬砌的弯矩绝对值要大于新黄土地层衬砌的弯矩，相比之下饱和软黄土地层中上覆土压力与新黄土地层、软黄土地层中的相差不大，但是饱和软黄土地层中的侧压力值要明显大于后两者地层中的相应值，故饱和软黄土中的弯矩绝对值最小。弯矩图上某点的切线斜率等于该点处剪力的大小[8]，从图 9（b）中可以看出在 45°、135°、225°及 315°处剪力出现极值，并且老黄土地层中衬砌的剪力绝对值要大于新黄土地层中的相应值，饱和软黄土中衬砌的剪力绝对值值最小。

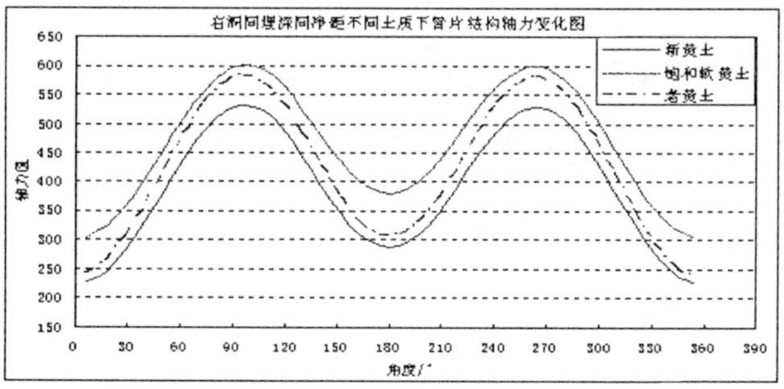

（a）衬砌轴力图

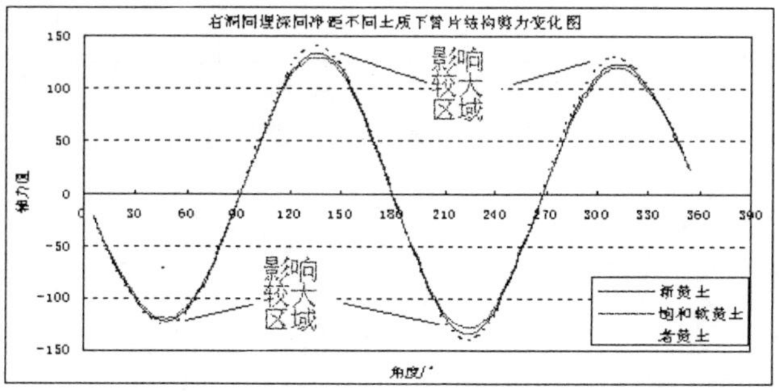

（b）衬砌剪力图

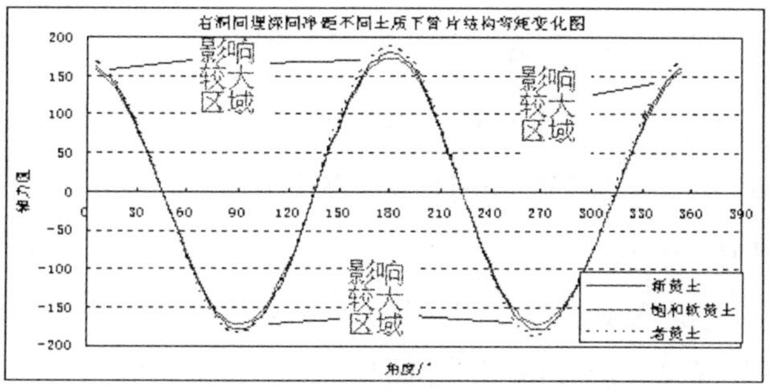

（c）衬砌弯矩图

图 9　不同土质下衬砌内力图

3.3 不同释放系数下结果分析

（1）不同释放系数下地表沉降槽分析

不同释放系数下地表沉降槽曲线如图 10 所示。开挖后应力释放阶段，地表产生的沉降占最终沉降值的绝大部分，本次模拟中以在开挖洞室周边加径向约束的方法来模拟应力释放，相当于施加了支护阻力 p_a，并且释放系数越大，对应的支护阻力 p_a 越小。支护阻力越大时，洞周径向位移越小，它所引起的地表位移也就越小。则如图 10 所示，释放系数越大，地表沉降值就越大，沉降槽开口宽度也越大。

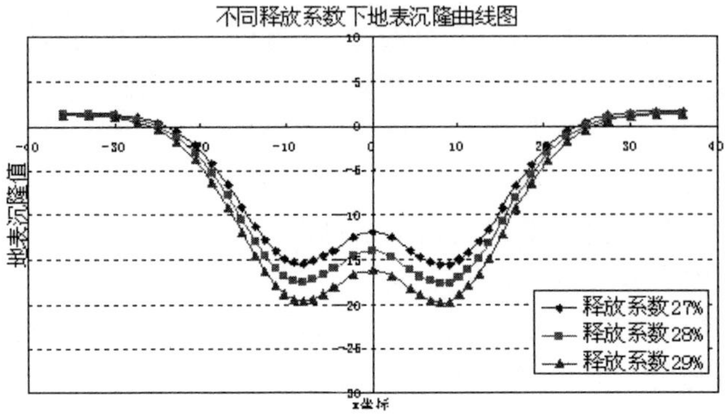

图 10　不同释放系数下地表沉降槽曲线

（2）不同释放系数下塑性区分析

释放系数越小，支护阻力越大，开挖洞室周围的塑性变形就越小，塑性区范围就越小，如图 11 所示。

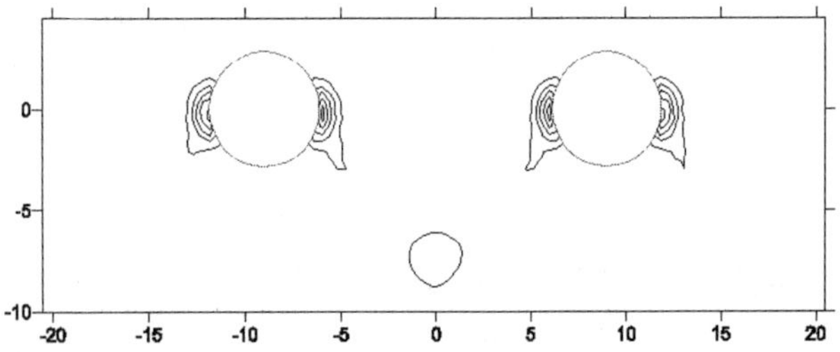

（a）释放系数 27% 时塑性区图

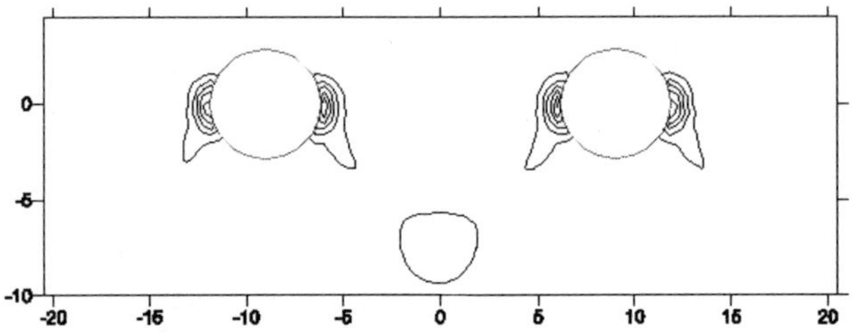

（b）释放系数 28% 时塑性区图

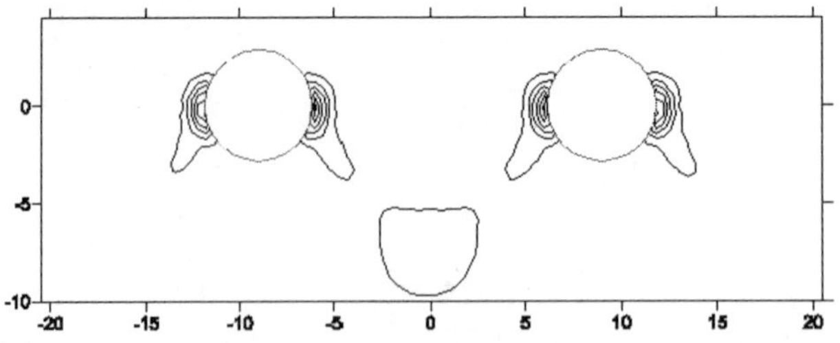

（c）释放系数 29% 时塑性区图

图 11　不同释放系数下塑性区图

（3）不同释放系数下结构内力分析

现代支护设计的作用荷载是岩体地应力，由围岩和支护共同承载[8]，在其他条件相同时，释放系数越大，在一定范围内围岩变形越大，那么围岩承担的荷载就越大，作用在衬砌结构上的荷载就越小，衬砌结构上的内力就越小。如图 12 所示。

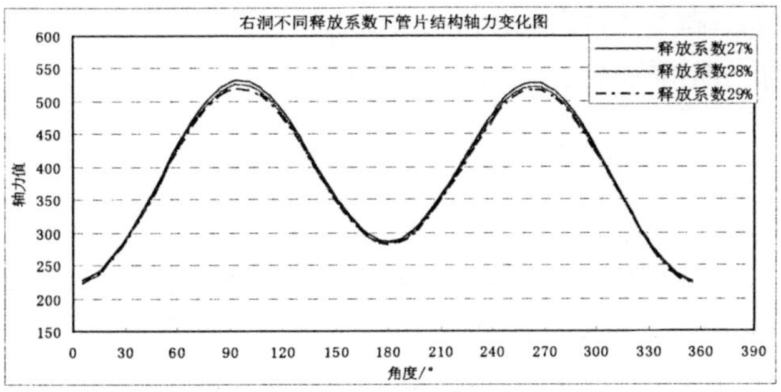

（a）衬砌结构轴力图

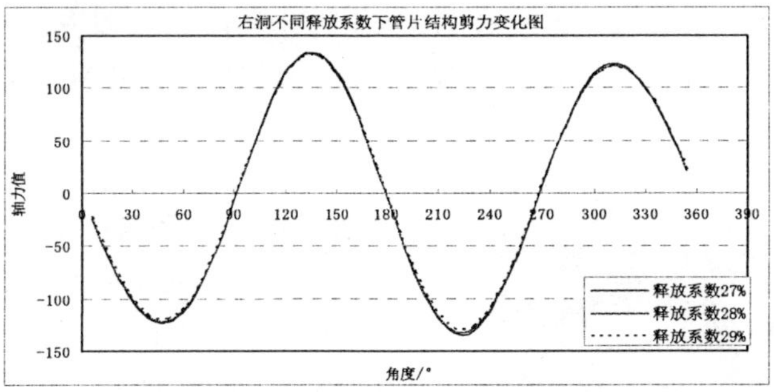

（b）衬砌结构轴力图

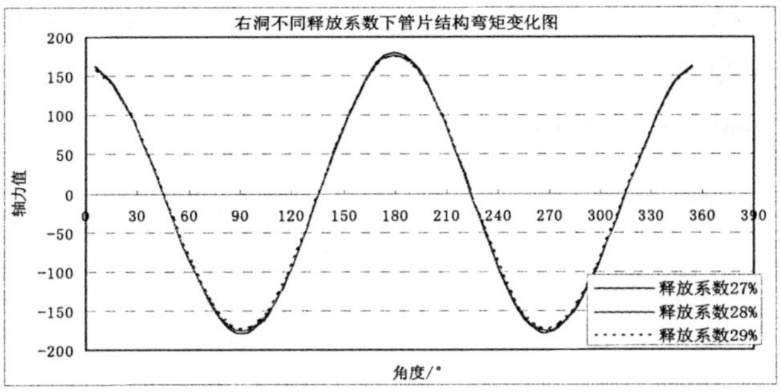

（c）衬砌结构轴力图

图 12　不同释放系数下衬砌结构内力图

4 结　论

（1）其他条件相同时，净距越大，地表发生沉降的范围越大，两洞中间处地表沉降值越小。净距较小时，地表最大沉降发生在两洞中间处；净距较大时，地表最大沉降值发生在各洞的正上方处。净距越大，两洞中间处地层塑性区范围越小，但是单洞开挖形成的塑性区范围较小的情况下，左洞左侧及右洞右侧地层的塑性区没有变化。净距越大，作用在衬砌上的内力越小。

（2）其他条件相同时，隧道穿越土层为老黄土时，地表沉降范围及沉降值最小，隧道开挖产生的塑性区也最小；隧道穿越土层为饱和软黄土时，地表沉降范围及沉降值最大，隧道开挖产生的塑性区也最大；隧道穿越土层为新黄土时，相应的值介于前述二者之间。饱和软黄土地层中的衬砌结构轴力值最大，新黄土中的最小，老黄土中的相应值介于二者之间。老黄土地层中衬砌结构的弯矩和剪力绝对值最大，新黄土地层中的次之，饱和软黄土中衬砌结构的弯矩和剪力绝对值最小。

（3）其他条件相同时，释放系数越大地表沉降值越大，地表沉降的范围越大，塑性区的范围越大，衬砌结构上内力越小。

参考文献（References）：

[1] 倪玉山，张华兵. 黄土隧道施工方案的数值分析[J]. 岩土力学，2006，27(supp)：22-26.

[2] 翁效林，王俊，张刚，武朝梁.黄土地区地铁开挖引起地表沉降试验分析[J]. 岩石力学与工程学报，2007，26（supp 2）：4348-4352.

[3] 李围. 隧道及地下工程 ANSYS 实例分析[M]. 北京：中国水利出版社，2008：402-424.

[4] British Standards Institution. Design of composite steel and concrete structures, Part1. 1: General rules and rules for buildings[S]. ENV 1994 - 1 - 1: 1992 Eurocode 4, London, 1992.

[5] 关宝树. 隧道力学概论[M]. 成都：西南交通大学出版社，1993：49-63.

[6] 张凤祥，朱合华，傅德明. 盾构隧道[M]. 北京：人民交通出版社，2004：325-332.

[7] 孙训方，方孝淑，关来泰. 材料力学：第 4 版[M]. 北京：高等教育出版社, 2002: 104.
[8] 李志业，曾艳华. 地下结构设计原理与方法[M]. 成都：西南交通大学出版社，2003: 11.

作者简介（Bio-data）：

高云龙，男，1985 年 3 月出生，2008 年毕业于西南交通大学，获得学士学位，现在在西南交通大学攻读硕士学位，主要研究方向为隧道工程。

Yunlong Gao (1985—), male, graduated from School of Civil Engineering, Southwest Jiaotong University in 2008 and obtained a Bachelor's degree in the same time. Now he is pursuing the master's degree in Southwest Jiaotong University. He specializes in tunnel engineering.

E-mail: swjtugaoyunlong@126.com

武汉长江隧道盾构下穿武九铁路沉降影响分析

季大雪
中铁第四勘察设计院集团有限公司，湖北　武汉　430063

【摘　要】　武汉长江隧道周边工程环境复杂，其中盾构下穿既有武九铁路是该工程的难点之一。本文分别采用经典的 Peck 法和有限元法计算了盾构推进对武九铁路的沉降影响，介绍了施工中所采取的保护措施和现场监测情况，为同类工程积累了经验。施工过程中的现场沉降监测结果大于计算结果，但未影响铁路的安全运行。由于列车运行的影响，下穿铁路引起的地表沉降槽宽度和深度均大于邻近的和平大道。
【关键词】　武汉长江隧道；盾构；武九铁路；沉降；现场监测

SETTLEMENT ANALYSIS OF WUHAN YANGTZE RIVER SHIELD TUNNEL CROSSING WUHAN-JIUJIANG RAILWAY

Daxue JI
China Railway Siyuan Survey and Design Group Co. Ltd., Wuhan 430063, Hubei, China

Abstract: The surrounding engineering environment of Wuhan Yangtze River Tunnel is complicated, and the shield crossing underground of the existing Wuhan-Jiujiang Railway is one of the difficult points in the project. This paper adopts the classical Peck Method and finite element method respectively to calculate the settlement influence on Wuhan-Jiujiang Railway which is caused by shield driving , introduces the protective measures taken during the construction and the onsite monitoring situation, thus accumulating experience for similar projects. The onsite monitoring result of the settlement is greater than the calculating result , but it doesn't affect the safe operation of the railway. Due to the impact of train operation, the surface settlement trough width and depth caused by the crossing railway are both greater than the adjacent Peace Road.
Key words: wuhanyangtze river tunnel; shield; wuhan-jiujiang railway; settlement; onsite monitoring

1　工程概况

武汉长江隧道工程位于武汉长江一桥、二桥之间，是一条解决内环线内主城区过江交通的城市主干道。隧道全长 3 630 m，其中盾构段长 2 550 m。隧道内设双向四车道，设计车速 50 km/h。该盾构隧道内径 10 m，外径 11 m，采用钢筋混凝土单层衬砌。盾构隧道管片环采用等分九块方式，为通用楔形环，管片环宽 2 m，厚 500 mm。

盾构隧道主要位于富含地下水的砂土层中，根据工程地质条件，盾构机选用复合式泥水平衡盾构，盾构机外径 11.38 m。

武九铁路自湖北省武汉市武昌站至江西省九江市庐山站，全长 261 km，是国家路网沿江通道的重要组成部分。铁路等级为一级复线，速度目标值 200 km/h，武汉市区段列车限速 80 km/h。

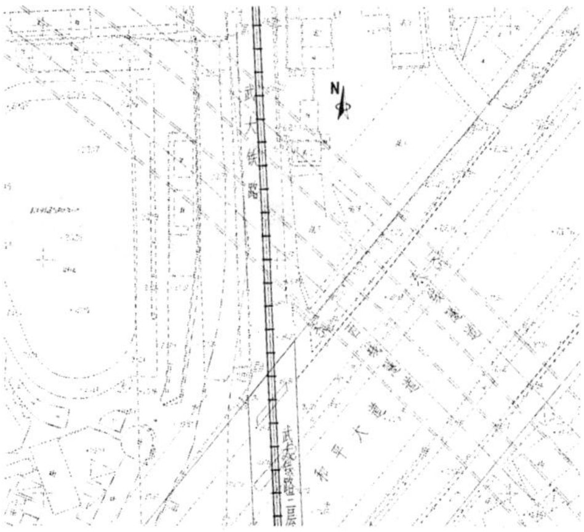

图 1　隧道与铁路平面关系图

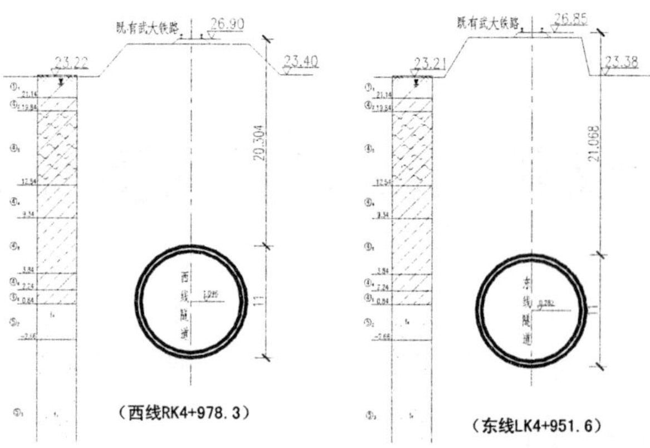

图 2　隧道与铁路立面关系图

武汉长江隧道在武昌侧和平大道附近斜穿武九铁路，夹角约 46 度。相交段长江隧道东、西线均位于半径 800 m 的圆曲线上，武九铁路位于直线上。图 1 为隧道与武九铁路平面关系图。其中东线隧道于 LK4＋951.6 处下穿武九铁路，隧道覆土厚度 21.068 m；西线隧道于 RK4＋978.3 处下穿武九铁路，覆土厚度 20.304 m，隧道下穿点武九铁路对应既有铁路里程约为 K4＋690，铁路线路为碎石道床，隧道下穿路基处断面如图 2 所示，主要地层物理力学性质见表 1。

表 1　主要地层物理力学参数

地层代号	土名	状态	重度 (kN/m^3)	内摩擦角	黏聚力 (kPa)	静止侧压力系数	压缩模量 (MPa)
①$_1$	杂填土	松散	18.6	18.0	8.0	0.64	3.0
④$_2$	粉质黏土	软塑	19.1	10.0	18.0	0.60	4.0
④$_4$	粉质黏土	软塑	18.8	8.0	14.0	0.61	4.5
④$_5$	淤泥质粉质黏土	流塑	18.0	6.0	10.0	0.65	3.2
④$_6$	粉土	中密	19.5	21.5	11.5	0.40	9.0
⑤$_2$	粉细砂	中密	19.6	32.0	0	0.35	16.0
⑤$_3$	粉细砂	密实	19.8	36.0	0	0.34	20.0

国内外研究[1, 2]表明，盾构隧道施工引起的地层变形主要原因是施工中的地层损失和隧道周围土体受扰动产生的再固结。引起地层损失的原因主要有以下几条：

① 开挖面土体的移动；

② 土体与管片衬砌的相互作用；

③ 盾构推进方向改变，超挖等。

目前用于预测盾构法掘进引起土体变形的主要方法有以现场实测资料为基础的经验公式法和部分考虑施工过程的数值模拟法。

2　Peck 法沉降估算

在武汉长江隧道所处的软弱地层中用盾构法施工，因地层损失和土体扰动，必然引起地表变形，具体表现在盾构掘进机的前方和顶部产生微量的隆起，盾尾脱离以后，地表开始下沉，并形成一定宽度的沉降槽地带，下沉的速率随时间而逐渐衰减，且与盾构所经过的地层、施工工况和地表荷载等有密切的关系，并表现出相当的差异性。

对于盾构隧道施工引起地面沉降预测，派克（Peck，1969 年）提出了地层损失的概念和估算方法。此后经过大量工程实践及修正完善，该方法成为最常用的估算盾构正常施工引起地面沉降的方法。该方法认为在不考虑土体排水固结与蠕变的条件下，盾构推进后地面横向沉降基本为似正态曲线，沉降槽体积等于地层损失的体积，具体地面沉降如下关系[2]:

$$S_x = \frac{V_l}{\sqrt{2\pi} i} e^{(-\frac{x^2}{2i^2})}$$

其中：Sx 为地面到盾构中心处埋深为 Z 的断面上，距离隧道中心线 x 处的沉降量；Vl 为地层损失量；i 为沉降槽宽度系数，是土壤条件、隧道半径、隧道中心埋深的函数。

按盾构隧道正常施工时 0.5% 的地层损失率进行计算，东线隧道先行掘进施工时，最大地面沉降位于东线隧道中心正上方，其值为 17.6 mm，当东线隧道施工完成，西线隧道施工对地面的影响累积后，其地面最大沉降位置出现在两盾构隧道施工的中间靠西线盾构侧正上方，最大沉降值为 25.95 mm。如图 3 所示。

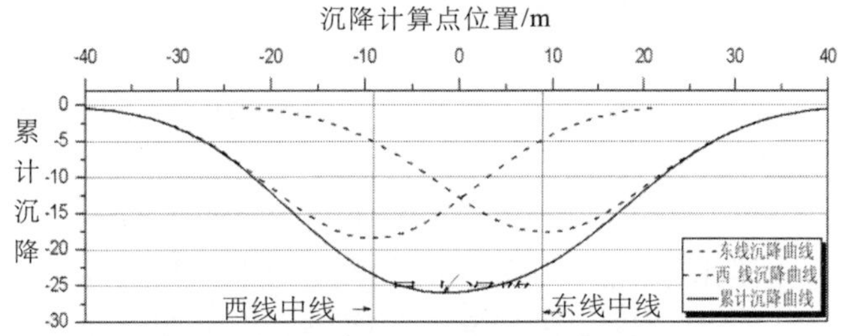

图 3 Peck 法计算的沉降槽

3 有限元分析

为进一步分析隧道施工对武九铁路的影响，除以上 Peck 理论分析外，同时进行了地层有限元分析。采用通用有限元软件 ANSYS 进行地层-结构模拟。模拟计算不考虑隧道纵向影响，取每延米隧道近似按平面应力应变问题处理。根据经验公式估算的地表沉降槽半宽度 w＝2.5i，双管隧道推进完成后地表沉降槽宽度应大于 28.8＋17.2＋28.8＝74.8 m。建立宽度 80 m，深度 50 m 的二维有限元计算模型，模型左右边界水平约束，底部边界竖直向约束，地层材料采用四节点平面单元模拟，管片采用二节点弹性梁单元。岩土材料屈服条件采用 Morh-Coulomb 准则。

根据隧道与铁路路基之间关系及工程地质条件，选取 LK4＋951.6 处隧道断面进行地层沉降有限元分析。

图 4 为东线隧道施工后，隧道周边地层沉降位移图，其中东线隧道中线处地面沉降最大值为 16.4 mm，地面沉降槽宽度约 54 m。图 5 为西线隧道施工完毕后隧道周边地层沉降位移图，其中地面最大沉降量 24.2 mm，位于东、西线隧道之间靠近西线隧道侧，地面沉降槽宽度约 76 m。

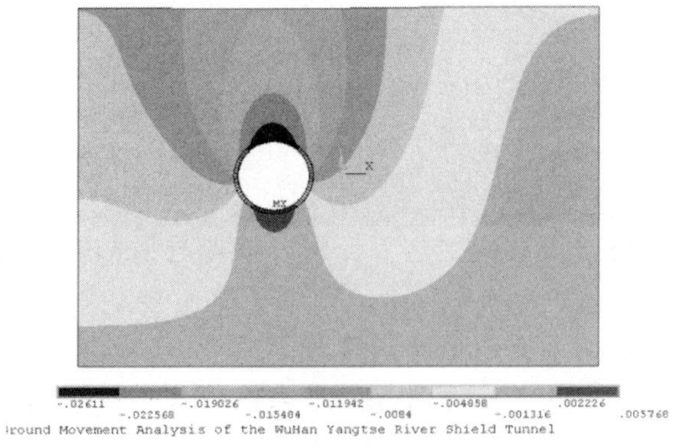

图 4 东线隧道下穿后地表沉降图

图 5 西线隧道下穿后地表沉降

从以上影响分析看，在盾构隧道正常施工时将对武九铁路产生一定的影响。该影响必须控制在不影响铁路运行安全的范围内。

经以上计算分析，盾构下穿铁路地段，地面最大沉降量约为 24.2 mm，地面最大曲率半径约 5 500 m。由于地下工程施工的不确定性，为确保铁路运行安全，在盾构隧道施工期间拟采取相应的保护措施。

4 保护措施

从以上计算分析看，在盾构隧道正常施工时将对武九铁路产生不可忽视的影响。施工期间结合现场监测情况，拟采取如下保护措施以保证铁路运营安全。

（1）扣轨加固线路

由于该沉降值非瞬时发生，而是随施工过程逐渐增加，施工过程中根据沉降监测情况随时补充道碴，保持轨面平顺性要求。为此，对隧道顶部 96 m（即左右线结构边线外各 25 m）范围内的铁路线路采用扣轨加固，并加强地表沉降观测，实行信息化施工。

（2）盾构施工保护措施

盾构在穿越武九铁路施工时将精心调整施工参数，控制泥水压力和推进速度，减少地层损失及对周边地层的扰动。具体施工措施为：

① 模拟推进，优化参数

在穿越铁路前 50 m 设立模拟试推进区，设置相应深度的土体垂直及水平位移监测点，地下水位及水压监测点，自始至终监测深层监测点的变化状况，紧密依靠地表变形监测数据，摸索不同盾构推进速度和泥水压力及盾构注浆工艺对地层的影响，精确测定地层的变形与盾构机泥水压力设定值、盾构掘进速度的实际值之间的关系，测得穿越武九铁路前最优施工参数，指导施工。

② 加强监测、控制沉降

在武九铁路通过地段沿线布置沉降及水平位移监测点，在施工穿越过程中连续监测并及时优化调整各种施工参数。

控制切口泥水压力和推进速度，严格控制泥水指标等施工参数，使切口泥水能更好地支护正面土体，减少盾构切口前方沉降。及时同步注浆，控制注浆参数，减少盾构通过时地面沉降及固结沉降。利用 Peck 公式、回归统计等对盾构推进过程中所产生的土体损失进行计算，在盾构推进过程中根据地面沉降情况，及时分析判断对注浆量、注浆部位和注浆压力进行调整，在施工中必要时进行补充注浆，控制后期沉降。

③ 信息化动态施工管理

盾构穿越武九铁路时，利用模拟推进积累的参数推进，并由专人昼夜对地面监测点进行沉降监测，及时、准确地将结构及轨道的变形情况反馈至盾构掘进工作面，指导盾构掘进参数及时优化调整。同时根据地面荷载的情况，及时重新计算泥水平衡设定值，并根据地面隆陷值加以调整，使盾构低速均匀推进，尽量缩短穿越时间，防止超挖和欠挖，减少对土体的扰动，最大限度地减少地层损失，将沉降控制在最小范围内，满足沉降要求。

5 实测结果

盾构推进时的地表监测十分重要，监测结果应及时反馈至盾构掘进工作面，以指导盾构掘进参数及时优化调整。

本盾构隧道下穿武九铁路时，在盾构区域内每隔 5 m 埋设一组铁路道轨沉降测点，盾构区域外每隔 10 m 埋设一组，东、西侧轨道共设置 15 组。盾构区域内每隔 5 m 埋设一个地表沉降测点，盾构区域外每隔 8 m 埋设一个测点。测点平面布置情况详见图 6。

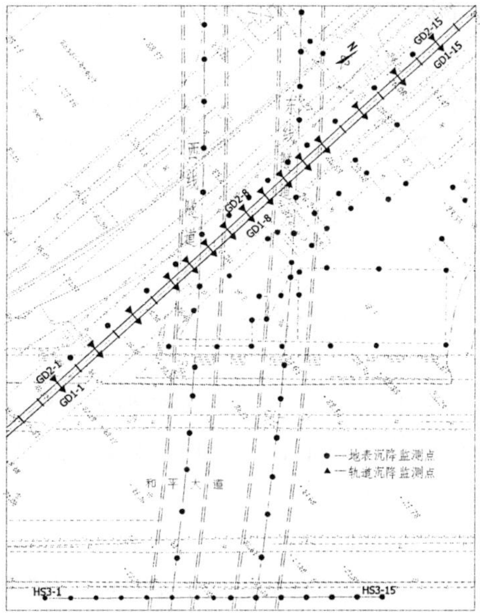

图 6　铁路附近沉降监测点平面布置

下穿铁路时对各测点进行连续监测，直至后续沉降趋于稳定时，根据累计沉降结果绘出铁路轨道沉降槽曲线如图 7 所示。图 8 为盾构下穿武昌和平大道的沉降槽曲线，二者穿越地层相似，下穿和平大道处盾构覆土更浅，但是沉降槽宽度、深度均小于下穿武九铁路的监测结果，除开盾构操作等因素以外，地面荷载对沉降的影响也是一个重要的影响因素。

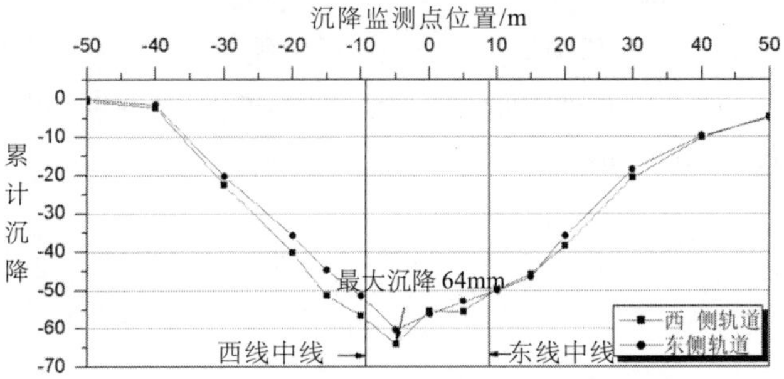

图 7　盾构下穿武九铁路实测沉降槽

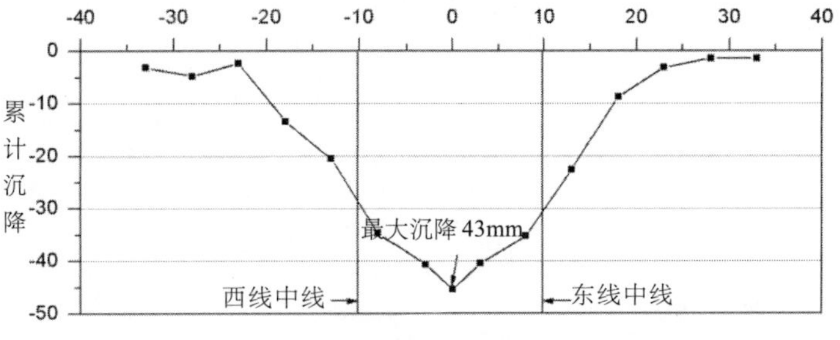

图 8　盾构下穿和平大道实测沉降槽

6　结　语

至 2007 年 6 月中旬，武九铁路后续沉降基本稳定，武汉长江隧道也于 2008 年 4 月成功实现双线贯通。下穿武九铁路过程中未出现灾害性地层损失[4]。总结本次下穿施工的经验，结合计算和实测情况，可以得到一些初步的结论：

（1）虽然实测累计沉降量远大于计算值，但是由于沉降量变化缓慢，该段铁路道床为碎石道床，在沉降槽宽度范围内的铁路运行并没有受到影响。如条件许可，盾构通过时地面列车应减速缓慢行驶。

（2）通过比较与铁路邻近的和平大道侧地表沉降监测数据可知，由于地面列车的影响，隧道下穿铁路引起的地表沉降比一般情况下盾构推进引起的地表沉降量大，沉降槽的深度和范围也更大。下穿铁路时，在盾构通过后较长一段时间后续沉降持续增大，后续沉降占总沉降的比重也更大。

（3）计算和监测结果都显示双线盾构最终沉降槽中心位于两条隧道之间并明显靠近后推进的隧道。

（4）盾构施工阶段引起地面沉降主要因素是施工导致地层损失，主要通过同步注浆和调整盾构施工参数来控制，因此在下穿铁路前一段距离，根据地面沉降监测情况，进行模拟推进，不断优化盾构施工的各种技术参数是必要的。

（5）根据本工程的经验，类似工程地质条件下，通过加强施工管理，合理设定泥水压力，熟练盾构机操作，控制泥水压力波动，保证适当的注浆量，地层损失可以减小到 0.5% 左右。

参考文献（References）：

[1] 吕培林，周顺华. 软土地区盾构隧道下穿铁路干线引起的线路沉降规律分析[J]. 中国铁道科学, 2007, 28(2).

[2] 刘建航，侯学渊. 盾构法隧道[M]. 北京：中国铁道出版社, 1991.

[3] 杜孔泽，严广艺. 近距离盾构隧道下穿铁路沉降分析[J]. 山西建筑, 2005, 31(14).

[4] 肖龙鸽，王超峰，赵运臣. 大直径泥水盾构施工引起的地表沉降分析和对策[J]. 现代隧道技术 2008, 45(5).

作者简介（Bio-data）：

季大雪，男，1978 年 12 月生，工程师，硕士研究生，主要从事交通隧道结构设计工作。

Daxue JI (1978—), male, engineer, master, engaged in the design of traffic tunnels.

Email: jidaxue@163.com

大型水下隧道水喷雾系统灭火的模拟分析

张玉春[1,2] 何 川[1] 曾艳华[1] 孙晓琴[2]
[1]西南交通大学 地下工程系，四川 成都 610031
[2]西南交通大学 消防工程系，四川 成都 610031

【摘 要】 为研究水喷雾系统实施对大型跨江海隧道火灾的影响，论文利用火灾动力模拟软件 FDS，以南京长江隧道为事例建立三维火灾数值模型，模拟了有/无水喷雾系统时隧道火灾的燃烧过程，通过水雾喷头不同雾化角大小以及不同水雾粒径直径的模拟，分析了不同水雾喷头不同雾化特征对隧道火灾的影响。研究表明，实施水喷雾系统后将降低隧道内火灾危险性，改善隧道环境，同时合理的水喷雾喷头参数设计，将提高水喷雾系统的灭火效果。

【关键词】 隧道；火灾；水喷雾；FDS；模拟

SIMULATION OF FIRE EXTINGUISHMENT BY WATER SPRAY SYSTEM OF LARGE-SCALE UNDERWATER TUNNEL

Yuchun ZHANG[1,2], Chuan HE[1], Yanhua ZENG[1], Xiaoqin SUN[2]
[1]*Department of Underground and Engineering, Southwest Jiaotong University, Chengdu 610031, Sichuan, China;*
[2]*Department of fire Engineering, Southwest Jiaotong University, Chengdu 610031, Sichuan, China*

Abstract: This paper established 3D fire simulation model of Nanjing Yangtze River Tunnel by means of Fire Dynamic Simulation Software (FDS), being in order to explore the influence on large-scale underwater tunnel. The model simulated the burning process of tunnel fire with or without water spray extinguishment system. Based on the simulation of spray nozzles on different water spray angle sizes and on different water spray particle diameters, the impacts on tunnel fires of different spray nozzles and water spray characteristics were analyzed. The study proved that water spray extinguishment system would decreased the fire risk in tunnel, improved tunnel circumstance, and the rational parameter design of spray nozzles would enhance the fire extinguishment efficiency of this system.

Key words: tunnel; fire; water spray; FDS; simulation

1 引 言

近年来，随着我国经济的不断发展，交通基础建设不断加大，出现了一大批大型跨江越海水下隧道，该批大型越江海隧道具有规模和投资巨大、超长、超大等特点[1]，一旦发生火灾并得到有效控制，将可能造成重大的人员伤亡、财产损失和社会影响。现阶段山岭公路隧道的火灾早期控制，以火灾烟气控制为主，一种为通过临界风速来控制火灾烟气蔓延方向的纵向通风排烟方式，另一种为在特长隧道顶部加设排烟通道的集中排烟方式[2-3]，该两种方式如果实施适当，能有效保证人员的生命安全，但烟气控制方式不能有效阻止火灾规模的发展，也不能有效扑灭火灾，只能依靠隧道内的消火栓系统和外部消防救援系统进行灭火。为提高大型跨江海隧道的消防能力，现阶段跨江海隧道除安装了消火栓系统和通风排烟

基金项目：863 计划（2006AA11Z116）

系统外，还实施了水成膜泡沫灭火系统和水喷雾灭火系统[4]。水灭火系统被认为是最有效的灭火设施，它经济、方便和高效，被广泛应用于各种建筑以保护生命和财产安全。本文以南京长江隧道为例，开展隧道水喷雾灭火的数值模拟研究，了解大型跨江海隧道水喷雾系统对火灾的影响，为水喷雾系统的设计提供参考。

2 水喷雾灭火系统

水喷雾灭火系统是利用水雾喷头在较高的水压作用下，将水流分离成细小的水雾滴，并喷向保护对象达到灭火或防护冷却的目的。水喷雾灭火系统由水源、供水设备、管道、雨淋阀组、过滤器和水雾喷头等组成。在大型跨江海隧道内水雾喷头分别交错布置在隧道侧墙上部，当隧道内火灾发生后，火灾探测器报警，启动该区域雨淋阀，水流动启动水流指示器报警，同时启动消防水泵，打开水雾喷头灭火或冷却。其中水喷雾灭火的系统的设计包括水雾喷头的流量、工作压力，系统设计流量、管道水力计算，以及喷头雾化角等参数的确定[5]，图 1 为跨江海隧道水雾喷头示意图。

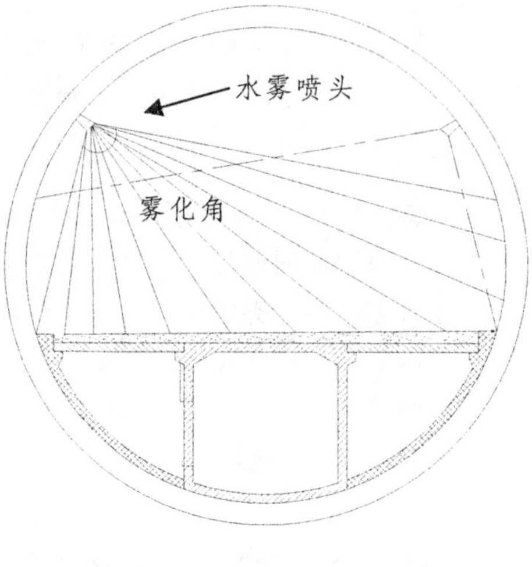

图 1 隧道水雾喷头示意

3 模型建立及火灾场景设置

本文以南京长江隧道为例，借助火灾动力模拟软件 FDS 对该隧道水喷雾灭火进行模拟分析。南京长江隧道为双向行车，每隧道设置三车道，设计行车速度为 80 km/h，盾构隧道内径 13.3 m，外径 14.5 m。依据南京长江隧道空间尺寸，建立了长 300 m、宽 14.5 m、高 14.5 m 的三维数值模型，火灾设置在隧道中部，最大热释放速率为 5 MW，按快速 t^2 米增长，水雾喷头交错布置在隧道侧墙上部，布置范围为 22.5 m，每侧每隔 2.25 m 布置一个，喷头设置参数如表 1 所示。图 2 为南京长江隧道的横断面图，图 3 为隧道的 FDS 三维模型。

表 1 水喷雾喷头的主要参数

喷水强度	工作压力	流量系数	流量
≥6 L/(m^2 · min)	0.35 MPa	134	250 L/min

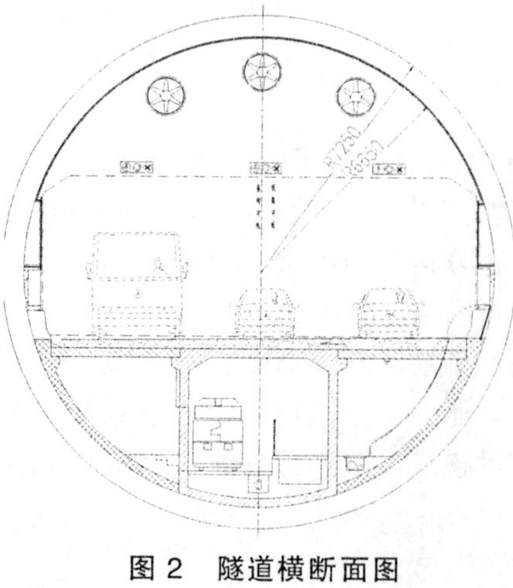

图 2 隧道横断面图

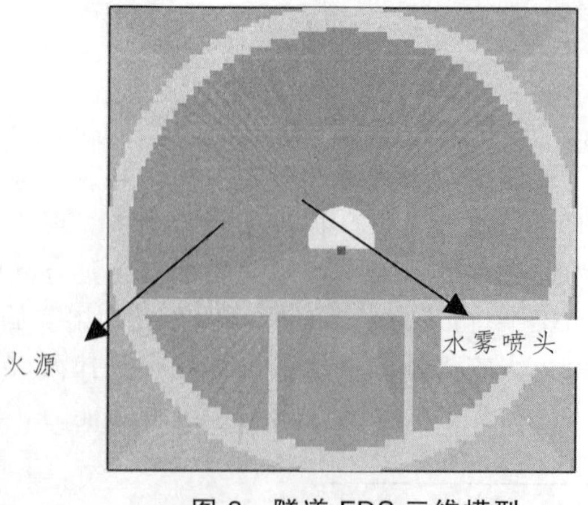

图 3 隧道 FDS 三维模型

4 水喷雾灭火的模拟分析

4.1 水喷雾灭火效果分析

图 4 为隧道实施水喷雾系统灭火过程，水喷雾系统采用雨淋系统，当火灾发生后，水喷雾系统是打开控制区内的所有水雾喷头已全湮没形式灭火或冷却，通过水雾喷头形成的雾化水对隧道内火灾进行冷却、窒息、冲击乳化和稀释实现灭火降温的作用。图 5 为隧道有/无水喷雾实施灭火时火源区拱顶处的温度和 CO 浓度变化曲线，通过对比两种方式的温度和 CO 浓度变化，当隧道发生火灾后通过实施水喷雾灭火作用后，隧道内的温度将降低，CO 浓度将下降，表明实施水喷雾系统后将降低隧道内火灾危险性，改善隧道内环境，更有利于人员疏散和结构设备的保护。

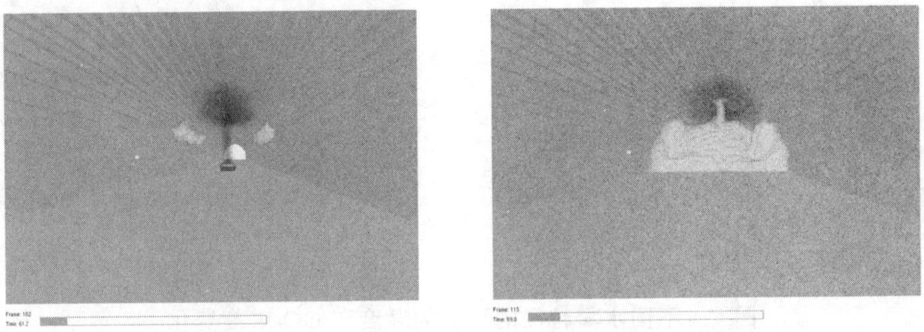

（a）水喷雾开始　　　　（b）水喷雾湮没火区

图 4　隧道水喷雾灭火过程

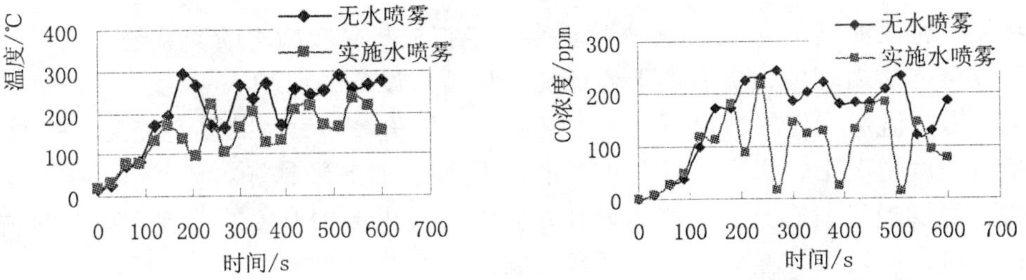

（a）温度变化曲线　　　　（b）CO 浓度变化曲线

图 5　隧道有/无水喷雾灭火的温度和 CO 浓度变化

4.2 水喷雾雾化特征参数分析

（1）喷头雾化角的影响

对雾化角为 60°、90°、120°三种水雾喷头的灭火效果进行了模拟，图 6 为不同雾化角的水喷雾系统最初喷雾的情况，如图所示，当雾化角为 60°时，水雾喷头的雾化角较小，喷射强度较大，有效射程相对越远；当雾化角为 120°时，由于水雾喷头压力不足，有效射程相对较近，保护半径相对较小。因此，水喷雾喷头的设计参考，应根据保护对象的范围，喷头的高度、角度以及水雾喷头的压力和流量综合考虑，保证水喷雾有效覆盖范围。

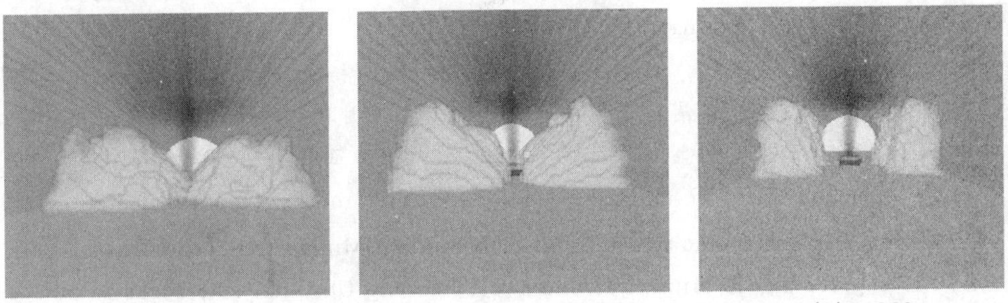

(a) 60°　　　　(b) 90°　　　　(c) 120°

图 6　不同雾化角的水雾特性

（2）水雾粒径大小的影响

对 600 μm、1 200 μm 两种不同的水雾粒径直径的灭火效果进行了模拟分析，如图 7 所示，600 μm 粒径水雾直径作用下的隧道火灾温度和 CO 浓度更低，600 μm 粒径明显好于 1 200 μm 粒径的水雾对隧道内的灭-控火效果，因此水喷雾液滴粒径的大小对隧道内的灭火效果有较大的影响，对比两种粒径，粒径越小水喷雾灭-控火效果更好，但当雾粒直径太小时，因雾滴质量很小，灭火时很难穿透火焰燃烧时产生的上升热气流，不能达到燃烧物质的表面，从而无法直接冷却正在燃烧的物质。同时太小的雾滴容易受隧道内环境的影响，如隧道内通风的影响，从而影响了灭火效果。

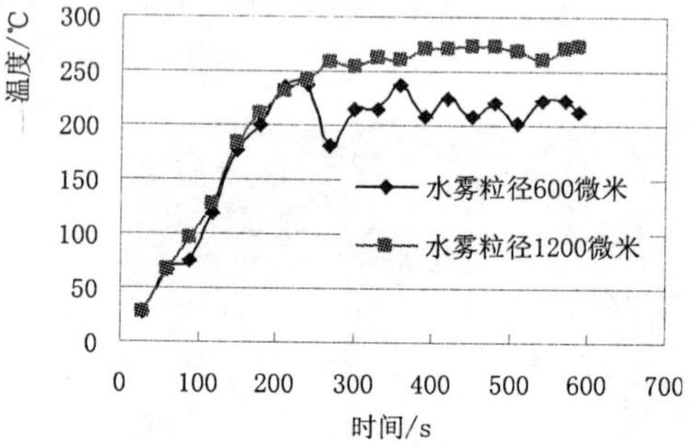

（a）温度变化曲线

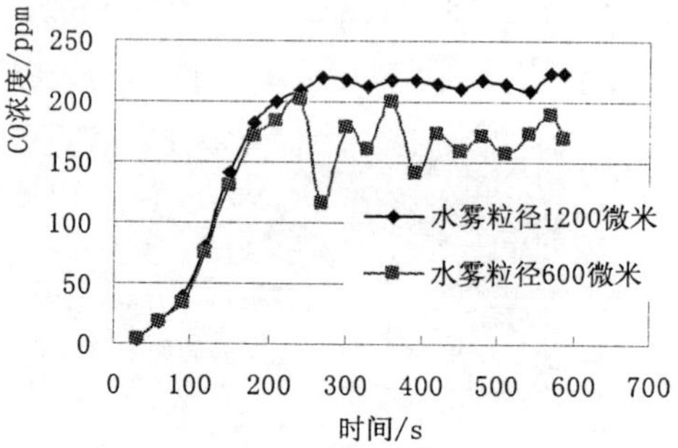

（b）CO 浓度变化曲线

图 7 不同水雾粒径的灭火的温度和 CO 浓度变化

5 结 论

（1）通过对大型跨江海隧道火灾有/无水喷雾系统模拟分析，实施水喷雾系统灭火后，将将降低隧道内火灾危险性，改善隧道内环境，更有利于人员疏散和结构设备的保护。

（2）在喷头压力和流量一定的情况下，水雾喷头的雾化角较小，喷射强度较大，有效射程相对越远；在保证喷头的喷射强度情况下，水雾粒径越小，水雾灭-控火的效果越好。

（3）大型跨江海隧道水喷雾灭火系统的设计，应综合考虑保护对象的范围，喷头的高度和角度，水雾喷头的压力、流量，以及水雾雾化特征等因素影响。

参考文献（References）：

[1] 苏宗贤. 超大断面水下盾构隧道原型结构试验及结构分析模型研究[D]. 西南交通大学，2008.

[2] JAE S R, HONG S R, DONG H K，critical velocity and burning rate in pool fire during longitudinal ventilation[J]. Tunnelling and Underground Space Technology, 2007(22): 262-271.

[3] 吴德兴，李伟平，郑国平. 苍岭隧道火灾条件下的通风排烟设计[J]. 公路，2008(5): 200-205.

[4] 黄盾. 南京长江隧道给排水、消防系统设计及若干问题讨论. 资源环境与工程, 2007, 21(5):579-581.

[5] 中华人民共和国公安部. GB50219—95 水喷雾灭火系统设计规范[S]. 北京：中国计划出版社，2007.

作者简介（Bio-data）：

张玉春，1980.2，男，硕士，讲师，2005 年毕业于中国矿业大学安全工程与技术专业，同年进入西南交通大学消防工程系工作，2007 年 3 月在职起攻读西南交通大学桥梁与隧道工程专业博士学位，主要从事地下及隧道工程防灾技术方面的研究、教学工作。

Yuchun ZHANG (1980.2—), male, lecturer, master, graduated from the major of safety engineering and technology in China University of Mining and Technology in 2005, later worked in fire engineering department of Southwest Jiaotong University. he began to pursue Ph.D degree of bridge and tunnel engineering of SWJTU in 2007; Main interests are covered in disaster prevention technology of underground and tunnel engineering.

越江盾构隧道纵向排烟的数值模拟研究

曾艳华 方伟 何川

西南交通大学 地下工程系，四川 成都 610031

【摘 要】 本文根据南京长江盾构隧道横断面及纵断面设计情况，采用火灾数值分析软件 FDS，对盾构隧道纵向排烟情况下不同位置处发生火灾进行了数值模拟，比较了火灾情况下不通风和控制不同风速下火灾烟流随时间的扩散场分布情况。模拟结果表明，在不通风情况下，火灾后烟流向上坡方向的蔓延速度远大于下坡方向，下坡隧道中控制烟流流动的速度应大于上坡隧道中控制烟流流动的速度。对于南京长江隧道，下坡段的临界风速为 3.5 m/s，上坡段的临界风速为 3.0 m/s，该风速与两种临界风速理论计算值均有差异。从工程应用的角度出发，火灾后下坡段控制风速可取为 2.5～3.0 m/s，而上坡段控制风速可取为 2.5～3.0 m/s，火灾通风设计可以该风速作为参考。

【关键词】 盾构隧道；纵向排烟；控制风速

中图分类号：U459.2 文献标识码：A

THE RESEARCH OF NUMERICAL SIMULATION FOR LONGITUDINAL SMOKE EXTRACTION IN RIVER-CROSSING SHIELD TUNNEL

Yanhua ZENG, Wei FANG, Chuan HE

Department of Underground Engineering, Southwest Jiaotong University, Chengdu 610031, Sichuan, China

Abstract: Based on the design of both cross-section and longitudinal section of Nanjing Yangtze River Tunnel, fire numerical simulation at different points in shield tunnel with longitudinal ventilation is carried out by use of the fire numerical analysis software (Fire Dynamic Simulator). The distribution of smoke diffusion field depending on the time without ventilation and with the controlled different velocity ventilation is compared. The result of numerical simulation indicates that, without ventilation, the fire smoke spread velocity along upgrade is faster than that along downgrade. The velocity of controlling smoke flow in downgrade tunnel should be greater than that in upgrade tunnel. About the Nanjing Yangtze River Tunnel, the critical wind velocity in downgrade section is 3.5m/s and in upgrade section is 3.0m/s. Both of the two wind velocities are different from the two theory calculating critical wind velocities. Starting from the point of engineering applications, controlled wind velocity in downgrade section may choose from 2.5m/s to 3.0m/s and in upgrade section may choose from 2.5m/s to 3.0m/s.The control wind velocity above can be a reference in fire ventilation design.

Keywords: shield tunnel; longitudinal smoke extraction; control wind velocity

南京长江隧道位于南京市区，长约 3 430 m，属特长市政工程隧道。隧道单向行车，两隧道间不设联络通道，隧道横断面分隔为两层（见图 1），上部为行车空间，下部为逃生通道及附属设施空间，隧道上下部空间通过间距为 100 m 的逃生口相连。隧道运营采用盾构竖井单吸分段纵向式通风，火灾时，将该井作为排烟井，隧道采用纵向排烟。

在单向行车的纵向通风隧道中，为保证人员及车辆的安全撤离，需要对隧道进行强制通风。如果

基金项目：863 计划（2006AA11Z116）

风量充足，则将使所有的火灾烟流向火灾下游。如果风量不足，火灾烟流将发生回流，危及上游的人员和车辆。因此，纵向排烟的公路隧道中，流向火源点风流速度的控制是火灾通风设计需要解决的关键问题。受地形限制，南京长江隧道采用“V”型坡，(见图 2)，其坡型复杂，受火灾在上坡位置和下坡位置的效应不同，各位置处控制火灾烟流流动的速度也将不同。本文将对不同坡率处发生火灾进行模拟，比较不同风速情况下火灾烟流的扩散情况，提出控制隧道内烟流流动的风速。模拟计算中火源功率取 30 MW。

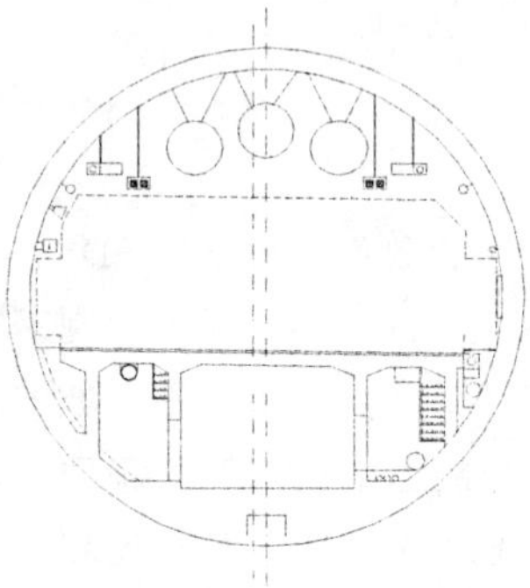

图 1　隧道横断面布置图

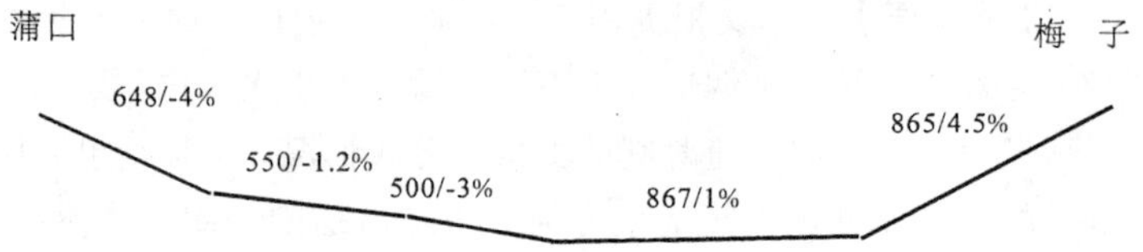

图 2　隧道纵断面坡型图

1　火灾临界风速的理论计算

火灾后不使火灾烟流发生回流的风速即称为临界风速，临界风速的大小受诸多因素的影响，包括火灾热释放率、隧道的坡率、几何形状等。

Heselden 和 Danziger、Kennedy 提出,临界风速可以根据以下方程组计算得出：

$$v_c = K_g K \left[\frac{gHQ}{\rho_0 c_p A T_p} \right]^{\frac{1}{3}} \tag{1}$$

$$T_p = T_0 + \frac{Q}{\rho_0 c_p A v_c} \tag{2}$$

其中，K_g 坡度修正系数,当火灾发生在隧道平坡或上坡段时，$K_g=1.0$；当火灾发生在隧道下坡段时，$K_g=1+0.0374(\tan\theta)^{0.8}$。

Oka 和 Atkinson 采用 1：10 缩尺的模型,研究水平隧道里的烟气运动状况，提出了用隧道水力直径作为特征长度，计算临界风速的新公式：

$$Q'' = \frac{Q}{\rho_0 c_p T_0 \sqrt{gD^5}} \tag{3}$$

$$v'' = \frac{v_{cr}}{\sqrt{gD}} \tag{4}$$

当 $Q''<0.20$ 时，$v''_{cr}=0.40*(0.2)^{-1/3}(Q'')^{1/3}$，当 $Q''\geqslant 0.20$ 时当 $v''_{cr}=0.40$。$0°-10°$ 倾角下坡隧道的坡度修正系数按下式计算：

$$v_{cr}(\theta) = v_{cr}(0)\cdot[1+0.014\cdot\theta] \tag{5}$$

根据南京长江隧道的坡率情况，计算了防止烟雾反向扩散的临界风速如表 1。计算结果表明，两种方法计算的临界风速不同，第 1 种方法计算的结果明显小于第 2 种方法的计算结果。

表 1 不同坡段发生火灾的临界风速（m/s）

项目 / 公式	东线下坡 (i = −4%)	东线下坡 (i = −1.2%)	东线下坡 (i = −3%)	上坡隧道
公式（1）、（2）	2.49	2.44	2.47	2.42
方法（3）、（4）	3.32	3.20	3.28	3.15

2 火灾风流控制速度的三维数值模拟

2.1 模型的建立及计算工况

根据图 1 中隧道的纵断面情况，建立了隧道路面以上全长三维计算模型（见图 3），对于不同坡度段，采用了不同计算区域叠加的方法来模拟纵向坡度的变化；盾构结构圆形内轮廓线，采用了矩形叠加逼近的方法。计算区域有 96 个。为了提高计算精度，在火源区对网格加密，采用 0.2 m*0.5 m*0.5 m 的网格，网格数共计约 644436 个。

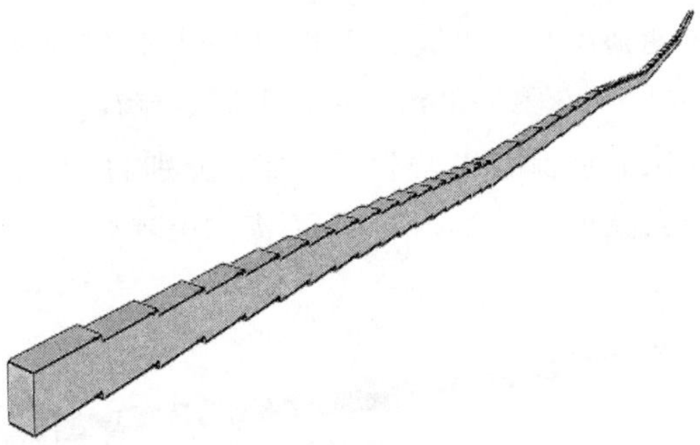

图 3 计算模型图

模拟中在不同坡率处设置火源，进行了 5 种位置的火灾数值模拟。为全面了解越江盾构隧道内火灾烟流的扩散情况，进行了以下的风流速度控制：① 隧道不通风，火源位置分别为下坡、上坡和“V”型坡的底部；② 下坡隧道风流速度分别为 2.5 m/s，3.0 m/s 和 3.5 m/s；③ 上坡隧道风流速度分别为 2.0 m/s，2.5 m/s，3.0 m/s。

2.2 火灾不通风情况模拟结果分析

在距离入口 480 m 下坡处、“V”型坡的底部和距离出口 860 m 处发生火灾，隧道不通风情况下烟流的扩散情况、温度场、速度场的分布分别如图 4 至图 6 所示，其中图 4 为火灾后 504 s 的分布图，图 5 为火灾后 564 s 的分布图，图 6 为火灾后 680 s 分布图。

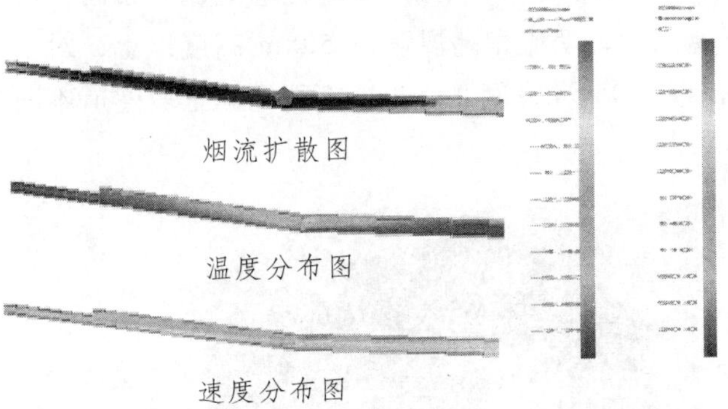

图 4 入口下坡隧道烟流扩散分布图

（不通风情况）

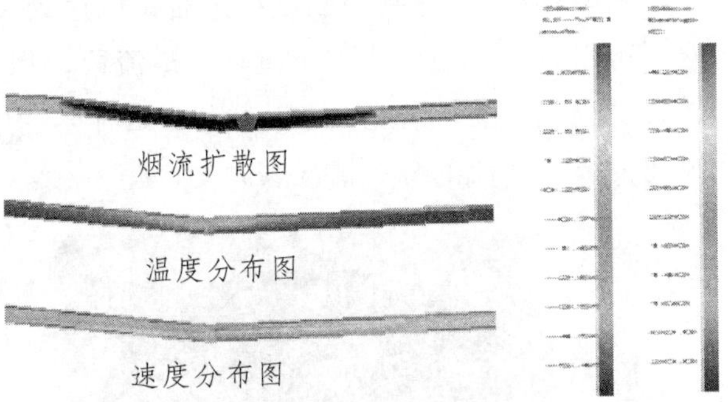

图 5 中部底部“V”隧道烟流扩散分布图

（不通风情况）

从图中可以看出，在不通风情况下，火灾后烟流向上坡方向扩散的速度远大于向下坡方向，由于火灾效应的作用，在一定时间后，隧道内将产生流动风速。当火灾发生在隧道入口 480 m 下坡处时，火灾后 504 s 火灾烟流已经向上坡方向扩散到隧道入口，而下坡方向扩散的距离为 252 m。当火灾发生“V”

型坡的底部时，火灾后 564 s 时，烟流向入口上坡方向扩散的距离为 540 m（坡率 3%），向出口上坡方向的扩散的距离为 470 m（坡率 3%），说明上坡坡率越大，同样的时间内烟流扩散的距离越大。当火灾发生在隧道距离出口上坡方向 860 m 时，火灾后 680 s 烟流到达出口，而向下坡方向的蔓延约为 220 m。

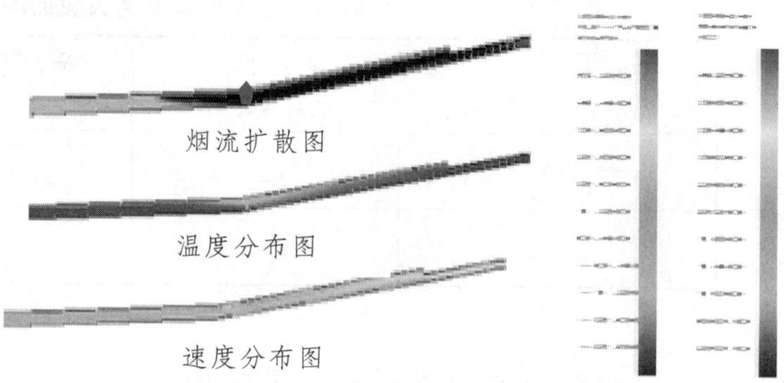

图 6 出口上坡隧道烟流扩散分布图（不通风情况）

2.3 下坡隧道不同风速模拟结果分析

当火灾发生在进口 4% 下坡位置时，不同风速情况下，火灾后 300 s 和燃烧稳定后烟流的扩散分别如图 7、图 8 所示。图中可以看出，当火灾风速为 2.5 m/s 和 3.0 m/s 时，火灾烟流存在逆流现象。当火灾后 300 s，逆流长度分别为 40 m，15 m，燃烧稳定后逆流长度略为有增加，分别为 75 m、35 m。当风流速度达到 3.5 m/s 后，基本不存在逆流情况，说明当隧道下坡率为 4%，火灾的临界风速应大于 3.5 m/s。

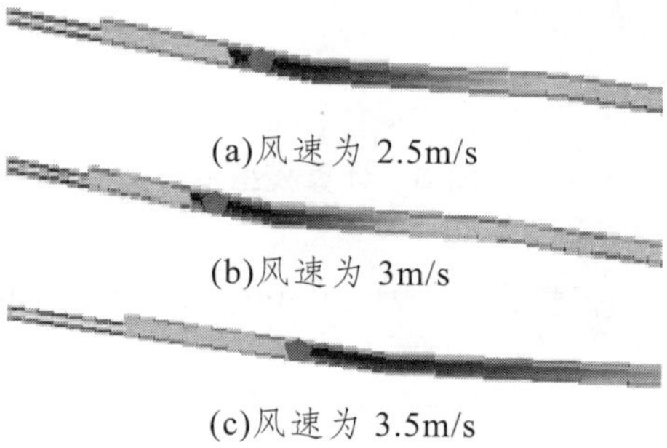

图 7 坡度为 4%，300 s 时烟流扩散图

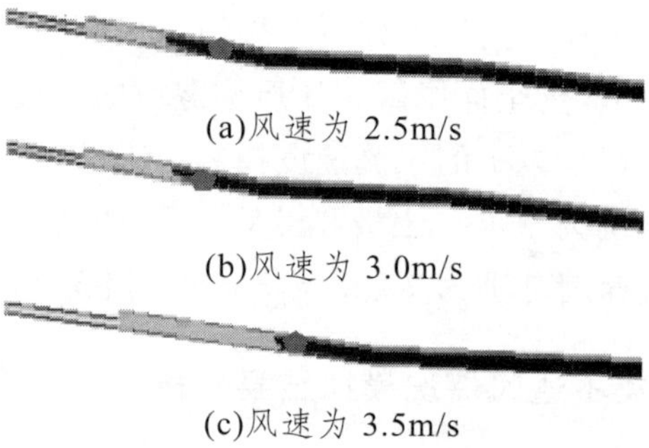

图 8 坡度为 4%，稳定后时烟流扩散图

图 9 和图 10 分别为燃烧稳定后，风速为 2.5 m/s 和 3.0 m/s 时处火灾上游 10 m 处的烟流分布图，从两图可以看出，虽然火灾上游存在逆流段，但在一定距离以后，烟流和高温仅在 5.0 m 高度以上，对上游人员构成威胁。因此，控制火灾的烟流速度可取 2.5 m/s～3.0 m/s 之间。表 2 是不同坡率上坡隧道不同风速情况下烟流的分布情况表。

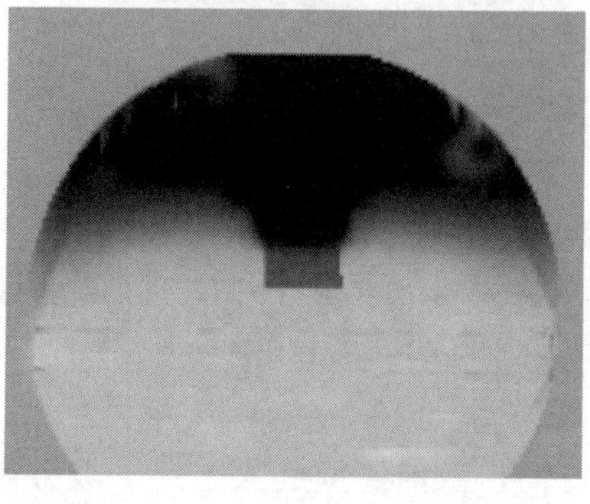

图 9 火源上游 10m 处烟流分布（风速 2.5m/s）

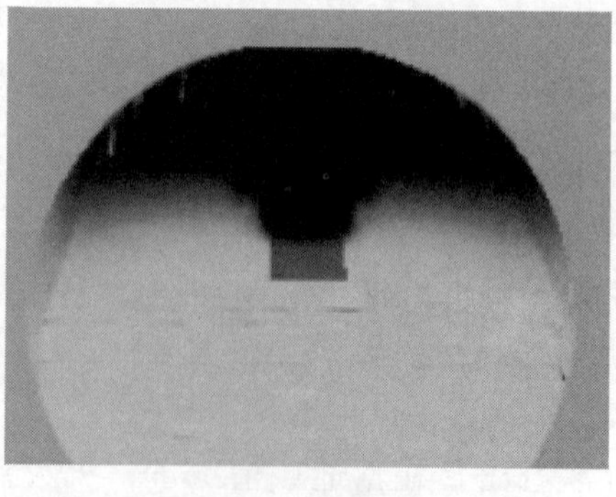

图 10 火源上游 10m 处烟流分布（风速 3.0m/s）

表 2　1.2% 和 3.0% 下坡不同风速情况烟流流动分布表

坡度	风速（m/s）	时间（s）	回流层长度（m）	下游蔓延距离（m）
－1.20%	2.5	300	26	450
		1 800	42	至隧道出口
	3	300	3	462
		1 800	7	至隧道出口
	3.5	300	0	496
		1 800	1	至隧道出口
－3.00%	2.5	300	32	472
		1 800	63	至隧道出口
	3	300	11	483
		1 800	23	至隧道出口
	3.5	300	0	506
		1 800	2	至隧道出口

2.4　上坡隧道不同风速模拟结果分析

当火灾发生在进口 1% 上坡位置时，不同风速情况下，火灾后 300 s 和燃烧稳定后烟流的扩散分别如图 10 和图 11 所示。

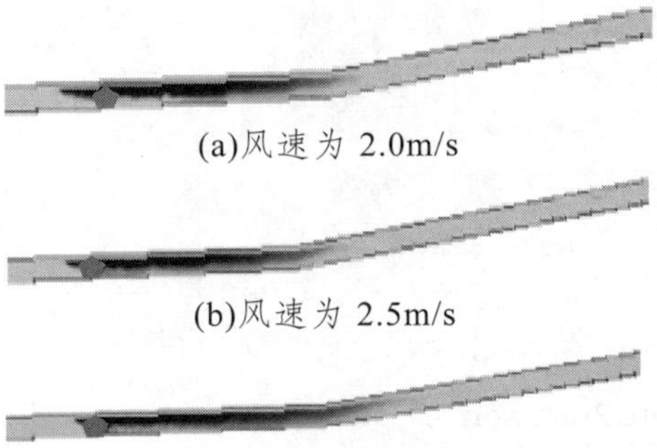

(a)风速为 2.0m/s

(b)风速为 2.5m/s

(c)风速为 3.0m/s

图 10　坡度为 1.0%，300 s 时烟流扩散图

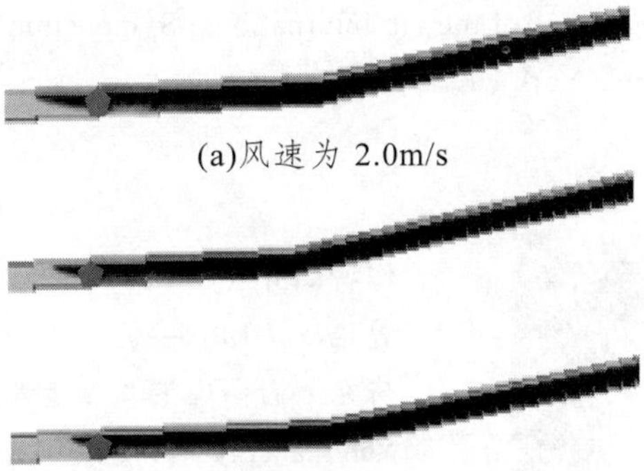

(a)风速为 2.0m/s

(c)风速为 3.0m/s

图 11　坡度为 1%，稳定后烟流扩散图

图中可以看出，当火灾风速为 2.0 m/s 和 2.5 m/s 时，火灾烟流存在逆流现象。当火灾后 300 s，逆流长度分别为 54 m，22 m，燃烧稳定后逆流长度略为有增加，分别为 81 m，43 m。当风流速度达到 3.0 m/s 后，基本不存在逆流情况，说明当隧道上坡坡率为 1%，火灾的临界风速应大于 3.0 m/s。燃烧稳定以后，风速为 2.0 m/s 和 2.5 m/s 时，火灾上游 60 m 和 30 m 的烟流分布情况与图 9、图 10 类似。

表 3　4.50% 上坡不同风速情况烟流流动分布表

坡度	风速（m/s）	时间（s）	回流层长度（m）	下游蔓延距离（m）
4.50%	2	300	46	522
		1 800	69	至隧道出口
	2.5	300	18	531
		1 800	38	至隧道出口
	3	300	0	542
		1 800	2	至隧道出口

3 结 论

通过南京长江盾构隧道火灾临界风速的理论计算和不同坡道处发生火灾的数值模拟，得到以下结论：

（1）当火灾不通风情况下，受火灾效应的影响，火灾烟流向上坡方向扩散的速度远大于向下坡方向的扩散速度。

（2）模拟结果表明，在下坡隧道和上坡隧道中火灾临界风速分别为 3.5 m/s 和 3 m/s。该值与理论计算值有差异，上、下坡隧道模拟结果值均大于公式（1）、（2）的计算值；与公式（3）、（4）的结果相比，下坡隧道模拟值大于理论计算值，而上坡隧道则小于理论计算值。

（3）由于在上游一定距离内，回流层的烟气分布高度对人员并不构成威胁，工程应用中可适当降低火灾烟流的控制速度，火灾后下坡段控制风速可取为 2.5～3.0 m/s，而上坡段控制风速可取为 2.5～3.0 m/s，火灾通风可以该数据作为参考。

参考文献（References）：

[1] 交通部重庆公路科学研究所. 公路隧道通风照明设计规范（JTJ 026.1-1999）[M]. 北京:人民交通出版社, 2000.

[2] 李元洲，霍然，易亮，等. 隧道火灾烟气发展的模拟计算研究[J]. 中国工程科学, 2004，6(2).

[3] 洪丽娟，刘传聚. 隧道火灾研究现状综述[J]. 地下空间与工程学报，2005，2(2): 149-155.

[4] 王海燕. FDS 数值模拟在隧道火灾中的应用[J]. 消防技术与产品信息，2008, 11: 5-8.

[5] Yasushi Oka,Atkinson GT.Control of smoke flow in tunnel fires[J]. Fire Safety Journal, 1995, 25(4): 305-322.

[6] Danziger N H, Kennedy W D. Longitudinal ventilation analysis for the Glenwood canyon tunnels[C]. In: Proeeedings of the 4th International Symposium Aerodynamics and Ventilation of Vehicle Tunnels.York,UK,1982:169-186.

作者简介（Bio-data）：

曾艳华（1968—），女，副教授，博士

研究方向：地下工程通风与防灾

Yanhua ZENG (1968—), female, Associate Professor，Doctor

Research Direction：Ventilation and Fire Prevention in Underground Engineering

E-mail: zengyhua@163.com

地铁盾构隧道下穿铁路桥结构安全分析

张 增 林 刚 张 庆

中国中铁二院工程集团有限责任公司，四川 成都 610031

【摘 要】 以成都地铁 2 号线西延线工程盾构下穿铁路桥为背景，通过数值计算的方法，研究盾构下穿铁路桥时对既有桥墩的影响以及盾构隧道管片结构的力学特征。通过研究表明，盾构近距离通过既有桥墩时，桥墩附近土体受到扰动，桥墩发生均匀沉降及倾斜，盾构管片内力相比普通地段增幅较大。采用合理的加固措施后，桥墩的沉降量明显减小，管片内力相应降低，从而降低盾构施工的风险。本文的研究对实际工程具有指导意义，并能作为其他工程设计参考。

【关键词】 地铁；盾构；数值模拟；沉降

ANALYSIS ON STRUCTURE SAFTY OF A SHIELD TUNNEL UNDER PASSING RAILWAY BRIDGE IN METRO CONSTRUCTION

Zeng ZHANG，Gang LIN，Qing ZHANG

China Railway Eryuan Engineering Group Co., Ltd. Chengdu 610031, Sichuan, China

Abstract: The paper is based on the shield tunnel construction beneath adjacent existing piers of railway bridge of West Extension project of Chengdu Metro Line #2. the analysis of mechanical behavior of the bridge piers and segment has been carried out by means of FEM. The results show that the surrounding soil has been serious disturbed while the shield under passing the existing piers foundations, at the same time the bridge piers developed an excessive settlement .The internal force of segment is much bigger than that in common earth. So reasonable reinforcement measures have been taken, and recalculation has been carried out. And then the settlement of bridge and internal force of segment have been cut down to an acceptable level, so it reduces the risk of shield construction. The paper is a guide to the exiting engineering and a useful reference to the other similar engineering.

Key words: metro; shield; numerical simulation; settlement

1 引 言

当前城市地铁建设发展呈现欣欣向荣的景象，由于线路需要，地铁修建过程中不可避免要近距离下穿建筑物、公路、铁路、桥梁以及各种通道，对于这些特殊情况的处理往往成为工程的技术难点。近距离下穿问题不仅加大了盾构掘进的风险，对上部建筑物也有较大的影响。目前国内遇到的类似工程较多，展开的研究也颇多。但是关于盾构隧道近距离穿越既有桥墩的理论研究在国内尚不成熟且可比性有限，有资料研究表明当盾构与桥墩的间距小于隧道半径，需要对于桥墩的沉降和倾斜量进行计算，并需加大掘进过程中同步注浆量及二次注浆量，施工的风险和成本都较高，如进行合理的处理措施既安全又经济。

2 工程概况

成都地铁 2 号线二期工程的西延伸线始于三环路北侧的成灌客运站，止于郫县的犀浦站；沿线经过了成都市高新西区、郫县，并在郫县的犀浦与成灌铁路换乘。线路通过路段基本处于城市主干道或既有建筑物下方，因而有多处与既有建（构）筑物发生空间上的交叉关系。

在互助站～信息路站区间 YCK20＋300 附近，盾构隧道下穿西环铁路桥。西环铁路桥上部为两跨简支梁结构，在平面上与盾构隧道斜交，夹角 45°；下部为扩大基础，基底距离隧顶最小约为 6.80 m。区间盾构为双洞双线，内径 5.4 m，外径 6 m，线间距为 13 m，盾构隧道覆土厚度 13.46 m。根据已有初勘资料显示，该区间段内均为第四系（Q_4）地层覆盖。地表多为第四系人工填筑土（Q_4^{ml}）；其下为第四系全新统冲积（Q_4^{al+pl}）粉质黏土，粉土，卵石土，部分地段夹中、细砂透镜体。

盾构隧道与西环铁路关系如图 1 所示。

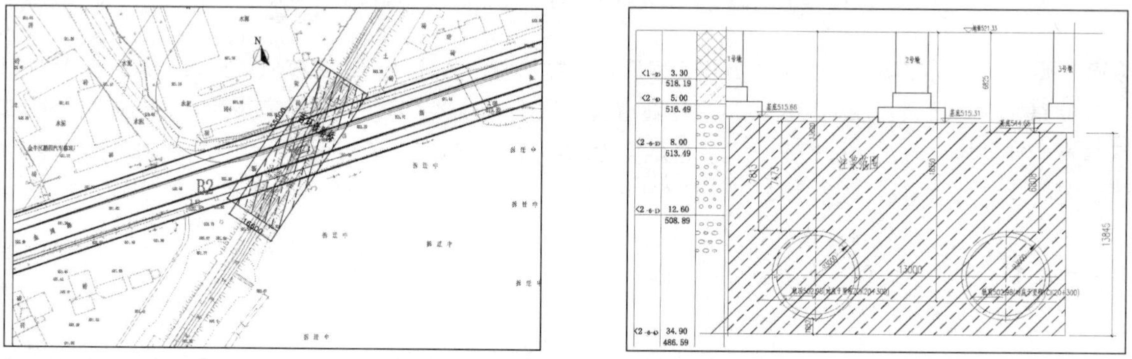

图 1　盾构隧道与西环铁路关系图

3　计算工况及模型

根据盾构隧道与西环铁路的关系，选取控制情况进行二维有限元模型进行计算.其中盾构距 1 桥#墩水平距离最小为 0.5 m，竖向距离 7.8 m，此时盾构掘进对于桥墩的影响大，选此断面作为控制工况一进行计算；2#桥墩位于盾构双线之间，左右洞的掘进对它均会产生显著的影响，因此选取盾构通过 2#桥墩的断面为控制工况二进行计算；3#桥墩基底距盾构隧道顶部垂直距离最小，仅为 6.8 m，左洞掘进过程中对于桥墩影响大，取该工况为控制工况三进行计算。模型中以平面实体单元模拟地层和桥梁基础，以梁单元模拟盾构隧道衬砌。模型的尺寸为水平方向 83 m，竖直方向 40.46 m。地应力场按自重应力场考虑，计算时在桥墩上部施加自重荷载以及列车活荷载。计算边界条件为：左右边界水平约束，下边界垂直方向约束，地表为自由面。

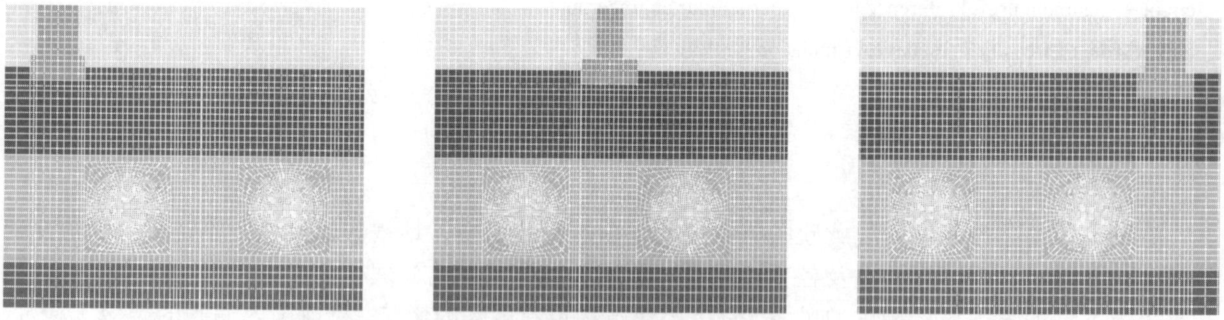

工况一　　工况二　　工况三

图 2　三种工况数值计算模型

4　未加固计算结果分析

4.1　地层位移场及主应力场分析

该工况为左线隧道与桥墩距离较近，左洞开挖对于桥墩的影响最大，左洞开挖产生的扰动效应比右洞明显。同时桥墩荷载作用使左洞洞周位移最大，拱顶最大沉降达到 70 mm，右洞拱顶沉降约为 64 mm，沉降形状为非对称。隧道底部向内鼓，最大值达到 47 mm，双洞之间土体下沉，并延伸到地表，沉降槽宽度约为 3.5D，沉降槽中心地表沉降量达到 36 mm。地层主应力场主要表现为压应力场（忽略应力集中造成的拉应力），最大主应力达到 0.24 MPa，隧道侧壁产生较大的压应力，拱顶处没有产生拉应力。双洞之间土体受压，压应力达到 0.2 MPa，桥墩底部由于开挖产出现受拉区域，表现为应力集中效应。

工况二左右洞位于桥墩两侧，左右洞的开挖对于桥墩都产生较大扰动，从竖向位移场云图上看，双洞贯通后地层位移基本对称，桥墩右侧土体产生的位移稍大，隧道上方土体受扰动效应明显，在位移场云图上桥墩附近的位移仅次于隧道拱顶。拱顶处沉降达到 75.6 mm，而桥墩附近土体达到 67.4 mm，桥墩均匀沉降量约为 42 mm，由此得出 2#墩是盾构下穿该铁路桥的最危险情况，应予提高监测密度和重视程度。双洞贯通后地层主应力最大值为 0.3 MPa，最大值位于围岩底部以及桥墩角部。隧道开挖没有产生应力集中效应，双线中部围岩的主应力为 0.24 MPa，墩台底部由于应力集中现象，部分区域产生拉应力。

工况三中对于桥墩影响最大的施工过称是右洞的开挖，地层位移场特征及主应力场特征与工况一反对称，分析过程类似，故不再详述。

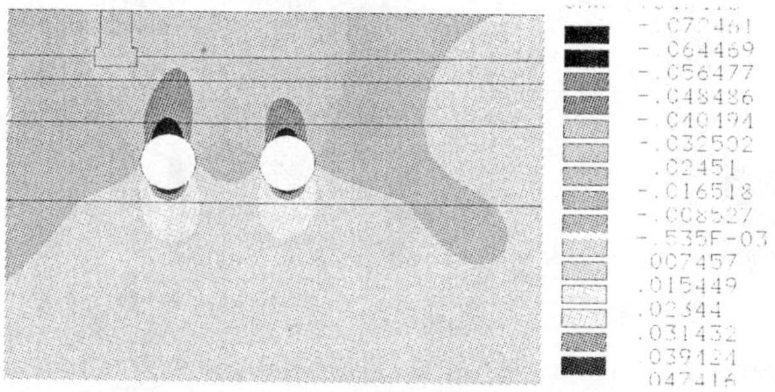

图 3　工况一地层竖向位移云图

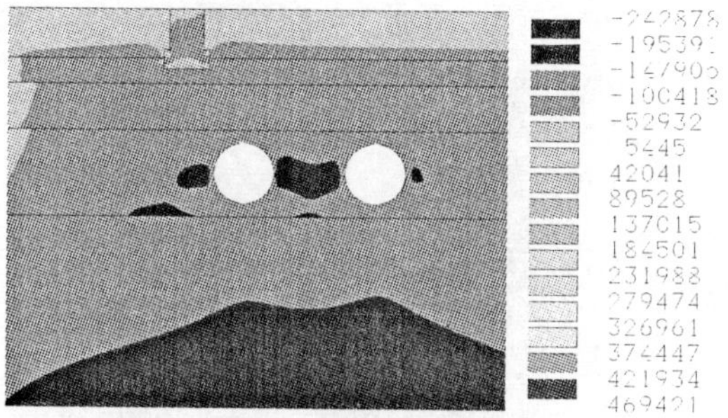

图 4　工况一地层主应力场云图

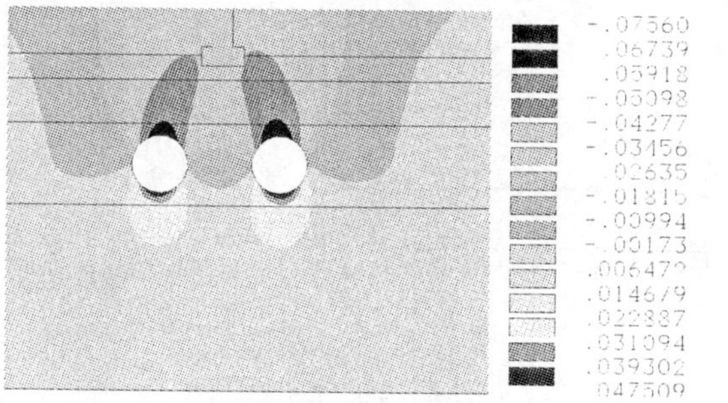

图 5　工况二地层竖向位移云图

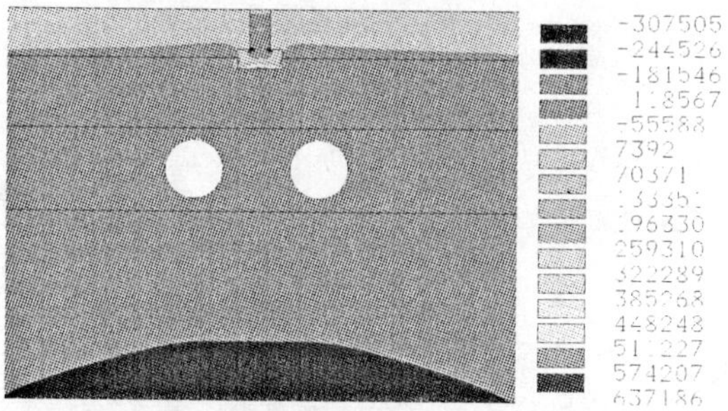

图 6　工况二地层主应力场云图

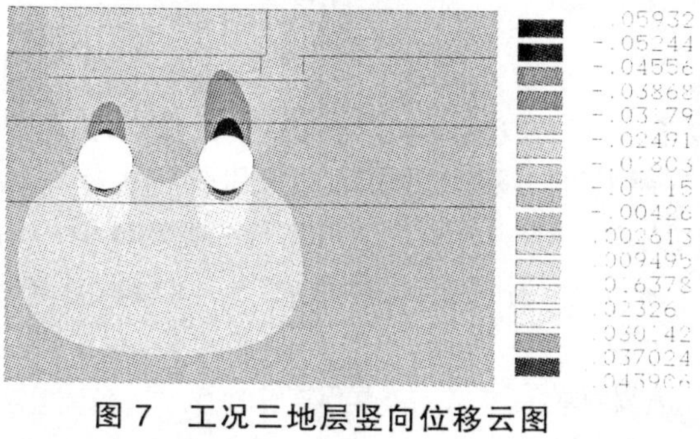

图 7　工况三地层竖向位移云图

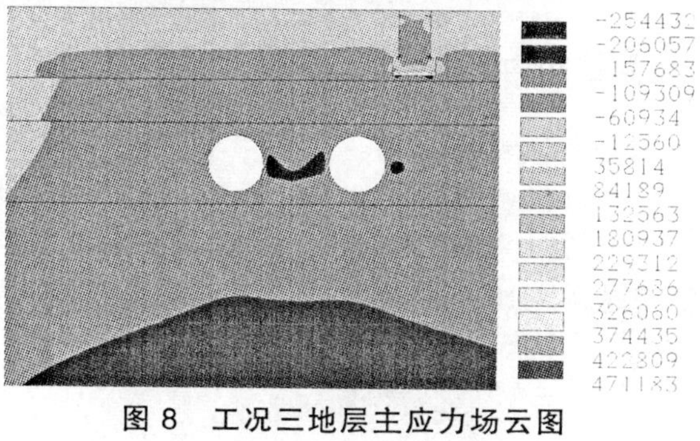

图 8　工况三地层主应力场云图

4.2　桥墩沉降分析

由于隧道与各个墩台之间的位置关系不同，使开挖过程对于墩台的影响不尽相同，结合图 10 可以看：由于 1#墩台位于左洞左侧，对于桥墩影响最大的施工步骤是左洞开挖，左洞开挖及管片拼装完成后，桥墩右侧产生 26.17 mm 的沉降，右洞开挖后，沉降虽在发展，但只增加了约 2.6 mm，最终双洞贯通后墩台左侧沉降 28.72 mm，右侧沉降约 18.12 mm，桥墩倾斜量为 10.6 mm。由于 2#墩台位于隧道两中间，左右动掘进对它都产生较为明显的影响。左洞施工完成后墩台左侧沉降量约为 24 mm，右侧约为 17 mm，墩台左右侧沉降差约为 7 mm，右洞开挖后桥墩沉降明显，且墩台左右侧的沉降差缩小，双洞贯通后，2#墩左侧沉降 42.29 mm，右侧 42.54 mm，几乎为均匀沉降。3#墩的沉降与 1#墩台反对称，由于左洞距离 3#墩台较远开挖对墩台产生的影响非常小，墩台沉降不足 2 mm，右洞开挖后墩台沉降明显约为 22 mm，墩台两侧不均匀沉降为 7 mm。

盾构通过时，2#墩台均匀沉降量最大，为 42.54 mm。1#墩台右侧与 2#墩台左侧的沉降差约为 13.58 mm，1#墩台均匀沉降与 2#墩台均匀沉降差约为 18.86 mm。3#墩台左侧与 2#墩台右侧的沉降差约为 20.64 mm，3#墩台与 2#墩台均匀沉降差约为 24.57 mm。根据《铁路桥涵地基和基础设计规范》（TB 1002.5—2005）中关于明桥面桥梁墩台的均匀沉降量不超过 40 mm，相邻墩台均匀沉降量之差不超过 20 mm 的规定，盾构通过时桥墩的沉降不能满足要求，须对桥墩周围土体进行加固。

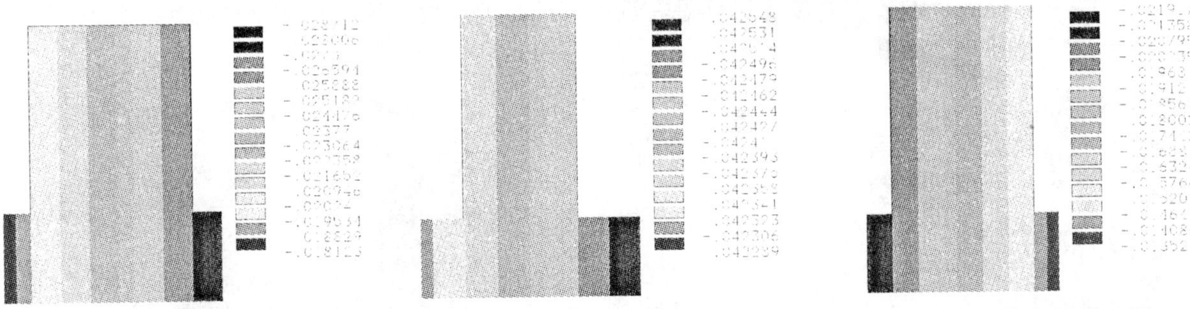

1#墩台沉降云图　　2#墩台沉降云图　　3#墩台沉降云图

图 9 各墩台沉降云图

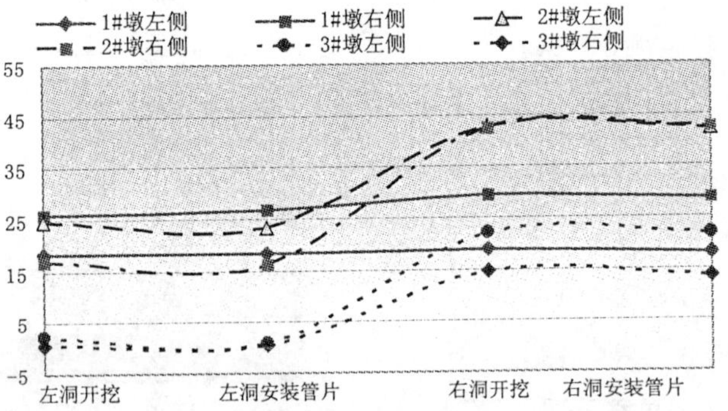

图 10 盾构隧道各施工过程墩台沉降量

4.3 管片结构内力分析

由于该桥跨度为 20 m，桥墩底部荷载较大，使得地层初始应力较相同埋深普通地层的围岩大。盾构开挖后围岩受到扰动释放部分荷载，剩余未释放部分作用在管片上。双洞贯通后，管片正弯矩最大值达到 151 kN · m，管片负弯矩最值达 145.9 kN · m，管片平均轴力 700 kN，与成都地铁 2 号线普通段管片相比管片配筋需提高约 10%，从经济及可行性出发需要加固地层，提高隧道围岩自身承载能力，可降低管片内力。

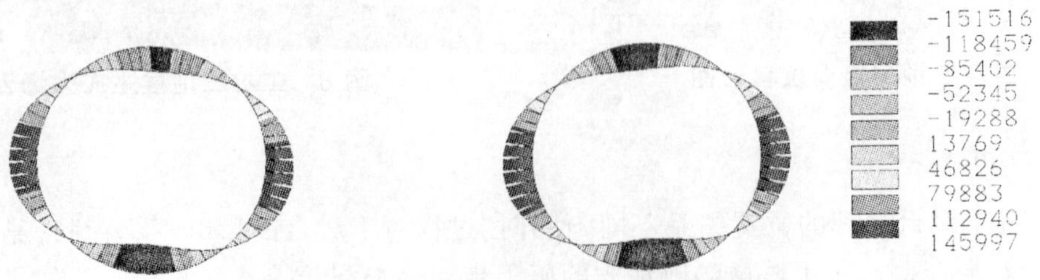

图 11 盾构隧道管片衬砌弯矩图（kN · m）

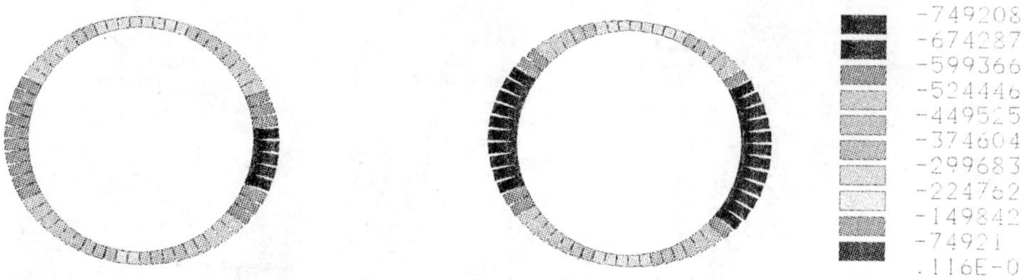

图 12　盾构隧道管片衬砌轴力图（kN）

5　加固后的数值分析结果

根据类似盾构隧道穿桥墩的施工经验，对于盾构隧道主要的影响区域进行地层加固。加固范围：竖直方向自墩台底部至隧道中心下 4.3 m，水平方向为左右线中心两侧各 6.5 m，加固后的地层参数相应提高，对加固后的模型进行计算。以下是工况一加固后的有限元模型图，其他工况加固范围基本相同。

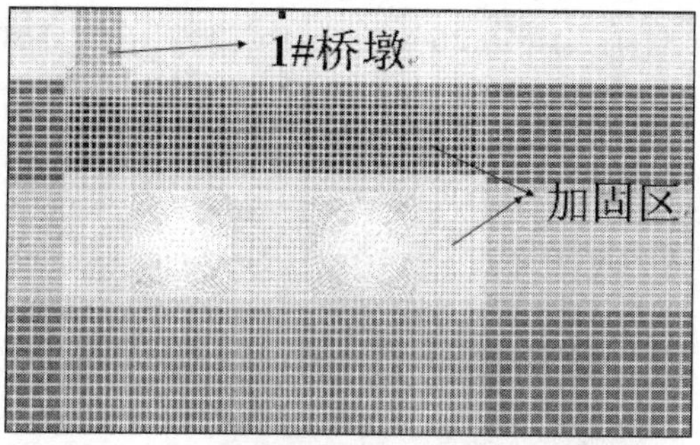

图 13 （1#桥墩）加固后有限元模型

5.1　地层位移场及主应力场

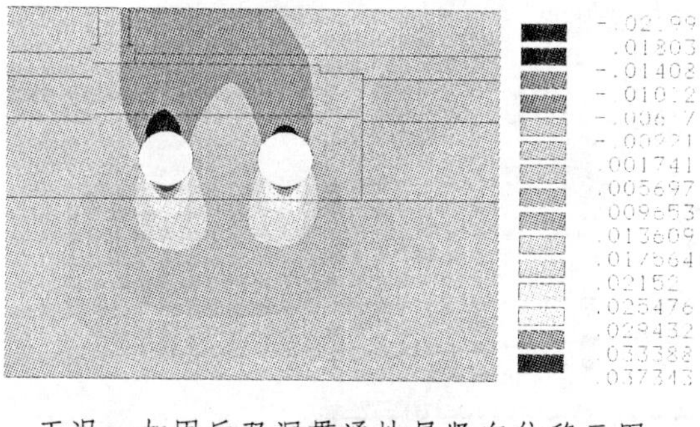

工况一加固后双洞贯通地层竖向位移云图

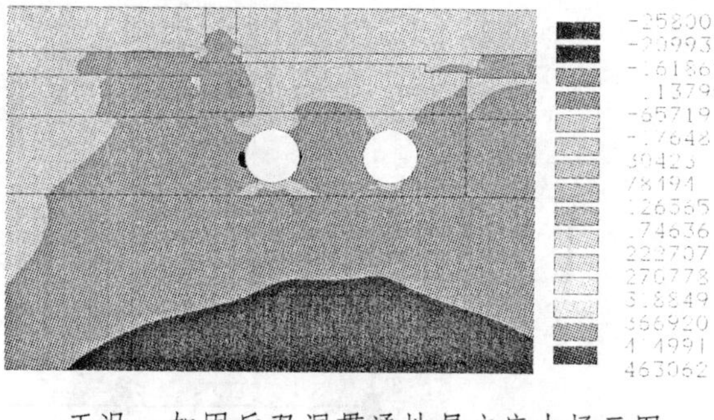

工况一加固后双洞贯通地层主应力场云图

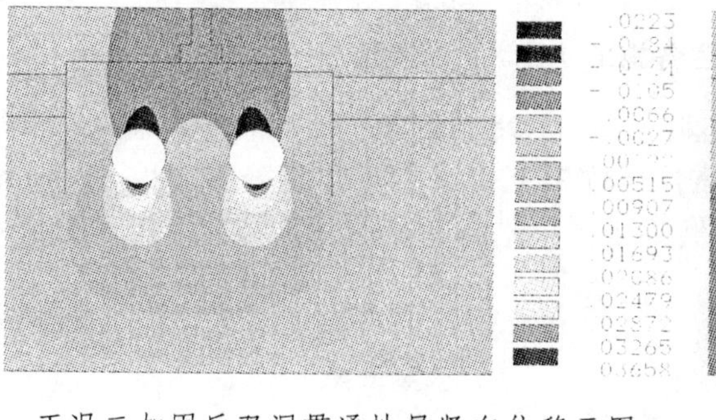

工况二加固后双洞贯通地层竖向位移云图

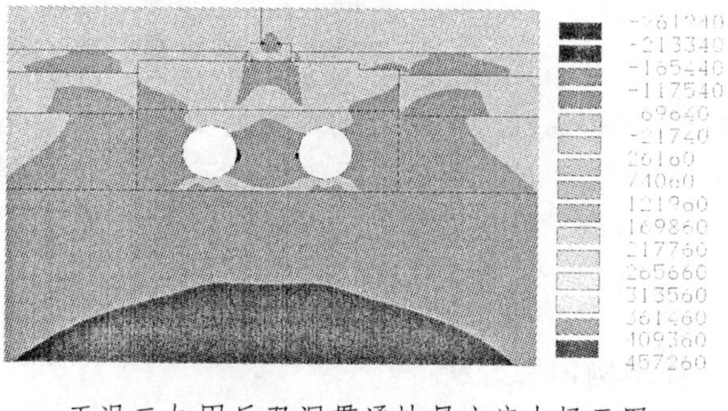

工况二加固后双洞贯通地层主应力场云图

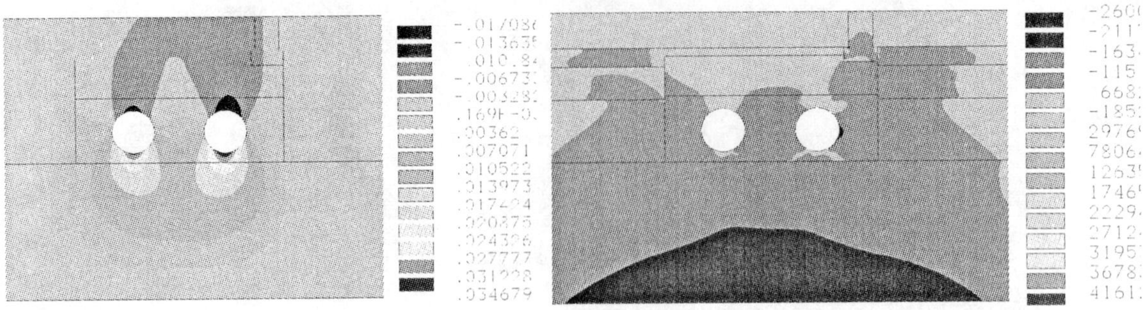

工况三加固后双洞贯通地层竖向位移云图　　工况三加固后双洞贯通地层主应力场云图

图 14　加固后地层位移场及主应力场云图

对于以上三种工况概括分析：由于采用了加固措施，有效地改善了围岩的应力状态，围岩承载能力有了一定提高，减小了隧道开挖对于桥墩附近的土体的扰动。从位移矢量云图上看，隧道贯通后沉降区域较为紧凑，开挖范围内扰动土体扩散效应较小，围岩自稳能力及自承能力增强。最大沉降量发生于拱顶部位，约为 22 mm，拱底向内鼓。三种工况中 2#沉降量最大，最大值约为 22 mm，地表沉降槽宽度与未加固前显著缩小，地表沉降量最大值为 15 mm，没有发生隆起，满足盾构开挖地表沉降要求。地层主应力场为压应力，相比未加固前略有减少，最大主应力为 0.26 MPa，比未加固前的 0.30 MPa 较少约 0.04 MPa。

5.2　墩台沉降分析

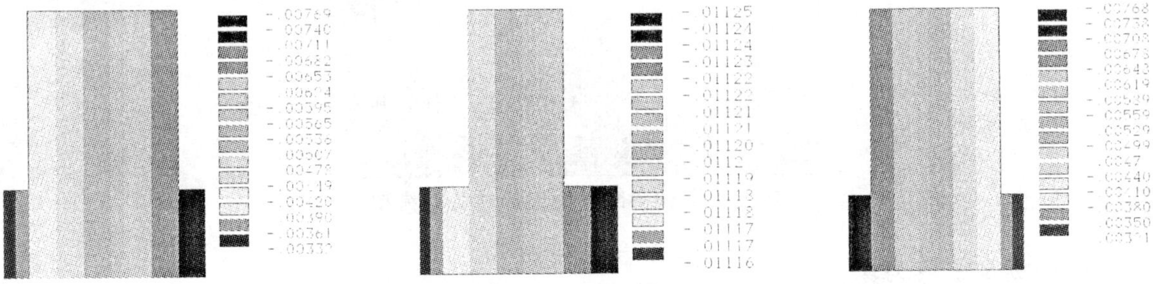

1#墩台沉降云图　　2#墩台沉降云图　　3#墩台沉降云图

图 15　各墩台沉降云图

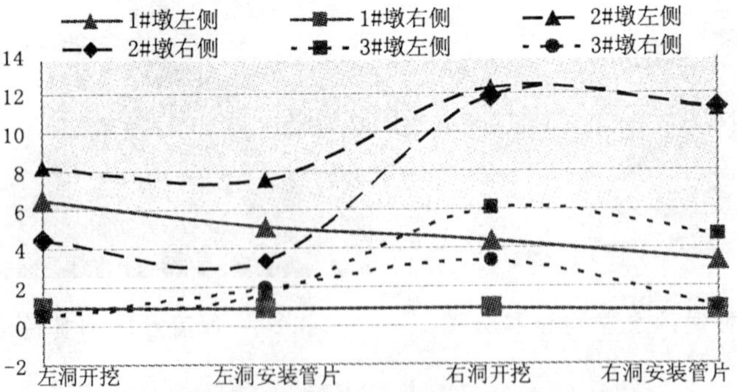

图 16　地层加固后盾构隧道各施工过程墩台沉降量

通过加固后墩台沉降最大的仍然是 2#墩，均匀沉降量为 11.25 mm,各个墩台自身倾斜最大值没有超过 5 mm，1#与 2#相邻墩台之间的均匀沉降约为 6 mm，2#与 3#相邻墩台均匀沉降差约为 5.6 mm。加固后墩台均匀沉降以及相邻墩台均与沉降差均能满足《铁路桥涵地基和基础设计规范》(TB 1002.5—2005)中关于墩台沉降的要求。

5.3　管片结构内力分析

通过加固盾构开挖范围内的围岩，围岩自承载能力得到提高，相应的作用在管片衬砌上的荷载有效地减少，管片内力降低。管片最大正弯矩从未加固前的 151 kN · m 降低到 127 kN · m，轴力变化不大。管片内力与普通段相比仍略显高，建议适当增加配筋量，以提高管片结构安全性。

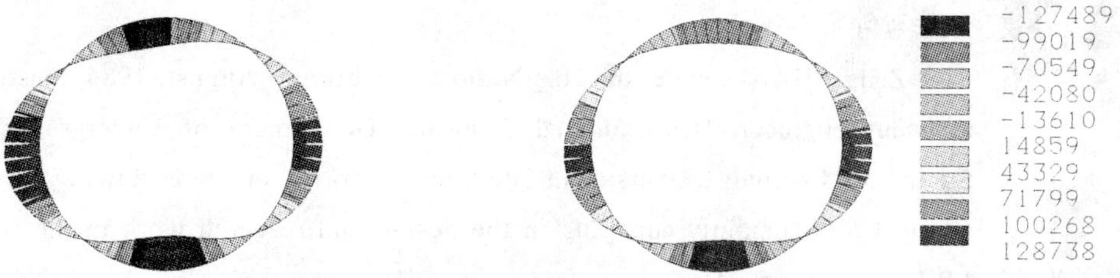

图 17 加固后管片衬砌弯矩图（kN · m）

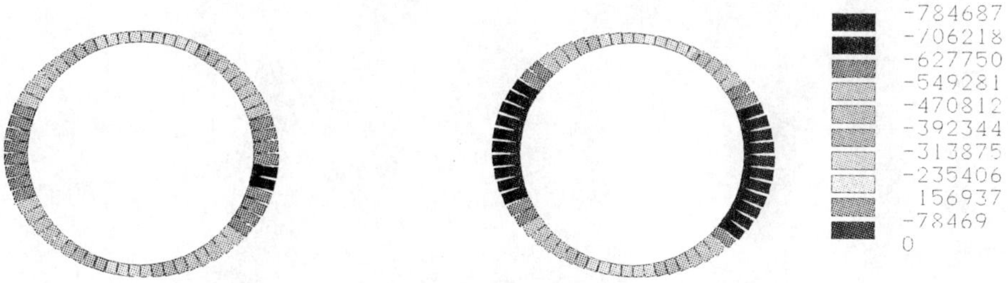

图 18 加固后管片衬砌轴力图（kN）

6 主要认识及结论

盾构下穿铁路桥墩时，施工造成隧道周围土体扰动，隧道上方土体发生沉降。处于双线隧道中间的墩台沉降量最大，墩台之间的不均匀沉降差显著。管片承受较大荷载，需对该段结构进行加强设计，同时对墩台与隧道间土体以及隧道开挖影响的一定范围内土体进行加固。加固后，地层自稳性及自承载能力增强，墩台沉降在可相关规范要求范围内，同时管片内力也有降低。为提高结构安全性，需对穿越桥墩段管片结构配筋率适当提高。

对其他类似工程，盾构下穿铁路桥时，视地层情况及隧道与墩台相互关系采取相应的技术措施。可采用的措施有：

（1）盾构通过时应进行地层加固。加固范围除墩台附近土体外，还需对隧道开挖范围内土体加固，以降低衬砌内力。

（2）增加管片配筋。盾构通过桥墩时，管片结构内力较大，建议提高管片配筋量，以提高管片结构的承载力。

（3）根据地质条件、周边环境调整盾构掘进参数和注浆参数。

（4）及时盾尾注浆、适时进行二次注浆，并适当加大注浆量。

（5）在盾构施工过程中，进行系统、全面的跟踪测量，实行信息化施工，必要时采取应急措施。

参考文献（References）：

[1] 张志强，何 川．地铁盾构隧道近接桩基的施工力学行为研究[J]．铁道学报，2003.2，25(1)：92-95.

[2] 张志强，何 川．南京地铁区间盾构隧道下穿玄武湖公路隧道施工的关键技术研究[J]．岩土力学，2005.11，26（11）：79-82.

[3] 贺美德,刘军,乐贵平，萧岩.地铁区间隧道下穿某桥数值模拟分析[A]．第二届全国岩土与工程学术大会，2006.

[4] 中铁二院工程集团有限责任公司、西南交通大学建筑勘察设计研究院，成都地铁 2 号线一期工程初步设计[R].

[5] 中铁二院工程集团有限责任公司，成都地铁 2 号线二期工程（西延伸线）初步设计[R].

作者简介（Bio-data）：

张增，男，汉族，1984 年 8 月生，工学硕士，助理工程师，2009 年毕业于西南交通大学地下工程系，现任职于中铁二院工程集团有限责任公司，主要从事地铁与轻轨的设计及研究工作。

Zeng ZHANG, male, the Han Nationality, born in August, 1984, master of engineering, assistant engineer. He graduated from the Department of Underground Engineering of Southwest Jiaotong University in 2009, now working in China Railway Eryuan Engineering Group Co.Ltd, mainly engaging in the design and research work in the field of Metro and LRT engineering.

E-mail: kingderzz@163.com

盾构超浅覆土近距离上穿运营地铁施工风险与对策

李 金[1] 廖少明[1, 2] 梁艳文[1]
[1]同济大学 地下建筑与工程系，上海 200092
[2]同济大学 岩土及地下工程教育部重点实验室，上海 200092

【摘 要】 本文结合上海轨道交通 9 号线某标段区间隧道超浅覆土近距离上穿越运营地铁的成功施工案例，对穿越中存在的超浅覆土及近距离上穿的叠加风险进行了分析，并提出了施工控制、压重、隧道加固和实时监测四个方面的技术对策，以保证地铁变形和地表沉降都控制在安全范围内。通过荷载计算，各种技术措施的弥补卸载量约占隧道开挖卸载量的 41%，可在一定程度上抑制地铁回弹变形。基于现场实测数据，对施工引起的运营地铁变形及地表沉降规律进行了分析，表明技术对策是有效的，可供类似工程借鉴。
【关键词】 盾构隧道；超浅覆土；上穿越；压重；卸载

CONSTRUCTION RISK AND COUTERMEASURES OF SHIELD TUNNELING CROSSING ABOVE RUNNING TUNNEL AT SHALLOW DEPTH

Jin LI[1], Shaoming LIAO[1, 2], Yanwen LIANG[1]
[1]Department of Geological Engineering, Tongji University, Shanghai 200092, China;
[2]Key Laboratory of Geotechnical and Underground Engineering of Ministry of Education, Tongji University, Shanghai 200092, China

Abstract: With regard to shield tunneling crossing above tunnel at shallow depth, the risk was analyzed, and corresponding technical countermeasures were put forward, including shield driving control, ballast weight, reinforcement of tunnel and real-time monitoring. These countermeasures were conducted to control the deformation and the settlement within the safety margin. Load calculation indicates that the ballast load of those countermeasures accounted for about 41% of total unloading, which can restrain the tunnel's heave to some extent. Based on the monitoring data, law of running tunnel deformation and ground settlement were also studied, which proves that the countermeasures are effective and can be used for reference in similar projects.
Key words: shield tunnel; shallow depth; crossing; ballast weight; unloading

1 引 言

随着上海城市轨道交通网络化建设的发展，新建盾构隧道穿越已运营地铁的情况日益频繁，同时一些特殊复杂的穿越情况也给施工带来了挑战，威胁到运营地铁的安全。多年来，很多学者对这类技术问题进行了相关研究。2000 年白延辉等人即初步总结和探讨了上海地铁 2 号线近距离穿越 1 号线的施工保护技术[1]。2004 年廖少明等人采用边界元法对盾构近距离穿越相邻隧道施工进行了数值分析，并提出盾构壳体也是影响周围地层变形的主要因素[2]。2005 年廖少明等人基于隧道受荷机理和弹性力学理论，对盾构近距离穿越施工时的土压力进行了理论研究，推导了理论公式，提出了土仓压力分步台阶控制方法[3]。邵华、陈亮等人则基于实测数据分别对盾构近距离下穿越和上穿越已运营地铁的沉降影响进行了定量的分析[4][5]。

以上研究多为中深埋盾构隧道上穿下穿的情形，而对于既为超浅覆土，又为近距离上穿越运营地铁的情形缺少研究。

2 工程背景

本区间隧道外径 6.2 m，内径 5.5 m，采用直径 6.34 m，长度 8.5 m 的土压平衡盾构机推进施工。盾构隧道上下行线均需上穿越运营地铁 1 号线，隧道穿越段剖面图如图 1(a)所示。两次穿越点相距约 90 m，相互影响可忽略不计。两隧道平面呈“井”字形交叉，交叉角为 46～49°，如图 1（b）所示。

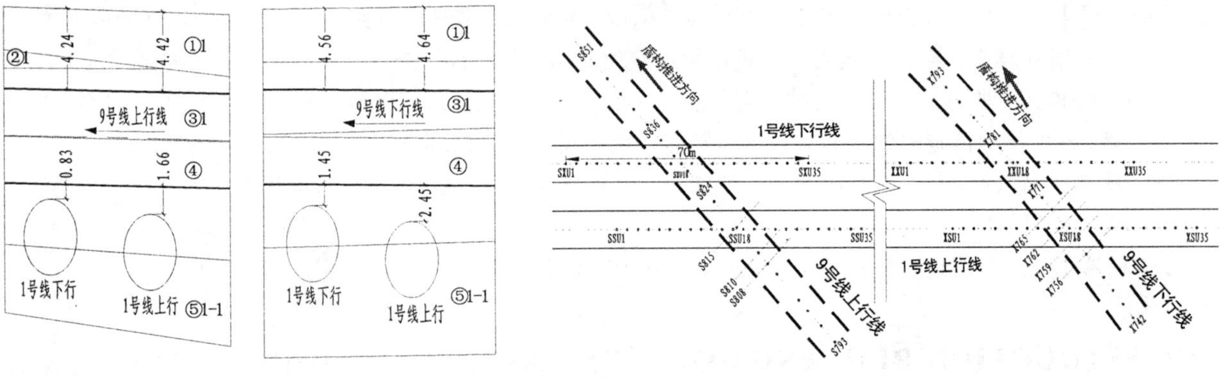

（a）剖面图　　　　（b）平面图

图 1　盾构与运营地铁相对位置关系图（单位：m）

盾构穿越地层为③$_1$灰色淤泥质粉质黏土层和④灰色淤泥质黏土层，由表 1 可知其含水量较高，孔隙比大，压缩模量小，土的强度指标低。盾构在此地层中穿越，周围土体结构容易破坏和变形，从而引起下方运营地铁和上方地表较大的沉降，穿越施工具有较高风险。

表 1　穿越地层物理力学指标

土层	含水量 W（%）	孔隙比 e	压缩模量 $Es_{0.1\text{-}0.2}$（MPa）	内聚力 C（kPa）	内摩擦角 ϕ（°）
③$_1$灰色淤泥质粉质黏土层	42.9	1.20	3.31	10	17.0
④灰色淤泥质黏土层	49.3	1.39	2.23	11	12.0

3 超浅覆土近距离穿越的风险与对策

3.1 超浅覆土近距离穿越的风险

盾构穿越运营地铁的工程经验已比较丰富，但超浅覆土近距离穿越运营地铁实属国内罕见，与以往穿越工程存在一定的差别。施工时，不仅需清楚超浅覆土穿越和近距离上穿越分别引起的风险，还应对两种高风险情况的叠加效应作深入分析。

3.1.1 超浅覆土穿越的风险

隧道在穿越段覆土为仅为 0.7 倍左右盾构直径，计算可知盾构推进所需土压力较小，仅约为 0.08～

0.1 MPa。因此，在此超浅覆土中推进，正面土压力难以维持稳定，且正面土舱压力和盾构姿态的变化对土体扰动更加敏感，容易引起路面较大沉降或隆起。而注浆压力和注浆量过大亦容易破坏土体结构，击穿上覆土层，导致浆液流失，地面冒浆，过小则注浆效果又不明显。总的来说，盾构超浅覆土穿越时，上方地表环境受盾构施工参数变化的影响具有较高的敏感性，施工风险较大。

3.1.2 近距离上穿越的风险

1 号线隧道覆土 13 m 左右，盾构隧道开挖后，两隧道交叠处的土体卸载量较大，土体应力释放大，隧道下方土体易产生较大的弹性和弹塑性隆起变形，从而引起下方运营地铁隧道上抬，威胁运营安全。此外，9 号线下行线距离 1 号线上行线最小净距仅 0.83 m，是目前为止穿越地铁工程中的最小间距。因此，盾构近距离上穿越时，下方运营地铁受上方土体卸载及盾构推进的影响很敏感，施工风险较大。

3.1.3 超浅覆土近距离上穿越的叠加风险

盾构超浅覆土近距离上穿越地铁时，一方面要保证上方地表建（构）筑物的安全，另一方面要保证下方运营地铁的安全。如图 2 所示，在浅覆土中推进，为防止地面开裂冒浆，盾构采用偏小的正面压力或注浆量，则下方运营地铁的隆起将较大，对抑制地铁回弹变形是不利的。而反过来，为抑制地铁回弹变形采取较高的正面压力或注浆量较大时，则易引起地表较大的隆起变形，甚至导致地面开裂或冒浆。因此，选择合理的施工参数以减少施工扰动，采取有效措施来抑制施工扰动的影响是降低穿越风险的两个重要出发点。

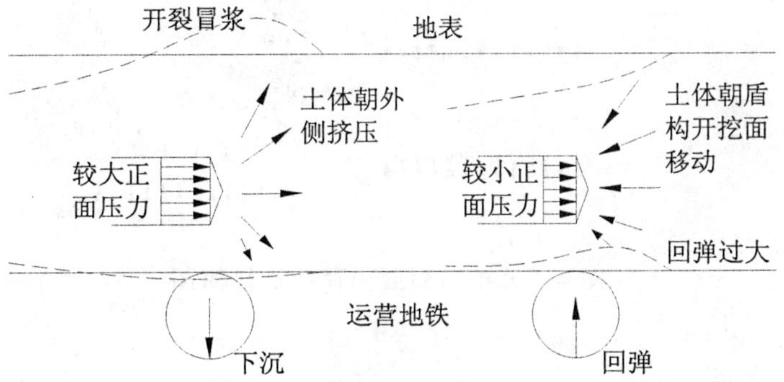

图 2 超浅覆土近距离穿越施工中的风险

3.2 工程技术对策

针对上述风险，参照以往穿越工程的施工技术经验，并根据本工程的具体情况作了深入的分析，提出了施工控制、压重、隧道加固、实时监控四个方面的技术措施。

3.2.1 施工参数控制

施工参数可根据“慢慢地推，分小段推；慢慢地转，均匀地转；顶住正面，调整压力；封住盾尾，合理注浆”的微扰动控制技术[6]，并结合工程具体情况来进行优化设置。根据风险分析，正面压力过大或过小均不宜。因此，根据隧道不同埋深，正面压力应维持在 0.08～0.1 MPa 左右，并保持压力波动小于 0.01 MPa，以保证切口前方土体稳定。推进速度应控制在 10 mm/min 左右，按每段 20～30 cm 进行推进，以缩小施工相关信息反馈的时间间隔，及时对参数进行优化调整。在慢推的基础上保证慢纠盾构姿态，盾构轴线水平向和垂直向偏角控制在 0.5‰～1‰ 以内，即水平和垂直向差值需控制在 4.25～8.5 mm 以内。同步注浆浆液采用高密度浆液，稠度为 9～10，注浆量为 4 m^3，以提高对盾构周围土体的填充和加固效果。9 号线下行线穿越 1 号线上行线施工过程中同步注浆量和千斤顶速度的变化如图 3 所示。

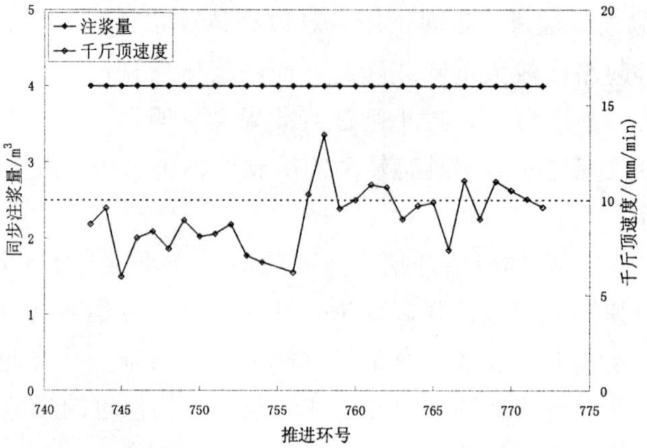

图 3 穿越施工过程中同步注浆量和千斤顶速度的变化

3.2.2 压 重

隧道开挖前后，竖向荷载计算简图如图 4 所示。

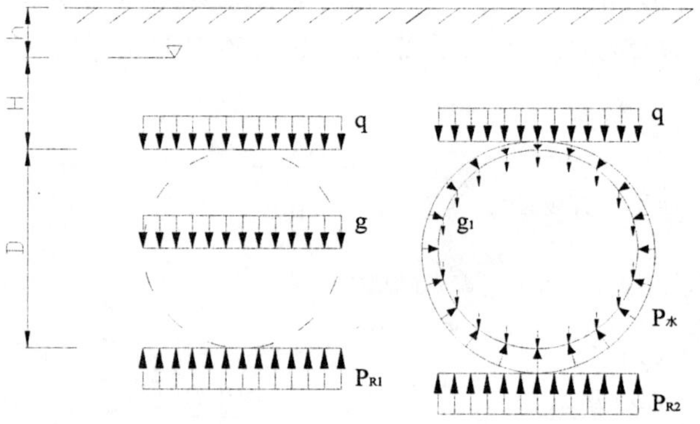

图 4 开挖前后竖向荷载计算简图

开挖前 $P_{R1}=q+g'$ (1)

开挖后 $P_{R2}=q+\pi g_1+P_{水}$ (2)

则式（1）、式（2）得到拱底反力变化量 $\Delta P=P_{R1}-P_{R2}=g'-\pi g_1+P_{水}=g-\pi g_1$ (3)

其中，P_{R1} 为假定隧道的拱底反力；q 为上覆土压；g' 为开挖土体浮重；P_{R2} 为开挖后隧道的拱底反力；g_1 为隧道结构自重；$P_{水}$ 为静水压；g 为开挖土体自重。

计算可得 $\Delta P=59.4$ kPa，即隧道开挖后，对下方地基的卸载量为 59.4 kPa。在超浅覆土中如此大的卸载量易引起下卧土层的回弹，导致下方运营地铁较大的隆起变形。为了将运营地铁最终隆起变形量控制在 5 mm 以内，一方面可采取临时压重来弥补穿越施工期间的卸载量，另一方面可通过注浆来加固土体，抵抗变形。各种技术措施实施方法及采取措施后压重效果分析如下所述。

（1）地面压重

地面穿越处上方路面铺设厚度 5 cm 厚钢板及 10 cm 厚沥青铺层，覆盖范围为衡山路路面穿越处 9 号线隧道边线以外 3 m 内，纵向约 16 m 长，均布荷载为 5.9 kPa，则路面压重正下方隧道顶部附加应力平均约为 4.8 kPa。

（2）隧道内压重

在作业空间允许的条件下，穿越范围内的 9 号线隧道施工轨道下方堆设每环 5t 的铅块压重，即均布荷载 6.7 kPa。压重作业与盾构掘进施工同步。在第一节车架与盾构本体之间有 9 环的距离，考虑到此范围内主要进行管片拼装和轨道、轨枕安装工作，可在靠近盾构本体约 5 环范围内堆载 2 层管片作为临时压重，之后再用铅块替代管片压重，以保证在施工可行的前提下尽量及时地进行压重。施工期间盾构车架自重以 5 t/m 计算，即 8.1 kPa。

（3）注浆加固

此外，考虑每环同步注浆使周围土体增重约 3.5 t，即 4.7 kPa。

综上可知，各种措施下的补偿卸载量总和 $P'=24.3$ kPa，约占总卸载量的 41%。

3.2.3 隧道加固

隧道加固措施可分别考虑对 1 号线和 9 号线隧道的加固，以增强隧道的整体刚度，减小盾构施工引起的隧道变形。对压重范围内的 9 号线隧道管片采用 20#槽钢进行纵向拉紧，与盾构掘进同步进行。槽钢可通过特殊连接件固定在管片拼装夹持孔上，断面内共计 5 道。1 号线隧道可在管片上打入膨胀螺栓，再利用槽钢进行固定连接。

3.2.4 实时监测

首先分别在 1 号线隧道四个被穿越段内布置电水平尺，每 2 m 布置一测点，监测范围约 70 m，用以 24 小时连续监测隧道的变形情况，并结合人工监测隧道沉降和收敛情况。其次对 1 号线隧道两侧各 10 环内（约 55 m）的 9 号线隧道进行沉降和水平位移监测，频率为 1 次/d。最后对盾构穿越范围内的地表加强监测，监测频率为 4 次/d。1 号线电水平尺监测、9 号线隧道纵向及横断面监测布置情况见图 1（b）。整个监测系统具备安全、全面、及时的特点，以保证穿越施工的安全。

4 穿越施工影响的实测分析

4.1 运营地铁的变形规律

根据盾构与运营地铁的相对位置，取 5 个关键施工工况，如图 5（a）所示。9 号线下行线上穿越 1 号线下行线的间距仅为 0.83 m，以此为例，对盾构推进期间运营地铁所受变形影响进行了分析，如图 5（b）所示（正值表示隆起，负值表示沉降，以下同）。

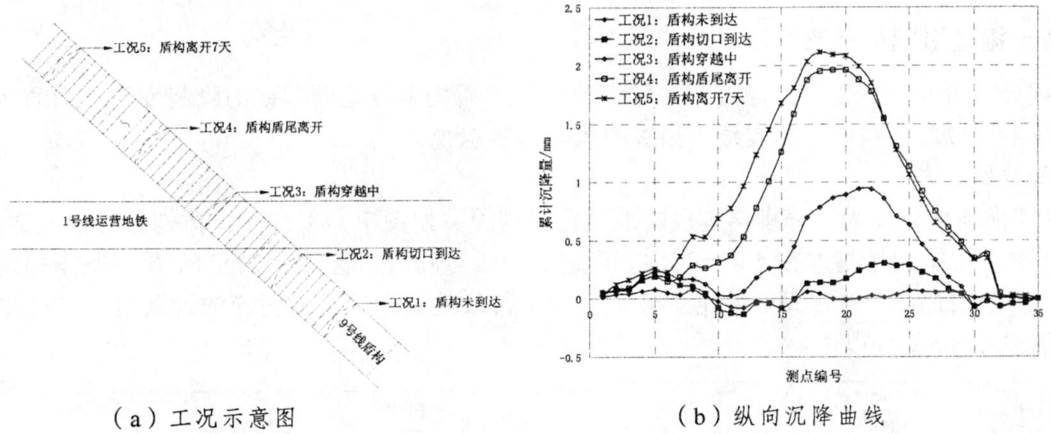

（a）工况示意图　　　　（b）纵向沉降曲线

图 5　盾构推进引起的地铁变形分析

工况 1 为盾构切口右端距离运营地铁水平距离 9.6 m（8 环），此时运营地铁受扰动影响不明显。工况 2 为盾构切口右端刚刚到达穿越的切入点，此时运营地铁已产生最大值为约 0.3 mm 隆起的显著影响。这阶段的隆起主要是由于盾构离运营地铁越近，对地铁附近土体的挤压效应增强引起的。工况 3 为盾构穿越中，可见运营地铁隆起量显著增大，其最大隆起量约为工况 2 最大隆起量的近 3 倍。工况 4 为盾构盾尾离开，运营地铁继续隆起，最大隆起量增至 2 mm。这主要由两个方面的原因造成的，一是盾构施工对周围土体的扰动影响，二是盾构推过后，土体卸载和盾构机重量的卸载影响。地铁两隧道轴线交叉点约位于电子水平尺测点 XXU18 附近，测点位置见图 1（b），但是穿越过程中，纵向沉降曲线轴线都显著偏离测点 XXU18，并且有逐渐靠近测点的趋势。这主要是由于盾构斜穿越，切口右端先切入，先引起右侧地铁的扰动。工况 3 后，盾构切口右端离开，切口左端推进扰动引起左侧地铁的明显隆起。工况 4 后 3～7 天，运营地铁隆起增量较小，隆起速率显著减缓。

本工程在穿越施工阶段，两隧道的 4 处交叠段最大隆起均小于 3 mm，地面未发生冒浆及过大隆起现象，最终隆起量控制在 4～5 mm 以内，基本达到要求。

4.2 隧道内压重卸载对地铁变形的影响

2009 年 2 月 8 号至 2 月 13 号先后完成下、上行线压重的全面卸载，此时下、上行线已分别经历后期沉降 2、4 个月。隧道内压重卸载后，由于应力释放的原因，原本稳定或变形缓慢的运营地铁会受到一定的影响。如图 6 所示为全面卸载引起的运营地铁电水平尺测点 SXU18 和 XSU18 的沉降变化情况，测点位置见图 1（b）。

从图中可以看出，当卸载施工开始后，趋于稳定的测点开始产生一定程度的隆起，但是，经过一段时间后，测点隆起量又回复到卸载之前的水平。这说明了卸载确实引起了土体扰动，但是这种扰动产生的土体变形是弹性可恢复的。此外，SXU18 测点的扰动影响显著大于 XSU18。

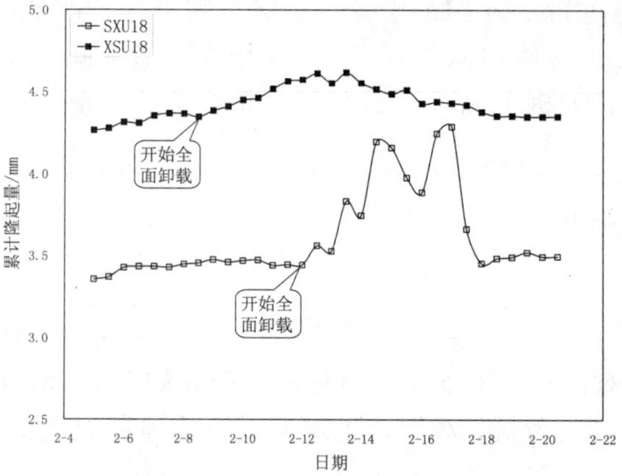

图 6 卸载影响曲线

4.3 浅覆土掘进引起的地表沉降

由上述分析可知，本工程穿越过程中较好地控制了盾构下方运营地铁的隆起变形。而盾构上方的地表沉降也得到了较好的控制，但浅覆土掘进的风险不容忽视。

4.3.1 良好控制状态

以 S815 横断面沉降为例分析穿越段的地表沉降规律，如图 7（a）所示。盾构穿越前或穿越过程中，地表呈微小隆起，隆起量基本在 5 mm 以内，穿越后一段时间内，地表持续沉降，最终基本稳定在 20 mm 以内。S815 横断面位于 9 号线上行线穿越 1 号线上行线的位置，与此对应的地铁电水平尺测点 SSU18 的最终隆起量在 3.5 mm 以内。

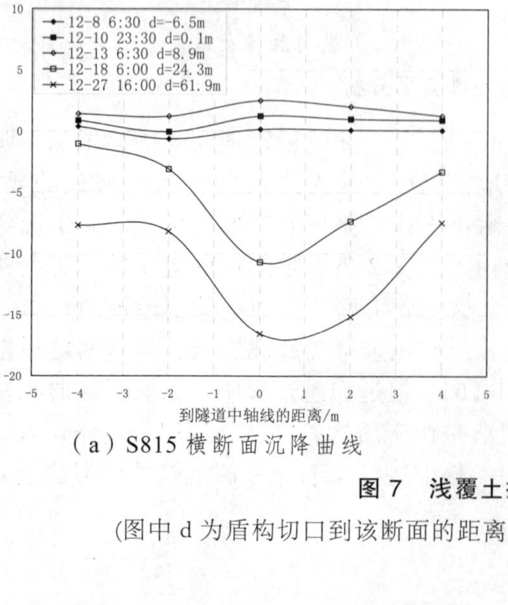

（a）S815 横断面沉降曲线

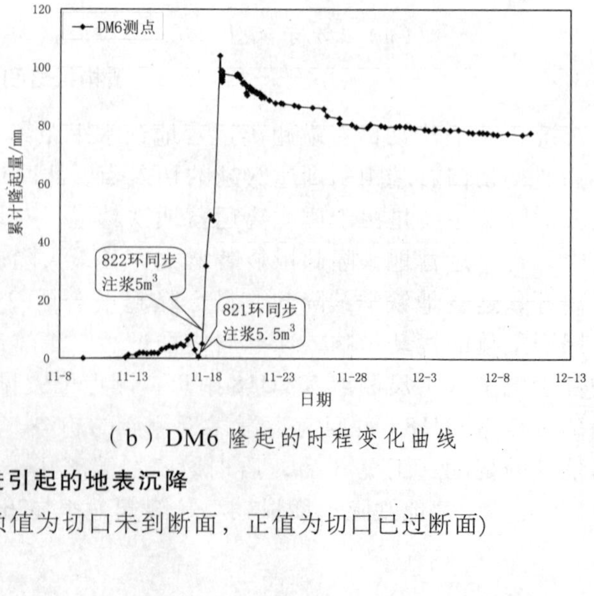

（b）DM6 隆起的时程变化曲线

图 7 浅覆土掘进引起的地表沉降

(图中 d 为盾构切口到该断面的距离，负值为切口未到断面，正值为切口已过断面)

4.3.2 不良控制状态

在浅覆土施工时，盾构施工参数变化对地层变形的影响是有高敏感性的，施工控制不当则易产生较大的地表变形。图 7（b）所示为测点 DM6 隆起的时程变化曲线，此时盾构已成功穿过运营地铁进入浅覆土穿越建筑群区域。11 月 7 日，测点发生突沉，为了防止地表建筑物的破坏，增加了同步注浆量 1～1.5 m^3，引起高达 10 cm 的隆起，导致上覆土体破坏，地表混凝土路面开裂，其裂缝延伸至路边的建筑物墙体。

5 讨 论

盾构穿越施工是土体变形及相关措施抑制其变形的一个综合过程。盾构穿越前布置好路面压重，一方面用以补偿隧道开挖的卸载量，抑制地面隆起和运营地铁隧道的隆起变形，另一方面可以增加上覆压力，防止注浆压力过大破坏上覆土体结构。穿越期间，盾构机车架及隧道拱底的铅块压重可以补偿一部分卸载量，同步注浆也增加了周围土体荷载。总的补偿卸载量约占总卸载量的 41%，从数值上来看这是偏小的。而事实上注浆不仅仅填充了盾构周围孔隙，也加固了周围土体，吸收了一定的回弹量，使隧道与周围土体整体刚度增加，抑制土体后期回弹。这在一定程度上也弥补了补偿卸载量的不足。此外，结合地面压重，可在压重两侧做桩，形成特殊结构整体。则地表不再是自由面，当隧道开挖卸载后，土体回弹将受到结构的限制，此时隧道隆起变形主要取决于结构间土体的压缩变形。由于穿越处地面位于交通要道，不便进行桩的施工，本工程仅实施了地面压重。

在穿越过程中，若 1 号线隆起值较大，超过警戒值，则表明补偿卸载量是严重不足的。此时，应采取应急措施，在穿越点上方路面临时封闭 1～2 车道以堆载压重，同时考虑在 1 号线隧道内压重。

盾构穿越后，首先车架重量开始卸载，其次再进行地面压重和隧道内压重的卸载。隧道内压重的卸载应在地铁变形趋于稳定的情况下进行。可考虑先进行压重的试验卸载，以判断卸载后地铁变形是否在可接受范围内。试验卸载安全的前提下，可进行全面的压重卸载施工。

6 结论与建议

本文对超浅覆土和近距离上穿越的叠加风险进行了分析，并据此提出了有效的工程技术对策，并对穿越施工的影响作了实测分析，得到了以下结论：

(1)盾构超浅覆土近距离上穿越运营地铁具有超浅覆土穿越和近距离上穿越两种高风险的叠加情形，施工过程中需通过盾构施工参数控制、压重、隧道加固、实时监测等技术措施来同时保证地铁变形和地表沉降控制在安全范围内。

(2) 本工程通过压重、注浆、隧道加固等措施来抑制卸载的影响，采用各种措施后的补偿卸载量约为总卸载量的 41%，成功将地铁变形控制在安全范围内。

(3) 穿越后，应在土体变形稳定后进行压重卸载施工。尽量选择分批卸载，以减小大范围内大量应力释放引起的扰动影响，保证土体变形以弹性可恢复为主。

(4) 超浅覆土穿越受盾构施工参数变化影响具有高敏感性，因此盾构参数宜维持在合理范围内，以防止地表发生突发性的隆起或沉降，威胁地表建（构）筑物的安全。

由于此类穿越工程的施工存在叠加风险，且运营期间地铁在浅覆土中运营，其长期振动的危害对今后地表建（构）筑物的规划建设与使用影响较大。因此，建议此类高风险工程应在规划设计时尽量予以避免。

7 致 谢

本文的研究得到了上海隧道工程股份有限公司顾春华、邓喜及地铁运营有限公司王如璐、邵华等单位及个人大力的支持，特此感谢。

参考文献（References）：

[1] 白延辉，尤旭东，李文勇. 盾构超近距离穿越地铁运营隧道的保护技术[J]. 地下工程与隧道，2000（3）：2-6.
[2] 廖少明，余炎，彭芳乐. 盾构近距离穿越相邻隧道施工的数值解析[J]. 岩土力学，2004，25（增 11）：223-226.
[3] 廖少明，杨俊龙，奚程磊，彭芳乐，侯学渊. 盾构近距离穿越施工的工作面土压力研究[J]. 岩土力学，2005，26（11）：1727-1730.
[4] 邵华，张子新. 盾构近距离穿越施工对已运营隧道的扰动影响分析[J]. 岩土力学，2004，25（增 1）：545-549.
[5] 陈亮，黄宏伟，王如路. 近距离上部穿越对原有隧道沉降的影响分析[J]. 土木工程学报，2006，39（6）：83-87.
[6] LIAO S M，GAO L Q，ZHU H H. Soft ground movement under small disturbance of shield driving[C]. Soil and Rock Behavior and Modeling—Proceedings of the GeoShanghai Conference. [S.l.]：ASCE，2006：62–69.

作者简介（Bio-data）：

李金，男，1986 年 4 月出生。2007 年 6 月毕业于中南大学。现就读于同济大学地下系攻读硕士学位，专业为隧道及地下建筑工程。曾参与过 7 号线穿越 1 号线、9 号线穿越 1 号线等工程的现场技术服务。主要从事盾构隧道穿越建（构）筑物的微扰动控制技术的研究。

Jin LI, male, was born in April 1986. I was graduated from Central South University in June 2007. And now, as an undergraduate master in Department of Geological Engineering of Tongji University, he specializes in Tunnel and Underground Engineering. He was involved in some engineering such as M7 crossing M1, M9 crossing M1 and supplied field technical service. My main research field is small disturbance control for shield crossing structures.

E-mail: leekim5230@163.com

软土盾构隧道渗漏水成因分析

芮 易[1] 李晓军[1] 尹 玫[1] 王 帅[2]
[1]同济大学 土木工程学院地下建筑与工程系，上海 200092
[2]同济大学 岩土工程重点实验室，上海 200092

【摘 要】 本文归纳了一般软土盾构隧道渗漏水的特征及其影响，运用故障树方法对其形成原因进行了初步分析。并进一步通过粗级方法，结合实际工程的现场调研，对软土盾构隧道渗漏水形成原因作了更深入的挖掘，得到影响隧道渗漏水的主要原因和生成规则，并对对今后的运营和养护提出了一些指导性的意见。
【关键词】 渗漏水；故障树；粗级方法；盾构隧道养护

CAUSE ANALYSIS OF SHIELD TUNNEL LEAKAGE IN SOFT SOIL

Yi RUI[1], Xiaojun LI[1], Mei YIN[1], Shuai WANG[2]
[1]*Department of Geotechnical Engineering, Tongji University, Shanghai 200092, China;*
[2]*Key Laboratory of Geotechnical and Underground Engineering of Ministry of Education, Tongji University, Shanghai 200092, China*

Abstract: Characteristics of the leakage and its impact for shield tunnel were summarized in this paper. Based on that, the fault-tree method was applied to perform a preliminary analysis of the causes of leakage. According to a rough set theory combined with actual on-site research on the shield tunnel in soft soil, the causes of leakage got more understanding. In the end, the main causes and generation rules were included and several guiding advices were proposed for the maintenance of shield tunnel in the future.
Key words: leakage fault; tree method; rough set theory; maintenance of shield tunnel

1 引 言

长期的自然环境和使用环境的双重作用下，已建软土盾构隧道会随着使用不同程度地出现裂缝以及渗漏水等病害[1,2]。根据对上海地铁隧道的初步调查，占相当比例的盾构隧道区段有渗漏水现象产生。但是在隧道的运营和养护方面，特别是盾构隧道方面针对盾构隧道病害的养护方法的知识和技术还不成熟。目前在制订盾构隧道病害处治对策和方案时，工程师一般结合隧道病害的大致特征及隧道所在地的地质、气候、水文等信息，根据经验判断病害成因，然后制订相应的加固方案和措施。实践表明，仅根据经验制定相关相互策略是不够的，缺乏系统和科学的隧道病害影响程度的理论、程序和方法，不可避免会导致不合理的治理措施和方案，所以展开对盾构隧道病害的研究是非常必要的。

本文主要针对渗漏水这一软土盾构隧道最主要的病害，结合实际工程，首先应用故障树方法对软土盾构隧道渗漏水可能病害进行挖掘[1]，通过粗级理论分析渗漏水产生的主要原因，从而为制定基于成因分析的盾构隧道养护策略提供依据。

2 渗漏水成因分析方法

2.1 渗漏水概述

渗漏水是软土盾构隧道最主要的病害。对隧道的稳定、洞内设施、行车安全、地面建筑和隧道周围水环境产生诸多不良影响甚至威胁。长期渗漏水容易使衬砌结构剥落、风化，隧道的使用可靠性将降低，如果渗漏水中含有侵蚀介质，将造成衬砌劣化，降低衬砌的承载能力。地下水向隧道区域汇集将浸泡腐蚀隧道周围地层，使地层强度和稳定性降低，冲淘衬砌背后地层形成空洞，影响周围地层和衬砌的长期稳定，形成巨大水压力，威胁衬砌安全。

此外在寒冷和严寒地区，水是影响隧道周围地层冻胀的重要因素。软土盾构隧道的渗漏水会造成衬砌冻胀开裂、酥落、剥落、拱部挂冰、边墙结冰，侵入隧道建筑限界等。

2.2 渗漏水成因分析

以下对软土盾构隧道渗漏水成因分析运用故障树分析法，这是一种图形演绎法，它能把盾构隧道渗漏水的故障与导致该故障的诸因素，包括自然灾害，水文地质，施工因素和运营因素，形象表现为故障谱；从上往下可得出系统故障与哪些影响因素有关，从下往上可得出各影响因素对系统故障的影响，从而分析故障产生的原因。故障树建立的主要步骤如下：

（1）选择和确定故障树的顶事件

顶事件是系统最不希望发生的事件，或是进行逻辑分析的故障事件。对于盾构隧道结构渗漏水成因分析来说，将隧道结构看作一个系统，故障树的顶事件即为隧道结构的渗漏。

（2）分析顶事件

寻找顶事件(盾构隧道结构的渗漏水)发生的直接的必要和充分原因，将顶事件(盾构隧道结构的渗漏水)作为输出事件，将所有直接原因作为输入事件，并根据这些事件的实际逻辑关系用适当的逻辑符号相联系。

（3）分析输入事件

分析每个与顶事件（盾构隧道结构的渗漏水)相联系的输入事件，若该事件能进一步分解，则将其作为下一级的输出事件，并将其按次级项事件进行处理。

（4）建立故障树

重复上述步骤，逐级向下分解，直到所有的输入事件不能再分解或不必再分解为止，这样即建成了故障树。

绘制故障树就是根据建立故障树时分析得到的逻辑关系，将顶事件与次级顶事件使用上述符号连接起来，对每一个次级顶事件再进行类似的分解，一直到不能再分解的基本事件为止。对于软土盾构隧道结构渗漏水成因分析来说，隧道结构渗漏水即为故障树的顶事件，根据收集的资料，对渗漏水产生原因进行逐级分析。建立故障树，从而分析得到渗漏水的可能原因。

2.3 渗漏水成因挖掘

由上述渗漏水成因的故障树分析法确定的渗漏水产生的可能原因带有一定的经验性和不确定性，而且含有冗余信息，从本质上讲只是一些理论上的可能原因。本研究通过对上海地铁隧道的实地调研，从结果上看主要发生在衬砌接缝和注浆孔处，而且在不同区段其渗漏水的发生也具有各自的特点。本文运用粗集理论[1]，进一步对产生渗漏水的可能原因进一步挖掘分析，结合实际工程，找出渗漏水产生的主要原因和规律。

渗漏水成因挖掘的粗集方法的主要步骤如下：

（1）建立渗漏水成因分析的原始数据信息表

对数据挖掘来说相关信息的收集、存储和查询具有十分重要的作用，是其基础和前提。根据领域知识和相关的先验知识，本文收集并统计了上海地铁遁构隧道的相关工程数据，主要包括水文地质条件、设计、施工、运行、管理等阶段的相关数据，并结合在实际调研中的渗漏水记录，确定条件属性(渗漏水的可能成因)集合和决策属性(是否产生渗漏水)集合，建立渗漏水成因分析的原始数据信息表。

(2) 连续属性离散化

渗漏水成因分析的原始数据信息表中的属性一般有两种类型：一种是连续性(定量)属性，另一种是离散性〔定性)属性。运用粗集理论处理决策表时，需要将相关连续属性进行离散化处理。

(3) 渗漏水成因分析的初始决策表

对原始数据信息表中的连续属性经过离散化处理后，构成渗漏水成因分析的初始决策表。

(4) 属性约简

在一个信息系统 $S=<U,A,V,f>$ 中，$U=(x_1,x_2,...,x_n)$ 是全部有限个处理对象(样本)的集合：$A=C\bigcup D$ 是全部有限个属性的集合，C 是条件属性集合，即渗漏水产生的各种可能原因所组成的集合，D 是决策属性集合，即是否产生渗漏水,为单决策属性，且 $C\bigcap D=\varnothing$。条件属性约简步骤如下：

① 首先，从 C 中去掉第 i 个条件属性 C_i，计算 $\gamma_{c-|c_i|}(D)$；

② 若 $\gamma_{c-|c_i|}(D)=\gamma_c(D)$，则 C_i 为冗余属性，从 C 中将该属性去除，$\gamma_c(D)$ 表示属性集合 C 对 C 的依赖程度。

③ 若 $\gamma_{c-|c_i|}(D)\neq\gamma_c(D)$，则保留该属性 C_i；

④ 对所有条件属性 $C_i(i=1-n)$ 均作上述判断后，即可得到约简条件属性 C'。

(5) 生成决策规则(主要成因)

设 $R(C')=\{x_1,x_2,...,x_n\}$ 是根据 d 的约简条件属性 C' 在 U 上划分的全部等价类集合，其中每个等价类 x_i 对应一个条件属性取值的序列，即等价类戈的描述可表示为：

$$Des(x_i)=\wedge_{a\in C}(a=f(x_i,a)) \tag{1}$$

式中：^表示“与”运算符；x_f 等是等价类 x_i 中的元素；a 是属性对象 x_f 对属性 a 的取值。

类似地，决策属性 d 的描述为：

$$Des(d)=(\beta=f(x_i,d)) \tag{2}$$

式中：β 是对象 x_i 对决策层属性 d 的取值。

这样，由粗集得到的一条决策规则为：

$$Des(x)\Rightarrow Des(d) \tag{3}$$

也可以描述为“if...then... ”的规则形式。

3 工程实例

3.1 工程概况

上海地铁一号线于 1993 年 5 月南段建成通车；1995 年 4 月全线投入试运营；1997 年 7 月，南延伸段贯通运营。2004 年 12 月，北延伸段开通试运营。由于建成并运营已有十余年，加上当时地铁建设经验不足，出现了许多结构病害，特别是渗漏水现象比较普遍。

3.2 隧道渗漏水成因分析

以隧道结构渗漏水作为故障树的顶事件，根据收集的资料，对渗漏水产生原因进行逐级分析。建立如下故障树。

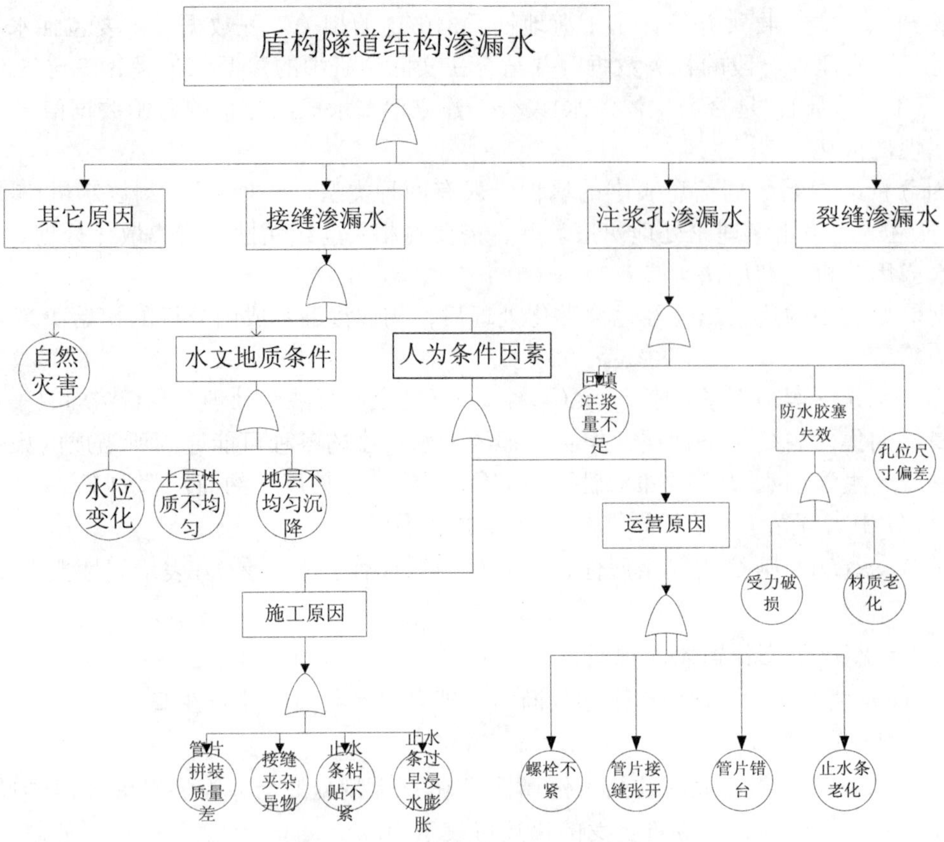

图 1 软土盾构隧道渗漏水故障树

运用前面介绍的粗集方法，对该隧道产生渗漏水的可能原因进一步挖掘分析。

（1）信息表条件属性选择

根据故障树的分析结果，信息表条件属性选为：地层不均匀沉降，管片拼装质量差，接缝夹杂异物，止水条粘贴不紧，管片接缝张开，管片错台，止水条老化失效，防水胶塞受力破损，防水胶塞材质老化失效，孔位尺寸偏差。分别用 $C_1 \sim C_{10}$ 表示。

（2）信息表决策属性选择

因为挖掘的目标是渗漏水的成因，因此决策属性选为是否产生渗漏水，为单决策属性，用 d 表示。

（3）初始策表

由以上分析得到条件属性集合:$C = \{C_1, C_2, C_3, C_4, C_5, C_6, C_7, C_8, C_9, C_{10}\}$[1]。值域为{0,1}，1 表示有该项因素，0 表示无该项因素。决策属性集合:$D = \{d\}$，决策属性的值域为{0,1}，1 表示出现渗漏水，0 表示未出现渗漏水。将该隧道 14 个区段作为样本，分别以 $X_1 \sim X_{14}$ 表示。最终得到如下初始决策表。

表 1 初始决策表

样本	C_1	C_2	C_3	C_4	C_5	C_6	C_7	C_8	C_9	C_{10}	d
X_1	0	1	0	0	1	1	0	0	0	0	1
X_2	0	0	0	1	0	1	0	1	0	0	1
X_3	1	1	0	0	0	0	0	0	0	0	1
X_4	1	1	0	0	1	0	1	0	1	0	1
X_5	1	0	0	0	1	1	0	0	0	0	1
X_6	1	0	0	0	0	1	0	0	0	0	1
X_7	1	0	0	0	1	1	0	0	0	0	1
X_8	1	1	0	0	1	0	0	0	0	0	1

续表 1

样本	C_1	C_2	C_3	C_4	C_5	C_6	C_7	C_8	C_9	C_{10}	d
X_9	1	1	0	0	1	1	0	0	0	0	1
X_{10}	1	1	1	0	0	0	0	0	0	0	1
X_{11}	0	0	0	0	0	0	0	0	0	0	1
X_{12}	1	1	0	1	0	0	1	0	1	0	1
X_{13}	1	0	0	0	1	1	0	0	0	0	1
X_{14}	0	0	0	0	0	0	0	0	0	1	1

（4）属性约简

通过对条件属性进行约简计算，得到 d 关于条件属性 C 的约简属性集 C' 如下：

$$C' = \{C_1, C_2, C_5, C_6\} \tag{4}$$

其中，C_1，C_2，C_5，C_6分别对应地层不均匀沉降，管片拼装质量差，管片接缝张开，管片错台。即各盾构隧道渗漏水的形成主要是受到地层不均匀沉降，管片拼装质量差，管片接缝张开，管片错台这四方面因素的影响。

（5）生成规则

if $f(X_i,C_1)=1$ and $f(X_i,C_2)=1$ and $f(X_i, C_5)=1$ and $f(X_i, C_6)=1$ then $f(X_i,d)=1$

4 结 语

对软土盾构隧道进行成因分析是采取合理有效的养护、维修加固措施的前提和依据，对于降低病害威胁、延长维护周期和隧道使用寿命具有重要的意义。本文在病害特征分析、病害成因分析方面展开研究，得出以下结论：

（1）在隧道日常检查中，对地层不均匀沉降量大，管片拼装质量差，管片接缝张开和管片错台量大的区段该重点观察。

（2）依据渗漏水的特性，在隧道施工过程中制定相适宜的施工方案，严把施工质量，特别是加强管片拼装质量是预防隧道渗漏的重要保证。

（3）在运营养护过程中，应该严密注意隧道所在地层的沉降动态，对临近工程施工造成的地层扰动应密切关注，及时采取有效措施，确保隧道不均匀沉降在可控范围之内。

参考文献（References）：

[1] 戴宏伟. 公路隧道渗漏水成因、危害机理和冻害问题研究. [硕士学位论文]，同济大学，2006.

[2] 王如路，周贤浩. 近年来上海地铁监护发现的问题及对策[C]. 中国土木工程学会隧道及地下工程学会地下铁道专业委员会第十四届学术交流会论文集，2001：239-242.

作者简介（Bio-data）：

芮易，男，1984 年 11 月，硕士在读。2007 获同济大学土木工程学院桥梁工程学士学位。现为同济大学土木工程学院地下建筑与工程系硕士。主要从事专业及研究方向：地下工程数字化技术研究，软土

Yi RUI, Male, Nov 23th, 1984, He graduated from Tongji University and got Bridge Engineering Bachelor Degree in 2007.Now he is studying for Geotechnical Engineering Master Degree in the same University.Major and Research Fields: digital technology，technology of maintenance for shield tunnel.

E-mail: ruiyi1123@126.com

世界最大級φ１4.27mの泥土圧シールドの適用

三浦 正昭　田中 淳一

三菱重工地中建機株式会社　兵庫　652-0863

2010年の上海万博に向けて、上海市内の地下鉄、高速道路などの交通網の整備が急速に進められている。このうち、上海で最も風光明媚な観光地として有名な外灘ウォータフロント地域の交通渋滞の解消と、観光地の再開発のために、このウォータフロント地域と並行して設けられている11車線の道路を地上と地下に分離し、交通渋滞の解消と観光地の再開発を実施する。地下化されるトンネル延長は3300mで、このうち重要建築物の多い1100m区間を世界最大級の土圧式シールドを適用して施工された。

本論文は、この工事に用いられた土圧式シールドマシンを中心にトンネル工事全体について報告するものである。

キーワード：外灘シールド；超大型泥土圧シールド

APPLICATION OFΦ14.27M LARGEST EARTH PRESSURE BALANCE SHIELD MACHINE TO THE WAITAN ROAD TUNNEL IN SHANGHAI CHINA

Masaaki MIURA，Junichi TANAKA

MITSUBIHI HAVEY INDUSTRIES TUNNELING MACHINERY & GEOTECHNOLOGY CO. LTD. HYOGO REF. 652-0863

Abstract: For Shanghai World Exposition of 2010, the maintenance of the transportation networks such as the subway and the highway of the Shanghai city are pushed forward rapidly. Of this, for the resolution of the traffic jam of WaiTan waterfront area where is famous as the sightseeing spot of scenic beauty in Shanghai and the redevelopment of the sightseeing spot, it needs to separate the road ground with underground of 11 traffic lanes which is established in parallel with WaiTan waterfront area and implement the resolution of the traffic jam and the redevelopment of the sightseeing spot. The underground of tunnel extension is 3300m, of this, one of the largest earth pressure shield machine in the world is applied and constructed in 1100m section with many important buildings.

This article reports it about the whole tunnel construction work mainly on an earth pressure shield machine used for this construction work.

Key words: WaiTan shield; largest earth pressure balance shield machine

1　はじめに

中国上海市で2010年に開催される万国博覧会に向けて、上海市の有数の観光地である外灘地区の再開発の一環として、外灘地区を南北に縦断する中山東一路を、地上部と外灘地区をバイパスする地下部に分離し、観光地における交通緩和を目的として施工されるトンネルである。

このトンネルは、上下二層式の6車線でトンネル内径は12.75 mあり、重要建築物の近接施工、低土被り部の施工、市街地における発進基地の確保等を考慮し、超大型シールドとしては中国国内で初めて採用された土圧式である。

本プロジェクト向けに、上海隧道股份有限公司と三菱重工地中建機株式会社により数々の検討を行い、両社の合作により製作されたφ14.27 m泥土圧シールドの工事について報告するものである。

2 外灘トンネル

外灘トンネルは、北側に虹口区、南側に黄浦区に連結されており、さらに福州路南側では上海市の主要高速道路の延安東路高架道路に連結される。この外灘トンネルは南側工区と北側工区の２工区に分かれており、南側工区は開削工事、北側工区はシールド工事により行なわれる。

特に、北側工区に関しては、歴史的重要建築物との近接施工、河川横断、工事期間中の交通渋滞緩和などの目的により、シールド工法が採用された。

本工事の主要概要は以下の通りである。

（1）施工者　上海隧道股份有限公司（略号 STEC）

（2）地　質　灰色粘质粉土夹粉质粘土、灰色淤泥质粉质粘土、灰色淤泥质粘土、灰色粘土、灰色粉质粘土、灰色粉质粘土夹粘质粉土

（3）トンネル緒元

① トンネル延長　1 102 m

② 土被り　8.52～23.5 m

③ 最小カーブ　平面 500 m R、縦断 2 000 m R

④ トンネル勾配　±50‰

⑤ 近接施工

最近接建築物離隔	水平距離	2.7 m
地下通路離隔	鉛直距離	0.675 m
地下鉄離隔	鉛直距離	1.463 m

⑥ セグメント

a．セグメント型式　コンクリートセグメント
　　軸挿入型ユニバーサルセグメント

b．セグメント外径　13 950 m m

c．セグメント内径　12 750 m m

d．セグメント幅　2 000 m m

e．分割及び重量　8＋1 分割、最大重量 15ton

トンネル路線は、図-1のトンネル平面図に示すように、外灘北端の天潼路発進立坑より発進し、上海ビルと浦江ホテルの間を通過したのち、外白渡橋下の蘇州川を横断する。河川横断後重要建築物の横を地下道、地下鉄の上下面を通過して福州路到達立坑まで施工する。

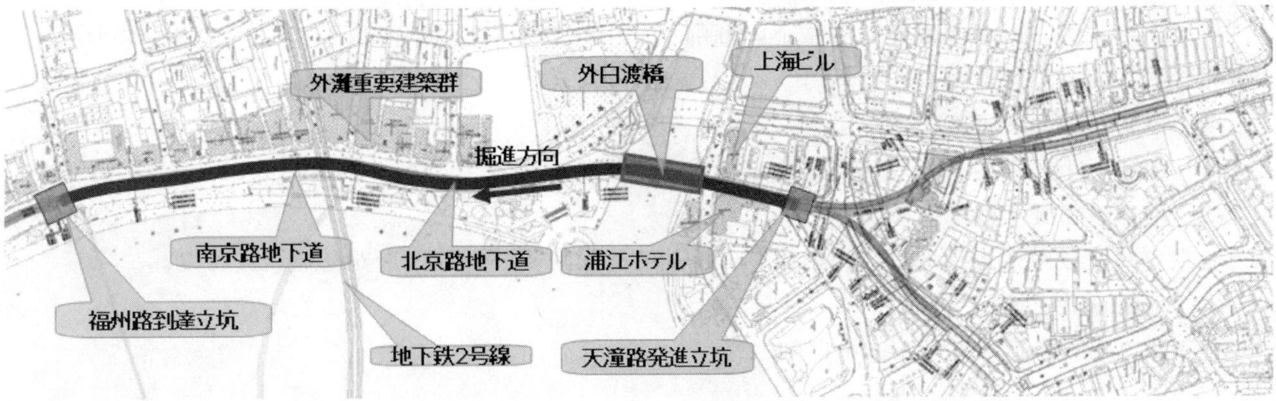

図-1　トンネル平面図

トンネルの縦断面図及び土質に関しては、図-2 に示すように発進立て坑より下り 50‰で蘇州川を通過し、上り 50‰で掘進した後、土被り 8.52 m の低土被り施工を実施する。一方、土質に関してはシールド勾配にあわせて互層の土質を掘削するが、基本的には粘性土で、上部はＮ値が低く下部ほどＮ値が高い。

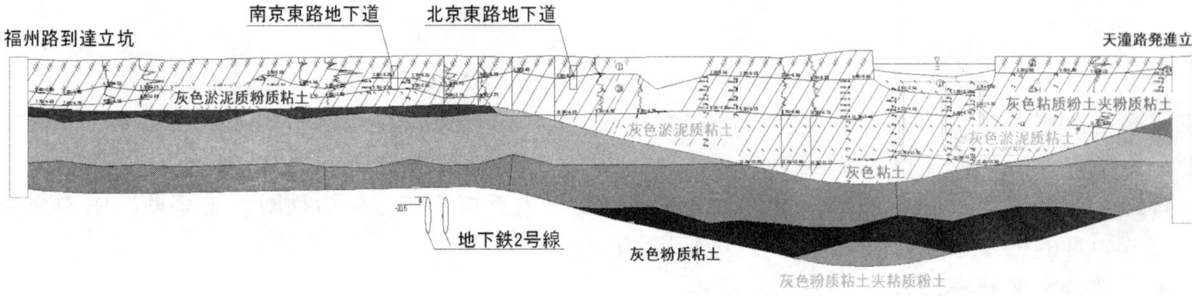

図-2 トンネル縦断面及び土質分布図

トンネル断面は図-3 に示す通り、三車線の上下二層式路面で、トンネル下面に電線通路、トンネル側面に避難通路を有し、照明設備、換気設備及び消火設備など限られたトンネル断面内を有効活用している。

また、道路の有効高さは 3.2 m、一車線の幅は 3 m で普通車の通行用として設計されている。

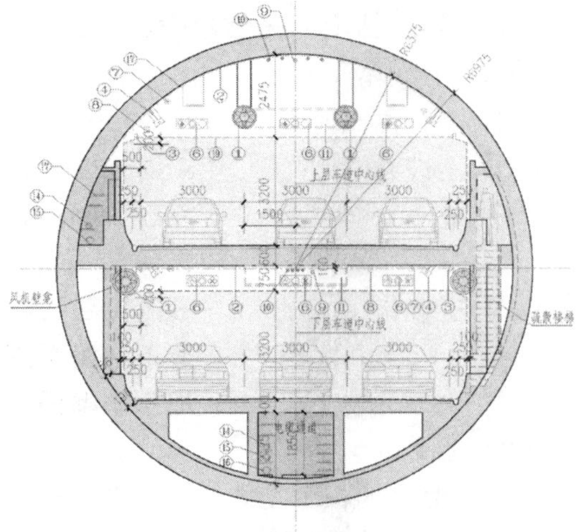

図-3 トンネル断面図

3 施工上の課題

外灘シールドを施工するに際し、施工上の主要な課題は、以下の通りである。

(1) 大断面勾配発進

シールド外径 ϕ 14.27 m における断面は 160 m^2 あり、発進勾配は下り 5% で切羽の崩落の問題がある。

(2) 低土被り

シールド計画路線の最低土被りは 8.52 m で、シールド径に対して約 0.6D と低土被りの施工となる。

(3) 河川下掘削と外白渡橋脚下掘削

河川下の掘削、河川両側の防護壁下の掘削及び中央部の橋脚下の掘削を行なうため、水圧に対する噴発、残地杭のへの対応が必要。

(4) 重要建築物近接施工

浦江飯店、上海大厦、外灘建築群などの重要建築物との最至近水平距離約 2.7 m の近接施工。

(5) 地下通路直下掘削

北京東路及び南京東路地下通路の直下 0.675 m を掘削及び、地下通路防護杭の掘削。

(6) 地下鉄直上掘削

地下鉄 2 号線の直上 1.463 m を掘削。

4 シールドマシン

本工事に採用されたシールドの全体図を図-4 に示す。

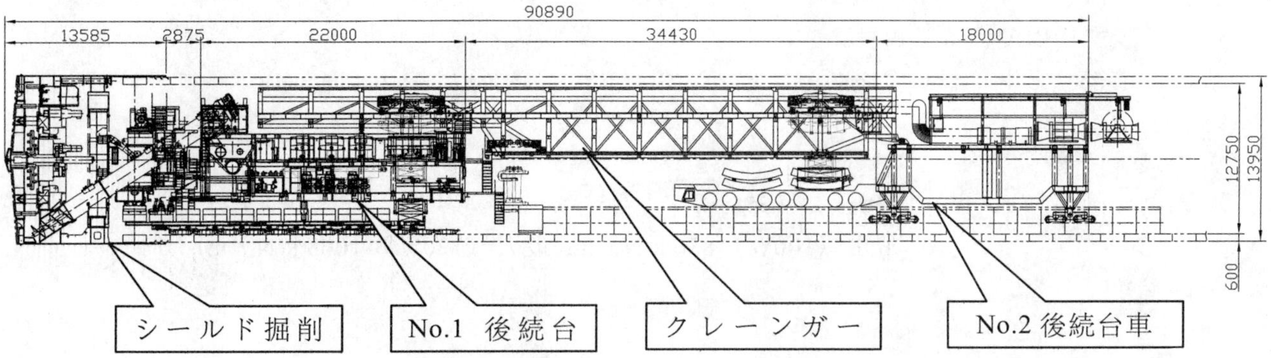

図-4 シールドマシン 全体図

4.1 シールド掘削機

(1) 型 式	Earth Pressure Balance Shield Machine (泥土圧シールド)
(2) シールド外径	ϕ14 270 mm
(3) シールド機長	13 595 mm
(4) 推力	
① 総推力	176 000 kN
② 単位面積当たり推力	1 100 kN/m2
③ シールドジャッキ	2 600 kN×3 050 mmST×68 本（34 組）
(5) カッタヘッド	
① 形式	円錐型面板式カッタヘッド
主スポーク 4 本＋補助スポーク 4 本	
② 開口率	約 38%
③ カッタ	カッタビット、センターカッタ、特殊先行ビット、
チャンバー内交換型特殊先行ビット	
④ コピーカッタ	370 kN×120 mmST×4 本
(6) カッタ駆動部	
① 駆動方式	電動駆動方式、インバータ制御
② 駆動部動力	2 640 kw（132 kw×20 台）
③ トルク	常用（100%）57 900 kN・m （α=19.9）
	最大（120%）69 481 kN・m （α=23.9）
④ 回転数	0.1～0.8rpm （最大周速 35.9m/min）
(7) スクリューコンベヤ	
① 型式	油圧駆動軸付きスクリューコンベヤ
② トラフ内径	ϕ1 500 mm
③ 回転数	1～10.3 rpm
④ トルク	最大 720 kN・m （α=213）
⑤ 搬送量	約 850 m^3/h（η=100%）
(8) エレクター	
① 型式	中空軸式エレクター

② 回転数 0.1～0.6 rpm

③ 押付け力 902 k N

④ 吊上げ力 902 k N

⑤ 把持方法 3 パッドバキューム式（センターパッド＋左右パッド）

⑥ グリップ自由度 6 自由度

（旋回、前後、上下、ピッチング、ローリング、ヨーイング）

(9) 中央アジテータ

① 型式 電動駆動

② 駆動部動力 220 k w （55 k w×4 台）

③トルク 常用（100%）836 k N・m, 最大（120%）1003 k N・m

④ 回転数 2.51 rpm

シールド掘削機を以下の図-5 に示す。

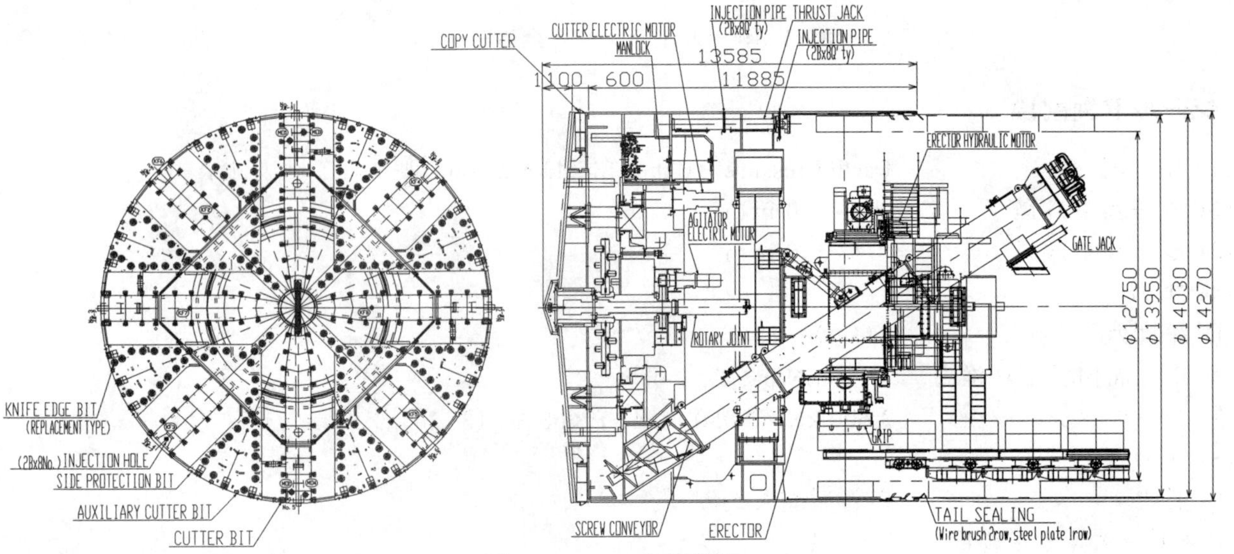

図-5 シールド掘削機

4.2 後続設備

本機に採用した後続設備は、下層床板を掘進と共に同時に布設する同時施工対応とし、工事期間短縮が可能な設備を導入する。一方、上層床板は後続台車通過後 200m の位置で施工する。

(1) セグメント供給設備

① セグメント搬送クレーン

地上から搬入されたセグメントは、坑内をトラックドーリーにて搬送し、クレーンガータに設置した 30ton クレーンにより 2 ピース毎のセグメントを供給装置上へ搬送する。搬送された 2 ピースのセグメントは、台車に設置した 15ton クレーンにより供給装置上に 1 ピース毎に配置される。また、下層床板の布設に関しては、20ton クレーンによって掘進とともに、No.1 後続台車と No.2 後続台車間に布設する。

② セグメント供給装置

供給装置は、1 リング分のセグメントを搭載できる長さを有しており、エレクター把持位置までセグメントを供給することができる。

(2) 排土装置

シールド機のスクリューコンベヤ以降の排土は、ミキシングホッパー、機内コンベヤ、連続コンベヤ及びクラムシェルを経由して、地上のホッパーへ搬送されるシステムである。

① ミキシングホッパー

大口径のスクリューコンベヤより排土された土砂は、多分に水を含み、スクリューの回転に伴う断続的な土砂の搬出が生じる。排土を適正に行なうために、スクリューコンベヤとベルトコンベヤの間に、排土された土砂の改良と連続搬送が行なえるミキシングホッパーを設置する。

② 機内コンベヤ

ベルトコンベヤは、ベルト幅 1 200 ｍｍ、最大速度 100 m/min の大型コンベヤを採用し、搬送量を約 750 m^3/h を確保した。また、本ベルトコンベヤは施工曲率に対応可能である。

③ 坑内連続コンベヤ

大断面の泥土圧シールドでは、排土効率を高めるために日本国内、欧米などで採用され始めてきた長距離対応の連続コンベヤを、中国のシールド工事として初めて採用した。ベルトコンベヤはベルト幅 1 000 ｍｍとし、シールド機の排土量に対応可能な大型連続コンベヤを採用。

④ 垂直搬送

坑内から地上への土砂の搬出は、3 台のクラムシェルにて行い、地上に設置したホッパーまで搬送する。

(3) 切羽注入設備

切羽注入設備としては、気泡注入設備及び加泥注入設備を装備しており、切羽への注入はカッタヘッド前面へ 7 箇所、カッタヘッド側面に 1 箇所行なえる。

(4) 裏込め注入設備

裏込め材は中粗砂、フライアッシュ、石灰、添加剤の一液注入を採用し、独立 6 系統で 6 箇所からの注入を行なう。

その他の設備として、圧気設備、給排水設備、受電設備、停電対策設備を有しており、それぞれの設備が No.1 後続台車及び No.2 後続台車に配置される。

5 施工実績

掘削は 2009 年 2 月より開始し、8 月上旬に到達した。進捗状況は、重要建築物及び地下鉄、地下通路との近接施工、低土被り施工などのデータを採取するために、初期推進は 19 リングを約 1 ヶ月間かけて掘進し、数々の掘進データを入手した。

初期掘進後の掘進は 4～6 リング/日で掘進を行い、当初懸念されていた歴史的重要構造物への影響、地下鉄営業線への影響、地下通路江の影響も無く無事通過することができた。

シールド機の掘進実績は、図-6 掘進速度と推力の関係図に示すように、本工区の推力は掘進速度との相関性は少なく、190R、220R の土被りの深さにより影響を受けている。

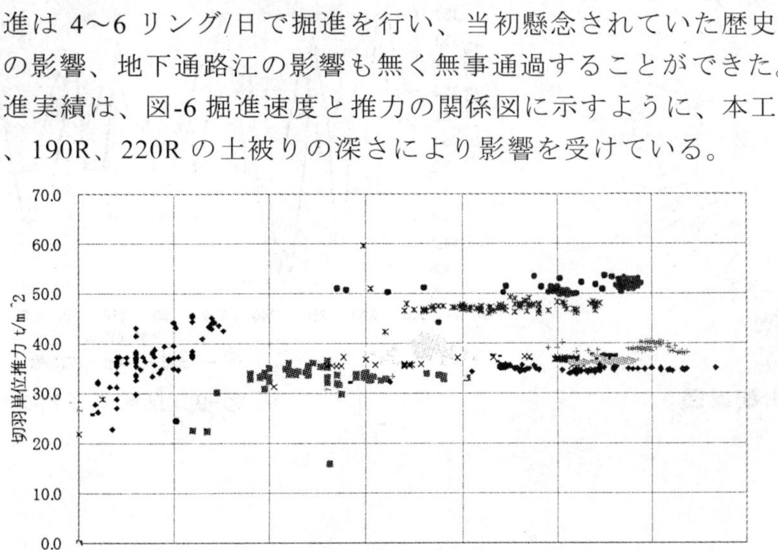

図-6　掘進速度と推力の関係図

一方、カッタトルクに関しては、図-7 掘進速度とカッタトルクの関係図に示すように、発進部の地盤改良部でトルク値が高くなっている他、トルク値は掘進速度に影響されていない。

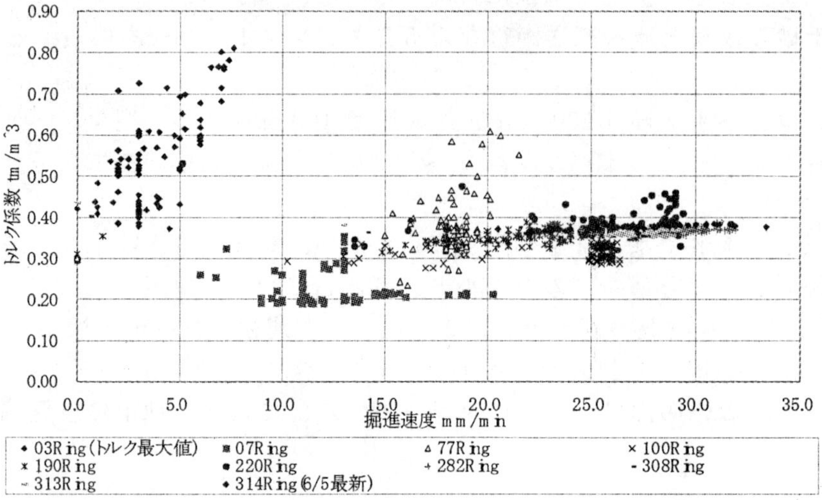

図-7 掘進速度とカッタトルクの関係図

地上への影響を最小限に抑えるために、切羽の土圧を適切に保つ必要がある。特に大断面泥土圧シールドにおいては、シールドの上部と下部ではその土圧に大きな差が出るが、地上部への影響を考慮し、バルクヘッドに装備している最上部、中央上部、中央下部、最下部に配置している土圧計のうち、地上への影響が最もでやすい最上部の土圧にて管理する。

一方、切羽土圧は常に最適に保つために自動土圧制御で施工し、制御は設定土圧に対して、土圧変動があった場合に、スクリューの回転数を増減させて制御するもので、制御結果は±0.55 kPa 程度の制御精度が確保されている。この制御精度は超大口径泥土圧シールドとしては極めて制御精度が高い制御である。

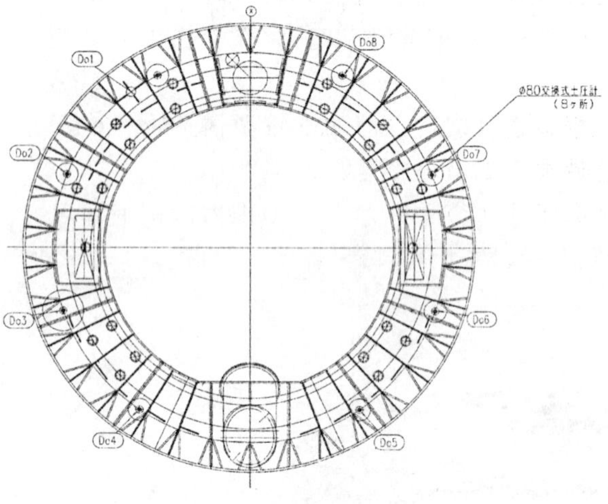

図-8 土圧計配置図

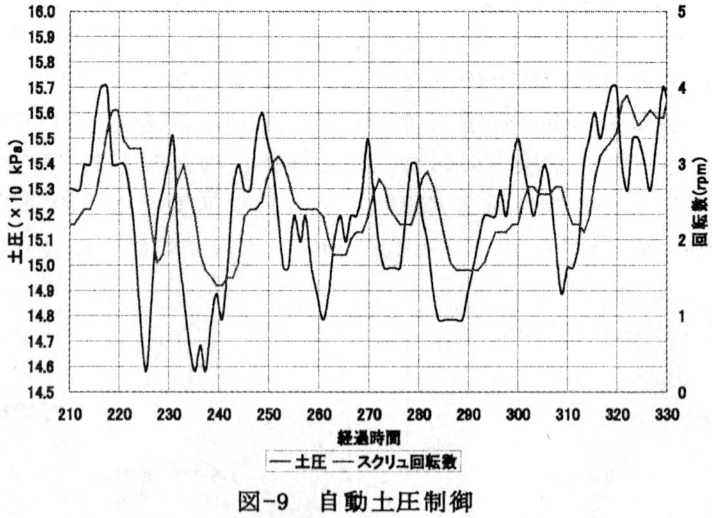

図-9 自動土圧制御

6 結 果

中国国内で初めて採用された世界最大級の ϕ 14.27 m 泥土圧シールドを採用し、当初の課題を克服して無事施工が行なえた。課題に対するシールドマシンの対応としては、

(1) 大断面勾配発進

発進時における切羽の崩落を防止するために、シールドジャッキの伸び速度を超低速領域で制御可能な微速回路を設置すると共に、カッタヘッドの回転数は、切羽の切り込み量を最適量とすることが可能な可変速を採用し、発進部における切羽の崩落に関する問題を克服した。

(2) 低土被り

低土被り施工を安全に行なうために、切羽部における掘削土の塑性流動性を確保する目的で、切羽への注入をカッタヘッド前面に 7 箇所、側面 1 箇所設け、切羽断面における塑性流動性及び、掘削外周部における土圧保持を行い、また、外周部に対して注入材と掘削土の撹拌性が劣る中央部に関しては中央アジテータを採用し、チャンバー内全体の塑性流動性を確保したことにより切羽部の崩落を防止した。

一方、裏込めに関しては、注入口を 6 カ所設け、それぞれ単独で注入することが可能な単独 6 系統の裏込め注入を採用し、各位置に於ける注入圧力と注入量を管理し、低土被り施工で問題となる地表面への影響を許容範囲以下で施工した。

(3) 河川下掘削と河川防護壁及び外白渡橋脚杭掘削

河川下掘削を行なう泥土圧シールドの問題点であるスクリューコンベヤからの噴発対策として、止水効果を確保するために、羽根ピッチを小さくし羽根のピッチ数を増やすことにより、スクリューコンベヤからの噴発を防止した。

また、防護壁及び橋脚杭掘削への対応として、カッタヘッドには特殊先行ビットを配置し、防護壁及び橋脚杭の掘削対応を行なった。

(4) 重要建築物近接施工

重要建築物との近接施工対応のために、切羽部への気泡、加泥、注水などが行なえる注入設備、裏込め注入の単独 6 系統における注入と共に、掘削時における緩み領域を減少させ、地上への影響を最小とすることが可能な大口径スクリューコンベヤの自動土圧制御システムを導入した。この結果、浦江飯店、上海大厦、外灘建築群などの重要建築物への影響はほとんど無く施工が行なえた。

(5) 地下通路直下掘削

施工中 2 箇所の地下通路の直下を施工に関し、地下通路の防護杭がシールド断面の上半に出現する計画で、この防護杭の掘削を前提としてカッタヘッドは円錐型を採用した。ビットに関しては、複数の防護杭を掘削するため、チャンバー内より安全に杭切り用特殊先行ビットの交換が可能な設備を採用した。但し、掘進開始直前にこの地下通路の防護杭が撤去されたが、一部残っていた残置杭の掘削となったため、ビットを交換することなく施工した。

(6) 地下鉄直上掘削

地下鉄の直上の掘削に対しては、切羽の塑性流動性を確保した土圧制御、適正な裏込め注入を実施することにより、シールド機の掘削は問題なく実施できた。

上記のように、河川下掘削、防護壁及び橋脚杭の掘削、歴史的建築物への影響、地下鉄営業線及び地下通路の近接施工などの課題を克服したことにより、超大口径土圧シールド工事が成功した。

この成功を足がかりとして、今後は超大口径の分野でも泥土圧の選択が可能となり、中国国内でも大型化するシールド工事において採用されるものと思われる。

最後に、本報告書を作成するにあたり、本プロジェクトを企画した中国上海市、外灘シールドの設計、製作に関して協力いただいた上海隧道股份有限公司機械製造所及び、高い技術力を持って施工を行なった上海隧道股份有限公司に感謝します。

著者紹介（Bio-data）：

三浦　正昭（E-mail　masaaki_miura@kbg.kobe.mhi.co.jp）

三菱重工地中建機株式会社　代表取締役社長

三菱重工業株式会社神戸造船所に入社後、シールドマシンの設計を経て、現在、三菱重工地中建機(株)代表取締役社長。本プロジェクトには、初期計画より参画した。

Masaaki MIURA

Mitsubishi Heavy Industries Tunneling Machinery & Geotechnology Co., Ltd, Present-Director.

I have engaged in the designing of the shield machine after joining the company of Mitsubishi Heavy Industries, Ltd. Kobe Shipyard & Machinery Works. Now I am a Present-Director of Mitsubishi Heavy Industries Tunneling Machinery & Geotechnology Co., Ltd, and from early planning I have been participated in this project.

田中　淳一(E-mail junichi_tanaka@kbg.kobe.mhi.co.jp)

三菱重工地中建機株式会社設計部　課長

三菱重工業株式会社神戸造船所に入社後、シールドマシンの設計に従事し、現在、日本国内及び中国向けにシールドマシンの設計を行なっている。

Junichi TANAKA

Mitsubishi Heavy Industries Tunneling Machinery & Geotechnology Co., Ltd, Designing Section Engineering Manager.

I have engaged in the designing of the shield machine after joining the company of Mitsubishi Heavy Industries, Ltd. Kobe Shipyard & Machinery Works, and I am designing the shield machine now for within Japan and China.

長距離・多急曲線シールド掘進の計画と実績

元永　隆章[1]　中野　修吾[2]

[1]株式会社間組　北陸支店，新潟　945-8601

[2]株式会社間組　関東土木支店，千葉　260-0024

千葉市内の浸水対策と合流式下水の水質改善を目的とした中央雨水幹線整備計画のひとつ，中央雨水1号貯留幹線2工区（管渠外径 6,300 mm，延長 2.6 km，土被り 25～30 m）を泥水式シールド工法にて施工するものである．高水圧かつ崩壊性の高い砂層において，円形立坑からの NOMST 発進，近接施工や支障物の存在，多数の急曲線を克服するために計画の段階で施した対応策と施工実績を報告するものである．

キーワード：泥水式シールド；急曲線；長距離掘進；近接施工；支障物；NOMST

PLANNING AND RECORDS OF SHIELD TUNNEL EXCAVATION WITH LONG DISTANCES AND MULTI CUTE CURVES

Takafumi MOTONAGA [1]，Shugo NAKANO[2]

[1]Hazama Co. Hokuriku Branch, Nigata 945-8601

[2]Kanto Branch, Tiba 260-0024

Abstract: As an improvement project of Chiba central sewer trunk line for flood countermeasure and improvement of sewer water quality of combination type sewerage, the storage trunk No. 2 section of Central Sewer Line 1 (out diameter 6,300 mm, length 2.6 km and cover height 25~30m) was constructed by using slurry type shield tunneling method. This paper presents the countermeasures for high water pressure, unstable ground, NOMST cutting in the vertical shaft, adjacent structures, obstacle and multi cute curves conducted at the planning stage and the construction records.

Key words: slurry type shield; cute curve; long distance excavation; adjacent construction; obstacle; NOMST

1　はじめに

千葉市では雨水管渠や貯留施設・ポンプ場等を計画的に整備してきたが，急速な都市化に伴い雨水が地下に浸透しにくくなり，結果として短時間で大量の雨水が下水道や河川に流入するようになった．特に近年，局地的な集中豪雨の発生頻度が増加しているため，雨水整備が一度完了した地域でも再び浸水するような事態が発生している．また中心市街地は合流式下水道を採用しており，雨天時に雨で希釈された汚水が河川や海に放流され，衛生面・景観面からも問題があった．そこで千葉市は新たに「中央雨水幹線整備計画」を策定し，市内路下に雨水を一時的に貯める貯留管の整備を行うとともに，放流水の水質改善のため中央雨水ポンプ場の建設を進めている（図－1）.

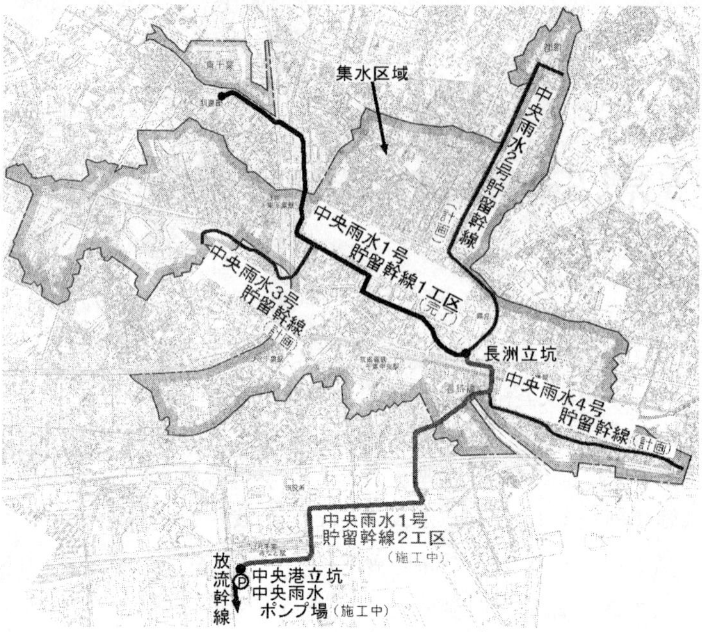

図-1　中央雨水幹線整備計画

本工事は貯留管の一つ，中央雨水 1 号貯留幹線（延長約 5 km）のうち，下流側の 2.6 km を泥水式シールド工法にて築造するものである．同幹線は既設構造物を回避する急曲線の多い複雑な線形で構成され，高水圧が作用し崩壊性の高い洪積砂層を掘進しなければならない．本稿ではこれら難条件下で長距離・多急曲線掘進のための計画と実績について報告する．

2　工事概要

工事名称：下水道排水施設工事（中央雨水 1 号貯留幹線 2 工区）
発 注 者：千葉市下水道局
施 工 者：間・東洋・飛島・京葉工管建設共同企業体
施工場所：千葉市中央区中央港 1 丁目地内他 6
工　　期：2005 年 10 月～平成 21 年 3 月
工事内容：一次覆工工事（泥水式シールド工法）
路線延長 2,620 m，曲線部 R=28 m～200 m 19 箇所　勾配　1.0‰～1.2‰
土被り　28～30 m（最大水圧 310 kPa）シールド機外径 φ6,450 mm　セグメント外径 φ6,300 mm

3　施工上の問題点

3.1　線形上の問題点

図－2 に路線平面図を示す．全長 2.6 km の路線中に曲線が 19 箇所あり，そのうちの 12 箇所が R=28～60 m の急曲線である．急曲線掘進を繰り返すことによりシールド機のテールブラシ・中折れパッキンに異常が生じる機械トラブルや，掘進時の施工時荷重によりセグメントが変形・破損することが懸念された．また急曲線が多くなると坑内基準点の基線長を長く取れなくなることから測量精度が下がると同時に，急曲線部でのシールド機・セグメントの制御は難易度が高いことから，線形管理基準値を超えてしまう可能性があった．

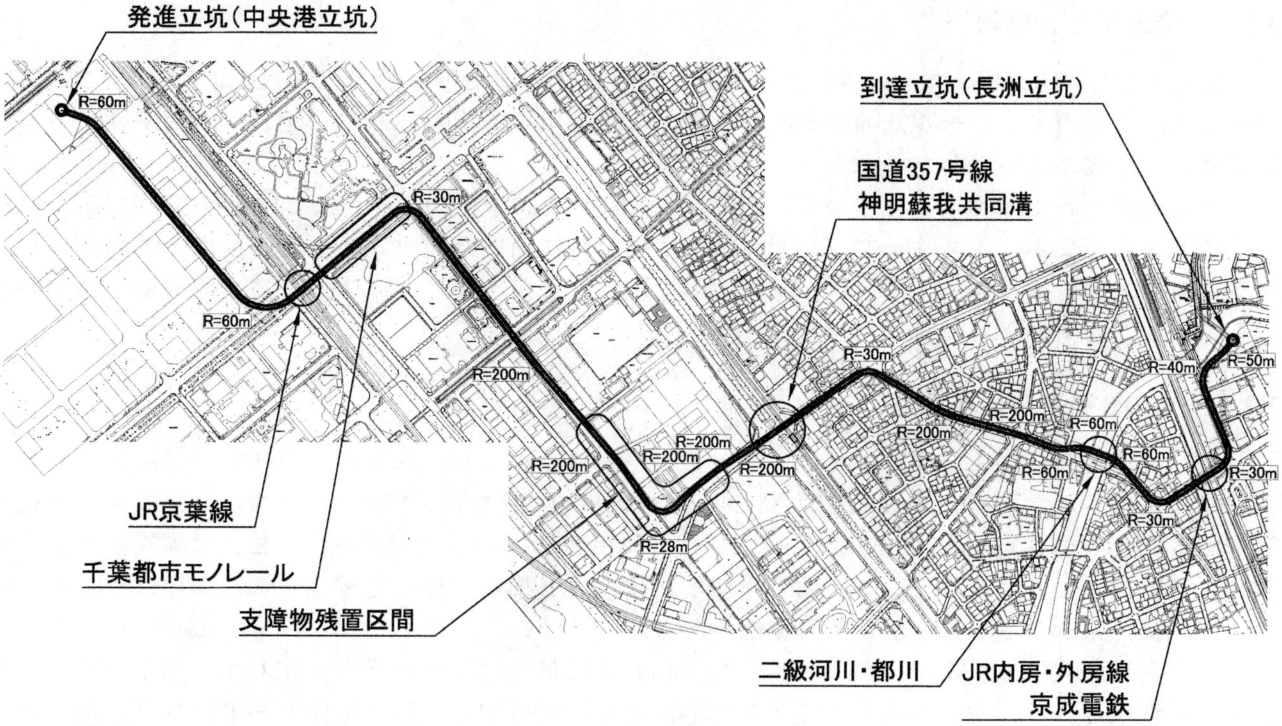

図-2　路線平面図

3.2　土質上の問題点

図－3 に土質想定図を示す．工事箇所は東京湾に面した千葉市海浜部の低地面に位置しており，シールド管渠は土被り 28～30 m，地下水圧が管渠中心で 310 kPa 程度の洪積細砂内に築造される．

N 値は 13～50 と幅があるが，概ね N=50 以上の値が測定されており，「非常に密な状態」の砂層と言える．粒度組成は粒径 75μm 以下のバインダー分が 3%～28%で，多くが 15%以下となっており少ない．均等係数 Uc は 2～7 で粒度分布が悪く，透水係数は 10^{-3} cm/s オーダーと中位である．以上のことから掘削対象地盤は粒子の揃ったさらさらの砂層であり，「地山としては安定しているが，切羽管理を誤ると非常に崩壊しやすい砂層」であることが予見された．そのため掘進時の異常出水時には水とともに土砂が噴発する可能性があった．

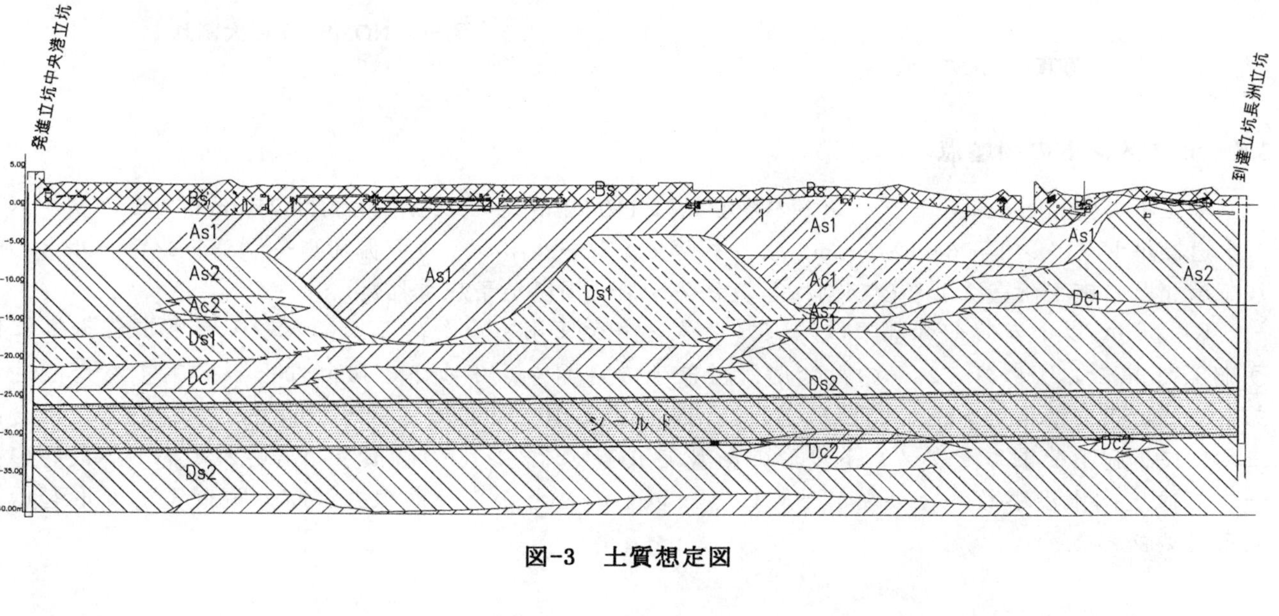

図-3　土質想定図

3.3　近接施工と支障物

図－1の路線平面図上に，近接施工の対象となる重要構造物等を示す．JR京葉線，内房・外房線，京成線，千葉都市モノレール，神明蘇我共同溝，二級河川・都川があり，いずれも離隔が1D程度で管理者との近接協議が必要となった．

また路線上の支障物調査を進めていたところ，BP+1,160～1,470 m付近，310 mの区間の路線付近に，隣接する千葉ポートスクエア（ハザマ施工）施工時に用いた除去式アースアンカーの高強度モルタル，シース管，先端金物（耐荷体）が残置していることが判明した．アースアンカーは総数400本にものぼり，対策が必要になった．

3.4　NOMST発進時の問題点

発進立坑となる中央港立坑は外径φ17.0 m，内径13.8 m，深さ36.1 mの円形立坑で圧入ケーソン工法にて築造された．発進坑口部は厚さ1.0 mのNOMST壁になっており，補強材としてCFRP格子筋（NEFMAC：□-250 mm×125 mm，C19，C13）が使用されている（写真－1）．これは縦筋と横筋を一体化させた網のような構造になっており，切削時に縦筋と横筋の接続を確実に切断しなければ面状に剥がれ，排泥系統の閉塞につながる可能性がある．

また円形立坑をNOMST発進する際，NOMST壁は最初にシールド機の左右から切削され，最後に中心が切削される．左右の切削が完了しても，シールド機中心付近の仮壁が弓形に残り，大割れし取込み不能になる可能性があった（図－4）．

写真-1　NOMST壁

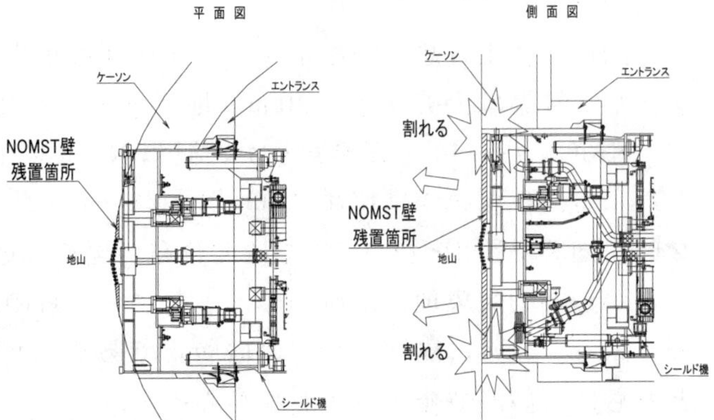

図-4　NOMST壁の大割れ

3.5　セグメントの問題点

本工事で使用したRCセグメントの鉄筋量は110 kg/m^{3}と少なく，桁高は250 mmでこのサイズの下水道標準セグメントC64（275 mm）よりも薄く，シールドジャッキ偏荷重やマシーンテールとのせり荷重などの施工荷重によりひび割れ等のセグメント損傷が予想された．

R≤60 m以下の急曲線部では鋼製セグメントを使用するが，ここにおいても急曲線掘進に伴う施工荷重によりセグメントの大変形，継ぎ手の目開き，ボルトの破断などが発生する可能性がある．また過去に事例として急曲線出入口，すなわちRCセグメントと鋼製セグメントとの接合部において，施工荷重やセグメント変形の影響でRCセグメントの破損が報告されており，最悪のケースでは坑内水没事故へとつながっている．以上のことから急曲線掘進時の編荷重・変形を低減する必要あった．

4　施工計画

4.1　シールド機

シールド機を設計・製作するにあたり，前項の問題点を留意事項として仕様を決定した．シールド機の全体図を図－5 に示す．

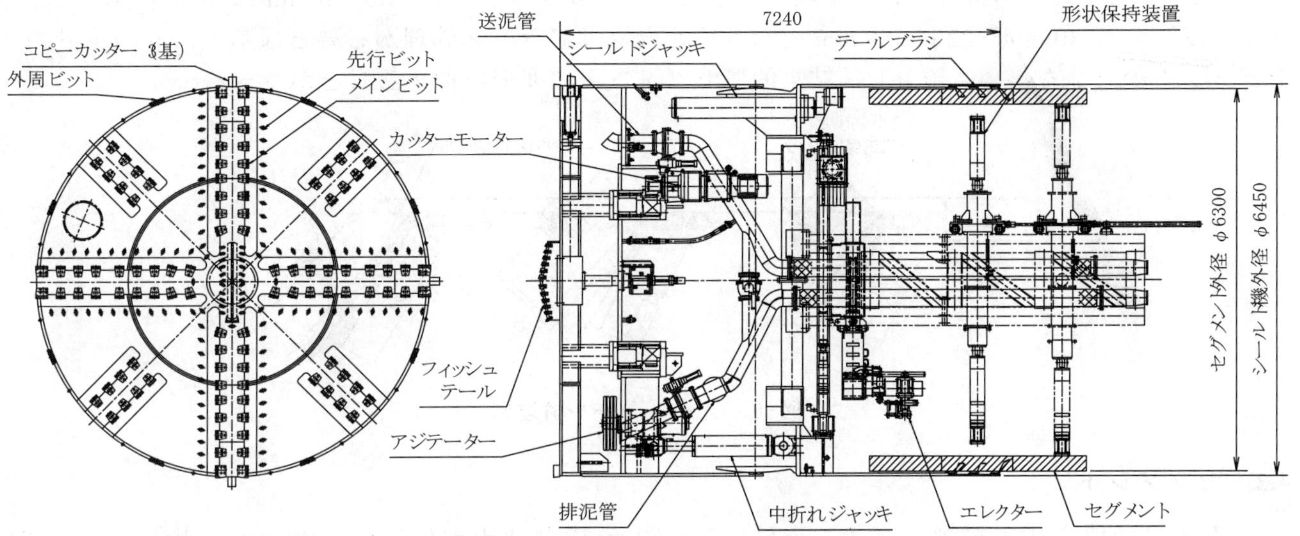

図-5　φ 6,450 泥水式シールド機構造図

(1) カッターヘッド

発進立坑にて NOMST 切削した後，洪積砂層を主とする地山を 2.6 km 掘進する．途中でのビット交換は非常に難しいことから，ビット摩耗検討結果よりチップ材として E5 を，母材には SKC24 を採用し，ビット交換なしでの到達を計画した（図－6）．

NOMST 切削時に CFRP 格子筋を確実に切断し，できるだけ仮壁を細かく切削するためのビット形状と配置を検討した．取込可能な格子筋の切断片の長さを最大 50 cm 程度に想定し，より小さく切断するため，高さが 15 mm 異なる先行ビットを 1/2 パスずらして千鳥配置した．高い先行ビットは切断を目的として鋭利な形状に，低い先行ビットは切削を目的とした平たい形状とした（図－7）．

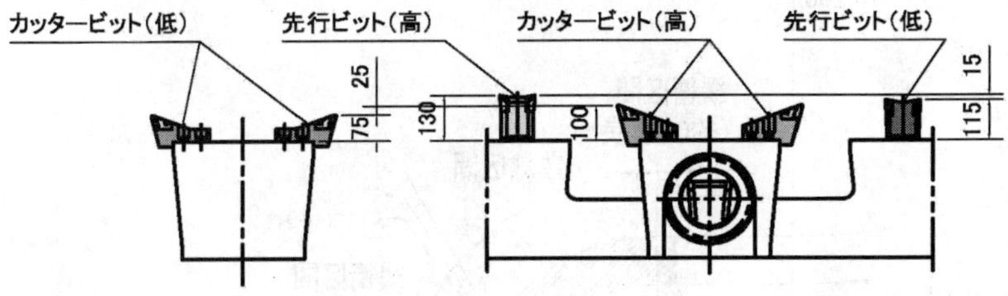

図-6　ビット配置図

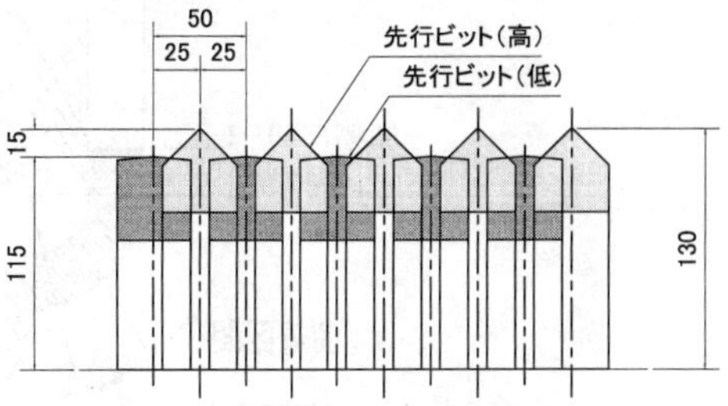

図-7　先行ビット配置図

泥水式であることからカッターヘッド形状は面盤型を採用している．崩壊しやすい砂層を掘進することからできる限り開口率を小さくし 21%とした．

(2)テールシール

高水圧および多急曲線施工での耐久性を考慮してテールブラシは 3 段とした．

急曲線部においてテールブラシ圧がセグメントに与える影響は大きい．さらに裏込め材がテールブラシの隙間に入り固結するとブラシ圧が上がると同時に柔軟性が失われセグメントの破損，異常出水の原因になる．そこでテールグリースが自動的に満遍なく供給されるようグリース注入管を 2 m（36°）ピッチに 10 系統，1 系統あたりブラシの隙間が 2 箇所あるため，計 20 本配置した．また材質はステンレス製とし，急曲線掘進時のテールクリアランスの大きな変動に柔軟に追従させると同時にブラシの反転を防止するため，長さを通常よりも 10% 程度長くした（1，2 段目は 230 mm，3 段目は 300 mm）．また裏込材がテールブラシの隙間に入らないよう，1,2 段目のブラシの密度を通常よりも高くし，3 段目のブラシについてはウレコンシールを施した．

テールクリアランス確保，セグメントの真円保持，テールブラシ保護のため，1 段目ブラシの前に，高さ 22 mm の真円保持リングを取り付けた．テールクリアランスは 30 mm であるから，実許容クリアランスは 30 mm－22 mm=8 mm となり緻密なクリアランス管理が必要となるが，シールド機とセグメントのせりを早めに予見し，結果的にセグメントの変形を抑えることができる．

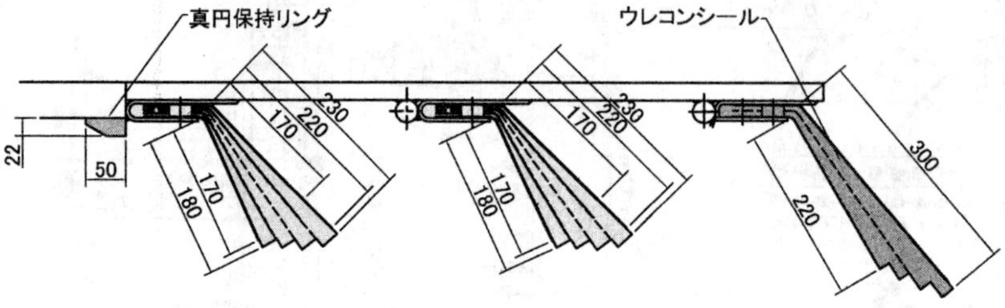

図-8　テールシール構造図

4.2　セグメント

急曲線で使用する鋼製セグメントは，R⩽60 m の急曲線部には幅 300 mm，出入口部の RC セグメントの接合部には幅 1,200 mm の鋼製セグメントとした．さらに R⩽40 m 以下の曲線部では外径 φ6,270 mm，幅 300 mm の縮径セグメント（縮径量 30 mm）を使用しテールクリアランスを確保した．

急曲線出口での RC セグメントの破損を防ぐ対策として，出入口前後の直線に鋼製セグメントを 1 機長～0.5 機長程度割り付け，緩衝区間とする方法がある．本工事においても設計にて R⩽30 m の急曲線出入口には 1 機長の緩衝区間が設定されていたが，使用する RC セグメントが薄く，R＞30 m の急曲線出入口においても破損が予想されたため，R=28～40 m に関しては 1 機長，R=50・60 m に関しては 0.5 機長の緩衝区間を設けるようセグメント割付を見直した．図－9 にセグメント割付図を示す．

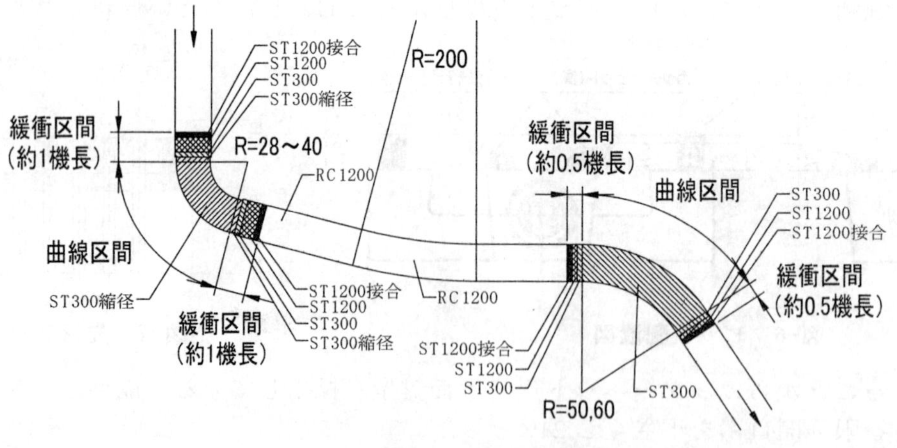

図-9　セグメント割付図

4.3　近接施工および支障物対策

近接施工協議の対象となる重要構造物対してシールド掘進が与える影響を事前に FEM 解析にて検討し，ほぼ影響なしという結果が得られていたため，管理者との協議の結果，トランシットとレベルによる変位観測にて監視することとなった．

一方，アースアンカーの残置物は，図面は残っているものの施工精度の観点から正確な位置を特定できないこと，有効な探査方法がないこと，残置物があまりにも多く撤去は事実上困難であることなどから，計画路線を支障物から十分な離隔を取って回避する路線に変更した（図－10）.

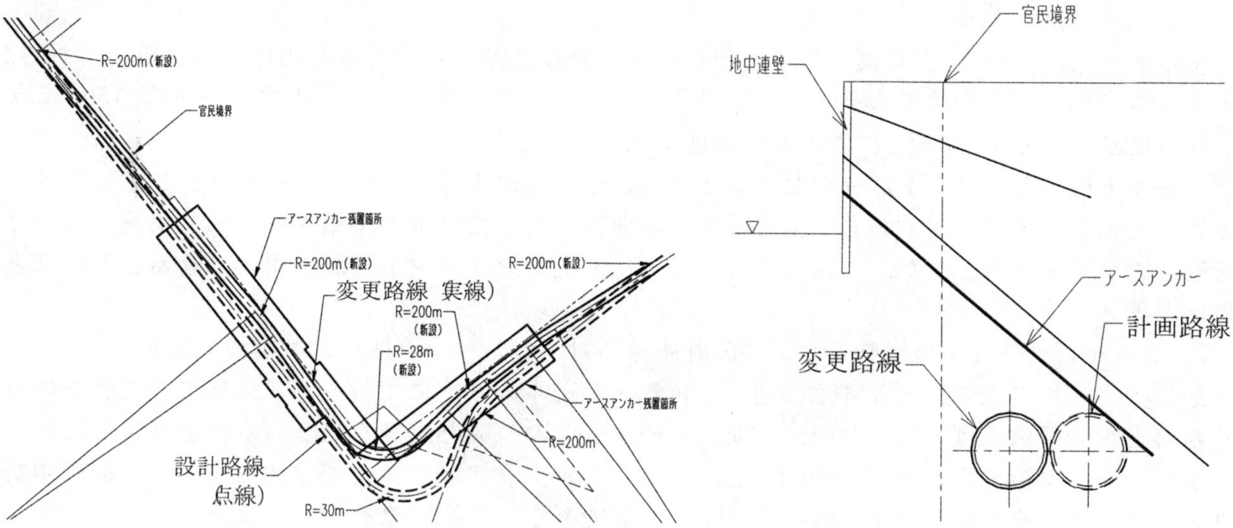

図-10　支障物回避のための路線変更

4.4　NOMST 発進対策

NOMST 切削については **4.1** にてシールド機の仕様を述べた．NOMST 壁の大割れを防ぐ対策としては，最終切削時にシールド機に押されて NOMST 壁が動かないよう背面の地山が堅固にする必要がある．発進箇所の地盤は N 値 50 前後の砂層であるが，立坑が圧入ケーソン工法にて築造されているためゆるみが生じている可能性があった．当初設計では発進防護工として薬液注入工（溶液型複相式）が計画されていたが，強度が期待できる高圧噴射撹拌工（Superjet-Midi 工法，以後 SJM 工法）に変更した（図－11）.

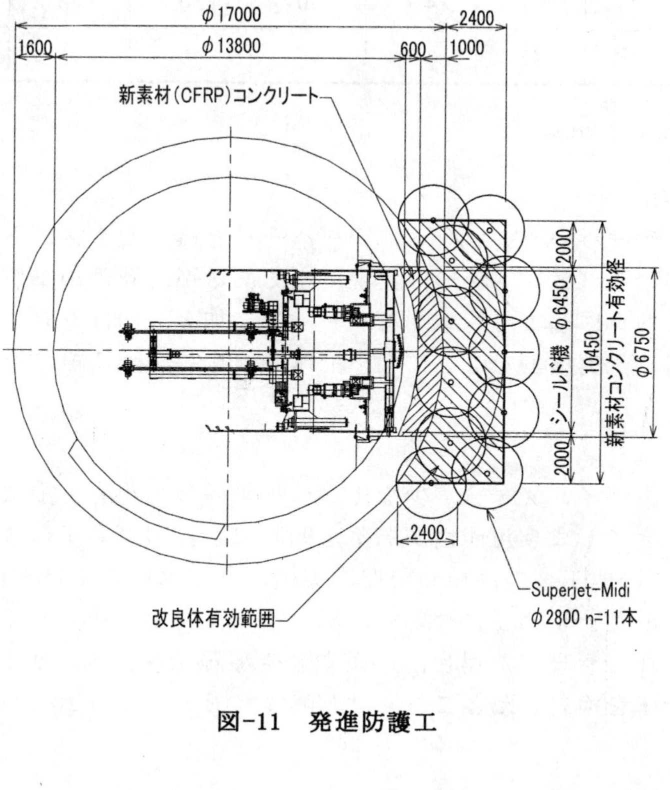

図-11　発進防護工

4.5 急曲線掘進対策

急曲線部の地盤は概ね N 値 25 以上であり良好であることから，過去の実績よりセグメント組立制御・シールド機の方向制御・裏込め注入の 3 つが適切になされれば，補助工法なしで十分に曲がりきれると判断した．

裏込め注入は，シールド管渠全体の変形を抑え十分な地盤反力を得るために非常に重要であるが，打ちすぎは余掘り部を埋めてしまうため，注入量が余掘りを見込んだテールボイド量の 130%になるか，注入圧が切羽圧＋200 kPa になるかで管理することとした．

シールド機とセグメントがせらないよう同調させて掘進することは，テールブラシやセグメントの保護のために極めて重要である．全ての曲率の曲線に対して以下の事項を確認し，実施工における線形管理の判断基準値とした．これに基づきシールド機とセグメントを制御すればせることはほとんど無いと考えた．

① 計画中折れ角度・余掘り量および設計基線に対するシールド機の理論位置の算定

通常，シールド機の線形管理は切羽・中折れ・テールの 3 点にて行うが，曲線ではこれらの点が描く軌跡と設計基線とは一致しない．事前にシールド機の軌跡と設計基線とのずれを検討した．

まずシールド機後胴の方向・回転中心およびテールクリアランスを規定することで，計画中折れ角度・余掘り量，そしてシールド機のずれ量が計算できる．計算結果を表－1 に示す．

表-1　シールド機線形管理規準値

曲率	余掘り (mm)	中折れ角 (°)	設計基線に対するシールド機の位置			テールクリアランス	
			切羽 (mm)	中折れ (mm)	テール (mm)	外側 (mm)	内側 (mm)
R=28m	98	8.0	64	64	20	12	78
R=30m	91	7.5	60	60	20	14	76
R=40m	61	5.6	45	45	15	22	68
R=50m	57	4.7	50	50	16	20	40
R=60m	48	3.9	46	46	16	25	35

注 1 :余掘りはカーブの内側。
注 2：シールド機はカーブの外側。

② セグメントの組立パターン

設計時に算出されるテーパーセグメントのテーパー量と標準セグメントとの使用比率と千鳥組パターンによって，曲線部のセグメント線形は実現可能であるが，管理規準値内に納めるためには詳細な検討が必要である．各曲率について基本的なパターンに加え，曲げをきつくするパターン，緩くするパターンを数種類検討し，実施工ではこれらを組み合わせて設計基線に乗せられるようにした．

4.6 切羽安定管理

今回掘進する砂層は，バインダー分が少なくかつ均等係数も小さく崩壊しやすいため，切羽安定管理を誤ると取り込みすぎてしまう可能性があると同時に，貝殻が若干含まれることから逸泥が予想された．そこで千葉県内での他工事の洪積砂層掘進実績より泥水比重 1.15～1.17，ファンネル粘性 23～25 s にて管理することとした．切羽圧については静止土圧，主働土圧，ゆるみ土圧に対して比較検討した．静止土圧・主働土圧で管理した場合，逸泥や噴発が懸念される．地山が良好で土被りが大きいことを考慮し，ゆるみ土圧を検討したところ，その値は水圧＋予備圧 20 kPa の値とほぼ一致した．逸泥を少しでも抑えたいため，管理水圧は水圧＋20 kPa を管理基準の下限値とし，地山の取込状況を監視のうえ調整することとした．

流体輸送設備の制御（流量・圧力）は自社の中央監視システムにて一元管理し，送排泥流量・比重をリアルタイムで計測して掘削乾砂量に換算する．リング毎の計測値を統計的に管理し，異常値の有無を常に監視すると同時に，実際の搬出土量と照らし合わせて取り込みすぎがないかを確認することにした．

5　施工実績

5.1　NOMST 発進

NOMST 切削は掘進速度 1.5 mm/min，切羽圧 50 kPa 程度に抑えて開始した（写真－3）．カッタートルクは切削範囲が広がるにつれて徐々に上昇したが，カッターヘッド全面で NOMST 壁の切削をした状態でも装備トルクの 35%～45%程度であった．切削中コンクリートを削る音が若干する程度で，シールド機の振動や立坑・地盤の振動は見受けられなかった．

排泥ラインに礫箱を取付け，ポンプ閉塞の原因となる 50 mm 超のコンクリート塊や CFRP 格子筋の回収を試みた．切削片の多くは砕石または再生砂のような状態で排出され，礫箱にはあまり引っかからなかった．CFRP 格子筋は 70 cm 程度で切断されたものがいくつか見受けられたが，ほとんどは細かく切断された状態で一次振動ふるいから排出された．縦筋と横筋がつながった網状で排出されたものはなく，今回のカッタービット配列が CFRP 格子筋を確実に切断したことを確認できた．また NOMST 壁が大割れすることもなく，SJM 工による防護が有効であったことも確認した（写真－4）．

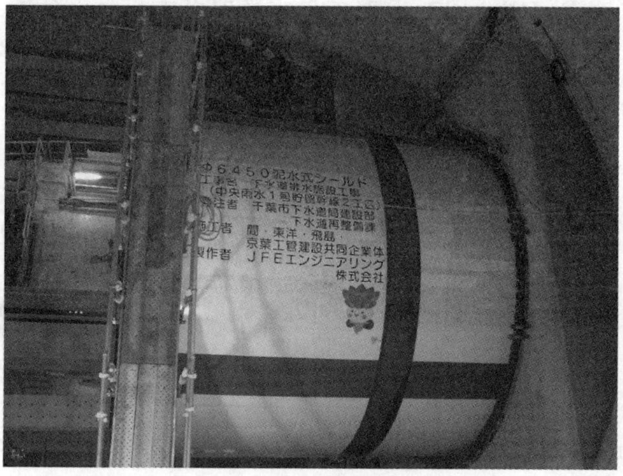

写真-3　発進状況

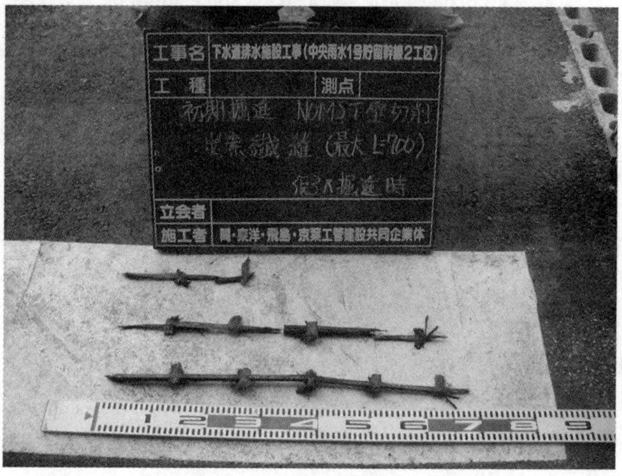

写真-4　CFRP 格子筋切断片

5.2　近接施工と支障物

近接重要構造物の変位は企業者と協議した管理値を下回り，掘進の影響は出なかった．アースアンカーの支障物区間に対しても順調に掘進を終え，残置物を完全にかわすことができたと考える．

5.3　急曲線掘進

(1) シールド機の方向制御

シールド機の方向制御は，以下のように行った（図－12）．

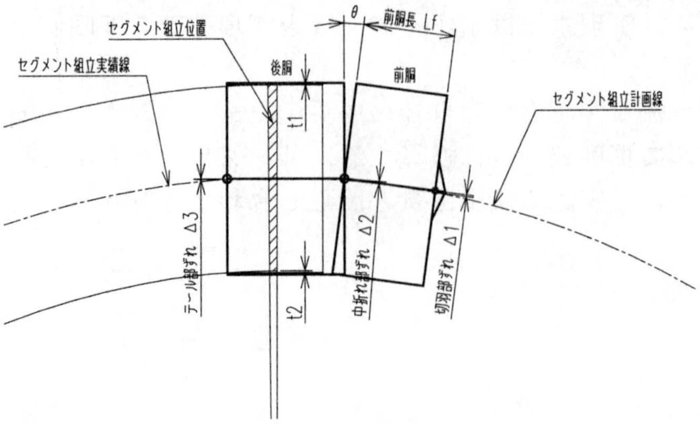

図-12　シールド機の方向制御

① 掘進完了後，シールド機とセグメントの位置を測量にて実測する．またクリアランス t1，t2 および中折れ角 θ を記録する．

② 現在のセグメントの位置・向きをもとに，今後の掘進で設計基線に近づくようなセグメント組立計画を立案し，計画線を決定する．

③ セグメントの組立実績線および計画線に対するシールド機の切羽・中折れ・テール部のずれ量 Δ1～Δ3 を計算する．

④ クリアランスとずれ量の数値が 4.5 で検討した管理基準値とほぼ同じであるかを評価し，ずれが生じた場合は，管理基準値に近づくように中折れやストローク量を調整する．

⑤ 前胴のずれが Δ1=Δ2 とならない場合，中折れを調整し前胴の方向をセグメントの方向に合わせる．調整角 Δθ1 は次式で求めた．

$$\Delta\theta 1=\tan^{-1}\left[(\Delta 1-\Delta 2)/Lf\right]$$　　Lf：シールド機前胴の長さ

Δ1～Δ3 が管理基準値と大幅に異なり，シールド機の位置そのものをずらす必要が生じた場合は，上乗せ調整角 Δθ2 を加える．この値はシールド機の動きを見ながら決定したが，概ね 0.1°～0.3°となった．よって，以後の掘進での中折れ角 θ'は次式のようになる．

$$\theta'=\theta+\Delta\theta 1+\Delta\theta 2$$

⑥ シールド機とセグメントの位置関係を維持させるため，原則としてシールド機のストローク変化量はセグメントのテーパー量と同じとした．またクリアランス調整のため，±15 mm（0.15°）程度の範囲でストローク変化量を増減した．

⑦ シールド機の掘進は，できるだけ全ジャッキによる掘進を基本とし，ストローク量の調整に必要なときだけ最小限のジャッキを抜くようにした．

⑧ 余掘り量はシールド機の曲がり具合を見ながら可能な限り小さくした．

この方向制御によりセグメントの水平変位も規格値の 50%以内に収まった．余掘り量ストローク量は計画値よりも 10～20 mm 少ない値で曲がれた．

問題の発生しやすい急曲線出入口部ではセグメントの変形・変位を低減するため，掘進を 1 日停止し裏込材の強度を上げるための養生期間とした．テールグリースは掘進に合わせ自動的に毎リング補充し，テールブラシの隙間に裏込材が入らないようにした．これによりテール部からの異常出水は発生していない．

(2) 急曲線部のセグメント変形

図－13 に R=28 m の急曲線掘進時の推力とセグメントリング間継手面の平面度を示す．この値はリング間継手面の不陸の最大値と最小値との差である．平面度が小さいほど変形が小さく理想的である．RC セグメント部では実績として平面度は 0～10 mm となったため，急曲線出入口部で変形量が 10 mm 以内であれば接合する RC セグメントに大きな影響を与えないと判断し管理基準値とした．

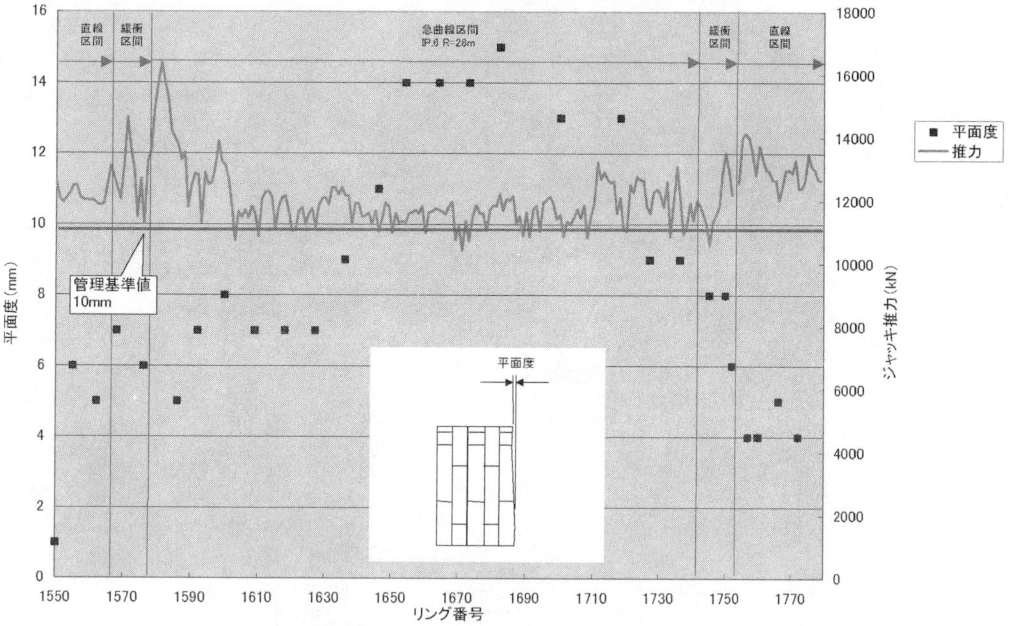

図-13　リング間継手平面度の推移

(3) で述べたとおりセグメントに極力負担をかけないように留意したが，平面度は次第に大きくなり管理基準値を超えてしまった．その変形の仕方は左右が上下よりも凹むことが多かった．

変形を抑える対策として，継手面の凹んでいる箇所に厚さ 5 mm のシール材を増し貼りした．掘進に伴いシール材はつぶれてしまうが，何リングも続けることで平面度の増加は抑えられ，出口付近および緩衝区間で大幅に小さくなり，結果として続く RC セグメントを破損させることなく組むことができた．

6　おわりに

着工前の綿密な調査と想定されるトラブルへの対策の検討，そして施工でのきめ細やかな管理により無事掘進を完了できた．2.6 km の掘進を終え到達したシールド機のカッタービットの摩耗はほとんどなく，さらに 2.6 km 掘進ができるような状態であった．到達精度は水平変位 11 mm，鉛直変位 4 mm と満足できるものであった．重要構造物が輻輳する都市部では，それらを回避するためより難条件，複雑な線形の長距離シールドを掘進する技術が要求される可能性がある．今回の実績をもとにさらに安全かつ合理的な施工法を検討していく所存ある．

最後に，本工事の計画・施工にあたりご指導，ご協力頂いた早稲田大学小泉教授，関係者各位にこの場を借りて厚く御礼申し上げるものである．

著者紹介（Bio-data）：
元永　隆章　課長
株式会社ハザマ　北陸支店
専門：シールドトンネル
Takafumi MOTONAGA　Supervisor
Kasiwazaki Branch Office, Hokuriku Branch, Hazama Corporation
Specialized field:　Shield Tunnel Engineering
E-mail: motonaga@hazama.co.jp

第五届中日盾构隧道技术交流会

部分主、参办单位介绍

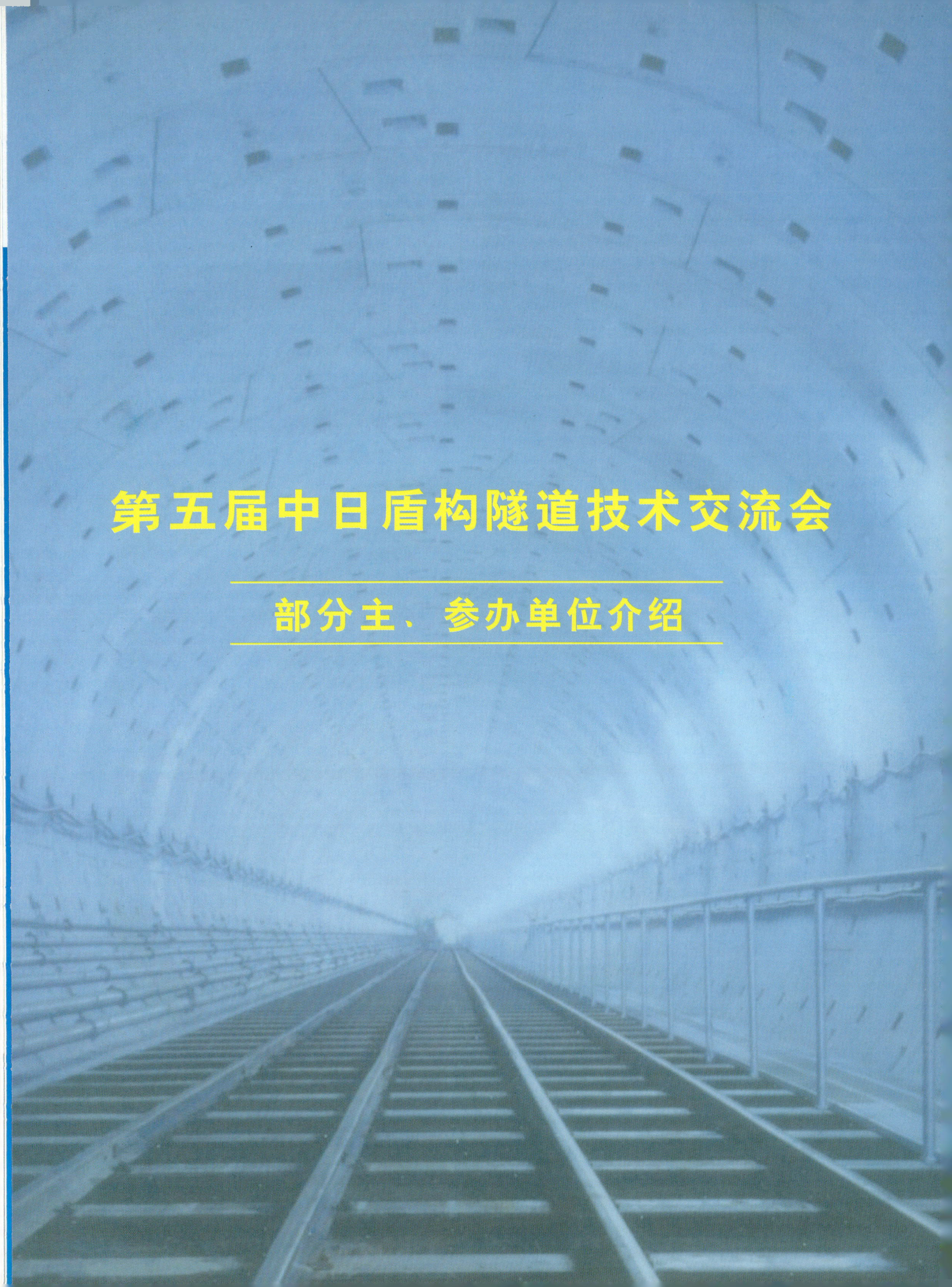

华隧建设本着“团结、诚信、廉洁、高效、奋进”的企业精神，经过多年的探索，在盾构施工技术的创新、盾构设备的改进等方面成果显著，掌握了泥水盾构施工的顶尖技术，不仅在华南地区、在全国范围内也是首屈一指，土压盾构施工技术在国内同行中也具有领先实力，已独立研发出多种施工方法，并先后获得多项国家级工法、省级工法、国家发明技术专利、省级科技进步奖等奖项，受到业内人士的高度关注。

盾构密闭接收装置

盾构密闭到达技术

盾构整体吊装技术

盾构暗挖始发技术

盾构暗挖到达技术

SEW工法盾构始发技术

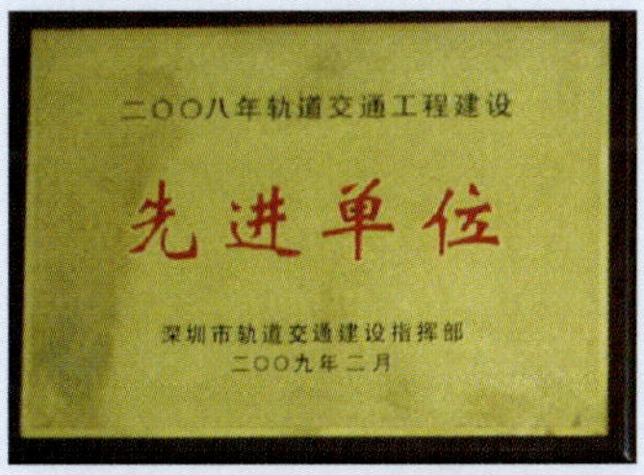

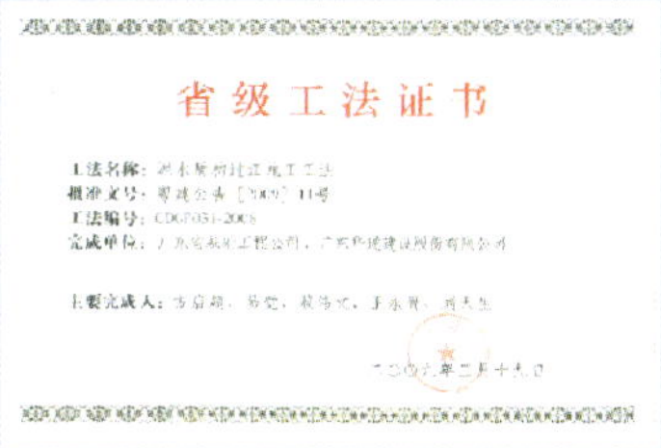

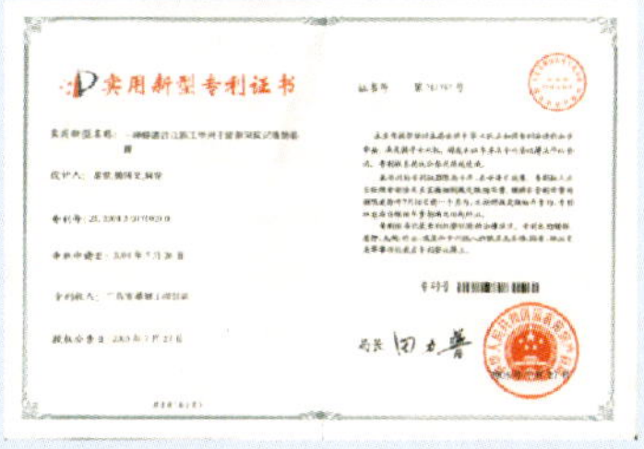

华隧建设凭借雄厚的技术力量和拥有的技术优势，加上严格、高效、优质的施工管理水平，使公司承建的工程项目得以高质、顺利完工并受到业主及社会各界的普遍好评，多次获得国家市政金杯奖，广东省优良样板工地、安全生产文明施工优良样板工地以及多项国家级优秀QC成果奖，在每年的“安康杯”竞赛中也取得优异的成绩。

“穿越无界、创建未来”，华隧建设将以饱满的热情、先进的技术、科学的管理、优质的服务致力于地下空间的开发和建设中，期待能与社会各界携手合作，再创辉煌！

公司地址：广东省广州市天河北路559号18楼1802-1805
联系电话：020-38105588
传　　真：020-85272530

中铁二十三局集团第五工程有限公司

中铁二十三局集团有限公司隶属于中国铁建股份有限公司，是一家综合型特大施工企业，具有铁路总承包特级资质，房屋建筑工程施工总承包壹级、公路工程施工总承包壹级、水利水电工程施工总承包壹级、市政公用工程施工总承包壹级、桥梁工程专业承包壹级、隧道工程专业承包壹级、城市轨道交通工程专业承包壹级。现有员工12681人，其中各类专业技术人员占员工总数的30.5%，中高级技工占员工总数的62.6%，一级建造师249人，拥有各类大中型设备3502台（套），总功率12.5万千瓦，年施工能力达100亿元以上。先后参加了上海磁悬浮、重庆轻轨、香港西铁东铁无碴轨道、郑西、厦深、贵广、石武、武广、向莆、南广等客运专线等一大批国内外工程。

中铁二十三局集团第五工程有限公司所在地上海浦东新区，主要从事地铁轨道交通及混凝土制品、钢结构、钢模开发、高铁轨道板研发、无碴轨道，参与了成都、上海、苏州、郑州地铁建设。2008年9月中标成都地铁2号线一期工程土建18标，区间隧道采用美国Robbins公司生产的EPB土压平衡盾构机施工。

拥有轨道技术专利的上海磁悬浮梁

↗ 铁道部总工程师何华武（左三）考察公司无碴轨道试验基地

↗ 管片堆场

车站基坑施工 ↖

↗ 900T箱梁运输

↙ 管片拼装

↙ 自行开发研究的管片钢模

中铁二十三局集团第五工程有限公司

↗铁道部总工程师何华武在中铁二十三局集团成都公司检查指导工作

↗全球化的起点——从上海发往非洲安哥拉的轨枕

公司发展战略：依托制品生产优势，向两端延伸产业链，长线与短线产品互补，打造国内一流城市轨道交通专业化施工企业.

↗中铁二十三局集团成都地铁盾构项目部

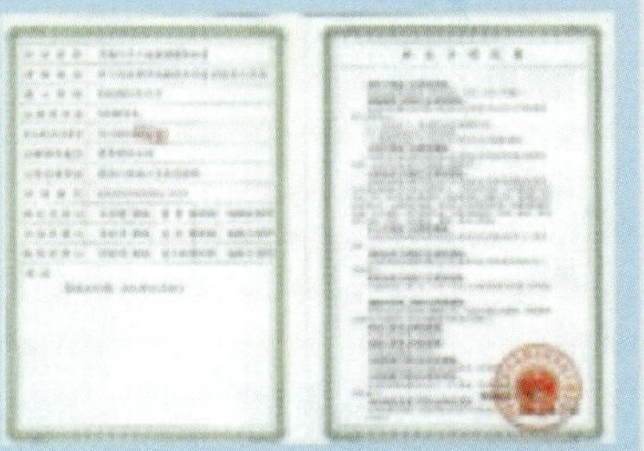

↗集团公司铁路施工总承包特级资质证书

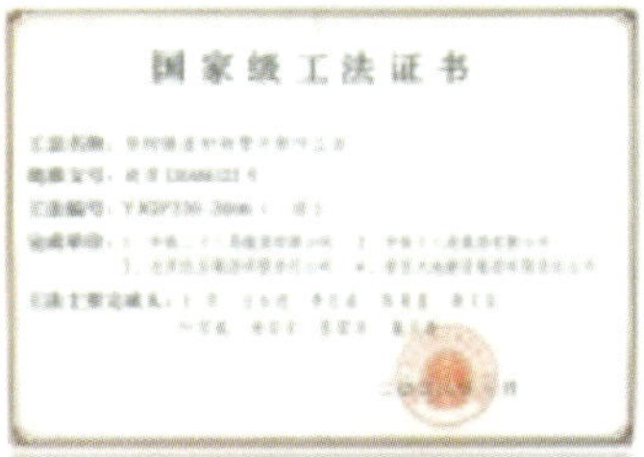

国家二级工法

中央企业先进集体

上海市科技进步奖

连续四年获得上海市文明场站

严谨治学　　严格要求　　竣实扬华　　自强不息

西南交通大學

Southwest Jiaotong University

西南交通大学创建于1896年，是我国近代建校最早的高等学府之一，是中国近代土木工程高等教育的发祥地，是首批进入“211工程”建设和设有研究生院的教育部直属全国重点高校。百年的历程铸就了“竢实扬华、自强不息”的交大精神和“严谨治学、严格要求”的办学传统。

西南交通大学是一所以工科为主，工、理、管、经、文、法等多学科协调发展的全国重点大学，拥有完整的学士-硕士-博士培养体系，拥有在世界交通领域有着重大影响的牵引动力国家重点实验室，拥有中国科学院院士4人，中国工程院院士3人，国家级教学名师3人，国家级有突出贡献专家7人，“长江学者”特聘教授和讲座教授7人，“973”首席科学家1人，第三届长江学者成就奖特等奖1人，国家杰出青年基金获得者8人，与20余个国家和地区、50余个科研机构开展了交流与合作，形成了“一校两地三校区”、开放式、国际化办学的局面。

近年来，学校紧紧围绕国家轨道交通事业的进步与发展，诞生了以“青藏铁路工程”、“高海拔地区大型公路隧道建设与运营关键技术及运用”、“万县长江大桥特大跨钢筋混凝土拱桥设计施工技术研究”、“机车车辆整车滚动振动试验台”、“高温超导磁悬浮试验车”等国家科技进步奖为代表的一系列标志性成果。

面向未来，学校将按照“育人为本、质量为先、结构合理、特色鲜明”的办学方针，以正在筹建的“轨道交通国家实验室”为创新平台和支撑平台，为建设具有交通特色的多学科协调发展的高水平研究型大学而奋斗。